Theory and Applications of Computability

In cooperation with the association Computability in Europe

For further volumes, go to
www.springer.com/series/8819

Books published in this series will be of interest to the research community and graduate students, with a unique focus on issues of computability. The perspective of the series is multidisciplinary, recapturing the spirit of Turing by linking theoretical and real-world concerns from computer science, mathematics, biology, physics, and the philosophy of science.

The series includes research monographs, advanced and graduate texts, and books that offer an original and informative view of computability and computational paradigms.

Rodney G. Downey • Denis R. Hirschfeldt

Algorithmic Randomness and Complexity

Springer

Rodney G. Downey
Victoria University of Wellington
School of Mathematics, Statistics
and Operations Research
Wellington, New Zealand
Rod.Downey@msor.vuw.ac.nz

Denis R. Hirschfeldt
University of Chicago
Department of Mathematics
Chicago, IL 60637
USA
drh@math.uchicago.edu

ISSN 2190-619X e-ISSN 2190-6203
ISBN 978-1-4939-3820-9 ISBN 978-0-387-68441-3 (eBook)
DOI 10.1007/978-0-387-68441-3
Springer New York Dordrecht Heidelberg London

Mathematics Subject Classification (2010): Primary: 03D32, Secondary: 03D25, 03D27, 03D30, 03D80, 68Q30

ACM Computing Classification (1998): F.1, F.2, F.4, G.3, H.1

Printed on acid-free paper

Springer is part of Springer Science+Business Media (www.springer.com)

Rod dedicates this book to his wife Kristin, and Denis to Larisa.

Contents

Preface xi

Acknowledgments xiv

Introduction xvii

I Background 1

1 Preliminaries **2**
- 1.1 Notation and conventions 2
- 1.2 Basics from measure theory 4

2 Computability Theory **7**
- 2.1 Computable functions, coding, and the halting problem . 7
- 2.2 Computable enumerability and Rice's Theorem 11
- 2.3 The Recursion Theorem 13
- 2.4 Reductions 15
  - 2.4.1 Oracle machines and Turing reducibility 16
  - 2.4.2 The jump operator and jump classes 18
  - 2.4.3 Strong reducibilities 19
  - 2.4.4 Myhill's Theorem 21
- 2.5 The arithmetic hierarchy 23
- 2.6 The Limit Lemma and Post's Theorem 24

2.7 The difference hierarchy 27
2.8 Primitive recursive functions 28
2.9 A note on reductions 29
2.10 The finite extension method 31
2.11 Post's Problem and the finite injury priority method . . 34
2.12 Finite injury arguments of unbounded type 39
2.12.1 The Sacks Splitting Theorem 39
2.12.2 The Pseudo-Jump Theorem 41
2.13 Coding and permitting 42
2.14 The infinite injury priority method 44
2.14.1 Priority trees and guessing 44
2.14.2 The minimal pair method 47
2.14.3 High computably enumerable degrees 53
2.14.4 The Thickness Lemma 56
2.15 The Density Theorem 58
2.16 Jump theorems 64
2.17 Hyperimmune-free degrees 67
2.18 Minimal degrees 70
2.19 Π_1^0 and Σ_1^0 classes 72
2.19.1 Basics 72
2.19.2 Π_n^0 and Σ_n^0 classes 75
2.19.3 Basis theorems 77
2.19.4 Generalizing the low basis theorem 81
2.20 Strong reducibilities and Post's Program 82
2.21 PA degrees 84
2.22 Fixed-point free and diagonally noncomputable functions 87
2.23 Array noncomputability and traceability 93
2.24 Genericity and weak genericity 100

3 Kolmogorov Complexity of Finite Strings 110
3.1 Plain Kolmogorov complexity 110
3.2 Conditional complexity 114
3.3 Symmetry of information 116
3.4 Information-theoretic characterizations of computability 117
3.5 Prefix-free machines and complexity 121
3.6 The KC Theorem 125
3.7 Basic properties of prefix-free complexity 128
3.8 Prefix-free randomness of strings 132
3.9 The Coding Theorem and discrete semimeasures 133
3.10 Prefix-free symmetry of information 134
3.11 Initial segment complexity of sets 136
3.12 Computable bounds for prefix-free complexity 137
3.13 Universal machines and halting probabilities 139
3.14 The conditional complexity of σ^* given σ 143
3.15 Monotone and process complexity 145

3.16 Continuous semimeasures and KM-complexity 150

4 Relating Complexities **154**
4.1 Levin's Theorem relating C and K 154
4.2 Solovay's Theorems relating C and K 155
4.3 Strong K-randomness and C-randomness 161
4.3.1 Positive results 161
4.3.2 Counterexamples 162
4.4 Muchnik's Theorem on C and K 168
4.5 Monotone complexity and KM-complexity 169

5 Effective Reals **197**
5.1 Computable and left-c.e. reals 197
5.2 Real-valued functions 202
5.3 Representing left-c.e. reals 203
5.3.1 Degrees of representations 203
5.3.2 Presentations of left-c.e. reals 206
5.3.3 Presentations and ideals 208
5.3.4 Promptly simple sets and presentations 215
5.4 Left-d.c.e. reals 217
5.4.1 Basics 217
5.4.2 The field of left-d.c.e. reals 219

II Notions of Randomness 225

6 Martin-Löf Randomness **226**
6.1 The computational paradigm 227
6.2 The measure-theoretic paradigm 229
6.3 The unpredictability paradigm 234
6.3.1 Martingales and supermartingales 234
6.3.2 Supermartingales and continuous semimeasures . 238
6.3.3 Martingales and optimality 239
6.3.4 Martingale processes 241
6.4 Relativizing randomness 245
6.5 Ville's Theorem 246
6.6 The Ample Excess Lemma 250
6.7 Plain complexity and randomness 252
6.8 n-randomness 254
6.9 Van Lambalgen's Theorem 257
6.10 Effective 0-1 laws 259
6.11 Infinitely often maximally complex sets 260
6.12 Randomness for other measures and degree-invariance . . 263
6.12.1 Generalizing randomness to other measures . . . 263
6.12.2 Computable measures and representing reals . . . 265

7 Other Notions of Algorithmic Randomness 269
7.1 Computable randomness and Schnorr randomness 270
7.1.1 Basics 270
7.1.2 Limitations 275
7.1.3 Computable measure machines 277
7.1.4 Computable randomness and tests 279
7.1.5 Bounded machines and computable randomness . 281
7.1.6 Process complexity and computable randomness . 282
7.2 Weak n-randomness 285
7.2.1 Basics 285
7.2.2 Characterizations of weak 1-randomness 290
7.2.3 Schnorr randomness via Kurtz null tests 293
7.2.4 Weakly 1-random left-c.e. reals 295
7.2.5 Solovay genericity and randomness 296
7.3 Decidable machines 298
7.4 Selection revisited 301
7.4.1 Stochasticity 301
7.4.2 Partial computable martingales and stochasticity 303
7.4.3 A martingale characterization of stochasticity . . 308
7.5 Nonmonotonic randomness 309
7.5.1 Nonmonotonic betting strategies 309
7.5.2 Van Lambalgen's Theorem revisited 313
7.6 Demuth randomness 315
7.7 Difference randomness 316
7.8 Finite randomness 318
7.9 Injective and permutation randomness 319

8 Algorithmic Randomness and Turing Reducibility 323
8.1 Π^0_1 classes of 1-random sets 324
8.2 Computably enumerable degrees 324
8.3 The Kučera-Gács Theorem 325
8.4 A "no gap" theorem for 1-randomness 327
8.5 Kučera coding 330
8.6 Demuth's Theorem 333
8.7 Randomness relative to other measures 334
8.8 Randomness and PA degrees 336
8.9 Mass problems 344
8.10 DNC degrees and subsets of random sets 347
8.11 High degrees and separating notions of randomness . . . 349
8.11.1 High degrees and computable randomness 349
8.11.2 Separating notions of randomness 350
8.11.3 When van Lambalgen's Theorem fails 357
8.12 Measure theory and Turing reducibility 358
8.13 n-randomness and weak n-randomness 360
8.14 Every 2-random set is GL_1 363

8.15 Stillwell's Theorem 364
8.16 DNC degrees and autocomplexity 366
8.17 Randomness and n-fixed-point freeness 370
8.18 Jump inversion 373
8.19 Pseudo-jump inversion 376
8.20 Randomness and genericity 378
8.20.1 Similarities between randomness and genericity . 378
8.20.2 n-genericity versus n-randomness 379
8.21 Properties of almost all degrees 381
8.21.1 Hyperimmunity 381
8.21.2 Bounding 1-generics 383
8.21.3 Every 2-random set is CEA 386
8.21.4 Where 1-generic degrees are downward dense . . 394

III Relative Randomness **403**

9 Measures of Relative Randomness **404**
9.1 Solovay reducibility 405
9.2 The Kučera-Slaman Theorem 408
9.3 Presentations of left-c.e. reals and complexity 411
9.4 Solovay functions and 1-randomness 412
9.5 Solovay degrees of left-c.e. reals 413
9.6 cl-reducibility and rK-reducibility 419
9.7 K-reducibility and C-reducibility 425
9.8 Density and splittings 427
9.9 Monotone degrees and density 432
9.10 Further relationships between reducibilities 433
9.11 A minimal rK-degree 437
9.12 Complexity and completeness for left-c.e. reals 439
9.13 cl-reducibility and the Kučera-Gács Theorem 441
9.14 Further properties of cl-reducibility 442
9.14.1 cl-reducibility and joins 442
9.14.2 Array noncomputability and joins 444
9.14.3 Left-c.e. reals cl-reducible to versions of Ω 447
9.14.4 cl-degrees of versions of Ω 454
9.15 K-degrees, C-degrees, and Turing degrees 456
9.16 The structure of the monotone degrees 459
9.17 Schnorr reducibility 462

10 Complexity and Relative Randomness for 1-Randoms Sets **464**
10.1 Uncountable lower cones in $\leqslant_K$ and $\leqslant_C$ 464
10.2 The K-complexity of Ω and other 1-random sets 466
10.2.1 $K(A \upharpoonright n)$ versus $K(n)$ for 1-random sets A 466
10.2.2 The rate of convergence of Ω and the α function . 467

10.2.3 Comparing complexities of 1-random sets 468
10.2.4 Limit complexities and relativized complexities . 471
10.3 Van Lambalgen reducibility 473
10.3.1 Basic properties of the van Lambalgen degrees . . 474
10.3.2 Relativized randomness and Turing reducibility . 475
10.3.3 vL-reducibility, K-reducibility, and joins 476
10.3.4 vL-reducibility and C-reducibility 478
10.3.5 Contrasting vL-reducibility and K-reducibility . . 479
10.4 Upward oscillations and $\leqslant_K$-comparable 1-random sets . 481
10.5 LR-reducibility 489
10.6 Almost everywhere domination 495

11 Randomness-Theoretic Weakness 500
11.1 K-triviality 500
11.1.1 The basic K-triviality construction 501
11.1.2 The requirement-free version 502
11.1.3 Solovay functions and K-triviality 504
11.1.4 Counting the K-trivial sets 505
11.2 Lowness 507
11.3 Degrees of K-trivial sets 511
11.3.1 A first approximation: wtt-incompleteness 511
11.3.2 A second approximation: impossible constants . . 512
11.3.3 The less impossible case 514
11.4 K-triviality and lowness 518
11.5 Cost functions 526
11.6 The ideal of K-trivial degrees 529
11.7 Bases for 1-randomness 531
11.8 ML-covering, ML-cupping, and related notions 534
11.9 Lowness for weak 2-randomness 536
11.10 Listing the K-trivial sets 538
11.11 Upper bounds for the K-trivial sets 541
11.12 A gap phenomenon for K-triviality 550

12 Lowness and Triviality for Other Randomness Notions 554
12.1 Schnorr lowness 554
12.1.1 Lowness for Schnorr tests 554
12.1.2 Lowness for Schnorr randomness 559
12.1.3 Lowness for computable measure machines 561
12.2 Schnorr triviality 564
12.2.1 Degrees of Schnorr trivial sets 564
12.2.2 Schnorr triviality and strong reducibilities 568
12.2.3 Characterizing Schnorr triviality 569
12.3 Tracing weak truth table degrees 576
12.3.1 Basics 576
12.3.2 Reducibilities with tiny uses 576

12.3.3 Anti-complex sets and tiny uses 578
12.3.4 Anti-complex sets and Schnorr triviality 580
12.4 Lowness for weak genericity and randomness 581
12.5 Lowness for computable randomness 586
12.6 Lowness for pairs of randomness notions 590

13 Algorithmic Dimension **592**
13.1 Classical Hausdorff dimension 592
13.2 Hausdorff dimension via gales 594
13.3 Effective Hausdorff dimension 596
13.4 Shift complex sets 601
13.5 Partial randomness 602
13.6 A correspondence principle for effective dimension 607
13.7 Hausdorff dimension and complexity extraction 608
13.8 A Turing degree of nonintegral Hausdorff dimension . . . 611
13.9 DNC functions and effective Hausdorff dimension 618
13.9.1 Dimension in h-spaces 619
13.9.2 Slow-growing DNC functions and dimension . . . 623
13.10 C-independence and Zimand's Theorem 627
13.11 Other notions of dimension 635
13.11.1 Box counting dimension 635
13.11.2 Effective box counting dimension 636
13.11.3 Packing dimension 638
13.11.4 Effective packing dimension 641
13.12 Packing dimension and complexity extraction 642
13.13 Clumpy trees and minimal degrees 645
13.14 Building sets of high packing dimension 648
13.15 Computable dimension and Schnorr dimension 654
13.15.1 Basics 654
13.15.2 Examples of Schnorr dimension 657
13.15.3 A machine characterization of Schnorr dimension 658
13.15.4 Schnorr dimension and computable enumerability 659
13.16 The dimensions of individual strings 662

IV Further Topics 667

14 Strong Jump Traceability **668**
14.1 Basics 668
14.2 The ideal of strongly jump traceable c.e. sets 672
14.3 Strong jump traceability and K-triviality: the c.e. case . 680
14.4 Strong jump traceability and diamond classes 689
14.5 Strong jump traceability and K-triviality: the general case 700

15 Ω as an Operator **705**

15.1 Introduction 705
15.2 Omega operators 707
15.3 A-1-random A-left-c.e. reals 709
15.4 Reals in the range of some Omega operator 711
15.5 Lowness for Ω 712
15.6 Weak lowness for K 713
15.6.1 Weak lowness for K and lowness for Ω 714
15.6.2 Infinitely often strongly K-random sets 715
15.7 When Ω^A is a left-c.e. real 716
15.8 Ω^A for K-trivial A 719
15.9 K-triviality and left-d.c.e. reals 722
15.10 Analytic behavior of Omega operators 722

16 Complexity of Computably Enumerable Sets 728
16.1 Barzdins' Lemma and Kummer complex sets 728
16.2 The entropy of computably enumerable sets 731
16.3 The collection of nonrandom strings 738
16.3.1 The plain and conditional cases 738
16.3.2 The prefix-free case 743
16.3.3 The overgraphs of universal monotone machines . 752
16.3.4 The strict process complexity case 761

References 767

Index 797

Preface

Though we did not know it at the time, this book's genesis began with the arrival of Cris Calude in New Zealand. Cris has always had an intense interest in algorithmic information theory. The event that led to much of the recent research presented here was the articulation by Cris of a seemingly innocuous question. This question goes back to Solovay's legendary manuscript [371], and Downey learned of it during a visit made to Victoria University in early 2000 by Richard Coles, who was then a postdoctoral fellow with Calude at Auckland University. In effect, the question was whether the Solovay degrees of left-computably enumerable reals are dense.

At the time, neither of us knew much about Kolmogorov complexity, but we had a distinct interest in it after Lance Fortnow's illuminating lectures [148] at Kaikoura[1] in January 2000. After thinking about Calude's question for a while, and eventually solving it together with André Nies [116], we began to realize that there was a huge and remarkably fascinating area of research, whose potential was largely untapped, lying at the intersection of computability theory and the theory of algorithmic randomness.

We also found that, while there is a truly classic text on Kolmogorov complexity, namely Li and Vitányi [248], most of the questions we were in-

[1]Kaikoura was the setting for a wonderful meeting on computational complexity. There is a set of lecture notes [112] resulting from this meeting, aimed at graduate students. Kaikoura is on the east coast of the South Island of New Zealand, and is famous for its beauty and for tourist activities such as whale watching and dolphin, seal, and shark swimming. The name "Kaikoura" is a Maori word meaning "eat crayfish", which is a fine piece of advice.

terested in either were open, were exercises in Li and Vitányi with difficulty ratings of about 40-something (out of 50), or necessitated an archaeological dig into the depths of a literature with few standards in notation[2] and terminology, marked by relentless rediscovery of theorems and a significant amount of unpublished material. Particularly noteworthy among the unpublished material was the aforementioned set of notes by Solovay [371], which contained absolutely fundamental results about Kolmogorov complexity in general, and about initial segment complexity of sets in particular. As our interests broadened, we also became aware of important results from Stuart Kurtz' PhD dissertation [228], which, like most of Solovay's results, seemed unlikely ever to be published in a journal. Meanwhile, a large number of other authors started to make great strides in our understanding of algorithmic randomness.

Thus, we decided to try to organize results on the relationship between algorithmic randomness and computability theory into a coherent book. We were especially thankful for Solovay's permission to present, in most cases for the first time, the details from his unpublished notes.[3] We were encouraged by the support of Springer in this enterprise.

Naturally, this project has conformed to Hofstadter's Law: It always takes longer than you expect, even when you take into account Hofstadter's Law. Part of the reason for this delay is that a large contingent of gifted researchers continued to relentlessly prove theorems that made it necessary to rewrite large sections of the book.[4] We think it is safe to say that the study of algorithmic randomness and dimension is now one of the most active areas of research in mathematical logic. Even in a book this size, much has necessarily been left out. To those who feel slighted by these omissions, or by inaccuracies in attribution caused by our necessarily imperfect historical knowledge, we apologize in advance, and issue a heartfelt invitation to write their own books. Any who might feel inclined to thank us will find a suggestion for an appropriate gift on page 517.

This is *not* a basic text on Kolmogorov complexity. We concentrate on the Kolmogorov complexity of sets (i.e., infinite sequences) and cover only as much as we need on the complexity of finite strings. There is quite a lot of background material in computability theory needed for some of the more sophisticated proofs we present, so we do give a full but, by necessity, rapid refresher course in basic "advanced" computability theory. This material

---

[2]We hope to help standardize notation. In particular, we have fixed upon the notation for Kolmogorov complexity used by Li and Vitányi: C for plain Kolmogorov complexity and K for prefix-free Kolmogorov complexity.

[3]Of course, Li and Vitányi used Solovay's notes extensively, mostly in the exercises and for quoting results.

[4]It is an unfortunate consequence of working on a book that attempts to cover a significant portion of a rapidly expanding area of research that one begins to hate one's most productive colleagues a little.

should not be read from beginning to end. Rather, the reader should dip into Chapter 2 as the need arises. For a fuller introduction, see for instance Rogers [334], Soare [366], Odifreddi [310, 311], or Cooper [79].

We will mostly avoid historical comments, particularly about events predating our entry into this area of research. The history of the evolution of Kolmogorov complexity and related topics can make certain people rather agitated, and we feel neither competent nor masochistic enough to enter the fray. What seems clear is that, at some stage, time was ripe for the evolution of the ideas needed for Kolmogorov complexity. There is no doubt that many of the basic ideas were implicit in Solomonoff [369], and that many of the fundamental results are due to Kolmogorov [211]. The measure-theoretic approach was pioneered by Martin-Löf [259]. Many key results were established by Levin in works such as [241, 242, 243, 425] and by Schnorr [348, 349, 350], particularly those using the measure of domains to avoid the problems of plain complexity in addressing the initial segment complexity of sets. It is but a short step from there to prefix-free complexity (and discrete semimeasures), first articulated by Levin [243] and Chaitin [58]. Schnorr's penetrating ideas, only some of which are available in their original form in English, are behind much modern work in computational complexity, as well as Lutz' approach to effective Hausdorff dimension in [252, 254], which is based on martingales and orders. As has often been the case in this area, however, Lutz developed his material without being too aware of Schnorr's work, and was apparently the first to explicitly connect orders and Hausdorff dimension. From yet another perspective, martingales, or rather supermartingales, are essentially the same as continuous semimeasures, and again we see the penetrating insight of Levin (see [425]).

We are particularly pleased to present the results of Kurtz and Solovay mentioned above, as well as hitherto unpublished material from Steve Kautz' dissertation [200] and the fundamental work of Antonin Kučera. Kučera was a real pioneer in connecting computability and randomness, and we believe that it is only recently that the community has really appreciated his deep intuition.

Algorithmic randomness is a highly active field, and still has many fascinating open questions and unexplored directions of research. Recent lists of open questions include Miller and Nies [278] and the problem list [2] arising from a workshop organized by Hirschfeldt and Miller at the American Institute of Mathematics in 2006. Several of the questions on these lists have already been solved, however, with many of the solutions appearing in this book. We will mention a number of open questions below, some specific, some more open ended. The pages on which these occur are listed in the index under the heading *open question*.

Acknowledgments

Our foremost acknowledgment is to the Marsden Fund of New Zealand. There is no question that this work would not have happened without its generous support. Hirschfeldt was Downey's Marsden Postdoctoral Fellow when the work that eventually led to this book began. George Barmpalias, Laurent Bienvenu, Richard Coles, Noam Greenberg (now a faculty member at VUW), Evan Griffiths, Geoff LaForte, Joe Miller, and Antonio Montalbán have also been Downey's Marsden Postdoctoral Fellows. Keng Meng Ng, Adam Day, and Andrew Fitzgerald were supported by the Marsden Fund as Downey's PhD students. Downey has also received direct Marsden support for the period of the writing of this book, as has André Nies, whose work appears throughout the text. As mentioned in the preface, our early interest in Kolmogorov complexity was stimulated by a talk given by Lance Fortnow at a conference in Kaikoura almost completely supported by the Marsden Fund, via the New Zealand Mathematical Research Institute.[5] Downey and Liang Yu have also been supported by the New Zealand

[5]This institute is a virtual one, and was the brainchild of Vaughan Jones. After receiving the Fields Medal, among other accolades, Vaughan has devoted his substantial influence to bettering New Zealand mathematics. The visionary NZMRI was founded with this worthy goal in mind. It runs annual workshops at picturesque locations, each devoted to a specific area of mathematics. These involve lecture series by overseas experts aimed at graduate students, and are fully funded for New Zealand attendees. The 2009 workshop, held in Napier, was devoted to algorithmic information theory, computability, and complexity, and Hirschfeldt was one of the speakers. The NZMRI is chaired by Vaughan Jones, and has as its other directors Downey and the uniformly excellent Marston Conder, David Gauld, and Gaven Martin.

Institute for Mathematics and its Applications, a recent CoRE (Centre of Research Excellence) that grew from the NZMRI, with Yu being Downey's postdoctoral fellow supported by the logic and computability programme of this CoRE. As a postdoctoral fellow, Guohua Wu was supported by the New Zealand Foundation for Research Science and Technology, having previously been supported by the Marsden Fund as Downey's PhD student. Stephanie Reid received similar support from the Marsden Fund for her MSc thesis. Finally, many visitors and temporary fellows at VUW have been supported by the Marsden Fund, and sometimes the ISAT Linkages programme, including Eric Allender, Veronica Becher, Peter Cholak, Barbara Csima, Carl Jockusch, Steffen Lempp, Andy Lewis, Jan Reimann, Ted Slaman, Sebastiaan Terwijn, and Rebecca Weber, among others.

Downey received a Maclaurin Fellowship from the NZIMA as part of the Logic and Computation programme, and a James Cook Fellowship from the New Zealand government for 2008–2010, both of which were important in supporting his work on this book.

We also owe substantial thanks to the National Science Foundation of the United States. Hirschfeldt's research has been supported by NSF grants throughout the period of the writing of this book, including a Focused Research Group grant on algorithmic randomness involving researchers from around a dozen institutions in the United States, who together have produced a significant portion of the research presented here. Among many activities, this FRG grant has funded important workshops in the area, in Chicago in 2008, Madison in 2009, and South Bend in 2010. The group of researchers involved in this project first came together at a workshop organized by Hirschfeldt and Joe Miller at the American Institute of Mathematics. The NSF has also funded many visitors to the University of Chicago, including Downey, who has also been funded by the NSF for visits to other institutions in the United States.

Many colleagues have helped us by sending in corrections and suggestions, by helping us with various aspects of the production of this book, and by generously sharing their results and ideas. Although errors and infelicities no doubt remain, and are entirely our responsibility, the text has benefited enormously from their assistance. With apologies to those we may have forgotten, we thank Eric Allender, Klaus Ambos-Spies, Bernie Anderson, Uri Andrews, Asat Arslanov, George Barmpalias, Veronica Becher, Laurent Bienvenu, Paul Brodhead, Cris Calude, Douglas Cenzer, Gregory Chaitin, Peter Cholak, Chi Tat Chong, Richard Coles, Chris Conidis, Barry Cooper, Barbara Csima, Adam Day, Ding Decheng, Jean-Paul Delahaye, David Diamondstone, Damir Dzhafarov, Santiago Figueira, Andrew Fitzgerald, Lance Fortnow, Johanna Franklin, Peter Gács, Noam Greenberg, Evan Griffiths, John Hitchcock, Carl Jockusch, Asher Kach, Bakh Khoussainov, Bjørn Kjos-Hanssen, Julia Knight, Antonin Kučera, Geoff LaForte, Steffen Lempp, Leonid Levin, Jack Lutz, Elvira Mayordomo, Wolfgang Merkle, Joe Mileti, Joe Miller, Antonio Montalbán, André Nies,

Keng Meng Ng, Chris Porter, Alex Raichev, Jan Reimann, Jeffrey Remmel, Alexander Shen, Richard Shore, Ted Slaman, Bob Soare, Robert Solovay, Frank Stephan, Jonathan Stephenson, Dan Turetsky, Nikolai Vereshchagin, Paul Vitányi, Rebecca Weber, Guohua Wu, Cathryn Young, Yang Yue, Liang Yu, Xizhong Zheng, and Marius Zimand.

We also thank the staff at Springer for all their help with the preparation of this book, and for their patience during this rather lengthy process. Particular thanks go to Ronan Nugent and Vaishali Damle. We are proud to inaugurate the CiE-Springer book series *Theory and Applications of Computability*, and thank the Computability in Europe Association, and particularly series editors Elvira Mayordomo and Barry Cooper. Finally, we thank the anonymous reviewers for their many valuable suggestions.

Introduction

What does it mean to say that an individual mathematical object such as an infinite binary sequence is random? Or to say that one sequence is more random than another? These are the most basic questions motivating the work we describe in this book. Once we have reasonable tools for measuring the randomness of infinite sequences, however, other questions present themselves: If we divide our sequences into equivalence classes of sequences of the same "degree of randomness", what does the resulting structure look like? How do various possible notions of randomness relate to each other and to the measures of complexity used in computability theory and algorithmic information theory, and to what uses can they be put? Should it be the case that high levels of randomness mean high levels of complexity or computational power, or low ones? Should the structures of computability theory such as Turing degrees and computably enumerable sets have anything to do with randomness? The material in this book arises from questions such as these. Much of it can be thought of as exploring the relationships between three fundamental concepts: relative computability, as measured by notions such as Turing reducibility; information content, as measured by notions such as Kolmogorov complexity; and randomness of individual objects, as first successfully defined by Martin-Löf (but prefigured by others, dating back at least to the work of von Mises). While some fundamental questions remain open, we now have a reasonable insight into many of the above questions, and the resulting body of work contains a number of beautiful and rather deep theorems.

When considering sequences such as

$$101010101010101010101010101010101010\ldots$$

and

$$101101011101010111100001010100010111\ldots,$$

none but the most contrarian among us would deny that the second (obtained by the first author by tossing a coin) is more random than the first. However, in measure-theoretic terms, they are both equally likely. Furthermore, what are we to make in this context of, say, the sequence obtained by taking our first sequence, tossing a coin for each bit in the sequence, and, if the coin comes up heads, replacing that bit by the corresponding one in the second sequence? There are deep and fundamental questions involved in trying to understand why some sequences should count as "random" and others as "lawful", and how we can transform our intuitions about these concepts into meaningful mathematical notions.

The roots of the study of algorithmic randomness go back to the work of Richard von Mises in the early 20th century. In his remarkable paper [402], he argued that a sequence should count as random if all "reasonable" infinite subsequences satisfy the law of large numbers (i.e., have the same proportion of 0's as 1's in the limit). This behavior is certainly to be expected of any intuitively random sequence. A sequence such as $1010101010\ldots$ should not count as random because, although it itself satisfies the law of large numbers, it contains easily described subsequences that do not. Von Mises wrote of "acceptable selection rules" for subsequences. Wald [403, 404] later showed that for any countable collection of selection rules, there are sequences that are random in the sense of von Mises, but at the time it was unclear exactly what types of selection rules should be acceptable. There seemed to von Mises to be no canonical choice.

Later, with the development of computability theory and the introduction of generally accepted precise mathematical definitions of the notions of algorithm and computable function, Church [71] made the first explicit connection between computability theory and randomness by suggesting that a selection rule be considered acceptable iff it is computable. In a sense, this definition of what we now call *Church stochasticity* can be seen as the birth of the theory of *algorithmic* randomness. A blow to the von Mises program was dealt by Ville [401], who showed that for any countable collection of selection rules, there is a sequence that is random in the sense of von Mises but has properties that make it clearly nonrandom. (In Ville's example, the ratio of 0's to 1's in the first n bits of the sequence is at least 1 for all n. If we flip a fair coin, we certainly expect the ratio of heads to tails not only to tend to 1, but also to be sometimes slightly larger and sometimes slightly smaller than 1.)

One might try to get around this problem by adding further specific statistical laws to the law of large numbers in the definition of randomness, but there then seems to be no reason not to expect Ville-like results from reappearing in this modified context. Just because a sequence respects laws A, B, and C, why should we expect it to respect law D? And law D may be one we have overlooked, perhaps one that is complicated to state, but clearly should be respected by any intuitively random sequence. Thus Ville's Theorem caused the situation to revert basically to what it had been before Church's work: intuitively, a sequence should be random if it passes all "reasonable" statistical tests, but how do we make this notion precise? Once again, the answer involved computability theory. In a sweeping generalization, Martin-Löf [259] noted that the particular statistical tests that had been considered (the law of large numbers, the law of iterated logarithms, etc.) were special cases of a general abstract notion of statistical test based on the notion of an "effectively null" set. He then defined a notion of randomness based on passing *all* such tests (or equivalently, not being in any effectively null set).

Martin-Löf's definition turned out to be not only foundationally well-motivated but mathematically robust and productive. Now known as *1-randomness* or *Martin-Löf randomness*, it will be the central notion of randomness in this book, but not the only one. There are certainly other reasonable choices for what counts as "effectively null" than the one taken by Martin-Löf, and many notions of randomness resulting from these choices will be featured here. Furthermore, one of the most attractive features of the notion of 1-randomness is that it can be arrived at from several other approaches, such as the idea that random sequences should be incompressible, and the idea that random sequences should be unpredictable (which was already present in the original motivation behind von Mises' definition). These approaches lead to equivalent definitions of 1-randomness in terms of, for example, prefix-free Kolmogorov complexity and computably enumerable martingales (concepts we will define and discuss in this book). Like Martin-Löf's original definition, these alternative definitions admit variations, again leading to other reasonable notions of algorithmic randomness that we will discuss. The evolution and clarification of many of these notions of randomness is carefully discussed in Michiel van Lambalgen's dissertation [397].

The first five chapters of this book introduce background material that we use throughout the rest of the text, but also present some important related results that are not quite as central to our main topics. Chapter 1 briefly covers basic notation, conventions, and terminology, and introduces a small amount of measure theory. Chapter 2 is a whirlwind tour of computability theory. It assumes nothing but a basic familiarity with a formalism such as Turing machines, at about the level of a first course on "theory of computation", but is certainly not designed to replace dedicated texts such as Soare [366] or Odifreddi [310, 311]. Nevertheless, quite sophisticated computability-theoretic methods have found themselves into the study of algorithmic randomness, so there is a fair amount of material in that chapter. It is probably best thought of as a reference for the rest of the text, possibly only to be scanned at a first reading.

Chapter 3 is an introduction to Kolmogorov complexity, focused on those parts of the theory that will be most useful in the rest of the book. We include proofs of basic results such as counting theorems, symmetry of information, and the Coding Theorem, among others. (A much more general reference is Li and Vitányi [248].) As mentioned above, Martin-Löf's measure-theoretic approach to randomness is not the only one. It can be thought of as arising from the idea that random objects should be "typical". As already touched upon above, two other major approaches we will discuss are through "unpredictability" and "incompressibility". The latter is perhaps the least obvious of the three, and also perhaps the most modern. Nowadays, with file compression a concept well known to many users of computers and other devices involving electronic storage or transmission, it is perhaps not so strange to characterize randomness via incompressibility, but it seems clear that typicality and unpredictability are even more intuitive properties of randomness. Nevertheless, the incompressibility approach had its foundations laid at roughly the same time as Martin-Löf's work, by Kolmogorov [211], and in a sense even earlier by Solomonoff [369], although its application to infinite sequences had to wait a while.

Roughly speaking, the Kolmogorov complexity of a finite string is the length of its shortest description. To formalize this notion, we use universal machines, thought of as "optimal description systems". We then get a good notion of randomness for finite strings: a string σ is random iff the Kolmogorov complexity of σ is no shorter than the length of σ (which we can think of as saying that σ is its own best description). Turning to infinite sequences, however, we have a problem. As we will see in Theorem 3.1.4, there is no infinite sequence all of whose initial segments are incompressible. We can get around this problem by introducing a different notion of Kolmogorov complexity, which is based on machines whose domains are antichains, and corresponds to the idea that if a string τ describes a string σ, then this description should be encoded entirely in the bits of τ, not in its length. In Section 3.5, we further discuss how this notion of *prefix-free* complexity can be seen as capturing the intuitive meaning of Kolmogorov complexity, arguably better than the original definition, and will briefly discuss its history. In Chapter 6 we use it to give a definition of randomness for infinite sequences equivalent to Martin-Löf's.

In Chapter 4, we present for the first time in published form the details of Solovay's remarkable results relating plain and prefix-free Kolmogorov complexity, and related results by Muchnik and Miller. We also present Gács' separation of two other notions of complexity introduced in Chapter 3, a surprisingly difficult result, and a significant extension of that result by Day. Most of the material in this chapter, although quite interesting in itself, will not be used in the rest of the book.

In Chapter 5 we discuss effective real numbers, in particular the left computably enumerable reals, which are those reals that can be computably approximated from below. These reals play a similar role in the theory of algorithmic randomness as the computably enumerable sets in classical computability theory. Many of the central objects in this book (Martin-Löf tests, Kolmogorov complexity, martingales, etc.) have naturally associated left-c.e. reals. A classic example is Chaitin's Ω, which is the measure of the domain of a universal prefix-free machine, and is the canonical example of a specific 1-random real (though, as we will see, it is in many ways not a "typical" 1-random real).

The next three chapters introduce most of the notions of algorithmic randomness we will study and examine their connections to computability theory.

Chapter 6 is dedicated to 1-randomness (and its natural generalization, n-randomness). We introduce the concepts of Martin-Löf test and of martingale, using them, as well as Kolmogorov complexity, to give definitions of randomness in the spirit of the three approaches mentioned above, and prove Schnorr's fundamental theorems that these definitions are equivalent. We also include some fascinating theorems by Miller, Yu, Nies, Stephan, and Terwijn on the relationship between plain Kolmogorov complexity and randomness. These include plain complexity characterizations of both 1-randomness and 2-randomness. We prove Ville's Theorem mentioned above, and introduce some of the most important tools in the study of 1-randomness and its higher level versions, including van Lambalgen's Theorem, effective 0-1 laws, and the Ample Excess Lemma of Miller and Yu. In the last section of this chapter, we briefly examine randomness relative to measures other than the uniform measure, a topic we return to, again briefly, in Chapter 8.

In Chapter 7 we introduce other notions of randomness, mostly based on variations on Martin-Löf's approach and on considering martingales with different levels of effectiveness. Several of these notions were originally motivated by what is now known as *Schnorr's critique*. Schnorr argued that 1-randomness is essentially a computably enumerable, rather than computable, notion and therefore too strong to capture the intuitive notion of randomness relative to "computable tests". We study various notions, including Schnorr randomness and computable randomness, introduced by Schnorr, and weak n-randomness, introduced by Kurtz. We discuss test set, martingale, and machine characterizations of these notions. We also return to the roots of the subject to discuss stochasticity, and study nonmonotonic randomness, which leads us to one of the most basic major open questions in the area: whether nonmonotonic randomness is strictly weaker than 1-randomness.

Chapter 8 is devoted to the interactions between randomness and computability. Highlights include the Kučera-Gács Theorem that any set can be coded into a 1-random set, and hence all degrees above $\mathbf{0}'$ contain 1-random sets; Demuth's Theorem relating 1-randomness and truth table reducibility; Stephan's dichotomy theorem relating 1-randomness and PA degrees; the result by Barmpalias, Lewis, and Ng that each PA degree is the join of two 1-random degrees; and Stillwell's Theorem that the "almost all" theory of the Turing degrees is decidable. We also examine how the ability to compute a fixed-point free function relates to initial segment complexity, discuss jump inversion for 1-random sets, and study the relationship between n-randomness, weak n-randomness, and genericity, among other topics. In addition, we examine the relationship between computational power and separating notions of randomness. For example, we prove the remarkable result of Nies, Stephan, and Terwijn that a degree contains a set that is Schnorr random but not computably random, or one that is computably random but not 1-random, iff it is high. We finish this chapter with Kurtz' results, hitherto available only in his dissertation, on "almost all" properties of the degrees, such as the fact that almost every set is computably enumerable in and above some other set, and versions of some of these results by Kautz (again previously unpublished) converting "for almost all sets" to "for all 2-random sets".

The next five chapters examine notions of relative randomness: What does it mean to say that one sequence is more random than another? Can we make precise the intuition that if we, say, replace the even bits of a 1-random sequence by 0's, the resulting sequence is "$\frac{1}{2}$-random"?

In Chapter 9 we study reducibilities that act as measures of relative randomness, focusing in particular, though not exclusively, on left-c.e. reals. For instance, we prove the result due to Kučera and Slaman that the 1-random left-c.e. reals are exactly the ones that are complete for a strong notion known as *Solovay reducibility*. These reals are also exactly the ones equal to Ω for some choice of universal prefix-free machine, so this result can be seen as an analog to the basic computability-theoretic result that all versions of the halting problem are essentially the same. We also prove that for a large class of reducibilities, the resulting degree structure on left-c.e. reals is dense and has other interesting properties, and discuss a natural but flawed strengthening of weak truth table reducibility known as *cl-reducibility*, and a better-behaved variation on it known as *rK-reducibility*.

In Chapter 10 we focus on reducibilities appropriate for studying the relative randomness of sets already known to be 1-random. We study K- and C-reducibility, basic measures of relative initial segment complexity introduced in the previous chapter, including results by Solovay on the initial segment complexity of 1-random sets, and later echoes of this work, as well as theorems on the structure of the K- and C-degrees. We introduce *van Lambalgen reducibility* and the closely related notion of *LR-reducibility*, and study their basic properties, established by Miller and Yu. We see that vL-reducibility is an excellent tool for studying the relative randomness of 1-random sets. It can be used to prove results about K- and C-reducibilities for which direct proofs seem difficult, and to establish theorems that help make precise the intuition that randomness should be antithetical to computational power. For instance, we show that if $A \leqslant_{\mathrm{T}} B$ are both 1-random, then if B is n-random, so is A. Turning to LR-reducibility (which agrees with vL-reducibility on the 1-random sets but not elsewhere), we introduce an important characterization due to Kjos-Hanssen, discuss structural results due to Barmpalias and others, and prove the equivalence between LR-reducibility and *LK-reducibility*, a result by Kjos-Hanssen, Miller, and Solomon related to the lowness notions mentioned in the following paragraph. We finish the chapter with a discussion of the quite interesting concept of *almost everywhere domination*, which arose in the context of the reverse mathematics of measure theory and turned out to have deep connections with algorithmic randomness.

Chapter 11 is devoted to one of the most important developments in recent work on algorithmic randomness: the realization that there is a class of "randomness-theoretically weak" sets that is as robust and mathematically interesting as the class of 1-random sets. A set A is *K-trivial* if its initial segments have the lowest possible prefix-free complexity (that is, the first n bits of A are no more difficult to describe than the number n itself). It is *low for 1-randomness* if every 1-random set is 1-random relative to A. It is *low for K* if the prefix-free Kolmogorov complexity of any string relative to A is the same as its unrelativized complexity, up to an additive constant. We show that there are noncomputable sets with these properties, and prove Nies' wonderful result that these three notions coincide. In other words, a set has lowest possible information content iff it has no derandomization power iff it has no compression power. We examine several other properties of the K-trivial sets, including the fact that they are very close to being computable, and provide further characterizations of them, in terms of other notions of randomness-theoretic weakness and the important concept of a *cost function*.

In Chapter 12 we study lowness and triviality for other notions of randomness, such as Schnorr and computable randomness. For instance, we prove results of Terwijn and Zambella, and Kjos-Hanssen, Nies, and Stephan, characterizing lowness for Schnorr randomness in terms of traceability, and Nies' result that there are no noncomputable sets that are low for computable randomness. We also study the analog of K-triviality for Schnorr randomness, including a characterization of Schnorr triviality by Franklin and Stephan.

Chapter 13 deals with algorithmic dimension. Lutz realized that Hausdorff dimension can be characterized using martingales, and used that insight to define a notion of *effective Hausdorff dimension*. This notion turns out to be closely related to notions of partial randomness that allow us to say, for example, that certain sets are $\frac{1}{2}$-random, and also has a pleasing and useful characterization in terms of Kolmogorov complexity. We also study *effective packing dimension*, which can also be characterized using Kolmogorov complexity, and can be seen as a dual notion to effective Hausdorff dimension. Algorithmic dimension is a large area of research in its own right, but in this chapter we focus on the connections with computability theory. For instance, we can formulate a computability-theoretic version of the quite natural question of whether randomness can be extracted from a partially random source. We prove Miller's result that there is a set of positive effective Hausdorff dimension that does not compute any set of higher effective Hausdorff dimension, the result by Greenberg and Miller that there is a degree of effective Hausdorff dimension 1 that is minimal (and therefore cannot compute a 1-random set), and the contrasting result by Zimand that randomness extraction *is* possible from two sufficiently independent sources of positive effective Hausdorff dimension. We also study the relationship between building sets of high packing dimension and array computability, and study the concept of *Schnorr dimension*. In the last section of this chapter, we look at Lutz' definition of dimension for finite strings and its relationship to Kolmogorov complexity.

The final three chapters cover further results relating randomness, complexity, and computability.

One of the byproducts of the theory of K-triviality has been an increased interest in notions of lowness in computability theory. Chapter 14 discusses the class of *strongly jump traceable* sets, a proper subclass of the K-trivials with deep connections to randomness. In the computably enumerable case, we show that the strongly jump traceable c.e. sets form a proper subideal of the K-trivial c.e. sets, and can be characterized as those c.e. sets that are computable from every ω-c.e. (or every superlow) 1-random set. We also discuss the general (non-c.e.) case, showing that, in fact, *every* strongly jump traceable set is K-trivial.

In Chapter 15 we look at Ω as an operator on Cantor space. In general, our understanding of operators that take each set A to a set that is c.e. relative to A but does not necessarily compute A (as opposed to the more usual "computably enumerable in and above" operators of computability theory) is rather limited. There had been a hope at some point that the Omega operator might turn out to be degree invariant, hence providing a counterexample to a long-standing conjecture of Martin that (roughly speaking) the only degree invariant operators on the degrees are iterates of the jump. However, among other results, we show that there are sets A and B that are equal up to finite differences, but such that Ω^A and Ω^B are relatively 1-random (and hence Turing incomparable). We also establish several other properties of Omega operators due to Downey, Hirschfeldt, Miller, and Nies, including the fact that almost every real is Ω^A for some A, and prove Miller's results that a set is 2-random iff it has infinitely many initial segments of maximal prefix-free Kolmogorov complexity.

Chapter 16 is devoted to the relationship between Kolmogorov complexity and c.e. sets. We prove Kummer's theorem characterizing the Turing degrees that contain c.e. sets of highest possible Kolmogorov complexity, Solovay's theorem relating the complexity of describing a c.e. set to its enumeration probability, and several results on the complexity of c.e. sets naturally associated with notions of Kolmogorov complexity, such as the set of nonrandom strings (in various senses of randomness for strings).

As mentioned in the preface, we have included several open questions and unexplored research directions in the text, which are referenced in the index under the heading *open question*.

Unlike the ideal machines computability theorists consider, authors are limited in both time and space. We have had to leave out many interesting results and research directions (and, of course, we are sure there are several others of which we are simply unaware). There are also entire areas of research that would have fit in with the themes of this book but had to be omitted. One of these is the uses of algorithmic randomness in reverse mathematics. Another, related one, is the growing body of results on converting classical "almost everywhere" results in areas such as probability and dynamical systems into "for all sufficiently random" results (often precise ones, saying, for instance, that a certain statement holds for all 2-random but not all 1-random real numbers). Others come from varying one of three ingredients of algorithmic randomness: the spaces we consider, the measures on those spaces, and the level of effectiveness of our notions. There has been a growing body of research in extending algorithmic randomness to spaces other than Cantor space, defining for example notions of random continuous functions and random closed sets. Even in the context of Cantor space, we only briefly discuss randomness for measures other than the uniform (or Lebesgue) measure (although, for computable continuous measures at least, much of the theory remains unaltered). The interaction between randomness and complexity theory is a topic that could easily fill a book this size by itself, but there are parts of it that are particularly close to the material we cover. Randomness in the context of effective descriptive set theory has also begun to be investigated.

Nevertheless, we hope to give a useful and rich account of the ways computability theorists have found to calibrate randomness for individual elements of Cantor space, and how these relate to traditional measures of complexity, including both computability-theoretic measures of relative computational power such as Turing reducibility and notions from algorithmic information theory such as Kolmogorov complexity. Most of the material we cover is from the last few years, when we have witnessed an explosion of wonderful ideas in the area. This book is our account of what we see as some of the highlights. It naturally reflects our own views of what is important and attractive, but we hope there is enough here to make it useful to a wide range of readers.

Part I

Background

1

Preliminaries

1.1 Notation and conventions

Most of our notation, terminology, and conventions will be introduced as we go along, but we set down here a few basic ones that are used throughout the book.

Strings. Unless specified otherwise, by a *string* we mean a finite binary string. We mostly use lowercase Greek letters toward the middle and end of the alphabet for strings. We denote the set of finite binary strings by $2^{<\omega}$, the set of binary strings of length n by 2^n, and the set of binary strings of length less than or equal to n by $2^{\leqslant n}$. We denote the empty string by λ, the length of a string σ by $|\sigma|$, and the concatenation of strings σ and τ by either $\sigma\tau$ or $\sigma^\frown\tau$.

The *length-lexicographic ordering* on $2^{<\omega}$ is defined by saying that σ is less than τ (written $\sigma <_{\mathrm{L}} \tau$) if either $|\sigma| < |\tau|$ or else both $|\sigma| = |\tau|$ and $\sigma(n) = 0$ for the least n such that $\sigma(n) \neq \tau(n)$.

Sets, sequences, and reals. Unless specified otherwise or clear from context, by a *set* we mean a set of natural numbers, by a *sequence* we mean an infinite binary sequence, and by a *real* we mean a real number in $[0, 1]$. For us, these three classes of objects are essentially the same, and we use them interchangeably. That is, we identify a set A with its characteristic function χ_A. (So, for instance, $A(n) = 1$ and $n \in A$ mean the same thing.) We then also identify A with the infinite binary sequence $A(0)A(1)\ldots$ and with the real $0.A(0)A(1)\ldots$. We mostly use uppercase Roman letters or lowercase Greek letters toward the beginning of the alphabet for sets.

R.G. Downey and D. Hirschfeldt, *Algorithmic Randomness and Complexity*, Theory and Applications of Computability, DOI 10.1007/978-0-387-68441-3_1,

The fact that there are reals with more than one binary expansion will for the most part not matter to us, but in any case we make the following convention, which saves some work in proofs where we do not want to treat the rational case in some nonuniform manner, and do not wish to fuss about nonunique representations. In all cases, dealing with the rational case is completely straightforward, and omitting it is just a matter of convenience.

Convention 1.1.1. Unless mentioned otherwise or clear from context, we assume that all reals are irrational, and hence have unique binary representations.

We denote the natural numbers by $\mathbb{N}$ or ω interchangeably, and the *Cantor space* of infinite binary sequences by 2^ω. We will discuss this space further in the next section.

We use standard set-theoretic notation, but mention here some notation that may be lesser-known. We write $A =^* B$ to mean that $A(n) = B(n)$ for all but finitely many n. We write $A \upharpoonright n$ to mean the restriction of A to its first n bits (that is, the string $A(0) \dots A(n-1)$), which we often identify with the finite set $\{m < n : m \in A\}$. More generally, $A \upharpoonright S$ is the restriction of A to the bits in S. We write $\overline{A}$ for the complement $\mathbb{N} \setminus A$ of A.

For a set A of pairs, the *domain* of A, denoted by $\operatorname{dom} A$, is the set of all x such that $(x, y) \in A$ for some y.

We fix a 1-1 function taking a sequence of natural numbers $(n_0, \dots, n_k)$ to a natural number $\langle n_0, \dots, n_k \rangle$, and a canonical listing $D_0, D_1, \dots$ of the finite sets. (The only thing that matters here is that we can effectively recover $(n_0, \dots, n_k)$ from $\langle n_0, \dots, n_k \rangle$ and D_n from n. That is, these functions are computable in the sense of the next chapter.)

When considering $\max S$ for a set S, we adopt the convention that the max of an empty set is 0.

We use the notation $[x, y]$ for a closed interval (in $\mathbb{N}$ or $\mathbb{R}$), (x, y) for an open interval, and $(x, y]$ and $[x, y)$ for half-open intervals.

Let $A^{[e]} = \{\langle e, n \rangle : \langle e, n \rangle \in A\}$. We call $A^{[e]}$ the *eth column* of A.

Functions. For a function f, we write $f^{(k)}$ to mean f composed with itself k many times. Thus, for example $\log^{(2)} n$ means $\log \log n$. By convention, $f^{(0)}$ is the identity function.

When we write $\log n$, we mean the base 2 logarithm of n, rounded up to the nearest larger integer. By convention, $\log 0 = 0$.

The *graph* of a function f is the set $\{(x, y) : f(x) = y\}$.

For functions $f, g, h : \mathbb{N} \to \mathbb{N}$, we write:

(i) $f(n) \leqslant g(n) + O(h(n))$ to mean that there is a constant c such that $f(n) \leqslant g(n) + c \cdot h(n)$ for all n,

(ii) $f(n) = g(n) \pm O(h(n))$ to mean that $f(n) \leqslant g(n) + O(h(n))$ and $g(n) \leqslant f(n) + O(h(n))$, and

(iii) $f(n) \leqslant g(n) + o(h(n))$ to mean that $\lim_n \frac{f(n)-g(n)}{h(n)} = 0$.

We say that f and g are *asymptotically equal* if $\lim_n \frac{f(n)}{g(n)} = 1$, and write $f \sim g$ to mean that $f(n) = O(g(n))$ and $g(n) = O(f(n))$.

Note that, in particular, $f(n) = O(h(n))$ means that there is a constant c such that $f(n) \leqslant c \cdot h(n)$ for all n. Similarly, $f(n) = o(h(n))$ means that $\lim_n \frac{f(n)}{h(n)} = 0$.

Sometimes, when we write an expression such as $f(n) \leqslant g(n) + O(h(n))$, there is an extra additive constant on the right-hand side. Such a constant is of course absorbed into the $O(h(n))$ term, but only if $h(n) > 0$. So we make it a convention that, even if $h(n) = 0$, the $O(h(n))$ term is at least $O(1)$, and hence still absorbs the constant.

We also use this notation for other kinds of functions, such as functions from $2^{<\omega}$ to $\mathbb{N}$, in an analogous way.

Logical notation. We will use standard logical notation, including the quantifiers $\exists^\infty$ for "there exist infinitely many", $\forall^\infty$ for "for all but finitely many", and $\exists^{\geqslant k}$ for "there exist at least k many". We also use the usual λ and μ notation: $\lambda x\, f(x, y_0, \ldots, y_n)$ is the function $x \mapsto f(x, y_0, \ldots, y_n)$ for fixed values $y_0, \ldots, y_n$ and $\mu n\, R(n)$ is the least n such that $R(n)$ holds.

Lattices. Let $(P, \leqslant)$ be a partial order. We say that $z \in P$ is the *join* of $x, y \in P$ if $x, y \leqslant z$ and $x, y \leqslant w \Rightarrow z \leqslant w$. The join of x and y is denoted by $x \vee y$. We say that $z \in P$ is the *meet* of $x, y \in P$ if $x, y \geqslant z$ and $x, y \geqslant w \Rightarrow z \geqslant w$. The meet of x and y is denoted by $x \wedge y$. If every pair of elements of P has a join, then $(P, \leqslant)$ is an *uppersemilattice*. If every pair of elements of P has a meet, then $(P, \leqslant)$ is a *lowersemilattice*. If both conditions obtain, then $(P, \leqslant)$ is a *lattice*. An *ideal* in an uppersemilattice $(P, \leqslant)$ is a subset of P that is closed downward and under joins.

1.2 Basics from measure theory

We assume familiarity with the basic concepts of measure theory as given in initial segments of texts such as Oxtoby [313], but review a few important facts in this section. For simplicity of presentation, we study the Cantor space 2^ω of infinite binary sequences. For $\sigma \in 2^{<\omega}$ we denote by $[\![\sigma]\!]$ the set of all extensions of σ in 2^ω. That is, $[\![\sigma]\!] = \{\sigma X : X \in 2^\omega\}$. For $A \subseteq 2^{<\omega}$ we let $[\![A]\!] = \bigcup_{\sigma \in A} [\![\sigma]\!]$. We say that A *generates* (or *is a set of generators of*) $[\![A]\!]$.

The (sub-)basic open sets of Cantor space are $[\![\sigma]\!]$ for $\sigma \in 2^{<\omega}$. In this topology these sets are clopen, and the clopen sets are finite unions of such basic open sets. Although the real unit interval is not homeomorphic to 2^ω with this topology, it is well known that the two spaces are isomorphic in the measure-theoretic sense. (See also Convention 1.1.1.)

The (uniform or Lebesgue) measure of a basic open set $[\![\sigma]\!]$ is $\mu([\![\sigma]\!]) = 2^{-|\sigma|}$. A sequence of basic open sets $\{[\![\sigma]\!] : \sigma \in A\}$ is said to *cover* a set $C \subseteq 2^\omega$ if $C \subseteq [\![A]\!]$. The *outer measure* of C is

$$\mu^*(C) = \inf\left\{\sum_n 2^{-|\sigma_n|} : \{[\![\sigma_n]\!] : n \in \mathbb{N}\} \text{ covers } C\right\}.$$

The *inner measure* of C is $\mu_*(C) = 1 - \mu^*(\overline{C})$, where $\overline{C}$ is the complement $2^\omega \setminus C$ of C. If C is measurable, then $\mu^*(C) = \mu_*(C)$, and we refer to this quantity as the *measure* $\mu(C)$ of C. *Null sets* are those that have measure 0. A set C has measure 0 iff there is a sequence of open covers of C whose measure goes to 0, that is, a collection $\{V_n\}_{n\in\omega}$ of open sets such that $\lim_n \mu(V_n) = 0$ and $C \subseteq \bigcap_n V_n$ We will later effectivize this notion when we look at Martin-Löf randomness in Chapter 6. We will also effectivize the following fact, known as the (First) Borel-Cantelli Lemma.

Theorem 1.2.1 (Borel-Cantelli Lemma). *Let $\{C_n\}_{n\in\omega}$ be a sequence of measurable sets such that $\sum_n \mu(C_n) < \infty$. Then $\mu(\{X : \exists^\infty n\,(X \in C_n)\}) = 0$.*

Proof. Let $D = \{X : \exists^\infty n\,(X \in C_n)\}$. Choose a sequence $n_0, n_1, \ldots$ such that $\sum_{j\geqslant n_i} \mu(C_j) \leqslant 2^{-i}$. For each i, we have $D \subseteq \bigcup_{j\geqslant n_i} C_j$, so D is a null set. □

The following (simplified version of a) classical fact from measure theory, known as the Lebesgue Density Theorem, will be used often in this book. It implies that for every set A of positive measure there are basic open sets within which the measure of A appears to be arbitrarily close to 1. As we will see, this is the critical fact allowing for the existence of 0-1 laws in degree theory. Our proof follows the one in Terwijn [387].

Definition 1.2.2. A measurable set A has *density d at $X \in 2^\omega$* if

$$\lim_n 2^n \mu(A \cap [\![X \upharpoonright n]\!]) = d.$$

Let $D(A) = \{X : A \text{ has density 1 at } X\}$.

Theorem 1.2.3 (Lebesgue Density Theorem). *If A is measurable then so is $D(A)$. Furthermore, the measure of the symmetric difference of A and $D(A)$ is 0, so $\mu(D(A)) = \mu(A)$.*

Thus, if $\mu(A) > 0$ then for any $q < 1$ there is a σ such that the relative measure $\frac{\mu(A\cap[\![\sigma]\!])}{\mu([\![\sigma]\!])}$ is greater than q.

Proof. It suffices to show that $A - D(A)$ is a null set, since $D(A) - A \subseteq \overline{A} - D(\overline{A})$ and $\overline{A}$ is measurable. For $\varepsilon \in \mathbb{Q}^+$, let

$$B_\varepsilon = \{X \in A : \liminf_n 2^n \mu(A \cap [\![X \upharpoonright n]\!]) < 1 - \varepsilon\}.$$

Then $A - D(A) = \bigcup_\varepsilon B_\varepsilon$, so it suffices to show that each B_ε is null.

Suppose for a contradiction that there is an ε such that B_ε is not null, that is, $\mu^*(B_\varepsilon) > 0$. It is easy to see that $\mu^*(B_\varepsilon) = \inf\{\mu(U) : B_\varepsilon \subseteq U \wedge U \text{ open}\}$, so there is an open set $U \supseteq B_\varepsilon$ such that $(1-\varepsilon)\mu(U) < \mu^*(B_\varepsilon)$. Let

$$I = \{\sigma : [\![\sigma]\!] \subseteq U \wedge \mu(A \cap [\![\sigma]\!]) < (1-\varepsilon)2^{-|\sigma|}\}.$$

Then the following facts hold.

(i) If $X \in B_\varepsilon$ then I contains $X \upharpoonright n$ for infinitely many n.

(ii) If $\sigma_0, \sigma_1, \ldots$ is a sequence of elements of I such that $[\![\sigma_i]\!] \cap [\![\sigma_j]\!] = \emptyset$ for $i \neq j$, then $\mu^*(B_\varepsilon - \bigcup_i [\![\sigma_i]\!]) > 0$.

Fact (i) holds because U is open and contains B_ε. Fact (ii) holds because

$$\mu^*\Big(B_\varepsilon \cap \bigcup_i [\![\sigma_i]\!]\Big) \leqslant \mu\Big(A \cap \bigcup_i [\![\sigma_i]\!]\Big) = \sum_i \mu(A \cap [\![\sigma_i]\!])$$
$$< \sum_i (1-\varepsilon)2^{-|\sigma_i|} \leqslant (1-\varepsilon).$$

Construct a sequence $\sigma_0, \sigma_1, \ldots$ as follows. Let σ_0 be any element of I. Given σ_i for $i \leqslant n$, let $I_n = \{\sigma \in I : [\![\sigma]\!] \cap [\![\sigma_i]\!] = \emptyset \text{ for all } i \leqslant n\}$. By (i) and (ii), I_n is infinite. Let $d_n = \sup\{2^{-|\sigma|} : \sigma \in I_n\}$ and let σ_{n+1} be an element of I_n such that $2^{-|\sigma_{n+1}|} > \frac{d_n}{2}$.

Let $X \in B_\varepsilon - \bigcup_i [\![\sigma_i]\!]$, which exists by (ii). By (i), there is a $\tau \in I$ with $X \in [\![\tau]\!]$. If $[\![\tau]\!]$ were disjoint from every $[\![\sigma_n]\!]$, and hence contained in every I_n, then we would have $2^{-|\tau|} \leqslant d_n < 2^{-|\sigma_n|+1}$ for every n, contradicting the fact that $\mu(\bigcup_n [\![\sigma_n]\!]) \leqslant 1$. So there is a least n such that $[\![\tau]\!] \cap [\![\sigma_n]\!] \neq \emptyset$. Then either $\tau \preccurlyeq \sigma_n$ or $\sigma_n \preccurlyeq \tau$. The minimality of n implies that $2^{-|\tau|} \leqslant d_{n-1} < 2^{-|\sigma_n|+1}$, so $|\tau| \geqslant |\sigma_n|$. Thus $\sigma_n \preccurlyeq \tau$, and hence $[\![\tau]\!] \subseteq [\![\sigma_n]\!]$. But then $X \in [\![\sigma_n]\!]$, contradicting the choice of X. □

A *tailset* is a set $A \subseteq 2^\omega$ such that for all $\sigma \in 2^{<\omega}$ and $X \in 2^\omega$, if $\sigma X \in A$ then $\tau X \in A$ for all τ with $|\tau| = |\sigma|$. An important corollary to the Lebesgue Density Theorem is the following theorem of Kolmogorov.

Theorem 1.2.4 (Kolmogorov's 0-1 Law). *If A is a measurable tailset, then either $\mu(A) = 0$ or $\mu(A) = 1$.*

Proof. Suppose that $\mu(A) > 0$. By Theorem 1.2.3, choose $X \in A$ such that A has density 1 at X. Let $\varepsilon > 0$. Choose n sufficiently large so that $2^n\mu(A \cap [\![X \upharpoonright n]\!]) > 1-\varepsilon$. Since A is a tailset, we know that $2^n\mu(A \cap [\![\sigma]\!]) > 1-\varepsilon$ for all σ of length n. Hence $\mu(A) > 1-\varepsilon$. Since ε is arbitrary, $\mu(A) = 1$. □

2
Computability Theory

In this chapter we will develop a significant amount of computability theory. Much of this technical material will not be needed until much later in the book, and perhaps in only a small section of the book. We have chosen to gather it in one place for ease of reference. However, as a result this chapter is quite uneven in difficulty, and we strongly recommend that one use most of it as a reference for later chapters, rather than reading through all of it in detail before proceeding. This is especially so for those unfamiliar with more advanced techniques such as priority arguments.

In a few instances we will mention, or sometimes use, methods or results beyond what we introduce in the present chapter. For instance, when we mention the work by Reimann and Slaman [327] on "never continuously random" sets in Section 6.12, we will talk about Borel Determinacy, and in a few places in Chapter 13, some knowledge of forcing in the context of computability theory could be helpful, although our presentations will be self-contained. Such instances will be few and isolated, however, and choices had to be made to keep the length of the book somewhat within reason.

2.1 Computable functions, coding, and the halting problem

At the heart of our understanding of algorithmic randomness is the notion of an *algorithm*. Thus the tools we use are based on classical computability

R.G. Downey and D. Hirschfeldt, *Algorithmic Randomness and Complexity*, Theory and Applications of Computability, DOI 10.1007/978-0-387-68441-3_2,

theory. While we expect the reader to have had at least one course in the rudiments of computability theory, such as a typical course on "theory of computation", the goal of this chapter is to give a reasonably self-contained account of the basics, as well as some of the tools we will need. We do, however, assume familiarity with the technical definition of computability via Turing machines (or some equivalent formalism). For more details see, for example, Rogers [334], Salomaa [347], Soare [366], Odifreddi [310, 311], or Cooper [79].

Our initial concern is with functions from A into $\mathbb{N}$ where $A \subseteq \mathbb{N}$, i.e., *partial* functions on $\mathbb{N}$. If $A = \mathbb{N}$ then the function is called *total*. Looking only at $\mathbb{N}$ may seem rather restrictive. For example, later we will be concerned with functions that take the set of finite binary strings or subsets of the rationals as their domains and/or ranges. However, from the point of view of classical computability theory (that is, where resources such as time and memory do not matter), our definitions naturally extend to such functions by *coding*; that is, the domains and ranges of such functions can be coded as subsets of $\mathbb{N}$. For example, the rationals $\mathbb{Q}$ can be coded in $\mathbb{N}$ as follows.

Definition 2.1.1. Let $r \in \mathbb{Q} \setminus \{0\}$ and write $r = (-1)^{\delta}\frac{p}{q}$ with $p, q \in \mathbb{N}$ in lowest terms and $\delta = 0$ or 1. Then define the *Gödel number* of r, denoted by $\#(r)$, as $2^{\delta}3^{p}5^{q}$. Let the Gödel number of 0 be 0.

The function $\#$ is an injection from $\mathbb{Q}$ into $\mathbb{N}$, and given $n \in \mathbb{N}$ we can decide exactly which $r \in \mathbb{Q}$, if any, has $\#(r) = n$. Similarly, if σ is a finite binary string, say $\sigma = a_1a_2 \ldots a_n$, then we can define $\#(\sigma) = 2^{a_1+1}3^{a_2+1} \ldots (p_n)^{a_n+1}$, where p_n denotes the nth prime. There are myriad other codings possible, of course. For instance, one could code the string σ as the binary number 1σ, so that, for example, the string 01001 would correspond to 101001 in binary. Coding methods such as these are called "effective codings", since they include algorithms for deciding the resulting injections, in the sense discussed above for the Gödel numbering of the rationals.

Henceforth, unless otherwise indicated, when we discuss computability issues relating to a class of objects, we will always regard these objects as (implicitly) effectively coded in some way.

Part of the philosophy underlying computability theory is the celebrated Church-Turing Thesis, which states that *the algorithmic (i.e., intuitively computable) partial functions are exactly those that can be computed by Turing machines on the natural numbers*. Thus, we formally adopt the definition of algorithmic, or *computable*, functions as being those that are computable by Turing machines, but argue informally, appealing to the intuitive notion of computability as is usual. Excellent discussions of the subtleties of the Church-Turing Thesis can be found in Odifreddi [310] and Soare [367].

There are certain important basic properties of the algorithmic partial functions that we will use throughout the book, often implicitly. Following the usual computability theoretic terminology, we refer to such functions as *partial computable functions.*

Proposition 2.1.2 (Enumeration Theorem – Universal Turing Machine). *There is an algorithmic way of enumerating all the partial computable functions. That is, there is a list $\Phi_0, \Phi_1, \ldots$ of all such functions such that we have an algorithmic procedure for passing from an index i to a Turing machine computing Φ_i, and vice versa. Using such a list, we can define a partial computable function $f(x, y)$ of two variables such that $f(x, y) = \Phi_x(y)$ for all x, y. Such a function, and any Turing machine that computes it, are called* universal.

To a modern computer scientist, this result is obvious. That is, given a program in some computer language, we can convert it into ASCII code, and treat it as a number. Given such a binary number, we can decode it and decide whether it corresponds to the code of a program, and if so execute this program. Thus a compiler for the given language can be used to produce a universal program.

Henceforth, we fix an effective listing $\Phi_0, \Phi_1, \ldots$ of the partial computable functions as above. We have an algorithmic procedure for passing from an index i to a Turing machine M_i computing Φ_i, and we identify each Φ_i with M_i.

For any partial computable function f, there are infinitely many ways to compute f. If Φ_y is one such algorithm for computing f, we say that y is an *index* for f.

The point of Proposition 2.1.2 is that we can pretend that we have all the machines $\Phi_1, \Phi_2, \ldots$ in front of us. For instance, to compute 10 steps in the computation of the 3rd machine on input 20, we can pretend to walk to the 3rd machine, put 20 on the tape, and run it for 10 steps (we write the result as $\Phi_3(20)[10]$). Thus we can *computably* simulate the action of computable functions. In many ways, Proposition 2.1.2 is the platform that makes undecidability proofs work, since it allows us to diagonalize over the class of partial computable functions *without leaving this class.* For instance, we have the following result, where we write $\Phi_x(y)\downarrow$ to mean that Φ_x is defined on y, or equivalently, that the corresponding Turing machine halts on input y, and $\Phi_x(y)\uparrow$ to mean that Φ_x is not defined on y.

Proposition 2.1.3 (Unsolvability of the halting problem). *There is no algorithm that, given x, y, decides whether $\Phi_x(y)\downarrow$. Indeed, there is no algorithm to decide whether $\Phi_x(x)\downarrow$.*

Proof. Suppose such an algorithm exists. Then by Proposition 2.1.2, it follows that the following function g is (total) computable:

$$g(x) = \begin{cases} 1 & \text{if } \Phi_x(x)\uparrow \\ \Phi_x(x) + 1 & \text{if } \Phi_x(x)\downarrow . \end{cases}$$

Again using Proposition 2.1.2, there is a y with $g = \Phi_y$. Since g is total, $g(y)\downarrow$, so $\Phi_y(y)\downarrow$, and hence $g(y) = \Phi_y(y) + 1 = g(y) + 1$, which is a contradiction. □

Note that we *can* define a *partial* computable function g via $g(x) = \Phi_x(x) + 1$ and avoid contradiction, as it will follow that, for any index y for g, we have $\Phi_y(y)\uparrow = g(y)\uparrow$. Also, the reason for the use of *partial* computable functions in Proposition 2.1.2 is now clear: The argument above shows that there is no computable procedure to enumerate all (and only) the total computable functions.

Proposition 2.1.3 can be used to show that many problems are algorithmically unsolvable by "coding" the halting problem into these problems. For example, we have the following result.

Proposition 2.1.4. *There is no algorithm to decide whether the domain of* Φ_x *is empty.*

To prove this proposition, we need a lemma, known as the *s-m-n* theorem. We state it for unary functions, but it holds for n-ary ones as well. Strictly speaking, the lemma below is the *s*-1-1 theorem. For the full statement and proof of the *s-m-n* theorem, see [366].

Lemma 2.1.5 (The *s-m-n* Theorem). *Let* $g(x, y)$ *be a partial computable function of two variables. Then there is a computable function* s *of one variable such that, for all* x, y,

$$\Phi_{s(x)}(y) = g(x, y).$$

Proof. Given a Turing machine M computing g and a number x, we can build a Turing machine N that on input y simulates the action of writing the pair (x, y) on M's input tape and running M. We can then find an index $s(x)$ for the function computed by N. □

Proof of Proposition 2.1.4. We code the halting problem into the problem of deciding whether $\text{dom}(\Phi_x) = \emptyset$. That is, we show that *if* we could decide whether $\text{dom}(\Phi_x) = \emptyset$ *then* we could solve the halting problem. Define a partial computable function of two variables by

$$g(x, y) = \begin{cases} 1 & \text{if } \Phi_x(x)\downarrow \\ \uparrow & \text{if } \Phi_x(x)\uparrow . \end{cases}$$

Notice that g ignores its second input.

Via the *s-m-n* theorem, we can consider $g(x, y)$ as a computable collection of partial computable functions. That is, there is a computable s such that, for all x, y,

$$\Phi_{s(x)}(y) = g(x, y).$$

Now

$$\mathrm{dom}(\Phi_{s(x)}) = \begin{cases} \mathbb{N} & \text{if } \Phi_x(x)\downarrow \\ \emptyset & \text{if } \Phi_x(x)\uparrow, \end{cases}$$

so if we could decide for a given x whether $\Phi_{s(x)}$ has empty domain, then we could solve the halting problem. □

We denote the result of running the Turing machine corresponding to Φ_e for s many steps on input x by $\Phi_e(x)[s]$. This value can of course be either defined, in which case we write $\Phi_e(x)[s]\downarrow$, or undefined, in which case we write $\Phi_e(x)[s]\uparrow$.

We will often be interested in the computability of families of functions. We say that $f_0, f_1, \ldots$ are *uniformly (partial) computable* if there is a (partial) computable function f of two variables such that $f(n, x) = f_n(x)$ for all n and x. It is not hard to see that $f_0, f_1, \ldots$ are uniformly partial computable iff there is a computable g such that $f_n = \Phi_{g(n)}$ for all n.

2.2 Computable enumerability and Rice's Theorem

We now show that the reasoning used in the proof of Proposition 2.1.4 can be pushed much further. First we wish to regard all problems as coded by subsets of $\mathbb{N}$. For example, the halting problem can be coded by

$$\emptyset' = \{x : \Phi_x(x)\downarrow\}$$

(or if we insist on the two-variable formulation, by $\{\langle x, y\rangle : \Phi_x(y)\downarrow\}$). Next we need some terminology.

Definition 2.2.1. A set $A \subseteq \mathbb{N}$ is called

(i) *computably enumerable* (*c.e.*) if $A = \mathrm{dom}(\Phi_e)$ for some e, and

(ii) *computable* if A and $\overline{A} = \mathbb{N} \setminus A$ are both computably enumerable.

A set is *co-c.e.* if its complement is c.e. Thus a set is computable iff it is both c.e. and co-c.e. Of course, it also makes sense to say that A is computable if its characteristic function χ_A is computable, particularly since, as mentioned in Chapter 1, we identify sets with their characteristic functions. It is straightforward to check that A is computable in the sense of Definition 2.2.1 if and only if χ_A is computable.

We let W_e denote the eth computably enumerable set, that is, $\mathrm{dom}(\Phi_e)$, and let $W_e[s] = \{x \leqslant s : \Phi_e(x)[s]\downarrow\}$. We sometimes write $W_e[s]$ as $W_{e,s}$.

We think of $W_e[s]$ as the result of performing s steps in the enumeration of W_e.

An *index* for a c.e. set A is an e such that $W_e = A$.

We say that a family of sets $A_0, A_1, \ldots$ is *uniformly computably enumerable* if $A_n = \text{dom}(f_n)$ for a family $f_0, f_1, \ldots$ of uniformly partial computable functions. It is easy to see that this condition is equivalent to saying that there is a computable g such that $A_n = W_{g(n)}$ for all n, or that there is a c.e. set A such that $A_n = \{x : \langle n, x \rangle \in A\}$ for all n. A family of sets $A_0, A_1, \ldots$ is *uniformly computable* if the functions $\chi_{A_0}, \chi_{A_1}, \ldots$ are uniformly computable, which is equivalent to saying that both $A_0, A_1, \ldots$ and $\overline{A_0}, \overline{A_1}, \ldots$ are uniformly c.e.

Definition 2.2.1 suggests that one way to make a set A noncomputable is by ensuring that A is coinfinite and for all e, if W_e is infinite then $A \cap W_e \neq \emptyset$. A c.e. set A with these properties is called *simple*. An infinite set that contains no infinite c.e. set is called *immune*. (So a simple set is a c.e. set whose complement is immune.) Not all noncomputable c.e. sets are simple, since given any noncomputable c.e. set A, the set $\{2n : n \in A\}$ is also c.e. and noncomputable, but is not simple.

The name *computably enumerable* comes from a notion of "effectively countable", via the following characterization, whose proof is straightforward.

Proposition 2.2.2. *A set A is computably enumerable iff either $A = \emptyset$ or there is a total computable function f from $\mathbb{N}$ onto A. (If A is infinite then f can be chosen to be injective.)*

Thus we can think of an infinite computably enumerable set as an effectively infinite list (but *not necessarily in increasing numerical order*). Note that computable sets correspond to decidable questions, since if A is computable, then either $A \in \{\emptyset, \mathbb{N}\}$ or we can decide whether $x \in A$ as follows. Let f and g be computable functions such that $f(\mathbb{N}) = A$ and $g(\mathbb{N}) = \overline{A}$. Now enumerate $f(0), g(0), f(1), g(1), \ldots$ until x occurs (as it must). If x occurs in the range of f, then $x \in A$; if it occurs in the range of g, then $x \notin A$.

It is straightforward to show that $\emptyset'$ is computably enumerable. Thus, by Proposition 2.1.3, it is an example of a computably enumerable set that is not computable. As we will show in Proposition 2.4.5, $\emptyset'$ is a *complete* computably enumerable set, in the sense that for any c.e. set A, there is an algorithm for computing A using $\emptyset'$. We will introduce another "highly knowledgeable" real, closely related to $\emptyset'$ and denoted by Ω, in Definition 3.13.6. Calude and Chaitin [48] pointed out that, in 1927, Émile Borel prefigured the idea of such knowledgeable reals by "defining" a real B such that the nth bit of B answers the nth question in an enumeration of all yes/no questions one can write down in French.

If A is c.e., then it clearly has a *computable approximation*, that is, a uniformly computable family $\{A_s\}_{s \in \omega}$ of sets such that $A(n) = \lim_s A_s(n)$ for all n. (For example, $\{W_e[s]\}_{s\in\omega}$ is a computable approximation of W_e.) In Section 2.6, we will give an exact characterization of the sets that have computable approximations. In the particular case of c.e. sets, we can choose the A_s so that $A_0 \subseteq A_1 \subseteq A_2 \subseteq \cdots$. In the constructions we discuss, whenever we are given a c.e. set, we assume we have such an approximation, and think of A_s as the set of numbers put into A by stage s of the construction. In general, whenever we have an object X that is being approximated during a construction, we denote the stage s approximation to X by $X[s]$.

An *index set* is a set A such that if $x \in A$ and $\Phi_x = \Phi_y$ then $y \in A$. For example, $\{x : \text{dom}(\Phi_x) = \emptyset\}$ is an index set. An index set can be thought of as coding a problem about computable functions (like the emptiness of domain problem) whose answer does not depend on the particular algorithm used to compute a function. Generalizing Proposition 2.1.4, we have the following result, which shows that nontrivial index sets are never computable. Its proof is very similar to that of Proposition 2.1.4.

Theorem 2.2.3 (Rice's Theorem [332]). *An index set A is computable (and so the problem it codes is decidable) iff $A = \mathbb{N}$ or $A = \emptyset$.*

Proof. Let $A \notin \{\emptyset, \mathbb{N}\}$ be an index set. Let e be such that $\text{dom}(\Phi_e) = \emptyset$. We may assume without loss of generality that $e \in \overline{A}$ (the case $e \in A$ being symmetric). Fix $i \in A$. By the *s-m-n* theorem, there is a computable $s(x)$ such that, for all $y \in \mathbb{N}$,

$$\Phi_{s(x)}(y) = \begin{cases} \Phi_i(y) & \text{if } \Phi_x(x)\downarrow \\ \uparrow & \text{if } \Phi_x(x)\uparrow . \end{cases}$$

If $\Phi_x(x)\downarrow$ then $\Phi_{s(x)} = \Phi_i$ and so $s(x) \in A$, while if $\Phi_x(x)\uparrow$ then $\Phi_{s(x)} = \Phi_e$ and so $s(x) \notin A$. Thus, if A were computable, $\emptyset'$ would also be computable. □

Of course, many nontrivial decision problems (such as the problem of deciding whether a natural number is prime, say) are not coded by index sets, and so can have decidable solutions.

2.3 The Recursion Theorem

Kleene's Recursion Theorem (also known as the Fixed Point Theorem) is a fundamental result in classical computability theory. It allows us to use an index for a computable function or c.e. set that we are building in a construction as part of that very construction. Thus it forms the theoretical underpinning of the common programming practice of having a routine make recursive calls to itself.

Theorem 2.3.1 (Recursion Theorem, Kleene [209]). *Let f be a total computable function. Then there is a number n, called a* fixed point *of f, such* *that*

$$\Phi_n = \Phi_{f(n)},$$

and hence

$$W_n = W_{f(n)}.$$

Furthermore, such an n can be computed from an index for f.

Proof. First define a total computable function d via the *s-m-n* Theorem so that

$$\Phi_{d(e)}(k) = \begin{cases} \Phi_{\Phi_e(e)}(k) & \text{if } \Phi_e(e)\downarrow \\ \uparrow & \text{if } \Phi_e(e)\uparrow . \end{cases}$$

Let i be such that

$$\Phi_i = f \circ d$$

and let $n = d(i)$. Notice that Φ_i is total. The following calculation shows that n is a fixed point of f.

$$\Phi_n = \Phi_{d(i)} = \Phi_{\Phi_i(i)} = \Phi_{f \circ d(i)} = \Phi_{f(n)}.$$

The explicit definition of n given above can clearly be carried out computably given an index for f. □

A longer but more perspicuous proof of the recursion theorem was given by Owings [312]; see also Soare [366, pp. 36–37].

There are many variations on the theme of the recursion theorem, such as the following one, which we will use several times below.

Theorem 2.3.2 (Recursion Theorem with Parameters, Kleene [209]). *Let f be a total computable function of two variables. Then there is a total computable function h such that $\Phi_{h(y)} = \Phi_{f(h(y),y)}$, and hence $W_{h(y)} = W_{f(h(y),y)}$, for all y. Furthermore, an index for h can be obtained effectively from an index for f.*

Proof. The proof is similar to that of the recursion theorem. Let d be a total computable function such that

$$\Phi_{d(x,y)}(k) = \begin{cases} \Phi_{\Phi_x(\langle x,y\rangle)}(k) & \text{if } \Phi_x(\langle x,y\rangle)\downarrow \\ \uparrow & \text{if } \Phi_x(\langle x,y\rangle)\uparrow . \end{cases}$$

Let i be such that

$$\Phi_i(\langle x,y\rangle) = f(d(x,y),y)$$

for all x and y, and let $h(y) = d(i,y)$. Then

$$\Phi_{h(y)} = \Phi_{d(i,y)} = \Phi_{\Phi_i(\langle i,y\rangle)} = \Phi_{f(d(i,y),y)} = \Phi_{f(h(y),y)}$$

for all y. The explicit definition of h given above can clearly be carried out computably given an index for f. □

It is straightforward to modify the above proof to show that if f is a partial computable function of two variables, then there is a total computable function h such that $\Phi_{h(y)} = \Phi_{f(h(y),y)}$ for all y such that $f(h(y), y)\downarrow$.

In Section 3.5, we will see that there is a version of the recursion theorem for functions computed by *prefix-free machines*, a class of machines that will play a key role in this book.

Here is a very simple application of the recursion theorem. We show that $\emptyset'$ is not an index set. Let f be a computable function such that $\Phi_{f(n)}(n)\downarrow$ and $\Phi_{f(n)}(m)\uparrow$ for all $m \neq n$. Let n be a fixed point for f, so that $\Phi_n = \Phi_{f(n)}$. Let $m \neq n$ be another index for Φ_n. Then $\Phi_n(n)\downarrow$ and hence $n \in \emptyset'$, but $\Phi_m(m)\uparrow$ and hence $m \notin \emptyset'$. So $\emptyset'$ is not an index set. Note that this example also shows that there is a Turing machine that halts only on its own index.

The following is another useful application of the recursion theorem.

Theorem 2.3.3 (Slowdown Lemma, Ambos-Spies, Jockusch, Shore, and Soare [7]). *Let $\{U_{e,s}\}_{e,s\in\omega}$ be a computable sequence of finite sets such that $U_{e,s} \subseteq U_{e,s+1}$ for all e and s. Let $U_e = \bigcup_s U_{e,s}$. There is a computable function g such that for all e, s, n, we have $W_{g(e)} = U_e$ and if $n \notin U_{e,s}$ then $n \notin W_{g(e),s+1}$.*

Proof. Let f be a computable function such that $W_{f(i,e)}$ behaves as follows. Given n, look for a least s such that $n \in U_{e,s}$. If such an s is found, ask whether $n \in W_{i,s}$. If not, then enumerate n into $W_{f(i,e)}$. By the recursion theorem with parameters, there is a computable function g such that $W_{g(e)} = W_{f(g(e),e)}$ for every e. If $n \notin U_{e,s}$, then $n \notin W_{g(e)}$. If $n \in U_{e,s}$ then for the least such s it cannot be the case that $n \in W_{g(e),s}$, since in that case we would have $n \notin W_{f(g(e),e)} = W_{g(e)}$. So $n \in W_{f(g(e),e)} = W_{g(e)}$ but $n \notin W_{g(e),s}$. □

We will provide the details of applications of versions of the recursion theorem for several results in this chapter, but will assume familiarity with their use elsewhere in the book.

2.4 Reductions

The key concept used in the proof of Rice's Theorem is that of *reduction*, that is, the idea that "if we can do B then this ability also allows us to do A". In other words, *questions about problem A are* reducible *to ones about problem B*. We want to use this idea to define partial orderings, known as *reducibilities*, that calibrate problems according to computational difficulty. The idea is to have $A \leqslant B$ if the ability to solve B allows us also to solve A, meaning that B is "at least as hard as" A. In this section, we introduce several ways to formalize this notion, beginning with the best-known one, Turing reducibility. For any reducibility $\leqslant_{\mathrm{R}}$, we write $A \equiv_{\mathrm{R}} B$, and say that A and B are *R-equivalent*, if $A \leqslant_R B$ and $B \leqslant_R A$. We write $A <_R B$ if $A \leqslant_R B$ and $B \nleqslant_R A$. Finally, we write $A \mid_R B$ if $A \nleqslant_R B$ and $B \nleqslant_R A$.

2.4.1 Oracle machines and Turing reducibility

An *oracle (Turing) machine* is a Turing machine with an extra infinite read-only *oracle tape*, which it can access one bit at a time while performing its computation. If there is an oracle machine M that computes the set A when its oracle tape codes the set B, then we say that A is *Turing reducible* to B, or B*-computable*, or *computable in* B, and write $A \leqslant_T B$.[1] Note that, in computing $A(n)$ for any given n, the machine M can make only finitely many queries to the oracle tape; in other words, it can access the value of $B(m)$ for at most finitely many m. The definition of relative computability can be extended to functions in the obvious way. We will also consider situations in which the oracle tape codes a finite string. In that case, if the machine attempts to make any queries beyond the length of the string, the computation automatically diverges. All the notation we introduce below for oracle tapes coding sets applies to strings as well.

For example, let $E = \{x : \text{dom}(\Phi_x) \neq \emptyset\}$. In the proof of Proposition 2.1.4, we showed that $\emptyset' \leqslant_T E$. Indeed the proof of Rice's Theorem demonstrates that, for a nontrivial index set I, we always have $\emptyset' \leqslant_T I$. On the other hand, the unsolvability of the halting problem implies that $\emptyset' \nleqslant_T \emptyset$. (Note that $X \leqslant_T \emptyset$ iff X is computable. Indeed, if Y is computable, then $X \leqslant_T Y$ iff X is computable.)

It is not hard to check that Turing reducibility is transitive and reflexive, and thus is a preordering on the subsets of $\mathbb{N}$. The equivalence classes of the form $\deg(A) = \{B : B \equiv_T A\}$ code a notion of equicomputability and are called *Turing degrees (of unsolvability)*, though we often refer to them simply as *degrees*. We always use boldface lowercase letters such as $\mathbf{a}$ for Turing degrees. A Turing degree is *computably enumerable* if it contains a computably enumerable set (which does not imply that all the sets in the degree are c.e.). The Turing degrees inherit a natural ordering from Turing reducibility: $\mathbf{a} \leqslant \mathbf{b}$ iff $A \leqslant_T B$ for some (or equivalently all) $A \in \mathbf{a}$ and $B \in \mathbf{b}$. We will relentlessly mix notation by writing, for example, $A <_T \mathbf{b}$, for a set A and a degree $\mathbf{b}$, to mean that $A <_T B$ for some (or equivalently all) $B \in \mathbf{b}$.

The Turing degrees form an uppersemilattice. The join operation is induced by $\oplus$, where $A \oplus B = \{2n : n \in A\} \cup \{2n+1 : n \in B\}$. Clearly $A, B \leqslant_T A \oplus B$, and if $A, B \leqslant_T C$, then $A \oplus B \leqslant_T C$. Furthermore, if

[1] We can also put resource bounds on our procedures. For example, if we count steps and ask that computations halt in a polynomial (in the length of the input) number of steps, then we arrive at the polynomial time computable functions and the notion of polynomial time (Turing) reducibility. We will not consider such reducibilities here; see Ambos-Spies and Mayordomo [10].

$A \equiv_T \widehat{A}$ and $B \equiv_T \widehat{B}$, then $A \oplus B \equiv_T \widehat{A} \oplus \widehat{B}$. Thus it makes sense to define the *join* $\mathbf{a} \vee \mathbf{b}$ of the degrees $\mathbf{a}$ and $\mathbf{b}$ to be the degree of $A \oplus B$ for some (or equivalently all) $A \in \mathbf{a}$ and $B \in \mathbf{b}$. Kleene and Post [210] showed that the Turing degrees are not a lattice. That is, not every pair of degrees has a greatest lower bound.

For sets $A_0, A_1, \ldots$, let $\bigoplus_i A_i = \{\langle i, n \rangle : n \in A_i\}$. Note that, while $A_j \leqslant_T \bigoplus_i A_i$ for all j, the degree of $\bigoplus_i A_i$ may be much greater than the degrees of the A_i's. For instance, for any function f, we can let $A_i = \{f(i)\}$, in which case each A_i is a singleton, and hence computable, but $\bigoplus_i A_i \equiv_T f$.

We let $\mathbf{0}$ denote the degree of the computable sets. Note that each degree is countable and has only countably many predecessors (since there are only countably many oracle machines), so there are continuum many degrees.

For an oracle machine Φ, we write Φ^A for the function computed by Φ with oracle A (i.e., with A coded into its oracle tape). The analog of Proposition 2.1.2 holds for oracle machines. That is, there is an effective enumeration $\Phi_0, \Phi_1, \ldots$ of all oracle machines, and a *universal oracle (Turing) machine* Φ such that $\Phi^A(x, y) = \Phi^A_x(y)$ for all x, y and all oracles A.

We had previously defined Φ_e to be the eth partial computable function. However, we have already identified partial computable functions with Turing machines, and we can regard normal Turing machines as oracle machines with empty oracle tape; in fact it is convenient to identify the eth partial computable function Φ_e with $\Phi^{\emptyset}_e$. Thus there is no real conflict between the two notations, and we will not worry about the double meaning of Φ_e.

When a set A has a computable approximation $\{A_s\}_{s \in \omega}$, we write $\Phi^A_e(n)[s]$ to mean the result of running Φ_e with oracle A_s on input n for s many steps.

We also think of oracle machines as determining *(Turing) functionals*, that is, partial functions from 2^ω to 2^ω (or ω^ω). The value of the functional Φ on A is Φ^A.

The *use* of a converging oracle computation $\Phi^A(n)$ is $x+1$ for the largest number x such that the value of $A(x)$ is queried during the computation. (If no such value is queried, then the use of the computation is 0.) We denote this use by $\varphi^A(n)$. In general, when we have an oracle computation represented by an uppercase Greek letter, its use function is represented by the corresponding lowercase Greek letter. Normally, we do not care about the exact position of the largest bit queried during a computation, and can replace the exact use function by any function that is at least as large. Furthermore, we may assume that an oracle machine cannot query its oracle's nth bit before stage n. So we typically adopt the following useful conventions on a use function φ^A.

1. The use function is strictly increasing where defined, that is, $\varphi^A(m) < \varphi^A(n)$ for all $m < n$ such that both these values are defined, and

similarly, when A is being approximated, $\varphi^A(m)[s] < \varphi^A(n)[s]$ for all $m < n$ and s such that both these values are defined.

2. When A is being approximated, $\varphi^A(n)[s] \leqslant \varphi^A(n)[t]$ for all n and $s < t$ such that both these values are defined.
3. $\varphi^A(n)[s] \leqslant s$ for all n and s such that this value is defined.

Although in a sense trivial, the following principle is quite important.

Proposition 2.4.1 (Use Principle). *Let $\Phi^A(n)$ be a converging oracle computation, and let B be a set such that $B \upharpoonright \varphi^A(n) = A \upharpoonright \varphi^A(n)$. Then $\Phi^B(n) = \Phi^A(n)$.*

Proof. The sets A and B give the same answers to all questions asked during the relevant computations, so the results must be the same. □

One important consequence of the use principle is that if A is c.e. and Φ^A is total, then A can compute the function f defined by letting $f(n)$ be the least s by which the computation of $\Phi^A(n)$ has settled, i.e., $\Phi^A(n)[t]\downarrow = \Phi^A(n)[s]\downarrow$ for all $t > s$. The reason is that $f(n)$ is the least s such that $\Phi^A(n)[s]\downarrow$ and $A \upharpoonright \varphi^A(n)[s] = A_s \upharpoonright \varphi^A(n)[s]$.

For a set A, let

$$A' = \{e : \Phi_e^A(e)\downarrow\}.$$

The set A' represents the halting problem *relativized* to A. The general process of extending a definition or result in the non-oracle case to the oracle case is known as *relativization*. For instance, Proposition 2.1.3 (the unsolvability of the halting problem) can be relativized with a completely analogous proof to show that $A' \not\leqslant_T A$ for all A. Two good (but not hard) exercises are to show that $A <_T A'$ and that if $A \leqslant_T B$ then $A' \leqslant_T B'$. Another important example of relativization is the concept of a set B being *computably enumerable in* a set A, which means that $B = \mathrm{dom}(\Phi_e^A)$ for some e. Most results in computability theory can be relativized in a completely straightforward way, and we freely use the relativized versions of theorems proved below when needed.

2.4.2 The jump operator and jump classes

We often refer to A' as the *(Turing) jump* of A. The *jump operator* is the function $A \mapsto A'$. The *nth jump* of A, written as $A^{(n)}$, is the result of applying the jump operator n times to A. So, for example, $A^{(2)} = A''$ and $A^{(3)} = A'''$. If $\mathbf{a} = \deg(A)$ then we write $\mathbf{a}'$ for $\deg(A')$, and similarly for the nth jump notation. This definition makes sense because $A \equiv_T B$ implies $A' \equiv_T B'$. Note that we have a hierarchy of degrees $\mathbf{0} < \mathbf{0}' < \mathbf{0}'' < \cdots$.

We also define the *ω-jump* of A as $A^{(\omega)} = \bigoplus_n A^{(n)}$. (We could continue to iterate the jump to define α-jumps for higher ordinals α, but we will not need these in this book.)

The halting problem, and hence the jump operator, play a fundamental role in much of computability theory. Closely connected to the jump operator, and also of great importance in computability theory, are the following *jump classes*.

Definition 2.4.2. A set A is *low$_n$* if $A^{(n)} \equiv_T \emptyset^{(n)}$. The low$_1$ sets are called *low*.

A set $A \leqslant_T \emptyset'$ is *high$_n$* if $A^{(n)} \equiv_T \emptyset^{(n+1)}$. The high$_1$ sets are called *high*. More generally, we call an arbitrary set A high if $A' \geqslant_T \emptyset''$.

These classes are particularly well suited to studying $\emptyset'$-computable sets. The following classes are sometimes better suited to the general case.

Definition 2.4.3. A set A is *generalized low$_n$* (*GL$_n$*) if $A^{(n)} \equiv_T (A \oplus \emptyset')^{(n-1)}$.

A set A is *generalized high$_n$* (*GH$_n$*) if $A^{(n)} \equiv_T (A \oplus \emptyset')^{(n)}$.

Note that if $A \leqslant_T \emptyset'$, then A is GL$_n$ iff it is low$_n$, and GH$_n$ iff it is high$_n$. A degree is low if the sets it contains are low, and similarly for other jump classes.

While jump classes are defined in terms of the jump operator, they often have more "combinatorial" characterizations. For example, we will see in Theorem 2.23.7 that a set A is high iff there is an A-computable function that dominates all computable functions, where f *dominates* g if $f(n) \geqslant g(n)$ for all sufficiently large n.

2.4.3 Strong reducibilities

The reduction used in the proof of Rice's Theorem is of a particularly strong type, since to decide whether $x \in \emptyset'$, we simply compute $s(x)$ and ask whether $s(x) \in A$. Considering this kind of reduction leads to the following definition.

Definition 2.4.4. We say that A is *many-one reducible* (*m-reducible*) to B, and write $A \leqslant_m B$, if there is a total computable function f such that for all x, we have $x \in A$ iff $f(x) \in B$.[2]

If B is $\emptyset$ or $\mathbb{N}$ then the only set m-reducible to B is B itself, but we will ignore these cases of the above definition. If the function f in the definition of m-reduction is injective, then we say that A is 1-*reducible* to B, and

[2]In the context of complexity theory, resource bounded versions of m-reducibility are at the basis of virtually all modern NP-completeness proofs. Although Cook's original definition of NP-completeness was in terms of polynomial time *Turing* reducibility, the Karp version in terms of polynomial time m-reducibility is most often used. It is still an open question of structural complexity theory whether there is a set A such that the polynomial time Turing degree of A collapses to a single polynomial time m-degree.

write $A \leqslant_1 B$. Note that if B is c.e. and $A \leqslant_{\mathrm{m}} B$ then A is also c.e. Also note that $\emptyset'$ is *m-complete*, and even 1-*complete*, in the following sense.

Proposition 2.4.5. *If A is c.e. then $A \leqslant_1 \emptyset'$.*

Proof. It is easy to define an injective computable function f such that for each n, the machine $\Phi_{f(n)}$ ignores its input and halts iff n enters A at some point. Then f witnesses the fact that $A \leqslant_1 \emptyset'$. □

It is not difficult to construct sets A and B such that $A \leqslant_{\mathrm{T}} B$ but $A \nleqslant_{\mathrm{m}} B$. For example, $\overline{\emptyset'} \leqslant_{\mathrm{T}} \emptyset'$, but $\overline{\emptyset'} \nleqslant_{\mathrm{m}} \emptyset'$, since $\overline{\emptyset'}$ is not c.e. It is also possible to construct such examples in which A and B are both c.e. Thus m-reducibility strictly refines Turing reducibility, and hence we say that m-reducibility is an example of a strong reducibility (which should not be confused with the notion of strong reducibility of mass problems introduced in Section 8.9). There are many other strong reducibilities. Their definitions depend on the types of oracle access used in the corresponding reductions. We mention two that will be important in this book.

One of the key aspects of Turing reducibility is that a Turing reduction may be adaptable, in the sense that the number and type of queries made of the oracle depends upon the oracle itself. For instance, imagine a reduction that works as follows: on input x, the oracle is queried as to whether it contains some power of x. That is, the reduction asks whether 1 is in the oracle, then whether x is in the oracle, then whether x^2 is in the oracle, and so on. If the answer is yes for some x^n, then the reduction checks whether the least such n is even, in which case it outputs 0, or odd, in which case it outputs 1.

Note that there is *no limit* to the number of questions asked of the oracle on a given input. This number depends on the oracle. Indeed, if the oracle happens to contain no power of x, then the computation on input x will not halt at all, and infinitely many questions will be asked.

Many naturally arising reductions do not have this adaptive property. One class of examples gives rise to the notion of *truth table reducibility.* A *truth table* on the variables $v_1, v_2, \ldots$ is a (finite) boolean combination σ of these variables. We write $A \vDash \sigma$ if σ holds with v_n interpreted as $n \in A$. For example, σ might be $((v_1 \wedge v_2) \vee (v_3 \rightarrow v_4)) \wedge v_5)$, in which case $A \vDash \sigma$ iff $5 \in A$ and either ($1 \in A$ and $2 \in A$) or ($3 \notin A$ or $4 \in A$) (or both). Let $\sigma_0, \sigma_1, \ldots$ be an effective list of all truth tables.

Definition 2.4.6. We say that A is *truth table reducible* to B, and write $A \leqslant_{\mathrm{tt}} B$, if there is a computable function f such that for all x,

$$x \in A \text{ iff } B \vDash \sigma_{f(x)}.$$

Notice that an m-reduction is a simple example of a tt-reduction. The relevant truth table for input n has a single entry $v_{f(n)}$, where f is the function witnessing the given m-reduction.

The following characterization follows easily from the compactness of 2^ω.

Proposition 2.4.7 (Nerode [293]). *A Turing reduction Φ is a truth table reduction iff Φ^X is total for all oracles X.*

This characterization is particularly useful in the context of effective measure theory, as it means that truth table reductions can be used to transfer measures from one space to another. Examples can be found in the work of Reimann and Slaman [327, 328, 329] and the proof of Demuth's Theorem 8.6.1 below.

Concepts defined using Turing reducibility often have productive analogs for strong reducibilities. The following is an example we will use below.

Definition 2.4.8. A set A is *superlow* if $A' \equiv_{\mathrm{tt}} \emptyset'$.

One way to look at a tt-reduction is that it is one in which the oracle queries to be performed on a given input are predetermined, independently of the oracle, and the computation halts for every oracle. Removing the last restriction yields the notion of *weak truth table reduction*, which can also be thought of as bounded Turing reduction, in the sense that there is a computable bound, independent of the oracle, on the amount of the oracle to be queried on a given input.

Definition 2.4.9. We say that A is *weak truth table reducible* (*wtt-reducible*) to B, and write $A \leqslant_{\mathrm{wtt}} B$, if there are a computable function f and an oracle Turing machine Φ such that $\Phi^B = A$ and $\varphi^B(n) \leqslant f(n)$ for all n.

Definitions and notations that we introduced for Turing reducibility, such as the notion of degree, also apply to these strong reducibilities. In particular, we have the notions of *truth table functional* and *weak truth table functional*. For a Turing functional Φ to be a wtt-functional, we require that there be a single computable function f such that for all oracles B, if $\Phi^B(n)\downarrow$ then $\varphi^B(n) \leqslant f(n)$. The best way to think of a tt-functional is as a total Turing functional, that is, a functional Φ such that Φ^B is total for all oracles B.

The reducibilities we have seen so far calibrate sets into degrees of greater and greater fineness, in the order T, wtt, tt, m, 1.

2.4.4 Myhill's Theorem

The definition of $\emptyset'$ depends on the choice of an effective enumeration of the partial computable functions. By Proposition 2.4.5, however, any two versions of $\emptyset'$ are 1-equivalent. The following result shows that they are in fact equivalent up to a computable permutation of $\mathbb{N}$.

Theorem 2.4.10 (Myhill Isomorphism Theorem [291]). *$A \equiv_1 B$ iff there is a computable permutation h of $\mathbb{N}$ such that $h(A) = B$.*

Proof. The "if" direction is immediate, so assume that $A \leqslant_1 B$ via f and $B \leqslant_1 A$ via g. We define h in stages. We will ensure that the finite partial function h_s defined at each stage is injective and such that $m \in A$ iff $h_s(m) \in B$ for all $m \in \operatorname{dom} h_s$.

Let $h_0 = \emptyset$. Suppose we have defined h_s for s even. Let m be least such that $h_s(m)$ is not defined. List $f(n), f \circ h_s^{-1} \circ f(n), f \circ h_s^{-1} \circ f \circ h_s^{-1} \circ f(n), \ldots$ until an element $k \notin \operatorname{rng} h_s$ is found. Note that each element of this list, and in particular k, is in B iff $n \in A$. Extend h_s to h_{s+1} by letting $h_{s+1}(m) = k$.

Now define h_{s+2} in the same way, with f, h_s, dom, and rng replaced by g, h_{s+1}^{-1}, rng, and dom, respectively.

Let $h = \bigcup_s h_s$. It is easy to check that h is a computable permutation of $\mathbb{N}$ and that $h(A) = B$. □

Myhill [291] characterized the 1-complete sets using the following notions.

Definition 2.4.11 (Post [316]). A set B is *productive* if there is a partial computable function h such that if $W_e \subseteq B$ then $h(e)\downarrow \in B \setminus W_e$.

A c.e. set A is *creative* if $\overline{A}$ is productive.

The halting problem is an example of a creative set, since $\overline{\emptyset'}$ is productive via the identity function.

Theorem 2.4.12 (Myhill's Theorem [291]). *The following are equivalent for a set A.*

(i) *A is creative.*

(ii) *A is m-complete (i.e., m-equivalent to $\emptyset'$).*

(iii) *A is 1-complete (i.e., 1-equivalent to $\emptyset'$).*

(iv) *A is equivalent to $\emptyset'$ up to a computable permutation of* $\mathbb{N}$.

Proof. The Myhill Isomorphism Theorem shows that (iii) and (iv) are equivalent, and (iii) obviously implies (ii). To show that (ii) implies (i), suppose that $\emptyset' \leqslant_m A$ via f. Let g be a computable function such that $W_{g(e)} = \{n : f(n) \in W_e\}$ for all e, and let $h(e) = f(g(e))$. If $W_e \subseteq \overline{A}$ then $W_{g(e)} \in \overline{\emptyset'}$, so $g(e) \in \overline{\emptyset'} \setminus W_{g(e)}$, and hence $h(e) \in \overline{A} \setminus W_e$. Thus A is creative via h.

To show that (i) implies (iii), we use the recursion theorem with parameters. Since A is c.e., we have $A \leqslant_1 \emptyset'$, so it is enough to show that $\emptyset' \leqslant_1 A$. Let h be a function witnessing that $\overline{A}$ is productive. Let f be a computable function such that $W_{f(n,k)} = \{f(n)\}$ if $k \in \emptyset'$ and $W_{f(n,k)} = \emptyset$ otherwise. By the recursion theorem with parameters, there is an injective computable function g such that $W_{g(k)} = W_{f(g(k),k)}$ for all k. Then

$$k \in \emptyset' \Rightarrow W_{g(k)} = \{f(g(k))\} \Rightarrow W_{g(k)} \nsubseteq \overline{A} \Rightarrow f(g(k)) \in A$$

and

$$k \notin \emptyset' \Rightarrow W_{g(k)} = \emptyset \Rightarrow W_{g(k)} \subseteq \overline{A} \Rightarrow f(g(k)) \in \overline{A}.$$

Thus $\emptyset' \leqslant_1 A$ via $f \circ g$. □

We will see a randomness-theoretic version of this result in Section 9.2.

2.5 The arithmetic hierarchy

We define the notions of Σ_n^0, Π_n^0, and Δ_n^0 sets as follows. A set A is Σ_n^0 if there is a computable relation $R(x_1, \ldots, x_n, y)$ such that $y \in A$ iff

$$\underbrace{\exists x_1 \, \forall x_2 \, \exists x_3 \, \forall x_4 \cdots Q_n x_n}_{n \text{ alternating quantifiers}} R(x_1, \ldots, x_n, y).$$

Since the quantifiers alternate, Q_n is $\exists$ if n is odd and $\forall$ if n is even. In this definition, we could have had n alternating quantifier *blocks*, instead of single quantifiers, but we can always collapse two successive existential or universal quantifiers into a single one by using pairing functions, so that would not make a difference.

The definition of A being Π_n^0 is the same, except that the leading quantifier is a $\forall$ (but there still are n alternating quantifiers in total). It is easy to see that A is Π_n^0 iff $\overline{A}$ is Σ_n^0.

Finally, we say a set is Δ_n^0 if it is both Σ_n^0 and Π_n^0 (or equivalently, if both it and its complement are Σ_n^0). Note that the Δ_0^0, Π_0^0, and Σ_0^0 sets are all exactly the computable sets. The same is true of the Δ_1^0 sets, as shown by Proposition 2.5.1 below.

These notions give rise to Kleene's *arithmetic hierarchy*, which can be pictured as follows.

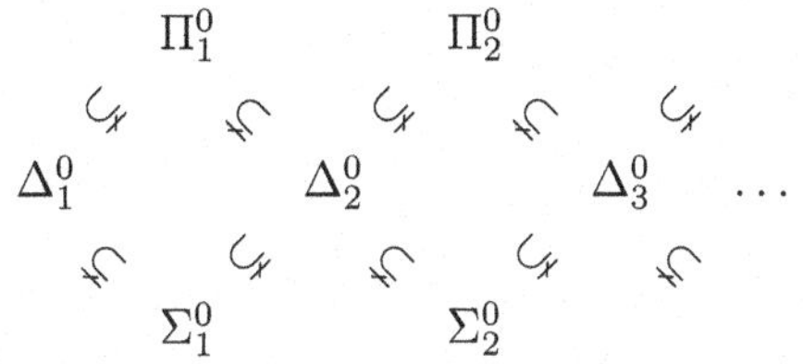

A set is *arithmetic* if it is in one of the levels of the arithmetic hierarchy.

As we will see in the next section, there is a strong relationship between the arithmetic hierarchy and enumeration. The following is a simple example at the lowest level of the hierarchy

Proposition 2.5.1 (Kleene [208]). *A set A is computably enumerable iff A is Σ_1^0.*

Proof. Suppose A is c.e. Then $A = \mathrm{dom}(\Phi_e)$ for some e, so $n \in A$ iff $\exists s \, \Phi_e(y)[s]\downarrow$. Thus A is Σ_1^0.

Conversely, if A is Σ_1^0 then for some computable R we have $n \in A$ iff $\exists x \, R(x, n)$. Define a partial computable function g by letting $g(n) = 1$ at stage s iff $s \geqslant n$ and there is an $x < s$ such that $R(x, n)$ holds. Then $n \in A$ iff $n \in \mathrm{dom}(g)$, so A is c.e. □

2.6 The Limit Lemma and Post's Theorem

There is an important generalization, due to Post, of Proposition 2.5.1. It ties in the arithmetic hierarchy with the degrees of unsolvability, and gives completeness properties of degrees of the form $\mathbf{0}^{(n)}$, highlighting their importance. In this section we will look at this and related characterizations, beginning with Shoenfield's Limit Lemma.

Saying that a set A is c.e. can be thought of as saying that A has a computable approximation that, for each n, starts out by saying that $n \notin A$, and then changes its mind at most once. More precisely, there is a computable binary function f such that for all n we have $A(n) = \lim_s f(n,s)$, with $f(n,0) = 0$ and $f(n,s+1) \neq f(n,s)$ for at most one s. Generalizing this idea, the limit lemma characterizes the sets computable from the halting problem as those that have computable approximations with *finitely many* mind changes, and hence are "effectively approximable". (In other words, the sets computable from $\emptyset'$ are exactly those that have computable approximations, as defined in Section 2.2.)

Theorem 2.6.1 (Limit Lemma, Shoenfield [354]). *For a set A, we have $A \leqslant_{\mathrm{T}} \emptyset'$ iff there is a computable binary function g such that, for all n,*

(i) $\lim_s g(n,s)$ *exists (i.e., $|\{s : g(n,s) \neq g(n,s+1)\}| < \infty$), and*

(ii) $A(n) = \lim_s g(n,s)$.

Proof. ($\Rightarrow$) Suppose $A = \Phi^{\emptyset'}$. Define g by letting $g(n,s) = 0$ if either $\Phi^{\emptyset'}[s]\uparrow$ or $\Phi^{\emptyset'}[s]\downarrow\neq 1$, and letting $g(n,s) = 1$ otherwise. Fix n, and let s be a stage such that $\emptyset'_t \upharpoonright \varphi^{\emptyset'}(n) = \emptyset' \upharpoonright \varphi^{\emptyset'}(n)$ for all $t \geqslant s$. By the use principle (Proposition 2.4.1), $g(n,t) = \Phi^{\emptyset'}(n)[t] = \Phi^{\emptyset'}(n) = A(n)$ for all $t \geqslant s$. Thus g has the required properties.

($\Leftarrow$) Suppose such a function g exists. Without loss of generality, we may assume that $g(n,0) = 0$ for all n. To show that $A \leqslant_{\mathrm{T}} \emptyset'$, it is enough to build a c.e. set B such that $A \leqslant_{\mathrm{T}} B$, since by Proposition 2.4.5, every c.e. set is computable in $\emptyset'$. We put $\langle n,k\rangle$ into B whenever we find that

$$|\{s : g(n,s) \neq g(n,s+1)\}| \geqslant k.$$

Now define a Turing reduction Γ as follows. Given an oracle X, on input n, search for the least k such that $\langle n,k\rangle \notin X$, and if one is found, then output 0 if k is even and 1 if k is odd. Clearly, $\Gamma^B = A$. □

As in the case of c.e. sets, whenever we are given a set A computable in $\emptyset'$, we assume that we have a fixed computable approximation $A_0, A_1, \ldots$ to A; that is, we assume we have a computable function g as in the limit lemma, and write A_s for the set of all n such that $g(n,s) = 1$. We may always assume without loss of generality that $A_0 = \emptyset$ and $A_s \subseteq [0,s]$.

Intuitively, the proof of the "if" direction of the limit lemma boils down to saying that, since (by Propositions 2.4.5 and 2.5.1) the set $\emptyset'$ can decide whether $\exists s > t\,(g(n,s) \neq g(n,s+1))$ for any n and t, it can also compute $\lim_s g(n,s)$.

Corollary 2.6.2. *For a set A, the following are equivalent.*

(i) $A \leqslant_{\mathrm{tt}} \emptyset'$.

(ii) $A \leqslant_{\mathrm{wtt}} \emptyset'$.

(iii) *There are a computable binary function g and a computable function h such that, for all n,*

(a) $|\{s : g(n,s) \neq g(n,s+1)\}| < h(n)$, *and*
(b) $A(n) = \lim_s g(n,s)$.

Proof. We know that (i) implies (ii). The proof that (ii) implies (iii) is essentially the same as that of the "if" direction of Theorem 2.6.1, together with the remark that if Φ is a wtt-reduction then we can computably bound the number of times the value of $\Phi^{\emptyset'}[s]$ can change as s increases. The proof that (iii) implies (i) is much the same as that of the "only if" direction of Theorem 2.6.1, except that we can now make Γ into a tt-reduction because we have to check whether $\langle n,k\rangle \notin X$ only for $k < h(n)$. □

Sets with the properties given in Corollary 2.6.2 are called *ω-c.e.*, and will be further discussed in Section 2.7.

As we have seen, we often want to relativize results, definitions, and proofs in computability theory. The limit lemma relativizes to show that $A \leqslant_{\mathrm{T}} B'$ iff there is a B-computable binary function f such that $A(n) = \lim_s f(n,s)$ for all n. Combining this fact with induction, we have the following generalization of the limit lemma.

Corollary 2.6.3 (Limit Lemma, Strong Form, Shoenfield [354]). *Let $k \geqslant 1$. For a set A, we have $A \leqslant_{\mathrm{T}} \emptyset^{(k)}$ iff there is a computable function g of $k+1$ variables such that $A(n) = \lim_{s_1} \lim_{s_2} \dots \lim_{s_k} g(n, s_1, s_2, \dots, s_k)$ for all n.*

We now turn to Post's characterization of the levels of the arithmetic hierarchy. Let $\mathcal{C}$ be a class of sets (such as a level of the arithmetic hierarchy). A set A is *$\mathcal{C}$-complete* if $A \in \mathcal{C}$ and $B \leqslant_{\mathrm{T}} A$ for all $B \in \mathcal{C}$. If in fact $B \leqslant_{\mathrm{m}} A$ for all $B \in \mathcal{C}$, then we say that A is $\mathcal{C}$ *m-complete*, and similarly for other strong reducibilities.

Theorem 2.6.4 (Post's Theorem [317]). *Let $n \geqslant 0$.*

(i) *A set B is Σ^0_{n+1} $\Leftrightarrow$ B is c.e. in some Σ^0_n set $\Leftrightarrow$ B is c.e. in some Π^0_n set.*

(ii) *The set $\emptyset^{(n)}$ is Σ^0_n m-complete.*

(iii) *A set B is Σ^0_{n+1} iff B is c.e. in $\emptyset^{(n)}$.*

(iv) *A set B is Δ^0_{n+1} iff $B \leqslant_{\mathrm{T}} \emptyset^{(n)}$.*

Proof. (i) First note that if B is c.e. in A then B is also c.e. in $\overline{A}$. Thus, being c.e. in a Σ^0_n set is the same as being c.e. in a Π^0_n set, so all we need to show is that B is Σ^0_{n+1} iff B is c.e. in some Π^0_n set.

The "only if" direction has the same proof as the corresponding part of Proposition 2.5.1, except that the computable relation R in that proof is now replaced by a Π^0_n relation R.

For the "if" direction, let B be c.e. in some Π^0_n set A. Then, by Proposition 2.5.1 relativized to A, there is an e such that $n \in B$ iff

$$\exists s\, \exists \sigma \prec A\, (\Phi^\sigma_e(n)[s]\downarrow). \tag{2.1}$$

The property in parentheses is computable, while the property $\sigma \prec A$ is a combination of a Π^0_n statement (asserting that certain elements are in A) and a Σ^0_n statement (asserting that certain elements are not in A), and hence is Δ^0_{n+1}. So (2.1) is a Σ^0_{n+1} statement.

(ii) We proceed by induction. By Propositions 2.4.5 and 2.5.1, $\emptyset'$ is Σ^0_1 m-complete. Now assume by induction that $\emptyset^{(n)}$ is Σ^0_n m-complete. Since $\emptyset^{(n+1)}$ is c.e. in $\emptyset^{(n)}$, it is Σ^0_{n+1}. Let C be Σ^0_{n+1}. By part (i), C is c.e. in some Σ^0_n set, and hence it is c.e. in $\emptyset^{(n)}$. As in the unrelativized case, it is now easy to define a computable function f such that $n \in C$ iff $f(n) \in \emptyset^{(n+1)}$. (In more detail, let e be such that $C = W^{\emptyset^{(n)}}_e$, and define f so that for all oracles X and all n and x, we have $\Phi^X_{f(n)}(x)\downarrow$ iff $n \in W^X_e$.)

(iii) By (i) and (ii), and the fact that if X is c.e. in Y and $Y \leqslant_T Z$, then X is also c.e. in Z.

(iv) The set B is Δ^0_{n+1} iff B and $\overline{B}$ are both Σ^0_{n+1}, and hence both c.e. in $\emptyset^{(n)}$ by (ii). But a set and its complement are both c.e. in X iff the set is computable in X. Thus B is Δ^0_{n+1} iff $B \leqslant_T \emptyset^{(n)}$. □

Note in particular that the Δ^0_2 sets are exactly the $\emptyset'$-computable sets, that is, the sets that have computable approximations.

There are many "natural" sets, such as certain index sets, that are complete for various levels of the arithmetic hierarchy. The following result gives a few examples.

Theorem 2.6.5. (i) *Fin* $= \{e : W_e$ *is finite*$\}$ *is* Σ^0_2 *m-complete.*

(ii) *Tot* $= \{e : \Phi_e$ *is total*$\}$ *and Inf* $= \{e : W_e$ *is infinite*$\}$ *are both* Π^0_2 *m-complete.*

(iii) *Cof* $= \{e : W_e$ *is cofinite*$\}$ *is* Σ^0_3 *m-complete.*

Proof sketch. None of these are terribly difficult. We do (i) as an example. We know that $\emptyset''$ is Σ^0_2 m-complete by Post's Theorem, and it is easy to check that Fin is itself Σ^0_2, so it is enough to m-reduce $\emptyset''$ to Fin. Using the *s-m-n* theorem, we can define a computable function f such that for all s and e, we have $s \in W_{f(e)}$ iff there is a $t \geqslant s$ such that either $\Phi^{\emptyset'}_e(e)[t]\uparrow$ or $\emptyset'_{t+1} \upharpoonright \varphi^{\emptyset'}_e(e)[t] \neq \emptyset'_t \upharpoonright \varphi^{\emptyset'}_e(e)[t]$. Then $f(e) \in$ Fin iff $\Phi^{\emptyset'}_e(e)\downarrow$ iff $e \in \emptyset''$.

Part (ii) is similar, and (iii) is also similar but more intricate. See Soare [366] for more details. □

2.7 The difference hierarchy

The arithmetic hierarchy gives us one way to extend the concept of computable enumerability. Another way to do so is via the *difference hierarchy*, which is defined as follows.

Definition 2.7.1. Let $n \geqslant 1$. A set A is *n-computably enumerable* (*n-c.e.*) if there is a computable binary function f such that for all x,

(i) $f(x,0) = 0$,

(ii) $A(x) = \lim_s f(x,s)$, and

(iii) $|\{s : f(x,s+1) \neq f(x,s)\}| \leqslant n$.

Thus the 1-c.e. sets are simply the c.e. sets. The 2-c.e. sets are often called *d.c.e.*, which stands for "difference of c.e.", because of the easily proved fact that A is 2-c.e. iff there are c.e. sets B and C such that $A = B \setminus C$.

We have seen the following definition in Section 2.6.

Definition 2.7.2. A set A is *ω-c.e.* if there are a computable binary function f and a computable unary function g such that for all x,

(i) $f(x,0) = 0$,

(ii) $A(x) = \lim_s f(x,s)$, and

(iii) $|\{s : f(x,s+1) \neq f(x,s)\}| \leqslant g(x)$.

In Corollary 2.6.2, we saw that the ω-c.e. sets are exactly those that are (w)tt-reducible to $\emptyset'$. The following fact was probably known before it was explicitly stated by Arslanov [14].

Proposition 2.7.3 (Arslanov [14]). *If A is ω-c.e. then there is a $B \equiv_{\mathrm{m}} A$ and a computable binary function h such that for all x,*

(i) $h(x,0) = 0$,

(ii) $B(x) = \lim_s h(x,s)$, *and*

(iii) $|\{s : h(x,s+1) \neq h(x,s)\}| \leqslant x$.

Proof. Let g be as in Definition 2.7.2. Without loss of generality, we may assume that g is increasing. Let $B = \{g(x) : x \in A\}$. Then B clearly has the desired properties. □

It is possible to define the concept of α-c.e. set for all computable ordinals α, forming what is known as the *Ershov hierarchy*. The details of the definition depend on ordinal notations. We will not use this concept in any significant way, so for simplicity we assume familiarity with the definition of a computable ordinal and Kleene's ordinal notations. For those unfamiliar with these concepts, we refer to Rogers [334] and Odifreddi [310, 311]. See Epstein, Haas, and Kramer [140] for more on α-c.e. sets and degrees.

Definition 2.7.4. Let α be a computable ordinal. A set A is *α-c.e.* relative to a computable system $\mathcal{S}$ of notations for α if there is a partial computable function f such that for all x, we have $A(x) = f(x, b)$ for the $\mathcal{S}$-least notation b such that $f(x, b)$ converges.

It is not hard to check that this definition agrees with the previous ones for $\alpha \leqslant \omega$, independently of the system of notations chosen.

As in the c.e. case, we say that a degree is n-c.e. if it contains an n-c.e. set, and similarly for ω-c.e. and α-c.e. degrees.

2.8 Primitive recursive functions

The class of *primitive recursive* functions is the smallest class of functions satisfying the following properties (where a 0-ary function is just a natural number).

(i) The function $n \mapsto n + 1$ is primitive recursive.

(ii) For each k and m, the function $(n_0, \ldots, n_{k-1}) \mapsto m$ is primitive recursive.

(iii) For each k and $i < k$, the function $(n_0, \ldots, n_{k-1}) \mapsto n_i$ is primitive recursive.

(iv) If f and $g_0, \ldots, g_{k-1}$ are primitive recursive, f is k-ary, and the g_i are all j-ary, then

$$(n_0, \ldots, n_{j-1}) \mapsto f(g_0(n_0, \ldots, n_{j-1}), \ldots, g_{k-1}(n_0, \ldots, n_{j-1}))$$

is primitive recursive.

(v) If the k-ary function g and the $(k + 2)$-ary function h are primitive recursive, then so is the function f defined by

$$f(0, n_0, \ldots, n_{k-1}) = g(n_0, \ldots, n_{k-1})$$

and

$$f(i + 1, n_0, \ldots, n_{k-1}) = h(n, f(i, n_0, \ldots, n_{k-1}), n_0, \ldots, n_{k-1}).$$

It is easy to see that every primitive recursive function is computable. However, it is also easy to see that the primitive recursive functions are total and can be effectively listed, so there are computable functions that are not primitive recursive.[3] A famous example is *Ackermann's function*

$$A(m,n) = \begin{cases} n+1 & \text{if } m = 0 \\ A(m-1,1) & \text{if } m > 0 \wedge n = 0 \\ A(m-1, A(m,n-1)) & \text{otherwise.} \end{cases}$$

Many natural computable functions are primitive recursive, though, and it is sometimes useful to work with an effectively listable class of total computable functions, so we will use primitive recursive functions in a few places below.

2.9 A note on reductions

There are several ways to describe a reduction procedure. Formally, $A \leqslant_{\mathrm{T}} B$ means that there is an e such that $\Phi_e^B = A$. In practice, though, we never actually build an oracle Turing machine to witness the fact that $A \leqslant_{\mathrm{T}} B$, but avail ourselves of the Church-Turing Thesis to informally describe a reduction Γ such that $\Gamma^B = A$. One such description is given in the proof of the $\Leftarrow$ direction of Shoenfield's Limit Lemma (Theorem 2.6.1). This proof gives an example of a *static* definition of a reduction procedure, in that the action of Γ is specified by a rule, rather than being defined during a construction. As an example of a *dynamic* definition of a reduction procedure, we reprove the $\Leftarrow$ direction of the limit lemma.

Recall that we are given a computable binary function g such that, for all n,

(i) $\lim_s g(n,s)$ exists and

(ii) $A(n) = \lim_s g(n,s)$.

We wish to show that $A \leqslant_{\mathrm{T}} \emptyset'$, by building a c.e. set B and a reduction $\Gamma^B = A$.

We simultaneously construct B and Γ in stages. We begin with $B_0 = \emptyset$. For each n, we leave the value of $\Gamma^B(n)$ undefined until stage n. At stage n, we let $\Gamma^B(n)[n] = g(n,n)$ with use $\gamma^B(n)[n] = \langle n, 0\rangle + 1$.

Furthermore, at stage $s > 0$ we proceed as follows for each $n < s$. If $g(n,s) = g(n,s-1)$, then we change nothing. That is, we let $\Gamma^B(n)[s] = \Gamma^B(n)[s-1]$ with the same use $\gamma^B(n)[s] = \gamma^B(n)[s-1]$. Otherwise, we enumerate $\gamma(n,s-1) - 1$ into B, which allows us to redefine $\Gamma^B(n)[s] = g(n,s)$, with use $\gamma^B(n)[s] = \langle n,k\rangle + 1$ for the least $\langle n,k\rangle \notin B$.

It is not hard to check that $\Gamma^B = A$, and that in fact this reduction is basically the same as that in the original proof of the limit lemma (if we

[3]We can obtain the partial computable functions by adding to the five items above an unbounded search scheme. See Soare [366] for more details and further discussion of primitive recursive functions.

assume without loss of generality that $g(n, n) = 0$ for all n), at least as far as its action on oracle B goes.

More generally, the rules for a reduction Δ^C to a c.e. set C are as follows, for each input n.

1. Initially $\Delta^C(n)[0]\uparrow$.

2. At some stage s we must define $\Delta^C(n)[s]\downarrow= i$ for some value i, with some use $\delta^C(n)[s]$. By this action, we are promising that $\Delta^C(n) = i$ unless $C \upharpoonright \delta^C(n)[s] \neq C_s \upharpoonright \delta^C(n)[s]$.

3. The convention now is that $\delta^C(n)[t] = \delta^C(n)[s]$ for $t > s$ unless $C_t \upharpoonright \delta^C(n)[s] \neq C_s \upharpoonright \delta^C(n)[t]$. Should we find a stage $t > s$ such that $C_t \upharpoonright \delta^C(n)[s] \neq C_s \upharpoonright \delta^C(n)[t]$, we then again have $\Delta^C(n)[t]\uparrow$.

4. We now again must have a stage $u \geqslant t$ at which we define $\Delta^C(n)[u]\downarrow= j$ for some value j, with some use $\delta^C(n)[u]$. We then return to step 3, with u in place of s.

5. If Δ^C is to be total, we have to ensure that we stay at step 3 permanently from some point on. That is, there must be a stage u at which we define $\Delta^C(n)[u]$ and $\delta^C(n)[u]$, such that $C \upharpoonright \delta^C(n)[u] = C_u \upharpoonright \delta^C(n)[u]$. One way to achieve this is to ensure that, from some point on, whenever we redefine $\delta^C(n)[u]$, we set it to the same value.

In some constructions, C will be given to us, but in others we will build it along with Δ. In this case, when we want to redefine the value of the computation $\Delta^C(n)$ at stage s, we will often be able to do so by putting a number less than $\delta^C(n)[s]$ into C (as we did in the limit lemma example above).

There is a similar method of building a reduction Δ^C when C is not c.e., but merely Δ^0_2. The difference is that now we must promise that if $\Delta^C(n)[s]$ is defined and there is a $t > s$ such that $C_t \upharpoonright \delta^C(n)[s] = C_s \upharpoonright \delta^C(n)[s]$, then $\Delta^C(n)[t] = \Delta^C(n)[s]$ and $\delta^C(n)[t] = \delta^C(n)[s]$.

A more formal view of a reduction is as a partial computable map from strings to strings obeying certain continuity conditions. In this view, a reduction $\Gamma^B = A$ is specified by a partial computable function $f : 2^{<\omega} \to 2^{<\omega}$ such that

1. if $\sigma \prec B$, then $f(\sigma) \prec A$;

2. for all $\sigma \prec \tau$, if both $f(\sigma)\downarrow$ and $f(\tau)\downarrow$, then $f(\sigma) \preccurlyeq f(\tau)$; and

3. for all $\tau \prec A$ there is a $\sigma \prec B$ such that $\tau \prec f(\sigma)$.

The reduction in the proof of the $\Leftarrow$ direction of the limit lemma can be viewed in this way by letting $f(\sigma)$ be the longest string τ such that, for all $n < |\tau|$, there is a k with $\sigma(\langle n, k\rangle) = 0$, and $\tau(n) = 0$ iff the first such k to be found is even.

Notice that this last method implies the following interesting observation: *A function $f : 2^{<\omega} \to 2^{<\omega}$ is continuous iff it is computable relative to some oracle.*

2.10 The finite extension method

In this section, we introduce one of the main techniques used in classical degree theory. We will refine this technique in the next section to what is known as the finite injury priority method.

The dynamic construction of a reduction from B to A in the limit lemma, discussed in the previous section, has much in common with many proofs in classical computability theory. We perform a construction where some object is built in stages. Typically, we have some overall goal that we break down into smaller subgoals that we argue are all met in the limit. In this case, the goal is to construct the reduction $\Gamma^B = A$. We break this goal into the subgoals of defining $\Gamma^B(n)$ for each n, and we accomplish these subgoals by using the information supplied by our "opponent", who is feeding us information about the universe, in this case the values $g(n, s)$.

As an archetype for such proofs, think of Cantor's proof that the collection of all infinite binary sequences is uncountable. One can conceive of this proof as follows. Suppose we could list the infinite binary sequences as $\mathcal{S} = \{S_0, S_1, \ldots\}$, with $S_e = s_{e,0}s_{e,1}\ldots$. It is our goal to construct a binary sequence $U = u_0u_1\ldots$ that is not on the list $\mathcal{S}$. We think of the construction as a game against our opponent who must supply us with $\mathcal{S}$. We construct u in stages, at stage t specifying only $u_0 \ldots u_t$, the initial segment of U of length $t+1$. Our list of *requirements* is the decomposition of the overall goal into subgoals of the form

$$\mathcal{R}_e : U \neq S_e.$$

There is one such requirement for each $e \in \mathbb{N}$. Of course, we know how to satisfy these requirements. At stage e, we simply ensure that $u_e \neq s_{e,e}$ by setting $u_e = 1 - s_{e,e}$. This action ensures that $U \neq S_e$ for all e; in other words, all the requirements are met. This fact contradicts the assumption that $\mathcal{S}$ lists all infinite binary sequences, as U is itself an infinite binary sequence.

Notice that if we define a real number to be *computable* if it has a computable binary expansion, then the above proof can be used to show that there is no computable listing of all the computable reals (modulo some unimportant technicalities involving nonunique representations of reals). We will return to the topic of effective real numbers in Chapter 5.

Clearly, the proof of the unsolvability of the halting problem can also be similarly recast, where this time the eth requirement asks us to invalidate the eth member of some supposed list of all algorithms deciding whether $\Phi_e(e)\downarrow$.

While later results will be more complicated than these easy examples, the overall structure of the above should be kept in mind: Our constructions will be in finite steps, where one or more objects are constructed stage by stage in finite pieces. These objects will be constructed to satisfy a list of requirements. The strategy we use will be dictated by how our opponent reveals the universe to us. Our overall goal is to satisfy all requirements in the limit.

To finish this section, we look at a slightly more involved version of this technique. While we know that there are uncountably many Turing degrees, the only ones we have seen so far are the iterates of the halting problem. Rice's Theorem 2.2.3 shows that all index sets are of degree $\geqslant \mathbf{0}'$. In 1944, Post [316] observed that all computably enumerable problems known at the time were either computable or of Turing degree $\mathbf{0}'$. He asked the following question.

Question 2.10.1 (Post's Problem). Does there exist a computably enumerable degree $\mathbf{a}$ with $\mathbf{0} < \mathbf{a} < \mathbf{0}'$?

As we will see in the next section, Post's Problem was finally given a positive answer by Friedberg [161] and Muchnik [284], using a new and ingenious method called the priority method. This method was an effectivization of an earlier method discovered by Kleene and Post [210]. The latter is called the finite extension method, and was used to prove the following result.

Theorem 2.10.2 (Kleene and Post [210]). *There are degrees* $\mathbf{a}$ *and* $\mathbf{b}$*, both below* $\mathbf{0}'$*, such that* $\mathbf{a} \mid \mathbf{b}$*. In other words, there are* $\emptyset'$*-computable sets that are incomparable under Turing reducibility.*[4]

Proof. We construct $A = \lim_s A_s$ and $B = \lim_s B_s$ in stages, to meet the following requirements for all $e \in \mathbb{N}$.

$$\mathcal{R}_{2e} : \Phi_e^A \neq B.$$
$$\mathcal{R}_{2e+1} : \Phi_e^B \neq A.$$

Note that if $A \leqslant_T B$ then there must be some procedure Φ_e with $\Phi_e^B = A$. Hence, if we meet all our requirements then $A \nleqslant_T B$, and similarly $B \nleqslant_T A$, so that A and B have incomparable Turing degrees. The fact that $A, B \leqslant_T \emptyset'$ will come from the construction and will be observed at the end.

The argument is by finite extensions, in the sense that at each stage s we specify a finite portion A_s of A and a finite portion B_s of B. These finite portions A_s and B_s will be specified as binary strings. The key invariant that we need to maintain throughout the construction is that $A_s \preccurlyeq A_u$ and

[4] The difference between the Kleene-Post Theorem and the solution to Post's Problem is that the degrees constructed in the proof of Theorem 2.10.2 are not necessarily computably enumerable, but merely Δ_2^0.

$B_s \preccurlyeq B_u$ for all stages $u \geqslant s$. Thus, after stage s we can only *extend* the portions of A and B that we have specified by stage s, which is a hallmark of the finite extension method.

Construction.
Stage 0. Let $A_0 = B_0 = \lambda$ (the empty string).

Stage $2e+1$. (Attend to $\mathcal{R}_{2e}$.) We will have specified A_{2e} and B_{2e} at stage $2e$. Pick some number x, called a *witness*, with $x \geqslant |B_{2e}|$, and ask whether there is a string σ properly extending A_{2e} such that $\Phi_e^\sigma(x)\downarrow$.

If such a σ exists, then let A_{2e+1} be the length-lexicographically least such σ. Let B_{2e+1} be the string of length $x+1$ extending B_{2e} such that $B_{2e+1}(n) = 0$ for all n with $|B_{2e}| \leqslant n < x$ and $B_{2e+1}(x) = 1 - \Phi_e^\sigma(x)$.

If no such σ exists, then let $A_{2e+1} = A_{2e}0$ and $B_{2e+1} = B_{2e}0$.

Stage $2e+2$. (Attend to $\mathcal{R}_{2e+1}$.) Define A_{2e+2} and B_{2e+2} by proceeding in the same way as at stage $2e+1$, but with the roles of A and B reversed.
End of Construction.

Verification. First note that we have $A_0 \prec A_1 \prec \cdots$ and $B_0 \prec B_1 \prec \cdots$, so A and B are well-defined.

We now prove that we meet the requirement $\mathcal{R}_n$ for each n; in fact, we show that we meet $\mathcal{R}_n$ at stage $n+1$. Suppose that $n = 2e$ (the case where n is odd being completely analogous). At stage $n+1$, there are two cases to consider. Let x be as defined at that stage.

If there is a σ properly extending A_n with $\Phi_e^\sigma(x)\downarrow$, then our action is to adopt such a σ as A_{n+1} and define B_{n+1} so that $\Phi_e^{A_{n+1}}(x) \neq B_{n+1}(x)$. Since A extends A_{n+1} and $\Phi_e^{A_{n+1}}(x)\downarrow$, it follows that A and A_{n+1} agree on the use of this computation, and hence $\Phi_e^A(x) = \Phi_e^{A_{n+1}}$. Since B extends B_{n+1}, we also have $B(x) = B_{n+1}(x)$. Thus $\Phi_e^A(x) \neq B(x)$, and $\mathcal{R}_n$ is met.

If there is no σ extending A_n with $\Phi_e^\sigma(x)\downarrow$, then since A is an extension of A_n, it must be the case $\Phi^A(x)\uparrow$, and hence $\mathcal{R}_n$ is again met.

Finally we argue that $A, B \leqslant_T \emptyset'$. Notice that the construction is in fact fully computable except for the decision as to which case we are in at a given stage. There we must decide whether there is a convergent computation of a particular kind. For instance, at stage $2e+1$ we must decide whether the following holds:

$$\exists \tau\, \exists s\, [\tau \succ A_{2e} \wedge \Phi_e^\tau(x)[s]\downarrow]. \qquad (2.2)$$

This is a Σ_1^0 question, uniformly in x, and hence can be decided by $\emptyset'$.[5] □

The reasoning at the end of the above proof is quite common: we often make use of the fact that $\emptyset'$ can answer any Δ_2^0 question, and hence any Σ_1^0 or Π_1^0 question.

[5]More precisely, we use the s-m-n theorem to construct a computable ternary function f such that for all e, σ, x, and z, we have $\Phi_{f(e,\sigma,x)}(z)\downarrow$ iff (2.2) holds. Then (2.2) holds iff $f(e, \sigma, x) \in \emptyset'$.

A key ingredient of the proof of Theorem 2.10.2 is the use principle (Proposition 2.4.1). In constructions of this sort, where we build objects to defeat certain oracle computations, a typical requirement will say something like "the reduction Γ is not a witness to $A \leqslant_{\mathrm{T}} B$." If we have a converging computation $\Gamma^B(n)[s] \neq A(n)[s]$ and we "preserve the use" of this computation by not changing B after stage s on the use $\gamma^B(n)[s]$ (and similarly preserve $A(n)$), then we will preserve this disagreement. But this use corresponds to only a finite portion of B, so we still have all the numbers bigger than it to meet other requirements. In the finite extension method, this use preservation is automatic, since once we define $B(x)$ we never redefine it, but in other constructions we will introduce below, this may not be the case, because we may have occasion to redefine certain values of B. In that case, to ensure that $\Gamma^B \neq A$, we will have to structure the construction so that, if Γ^B is total, then there are n and s such that $\Gamma^B(n)[s] \neq A(n)[s]$ and, from stage s on, we preserve both $A(n)$ and $B \upharpoonright \gamma^B(n)[s]$.

2.11 Post's Problem and the finite injury priority method

A more subtle technique than the finite extension method is the *priority method.* We begin by looking at the simplest incarnation of this elegant technique, the *finite injury priority method.* This method is somewhat like the finite extension method, but with backtracking.

The idea behind it is the following. Suppose we must again satisfy requirements $\mathcal{R}_0, \mathcal{R}_1, \ldots$, but this time we are constrained to some sort of effective construction, so we are not allowed to ask questions of a noncomputable oracle during the construction. As an illustration, let us reconsider Post's Problem (Question 2.10.1). Post's Problem asks us to find a c.e. degree strictly between $\mathbf{0}$ and $\mathbf{0}'$. It is clearly enough to construct c.e. sets A and B with incomparable Turing degrees. The Kleene-Post method does allow us to construct sets with incomparable degrees below $\mathbf{0}'$, using a $\emptyset'$ oracle question at each stage, but there is no reason to expect these sets to be computably enumerable. To make A and B c.e., we must have a *computable* (rather than merely $\emptyset'$-computable) construction where elements go into the sets A and B but never leave them. As we will see, doing so requires giving up on satisfying our requirements in order. The key idea, discovered independently by Friedberg [161] and Muchnik [284], is to pursue multiple strategies for each requirement, in the following sense.

In the proof of the Kleene-Post Theorem, it appears that, in satisfying the requirement $\mathcal{R}_{2e}$, we need to know whether or not there is a σ extending A_{2e} such that $\Phi_e^{\sigma}(x)\downarrow$, where x is our chosen witness. Now our idea is to first *guess* that no such σ exists, which means that we do nothing for $\mathcal{R}_{2e}$

other than keep x out of B. If at some point we find an appropriate σ, we then make A extend σ and put x into B if necessary, as in the Kleene-Post construction.

The only problem is that putting x into B may well upset the action of other requirements of the form $\mathcal{R}_{2i+1}$, because such a requirement might need B to extend some string τ (for the same reason that $\mathcal{R}_{2e}$ needs A to extend σ), which may no longer be possible. If we nevertheless put x into B, we say that we have *injured* $\mathcal{R}_{2i+1}$. Of course, $\mathcal{R}_{2i+1}$ can now choose a new witness and start over from scratch, but perhaps another requirement may injure it again later. So we need to somehow ensure that, for each requirement, there is a stage after which it is never injured.

To make sure that this is the case, we put a *priority ordering* on our requirements, by stating that $\mathcal{R}_j$ has stronger priority than $\mathcal{R}_i$ if $j < i$, and allow $\mathcal{R}_j$ to injure $\mathcal{R}_i$ only if $\mathcal{R}_j$ has stronger priority than $\mathcal{R}_i$. Thus $\mathcal{R}_0$ is never injured. The requirement $\mathcal{R}_1$ may be injured by the action of $\mathcal{R}_0$. However, once this happens $\mathcal{R}_0$ will never act again, so if $\mathcal{R}_1$ is allowed to start over at this point, it will succeed. This process of starting over is called *initialization*. Initializing $\mathcal{R}_1$ means that we restart its action with a new witness, chosen to be larger than any number previously seen in the construction, and hence larger than any number $\mathcal{R}_0$ cares about. This new incarnation of $\mathcal{R}_1$ is guaranteed never to be injured. It should now be clear that, by induction, each requirement will eventually reach a point, following a finite number of initializations, after which it will never be injured and hence will succeed in reaching its goal.

We may think of this kind of construction as a game between a team of industrialists (each possibly trying to erect a factory) and a team of environmentalists (each possibly trying to build a park). In the end we want the world to be happy. In other words, we want all desired factories and parks to be built. However, some of the players may get distracted by other activities and never decide to build anything, so we cannot simply let one player build, then the next, and so on, because we might then get permanently stuck waiting for a player who never decides to build. Members of the two teams have their own places in the pecking order. For instance, industrialist 6 has stronger priority than all environmentalists except the first six, and therefore can build anywhere except on parks built by the first six environmentalists. So industrialist 6 may choose to build on land already demarcated by environmentalist 10, say, who would then need to find another place to build a park. Of course, even if this event happens, a higher ranked environmentalist, such as number 3, for instance, could later lay claim to that same land, forcing industrialist 6 to find another place to build a factory. Whether the highest ranked industrialist has priority over the highest ranked environmentalist or vice versa is irrelevant to the construction, so we leave that detail to each reader's political leanings.

For each player, there are only finitely many other players with stronger priority, and once all of these have finished building what they desire, the given player has free pick of the remaining land (which is infinite), and can build on it without later being forced out.

In general, in a finite injury priority argument, we have a list of requirements in some priority ordering. There are several different ways to meet each individual requirement. Exactly which way will be possible to implement depends upon information that is not initially available to us but is "revealed" to us during the construction. The problem is that a requirement cannot wait for others to act, and hence must risk having its work destroyed by the actions of other requirements. We must arrange things so that only requirements of stronger priority can injure ones of weaker priority, and we can always restart the ones of weaker priority once they are injured. In a finite injury argument, any requirement *requires attention* only finitely often, and we argue by induction that each requirement eventually gets an environment wherein it can be met. As we will later see, there are much more complex infinite injury arguments where one requirement might injure another infinitely often, but the key there is that the injury is somehow controlled so that it is still the case that each requirement eventually gets an environment wherein it can be met. Of course, imposing this coherence criterion on our constructions means that each requirement must ensure that its action does not prevent weaker requirements from finding appropriate environments (a principle known as Harrington's "golden rule").

For a more thorough account of these beautiful techniques and their uses in modern computability theory, see Soare [366].

We now turn to the formal description of the solution to Post's Problem by Friedberg and Muchnik, which was the first use of the priority method. In Chapter 11, we will return to Post's Problem and explore its connections with the notion of Kolmogorov complexity.

Theorem 2.11.1 (Friedberg [161], Muchnik [284]). *There exist computably enumerable sets A and B such that A and B have incomparable Turing degrees.*

Proof. We build $A = \bigcup_s A_s$ and $B = \bigcup_s B_s$ in stages to satisfy the same requirements as in the proof of the Kleene-Post Theorem. That is, we make A and B c.e. while meeting the following requirements for all $e \in \mathbb{N}$.

$$\mathcal{R}_{2e} : \Phi_e^A \neq B.$$

$$\mathcal{R}_{2e+1} : \Phi_e^B \neq A.$$

The strategy for a single requirement. We begin by looking at the strategy for a single requirement $\mathcal{R}_{2e}$. We first pick a witness x to *follow* $\mathcal{R}_{2e}$. This *follower* is targeted for B, and, of course, we initially keep it out of B. We then wait for a stage s such that $\Phi_e^A(x)[s]\downarrow = 0$. If such a stage does not occur, then either $\Phi_e^A(x)\uparrow$ or $\Phi_e^A(x)\downarrow \neq 0$. In either case, since we keep x out of B, we have $\Phi_e^A(x) \neq 0 = B(x)$, and hence $\mathcal{R}_{2e}$ is satisfied.

If a stage s as above occurs, then we put x into B and *protect* A_s. That is, we try to ensure that any number entering A from now on is greater than any number seen in the construction thus far, and hence in particular greater than $\varphi_e^A(x)[s]$. If we succeed then, by the use principle, $\Phi_e^A(x) = \Phi_e^A(x)[s] = 0 \neq B(x)$, and hence again $\mathcal{R}_{2e}$ is satisfied. We refer to this action of protecting A_s as imposing *restraint* on weaker priority requirements.

Note that when we take this action, we might injure a requirement $\mathcal{R}_{2i+1}$ that is trying to preserve the use of a computation $\Phi_i^B(x')$, since x may be below this use. As explained above, the priority mechanism will ensure that this can happen only if $2i + 1 > 2e$.

We now proceed with the full construction. We will denote by A_s and B_s the sets of elements enumerated into A and B, respectively, by the end of stage s.

Construction.

Stage 0. Declare that no requirement currently has a follower.

Stage $s + 1$. Say that $\mathcal{R}_j$ *requires attention* at this stage if one of the following holds.

(i) $\mathcal{R}_j$ currently has no follower.

(ii) $\mathcal{R}_j$ has a follower x and, for some e, either

  (a) $j = 2e$ and $\Phi_e^A(x)[s]\downarrow = 0 = B_s(x)$ or
  (b) $j = 2e + 1$ and $\Phi_e^B(x)[s]\downarrow = 0 = A_s(x)$.

Find the least $j \leqslant s$ with $\mathcal{R}_j$ requiring attention. (If there is none, then proceed to the next stage.) We suppose that $j = 2e$, the odd case being symmetric. If $\mathcal{R}_{2e}$ has no follower, then let x be a *fresh large* number (that is, one larger than all numbers seen in the construction so far) and appoint x as $\mathcal{R}_{2e}$'s follower.

If $\mathcal{R}_{2e}$ has a follower x, then it must be the case that $\Phi_e^A(x)[s]\downarrow = 0 = B_s(x)$. In this case, enumerate x into B and *initialize* all $\mathcal{R}_k$ with $k > 2e$ by canceling all their followers.

In either case, we say that $\mathcal{R}_{2e}$ *receives attention* at stage s.

End of Construction.

Verification. We prove by induction that, for each j,

(i) $\mathcal{R}_j$ receives attention only finitely often, and

(ii) $\mathcal{R}_j$ is met.

Suppose that (i) holds for each $k < j$ in place of j. Suppose that $j = 2e$ for some e, the odd case being symmetric. Let s be the least stage such that for all $k < j$, the requirement $\mathcal{R}_k$ does not require attention after stage s. By the minimality of s, some requirement $\mathcal{R}_k$ with $k < j$ received attention at stage s (or $s = 0$), and hence $\mathcal{R}_j$ does not have a follower at the beginning of stage $s+1$. Thus, $\mathcal{R}_j$ requires attention at stage $s+1$, and is appointed a follower x. Since $\mathcal{R}_j$ cannot have its follower canceled unless some $\mathcal{R}_k$ with $k < j$ receives attention, x is $\mathcal{R}_j$'s permanent follower.

It is clear by the way followers are chosen that x is never any other requirement's follower, so x will not enter B unless $\mathcal{R}_j$ acts to put it into B. So if $\mathcal{R}_j$ never requires attention after stage $s+1$, then $x \notin B$, and we never have $\Phi_e^A(x)[t]\downarrow= 0$ for $t > s$, which implies that either $\Phi_e^A(x)\uparrow$ or $\Phi_e^A(x)\downarrow\neq 0$. In either case, $\mathcal{R}_j$ is met.

On the other hand, if $\mathcal{R}_j$ requires attention at a stage $t+1 > s+1$, then $x \in B$ and $\Phi_e^A(x)[t]\downarrow= 0$. The only requirements that put numbers into A after stage $t+1$ are ones weaker than $\mathcal{R}_j$ (i.e., requirements $\mathcal{R}_k$ for $k > j$). Each such strategy is initialized at stage $t+1$, which means that, when it is later appointed a follower, that follower will be bigger than $\varphi_e^A(x)[t]$. Thus no number less than $\varphi_e^A(x)[t]$ will ever enter A after stage $t+1$, which implies, by the use principle, that $\Phi^A(x)\downarrow= \Phi_e^A(x)[t] = 0 \neq B(x)$. So in this case also, $\mathcal{R}_j$ is met. Since $x \in B_{t+2}$ and x is $\mathcal{R}_j$'s permanent follower, $\mathcal{R}_j$ never requires attention after stage $t+1$. □

The above proof is an example of the simplest kind of finite injury argument, what is called a *bounded injury* construction. That is, we can put a computable bound *in advance* on the number of times that a given requirement $\mathcal{R}_j$ will be injured. In this case, the bound is $2^j - 1$.

We give another example of this kind of construction, connected with the important concept of lowness. It is natural to ask what can be said about the jump operator beyond the basic facts we have seen so far. The next theorem proves that the jump operator on degrees is not injective. Indeed, injectivity fails in the first place it can, in the sense that there are noncomputable sets that the jump operator cannot distinguish from $\emptyset$.

Theorem 2.11.2 (Friedberg). *There is a noncomputable c.e. low set.*

Proof. We construct our set A in stages. To make A noncomputable we need to meet the requirements

$$\mathcal{P}_e : \overline{A} \neq W_e.$$

To make A low we meet the requirements

$$\mathcal{N}_e : (\exists^\infty s\, \Phi_e^A(e)[s]\downarrow) \Rightarrow \Phi_e^A(e)\downarrow.$$

To see that such requirements suffice, suppose they are met and define the computable binary function g by letting $g(e,s) = 1$ if $\Phi_e^A(e)[s]\downarrow$ and $g(e,s) = 0$ otherwise. Then $g(e) = \lim_s g(e,s)$ is well-defined, and by the limit lemma, $A' = \{e : g(e) = 1\} \leqslant_{\mathrm{T}} \emptyset'$.

The strategy for $\mathcal{P}_e$ is simple. We pick a fresh large follower x, and keep it out of A. If x enters W_e, then we put x into A. We meet $\mathcal{N}_e$ by an equally simple conservation strategy. If we see $\Phi_e^A(e)[s]\downarrow$ then we simply try to ensure that $A \upharpoonright \varphi_e^A(e)[s] = A_s \upharpoonright \varphi_e^A(e)[s]$ by initializing all weaker priority requirements, which forces them to choose fresh large numbers as followers. These numbers will be too big to injure the $\Phi_e^A(e)[s]$ computation after stage s. The priority method sorts the actions of the various strategies out. Since $\mathcal{P}_e$ picks a fresh large follower each time it is initialized, it cannot injure any $\mathcal{N}_j$ for $j < e$. It is easy to see that any $\mathcal{N}_e$ can be injured at most e many times, and that each $\mathcal{P}_e$ is met, since it is initialized at most 2^e many times. □

Actually, the above proof constructs a noncomputable c.e. set that is superlow. (Recall that a set A is superlow if $A' \equiv_{tt} \emptyset'$.)

2.12 Finite injury arguments of unbounded type

2.12.1 The Sacks Splitting Theorem

There are priority arguments in which the number of injuries to each requirement, while finite, is not bounded by any computable function. One example is the following proof of the Sacks Splitting Theorem [342]. We write $A = A_0 \sqcup A_1$ to mean that $A = A_0 \cup A_1$ and $A_0 \cap A_1 = \emptyset$. Turing incomparable c.e. sets A_0 and A_1 such that $A = A_0 \sqcup A_1$ are said to form a *c.e. splitting* of A.

Theorem 2.12.1 (Sacks Splitting Theorem [342]). *Every noncomputable c.e. set has a c.e. splitting.*

Proof. Let A be a noncomputable c.e. set. We build $A_i = \bigcup_s A_{i,s}$ in stages by a priority argument to meet the following requirements for all $e \in \mathbb{N}$ and $i = 0, 1$, while ensuring that $A = A_0 \sqcup A_1$.

$$\mathcal{R}_{e,i} : \Phi_e^{A_i} \neq A.$$

These requirements suffice because if $A_{1-i} \leqslant_T A_i$ then $A \leqslant_T A_i$.

Without loss of generality, we assume that we are given an enumeration of A so that exactly one number enters A at each stage. We must put this number $x \in A_{s+1} \setminus A_s$ into exactly one of A_0 or A_1, to ensure that $A = A_0 \sqcup A_1$.

To meet $\mathcal{R}_{e,i}$, we define the *length of agreement function*

$$l(e,i,s) = \max\{n : \forall k < n\,(\Phi_e^{A_i}(k)[s] = A(k)[s])\}$$

and an associated use function

$$u(e,i,s) = \varphi_e^{A_i}(l(e,i,s) - 1)[s],$$ [6]

using the convention that use functions are monotone increasing (with respect to the position variable) where defined.

[6] Of course, in defining this set we ignore s's such that $l(e,i,s) = 0$. We will do the same without further comment below. Here and below, we take the maximum of the empty set to be 0.

The main idea of the proof is perhaps initially counterintuitive. Let us consider a single requirement $\mathcal{R}_{e,i}$ in isolation. At each stage s, although we want $\Phi_e^{A_i} \neq A$, instead of trying to destroy the agreement between $\Phi_e^{A_i}[s]$ and $A[s]$ represented by $l(e,i,s)$, we try to *preserve* it (a method sometimes called the *Sacks preservation strategy*). The way we implement this preservation is to put numbers entering $A \upharpoonright u(e,i,s)$ after stage s into A_{1-i} and *not* into A_i. By the use principle, since this action freezes the A_i side of the computations involved in the definition of $l(e,i,s)$, it ensures that $\Phi_e^{A_i}(k) = \Phi_e^{A_i}(k)[s]$ for all $k < l(e,i,s)$.

Now suppose that $\limsup_s l(e,i,s) = \infty$, so for each k we can find infinitely many stages s at which $k < l(e,i,s)$. For each such stage, $\Phi_e^{A_i}(k) = \Phi_e^{A_i}(k)[s] = A(k)[s]$. Thus $A(k) = A(k)[s]$ for any such s. So we can compute $A(k)$ simply by finding such an s, which contradicts the noncomputability of A. Thus $\limsup_s l(e,i,s) < \infty$, which clearly implies that $\mathcal{R}_{e,i}$ is met.

In the full construction, of course, we have competing requirements, which we sort out by using priorities. That is, we establish a priority list of our requirements (for instance, saying that $\mathcal{R}_{e,i}$ is stronger than $\mathcal{R}_{e',i'}$ iff $\langle e,i\rangle < \langle e',i'\rangle$). At stage s, for the single element x_s entering A at stage s, we find the strongest priority $\mathcal{R}_{e,i}$ with $\langle e,i\rangle < s$ such that $x_s < u(e,i,s)$ and put x_s into A_{1-i}. We say that $\mathcal{R}_{e,i}$ *acts* at stage s. (If there is no such requirement, then we put x_s into A_0.)

To verify that this construction works, we argue by induction that each requirement eventually stops acting and is met. Suppose that all requirements stronger than $\mathcal{R}_{e,i}$ eventually stop acting, say by a stage $s > \langle e,i\rangle$. At any stage $t > s$, if $x_t < u(e,i,t)$, then x_t is put into A_{1-i}. The same argument as in the one requirement case now shows that if $\limsup_s l(e,i,s) = \infty$ then A is computable, so $\limsup_s l(e,i,s) < \infty$. Our preservation strategy then ensures that $\limsup_s u(e,i,s) < \infty$. Thus $\mathcal{R}_{e,i}$ eventually stops acting and is met. □

In the above construction, injury to a requirement $\mathcal{R}_{e,i}$ happens whenever $x_s < u(e,i,s)$ but x_s is nonetheless put into A_i, at the behest of a stronger priority requirement. How often $\mathcal{R}_{e,i}$ is injured depends on the lengths of agreement attached to stronger priority requirements, and thus cannot be computably bounded.

Note that, for any noncomputable c.e. set C, we can easily add requirements of the form $\Phi_e^{A_i} \neq C$ to the above construction, satisfying them in the same way that we did for the $\mathcal{R}_{e,i}$. Thus, as shown by Sacks [342], in addition to making $A_0 \mid_{\mathrm{T}} A_1$, we can also ensure that $A_i \not\geqslant_{\mathrm{T}} C$ for $i = 0, 1$.

Note also that the computable enumerability of A is not crucial in the above argument. Indeed, a similar argument works for any set A that has a computable approximation, that is, any Δ_2^0 set A. Such an argument shows that if A and C are noncomputable Δ_2^0 sets, then there exist Turing incomparable Δ_2^0 sets A_0 and A_1 such that $A = A_0 \sqcup A_1$ and $A_i \not\geqslant_{\mathrm{T}} C$

for $i = 0, 1$. Checking that the details of the proof still work in this case is a good exercise for those unfamiliar with priority arguments involving Δ^0_2 sets.

2.12.2 The Pseudo-Jump Theorem

Another basic construction using the finite injury method was discovered by Jockusch and Shore [193]. It involves what are called *pseudo-jump operators*.

Definition 2.12.2 (Jockusch and Shore [193]). For an index e, let the *pseudo-jump operator* V_e be defined by $V_e^A = A \oplus W_e^A$ for all oracles A. We say that V_e is *nontrivial* if $A <_{\mathrm{T}} V_e^A$ for all oracles A.

The jump operator is itself a nontrivial pseudo-jump operator (up to degree). The following pseudo-jump inversion theorem is an important tool in the theory of pseudo-jump operators.

Theorem 2.12.3 (Jockusch and Shore [193]). *For any nontrivial pseudo-jump operator V, there is a noncomputable c.e. set A with $V^A \equiv_{\mathrm{T}} \emptyset'$.*

Proof. We build $A = \bigcup_s A_s$ in stages. Let k be such that $V^X = X \oplus W_k^X$ for all X.

To ensure that $V^A \leqslant_{\mathrm{T}} \emptyset'$, we meet the requirements

$$\mathcal{N}_n : \exists^\infty s\,(n \in W_k^A[s]) \;\Rightarrow\; n \in W_k^A,$$

which imply that W_k^A is Π^0_2. Since W_k^A is necessarily Σ^0_2 and V^A is the join of W_k^A with a c.e. set, these requirements suffice to ensure that V^A is Δ^0_2. To satisfy $\mathcal{N}_n$, we have a *restraint function* $r(n,s)$, which we define as follows. If $n \in W_k^A[s]$, then $r(n,s)$ is the use of the computation ensuring this fact (that is, $\varphi_k^A(n)[s]$). Otherwise, $r(n,s) = 0$.

Let $\gamma(n,s)$ be the least element of $\mathbb{N}^{[n]}$ greater than or equal to $r(m,s)$ for all $m \leqslant n$. We use these numbers both to make A noncomputable and to ensure that $\emptyset' \leqslant_{\mathrm{T}} V^A$. We will make sure that $\gamma(n) = \lim_s \gamma(n,s)$ exists for all n.

To make A noncomputable, we meet the requirements

$$\mathcal{R}_e : \overline{W_e} \neq A,$$

by putting $\gamma(2e,s)$ into A if we have not yet satisfied $\mathcal{R}_e$ and $\gamma(2e,s) \in W_e[s]$.

To have $\emptyset' \leqslant_{\mathrm{T}} V^A$, we ensure that, for each n, we can V^A-computably determine a stage u such that $\gamma(n,s) = \gamma(n,u)$ for all $s \geqslant u$, and satisfy

$$\mathcal{P}_n : n \in \emptyset' \;\Leftrightarrow\; \exists s\,(\gamma(2n+1,s) \in A).$$

To satisfy $\mathcal{P}_n$, if n enters $\emptyset'$ at stage s, then we put $\gamma(2n+1,s)$ into A.

Thus the full construction proceeds as follows at stage s: For each e such that $W_e[s] \cap A[s] = \emptyset$ and $\gamma(2e, s) \in W_e[s]$, put $\gamma(2e, s)$ into A. For each n entering $\emptyset'$ at stage s, put $\gamma(2n+1, s)$ into A.

We put at most one number into A for the sake of a given $\mathcal{R}$- or $\mathcal{P}$-requirement. By the definition of the γ function, for each n there is an s such that, for all $t \geqslant s$, no number less than $r(n, t)$ is put into A at stage t. It follows that $\lim_t r(n, t)$ exists, and $\mathcal{N}_n$ is satisfied.

Thus $\gamma(n) = \lim_s \gamma(n, s)$ exists for all n, and the construction ensures that if $W_e \cap A = \emptyset$ then $\gamma(2e) \in A$ iff $\gamma(2e) \in W_e$, so that $\mathcal{R}_e$ is satisfied.

It is also clear that each $\mathcal{P}$-requirement is satisfied by the construction, so we are left with showing that for each n, we can V^A-computably determine a stage u such that $\gamma(n, s) = \gamma(n, u)$ for all $s \geqslant u$. Assume by induction that we have determined a stage t such that $\gamma(m, s) = \gamma(m, t)$ for all $m < n$ and $s \geqslant t$. Let $u > t$ be a stage such that for all $m \leqslant n$, if $m \in W_k^A$ then $m \in W_k^A[u]$. Clearly, such a u can be found V^A-computably. Let $m \leqslant n$. If $m \in W_k^A$ then $r(m, s) = r(m, u)$ for all $s \geqslant u$, since no number less than $r(m, u)$ enters A during or after stage u. Now suppose that $m \notin W_k^A$. For each $s \geqslant u$, no number less than $r(m, s)$ enters A during or after stage s, so if m were in $W_k^A[s]$ then it would be in W_k^A, and hence $m \notin W_k^A[s]$. Thus in this case $r(m, s) = 0$ for all $s \geqslant u$. So we see that $r(m, s) = r(m, u)$ for all $m \leqslant n$ and $s \geqslant u$, and hence $\gamma(n, s) = \gamma(n, u)$ for all $s \geqslant u$. □

Jockusch and Shore [193, 194] used the pseudo-jump machinery to establish a number of results. One application is a finite injury proof that there is a high incomplete c.e. Turing degree, a result first proved using the infinite injury method, as we will see in Section 2.14.3. The Jockusch-Shore proof of the existence of a high incomplete c.e. degree in fact produces a superhigh degree (where a set X is *superhigh* if $\emptyset'' \leqslant_{\mathrm{tt}} X'$), and runs as follows. Relativize the original Friedberg theorem that there is a noncomputable set W_e of low (or even superlow) Turing degree, to obtain an operator V_e such that for all Y we have that $Y <_{\mathrm{T}} V_e^Y$ and V_e^Y is (super)low over Y. Then use Theorem 2.12.3 to obtain a c.e. set A with $V_e^A \equiv_{\mathrm{T}} \emptyset'$. Then $\emptyset'$ is (super)low over A and $A <_{\mathrm{T}} \emptyset'$, and hence A is (super)high and incomplete. We will use this pseudo-jump technique again in Section 11.8. See Jockusch and Shore [193, 194], Downey and Shore [132], and Coles, Downey, Jockusch, and LaForte [73] for more on the general theory of pseudo-jump operators.

2.13 Coding and permitting

Coding and permitting are two basic methods for controlling the degrees of sets we build. Coding is a way of ensuring that a set A we build has degree at least that of a given set B. As the name implies, it consists of encoding the bits of B into A in a recoverable way. One simple way to to do this is to build A to equal $B \oplus C$ for some C, but in some cases we need to employ a more elaborate coding method. We will see an example in Proposition 2.13.1 below.

Permitting is a way of ensuring that a set A we build has degree at most that of a given set B. We will describe the basic form of c.e. permitting. For more elaborate forms of c.e. permitting, see Soare [366]. For a thorough exposition of the Δ_2^0 permitting method, see Miller [281].

Let B be a noncomputable c.e. set, and suppose we are building a c.e. set A to satisfy certain requirements while also ensuring that $A \leqslant_T B$. At a stage s in the construction, we may want to put a number n into A. But instead of putting n into A immediately, we wait for a stage $t \geqslant s$ such that $B_{t+1} \upharpoonright n \neq B_t \upharpoonright n$. At that stage, we say that B *permits* us to put n into A. If we always wait for permissions of this kind before putting numbers into A, then we can compute A from B as follows. Given n, look for an s such that $B_s \upharpoonright n = B \upharpoonright n$. Then $n \in A$ iff $n \in A_s$. Of course, one has to worry whether a particular requirement can live with this permitting strategy. But suppose that we have a requirement $\mathcal{R}$ that provides us with infinitely many followers n, and will be satisfied as long as one such n enters A. Suppose that we never get a permission to put such an n into A. Then we can compute B as follows. Given m, wait for a stage s such that $\mathcal{R}$ provides us with a follower $n > m$. Since we are assuming we are never permitted to put n into A, we have $B \upharpoonright n = B_s \upharpoonright n$. In particular, $m \in B$ iff $m \in B_s$. Since we are assuming that B is noncomputable, some follower must eventually be permitted to enter A, and hence $\mathcal{R}$ is satisfied.

The following proof illustrates both coding and permitting. Recall that a coinfinite c.e. set A is simple if its complement does not contain any infinite c.e. set.

Proposition 2.13.1. *Every nonzero c.e. degree contains a simple set.*

Proof. Let B be a noncomputable c.e. set. We may assume that exactly one element x_s enters B at each stage s. We build a c.e. set $A \equiv_T B$ to satisfy the simplicity requirements

$$\mathcal{R}_e : |W_e| = \infty \;\Rightarrow\; W_e \cap A \neq \emptyset.$$

At stage s, let $a_0^s < a_1^s < \cdots$ be the elements of $\overline{A_s}$. For each $e < s$, if $W_{e,s} \cap A_s = \emptyset$ and there is an $n \in W_{e,s}$ with $n > 3e$ and $n > x_s$, then put n into A. Also, put $a_{3x_s}^s$ into A.

The set A is clearly c.e. Each $\mathcal{R}_e$ puts at most one number into A, and this number must be greater than $3e$, while for each $x \in B$, the coding of B puts only one number into A, and this number is at least $3x$. Thus A is coinfinite.

For each n, if $B_s \upharpoonright n+1 = B \upharpoonright n+1$, then $n < x_t$ for all $t > s$, so n cannot enter A after stage s. As explained above, it follows that $A \leqslant_T B$.

Given x, the set A can compute a stage s such that $a_i^s \in \overline{A}$ for all $i \leqslant 3x$. Then $a_{3x}^t = a_{3x}^s$ for all $t \geqslant s$, so $x \in B$ iff either $x \in B_s$ or $a_{3x}^s \in A$. Thus $B \leqslant_T A$.

Finally, we need to show that each $\mathcal{R}_e$ is met. Suppose that W_e is infinite but $W_e \cap A = \emptyset$. Then we can computably find $3e < n_0 < n_1 < \cdots$ and $e \leqslant s_0 < s_1 < \cdots$ such that $n_i \in W_{e,s_i}$ for all i. None of the n_i are ever permitted by B, that is, $n_i \leqslant x_t$ for all i and $t \geqslant s_i$. So $B \upharpoonright n_i = B_{s_i} \upharpoonright n_i$ for all i, and hence B is computable, contrary to hypothesis. Thus each requirement is met, and hence A is simple. □

2.14 The infinite injury priority method

In this section, we introduce the infinite injury priority method. We begin by discussing the concept of priority trees, then give a few examples of constructions involving such trees. See Soare [366] for further examples.

2.14.1 Priority trees and guessing

The Friedberg-Muchnik construction used to prove Theorem 2.11.1 can be viewed another way. Instead of having a single strategy for each requirement, which is restarted every time a stronger priority requirement acts, we can attach multiple versions of each requirement to a *priority tree*, in this case the full binary tree $2^{<\omega}$.

Recall that the relevant requirements are the following.

$$\mathcal{R}_{2e} : \Phi_e^A \neq B.$$

$$\mathcal{R}_{2e+1} : \Phi_e^B \neq A.$$

Attached to each node σ is a "version" R_σ of $\mathcal{R}_{|\sigma|}$. We call such a version a *strategy* for $\mathcal{R}_{|\sigma|}$, and refer to σ itself as a *guess*, for reasons that will soon become clear. Thus there are 2^e separate strategies for $\mathcal{R}_e$.

Each strategy R_σ has two *outcomes*, 0 and 1. The outcome 1 indicates that R_σ appoints a follower but never enumerates this follower into its target set. The outcome 0 indicates that R_σ actually enumerates its follower into its target set. At a stage s, we have a guess as to which outcome is correct, depending on whether or not R_σ has enumerated its follower into its target set. If this guess is ever 0, then we immediately know that 0 is indeed the correct outcome, so we regard the 0 outcome as being stronger than the 1 outcome. We order our guesses lexicographically, and hence if σ is to the left of τ, then we think of σ as being stronger than τ.

Figure 2.1 shows the above setup. For comparison, it also shows the setup for the Minimal Pair Theorem, which will be discussed in the next subsection.

Here is how this mechanism is used. Consider $\mathcal{R}_1$. We have two strategies for this requirement. One, which in this paragraph we write as $R_{\langle 0 \rangle}$ rather than R_0 to avoid confusion with $\mathcal{R}_0$, is below the 0 outcome of R_λ and the other, $R_{\langle 1 \rangle}$, is below the 1 outcome of R_λ. We think of these versions

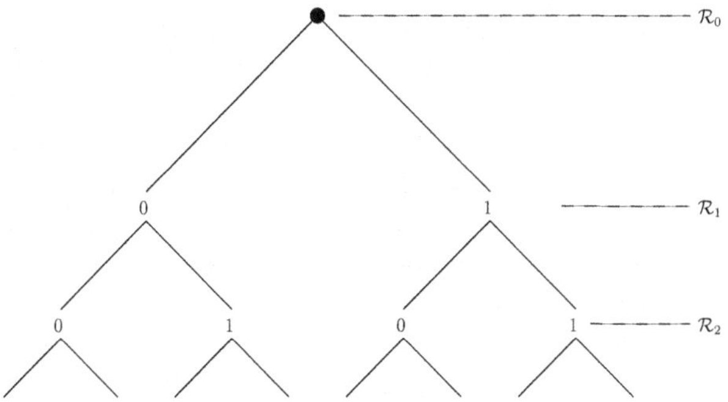

For the Friedberg-Muchnik Theorem

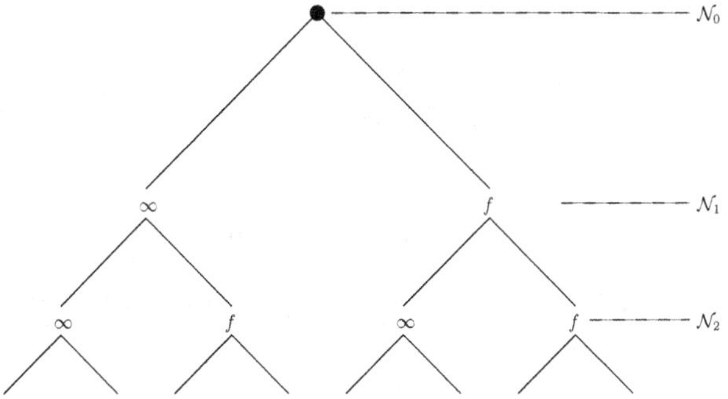

For the Minimal Pair Theorem

Figure 2.1. The assignment of priorities and outcomes

as guessing that R_λ's outcome is 0 and 1, respectively. The strategy $R_{\langle 1\rangle}$ believes that R_λ will appoint a follower, but will never enumerate it into its target set. Thus its action is simply to act immediately after its guess appears correct, that is, once R_λ appoints its follower. At this point, $R_{\langle 1\rangle}$ can appoint its own follower, and proceed to act as $\mathcal{R}_1$ would have acted in the original proof of the Friedberg-Muchnik Theorem. Its belief may turn out to be false (i.e., R_λ may enumerate its follower into its target set), in which case its action may be negated, but in that case we do not care about $R_{\langle 1\rangle}$. Indeed, in general, we only care about strategies whose guesses about the outcomes of strategies above them in the tree are correct. So we have the "back-up" strategy $R_{\langle 0\rangle}$, which believes that R_λ will enumerate its follower into its target set. This strategy will act only once its guess appears correct, i.e., after R_λ enumerates its follower into its target set. Then and only then does this strategy wake up and appoint its follower.

The above is extended inductively on the tree of strategies in a natural way. For instance, for $\sigma = 0110$, there is a strategy R_σ for $\mathcal{R}_4$, which guesses that R_λ and R_{011} do not enumerate their followers, but R_0 and R_{01} do.

This strategy waits for R_λ and R_{011} to appoint followers, and for R_0 and R_{01} to both appoint followers and then enumerate them. Once all of these conditions are met, it appoints its own follower and proceeds to act as $\mathcal{R}_4$ would have acted in the original proof of the Friedberg-Muchnik Theorem.

More precisely, at stage s, we have a guess σ_s of length s, which is defined inductively. Only those strategies R_τ with $\tau \preccurlyeq \sigma_s$ get to act at stage s. We say that such τ are *visited* at stage s. Suppose we have defined $\sigma_s \upharpoonright n$. Let $\tau = \sigma_s \upharpoonright n$. Then we allow R_τ to act as follows. Let us suppose that $n = 2e$, the odd case being symmetric. If R_τ has previously put a number into B, then it does nothing. In this case, if $n < s$ then $\sigma(n) = 0$. Otherwise, R_τ acts in one of three ways.

1. If R_τ does not currently have a follower, then it appoints a follower x_τ greater than any number seen in the construction so far. In this case, if $n < s$ then $\sigma_s(n) = 1$.

2. Otherwise, if $\Phi_e^A(x_\tau)[s]\downarrow = 0 = B_s(x_\tau)$, then R_τ enumerates x_τ into B. In this case, if $n < s$ then $\sigma_s(n) = 0$.

3. Otherwise, R_τ does nothing. In this case, if $n < s$ then $\sigma_s(n) = 1$.

The strategy R_λ has a *true outcome* i, which is 0 if it eventually enumerates its witness into B, and 1 otherwise. Similarly, R_i has a true outcome. The *true path* TP of the construction is the unique path such that $\mathrm{TP}(n)$ is the true outcome of $R_{\mathrm{TP}\upharpoonright n}$. Note that, in the above construction, $\mathrm{TP}(n) = \lim_s \sigma_s(n)$, but with an eye to more complicated tree constructions, we in general define the true path of such a construction as the leftmost path visited infinitely often (that is, the path extending those guesses τ such that τ is the leftmost guess of length $|\tau|$ that is visited infinitely often). The idea behind this definition is that the strategies on the true path are the ones that actually succeed in meeting their respective requirements.

In the construction described above, it is easy to verify that this is indeed the case. Let $\tau \in \mathrm{TP}$. Again, let us assume that $|\tau| = 2e$, the odd case being symmetric. At the first stage s at which τ is visited, a follower x_τ is appointed. Since followers are always chosen to be fresh large numbers, x_τ will not be enumerated into B by any strategy other than R_τ. So if $\Phi_e^A(x_\tau)\uparrow$ or $\Phi_e^A(x_\tau)\downarrow = 1$, then $\mathcal{R}_{|\tau|}$ is met. Otherwise, there is a stage $t > s$ such that $\Phi_e^A(x_\tau)[t]\downarrow = 0 = B_t(x_\tau)$ and τ is visited at stage t. Then R_τ enumerates x_τ into B.

Nodes to the right of $\tau 0$ will never again be visited, so the corresponding strategies will never again act. Nodes to the left of τ are never visited at all, so the corresponding strategies never act. Nodes extending $\tau 0$ will not have been visited before stage t, so the corresponding strategies will pick followers greater than $\varphi_e^A(x_\tau)[t]$. If $n < |\tau|$ then there are two possibilities. If $\tau(n) = 1$ then 1 is the true outcome of $R_{\tau\upharpoonright n}$, and hence that strategy never enumerates its witness. If $\tau(n) = 0$ then $R_{\tau\upharpoonright n}$ must have already enumerated its witness by stage s, since otherwise τ would not have been visited at that stage. In either case, we see that strategies corresponding to nodes extended by τ do not enumerate numbers during or after stage t.

The upshot of the analysis in the previous paragraph is that no strategy enumerates a number less than $\varphi_e^A(x_\tau)[t]$ into A during or after stage t, so by the use principle, $\Phi_e^A(x_\tau)\downarrow = 0 \neq B(x_\tau)$, and hence $\mathcal{R}_\tau$ is met.

It is natural to wonder why we should introduce all this machinery. For the Friedberg-Muchnik Theorem itself, as well as for most finite injury arguments, the payoff in new insight provided by this reorganization of the construction does not really balance the additional notational and conceptual burden. However, the above concepts were developed in the past few decades to make *infinite* injury arguments comprehensible.

The key difference between finite injury and infinite injury arguments is the following. In an infinite injury argument, the action of a given requirements $\mathcal{R}$ may be infinitary. Obviously, we cannot simply restart weaker priority requirements every time $\mathcal{R}$ acts. Instead, we can have multiple strategies for weaker priority requirements, depending on whether or not $\mathcal{R}$ acts infinitely often. Thus, in a basic setup of this sort, the left outcome of $\mathcal{R}$, representing the guess that $\mathcal{R}$ acts infinitely often, is visited each time $\mathcal{R}$ acts.

In the Friedberg-Muchnik argument, the approximation to the true path moves only to the left as time goes on, since the guessed outcome of a strategy can change from 1 to 0, but never the other way. Thus, the true path is computable in $\emptyset'$. In infinite injury arguments, the approximation to the true path can move both left and right. Assuming that the tree is finitely branching, this possibility means that, in general, the true path is computable only in $\emptyset''$. It clearly is computable in $\emptyset''$ because, letting TP_s be the unique string of length s visited at stage s,

$$\sigma \prec \mathrm{TP} \text{ iff } \exists^\infty s\, (\sigma \prec \mathrm{TP}_s) \wedge \exists^{<\infty} s\, (\mathrm{TP}_s <_{\mathrm{lex}} \sigma).$$

In the following sections, we will give examples of infinite injury priority tree constructions to illustrate the application of this mechanism.

2.14.2 The minimal pair method

Our first example of infinite injury argument is the construction of a minimal pair of c.e. degrees. A pair of noncomputable degrees $\mathbf{a}$ and $\mathbf{b}$ is a *minimal pair* if the only degree below both $\mathbf{a}$ and $\mathbf{b}$ is $\mathbf{0}$.

Theorem 2.14.1 (Lachlan [231], Yates [408]). *There is a minimal pair of c.e. degrees.*

Proof. We build noncomputable c.e. sets A and B such that every set computable in both A and B is computable. We construct A and B in stages to satisfy the following requirements for each e.

$$\mathcal{R}_e : \overline{A} \neq W_e.$$

$$\mathcal{Q}_e : \overline{B} \neq W_e.$$

$$\mathcal{N}_e : \Phi_e^A = \Phi_e^B \text{ total } \Rightarrow \Phi_e^A \text{ computable.}^7$$

We arrange these requirements in a priority list as in previous constructions.

We meet the $\mathcal{R}$- and $\mathcal{Q}$-requirements by a Friedberg-Muchnik type strategy. For instance, to satisfy $\mathcal{R}_e$, we pick a follower x, targeted for A, and wait until x enters W_e. If this event never happens, then $x \in \overline{A} \cap \overline{W_e}$, so $\mathcal{R}_e$ is met. If x does enter W_e, then we put x into A, thus again meeting $\mathcal{R}_e$.

The $\mathcal{N}$-requirements are trickier to meet. We first discuss how to meet a single $\mathcal{N}_e$ in isolation, and then look at the coherence problems between the various requirements and the solution to these provided by the use of a tree of strategies.

We follow standard conventions, in particular assuming that all uses at stage s are bounded by s. As in the proof of the Sacks Splitting Theorem 2.12.1, we have a length of agreement function

$$l(e,s) = \max\{n : \forall k < n\, (\Phi_e^A(k)[s]\downarrow = \Phi_e^B(k)[s]\downarrow)\}$$

and an associated use function

$$u(e,s) = \max\{\varphi_e^A(l(e,t)-1)[t],\ \varphi_e^B(l(e,t)-1)[t] : t \leqslant s\},$$

using the convention that use functions are monotone increasing where defined. We now also have a maximum length of agreement function

$$m(e,s) = \max\{l(e,t) : t \leqslant s\},$$

which can be thought of as a high water mark for the length of agreements seen so far. We say that a stage s is *e-expansionary* if $l(e,s) > m(e,s-1)$, that is, if the current length of agreement surpasses the previous high water mark.

The key idea for meeting $\mathcal{N}_e$ is the following. Suppose that $n < l(e,s)$, so that $\Phi_e^A(n)[s]\downarrow = \Phi_e^B(n)[s]\downarrow$. Now suppose that we allow numbers to enter A at will, but "freeze" the computation $\Phi_e^B(n)[s]$ by not allowing

---

[7] Clearly, meeting the $\mathcal{R}$- and $\mathcal{Q}$-requirements is enough to ensure that A and B are noncomputable. As for the $\mathcal{N}$-requirements, it might seem at first glance that we need stronger requirements, of the form $\Phi_i^A = \Phi_j^B$ total $\Rightarrow$ Φ_i^A computable. However, suppose that we are able to meet the $\mathcal{N}$-requirements. Then we cannot have $A = B$, since the $\mathcal{N}$-requirements would then force A and B to be computable. So there is an n such that $A(n) \neq B(n)$. Let us assume without loss of generality that $n \in B$. If $f \leqslant_T A, B$ then there are i and j such that $\Phi_i^A = \Phi_j^B = f$. But also, there is an e such that, for all oracles X, we have $\Phi_e^X = \Phi_i^X$ if $n \notin X$ and $\Phi_e^X = \Phi_j^X$ if $n \in X$. For this e, we have $\Phi_e^A = \Phi_e^B = f$. So if such an f is total, then $\mathcal{N}_e$ ensures that it is computable. This argument is known as *Posner's trick*. It is, of course, merely a notational convenience.

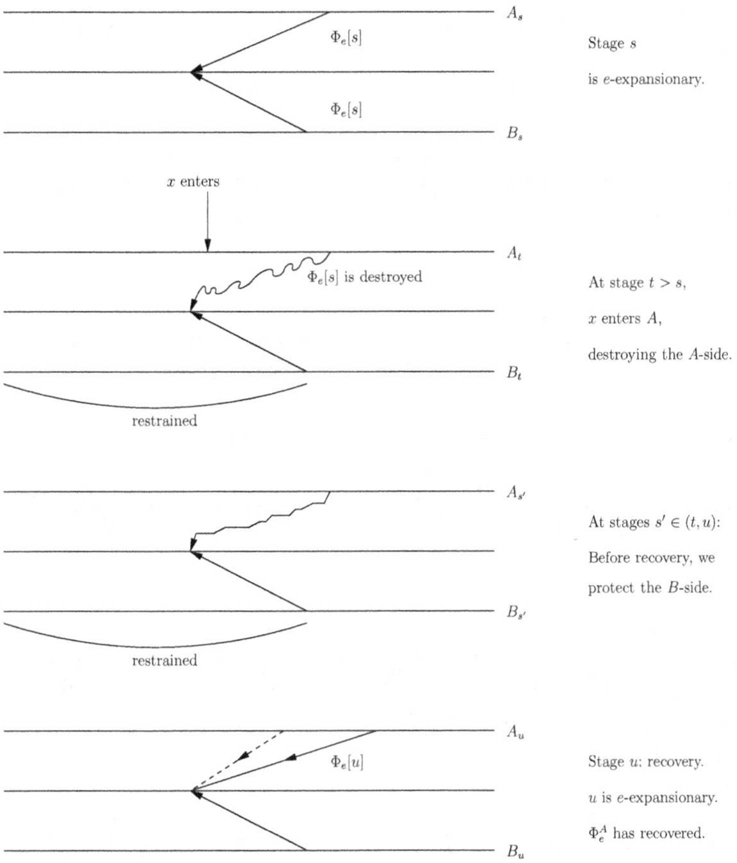

Figure 2.2. The $\mathcal{N}_e$ strategy

any number to enter B below $\varphi_e^B(n)[s]$ until the next e-expansionary stage $t > s$. At this stage t, we again have $\Phi_e^A(n)[t] \downarrow = \Phi_e^B(n)[t] \downarrow$. But we also have $\Phi_e^B(n)[t] = \Phi_e^B(n)[s]$, by the use principle. Now suppose that we start allowing numbers to enter B at will, but freeze the computation $\Phi_e^A(n)[t]$ by not allowing any number to enter A below $\varphi_e^A(n)[t]$ until the next e-expansionary stage $u > t$. Then again $\Phi_e^A(n)[u] \downarrow = \Phi_e^B(n)[u] \downarrow$, but also $\Phi_e^A(n)[u] = \Phi_e^A(n)[t] = \Phi_e^B(n)[t] = \Phi_e^B(n)[s] = \Phi_e^A(n)[s]$. (Note that we are not saying that these *computations* are the same, only that they have the same *value*. It may well be that $\varphi_e^A(n)[u] > \varphi_e^A(n)[s]$, for example.) So if we keep to this strategy, alternately freezing the A-side and the B-side of our agreeing computations, then we ensure that, if $\Phi_e^A = \Phi_e^B$ is total (which implies that there are infinitely many e-expansionary stages), then $\Phi_e^A(n) = \Phi_e^A(n)[s]$. Thus, if we follow this strategy for all n, then we can compute Φ_e^A, and hence $\mathcal{N}_e$ is met. Figure 2.2 illustrates this idea.

In summary, the strategy for meeting $\mathcal{N}_e$ is to wait until an e-expansionary stage s, then impose a restraint $u(e, s)$ on A, then wait until the next e-expansionary stage t, lift the restraint on A, and impose a restraint $u(e, t)$ on B, and then continue in this way, alternating which set is restrained at each new e-expansionary stage. Note that there is an important difference between this strategy and the one employed in the proof of the Sacks Splitting Theorem. There we argued that the length of agreement associated with a given requirement could not go to infinity. Here, however, it may well be the case that $\lim_s l(e, s) = \infty$, and hence $\lim_s u(e, s) = \infty$. Thus, the restraints imposed by the strategy for $\mathcal{N}_e$ may tend to infinity.

How do the $\mathcal{R}$- and $\mathcal{Q}$-requirements of weaker priority deal with this possibility? Consider a requirement $\mathcal{R}_i$ weaker than $\mathcal{N}_e$. We have two strategies for $\mathcal{R}_i$. One strategy guesses that there are only finitely many e-expansionary stages. This strategy picks a fresh large follower. Each time a new e-expansionary stage occurs, the strategy is *initialized*, which means that it must pick a new fresh large follower. Otherwise, the strategy acts exactly as described above. That is, it waits until its current follower x enters W_i, if ever, then puts x into A.

The other strategy for $\mathcal{R}_i$ guesses that there are infinitely many e-expansionary stages. It picks a follower x. If x enters W_i at stage s, then it wants to put x into A, but it may be restrained from doing so by the strategy for $\mathcal{N}_e$. However, if its guess is correct then there will be an e-expansionary stage $t \geqslant s$ at which the restraint on A is dropped. At that stage, x can be put into A.

Coherence. When we consider multiple $\mathcal{N}$-requirements, we run into a problem. Consider two requirements $\mathcal{N}_e$ and $\mathcal{N}_i$, with the first having stronger priority. Let $s_0 < s_1 < \cdots$ be the e-expansionary stages and $t_0 < t_1 < \cdots$ be the i-expansionary stages. During the interval $[s_0, s_1)$, weaker strategies are prevented from putting certain numbers into A by $\mathcal{N}_e$. At stage s_1, this restraint is lifted, but if $t_0 \leqslant s_1 < t_1$, then at stage s_1 it will be $\mathcal{N}_i$ that prevents weaker strategies from putting certain numbers into A. When $\mathcal{N}_i$ drops that restraint at stage t_1, we may have a new restraint on A imposed by $\mathcal{N}_e$ (if say $s_2 \leqslant t_1 < s_3$). Thus, although individually $\mathcal{N}_e$ and $\mathcal{N}_i$ each provide infinitely many stages at which they allow weaker strategies to put numbers into A, the two strategies *together* may conspire to block weaker strategies from *ever* putting numbers into A.

This problem is overcome by having two strategies for $\mathcal{N}_i$. The one guessing that there are only finitely many e-expansionary stages has no problems. The one guessing that there are infinitely many e-expansionary stages acts only at such stages, and in particular calculates its expansionary stages based only on such stages, which forces its expansionary stages to be nested within the e-expansionary stages. Thus the actions of $\mathcal{N}_e$ and $\mathcal{N}_i$ are forced to cohere.

We now turn to the formal details of the construction. These details may at first appear somewhat mysterious, in that it may be unclear how they actually implement the strategies described above. However, the verification section should clarify things.

The Priority Tree. We use the tree $\mathcal{T} = \{\infty, f\}^{<\omega}$. (Of course, this tree is the same as $2^{<\omega}$, but renaming the nodes should help in understanding the construction.) To each $\sigma \in \mathcal{T}$, we assign strategies N_σ, R_σ, and Q_σ for $\mathcal{N}_{|\sigma|}$, $\mathcal{R}_{|\sigma|}$, and $\mathcal{Q}_{|\sigma|}$, respectively. (It is only the $\mathcal{N}$-requirements that really need to be on the tree, since only they have outcomes we care about, but this assignment is notationally convenient.) Again we use lexicographic ordering, with ∞ to the left of f.

Definition 2.14.2. We define the notions of *σ-stage*, $m(\sigma, s)$, and *σ-expansionary stage* by induction on $|\sigma|$.

(i) Every stage is a λ-stage.

(ii) Suppose that s is a τ-stage. Let $e = |\tau|$. Let

$$m(\tau, s) = \max\{l(e,t) : t < s \text{ is a } \tau\text{-stage}\}.$$

If $l(e, s) > m(\tau, s)$ then we say that s is τ-expansionary and declare s to be a $\tau^\frown\infty$-stage. Otherwise, we declare s to be a $\tau^\frown f$-stage.

Let TP_s be the unique σ of length s such that s is a σ-stage.

Definition 2.14.3. We say that R_σ *requires attention* at a σ-stage $s > |\sigma|$ if $W_{|\sigma|,s} \cap A_s = \emptyset$ and one of the following holds.

(i) R_σ currently has no follower.

(ii) R_σ has a follower $x \in W_{|\sigma|,s}$.

The definition of Q_σ requiring attention is analogous.

Construction. At stage s, proceed as follows.
Step 1. Compute TP_s. Initialize all strategies attached to nodes to the right of TP_s. For the R- and Q-strategies, this initialization means that their followers are canceled.
Step 2. Find the strongest priority $\mathcal{R}$- or $\mathcal{Q}$-requirement that has a strategy requiring attention at stage s. Let us suppose that this requirement is $\mathcal{R}_e$ (the $\mathcal{Q}$-requirement case being analogous), and that R_σ is the corresponding strategy requiring attention at stage s. (Note that s must be a σ-stage.) We say that R_σ *acts* at stage s. Initialize all strategies attached to nodes properly extending σ. If R_σ does not currently have a follower, appoint a fresh large follower for R_σ. Otherwise, enumerate R_σ's follower into A.
End of Construction.

Verification. Let the true path TP be the leftmost path of $\mathcal{T}$ visited infinitely often. In other words, let TP be the unique path of $\mathcal{T}$ such that

$$\sigma \prec \text{TP iff } \exists^\infty s\,(\sigma \prec \text{TP}_s) \wedge \exists^{<\infty} s\,(\text{TP}_s <_{\text{lex}} \sigma).$$

We write $\tau \leqslant \text{TP}$ to mean that τ is either on or to the left of the true path.

Lemma 2.14.4. *Each $\mathcal{R}$- and $\mathcal{Q}$-requirement is met.*

Proof. Consider $\mathcal{R}_e$ (the $\mathcal{Q}$-requirement case being analogous). Let $\sigma = \mathrm{TP} \upharpoonright e$. Assume by induction that the strategies attached to proper prefixes of σ act only finitely often, and let s be the least stage such that

1. no strategy attached to a proper prefix of σ acts after stage s and

2. TP_t is not to the left of σ for all $t > s$.

By the minimality of s, it must be the case that R_σ is initialized at stage s. Thus, at the next σ-stage $t > s$, it will be assigned a follower x. Since R_σ cannot be initialized after stage t, this follower is permanent. By the way followers are chosen, x will not be put into A unless x enters W_e. If x enters W_e at stage $u > t$, then at the first σ-stage $v \geqslant u$, the strategy R_σ will act, and x will enter A. In any case, R_σ succeeds in meeting $\mathcal{R}_e$. Note that R_σ acts at most twice after stage s, and hence the induction can continue. □

Lemma 2.14.5. *Each $\mathcal{N}$-requirement is met.*

Proof. Consider $\mathcal{N}_e$. Let $\sigma = \mathrm{TP} \upharpoonright e$. If $\sigma^\frown f \prec TP$ then there are only finitely many e-expansionary stages, so $\Phi_e(A) \neq \Phi_e(B)$, and hence $\mathcal{N}_e$ is met.

So suppose that $\sigma^\frown\infty \prec TP$ and that Φ_e^A is total. We will show that Φ_e^A is computable. Let s be the least stage such that

1. no strategy attached to a prefix of σ (including σ itself) acts after stage s and

2. TP_t is not to the left of σ for all $t > s$.

To compute $\Phi_e^A(n)$, find the least $\sigma^\frown\infty$-stage $t_0 > s$ such that $l(e,s) > n$. We claim that $\Phi_e^A(n) = \Phi_e^A(n)[t_0]$.

Let $t_0 < t_1 < \cdots$ be the $\sigma^\frown\infty$-stages greater than or equal to t_0. Each such stage is e-expansionary, so we have $\Phi_e^A(n)[t_i] = \Phi_e^B(n)[t_i]$ for all i. We claim that, for each i, we have either $\Phi_e^A(n)[t_{i+1}] = \Phi_e^A(n)[t_i]$ or $\Phi_e^B(n)[t_{i+1}] = \Phi_e^B(n)[t_i]$. Assuming this claim, it follows easily that $\Phi_e^A(n)[t_0] = \Phi_e^A(n)[t_1] = \cdots$, which implies that $\Phi_e^A(n) = \Phi_e^A(n)[t_0]$.

To establish the claim, fix i. At stage t_i, we initialize all strategies to the right of $\sigma^\frown\infty$. Thus, any follower of such a strategy appointed after stage t_i must be larger than any number seen in the construction by stage t_i, and in particular larger than $\varphi_e^A(n)[t_i]$ and $\varphi_e^B(n)[t_i]$. By the choice of s, strategies above or to the left of σ do not act after stage s. Thus, the only strategies that can put numbers less than $\varphi_e^A(n)[t_i]$ into A or numbers less than $\varphi_e^B(n)[t_i]$ into B between stages t_i and t_{i+1} are the ones associated with extensions of $\sigma^\frown\infty$. But such a strategy cannot act except at a $\sigma^\frown\infty$-stage, and at each stage at most one strategy gets to act. Thus, at most one strategy associated with an extension of $\sigma^\frown\infty$ can act between stages t_i

and t_{i+1}, and hence only one of $A \upharpoonright \varphi_e^A(n)[t_i]$ and $B \upharpoonright \varphi_e^B(n)[t_i]$ can change between stages t_i and t_{i+1}. So either $A \upharpoonright \varphi_e^A(n)[t_{i+1}] = A \upharpoonright \varphi_e^A(n)[t_i]$ or $B \upharpoonright \varphi_e^B(n)[t_{i+1}] = B \upharpoonright \varphi_e^B(n)[t_i]$, which implies that either $\Phi_e^A(n)[t_{i+1}] = \Phi_e^A(n)[t_i]$ or $\Phi_e^B(n)[t_{i+1}] = \Phi_e^B(n)[t_i]$. As mentioned above, it follows that $\Phi_e^A(n) = \Phi_e^A(n)[t_0]$. □

These two lemmas show that all requirements are met, which concludes the proof of the theorem. □

Giving a full proof of the following result is a good exercise for those unfamiliar with the methodology above.

Theorem 2.14.6 (Ambos-Spies [5], Downey and Welch [135]). *There is a noncomputable c.e. set A such that if $C \sqcup D = A$ is a c.e. splitting of A, then the degrees of C and D form a minimal pair.*

Proof sketch. The proof is similar to that of Theorem 2.14.1, using the length of agreement function

$$l(i,j,k,m,s) = \max\{x : \forall y < x\, [\Phi_i^{W_k}(y)[s]\downarrow = \Phi_j^{W_m}(y)[s]\downarrow \\ \wedge\ \forall z \leqslant \varphi_i^{W_k}(y)[s], \varphi_j^{W_m}(y)[s]\ (W_k[s] \upharpoonright z \sqcup W_m[s] \upharpoonright z = A_s \upharpoonright z)]\}.$$

□

2.14.3 High computably enumerable degrees

Another example of an infinite injury argument is the construction of an incomplete high c.e. degree. Recall that a c.e. degree $\mathbf{a}$ is high if $\mathbf{a}' = \mathbf{0}''$. We begin with a few definitions. Recall that $A^{[e]}$ denotes the eth column $\{\langle e,n\rangle : \langle e,n\rangle \in A\}$ of A.

Definition 2.14.7. A set A is *piecewise trivial* if for all e, the set $A^{[e]}$ is either finite or equal to $\mathbb{N}^{[e]}$.

A subset B of A is *thick* if for all e we have $A^{[e]} =^* B^{[e]}$ (i.e., the symmetric difference of $A^{[e]}$ and $B^{[e]}$ is finite).

Lemma 2.14.8. (i) *There is a piecewise trivial c.e. set A such that $A^{[e]}$ is infinite iff Φ_e is total.*

(ii) *If B is a thick subset of such a set A, then B is high.*

Proof. (i) Let $A = \{\langle e,n\rangle : e \in \mathbb{N} \wedge \forall k \leqslant n\, \Phi_e(k)\downarrow\}$. Then A is c.e., and clearly $A^{[e]}$ is infinite iff $A^{[e]} = \mathbb{N}^{[e]}$ iff Φ_e is total.

(ii) Define a reduction Γ by letting $\Gamma^X(e,s) = 1$ if $\langle e,s\rangle \in X$ and $\Gamma^X(e,s) = 0$ otherwise. If Φ_e is total then $A^{[e]} = \mathbb{N}^{[e]}$, so $B^{[e]}$ is coinfinite, which implies that $\lim_s \Gamma^B(e,s) = 1$. On the other hand, if Φ_e is not total then $A^{[e]}$ is finite, so $B^{[e]}$ is finite, which implies that $\lim_s \Gamma^B(e,s) = 0$.

Thus, the function f defined by $f(e) = \lim_s \Gamma^B(e, s)$ is total. By the relativized form of the limit lemma, $f \leqslant_T B'$. So B' can decide whether a given Φ_e is total or not. By Theorem 2.6.5, $\emptyset'' \leqslant_T B'$. □

Thus, to construct an incomplete high c.e. degree, it suffices to prove the following result, which is a weak form of the Thickness Lemma discussed in the next section.

Theorem 2.14.9 (Shoenfield [355]). *Let C be a noncomputable c.e. set, and let A be a piecewise trivial c.e. set. Then there is a c.e. thick subset B of A such that $C \nleqslant_T B$.*

Proof. We construct $B \subseteq A$ to meet the following requirements for all e.

$$\mathcal{R}_e : |A^{[e]} \setminus B^{[e]}| < \infty.$$
$$\mathcal{N}_e : \Phi_e^B \neq C.$$

We give the intuition and formal details of the construction, and sketch out its verification, leaving some details to the reader.

To meet $\mathcal{R}_e$, we must make sure that almost all of the eth column of A gets into B. To meet $\mathcal{N}_e$, we use the strategy already employed in the proof of the Sacks Splitting Theorem 2.12.1. That is, we measure the length of agreement

$$l(e, s) = \max\{n : \forall k < n\,(\Phi_e^B(k)[s] = C_s(k))\},$$

with the idea of preserving B_s on the use $\varphi_e^B(n)[s]$ for all $n < l(e, s)$.

The problem comes from the interaction of this preservation strategy with the strategies for stronger priority $\mathcal{R}$-requirements, since these may be infinitary. It might be the case that we infinitely often try to preserve an agreeing computation $\Phi_e^B(n)[s] = C_s(n)$, only to have some $\langle i, x\rangle$ enter A with $i < e$ and $\langle i, x\rangle < \varphi_e^B(n)[s]$. Since we must put almost every such pair into B to meet $\mathcal{R}_i$, our strategy for meeting $\mathcal{N}_e$ might be injured infinitely often.

On the other hand, we do know that $\mathcal{R}_i$ can do only one of two things. Either $A^{[i]}$ is finite, and hence $\mathcal{R}_i$ stops injuring $\mathcal{N}_e$ after some time, or almost all of $A^{[i]}$ is put into B. In the latter case, the numbers put into B for the sake of $\mathcal{R}_i$ form a computable set (since A is piecewise trivial). It is easy to adapt the strategy for $\mathcal{N}_e$ to deal with this case. Let S be the computable set of numbers put into B for the sake of $\mathcal{R}_i$. We can then proceed with the Sacks preservation strategy, except that we do not believe a computation $\Phi_e^B(k)[s]$ unless B_s already contains every element of $S \upharpoonright \varphi_e^B(k)[s]$. This modification prevents the action taken for $\mathcal{R}_i$ from ever injuring the strategy for meeting $\mathcal{N}_e$.

Of course, we do not know which of the two possibilities for the action of $\mathcal{R}_i$ actually happens, so, as before, we will have multiple strategies for $\mathcal{N}_e$, representing guesses as to whether or not $A^{[i]}$ is finite. There are several ways to organize this argument as a priority tree construction.[8] We give the details of one such construction.

The N-strategies do not have interesting outcomes, so we use the same tree $\mathcal{T} = \{\infty, f\}^{<\omega}$ as in the proof of the Minimal Pair Theorem 2.14.1, with the same lexicographic ordering as before (i.e., the ordering induced by regarding ∞ as being to the left of f). To each $\sigma \in \mathcal{T}$ of length e we associate strategies R_σ and N_σ for meeting $\mathcal{R}_e$ and $\mathcal{N}_e$, respectively.

Definition 2.14.10. We define the notions of *σ-stage, σ-believable computation, σ-restraint $r(\sigma, s)$, σ-expansionary stage*, and *σ-length of agreement $l(\sigma, s)$* by induction on $|\sigma|$ and s as follows.

Every stage is a λ-stage, and $r(\sigma, 0) = 0$ for all σ. As usual, if we do not explicitly define $r(\sigma, s)$ at stage s, then $r(\sigma, s) = r(\sigma, s-1)$.

Suppose that $s > 0$ is a σ-stage, and let $e = |\sigma|$. A computation $\Phi_e^B(k)[s] = C_s(k)$ is σ-believable if for all $\tau^\frown\infty \preccurlyeq \sigma$ and all x, if $r(\tau, s) < \langle|\tau|, x\rangle < \varphi_e^B(k)[s]$, then $\langle|\tau|, x\rangle \in B_s$. Let

$$l(\sigma, s) = \max\{n : \forall k < n\, (\Phi_e^B(k)[s] = C_s(k) \text{ via a } \sigma\text{-believable computation})\}.$$

Say that s is σ-expansionary if $l(\sigma, s) > \max\{l(\sigma, t) : t < s\}$. Let

$$r(\sigma, s) = \max(\{r(\tau, s) : \tau <_{\text{lex}} \sigma\} \cup \{\varphi_e^B(k)[s] : k < l(\sigma, s)\}).$$

Let t be the last σ-stage before s, or 0 if there have been no such stages. If $|A_s^{[e]}| > |A_t^{[e]}|$ then s is a $\sigma^\frown\infty$-stage. Otherwise, s is a $\sigma^\frown f$-stage.

Construction. The construction is now rather simple. At stage s, let σ_s be the unique string of length s such that s is a σ_s-stage. For each $e < s$ and each $\langle e, x\rangle \in A_s$ that is not yet in B_s, if $\langle e, x\rangle > r(\sigma_s \upharpoonright i, s)$ then put $\langle e, x\rangle$ into B.

End of Construction.

We now sketch the verification that this construction succeeds in meeting all requirements. As usual, the true path TP of the construction is the leftmost path visited infinitely often.

Let $\sigma \in$ TP, let $e = |\sigma|$, and assume by induction that $\lim_t r(\tau, t)$ is well-defined for all $\tau \prec \sigma$. Let s be a stage such that

1. $r(\tau, t)$ has reached a limit $r(\tau)$ by stage s for every $\tau \prec \sigma$,
2. the construction never moves to the left of σ after stage s,
3. $B \upharpoonright r(\tau) = B_s \upharpoonright r(\tau)$ for every $\tau \prec \sigma$, and

[8]It is often the case in an infinite injury construction that we have substantive choices in defining the priority tree. In particular, some authors prefer to encode as much information as possible about the behavior of a strategy into its outcomes, while others prefer to encode only the information that weaker strategies need to have. It is worth keeping this fact in mind when reading such constructions.

4. $B_s^{[i]} = B^{[i]}$ for all $i < e$ such that $\sigma(i) = f$.

Note that item 4 makes sense because if $\sigma \in \text{TP}$ and $\sigma(i) = f$, then there is a τ of length i such that $\tau^\frown f \in \text{TP}$, which means that $A^{[i]}$ is finite, and hence so is $B^{[i]}$.

It is now not hard to argue, as in the proof of the Sacks Splitting Theorem, that if $t > s$ is a σ-stage and $n < l(\sigma, t)$, then the computation $\Phi_e^B(n)[s]$ is preserved forever. (The key fact is that this computation is σ-believable, and hence cannot be injured by stronger priority strategies.) Again as in the proof of the Sacks Splitting Theorem, it must be the case that $\lim_t l(\sigma, t)$ exists, and hence $\mathcal{N}_e$ is met.

It is also not hard to argue now that $r(\sigma) = \lim_t r(\sigma, t)$ is well-defined. Let u be a stage by which this limit has been reached. Then every $\langle e, x\rangle > r(\sigma)$ that enters A after stage u is eventually put into B, and hence $\mathcal{R}_e$ is met. □

A good exercise for those new to the techniques presented in this section is to combine the constructions of this subsection and the previous one to build a minimal pair of high c.e. degrees.

2.14.4 The Thickness Lemma

Theorem 2.14.9 is only a weak form of the real Thickness Lemma of Shoenfield [355]. To state the full version, we need a new definition.

Definition 2.14.11. A set A is *piecewise computable* if $A^{[e]}$ is computable for each e.

Theorem 2.14.12 (Thickness Lemma, Shoenfield [355]). *Let C be a noncomputable c.e. set, and let A be a piecewise computable c.e. set. Then there is a c.e. thick subset B of A such that $C \not\leqslant_T B$.*

Proof Sketch. We briefly sketch how to modify the proof of Theorem 2.14.9. Recall that in that result, we assumed that A was piecewise trivial. Now we have the weaker assumption that A is piecewise computable, that is, every column of A is computable. Thus, for each e, there is a c.e. set $W_{g(e)} \subseteq \mathbb{N}^{[e]}$ such that $W_{g(e)}$ is the complement of $A^{[e]}$ in $\mathbb{N}^{[e]}$ (meaning that $W_{g(e)} \sqcup A^{[e]} = \mathbb{N}^{[e]}$).

The key to how we used the piecewise triviality of A in Theorem 2.14.9 was in the definition of σ-believable computation. Recall that for σ with $e = |\sigma|$, we said that a computation $\Phi_e^B(k)[s] = C_s(k)$ at a σ-stage s was σ-believable if for all $\tau^\frown\infty \preccurlyeq \sigma$ and all x, if $r(\tau, s) < \langle|\tau|, x\rangle < \varphi_e^B(k)[s]$, then $\langle|\tau|, x\rangle \in B_s$. This definition relied on the fact that, if $\tau^\frown\infty \in \text{TP}$, then every $\langle|\tau|, x\rangle > r(\tau, s)$ was eventually put into B. The corresponding fact here is that every $\langle|\tau|, x\rangle > r(\tau, s)$ that is not in $W_{g(|\tau|)}$ is eventually put into B.

So in order to adjust the definition of σ-believable computation, for each $\tau \prec \sigma$, we need to know an index j such that $W_j = W_{g(|\tau|)}$. Since we cannot compute such a j from $|\tau|$, we must guess it along the tree of strategies. That is, for each τ, instead of the outcomes ∞ and f, we now have an outcome j for each $j \in \mathbb{N}$, representing a guess that $W_j = W_{g(|\tau|)}$. The outcome j is taken to be correct at a stage s if j is the least number for which we see the length of agreement between $\mathbb{N}^{[e]}$ and $A^{[e]} \sqcup W_j$ increase at stage s.

Now a computation $\Phi_e^B(k)[s] = C_s(k)$ at a σ-stage s is σ-believable if for all $\tau^\frown j \preccurlyeq \sigma$ and all x, if $r(\tau, s) < \langle |\tau|, x\rangle < \varphi_e^B(k)[s]$, then $\langle |\tau|, x\rangle \in B_s \cup W_j$. The rest of the construction is essentially the same as before. One important point is that, because the tree of strategies is now infinitely branching, the existence of the true path is no longer automatically guaranteed. However, if τ is visited infinitely often then $\tau^\frown j$ is visited infinitely often for the least j such that $W_j = W_{g(|\tau|)}$, from which it follows that TP is well-defined. There are infinite injury constructions in which showing that TP is well-defined requires a careful proof. □

We make some remarks for those who, like the senior author, were brought up with the "old" techniques using the "hat trick" and the "window lemma" of Soare [366]. It is rather ironic that the very first result that used the infinite injury method in its proof was the Thickness Lemma, since, like the Density Theorem of the next section, it has a proof *not* using priority trees that is combinatorially much easier to present. In a sense, this fact shows an inherent shortcoming of the tree technique in that often more information needs to be represented on the tree than is absolutely necessary for the proof of the theorem. To demonstrate this point, and since it is somewhat instructive, we now sketch the original proof of the Thickness Lemma.

We have the same requirements, but we define $\widehat{\Phi}^B(n)[s]$ to be $\Phi^B(n)[s]$ unless some number less than $\varphi^B(n)[s]$ enters B at stage s, in which case we declare that $\widehat{\Phi}^B(n)[s]\uparrow$. This is called the *hat convention*. Using this convention, we can generate the hatted length of agreement $\widehat{l}(e, s)$ with $\widehat{\Phi}$ in place of Φ, and so forth. Finally, we define the *restraint function*

$$\widehat{r}(e, s) = \max\{\widehat{\varphi}^B(n)[s] : n < \widehat{l}(e, s)\}.$$

The construction is to put $\langle e, x\rangle \in A_s$ into B at stage s if it is not yet there and $\langle e, x\rangle > \max\{\widehat{r}(j, s) : j \leqslant e\}$.

To verify that this construction succeeds in meeting all our requirements, it is enough to show that, for each e, the *injury set*

$$\widehat{I}_{e,s} = \{x : \exists v \leqslant s\,(x \leqslant \widehat{r}(e, v) \wedge x \in B_{s+1} \setminus B_v)\}$$

is computable, $B^{[e]} =^* A^{[e]}$, and $\mathcal{N}_e$ is met, all by simultaneous induction, the key idea being the "window lemma", which states that the liminf of the restraint $\widehat{R}(e, s) = \max\{\widehat{r}(j, s) : j \leqslant e\}$ is finite. The key point is that to verify these facts we do not actually need to know during the construction what the complement of $A^{[e]}$ is. This knowledge is used only in the verification. See Soare [366, Theorem VIII.1.1] for more details.

There is a strong form of the Thickness Lemma that is implicit in the work of Lachlan, Robinson, Shoenfield, Sacks, Soare, and others. We write $A^{[<e]}$ for $\bigcup_{i<e} A^{[i]}$.

Theorem 2.14.13 (Strong Thickness Lemma, see Soare [366]). *Let C be such that $\emptyset <_{\mathrm{T}} C \leqslant \emptyset'$ and let A be c.e. There is a c.e. set $B \subseteq A$ such that $B \leqslant_{\mathrm{T}} A$ and for all e, if $C \nleqslant_{\mathrm{T}} A^{[<e]}$ then for all $j \leqslant e$ we have $C \neq \Phi_j^B$ and $B^{[j]} =^* A^{[j]}$. It follows that if $C \nleqslant_{\mathrm{T}} A^{[<e]}$ for all e then $C \nleqslant_{\mathrm{T}} B$ and B is a thick subset of A. Furthermore, an index for B can be obtained uniformly from indices for A and C.*

Theorem 2.14.13 can be proved with much the same methods as those used to prove the Thickness Lemma. Soare [366] showed that many results of classical computability theory can be obtained from the Strong Thickness Lemma. Here is an example.

Corollary 2.14.14 (Sacks [342]). *Let $\mathbf{a}_0 < \mathbf{a}_1 < \cdots$ be an infinite ascending sequence of uniformly c.e. degrees. Then there is an incomplete c.e. degree $\mathbf{b}$ such that $\mathbf{a}_0 < \mathbf{a}_1 < \cdots < \mathbf{b}$. Thus $\mathbf{0}'$ is not a minimal upper bound for any such sequence of degrees.*

Proof. Let h be a computable function such that $\mathbf{a}_i = \deg(W_{h(i)})$ for all i. Let $A = \{\langle i, n \rangle : n \in W_{h(i)}\}$. Let $C = \emptyset'$ and apply the Strong Thickness Lemma to get a c.e. set $B \subseteq A$ such that $C \nleqslant_{\mathrm{T}} B$ and $B^{[i]} =^* A^{[i]}$ (which implies that $\deg(B^{[i]}) = \mathbf{a}_i$) for all i. Let $\mathbf{b} = \deg(B)$. □

2.15 The Density Theorem

One of the classic applications of the infinite injury method is to extend the Friedberg-Muchnik Theorem to show that not only are there intermediate c.e. degrees, but in fact the c.e. degrees form a dense partial ordering. It is possible to give a short and elegant proof of this result without using priority trees (see [366]), but it is quite hard to understand how that proof works. Therefore, in this section we give a proof using trees.

Theorem 2.15.1 (Sacks Density Theorem [344]). *For any c.e. sets $B <_{\mathrm{T}} C$, there are c.e. sets $A_0 \mid_{\mathrm{T}} A_1$ such that $B <_{\mathrm{T}} A_i <_{\mathrm{T}} C$ for $i = 0, 1$.*

Proof. We will construct A_0, A_1 satisfying the following requirements for all e.

$$\mathcal{R}_{2e} : \Phi_e^{A_0} \neq A_1.$$
$$\mathcal{R}_{2e+1} : \Phi_e^{A_1} \neq A_0.$$

Additionally, we must meet the global permitting requirement

$$A_0, A_1 \leqslant_{\mathrm{T}} C$$

and the global coding requirement

$$B \leqslant_{\mathrm{T}} A_0, A_1.$$

Together with the incomparability of the A_i, these global requirements imply that $B <_{\mathrm{T}} A_i <_{\mathrm{T}} C$ for $i = 0, 1$.

To satisfy the coding requirement, we simply code B into the even bits of each A_i. That is, whenever n enters B, we put $2n$ into A_i, and we ensure that all other numbers entering A_i are odd.

To satisfy the $\mathcal{R}$-requirements, we adopt a Friedberg-Muchnik type strategy, which we later modify to cope with the coding and permitting requirements. Consider the satisfaction of $\mathcal{R}_{2e}$. We pick an odd follower n, wait until $\Phi_e^{A_0}(n)[s]\downarrow= 0$, and if that ever happens, put n into A_1 and attempt to preserve $A_0 \upharpoonright \varphi_e^{A_0}(n)[s]$. This strategy is not correct as stated, but will serve as a basis for future modifications. The basic problems are that we cannot control B and that we can put numbers into A_1 only when permitted to do so by C. We deal with the latter issue first.

In place of a single follower n, we will use a potentially infinite collection $\{n(i) : i \in \mathbb{N}\}$ of followers or *coding markers*, picked inductively as follows. Suppose that we have already chosen $n(j)$ for $j < i$, and that all of these have been realized (a concept that will be defined below). We choose a large fresh odd follower $n(i)$ targeted for A_1. Now we wait until $\Phi_e^{A_0}(n(i))[s]\downarrow= 0$. If that ever happens, we declare $n(i)$ to be *realized*, attempt to preserve $\varphi_e^{A_0}(n(i))[s]$ by initializing weaker priority requirements, and repeat this procedure for $i + 1$.

We keep to this procedure until i enters C for some realized $n(i)$, at which point we put $n(i)$ into A_1. Without considering the effect of B or stronger priority strategies, this strategy will be successful, because if infinitely many followers are realized, then eventually C must permit us to put one of them into A_1, since otherwise we could compute C.

Now let us consider the effect of the coding of B into A_0. After we realize a follower $n(i)$ at stage s, we could be forced to change $A_0 \upharpoonright \varphi_e^{A_0}(n(i))[s]$ by a change in B. We could attempt to cope with this possibility by simply declaring $n(i)$ to be unrealized and waiting for a new stage t such that $\Phi_e^{A_0}(n(i))[t]\downarrow= 0$. We could then declare $n(i)$ to be once again realized and attempt to preserve $\varphi_e^{A_0}(n(i))[t]$ by initializing weaker priority requirements. The problem is that again we could be forced to change $A_0 \upharpoonright \varphi_e^{A_0}(n(i))[t]$ by a change in B. (Notice that $\varphi_e^{A_0}(n(i))[t]$ could be much larger than $\varphi_e^{A_0}(n(i))[s]$.) If we keep to this strategy, we could infinitely often realize $n(i)$, then unrealize it, then realize it again, and so on. Of course, in this case, $\mathcal{R}_{2e}$ is satisfied because $\Phi_e^{A_0}(n(i))\uparrow$. Unfortunately, weaker strategies are in trouble, as they are initialized infinitely often. In other words, we have won the $\mathcal{R}_{2e}$-battle, but lost the war.

The solution to this dilemma is to notice that this ugly situation can happen only if the values of $\varphi_e^{A_0}(n(i))[s]$ are unbounded for some i. If we *knew* this to be the case, then we could do the construction ignoring $\mathcal{R}_{2e}$, as it would automatically be satisfied. Obviously, though, we cannot know whether this situation happens ahead of time. However, we can have an infinitary outcome for $\mathcal{R}_{2e}$, which *guesses* that this use is unbounded. The trick is to make the effect on the construction of this outcome computable, hence allowing strategies below it to live with the action of $\mathcal{R}_{2e}$ if it truly has this infinitary outcome.

To make this idea more precise, we begin by presenting the basic module for the $\mathcal{R}_{2e}$ strategy described above, in the absence of stronger priority requirements. (Thus the single strategy for $\mathcal{R}_0$, the strongest requirement, acts exactly as follows.) The basic module for $\mathcal{R}_{2e+1}$ strategies is of course symmetric.

1. If all currently defined followers are realized, then choose a large fresh odd follower $n(i)$.

2. If $\Phi_e^{A_0}(n(i))[s]\downarrow= 0$, then declare $n(i)$ to be realized and initialize weaker strategies.

3. If $n(i)$ is realized and i enters C, then put $n(i)$ into A_1. In this case, stop choosing new followers unless $n(i)$ later becomes unrealized.

4. If $n(i)$ is realized and the coding of B causes A_0 to change below $\varphi_e^{A_0}(n(i))[t]$ at stage t, then, for the least i for which this is the case at this stage, cancel all $n(j)$ for $j > i$ (which will have different values if defined again later) and declare $n(i)$ to be unrealized.

Note that at each stage s, the strategy for $\mathcal{R}_{2e}$ has realized followers $n(0), \dots, n(i-1)$ and an unrealized follower $n(i)$. For each realized follower $n(j)$, we have $\Phi_e^{A_0}(n(j))[s]\downarrow$.

To see that the above module succeeds in satisfying a single requirement $\mathcal{R}_{2e}$, suppose not, so that $\Phi_e^{A_0} = A_1$. Then each $n(i)$ is eventually defined and reaches a final value, since all uses of the form $\varphi_e^{A_0}(n(i))$ eventually settle. Moreover, we can compute these final values using B, since it is only the coding of B into A_0 that can change these uses. Now we claim that B can compute C, contrary to hypothesis. Given i, we can use B to compute a stage s at which $n(i)$ reaches its final value and becomes permanently realized. If i were to enter C after stage s, then $n(i)$ would enter A_1, ensuring that $\Phi_e^{A_0} \neq A_1$. Thus $i \in C$ iff $i \in C_s$.

The above also shows that this module has two possible kinds of outcomes. Either $\varphi_e^{A_0}(n(i))$ is unbounded for some i, or $\Phi_e^{A_0}(n(i)) \neq A_1(n(i))$. We denote the former outcome by (i, u) and the latter by (i, f). We use these outcomes to generate the priority tree $T = \{(i,u), (i,f) : i \in \mathbb{N}\}^{<\omega}$, with a lexicographic ordering inherited from the ordering of outcomes $(i,u) <_L (i,f) <_L (i+1,u)$.

We now discuss how weaker priority requirements can live in the environments provided by $\mathcal{R}_{2e}$, by considering the case $e = 0$. The markers $n(i)$ for the $\mathcal{R}_0$ strategy will now be denoted by $n(\lambda, i)$ (since that strategy is associated with the empty sequence in $\mathcal{T}$). There are infinitely many strategies for $\mathcal{R}_1$, one for each outcome. We denote the strategy below outcome σ by R_σ and its markers by $n(\sigma, i)$.

A strategy living below (i, f) guesses that the strategy for $\mathcal{R}_0$ has finite action. Hence it can be initialized each time we realize $n(\lambda, j)$ for $j \leqslant i$, and simply implements the basic module.

A strategy R_σ living below $\sigma = (i, u)$ guesses that $n(\lambda, i)$ comes to a final value but no $n(\lambda, j)$ for $j > i$ does, because we keep changing A_0 below $\varphi_0^{A_0}(n(\lambda, i))[s]$ for the sake of coding B. As in the Thickness Lemma, this strategy will believe a $\Phi_0^{A_1}$-computation only if the current value of $n(\lambda, i+1)$ (and hence every $n(\lambda, j)$ for $j > i$) is greater than the use of that computation.

However, there is a problem here. The strategy R_σ may want to put numbers into A_0 smaller than uses that the $\mathcal{R}_0$ strategy is trying to preserve. For instance, say a follower $n(\sigma, j)$ is appointed, then followers $n(\lambda, k)$ with $k > i$ are appointed and become realized with corresponding uses larger than $n(\sigma, j)$, then $n(\sigma, j)$ becomes realized and permitted by C. If the guess that (i, u) is the true outcome of the $\mathcal{R}_0$ strategy is correct, then there is no problem. We can put $n(\sigma, j)$ into A_0 and still satisfy $\mathcal{R}_0$. But otherwise, we cannot afford to allow the enumeration of $n(\sigma, j)$ to injure $\mathcal{R}_0$.

We now come to the main idea of this proof, Sacks' notion of *delayed permitting*: Since R_σ is guessing that (i, u) is the true outcome of the $\mathcal{R}_0$ strategy, it believes that any use larger than $n(\sigma, j)$ that the $\mathcal{R}_0$ strategy is trying to preserve will eventually be violated by the coding of B into A_0. So once $n(\sigma, j)$ is realized and C-permitted, instead of immediately putting $n(\sigma, j)$ into A_0, we merely promise to put it there if these uses do go away; that is, if R_σ becomes accessible again before $n(\sigma, j)$ is initialized.

This delayed permitting still allows C to compute A_0, because C can compute B, and hence know whether the relevant uses will ever be violated. That is, given a realized follower $n(\sigma, j)$, the set C knows whether $j \in C$. If not, then $n(\sigma, j)$ never enters A_0. Otherwise, C can check what the B-conditions are for R_σ to be accessible again, find out whether these conditions will ever obtain, and if so, go to that stage of the construction to check whether $n(\sigma, j)$ has not been initialized in the meantime, which is the only case in which $n(\sigma, j)$ enters A_0.

It is a subtle fact that, while the true path of the construction remains computable only from $\mathbf{0}''$, the fate of a particular follower is always computable from C. Furthermore, we can still argue that, if $\sigma = (i, u)$ is in fact the true outcome of $\mathcal{R}_0$ strategy and R_σ fails, then B can compute C, in much the same way as before, since every C-permitted follower eventually has no restraint placed on it.

Construction.

We code B by enumerating $2n$ into A_0 and A_1 whenever n enters B.

At a stage s, the construction proceeds in substages $t \leqslant s$. At each substage t, some node $\alpha(s,t)$ of $\mathcal{T}$ will be accessible, beginning with $\alpha(s,0) = \lambda$. At the end of the stage (which might come before substage s), we will have defined a node α_s. At substage t, the strategy $R_{\alpha(s,t)}$ for $\mathcal{R}_t$ will act. Let us assume that $t = 2e$, the odd case being symmetric, and let $\alpha = \alpha(s,t)$. We say that s is an *α-stage.*

If $n(\alpha,0)$ is currently undefined, then proceed as follows. Define $n(\alpha,0)$ to be a fresh large odd number. Let $\alpha_s = \alpha(s,t+1) = \alpha(s,t)^\frown(0,f)$, initialize all $\tau \nleq_{\mathrm{L}} \alpha_s$, and end the stage.

We say that the computation $\Phi_e^{A_0}(x)[s]$ is *α-correct* if for all $\beta^\frown(j,u) \preccurlyeq \alpha$, if $n(\beta,j)$ is currently defined, then it is greater than $\varphi_e^{A_0}[s]$. Let $\ell(\alpha,s)$ be the α-correct length of agreement at stage s, that is, the largest m such that for all $x < m$, we have $\Phi_e^{A_0}(x)[s] = A_1(x)[s]$ via an α-correct computation. Adopt the first among the following cases that obtains.

1. For some i with $n(\alpha,i)$ realized (defined below), i has entered C since the last α-stage, and the α-correct length of agreement has exceeded $n(\alpha,i)$ since the last α-stage. Fix the least such i. Let $\alpha_s = \alpha(s,t+1) = \alpha(s,t)^\frown(i,f)$, and initialize all $\tau \nleq_{\mathrm{L}} \alpha_s$. Put $n(\alpha,i)$ into A_0 and end the stage.

2. For some i with $n(\alpha,i)$ realized, the computation $\Phi_e^{A_0}(n(\alpha,i))$ has been injured since the previous α-stage. Fix the least such i. Declare $n(\alpha,i)$ to be unrealized. Cancel all $n(\alpha,j)$ for $j > i$. Let $\alpha(s,t+1) = \alpha^\frown(i,u)$. Initialize all τ with $\tau \nleq_{\mathrm{L}} \alpha(s,t+1)$ and $\alpha(s,t+1) \not\preccurlyeq \tau$. If $t < s$ then proceed to the next substage. Otherwise let $\alpha_s = \alpha(s,t+1)$ and end the stage.

3. For some unrealized $n(\alpha,i)$, we have $\ell(\alpha,s) > n(\alpha,i)$. Fix the least such i. Declare $n(\alpha,i)$ to be realized, define $n(\alpha,i+1)$ to be a fresh large odd number, and cancel all $n(\alpha,j)$ for $j > i+1$. Let $\alpha_s = \alpha(s,t+1) = \alpha^\frown(i+1,f)$. Initialize all $\tau \nleq_{\mathrm{L}} \alpha_s$ and end the stage.

4. Otherwise. Find the least (necessarily unrealized) $n(\alpha,i)$ that is defined. Let $\alpha(s,t+1) = \alpha^\frown(i,f)$. Initialize all τ with $\tau \nleq_{\mathrm{L}} \alpha(s,t+1)$ and $\alpha(s,t+1) \not\preccurlyeq \tau$. If $t < s$ then proceed to the next substage. Otherwise let $\alpha_s = \alpha(s,t+1)$ and end the stage.

End of Construction.

Verification. We first show that the true path of the construction is well-defined, and all requirements are met. We say that α is on the *true path* if there are infinitely many α-stages but only finitely many s with $\alpha_s <_{\mathrm{L}} \alpha$.

If there are infinitely many α stages, then the *true outcome* of R_α is the leftmost outcome γ such that there are infinitely many α-stages s with $\alpha(s,|\alpha|+1) = \alpha^\frown\gamma$.

Lemma 2.15.2. *Let α be on the true path, and let γ be its true outcome. Then R_α succeeds in meeting $\mathcal{R}_{|\alpha|}$, there are infinitely many α-stages where the stage does not end at substage $|\alpha|$, and R_α initializes strategies below $\alpha^\frown\gamma$ only finitely often.*

Proof. Assume by induction that the lemma holds for strategies above α. Then, since α can be initialized only when $\alpha_s <_{\mathrm{L}} \alpha$ or when a strategy above it initializes it, there is a stage s_0 such that α is not initialized after stage s_0. After this stage, no $n(\alpha, i)$ is canceled except for the sake of an $n(\alpha, j)$ with $j < i$. Now we can argue as in the basic module, but using α-correct computations at α-stages, to show that R_α succeeds in meeting $\mathcal{R}_{|\alpha|}$.

If $\gamma = (i, u)$ then R_α does not initialize strategies below $\alpha^\frown\gamma$, and at every stage $s > |\alpha|$ at which $\alpha(s, |\alpha| + 1) = \alpha^\frown\gamma$, the stage does not end at substage $|\alpha|$.

If $\gamma = (i, f)$, then the R_α-module acts only finitely often. □

Thus, by induction, for each e there is an α of length e such that there are infinitely many α-stages but only finitely many s with $\alpha_s <_{\mathrm{L}} \alpha$, whence R_e is met.

Lemma 2.15.3. $A_0, A_1 \leqslant_{\mathrm{T}} C$.

Proof. We do the A_0 case, the A_i case being symmetric.

If $n \in A_0$, then n must be chosen by stage n as $n(\alpha, i)$ for some α and i with $|\alpha|$ even and $i \in C$. If that is the case, let s be the stage at which i enters C. Then n will be in A_0 iff there is an α-stage $t \geqslant s$ at which $n(\alpha, i)$ is still equal to n. So we may assume that s is not itself an α-stage and $n(\alpha, i)$ is not canceled at stage s, since otherwise we would already know whether $n \in A_0$ at stage s. Thus $\alpha <_{\mathrm{L}} \alpha_s$. Let β be the longest common initial segment of α and α_s. We have two cases.

First suppose that $\beta^\frown(k, f) \preccurlyeq \alpha$ for some k. Then $\beta^\frown(j, o) \preccurlyeq \alpha_s$ for some $j > k$ and $o \in \{f, u\}$. Suppose there is a least $\beta^\frown(k, f)$-stage $t > s$. If the construction moves to the left of $\beta^\frown(k, f)$ between stages s and t then α is initialized, so $n \notin A_0$. Otherwise, either case 1 or case 3 above holds for β at stage t, so again α is initialized and $n \notin A_0$. Of course, if there is no $\beta^\frown(k, f)$-stage after s, then $n \notin A_o$. Thus, in this case, we know that $n \notin A_0$ no matter what happens after stage s.

Now suppose that $\beta^\frown(k, u) \preccurlyeq \alpha$ for some k. After stage s, there can be an α-stage only if there is a $\beta^\frown(k, u)$-stage. Now C can use B to figure out whether the use of the relevant computation $\Phi_e^{A_i}(n(\beta, k))$ is B-correct. If it is B-correct, then $n \notin A_0$, since the only way for there to be a further $\beta^\frown(k, u)$-stage is for a strategy above or to the left of $\beta^\frown(k, u)$ to enumerate something into A_i, which causes α to be initialized. If not, then go to a stage t where B changes below this use. If t is not a $\beta^\frown(k, u)$-stage and $n(\alpha, i)$ is not canceled at stage t, then $\alpha_t <_{\mathrm{L}} \beta$. Let β' be the longest common initial segment of β and α_t. We can now repeat the above argument with β' in place of β.

It is a straightforward exercise to show that, proceeding in this manner, we eventually reach a stage at which we either can be sure that $n \notin A_0$, or we have an α-stage, at which point n enters A_0. Since we do so using B and $B \leqslant_{\mathrm{T}} C$, we have $A_0 \leqslant_{\mathrm{T}} C$. □

The two lemmas above complete the proof of the theorem. □

2.16 Jump theorems

We will see that the jump operator plays an important role in the study of algorithmic randomness. In this section, we look at several classic results about the range of the jump operator, whose proofs are combinations of techniques we have already seen. Of course, if $\mathbf{d} = \mathbf{a}'$ then $\mathbf{d} \geqslant \mathbf{0}'$. The following result is a converse to this fact.

Theorem 2.16.1 (Friedberg Completeness Criterion [160]). *If* $\mathbf{d} \geqslant \mathbf{0}'$ *then there is a degree* $\mathbf{a}$ *such that* $\mathbf{a}' = \mathbf{a} \vee \mathbf{0}' = \mathbf{d}$.

Proof. This is a finite extension argument. Let $D \in \mathbf{d}$. We construct a set A in stages, and let $\mathbf{a} = \deg(A)$. At stage 0, let $A_0 = \lambda$.

At odd stages $s = 2e+1$, we force the jump (i.e., decide whether $e \in A'$). We ask $\emptyset'$ whether there is a $\sigma \succ A_{s-1}$ such that $\Phi_e^{\sigma}(e)\downarrow$. If so, we search for such a σ and let $A_s = \sigma$. If not, we let $A_s = A_{s-1}$. Note that, in this case, we have ensured that $\Phi_e^{A}(e)\uparrow$.

At even stages $s = 2e+2$, we code $D(e)$ into A by letting $A_s = A_{s-1}D(e)$.

This concludes the construction. We have $A \oplus \emptyset' \leqslant_{\mathrm{T}} A'$ (which is always the case for any set A), so we can complete the proof by showing that $A' \leqslant_{\mathrm{T}} D$ and $D \leqslant_{\mathrm{T}} A \oplus \emptyset'$.

Since $\emptyset' \leqslant_{\mathrm{T}} D$, we can carry out the construction computably in D. To decide whether $e \in A'$, we simply run the construction until stage $2e+1$. At this stage, we decide whether $e \in A'$. Thus $A' \leqslant_{\mathrm{T}} D$.

A $\emptyset'$ oracle can tell us how to obtain A_{2e+1} given A_{2e}, while an A oracle can tell us how to obtain A_{2e+2} given A_{2e+1}, so using $A \oplus \emptyset'$, we can compute A_{2n+2} for any given n. Since $D(n)$ is the last element of A_{2n+2}, we can compute $D(n)$ using $A \oplus \emptyset'$. Thus $D \leqslant_{\mathrm{T}} A \oplus \emptyset'$. □

The above proof should be viewed as a combination of a coding argument and the construction of a low set, done simultaneously. This kind of combination is a recurrent theme in the proofs of results such as the ones in this section.

The following extension of the above result is due to Posner and Robinson [315]. We give a proof due to Jockusch and Shore [194].

Theorem 2.16.2 (Posner and Robinson [315]). *r If* $\mathbf{c} > \mathbf{0}$ *and* $\mathbf{d} \geqslant \mathbf{0}' \vee \mathbf{c}$ *then there is a degree* $\mathbf{a}$ *such that* $\mathbf{a}' = \mathbf{a} \vee \mathbf{c} = \mathbf{d}$.

Proof. By Proposition 2.13.1, there is an immune $C \in \mathbf{c}$. (Recall that the complement of a simple set is immune.) Let $D \in \mathbf{d}$. We build a set A by finite extensions.

Let $A_0 = \lambda$. Given A_n, proceed as follows. Let $S_n = \{x : \exists \sigma \succcurlyeq A_n 0^x 1\, (\Phi_n^\sigma(n) \downarrow)\}$. If S_n is finite then there is an $x \in C \setminus S_n$. In this case, let $A_{n+1} = A_n 0^x 1 D(n)$. If S_n is infinite then, since S_n is c.e. and C is immune, there is an $x \in S_n \setminus C$. In this case, let s be least such that $\exists \sigma \succcurlyeq A_n 0^x 1\, (\Phi_n^\sigma(n)[s] \downarrow)$, let σ be the length-lexicographically least string witnessing this existential, and let $A_{n+1} = \sigma D(n)$.

It is easy to see that from the sequence $A_0, A_1, \ldots$ we can compute the set A', the set $A \oplus C$, and the set D. Thus, it is enough to show that this sequence can be computed from each of these three sets. Suppose we have computed A_n.

Since $D \geqslant_{\mathrm{T}} \emptyset' \oplus C$, using D we can compute S_n and C and hence determine A_{n+1}.

If we have A', then we have A, so we can determine the x such that $A_n 0^x 1 \prec A$. Then using $\emptyset'$ we can determine whether $x \in S_n$, and hence determine A_{n+1}.

If we have $A \oplus C$, then again we can determine the x such that $A_n 0^x 1 \prec A$. By construction, $x \in S_n$ iff $x \notin C$, so we can then use C to determine A_{n+1}. □

It is not hard to show that if $A \leqslant_{\mathrm{T}} \emptyset'$ then A' is c.e. in $\emptyset'$. Since also $\emptyset' \leqslant_{\mathrm{T}} A'$, we say that A' is *computably enumerable in and above* $\emptyset'$, abbreviated by CEA($\emptyset'$). The following theorem is an elaboration of Theorem 2.16.1.

Theorem 2.16.3 (Shoenfield Jump Inversion Theorem [354]). *If* D *is CEA(*$\emptyset'$*) then there is an* $A \leqslant_{\mathrm{T}} \emptyset'$ *such that* $A' \equiv_{\mathrm{T}} D$.

We will briefly sketch a proof of the following stronger result. (We restrict ourselves to a sketch because, from a modern viewpoint, the proof contains no new ideas beyond what we have seen so far. See Soare [366] for a full proof.)

Theorem 2.16.4 (Sacks Jump Inversion Theorem [341]). *If* D *is CEA(*$\emptyset'$*) then there is a c.e. set* A *such that* $A' \equiv_{\mathrm{T}} D$.

Proof sketch. Let D be CEA($\emptyset'$). Then D is Σ_2^0, so there is an approximation $\{D_s\}_{s \in \omega}$ such that $n \in D$ iff there is an s such that $n \in D_t$ for all $t > s$. Arguing as in the proof of Lemma 2.14.8, we have a c.e. set B such that $B^{[e]}$ is an initial segment of $\mathbb{N}^{[e]}$ and equals $\mathbb{N}^{[e]}$ iff $e \notin D$.

We need to make the jump of A high enough to compute D, which we do by meeting for each e the requirement

$$\mathcal{P}_e : A^{[e]} =^* B^{[e]}.$$

As in Lemma 2.14.8, this action ensures that A' can compute D. We also need to keep the jump of A computable in D, which we do by controlling the jump as in Theorem 2.11.2.

For $\mathcal{P}_e$, we enumerate all elements of $B^{[e]}$ into A as long as we are not restrained from doing so. This requirement has nodes on the priority tree $\mathcal{T}$ with outcomes $\{\infty, f\}$. The first outcome corresponds to the case $B^{[e]} = \mathbb{N}^{[e]}$, and the second to the case $B^{[e]} =^* \emptyset$. Naturally, in the end we need to argue that if the outcome on the true path is $\nu^\frown\infty$, then almost all of $B^{[e]}$ is enumerated into A. We refer to $\mathcal{P}_e$ nodes as *coding nodes.*

A strategy N corresponding to a lowness requirement has a finite number of coding nodes above it with which it needs to contend. The strategy N does not have to worry about coding nodes with outcome f above it. But suppose there is a coding node P corresponding to $\mathcal{P}_e$ outcome ∞ above N. Then N assumes that all of $\mathbb{N}^{[e]}$ enters A, except for numbers below the maximum r of the restraints imposed by strategies above P. Thus N does not believe any computation until it has seen all numbers in $\mathbb{N}^{[e]}$ between r and the use of the computation enter $A^{[e]}$.

The full construction works in the standard inductive way. As with the density theorem, while D cannot figure out the true path of the construction, it can sort out the fate of a given coding marker, by deciding whether a particular restraint is B-correct. □

The above result can be extended to higher jumps as follows.

Theorem 2.16.5 (Sacks [341]). *If D is CEA($\emptyset^{(n)}$) then there is a c.e. set A such that $A^{(n)} \equiv_T D$.*

Proof. This result is proved by induction. Suppose that D is CEA($\emptyset^{(n+1)}$). Then we know that there is a set B that is CEA($\emptyset^{(n)}$) with $B' \equiv_T D$, by the relativized form of Theorem 2.16.4. By induction, there is a c.e. set A with $A^{(n)} \equiv_T B$. Then $A^{(n+1)} \equiv_T D$. □

There are even extensions of the above result to transfinite ordinals in place of n.

We will later have occasion to use the fact that the proof of the Sacks Jump Inversion Theorem is uniform. That is, an index for the set A in Theorem 2.16.5 can be found effectively from an index for the c.e. operator enumerating D from $\emptyset^{(n)}$.

The Sacks Jump Inversion and Density Theorems have been extraordinarily influential. They have been extended and generalized in many ways. Roughly speaking, any "reasonable" set of requirements on the ordering of a collection of c.e. degrees and their jumps that does not explicitly contradict obvious partial ordering considerations (such as $\mathbf{a} \leqslant \mathbf{b} \Rightarrow \mathbf{a}' \leqslant \mathbf{b}'$) is realizable. Here is one example.

Theorem 2.16.6 (Jump Interpolation Theorem, Robinson [333]). *Let C and D be c.e. sets with $C <_T D$, and let S be CEA(D) with $C' \leqslant_T S$. Then there is a c.e. set A such that $C <_T A <_T D$ and $A' \equiv_T S$.*

The methods for proving the Jump Interpolation Theorem are much the same as the ones we have seen. One can even prove vast generalizations for n-jumps with additional ordering requirements. For the latest word on this subject, see Lempp and Lerman [238, 239].

2.17 Hyperimmune-free degrees

The notions of hyperimmune and hyperimmune-free degree have many applications in the study of computability theory and its interaction with algorithmic randomness. There are several ways to define these notions. We will adopt what is probably the simplest definition, using the concept of domination. Recall that a function f dominates a function g if $f(n) \geqslant g(n)$ for almost all n. It is sometimes technically useful to work with the following closely related concept. A function f *majorizes* a function g if $f(n) \geqslant g(n)$ for *all* n.

Definition 2.17.1 (Miller and Martin [282]). A degree $\mathbf{a}$ is *hyperimmune* if there is a function $f \leqslant_T \mathbf{a}$ that is not dominated by any computable function (or, equivalently, not majorized by any computable function). Otherwise, $\mathbf{a}$ is *hyperimmune-free*.

While $\mathbf{0}$ is clearly hyperimmune-free, all other Δ_2^0 degrees are hyperimmune, as shown by the following result.

Proposition 2.17.2 (Miller and Martin [282]). *If $\mathbf{a} < \mathbf{b} \leqslant \mathbf{a}'$ for some $\mathbf{a}$, then $\mathbf{b}$ is hyperimmune. In particular, every nonzero degree below $\mathbf{0}'$, and hence every nonzero c.e. degree, is hyperimmune.*

Proof. We do the proof for the case $\mathbf{a} = \mathbf{0}$. The general result follows by a straightforward relativization. Let B be a set such that $\emptyset <_T B \leqslant_T \emptyset'$. Let $g(n) = \mu s \geqslant n\,(B_s \upharpoonright n = B \upharpoonright n)$. Notice that $g(n)$ is *not* the stage s by which the approximation to $B \upharpoonright n$ has stabilized (so that $B_t \upharpoonright n$ is correct for all $t \geqslant s$), but rather the first stage s at which $B_s \upharpoonright n$ is correct. Clearly, $g \leqslant_T B$.

We claim that no computable function majorizes g. Suppose that h is computable and majorizes g. Then we claim that B is computable. To compute $B \upharpoonright m$, search for an $n > m$ such that $B_t \upharpoonright m = B_n \upharpoonright m$ for all $t \in [n, h(n)]$. Such an n must exist because there is a stage at which the approximation to $B \upharpoonright m$ stabilizes. By the definition of g and the choice of h, we have $g(n) \in [n, h(n)]$, so $B \upharpoonright m = B_{g(n)} \upharpoonright m = B_n \upharpoonright m$. Thus B is computable, which is a contradiction. □

On the other hand, there do exist nonzero hyperimmune-free degrees.

Theorem 2.17.3 (Miller and Martin [282]). *There is a nonzero hyperimmune-free degree.*

Proof. We define a noncomputable set A of hyperimmune-free degree, using a technique known as *forcing with computable perfect trees*. A *function tree* is a function $T : 2^{<\omega} \to 2^{<\omega}$ such that $T(\sigma 0)$ and $T(\sigma 1)$ are incompatible extensions of $T(\sigma)$. For a function tree T, let $[T]$ be the collection of all X for which there is a $B \in 2^\omega$ such that $T(\sigma) \prec X$ for all $\sigma \prec B$. We build a sequence $\{T_i\}_{i \in \omega}$ of computable function trees such that $[T_0] \supseteq [T_1] \supseteq [T_2] \supseteq \cdots$. Since each $[T_i]$ is closed, $\bigcap_n [T_n] \neq \emptyset$. We will take A to be any element of this intersection. At stage $2e+1$, we ensure that $A \neq W_e$, while at stage $2e+2$, we ensure that Φ_e^A is majorized by a computable function.

At stage 0, we let T_0 be the identity map.

At stage $2e+1$, we are given T_{2e}. Let $i \in \{0,1\}$ be such that $T_{2e}(i) \neq W_e \upharpoonright |T_{2e}(i)|$. Since $T_{2e}(0)$ and $T_{2e}(1)$ are incompatible, such an i must exist. Now define T_{2e+1} by letting $T_{2e+1}(\sigma) = T_{2e}(i\sigma)$. Notice that $[T_{2e+1}]$ consists exactly of those elements of $[T_{2e}]$ that extend $T_{2e}(i)$, and hence, if $A \in [T_{2e+1}]$ then $A \neq W_e$.

At stage $2e+2$, we are given a computable function tree T_{2e+1}. It suffices to build T_{2e+2} to ensure that either

(i) if $A \in [T_{2e+2}]$ then Φ_e^A is not total, or

(ii) there is a computable function f such that if $A \in [T_{2e+2}]$ then $\Phi_e^A(n) \leqslant f(n)$ for all n.

First suppose there are n and σ such that $\Phi_e^{T_{2e+1}(\tau)}(n)\uparrow$ for all $\tau \succcurlyeq \sigma$. Then define T_{2e+2} by letting $T_{2e+2}(\nu) = T_{2e+1}(\sigma\nu)$. This definition clearly ensures that if $A \in [T_{2e+2}]$ then $\Phi_e^A(n)\uparrow$.

Now suppose there are no such n and σ. Then define T_{2e+2} as follows. For the empty string λ, search for a σ_λ such that $\Phi_e^{T_{2e+1}(\sigma_\lambda)}(0)\downarrow$ and define $T_{2e+2}(\lambda) = T_{2e+1}(\sigma_\lambda)$. Having defined σ_τ, search for incompatible extensions $\sigma_{\tau 0}$ and $\sigma_{\tau 1}$ of σ_τ such that $\Phi_e^{T_{2e+1}(\sigma_{\tau i})}(|\tau|)\downarrow$ for $i = 0, 1$, and define $T_{2e+2}(\tau i) = T_{2e+1}(\sigma_{\tau i})$. This process ensures that for all n and all τ of length n, we have $\Phi_e^{T_{2e+2}(\tau)}(n)\downarrow$. Furthermore, it ensures that T_{2e+2} is computable, so that we can define a computable function f by letting $f(n) = \max\{\Phi_e^{T_{2e+2}(\tau)}(n) : |\tau| = n\}$. Thus if $A \in [T_{2e+2}]$ then $\Phi_e^A(n) \leqslant f(n)$. □

Note that the above construction can be carried out effectively using $\emptyset''$ as an oracle, so there are nonzero Δ_3^0 hyperimmune-free degrees. It is also possible to adapt the construction to prove the following result.

Theorem 2.17.4 (Miller and Martin [282]). *There are continuum many hyperimmune-free degrees.*

On the other hand, we will see in Section 8.21.1 that the class of sets of hyperimmune-free degree has measure 0.

The name "hyperimmune degree" comes from the notion of a hyperimmune set, which we now define.[9] A *strong array* is a computable collection of pairwise disjoint finite sets $\{F_i\}_{i\in\mathbb{N}}$ (which means not only that the F_i are uniformly computable, but also that the function $i \mapsto \max F_i$ is computable). An infinite set A is *hyperimmune* if for all strong arrays $\{F_i\}_{i\in\mathbb{N}}$, there is an i such that $F_i \subset \overline{A}$. A c.e. set is *hypersimple* if its complement is hyperimmune.

Given the terminology, one would expect that a hyperimmune degree is one that contains a hyperimmune set. We will show that this is indeed the case by first introducing another equivalent characterization of the hyperimmune degrees. The *principal function* of a set $A = \{a_0 < a_1 < \cdots\}$ is the function p_A defined by $p_A(n) = a_n$.

Lemma 2.17.5 (Miller and Martin [282]). *A degree* **a** *is hyperimmune iff* **a** *contains a set A such that p_A is not majorized by any computable function.*

Proof. Since $p_A \leqslant_T A$, the "if" direction is obvious. For the other direction, suppose that there is a function $f \leqslant_T \mathbf{a}$ that is not majorized by any computable function. We may assume that f is increasing. Let $B \in \mathbf{a}$ and let $b_0 < b_1 < \cdots$ be the elements of B. Let $A = \{f(b_n) : n \in \mathbb{N}\}$. Using the fact that f is increasing, it is easy to show that $A \equiv_T B$. Thus $A \in \mathbf{a}$, and $p_A(n) \geqslant f(n)$ for all n, so p_A is not majorized by any computable function. □

Theorem 2.17.6 (Kuznecov [230], Medvedev [264], Uspensky [393]). *A degree is hyperimmune iff it contains a hyperimmune set.*

Proof. Suppose that A is not hyperimmune. Then there is a strong array $\{F_i\}_{i\in\mathbb{N}}$ such that $A \cap F_i \neq \emptyset$ for all i. Let $f(n) = \max \bigcup_{i\leqslant n} F_i$. Then f is computable, and $p_A(n) \leqslant f(n)$ for all n. So if no set in **a** is hyperimmune, then it follows from Lemma 2.17.5 that **a** is not hyperimmune.

Now suppose that **a** is not hyperimmune and let $A \in \mathbf{a}$. By Lemma 2.17.5, there is a computable function f such that $p_A(n) \leqslant f(n)$ for all n. Let $F_0 = [0, f(0)]$. Given F_i, let $k_i = \max F_i + 1$ and let $F_{i+1} = [k_i, f(k_i)]$. Then $p_A(k_i) \in A \cap F_i$ for all i, so A is not hyperimmune. □

The following is a useful characterization of the hyperimmune-free degrees.

[9] Some authors have argued that the adoption of the term "hyperimmune-free degree" is a historical accident, and that a more descriptive one, based on domination properties, should be used. Nies, Barmpalias, and Soare, for example, have all used the term *computably dominated*. Earlier, authors such as Gasarch and Simpson used the term *almost recursive*.

Proposition 2.17.7 (Jockusch [187], Martin [unpublished]). *The following are equivalent for a set A.*

(i) *A has hyperimmune-free degree.*

(ii) *For all functions f, if $f \leqslant_T A$ then $f \leqslant_{tt} A$.*

(iii) *For all sets B, if $B \leqslant_T A$ then $B \leqslant_{tt} A$.*

Proof. To show that (i) implies (ii), suppose that A has hyperimmune-free degree and $f = \Phi_e^A$, and let $g(n)$ be the number of steps taken by the computation $\Phi_e^A(n)$. Then $g \leqslant_T A$, so there is a computable function h that majorizes g. Let Ψ be the functional defined as follows. On oracle X and input n, run the computation $\Phi_e^X(n)$ for $h(n)$ many steps. If this computation converges, then output its value, and otherwise output 0. Then Ψ is a truth table functional, and $\Psi^A = \Phi_e^A = f$.

Clearly (ii) implies (iii). To show that (iii) implies (i), assume that A does not have hyperimmune-free degree and let $g \leqslant_T A$ be a function not dominated by any computable function. We build a set $B \leqslant_T A$ such that $B \not\leqslant_{tt} A$. Let $\sigma_0, \sigma_1, \ldots$ be an effective list of all truth tables. For each e and n, proceed as follows. If $\Phi_e(\langle e, n\rangle)[g(n)]\downarrow$ then let $\langle e, n\rangle \in B$ iff $A \nvDash \sigma_{\Phi_e(\langle e,n\rangle)}$. Note that this definition ensures that Φ_e does not witness a truth table reduction from A to B. If $\Phi_e(\langle e, n\rangle)[g(n)]\uparrow$ then let $\langle e, n\rangle \in B$. Clearly $B \leqslant_T A$. Assume for a contradiction that $B \leqslant_{tt} A$. Then there is an e such that Φ_e witnesses this fact. This Φ_e is total, so there is a computable function h such that $\Phi_e(\langle e, n\rangle)[h(n)]\downarrow$ for all n. Since h does not dominate g, there is an n such that $\Phi_e(\langle e, n\rangle)[g(n)]\downarrow$. For this n, we have $\langle e, n\rangle \in B$ iff $A \nvDash \sigma_{\Phi_e(\langle e,n\rangle)}$, contradicting the choice of e. □

The above result cannot be extended to wtt-reducibility. Downey [99] constructed a noncomputable c.e. set A such that for all sets B, if $B \leqslant_T A$ then $B \leqslant_{wtt} A$. Since A is noncomputable and c.e., it has hyperimmune degree.

2.18 Minimal degrees

The proof of Theorem 2.17.3 uses ideas that go back to a fundamental theorem of Spector [374].

Definition 2.18.1. A degree $\mathbf{a} > \mathbf{0}$ is *minimal* if there is no degree $\mathbf{b}$ with $\mathbf{0} < \mathbf{b} < \mathbf{a}$.

Theorem 2.18.2 (Spector [374]). *There is a minimal degree below $\mathbf{0}''$.*

Proof. As with Theorem 2.17.3, the proof uses forcing with computable perfect trees. As before, we build a sequence $\{T_i\}_{i\in\omega}$ of computable function trees such that $[T_0] \supseteq [T_1] \supseteq [T_2] \supseteq \cdots$, and take our set A of minimal degree to be any element of $\bigcap_n [T_n]$.

At stage 0, we let T_0 be the identity map.

The action at stage $2e+1$ is exactly the same as in the proof of Theorem 2.17.3. That is, we let $i \in \{0,1\}$ be such that $T_{2e}(i) \neq W_e \upharpoonright |T_{2e}(i)|$ and define T_{2e+1} by letting $T_{2e+1}(\sigma) = T_{2e}(i\sigma)$. As before, this action ensures that $A \neq W_e$.

At stage $2e+2$, we are given T_{2e+1} and want to meet the requirement

$$\mathcal{R}_e : \Phi_e^A \text{ total} \Rightarrow \Phi_e^A \equiv_T \emptyset \vee A \leqslant_T \Phi_e^A.$$

The first thing we do is follow the method used in the proof of Theorem 2.17.3 to try to force the nontotality of Φ_e^A. We ask $\emptyset''$ whether there are n and σ such that $\Phi_e^{T_{2e+1}(\tau)}(n)\uparrow$ for all $\tau \succcurlyeq \sigma$. If so, we define T_{2e+2} by letting $T_{2e+2}(\nu) = T_{2e+1}(\sigma\nu)$. This definition clearly ensures that $\Phi_e^A(n)\uparrow$, and hence that $\mathcal{R}_e$ is met.

If there are no such n and σ, then we try to ensure that if Φ_e^A is total then it is computable. The critical question to ask $\emptyset''$ is whether there is a σ such that for all n and all $\tau_0, \tau_1 \succcurlyeq \sigma$, if $\Phi_e^{T_{2e+1}(\tau_i)}(n)\downarrow$ for $i = 0, 1$, then $\Phi_e^{T_{2e+1}(\tau_0)}(n) = \Phi_e^{T_{2e+1}(\tau_1)}(n)$. If this question has a positive answer, then we define T_{2e+2} by letting $T_{2e+2}(\nu) = T_{2e+1}(\sigma\nu)$. Then, to compute $\Phi_e^A(n)$ (assuming $\Phi_e^A(n)\downarrow$), we simply need to find a μ such that $\Phi_e^{T_{2e+2}(\mu)}(n)\downarrow$, and we are guaranteed that $\Phi_e^A(n) = \Phi_e^{T_{2e+2}(\mu)}(n)$. Thus, in this case, Φ_e^A is computable if total, and hence $\mathcal{R}_e$ is met.

If the answer to the above question is negative, then we need to ensure that $A \leqslant_T \Phi_e^A$. The crucial new idea is Spector's notion of an *e-splitting tree.*[10]

Definition 2.18.3. We say that a function tree T is *e-splitting* if for each σ, there is an n such that $\Phi_e^{T(\sigma 0)}(n)\downarrow \neq \Phi_e^{T(\sigma 1)}(n)\downarrow$.

The crucial fact about e-splitting trees is the following.

Lemma 2.18.4. *Let T be e-splitting and let $B \in [T]$. If Φ_e^B is total then $\Phi_e^B \geqslant_T B$.*

Proof. Suppose we are given Φ_e^B, and that Φ_e^B is total. Search for an n_0 such that $\Phi_e^{T(0)}(n_0)\downarrow \neq \Phi_e^{T(1)}(n_0)\downarrow$. Let i be such that $\Phi_e^B(n_0) = \Phi_e^{T(i)}(n_0)$. Then we know that $T(i) \prec B$. Now find an n_1 such that $\Phi_e^{T(i0)}(n_1)\downarrow \neq \Phi_e^{T(i1)}(n_1)\downarrow$. Let j be such that $\Phi_e^B(n_1) = \Phi_e^{T(ij)}(n_1)$. Then $T(ij) \prec B$. Continuing in this way, we can compute more and more of B. Thus $B \leqslant_T \Phi_e^B$. □

So to meet $\mathcal{R}_e$, it is enough to ensure that T_{2e+2} is e-splitting. But recall that we are now in the case in which for each σ there are n and

[10] We are being a bit free and easy with history. The notion of being e-splitting was first used by Spector, but the influential use of *trees* in the construction of a minimal degree actually first occurred in Shoenfield's book [356].

$\tau_0, \tau_1 \succ \sigma$ such that $\Phi_e^{T_{2e+1}(\tau_0)}(n)\downarrow \neq \Phi_e^{T_{2e+1}(\tau_1)}(n)\downarrow$. So we can define T_{2e+2} as follows. Let $T_{2e+2}(\lambda) = T_{2e+1}(\lambda)$. Suppose we have defined $T_{2e+2}(\mu)$ to equal $T_{2e+1}(\sigma)$ for some σ. Search for τ_0 and τ_1 as above and define $T_{2e+2}(\mu i) = T_{2e+1}(\tau_i)$ for $i = 0, 1$. Then T_{2e+2} is computable and e-splitting. □

As with hyperimmune-free degrees, there are in fact continuum many minimal degrees. A crucial difference between hyperimmune-free degrees and minimal degrees is given by the following result. (We say that a degree **b** *bounds* a degree **a** if $\mathbf{a} \leqslant \mathbf{b}$.)

Theorem 2.18.5 (Yates [410], Cooper [76]). *Every nonzero c.e. degree bounds a minimal degree.*

In particular, there are minimal degrees below $\mathbf{0}'$ (which was first shown by Sacks [342]), and hence hyperimmune minimal degrees. The method used to prove Theorem 2.18.5, known as the *full approximation method*, is quite involved and would take us a little too far afield. See Lerman [240] or Odifreddi [311] for more details.

Minimal degrees form a very interesting class. We finish by quoting two important results about their possible Turing degrees.

Theorem 2.18.6 (Jockusch and Posner [192]). *All minimal degrees are GL_2. That is, if* **a** *is a minimal degree then* $\mathbf{a}'' \leqslant (\mathbf{a} \vee \mathbf{0}')'$.

This result improved an earlier one by Cooper [77], who showed that no minimal degree below $\mathbf{0}'$ can be high. (There are low minimal degrees, as well as minimal degrees below $\mathbf{0}'$ that are not low; see [192] for a discussion of these and related results.) Cooper [77] also proved the following definitive result.

Theorem 2.18.7 (Cooper [77]). *If* $\mathbf{b} \geqslant \mathbf{0}'$ *then there is a minimal degree* **a** *with* $\mathbf{a}' = \mathbf{b}$.

Thus there is an analog of the Friedberg Completeness Criterion (Theorem 2.16.1) for minimal degrees. It is not possible to prove an analog of the Shoenfield Jump Inversion Theorem since Downey, Lempp, and Shore [124] showed that there are degrees CEA($\emptyset'$) and low over $\mathbf{0}'$ that are not jumps of minimal degrees below $\mathbf{0}'$. Cooper [78] claimed a characterization of the degrees CEA($\emptyset'$) that are jumps of minimal degrees below $\mathbf{0}'$, but no details were given.

2.19 Π_1^0 and Σ_1^0 classes

2.19.1 Basics

A *tree* is a subset of $2^{<\omega}$ closed under initial segments. A *path* through a tree T is an infinite sequence $P \in 2^\omega$ such that if $\sigma \prec P$ then $\sigma \in T$. The collection of paths through T is denoted by $[T]$. A subset of 2^ω is a Π^0_1 *class* if it is equal to $[T]$ for some computable tree T.[11]

An equivalent formulation is that C is a Π^0_1 class if there is a computable relation R such that

$$C = \{A \in 2^\omega : \forall n\, R(A \upharpoonright n)\}.$$

It is not hard to show that this definition is equivalent to the one via computable trees.

There is a host of natural examples of important Π^0_1 in several branches of logic. For example, let A and B be disjoint c.e. sets. The collection of *separating sets* $\{X : X \supseteq A \wedge X \cap B = \emptyset\}$ is a Π^0_1 class. An important special case is an *effectively inseparable* pair, that is, a pair of disjoint c.e. sets A and B for which there is a computable function f such that for all disjoint c.e. $W_e \supseteq A$ and $W_j \supseteq B$, we have $f(e,j) \notin W_e \cup W_j$. This is the two variable version of a creative set. One example of an effectively inseparable pair is the sets $\{e : \Phi_e(e)\downarrow= 0\}$ and $\{e : \Phi_e(e)\downarrow= 1\}$. The function f witnessing the effective inseparability of this pair is not hard to build: given e and j, using the recursion theorem we can find an i such that $\Phi_i(i)\downarrow= 1$ if $i \in W_e$ and $\Phi_i(i)\downarrow= 0$ if $i \in W_j$.[12] We then let $f(e,j) = i$.

Another example of a Π^0_1 class is the class of (codes of) extensions of a complete consistent theory. By the proof of Gödel's Incompleteness Theorem (see e.g. [139]), for a theory such as Peano Arithmetic (PA), the set A of sentences provable from PA and the set B of sentences refutable from PA form an effectively inseparable pair.

It is easy to check that the intersection of two Π^0_1 classes is again a Π^0_1 class, as is their union.

The complement of a Π^0_1 class is a Σ^0_1 *class*. Thus C is a Σ^0_1 class iff there is a computable relation R such that

$$C = \{A : \exists n\, R(A \upharpoonright n)\}.$$

We can think of Σ^0_1 classes as the analogs for infinite sequences of c.e. sets of finite strings. Indeed, an important fact about Σ^0_1 classes is that they are exactly the subsets of 2^ω generated by c.e. sets of finite strings, in the following sense. (Here we use the notation of Section 1.2.)

---

[11] Sometimes a Π^0_1 class is defined to be the set of paths through a computable subtree T of $\omega^{<\omega}$. Such a class is *computably bounded* if there is a computable function f such that for each $\sigma \in T$, if $\sigma n \in T$ then $n \leqslant f(\sigma)$. The study of computably bounded Π^0_1 classes reduces to the study of the special case of Π^0_1 subclasses of 2^ω, since every computably bounded Π^0_1 class is computably equivalent to a Π^0_1 subclass of 2^ω. We will restrict our attention to such classes, so for us a Π^0_1 class will mean a Π^0_1 subclass of 2^ω.

[12] In greater detail: Let g be a computable function such that for each k, the machine $\Phi_{g(k)}$ ignores its input and waits until k enters either W_e or W_j, at which point the machine returns 0 if $k \in W_e$ and 1 if $k \in W_j$ (while if $k \notin W_e \cup W_j$ then the machine does not return). By the recursion theorem, there is an i such that $\Phi_i = \Phi_{g(i)}$. For this i, we have $\Phi_i(i)\downarrow= 1$ if $i \in W_e$ and $\Phi_i(i)\downarrow= 0$ if $i \in W_j$.

Definition 2.19.1. A set $A \subseteq 2^{<\omega}$ is *prefix-free* if it is an antichain with respect to the natural partial ordering of $2^{<\omega}$; that is, for all $\sigma \in A$ and all τ properly extending σ, we have $\tau \notin A$.

Prefix-free sets will play an important role in this book, for example in the definition of prefix-free Kolmogorov complexity given in Section 3.5. Clearly, a set $C \subseteq 2^\omega$ is open iff it is of the form $[\![A]\!]$ for some prefix-free $A \subseteq 2^{<\omega}$. The following result is the effective analog of this fact.

Proposition 2.19.2. *A set $C \subseteq 2^\omega$ is a Σ^0_1 class iff there is a c.e. set $W \subseteq 2^{<\omega}$ such that $C = [\![W]\!]$. This fact remains true if we require W to be prefix-free.*

Proof. Given a Σ^0_1 class C, let T be a computable tree such that $\overline{C} = [T]$. Let W be the set of minimal elements of $\overline{T}$, that is, strings $\sigma \notin T$ such that every proper substring of σ is in T. Then W is prefix-free and $C = [\![W]\!]$.

Conversely, let $W \subseteq 2^{<\omega}$ be a c.e. set. Then $[\![W]\!] = \{A : \exists \langle n, s\rangle\, (A \upharpoonright n \in W_s)\}$, so $[\![W]\!]$ is a Σ^0_1 class. □

Thus we can think of Σ^0_1 classes as effectively open sets, and of Π^0_1 classes as effectively closed sets. So when we have a Σ^0_1 class C, we assume that we have fixed a c.e. set $W \subseteq 2^{<\omega}$ such that $C = [\![W]\!]$ and let $C[s] = [\![W[s]]\!]$. Similarly, for the Π^0_1 class $P = \overline{C}$, we let $P[s] = \overline{C[s]}$.

It is a potentially confusing fact that Proposition 2.19.2 remains true if we require W to be computable, rather than merely c.e. The reason for this fact is that if $W \subset 2^{<\omega}$ is prefix-free and c.e., then

$$V = \{\sigma : \exists \tau \in W_{|\sigma|+1} \setminus W_{|\sigma|}\, (\tau \preccurlyeq \sigma)\}$$

is computable and prefix-free, and $[\![V]\!] = [\![W]\!]$.

We say that the Σ^0_1 classes $C_0, C_1, \ldots$ are *uniformly* Σ^0_1, and their complements are *uniformly* Π^0_1, if there are uniformly c.e. sets $V_0, V_1, \ldots \subseteq 2^{<\omega}$ such that $C_i = [\![V_i]\!]$ for all i. It is not hard to see that $P_0, P_1, \ldots$ are uniformly Π^0_1 classes iff there are uniformly computable trees $T_0, T_1, \ldots$ such that $P_i = [T_i]$ for all i.

As one might imagine, a Δ^0_1 *class* is one such that both it and its complement are Σ^0_1. It is not hard to see that C is a Δ^0_1 class iff $C = [\![F]\!]$ for some finite $F \subset 2^{<\omega}$, so a Δ^0_1 class is just a clopen subset of 2^ω. The classes $C_0, C_1, \ldots$ are *uniformly* Δ^0_1 if there are uniformly computable finite sets $F_0, F_1, \ldots \subset 2^{<\omega}$ such that $C_i = [\![F_i]\!]$ for all i.

We will not need all that much of the extensive theory of Π^0_1 and Σ^0_1 classes, but a few facts will be important, such as the following bits of folklore. For more on the subject, see for instance Cenzer [55] or Cenzer and Remmel [57].

A path P through a tree T is *isolated* if there is a $\sigma \prec P$ such that no other path through T extends σ.

Proposition 2.19.3. *Let T be a computable tree and let P be an isolated path through T. Then P is computable.*

Proof. Let $\sigma \prec P$ be such that no path through T other than P extends σ. For any $n > |\sigma|$, there is exactly one $\tau \succ \sigma$ such that the portion of T above τ is infinite (by König's Lemma, which says that if a finitely branching tree is infinite, then it has a path). So to compute $P \upharpoonright n$ for $n > |\sigma|$, we look for an $m \geqslant n$ such that exactly one $\tau \succ \sigma$ of length n has an extension of length m in T. Then $P \upharpoonright n = \tau$. □

Corollary 2.19.4. *Let C be a Π_1^0 class with only finitely many members. Then every member of C is computable.*

Proof. Let T be a computable tree such that $C = [T]$. Then T has only finitely many paths, so every path through T is isolated. □

Proposition 2.19.5. *Let C be a nonempty Π_1^0 class with no computable members. Then $|C| = 2^{\aleph_0}$.*

Proof. Let T be a computable tree such that $C = [T]$. Let S be the set of *extendible* elements of T, that is, those σ such that there is an extension of σ in $[T]$. If every $\sigma \in S$ has two incompatible extensions in S, then it is easy to show that there are continuum many paths through T. Otherwise, there is a $\sigma \in S$ with a unique extension $P \in [T]$. As in the previous proof, P is computable. □

Note also that the question of whether a given computable tree T is finite is an existential one, since it amounts to asking whether there is an n such that no string of length n is in T, and hence it can be decided by $\emptyset'$.

The *Cantor-Bendixson derivative* of a Π_1^0 class C is the class C' obtained from C by removing the isolated points of C (i.e., those elements $X \in C$ such that for some n, we have $[\![X \upharpoonright n]\!] \cap C = \{X\}$). Let $C^{(0)} = C$. For an ordinal δ, let $C^{(\delta+1)} = (C^{\delta})'$, and for a limit ordinal δ, let $C^{(\delta)} = \bigcap_{\gamma<\delta} C^{(\gamma)}$. The *rank* of $X \in C$ is the least δ such that $X \in C^{(\delta)} \setminus C^{(\delta+1)}$, if such a δ exists. Note that, by Proposition 2.19.3, if X has rank 0, then it is computable. If all the elements of C have ranks, then the *rank* of C is the supremum of the ranks of its elements (or, equivalently, the least δ such that $C^{(\delta+1)} = \emptyset$).

2.19.2 Π_n^0 and Σ_n^0 classes

There is a hierarchy of classes, akin to the arithmetic hierarchy of sets.

Definition 2.19.6. A set $C \subseteq 2^\omega$ is a Π_n^0 *class* if there is a computable relation R such that

$$C = \{A : \forall k_1 \, \exists k_2 \cdots Qk_n \, R(A \upharpoonright k_1, A \upharpoonright k_2, \ldots, A \upharpoonright k_n)\},$$

where the quantifiers alternate and hence $Q = \forall$ if n is odd and $Q = \exists$ if n is even.

The complement of a Π^0_n class is a Σ^0_n *class*.

These definitions can be relativized to a given set X (by letting R be X-computable) to obtain the notions of $\Pi^{0,X}_n$ class and $\Sigma^{0,X}_n$ class. A Π^0_{n+1} class is also a $\Pi^{0,\emptyset^{(n)}}_1$ class, since every predicate of the form $\exists k_2 \cdots Q k_n\, R(A \upharpoonright k_1, A \upharpoonright k_2, \ldots, A \upharpoonright k_n)$ with R computable is computable in $\emptyset^{(n)}$. Similarly, every Σ^0_{n+1} class is also a $\Sigma^{0,\emptyset^{(n)}}_1$ class. The converse, however, is not always true, because every $\Pi^{0,\emptyset'}_1$ class is closed (indeed, every $\Pi^{0,X}_1$ class is closed for any X), but there are Π^0_2 classes that are not closed, such as the class C of all A with $A(m) = 1$ for infinitely many m, which can be written as $\{A : \forall k\, \exists m\, (m > k \,\wedge\, A(m) = 1)\}$.

Indeed, even a *closed* Π^0_2 class can fail to be a $\Pi^{0,\emptyset'}_1$ class. Doug Cenzer [personal communication] provided us the following example. It is not hard to build a computable subtree T of $\mathbb{N}^{<\omega}$ with a single infinite path $f \not\leqslant_{\mathrm{T}} \emptyset'$. Let $\widehat{T} = \{1^{n_0+1}01^{n_1+1}0 \ldots 1^{n_k+1}0^m : (n_0, \ldots, n_k) \in T,\ m \in \mathbb{N}\}$. It is easy to check that $\widehat{T}$ is a computable subtree of $2^{<\omega}$. Let $P = [\widehat{T}] \cap C$, where C is as in the previous paragraph. Then P is a Π^0_2 class (because, as with Π^0_1 classes, the intersection of two Π^0_n classes is again a Π^0_n class, as is their union). Furthermore, P has a single member $A = 1^{f(0)+1}01^{f(1)+1}0 \ldots$. But $A \equiv_{\mathrm{T}} f$, so $A \not\leqslant_{\mathrm{T}} \emptyset'$. Thus P cannot be a $\Pi^{0,\emptyset'}_1$ class by the relativized form of Corollary 2.19.4.

Since $\Sigma^{0,\emptyset^{(n)}}_1$ *sets* are the same as Σ^0_n sets, the relativized form of Proposition 2.19.2 says that a class is $\Sigma^{0,\emptyset^{(n)}}_1$ iff it is of the form $[\![W]\!]$ for some Σ^0_n set $W \subseteq 2^{<\omega}$.

We fix effective listings $S^n_0, S^n_1, \ldots$ of the Σ^0_n classes by letting $S^n_e = \{A : \exists k_1\, \forall k_2 \cdots Q k_n\, R(A \upharpoonright k_1, A \upharpoonright k_2, \ldots, A \upharpoonright k_n)\}$ where e is a code for the n-ary computable relation R. By an *index* for a Σ^0_n class S we mean an i such that $S = S^n_i$. Similarly, by an index for a Π^0_n class P we mean an i such that $P = \overline{S^n_i}$. We do the same for relativized classes in the natural way. We then say that the classes $C_0, C_1, \ldots$ are *uniformly* Σ^0_n if there is a computable function f such that $C_i = S^n_{f(i)}$ for all i, and *uniformly* Π^0_n if their complements are uniformly Σ^0_n. This definition agrees with the definition of uniformly Σ^0_1 classes given in the previous section because the proof of Proposition 2.19.2 is effective, as we now note.

Proposition 2.19.7. *From an index for a Σ^0_1 class C, we can computably find an index for a (prefix-free) c.e. set $W \subseteq 2^{<\omega}$ such that $C = [\![W]\!]$, and vice versa.*

Another way to look at this hierarchy of classes is in terms of effective unions and intersections. For example, in the same way that Π^0_1 and Σ^0_1 classes are the effective analogs of closed and open sets, respectively, Π^0_2

and Σ^0_2 classes are the effective analogs of G_δ and F_σ sets, respectively (where a set is G_δ if it is a countable intersection of open sets and F_σ if it is a countable union of closed sets). More precisely, C is a Π^0_2 class iff there are uniformly Σ^0_1 classes $U_0, U_1, \ldots$ such that $C = \bigcap_n U_n$. Similarly, C is a Σ^0_2 class iff there are uniformly Π^0_1 classes $P_0, P_1, \ldots$ such that $C = \bigcup_n P_n$. The same is true for any n in place of 1 and $n+1$ in place of 2. It is also easy to check that we can take $U_0 \supseteq U_1 \supseteq \cdots$ and $P_0 \subseteq P_1 \subseteq \cdots$ if we wish.

2.19.3 Basis theorems

A *basis* for the Π^0_1 classes is a collection of sets $\mathcal{C}$ such that every nonempty Π^0_1 class has an element in $\mathcal{C}$. One of the most important classes of results on Π^0_1 classes is that of basis theorems. A *basis theorem* for Π^0_1 classes states that every nonempty Π^0_1 class has a member of a certain type. (Henceforth, all Π^0_1 classes will be taken to be nonempty without further comment.) For instance, it is not hard to check that the lexicographically least element of a Π^0_1 class C (i.e., the leftmost path of a computable tree T such that $[T] = C$) has c.e. degree.[13] This fact establishes the Computably Enumerable Basis Theorem of Jockusch and Soare [195], which states that every Π^0_1 class has a member of c.e. degree, and is a refinement of the earlier Kreisel Basis Theorem, which states that every Π^0_1 class has a Δ^0_2 member.

The following is the most famous and widely applicable basis theorem.

Theorem 2.19.8 (Low Basis Theorem, Jockusch and Soare [196]). *Every Π^0_1 class has a low member.*

Proof. Let $C = [T]$ with T a computable tree. We define a sequence $T = T_0 \supseteq T_1 \supseteq \cdots$ of infinite computable trees such that if $P \in \bigcap_e [T_e]$ then P is low. (Note that there must be such a P, since each $[T_e]$ is closed.)

We begin with $T_0 = 2^{<\omega}$. Suppose that we have defined T_e, and let

$$U_e = \{\sigma : \Phi^\sigma_e(e)[|\sigma|]\uparrow\}.$$

Then U_e is a computable tree. If $U_e \cap T_e$ is infinite, then let $T_{e+1} = T_e \cap U_e$. Otherwise, let $T_{e+1} = T_e$. Note that either $\Phi^P_e(e)\uparrow$ for all $P \in [T_{e+1}]$ or $\Phi^P_e(e)\downarrow$ for all $P \in [T_{e+1}]$.

Now suppose that $P \in \bigcap_e [T_e]$. We can perform the above construction computably in $\emptyset'$, since $\emptyset'$ can decide the question of whether $U_e \cap T_e$ is finite. Thus $\emptyset'$ can decide whether $\Phi^P_e(e)\downarrow$ for any given e, and hence P is low. □

The above proof has a consequence that will be useful below. Recall that a set A is superlow if $A' \equiv_{tt} \emptyset'$. Marcus Schaefer observed that the proof of the low basis theorem actually produces a superlow set.

[13]Such an element is in fact a *left-c.e. real*, a concept we will define in Chapter 5.

Corollary 2.19.9 (Jockusch and Soare [196], Schaefer). *Every Π^0_1 class has a superlow member.*

The following variation on the low basis theorem will be useful below.

Theorem 2.19.10 (Jockusch and Soare [196]). *Let C be a Π^0_1 class and let X be a noncomputable set. Then there is an $A \in C$ such that $X \nleqslant_T A$ and $A' \leqslant_T X \oplus \emptyset'$.*

Proof. Let $C = [T]$ with T a computable tree. As in the proof of the low basis theorem, we define a sequence $T = T_0 \supseteq T_1 \supseteq \cdots$ of infinite computable trees.

We begin with $T_0 = 2^{<\omega}$. Suppose that we have defined T_{2e} to be a computable tree. We first proceed as in the proof of the low basis theorem. Let $U_e = \{\sigma : \Phi^\sigma_e(e)[|\sigma|]\uparrow\}$. If $U_e \cap T_{2e}$ is infinite, then let $T_{2e+1} = T_{2e} \cap U_e$. Otherwise, let $T_{2e+1} = T_{2e}$. As before, T_{2e+1} is a computable tree.

We now handle cone-avoidance as follows. We $X \oplus \emptyset'$-computably search until we find that one of the following holds.

1. There are an n and an extendible $\sigma \in T_{2e+1}$ such that $\Phi^\sigma_e(n)\downarrow \neq X(n)$.

2. There is an n such that $T_{2e+1} \cap \{\sigma : \Phi^\sigma_e(n)\uparrow\}$ is infinite.

We claim one of the above must hold. Suppose not, and fix n. The fact that 2 does not hold means that we can find a k such that $\Phi^\sigma_e(n)\downarrow$ for all $\sigma \in T_{2e+1} \cap 2^k$. The fact that 1 does not hold means that, for each such σ, if $\Phi^\sigma_e(n) \neq X(n)$, then T_{2e+1} is finite above σ. Thus we can compute $X(n)$ by searching for a j such that for all $\sigma, \tau \in T_{2e+1} \cap 2^j$, we have $\Phi^\sigma_e(n)\downarrow = \Phi^\tau_e(n)\downarrow$, which by the above must exist. Since X is noncomputable, either 1 or 2 must hold. If we find that 1 holds, then let $T_{2e+2} = T_{2e+1} \cap \{\tau : \sigma \preccurlyeq \tau\}$. Otherwise, let $T_{2e+2} = T_{2e+1} \cap \{\sigma : \Phi^\sigma_e(n)\uparrow\}$.

Now let $A \in \bigcap_e [T_e]$. It is easy to check that we can perform the above construction computably in $X \oplus \emptyset'$, so as in the proof of the low basis theorem, we have $A' \leqslant_T X \oplus \emptyset'$. Furthermore, the definition of the trees T_{2e+2} ensures that $X \nleqslant_T A$. □

Corollary 2.19.9 and Theorem 2.19.10 cannot be combined. That is, there are a Π^0_1 class C and a noncomputable set X such that X is computable from every superlow member of C. We will see examples in Section 14.4.

Another important basis theorem is provided by the hyperimmune-free degrees.

Theorem 2.19.11 (Hyperimmune-Free Basis Theorem, Jockusch and Soare [196]). *Every Π^0_1 class has a member of hyperimmune-free degree.*

Proof. Let C be a Π^0_1 class, and let T be a computable tree such that $C = [T]$. We can carry out a construction like that in the proof of Miller and Martin's Theorem 2.17.3 within T. We begin with $T_0 = T$. We do not need the odd stages of that construction since we do not need to force noncomputability (as $\mathbf{0}$ is hyperimmune-free). Thus we deal with Φ_e at stage $e+1$.

We are given T_e and we want to build T_{e+1} to ensure that either

(i) if $A \in [T_{e+1}]$ then Φ_e^A is not total, or

(ii) there is a computable function f such that if $A \in [T_{e+1}]$ then $\Phi_e^A(n) \leqslant f(n)$ for all n.

Let

$$U_e^n = \{\sigma : \Phi_e^\sigma(n)\uparrow\}.$$

There are two cases.

If there is an n such that $U_e^n \cap T_e$ is infinite, then let $T_{e+1} = U_e^n \cap T_e$. In this case, if $A \in [T_{e+1}]$ then $\Phi_e^A(n)\uparrow$.

Otherwise, let $T_{e+1} = T_e$. In this case, for each n we can compute a number $l(n)$ such that no string $\sigma \in T_e$ of length $l(n)$ is in U_e^n. For any such σ, we have $\Phi_e^\sigma(n)\downarrow$. Define the computable function f by

$$f(n) = \max\{\Phi_e^\sigma(n) : \sigma \in T_e \wedge |\sigma| = l(n)\}.$$

Then $A \in [T_{e+1}]$ implies that $\Phi_e^A(n) \leqslant f(n)$ for all n.

So if we let $A \in \bigcap_e [T_e]$, then A is a member of C and has hyperimmune-free degree. □

In the above construction, if $[T]$ has no computable members, then Proposition 2.19.5 implies that each T_e must have size $2^{\aleph_0}$. It is not hard to adjust the construction in this case to obtain continuum many members of C of hyperimmune-free degree. Thus, a Π^0_1 class with no computable members has continuum many members of hyperimmune-free degree.

The following result is an immediate consequence of the hyperimmune-free basis theorem and Theorem 2.17.2, but it was first explicitly articulated by Kautz [200], who gave an interesting direct proof. Recall that a set A is computably enumerable in and above a set X (CEA(X)) if A is c.e. in X and $X \leqslant_T A$. A set A is *CEA* if it is CEA(X) for some $X <_T A$.

Corollary 2.19.12 (Jockusch and Soare [196], Kautz [200]). *Every Π^0_1 class has a member that is not CEA.*

Although the existence of minimal degrees (Theorem 2.18.2) was proved by techniques similar to those used to prove the hyperimmune-free basis theorem, there is no "minimal basis theorem", since there are Π^0_1 classes with no members of minimal degree. An example is the Π^0_1 class of all complete extensions of Peano Arithmetic, by Theorem 2.21.9 below. However, using techniques beyond the scope of this book, Groszek and Slaman [173] proved the following elegant result.

Theorem 2.19.13 (Groszek and Slaman [173]). *There is a Π^0_1 class such that every member either is c.e. and noncomputable, or has minimal degree.*

We end this section by looking at examples of *nonbasis* theorems.

Proposition 2.19.14. *The intersection of all bases for the Π^0_1 classes is the collection of computable sets, and hence there is no minimal basis.*

Proof. If A is a computable set then $\{A\}$ is a Π^0_1 class, so every basis for the Π^0_1 classes must include A. On the other hand, if B is noncomputable then, by Corollary 2.19.4, $\{B\}$ is not a Π^0_1 class, so every Π^0_1 class must contain a member other than B, and hence the collection of all sets other than B is a basis for the Π^0_1 classes.[14] □

For our next result, we will need the following definition and lemma.

Definition 2.19.15. An infinite set A is *effectively immune* if there is a computable function f such that for all e, if $W_e \subseteq A$ then $|W_e| \leqslant f(e)$.

Post gave the following construction of an effectively immune co-c.e. set A. At stage s, for each $e < s$, if $W_e[s] \subseteq A_s$ and there is an $x \in W_e[s]$ such that $x > 2e$, then put the least such x into $\overline{A}$. Then A is infinite, and is effectively immune via the function $e \mapsto 2e$.

Lemma 2.19.16 (Martin [258]). *If a c.e. set B computes an effectively immune set, then B is Turing complete.*

Proof. Let B be c.e., and let $A \leqslant_{\mathrm{T}} B$ be effectively immune, as witnessed by the computable function f. Let Γ be a reduction such that $\Gamma^B = A$.

For each k we build a c.e. set $W_{h(k)}$, where the computable function h is given by the recursion theorem with parameters. Initially, $W_{h(k)}$ is empty. If k enters $\emptyset'$ at stage t then we wait until a stage $s \geqslant t$ at which there is a q such that $\Gamma^B(n)[s]\downarrow$ for all $n < q$ and there are more than $f(h(k))$ many numbers in $\Gamma^B[s] \upharpoonright q$. We then let $W_{h(k)} = \Gamma^B[s] \upharpoonright q$.[15] This action ensures that $|W_{h(k)}| > f(h(k))$, so we must have $W_{h(k)} \not\subseteq A$. Thus,

$$\Gamma^B[s] \upharpoonright q = W_{h(k)} \neq A \upharpoonright q = \Gamma^B \upharpoonright q.$$

So to compute $\emptyset'(k)$ from B, we simply look for a stage s at which there is a q such that $B_s \upharpoonright \gamma^B(n)[s] = B \upharpoonright \gamma^B(n)[s]$ for all $n < q$ and there are more than $f(h(k))$ many numbers in $\Gamma^B[s] \upharpoonright q$. If k is not in $\emptyset'$ by stage s, it cannot later enter $\emptyset'$. □

---

[14]Another way to prove this fact is to note that, by Theorem 2.17.2, the only sets that are both low and hyperimmune-free are the computable ones.

[15]In greater detail: For each i and k, we define a c.e. set $C_{i,k}$ as follows. Initially, $C_{i,k}$ is empty. If k enters $\emptyset'$ at stage t then we wait until a stage $s \geqslant t$ at which there is a q such that $\Gamma^B(n)[s]\downarrow$ for all $n < q$ and there are more than $f(i)$ many numbers in $\Gamma^B[s] \upharpoonright q$. We then let $C_{i,k} = \Gamma^B[s] \upharpoonright q$. It is easy to see that there is a computable function g such that $g(i, k)$ is an index for $C_{i,k}$ for all i and k. By the recursion theorem with parameters, there is a computable function h such that $W_{h(k)} = W_{g(h(k),k)}$ for all k. This h has the required properties.

Theorem 2.19.17 (Jockusch and Soare [195]). (i) *The incomplete c.e. degrees do not form a basis for the Π^0_1 classes.*

(ii) *Let* $\mathbf{a}$ *be an incomplete c.e. degree. Then the degrees less than or equal to* $\mathbf{a}$ *do not form a basis for the Π^0_1 classes.*

Proof. By Lemma 2.19.16, to prove both parts of the theorem, it is enough to find a Π^0_1 class whose members are all effectively immune. Let A be Post's effectively immune set described after Definition 2.19.15. An infinite subset of an effectively immune set is clearly also effectively immune, so it is enough to find a Π^0_1 class all of whose members are infinite subsets of A.

It is clear from the construction of A that $|\overline{A} \upharpoonright 2e| \leqslant e$ for all e. Thus $A \cap [2^k - 1, 2^{k+1} - 2] \neq \emptyset$ for all k.[16] Let

$$\mathcal{P} = \{B : B \subseteq A \wedge \forall k\, (B \cap [2^k - 1, 2^{k+1} - 2] \neq \emptyset)\}.$$

Since A is co-c.e., $\mathcal{P}$ is a Π^0_1 class, and it is nonempty because $A \in \mathcal{P}$. Furthermore, every element of $\mathcal{P}$ is an infinite subset of A. As explained in the previous paragraph, these facts suffice to establish the theorem. □

2.19.4 Generalizing the low basis theorem

We would like to extend the low basis theorem to degrees above $\mathbf{0}'$. Of course, we cannot hope to prove that for every degree $\mathbf{a} \geqslant \mathbf{0}'$, every Π^0_1 class has a member whose jump has degree $\mathbf{a}$, since there are Π^0_1 classes whose members are all computable. We can prove this result, however, if we restrict our attention to *special* Π^0_1 classes, which are those with no computable members.

Theorem 2.19.18 (Jockusch and Soare [196]). *If C is a Π^0_1 class with no computable members and $\mathbf{a} \geqslant \mathbf{0}'$, then there is a $P \in C$ such that* $\deg(P') = \deg P \oplus \emptyset' = \mathbf{a}$.

Proof. Let $C = [T]$ with T a computable tree and let $A \in \mathbf{a}$. By Proposition 2.19.5, T has $2^{\aleph_0}$ many paths. We A-computably define an infinite sequence of computable trees $T_0 \supseteq T_1 \supseteq \cdots$, each with $2^{\aleph_0}$ many paths. We begin with $T_0 = T$.

Given T_{2e}, let

$$U_{2e} = \{\sigma \in T_{2e} : \Phi^\sigma_e(e)[|\sigma|]\uparrow\}.$$

If U_{2e} is finite then let $T_{2e+1} = T_{2e}$. Otherwise, since U_{2e} is a subtree of T, it has no computable paths, and hence has $2^{\aleph_0}$ many paths. In this case, let $T_{2e+1} = U_{2e}$. Notice that we can A-computably decide which case we are in because $A \geqslant_{\mathrm{T}} \emptyset'$.

---

[16] Notice that this fact shows that A is not hyperimmune. In fact, it is not hard to show that a co-c.e. set X is not hyperimmune iff there is a Π^0_1 class all of whose members are infinite subsets of X.

Now let $\sigma_0 <_L \sigma_1$ be the length-lexicographically least pair of incomparable strings in T_{2e+1} such that for each $i < 2$, the subtree of T_{2e+1} above σ_i is infinite (and hence has $2^{\aleph_0}$ many paths). Notice that we can find σ_0, σ_1 using A, again because $A \geqslant_T \emptyset'$. Let T_{2e+2} be the subtree of T_{2e+1} above $\sigma_{A(e)}$.

Having defined the T_e, let $P \in \bigcap_e [T_e]$. The choice of T_{2e+1} determines whether $\Phi_e^P(e)\downarrow$, so, since the entire construction is A-computable, $P' \leqslant_T A$. On the other hand, we can also perform the construction $(P \oplus \emptyset')$-computably, since all the steps can be done $\emptyset'$-computably, except the choice of which σ_i to extend in defining T_{2e+2}, which can be done P-computably, since the σ_i we choose at that stage is the one extended by P. Furthermore, that choice determines the eth bit of A. Thus $A \leqslant_T P \oplus \emptyset' \leqslant_T P'$, and hence $P' \equiv_T P \oplus \emptyset' \equiv_T A$. □

Corollary 2.19.19 (Jockusch and Soare [196]). *For each* $\mathbf{a} \geqslant \mathbf{0}'$, *the sets with degrees in* $\{\mathbf{b} : \mathbf{b}' = \mathbf{a}\} \cup \{\mathbf{0}\}$ *form a basis for the* Π^0_1 *classes.*

2.20 Strong reducibilities and Post's Program

The concept of hypersimplicity, which we defined in Section 2.17, was introduced by Post [316] as part of an attempt to solve Post's Problem. Although hypersimple sets can be Turing complete, Post [316] showed that no hypersimple set can be tt-complete. Later, Friedberg and Rogers [162] proved that no hypersimple set can be wtt-complete. This result has been extended as follows. A set A is *wtt-cuppable* if there is a c.e. set $W <_{\text{wtt}} \emptyset'$ such that $A \oplus W \geqslant_{\text{wtt}} \emptyset'$.

Theorem 2.20.1 (Downey and Jockusch [119]). *No hypersimple set is wtt-cuppable.*

Proof. Suppose that A is hypersimple, W is c.e., $W \leqslant_{\text{wtt}} \emptyset'$, and $A \oplus W \geqslant_{\text{wtt}} \emptyset'$. We show that $W \geqslant_{\text{wtt}} \emptyset'$. We will build a c.e. set B. By the recursion theorem, we may assume that we have a wtt-reduction $\Gamma^{A \oplus W} = B$ with computable use g.[17] Without loss of generality, we may assume that $g(n)$ is increasing and even for all n and write $h(n)$ for $\frac{g(n)}{2}$.

We define a strong array $\{F_i\}_{i \in \mathbb{N}}$ as follows, writing $m(i)$ for $\max F_i$. Let $F_0 = [0, h(0)]$. Given F_i, pick $m(i) + 1$ many fresh large numbers $b_0^{i+1} < \cdots < b_{m(i)}^{i+1}$ and let $F_{i+1} = (\max F_i, h(b_{m(i)}^{i+1})]$. Since the F_i form a strong array, there are infinitely many i with $F_i \subseteq A$. We can therefore

---

[17] In greater detail: We can think of the ensuing construction as building a c.e. set $W_{f(e)}$ given a parameter e, taking as Γ a wtt-functional such that $\Gamma^{A \oplus W} = W_e$. (It is not hard to see that indices for Γ and for a computable function bounding its use can be found effectively from e.) By the recursion theorem, there is an e such that $W_e = W_{f(e)}$, and we let $B = W_e$.

enumerate an increasing computable sequence $i_0 < i_1 < \cdots$ such that $F_{i_k+1} \subseteq A$ for all k.

Now for each k, we act as follows. Let $b = b^{i_k+1}_{m(i_k)}$. We wait until a stage s_k such that $F_{i_k+1} \subseteq A_{s_k}$. If k enters $\emptyset'$ at a stage $t_k \geqslant s_k$, we wait for a stage s such that $\Gamma^{A\oplus W}[s] \upharpoonright (b+1) = B_s \upharpoonright (b+1)$, then put $b^{i_k+1}_0$ into B. If later A changes below $h(b)$, we again wait for a stage s such that $\Gamma^{A\oplus W}[s] \upharpoonright (b+1) = B_s \upharpoonright (b+1)$, then put $b^{i_k+1}_1$ into B. We continue in this manner, enumerating one more $b^{i_k+1}_j$ into B each time A changes below $h(b)$ and the computation $\Gamma^{A\oplus W} \upharpoonright (b+1)$ recovers. Since $F_{i_k+1} \subseteq A_{s_k}$, we cannot have more than $m(i_k)+1$ many changes in A below $h(b)$ after stage s_k, so we never run out of $b^{i_k+1}_j$'s. Since we change $B \upharpoonright (b+1)$ after the last time $A \upharpoonright h(b)$ changes, $W \upharpoonright h(b)$ must change at that point to ensure that $\Gamma^{A\oplus W} \upharpoonright (b+1) = B \upharpoonright (b+1)$.

Thus $W \upharpoonright h(b)$ changes at least once after stage t_k, so we can wtt-compute $\emptyset'$ using W as follows. Given k, wait for a stage $s \geqslant s_k$ such that $W_s \upharpoonright h(b) = W \upharpoonright h(b)$. Then $k \in \emptyset'$ iff $k \in \emptyset'_s$. □

Post's original program for solving Post's Problem was to find a "thinness" property of the lattice of supersets of a c.e. set (under inclusion) guaranteeing Turing incompleteness of the given set. It was eventually shown that this approach could not succeed. Although Sacks [343] constructed a *maximal set* (i.e., a coinfinite c.e. set M such that if $W \supseteq M$ is c.e. then either W is cofinite or $W \setminus M$ is finite) that is Turing incomplete, it is also possible to construct Turing complete maximal sets. Indeed, Soare [365] showed that the maximal sets form an orbit of the automorphisms of the lattice of c.e. sets under inclusion, and hence there is no definable property that can be added to maximality to guarantee incompleteness. Eventually, Cholak, Downey, and Stob [66] showed that no property of the lattice of c.e. supersets of a c.e. set can by itself guarantee incompleteness. Finally, Harrington and Soare [176] did find an elementary property of c.e. sets (that is, one that is first-order definable in the language of the lattice of c.e. sets) that guarantees incompleteness. There is a large amount of fascinating material related to this topic. For instance, Cholak and Harrington [68] have shown that one can define all "double jump" classes in the lattice of c.e. sets using infinitary formulas. The methods are intricate and rely on analyzing the failure of the "automorphism machinery" first developed by Soare and later refined by himself and others, particularly Cholak and Harrington.

Properties like simplicity (defined in Section 2.2) and hypersimplicity do have implications for the degrees of sets related to a given c.e. set. For instance, Stob [383] showed that a c.e. set is simple iff it does not have c.e. supersets of all c.e. degrees. Downey [100] showed that if A is hypersimple then there is a c.e. degree $\mathbf{b} \leqslant \deg(A)$ such that if $A_0 \sqcup A_1$ is a c.e. splitting of A, then neither of the A_i has degree $\mathbf{b}$.

2.21 PA degrees

In this section, we assume familiarity with basic concepts of mathematical logic, such as the notion of a first-order theory, the formal system of Peano Arithmetic, and Gödel's Incompleteness Theorem, as may be found in an introductory text such as Enderton [139]. Those unfamiliar with this material may take Corollary 2.21.4 below as a definition of the notion of a PA degree (which makes Theorem 2.21.3 immediate).

The class of complete extensions of a given computably axiomatizable first-order theory is a Π^0_1 class. (We assume here that all theories are consistent.) Jockusch and Soare [195, 196] showed that, in fact, for every Π^0_1 class P there is a computably axiomatizable first-order theory T such that the class of degrees of members of P coincides with the class of degrees of complete extensions of T. (This result was later extended by Hanf [174] to finitely axiomatizable theories.) As we will see, there are Π^0_1 classes P that are *universal*, in the sense that any set that can compute an element of P can compute an element of any nonempty Π^0_1 class. A natural example of such a class is the class of complete extensions of Peano Arithmetic. The degrees of elements of this class are known as *PA degrees*.

Definition 2.21.1. A degree $\mathbf{a}$ is a *PA degree* if it is the degree of a complete extension of Peano Arithmetic.

Theorem 2.21.2 (Scott Basis Theorem [352]). *If $\mathbf{a}$ is a PA degree then the sets computable from $\mathbf{a}$ form a basis for the Π^0_1 classes.*

Proof. Let S be a complete extension of PA of degree $\mathbf{a}$.[18] Let T be an infinite computable tree. We compute a path through T using S by defining a sequence $\sigma_0 \prec \sigma_1 \prec \cdots \in T$.

Let $\sigma_0 = \lambda$. Suppose that σ_n has been defined in such a way that there is a path through T extending σ_n. If there is a unique i such that $\sigma_n i \in T$, then let $\sigma_{n+1} = \sigma_n i$. Otherwise, both $\sigma_n 0$ and $\sigma_n 1$ are in T. For $i = 0, 1$, let θ_i be the sentence

$$\exists m\,(\sigma_n i \text{ has an extension of length } m \text{ in } T \text{ but } \sigma_n(1-i) \text{ does not}).$$

These sentences can be expressed in the language of first-order arithmetic, by the kind of coding used in the proof of Gödel's Incompleteness Theorem.

Within PA, we can argue as follows. Suppose that θ_0 and θ_1 both hold. Then for each $i = 0, 1$, there is a least m_i such that $\sigma_n i$ has an extension of length m_i in T but $\sigma_n(1-i)$ does not. Let i be such that $m_i \geqslant m_{1-i}$. Then $\sigma_n(1-i)$ has an extension of length m_{1-i}, and hence one of length m_i, which contradicts the choice of m_i.

[18] We do not actually need S to be complete, but only consistent and deductively closed.

Thus PA $\vDash \neg(\theta_0 \wedge \theta_1)$, so there is a least i such that $\theta_{1-i} \notin S$. Let $\sigma_{n+1} = \sigma_n i$. There must be a path through T extending σ_{n+1}, since otherwise we would have PA $\vDash \theta_{1-i}$, and hence $\theta_{1-i} \in S$. □

In unpublished work, Solovay showed that, in fact, the property in Theorem 2.21.2 exactly characterizes the PA degrees. This fact, which we will state as Corollary 2.21.4 below, follows immediately from the following result, which is important in its own right.

Theorem 2.21.3 (Solovay [unpublished]). *The class of PA degrees is closed upwards.*

Proof. Let A be the set of (Gödel numbers of) sentences provable in PA and B the set of (Gödel numbers of) sentences refutable from PA. We follow the proof in Odifreddi [310], which uses the fact that A and B form an effectively inseparable pair of c.e. sets (which recall means that there is a computable function f such that for all disjoint c.e. $W_e \supseteq A$ and $W_i \supseteq B$, we have $f(e,i) \notin W_e \cup W_i$).

Let T be a complete extension of PA computable in a set X. Using T, we will build finite extensions F_σ of PA for $\sigma \in 2^{<\omega}$ so that $\bigcup_{\sigma \prec X} F_\sigma$ is a complete extension of PA with the same degree as X.

Let $\varphi_0, \varphi_1, \ldots$ be an effective listing of the sentences of arithmetic. Let $F_\lambda =$ PA. Suppose that we have defined F_σ to be a finite consistent extension of PA. Let ψ_0 be an existential sentence of arithmetic expressing the statement that

$$\exists m\,(m \text{ codes a proof of } \varphi_n \text{ in } F_\sigma \text{ and no } k < m \text{ codes a proof of } \neg\varphi_n \text{ in } F_\sigma).$$

Let ψ_1 be the same with the roles of φ_n and $\neg\varphi_n$ interchanged.

We have $\psi_i \in T$ iff ψ_i is true, and at most one ψ_i is true. If $\psi_0 \in T$ then let $F'_\sigma = F_\sigma \cup \{\varphi_n\}$ and otherwise let $F'_\sigma = F_\sigma \cup \{\neg\varphi_n\}$.

Let C be the sentences provable in F'_σ and D the sentences refutable from F'_σ. Then C and D are c.e. sets containing A and B, respectively, and we can effectively find indices for C and D. Since A and B form an effectively inseparable pair, we can compute a sentence $\nu \notin C \cup D$. Let $F_{\sigma 0} = F'_\sigma \cup \{\nu\}$ and $F_{\sigma 1} = F'_\sigma \cup \{\neg\nu\}$.

Let $S = \bigcup_{\sigma \prec X} F_\sigma$. Then S is a complete extension of PA, and is X-computable, since T is X-computable. Given S, we can compute X as follows. Assume by induction that we have computed $X \upharpoonright n$ and $F_{X \upharpoonright n}$. We know which of φ_n and $\neg\varphi_n$ is in S, so we know $F'_{X \upharpoonright n}$. Thus we can compute ν. We know which of ν and $\neg\nu$ is in S, so we know $X \upharpoonright n+1$ and $F_{X \upharpoonright n+1}$. Thus $S \equiv_{\mathrm{T}} X$. □

Since the complete extensions of PA form a Π^0_1 class, if the sets computable from a degree **a** form a basis for the Π^0_1 classes, then in particular

a computes a complete extension of PA, and hence, by the above theorem, is itself a PA degree. Thus we have the following result.

Corollary 2.21.4 (Solovay). *A degree is PA iff the sets computable from it form a basis for the Π^0_1 classes.*

A useful way to restate this corollary is that a degree **a** is PA iff every computable infinite subtree of $2^{<\omega}$ has an **a**-computable path.

Another way to characterize PA degrees is via effectively inseparable pairs of c.e. sets. Let A and B form such a pair. As previously mentioned, the class of all sets that separate A and B is a Π^0_1 class, so every PA degree computes such a set. Conversely, given a set C separating A and B, we can use the following useful lemma to obtain a C-computable complete extension of PA.

Lemma 2.21.5 (Muchnik [285], Smullyan [362]). *Let C be a separating set for an effectively inseparable pair of c.e. sets A and B, and let X and Y be disjoint c.e. sets. Then there is a C-computable set separating X and Y.*

Proof. Let f be a total function witnessing the effective inseparability of A and B. It is not hard to see that we may assume that f is 1-1. Using the recursion theorem with parameters, we can define computable 1-1 functions g and h such that for all n we have

$$W_{g(n)} = \begin{cases} A \cup \{f(g(n), h(n))\} & \text{if } n \in Y \\ A & \text{otherwise} \end{cases}$$

and

$$W_{h(n)} = \begin{cases} B \cup \{f(g(n), h(n))\} & \text{if } n \in X \\ B & \text{otherwise.}^{19} \end{cases}$$

Let $D = \{n : f(g(n), h(n)) \in C\}$. If $n \in X$ then $f(g(n), h(n)) \in W_{g(n)} \cup W_{h(n)}$, so $W_{g(n)}$ and $W_{h(n)}$ cannot be disjoint. It follows that $f(g(n), h(n)) \in A \subseteq C$, so $n \in D$. The same argument shows that if $n \in Y$ then $f(g(n), h(n)) \in B$, so $n \notin D$. Thus D is a separating set for X and Y. □

Theorem 2.21.6 (Jockusch and Soare [196]). *If C is a separating set for an effectively inseparable pair then C has PA degree. Thus a degree is PA iff it computes a separating set for an effectively inseparable pair.*

Proof. Let X be the set of sentences provable in PA and Y the set of sentences refutable from PA. By the above lemma, there is a C-computable set D separating X and Y. Let $\varphi_0, \varphi_1, \ldots$ be an effective listing of the

[19] It is a useful exercise to work out the full details of the application of the recursion theorem in this case.

sentences of arithmetic. Let $T_0 = \emptyset$. Suppose we have defined the finite set of sentences T_n. Let $\psi = (\bigwedge_{\varphi \in T_n} \varphi) \rightarrow \varphi_n$. If $\psi \in D$ then we know ψ is not refutable from PA, so $(\bigwedge_{\varphi \in T_n} \varphi) \rightarrow \neg\varphi_n$ is not provable from PA, and we can let $T_{n+1} = T_n \cup \{\varphi_n\}$. Otherwise, ψ is not provable from PA, so we can let $T_{n+1} = T_n \cup \{\neg\varphi_n\}$. Let $T = \bigcup_n T_n$. It is easy to check that T is a D-computable (and hence C-computable) complete extension of PA. □

The following result follows immediately from the Low Basis Theorem 2.19.8. (Indeed, this result was Jockusch and Soare's first application of their theorem.)

Theorem 2.21.7 (Jockusch and Soare [196]). *There is a low PA degree.*

By upward closure, $\mathbf{0}'$ is a PA degree. However, combining Theorems 2.19.17 and 2.21.2, we see that it is the only c.e. PA degree.

Theorem 2.21.8 (Jockusch and Soare [195]). *No incomplete c.e. degree is PA.*

The following is another useful fact about the distribution of PA degrees.

Theorem 2.21.9 (Scott and Tennenbaum [351]). *A PA degree cannot be minimal.*

Proof. Let $P = \{A \oplus B : \forall e\,(A(e) \neq \Phi_e(e) \wedge B(e) \neq \Phi_e^A(e))\}$. If a set S has PA degree then there is an $A \oplus B \in P$ such that $A \oplus B \leqslant_{\mathrm{T}} S$. It follows from the definition of P that $0 <_{\mathrm{T}} A <_{\mathrm{T}} A \oplus B \leqslant_{\mathrm{T}} S$, so S does not have minimal degree. □

2.22 Fixed-point free and diagonally noncomputable functions

A total function f is *fixed-point free* if $W_{f(e)} \neq W_e$ for all e. By the recursion theorem, no computable function is fixed-point free, and indeed the fixed-point free functions can be thought of as those that avoid having fixed points in the sense of the recursion theorem. As we will see (in Section 8.17, for example), fixed-point free functions have interesting ramifications in both classical computability theory and the theory of algorithmic randomness. A related concept is that of a *diagonally noncomputable* (*DNC*) function, where the total function g is DNC if $g(e) \neq \Phi_e(e)$ for all e. A degree is diagonally noncomputable if it computes a DNC function.

Theorem 2.22.1 (Jockusch, Lerman, Soare, and Solovay [191]). *The following are equivalent.*

(i) *The set A computes a fixed-point free function.*

(ii) *The set A computes a total function h such that $\Phi_{h(e)} \neq \Phi_e$ for all e.*

(iii) *The set A computes a DNC function.*

(iv) *For each e there is a total function $h \leqslant_T A$ such that $h(n) \neq \Phi_e(n)$ for all n.*

(v) *For each total computable function f there is an index i with Φ_i^A total and $\Phi_i^A(n) \neq \Phi_{f(i)}(n)$ for all n.*

Proof. We begin by proving the equivalence of (i)–(iii).

Clearly (i) implies (ii), since if $W_{h(e)} \neq W_e$ then $\Phi_{h(e)} \neq \Phi_e$.

To show that (ii) implies (iii), suppose that h is as in (ii). Define $\Phi_{d(u)}$ as in the proof of the recursion theorem. That is, $\Phi_{d(u)}(z)$ is $\Phi_{\Phi_u(u)}(z)$ if $\Phi_u(u)\downarrow$, and $\Phi_{d(u)}(z)\uparrow$ otherwise. As we have seen, we can choose d to be a total computable function. Let $g = h \circ d$. Note that $g \leqslant_T A$. Suppose that $g(e) = \Phi_e(e)$. Then by (ii) we have

$$\Phi_{d(e)} \neq \Phi_{h(d(e))} = \Phi_{g(e)} = \Phi_{\Phi_e(e)} = \Phi_{d(e)},$$

which is a contradiction. So g is DNC.

To show that (iii) implies (i), fix a partial computable function ψ such that, for all e, if $W_e \neq \emptyset$ then $\psi(e) \in W_e$, and let q be partial computable with $\Phi_{q(e)}(q(e)) = \psi(e)$ for all e. Let $g \leqslant_T A$ be DNC, and define $f \leqslant_T A$ so that $W_{f(e)} = \{g(q(e))\}$. Suppose that $W_e = W_{f(e)}$. Then $W_e \neq \emptyset$, so $\psi(e) \in W_e$, which implies that $\psi(e) = g(q(e))$. But g is DNC, so $g(q(e)) \neq \Phi_{q(e)}(q(e)) = \psi(e)$, which is a contradiction. So f is fixed-point free.

We now prove the equivalence of (iv) and (v).

To show that (iv) implies (v), let f be a computable function, and let e be such that $\Phi_e(\langle i,j\rangle) = \Phi_{f(i)}(j)$. Fix $h \leqslant_T A$ satisfying (iv) for this e. For all i and n, let $h_i(n) = h(\langle i,n\rangle)$. Then there is a total computable function p with $\Phi_{p(i)}^A = h_i$ for all i. By the relativized form of the recursion theorem, there is an i such that $\Phi_{p(i)}^A = \Phi_i^A$. Then Φ_i^A is total, and

$$\Phi_i^A(n) = \Phi_{p(i)}^A(n) = h(\langle i,n\rangle) \neq \Phi_e(\langle i,n\rangle) = \Phi_{f(i)}(n).$$

To show that (v) implies (iv), assume that (iv) fails for some e. Let $f(i) = e$ for all i. Then for all i such that Φ_i^A is total, there is an n such that $\Phi_i^A(n) = \Phi_e(n) = \Phi_{f(i)}(n)$, so (v) fails.

Finally, we show that (iii) and (iv) are equivalent.

To show that (iii) implies (iv), given e, let f be a total computable function such that $\Phi_{f(n)}(x) = \Phi_e(n)$ for all n and x. Let $g \leqslant_T A$ be DNC and let $h = g \circ f$. Then

$$\Phi_e(n) = \Phi_{f(n)}(f(n)) \neq g(f(n)) = h(n).$$

To show that (iv) implies (iii), let e be such that $\Phi_e(n) = \Phi_n(n)$ for all n, and let h be as in (iv). Then $h(n) \neq \Phi_e(n) = \Phi_n(n)$ for all n, so h is DNC. □

Further results about DNC functions, including ones relating them to Kolmogorov complexity, will be discussed in Chapter 8, particularly in Theorem 8.16.8.

For DNC functions with range $\{0, 1\}$, we have the following result.

Theorem 2.22.2 (Jockusch and Soare [195], Solovay [unpublished]). *A degree is PA iff it computes a $\{0,1\}$-valued DNC function.*

Proof. It is straightforward to define a Π^0_1 class $\mathcal{P}$ such that the characteristic function of any element of $\mathcal{P}$ is a $\{0, 1\}$-valued DNC function. So by the Scott Basis Theorem 2.21.2, every PA degree computes a $\{0, 1\}$-valued DNC function.

Now let A compute a $\{0, 1\}$-valued DNC function g. Then g is the characteristic function of a set separating the effectively inseparable pair $\{e : \Phi_e(e) = 0\}$ and $\{e : \Phi_e(e) = 1\}$. So by Lemma 2.21.6, g has PA degree. Since the class of PA degrees is closed upwards, so does A. □

The following is a classic result on the interaction between fixed-point free functions and computable enumerability.

Theorem 2.22.3 (Arslanov's Completeness Criterion [13]). *A c.e. set is Turing complete iff it computes a fixed-point free function.*

Proof. It is easy to define a total $\emptyset'$-computable fixed-point free function. For the nontrivial implication, let A be a c.e. set that computes a fixed-point free function f. By speeding up the enumeration of A, we may assume we have a reduction $\Gamma^A = f$ such that $\Gamma^A(n)[s]\downarrow$ for all s and $n \leqslant s$.

For each n we build a set $W_{h(n)}$, with the total computable function h given by the recursion theorem with parameters. Initially, $W_{h(n)} = \emptyset$. If $n \in \emptyset'_s$ then for every $x \in W_{\Gamma^A(h(n))[s]}[s]$, we put x into $W_{h(n)}$ if it is not already there. (The full details of the application of the recursion theorem are much as in the footnote to the proof of Theorem 2.19.16.)

We claim we can compute $\emptyset'$ from A using h. To prove this claim, fix n. If $n \in \emptyset'$, then consider the stage s at which n enters $\emptyset'$. If the computation $\Gamma^A(h(n))$ has settled by stage s, then every $x \in W_{\Gamma^A(h(n))}$ is eventually put into $W_{h(n)}$, while no other x ever enters $W_{h(n)}$. So $W_{f(h(n))} = W_{\Gamma^A(h(n))} = W_{h(n)}$, contradicting the choice of f. Thus it must be the case that the computation $\Gamma^A(h(n))$ has not settled by stage s.

So, to decide whether $n \in \emptyset'$, we simply look for a stage s by which the computation $\Gamma^A(h(n))$ has settled (which we can do computably in A because A is c.e.). Then $n \in \emptyset'$ iff $n \in \emptyset'_s$. □

The above argument clearly works for wtt-reducibility as well, so a c.e. set is wtt-complete iff it wtt-computes a fixed-point free function. Arslanov [14] has investigated similar completeness criteria for other reducibilities such as tt-reducibility.

Antonin Kučera realized that fixed-point free functions have much to say about c.e. degrees, even beyond Arslanov's Completeness Criterion, and, as we will later see, about algorithmic randomness. In particular, in [216] he showed that if $f \leqslant_T \emptyset'$ is fixed-point free, then there is a noncomputable c.e. set $B \leqslant_T f$. We will prove this result in a slightly stronger form after introducing the following notion.

Definition 2.22.4 (Maass [256]). A coinfinite c.e. set A is *promptly simple* if there are a computable function f and an enumeration $\{A_s\}_{s\in\omega}$ of A such that for all e,

$$|W_e| = \infty \Rightarrow \exists^\infty x\, \exists s\, (x \in W_e[s] \setminus W_e[s-1] \wedge x \in A_{f(s)}).$$

The idea of this definition is that x needs to enter A "promptly" after it enters W_e. We will say that a degree is promptly simple if it contains a promptly simple set. The usual simple set constructions (such as that of Post's hypersimple set) yield promptly simple sets.

We can now state the stronger form of Kučera's result mentioned above.

Theorem 2.22.5 (Kučera [216]). *If $f \leqslant_T \emptyset'$ is fixed-point free then there is a promptly simple c.e. set $B \leqslant_T f$.*

Proof. Let $f \leqslant_T \emptyset'$ be fixed-point free. We build $B \leqslant_T f$ to satisfy the following requirements for all e:

$$\mathcal{R}_e : |W_e| = \infty \Rightarrow \exists x\, \exists s\, (x \in W_e[s] \setminus W_e[s-1] \wedge x \in B_s).$$

To see that these requirements suffice to ensure the prompt simplicity of B (assuming that we also make B c.e. and coinfinite), notice that it is not hard to define a computable function g such that for all e and sufficiently large n, there is an i such that $W_i = W_e \cap \{n, n+1, \ldots\}$ and for $x \geqslant n$, if $x \in W_e[s] \setminus W_e[s-1]$ then $x \in W_i[g(s)] \setminus W_i[g(s)-1]$. So if the requirements are satisfied, then for each e and n,

$$|W_e| = \infty \Rightarrow \exists x > n\, \exists s\, (x \in W_e[s] \setminus W_e[s-1] \wedge x \in B_{g(s)}).$$

During the construction, we will define an auxiliary computable function h using the recursion theorem with parameters. (We will give the details of this somewhat subtle application of the recursion theorem after outlining the construction.)

At stage s, act as follows for each $e \leqslant s$ such that

1. $\mathcal{R}_e$ is not yet met,
2. some $x > \max\{2e, h(e)\}$ is in $W_e[s] \setminus W_e[s-1]$, and
3. $f_s(h(e)) = f_t(h(e))$ for all t with $x \leqslant t \leqslant s$.

Enumerate x into B (which causes $\mathcal{R}_e$ to be met). Using the recursion theorem with parameters, let $W_{h(e)} = W_{f_s(h(e))}$.

In greater detail, we think of the construction as having a parameter i and enumerating a set B_i. We define an auxiliary partial computable function g, which we then use to define h.

At stage s, act as follows for each $e \leqslant s$ such that

1. $\mathcal{R}_e$ is not yet met (with B_i in place of B),
2. some $x > \max\{2e, i\}$ is in $W_e[s] \setminus W_e[s-1]$, and
3. $f_s(i) = f_t(i)$ for all t with $x \leqslant t \leqslant s$.

Enumerate x into B_i (which causes $\mathcal{R}_e$ to be met) and let $g(i,e) = f_s(i)$. Using the recursion theorem with parameters (in the version for partial computable functions mentioned following the proof of Theorem 2.3.2), let h be a total computable function such that $W_{h(e)} = W_{g(h(e),e)}$ whenever $g(h(e),e)\downarrow$. Let $B = B_{h(e)}$. It is not hard to check that h is as above.

Having concluded the construction, we first verify that B is promptly simple. Clearly, B is c.e., and it is coinfinite because at most one number is put into B for the sake of each $\mathcal{R}_e$, and that number must be greater than $2e$. As argued above, it is now enough to show that each $\mathcal{R}_e$ is met. So suppose that $|W_e| = \infty$. Let u be such that $f_t(h(e)) = f(h(e))$ for all $t \geqslant u$. There must be some $x > \max\{2e, h(e), u\}$ and some s such that $x \in W_e[s] \setminus W_e[s-1]$. If $\mathcal{R}_e$ is not yet met at stage s, then x will enter B at stage s, thus meeting $\mathcal{R}_e$.

We now show that $B \leqslant_T f$. Let

$$q(x) = \mu u > x \, \forall y \leqslant x \, (f_u(y) = f(y)).$$

Then $q \leqslant_T f$. We claim that $x \in B$ iff $x \in B_{q(x)}$. Suppose for a contradiction that $x \in B \setminus B_{q(x)}$. Then x must have entered B for the sake of some $\mathcal{R}_e$ at some stage $s > q(x)$. Thus $f_s(h(e)) = f_t(h(e))$ for all t with $x \leqslant t \leqslant s$. However, $x < q(x) < s$, so $W_{h(e)} = W_{f_s(h(e))} = W_{f_{q(x)}(h(e))} = W_{f(h(e))}$, contradicting the fact that f is fixed-point free. □

As Kučera [216] noted, Theorem 2.22.5 can be used to give a priority-free solution to Post's Problem: Let A be a low PA degree (which exists by the low basis theorem). By Theorem 2.22.2, A computes a DNC function, so by Theorem 2.22.1, A computes a fixed-point free function. Thus A computes a promptly simple c.e. set, which is noncomputable and low, and hence a solution to Post's Problem.

Prompt simplicity also has some striking structural consequences. A c.e. degree $\mathbf{a}$ is *cappable* if there is a c.e. degree $\mathbf{b} > \mathbf{0}$ such that $\mathbf{a} \cap \mathbf{b} = \mathbf{0}$. Otherwise, $\mathbf{a}$ is *noncappable*.

Theorem 2.22.6 (Ambos-Spies, Jockusch, Shore, and Soare [7]). *Every promptly simple degree is noncappable.*

Proof. Let A be promptly simple, with witness function f. Let B be a noncomputable c.e. set. We must build $C \leqslant_T A, B$ meeting

$$\mathcal{R}_e : W_e \neq \overline{C}$$

for all e. To do so we build auxiliary c.e. sets $V_e = W_{h(e)}$ with indices $h(e)$ given by the recursion theorem with parameters. Analyzing the proof of the recursion theorem, we see that there is a computable function g such that for almost all n, if we decide to put n into V_e at a stage s, then n enters $W_{h(e)}$ before stage $g(s)$.

Our strategy for meeting $\mathcal{R}_e$ is straightforward. We pick a follower n targeted for C. If we ever see a stage s such that $n \in W_{e,s}$, we declare n to be *active*. If $W_e \cap C_s = \emptyset$, then we pick a new follower $n' > n$. For an active n, if some number less than n enters B at a stage t, we enumerate n into V_e. If $n \in A_{f(g(t))}$ then we put n into C. In any case, we declare n to be inactive.

Assume for a contradiction that $W_e = \overline{C}$. Then infinitely many followers become active during the construction. Since B is noncomputable, infinitely many of these enter $W_{h(e)}$, so by the prompt simplicity of A, some active follower enters C, whence $W_e \neq \overline{C}$.

The strategies for different requirements act independently, choosing followers in such a way that no two strategies ever have the same follower. Thus all requirements are met. Whenever we enumerate n into C at a stage t, this action is permitted by a change in B below n at stage t and by n itself entering A by stage $f(g(t))$. Since f is computable, $C \leqslant_{\mathrm{T}} A, B$. □

Ambos-Spies, Jockusch, Shore, and Soare [7] extended the above result by showing that the promptly simple degrees and the cappable degrees form an algebraic decomposition of the c.e. degrees into a strong filter and an ideal. (See [7] for definitions.) Furthermore, they showed that the promptly simple degrees coincide with the low cuppable degrees, where $\mathbf{a}$ is *low cuppable* if there is a low c.e. degree $\mathbf{b}$ such that $\mathbf{a} \cup \mathbf{b} = \mathbf{0}'$. The proofs of these results are technical, and would take us too far afield.

Corollary 2.22.7 (Kučera [216]). *Let* $\mathbf{a}$ *and* $\mathbf{b}$ *be* Δ^0_2 *degrees both of which compute fixed-point free functions. Then* $\mathbf{a}$ *and* $\mathbf{b}$ *do not form a minimal pair.*

Proof. By Theorem 2.22.5, each of $\mathbf{a}$ and $\mathbf{b}$ bounds a promptly simple degree. By Theorem 2.22.6, these promptly simple degrees are noncappable, and hence do not form a minimal pair. Thus neither do $\mathbf{a}$ and $\mathbf{b}$.[20] □

Kučera [217] introduced the following variation of the notion of DNC function.

Definition 2.22.8 (Kučera [217]). A total function f is *generally noncomputable* (*GNC*) if $f(\langle e, n\rangle) \neq \Phi_e(n)$ for all e and n.

We can argue as before to show that the degrees computing $\{0,1\}$-valued GNC functions are exactly the degrees computing $\{0,1\}$-valued DNC functions, that is, the PA degrees.

[20] Kučera's original proof of this result was direct, in the style of the proof of Theorem 2.22.5, and used the (double) recursion theorem.

Theorem 2.22.9 (Kučera [217]). *Let A be a Π^0_1 class whose elements are all $\{0,1\}$-valued GNC functions, and let C be a set. There is a function $g \in A$ and an index e such that $g(\langle e, n \rangle) = C(n)$ for all n. Furthermore, e can be found effectively from an index for A.*

Proof. Using the recursion theorem, choose e such that $\Phi_e(n)$ is defined as follows. Suppose there is a $\tau \in 2^{<\omega}$ such that

$$A \cap \{f : \forall n < |\tau| \, (f(\langle e, n \rangle) = \tau(n))\} = \emptyset.$$

This condition is c.e., so we can choose the first τ we see satisfying it and let $\Phi_e(n) = 1 - \tau(n)$ for $n < |\tau|$ and $\Phi_e(n) = 0$ for $n \geqslant |\tau|$. If there is no such τ, then let $\Phi_e(n)\uparrow$ for all n.

If there is such a τ, then for each $\{0,1\}$-valued GNC function f we have $f(\langle e, n \rangle) = \tau(n)$ for all $n < |\tau|$, and hence $A \cap \{f : \forall n < |\tau| \, (f(\langle e, n \rangle) = \tau(n))\} = A \neq \emptyset$, contradicting the definition of τ. Thus there is no such τ, and hence for every σ there is a $g \in A$ such that $g(\langle e, n \rangle) = \sigma(n)$ for all $n < |\sigma|$. By compactness, there is a $g \in A$ such that $g(\langle e, n \rangle) = C(n)$ for all n. □

Kučera [217] remarked that the use of $\langle e, n \rangle$ with $\Phi_e(n)\uparrow$ for all n is an analog of the use of what are known as flexible formulas in axiomatizable theories, first introduced and studied by Mostowski [283] and Kripke [214], in connection with Gödel's Incompleteness Theorem.

In unpublished work,[21] Kučera also noted that the above proof can be combined with the proof of the low basis theorem to show that if $\mathbf{c}$ is a low degree then there is a low PA degree $\mathbf{a} \geqslant \mathbf{c}$. Combining this result with Kučera's priority-free solution to Post's Problem, we see that for any low degree $\mathbf{c}$ there is a c.e. degree $\mathbf{b}$ such that $\mathbf{b} \cup \mathbf{c}$ is low. This result is particularly interesting in light of the fact that Lewis [245] has constructed a minimal (and hence low$_2$) degree $\mathbf{c}$ such that $\mathbf{b} \cup \mathbf{c} = \mathbf{0}'$ for every nonzero c.e. degree $\mathbf{b}$. Kučera has also used the above method to construct PA degrees in various jump classes.

2.23 Array noncomputability and traceability

In this section, we discuss the *array noncomputable degrees* introduced by Downey, Jockusch, and Stob [120, 121]. The original definition of this class was in terms of *very strong arrays.* Recall that a strong array is a computable collection of pairwise disjoint finite sets $\{F_n : n \in \mathbb{N}\}$ (which recall means not only that the F_n are uniformly computable, but also that the function $i \mapsto \max F_i$ is computable).

[21] This work is now mentioned as example 2.1 in Kučera and Slaman [222]. In unpublished work, Kučera and Slaman have also shown that there is a low$_2$ degree that joins all Δ^0_2 fixed-point free degrees to $\mathbf{0}'$.

Definition 2.23.1 (Downey, Jockusch, and Stob [120]).

(i) A strong array $\{F_n : n \in \mathbb{N}\}$ is a *very strong array* if $|F_n| > |F_m|$ for all $n > m$.

(ii) For a very strong array $\mathcal{F} = \{F_n : n \in \mathbb{N}\}$, we say that a c.e. set A is *$\mathcal{F}$-array noncomputable* (*$\mathcal{F}$-a.n.c.*) if for each c.e. set W there is a k such that $W \cap F_k = A \cap F_k$.

Notice that for any c.e. set W and any k there is a c.e. set $\widehat{W}$ such that $W \cap F_k \neq \widehat{W} \cap F_k$ but $W(n) = \widehat{W}(n)$ for $n \notin F_k$. From this observation it follows that if A is $\mathcal{F}$-a.n.c. then for each c.e. set W there are infinitely many k such that $W \cap F_k = A \cap F_k$.

This definition was designed to capture a certain kind of multiple permitting construction. The intuition is that for A to be $\mathcal{F}$-a.n.c., A needs $|F_k|$ many permissions to agree with W on F_k. As we will see below, up to degree, the choice of very strong array does not matter. Downey, Jockusch, and Stob [120] used multiple permitting to show that several properties are equivalent to array noncomputability. For example, the a.n.c. c.e. degrees are precisely those that bound c.e. sets A_1, A_2, B_1, B_2 such that $A_1 \cap A_2 = B_1 \cap B_2 = \emptyset$ and every separating set for A_1, A_2 is Turing incomparable with every separating set for B_1, B_2. (There are a number of other characterizations of the array noncomputable c.e. degrees in [120, 121].) We will see two examples of this technique connected with algorithmic randomness in Theorems 9.14.4 and 9.14.7 below.

In Downey, Jockusch, and Stob [121], a new definition of array noncomputability was introduced, based on domination properties of functions and not restricted to c.e. sets.

Definition 2.23.2 (Downey, Jockusch, and Stob [121]). A degree $\mathbf{a}$ is *array noncomputable* (*a.n.c*) if for each $f \leqslant_{\mathrm{wtt}} \emptyset'$ there is a function g computable in $\mathbf{a}$ such that $g(n) \geqslant f(n)$ for infinitely many n. Otherwise, $\mathbf{a}$ is *array computable*.

Note that, using this definition, the a.n.c. degrees are clearly closed upwards. The following results give further characterizations of array noncomputability. They also show that, for c.e. sets, the two definitions of array noncomputability coincide and the first definition is independent of the choice of very strong array up to degree. Let $m_{\emptyset'}(n)$ be the least s such that $\emptyset' \upharpoonright n = \emptyset'_s \upharpoonright n$.

Theorem 2.23.3 (Downey, Jockusch, and Stob [121]). *Let* $\mathbf{a}$ *be a degree, and let* $\{F_n\}_{n \in \omega}$ *be a very strong array. The following are equivalent.*

(i) *The degree* $\mathbf{a}$ *is a.n.c.*

(ii) *There is a function* h *computable in* $\mathbf{a}$ *such that* $h(n) \geqslant m_{\emptyset'}(n)$ *for infinitely many* n.

(iii) *There is a function g computable in* $\mathbf{a}$ *such that for each e there is an n for which $W_e \cap F_n = W_{e,g(n)} \cap F_n$.*

Proof. To prove that (i) → (iii), let $f(n) = \mu s\, \forall e \leqslant n\, (W_e \cap F_n = W_{e,s} \cap F_n)$. Then $f \leqslant_{\text{wtt}} \emptyset'$, so there is an $\mathbf{a}$-computable function g such that $g(n) \geqslant f(n)$ for infinitely many n.

To prove that (ii) → (i), let $f \leqslant_{\text{wtt}} \emptyset'$, and let h satisfy (ii). Fix e and a computable function b such that $f(n) = \Phi_e^{\emptyset'}(n)$ with use at most $b(n)$ for all n. We may assume without loss of generality that h and b are increasing. We define a function g such that $g(n) \geqslant f(n)$ for infinitely many n as follows. Given n, let s be minimal such that $s > h(b(n+1))$ and $\Phi_e^{\emptyset'}(n)[s]\downarrow$ with use at most $b(n)$, and let $g(n) = \Phi_e^{\emptyset'}(n)[s]$. Clearly g is computable in $\mathbf{a}$. Let n and k be such that $b(n) \leqslant k \leqslant b(n+1)$ and $h(k) \geqslant m_{\emptyset'}(k)$, and let s be as in the definition of $g(n)$. We have $s \geqslant h(b(n+1)) \geqslant h(k) \geqslant m_{\emptyset'}(k) \geqslant m_{\emptyset'}(b(n))$, so $\emptyset'_s \upharpoonright \varphi_e^{\emptyset'}(n)[s] = \emptyset' \upharpoonright \varphi_e^{\emptyset'}(n)[s]$, and hence $g(n) = f(n)$. Since there are infinitely many j with $h(j) \geqslant m_{\emptyset'}(j)$, there are infinitely many n for which there is a k as above, and hence $g(n) = f(n)$ for infinitely many n.

It remains to show that (iii) → (ii). Let g be as in (iii). We claim that for each e there are infinitely many n with $W_e \cap F_n = W_{e,g(n)} \cap F_n$. Suppose otherwise. Let i be such that Φ_i is defined as follows. If $x \in F_n$ for one of the finitely many n such that $W_e \cap F_n = W_{e,g(n)} \cap F_n$, then let $\Phi_i(x)$ converge in strictly more than $g(n)$ steps. Otherwise, if $\Phi_e(x)\downarrow$ then let $\Phi_i(x)$ converge in at least the same number of steps as $\Phi_e(x)$, and if $\Phi_e(x)\uparrow$ then let $\Phi_i(x)\uparrow$. Then there is no n such that $W_i \cap F_n = W_{i,g(n)} \cap F_n$, contradicting the choice of g. Thus the claim holds, so it suffices to show that there is an e such that $\mu s\,(W_{e,s} \cap F_{n+1} = W_e \cap F_{n+1}) \geqslant m_{\emptyset'}(n)$ for all n, since it then follows that (ii) holds with $h(n) = g(n+1)$.

Define a c.e. set V as follows. At stage s, let $c_{n,s}$ be the least element (if any) of $F_{n+1} \setminus V_s$. For each $n < s$, if $\emptyset'_{s+1} \upharpoonright n \neq \emptyset'_s \upharpoonright n$ then enumerate $c_{n,s}$ into V. Also enumerate $c_{s,s}$ into V.

Note that $|F_{n+1} \cap V| \leqslant |\{s : \exists i < n\,(i \in \emptyset'_{s+1} \setminus \emptyset'_s)\}| + 1 \leqslant n+1 < |F_{n+1}|$, so $c_{n,s}$ is defined for all n and s. It follows that $\mu s\,(V_s \cap F_{n+1} = V \cap F_{n+1}) \geqslant m_{\emptyset'}(n)$. By Theorem 2.3.3, there is an e such that $W_e = V$ and $W_{e,s} \subseteq V_s$ for all s. Then $\mu s\,(W_{e,s} \cap F_{n+1} = W_e \cap F_{n+1}) \geqslant \mu s\,(V_s \cap F_{n+1} = V \cap F_{n+1}) \geqslant m_{\emptyset'}(n)$ for all n, as required. □

Since the truth of item (i) in Theorem 2.23.3 does not depend on a choice of very strong array, neither does the truth of item (iii).

Theorem 2.23.4 (Downey, Jockusch, and Stob [120, 121]). *Let* $\mathbf{a}$ *be a c.e. degree and let $\mathcal{F} = \{F_n\}_{n \in \mathbb{N}}$ be a very strong array. Then* $\mathbf{a}$ *is a.n.c. in the sense of Definition 2.23.2 iff there is an $\mathcal{F}$-a.n.c. c.e. set $A \in$* $\mathbf{a}$.

Proof. (⇐) Let $A \in \mathbf{a}$ be an $\mathcal{F}$-a.n.c. c.e. set. We show that item (iii) in Theorem 2.23.3 holds with $g(n) = \mu s\,(A_s \cap F_n = A \cap F_n)$. For each e, let $V_e = \{x : \exists s\,(x \in W_{e,s} \setminus A_s)\}$. Each V_e is c.e., so there is an n such that $A \cap F_n = V_e \cap F_n$. If x enters $W_e \cap F_n$ after stage $g(n)$, then we have two cases: if $x \in A$ then $x \in A_{g(n)}$, so $x \notin V_e$, while if $x \notin A$ then $x \in V_e$. Both these possibilities contradict the fact that $A \cap F_n = V_e \cap F_n$, so $W_e \cap F_n = W_{e,g(n)} \cap F_n$.

($\Rightarrow$) Let **a** be an a.n.c. c.e. degree and let $\{F_n\}_{n \in \mathbb{N}}$ be a very strong array. Let $f(n) = \mu s \, \forall e \leqslant n \, (W_{e,s} \cap F_{\langle e+1,n \rangle} = W_e \cap F_{\langle e+1,n \rangle})$. Clearly $f \leqslant_{\text{wtt}} \emptyset'$, so there is an **a**-computable g such that $g(n) \geqslant f(n)$ for infinitely many n. Since g is **a**-computable and **a** is c.e., there is a computable function $h(n, s)$ and an **a**-computable function p such that $g(n) = h(n, s)$ for all $s \geqslant p(n)$. We now define the c.e. set A.

First, we let $B \in \mathbf{a}$ be c.e. and put $\bigcup_{n \in B} F_{\langle 0,n \rangle}$ into A. We will not put any other elements of any $F_{\langle 0,n \rangle}$ into A, so this action ensures that A has degree at least **a**.

Now it suffices to ensure that if $n \geqslant e$ and $g(n) \geqslant f(n)$, then $A \cap F_{\langle e+1,n \rangle} = W_e \cap F_{\langle e+1,n \rangle}$. Whenever $h(n, s) \neq h(n, s+1)$ and $e \leqslant n \leqslant s$, we put all elements of $W_{e,h(n,s+1)} \cap F_{\langle e+1,n \rangle}$ into A at stage s.

The definition of A ensures that if $x \in A \cap F_{\langle e+1,n \rangle}$ then $x \in A_{p(n)}$, so A is computable in p and hence $A \in \mathbf{a}$. Suppose now that $n \geqslant e$ and $g(n) \geqslant f(n)$. It follows from the definition of f that $W_{e,g(n)} \cap F_{\langle e+1,n \rangle} = W_e \cap F_{\langle e+1,n \rangle}$. Choose s as large as possible so that $h(n, s) \neq h(n, s+1)$. (There is no loss of generality in assuming there is at least one such $s \geqslant n$.) Then $h(n, s+1) = g(n)$ and so

$$A_{s+1} \cap F_{\langle e+1,n \rangle} = W_{e,h(n,s+1)} \cap F_{\langle e+1,n \rangle}$$
$$= W_{e+1,g(n)} \cap F_{\langle e+1,n \rangle} = W_e \cap F_{\langle e+1,n \rangle}.$$

Furthermore, by the maximality of s, no elements of $F_{\langle e+1,n \rangle}$ enter A after stage $s+1$, so $A \cap F_{\langle e+1,n \rangle} = W_e \cap F_{\langle e+1,n \rangle}$. □

Corollary 2.23.5 (Downey, Jockusch, and Stob [120, 121]). *Let $\mathcal{F}$ and $\mathcal{G}$ be very strong arrays. Then a degree contains an $\mathcal{F}$-a.n.c. c.e. set iff it contains a $\mathcal{G}$-a.n.c. c.e. set.*

We do not need to consider all wtt-reductions in the definition of array noncomputability, but can restrict ourselves to reductions with use bounded by the identity function.

Proposition 2.23.6 (Downey and Hirschfeldt, generalizing [120]). *A degree* **a** *is a.n.c. iff for every f that is computable from $\emptyset'$ via a reduction with use bounded by the identity function, there is an* **a***-computable function g such that $g(n) \geqslant f(n)$ for infinitely many n.*

Proof. The "only if" direction is obvious. We prove the "if" direction. Suppose that $\Gamma^{\emptyset'} = f$ with use bounded by the increasing computable function p. Let $\Phi^{\emptyset'}(n) = \max\{\Gamma^{\emptyset'}(m) : p(m) \leqslant n\}$. Then $\varphi^{\emptyset'}(n) \leqslant n$, so there is an **a**-computable increasing function g such that $g(n) \geqslant \Phi^{\emptyset'}(n)$ for infinitely many n. Let $\widehat{g}(m) = g(p(m+1))$. Since p is computable, $\widehat{g} \leqslant_{\mathrm{T}} A$. Furthermore, if $g(n) \geqslant \Phi^{\emptyset'}(n)$ then for the largest m such that $p(m) \leqslant n$, we have $\widehat{g}(m) = g(p(m+1)) > g(n) \geqslant \Phi^{\emptyset'}(n) \geqslant \Gamma^{\emptyset'}(m) = f(m)$, so $\widehat{g}(m) \geqslant f(m)$ for infinitely many m. □

Martin [258] gave a characterization of the GL_2 sets quite close to the definition of array computability, as a consequence of the following result. Recall that a function f dominates a function g if $f(n) \geqslant g(n)$ for all sufficiently large n. A function is *dominant* if it dominates all computable functions.

Theorem 2.23.7 (Martin [258]). *A set A is high iff there is a dominant function $f \leqslant_T A$.*

Proof. Recall that $\text{Tot} = \{e : \Phi_e \text{ is total}\}$. This set has degree $\emptyset''$, so A is high iff $\text{Tot} \leqslant_T A'$ iff there is an A-computable function h such that $\lim_s h(e,s) = \text{Tot}(e)$ for all e.

Suppose that A is high, and let h be as above. Define an A-computable f as follows. Given n, for each $e \leqslant n$, look for an $s \geqslant n$ such that either

1. $\Phi_e(n)[s]\downarrow$ or
2. $h(e,s) = 0$.

For each $e \leqslant n$, one of the two must happen. Define $f(n)$ to be larger than $\Phi_e(n)$ for all $e \leqslant n$ such that 1 holds. If Φ_e is total then $h(e,s) = 1$ for all sufficiently large s, so $f(n) > \Phi_e(n)$ for all sufficiently large n. Thus f dominates all computable functions.

Now suppose that there is a function $f \leqslant_T A$ that dominates all computable functions. Define $h \leqslant_T A$ as follows. Given e and s, check whether $\Phi_e(n)[f(s)]\downarrow$ for all $n \leqslant s$. If so, let $h(e,s) = 1$, and otherwise let $h(e,s) = 0$. If $e \notin \text{Tot}$ then clearly $h(e,s) = 0$ for all sufficiently large s. If $e \in \text{Tot}$ and s is sufficiently large then $f(s)$ is greater than the stage by which $\Phi_e(n)$ converges for all $n \leqslant s$, since the latter is a computable function of s. So $h(e,s) = 1$ for all sufficiently large s. Thus $\lim_s h(e,s) = \text{Tot}(e)$ for all e. □

Corollary 2.23.8 (Martin [258]). *A set A is GL_2 iff there is a function $f \leqslant_T A \oplus \emptyset'$ that dominates all A-computable functions.*

Proof. A set A is GL_2 iff $(A \oplus \emptyset')' \equiv_T A''$ iff $A \oplus \emptyset'$ is high relative to A. Thus the corollary follows by relativizing Theorem 2.23.7 to A. □

By Corollary 2.23.8, if a set A is not GL_2 then for each function $f \leqslant_T A \oplus \emptyset'$ there is a function $g \leqslant_T A$ such that $g(n) \geqslant f(n)$ for infinitely many n. Thus if a degree is not GL_2 then it is a.n.c. In particular, every array computable Δ^0_2 degree is low_2. In [121], Downey, Jockusch, and Stob demonstrated that many results previously proved for non-GL_2 degrees extend to a.n.c. degrees. However, the a.n.c degrees do not coincide with the non-GL_2 degrees, nor do the a.n.c. c.e. degrees coincide with the nonlow$_2$ c.e. degrees.

Theorem 2.23.9 (Downey, Jockusch, and Stob [120]). *There is a low a.n.c. c.e. degree.*

Proof. The proof is a straightforward combination of lowness and array noncomputability requirements. Let $\mathcal{F} = \{F_n : n \in \mathbb{N}\}$ be a very strong array with $|F_n| = n + 1$. We build a c.e. set A to satisfy the requirements

$$\mathcal{R}_e : \exists n \, (W_e \cap F_n = A \cap F_n)$$

and

$$\mathcal{N}_e : \exists^\infty s \, \Phi_e^A(e)[s]\downarrow \; \Rightarrow \; \Phi_e^A(e)\downarrow .$$

For the sake of $\mathcal{R}_e$ we simply pick a fresh n to devote to making $W_e \cap F_n = A \cap F_n$. We do so in the obvious way: Whenever a new element enters $W_e \cap F_n$, we put it into A. Such enumerations will happen at most $n+1$ many times. Each time one happens we initialize the weaker priority $\mathcal{N}$-requirements. Similarly, each time we see a computation $\Phi_e^A(e)[s]\downarrow$ we initialize the weaker priority $\mathcal{R}$-requirements, which now must pick their n's to be above the use of this computation. The result follows by the usual finite injury argument. □

On the other hand, an easy modification of Martin's proofs above shows that if A is superlow then there is a function wtt-computable in $\emptyset'$ that dominates every A-computable function, and hence A is array computable.

Array computability is also related to hyperimmunity.

Proposition 2.23.10 (Folklore). *If* **a** *is hyperimmune-free then* **a** *is array computable.*

Proof. If A is of hyperimmune-free degree then every $f \leqslant_\mathrm{T} A$ is dominated by some total computable function. It is easy to construct a function $g \leqslant_{\mathrm{wtt}} \emptyset'$ that is a uniform bound for all partial computable functions. (That is, for each e, we have $\Phi_e(n) \leqslant h(n)$ for almost all n such that $\Phi_e(n)\downarrow$.) Then every function $f \leqslant_\mathrm{T} A$ is dominated by g, and hence A is array computable. □

The following concept, closely related to both hyperimmune-freeness and array computability, is quite useful in the study of algorithmic randomness.

Definition 2.23.11 (Zambella [416], see [386], also Ishmukhametov [184]). A set A, and the degree of A, are *c.e. traceable* if there is a computable function p (called a *bound*) such that, for each function $f \leqslant_\mathrm{T} A$, there is a computable function h (called a *trace* for f) satisfying, for all n,

(i) $|W_{h(n)}| \leqslant p(n)$ and

(ii) $f(n) \in W_{h(n)}$.

Since one can uniformly enumerate all c.e. traces for a fixed bound p, there is a universal trace with bound p^2, say. By a *universal trace* we mean one that traces each function $f \leqslant_T A$ on almost all inputs. As the following result shows, the above definition does not change if we replace "there is a computable function p" by "for every unbounded nondecreasing computable function p such that $p(0) > 0$".

Proposition 2.23.12 (Terwijn and Zambella [389]). *Let A be c.e. traceable and let q be an unbounded nondecreasing computable function such that $q(0) > 0$. Then A is c.e. traceable with bound q.*

Proof. Let A be c.e. traceable with some bound p. Let $g \leqslant_T A$. For each m, let r_m be such that $q(r_m) \geqslant p(m+1)$, and let $f(m) = \langle g(0), \dots, g(r_m)\rangle$. Let h be as in Definition 2.23.11. Let $\widehat{h}$ be a computable function such that $W_{\widehat{h}(n)}$ is defined as follows. For each m, if $r_m \leqslant n < r_{m+1}$, then enumerate into $W_{\widehat{h}(n)}$ all the nth coordinates of elements of $W_{h(m+1)}$. Then $|W_{\widehat{h}(n)}| \leqslant |W_{h(m+1)}| \leqslant p(m+1) \leqslant q(r_m) \leqslant q(n)$. Furthermore, $g(n)$ is the nth coordinate of $f(m+1)$, and $f(m+1) \in W_{h(m+1)}$, so $g(n) \in W_{\widehat{h}(n)}$. We have not yet defined $W_{\widehat{h}(n)}$ for $n < r_0$, but since there are only finitely many such n, we can define $W_{\widehat{h}(n)} = \{g(n)\}$ for such n. Then for all n we have $|W_{\widehat{h}(n)}| \leqslant q(n)$ and $g(n) \in W_{\widehat{h}(n)}$, as required. □

Ishmukhametov [184] gave the following characterization of the array computable c.e. degrees.

Theorem 2.23.13 (Ishmukhametov [184]). *A c.e. degree is array computable iff it is c.e. traceable.*

Proof. Let A be a c.e. traceable c.e. set. Let $f \leqslant_T A$. Let p and h be as in Definition 2.23.11. Let $g(n) = \max W_{h(n)}$. Then $g \leqslant_{wtt} \emptyset'$, since we can use $p(n)$ to bound the $\emptyset'$-oracle queries needed to compute $g(n)$, and g dominates f. Since f is arbitrary, A is array computable.

Now let A be an array computable c.e. set. By Proposition 2.23.6, there is a function g computable from $\emptyset'$ with use bounded by the identity that dominates every A-computable function. Let $f = \Phi_e^A$. Let $F(n)$ be the least s such that $\Phi_e^A(n)[t] = \Phi_e^A(n)[s]$ for all $t > s$. Then $F \leqslant_T A$, so by modifying g at finitely many places, we obtain a function G that is computable in $\emptyset'$ with use bounded by the identity function and such that $G(n) > F(n)$ for all n. Since $\emptyset' \upharpoonright n$ can change at most n many times during the enumeration of $\emptyset'$, there is a computable approximation $G_0, G_1, \dots$ to G that changes value at n at most n times. Let h be a computable function such that $W_{h(n)} = \{\Phi_e^A(n)[G_s(n)] : s \in \mathbb{N} \wedge \Phi_e^A(n)[G_s(n)]\downarrow\}$. Then $|W_{h(n)}| \leqslant n$ and $f(n) \in W_{h(n)}$. Since f is arbitrary, A is c.e. traceable. □

Using this characterization, Ishmukhametov proved the following remarkable theorem, which shows that if the c.e. degrees are definable in the global structure of the degrees, then so are the a.n.c. c.e. degrees. A degree $\mathbf{m}$ is a *strong minimal cover* of a degree $\mathbf{a} < \mathbf{m}$ if for all degrees $\mathbf{d} < \mathbf{m}$, we have $\mathbf{d} \leqslant \mathbf{a}$.

Theorem 2.23.14 (Ishmukhametov [184]). *A c.e. degree is array computable iff it has a strong minimal cover.*

Definition 2.23.11 can be strengthened as follows. Recall that $D_0, D_1, \ldots$ is a canonical listing of finite sets, as defined in Chapter 1.

Definition 2.23.15 (Terwijn and Zambella [389]). A set A, and the degree of A, are *computably traceable* if there is a computable function p such that, for each function $f \leqslant_T A$, there is a computable function h satisfying, for all n,

(i) $|D_{h(n)}| \leqslant p(n)$ and

(ii) $f(n) \in D_{h(n)}$.

As with c.e. traceability, the above definition does not change if we replace "there is a computable function p" by "for every unbounded nondecreasing computable function p such that $p(0) > 0$".

If A is computably traceable then each function $g \leqslant_T A$ is dominated by the function $f(n) = \max D_{h(n)}$, where h is a trace for f. Thus, every computably traceable degree is hyperimmune-free. One may think of computable traceability as a uniform version of hyperimmune-freeness. Terwijn and Zambella [389] showed that a simple variation of the standard construction of hyperimmune-free sets by Miller and Martin [282] (Theorem 2.17.3) produces continuum many computably traceable sets. Indeed, the proof we gave of Theorem 2.17.3 produces a computably traceable set.

2.24 Genericity and weak genericity

The notion of genericity arose in the context of set-theoretic forcing. It was subsequently "miniaturized" to obtain a notion of n-genericity appropriate to computability theory. Although the original definition of n-genericity was in terms of forcing, the following more modern definition is the one that is now generally used.[22] Let $S \subseteq 2^{<\omega}$. A set A *meets* S if there is an

[22]The original definition of n-genericity, dating back to Feferman [143], is as follows. Let $\mathcal{L}$ be the usual first-order language of number theory together with a set constant X and the membership relation $\in$. Let $\sigma \in 2^{<\omega}$. For sentences ψ in $\mathcal{L}$, we define the notion "σ *forces* φ", written $\sigma \Vdash \psi$, by recursion on the structure of ψ as follows.

(i) If ψ is atomic and does not contain X, then $\sigma \Vdash \psi$ iff ψ is true in arithmetic.

(ii) $\sigma \Vdash n \in X$ iff $\sigma(n) = 1$.

(iii) $\sigma \Vdash \psi_0 \vee \psi_1$ iff $\sigma \Vdash \psi_0$ or $\sigma \Vdash \psi_1$.

(iv) $\sigma \Vdash \neg\psi$ iff $\forall \tau \succcurlyeq \sigma\, (\tau \nVdash \psi)$.

n such that $A \upharpoonright n \in S$. A set A *avoids* S if there is an n such that for all $\tau \succcurlyeq A \upharpoonright n$, we have $\tau \notin S$.

Definition 2.24.1 (Jockusch and Posner, see Jockusch [188]). A set is *n-generic* if it meets or avoids each Σ^0_n set of strings.

A set is *arithmetically generic* if it is n-generic for all n.

It is easy to construct n-generic Δ^0_{n+1} sets, and arithmetically generic sets computable from $\emptyset^{(\omega)}$. Indeed, it does not require much computational power to build a 1-generic set.

Proposition 2.24.2. *Every noncomputable c.e. set computes a 1-generic set.*

Proof. The proof is a standard permitting argument. Let $S_0, S_1, \ldots$ be an effective listing of the c.e. sets of strings. We build $G \leqslant_T A$ to satisfy the requirements

$$R_e : G \text{ meets or avoids } S_e.$$

Associated with each R_e is a restraint r_e, initially set to 0. We say that R_e requires attention through n at stage s if $n > r_e$ and $G_s \upharpoonright n$ has an extension in $S_e[s]$. For each e, we also have a set M_e of numbers through which R_e has required attention.

Initially, we have $G_0 = \emptyset$. At stage s, let $e \leqslant s$ be least such that R_e is not currently satisfied and either

1. there is an $n > r_e$ such that $G_s \upharpoonright n$ has an extension σ in $S_e[s]$ and $A_{s+1} \upharpoonright n \neq A_s \upharpoonright n$ or
2. R_e requires attention through some n not currently in M_e.

(If there is no such e then let $G_{s+1} = G_s$ and proceed to the next stage.) In the first case, let G_{s+1} extend σ and declare R_e to be satisfied. In the second, put n into M_e and let $G_{s+1} = G_s$. In either case, for all $i > e$, declare R_i to be unsatisfied, empty M_i, and let r_i be a fresh large number. We say we have acted for e.

Let $G = \lim_s G_s$. Once numbers less than n have stopped being enumerated into A, we cannot change G below n, so G is well-defined and A-computable. Assume by induction that there is a stage s after which we never act for any $i < e$. If we ever act for e after stage s and are in case 1

(v) $\sigma \Vdash \exists z\, \psi(z)$ iff there is an $n \in \mathbb{N}$ such that $\sigma \Vdash \psi(n)$.

For a set A, we have $A \Vdash \psi$ iff there is some $\sigma \prec A$ such that $\sigma \Vdash \psi$.

A set A is *n-generic* if for each Σ^0_n sentence ψ of $\mathcal{L}$, either $A \Vdash \psi$ or $A \Vdash \neg\psi$. As Jockusch and Posner showed (see Jockusch [188]), it is not hard to see that this definition is equivalent to the one in Definition 2.24.1 using the result due to Matijacevic [261] that each Σ^0_n subset of $\mathbb{N}$ is defined by a Σ^0_n formula in $\mathcal{L}$.

of the construction, we permanently satisfy R_e by ensuring that G meets S_e. In that case, R_e never again acts, so the induction can proceed.

So suppose we never act for e in case 1 of the construction after stage s. Assume for a contradiction that we act infinitely often for e. At each stage $t > s$ at which we act for e, we find a new n such that $G_t \upharpoonright n$ has an extension in $S_e[t]$. Since we then increase all restraints for weaker priority requirements, $G \upharpoonright n = G_t \upharpoonright n$. Since we never reach case 1 of the construction for e, we must have $A \upharpoonright n = A_t \upharpoonright n$. From this fact it is easy to see that A is computable, which is a contradiction.

Thus we act only finitely often for e. But if $G \upharpoonright n$ has an extension in S_e, then R_e requires attention through n at all large enough stages t. Thus no sufficiently long initial segment of G has an extension in S_e, so G avoids S_e. ☐

A degree is n-generic if it contains an n-generic set, and arithmetically generic if it contains an arithmetically generic set. An interesting fact about arithmetically generic degrees, shown by Jockusch [188], is that if $\mathbf{a}$ and $\mathbf{b}$ are arithmetically generic, then the structures of the degrees below $\mathbf{a}$ and of the degrees below $\mathbf{b}$ are elementarily equivalent. There is a wealth of results on n-generic sets and degrees, many of which are discussed in the survey Jockusch [188]. Kumabe [224] also contains several results on n-genericity.

The following is an important property of n-generic sets.

Theorem 2.24.3 (Jockusch [188]). *If A is n-generic then $A^{(n)} \equiv_T A \oplus \emptyset^{(n)}$. In particular, every 1-generic set is GL_1.*

Proof. Assume by induction that the theorem is true for $n-1$. (The base case $n = 0$ is trivial, as it says that $A \equiv_T A \oplus \emptyset$ for all A.) Let A be n-generic. By the inductive hypothesis, it is enough to show that $(A \oplus \emptyset^{(n-1)})' \equiv_T A \oplus \emptyset^{(n)}$. One direction of this equivalence is immediate, so we are left with showing that $(A \oplus \emptyset^{(n-1)})' \leqslant_T A \oplus \emptyset^{(n)}$.

Let $R_e = \{\sigma : \Phi_e^{\sigma \oplus (\emptyset^{(n-1)} \upharpoonright |\sigma|)}(e)\downarrow\}$ and $S_e = \{\sigma : \forall \tau \succcurlyeq \sigma\, (\tau \notin R_e)\}$. The R_e are c.e. in $\emptyset^{(n-1)}$ and hence are Σ^0_n. So for each e, we have $e \in (A \oplus \emptyset^{(n-1)})'$ iff A meets R_e iff A does not meet S_e, the last equivalence following by n-genericity. But it is easy to check that the R_e and S_e are uniformly $\emptyset^{(n)}$-computable, so using $A \oplus \emptyset^{(n)}$, we can compute $(A \oplus \emptyset^{(n-1)})'$. ☐

The above result is an example of the phenomenon that, in many cases, a construction used to show that a set with a certain property (such as being GL_1) exists actually shows that the given property holds of all sufficiently generic sets. For example, the requirements of a finite extension argument are usually ones that ask that the set being constructed meet or avoid some open set of conditions.

A related phenomenon is the fact that genericity requirements can often be added to finite extension constructions. For instance, it is straightforward to modify the construction in the proof of Theorem 2.16.2 to obtain the following result.

Theorem 2.24.4. *If $C > 0$ and $D \geqslant_T \emptyset' \oplus C$ then there is a 1-generic set A such that $A' \equiv_T A \oplus C \equiv_T D$.*

The following result exemplifies the fact that generic sets are quite computationally weak.

Theorem 2.24.5 (Demuth and Kučera [96]). *If a set is 1-generic then it does not compute a DNC function.*

Proof. Let G be 1-generic and let $\Phi^G = f$. Let

$$S = \{\sigma \in \omega^{<\omega} : \forall n < |\sigma| \, (\sigma(n) \neq \Phi_n(n))\}.$$

Note that S is co-c.e. Let

$$X = \{\tau : \exists \sigma \, (\Phi^\tau \upharpoonright |\sigma| \downarrow = \sigma \, \wedge \, \sigma \notin S)\}.$$

Then X is c.e., so G either meets or avoids X. If G meets X then there is a $\tau \prec G$ and a $\sigma \in \omega^{<\omega}$ such that $\Phi^\tau \upharpoonright |\sigma| \downarrow = \sigma$ and $\sigma \notin S$. Since $\Phi^G = f$, we have $\sigma \prec f$, and hence f is not DNC. Thus it is enough to assume that G avoids X and derive a contradiction.

Let $\nu \prec G$ be such that if $\tau \in X$ then $\nu \not\prec \tau$. Let

$$Y = \{\sigma : \exists \rho \, (\nu \prec \rho \, \wedge \, \Phi^\rho \upharpoonright |\sigma| \downarrow = \sigma)\}.$$

Then Y is a c.e. subset of S, and it is infinite because every initial segment of f is in Y. So we can computably find $\sigma_0, \sigma_1, \ldots \in S$ such that $|\sigma_i| > i$. Let $g(i) = \sigma_i(i)$. Then g is computable and, by the definition of S, it is DNC, which is a contradiction. □

By Theorem 2.22.2, we have the following result.

Corollary 2.24.6. *No PA degree is computable from a 1-generic degree.*

Since the hyperimmune-free basis theorem implies that there is a DNC function of hyperimmune-free degree, we have the following.

Corollary 2.24.7 (Downey and Yu [137]). *There is a hyperimmune-free degree not computable from any 1-generic degree.*

Corollary 2.24.7 should be contrasted with the following result, whose proof uses a special notion of perfect set forcing.

Theorem 2.24.8 (Downey and Yu [137]). *There is a hyperimmune-free degree computable from a 1-generic degree.*

Recall that a set A is CEA if it is computably enumerable in some $X <_T A$. By Theorem 2.17.2, no set of hyperimmune-free degree can be CEA. There are also noncomputable Δ^0_2 sets that are not CEA. For example, let A be co-c.e. If A is c.e. in X, then A is computable in X, so A is not CEA.

The following result will be of interest in Section 8.21.3, where we show that being CEA is in fact a property of almost all sets, in the measure-theoretic sense.

Theorem 2.24.9 (Jockusch [188]). *Every 1-generic set is CEA.*

Proof.[23] Let A be 1-generic. Let $X = \{2\langle i,j\rangle : i \in A \wedge 2\langle i,j\rangle \notin A\}$. Clearly, $X \leqslant_T A$. For each i, the set $\{\sigma : \exists j\,(\sigma(2\langle i,j\rangle) = 0)\}$ is computable and dense, so for each i there is a j such that $2\langle i,j\rangle \notin A$. Thus $i \in A$ iff $\exists j\,(2\langle i,j\rangle \in X)$, whence A is c.e. in X. So A is CEA(X), and thus we are left with showing that $A \nleqslant_T X$.

Let $\widehat{\sigma}$ be the unique string of length $|\sigma|$ such that $\widehat{\sigma}(n) = 1$ iff $n = 2\langle i,j\rangle$ for i and j such that $\sigma(i) = 1$ and $\sigma(2\langle i,j\rangle) = 0$. We claim that if $\nu \preccurlyeq \sigma$ and $n \geqslant |\nu|$ is odd, then there is a string $\tau \succcurlyeq \nu$ such that $\tau(n) = 1$ and $\widehat{\sigma} \preccurlyeq \widehat{\tau}$.

If $\sigma(n) = 1$ then we can take $\tau = \sigma$, and if $n \geqslant |\sigma|$ then we can take any $\tau \succ \sigma$ such that $\tau(n) = 1$. So suppose that $\sigma(n) = 0$. Let S be the smallest set under inclusion such that $n \in S$, and if $i \in S$, then $2\langle i,j\rangle \in S$ if $\sigma(i) = 0$ and $2\langle i,j\rangle < |\sigma|$. Let τ be the string of length $|\sigma|$ such that $\tau(k) = 1$ iff either $\sigma(k) = 1$ or $k \in S$. Then $\nu \preccurlyeq \tau$. We need to show that $\widehat{\sigma} \preccurlyeq \widehat{\tau}$. Let $k \leqslant |\sigma|$. If k is odd then $\widehat{\sigma}(k) = \widehat{\tau}(k) = 0$, so assume that $k = 2\langle i,j\rangle$ for some i and j.

If $\widehat{\sigma}(k) = 0$, then either $\sigma(i) = 0$ or $\sigma(2\langle i,j\rangle) = 1$. In the latter case, $\tau(2\langle i,j\rangle) = 1$, so $\widehat{\tau}(2\langle i,j\rangle) = 0$. Now suppose that $\sigma(i) = 0$. If $i \in S$, then $2\langle i,j\rangle \in S$, so $\tau(2\langle i,j\rangle) = 1$, and hence $\widehat{\tau}(2\langle i,j\rangle) = 0$. If $i \notin S$, then $\tau(i) = 0$ and hence $\widehat{\tau}(2\langle i,j\rangle) = 0$.

If $\widehat{\sigma}(k) = 1$, then $\sigma(i) = 1$ and $\sigma(2\langle i,j\rangle) = 0$. Since $\sigma(i) = 1$, we have $\tau(i) = 1$. Furthermore, it follows easily by induction that S contains no numbers of the form $2\langle d,q\rangle$ with $\sigma(d) = 1$. Since $\sigma(2\langle i,j\rangle) = 0$ and $2\langle i,j\rangle \notin S$, we have $\tau(2\langle i,j\rangle) = 0$, and hence $\widehat{\tau}(k) = 1$.

We have established our claim. Now assume for a contradiction that $\Phi^X = A$ for some Turing functional Φ. Let $V = \{\sigma : \sigma \mid \Phi^{\widehat{\sigma}}\}$. Then V is c.e. and A extends no string in V, so, since A is 1-generic, there is a $\nu \prec A$ such that no extension of ν is in V. Let $n \geqslant |\nu|$ and $\sigma \succcurlyeq \nu$ be such that n is odd and $\Phi^{\widehat{\sigma}}(n) = 0$. (Such a σ must exist because $\{\rho : \exists n \geqslant |\nu|\,(n \text{ odd} \wedge \rho(n) = 0)\}$ is computable and dense, so there is an odd $n \geqslant |\nu|$ such that $\Phi^X(n) = A(n) = 0$.) Then there is a $\tau \succcurlyeq \nu$ such that $\tau(n) = 1$ and $\widehat{\sigma} \preccurlyeq \widehat{\tau}$. We have $\Phi^{\widehat{\tau}}(n) = 0$ and $\tau(n) = 1$, so $\tau \in V$, contradicting the choice of ν. □

We now consider a weaker notion of genericity. A set of strings D is *dense* if every string has an extension in D. Recall that a set A meets D if there is a $\sigma \in D$ such that $\sigma \prec A$. Similarly, a string τ meets D if there is a

[23] Jockusch [188] attributes the idea behind this proof to Martin.

$\sigma \in D$ such that $\sigma \preccurlyeq \tau$. Given the set-theoretic definition of genericity in terms of meeting dense sets, the following definition is natural.

Definition 2.24.10 (Kurtz [228, 229]). A set is *weakly n-generic* if it meets all dense Σ^0_n sets of strings. A degree is weakly n-generic if it contains a weakly n-generic set.

As noted by Jockusch (see [228, 229]), it is not hard to show that A is weakly $(n+1)$-generic iff A meets all dense Δ^0_{n+1} sets of strings iff A meets all dense Π^0_n sets of strings.

Clearly, if a set is n-generic then it is weakly n-generic. The following result is slightly less obvious.

Theorem 2.24.11 (Kurtz [228, 229]). *Every weakly $(n+1)$-generic set is n-generic.*

Proof. Let A be weakly $(n+1)$-generic. Let S be a Σ^0_n set of strings. Let $R = \{\sigma : \sigma \in S \vee \forall \tau \succcurlyeq \sigma\, (\tau \notin S)\}$. Then R is a dense Σ^0_{n+1} set of strings, and hence A meets R, which clearly implies that A meets or avoids S. Thus A is n-generic. □

Thus we have the following hierarchy: weakly 1-generic $\Leftarrow$ 1-generic $\Leftarrow$ weakly 2-generic $\Leftarrow$ 2-generic $\Leftarrow$ weakly 3-generic $\Leftarrow \cdots$. We now show that none of these implications can be reversed, even for degrees, by exploring the connection between weak genericity and hyperimmunity. Recall that a degree $\mathbf{a}$ is hyperimmune relative to a degree $\mathbf{b}$ if there is an $\mathbf{a}$-computable function that is not majorized by any $\mathbf{b}$-computable function.

Theorem 2.24.12 (Kurtz [228, 229]). *If A is weakly $(n+1)$-generic, then the degree of A is hyperimmune relative to $\mathbf{0^{(n)}}$.*

Proof. Let p_A be the principal function of A. (That is, $p_A(n)$ is the nth element of A in the natural order.) We show that no $\mathbf{0^{(n)}}$-computable function majorizes p_A. Let f be a $\mathbf{0^{(n)}}$-computable function. For a string σ, let p_σ be the principal function of $\{n < |\sigma| : \sigma(n) = 1\}$ (which is a partial function, of course). Let $S_f = \{\sigma : \exists n\, (p_\sigma(n)\downarrow > f(n))\}$. Then S_f is a dense Δ^0_{n+1} set, so A meets S_f, and hence f does not majorize p_A. □

Corollary 2.24.13 (Kurtz [228, 229]). *There is an n-generic degree that is not weakly $(n+1)$-generic.*

Proof. There is an n-generic degree that is below $\mathbf{0^{(n)}}$, and hence not hyperimmune relative to $\mathbf{0^{(n)}}$. □

Theorem 2.24.14 (Kurtz [228, 229]). *A degree $\mathbf{b}$ is the nth jump of a weakly $(n+1)$-generic degree iff $\mathbf{b} > \mathbf{0^{(n)}}$ and $\mathbf{b}$ is hyperimmune relative to $\mathbf{0^{(n)}}$.*

Proof. Suppose that $\mathbf{b} = \mathbf{a^{(n)}}$ with $\mathbf{a}$ weakly $(n+1)$-generic. By Theorem 2.24.12, $\mathbf{a}$ is hyperimmune relative to $\mathbf{0^{(n)}}$, and the class of degrees that are hyperimmune relative to $\mathbf{0^{(n)}}$ is clearly closed upwards. Thus $\mathbf{b}$ is hyperimmune relative to $\mathbf{0^{(n)}}$. Clearly, $\mathbf{b} \geqslant \mathbf{0^{(n)}}$, so in fact $\mathbf{b} > \mathbf{0^{(n)}}$.

The proof of the converse is a variant of the proof of the Friedberg Completeness Criterion (Theorem 2.16.1). Let $\mathbf{b} > \mathbf{0^{(n)}}$ be hyperimmune with respect to $\mathbf{0^{(n)}}$. Let h be a $\mathbf{b}$-computable function that is not majorized by any $\mathbf{0^{(n)}}$-computable function. We may assume that h is increasing and has degree exactly $\mathbf{b}$, and let $B = \operatorname{rng} h$, so that $h = p_B$ and $\deg(B) = \mathbf{b}$. Let $f_0, f_1, \ldots$ be uniformly $\mathbf{0^{(n)}}$-computable functions such that $\{\operatorname{rng} f_i : i \in \mathbb{N}\}$ is the collection of all nonempty Σ^0_{n+1} sets of strings. Let $S_i = \operatorname{rng} f_i$ and let $S_i^s = \{\sigma : \exists k \leqslant p_B(s)\, (f_i(k) = \sigma)\}$.

We build a set A by finite extensions $\sigma_0 \preccurlyeq \sigma_1 \preccurlyeq \cdots$ so that $A^{(n)} \equiv_{\mathrm{T}} B$ and A is weakly $(n+1)$-generic. We meet the requirements

$$\mathcal{R}_e : \text{If } S_e \text{ is dense then } A \text{ meets } S_e.$$

We say that $\mathcal{R}_e$ *requires attention* at stage s if σ_s does not meet S_e^s, but there is a string $\tau \succcurlyeq \sigma_s 01^{e+1}0$ that meets S_e^s. Our construction is done relative to B, which can compute $\emptyset^{(n)}$, and hence we can test whether a given requirement requires attention at a given stage.

The peculiar form that τ must have comes from the coding of B into $A^{(n)}$. The number e encodes which requirement is being addressed, which will allow us to "unwind" the construction to recover the coding. We will say that a stage s is a *coding stage* if we act to code information about B into A at stage s. Let $c(s)$ denote the number of coding stages before s.

At stage 0, declare that 0 is a coding stage and let $\sigma_0 = B(0)$.

At stage $s+1$, if no requirement $\mathcal{R}_e$ with $e \leqslant s+1$ requires attention then let $\sigma_{s+1} = \sigma_s$ and declare that $s+1$ is not a coding stage. Otherwise, let $\mathcal{R}_e$ be the strongest priority requirement requiring attention. Let m_0 be the least m such that $f_e(m) \succcurlyeq \sigma_s 01^{e+1}0$. If $|f_e(m_0)| > s+1$, then let $\sigma_{s+1} = \sigma_s$ and declare that $s+1$ is not a coding stage. Otherwise, let $\sigma_{s+1} = f_e(m_0)^\frown B(c(s+1))$ and declare that $s+1$ is a coding stage.

Let $A = \bigcup_s \sigma_s$.

Lemma 2.24.15. *$\mathcal{R}_e$ requires attention only finitely often.*

Proof. Assume by induction that there is a stage s after which no requirement stronger than $\mathcal{R}_e$ requires attention. Suppose $\mathcal{R}_e$ requires attention at a stage $t+1 > s$, and let m_0 be the least m such that $f_e(m) \succcurlyeq \sigma_t 01^{e+1}0$. If $|f_e(m_0)| \leqslant s+1$ then $\mathcal{R}_e$ is met at stage $t+1$ and hence never again requires attention. Otherwise, $\mathcal{R}_e$ continues to be the strongest priority requirement requiring attention until stage $|f_e(m_0)| - 1$, at which point it is met, and never again requires attention. □

Lemma 2.24.16. *A is weakly $(n+1)$-generic.*

Proof. Assume that S_e is dense. Let $g(s)$ be the least k such that for each $\sigma \in 2^{\leqslant s+1}$ there is a $j \leqslant k$ such that $f_e(j)$ extends $\sigma 01^{e+1}0$. Then $g \leqslant_{\mathrm{T}} \emptyset^{(n)}$. Let s be a stage after which no requirement stronger than $\mathcal{R}_e$ ever requires attention. Since p_B is not majorized by any $\emptyset^{(n)}$-computable function, there is a $t > s$ such that $p_B(t) > g(t)$. At stage t, the requirement $\mathcal{R}_e$ requires attention unless it is already met, and continues to be the strongest priority requirement requiring attention from that stage on until it is met. □

Lemma 2.24.17. $A^{(n)} \leqslant_T B$.

Proof. Since $\emptyset^{(n)} \leqslant_T B$, the construction of A is computable from B. By the previous lemma, A is weakly $(n+1)$-generic and hence n-generic, so by Theorem 2.24.3, $A^{(n)} \equiv_T A \oplus \emptyset^{(n)} \leqslant_T A \oplus B \equiv_T B$. □

Lemma 2.24.18. $B \leqslant_T A^{(n)}$.

Proof. Note that A is infinite, as it is weakly $(n+1)$-generic. Elements are added to A only during coding stages, and there are thus infinitely many such stages $s_0 < s_1 < \cdots$. During stage s_k we define σ_{s_k} so that $\sigma_{s_k}(|\sigma_{s_k}| - 1) = B(k)$. Thus it is enough to show that the function g defined by $g(k) = |\sigma_{s_k}|$ is computable from $A^{(n)}$.

We have $g(0) = 1$. Assume that we have computed $g(k)$ using $A^{(n)}$. We know that $\sigma_{s_{k+1}} \succcurlyeq \sigma_{s_k}01^{e+1}0$ for some e, and we can determine this e from A, since $(A \upharpoonright g(k))^\frown 01^{e+1}0 \prec A$. Since $\emptyset^{(n)} \leqslant A^{(n)}$, we can compute from $A^{(n)}$ the least m such that $f_e(m) \succcurlyeq \sigma_{s_k}01^{e+1}0$, which must exist. By construction, $g(k+1) = |f_e(m)| + 1$. □

Together, the three previous lemmas imply the theorem. □

Taking $n = 0$ in the theorem above, we have the following special case, which will be useful below.

Corollary 2.24.19 (Kurtz [228, 229]). *A degree is weakly 1-generic iff it is hyperimmune.*

Corollary 2.24.20 (Kurtz [228, 229]). *There is a weakly $(n+1)$-generic degree that is not $(n+1)$-generic.*

Proof. By the theorem, there is a weakly $(n+1)$-generic degree $\mathbf{a}$ such that $\mathbf{a}^{(\mathbf{n})} = \mathbf{0}^{(\mathbf{n+1})}$, so that $\mathbf{a}^{(\mathbf{n+1})} = \mathbf{0}^{(\mathbf{n+2})}$. Since $\mathbf{a} < \mathbf{0}^{(\mathbf{n+1})}$, we have $\mathbf{a}^{(\mathbf{n+1})} > \mathbf{a} \vee \mathbf{0}^{(\mathbf{n+1})}$, so by Theorem 2.24.3, $\mathbf{a}$ is not 1-generic. □

Downey, Jockusch, and Stob [121] introduced a new notion of genericity related to array computability. Let $f \leqslant_{\mathrm{pb}} C$ mean that f can be computed from oracle C by a reduction procedure with a primitive recursive bound on the use function. It is easy to show that $f \leqslant_{\mathrm{pb}} \emptyset'$ iff there is a computable function $\widehat{f}(n, s)$ and a primitive recursive function p such that $\lim_s \widehat{f}(n, s) = f(n)$ and $|\{s : \widehat{f}(n, s) \neq \widehat{f}(n, s+1)\}| \leqslant p(n)$. Most proofs yielding results about array noncomputable degrees that use functions $f \leqslant_{\mathrm{wtt}} \emptyset'$ actually use functions $f \leqslant_{\mathrm{pb}} \emptyset'$.

Definition 2.24.21 (Downey, Jockusch, and Stob [121]). (i) A set of strings S is *pb-dense* if there is a function $f \leqslant_{\mathrm{pb}} \emptyset'$ such that $f(\sigma) \succcurlyeq \sigma$ and $f(\sigma) \in S$ for all σ.

(ii) A set is *pb-generic* if it meets every pb-dense set of strings. A degree is pb-generic if it contains a pb-generic set.

For every e, the set $\{\sigma : \sigma \in W_e \vee \forall \tau \succcurlyeq \sigma\,(\tau \notin W_e)\}$ is pb-dense, so every pb-generic set is 1-generic. If $f \leqslant_{\mathrm{pb}} \emptyset'$, then the range of f is Σ^0_2, so every 2-generic set is pb-generic.

The main result about pb-genericity of relevance to us is the following.

Theorem 2.24.22 (Downey, Jockusch, and Stob [121]).

(i) *If* $\mathbf{a}$ *is a.n.c., then there is a pb-generic set* $A \leqslant_{\mathrm{T}} \mathbf{a}$.

(ii) *If* A *is pb-generic, then* $\deg(A)$ *is a.n.c.*

To prove this theorem, we need a lemma. A sequence $\{S_n\}_{n \in \omega}$ of sets of strings is *uniformly wtt-dense* if there is a function $d \leqslant_{\mathrm{wtt}} \emptyset'$ such that $d(n, \sigma) \succcurlyeq \sigma$ and $d(n, \sigma) \in S_n$ for all n and σ.

Lemma 2.24.23 (Downey, Jockusch, and Stob [121]). *If* $\mathbf{a}$ *is a.n.c. and* $\{S_n\}_{n \in \omega}$ *is uniformly wtt-dense, then there is an* $A \leqslant_{\mathrm{T}} \mathbf{a}$ *that meets each* S_n.

Proof. Let $d(n, \sigma)$ witness the uniform wtt-density of the S_n. Let $\widehat{d}$ and b be computable functions such that $\lim_s \widehat{d}(n, \sigma, s) = d(n, \sigma)$ and $|\{s : \widehat{d}(n, \sigma, s) \neq \widehat{d}(n, \sigma, s+1)\}| \leqslant b(n, \sigma)$. We may assume that $\widehat{d}(n, \sigma, s) \succcurlyeq \sigma$ for all σ, n, and s. Let $h(n, \sigma) = \mu s\, \forall t \geqslant s\, (\widehat{d}(n, \sigma, t) = \widehat{d}(n, \sigma, s))$. Let $f(n) = \max\{h(e, \sigma) : e, |\sigma| \leqslant n\}$. We have $f \leqslant_{\mathrm{wtt}} \emptyset'$, since $d \leqslant_{\mathrm{wtt}} \emptyset'$. Fix a function g computable in $\mathbf{a}$ such that $g(n) \geqslant f(n)$ for infinitely many n.

We obtain A as $\bigcup_s \sigma_s$, where $|\sigma_s| = s$. The basic strategy for n at a stage $s > n$ is to let $\sigma_t = \widehat{d}(n, \sigma_s, g(s)) \upharpoonright t$ for all t such that $s < t \leqslant |\widehat{d}(n, \sigma_s, g(s))|$, at which point we declare S_n to be satisfied. If at any stage $u > s$ we find that for some $t \in (g(s), g(u)]$, we have $\widehat{d}(n, \sigma_s, t) \neq \widehat{d}(n, \sigma_s, g(s))$, then we declare S_n to be unsatisfied and repeat the strategy. This strategy can be interrupted at any point by the strategy for an S_m with $m < n$. If this situation happens, we wait until S_m is satisfied and repeat the strategy.

Clearly, $A \leqslant_{\mathrm{T}} \mathbf{a}$, and if S_n is eventually permanently satisfied, then A meets S_n. To see that every S_n is indeed eventually permanently satisfied, assume by induction that there is a least stage $s_0 > n$ by which all S_m with $m < n$ are permanently satisfied. Let $s > s_0$ be such that $g(s) \geqslant f(s)$. If an iteration of the strategy for S_n begins at stage s, then it will clearly lead to S_n becoming permanently satisfied. Otherwise, there must be a stage $v \in [s_0, s)$ such that a strategy for S_n is started at stage v and for all $t \in$

$(g(v), g(s)]$, we have $\widehat{d}(n, \sigma_v, t) = \widehat{d}(n, \sigma_v, g(v))$. But then $g(v) \geqslant h(n, \sigma_v)$, so S_n is again permanently satisfied. $\square$

Proof of Theorem 2.24.22. (i) Let $p_0, p_1, \ldots$ be a uniformly computable listing of the primitive recursive functions. If $\Phi_e^{\emptyset'}(m) \downarrow$ with use at most $p_i(m)$ for all $m \leqslant n$, then let $g(e, i, n) = \Phi_e^{\emptyset'}(n)$. Otherwise, let $g(e, i, n) = 0$. Clearly, $g \leqslant_{\mathrm{wtt}} \emptyset'$ and each function $f \leqslant_{\mathrm{pb}} \emptyset'$ has the form $n \mapsto g(e, i, n)$ for some e and i. Let $\sigma_0, \sigma_1, \ldots$ be an effective listing of $2^{<\omega}$. Let $h(e, i, n) = g(e, i, n)$ if $\sigma_{g(e,i,n)} \supseteq \sigma_n$, and otherwise let $h(e, i, n) = n$. Let $S_{e,i} = \{\sigma_{h(e,i,n)} : n \in \mathbb{N}\}$. Then the sets $S_{e,i}$ are uniformly wtt-dense, and every pb-dense set is equal to $S_{e,i}$ for some e and i. By Lemma 2.24.23, there is a set A computable in $\mathbf{a}$ that meets each $S_{e,i}$, which makes A pb-generic.

(ii) Let $A = \{a_0 < a_1 < \cdots\}$ be pb-generic. Recall that the principal function p_A of A is defined by $p_A(n) = a_n$, and that $m_{\emptyset'}(n)$ is the least s such that $\emptyset' \upharpoonright n = \emptyset'_s \upharpoonright n$. We show that $p_A(n) \geqslant m_{\emptyset'}(n)$ for infinitely many n, which by Theorem 2.23.3 suffices to conclude that $\deg(A)$ is a.n.c. For a string σ, let $i_0 < i_1 < \cdots < i_{j_\sigma - 1}$ be all the numbers such that $\sigma(i_n) = 1$. Let $p_\sigma(n) = i_n$ if $n < j_\sigma$ and let $p_\sigma(n) \uparrow$ otherwise. Fix k. We show that there is an $n \geqslant k$ such that $p_A(n) \geqslant m_{\emptyset'}(n)$. Let

$$S = \{\sigma : \exists n \geqslant k\, (p_\sigma(n) \geqslant m_{\emptyset'}(n))\}.$$

Then S is pb-dense, as witnessed by the function f defined by $f(\sigma) = \sigma 1^k 0^{m_{\emptyset'}(j_\sigma + k)} 1$. Thus A meets S, which means that there is a σ such that $f(\sigma) \prec A$. Then $p_A(j_\sigma + k) \geqslant m_{\emptyset'}(j_\sigma + k)$. $\square$

Since each nonzero c.e. degree bounds a 1-generic degree, but no 2-generic degree is below $\mathbf{0}'$, pb-genericity is an intermediate notion between 1- and 2-genericity.

Corollary 2.24.24 (Downey, Jockusch, and Stob [121]). *There is a 1-generic degree that is not pb-generic, and a pb-generic degree that is not 2-generic.*

3

Kolmogorov Complexity of Finite Strings

This chapter is a brief introduction to Kolmogorov complexity and the theory of algorithmic randomness for finite strings. We will concentrate on a few fundamental aspects, in particular ones that will be useful in dealing with our main topic, the theory of algorithmic randomness for infinite sequences. A much fuller treatment of Kolmogorov complexity can be found in Li and Vitányi [248]. We will not discuss the philosophical roots of Kolmogorov complexity. See Li and Vitányi [248] and van Lambalgen [397, 398] for a thorough discussion of the foundations of the subject.

We will mainly deal with two kinds of Kolmogorov complexity: plain and prefix-free (both defined below). There are two notational traditions in algorithmic information theory. One uses C for plain Kolmogorov complexity and K for prefix-free Kolmogorov complexity (sometimes referred to as prefix Kolmogorov complexity). The other uses K for plain Kolmogorov complexity and H for prefix-free Kolmogorov complexity. In line with [248], we adopt the former convention.

3.1 Plain Kolmogorov complexity

The main idea behind the theory of algorithmic randomness for finite strings is that a string σ is random if and only if it is "incompressible", that is, the only way to generate σ by an algorithm is to essentially hardwire σ into the algorithm, so that the minimal length of a program to generate σ is essentially the same as that of σ itself. For instance, $0^{1000000}$ can be

R.G. Downey and D. Hirschfeldt, *Algorithmic Randomness and Complexity*, Theory and Applications of Computability, DOI 10.1007/978-0-387-68441-3_3,

described by saying that we should repeat 0 1000000 times, an algorithm that can easily be described in less than 1000000 bits. On the other hand, if we were to toss a coin 1000000 times and record the outcome as a binary string, we would not expect this string to have a very short description.

We formalize this notion, in a sense first due to Solomonoff [369], but independently to Kolmogorov [211], as follows. Let $f : 2^{<\omega} \to 2^{<\omega}$ be a partial computable function. The *Kolmogorov complexity* of a string σ with respect to f is

$$C_f(\sigma) = \min\{|\tau| : f(\tau) = \sigma\},$$

where this minimum is taken to be ∞ if the set is empty. We say that σ is *random relative to* f if $C_f(\sigma) \geqslant |\sigma|$.

Here we think of f as a "description system". Relative to this system, the string described (or generated) by a given string τ is $f(\tau)$ (if this value is defined). Thus σ is random relative to f if and only if it has no descriptions shorter than itself, relative to the description system f.

We would like to get rid of the dependence on f by choosing a *universal* description system. Such a system should be able to simulate any other description system with at most a small increase in the length of descriptions. Thus we fix a partial computable function $U : 2^{<\omega} \to 2^{<\omega}$ that is *universal* in the sense that, for each partial computable function $f : 2^{<\omega} \to 2^{<\omega}$, there is a string ρ_f such that

$$\forall\sigma\, [U(\rho_f\sigma) = f(\sigma)].$$ [1]

We call ρ_f the *coding string* and $|\rho_f|$ the *coding constant* of f in U. As usual, we identify partial computable functions and Turing machines, and hence often refer to U as a universal (Turing) machine. (These definitions of universal partial computable function and universal Turing machine are not exactly the same as the ones given in Proposition 2.1.2, but are essentially equivalent to those, so we do not bother to make a distinction.)

It is easy to check that for any partial computable function $f : 2^{<\omega} \to 2^{<\omega}$, we have

$$C_U(x) \leqslant C_f(x) + |\rho_f|,$$

so U is a universal description system in the sense discussed above. Thus, it makes sense to define the *(plain) Kolmogorov complexity* (or *C-complexity*) of a binary string σ to be

$$C(\sigma) = C_U(\sigma).$$

[1] Such a function, and the corresponding Turing machine, are sometimes called *universal by adjunction*, to distinguish them from a more general notion of universality, where we say that U is universal if for each partial computable $f : 2^{<\omega} \to 2^{<\omega}$ there is a c such that for each $\sigma \in \mathrm{dom}(f)$ there is a τ with $|\tau| \leqslant |\sigma| + c$ and $U(\tau) = f(\sigma)$. The distinction between these two notions is irrelevant in most cases, but not always, and it should be kept in mind that it is the stronger one that we adopt.

Of course, a different choice of U would yield a different definition of C, but the two definitions would agree up to an additive constant.

The following results are not hard to prove.

Proposition 3.1.1 (Kolmogorov [211]).

(i) $C(\sigma) \leqslant |\sigma| + O(1)$.

(ii) $C(\sigma\sigma) \leqslant C(\sigma) + O(1)$.

(iii) *If* $h : 2^{<\omega} \to 2^{<\omega}$ *is computable then* $C(h(\sigma)) \leqslant C(\sigma) + O(1)$.

To prove (i), let $f : 2^{<\omega} \to 2^{<\omega}$ be the identity function. Then $C(\sigma) \leqslant C_f(\sigma) + O(1) = |\sigma| + O(1)$. The other two parts of the lemma are equally straightforward to prove.

We can think of $n \in \mathbb{N}$ as a binary string σ (namely, its representation in binary), and define $C(n) = C(\sigma)$. By part (iii) of Proposition 3.1.1, it would not really matter if we chose to define $C(n)$ to be $C(0^n)$, say. Note that $C(n) \leqslant \log n + O(1)$, since the length of the binary representation of n is $\log n$.

We will denote $C(\langle\sigma, \tau\rangle)$ by $C(\sigma, \tau)$. By part (iii) of Proposition 3.1.1, the particular choice of pairing function does not matter, up to an additive constant.

Suppose that $C(\sigma) = k$. Then there is a first string τ of length k such that the computation of $U(\tau)$ converges with value σ. More precisely, there is a least stage s such that $U(\tau)[s]\downarrow= \sigma$ for one or more strings τ of length k. We fix the lexicographically least such τ and denote it by σ^*_C.

The following fact is easy to check, since from σ^*_C we can compute both σ and $C(\sigma) = |\sigma^*_C|$, and from $C(\sigma)$ and σ we can compute σ^*_C.

Proposition 3.1.2. $C(\sigma, C(\sigma)) = C(\sigma^*_C) \pm O(1)$.

We wish to say that a binary string σ is C-random if it is random relative to U, that is, $C(\sigma) \geqslant |\sigma|$. However, it is more convenient (and reasonable, given the arbitrary choice of U) to relax this definition a little by fixing a constant d and defining σ to be *C-random* if $C(\sigma) \geqslant |\sigma| - d$. The following result says that C-random strings exist.

Proposition 3.1.3 (Solomonoff [369], Kolmogorov [211]). *For each n there exists a σ with $|\sigma| = n$ and $C(\sigma) \geqslant n$.*

Proof. There are only $2^n - 1$ binary strings of length less than n, so there are at most $2^n - 1$ binary strings with Kolmogorov complexity less than n. □

Notice that the same kind of counting argument shows that, for any k and n,

$$|\{\sigma \in 2^n : C(\sigma) \geqslant |\sigma| - k\}| > 2^n(1 - 2^{-k}).$$

For instance, the number of strings of length 1000 that are "half-random" (i.e., those with Kolmogorov complexity at least 500) is greater than $2^{1000}(1 - 2^{-500})$. Thus, heuristically, almost every string is half-random.

We would like to have $C(\sigma\tau) \leqslant C(\sigma) + C(\tau) + O(1)$, but this is not the case. The problem is that we cannot simply concatenate descriptions of σ and τ, since we would have no way of knowing where one description ends and the other begins. In fact, sufficiently long strings always have fairly compressible initial segments, as we now see.

Theorem 3.1.4 (Martin-Löf, see Kolmogorov [212] and Li and Vitányi [248]). *Fix k. If μ is sufficiently long then there is an initial segment σ of μ such that $C(\sigma) < |\sigma| - k$. Thus, for any fixed d, we have $\mu = \sigma\tau$ such that $C(\mu) > C(\sigma) + C(\tau) + d$.*

Proof. Let ν be an initial segment of μ, and let n be such that ν is the nth string in the length-lexicographic ordering of $2^{<\omega}$. Let ρ be the string consisting of the next n bits of μ following ν, and let $\sigma = \nu\rho$. To generate σ we need only know ρ, since the length n of ρ will then give us ν, so there is a constant c such that $C(\sigma) \leqslant |\rho| + c$, where c does not depend on the choice of μ or ν.[2] On the other hand, $|\sigma| = |\nu| + |\rho|$, so if we choose ν so that $|\nu| > c + k$, then $C(\sigma) < |\sigma| - k$.

For the second part of the lemma, let c be such that $C(\tau) \leqslant |\tau| + c$ for all τ, and let $k = c + d$. Let μ be a sufficiently large string such that $C(\mu) \geqslant |\mu|$. By the first part of the lemma, we can write $\mu = \sigma\tau$ so that $C(\sigma) < |\sigma| - k$. Then $C(\mu) \geqslant |\mu| = |\sigma| + |\tau| > C(\sigma) + k + C(\tau) - c = C(\sigma) + C(\tau) + d$. □

On the other hand, we do have the following bound, which has been shown to be fairly sharp, using techniques like that in the proof of Theorem 3.1.4.

Proposition 3.1.5. $C(\sigma\tau) \leqslant C(\sigma, \tau) \leqslant C(\sigma) + C(\tau) + 2\log C(\sigma) + O(1)$.

Proof. That $C(\sigma\tau) \leqslant C(\sigma, \tau)$ is clear, since if we know both σ and τ then we know $\sigma\tau$.

For a string $\nu = a_0 a_1 \dots a_m$, let $\overline{\nu} = a_0 a_0 a_1 a_1 \dots a_m a_m 01$. That is, $\overline{\nu}$ is the result of doubling each bit of ν and adding 01 to the end. Intuitively, the second inequality in the lemma follows because we can describe σ and τ by giving σ^*_C and τ^*_C together with the length of σ^*_C, that is, $C(\sigma)$. If we code this length as a binary string ρ, then we can give this length in an unambiguous way as $\overline{\rho}$, because each string μ has at most one initial segment of the form $\overline{\nu}$ for some ν, so $\overline{\rho}\sigma^*_C\tau^*_C$ unambiguously describes $\langle\sigma, \tau\rangle$.

---

[2]It may be useful to those unfamiliar with this kind of argument to give a more detailed justification here: For a string τ, let $m = |\tau|$ and let $f(\tau) = \zeta\tau$, where ζ is the mth string in the length-lexicographic ordering of $2^{<\omega}$. Then f is a computable function and $f(\rho) = \nu\rho = \sigma$. So $C_f(\sigma) \leqslant |\rho|$, and hence $C(\sigma) \leqslant |\rho| + c$, where c is the coding constant of f in our fixed universal function U.

More formally, let $f : 2^{<\sigma} \to 2^{<\sigma}$ be defined as follows. On input μ, search for $\mu_0, \mu_1, \mu_2, \rho$ such that

1. $\mu = \mu_0\mu_1\mu_2$,

2. $\mu_0 = \overline{\rho}$,

3. ρ is the binary representation of $|\mu_1|$,

4. $U(\mu_1)\downarrow$, and $U(\mu_2)\downarrow$.

If these strings are found then let $f(\mu) = \langle U(\mu_1), U(\mu_2)\rangle$.

Letting ρ be the binary representation of $C(\sigma)$, we have $f(\overline{\rho}\sigma^*_C\tau^*_C) = \langle \sigma, \tau\rangle$, so $C(\sigma, \tau) \leqslant |\overline{\rho}\sigma^*_C\tau^*_C| + O(1) = C(\sigma) + C(\tau) + 2\log C(\sigma) + O(1)$. □

We will use Kolmogorov complexity to study issues related to the relative algorithmic randomness of infinite sequences, but it has also found many other applications. For instance, there is a well-developed theory applying incompressibility to avoid counting in combinatorial arguments. This method is extensively used for lower bound arguments in complexity theory, and is one of the principal reasons for much of the interest in C-complexity. We will not dwell on such applications of Kolmogorov complexity here, since they are not directly related to our central theme, but will give a short but interesting example: the construction of an immune set, that is, a set with no infinite c.e. subset. For more on applications of Kolmogorov complexity, see Chapter 6 of [248].

Let $A = \{\sigma : C(\sigma) \geqslant \frac{|\sigma|}{2}\}$. Then A is immune. Indeed, suppose that A has an infinite c.e. subset B. Let $h(n)$ be the first string of length greater than n to enter B. Then $C(h(n)) \geqslant \frac{|h(n)|}{2} > \frac{n}{2}$, since $h(n) \in A$, but we can generate $h(n)$ given n simply by running the enumeration of B until a string of length greater than n appears, so $C(h(n)) \leqslant C(n) + O(1) \leqslant \log n + O(1)$. For large enough n, this is a contradiction.

3.2 Conditional complexity

It is often useful to measure the compressibility of a string *given another string*. To do so, we fix a *universal oracle machine*, that is, an oracle Turing machine U such that for each oracle Turing machine M there is a coding string ρ_M such that

$$\forall X\, \forall \sigma\, [U^X(\rho_M\sigma) = M^X(\sigma)],$$

where X ranges over all oracles, both finite and infinite. For strings σ and τ, the *(plain) Kolmogorov complexity of σ given τ* is

$$C(\sigma \mid \tau) = \min\{|\mu| : U^{\tau}(\mu) = \sigma\},$$

where $\overline{\tau}$ is as defined in the proof of Proposition 3.1.5. (The reason we use $\overline{\tau}$ instead of τ is the following. By the way we have defined the action of oracle machines on finite oracles in Section 2.4.1, for any such machine M and any μ, the set of oracles ρ such that $M^{\rho}(\mu)\downarrow$ is prefix-free, as defined in Definition 2.19.1. It is not hard to use this fact to show that $\min\{|\mu| : U^{\tau}(\mu) = \sigma\}$ does not behave as we would expect conditional complexity to behave. For example, $\min\{|\mu| : U^{\sigma}(\mu) = \sigma\}$ is not bounded by a constant, but we of course want to have $C(\sigma \mid \sigma) \leqslant O(1)$. With the definition we have given, we do have this property, since it is easy to define an oracle Turing machine M such that $M^{\overline{\sigma}}(\lambda) = \sigma$ for all σ.)

Notice that this notion of conditional Kolmogorov complexity reduces to unconditional Kolmogorov complexity by letting $\tau = \lambda$, the empty string. That is, $C(\sigma) = C(\sigma \mid \lambda) \pm O(1)$.

In Proposition 3.1.2, we saw that $C(\sigma^*_C) = C(\sigma, C(\sigma)) \pm O(1)$. We can say a little more using conditional complexity.

Proposition 3.2.1. $C(\sigma^*_C \mid \sigma) = C(C(\sigma) \mid \sigma) \pm O(1)$.

The proof is essentially the same as that of Proposition 3.1.2.

Easy counting arguments give us the following basic result relating the size of a finite set to the complexity of its elements.

Theorem 3.2.2 (Kolmogorov [211]).

(i) *Let $A \subset 2^{<\omega}$ be finite. Then for each τ there is a $\sigma \in A$ such that $C(\sigma \mid \tau) \geqslant \log |A|$.*

(ii) *Let $B \subseteq 2^{<\omega} \times 2^{<\omega}$ be an infinite computably enumerable set such that each set of the form $B_\tau = \{\sigma : \langle \sigma, \tau \rangle \in B\}$ is finite. Then for every τ and every $\sigma \in B_\tau$, we have $C(\sigma \mid \tau) \leqslant \log |B_\tau| + O(1)$, where the constant term is independent of both σ and τ.*

Proof. Part (i) is a counting argument, as in the proof of Proposition 3.1.3. For part (ii), given τ, we can describe $\sigma \in B_\tau$ by giving its position in the enumeration of B_τ derived from a fixed enumeration of B. This position is less than or equal to $|B_\tau|$, and hence can be coded by a string of length less than or equal to $\log |B_\tau|$. □

Universal oracle machines also allow us to relativize the notion of plain Kolmogorov complexity to any oracle A, by letting U be such a machine and defining $C^A(\sigma) = \min\{|\tau| : U^A(\tau) = \sigma\}$. All the basic properties of plain complexity continue to hold in the relativized case, with the same proofs. It is also easy to show that if $B \geqslant_{\mathrm{T}} A$ then $C^B(\sigma) \leqslant C^A(\sigma) + O(1)$.

3.3 Symmetry of information

The *(plain) information content* of a string τ in a string σ is defined as

$$I_C(\sigma : \tau) = C(\tau) - C(\tau \mid \sigma).$$

This notion is meant to capture the difference between the intrinsic difficulty of producing τ given σ and that of producing τ *without* σ. The following famous result expresses concisely the relationship between $I_C(\sigma : \tau)$ and $I_C(\tau : \sigma)$.

Theorem 3.3.1 (Symmetry of Information, Levin and Kolmogorov, see [425]).

$$I_C(\sigma : \tau) = I_C(\tau : \sigma) \pm O(\log C(\sigma, \tau)).$$

Note that it follows immediately from this result that $I_C(\sigma : \tau) = I_C(\tau : \sigma) \pm O(\log n)$, where $n = \max\{|\tau|, |\sigma|\}$.

Theorem 3.3.1 follows easily from the following restated version.

Theorem 3.3.2 (Symmetry of Information, Restated).

$$C(\sigma, \tau) = C(\tau \mid \sigma) + C(\sigma) \pm O(\log C(\sigma, \tau)).$$

To obtain Theorem 3.3.1 from Theorem 3.3.2, we argue as follows. We have

$$C(\sigma, \tau) = C(\tau \mid \sigma) + C(\sigma) \pm O(\log C(\sigma, \tau))$$

and

$$C(\tau, \sigma) = C(\sigma \mid \tau) + C(\tau) \pm O(\log C(\tau, \sigma)).$$

But $C(\sigma, \tau) = C(\tau, \sigma) \pm O(1)$, so

$$\begin{aligned} I_C(\sigma : \tau) = C(\tau) - C(\tau \mid \sigma) = C(\sigma) - C(\sigma \mid \tau) \pm O(\log C(\sigma, \tau)) \\ = I_C(\tau : \sigma) \pm O(\log C(\sigma, \tau)). \end{aligned}$$

We now proceed with the proof of Theorem 3.3.2, which follows that given by Li and Vitányi [248].

Proof of Theorem 3.3.2. It is easy to see that

$$C(\sigma, \tau) \leqslant C(\sigma) + C(\tau \mid \sigma) + O(\log C(\sigma, \tau)),$$

since we can describe $\langle \sigma, \tau \rangle$ via a description of σ, a description of τ given σ, and an indication of where to delimit the two descriptions, as in Proposition 3.1.5.

For the other direction, let

$$A = \{(\mu, \nu) : C(\mu, \nu) \leqslant C(\sigma, \tau)\}$$

and

$$A_\mu = \{\nu : (\mu, \nu) \in A\}.$$

The set A is finite, and there is a uniform procedure (over all choices of σ and τ) for enumerating it given $C(\sigma, \tau)$. Similarly, the sets A_μ are finite and there is a uniform procedure (again over all choices of σ and τ) for enumerating them given $C(\sigma, \tau)$ and μ. Hence, one can describe τ given σ and $C(\sigma, \tau)$, along with τ's place in the enumeration order of A_σ. Thus

$$C(\tau \mid \sigma) \leqslant \log |A_\sigma| + 2 \log C(\sigma, \tau) + O(1).$$

Let $N = 2^{\log |A_\sigma| - 1}$. (Recall our convention that when we write $\log n$, we mean the base 2 logarithm of n, rounded up to the nearest integer. Thus we do not necessarily have $N = |A_\sigma|/2$. However, it is the case that $N \leqslant |A_\sigma|$.) Since $\log N = \log |A_\sigma| - 1$,

$$C(\tau \mid \sigma) \leqslant \log N + O(\log C(\sigma, \tau)). \tag{3.1}$$

Now consider the set $B = \{\mu : |A_\mu| \geqslant N\}$. We have $\sigma \in B$. Furthermore, there is a uniform procedure (over all choices of σ and τ) for enumerating B given $C(\sigma, \tau)$ and N, and $|B| \leqslant \frac{|A|}{N} \leqslant \frac{2^{C(\sigma,\tau)}}{N}$. Thus, to describe σ, we need only give $C(\sigma, \tau)$ and N, along with σ's place in the enumeration order of B. Now, N can be specified with $\log \log |A_\sigma|$ many bits, so

$$C(\sigma) \leqslant \log \frac{2^{C(\sigma,\tau)}}{N} + 2 \log \log |A_\sigma| + 2 \log C(\sigma, \tau) + O(1).$$

But $|A_\sigma| \leqslant 2^{C(\sigma,\tau)}$, so

$$C(\sigma) \leqslant C(\sigma, \tau) - \log N + O(\log C(\sigma, \tau)). \tag{3.2}$$

Combining (3.1) and (3.2), we have

$$C(\sigma) + C(\tau \mid \sigma) \leqslant C(\sigma, \tau) + O(\log C(\sigma, \tau)),$$

as required. □

3.4 Information-theoretic characterizations of computability

In this section, we establish some combinatorial facts about the number of strings of a specified complexity, and show that one can use Kolmogorov complexity to provide information-theoretic characterizations of computability. We begin with a result of Loveland [250]. If A is a computable set then we can generate $A \upharpoonright n$ simply by running the computation of $A(i)$ for all $i < n$. Thus $C(A \upharpoonright n \mid n) = O(1)$, where the constant depends on A. Loveland's result is a converse to this fact.

Theorem 3.4.1 (Loveland [250]). *Let X be an infinite computable set. For each e, there are only finitely many sets A such that $C(A \upharpoonright n \mid n) \leqslant e$ for all $n \in X$, and each such A is computable.*

Proof. Let U be our universal Turing machine. Fix e. For each n, let $k_n = |\{\tau \in 2^{\leqslant e} \mid U^n(\tau)\downarrow\}|$. Since $k_n < 2^{e+1}$ for all n, there is a largest m such that $k_n = m$ for infinitely many $n \in X$, and there is an l such that $k_n \leqslant m$ for all $n \in X$ with $n \geqslant l$. Furthermore, there is a computable sequence $n_0 < n_1 < \cdots \in X$ such that $n_0 \geqslant l$ and $k_{n_i} = m$ for all i. Note that the sets

$$S_i = \{\mu \mid C(\mu \mid n_i) \leqslant e\}$$

are uniformly computable, since for each i we can wait until we see m strings $\tau \in 2^{\leqslant e}$ with $U^{n_i}(\tau)\downarrow$, at which point we know that S_i is exactly the collection of values of $U^{n_i}(\tau)$ for such τ.

Let T be the tree consisting of all σ such that

$$\forall n_i \leqslant |\sigma| \, (\sigma \upharpoonright n_i \in S_i).$$

If $C(A \upharpoonright n \mid n) \leqslant e$ for all $n \in X$ then in particular $A \upharpoonright n_i \in S_i$ for all i, so A is a path of T. But the tree T is computable, and has width at most m, since for each n_i there are at most m strings of length n_i on T, so T has only finitely many paths, which means that each path of T is computable. □

It is interesting to note that Loveland [250] also showed that one cannot weaken the hypothesis of the above theorem to simply say that $C(A \upharpoonright n \mid n) \leqslant e$ for infinitely many n. The key fact here is the following. Let $\#(\sigma)$ denote the position of σ in the length-lexicographic ordering of $2^{<\omega}$, and let $\widehat{\sigma} = \sigma 0^{\#(\sigma)-|\sigma|}$. Then for any σ, given $|\widehat{\sigma}| = \#(\sigma)$ we know σ, and hence $\widehat{\sigma}$. Thus there is an e such that $C(\widehat{\sigma} \mid |\widehat{\sigma}|) \leqslant e$ for all σ. Now for any set B we can form a sequence $\sigma_0 \prec \sigma_1 \prec \cdots$ by taking $\sigma_0 = \lambda$ and $\sigma_{i+1} = \widehat{\sigma_i}B(i)$. Letting $A = \bigcup_i \sigma_i$, we have $C(A \upharpoonright n \mid n) \leqslant e$ for infinitely many n. But because the choice of B was arbitrary, there are continuum many such A.

One of the keys to Theorem 3.4.1 is the uniformity implicit in having $C(A \upharpoonright n \mid n)$ bounded by a constant. We now turn to a more interesting theorem, due to Chaitin [60], which also gives an information-theoretic characterization of computability, but at the same time indicates a hidden uniformity in plain complexity. We begin with two lemmas of independent interest.

Let $D : 2^{<\omega} \to 2^{<\omega}$ be partial computable. Then τ is a *D-description* of σ, or a *D-program* for σ, if $D(\tau) = \sigma$.

Lemma 3.4.2 (Chaitin [60]). *Let $D : 2^{<\omega} \to 2^{<\omega}$ be partial computable. There is a constant c such that letting $h(d) = 2^{(d+c)}$, for each $\sigma \in 2^{<\omega}$,*

$$|\{\tau : D(\tau) = \sigma \wedge |\tau| \leqslant C(\sigma) + d\}| < h(d).$$

That is, the number of D-descriptions of σ of length at most $C(\sigma) + d$ is $O(2^d)$.

Proof. The intuition behind this proof is that if there are too many short D-descriptions of σ, then using a listing of these we can give a description of σ shorter than $C(\sigma)$, which is impossible.

For each m and k, let L^k_m be the set of all τ that have at least 2^m many D-descriptions of length at most k. Then $|L^k_m| < 2^{k-m}$, and the L^k_m are uniformly c.e. Thus we can describe any element of L^k_m by giving m and a string of length 2^{k-m}, indicating its position in the enumeration of L^k_m. Such a description can be given in at most $2\log m + k - m + O(1)$ many bits, where the constant term depends only on D. So there is a c such that if $\sigma \in L^k_m$ then $C(\sigma) \leqslant 2\log m + k - m + c$. We may assume that $c > 3$. Let $h(d) = 2^{d+c}$.

Let $m = h(d)$ and $k = C(\sigma) + d$. If $\sigma \in L^k_m$ then $C(\sigma) \leqslant 2\log h(d) + C(\sigma) + d - h(d) + c$, and hence $h(d) \leqslant 2\log h(d) + d + c = 3(d+c)$, which is not the case. Thus $\sigma \notin L^k_m$. In other words, the number of D-descriptions of σ of length at most $C(\sigma) + d$ is less than $h(d)$. □

Lemma 3.4.3 (Chaitin [60]). *There is a computable function h with $h(d) = O(2^d)$ such that, for all n and d,*

$$|\{\sigma \in 2^n : C(\sigma) \leqslant C(n) + d\}| \leqslant h(d).$$

Proof. Let D be the partial computable function defined by $D(\tau) = 1^{|U(\tau)|}$, where U is our universal Turing machine, and let h be as in Lemma 3.4.2. If $C(\sigma) \leqslant C(n)+d$ then σ^*_C is a D-description of n of length at most $C(n)+d$. There are at most $h(d)$ many such descriptions, and hence at most $h(d)$ many σ with $C(\sigma) \leqslant C(n) + d$. □

Thus, although one might expect that, as the size of σ increases, the number of descriptions of σ of length close to $C(\sigma)$ would grow, we see that this is not the case.

Theorem 3.4.4 (Chaitin [60]). *A set A is computable iff $C(A \upharpoonright n) \leqslant C(n) + O(1)$. Furthermore, for each k there are only $O(2^d)$ many A such that $C(A \upharpoonright n) \leqslant C(n) + d$.*

Proof. If A is computable, then clearly $C(A \upharpoonright n) \leqslant C(n) + O(1)$. Now let e be such that $C(n) \leqslant \log n + e$ for all n. Fix d and let

$$T = \{\sigma : \forall \tau \preccurlyeq \sigma\, (C(\tau) \leqslant \log|\tau| + d + e)\}.$$

The tree T is c.e. We want to transform it into a computable tree. We assume we have an enumeration of T such that each T_s is closed under substrings.

Let I_k be the interval $(2^k, 2^{k+1}]$, and let $m_k = \min\{|2^n \cap T| : n \in I_k\}$. Each I_k contains some n such that $C(n) \geqslant \log n$. For this n, we have $|2^n \cap T| \leqslant h(d+e)$, so $m_k \leqslant h(d+e)$ for all k. Let $c \leqslant h(d+e)$ be the largest number such that $m_k = c$ for infinitely many k, and let l be such that $m_k \leqslant c$ for all $k > l$. Let $l < k_0 < k_1 < \cdots$ and $s_0, s_1, \ldots$ be computable sequences such that for each i we have $|2^n \cap T_{s_i}| \geqslant c$ for all

$n \in I_{k_i}$. Let a_i be the least element of I_{k_i} such that $|2^n \cap T_{s_i}| = c$, which must exist since $m_{k_i} = c$.

Let

$$S = \{\sigma : \forall a_i < |\sigma| \, (\sigma \upharpoonright a_i \in T_{s_i})\}.$$

Then S is a computable tree. If $P \in [S]$ then $P \upharpoonright a_i \in T$ for all i, so $P \in [T]$. Conversely, suppose that a string σ of length a_i is not in T_{s_i}. Let $n \in I_{k_i}$ be such that $|2^n \cap T| = c$. Then $n \geqslant a_i$, and there is no extension of σ of length n in T. So if $P \in [T]$ then $P \upharpoonright a_i \in T_{s_i}$ for all i, and hence $P \in [S]$. Thus $[S] = [T]$.

If $C(A \upharpoonright n) \leqslant C(n) + d$ for all n then $A \in [T]$, so $A \in [S]$. But S has width $c \leqslant h(d + e) = O(2^d)$, so there are only $O(2^d)$ many such A, and they are all computable. □

Note that the above theorem remains true (with a similar proof) if we weaken the latter condition by requiring that $C(A \upharpoonright n) \leqslant C(n) + O(1)$ only for an infinite computable set of n, or if we replace it by $C(A \upharpoonright n) \leqslant \log n + O(1)$ (for all n or for an infinite computable set of n), since if $C(A \upharpoonright n) \leqslant \log n + d$ for all n then $A \in [T]$ for the tree T defined in the above proof. We record the former variation for later use.

Theorem 3.4.5 (Chaitin [60]). *A set A is computable iff there is an infinite computable set S such that $C(A \upharpoonright n) \leqslant C(n) + O(1)$ for all $n \in S$.*

Merkle and Stephan [270] observed that this theorem relativizes to show that, for any infinite S, if $C(A \upharpoonright n) \leqslant C(n) + O(1)$ for all $n \in S$ then $A \leqslant_T S$.

There are several other counting results along the lines of Lemma 3.4.3, many due to the Moscow school of algorithmic information theory. We prove one that will be useful below. (It is possible this result was known earlier than the given reference.)

Theorem 3.4.6 (Figueira, Nies, and Stephan [147]). *Let $\sigma \in 2^{<\omega}$. Then $|\{\tau : C(\sigma, \tau) \leqslant C(\sigma) + d\}| \leqslant O(d^4 2^d)$, where the constant does not depend on σ.*

Proof. Let n_σ be the position of σ in a fixed effective enumeration of $2^{<\omega}$. Let c be such that $C(\sigma) \leqslant n_\sigma + c$ for all σ. Let $f(\sigma, \tau, d)$ be a partial computable function defined as follows. Given σ, τ, and d, enumerate all the strings $\mu_0, \mu_1, \ldots$ with $C(\mu_i) \leqslant n_\sigma + d + c$. If there is an i such that $\mu_i = \tau$, let ν be a binary representation of i with enough initial zeroes so that $|\nu| = n_\sigma + d + c + 1$. Such a ν must exist because there are at most $2^{n_\sigma + d + c + 1}$ many μ_j. Let $f(\sigma, \tau, d) = \nu$. Of course, if $C(\tau) > n_\sigma + d + c$ then $f(\sigma, \tau, d)\uparrow$.

Now suppose that $C(\sigma,\tau) \leqslant C(\sigma) + d$. Then $C(\sigma,\tau) \leqslant n_\sigma + d + c$, so $f(\sigma,\tau,d)\downarrow$. We have

$$\begin{aligned} C(f(\sigma,\tau,d)) &\leqslant C(\sigma,\tau) + 2\log d + O(1) \\ &\leqslant C(\sigma) + d + 2\log d + O(1) \\ &\leqslant C(n_\sigma + d + c + 1) + d + 4\log d + O(1). \end{aligned}$$

(The last inequality follows since we can compute σ from $n_\sigma + d + c + 1$ and d.) For fixed σ and d, the map $\tau \mapsto f(\sigma,\tau,d)$ is injective, so

$$\begin{aligned} &|\{\tau : C(\sigma,\tau) \leqslant C(\sigma) + d\}| \\ &\leqslant |\{\sigma \in 2^{n_\sigma+d+c+1} : C(\sigma) \leqslant C(n_\sigma + d + c + 1) + d + 4\log d + O(1)\}| \\ &\leqslant O(d^4 2^d), \end{aligned}$$

the last inequality following by Lemma 3.4.3. □

3.5 Prefix-free machines and complexity

In this section, we introduce the notion of prefix-free Kolmogorov complexity. Our main reason for working with this notion is to use it in studying algorithmic randomness of infinite sequences. However, some have argued that prefix-free complexity is *the* correct notion of descriptive complexity even for finite strings.

One argument for the inadequacy of plain Kolmogorov complexity is the following. The intended meaning in saying that τ is a description of σ is that the bits of τ contain all the information necessary to obtain σ. But a Turing machine M might produce σ by using not only the bits of τ but also its length. In this way, τ actually represents $|\tau| + \log|\tau|$ many bits of information. Indeed, this fact was exploited in the proof of Theorem 3.1.4.

Another way to make this argument is that, if M is allowed to use the length of τ in computing σ, then there must be some kind of *termination symbol* T (such as a blank space) on M's input tape following the bits of τ. Thus, to output a word in the alphabet $\{0,1\}$, our machine uses an input in the alphabet $\{0,1,T\}$, which we may view as cheating. If one accepts this argument then one ought to try to circumvent this shortcoming of plain Kolmogorov complexity. First Levin [241, 243] and later Chaitin [58] suggested using *prefix-free machines* to do so.

Recall from Definition 2.19.1 that a set $A \subseteq 2^{<\omega}$ is prefix-free if it is an antichain with respect to the natural partial ordering of $2^{<\omega}$, that is, if for all $\sigma \in A$ and all τ properly extending σ, we have $\tau \notin A$. Joe Miller has pointed out that the set of valid telephone numbers is a real-world example of a prefix-free set. Note that this prefix-freeness allows us to give a phone number using only the alphabet $\{0,\ldots,9\}$. Anil Nerode has remarked that there have been phone numbering systems in the past that were not prefix-free. In such a system, to give a phone number, we also need a termination symbol, such as a blank space.

A *prefix-free function* is one whose domain is prefix-free. Similarly, a *prefix-free (Turing) machine* is one whose domain is prefix-free. It is usual to consider such a machine as being *self-delimiting*, which means that it has a one-way read head that halts when the machine accepts the string described by the bits read so far. The point is that such a machine is forced to accept strings without knowing whether there are any more bits written on the input tape. This is a purely technical device that forces the machine to have a prefix-free domain, but it also highlights how using prefix-free machines circumvents the use of the length of a string to gain more information than is present in the bits of the string.[3] To highlight the role of machines in the definition of Kolmogorov complexity, we will sometimes refer to general Turing machines as *plain machines.*

A partial computable prefix-free function U is *universal* if for each partial computable prefix-free function $f : 2^{<\omega} \to 2^{<\omega}$, there is a string ρ_f such that

$$\forall\sigma\,[U(\rho_f\sigma) = f(\sigma)].$$

As in the non-prefix-free case, we call ρ_f the *coding string* and $|\rho_f|$ the *coding constant* of f in U. As the following result shows, we can identify partial computable prefix-free functions and prefix-free machines, and hence often refer to U as a *universal prefix-free machine.*[4]

Proposition 3.5.1. (i) *If Φ is a prefix-free partial computable function, then there is a prefix-free (self-delimiting) machine M such that M computes Φ.*

(ii) *There is a universal (self-delimiting) prefix-free machine.*

[3]Another way to achieve this goal is to require the complexity measure to be "continuous". This requirement gives rise to the notions of monotone complexity and process complexity, which we will discuss in Section 3.15. Another related notion, which we will not discuss in this book, is uniform complexity; see Li and Vitányi [248] and Barzdins [29] for more details. Another example of a notion of complexity that we will not discuss is Loveland's decision complexity Kd. It is defined by considering a machine as a c.e. collection of pairs (σ, τ), thinking of σ as a description of τ, but now insisting that if (σ, τ) occurs in our collection, then so does (σ, ρ) for all $\rho \prec \tau$. As with most complexities, Loveland's variant gives further insight into descriptional complexity. See [250] for more details. Notice that $Kd(\sigma) \leqslant C(\sigma) + O(1)$, and in fact it is possible to have $Kd(\sigma)$ be much less than $C(\sigma)$, so C is not the minimal complexity measure to have been studied. For more on this topic see Uspensky and Shen [396]. Notions such as decision complexity and uniform complexity have much less developed theories than prefix-free complexity and plain complexity.

[4]As in the non-prefix-free case, we sometimes refer to these functions and machines as *universal by adjunction*. See footnote 1 on page 111.

Proof. (i) Let Φ be partial computable and prefix-free. We build a self-delimiting machine M in stages. Initially, M works on the empty string. At a given point in the action of M, let σ be the string consisting of the bits read by M so far. The read head does not scan the next symbol unless it sees some extension τ of σ such that $\Phi(\tau)\downarrow$. At this point, M scans the next symbol i on the read tape. If the string $\sigma' = \sigma i$ remains an initial segment of τ, then M reads the next symbol and repeats the above process with σ' in place of σ. Otherwise, M goes back to waiting for a string τ' extending σ' upon which Φ halts. Of course, if the string σ consisting of the bits read by M so far is ever such that $\Phi(\sigma)\downarrow$, then M simply outputs $\Phi(\sigma)$.

(ii) Let Ψ_e be the partial computable function defined by letting $\Psi_e[s] = \Phi_e[s]$ if $\operatorname{dom}\Phi_e[s]$ is prefix-free and $\Psi_e[s] = \Psi_e[s-1]$ otherwise. Then $\{\Psi_e\}_{e\in\omega}$ is an enumeration of all (and only) the prefix-free partial computable functions. We can then define

$$\Psi(1^e0\sigma) = \Psi_e(\sigma),$$

which is evidently prefix-free and universal. By part (i), there is a self-delimiting machine computing Ψ. □

By the same argument as above, there is a *universal prefix-free oracle machine* U, that is, one such that for each prefix-free oracle machine M, there is a coding string ρ_M such that for every oracle X, we have $\forall\sigma\,[U^X(\rho_M\sigma) = m^X(\sigma)]$ (where X is either a finite or an infinite oracle).

Definition 3.5.2. Henceforth in this book, we fix a universal prefix-free oracle machine $\mathcal{U}$. We write $\mathcal{U}(\sigma)$ for $\mathcal{U}^{\emptyset}(\sigma)$, and thus also think of $\mathcal{U}$ as a universal prefix-free machine in the unrelativized case. All our results will be independent of the choice of $\mathcal{U}$.

Fix the enumeration $\Psi_0, \Psi_1, \dots$ of prefix-free partial computable functions given in the proof of Proposition 3.5.1. We will use the following version of the recursion theorem below.

Theorem 3.5.3 (Recursion Theorem for Prefix-Free Machines)**.** *Let $h : 2^{<\omega} \times \mathbb{N} \to 2^{<\omega}$ be a partial computable function such that for each e, the function $\lambda\sigma.h(\sigma, e)$ is prefix-free. From an index for h, we can compute an index e such that $\Psi_e = \lambda\sigma.h(\sigma, e)$.*

Proof. Let f be a total computable function such that $\Phi_{f(e)} = \lambda\sigma.h(\sigma, e)$ for all e. By the recursion theorem, there is an e (which can be computed from an index for f, and hence from an index for h) such that $\Phi_{f(e)} = \Phi_e$. Since $\Phi_{f(e)}$ is prefix-free, so is Φ_e, and hence $\Psi_e = \Phi_e$. Thus we have $\Psi_e = \Phi_{f(e)} = \lambda\sigma.h(\sigma, e)$. □

The machine $\mathcal{U}$ is minimal, in the sense that, if M is any prefix-free machine, then $C_{\mathcal{U}}(\sigma) \leqslant C_M(\sigma) + O(1)$. Thus we can define the *prefix-free*

Kolmogorov complexity of a string σ to be

$$K(\tau) = C_{\mathcal{U}}(\sigma).$$

Similarly, we can define the prefix-free Kolmogorov complexity $K(\sigma \mid \tau)$ of σ given τ and the prefix-free Kolmogorov complexity $K^A(\sigma)$ of σ relative to A as we did for plain complexity. As in the case of plain complexity, the choice of universal prefix-free machine does not affect the definition of K, up to an additive constant.

When M is a prefix-free machine, we will sometimes write K_M instead of C_M.

As we did for plain complexity, we associate a natural number n with its binary representation σ and let $K(n) = K(\sigma)$, and similarly for other notation introduced in the case of plain complexity.

As was the case for plain complexity, we have the following simple but important result.

Proposition 3.5.4. *If $h : 2^{<\omega} \to 2^{<\omega}$ is computable then $K(h(\sigma)) \leqslant K(\sigma) + O(1)$.*

Suppose that $K(\sigma) = n$. Then there is a first string τ of length n such that the computation of $\mathcal{U}(\tau)$ converges with value σ. More precisely, there is a least stage s such that $\mathcal{U}(\tau)[s]\downarrow = \sigma$ for one or more strings τ of length n. We fix the lexicographically least such τ and denote it by σ^*.

One of the most important facts about K is that it can be approximated from above. Specifically, let $K_s(\sigma) = \min\{|\tau| : \mathcal{U}(\tau)[s]\downarrow = \sigma\}$. In other words, $K_s(\sigma)$ is the length of the shortest description of σ provided by $\mathcal{U}$ in at most s many steps. Of course, there may be no such description. However, it will be technically useful to assume that $K_s(\sigma)$ is always defined. It is easy to show that there is a c such that $K(\sigma) \leqslant 2|\sigma| + c$ for all σ. (We will give much better upper bounds below.) Thus, if there is no τ with $\mathcal{U}(\tau)[s]\downarrow = \sigma$, then let $K_s(\sigma) = 2|\sigma| + c$. The important properties of this approximation are that

1. The function $(s, \sigma) \mapsto K_s(\sigma)$ is computable,
2. $K_s(\sigma) \geqslant K_{s+1}(\sigma)$ for all s and σ, and
3. $K(\sigma) = \lim_s K_s(\sigma)$ for all σ.

On the other hand, we have the following fact (which is also true for plain complexity, with the same proof).

Proposition 3.5.5. *There is no partial computable f with unbounded range such that $f(\sigma) \leqslant K(\sigma)$ whenever $f(\sigma)$ is defined.*

Proof. Define a prefix-free machine M as follows. For each k, look for a σ_k such that $f(\sigma_k) \geqslant 2k$ and let $M(0^k1) = \sigma_k$. Then $K(\sigma_k) \leqslant C_M(\sigma_k) + O(1) \leqslant k + O(1) < 2k \leqslant f(\sigma_k) \leqslant K(\sigma_k)$ for all sufficiently large k, which is a contradiction. □

We will develop some further basic properties of prefix-free Kolmogorov complexity after discussing an important indirect way to build prefix-free machines in the next section.

3.6 The KC Theorem

A central tool in building prefix-free machines is an effective interpretation of an inequality of Kraft [213].[5] If $S_0, S_1, \ldots \subset 2^\omega$ are disjoint measurable sets then $\mu(\bigcup_n S_n) = \sum_n \mu(S_n)$, so if $A \subset 2^{<\omega}$ is prefix-free then $\sum_{\sigma\in A} 2^{-|\sigma|} = \mu(\llbracket A \rrbracket) \leqslant 1$. Conversely, suppose that we have a sequence $\{d_i\}_{i\in\omega}$ of natural numbers such that $\sum_i 2^{-d_i} \leqslant 1$. Since we are not arguing effectively, by rearranging the d_i if necessary, we may assume that $d_0 \leqslant d_1 \leqslant d_2 \leqslant \cdots$. Let σ_i be the leftmost string of length d_i that does not extend any σ_j with $j < i$. An easy induction shows that such a string always exists. Thus we see that, for any sequence $\{d_i\}_{i\in\omega}$ of natural numbers such that $\sum_i 2^{-d_i} \leqslant 1$, there is a prefix-free sequence $\{\sigma_i\}_{i\in\omega}$ of strings such that $|\sigma_i| = d_i$ for all i. The KC Theorem is an effectivization of this fact.

Theorem 3.6.1 (KC Theorem, Levin [241], Schnorr [350], Chaitin [58]). *Let $(d_i, \tau_i)_{i\in\omega}$ be a computable sequence of pairs (which we call* requests*), with $d_i \in \mathbb{N}$ and $\tau_i \in 2^{<\omega}$, such that $\sum_i 2^{-d_i} \leqslant 1$. Then there is a prefix-free machine M and strings σ_i of length d_i such that $M(\sigma_i) = \tau_i$ for all i and* $\operatorname{dom} M = \{\sigma_i : i \in \omega\}$. *Furthermore, an index for M can be obtained effectively from an index for our sequence of requests.*

Proof. It is enough to define effectively a prefix-free sequence of strings $\sigma_0, \sigma_1, \ldots$ with $|\sigma_n| = d_n$. The following organizational device is due to Joe Miller. For each n, let $x^n = x_1^n \ldots x_m^n$ be a binary string such that $0.x_1^n \ldots x_m^n = 1 - \sum_{j\leqslant n} 2^{-d_j}$. We will define the σ_n so that the following holds for each n: for each m with $x_m^n = 1$ there is a string μ_m^n of length m so that $S_n = \{\sigma_i : i \leqslant n\} \cup \{\mu_m^n : x_m^n = 1\}$ is prefix-free.

[5]This result is usually known as the *Kraft-Chaitin Theorem*, as it appears in Chaitin [58], but it appeared earlier in Levin's dissertation [241], as stated in Levin [243], where it is proved using Shannon-Fano codes (giving slightly weaker constants). There is also a version of it in Schnorr [350, Lemma 1, p. 380]. In Chaitin [58], where the first proof explicitly done for prefix-free complexity seems to appear, the key idea of that proof is attributed to Nick Pippinger. Thus perhaps we should refer to the theorem by the rather unwieldy name of Kraft-Levin-Schnorr-Pippinger-Chaitin Theorem. Instead, we will refer to it as the KC Theorem. Since it is an effectivization of Kraft's inequality, one should feel free if one wishes to regard the initials as coming from "Kraft's inequality (Computable version)". Recently, some authors such as Nies have referred to this result as the Bounded Request Theorem, and to what we call a KC set as a *bounded request set.*

We begin by letting σ_0 be 0^{d_0}. Notice that $x^0_m = 1$ iff $0 < m \leqslant d_0$, so if we define $\mu^0_m = 0^{m-1}1$, then $\{\sigma_0\} \cup \{\mu^0_m : x^0_m = 1\}$ is prefix-free.

Now assume we have defined $\sigma_0, \ldots, \sigma_n$ and μ^n_m for $x^n_m = 1$ so that $S_n = \{\sigma_i : i \leqslant n\} \cup \{\mu^n_m : x^n_m = 1\}$ is prefix-free.

If $x^n_{d_{n+1}} = 1$ then x^{n+1} is the same as x^n except that $x^{n+1}_{d_{n+1}} = 0$. So we can let $\sigma_{n+1} = \mu^n_{d_{n+1}}$ and $\mu^{n+1}_m = \mu^n_m$ for all $m \neq d_{n+1}$, and then $S_{n+1} = \{\sigma_i : i \leqslant n+1\} \cup \{\mu^{n+1}_m : x^{n+1}_m = 1\}$ is equal to S_n, and hence is prefix-free.

Otherwise, find the largest $j < d_{n+1}$ such that $x^n_j = 1$. Such a j must exist since otherwise $1 - \sum_{j \leqslant n} 2^{-d_j} < 2^{-d_{n+1}}$, which would mean that $\sum_{j \leqslant n+1} 2^{-d_j} > 1$. In this case x^{n+1} is the same as x^n except for positions $j, \ldots, d_{n+1}$, where we have $x^{n+1}_j = 0$ and $x^{n+1}_m = 1$ for $j < m \leqslant d_{n+1}$. Let $\sigma_{n+1} = \mu^n_j 0^{d_{n+1}-j}$. For $m < j$ or $m > d_{n+1}$, let $\mu^{n+1}_m = \mu^n_m$, and for $j < m \leqslant d_{n+1}$, let $\mu^{n+1}_m = \mu^n_j 0^{m-j-1}1$. Then $S_{n+1} = \{\sigma_i : i \leqslant n+1\} \cup \{\mu^{n+1}_m : x^{n+1}_m = 1\}$ is the same as S_n except that μ^n_j is replaced by a pairwise incomparable set of superstrings of μ^n_j. This fact clearly ensures that S_{n+1} is prefix-free.

This completes the definition of the σ_i. Each finite subset of $\{\sigma_0, \sigma_1, \ldots\}$ is contained in some S_n, and hence is prefix-free. Thus the whole set is prefix-free. Since the σ_i are chosen effectively, we can define a prefix-free machine M by letting $M(\sigma_i) = \tau_i$ for each i. □

The *weight* of a request (d, τ) is $2^{-|\tau|}$. The *weight* of a computable sequence of requests $(d_i, \tau_i)_{i \in \omega}$ is the sum of the weights of the requests, i.e., $\sum_i 2^{-d_i}$. If this weight is less than or equal to 1, then we say that this sequence is a *KC set*. The beauty of using the KC Theorem to define a prefix-free machine is that we need only build a KC set, issuing requests and ensuring that the weight is kept less than or equal to 1; the prefix-free machine itself is built implicitly for us.

The following is a very useful immediate consequence of the KC Theorem. (Recall that we denote the measure of $A \subseteq 2^\omega$ by $\mu(A)$.)

Corollary 3.6.2. *Let $(d_i, \tau_i)_{i \in \omega}$ be a KC set. Then $K(\tau_i) \leqslant d_i + O(1)$.*

Proof. Let M be as in the KC Theorem. Then $K(\tau_i) \leqslant K_M(\tau_i) + O(1) \leqslant d_i + O(1)$. □

If a computable sequence of requests $(d_i, \tau_i)_{i \in \omega}$ has finite weight, then there is a c such that $(d_i + c, \tau_i)_{i \in \omega}$ has weight less than or equal to 1, and hence is a KC set. Thus Corollary 3.6.2 still holds for such a sequence. We will sometimes abuse terminology and refer to such a sequence as a KC set.

A simple application of the KC Theorem is the following. Let $\tau_0, \tau_1, \ldots$ be an effective enumeration of $2^{<\omega}$, with τ_0 being the empty string. Let

$d_0 = 2$ and for $i > 0$ let $d_i = |\tau_i| + 2\log|\tau_i| + 3$. Then

$$\sum_i 2^{-d_i} \leqslant \frac{1}{4} + \sum_{i>0} \frac{2^{-|\tau_i|}}{3|\tau_i|^2} = \frac{1}{4} + \sum_{n>0} 2^n \frac{2^{-n}}{3n^2} = \frac{1}{4} + \frac{1}{3}\sum_{n>0}\frac{1}{n^2} < 1.$$

Thus $\{(d_i, \tau_i)\}_{i\in\omega}$ is a KC set, so we have the following upper bound on $K(\tau)$, which we will improve on in Theorem 3.7.4 below.

Proposition 3.6.3. $K(\tau) \leqslant |\tau| + 2\log|\tau| + O(1)$.

The following is another useful application of the KC Theorem.

Proposition 3.6.4. *Let $A_0, A_1, \ldots \subset 2^{<\omega}$ be nonempty, pairwise disjoint, and uniformly c.e. Then $K(n) \leqslant -\log \sum_{\sigma\in A_n} 2^{-|\sigma|} + O(1)$.*

Proof. Let $f(n) = \sum_{\sigma\in A_n} 2^{-|\sigma|}$ and $f(n,s) = \sum_{\sigma\in A_{n,s}} 2^{-|\sigma|}$, where $A_{n,s}$ is the stage s approximation to A_n. Note that because the A_n are pairwise disjoint, $\sum_n f(n) \leqslant 1$.

Build a KC set L as follows. For each n and k, if there is an s such that $f(n,s) \geqslant 2^{-k}$, then enumerate a request $(k+1, n)$ into L. The weight of L is bounded by

$$\sum_n \sum_{k\leqslant -\log f(n)} 2^{-(k+1)} \leqslant \sum_n f(n) \leqslant 1,$$

so L is indeed a KC set.

For each n there is an s such that $f(n,s) \geqslant \frac{f(n)}{2}$, so L contains a request $(k+1, n)$ with $k \leqslant -\log f(n) + 1$, which implies, by Corollary 3.6.2, that $K(n) \leqslant -\log f(n) + O(1)$. ☐

Corollary 3.6.5. *Let $C_0, C_1, \ldots$ be nonempty, pairwise disjoint uniformly Σ^0_1 classes. Then $K(n) \leqslant -\log \mu(C_n) + O(1)$.*

Corollary 3.6.6. *Let $B_0, B_1, \ldots \subseteq 2^{<\omega}$ be nonempty, pairwise disjoint, and uniformly c.e. Then $K(n) \leqslant -\log \sum_{\tau\in B_n} 2^{-K(\tau)} + O(1)$.*

Proof. Let $A_n = \{\sigma : \mathcal{U}(\sigma) \in B_n\}$. The A_n are nonempty, pairwise disjoint, and uniformly c.e. Since $\tau^* \in A_n$ for all $\tau \in B_n$,

$$K(n) \leqslant -\log \sum_{\sigma\in A_n} 2^{-|\sigma|} + O(1) \leqslant -\log \sum_{\tau\in B_n} 2^{-|\tau^*|} + O(1)$$
$$= -\log \sum_{\tau\in B_n} 2^{-K(\tau)} + O(1).$$

☐

One technique that we will employ several times is to build a KC set and assume, by the recursion theorem, that we have an index for the corresponding prefix-free machine. The legitimacy of this assumption requires a brief comment. It is certainly the case that, when we enumerate a c.e. set of requests L, we can use the recursion theorem to assume that we have an index for L. If L is a KC set, then the KC Theorem tells us that from this index we can effectively pass to an index for the corresponding prefix-free machine. But if L is not a KC set, then there is no corresponding machine, so we have a problem unless we can ensure that our construction always builds a KC set, regardless of the parameter it is provided. Fortunately, this issue is easily bypassed. Whenever we say that we are building a KC set L using the recursion theorem, we have an additional unstated rule that if we ever wish to add a request to L that would drive its weight above 1, we do not do so, and immediately halt the construction. A construction with this rule always produces a KC set, no matter what the parameter, and in the constructions below, we will always implicitly show that the construction never halts if provided with the correct parameter (i.e., with an index for the machine corresponding to the KC set it builds).

3.7 Basic properties of prefix-free complexity

We begin with the following simple but quite fundamental result.

Proposition 3.7.1. $\sum_{\sigma \in 2^{<\omega}} 2^{-K(\sigma)} \leqslant 1$.

Proof. Since $\mathcal{U}$ is prefix-free, $\sum_{\sigma \in 2^{<\omega}} 2^{-K(\sigma)} < \sum_{\tau \in \operatorname{dom} \mathcal{U}} 2^{-|\tau|} \leqslant 1$. □

We now show that the upper bound in Proposition 3.6.3 cannot be improved too much.

Proposition 3.7.2. *For any d, there are σ with $K(\sigma) > |\sigma| + \log |\sigma| + d$.*

Proof. Suppose that $K(\sigma) \leqslant |\sigma| + \log |\sigma| + d$ for all σ. Then

$$\sum_{\sigma} 2^{-K(\sigma)} \geqslant \sum_{|\sigma|>0} \frac{2^{-|\sigma|-d}}{|\sigma|} = \sum_{n>0} 2^n \frac{2^{-n-d}}{n} = 2^{-d} \sum_{n>0} \frac{1}{n} = \infty,$$

contradicting Proposition 3.7.1. □

In fact, the argument in the above proof shows the following.

Corollary 3.7.3. *Let $f : 2^{<\omega} \to \mathbb{N}$ be such that $\sum_{\sigma \in 2^{<\omega}} 2^{-f(\sigma)} = \infty$. Then $K(\sigma) > |\sigma| + f(|\sigma|)$ for infinitely many σ.*

The most precise bound on $K(\sigma)$ is given by the following result.

Theorem 3.7.4 (Chaitin [58]). $K(\sigma) \leqslant |\sigma| + K(|\sigma|) + O(1)$.

Proof. Consider the prefix-free machine M that, on input μ, searches for strings σ and τ such that $\mu = \tau\sigma$ and $\mathcal{U}(\tau)\downarrow = |\sigma|$, and, if such a pair is found, outputs σ. Note that, since $\mathcal{U}$ is prefix-free, there can be at most one such pair σ, τ for any given μ. Furthermore, it is easy to check that M

is prefix-free. Thus, letting ν_σ be a minimal-length $\mathcal{U}$-program for $|\sigma|$, we have

$$K(\sigma) \leqslant C_M(\sigma) + O(1) = |\nu_\sigma| + |\sigma| + O(1) = K(|\sigma|) + |\sigma| + O(1).$$

□

This result immediately gives us the bound of Proposition 3.6.3, but we can do better by proceeding iteratively. That is, letting $||\sigma||$ be the length of the binary representation of $|\sigma|$, we have $K(\sigma) \leqslant |\sigma| + ||\sigma|| + K(||\sigma||) + O(1) \leqslant |\sigma| + \log|\sigma| + 2\log\log|\sigma| + O(1)$. Continuing in this way, we have the following.

Corollary 3.7.5. *For any k and $\varepsilon > 0$, we have $K(\sigma) \leqslant |\sigma| + \log|\sigma| + \log\log|\sigma| + \cdots + (1+\varepsilon)\log^{(k)}|\sigma| + O(1)$.*

Chaitin [58] showed that the bound given in Theorem 3.7.4 is tight, as part of the following result.

Theorem 3.7.6 (Counting Theorem, Chaitin [58]).

(i) $\max\{K(\sigma) : |\sigma| = n\} = n + K(n) \pm O(1)$.

(ii) $|\{\sigma : |\sigma| = n \wedge K(\sigma) \leqslant n + K(n) - r\}| \leqslant 2^{n-r+O(1)}$, *where the constant does not depend on n and r.*

Of course, part (i) of the Counting Theorem follows from part (ii). The most elegant way to prove part (ii) was given by Chaitin [63], and works by way of the minimality of K as an information content measure, as we now explain. The concept of information content measure is more or less the same as the earlier one of *computably enumerable discrete semimeasure*, introduced by Levin [243], as we will see in Section 3.9.

Definition 3.7.7 (Chaitin [63], after Levin [243]). An *information content measure (i.c.m.)* is a partial function $F : 2^{<\omega} \to \mathbb{N}$ such that

1. $\sum_{F(\sigma)\downarrow} 2^{-F(\sigma)} \leqslant 1$ and
2. $\{(\sigma, k) : F(\sigma) \leqslant k\}$ is c.e.

Notice that K is an information content measure.

As with prefix-free machines, we can enumerate the information content measures as $F_0, F_1, \ldots$ in such a way that the corresponding sets given in item 2 of Definition 3.7.7 are uniformly c.e. We can then define a *minimal information content measure*

$$\widehat{K}(\sigma) = \min_{F_k(\sigma)\downarrow}\{F_k(\sigma) + k + 1\}.$$

It is easy to check that $\widehat{K}$ is indeed an information content measure, and that it is minimal in the sense that, for any information content measure F, we have $\widehat{K}(\sigma) \leqslant F(\sigma) + O(1)$ for $\sigma \in \operatorname{dom} F$. In particular, $\widehat{K}(\sigma) \leqslant K(\sigma) + O(1)$.

On the other hand, we can easily translate information content measures to prefix-free machines, using the KC Theorem. That is, given an information content measure F, the set $\{(k+1,\sigma) : F(\sigma) \leqslant k\}$ is a KC set, so there is a prefix-free machine M such that for each σ there is a τ of length $F(\sigma)+1$ with $M(\tau) = \sigma$. In particular, this fact holds for $F = \widehat{K}$, so $K(\sigma) \leqslant \widehat{K}(\sigma) + O(1)$. Thus we see that K and $\widehat{K}$ are the same up to an additive constant, and so we will henceforth identify K and $\widehat{K}$ without further comment. We note the result we have just proved for future reference.

Theorem 3.7.8 (Chaitin [63]). *Let F be an information content measure. Then $K(\sigma) \leqslant F(\sigma) + O(1)$ for $\sigma \in \operatorname{dom} F$.*

Chaitin found some clever proofs exploiting the minimality of K. Before turning to the proof of the Counting Theorem, we give an example, Chaitin's proof of Theorem 3.7.4. Since

$$\sum_{\sigma} 2^{-(|\sigma|+K(|\sigma|))} = \sum_{n} 2^{n} 2^{-(n+K(n))} = \sum_{n} 2^{-K(n)} \leqslant 1,$$

the map $\sigma \mapsto |\sigma| + K(|\sigma|)$ is an information content measure, so $K(\sigma) \leqslant |\sigma| + K(|\sigma|) + O(1)$ by the minimality of K.

Proof of Theorem 3.7.6. As mentioned above, it is enough to prove part (ii). Let $F(n) = \lceil -\log(\sum_{\sigma\in 2^n} 2^{-K(\sigma)})\rceil$. Then

$$\sum_{n} 2^{-F(n)} \leqslant \sum_{n} \sum_{\sigma\in 2^n} 2^{-K(\sigma)} = \sum_{\sigma\in 2^{<\omega}} 2^{-K(\sigma)} \leqslant 1,$$

and $\{(n,k) : F(n) \leqslant k\}$ is c.e. Thus F is an information content measure. (Here we are thinking of n as a binary string by identifying it with its binary representation.) So, by the minimality of K, there are c and $\varepsilon > 0$ such that

$$2^{-K(n)} \geqslant 2^{-F(n)-c} = \varepsilon \sum_{\sigma\in 2^n} 2^{-K(\sigma)}.$$

Now suppose that there are more than $2^{n-r+O(1)}$ strings of length n with $K(\sigma) \leqslant n + K(n) - r$. In other words, suppose that there exists an unbounded binary function f such that, for

$$S_{n,r} = \{\sigma \in 2^n : K(\sigma) \leqslant n + K(n) - r\},$$

we have $|S_{n,r}| \geqslant f(n,r)2^{n-r}$ for all n and r. Then for each n and r,

$$\begin{aligned} 2^{-K(n)} &\geqslant \varepsilon \sum_{\sigma\in 2^n} 2^{-K(\sigma)} \geqslant \varepsilon \sum_{\sigma\in S_{n,r}} 2^{-K(\sigma)} \\ &\geqslant \varepsilon f(n,r) 2^{n-r} 2^{-n-K(n)+r} = \varepsilon f(n,r) 2^{-K(n)}. \end{aligned}$$

Since $f(n,r)$ is unbounded, we have a contradiction.[6] □

Notice that the proof above also establishes the following.

Corollary 3.7.9 (Chaitin [63]). *There is a constant c such that $2^{-K(n)+c} \geqslant \sum_{\sigma \in 2^n} 2^{-K(\sigma)}$ for all n.*

Miller and Yu [279] gave an extension of the Counting Theorem, though for all applications the authors are aware of, the original counting theorem suffices.

Theorem 3.7.10 (Miller and Yu [279]). $|\{\sigma \in 2^n : K(\sigma) < n + K(n) - m\}| \leqslant 2^{n-m-K(m|n^*)+O(1)}$.

Proof. Let c be as in Corollary 3.7.9 and define

$$\widehat{K}(m \mid \tau) = \begin{cases} n + c - m - \log(|\{\sigma \in 2^n : K(\sigma) < n + |\tau| - m\}|) & \text{if } U(\tau)\downarrow = n \\ \infty & \text{otherwise.} \end{cases}$$

Note that $\{(k,m) : \widehat{K}(m \mid \tau) < k\}$ is c.e., uniformly in τ. Furthermore,

$$\begin{aligned} \sum_m 2^{-\widehat{K}(m|n^*)} &= 2^{-n-c} \sum_m 2^m |\{\sigma \in 2^n : K(\sigma) < n + K(n) - m\}| \\ &= 2^{-n-c} \sum_{\sigma \in 2^n} \sum_{m < n+K(n)-K(\sigma)} 2^m \leqslant 2^{-n-c} \sum_{\sigma \in 2^n} 2^{n+K(n)-K(\sigma)} \\ &= 2^{K(n)-c} \sum_{\sigma \in 2^n} 2^{-K(\sigma)} \leqslant 1, \end{aligned}$$

where the last inequality follows from Corollary 3.7.9. Therefore, there is a d such that $\forall n \, \forall m \, (K(m \mid n^*) \leqslant \widehat{K}(m \mid n^*) + d)$. So for all n and m,

$$2^{-K(m|n^*)} \geqslant 2^{-\widehat{K}(m|n^*)-d} = 2^{-n+m-c-d} \, |\{\sigma \in 2^n : K(\sigma) < n+K(n)-m\}|.$$

Multiplying both sides by $2^{n-m+c+d}$ completes the proof. □

Miller and Yu [279] showed that their Improved Counting Theorem is tight up to a multiplicative constant.

Theorem 3.7.11 (Miller and Yu [279]). $|\{\sigma \in 2^n : K(\sigma) < n + K(n) - m\}| \geqslant 2^{n-m-K(m|n^*)-O(1)}$.

To prove this theorem, we need the following lemma.

[6] It would also be possible to prove this result using the KC Theorem. The key step in the above proof is showing that $2^{-K(n)} \geqslant O(\sum_{\sigma \in 2^n} 2^{-K(\sigma)})$. We can do this by monitoring $\lceil -\log(\sum_{\sigma \in 2^n} 2^{-K(\sigma)}) \rceil$, and each time this value drops to a new low p, enumerating a KC request (p, n). The details are straightforward.

Lemma 3.7.12. *There is a c such that if* $\delta \in 2^n$ *ends in at least* $m+K(m \mid n^*)+c$ *many zeroes, then* $K(\delta) < n + K(n) - m$.

Proof. We define a prefix-free machine M. By the recursion theorem, we may assume that we know in advance the prefix ρ by which our universal prefix-free machine U simulates M. Let $c = |\rho| + 1$. The domain of M consists of strings $\sigma\tau\nu$ for which there are $n, m \in \omega$ with $|\nu| = n-m-|\tau|-c$ such that $U(\sigma)\downarrow = n$ and $U(\tau \mid \sigma)\downarrow = m$. Note that the set of all such strings is prefix-free. For $\sigma\tau\nu$ and n, m as above, define $M(\sigma\tau\nu) = \nu 0^{n-|\nu|}$.

Now fix $n, m \in \omega$ and let $\delta = \nu 0^{m+K(m|n^*)+c}$ be a string of length n. Let $\sigma = n^*$ and let τ be a minimal program for m given n^*. Note that $|\nu| = n - m - |\tau| - c$, so we have $M(\sigma\tau\nu) = \nu 0^{n-|\nu|} = \delta$. Therefore, $K(\delta) \leqslant |\sigma\tau\nu|+c-1 = K(n)+|\tau|+(n-m-|\tau|-c)+c-1 = n+K(n)-m-1$, as required. □

Proof of Theorem 3.7.11. Let c be the constant from Lemma 3.7.12. That lemma guarantees that there are $2^{n-m-K(m|n^*)-c}$ many distinct strings of length n with complexity less than $n + K(n) - m$ (assuming that $n - m - K(m \mid n^*) - c \geqslant 0$). □

Thus we see that in certain aspects, such as upper bounds, prefix-free complexity is more difficult to deal with than plain complexity. There are trade-offs, however, in that prefix-free complexity simplifies certain results, such as the following (cf. the discussion beginning in the paragraph before Theorem 3.1.4).

Proposition 3.7.13. $K(\sigma\tau) \leqslant K(\sigma, \tau) \leqslant K(\sigma) + K(\tau) + O(1)$.

This property of prefix-free complexity is known as *subadditivity*. Proving that it holds is not difficult, but can be a useful exercise. For this and similar facts about prefix-free complexity, see Li and Vitányi [248] or Fortnow [148]. We will sharpen the estimate of Proposition 3.7.13 when we consider symmetry of information in Theorem 3.10.2.

3.8 Prefix-free randomness of strings

There are two possibilities for defining prefix-free randomness of strings. One is to regard σ as random if it is random relative to $\mathcal{U}$ in the sense of Section 3.1, that is, if $K(\sigma) \geqslant |\sigma|$. As with C-randomness, we relax this condition a bit by choosing a constant d and calling σ *weakly K-random* if $K(\sigma) \geqslant |\sigma| - d$.

The other possibility is to regard σ as random if its shortest description is essentially as large as possible, that is, if for a fixed d, we have $K(\sigma) \geqslant |\sigma| + K(|\sigma|) - d$. We call such σ *strongly K-random*.

We will see below that there is a real difference between these two notions of prefix-free randomness. Since every prefix-free machine is a plain machine, every C-random string is weakly K-random for some choice of constant. The converse is definitely not true. In fact, in Corollary 6.6.5, we will see that there are infinitely many strings σ such that $K(\sigma) \geqslant |\sigma|$ but $C(\sigma) \leqslant |\sigma| - \log|\sigma|$. On the other hand, in Corollary 4.3.3 we will see that every strongly K-random string is C-random for some choice of constant.

3.9 The Coding Theorem and discrete semimeasures

Chaitin's information content measures are more or less the same as the computably enumerable discrete semimeasures introduced by Levin [243] (see also Gács [164]), and in a sense Solomonoff [369].

Definition 3.9.1 (Levin [243] (see also Gács [164]), Solomonoff [369]). A *discrete semimeasure* is a function $m : 2^{<\omega} \to \mathbb{R}^{\geqslant 0}$ such that $\sum_{\sigma \in 2^{<\omega}} m(\sigma) \leqslant 1$.

A discrete semimeasure m is *computably enumerable* if it is approximable from below; that is, there are uniformly computable functions $m_s : 2^{<\omega} \to \mathbb{Q}$ such that for all s and σ we have $m_{s+1}(\sigma) \geqslant m_s(\sigma)$ and $\lim_s m_s(\sigma) = m(\sigma)$.[7]

A c.e. discrete semimeasure m is *maximal* if $m(\sigma) \geqslant O(\widehat{m}(\sigma))$ for each c.e. discrete semimeasure $\widehat{m}$.

Theorem 3.9.2 (Levin [243]). *There is a maximal c.e. discrete semimeasure.*

Proof. It is not hard to see that there is an effective enumeration $m_0, m_1, \ldots$ of the c.e. discrete semimeasures, and that $m(\sigma) = \sum_n 2^{-n} m_n(\sigma)$ is a maximal c.e. discrete semimeasure. □

The Coding Theorem, due to Levin [241, 243] and Chaitin [58] (and in a sense Solomonoff [369]), relates prefix-free Kolmogorov complexity and maximal c.e. discrete semimeasures. We present it in a stronger form, which also involves the probability that $\mathcal{U}$ outputs a given string. Fix a maximal c.e. discrete semimeasure m.

Definition 3.9.3. For a prefix-free machine M, let $Q_M(\sigma) = \mu([\![\{\tau : M(\tau)\downarrow = \sigma\}]\!])$. That is, $Q_M(\sigma)$ is the probability that M outputs σ. We write $Q(\sigma)$ for $Q_{\mathcal{U}}(\sigma)$.

Theorem 3.9.4 (Coding Theorem, Solomonoff [369], Levin [241, 243], Chaitin [58], see also Gács [164]). $K(\sigma) = -\log m(\sigma) \pm O(1) = -\log Q(\sigma) \pm O(1)$.

[7] In the terminology of Definition 5.2.1 below, a discrete semimeasure is c.e. if it is c.e. as a function.

Proof. The function Q is a c.e. discrete semimeasure, so $m(\sigma) \geqslant O(Q(\sigma))$, whence $-\log m(\sigma) \leqslant -\log Q(\sigma)$. Since $\mathcal{U}(\sigma^*) = \sigma$, we have $Q(\sigma) \geqslant 2^{-|\sigma^*|} = 2^{-K(\sigma)}$, so $-\log Q(\sigma) \leqslant K(\sigma)$. Finally, $\lceil -\log m(\sigma) \rceil$ is an information content measure, so $K(\sigma) \leqslant \lceil -\log m(\sigma) \rceil + O(1) \leqslant -\log m(\sigma) + O(1)$.[8] □

One informal interpretation of the Coding Theorem is that if a string has many long descriptions then it also has a short description.

3.10 Prefix-free symmetry of information

As with plain complexity, we can explore the notion of symmetry of information for prefix-free Kolmogorov complexity. In the same spirit as for C, we may define the *prefix-free information content* of τ in σ as

$$I_K(\sigma : \tau) = K(\tau) - K(\tau \mid \sigma).$$

For the rest of the section, we will drop the subscript K from I_K.

First note that the results of Section 3.3 hold for K in place of C, since K and C agree up to a log factor. In addition, we have the following.

Theorem 3.10.1 (Symmetry of Information, Levin and Gács [164], Chaitin [58]). $I(\langle\sigma, K(\sigma)\rangle : \tau) = I(\langle\tau, K(\tau)\rangle : \sigma) \pm O(1)$.

Note that given the relationship $K(\rho, K(\rho)) = K(\rho^*) \pm O(1)$, the Symmetry of Information Theorem for prefix-free complexity may be neatly rewritten as

$$I(\sigma^* : \tau) = I(\tau^* : \sigma).$$

As with the C case, the Symmetry of Information Theorem follows from a reformulated version.

Theorem 3.10.2 (Symmetry of Information, Restated). $K(\sigma, \tau) = K(\sigma) + K(\tau \mid \sigma, K(\sigma)) \pm O(1) = K(\sigma) + K(\tau \mid \sigma^*) \pm O(1)$.

Theorem 3.10.2 gives us Theorem 3.10.1 as follows:

$$\begin{aligned} K(\sigma) + K(\tau \mid \sigma, K(\sigma)) &= K(\sigma, \tau) \pm O(1) \\ &= K(\tau, \sigma) \pm O(1) = K(\tau) + K(\sigma \mid \tau, K(\tau)) \pm O(1), \end{aligned}$$

and hence,

$$K(\tau) - K(\tau \mid \sigma, K(\sigma)) = K(\sigma) - K(\sigma \mid \tau, K(\tau)) \pm O(1).$$

We now turn to the proof of Theorem 3.10.2.

[8] Technically, $\lceil -\log m(\sigma) \rceil$ may not quite be an i.c.m., since we might not have $\lim_s \lceil -\log m_s(\sigma) \rceil = \lceil -\log m(\sigma) \rceil$ if $-\log m(\sigma)$ is an integer. But the function that takes σ to $1 + \lim_s \lceil -\log m_s(\sigma) \rceil$ is an i.c.m., and is within $O(1)$ of $-\log m(\sigma)$.

Proof of Theorem 3.10.2. The second equality is clear, so it is enough to show that $K(\sigma,\tau)=K(\sigma)+K(\tau\mid\sigma^*)\pm O(1)$.

We first prove that

$$K(\sigma,\tau)\leqslant K(\sigma)+K(\tau\mid\sigma^*)+O(1).$$

Let ρ be a minimal length description of τ given σ^*. Then we can construct a prefix-free machine M that, on input $\sigma^*\rho$, first computes σ from σ^*, then computes τ from σ^* and ρ, and finally outputs $\langle\sigma,\tau\rangle$.

We now prove that

$$K(\sigma,\tau)\geqslant K(\sigma)+K(\tau\mid\sigma^*)-O(1).$$

To do this, we prove that

$$K(\tau\mid\sigma^*)\leqslant K(\sigma,\tau)-K(\sigma)+O(1).$$

Let $\nu_0,\nu_1,\dots$ be a computable ordering of the domain of $\mathcal{U}$ and let σ_s and τ_s be such that $\nu_s=\langle\sigma_s,\tau_s\rangle$. Let $W_\sigma=\{s:\sigma_s=\sigma\}$. Given n and σ, build a KC set by enumerating requests $(|\nu_s|-n,\tau_s)$ for $s\in W_\sigma$, as long as the weight of these requests does not exceed 1. Call the resulting prefix-free machine $M_{n,\sigma}$.

By the Coding Theorem 3.9.4, there is a constant c such that

$$2^{K(\sigma)-c}\sum_\tau Q(\langle\sigma,\tau\rangle)\leqslant 1$$

for all σ, where Q is as in Definition 3.9.3. (To see this, consider the machine V that has $V(\nu)=\sigma$ whenever $\mathcal{U}(\nu)=\langle\sigma,\tau\rangle$ for some τ. Then $Q_V(\sigma)=\sum_\tau Q(\langle\sigma,\tau\rangle)$, so $\sum_\tau Q(\langle\sigma,\tau\rangle)\leqslant Q(\sigma)+O(1)$.) Since

$$\sum_{s\in W_\sigma}2^{-(|\nu_s|-|\sigma^*|+c)}=2^{K(\sigma)-c}\sum_\tau Q(\langle\sigma,\tau\rangle)\leqslant 1,$$

all relevant requests will be enumerated for the machine $M_{K(\sigma)-c,\sigma}$.

Now define the oracle prefix-free machine M as follows. With ρ on the oracle tape, M first looks for a σ such that $\mathcal{U}(\rho)=\sigma$. Then it simulates $M_{|\rho|-c,\sigma}$.

If M has σ^* on its oracle tape, then it will simulate $M_{K(\sigma)-c,\sigma}$. Since there is an $s\in W_\sigma$ such that $\nu_s=\langle\sigma,\tau\rangle^*$, the KC set defining this machine has as one of its requests $(K(\sigma,\tau)-K(\sigma)+c,\tau)$, so

$$K(\tau\mid\sigma^*)\leqslant K_M(\tau\mid\sigma^*)\leqslant K(\sigma,\tau)-K(\sigma)+O(1).$$

□

It is sometimes useful to apply symmetry of information to $\sigma\tau$ rather than $\langle\sigma,\tau\rangle$. By Theorem 3.10.2, $K(\sigma,\tau)=K(\sigma,\sigma\tau)\pm O(1)=K(\sigma\tau)+K(\sigma\mid(\sigma\tau)^*)\pm O(1)$, so we have the following.

Corollary 3.10.3. $K(\sigma\tau)=K(\sigma,\tau)-K(\sigma\mid(\sigma\tau)^*)\pm O(1)=K(\sigma)+K(\sigma\mid\tau^*)-K(\sigma\mid(\sigma\tau)^*)\pm O(1)$.

A similar result holds for C in place of K.

We finish this section with a useful "mixed" theorem for the complexity of $\sigma\tau$, relating C and K in the spirit of Chapter 4.

Proposition 3.10.4 (Folklore, see [308]). $C(\sigma\tau) \leqslant K(\sigma) + C(\tau) + O(1)$.

Proof. Let $\mathcal{V}$ be a universal plain machine. Define a plain machine M as follows. On input ρ, look for ρ_0 and ρ_1 such that $\rho_0\rho_1 = \rho$ and both $\mathcal{U}(\rho_0)\downarrow$ and $\mathcal{V}(\rho_1)\downarrow$. If found, then output $\mathcal{U}(\rho_0)\mathcal{V}(\rho_1)$. Then $C(\sigma\tau) \leqslant C_M(\sigma\tau) + O(1) \leqslant K(\sigma) + C(\tau) + O(1)$. □

3.11 Initial segment complexity of sets

It follows from Theorem 3.1.4 that there is no set A such that $C(A \upharpoonright n) \geqslant n - O(1)$. Recall that the idea of the proof of Theorem 3.1.4 was to take a string $\sigma\tau$ such that the length of τ codes σ, and use τ alone to describe $\sigma\tau$. This reasoning is refined in the following results of Martin-Löf [260], the proofs here being drawn from Li and Vitányi [248].

Lemma 3.11.1 (Martin-Löf [260], see Li and Vitányi [248] and Staiger [376]). *Let f be a computable function such that $\sum_n 2^{-f(n)} = \infty$. Then for any set A there are infinitely many n such that $C(A \upharpoonright n \mid n) \leqslant n - f(n)$.*

Proof. Let g be a computable function such that $\sum_n 2^{-g(n)} = \infty$ and $\lim_n g(n) - f(n) = \infty$. It is easy to see that such a function must exist. Let $G(n) = \sum_{i \leqslant n} 2^{-g(n)}$. Think of $[0, 1]$ as a circle with 0 and 1 identified and let I_n be the interval $[G(n), G(n+1))$ mod 1 on this circle. Let $C_n = \{\sigma \in 2^n : [\![\sigma]\!] \cap I_n \neq \emptyset\}$, where we think of $[\![\sigma]\!]$ as a subset of $[0, 1]$. Note that the C_n are uniformly computable and $|C_n| \leqslant 2^n(G(n+1) - G(n))$.

Thinking of A as a real, there are infinitely many n such that $A \in I_n$, since $\lim_n G(n) = \infty$. Thus there are infinitely many n such that $A \upharpoonright n \in C_n$. Given n, we can describe any element of C_n by its position in C_n, ordered lexicographically. Thus there are infinitely many n such that

$$C(A \upharpoonright n \mid n) \leqslant \log |C_n| + O(1) \leqslant \log(2^n(G(n+1) - G(n))) + O(1)$$
$$= n - g(n) + O(1).$$

For all such n that are sufficiently large, $C(A \upharpoonright n \mid n) \leqslant n - f(n)$. □

Theorem 3.11.2 (Li and Vitányi [248], after Martin-Löf [260]). *Let f be a computable function such that $\sum_n 2^{-f(n)} = \infty$ and $C(n \mid n - f(n)) = O(1)$. Then for any set A there are infinitely many n such that $C(A \upharpoonright n) \leqslant n - f(n)$.*

Proof. It is enough to show that there are infinitely many n such that $C(A \upharpoonright n) \leqslant n - f(n) + O(1)$, where the constant term does not depend on f, because if f satisfies the hypotheses of the theorem, then so does $n \mapsto f(n) - c$ for any constant c.

Let σ_n be a minimal length $\mathcal{U}^n$-program from $A \upharpoonright n$. Let τ_n be a minimal length $\mathcal{U}^{n-f(n)}$-program for n, and let t_n be the position of τ_n in a fixed effective list of finite strings. Let $\mu_n = 1^{t_n}0\sigma_n$. By Lemma 3.11.1, there are infinitely many n such that $|\sigma_n| \leqslant n - f(n)$. Since t_n is bounded, there is a constant c and infinitely many n such that $|\mu_n| \leqslant n - f(n) + c$. For such n, let $\nu_n = 0^{n-f(n)+c-|\mu_n|}\mu_n$. Then $|\nu_n| = n - f(n) + c$.

We can now easily define a Turing machine, which does not depend on f, that on input ν_n first obtains $n - f(n)$ from $|\nu_n|$, then decodes τ_n and obtains n, then decodes σ_n and obtains $A \upharpoonright n$. Thus there are infinitely many n such that $C(A \upharpoonright n) \leqslant |\nu_n| + O(1) = n - f(n) + O(1)$, where the constant term does not depend on f. □

Corollary 3.11.3. *For any set A there are infinitely many n such that $C(A \upharpoonright n) \leqslant n - \log n$.*

Proof. The function $n - \log n \mapsto n$ is computable, so $C(n \mid n - \log n) = O(1)$. Furthermore, $\sum_n 2^{-\log n} = \infty$, so we can apply Theorem 3.11.2. □

There has been much work on C-complexity oscillations related to the above results. See Li and Vitányi [248, page 138] for more on this topic.

The following is a prefix-free analog of the above results.

Theorem 3.11.4 (after Solovay [371]). *If g is computable and $\sum_n 2^{-g(n)} = \infty$, then for every set X there are infinitely many n such that $K(X \upharpoonright n) \leqslant n + K(n) - g(n) + O(1)$.*

Proof. Let $I_0, I_1, \ldots \subset \mathbb{N}$ be a uniformly computable sequence of pairwise disjoint finite sets such that $\sum_{n \in I_j} 2^{-g(n)} \geqslant 1$ for all n. Let $m_j = \max\{g(n) : n \in I_j\}$. Effectively split 2^{m_j} into (not necessarily pairwise disjoint) sets S_n^j for $n \in I_j$ so that $|S_n^j| = 2^{m_j - g(n)}$ and every element of 2^{m_j} is in at least one S_n^j. For a given X and j, let n be such that X extends a string in S_n^j. Then we can describe $X \upharpoonright n$ given n by specifying which of the $2^{m_j - g(n)}$ many strings in S_n^j is extended by X, and then giving $X \upharpoonright [m_j, n)$. Thus $K(X \upharpoonright n \mid n) \leqslant m_j - g(n) + n - m_j + O(1) = n - g(n) + O(1)$, and hence $K(X \upharpoonright n) \leqslant n + K(n) - g(n) + O(1)$. □

3.12 Computable bounds for prefix-free complexity

Ignoring additive constants, we have seen that for plain complexity, there is a computable upper bound on $C(\sigma)$, namely $|\sigma|$, that is achieved infinitely often. The analogous bound on $K(\sigma)$, however, is $|\sigma| + K(|\sigma|)$, which is not computable, and approximations to this bound, such as $|\sigma| + 2\log|\sigma|$ or $|\sigma| + \log|\sigma| + 2\log^{(2)}|\sigma|$, are not achieved infinitely often. It is tempting to conjecture that there is no computable upper bound on $K(\sigma)$ that is achieved infinitely often. This conjecture is false, however.

Theorem 3.12.1 (Solovay [371], see also Gács [163]). *There is a computable function* $g : 2^{<\omega} \to \mathbb{N}$ *such that*

(i) $K(\sigma) \leqslant g(\sigma)$ *for all* σ, *and*

(ii) $K(\sigma) = g(\sigma)$ *for infinitely many* σ.

Proof. It will be notationally convenient to build $g : \mathbb{N} \to \mathbb{N}$ so that $K(n) \leqslant g(n)$ for almost all n and $K(n) = g(n)$ for infinitely many n. Since we can identify binary strings with natural numbers via Gödel numbers, this construction will be enough to establish the theorem. We will in fact first build an auxiliary function $\widehat{g}$, then modify it slightly to obtain g.

We can construct a prefix-free machine M such that, for each τ and n, if s is least such that $\mathcal{U}(\tau)[s]\downarrow= n$, then $M(\tau)\downarrow= \langle n, s\rangle$. Since $\mathcal{U}$ is universal, there is a constant c such that, for each such τ, n, s, we have $\mathcal{U}(\mu)\downarrow= \langle n, s\rangle$ for some μ with $|\mu| \leqslant |\tau|+c$. We can now define a computable function f such that for all τ, n, s, if s is least such that $\mathcal{U}(\tau)[s]\downarrow= n$, then $\mathcal{U}(\mu)[f(s)]\downarrow= \langle n, s\rangle$ for some μ with $|\mu| \leqslant |\tau| + c$. Thus, if s is least such that $K(n) = K_s(n)$, then $K_{f(s)}(\langle n, s\rangle) \leqslant K(n) + c$.

Now define $\widehat{g}$ as follows. Given x, find the unique n and s such that $x = \langle n, s\rangle$, and let $\widehat{g}(x) = K_{f(s)}(x)$. Clearly, $K(x) \leqslant \widehat{g}(x)$ for all x.

On the other hand, suppose that x is one of the infinitely many integers of the form $\langle n, s\rangle$ where s is least such that $K(n) = K_s(n)$. Then $\widehat{g}(x) = K_{f(s)}(x) \leqslant K(n) + O(1) \leqslant K(x) + O(1)$, the latter inequality coming from the fact that the function $\langle n, s\rangle \mapsto n$ is computable. Thus there is a constant $d \in \mathbb{N}$ such that $K(x) = \widehat{g}(x) - d$ for infinitely many x and $K(x) \leqslant \widehat{g}(x) - d$ for all but finitely many x. Define $g(m) = \widehat{g}(m) - d$, then modify finitely many values of g to ensure that $K(m) \leqslant g(m)$ for all m. □

Note that there is a critical difference between the computable bound $|\sigma| + O(1)$ for $C(\sigma)$ and the computable bound $g(\sigma)$ of Theorem 3.12.1. For the appropriate choice of constant c, we know that for each n there is some string σ of length n with $C(\sigma) = |\sigma| + c$. For g, however, we know only that there are infinitely many σ with $K(\sigma) = g(\sigma)$, and apparently only $\emptyset'$ can figure out where these σ are. This difference will be important, especially in Chapter 11, where we discuss a class of sets (the *K-trivial* sets) that show that Chaitin's Theorem 3.4.4 fails for K in place of C.

Bienvenu, Downey, and Merkle [39, 40] began a systematic study of computable upper bounds for K. These bounds admit a simple characterization.

Lemma 3.12.2 (Bienvenu and Downey [39]). *Let* $f : \mathbb{N} \to \mathbb{N}$ *be computable. The following are equivalent:*

(i) $K(n) \leqslant f(n) + O(1)$.

(ii) $\sum_n 2^{-f(n)} < \infty$.

Proof. (i) $\Rightarrow$ (ii) is trivial, as $\sum_n 2^{-K(n)} \leqslant 1$. The other direction follows by the minimality of K as an information content measure, Theorem 3.7.8. ☐

Definition 3.12.3 (Bienvenu and Merkle [40]). A computable function f is a *Solovay function* if $\sum_n 2^{-f(n)} < \infty$ and $\liminf_n f(n) - K(n) < \infty$ (in other words, there is a c such that $f(n) \leqslant K(n) + c$ for infinitely many n).

As we will see in Theorem 9.4.1, Solovay functions are exactly those computable functions f for which $\sum_n 2^{-f(n)}$ is a 1-random real, as defined in Chapter 6. They will play a part in several chapters below. We will refer to the Solovay function built in the proof of Theorem 3.12.1 as "Solovay's Solovay function".

For a computable function t, the *prefix-free Kolmogorov complexity of σ with time bound t*, denoted by $K^t(\sigma)$, is $\min\{|\tau| : U(\tau)[t(|\sigma|)]\downarrow = \sigma\}$, where U is a universal prefix-free function that efficiently simulates every partial computable prefix-free function f, in the sense that there are a string ρ_f and a constant c_f such that for all σ and s, if $f(\sigma)[s]\downarrow$ then $U(\rho_f\sigma)[c_f s]\downarrow = f(\sigma)$, while if $f(\sigma)\uparrow$ then $U(\rho_f\sigma)\uparrow$. Letting $\tilde{K}$ be the function $K_{f(s)}$ from the proof of Theorem 3.12.1, we see that there is a quadratic time version[9] $\tilde{K}$ of K such that $K(n) = \tilde{K}(n)$ for infinitely many n. Hölzl, Kräling, and Merkle [183] showed that this fact has the following consequence, whose proof is along the lines of that of Theorem 3.12.1.

Theorem 3.12.4 (Hölzl, Kräling, and Merkle [183]). *If t is any superlinear time bound, then the time-bounded version K^t of K is always a Solovay function.*

3.13 Universal machines and halting probabilities

In this section, we prove results of Solovay [371] giving estimates of the sizes of some basic sets associated with $\mathcal{U}$. Recall that σ^* is the first string τ of length $K(\sigma)$ such that $\mathcal{U}(\tau)\downarrow = \sigma$. (A more precise definition was given in Section 3.5.) Recall also that we write $f \sim g$ to mean that $f(n) = O(g(n))$ and $g(n) = O(f(n))$. We slightly abuse notation by writing, for instance, $f(n) \sim 2^n$ to mean that $f \sim n \mapsto 2^n$. We begin with the following fixed-point result for $\mathcal{U}$.

Lemma 3.13.1 (Solovay [371]). *For each n there are at least $O(2^{n-K(n)})$ many strings σ of length n such that $\mathcal{U}(\sigma)\downarrow = \sigma$.*

Proof. We define a prefix-free machine M with coding string ρ given by the recursion theorem. On input σ, the machine M looks for $\tau \in \operatorname{dom}\mathcal{U}$

[9] Superlinear would work as well.

and μ such that $\sigma = \tau\mu$. Then M interprets $\mathcal{U}(\tau)$ as a natural number n. If $|\mu| < n - |\rho| - |\tau|$ then M does not halt. Otherwise, M outputs $\rho\tau(\mu \upharpoonright (n - |\rho| - |\tau|))$.

Given n, let $S_n = \{\rho n^*\nu : |\nu| = n - |\rho| - K(n)\}$. If $\rho n^*\nu \in S_n$ then $\mathcal{U}(\rho n^*\nu) = M(n^*\nu) = \rho n^*\nu$, and $|S_n| = 2^{n-|\rho|-K(n)} = O(2^{n-K(n)})$. □

Theorem 3.13.2 (Solovay [371]). *Let*

(i) $p(n) = |\{\sigma \in 2^n : \mathcal{U}(\sigma)\downarrow\}|$,

(ii) $P(n) = |\{\sigma \in 2^{\leqslant n} : \mathcal{U}(\sigma)\downarrow\}|$,

(iii) $p'(n) = |\{\sigma : K(\sigma) = n\}|$, *and*

(iv) $d(n) = |\{\sigma : K(\sigma) \leqslant n\}|$.

Then $p(n) \sim P(n) \sim d(n) \sim 2^{n-K(n)}$. *Furthermore, there is a number k such that* $\sum_{n \leqslant j \leqslant n+k} p'(j) \sim 2^{n-K(n)}$.[10]

Proof. Let $A_n = \{\sigma \in 2^n : \mathcal{U}(\sigma)\downarrow\}$. The A_n are pairwise disjoint, uniformly c.e. subsets of the prefix-free set dom$\mathcal{U}$. By Proposition 3.6.4,

$$K(n) \leqslant -\log \sum_{\sigma \in A_n} 2^{-|\sigma|} + O(1) = -\log(p(n)2^{-n}) + O(1),$$

so $p(n) \leqslant O(2^{n-K(n)})$. By Lemma 3.13.1, in fact $p(n) = O(2^{n-K(n)})$.

Since $p(n) \leqslant P(n)$, we have the lower bound $P(n) \geqslant O(2^{n-K(n)})$. For the upper bound, first notice that there is a c such that

$$P(n) = \sum_{j \leqslant n} p(n-j) \leqslant \sum_{j \leqslant n} c2^{n-j-K(n-j)}.$$

Now, $K(n) \leqslant K(n-j)+K(j)+O(1)$, so $-K(n-j) \leqslant -K(n)+2\log j+O(1)$. Thus there is a c' such that

$$P(n) \leqslant \sum_{j \leqslant n} c'2^{n-j-K(n)+2\log j} = c'2^{n-K(n)} \sum_j j^2 2^{-j} = O(2^{n-K(n)}),$$

as $\sum_j j^2 2^{-j}$ converges. So $P(n) = O(2^{n-K(n)})$.

Clearly, $d(n) \leqslant P(n) \leqslant O(2^{n-K(n)})$, and it follows from Lemma 3.13.1 that $d(n) \geqslant O(2^{n-K(n)})$, so $d(n) = O(2^{n-K(n)})$.

Finally, we consider $p(n)'$. For a fixed k, we have the upper bound $\sum_{n \leqslant j \leqslant n+k} p'(j) \leqslant P(n+k) = O(2^{n+k-K(n+k)}) = O(2^{n-K(n)})$. We now establish the necessary lower bound.

---

[10]Solovay remarked that the machine-dependence of the definition of $p(n)'$ means that we cannot have an estimate such as $p(n)' \sim 2^{n-K(n)}$ in general. For instance, it is easy to define a universal prefix-free machine relative to which $K(\sigma)$ is always odd. Solovay also remarked that he did not know of a natural universal prefix-free machine relative to which $p(n)' \sim 2^{n-K(n)}$.

Since $d(n+k) = O(2^{n+k-K(n+k)})$, there is a c such that, for any n and k, we have $d(n+k) \geqslant c2^{n+k-K(n)-O(\log k)}$. Also, there is a c' such that $d(n) \leqslant c'2^{n-K(n)}$ for all n. Let k be large enough so that $c2^{k-O(\log k)} \geqslant 2c'$. Then $d(n+k) \geqslant d(n)+c'2^{n-K(n)}$ for all n. Thus, there are at least $c'2^{n-K(n)}$ many strings σ for which $n < K(\sigma) \leqslant n+k$, and hence $\sum_{n \leqslant j \leqslant n+k} p(j)' \geqslant c'2^{n-K(n)}$. □

As pointed out by Solovay, there is another way to look at the last part of Theorem 3.13.2. First we need a lemma.

Lemma 3.13.3. *There is a c such that if $m \geqslant c$, then for each σ there is a $\tau \in 2^{K(\sigma)+m}$ with $\mathcal{U}(\tau) = \sigma$.*

Proof. We define a prefix-free machine M with coding string ρ given by the recursion theorem. On input σ, the machine M looks for $\tau, \mu \in \operatorname{dom} \mathcal{U}$ and ν such that $\sigma = \tau\mu\nu$. Then M interprets $\mathcal{U}(\mu)$ as a natural number m. If $|\nu| \neq m - |\mu| - |\rho|$, then M does not halt. Otherwise, M outputs $\mathcal{U}(\tau)$.

Let c be large enough so that $m \geqslant K(m) + |\rho|$ for all $m \geqslant c$. Then if $m \geqslant c$ and ν is any string of length $m - K(m) - |\rho|$, we have $|\rho\sigma^* m^* \nu| = |\rho| + K(\sigma) + K(m) + (m - K(m) - |\rho|) = K(\sigma) + m$ and $\mathcal{U}(\rho\sigma^* m^* \nu) = M(\sigma^* m^* \nu) = \sigma$. □

Say that τ is a *d-minimal program* for σ if $\mathcal{U}(\tau) = \sigma$ and $|\tau| \leqslant K(\sigma) + d$, and that τ is a d-minimal program if it is a d-minimal program for some σ. We claim that there is a d such that the number of d-minimal programs of length n is $O(2^{n-K(n)})$. This number is bounded above by the function $p(n)$ from Theorem 3.13.2, and hence is no greater than $O(2^{n-K(n)})$. Now let c be as in Lemma 3.13.3 and let k be such that $\sum_{n \leqslant j \leqslant n+k} p'(j) \sim 2^{n-K(n)}$, as in Theorem 3.13.2. If $n \leqslant K(\sigma) \leqslant n+k$, then by Lemma 3.13.3 there is a $\mathcal{U}$-program for σ of length exactly $n+k+c$. Each one of these programs is $(k+c)$-minimal. So the claim holds with $d = k+c$.

We now turn to further results of Solovay [371] concerning the sets $\mathcal{D}_n = \{\sigma \in 2^{\leqslant n} : \mathcal{U}(\sigma)\downarrow\}$. We have $P(n) = |\mathcal{D}_n|$ as in Theorem 3.13.2. Since the $\mathcal{D}_n$ are uniformly c.e., we can uniformly compute $\mathcal{D}_n$ given n and $P(n)$. Thus

$$K(\mathcal{D}_n) \leqslant K(n, P(n)) + O(1) \leqslant K(n) + K(P(n) \mid n^*) + O(1).$$[11]

By Theorem 3.13.2, there is a c such that $P(n) \leqslant 2^{n-K(n)+c}$, so if we know $n - K(n)$ then we can describe $P(n)$ with a string of length $n - K(n) + c$. Furthermore, $K(n - K(n) \mid n^*) = O(1)$, so

$$K(P(n) \mid n^*) \leqslant n - K(n) + K(n - K(n) \mid n^*) + O(1) = n - K(n) + O(1).$$

Thus $K(\mathcal{D}_n) \leqslant K(n) + n - K(n) + O(1) = n + O(1)$. We now show that this estimate is sharp.

[11]For a finite set F, we can take $K(F)$ to be the minimum of $K(n)$ over all n such that F is equal to the canonical finite set D_n. We can similarly define F^*.

Theorem 3.13.4 (Solovay [371]). $K(\mathcal{D}_n) = n \pm O(1)$.

Proof. By the above argument, it is enough to show that $K(\mathcal{D}_n) \geqslant n - O(1)$. We define a prefix-free machine M with coding string ρ given by the recursion theorem. On input σ, the machine M looks for $\tau \in \operatorname{dom}\mathcal{U}$ and μ such that $\sigma = \tau\mu$. Then it interprets $\mathcal{U}(\tau)$ as a finite set of strings E (via a fixed encoding of finite sets of strings into strings). Let m be the length of the longest string in E. If $m - |\rho| - |\tau| < 0$ or $|\mu| < m - |\rho| - |\tau|$, then M does not halt. Otherwise, M checks whether $\rho\tau(\mu \upharpoonright (m - |\rho| - |\tau|)) \in E$. If not, then M outputs 0, and otherwise M does not halt.

Suppose that $K(\mathcal{D}_n) \leqslant n - |\rho|$, let $\tau = (\mathcal{D}_n)^*$, and let μ be a string of length $n - |\rho| - K(\mathcal{D}_n)$. Then $\rho\tau\mu \in \mathcal{D}_n$ iff $\tau\mu \in \operatorname{dom} M$ iff $\rho\tau\mu \notin E$ iff $\rho\tau\mu \notin \mathcal{D}_n$, which is a contradiction. Thus $K(\mathcal{D}_n) \geqslant n - |\rho|$ for all n. □

Corollary 3.13.5 (Solovay [371]). $K((\mathcal{D}_n)^* \mid \mathcal{D}_n) = O(1)$.

Proof. We can determine $(\mathcal{D}_n)^*$ given $K(\mathcal{D}_n)$ and n, so $K((\mathcal{D}_n)^* \mid \mathcal{D}_n) \leqslant K(K(\mathcal{D}_n) \mid \mathcal{D}_n) + O(1)$. But $K(\mathcal{D}_n) = n \pm O(1)$, so $K(K(\mathcal{D}_n) \mid \mathcal{D}_n) = K(n \mid \mathcal{D}_n) \pm O(1) = O(1)$, since n is the length of the longest string in $\mathcal{D}_n$, and hence we can determine n given $\mathcal{D}_n$. □

The sets $\mathcal{D}_n$ are closely related to Chaitin's famous number Ω, whose properties we will further explore in Section 6.1. (See Calude and Chaitin [48] for an expository discussion of this number.)

Definition 3.13.6 (Chaitin [58]). The *halting probability* Ω of $\mathcal{U}$ is $\mu([\![\operatorname{dom}\mathcal{U}]\!]) = \sum_{\sigma\in\operatorname{dom}\mathcal{U}} 2^{-|\sigma|}$.

Of course, the value of Ω depends on the choice of $\mathcal{U}$, much as $\emptyset'$ depends on the choice of enumeration of the partial computable functions. We have seen in Myhill's Theorem 2.4.12 that all versions of $\emptyset'$ are the same up to computable permutations of $\mathbb{N}$. In Section 9.2 we will see that, as with $\emptyset'$, all versions of Ω are quite closely related, and it does make sense to ignore the machine-dependence of Ω in most circumstances. Let $\Omega_s = \sum_{\sigma\in\operatorname{dom}\mathcal{U}[s]} 2^{-|\sigma|}$. Note that $\Omega = \lim_s \Omega_s$.

Theorem 3.13.7 (Solovay [371]).

(i) $K(\mathcal{D}_n \mid \Omega \upharpoonright n) = O(1)$. *(Indeed, $\mathcal{D}_n$ can be computed from $\Omega \upharpoonright n$.)*

(ii) $K(\Omega \upharpoonright n \mid \mathcal{D}_{n+K(n)}) = O(1)$.

Proof. (i) It is easy to see that Ω is not computable (since otherwise we would be able to compute the domain of $\mathcal{U}$). So in particular $\Omega \notin \mathbb{Q}$, which implies that, for each n, we must have $\Omega_s \upharpoonright n = \Omega \upharpoonright n$ for some s. Given $\Omega \upharpoonright n$, look for such an s. Then $\sigma \in \mathcal{D}_n$ iff $\sigma \in \operatorname{dom}\mathcal{U}[s]$.

(ii) Given n, let $D = \mathcal{D}_{n+K(n)}$. We may assume that n is large enough so that $D \neq \emptyset$. Using D, we can find the least j such that $j + K(j) = n + K(n)$. We have $|n - j| = |K(n) - K(j)| \leqslant K(|n - j|) + O(1) \leqslant 2\log|n - j| + O(1)$, so $|n - j| + O(1)$. Thus $K(n \mid D) = O(1)$.

We define a prefix-free machine M with coding string ρ given by the recursion theorem. On input σ, the machine M looks for $\tau \in \operatorname{dom}\mathcal{U}$ and μ such that $\sigma = \tau\mu$. Then M interprets $\mathcal{U}(\tau)$ as a number n. If $|\mu| \neq n$ then M does not halt. Otherwise, M interprets τ as a number $m \in [0, 2^{n-1})$ and looks for an s such that $\Omega_s \geqslant m2^{-n}$. If such an s is found, then M outputs 0, and otherwise M does not halt.

Let c be such that $|\rho| + K(n-c) + n - c \leqslant n + K(n)$ for all sufficiently large n, which must exist because $K(n-d) \leqslant K(n) + O(\log d)$. Then $\Omega \geqslant m2^{-(n-c)}$ iff $(n-c)^*\mu \in \operatorname{dom} M$, where $\mu \in 2^{n-c}$ codes m as a number in $[0, 2^{n-c-1})$. Since $|\rho(n-c)^*\mu| = |\rho| + K(n-c) + n - c \leqslant n + K(n)$, it follows that $\Omega \geqslant m2^{-(n-c)}$ iff $\rho(n-c)^*\mu \in D$. Since $K(n \mid D) = O(1)$, we have $K(\Omega \upharpoonright (n-c) \mid D) = O(1)$, so $K(\Omega \upharpoonright n \mid D) = O(1)$. □

3.14 The conditional complexity of σ^* given σ

In this section, we investigate how difficult it is to produce σ^* given σ. This question is equivalent to asking how difficult it is to produce $K(\sigma)$ given σ, as shown by the following lemma, which has the same proof as the analogous Proposition 3.2.1.

Proposition 3.14.1. $K(\sigma^* \mid \sigma) = K(K(\sigma) \mid \sigma) \pm O(1)$.

It follows from this result that $K(\sigma^* \mid \sigma) \leqslant \log|\sigma| + O(\log^{(2)}|\sigma|)$. The following result shows that this bound is not too far from optimal.

Theorem 3.14.2 (Gács [164], Solovay [371]). *For all sufficiently large n, there is a $\sigma \in 2^n$ such that*

$$K(\sigma^* \mid \sigma) \geqslant \log n - \log^{(2)} n - 3.$$

Before proving this theorem, we need a combinatorial lemma. To simplify notation, for the remainder of this section, we let $k(n) = \log n - \log^{(2)} n - 3$, and assume that n is sufficiently large for $k(n)$ to be positive.

Lemma 3.14.3. $\sum_{i<2^{k(n)}} n^{4i} < 2^n$.

Proof. Let $M = \sum_{i<2^{k(n)}} n^{4i}$. Then $M < \sum_{j<2^{k(n)+2}} n^j < n^{2^{k(n)+2}}$, so $\log M \leqslant 2^{k(n)+2} \log n$, and hence $\log^{(2)} M \leqslant k(n) + 2 + \log^{(2)} n = \log n - 1$. Thus $M < 2^n$. □

Corollary 3.14.4. *Suppose that 2^n is divided into $2^{k(n)}$ disjoint pieces $A_0, \ldots, A_{2^{k(n)}-1}$. Then there is an $i < 2^{k(n)}$ such that $|A_i| > n^{4i}$.*

For the least such i, we have $\sum_{j<i} |A_j| = O(n^{4(i-1)})$.

Proof. If $|A_i| \leqslant n^{4i}$ for all i, then $2^n = \sum_{i<2^{k(n)}} |A_i| \leqslant \sum_{i<2^{k(n)}} n^{4i} < 2^n$.

Now let i be least such that $|A_i| > n^{4i}$. Then $\sum_{j<i} |A_j| \leqslant \sum_{j<i} n^{4j} = O(n^{4(i-1)})$. □

Proof of Theorem 3.14.2. Assume for a contradiction that $K(\sigma^* \mid \sigma) < k(n)$ for all $\sigma \in 2^n$.

We say that $\tau \in 2^{<k(n)}$ is *active for* σ if there is a μ such that $\mathcal{U}^\sigma(\tau) = \mu$ and $\mathcal{U}(\mu) = \sigma$. Note that for each $\sigma \in 2^n$, there is a τ that is active for σ such that $\mathcal{U}^\sigma(\tau) = \sigma^*$.

Since the active strings all have length less than $k(n)$, the number of strings that are active for a given σ is in $[1, 2^{k(n)})$. Let

$$A_i = \{\sigma \in 2^n : \text{there are exactly } 2^{k(n)} - i \text{ many strings active for } \sigma\},$$

and let $S_i = \bigcup_{j<i} A_j$. Note that the S_i are uniformly c.e. (More precisely, we have a different collection of S_i for each n. All of these collections together are uniformly c.e.) Let $S_{i,s}$ be the stage s approximation to S_i.

By Corollary 3.14.4, there is a least i such that $|A_i| > n^{4i}$, and for this i we have $|S_i| = O(n^{4(i-1)})$.

Since $|A_i| > n^{4i}$, there must be a $\sigma \in A_i$ such that $K(\sigma) \geqslant 4i \log n$. Now suppose that we know the parameters i, $|S_i|$, and n. Then we can wait until a stage s such that $S_{i,s} = S_i$, and hence compute S_i. Every string entering S_{i+1} that is not in S_i is in A_i, so we can computably enumerate A_i. But once we know that $\sigma \in A_i$, we can find the $2^{k(n)} - i$ many strings τ active for σ, and compute $\mathcal{U}^\sigma(\tau)$ for all such τ. One of these computations will produce σ^*, and hence we can determine $K(\sigma)$. Let σ be the first string to enter our enumeration of A_i with $K(\sigma) \geqslant 4i \log n$. We have just argued that we can compute σ given i, $|S_i|$, and n. Thus $K(\sigma) \leqslant K(i) + K(|S_i|) + K(n) + O(1)$, so to arrive at a contradiction, it is enough to show that $4i \log n \nleqslant K(i) + K(|S_i|) + K(n) + O(1)$ if n is sufficiently large.

Now, $K(n) \leqslant \log n + O(\log^{(2)} n)$, and $i < 2^{k(n)}$, so

$$\begin{aligned} K(i) &\leqslant k(n) + O(\log k(n)) \\ &= \log n - \log^{(2)} n - 3 + O(\log(\log n - \log^{(2)} n - 3)) \\ &\leqslant \log n + O(\log^{(2)} n). \end{aligned}$$

Finally, $|S_i| = O(n^{4(i-1)})$, so

$$K(|S_i|) \leqslant \log(|S_i|) + O(\log^{(2)} |S_i|) \leqslant 4(i-1) \log n + O(\log^{(2)} n).$$

Thus $K(i) + K(|S_i|) + K(n) = (4i - 2) \log n + O(\log^{(2)} n)$, and hence $4i \log n \nleqslant K(i) + K(|S_i|) + K(n) + O(1)$ for sufficiently large n, as desired. □

The same proof also gives the analogous result for plain complexity.

Theorem 3.14.5 (Gács [164], Solovay [371]). *For all sufficiently large n, there is a $\sigma \in 2^n$ such that $C(C(\sigma) \mid \sigma) \geqslant \log n - \log^{(2)} n - 3$.*

Note that this lower bound is close to the obvious upper bound $C(C(\sigma) \mid \sigma) \leqslant C(C(\sigma)) + O(1) \leqslant \log |\sigma| + O(1)$.

Chaitin conjectured the following, which implies the above and was also conjectured correct by Solovay.

Conjecture 3.14.6. There is an infinite sequence $\sigma_0, \sigma_1, \ldots$ such that

(i) $|\sigma_n| = n$,

(ii) $K(\sigma_n) \sim n$, and

(iii) $K(\sigma_n^* \mid \sigma_n) \sim \log n$.

Solovay pointed out that these σ_n might well satisfy $K(\sigma_n) \leqslant \frac{n}{\log^{(2)} n}$, say.

3.15 Monotone and process complexity

The original machine characterization of randomness was due to Levin [241, 242], and involved what are called *monotone machines*, and a resulting notion of *monotone complexity*. A related notion is the *process complexity* of Schnorr [350], which uses a different kind of monotone machine.[12] We will discuss both of these concepts in this section.

Here, we are viewing Cantor space as a continuous sample space, and thinking of a sequence as a limit of computable sequences, rather than a limit of strings.

Levin [241, 242] considered machines with possibly infinite outputs. On a given input σ, such a machine M either halts with a finite output or computes forever, producing a potentially infinite sequence. (So, given a fixed input, if at some stage M outputs some τ, and then at a later stage it outputs $\widehat{\tau}$, then $\tau \preccurlyeq \widehat{\tau}$.) We write $M(\sigma)\downarrow$ if M has either of these behaviors after reading exactly σ from its input tape. For a standard Turing machine M (which we will call a *discrete* machine in this section), we may always assume that if M halts on input σ, then M reads all of σ from its input tape, and then ceases activity, so this notation agrees with our usual notation in the discrete case. Following Levin [241, 242], we call a machine *monotone* if its action is continuous, that is, for all $\sigma \prec \tau$, if $M(\sigma)\downarrow$ and $M(\tau)\downarrow$ then $M(\sigma) \preccurlyeq M(\tau)$.[13] Another way of thinking of such machines is to define them as a computably enumerable W collection of pairs of strings

[12] A concept similar to monotone machines was also introduced by Solomonoff [369].

[13] It is perhaps helpful to have a particular machine model for discrete machines in mind. We can think of them as machines with a one-way read-only input tape, a one-way write-only output tape, and work tapes. The input is read one bit at a time, and the output written one bit at a time, with the one-way nature of the output tape allowing no revisions. For such a machine M, we have $M(\sigma)\downarrow = \alpha$, where $\sigma \in 2^{<\omega}$ and $\alpha \in 2^{<\omega} \cup 2^{\omega}$, if either M halts after reading the bits of σ from the input tape, and α is what is on the output tape at that point, or M computes forever after reading exactly the bits of σ, and α is what is on the output tape in the limit.

(σ, τ) such that for all pairs (σ, τ) and $(\widehat{\sigma}, \widehat{\tau})$ in W, if $\sigma \preccurlyeq \widehat{\sigma}$, then τ is compatible with $\widehat{\tau}$. Note that this allows for the possibility that $\sigma = \widehat{\sigma}$ yet $\tau \prec \widehat{\tau}$ for infinitely many $\widehat{\tau}$. Note that (discrete) prefix-free machines are monotone; their definition simply asks that for each σ there be at most one τ with $(\sigma, \tau) \in W$. Discrete monotone machines are also known as *process machines*.

A simple but important fact is that we can enumerate all monotone machines, and hence use the standard method of constructing a universal one. We fix a universal monotone machine $\mathcal{M}$ and a universal discrete monotone machine $\mathcal{D}$. Using these machines we can define two varieties of monotone Kolmogorov complexity.

Definition 3.15.1 (Levin [241, 242], Schnorr [349, 350]).

(i) The *monotone complexity* of σ is $Km(\sigma) = \min\{|\tau| : \sigma \preccurlyeq \mathcal{M}(\tau)\downarrow\}$.

(ii) The *process complexity* of σ is $Km_D(\sigma) = \min\{|\tau| : \mathcal{D}(\tau)\downarrow= \sigma\}$.

The latter notion was introduced by Schnorr in [349] and further developed by him in [350], where process complexity was used to obtain a characterization of 1-randomness. Schnorr called it process complexity because he regarded information as being given with a direction. As he put it in [350], "he who wants to understand a book will not read it backwards, since the comments or facts which are given in its first part will help him to understand subsequent chapters (this means they help him to find regularities in the rest of the book). Hence anyone who tries to detect regularities in a process (for example an infinite sequence or an extremely long finite sequence) proceeds in the direction of the process. Regularities that have ever been found in an initial segment of the process are regularities for ever. Our main argument is that the interpretation of a process (for example to measure the complexity) is a process itself that proceeds in the same direction."

It is interesting to note that, even earlier and echoing work of Solomonoff [369], Levin had also developed a notion of process complexity, as can be seen in Zvonkin and Levin [425]. To make things clear, we will use the term *strict process machine* for Levin's definition.

Definition 3.15.2 (Levin, see [425], Solomonoff [369]). A *strict process machine* is a partial computable function $M : 2^{<\omega} \to 2^{<\omega}$ such that if $\tau \in \mathrm{dom}(M)$ and $\tau' \preccurlyeq \tau$, then $\tau' \in \mathrm{dom}(M)$ and $M(\tau') \preccurlyeq M(\tau)$.

Let U be a universal strict process machine. The *strict process complexity* $Km_S(\sigma)$ of σ is $C_U(\sigma)$.

As pointed out by Adam Day, a natural model corresponding to Levin's definition is almost identical to one described in the first paper on algorithmic randomness by Solomonoff [369]. Take a three-tape Turing machine M with a read-only one-way input tape, a one-way write-once output tape, and a work tape. The first square of the input tape is blank and the input head starts on that square. Let the machine run. If at any stage M wants to move the input head of the tape, we first define $M(\tau) = \sigma$, where τ is the input string read so far and σ is the current output on the output tape.

The distinction between a strict process machine and a process machine is almost completely unimportant in this book save for a theorem of Day [88] on the complexity of collections of non-random strings, Theorem 16.3.31. Until we reach that section, all theorems we state hold for both measures, and we will stick to Schnorr's definition. Little is known about the relationship between Schnorr's and Levin's complexities.

We now give some results relating Km and Km_D to C and K. The precise nature of the interaction between these notions is not fully known. Some results can be found in Uspensky and Shen [396], but there are no sharp estimates akin to those of Solovay's relating C to K, which we will discuss in Chapter 4.

Clearly, $Km(\sigma) \leqslant Km_D(\sigma)+O(1) \leqslant K(\sigma)+O(1)$ and $C(\sigma) \leqslant Km_D(\sigma)+O(1)$. Furthermore, the identity machine is monotone, so $Km_D(\sigma) \leqslant |\sigma| + O(1)$.

The following easy result was noted by several authors, including Gács (implicit in [166]) and Calhoun [46].

Proposition 3.15.3. $Km(0^n1) = Km_D(0^n1) \pm O(1) = K(1^n) \pm O(1)$.

Proof. We have observed that $Km(\sigma) \leqslant Km_D(\sigma) + O(1) \leqslant K(\sigma) + O(1)$ for all σ, and clearly $K(0^n1) = K(1^n) \pm O(1)$, so it is enough to show that $K(1^n) \leqslant Km(0^n1) + O(1)$. The minimal-length $\mathcal{M}$-descriptions of 0^n1 over all n form a prefix-free set, so if we let $L = \{(k+1, 1^n) : \exists\tau \in 2^k\, (0^n1 \preccurlyeq \mathcal{M}(\tau))\}$, then L is c.e. and

$$\sum_{(k+1,1^n)\in L} 2^{-(k+1)} \leqslant \sum_n \sum_{k \geqslant Km(0^n1)} 2^{-(k+1)} = \sum_n 2^{-Km(0^n1)} \leqslant 1,$$

so L is a KC set. Furthermore, $(Km(0^n1)+1, 1^n) \in L$ for all n, so $K(1^n) \leqslant Km(0^n1) + O(1)$. □

Since $C(\sigma) \leqslant Km_D(\sigma) + O(1) \leqslant K(\sigma) + O(1)$, some results come for free. For instance, the estimate in Lemma 4.2.1 below shows that for any σ and $\varepsilon > 0$, we have $K(\sigma) \leqslant Km_D(\sigma) + \log|\sigma| + \log\log(|\sigma|) + \cdots + (1+\varepsilon)\log^{(k)}(|\sigma|)$. Actually, the strengthening of this result to Km is also true.

Theorem 3.15.4 (Uspensky and Shen [396]). *For any σ and $\varepsilon > 0$, we have $K(\sigma) \leqslant Km(\sigma) + \log|\sigma| + \log\log(|\sigma|) + \cdots + (1+\varepsilon)\log^{(k)}(|\sigma|)$.*

Proof. The proof uses a device introduced in the proof of Proposition 3.1.5. As in that proposition, for a string $\nu = a_0a_1\ldots a_m$, let $\overline{\nu} = a_0a_0a_1a_1\ldots a_ma_m01$. This encoding is a prefix-free representation of ν of length $2|\nu| + O(1)$. To improve on it, we can represent ν as $\overline{|\nu|}\nu$, which has length $|\nu| + 2\log|\nu| + O(1)$, or as $\overline{||\nu||}|\nu|\nu$ (where $||\nu||$ is the length of the binary representation of the length of ν), which has length

$|\nu| + \log|\nu| + 2\log\log|\nu| + O(1) \leqslant |\nu| + (1+\varepsilon)\log|\nu|$ for any $\varepsilon > 0$. So for any k, we have a prefix-free representation $r(\nu)$ of ν of length $\log|\sigma| + \log\log|\sigma| + \cdots + (1+\varepsilon)\log^{(k)}|\sigma|$.

Now let N be a prefix-free machine defined as follows. On input τ, look for τ_0 and τ_1 with $\tau = \tau_0\tau_1$ and such that $\tau_0 = r(|\sigma|)$ for some $\sigma \preccurlyeq \mathcal{M}(\tau_1)$. If these are found, then output σ. If ρ is a minimal-length program such that $\sigma \preccurlyeq \mathcal{M}(\rho)$, then $N(r(|\sigma|)\rho) = \sigma$. □

In some ways, the theory of monotone complexity is smoother than those of plain complexity and prefix-free complexity. For example, we have the following simpler version of Chaitin's Theorem 3.4.4.

Proposition 3.15.5. *A set A is computable iff $Km(A \upharpoonright n) = O(1)$.*

Proof. If A is computable then there is a monotone machine that on input λ outputs A, so $Km(A \upharpoonright n) = O(1)$. Conversely, if $Km(A \upharpoonright n) = O(1)$ then there are computable sets $B_0, \ldots, B_k$ such that for each n there is an $i \leqslant k$ for which $A \upharpoonright n \prec B_i$. But that clearly implies that $A = B_i$ for some $i \leqslant k$, so A is computable. □

For process complexity, we have the following analogous result.

Theorem 3.15.6. *A set A is computable iff $Km_D(A \upharpoonright n) \leqslant Km_D(1^n) + O(1)$ for all n.*

Proof. Let M be a machine such that for each σ we have $M(\sigma)\downarrow = 1^n$ where n is the position of σ in the length-lexicographic ordering of $2^{<\omega}$. Then M is a discrete monotone machine, so $Km_D(1^n) \leqslant \log n + O(1)$. Since monotone machines are Turing machines, at C-random n we have $Km_D(1^n) = \log n \pm O(1)$. Now we simply follow the proof of Theorem 3.4.4. □

We have $Km(1^n) = O(1)$ and $Km(0^n) = O(1)$ for all n, but for each c we can find an n such that $Km(0^n1^n) > c$, so Km is not subadditive. However, it is possible to recover a mild form of subadditivity by mixing complexities.

Theorem 3.15.7. *$Km(\sigma\tau) \leqslant K(\sigma) + Km(\tau) + O(1)$.*

Proof. Let N be a machine defined as follows. On input ρ, the machine N looks for μ and ν such that $\rho = \mu\nu$ and $\mathcal{U}(\mu)\downarrow$. Then N computes $\mathcal{U}(\mu)\mathcal{M}(\nu)$. (In other words, N writes $\mathcal{U}(\mu)$ on its output tape, then proceeds to emulate $\mathcal{M}$ on input ν.) The machine N is monotone. If μ is a minimal-length $\mathcal{U}$-program for σ and ν is a minimal-length $\mathcal{M}$-program such that $\tau \preccurlyeq \mathcal{M}(\nu)\downarrow$, then $\sigma\tau \preccurlyeq N(\mu\nu)\downarrow$, so $Km(\sigma\tau) \leqslant |\mu\nu| + O(1) = K(\sigma) + Km(\tau) + O(1)$. □

Process complexity is also not subadditive. The usual argument for plain complexity uses complexity oscillations applied to a long random string.

This argument is not available for process complexity, but it is nevertheless possible to show that subadditivity fails.

Theorem 3.15.8 (Day [90]). *For any d there are σ and τ such that $Km_D(\sigma\tau) > Km_D(\sigma) + Km_D(\tau) + d$.*

We will prove this theorem by giving short descriptions to many strings, and arguing combinatorially that one of these strings σ must have an extension $\sigma\tau$ with the desired property. The following lemma expresses a basic combinatorial fact about process machines.

Lemma 3.15.9 (Day [90]). *If $A \subseteq 2^{<\omega}$ is prefix-free then*

$$\sum_{\sigma \in A} 2^{-Km_D(\sigma)} \leqslant 1.$$

Proof. Let $B = \{\tau_\sigma : \sigma \in A\}$, where τ_σ is a minimal-length description of σ with respect to the fixed universal discrete monotone machine $\mathcal{D}$. If τ_1 and τ_2 are distinct elements of B, then $\mathcal{D}(\tau_1)$ and $\mathcal{D}(\tau_2)$ are incompatible, so B is also prefix-free. Thus $\sum_{\sigma\in A} 2^{-Km_D(\sigma)} = \sum_{\tau \in B} 2^{-|\tau|} = \mu([\![B]\!]) \leqslant 1$. □

For $\sigma = a_0, \ldots, a_{n-1}$, let $M(\sigma) = a_0a_0a_1a_1 \ldots a_{n-1}a_{n-1}$. Let $A_n = \{M(\sigma) : \sigma \in 2^n\}$. Since M is a discrete monotone machine, there is a c such that for all $\tau \in A_n$, we have $Km_d(\tau) \leqslant K_M(\sigma) + c = n + c$.

For all n and $m \geqslant 2n+2$, let $B_n^m = \{\sigma \in 2^m : \exists \rho \in A_i \, (\rho 01 \preccurlyeq \sigma \vee \rho 10 \preccurlyeq \sigma)\}$. Note that if $n \neq n'$ then $B_n^m \cap B_{n'}^m = \emptyset$, and $|B_n^m| = 2 \cdot 2^{m-2n-2}|A_n| = 2^{m-n-1}$. We will use the following lemma to find the extension we want.

Lemma 3.15.10 (Day [90]). *For each e there are m, n, and $\sigma \in B_n^m$ such that $Km_D(\sigma) > |\sigma| - n + e$.*

Proof. Let $m = 2^{e+3}$ and assume that no such n and σ exist. Then

$$\sum_{\sigma \in 2^m} 2^{-Km_D(\sigma)} \geqslant \sum_{n<\frac{m}{2}} \sum_{\sigma \in B_n^m} 2^{-Km_D(\sigma)} \geqslant \sum_{n<\frac{m}{2}} \sum_{\sigma \in B_n^m} 2^{-|\sigma|+n-e}$$
$$= \sum_{n<\frac{m}{2}} |B_n^m| 2^{-m+n-e} = \sum_{n<\frac{m}{2}} 2^{m-n-1}2^{-m+n-e} = \frac{m}{2}2^{-e-1} > 1,$$

which contradicts Lemma 3.15.9. □

Proof of Theorem 3.15.8. Let c be as above, and let d be such that $Km_D(\tau) \leqslant |\tau| + d$ for all τ. Fix k and let $e = k + c + d$. By the previous lemma, there exist m, n, and $\upsilon \in B_n^m$ such that $Km_D(\upsilon) > |\upsilon| - n + e$. Let $\sigma = \upsilon \upharpoonright 2n$. Then $\sigma \in A_n$, so $Km_D(\sigma) \leqslant |\sigma| - n + c$. Let τ be such that $\sigma\tau = \upsilon$. Then

$$Km_D(\sigma) + Km_D(\tau) + k \leqslant |\sigma| - n + c + |\tau| + d + k$$
$$= |\sigma\tau| - n + e < Km_D(\sigma\tau).$$

□

There is comparatively little known about process and monotone complexity; their study seems to be a fertile area of research, particularly in view of the basic natural intuition behind them.

3.16 Continuous semimeasures and *KM*-complexity

In Section 3.9, we defined the notion of a discrete semimeasure. This notion is not compatible with the usual measure on Cantor space. Its continuous analog is the following.

Definition 3.16.1. A *continuous semimeasure* is a function $\delta : \{[\![\sigma]\!] : \sigma \in 2^{<\omega}\} \to \mathbb{R}^{\geqslant 0}$ such that

(i) $\delta([\![\lambda]\!]) \leqslant 1$ and

(ii) $\delta([\![\sigma]\!]) \geqslant \delta([\![\sigma 0]\!]) + \delta([\![\sigma 1]\!])$ for all σ.

To simplify notation, we often think of δ as a function from $2^{<\omega}$ to $\mathbb{R}^{\geqslant 0}$ and write $\delta(\sigma)$ for $\delta([\![\sigma]\!])$.

Of course, there is a big difference between continuous semimeasures and the discrete semimeasures of Section 3.9. For example, if we let $\delta([\![0^k]\!]) = 1$ for all k and $\delta([\![\sigma]\!]) = 0$ for all other $\sigma \in 2^{<\omega}$, then δ is a continuous semimeasure, but $\sum_\sigma \delta([\![\sigma]\!]) = \infty$.

Continuous semimeasures are closely connected to the important notion of supermartingale, which we discuss in Chapter 6 (see in particular Section 6.3.2).

In the words of Li and Vitányi [248], a continuous semimeasure is a "defective" measure, as it is only subadditive. Of course, we can define effective continuous semimeasures (and hence "effective defective measures"...), such as c.e. continuous semimeasures, as we did for discrete semimeasures. A continuous semimeasure δ is *computably enumerable* if it is approximable from below; that is, there are uniformly computable functions $\delta_s : 2^{<\omega} \to \mathbb{Q}$ such that for all s and σ we have $\delta_{s+1}([\![\sigma]\!]) \geqslant \delta_s([\![\sigma]\!])$ and $\lim_s \delta_s([\![\sigma]\!]) = \delta([\![\sigma]\!])$.

A c.e. continuous semimeasure δ is *optimal* if for every c.e. continuous semimeasure δ', we have $\delta[\![\sigma]\!] \geqslant O(\delta'([\![\sigma]\!]))$. Levin, see [425], showed that there is an optimal c.e. continuous semimeasure, as we will see in Theorem 3.16.2. Given this fact, we can associate a version of Kolmogorov complexity to a continuous semimeasure. Fix an optimal c.e. continuous semimeasure δ and let $KM(\sigma) = -\log \delta([\![\sigma]\!])$. This notion is called the *a priori entropy* of $[\![\sigma]\!]$; we will also refer to it as the *KM-complexity* of σ.

Along the lines of the Coding Theorem 3.9.4, but for continuous semimeasures, we can show that *KM* corresponds to the probability that a string is output by a given universal monotone machine. The following result is due to Levin (see [425]), but, while the theorem is referred to in the literature, only a sketch of its proof appeared in [425]. We give a proof due to Day [87].

If L is a monotone machine, then let the function $M_L : 2^{<\omega} \to \mathbb{R}^{\geqslant 0}$ be defined by $M_L(\sigma) = \mu([\![\{\tau : \exists \sigma' \succcurlyeq \sigma \, ((\tau, \sigma') \in L)\}]\!])$.

Theorem 3.16.2 (Levin, see [425]).

(i) *If L is a monotone machine, then M_L is a c.e. continuous semimeasure.*

(ii) *If m is a c.e. continuous semimeasure, then there exists a monotone machine L such that $M_L = m$.*

(iii) *If $\mathcal{M}$ is a universal monotone machine, then $M_{\mathcal{M}}$ is an optimal c.e. continuous semimeasure, so $KM(\sigma) = -\log(M_{\mathcal{M}}(\sigma)) \pm O(1)$.*

Proof. As discussed in Section 3.15, we think of a monotone machine L as given by axioms of the form (σ, τ), where $(\sigma, \tau) \in L$ means that on input σ, the machine $\mathcal{M}$ writes at least τ on its output tape. We write $\sigma \approx \tau$ to mean that $\sigma \preccurlyeq \tau$ or $\tau \preccurlyeq \sigma$. We prove (i) and (ii). Then (iii) follows immediately by the definition of M_L.

(i) Clearly $M_L(\lambda) \leqslant 1$. Furthermore,

$$[\![\{\tau : \exists \sigma' \succcurlyeq \sigma((\tau, \sigma') \in L)\}]\!] \supseteq [\![\{\tau : \exists \sigma' \succcurlyeq \sigma 0((\tau, \sigma') \in L)\}]\!] \cup [\![\{\tau : \exists \sigma' \succcurlyeq \sigma 1((\tau, \sigma') \in L)\}]\!],$$

and

$$[\![\{\tau : \exists \sigma' \succcurlyeq \sigma 0((\tau, \sigma') \in L)\}]\!] \cap [\![\{\tau : \exists \sigma' \succcurlyeq \sigma 1((\tau, \sigma') \in L)\}]\!] = \emptyset,$$

because L is a monotone machine. It follows that $M_L(\sigma) \geqslant M_L(\sigma 0) + M_L(\sigma 1)$ for all σ. Finally, M_L is approximable from below, since $M_L(\sigma) = \lim_t M_{L_t}(\sigma)$, and $M_{L_t}(\sigma)$ is rational and nondecreasing in t.

(ii) We will use the following lemma.

Lemma 3.16.3. *If $T, S \subseteq 2^{\leqslant l}$ then there exists $R \subseteq 2^l$ such that $[\![R]\!] = [\![T]\!] \setminus [\![S]\!]$.*

Proof. Let $R = \{\sigma \in 2^l : [\![\sigma]\!] \subseteq [\![T]\!] \wedge [\![\sigma]\!] \cap [\![S]\!] = \emptyset\}$. Then $[\![R]\!] \subseteq [\![T]\!]$ and $[\![R]\!] \cap [\![S]\!] = \emptyset$, so $[\![R]\!] \subseteq [\![T]\!] \setminus [\![S]\!]$. If $\alpha \in [\![T]\!] \setminus [\![S]\!]$ then $[\![\alpha \upharpoonright l]\!] \subseteq [\![T]\!]$ because there must be some string of length $\leqslant l$ in T extended by α. No string in S is extended by α, and as all strings in S have length less than or equal to l, we have $[\![\alpha \upharpoonright l]\!] \cap [\![S]\!] = \emptyset$. Hence $\alpha \upharpoonright l \in R$ and so $[\![T]\!] \setminus [\![S]\!] \subseteq [\![R]\!]$. □

Let m be a c.e. semimeasure. We can choose a monotone approximation $m(\sigma, s)$ of m whose values are dyadic rationals and such that the following hold for all t.

(i) If $|\sigma| \geqslant t$ then $m(\sigma, t) = 0$.

(ii) There is at most one σ such that $m(\sigma, t+1) \neq m(\sigma, t)$.

(iii) If $m(\sigma, t+1) \neq m(\sigma, t)$, then $m(\sigma, t+1) = m(\sigma, t) + n2^{-(t+1)}$ for some n.

(iv) For all σ, we have $m(\sigma, t) \geqslant m(\sigma 0, t) + m(\sigma 1, t)$.

We build a monotone machine L via an enumeration with certain properties, which we now describe. Letting $D_t(\sigma) = \{\tau : (\tau, \sigma) \in L_t\}$, we will ensure that the following hold for all σ and t.

(i) L_t is a monotone machine.

(ii) $D_t(\sigma)$ is a prefix-free set.

(iii) $\mu([\![D_t(\sigma)]\!]) = m(\sigma, t)$.

(iv) If $\tau \in D_t(\sigma)$ then $|\tau| \leqslant t$.

(v) If $\sigma \prec \sigma'$ then $[\![D_t(\sigma)]\!] \supseteq [\![D_t(\sigma')]\!]$.

The construction of L proceeds as follows. Let $L_0 = \emptyset$. Notice that L_0 has the desired properties trivially.

Assume that L_t has the desired properties. At stage $t+1$, if $m(\sigma, t+1) = m(\sigma, t)$ for all σ such that $|\sigma| < t$, then let $L_{t+1} = L_t$. That is, if the semimeasure does not change then do not change the machine. Otherwise, let σ be the unique string such that $m(\sigma, t+1) \neq m(\sigma, t)$. Let n be such that $m(\sigma, t+1) = m(\sigma, t) + n2^{-(t+1)}$.

If $\sigma \neq \lambda$ then let $\rho = \sigma \upharpoonright (|\sigma| - 1)$. By the assumption on L_t,

$$\begin{aligned} &\mu([\![D_t(\rho)]\!] \setminus ([\![D_t(\rho 0)]\!] \cup [\![D_t(\rho 1)]\!])) \\ &\qquad = \mu([\![D_t(\rho)]\!]) - \mu([\![D_t(\rho 0)]\!]) - \mu([\![D_t(\rho 1)]\!]) \\ &\qquad\qquad = m(\rho, t) - m(\rho 0, t) - m(\rho 1, t) \geqslant n2^{-(t+1)}. \end{aligned}$$

The first equality holds because $[\![D_t(\rho 0)]\!] \cup [\![D_t(\rho 1)]\!] \subseteq [\![D_t(\rho)]\!]$, and as L_s is a monotone machine, $[\![D_t(\rho 0)]\!] \cap [\![D_t(\rho 1)]\!] = \emptyset$.

By Lemma 3.16.3, there is a set R of strings of length $t+1$ such that $[\![R]\!] = [\![D_t(\rho)]\!] \setminus ([\![D_t(\rho 0)]\!] \cup [\![D_t(\rho 1)]\!])$. So $\mu([\![R]\!]) \geqslant n2^{-(t+1)}$. Choose n strings of length $t+1$ from R and let this set be T_t. If $\sigma = \lambda$ then find a set $R \subseteq 2^{t+1}$ such that $[\![R]\!] = [\![\lambda]\!] \setminus [\![D_t(\lambda)]\!]$, and let T_t consist of n strings from this R.

Let $L_{t+1} = L_t \cup \{(\tau, \sigma) : \tau \in T_t\}$. We show that L_{t+1} has the desired properties.

First we show that L_{t+1} is a monotone machine. If $\sigma = \lambda$ then there is nothing to check, as λ is comparable with any string. If $\sigma \neq \lambda$, then take any $\tau \in T_t$ and consider any $\upsilon \prec \tau$ such that $(\upsilon, \pi) \in L_t$. We will show that $\pi \prec \sigma$. First note that, by the choice of τ, there is some $\tau' \prec \tau$ with $(\tau', \rho) \in L_t$ for some ρ. Then $\tau' \approx \upsilon$, so $\pi \approx \rho$. If $\pi \succcurlyeq \rho 0$ or $\pi \succcurlyeq \rho 1$, then $[\![\upsilon]\!] \subseteq ([\![D_t(\rho 0)]\!] \cup [\![D_s(\rho 1)]\!])$, and so $\tau \notin L_t$. Hence $\pi \preccurlyeq \rho \prec \sigma$.

The set $D_{t+1}(\sigma)$ is prefix-free because $D_t(\sigma)$ and T_t are prefix-free and none of the elements of T_t extend elements of $D_t(\sigma)$. We have $\mu(\llbracket D_{t+1}(\sigma)\rrbracket) = \mu(\llbracket D_t(\sigma)\rrbracket) + \mu(\llbracket T_t\rrbracket) = m(\sigma,t) + n2^{-(t+1)} = m(\sigma,t+1)$. The final two properties hold by construction.

Since each L_t is a monotone machine, it follows that L is a monotone machine. By property (v), $M_{L_t}(\sigma) = \mu(\llbracket D_t(\sigma)\rrbracket)$, so for all σ,

$$M_L(\sigma) = \lim_t M_{L_t}(\sigma) = \lim_t \mu(\llbracket D_t(\sigma)\rrbracket) = \lim_t m(\sigma,t) = m(\sigma).$$

□

It was a long-standing open question whether KM and Km are the same, that is, whether a natural analog of the Coding Theorem 3.9.4 holds for continuous semimeasures. In one direction, we saw in Theorem 3.16.2 that $KM(\sigma) = -\log(M_{\mathcal{M}}(\sigma)) \pm O(1)$. But $M_{\mathcal{M}}(\sigma) = \mu(\llbracket\{\tau : \exists\sigma' \succcurlyeq \sigma((\tau,\sigma') \in \mathcal{M})\}\rrbracket) \geqslant 2^{-Km(\sigma)}$. Thus $KM(\sigma) \leqslant Km(\sigma) + O(1)$. In Section 4.5, we will see results by Gács [166] and Day [87] showing that the converse does not hold, although proving that fact is remarkably difficult.

4
Relating Complexities

In this chapter, we look at some of the fundamental relationships between flavors of Kolmogorov complexity. The first four sections explore relationships between plain and prefix-free complexity, while the last deals with the relationship between Km and KM. Most of this material, although of independent interest, will not be used directly in the rest of this book. Exceptions are Corollaries 4.3.3 and 4.3.8, which will be relevant in the discussion of sets with infinitely many initial segments of highest possible complexity in Chapter 6.

Throughout this chapter, in addition to our fixed universal prefix-free machine $\mathcal{U}$, we fix a universal Turing machine $\mathcal{V}$ and define C using this machine.

4.1 Levin's Theorem relating C and K

Our first results relating K and C are due to Levin. They appeared in his dissertation [241]; the first published proofs were in Gács [165].

Theorem 4.1.1 (Levin [241], see Gács [165]).

(i) $C(\sigma) = \min\{n : K(\sigma \mid n) \leqslant n\} \pm O(1)$.

(ii) $C(\sigma) = K(\sigma \mid C(\sigma)) \pm O(1)$.

Proof. Let $m_\sigma = \min\{n : K(\sigma \mid n) \leqslant n\}$.

Part (i). Consider a prefix-free oracle machine M, with coding constant c given by the recursion theorem, such that $M^n(\tau) = \mu$ iff $|\tau| = n - c$ and

R.G. Downey and D. Hirschfeldt, *Algorithmic Randomness and Complexity*, Theory and Applications of Computability, DOI 10.1007/978-0-387-68441-3_4,

$\mathcal{V}(\tau) = \mu$. Given σ, let τ be a minimal-length $\mathcal{V}$-program for σ. On input τ and oracle $C(\sigma) + c$, this machine will output σ. Thus $K(\sigma \mid C(\sigma) + c) \leqslant |\tau| + c = C(\sigma) + c$, and hence $C(\sigma) \geqslant m_\sigma - O(1)$.

Now consider a plain machine N that, on input τ, searches for $\mu \preccurlyeq \tau$ such that $\mathcal{U}^{|\tau|}(\mu)\downarrow$, and if such a μ is found, outputs $\mathcal{U}^{|\tau|}(\mu)$. Note that, by the prefix-freeness of $\mathcal{U}$, such a μ, if it exists, is unique. Suppose that $K(\sigma \mid n) \leqslant n$, and let μ be a minimal-length $\mathcal{U}$-program for σ given n. Note that $|\mu| \leqslant n$. Let $\tau = \mu 0^{n-|\mu|}$. Then $N(\tau) = \mathcal{U}^n(\mu) = \sigma$, so $C(\sigma) \leqslant |\tau| + O(1) = n + O(1)$. Thus $C(\sigma) \leqslant m_\sigma + O(1)$.

Part (ii). We have $K(\sigma \mid m_\sigma - 1) \geqslant m_\sigma - 1$, so $K(\sigma \mid m_\sigma) \geqslant K(\sigma \mid m_\sigma - 1) - O(1) \geqslant m_\sigma - O(1)$. But also $K(\sigma \mid m_\sigma) \leqslant m_\sigma$, so in fact $K(\sigma \mid m_\sigma) = m_\sigma \pm O(1)$. Now part (i) gives us

$$K(\sigma \mid C(\sigma)) = K(\sigma \mid m_\sigma) \pm O(1) = m_\sigma \pm O(1) = C(\sigma) \pm O(1).$$

□

4.2 Solovay's Theorems relating C and K

In this section and the next, we look at the beautiful unpublished material of Solovay [371] relating C and K. The positive results involve simulations of Turing machines by prefix-free machines and vice versa. The negative ones involve the construction of an infinite sequence of strings whose plain and prefix-free complexities behave very differently in the limit. These results also have a bearing on the relationship between C-randomness and strong K-randomness (as defined in Sections 3.1 and 3.8, respectively). In Section 4.4, we give applications of Solovay's results due to Miller [272] to obtain a result of An. A. Muchnik, see [288], and an improvement thereof.

As the following result shows, it is not hard to give upper bounds on $K(\sigma)$ in terms of $C(\sigma)$. Recall that, for a function f, we write $f^{(n)}$ for the result of composing f with itself n many times.

Proposition 4.2.1 (Solovay [371]). *$K(\sigma) \leqslant C(\sigma) + C^{(2)}(\sigma) + \cdots + C^{(n)}(\sigma) + O(C^{(n+1)}(\sigma))$ for any n.*

Proof. This lemma follows from Lemma 4.2.3 below by an easy induction, but we give a direct proof here.

Recall the following idea from Proposition 3.1.5 and Lemma 3.15.4. For a string $\sigma = a_0 a_1 \ldots a_m$, let $\overline{\sigma} = a_0 a_0 a_1 a_1 \ldots a_m a_m 01$. That is, $\overline{\sigma}$ is the result of doubling each bit of σ and adding 01 to the end. The key fact about this operation is that if $\sigma \neq \tau$ then $\overline{\sigma}$ and $\overline{\tau}$ are incompatible.

Thus there is a prefix-free machine M such that $M(\overline{\tau}) = \mathcal{V}(\tau)$ for each τ. Taking τ to be a minimal-length $\mathcal{V}$-program for σ, this fact shows that $K(\sigma) \leqslant |\overline{\tau}| + O(1) = O(C(\sigma))$, thus proving the lemma for $n = 0$.

But we can also build a prefix-free machine M so that for each τ we have $M(\overline{\tau'}\tau) = \mathcal{V}(\tau)$, where τ' is a minimal-length $\mathcal{V}$-program for

$|\tau|$. On input μ, the machine M simply looks for a splitting $\mu = \mu_1\mu_2$ such that $\mu_1 = \overline{\nu}$ for some ν, then computes $\mathcal{V}(\nu)$, and if that halts and equals $|\mu_2|$, computes $\mathcal{V}(\mu_2)$ and outputs the result if any. Taking τ to be a minimal-length $\mathcal{V}$-program for σ, this construction shows that $K(\sigma) \leqslant |\overline{\tau'}\tau| = C(\sigma) + O(C^{(2)}(\sigma))$, thus proving the lemma for $n = 1$.

It should now be clear how to build a prefix-free machine M so that for each τ we have $M(\overline{\tau''}\tau'\tau) = \mathcal{V}(\tau)$, where τ'' is a minimal-length $\mathcal{V}$-program for $|\tau'|$, which proves the lemma for $n = 2$, and how to iterate this process to prove the lemma in general. □

The more precise relationships between C and K are as follows.

Theorem 4.2.2 (Solovay [371]).

$$K(\sigma) = C(\sigma) + C^{(2)}(\sigma) \pm O(C^{(3)}(\sigma)). \tag{4.1}$$

and

$$C(\sigma) = K(\sigma) - K^{(2)}(\sigma) \pm O(K^{(3)}(\sigma)). \tag{4.2}$$

Proof. It is useful to recall what the O-notation means here. For example, (4.1) means that there is a d such that

$$C(\sigma) + C^{(2)}(\sigma) - dC^{(3)}(\sigma) \leqslant K(\sigma) \leqslant C(\sigma) + C^{(2)}(\sigma) + dC^{(3)}(\sigma)$$

for all σ. We have already seen that the second inequality holds for some d. The difficulty comes in proving the first inequality.

One might expect (4.1) and (4.2) to be part of an infinite sequence of approximations involving increasing numbers of iterations of C and K, respectively, as in Proposition 4.2.1. In the next section we will see that, remarkably, this is not the case.

As Solovay observed, (4.1) and (4.2) are in fact equivalent. Indeed, we will also prove that

$$K^{(2)}(\sigma) - C^{(2)}(\sigma) = O(K^{(3)}(\sigma)) \tag{4.3}$$

and

$$K^{(3)}(\sigma) \text{ is asymptotically equal to } C^{(3)}(\sigma). \tag{4.4}$$

Granted these two facts, (4.1) and (4.2) are clearly equivalent.

The proof of the above equations proceeds in two stages. First we prove that

$$K(\sigma) \leqslant C(\sigma) + K(C(\sigma)) + O(1), \tag{4.5}$$

which is not too difficult. Then we prove the more difficult inequality

$$C(\sigma) \leqslant K(\sigma) - K^{(2)}(\sigma) + K^{(3)}(\sigma) + O(1). \tag{4.6}$$

Note that (4.5) and (4.6) are close to (4.2), the problem being that (4.5) has the term KC rather than $K^{(2)}$. It turns out that we can use the estimate on $K - C$ to get one on $K^{(2)} - KC$ to establish (4.2). After doing so, it will remain to prove (4.3) and (4.4) to get (4.1).

We begin by establishing (4.5).

Lemma 4.2.3. $K(\sigma) \leqslant C(\sigma) + K(C(\sigma)) + O(1)$.

Proof. Define a prefix-free machine M as follows. On input μ, first attempt to simulate $\mathcal{U}$ by searching for $\mu_1 \preccurlyeq \mu$ such that $\mathcal{U}(\mu_1)\downarrow$. If such a string is found then let μ_2 be such that $\mu = \mu_1\mu_2$ and check whether $|\mu_2| = \mathcal{U}(\mu_1)$. If so, output $\mathcal{V}(\mu_2)$ (if this value is defined).

Notice that M is prefix-free, since, firstly, $\mathcal{U}$ is prefix-free, and, secondly, if M halts on μ then $\mu = \mu_1\mu_2$ with $\mathcal{U}(\mu_1)\downarrow$ and $|\mu| = |\mu_1| + |\mathcal{U}(\mu_1)|$, which means that all extensions of μ_1 on which M halts have the same length, and hence are pairwise incompatible.

Given σ, let τ_2 be a minimal-length $\mathcal{V}$-program for σ and let τ_1 be a minimal-length $\mathcal{U}$-program for $C(\sigma) = |\tau_2|$. Then $M(\tau_1\tau_2) = \mathcal{V}(\tau_2) = \sigma$, and hence $K(\sigma) \leqslant |\tau_2| + |\tau_1| + O(1) = C(\sigma) + K(C(\sigma)) + O(1)$. □

We now establish (4.6). The idea of the proof is the following. Fix a computable enumeration of $\operatorname{dom}\mathcal{U}$ and let L_n be the list of strings $\tau \in \operatorname{dom}\mathcal{U}$ such that $|\tau| = n$, ordered according to this enumeration. We will show that there is a c such that $|L_{K(x)}| \leqslant 2^{K(x)-K^{(2)}(x)+c}$. We will then argue as follows (in the proof of Lemma 4.2.6). Given σ, let τ be a minimal-length $\mathcal{U}$-program for σ. Let μ_1 be a minimal-length $\mathcal{U}$-program for $K^{(2)}(\sigma)$ and let μ_2 be a string of length $K(\sigma) - K^{(2)}(\sigma) + c$ encoding the position of τ on the list $L_{K(\sigma)}$. The strings μ_1 and μ_2 together allow us to compute both $K(\sigma) = \mathcal{U}(\mu_1) + |\mu_2| - c$ and the position of τ on the list $L_{K(\sigma)}$, and hence allow us to compute σ. Since $\mathcal{U}$ is prefix-free, the string $\mu_1\mu_2$ is enough to allow us to compute σ, whence $C(\sigma) \leqslant |\mu_1\mu_2| + O(1) = K(\sigma) - K^{(2)}(\sigma) + K^{(3)}(\sigma) + O(1)$.

We now give the details of this argument.

Lemma 4.2.4. $|L_n| \leqslant 2^{n-K(n)+O(1)}$.

Proof. We wish to apply the KC Theorem 3.6.1 to build a prefix-free machine M as follows. We enumerate the L_n simultaneously. Whenever we first see that $|L_n| \geqslant 2^k$, we enumerate a request $(n - k + 1, n)$. We claim that these requests form a KC set. Assume this claim for now, and let k_n be the largest k such that $|L_n| \geqslant 2^k$. Then $K(n) \leqslant n - k_n + O(1)$, so $2^{K(n)} \leqslant 2^{n-k_n+O(1)}$. Thus $|L_n| < 2^{k_n+1} \leqslant 2^{n-K(n)+O(1)}$.

So we are left with establishing the claim. Defining k_n as above, this task amounts to showing that

$$\sum_n \sum_{i \leqslant k_n} 2^{-(n-i+1)} \leqslant 1.$$

To show that the above inequality holds, first note that

$$\sum_{i \leqslant k_n} 2^{-(n-i+1)} = \sum_{j=n-k_n+1}^{n+1} 2^{-j} \leqslant \sum_{j \geqslant n-k_n+1} 2^{-j} = 2^{k_n - n}.$$

Since $2^{k_n} \leqslant |L_n|$, we now have

$$\sum_{i \leqslant k_n} 2^{-(n-i+1)} \leqslant 2^{-n}|L_n|,$$

and hence

$$\sum_n \sum_{i \leqslant k_n} 2^{-(n-i+1)} \leqslant \sum_n 2^{-n}|L_n| = \sum_n \sum \{2^{-|\sigma|} : \sigma \in \operatorname{dom} \mathcal{U} \wedge |\sigma| = n\}$$
$$= \sum \{2^{-|\sigma|} : \sigma \in \operatorname{dom} \mathcal{U}\} \leqslant 1.$$

This fact establishes the claim and completes the proof. □

Corollary 4.2.5. $|L_{K(\sigma)}| \leqslant 2^{K(\sigma) - K^{(2)}(\sigma) + O(1)}$.

We now establish (4.6).

Lemma 4.2.6. $C(\sigma) \leqslant K(\sigma) - K^{(2)}(\sigma) + K^{(3)}(\sigma) + O(1)$.

Proof. Let c be such that $|L_{K(\sigma)}| \leqslant 2^{K(\sigma) - K^{(2)}(\sigma) + c}$ for all σ. We define a machine M as follows.

On input μ, first attempt to simulate $\mathcal{U}$ by searching for $\mu_1 \preccurlyeq \mu$ such that $\mathcal{U}(\mu_1)\downarrow$. If such a string is found then let μ_2 be such that $\mu = \mu_1\mu_2$. Let $n = |\mu_2| + \mathcal{U}(\mu_1) - c$ and interpret μ_2 as a number j in the interval $[1, 2^{|\mu_2|}]$ in the natural way. Enumerate L_n until its jth element appears, if ever. If such an element τ appears, output $\mathcal{U}(\tau)$ (if this value is defined).

Given σ, let τ be a minimal-length $\mathcal{U}$-program for σ and let ν_2 be a string of length $K(\sigma) - K^{(2)}(\sigma) + c$ encoding the position j of τ on the list $L_{K(\sigma)}$. Let ν_1 be a minimal-length $\mathcal{U}$-program for $K^{(2)}(\sigma)$. If we run M on input $\nu_1\nu_2$ then M will set $n = |\nu_2| + \mathcal{U}(\nu_1) - c = K(\sigma) - K^{(2)}(\sigma) + c + K^{(2)}(\sigma) - c = K(\sigma)$ and will proceed to search the list L_n for its jth element, namely τ. It will then output $\mathcal{U}(\tau) = \sigma$.

Since $|\nu_1\nu_2| = K^{(3)}(\sigma) + K(\sigma) - K^{(2)}(\sigma) + c$, the result follows. □

We are now ready to show that (4.2) holds. Let m and n range over the integers. It is easy to check that

$$K(|m+n|) \leqslant K(|m|) + K(|n|) + O(1).$$

(Here $|\cdot|$ denotes absolute value.) Also,

$$K(|m|) \leqslant K(|m-n|) + K(|n|) + O(1)$$

and similarly with m and n interchanged, from which it follows that

$$|K(|m|) - K(|n|)| \leqslant K(|m-n|) + O(1).$$

Lemma 4.2.7. $C(\sigma) = K(\sigma) - K^{(2)}(\sigma) \pm O(K^{(3)}(\sigma))$.

Proof. Let $D(\sigma) = K(\sigma) - C(\sigma) - K^{(2)}(\sigma)$. We need to show that $|D(\sigma)| = O(K^{(3)}(\sigma))$.

By Lemma 4.2.6, $D(\sigma) \geqslant -K^{(3)}(\sigma) - O(1)$.

By Lemma 4.2.3, $D(\sigma) \leqslant K(C(\sigma)) - K^{(2)}(\sigma) + O(1)$. By the facts about the relationship between K-complexity and addition and subtraction of integers mentioned above,

$$\begin{aligned}|K(C(\sigma)) - K^{(2)}(\sigma)| &\leqslant K(|C(\sigma) - K(\sigma)|) + O(1)\\ &= K(|D(\sigma) + K^{(2)}(\sigma)|) + O(1) \leqslant K(|D(\sigma)|) + K^{(3)}(\sigma) + O(1).\end{aligned}$$

Thus $D(\sigma) \leqslant K(|D(\sigma)|) + K^{(3)}(\sigma) + O(1)$.

Putting the two previous paragraphs together, we see that

$$|D(\sigma)| \leqslant K^{(3)}(\sigma) + K(|D(\sigma)|) + O(1).$$

For k ranging over the natural numbers, $K(k) = o(k)$, so

$$|D(\sigma)| - o(|D(\sigma)|) \leqslant K^{(3)}(\sigma),$$

whence $|D(\sigma)| = O(K^{(3)}(\sigma))$. □

We now turn to (4.3), from which (4.4) and (4.1) will follow easily.

Lemma 4.2.8. $|K^{(2)}(\sigma) - C^{(2)}(\sigma)| = O(K^{(3)}(\sigma))$.

Proof. By Lemma 4.2.7, $C(\sigma)$ and $K(\sigma)$ differ by $O(K^{(2)}(\sigma))$, and hence their K-complexities differ by $O(K^{(3)}(\sigma))$. That is,

$$K(C(\sigma)) = K^{(2)}(\sigma) \pm O(K^{(3)}(\sigma)). \tag{4.7}$$

Likewise, (4.7) shows that $K^{(2)}(C(\sigma))$ and $K^{(3)}(\sigma)$ differ by $o(K^{(3)}(\sigma))$, whence

$$K^{(2)}(C(\sigma)) = O(K^{(3)}(\sigma)). \tag{4.8}$$

Replacing σ by $C(\sigma)$ in (4.2), we have

$$C^{(2)}(\sigma) = K(C(\sigma)) - K^{(2)}(C(\sigma)) \pm O(K^{(3)}(C(\sigma))).$$

By (4.8), this equation gives us

$$C^{(2)}(\sigma) = K(C(\sigma)) \pm O(K^{(3)}(\sigma)). \tag{4.9}$$

Combining this equation with (4.7) establishes the lemma. □

Corollary 4.2.9. *$K^{(3)}(\sigma)$ is asymptotically equal to $C^{(3)}(\sigma)$.*

Proof. By Lemma 4.2.8, $K^{(2)}(\sigma)$ and $C^{(2)}(\sigma)$ differ by $O(K^{(3)}(\sigma))$, so $|K^{(3)}(\sigma) - K(C^{(2)}(\sigma))| = o(K^{(3)}(\sigma))$, and hence $K^{(3)}$ and $KC^{(2)}$ are asymptotically equal. But K and C are asymptotically equal, so $KC^{(2)}$ and $C^{(3)}$ are asymptotically equal. □

Corollary 4.2.10. $K(\sigma) = C(\sigma) + C^{(2)}(\sigma) \pm O(C^{(3)}(\sigma))$.

Proof. From Lemma 4.2.7 we have $K(\sigma) = C(\sigma) + K^{(2)}(\sigma) \pm O(K^{(3)}(\sigma))$. Using Corollary 4.2.8 we then have $K(\sigma) = C(\sigma) + C^{(2)}(\sigma) \pm O(K^{(3)}(\sigma))$. By Corollary 4.2.9, it follows that $K(\sigma) = C(\sigma) + C^{(2)}(\sigma) \pm O(C^{(3)}(\sigma))$. □

This result completes the proof of Theorem 4.2.2. □

The following corollary of the previous results will be useful below.

Corollary 4.2.11 (Solovay [371]). $K(\sigma) = C(\sigma) + K(C(\sigma)) \pm O(C^{(3)}(\sigma))$.

Proof. Combine Corollaries 4.2.9 and 4.2.10 with (4.9). □

The results above all have relativized forms. For instance, we have the following.

Corollary 4.2.12 (Solovay [371]).

$$K(\sigma \mid \tau) = C(\sigma \mid \tau) + C^{(2)}(\sigma \mid \tau) \pm O(C^{(3)}(\sigma \mid \tau)),$$

$$C(\sigma \mid \tau) = K(\sigma \mid \tau) - K^{(2)}(\sigma \mid \tau) \pm O(K^{(3)}(\sigma \mid \tau)),$$

and

$$C(\sigma \mid \tau) \leqslant K(\sigma \mid \tau) + O(1) \leqslant C(\sigma \mid \tau) + K(C(\sigma \mid \tau)) + O(1).$$

Another point worth noticing is that the upper bound on the size of $L_{K(\sigma)}$ given in Corollary 4.2.5 is strict, as shown by the following result.

Proposition 4.2.13 (Solovay [371]). $|L_{K(\sigma)}| \geqslant 2^{K(\sigma) - K^{(2)}(\sigma) + O(1)}$.

Proof. Suppose otherwise. Define the prefix-free machine M as follows. By the recursion theorem, we may assume we know the coding constant c of M. On input μ, search for a splitting $\mu = \mu_1\mu_2$ such that $\mathcal{U}(\mu_1)\downarrow$ and $|\mu_2| = \mathcal{U}(\mu_1) - |\mu_1| - (c+1)$. If such a splitting is found then let k be the element of $[1, 2^{|\mu_2|}]$ coded by μ_2, and search for the kth element enumerated into $L_{\mathcal{U}(\mu_1)}$. If such an element τ is found, compute $\mathcal{U}(\tau)$ and output the result, if any.

By assumption, there is a σ such that $|L_{K(\sigma)}| \leqslant 2^{K(\sigma) - K^{(2)}(\sigma) - (c+1)}$. Let τ be a minimal-length $\mathcal{U}$-program for σ and let μ_1 be a minimal-length $\mathcal{U}$-program for $K(\sigma) = |\tau|$. Let μ_2 be a string of length $K(\sigma) - K^{(2)}(\sigma) - (c+1)$ coding the position of τ in $L_{K(\sigma)}$. Then $M(\mu_1\mu_2)\downarrow = \sigma$. But $|\mu_1\mu_2| = K^{(2)}(\sigma) + K(\sigma) - K^{(2)}(\sigma) - (c+1) = K(\sigma) - (c+1)$, so $K_M(\sigma) = K(\sigma) - (c+1)$. But c is the coding constant of M, so $K(\sigma) \leqslant K(\sigma) - 1$, which is a contradiction. □

4.3 Strong K-randomness, C-randomness, and limitations on the results of the previous section

In this section, we will present Solovay's theorem from [371] that, roughly speaking, every strongly K-random string is C-random, but the converse is not true. One intuitive explanation for this difference between the two notions of randomness is the following. Suppose we know a string σ. If σ is C-random then also knowing $C(\sigma)$ gives us no additional information, but if σ is strongly K-random then also knowing $K(\sigma)$ gives us $K(|\sigma|)$. Thus there is more information in the prefix-free complexity of a strongly K-random string than in the plain complexity of a C-random string. Indeed, this extra amount of information is exploited in the proof of Theorem 4.3.7 below, which has as an immediate corollary that not every C-random string is strongly K-random.

The existence of C-random but not strongly K-random strings will also allow us to show that the main results of the previous section cannot be improved. For instance, in the previous section we established identity (4.1): $K(\sigma) = C(\sigma) + C^{(2)}(\sigma) \pm O(C^{(3)}(\sigma))$. At first glance, one would expect this identity to be part of an infinite sequence of identities with decreasing O-terms (as in Proposition 4.2.1). However, the methods of this section will show that the identity $K(\sigma) = C(\sigma) + C^{(2)}(\sigma) + C^{(3)}(\sigma) \pm O(C^{(4)}(\sigma))$ is *not* true, and hence (4.1) is as sharp as possible.

4.3.1 Positive results

The following proposition combines some information about plain and prefix-free complexity from Chapter 3.

Proposition 4.3.1. *There are constants c_C and c_K such that*

(i) $C(\sigma) \leqslant |\sigma| + c_C$,

(ii) $|\{\sigma \in 2^n : C(\sigma) \leqslant n + c_C - j\}| = O(2^{n-j})$,

(iii) $K(\sigma) \leqslant |\sigma| + K(|\sigma|) + c_K$, *and*

(iv) $|\{\sigma \in 2^n : K(\sigma) \leqslant n + K(n) + c_K - j\}| = O(2^{n-j})$.

Let

$$m_C(\sigma) = |\sigma| + c_C - C(\sigma)$$

and

$$m_K(\sigma) = |\sigma| + K(|\sigma|) + c_K - K(\sigma).$$

In light of Proposition 4.3.1, we see that these values measure how far the complexity of σ falls from its potential maximum. For either version of randomness, the random strings are those strings σ for which the corresponding $m(\sigma)$ is small.

Recall that, for fixed constants c and d, we say that σ is C-random if $C(\sigma) \geqslant |\sigma| - c$ and strongly K-random if $K(\sigma) \geqslant |\sigma| + K(|\sigma|) - d$. As we will see, the following theorem implies that every strongly K-random string is C-random for some constant.

Theorem 4.3.2 (Solovay [371]). $m_K(\sigma) \geqslant m_C(\sigma) - O(\log m_C(\sigma))$.

Proof. Since $C(\sigma) = |\sigma| - m_C(\sigma) + O(1)$,

$$K(C(\sigma)) = K(|\sigma| - m_C(\sigma) + O(1)) \leqslant K(|\sigma|) + K(m_C(\sigma) + O(1)) \leqslant K(|\sigma|) + O(\log m_C(\sigma)).$$

By Lemma 4.2.3, $K(\sigma) \leqslant C(\sigma) + K(C(\sigma)) + O(1)$. Consequently,

$$K(\sigma) \leqslant |\sigma| - m_C(\sigma) + K(|\sigma|) + O(\log m_C(\sigma)).$$

Rearranging this inequality, we get

$$|\sigma| + K(|\sigma|) - K(\sigma) \geqslant m_C(\sigma) - O(\log m_C(\sigma)).$$

Since the left-hand side of this inequality is $m_K(\sigma)$ (up to the constant c_K), it follows that $m_K(\sigma) \geqslant m_C(\sigma) - O(\log m_C(\sigma))$. □

Corollary 4.3.3 (Solovay [371]). *Every strongly K-random string is C-random for some constant.*

Proof. If σ is strongly K-random then $m_K(\sigma) \leqslant c$ for some fixed c (independent of σ). By Theorem 4.3.2, $m_C(\sigma) - d \log m_C(\sigma) \leqslant c$ for some fixed d, which clearly implies that $m_C(\sigma) \leqslant c'$ for some fixed c'. □

4.3.2 Counterexamples

We now turn to counterexamples. We will present Solovay's construction of an infinite sequence of strings whose plain complexities behave "as differently as possible" from their prefix-free complexities, and examine the consequences of the existence of such sequences.

We begin with a few lemmas that will be useful below. The first says that if τ is C-random given n, then there are many μ's of length n such that $\tau\mu$ is C-random (though for a different constant).

Lemma 4.3.4 (Solovay [371]). *For each c there is a d such that, for all n and τ, if*

$$C(\tau \mid n) \geqslant |\tau| - c \tag{4.10}$$

then

$$|\{\mu \in 2^n : C(\tau\mu) \leqslant |\tau| + n - d\}| \leqslant 2^{n-c}. \tag{4.11}$$

Proof. Fix c. We build a machine that, for each d, τ, and n not satisfying (4.11), provides a short C-program for τ given n. The length of this program will depend on d, and we will show that, for large enough d, this program is shorter than $|\tau| - c$, so that any τ and n not satisfying (4.11) for any d also fail to satisfy (4.10).

For each d, m, and n, let $S_{d,m,n}$ be a list of all $\sigma \in 2^m$ such that $|\{\mu \in 2^n : C(\sigma\mu) \leqslant m + n - d\}| > 2^{n-c}$. Notice that the $S_{d,m,n}$ are uniformly c.e. Furthermore, there are at most $2^{m+n-d+1}$ many pairs (σ, μ) such that $|\sigma| = m$ and $C(\sigma\mu) \leqslant m + n - d$, whence $|S_{d,m,n}| \leqslant 2^{m+c-d+1}$.

Define the (plain) machine M as follows. On input (σ, n), search for $\sigma_1, \sigma_2, \sigma_3$ such that $\sigma_1, \sigma_2 \in \operatorname{dom}\mathcal{U}$ and $\sigma = \sigma_1\sigma_2\sigma_3$. If such σ_i exist, then let $d = \mathcal{U}(\sigma_1)$ and $m = \mathcal{U}(\sigma_2) + |\sigma_3|$. Interpret σ_3 as a number j in the interval $[1, 2^{|\sigma_3|}]$ and output the jth element of $S_{d,m,n}$, if any.

Consider d, n, and τ not satisfying (4.11), and let $m = |\tau|$. Then $\tau \in S_{d,m,n}$. Let $\sigma_1, \sigma_2, \sigma_3$ be strings of minimal length such that $\mathcal{U}(\sigma_1) = d$ and $\mathcal{U}(\sigma_2) = d - c + 1$, and σ_3 has length $m + c - d + 1$ and codes the position of τ in $S_{d,m,n}$. Then $M(\sigma_1\sigma_2\sigma_3, n) = \tau$, so

$$\begin{aligned} C(\tau \mid n) &\leqslant K(d) + K(d - c + 1) + m + c - d + 1 + O(1) \\ &\leqslant m - d + O(\log d) = |\tau| - d + O(\log d), \end{aligned}$$

where the O constant does not depend on τ or n. Choosing d large enough, we see that if n and τ do not satisfy (4.11) then $C(\tau \mid n) \leqslant |\tau| - c$, so n and τ do not satisfy (4.10). □

Combining Lemma 4.3.4 with part (iv) of Lemma 4.3.1, we have the following corollary, which says that if τ is C-random given n, then, since there are many μ's of length n such that $\tau\mu$ is C-random, there is such a μ that is strongly K-random.

Corollary 4.3.5 (Solovay [371]). *For each c there is a d such that, for all n and τ, if $C(\tau \mid n) \geqslant |\tau| - c$ then there is a $\mu \in 2^n$ with $C(\tau\mu) \geqslant |\tau| + n - d$ and $K(\mu) \geqslant n + K(n) - d$.*

The next lemma says that, given any n, we can find an m such that the prefix-free complexity of the strongly K-random strings of length m is close to n.

Lemma 4.3.6 (Solovay [371]). *There is a c such that for each n there is an m with $|m + K(m) - n| \leqslant c$.*

Proof. If d is large enough then $|K(m+d) - K(m)| \leqslant K(d) + O(1) < d$. Let $f(m) = m + K(m)$. Then $f(m+d) - f(m) = m + d + K(m+d) - m - K(m) = d + K(m+d) - K(m)$, so $0 < f(m+d) - f(m) < 2d$. Let $c = 2d$ and, given n, choose m such that $|f(m) - n|$ is minimal. Then $|f(m) - n| \leqslant c$, since otherwise one of $f(m+d)$ or $f(m-d)$ would be closer to n than $f(m)$. □

We are now ready to prove the main theorem of this section.

Theorem 4.3.7 (Solovay [371]). *There is an infinite sequence of strings* ν_i *such that*

(i) $\lim_i |\nu_i| = \infty$,

(ii) $C(\nu_i) = |\nu_i| \pm O(1)$, *and*

(iii) $\lim_i \frac{m_K(\nu_i)}{\log^{(2)} |\nu_i|} = 1$.

Before proceeding with the proof, we note the following consequence. By item (i) in Theorem 4.3.7, each ν_i is C-random. By item (iii), ν_i is not strongly K-random for large enough i. Hence the converse to Corollary 4.3.3 does not hold.

Corollary 4.3.8 (Solovay [371]). *There is a c such that, for all d, there are infinitely many strings that are C-random with constant c but not strongly K-random with constant d.*

Proof of Theorem 4.3.7. The idea of the proof is to find τ_i and n_i such that τ_i is hard to describe given n_i, but easy given $K(n_i)$. Then Corollary 4.3.5 implies that there is a μ_i of length n_i that is random enough so that from $K(\mu_i)$ we can compute $K(n_i)$ (so τ_i is easy to describe given $K(\mu_i)$), but at the same time $\tau_i\mu_i$ is C-random. Letting $\nu_i = \tau_i\mu_i$, we have that $K(\nu_i)$ is not much larger than $K(\mu_i)$, but $C(\nu_i)$ is as large as possible. By carefully choosing τ_i and n_i so that ν_i is sufficiently longer than μ_i, we will be able to satisfy the requirements of the theorem.

We now proceed with the details of the proof. Recall that σ^* is the first $\mathcal{U}$-program of length $K(\sigma)$ to converge with output σ. Recall also that by $\log n$ we mean the base 2 logarithm of n, rounded up to the nearest integer.

By Theorem 3.14.2, we can select $n_0, n_1, \ldots$ such that $\log n_i = 2^{2^i}$ and $K(n_i^* \mid n_i) \geqslant 2^i - O(i)$. By Proposition 3.14.1,

$$K(n_i^* \mid n_i) = K(K(n_i) \mid n_i) \pm O(1) \leqslant K^{(2)}(n_i) + O(1)$$
$$\leqslant \log 2^{2^i} + O(\log^{(2)} 2^{2^i}) = 2^i + O(i),$$

so $K(n_i^* \mid n_i) = 2^i \pm O(i)$. Thus $K^{(2)}(n_i^* \mid n_i) = O(i)$ (and hence, of course, $K^{(3)}(n_i^* \mid n_i) = o(i)$), so by Corollary 4.2.12,

$$C(n_i^* \mid n_i) = K(n_i^* \mid n_i) - K^{(2)}(n_i^* \mid n_i) \pm O(K^{(3)}(n_i^* \mid n_i)) = 2^i \pm O(i).$$

Let τ_i be the first to halt among the minimal-length $\mathcal{V}$-programs for n_i^* given n_i. (That is, τ_i is $(n_i^*)^*_C$, where the second star is defined with respect to $\mathcal{V}^{n_i}$.) Then $|\tau_i| = C(n_i^* \mid n_i) = 2^i \pm O(i)$. Also, by the minimality of τ_i, $C(\tau_i \mid n_i) = |\tau_i| \pm O(1)$. (That is, $|\tau_i| = C(n_i^* \mid n_i) \leqslant C(\tau_i \mid n_i) + O(1) \leqslant |\tau_i| + O(1)$. Thus it follows that τ_i is hard to describe given n_i, but as we will see below, τ_i is relatively easy to describe given n_i^*, and hence given n_i and $K(n_i)$.)

By Corollary 4.3.5, there is a $\mu_i \in 2^{n_i}$ such that $C(\tau_i\mu_i) = |\tau_i| + n_i \pm O(1)$ and $K(\mu_i) = n_i + K(n_i) \pm O(1)$. Let $\nu_i = \tau_i\mu_i$. Then $\lim_i |\nu_i| = \infty$, and each ν_i is C-random, since $C(\nu_i) = |\tau_i| + n_i \pm O(1) = |\nu_i| \pm O(1)$. So we are left with showing that $\lim_i \frac{m_K(\nu_i)}{\log^{(2)}|\nu_i|} = 1$.

We begin by computing $K(|\nu_i|)$. First,

$$K(|\nu_i|) = K(|\tau_i| + n_i \pm O(1)) = K(n_i) \pm O(K(|\tau_i|)).$$

Now,

$$K(|\tau_i|) = K(2^i \pm O(i)) = K(2^i) \pm O(\log i) = O(\log i),$$

since $K(2^i) = K(i) \pm O(1) = O(\log i)$. Therefore, $K(|\nu_i|) = K(n_i) \pm O(\log i)$.

We now need an upper bound on $K(\nu_i)$. If we have a $\mathcal{U}$-program σ for μ_i and a $\mathcal{U}$-program σ' for τ_i given σ, then we can easily obtain a $\mathcal{U}$-program for $\nu_i = \tau_i\mu_i$ of length roughly $|\sigma\sigma'|$. Thus,

$$K(\nu_i) \leqslant K(\mu_i) + K(\tau_i \mid \mu_i^*) + O(1) = n_i + K(n_i) + K(\tau_i \mid \mu_i^*) \pm O(1).$$

So we will obtain our bound on $K(\nu_i)$ by bounding $K(\tau_i \mid \mu_i^*)$.

Now, $n_i = |\mu_i|$, so $K(n_i \mid \mu_i^*) = O(1)$. Since $|\mu_i^*| = K(\mu_i) = n_i + K(n_i) \pm O(1)$, we have $K(K(n_i) \mid \mu_i^*) = O(1)$. By Proposition 3.14.1, $K(n_i^* \mid n_i, K(n_i)) = O(1)$. Thus,

$$K(n_i^* \mid \mu_i^*) \leqslant K(K(n_i) \mid \mu_i^*) + K(n_i \mid \mu_i^*) + K(n_i^* \mid n_i, K(n_i)) + O(1) = O(1).$$

So $K(\tau_i \mid \mu_i^*) \leqslant K(\tau_i \mid n_i^*) + K(n_i^* \mid \mu_i^*) + O(1) = K(\tau_i \mid n_i^*) + O(1)$.

Recall that τ_i is the first to halt among the minimal-length $\mathcal{V}$-programs for n_i^* given n_i. By the relativized version of Proposition 3.2.1,

$$K(\tau_i \mid n_i^*) \leqslant K(|\tau_i| \mid n_i^*) + O(1) = O(\log |\tau_i|) = O(i),$$

so $K(\tau_i \mid \mu_i^*) = O(i)$.

Putting the last three paragraphs together, we have

$$K(\nu_i) \leqslant n_i + K(n_i) + O(i).$$

Together with the computation of $K(|\nu_i|)$ above, this bound implies that

$$\begin{aligned} m_K(\nu_i) &= |\nu_i| + K(|\nu_i|) - K(\nu_i) \\ &\geqslant 2^i + n_i + K(n_i) - O(i) - [n_i + K(n_i) + O(i)] \\ &= 2^i - O(i) = \log^{(2)}|\nu_i| - O(\log^{(3)}|\nu_i|). \end{aligned}$$

(The last equality holds because $|\nu_i| = |\mu_i| + |\tau_i| = n_i + 2^i \pm O(i)$, and $\log n_i = 2^{2^i}$.) Thus

$$\liminf_i \frac{m_K(\nu_i)}{\log^{(2)}|\nu_i|} \geqslant 1. \tag{4.12}$$

On the other hand, it is easy to get an upper bound on $m_K(\nu_i)$ using the results of Section 4.2. Recall that $C(\nu_i) = |\nu_i| \pm O(1)$. Also, by Corollary

4.2.11, $K(\nu_i) = C(\nu_i) + K(C(\nu_i)) \pm O(C^{(3)}(\nu_i))$, so

$$\begin{aligned} m_K(\nu_i) &= |\nu_i| + K(|\nu_i|) - K(\nu_i) \\ &= C(\nu_i) + K(C(\nu_i)) \pm O(1) - [C(\nu_i) + K(C(\nu_i)) \pm O(C^{(3)}(\nu_i))] \\ &\qquad = O(C^{(3)}(\nu_i)) = O(\log^{(2)} |\nu_i|). \end{aligned}$$

Thus $m_K(\nu_i) = O(\log^{(2)} |\nu_i|)$, but we are not quite done because of the multiplicative constant that might be hidden in the O-term. The following method of finishing the proof was suggested by Joe Miller.

Lemma 4.3.9. $K(|\nu_i|) \leqslant K^{(2)}(\nu_i) + K(m_K(\nu_i)) + O(1)$.

Proof. Assume that $c_i = K(|\nu_i|) - K^{(2)}(\nu_i) - K(m_K(\nu_i))$ is positive, since otherwise we are done. From minimal-length $\mathcal{U}$-programs for $K(\nu_i)$, for $m_K(\nu_i)$, and for c_i, we can compute $K(|\nu_i|)$, and hence can compute $|\nu_i| = m_K(\nu_i) + K(\nu_i) - K(|\nu_i|)$. Thus,

$$\begin{aligned} K(|\nu_i|) &\leqslant K^{(2)}(\nu_i) + K(m_K(\nu_i)) + K(c_i) + O(1) \\ &\qquad = K(|\nu_i|) - c_i + K(c_i) + O(1). \end{aligned}$$

So $c_i \leqslant K(c_i) + O(1)$, whence $c_i = O(1)$. □

To finish the proof of the theorem given this lemma, we have the following inequality.

$$\begin{aligned} m_K(\nu_i) &= |\nu_i| + K(|\nu_1|) - K(\nu_i) \\ &= C(\nu_i) + K(|\nu_i|) - K(\nu_i) \pm O(1) \\ &\leqslant K(|\nu_i|) - K^{(2)}(\nu_i) + K^{(3)}(\nu_i) + O(1) && \text{by Lemma 4.2.6} \\ &\leqslant K(m_K(\nu_i)) + K^{(3)}(\nu_i) + O(1) && \text{by Lemma 4.3.9} \\ &\leqslant K(m_K(\nu_i)) + \log^{(2)} |\nu_i| + o(\log^{(2)} |\nu_i|). \end{aligned}$$

By the crude bound $m_K(\nu_i) = O(\log^{(2)} |\nu_i|)$ established above, we have $K(m_K(\nu_i)) = o(\log^{(2)} |\nu_i|)$, so $m_K(\nu_i) \leqslant \log^{(2)} |\nu_i| + o(\log^{(2)} |\nu_i|)$, whence

$$\limsup_i \frac{m_K(\nu_i)}{\log^{(2)} |\nu_i|} \leqslant 1.$$

Together with (4.12), this inequality implies that $\lim_i \frac{m_K(\nu_i)}{\log^{(2)} |\nu_i|} = 1$, completing the proof of the theorem. □

The following theorem, whose proof is based on Theorem 4.3.7, has as a corollary that the identities (4.1) and (4.2) cannot be improved, and the inequality (4.5) cannot be reversed.

Theorem 4.3.10 (Solovay [371]). *There are infinite sequences of strings ν_i, τ_i, and μ_i such that*

(i) $\lim_i |\nu_i| = \infty$,

(ii) $C(\tau_i) = C(\nu_i) + O(1)$,

(iii) $\lim_i \frac{K(\tau_i)-K(\nu_i)}{\log^{(2)} |\nu_i|} = 1$,

(iv) $K(\mu_i) = K(\nu_i) + O(1)$, *and*

(v) $\lim_i \frac{C(\nu_i)-C(\mu_i)}{\log^{(2)} |\nu_i|} = 1$.

Proof. Let ν_i be as in Theorem 4.3.7. For each i, let τ_i be a strongly K-random string of length $|\nu_i|$. By Corollary 4.3.3, $C(\tau_i) = |\nu_i| \pm O(1) = C(\nu_i) \pm O(1)$. The choice of τ_i implies that $K(\tau_i) = |\nu_i| + K(|\nu_i|) \pm O(1)$, so

$$\begin{aligned} K(\tau_i) - K(\nu_i) &= |\nu_i| + K(|\nu_i|) - [|\nu_i| + K(|\nu_i|) - m_K(\nu_i)] \pm O(1) \\ &= m_K(\nu_i) \pm O(1). \end{aligned}$$

By Theorem 4.3.7, $\lim_i \frac{K(\tau_i)-K(\nu_i)}{\log^{(2)} |\nu_i|} = \lim_i \frac{m_K(\nu_i)}{\log^{(2)} |\nu_i|} = 1$.

By Lemma 4.3.6, there exist m_i such that $|m_i + K(m_i) - K(\nu_i)| = O(1)$. For each i, let μ_i be a strongly K-random string of length m_i. Then $K(\mu_i) = m_i + K(m_i) \pm O(1) = K(\nu_i) \pm O(1)$. Furthermore, by Lemma 4.3.3, $C(\mu_i) = m_i \pm O(1)$, and by Theorem 4.3.7, $C(\nu_i) = |\nu_i| \pm O(1)$. Thus, to establish item 5, it is enough to show that $\lim_i \frac{|\nu_i|-m_i}{\log^{(2)} |\nu_i|} = 1$.

Let $r_i = |\nu_i| - m_i$. Then $K(m_i) = K(|\nu_i|) \pm O(\log r_i)$, so

$$\begin{aligned} r_i \pm O(\log(r_i)) &= |\nu_i| + K(|\nu_i|) - (m_i + K(m_i)) \\ &= |\nu_i| + K(|\nu_i|) - K(\nu_i) \pm O(1) = m_K(\nu_i) \pm O(1). \end{aligned}$$

By Theorem 4.3.7, $\lim_i \frac{r_i}{\log^{(2)} |\nu_i|} = \lim_i \frac{m_K(\nu_i)}{\log^{(2)} |\nu_i|} = 1$. □

Corollary 4.3.11 (Solovay [371]). *None of the following relations hold in general.*

$$K(\sigma) = C(\sigma) + C^{(2)}(\sigma) + C^{(3)}(\sigma) \pm O(C^{(4)}(\sigma)).$$
$$C(\sigma) = K(\sigma) - K^{(2)}(\sigma) + K^{(3)}(\sigma) \pm O(K^{(4)}(\sigma)).$$
$$K(\sigma) = C(\sigma) + K(C(\sigma)) \pm O(1).$$

Proof. Let ν_i, τ_i, and μ_i be as in Theorem 4.3.10.

If the first equation were true then, since $C(\nu_i) = C(\tau_i) \pm O(1)$, we would have $K(\nu_i) - K(\tau_i) = O(C^{(4)}(\nu_i)) = O(\log^{(3)} |\nu_i|)$. But then $\lim_i \frac{K(\nu_i)-K(\tau_i)}{\log^{(2)} |\nu_i|} = 0$, contradicting Theorem 4.3.10.

The argument for the second equation is the same, with μ_i in place of τ_i and K and C interchanged.

Similarly, if the third equation were true then we would have $K(\nu_i) - K(\tau_i) = O(1)$, which would lead to the same contradiction as before. □

4.4 Muchnik's Theorem on C and K

In [288], Muchnik proved the following interesting result on the relationship between prefix-free complexity and plain complexity. The proof we give, which is based on Solovay's results discussed above, is due to Miller [272].

Theorem 4.4.1 (Muchnik, see [288]). *For each d there are strings σ and τ such that $K(\sigma) > K(\tau) + d$ and $C(\tau) > C(\sigma) + d$.*

Proof. Let $\{\nu_i\}_{i\in\omega}$ be the sequence constructed in Theorem 4.3.7. For each i, take ρ_i to be a strongly K-random string of length $|\nu_i| - \frac{\log^{(2)}|\nu_i|}{2}$. (Here we slightly abuse notation by writing $\frac{\log^{(2)}|\nu_i|}{2}$ to mean $\lfloor\frac{\log^{(2)}|\nu_i|}{2}\rfloor$.) First note that

$$\begin{aligned}K(\rho_i) - K(\nu_i) &= |\rho_i| + K(|\rho_i|) - K(\nu_i) \pm O(1)\\ &= |\nu_i| - \frac{\log^{(2)}|\nu_i|}{2} + K(|\nu_i| - \frac{\log^{(2)}|\nu_i|}{2}) - K(\nu_i) \pm O(1)\\ &= |\nu_i| - \frac{\log^{(2)}|\nu_i|}{2} + K(|\nu_i|) - K(\nu_i) \pm O(\log^{(3)}|\nu_i|)\\ &= m_K(\nu_i) - \frac{\log^{(2)}|\nu_i|}{2} \pm O(\log^{(3)}|\nu_i|).\end{aligned}$$

Therefore,

$$\lim_i \frac{K(\rho_i) - K(\nu_i)}{\log^{(2)}|\nu_i|} = \lim_i \frac{m_K(\nu_i) - \frac{\log^{(2)}|\nu_i|}{2}}{\log^{(2)}|\nu_i|} = 1 - \frac{1}{2} = \frac{1}{2}.$$

By Theorem 4.3.3, ρ_i is C-random, so $C(\nu_i) - C(\rho_i) = |\nu_i| - |\rho_i| \pm O(1) = \frac{\log^{(2)}|\nu_i|}{2} \pm O(1)$, and hence

$$\lim_i \frac{C(\nu_i) - C(\rho_i)}{\log^{(2)}|\nu_i|} = \lim_i \frac{\frac{\log^{(2)}|\nu_i|}{2} \pm O(1)}{\log^{(2)}|\nu_i|} = \frac{1}{2}.$$

So for any d we can take i large enough so that $K(\rho_i) - K(\nu_i) \geqslant d$ and $C(\nu_i) - C(\rho_i) \geqslant d$. □

Miller's methods allow an additional improvement to the previous result, namely that we can choose σ and τ to have the same length.

Theorem 4.4.2 (Miller [272]). *For each d there are strings σ and τ of the same length such that $K(\sigma) \geqslant K(\tau) + d$ and $C(\tau) \geqslant C(\sigma) + d$.*

Proof. We extend the proof above. For each i, define $\tau_i = \rho_i 0^{\frac{\log^{(2)}|\nu_i|}{2}}$. Then $|\tau_i| = |\nu_i|$. Furthermore, $K(\tau_i) = K(\rho_i) \pm O(\log^{(3)}|\nu_i|)$ and $C(\tau_i) = C(\rho_i) \pm O(\log^{(3)}|\nu_i|)$. Thus

$$\lim_i \frac{K(\tau_i) - K(\nu_i)}{\log^{(2)}|\nu_i|} = \frac{1}{2} = \lim_i \frac{C(\nu_i) - C(\tau_i)}{\log^{(2)}|\nu_i|}.$$

As above, for any d we can take i large enough so that $K(\tau_i) - K(\nu_i) \geqslant d$ and $C(\nu_i) - C(\tau_i) \geqslant d$. □

Miller observed that the estimates used in both proofs can be improved. It is not hard to show that $K(|\nu_i| - \frac{\log^{(2)} |\nu_i|}{2}) = K(|\nu_i|) \pm O(1)$, and from this fact, that $K(\tau_i) = K(\rho_i) \pm O(1)$ and $C(\tau_i) = C(\rho_i) \pm O(1)$. The weaker estimates above were used because they are sufficient for our purposes and require no explanation.

4.5 Monotone complexity and KM-complexity

As mentioned in Section 3.16, it was a long-standing open question whether KM and Km are the same. We saw in that section that $KM(\sigma) \leqslant Km(\sigma) + O(1)$. Levin [242] conjectured that in fact $Km(\sigma) = KM(\sigma) \pm O(1)$. This conjecture was finally refuted by Gács [166].

Theorem 4.5.1 (Gács [166]). *There exists a function f with $\lim_n f(n) = \infty$ such that $Km(\sigma) - KM(\sigma) \geqslant f(|\sigma|)$ for infinitely many σ. Indeed, we may choose f to be the inverse of Ackermann's function.*

Although we will not discuss reducibilities arising from measures of complexity until later, the following corollary to Gács' Theorem is worth noting here. A natural question given Gács' Theorem is whether the corresponding reducibilities are different. That is, let $A \leqslant_{KM} B$ if $KM(A \upharpoonright n) \leqslant KM(B \upharpoonright n) + O(1)$, and similarly for Km (Km-reducibility is also known as *monotone reducibility*). Then is $\leqslant_{KM}$ different from $\leqslant_{Km}$? Miller observed that this question is easily settled using Gács Theorem.

Corollary 4.5.2 (Miller [personal communication]). *The reducibilities $\leqslant_{KM}$ and $\leqslant_{Km}$ are different.*

Proof. We define $A = \bigcup_s \alpha_s$ in stages, with each α_s a finite string. Let α_0 be such that $Km(\alpha_0) - KM(\alpha_0) > 1$. Now suppose we have defined α_s. For a string τ of length at least $|\alpha_s| + 1$, let $\widehat{\tau}$ be obtained by replacing the initial segment of τ of length $|\alpha_s|$ by α_s. Then it is easy to check that $Km(\widehat{\tau}) = Km(\tau) \pm O(1)$ and $KM(\widehat{\tau}) = KM(\tau) \pm O(1)$, where the constants depend only on α_s. So we can choose a τ such that $Km(\widehat{\tau}) - KM(\widehat{\tau}) > s+1$ and let $\alpha_{s+1} = \widehat{\tau}$. □

Returning to Theorem 4.5.1, we see that, while Gács proved that KM and Km do not agree within an additive constant, it seemed possible that the difference might be very slight. As we will discuss in this section, Adam Day [87] established a strong extension of Gács Theorem with a proof significantly extending and clarifying the original.

How different can these two complexities be? The following theorem gives an upper bound on their difference.

Theorem 4.5.3 (Gács [166], Uspensky and Shen [396]). *$K(\sigma) \leqslant KM(\sigma) + K(|\sigma|) + O(1)$. Thus, for any $k \geqslant 1$ and $\varepsilon > 0$,*

$$\begin{aligned} Km(\sigma) &\leqslant KM(\sigma) + K(|\sigma|) + O(1) \\ &\leqslant KM(\sigma) + \log|\sigma| + \log\log|\sigma| + \cdots + (1+\varepsilon)\log^{(k)}|\sigma| + O(1). \end{aligned}$$

Proof. For each n, we have $\sum_{\sigma \in 2^n} 2^{-KM(\sigma)} \leqslant 1$, by the definition of KM. Thus

$$\sum_{\sigma} 2^{-KM(\sigma) - K(|\sigma|)} = \sum_{n} 2^{-K(n)} \sum_{\sigma \in 2^n} 2^{-KM(\sigma)} \leqslant \sum_{n} 2^{-K(n)} < 1.$$

So $\{(k+1, \sigma) : \sigma \in 2^{<\omega} \wedge k \geqslant KM(\sigma) + K(|\sigma|)\}$ is a KC set. □

Given the upper bound provided by Theorem 4.5.3, the following result, which brings Gács inverse Ackermann function up to two logs, is not far from optimal. (Indeed, since the upper bound in Theorem 4.5.3 holds for K as well as Km, it would be surprising if it were tight, as that would imply that, in a sense, a prefix-free machine is just as good at approximating KM as a monotone machine.)

Theorem 4.5.4 (Day [87]). *Let $c < \frac{1}{2}$. Then there exist infinitely many σ such that $Km(\sigma) > KM(\sigma) + c \log\log|\sigma|$.*

We follow Day's presentation of his complex proof, which is included with his permission. Let $\mathcal{M}$ be a fixed universal monotone machine. We think of this machine as given by axioms of the form (σ, τ), and write $(\sigma, \tau) \in \mathcal{M}$ to mean that on input σ, the machine $\mathcal{M}$ writes at least τ on its output tape. In this section, we write $\sigma \approx \tau$ to mean that $\sigma \preccurlyeq \tau$ or $\tau \preccurlyeq \sigma$. In this case, we say that σ and τ are *comparable*, and otherwise that they are *incomparable*. (We have been using the term "incompatible" for this concept, but want to avoid confusion with the concept of "$\mathcal{M}$-incompatible" strings introduced below.)

To show that the above theorem holds, we will develop a proof that monotonic descriptional complexity and monotonic algorithmic probability do not agree to within an additive constant. The improvement in the lower bound follows from the construction used in the proof. This proof builds on the original work of Gács but is more intricate. A main point of difference is that the algorithm at the heart of the new proof works on sets of strings as opposed to individual strings. It is fair to say that Gács' Theorem is not well understood. We hope that the new proof, as well as improving the bound, clarifies the main reasons why Km and KM are different.

From now on we will refer to a c.e. continuous semimeasure as just a c.e. semimeasure. We will also drop the word monotonic and just talk about descriptional complexity and algorithmic probability. We know that $M_{\mathcal{M}}$ (as defined in Theorem 3.16.2) majorizes all c.e. semimeasures. So, if it were true that $Km(\sigma) = KM(\sigma) + O(1)$, then for any c.e. semimeasure m that we could construct, there would be some constant c such that

$Km(\sigma) \leqslant -\log(m(\sigma)) + c$. The general approach of the proof will be to build a c.e. semimeasure for which this is false, which means constructing a c.e. semimeasure m with the property that for all c there is a σ such that $Km(\sigma) > -\log(m(\sigma)) + c$.

Of course, we want to do more, and prove Theorem 4.5.4. This result will come out of the construction used in the proof. For now we will focus just on showing that Km and KM are different. We will leave the analysis of the size of the difference until later.

Another way to look at this problem is to consider whether for any n, we can construct a semimeasure m such that $m(\lambda) \leqslant 2^{-n}$ and there exists a σ such that $Km(\sigma) > -\log(m(\sigma))$. Viewing the problem this way helps simplify the proof a little, because we can build a c.e. semimeasure $a(\sigma)$ such that for all i,

1. $a(0^i1) \leqslant 2^{-2i-1}$,
2. $a(0^i) = \sum_j a(0^{i+j}1)$, and
3. there exists a σ such that $Km(0^i1\sigma) > -\log(a(0^i1\sigma))$.

Then we can *scale* the semimeasure a to construct a new semimeasure m with the desired properties.

Proposition 4.5.5. *If a semimeasure a with the above properties exists, then Theorem 4.5.1 holds.*

Proof. From a we can define a c.e. semimeasure m by letting $m(0^i1\sigma) = 2^i a(0^i1\sigma)$ and $m(0^i) = \sum_j m(0^{i+j}1)$. Then $m(\sigma) \geqslant m(\sigma 0) + m(\sigma 1)$ for all σ, and

$$m(\lambda) = \sum_i m(0^i1) = \sum_i 2^i a(0^i1) \leqslant \sum_i 2^i 2^{-2i-1} \leqslant 1,$$

so m is a c.e. semimeasure.

As $M_{\mathcal{M}}$ majorizes all c.e. semimeasures, there is some d such that $M_{\mathcal{M}}(\sigma) \geqslant 2^{-d}m(\sigma)$. Thus $KM(\sigma) \leqslant -\log(2^{-d}m(\sigma)) = -\log(m(\sigma)) + d$.

Now given any c, let $i \geqslant c + d$. By our hypothesis on a, there is some σ such that

$$\begin{aligned} Km(0^i1\sigma) &> -\log(a(0^i1\sigma)) = -\log(2^{-i}m(0^i1\sigma)) \\ &= -\log(m(0^i1\sigma)) + i \geqslant -\log(m(0^i1\sigma)) + c + d \geqslant KM(0^i1\sigma) + c. \end{aligned}$$

□

Note that we could use the recursion theorem to determine the constant d in the above proof. However, doing so is not necessary for our construction.

Since we want a to be c.e., we can construct it in stages depending on some computable enumeration of the universal monotone machine $\mathcal{M}$. We will start with $a(\sigma, 0) = 0$ for all σ. At each stage $t+1$, we have the option of choosing a single string ρ and a positive integer x such that $a(\lambda, t)+2^{-x} \leqslant 1$, and defining $a(\sigma, t+1)$ as follows:

$$a(\sigma, t+1) = \begin{cases} a(\sigma, t) + 2^{-x} & \text{if } \sigma \preccurlyeq \rho \\ a(\sigma, t) & \text{otherwise.} \end{cases}$$

In the rest of the proof we will write simply $a(\rho, t+1) = a(\rho, t) + 2^{-x}$ to refer to this process. If we select ρ at stage $t+1$ and $a(\rho, t) = 0$, we will simplify the notation further and write $a(\rho, t+1) = 2^{-x}$. If no such ρ is chosen for a stage $t+1$ then this simply means that $a(\sigma, t+1) = a(\sigma, t)$ for all σ.

Our objective is to construct a c.e. semimeasure a that meets the following requirements for all i.

$R_i : a(0^i 1) \leqslant 2^{-2i-1}$ and there is a σ s.t. $Km(0^i 1\sigma) > -\log(a(0^i 1\sigma))$

For most of this proof we will focus on meeting a single requirement R_i for some arbitrary i. Once we can achieve a single requirement, it will be relatively easy to meet all requirements.

A natural way to view this construction is as a game between us constructing the semimeasure and an opponent constructing the universal monotone machine. For example, to meet the requirement that there is some string 1σ such that $Km(1\sigma) > -\log(a(1\sigma))$, we could choose a string σ and set $a(1\sigma, 1) = 2^{-r}$. Then we could wait and see whether a pair $(\tau, 1\sigma')$ is enumerated into $\mathcal{M}$ where $|\tau| \leqslant r$ and $\sigma \preccurlyeq \sigma'$. If such a pair is not enumerated into $\mathcal{M}$ then the requirement is met because $Km(1\sigma) > r = -\log(a(1\sigma))$. If such a pair is enumerated into $\mathcal{M}$ then we can make another change to a at some future stage.

We need to develop a construction of a such that no matter how the opponent enumerates $\mathcal{M}$, the requirements on a are met. We have only a finite amount of measure that we can use, and similarly, the opponent has only a finite number of descriptions of any given length. Our goal is make the opponent run out of suitable descriptions before we run out of measure. There are some fundamental concepts used by Gács in his proof of Theorem 4.5.1 that we will make use of. We will introduce one of these with the following example.

Example 4.5.6. We choose a string σ and set $a(\sigma, 1) = 2^{-4}$. Now the opponent must respond by ensuring that $Km(\sigma) \leqslant 4$. To do so, the opponent must enumerate some pair (τ, σ') into $\mathcal{M}$, where $|\tau| \leqslant 4$ and $\sigma' \succcurlyeq \sigma$. Let us suppose that the opponent enumerates $(0000, \sigma)$ into $\mathcal{M}$. Then either it is possible for the opponent to add $(000, \sigma)$ into $\mathcal{M}$ or not. If not, we can set $a(\sigma, 2) = a(\sigma, 1) + 2^{-4} = 2^{-3}$. Now, as it is not possible for the opponent to add $(000, \sigma)$ to $\mathcal{M}$, the opponent must find a new string, say 001, and add $(001, \sigma)$ to $\mathcal{M}$. However, in this case, the opponent has used both 0000 and 001 to describe σ, a waste of resources. Alternatively, assume that the opponent can enumerate $(000, \sigma)$ into $\mathcal{M}$. We can think of the opponent as holding 000 as a description in reserve for σ. Now we make this reservation useless, by

1. never again adding measure to a string comparable with σ, and
2. using only units of measure of size at least 2^{-3} from now on.

As we are using increments of measure of size 2^{-3} or more, the opponent must always respond with strings of length at most 3. However, the opponent cannot use 000 because 000 can be used only to describe a string comparable with σ. Hence, if we never increase the measure on a string comparable with σ, the opponent can never use 000. In this case, 0001 is a *gap* in the domain of $\mathcal{M}$, as it cannot be used to respond to any of our increments in measure, which again is a waste of the opponent's resources.

A proof of Theorem 4.5.1 can be developed by generalizing the approach of this example. A first step toward this generalization is the following. We take a string σ. We have two integer parameters r, g with $0 < r < g$. We want to increase the measure on σ in increments of 2^{-g}. Each time we increase the measure we want the opponent to respond. To do so, we do not increase the measure on σ directly but on some extension of σ. Let $\Xi = \{\sigma\tau : \tau \in 2^{g-r}\}$. We will take some $\xi \in \Xi$ and increase the measure on ξ instead of on σ. A first attempt at the algorithm we need is as follows.

Algorithm 1.

> Let t be the current stage in the enumeration of $\mathcal{M}$. Choose some $\xi \in \Xi$ that has not been used before (so that $a(\xi, t) = 0$). If there is some description of a string σ' with $\sigma' \succcurlyeq \sigma$ in the domain of $\mathcal{M}_t$ that can be shortened to a description of length r, then terminate the algorithm. Otherwise, increase the measure on ξ by 2^{-g}, and wait until a stage t' at which the opponent describes ξ with a string of length at most g. If we have not used all the elements of Ξ, then let $t = t'$ and repeat. If we have used all the elements of Ξ, then the measure on σ must be $|\Xi|2^{-g} = 2^{-r}$, so wait until the opponent uses a string of length r to describe σ.

If we apply this algorithm, then the opponent must either use a string of length r to describe σ, or have some string that describes a string comparable with σ that can be shortened to a string of length r. The crucial fact is that, at some point, we increased the measure on σ by *just* 2^{-g}, and the opponent had to respond by finding a *new* string of length r. The string is new in the sense that it is not just some initial segment of a string already used.

As it stands, this algorithm can make only a small gap between Km and KM. The hard part is amplifying this gap. Amplification can be done by using the algorithm recursively. In the algorithm above, we act by setting

$a(\xi, t) = 2^{-g}$ for some ξ at some stage t. However, rather than just directly increasing the measure on ξ, we could instead run the algorithm again on some *extension* of ξ. This action would have the effect of increasing the measure on ξ while forcing the opponent to waste even more resources. However, to implement this strategy, a number of issues need to be dealt with:

1. We want to make sure our algorithm increases the measure enough. Algorithm 1 will increase the measure on σ somewhere between 2^{-g} and 2^{-r}, which is too great a range.

2. We need to ensure that any gaps the algorithm makes in the domain of $\mathcal{M}$ are never used again. The algorithm above does not address this.

3. Each time we use an extension of a string, we go deeper into the tree of binary strings. We would like to minimize the depth that we go to in order to get the best possible lower bound on the difference between Km and KM.

The concepts in Example 4.5.6 and Algorithm 1 were used by Gács in his original proof of Theorem 4.5.1.[1] The approach of this proof is still based on these ideas but differs from that of Gács in how the problems listed above are addressed.

The algorithm that we will present will make decisions based on the domain of $\mathcal{M}$. The question of whether there is a description of σ that can be shortened will be crucial (e.g., whether or not 0000 could be shortened to 000 in example 4.5.6). First we will define certain subsets of the domain of $\mathcal{M}$. We will prove some technical lemmas about how these sets change as the parameters defining them change. These lemmas will be crucial to the verification of the proof. Then we will present the algorithm that establishes a gap between Km and KM. After that, we will verify that the algorithm works. Finally, we will analyze the algorithm to show how it improves the lower bound.

At any stage t, the approximation $\mathcal{M}_t$ tells us the options the opponent has left. In particular, $\mathcal{M}_t$ tells us what the opponent can and cannot use certain strings for. We need a more exact notion for the idea of the opponent shortening an existing description. In his original proof, Gács came up with the notion of a string τ being *reserved* as a description for σ. The idea is not just that the opponent can use τ to describe σ, but additionally that the opponent cannot use τ to describe a string incomparable with σ. For τ to be reserved for σ, the opponent must have already used a string comparable with τ to describe an extension of σ.

[1]At the time of writing, an extended version of the original proof is available from Gács' homepage.

There are really two ideas in this definition that are worth separating out and making more explicit. First we will say that a string τ is *fragmented* by σ if some string comparable to τ describes an extension of σ, which means the opponent cannot use τ to describe a string incomparable with σ (as otherwise $\mathcal{M}$ would not be a monotone machine). Second, a string τ is $\mathcal{M}$*-incompatible* with σ if some string comparable with τ describes a string incomparable with σ. This means that τ cannot be used to describe σ. Hence another way of saying a string τ is reserved for σ is that τ is fragmented by σ but τ is not $\mathcal{M}$-incompatible with σ. As we are not so much interested in particular descriptions, but descriptions of a certain length, we will make the following definitions.

Definition 4.5.7. (i) The strings of length r *fragmented* by σ at stage t are those in the set

$$F_r(\sigma, t) = \{\tau \in 2^r : \exists(\tau', \sigma') \in \mathcal{M}_t\,(\tau' \approx \tau \wedge \sigma \preccurlyeq \sigma')\}.$$

(ii) The strings of length r $\mathcal{M}$*-incompatible* with σ at stage t are those in the set

$$I_r(\sigma, t) = \{\tau \in 2^r : \exists(\tau', \sigma') \in \mathcal{M}_t\,(\tau' \approx \tau \wedge \sigma \mid \sigma')\}.$$

(iii) The strings of length r *reserved* for σ at stage t are those in the set

$$R_r(\sigma, t) = F_r(\sigma, t) \setminus I_r(\sigma, t).$$

Example 4.5.8. Suppose that

$$\mathcal{M}_t = \{(00, 11), (000, 1), (000, 11), (001, 11), \\ (011, 01), (100, 01), (110, 011), (111, 1)\}.$$

If we consider the strings of length 2, working through the above definitions establishes that $F_2(01, t) = \{01, 10, 11\}$, that $I_2(01, t) = \{00, 11\}$, and that $R_2(01, t) = \{01, 10\}$.

The definitions given for F_r and I_r can be extended to sets of strings.

Definition 4.5.9. If Σ is a set of finite strings, then

(i) $F_r(\Sigma, t) = \bigcup_{\sigma \in \Sigma} F_r(\sigma, t)$ and

(ii) $I_r(\Sigma, t) = \bigcap_{\sigma \in \Sigma} I_r(\sigma, t)$.

We will explain later why we take the intersection in the definition of $I_r(\Sigma, t)$. The following lemmas show how the sets $F_r(\sigma, t)$, $I_r(\sigma, t)$, $F_r(\Sigma, t)$, and $I_r(\Sigma, t)$ change as the parameters that define them vary.

Lemma 4.5.10. (i) *If* $r_0 \leqslant r_1$ *then* $[\![F_{r_0}(\sigma, t)]\!] \supseteq [\![F_{r_1}(\sigma, t)]\!]$ *and* $[\![I_{r_0}(\sigma, t)]\!] \supseteq [\![I_{r_1}(\sigma, t)]\!]$.

(ii) *If* $\sigma_0 \preccurlyeq \sigma_1$ *then* $[\![F_r(\sigma_0, t)]\!] \supseteq [\![F_r(\sigma_1, t)]\!]$ *and* $[\![I_r(\sigma_0, t)]\!] \subseteq [\![I_r(\sigma_1, t)]\!]$.

(iii) *If* $t_0 \leqslant t_1$ *then* $[\![F_r(\sigma, t_0)]\!] \subseteq [\![F_r(\sigma, t_1)]\!]$ *and* $[\![I_r(\sigma, t_0)]\!] \subseteq [\![I_r(\sigma, t_1)]\!]$.

Proof. (i) If $\alpha \in [\![F_{r_1}(\sigma,t)]\!]$ then $\alpha \upharpoonright r_1 \in F_{r_1}(\sigma,t)$, so there exist $\tau \approx \alpha \upharpoonright r_1$ and $\sigma' \succcurlyeq \sigma$ such that $(\tau,\sigma') \in \mathcal{M}_t$. Since $r_0 \leqslant r_1$, we have $\tau \approx \alpha \upharpoonright r_0$, so $\alpha \upharpoonright r_0 \in F_{r_0}(\sigma,t)$, and hence $\alpha \in [\![F_{r_0}(\sigma,t)]\!]$. Similarly, $[\![I_{r_0}(\sigma,t)]\!] \supseteq [\![I_{r_1}(\sigma,t)]\!]$.

(ii) If $\tau \in F_r(\sigma_1,t)$ then there exist $\tau' \approx \tau$ and $\sigma \succcurlyeq \sigma_1$ such that $(\tau',\sigma) \in \mathcal{M}_t$. As $\sigma \succcurlyeq \sigma_1 \succcurlyeq \sigma_0$, we have $\tau \in F_r(\sigma_0,t)$. If $\tau \in I_r(\sigma_0,t)$ then there are $\tau' \approx \tau$ and $\rho \mid \sigma_0$ such that $(\tau',\rho) \in \mathcal{M}_t$. As $\sigma_1 \succcurlyeq \sigma_0$, we have $\sigma_1 \mid \rho$, and thus $\tau \in I_r(\sigma_1,t)$.

(iii) follows because $\mathcal{M}_{t_0} \subseteq \mathcal{M}_{t_1}$. □

In summary, $[\![F_r(\sigma,t)]\!]$ and $[\![I_r(\sigma,t)]\!]$ are both increasing in t and decreasing in r. In the length of σ, we have that $[\![F_r(\sigma,t)]\!]$ is decreasing and $[\![I_r(\sigma,t)]\!]$ is increasing. To establish similar results for $F_r(\Sigma,t)$, and $I_r(\Sigma,t)$, we need to define a relationship $\preccurlyeq$ between sets of strings.

Definition 4.5.11. If $\Sigma_0, \Sigma_1 \subseteq 2^{<\omega}$, then $\Sigma_0 \preccurlyeq \Sigma_1$ if for all $\sigma_1 \in \Sigma_1$, there exists a $\sigma_0 \in \Sigma_0$ such that $\sigma_0 \preccurlyeq \sigma_1$.

Lemma 4.5.12. (i) *If* $r_0 \leqslant r_1$ *then* $[\![F_{r_0}(\Sigma,t)]\!] \supseteq [\![F_{r_1}(\Sigma,t)]\!]$ *and* $[\![I_{r_0}(\Sigma,t)]\!] \supseteq [\![I_{r_1}(\Sigma,t)]\!]$.

(ii) *If* $\Sigma_0 \preccurlyeq \Sigma_1$ *then* $[\![F_r(\Sigma_0,t)]\!] \supseteq [\![F_r(\Sigma_1,t)]\!]$ *and* $[\![I_r(\Sigma_0,t)]\!] \subseteq [\![I_r(\Sigma_1,t)]\!]$.

(iii) *If* $t_0 \leqslant t_1$ *then* $[\![F_r(\Sigma,t_0)]\!] \subseteq [\![F_r(\Sigma,t_1)]\!]$ *and* $[\![I_r(\Sigma,t_0)]\!] \subseteq [\![I_r(\Sigma,t_1)]\!]$.

Proof. (i) If $\tau \in F_{r_1}(\Sigma,t)$, then for some $\sigma \in \Sigma$, we have $\tau \in F_{r_1}(\sigma,t)$, so by the previous lemma, $\tau \in F_{r_0}(\sigma,t) \subseteq F_{r_0}(\Sigma,t)$.

If $\tau \in I_{r_1}(\Sigma,t)$, then for all $\sigma \in \Sigma$, we have $\tau \in I_{r_1}(\sigma,t)$, so by the previous lemma, $\tau \in \bigcap_{\sigma\in\Sigma} I_{r_0}(\sigma,t) = I_{r_0}(\Sigma,t)$.

(ii) If $\alpha \in [\![F_r(\Sigma_1,t)]\!]$ then for some $\sigma_1 \in \Sigma_1$, we have $\alpha \in [\![F_r(\sigma_1,t)]\!]$. There exists $\sigma_0 \in \Sigma_0$ such that $\sigma_0 \preccurlyeq \sigma_1$, so by the previous lemma, $\alpha \in [\![F_r(\sigma_0,t)]\!] \subseteq [\![F_r(\Sigma_0,t)]\!]$.

If $\alpha \in [\![I_r(\Sigma_0,t)]\!]$ then for all $\sigma_0 \in \Sigma_0$, we have $\alpha \in [\![I_r(\sigma_0,t)]\!]$. Now, if $\sigma_1 \in \Sigma_1$ then for some $\sigma_0 \in \Sigma_0$, we have $\sigma_0 \preccurlyeq \sigma_1$. Since $\alpha \in [\![I_r(\sigma_0,t)]\!]$, by the previous lemma, $\alpha \in [\![I_r(\sigma_1,t)]\!]$. Thus $\alpha \in \bigcap_{\sigma_1\in\Sigma_1} [\![I_r(\sigma_1,t)]\!] = [\![I_r(\Sigma_1,t)]\!]$.

(iii) If $\tau \in F_r(\Sigma,t_0)$, then for some $\sigma \in \Sigma$, we have $\tau \in F_r(\sigma,t_0)$, so by the previous lemma, $\tau \in F_r(\sigma,t_1) \subseteq F_r(\Sigma,t_1)$.

If $\tau \in I_r(\Sigma,t_0)$, then for all $\sigma \in \Sigma$, we have $\tau \in I_r(\sigma,t)$, so by the previous lemma, $\tau \in \bigcap_{\sigma\in\Sigma} I_r(\sigma,t_1) = I_r(\Sigma,t_1)$. □

We are going to describe an algorithm that can be used to prove Theorems 4.5.1 and 4.5.4. The algorithm will be allocated a certain amount of measure to spend on the construction of the c.e. semimeasure a. It will also be given a set of strings Σ, and it will be able to increase the measure only on extensions of these strings. Ultimately we want the algorithm to establish some difference between $Km(\rho)$ and $-\log(a(\rho))$ for some string ρ that extends some element of Σ. We will argue that if this does not happen, then some contradiction must ensue. The basic idea is to make the opponent run out of short descriptions. Formalizing this idea is a little difficult. We want to be able to say that if we spend 2^{-r} much measure on extensions of Σ, and we do not establish a difference between Km and $-\log(a)$, then we can cause x amount of something to happen to $\mathcal{M}$ (where $\mathcal{M}$ is the universal machine controlled by the opponent). We will refer to this x, whatever it is, as the gain made by the algorithm.

Now, the most obvious measurement to use would be $\mu([\![\pi_1(\mathcal{M}_t)]\!])$ (where $\pi_1(\mathcal{M}_t)$ is the projection of $\mathcal{M}_t$ onto the first coordinate), because this projection is analogous to the domain of $\mathcal{M}_t$. However, remember that part of the idea is to leave gaps in $\mathcal{M}$ that the opponent cannot do anything useful with. The problem with this measurement is that it does not account for gaps. An alternative is the size of $F_r(\Sigma, t)$, the set of strings of length r that are fragmented by elements of Σ. This measurement will count gaps, and is almost what we need. The size of $F_r(\Sigma, t)$ is at most 2^r, so if the algorithm ends at stage t_1, and we could ensure that $|F_r(\Sigma, t_1)| \geqslant k$ for an arbitrary k, we would be done. However, the actual situation is still more complicated. We will end up using the algorithm we define recursively. When verifying the algorithm, we do not want to double-count any gain made. To make the verification possible, we will subtract $[\![I_{r'}(\Sigma, t_0)]\!]$ from $[\![F_r(\Sigma, t_1)]\!]$, where $r' \geqslant r$ and t_0 is the time the algorithm starts. This measurement is what we will use to determine the gain made by the algorithm. The following definition, where G is for gain, codifies this idea.

Definition 4.5.13. If $\Sigma \subseteq 2^{<\omega}$, and $r, r', t_0, t_1 \in \mathbb{N}$ are such that $r \leqslant r'$ and $t_0 \leqslant t_1$, then

$$G_r^{r'}(\Sigma; t_0, t_1) = [\![F_r(\Sigma, t_1)]\!] \setminus [\![I_{r'}(\Sigma, t_0)]\!].$$

The value $G_r^{r'}(\Sigma; t_0, t_1)$ can be thought of as the gain the algorithm obtains using the strings in Σ between stages t_0 and t_1, and using units of measure between r and r'. With this definition in hand, we can define what sort of algorithm is needed. The following definition is complicated, so we will take some time to explain it after giving it. Note that we describe an algorithm that works on a set of strings, which is a new feature of this proof.

Definition 4.5.14. If $r, b \in \mathbb{N}$, and Σ is a finite prefix-free subset of $2^{<\omega}$, then an (r, b, Σ)*-strategy* is an algorithm that, if implemented at stage t_0, ensures that one of the following holds.

(i) (a) There is a $\sigma \in \Sigma$ such that for some σ' extending σ, we have $Km(\sigma') > -\log(a(\sigma'))$, and
  (b) for all stages t and all $\sigma \in \Sigma$, we have $a(\sigma, t) < \frac{5}{4}2^{-r}$; or

(ii) at some stage t_1, for some $r' \geqslant r$ computable from (r, b),
  (a) for all $\sigma \in \Sigma$, we have $2^{-r} \leqslant a(\sigma, t_1) < \frac{5}{4}2^{-r}$,

(b) $\mu(G_r^{r'}(\Sigma; t_0, t_1)) \geqslant \left(1 + \frac{b}{2}\right) a(\Sigma, t_1)$, and

(c) for all $\widehat{\Sigma} \subseteq \Sigma$, we have

$$\mu(G_r^{r'}(\widehat{\Sigma}; t_0, t_1)) \geqslant \left(1 + \frac{b}{2}\right) a(\Sigma, t_1) - 2^{-r} D(b) |\Sigma \setminus \widehat{\Sigma}|,$$

where $D(b) = 5\left(\frac{5}{4}\right)^b - 4$ and $a(\Sigma, t) = \sum_{\sigma \in \Sigma} a(\sigma, t)$.

The input parameters for the strategy are r, b, and Σ. The set Σ is a finite prefix-free set of binary strings. These are the strings that the algorithm will work on. The r parameter determines the measure that the algorithm should spend on *every* string in Σ. The b parameter determines the amount of gain that the algorithm should make. First we will establish the existence of an $(r, 0, \Sigma)$-strategy for any appropriate r, then we will inductively establish the existence of $(r, b+1, \Sigma)$-strategies assuming the existence of (r, b, Σ)-strategies.

The definition gives two possible outcomes to a strategy. Outcome (i) is the preferred outcome. If outcome (i) occurs, then we have established a difference between Km and KM. However, if we do not achieve this outcome, then outcome (ii) is at least a step in the right direction. Provided $b > 0$, outcome (ii) ensures that some difference between $\mu(G_r^{r'}(\Sigma; t_0, t_1))$ and $a(\Sigma, t_1)$ is created.

In outcome (ii), condition (b) says that the gain on the set of strings Σ is bounded below. We do not want the gain to be too concentrated on some particular subset of Σ. The gain achieved need not be evenly distributed among the elements of Σ, but it is important that this distribution not be too skewed. This is the reason for condition (c). Condition (c) ensures that no individual string in Σ contributes too much to the overall gain made. We need condition (c) because when we use the algorithm recursively, we will not be able to count the gain that occurs on certain individual elements of Σ. Hence we do not want an individual element of Σ providing too much of the overall gain. Note that (c) implies (b) by taking $\widehat{\Sigma} = \Sigma$.

It is also important to observe that for all $\sigma \in \Sigma$, if the strategy is running at stage t, then $a(\sigma, t)$ is bounded above in outcomes (i) and (ii). In outcome (ii) there is also a lower bound for $a(\sigma, t_1)$. This lower bound is essential for using strategies recursively because we want these strategies to increase the measure on strings, as well as establish some gain. The function $D(b)$ is chosen because it has the properties that $D(0) = 1$ and $D(b+1) = \frac{5}{4} D(b) + 1$.

If we can implement an (r, b, Σ)-strategy with an arbitrarily high b then (ii) is not a possible outcome as the measure would be greater than 1. This situation would force outcome (i) to occur.

The other value in the above definition to discuss is r'. The value r' dictates where the strategy should make its gain. In practice, what it will mean is that $2^{-r'}$ will be the minimum-sized increment in measure that the strategy will make to a. In other words, each time the strategy increases the measure on some string, the amount increased will be at least $2^{-r'}$. The idea is that if any previous strategy has created a gap of measure less that $2^{-r'}$, then the current strategy will not interfere with that gap.

The idea behind the basic $(r, 0, \Sigma)$-strategy is simple. For every $\sigma \in \Sigma$ we set $a(\sigma) = 2^{-r}$. The opponent is then forced to respond by setting $Km(\sigma) \leqslant r$. To do this, the opponent must find some string τ of length at most r and enumerate (τ, σ) into $\mathcal{M}$. The only difficulty is in showing that this basic idea meets our rather elaborate definition of a strategy.

Proposition 4.5.15. *Let $r \in \mathbb{N}$ and let Σ be a finite prefix-free subset of $2^{<\omega}$ such that $|\Sigma| \leqslant 2^r$. If t_0 is the current stage in the construction of a and $a(\Sigma, t_0) = 0$, then we can implement an $(r, 0, \Sigma)$-strategy with $r' = r$.*

Proof. Let $\Sigma = \{\sigma_1, \ldots, \sigma_n\}$. The desired strategy can be implemented as follows. First, let $a(\sigma_i, t_0 + i) = 2^{-r}$ for all i such that $1 \leqslant i \leqslant n$. (We know that $a(\sigma_i, t_0 + i - 1) = 0$ because Σ is prefix-free.) This definition ensures that $a(\Sigma, t_0 + n) = |\Sigma| 2^{-r}$. The second step is to wait until a stage t_1, when the opponent responds by setting $Km_{t_1}(\sigma) \leqslant r$ for all $\sigma \in \Sigma$. If this response never happens, then for some $\sigma \in \Sigma$, we have $Km(\sigma) > r = -\log(2^{-r}) = -\log(\lim_t a(\sigma, t)) = -\log(a(\sigma))$, so outcome (i) occurs.

If at some stage t_1, we have $Km_{t_1}(\sigma) \leqslant r$ for all $\sigma \in \Sigma$, then for each i such that $1 \leqslant i \leqslant n$, the opponent must have enumerated some (τ_i, σ_i') into $\mathcal{M}_{t_1}$, where $s_i = |\tau_i| \leqslant r$ and $\sigma_i' \succcurlyeq \sigma_i$. In this case we will show that outcome (ii) occurs. First, (a) holds as $a(\Sigma, t_1) = a(\Sigma, t_0 + n)$.

For any i, let τ_r be any extension of τ_i of length r. By definition, $\tau_r \in F_r(\sigma_i, t_1)$, so $\tau_r \in \bigcup_{\sigma \in \Sigma} F_r(\sigma, t_1) = F_r(\Sigma, t_1)$. If $\tau_r \in I_r(\sigma_i, t_0)$, then for some τ' comparable with τ_r and some ρ incomparable with σ_i, we have $(\tau', \rho) \in \mathcal{M}_{t_0} \subseteq \mathcal{M}_{t_1}$, which contradicts the definition of a monotone machine, as it implies that both $\tau' \approx \tau_i$ and $\rho \mid \sigma_i'$. So $\tau_r \notin I_r(\sigma_i, t_0)$ and thus $\tau_r \notin \bigcap_{\sigma_i \in \Sigma} I_r(\sigma_i, t_0) = I_r(\Sigma, t_0)$. Hence $G_r^r(\Sigma; t_0, t_1)$, which by definition is $[\![F_r(\Sigma, t_1)]\!] \setminus [\![I_r(\sigma, t_0)]\!]$, contains all infinite extensions of τ_r and hence all infinite extensions of τ_i. So $[\![\tau_i]\!] \subseteq G_r^r(\Sigma; t_0, t_1)$.

Now if $i \neq j$ then $[\![\tau_i]\!] \cap [\![\tau_j]\!] = \emptyset$, because otherwise σ_i and σ_j must be comparable, but Σ is a prefix-free set. Thus

$$\begin{aligned} \mu(G_r^r(\Sigma; t_0, t_1)) &\geqslant \sum_{i=1}^{n} \mu([\![\tau_i]\!]) = \sum_{i=1}^{n} 2^{-s_i} \\ &\geqslant \sum_{i=1}^{n} 2^{-r} = |\Sigma| 2^{-r} = a(\Sigma, t_1) = (1 + \tfrac{0}{2}) a(\Sigma, t_1). \end{aligned}$$

Hence (b) holds.

Let $\widehat{\Sigma} \subseteq \Sigma$. Let $I = \{1, \ldots, n\}$ and $J = \{i \in I : \sigma_i \in \widehat{\Sigma}\}$. By the same logic as above,

$$\mu(G_r^r(\widehat{\Sigma}; t_0, t_1)) \geqslant \sum_{j \in J} 2^{-r} = |I|2^{-r} - (|I \setminus J|)2^{-r}$$
$$= (1 + \tfrac{0}{2})a(\Sigma, t_1) - (|\Sigma \setminus \widehat{\Sigma}|)2^{-r}(1 + \tfrac{0}{2})a(\Sigma, t_1) - 2^{-r}D(0)|\Sigma \setminus \widehat{\Sigma}|.$$

So (c) holds, and outcome (ii) occurs. □

We are going to work up to developing an $(r, b + 1, \Sigma)$-strategy, using (r, b, Σ)-strategies. Before we present the main algorithm that does so, there is some more preparatory work to do. Ideally, when we implement a strategy, we want to achieve outcome (i). However, if this outcome does not occur then at some stage the strategy will terminate and we can start a new strategy. We want to ensure that if the second strategy also achieves outcome (ii), then the gain of running the strategies sequentially is at least the sum of the minimum gain expected from the strategies individually. The definition of the (r, b, Σ)-strategy is designed to allow this to be the case, as Proposition 4.5.17 will show. Before proving this proposition, we need the following lemma.

Lemma 4.5.16. *If $\sigma_0 \mid \sigma_1$ then $F_p(\sigma_0, t) \subseteq I_p(\sigma_1, t)$.*

Proof. If $\tau \in F_p(\sigma_0, t)$ then there exists $(\tau', \sigma_0') \in \mathcal{M}_t$ such that $\tau' \approx \tau$ and $\sigma_0' \succcurlyeq \sigma_0$, which implies that $\sigma_0' \mid \sigma_1$. Thus $\tau \in I_p(\sigma_1, t)$. □

Proposition 4.5.17. *If $r_0 \leqslant r_1 \leqslant \cdots \leqslant r_n$ and $t_0 \leqslant t_1 \leqslant \cdots \leqslant t_n$ are sequences of natural numbers, and $\Sigma_0, \Sigma_1, \ldots, \Sigma_{n-1}$ are pairwise disjoint prefix-free subsets of $2^{<\omega}$ such that $\Sigma = \Sigma_0 \cup \Sigma_1 \cup \cdots \cup \Sigma_{n-1}$ is also prefix-free, then*

$$\mu(G_{r_0}^{r_n}(\Sigma; t_0, t_n)) \geqslant \sum_{i<n} \mu(G_{r_{n-1-i}}^{r_{n-i}}(\Sigma_i; t_i, t_{i+1})).$$

Proof. First, if $i < n$ then $\Sigma \preccurlyeq \Sigma_i$, so by chaining together applications of Lemma 4.5.12, we have

$$[\![F_{r_{n-i-1}}(\Sigma_i, t_{i+1})]\!] \subseteq [\![F_{r_0}(\Sigma_i, t_{i+1})]\!] \subseteq [\![F_{r_0}(\Sigma, t_{i+1})]\!] \subseteq [\![F_{r_0}(\Sigma, t_n)]\!]$$

and

$$[\![I_{r_n}(\Sigma, t_0)]\!] \subseteq [\![I_{r_n}(\Sigma, t_i)]\!] \subseteq [\![I_{r_n}(\Sigma_i, t_i)]\!] \subseteq [\![I_{r_{n-i}}(\Sigma_i, t_i)]\!].$$

Hence $[\![F_{r_0}(\Sigma, t_n)]\!] \setminus [\![I_{r_n}(\Sigma, t_0)]\!] \supseteq [\![F_{r_{n-i-1}}(\Sigma_i, t_{i+1})]\!] \setminus [\![I_{r_{n-i}}(\Sigma_i, t_i)]\!]$, which by definition means that $G_{r_0}^{r_n}(\Sigma; t_0, t_n) \supseteq G_{r_{n-i-1}}^{r_{n-i}}(\Sigma_i; t_i, t_{i+1})$.

Now let $i < j < n$. Then

$$[\![F_{r_{n-i-1}}(\Sigma_i, t_i)]\!] \subseteq [\![F_{r_{n-j}}(\Sigma_i, t_j)]\!] \subseteq [\![I_{r_{n-j}}(\Sigma_j, t_j)]\!].$$

The first inclusion is by Lemma 4.5.12. The second inclusion follows because if $\tau \in F_{r_{n-j}}(\Sigma_i, t_j)$, then $\tau \in F_{r_{n-j}}(\sigma_i, t_j)$ for some $\sigma_i \in \Sigma_i$. But if $\sigma_j \in \Sigma_j$

then σ_j is incomparable with σ_i. So $\tau \in I_{r_{n-j}}(\sigma_j, t_j)$ by Lemma 4.5.16. Thus $\tau \in \bigcap_{\sigma_j \in \Sigma_j} I_{r_{n-j}}(\sigma_j, t_j) = I_{r_{n-j}}(\Sigma_j, t_j)$. So we can conclude that

$$([\![F_{r_{n-i-1}}(\Sigma_i, t_{i+1})]\!] \setminus [\![I_{r_{n-i}}(\Sigma_i, t_i)]\!]) \\ \cap ([\![F_{r_{n-j-1}}(\Sigma_j, t_{j+1})]\!] \setminus [\![I_{r_{n-j}}(\Sigma_j, t_j)]\!]) = \emptyset,$$

which again by definition means that

$$G^{r_{n-i}}_{r_{n-i-1}}(\Sigma_i; t_i, t_{i+1}) \cap G^{r_{n-j}}_{r_{n-j-1}}(\Sigma_j; t_j, t_{j+1}) = \emptyset.$$

□

Buried in the above proof is the reason we define $I_r(\Sigma, t)$ to be the intersection of $I_r(\sigma, t)$ for all $\sigma \in \Sigma$: Take Σ_0 and Σ_1 to be disjoint sets whose union is prefix-free. If $\tau \in F_r(\Sigma_0, t)$ then τ is fragmented by some string in Σ_0. As all strings in Σ_0 are incomparable with all strings in Σ_1, we have $\tau \in I_r(\Sigma_1, t)$. This is the reason the above proposition works, as it avoids double-counting any gains.

Example 4.5.18. To illustrate why this proposition is useful, we will show how we can use it to gradually increase the measure on a string without losing any gain made along the way. Consider the following implementation of three strategies in sequence and assume that they all have outcome (ii). Take some $r_0 \in \mathbb{N}$. Fix a $b \in \mathbb{N}$ and assume we have an (r, b, Σ) strategy for any appropriate r and Σ. Let r_1 be the r' computable from (r_0, b), as in Definition 4.5.14. Similarly, let r_2 be the r' computable from (r_1, b), and let r_3 be the r' computable from (r_2, b). Take any string σ and let $\Sigma_2 = \{\sigma 00\}$, let $\Sigma_1 = \{\sigma 01\tau : \tau \in 2^{r_1 - r_0}\}$, let $\Sigma_0 = \{\sigma 1\tau : \tau \in 2^{r_2 - r_0}\}$, and let $\Sigma = \Sigma_0 \cup \Sigma_1 \cup \Sigma_2$.

Starting at stage t_0, we first implement an (r_2, b, Σ_0)-strategy. When this strategy finishes at stage t_1, we implement an (r_1, b, Σ_1)-strategy. Finally, when this strategy finishes at stage t_2, we implement an (r_0, b, Σ_2)-strategy. Let t_3 be the stage at which this final strategy finishes. By Proposition 4.5.17,

$$\mu(G^{r_3}_{r_0}(\Sigma; t_0, t_3)) \geqslant \sum_{i \leqslant 2} \mu(G^{r_{3-i}}_{r_{3-1-i}}(\Sigma_i; t_i, t_{i+1})) \\ \geqslant \sum_{i \leqslant 2} \left(1 + \frac{b}{2}\right) a(\Sigma_i, t_{i+1}) = \left(1 + \frac{b}{2}\right) a(\Sigma, t_3).$$

The last step follows provided we do not increase the measure on any other string comparable with a string in Σ except as required by the strategies. Now $a(\sigma) \geqslant a(\Sigma) \geqslant |\Sigma_0| 2^{-r_2} + |\Sigma_1| 2^{-r_1} + |\Sigma_2| 2^{-r_0} = 3 \cdot 2^{-r_0}$. This approach has allowed us to use strategies to increase the measure on σ in three increments of 2^{-r_0} without losing any of the gain made by the three strategies individually. This ability to increase the measure on a string in small increments will be exploited in the main proof.

We have seen that we can use strategies sequentially without losing any of their individual gains. However, we need to do better: we need to be able to combine strategies in such a way as to *increase* our gain. To do so, we will make use of reservations. Our goal is to implement an $(r, b+1, \Sigma)$-strategy using a finite sequence of (r_i, b, Σ_i)-strategies.

We will improve Algorithm 1. The basic idea remains the same. When we assign measure to a string, say when at stage t_0 we set $a(\sigma, t_0) = 2^{-g}$, the opponent has to respond by allocating a string of length at most g to describe σ. Say that in response to our setting $a(\sigma, t_0) = 2^{-g}$, the opponent enumerates (τ, σ) into $\mathcal{M}_{t_1}$, where $|\tau| = g$. Take $p < g$ and let τ_p be the first p bits of τ. If $\tau_p \notin R_p(\sigma, t)$, then $\tau_p \in I_p(\sigma, t)$, so the opponent can never enumerate (τ_p, σ) into $\mathcal{M}$. So if we set $a(\sigma, t_1) = 2^{-p}$, the opponent must find some new string v of length at most p to describe σ. The original τ description of σ is effectively a waste of resources.

On the other hand, while $\tau_p \in R_p(\sigma, t)$, we also have a gain because the opponent can use τ_p only to describe a string comparable with σ. If we increase measure only on strings incomparable with σ, then the opponent cannot use τ_p in response. If we use only increments of measure of size at least 2^{-p}, then the opponent cannot make use of any extension of τ_p (as it would be too long to be useful). Note that this is why we need an r' in the definition of an (r, b, Σ)-strategy. The r' is the smallest amount of measure this strategy needs. Being able to compute r' means we know how much space strategies need in terms of units of measure. With this knowledge, we can ensure that the smallest measure needed by a strategy will not interfere with any reservations established by previous strategies.

We noted earlier that part of the problem with Algorithm 1 was that the amount of measure that it assigned to a string ranged between 2^{-g} and 2^{-r}. This range was too great to allow the algorithm to be used recursively. Hence our new algorithm has two objectives: to create a certain amount of gain, and to ensure a certain amount of measure is allocated. These two objectives will be achieved by splitting the algorithm into two phases. In the first, the *advantage phase*, the objective will be to force the opponent to reserve a number of strings of length p. We do not know how much measure we will need to use before the opponent makes this many reservations. If we do not use enough measure, then we proceed with the second phase, the *spend phase*. The spend phase is where we make sure that we have placed enough measure on each string so that the strategies can be used recursively. The use of these two phases is another new feature of this proof.

The spend phase must occur after the advantage phase, because only then will we know how much more measure we need to allocate. Accordingly, the spend phase will use larger units of measure than the advantage phase. From r we will compute a p, q, and r' such that $r < p < q < r'$. The advantage phase will use units of measure between q and r' while the spend phase will use units of measure between r and p (see Figure 4.2). This fact gives us a bit of a problem. During the advantage phase we can require only reservations of length at most p. If p is much larger than r, then we will need to make many reservations to achieve anything. To get around this problem, we define $\Upsilon = \{\sigma 0 \tau : \sigma \in \Sigma \wedge \tau \in 2^{p-r}\}$ (where Σ is the set of input strings for the algorithm). Note that the purpose of the 0 in the definition of Υ is just to separate the strings used by the advantage phase from those used by the spend phase. We will run the algorithm on the strings in Υ until enough of these have a reservation of length p.

As in Algorithm 1, we will not increase the measure on the elements of Υ directly, but rather will make a series of small increments of measure on some extensions of them. We will let $\Xi = \{\upsilon\tau : \upsilon \in \Upsilon \wedge \tau \in 2^e\}$ (where e depends on b and will be defined shortly). The idea is the following. If $\upsilon \in \Upsilon$ and $\xi_0, \ldots \xi_{2^e-1}$ are the elements of Ξ that extend υ, then we will sequentially set the measure of each ξ_i to 2^{-p-e} until a reservation of size p occurs for υ. If we do so for all such ξ_i, then the measure on υ will be 2^{-p}, and the opponent must allocate a string of length p to describe υ. However, it is not quite that simple. We want to increase the measure on ξ_i by running some strategy on it. Every time we run a strategy we need to use larger units of measure. So instead, what we will do is take many extensions of ξ_0. Then we can run our first strategy on all these extensions, spending a little bit of measure on each. Then we will take slightly fewer extensions of ξ_1 and run a strategy that spends a little more measure on each of these extensions, and so on. This procedure is just like what we did in Example 4.5.18. It gives us sets $\Psi_0, \Psi_1, \ldots$, where Ψ_i is the ith set of extensions of elements of Ξ on which we want to increase measure. The sets used by the advantage phase are shown in Figure 4.1. In this figure arrows represent extensions of strings.

The algorithm would ideally achieve a reservation of length p for each element of Υ, but there is a problem. Once a reservation is achieved for some $\upsilon \in \Upsilon$, we do not want to increase the measure on that υ. However, reservations are not monotonic; they can appear at one stage and then disappear at the next. Consider $\upsilon_1, \upsilon_2 \in \Upsilon$. Say we increase the measure on both υ_1 and υ_2 by 2^{-p-e}, and then the opponent responds by giving a p reservation to υ_1, but not to υ_2. Then we could increase the measure on υ_2, and the opponent might respond by giving a p reservation to υ_2 but taking away the p reservation from υ_1. By adopting this sort of tactic, the opponent could force us to make many separate increases in measure to achieve reservations for all elements of Υ. Every time we increase the measure on some subset of Υ, we need a new Ψ_i. The more Ψ_i's we need, the deeper we need to go into the binary tree. To improve the lower bound, we want to limit the number of Ψ_i's we need. To do so, we will wait until we have a reservation for three-quarters of the elements of Υ. Thus, any time we increase the measure, we must be increasing the measure on at least one-quarter of the elements of Υ.

The spend phase is similar but simpler. In this phase we will identify those elements $\sigma \in \Sigma$ that do not have enough measure. We will increase

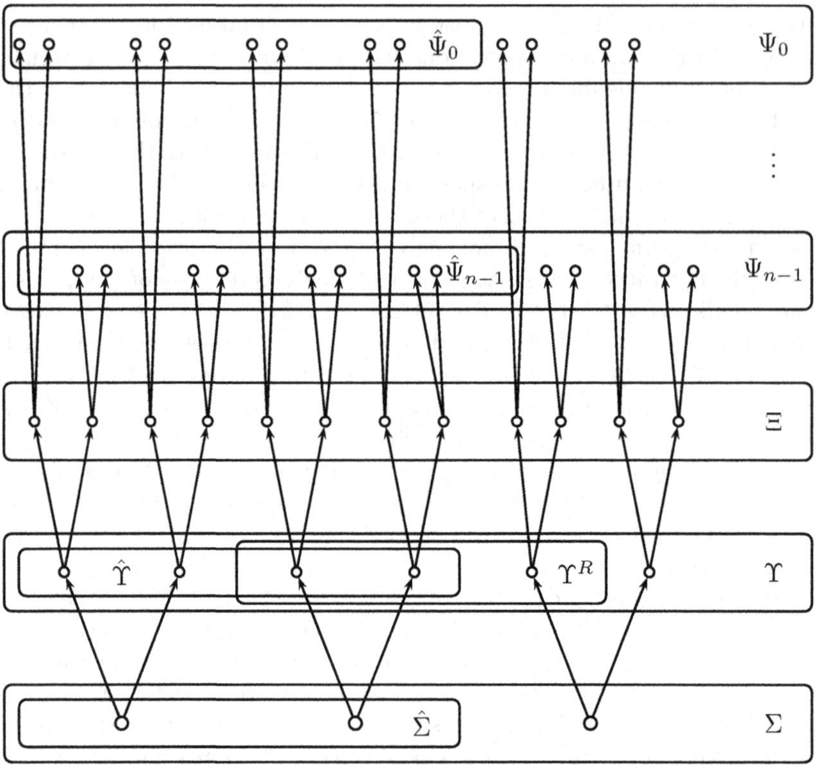

Figure 4.1. Algorithm strings

the measure on such σ in increments of 2^{-r-3}, until we have exceeded 2^{-r}. Again like in Example 4.5.18, we will not increase the measure directly on σ but rather on some set of extensions of it. These extensions will form the sets $\Phi_0, \ldots, \Phi_7$.

The length of extensions that we take to form the sets Ψ_i and Φ_i is governed by the space that a strategy needs to run, in terms of quantities of measure. The function $S(b)$ is used to determine this space. We will show that there exist (r, b, Σ)-strategies such that $r' = r + S(b)$. From our base strategy we can set $S(0) = 0$ because in this case $r = r'$.

In the process of determining $S(b+1)$ we will also compute all the other variables we need for the main algorithm. These variables are illustrated in Figure 4.2. To determine $S(b+1)$, first we compute an increasing sequence $r_0 \leqslant r_1 \leqslant \cdots \leqslant r_8$ by $r_0 = r+3$ and $r_{i+1} = r_i + S(b)$. This sequence gives us room for the spend phase. Let $p = r_8$. Let $e = b+6$. The number e is chosen so that $D(b)2^{-e} = (5(\frac{5}{4})^b - 4)2^{-b-6} < 4(\frac{5}{4})^{b+1}2^{-b-6} < 4 \cdot 2^{b+1}2^{-b-6} = \frac{1}{8}$.

Let $q = p + e$. Now compute an increasing sequence $r_0^* \leqslant r_1^* \leqslant \cdots \leqslant r_n^*$, where $r_0^* = q$ and $n = 2^{e+2}$, and $r_{i+1}^* = r_i^* + S(b)$. This sequence gives us room for the advantage phase. Finally let $r' = r_n^*$, and $S(b+1) = r' - r$.

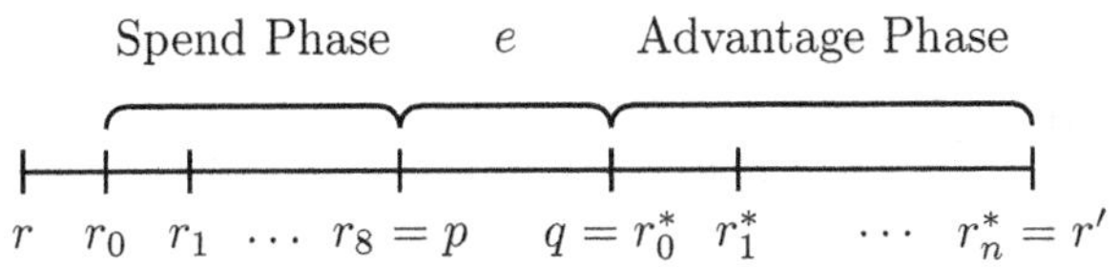

Figure 4.2. Algorithm parameters

This value is well-defined as $S(b+1)$ does not depend on the initial choice of r.

It is possible to unravel the above definition to determine that S can be defined as follows: $S(0) = 0$ and $S(b+1) = (8 + 2^{b+8})S(b) + b + 9$.

We are finally ready to present the main algorithm. We are given $r, b \in \mathbb{N}$ and a prefix-free set of strings Σ such that $|\Sigma|\frac{5}{4}2^{-r} \leqslant 1$. We let t_0 be the stage that the algorithm starts and we require that $a(\Sigma, t_0)$=0. To implement an $(r, b+1, \Sigma)$-strategy, we first determine all the values $n, p, q, e, r_i, r_i^*, r'$, as shown in Figure 4.2. In the algorithm, Υ' represents those elements of Υ whose measure we will increase in the current pass through the advantage phase of the algorithm. Now, with all the values that we need computed, the algorithm that we will use to implement an $(r, b+1, \Sigma)$-strategy is as follows.

Advantage Phase.

> Let t be the current stage. Let $\Upsilon = \{\sigma 0 \tau : \sigma \in \Sigma \wedge \tau \in 2^{p-r}\}$. Let $\Xi = \{\upsilon\rho : \upsilon \in \Upsilon \wedge \rho \in 2^e\}$. Let $\Upsilon' = \{\upsilon \in \Upsilon : R_p(\upsilon, t) = \emptyset\}$. If $|\Upsilon'| < \frac{1}{4}|\Upsilon|$, then move to the spend phase.
> For each $\upsilon \in \Upsilon'$, choose a $\xi_\upsilon \in \Xi$ such that $\xi_\upsilon \succcurlyeq \upsilon$ and $a(\xi_\upsilon, t) = 0$. Let $\Xi' = \{\xi_\upsilon : \upsilon \in \Upsilon'\}$. Choose the least $i < n-1$ that has not been used previously. Let $\Psi_i = \{\xi\tau : \xi \in \Xi' \wedge \tau \in 2^{r^*_{n-i-1}-q}\}$ and implement an (r^*_{n-i-1}, b, Ψ_i)-strategy. If this strategy finishes at stage t', then wait until stage t'' such that $K_{m,t''}(\upsilon) \leqslant p$ for all $\upsilon \in \Upsilon$ such that $a(\upsilon, t') \geqslant 2^{-p}$. Repeat the advantage phase.

Spend Phase.

> Let t be the current stage. Let $\Sigma' = \{\sigma \in \Sigma : a(\sigma, t) < 2^{-r}\}$. If $\Sigma' = \emptyset$ then terminate the algorithm. Otherwise choose the least $i < 8$ such that i has not been used previously in the spend phase. Let $\Phi_i = \{\sigma 1 0^1 1 \tau : \sigma \in \Sigma' \wedge \tau \in 2^{r_{7-i}-r-3}\}$ and run a (r_{7-i}, b, Φ_i)-strategy. Repeat the spend phase.

We now verify the correctness of this algorithm. The algorithm starts at stage t_0. We will define the following parameters assuming that the algorithm terminates at some stage t_1. Let n_a be the number of times the advantage phase is run. Let n_s be the number of times the spend phase is run. For all $i < n_a$, let t_i^* be the stage the ith strategy in the advantage phase begins (starting with $i = 0$). Let t_{mid} be the stage at which the algorithm completes the advantage phase and let $t^*_{n_a} = t_{\text{mid}}$. For all $0 \leqslant i < n_s$, let t'_i be the stage the ith strategy in the spend phase begins (starting with $i = 0$). Let $t'_{n_s} = t_1$. Let $\Phi = \Phi_0 \cup \cdots \cup \Phi_{n_s - 1}$ and $\Psi = \Psi_0 \cup \cdots \cup \Psi_{n_a - 1}$. Let $\widehat{\Sigma} \subseteq \Sigma$.

The first step in the verification is to prove that the algorithm runs without error. To prove this, we need to show that each time we "choose" something in the algorithm, there is something valid to choose. First we note that the opponent cannot add a description of σ of length $\leqslant p$ without making a reservation of length p.

Lemma 4.5.19. *If t, p, and σ are such that $K_{m,t}(\sigma) \leqslant p$, then $R_p(\sigma, t) \neq \emptyset$.*

Proof. If $K_{m,t}(\sigma) \leqslant p$, then there exists $(\tau, \sigma') \in \mathcal{M}_t$ such that $s = |\tau| \leqslant p$ and $\sigma' \succcurlyeq \sigma$. Consider $\tau' = \tau 0^{p-s}$. As $|\tau'| = p$ and $\tau \preccurlyeq \tau'$, and $\sigma' \succcurlyeq \sigma$, we have $\tau' \in F_p(\sigma, t)$. If $\tau' \in I_p(\sigma, t)$ then there would exist $\tau'' \approx \tau'$ and $\rho \mid \sigma$ such that $(\tau'', \rho) \in \mathcal{M}_t$. However, then $\tau'' \approx \tau$ and $\rho \mid \sigma'$, so this fact would contradict the definition of a monotone machine. Thus $\tau' \notin I_p(\sigma, t)$, and so $\tau' \in R_p(\sigma, t)$. □

Proposition 4.5.20. *The advantage phase of the algorithm never runs out of choices for ξ_υ or i, and the spend phase never runs out of choices for i.*

Proof. First we see that there is always a choice for ξ_υ. Take any $\upsilon \in \Upsilon$ and any $j < n_a$. Assume that at stage t^*_j for any $\xi \in \Xi$ such that $\xi \succcurlyeq \upsilon$, we have $a(\xi, t^*_j) \neq 0$. Then, given any $\xi \in \Xi$ such that $\xi \succcurlyeq \upsilon$, there is some $i < j$ such that an (r^*_{n-i-1}, b, Ψ_i)-strategy has been implemented with $\{\xi\sigma : \sigma \in 2^{r^*_{n-i-1} - q}\} \subseteq \Psi_i$. There are $2^{r^*_{n-i-1} - q}$ many extensions of ξ in Ψ_i, so

$$a(\xi, t^*_j) \geqslant 2^{r^*_{n-i-1} - q} 2^{-r^*_{n-i-1}} = 2^{-q}.$$

Hence $a(\upsilon, t^*_j) \geqslant 2^e 2^{-q} = 2^{-p}$, because there are 2^e many extensions of υ in Ξ. Thus, at the end of the iteration of the previous advantage phase, the algorithm waits until a stage t when the opponent uses a string of length at most p to describe υ before running the advantage phase again. As this fact implies that $R_p(\upsilon, t^*_j) \neq \emptyset$, by Lemma 4.5.19, it follows that no choice of ξ_υ will be needed.

The advantage phase stops if $|\Upsilon'| < \frac{1}{4}|\Upsilon|$. So each time the phase is run, at least $\frac{1}{4}|\Upsilon|$ many elements of Ξ are selected, which can happen only $4 \cdot 2^e = 2^{e+2}$ many times (as otherwise the algorithm would run out of choices for some ξ_υ), so there is always a choice for i.

The spend phase will terminate if $a(\sigma, t'_i) \geqslant 2^{-r}$ for all $\sigma \in \Sigma$. During each iteration through the phase, $a(\sigma, t'_{i+1}) \geqslant a(\sigma, t'_i) + 2^{-r-3}$ (if it is not greater than 2^{-r} already), so after a maximum of 8 steps, $a(\sigma, t) \geqslant 2^{-r}$ for all $\sigma \in \Sigma$, and hence the algorithm will not run out of choices for i. □

The next step in the verification is to show that the required bounds on the measure that the algorithm uses are met.

Proposition 4.5.21. *For all $\sigma \in \Sigma$, if the algorithm terminates at stage t_1, then $2^{-r} \leqslant a(\sigma, t_1) < \frac{5}{4}2^{-r}$.*

Proof. As $a(\sigma, t_0) = 0$, any measure placed on σ by stage t_{mid} must be due to an increase of measure on some $\psi \in \Psi$ where $\psi \succcurlyeq \sigma$. Hence, for any $\sigma \in \Sigma$, we have $a(\sigma, t_{\text{mid}}) = \sum_{\psi \in \Psi, \psi \succcurlyeq \sigma} a(\psi, t_{\text{mid}})$. If $\psi \in \Psi_i$, then we increase the measure on ψ by less than $\frac{5}{4}2^{-r^*_{n-i-1}}$. Now if $\psi \succcurlyeq \sigma$ then $|\psi| = |\sigma| + 1 + p - r + e + r^*_{n-i-1} - q = |\sigma| + 1 - r + r^*_{n-i-1}$, so $r^*_{n-i-1} = |\psi| - |\sigma| - 1 + r$. Thus $a(\psi, t_{\text{mid}}) < \frac{5}{4}2^{-(|\psi| - |\sigma| - 1 + r)}$.

All such ψ form a prefix-free set of extensions of $\sigma 0$, so

$$\begin{aligned} a(\sigma, t_{\text{mid}}) = a(\sigma 0, t_{\text{mid}}) &= \sum_{\psi \in \Psi,\ \psi \succcurlyeq \sigma 0} a(\psi, t_{\text{mid}}) \\ &< \sum_{\psi \in \Psi,\ \psi \succcurlyeq \sigma 0} \frac{5}{4} 2^{-|\psi| + |\sigma 0| - r} \leqslant \frac{5}{4} 2^{-r}. \end{aligned}$$

The spend phase will run only if $a(\sigma) < 2^{-r}$. Each iteration of the spend phase increases the measure on σ by less than $\frac{5}{4}2^{-r-3} < 2^{-r-2}$, so at the end of the spend phase, $2^{-r} \leqslant a(\sigma, t_1) < 2^{-r} + 2^{-r-2} = \frac{5}{4}2^{-r}$. ☐

Note that as $a(\Sigma, t_1) < |\Sigma| \frac{5}{4} 2^{-r} \leqslant 1$, we do not run out of measure. There are two possible outcomes to an $(r, b+1, \Sigma)$-strategy, related to whether or not the algorithm terminates.

Proposition 4.5.22. *If the algorithm does not terminate then outcome (i) is achieved.*

Proof. The number of times any phase is repeated is bounded, so if the algorithm does not terminate, then this fact must be caused by waiting for a response from the opponent or by waiting for another strategy to finish. Using the basic strategy as an inductive base case, this situation can occur only if for some $\sigma \in \Sigma$, there is a $\sigma' \succcurlyeq \sigma$ with $Km(\sigma') > -\log(a(\sigma'))$. Hence (i) (a) holds. Now (i) (b) holds by Proposition 4.5.21, because if the algorithm does not exceed the measure upper bound when it terminates, then it will not exceed the upper bound if it takes no action from some point onwards. ☐

We now proceed to the more difficult stage of the verification. Let us examine what happens if the algorithm does terminate. We are going to look at the gain made during the advantage phase and the spend phase separately. We do so because we know from Proposition 4.5.17 that the overall gain is at least the sum of the gains that occur during these phases. That is, letting $\widehat{\Sigma}\{i\} = \{\sigma i : \sigma \in \widehat{\Sigma}\}$,

$$\mu(G_r^{r'}(\widehat{\Sigma}; t_0, t_1)) \geqslant \mu(G_p^{r'}(\widehat{\Sigma}\{0\}; t_0, t_{\text{mid}})) + \mu(G_r^p(\widehat{\Sigma}\{1\}; t_{\text{mid}}, t_1)).$$

We know what we can expect from the spend phase of the algorithm because it is just a series of (r, b, Φ_i)-strategies. However, in the advantage phase we have to show that the overall gain is increased by the fact that some reservations of length p are made; i.e., for some $\upsilon \in \Upsilon$, we have $R_p(\upsilon, t_{\text{mid}}) \neq \emptyset$.

First let us look at the spend phase. For all $i < n_s$, let $\widehat{\Phi}_i = \{\varphi \in \Phi_i : \exists\sigma \in \widehat{\Sigma}\,(\varphi \succcurlyeq \sigma)\}$. Note that $\widehat{\Sigma}\{1\} \preccurlyeq \widehat{\Phi}_i$. Let $\widehat{\Phi} = \widehat{\Phi}_0 \cup \cdots \cup \widehat{\Phi}_{n_s-1}$.

Proposition 4.5.23. *If the algorithm terminates then*

$$\mu(G_r^p(\widehat{\Sigma}\{1\}; t_{mid}, t_1)) \geqslant (1 + \tfrac{b}{2})a(\Sigma\{1\}, t_1) - a(\Sigma\{1\} \setminus \widehat{\Sigma}\{1\}, t_1)D(b).$$

Proof. From Proposition 4.5.17 and the inductive hypothesis of the existence of (r, b, Σ)-strategies, we know that

$$\begin{aligned}\mu(G_r^p(\widehat{\Sigma}\{1\}; t_{\text{mid}}, t_1)) &\geqslant \sum_{i<n_s} \mu(G_{r_{7-i}}^{r_{8-i}}(\widehat{\Phi}_i; t_i', t_{i+1}')) \\ &\geqslant \sum_{i<n_s} ((1 + \tfrac{b}{2})a(\Phi_i, t_{i+1}') - 2^{r_{7-i}} D(b)|\Phi_i \setminus \widehat{\Phi}_i|).\end{aligned}$$

The second inequality is a consequence of condition (c) of outcome (ii).

Now, because this is the only way we increase measure on extensions of $\Sigma\{1\}$, it follows that

$$\sum_{i<n_s} (1 + \tfrac{b}{2})a(\Phi_i, t_{i+1}') = \sum_{i<n_s} (1 + \tfrac{b}{2})a(\Phi_i, t_1) = (1 + \tfrac{b}{2})a(\Sigma\{1\}, t_1).$$

The (r_{7-i}, b, Φ_i) strategy run guarantees that

$$a(\Phi_i \setminus \widehat{\Phi}_i, t_1) \geqslant 2^{r_{7-i}}|\Phi_i \setminus \widehat{\Phi}_i|,$$

so

$$\begin{aligned}\sum_{i<n_s} 2^{r_{7-i}} D(b)|\Phi_i \setminus \widehat{\Phi}_i| &\leqslant \sum_{i<n_s} a(\Phi_i \setminus \widehat{\Phi}_i, t_1)D(b) \\ &= a(\Sigma\{1\} \setminus \widehat{\Sigma}\{1\}, t_1)D(b).\end{aligned}$$

The result follows by combining these inequalities. □

Before we examine the advantage phase, we need some more definitions. We need to define those subsets of Υ that have p reservations, or extend elements of $\widehat{\Sigma}$, or both.

1. Let $\Upsilon^R = \{\upsilon \in \Upsilon : R_p(\upsilon, t_{\text{mid}}) \neq \emptyset\}$.
2. Let $\widehat{\Upsilon} = \{\upsilon \in \Upsilon : \exists\sigma \in \widehat{\Sigma}\,(\upsilon \succcurlyeq \sigma)\}$.
3. Let $\widehat{\Upsilon}^R = \Upsilon^R \cap \widehat{\Upsilon}$.

Note that $|\Upsilon^R| \geqslant \frac{3}{4}|\Upsilon| = \frac{3}{4}|\Sigma|2^{p-r}$, as this is the condition for the algorithm to move to the spend phase. Additionally, $|\Upsilon \setminus \widehat{\Upsilon}| = |\Sigma \setminus \widehat{\Sigma}|2^{p-r}$. Hence,

$$\begin{aligned}|\widehat{\Upsilon}^R| &= |\Upsilon^R| + |\widehat{\Upsilon}| - |\Upsilon^R \cup \widehat{\Upsilon}| \geqslant |\Upsilon^R| + |\widehat{\Upsilon}| - |\Upsilon| \\ &= |\Upsilon^R| - |\Upsilon \setminus \widehat{\Upsilon}| \geqslant \frac{3}{4}|\Sigma|2^{p-r} - |\Sigma \setminus \widehat{\Sigma}|2^{p-r} = (\frac{3}{4}|\Sigma| - |\Sigma \setminus \widehat{\Sigma}|)2^{p-r}.\end{aligned}$$

For each $\upsilon \in \Upsilon^R$, we choose a specific τ_υ in $R_p(\upsilon, t_{\mathrm{mid}})$. The following lemma establishes that these τ_υ's must be distinct.

Lemma 4.5.24. *If $\upsilon_0, \upsilon_1 \in \Upsilon^R$ and $\upsilon_0 \neq \upsilon_1$ then $\tau_{\upsilon_0} \neq \tau_{\upsilon_1}$.*

Proof. If $\upsilon_0 \neq \upsilon_1$ then $\upsilon_0 \mid \upsilon_1$ because Υ^R is a prefix-free set. If $\tau_{\upsilon_0} \in R_p(\upsilon_0, t_{\mathrm{mid}})$, then $\tau_{\upsilon_0} \in F_p(\upsilon_0, t_{\mathrm{mid}})$, so $\tau_{\upsilon_0} \in I_p(\upsilon_1, t_{\mathrm{mid}})$ by Lemma 4.5.16. Hence $\tau_{\upsilon_0} \notin R_p(\upsilon_1, t_{\mathrm{mid}})$, and so $\tau_{\upsilon_0} \neq \tau_{\upsilon_1}$. □

The gain made during the advantage phase can be broken down into two parts. Firstly, for every $\upsilon \in \widehat{\Upsilon}^R$, we have $[\![\tau_\upsilon]\!] \subseteq G_p^{r'}(\widehat{\Sigma}\{0\}; t_0, t_{\mathrm{mid}})$. This is the case because $\tau_\upsilon \in R_p(\upsilon, t_{\mathrm{mid}}) = F_p(\upsilon, t_{\mathrm{mid}}) \setminus I_p(\upsilon, t_{\mathrm{mid}})$. In the following argument we will make use of Lemmas 4.5.10 and 4.5.12. As $\upsilon \succcurlyeq \sigma 0$ for some $\sigma \in \widehat{\Sigma}$, we have $\tau_\upsilon \in F_p(\sigma 0, t_{\mathrm{mid}}) \subseteq F_p(\widehat{\Sigma}\{0\}, t_{\mathrm{mid}})$. Additionally, $\tau_\upsilon \notin I_p(\sigma 0, t_{\mathrm{mid}})$, so $\tau_\upsilon \notin I_p(\widehat{\Sigma}\{0\}, t_{\mathrm{mid}}) \supseteq I_p(\widehat{\Sigma}\{0\}, t_0)$. Now, $[\![I_p(\widehat{\Sigma}\{0\}, t_0)]\!] \supseteq [\![I_{r'}(\widehat{\Sigma}\{0\}, t_0)]\!]$, so $[\![\tau_\upsilon]\!] \cap [\![I_{r'}(\widehat{\Sigma}\{0\}, t_0)]\!] = \emptyset$. Thus,

$$[\![\tau_\upsilon]\!] \subseteq [\![F_p(\widehat{\Sigma}\{0\}, t_{\mathrm{mid}})]\!] \setminus [\![I_{r'}(\widehat{\Sigma}\{0\}, t_0)]\!] = G_p^{r'}(\widehat{\Sigma}\{0\}; t_0, t_{\mathrm{mid}}).$$

Secondly, we can count the gains made by the recursive use of the strategies in the advantage phase as

$$\bigcup_{i<n_{\mathrm{a}}} G_{r^*_{n-i-1}}^{r^*_{n-i}}(\widehat{\Psi}_i; t^*_i, t^*_{i+1}) \subseteq G_p^{r'}(\widehat{\Sigma}\{0\}; t_0, t_{\mathrm{mid}}).$$

We would like to combine the above to have

$$\mu(G_p^{r'}(\widehat{\Sigma}\{0\}; t_0, t_{\mathrm{mid}})) \geqslant \mu\Bigg(\bigcup_{\upsilon \in \widehat{\Upsilon}^R} [\![\tau_\upsilon]\!]\Bigg) + \mu\Bigg(\bigcup_{i<n_{\mathrm{a}}-1} G_{r^*_{n-i-1}}^{r^*_{n-i}}(\widehat{\Psi}_i; t^*_i, t^*_{i+1})\Bigg).$$

However, we cannot do so, as $\bigcup_{\upsilon \in \widehat{\Upsilon}^R} [\![\tau_\upsilon]\!]$ and $\bigcup_{i=0}^{n_{\mathrm{a}}-1} G_{r^*_{n-i-1}}^{r^*_{n-i}}(\widehat{\Psi}_i; t^*_i, t^*_{i+1})$ are not necessarily disjoint. Our goal is to find some subset $\Psi^R \subseteq \Psi$ that we can subtract from any $\widehat{\Psi}_i$ so that $\bigcup_{\upsilon \in \widehat{\Upsilon}^R} [\![\tau_\upsilon]\!]$ and $\bigcup_{i=0}^{n_{\mathrm{a}}-1} G_{r^*_{n-i-1}}^{r^*_{n-i}}(\widehat{\Psi}_i \setminus \Psi^R; t^*_i, t^*_{i+1})$ are disjoint. We use the superscript R in Ψ^R because we will construct the set so that $\Upsilon^R \preccurlyeq \Psi^R$.

How do we find Ψ^R? For each $\upsilon \in \Upsilon^R$, we show that there is at most one i such that $\tau_\upsilon \in F_p(\Psi_i, t^*_{i+1})$. Call this i, if it exists, i_υ. We will show that all elements of Ψ_{i_υ} that extend υ actually extend some unique $\xi \in \Xi$. We denote this ξ by ξ_υ. We can form Ψ^R by taking all extensions of ξ_υ in Ψ for all υ.

To show how to implement the above in detail, first note that, while $R_p(\sigma, t)$ is not monotonic in t, if some τ is in $R_p(\sigma, t_i)$ but is not in $R_p(\sigma, t_j)$, with $t_j > t_i$, then it must be that $\tau \in I_p(\sigma, t_j)$, so $\tau \notin R_p(\sigma, t)$ for all $t \geqslant t_j$.

Proposition 4.5.25. *If $\upsilon \in \Upsilon^R$ then there is at most one $i < n_{\mathrm{a}}$ such that $\tau_\upsilon \in F_p(\Psi_i, t^*_{i+1})$.*

Proof. If no such i exists then the lemma holds trivially. Otherwise, let i be the least element of $\{0, \dots, n_{\mathrm{a}} - 1\}$ such that $\tau_\upsilon \in F_p(\Psi_i, t^*_{i+1})$. For some $\psi \in \Psi_i$, we have $\tau_\upsilon \in F_p(\psi, t^*_{i+1})$. It follows that $\upsilon \preccurlyeq \psi$, because if not, then $\psi \mid \upsilon$, and so by Lemma 4.5.16, $\tau_\upsilon \in I_p(\upsilon, t^*_{i+1})$, whence $\tau_\upsilon \notin R_p(\upsilon, t_{\mathrm{mid}})$, which is a contradiction.

Hence, as $\upsilon \preccurlyeq \psi$, by Lemma 4.5.10, $\tau_\upsilon \in F_p(\upsilon, t^*_{i+1})$. Thus $\tau_\upsilon \in R_p(\upsilon, t^*_{i+1})$, because $\tau_\upsilon \notin I_p(\upsilon, t)$ for all $t \leqslant t_{\mathrm{mid}}$. Now for all t such that $t^*_{i+1} \leqslant t \leqslant t_{\mathrm{mid}}$, we have that τ_υ must remain in $R_p(\upsilon, t)$. Thus $R_p(\upsilon, t) \neq \emptyset$, and so if $j > i$, then there is no $\psi \succcurlyeq \upsilon$ in Ψ_j, because the algorithm chooses only ψ that extend elements of $\upsilon' \in \Upsilon$ for which $R_p(\upsilon', t^*_j)$ is empty. Hence, for all $\psi' \in \Psi_j$, we have $\psi' \mid \upsilon$. If $\tau_\upsilon \in F_p(\psi', t^*_{j+1})$ then $\tau_\upsilon \in I_p(\upsilon, t_{\mathrm{mid}})$ (again by Lemma 4.5.16), which is false as $\tau_\upsilon \in R_p(\upsilon, t_{\mathrm{mid}})$. Hence, $\tau_\upsilon \notin F_p(\Psi_j, t^*_{j+1})$. □

Now, by construction, for any $\upsilon \in \Upsilon$ and any $i < n_{\mathrm{a}}$, there is a single $\xi \in \Xi$ such that any $\psi \in \Psi_i$ that extends υ also extends ξ; i.e., $\upsilon \preccurlyeq \xi \preccurlyeq \psi$. Hence we can define ξ_υ for all $\upsilon \in \Upsilon^R$ as follows. Let i be the unique element of $\{0, \dots, n_{\mathrm{a}} - 1\}$ such that there exists a $\psi \in \Psi_i$ and $\tau_\upsilon \in F_p(\psi, t^*_{i+1})$ (assuming such an i exists), and define ξ_υ to be that element of Ξ such that all $\psi \in \Psi_i$ that extend υ also extend ξ_υ. If no such i exists then let $\xi_\upsilon = \upsilon 0^e$.

Let $\Psi^R = \{\psi \in \Psi : \psi \succcurlyeq \xi_\upsilon \text{ for some } \upsilon \in \Upsilon^R\}$. The following lemma shows us that this Ψ^R is really what we want.

Lemma 4.5.26. *For any $i < n_{\mathrm{a}}$ and any $\upsilon \in \Upsilon^R$,*

$$[\![\tau_\upsilon]\!] \cap G^{r^*_{n-i}}_{r^*_{n-i-1}}(\Psi_i \setminus \Psi^R; t^*_i, t^*_{i+1}) = \emptyset.$$

Proof. Take any such i and υ. We have shown that if $\psi \in \Psi_i$ and $\tau_\upsilon \in F_p(\psi, t_{\mathrm{mid}})$, then $\psi \succcurlyeq \xi_\upsilon$ and hence $\psi \in \Psi^R$. Thus $\tau_\upsilon \notin F_p(\Psi_i \setminus \Psi^R, t_{\mathrm{mid}})$, and so $\tau_\upsilon \notin F_p(\Psi_i \setminus \Psi^R, t^*_{i+1})$. Hence, $[\![\tau_\upsilon]\!] \cap [\![F_p(\Psi_i \setminus \Psi^R, t^*_{i+1})]\!] = \emptyset$.

The lemma now follows, as

$$G^{r^*_{n-i}}_{r^*_{n-i-1}}(\Psi_i \setminus \Psi^R; t^*_i, t^*_{i+1}) \subseteq [\![F_{r^*_{n-i-1}}(\Psi_i \setminus \Psi^R, t^*_{i+1})]\!] \subseteq [\![F_p(\Psi_i \setminus \Psi^R, t^*_{i+1})]\!].$$

□

The remainder of the proof is essentially book-keeping. We need to show that breaking the gain into the above two components gives us what we need.

Proposition 4.5.27. *If the algorithm terminates and* $\widehat{\Sigma} \subseteq \Sigma$, *then*

$$\mu(G_p^{r'}(\widehat{\Sigma}\{0\}; t_0, t_{mid})) \geqslant \frac{5}{8}|\Sigma|2^{-r} - |\Sigma \setminus \widehat{\Sigma}|2^{-r} + (1 + \tfrac{b}{2})a(\Sigma\{0\}, t_1) - a(\Sigma\{0\} \setminus \widehat{\Sigma}\{0\}, t_{mid})D(b).$$

Proof. The previous lemma shows that the sets $\bigcup_{\upsilon \in \widehat{\Upsilon}^R} [\![\tau_\upsilon]\!]$ and

$$\bigcup_{i=1}^{n} G_{r^*_{n-i}}^{r^*_{n-1+1}}(\widehat{\Psi}_i \setminus \Psi^R; t_i, t_{i+1})$$

are disjoint, so

$$\mu(G_p^{r'}(\widehat{\Sigma}\{0\}; t_0, t_{\mathrm{mid}})) \geqslant \sum_{\upsilon \in \widehat{\Upsilon}^R} \mu([\![\tau_\upsilon]\!]) + \sum_{i<n} \mu(G_{r^*_{n-i-1}}^{r^*_{n-i}}(\widehat{\Psi}_i \setminus \Psi^R; t_i^*, t_{i+1}^*)).$$

At this point, we use part (c) of outcome (ii). We know that the amount of gain that occurs on Ψ^R is bounded. So if we subtract it from $\widehat{\Psi}_i$, we can determine the maximum amount we can lose. Note that as $\widehat{\Psi}_i \subseteq \Psi_i$, it follows that

$$\begin{aligned}|\Psi_i \setminus (\widehat{\Psi}_i \setminus \Psi^R)| &= |\Psi_i| - |\widehat{\Psi}_i \setminus \Psi^R| \\ &= |\Psi_i| - (|\widehat{\Psi}_i| - |\widehat{\Psi}_i \cap \Psi^R|) = |\Psi_i \setminus \widehat{\Psi}_i| + |\widehat{\Psi}_i \cap \Psi^R|.\end{aligned}$$

With this identity we can determine that

$$\begin{aligned}&\mu(G_{r^*_{n-i-1}}^{r^*_{n-i}}(\widehat{\Psi}_i \setminus \Psi^R; t_i^*, t_{i+1}^*)) \\ &\qquad \geqslant (1 + \tfrac{b}{2})a(\Psi_i, t_{i+1}^*) - |\Psi_i \setminus (\widehat{\Psi}_i \setminus \Psi^R)|D(b)2^{-r^*_{n-i-1}} \\ &= (1 + \tfrac{b}{2})a(\Psi_i, t_{i+1}^*) - |\Psi_i \setminus \widehat{\Psi}_i|D(b)2^{-r^*_{n-i-1}} - |\Psi^R \cap \widehat{\Psi}_i|D(b)2^{-r^*_{n-i-1}}.\end{aligned}$$

The first inequality comes from part (c) of outcome (ii) applied to our (r, b, Ψ_i)-strategies.

Now we can combine these results along with the facts that $a(\Psi_i, t_{i+1}^*) = a(\Psi_i, t_1)$ and $\sum_{\upsilon \in \widehat{\Upsilon}^R} \mu([\![\tau_\upsilon]\!]) = |\widehat{\Upsilon}^R|2^{-p}$ to get that

$$\begin{aligned}\mu(G_r^p(\widehat{\Sigma}\{0\}; t_0, t_{\mathrm{mid}})) &\geqslant |\widehat{\Upsilon^R}|2^{-p} + \sum_{i<n_{\mathrm{a}}} (1 + \tfrac{b}{2})a(\Psi_i, t_1) \\ &\quad - \sum_{i<n_{\mathrm{a}}} |\Psi_i \setminus \widehat{\Psi}_i|D(b)2^{-r^*_{n-i-1}} - \sum_{i<n_{\mathrm{a}}} |\Psi^R \cap \widehat{\Psi}_i|D(b)2^{-r^*_{n-i-1}}.\end{aligned}$$

These terms can be simplified. First,

$$\sum_{i<n_{\mathrm{a}}} (1 + \tfrac{b}{2})a(\Psi_i, t_1) = (1 + \tfrac{b}{2})a(\Sigma\{0\}, t_1).$$

Now define $\widehat{\Upsilon}_i^R = \{\upsilon \in \widehat{\Upsilon}^R : \exists \psi \succcurlyeq \upsilon\,(\psi \in \Psi^R \cap \widehat{\Psi}_i)\}$. Because any $\psi \in \Psi^R \cap \widehat{\Psi}_i$ extends some $\upsilon \in \Upsilon^R$, by the construction of Ψ^R, we have

$\psi \succcurlyeq \xi_v$. It follows that $|\Psi^R \cap \widehat{\Psi}_i| \leqslant |\widehat{\Upsilon}_i^R| 2^{r^*_{n-i-1}-q}$. Hence

$$\sum_{i<n_a} |\Psi^R \cap \widehat{\Psi}_i| D(b) 2^{-r^*_{n-i-1}} \leqslant \sum_{i<n_a} |\widehat{\Upsilon}_i^R| D(b) 2^{-q} \leqslant |\widehat{\Upsilon}^R| D(b) 2^{-q}.$$

The second inequality is a consequence of the following lemma.

Lemma 4.5.28. *The sets $\widehat{\Upsilon}_0^R, \ldots, \widehat{\Upsilon}_{n_a-1}^R$ are pairwise disjoint.*

Proof. Assume $v \in \widehat{\Upsilon}_i^R \cap \widehat{\Upsilon}_j^R$. By definition, there exist ψ_0 and ψ_1, both extending v, such that $\psi_0 \in \Psi^R \cap \widehat{\Psi}_i \subseteq \Psi_i$ and $\psi_1 \in \Psi^R \cap \widehat{\Psi}_j \subseteq \Psi_j$. As both ψ_0 and ψ_1 are in Ψ^R, they both must extend ξ_v. But the algorithm construction then ensures that $i = j$. □

The (r^*_{n-i-1}, b, Ψ_i)-strategy run guarantees that

$$a(\Psi_i \setminus \widehat{\Psi}_i, t_{\mathrm{mid}}) \geqslant 2^{-r^*_{n-i-1}} |\Psi_i \setminus \widehat{\Psi}_i|,$$

which shows that

$$\begin{aligned}\sum_{i=0}^{n_a-1} |\Psi_i \setminus \widehat{\Psi}_i| D(b) 2^{-r^*_{n-i-1}} &\leqslant \sum_{i=0}^{n_a-1} a(\Psi_i \setminus \widehat{\Psi}_i, t_{\mathrm{mid}}) D(b) \\ &= a(\Sigma\{0\} \setminus \widehat{\Sigma}\{0\}, t_{\mathrm{mid}}) D(b).\end{aligned}$$

Putting these inequalities together shows that

$$\begin{aligned}&\mu(G_p^{r'}(\widehat{\Sigma}\{0\}; t_0, t_{\mathrm{mid}})) \\ &\geqslant |\widehat{\Upsilon^R}| 2^{-p} - |\widehat{\Upsilon}^R| D(b) 2^{-q} + (1+\tfrac{b}{2}) a(\Sigma\{0\}, t_1) - a(\Sigma\{0\} \setminus \widehat{\Sigma}\{0\}, t_{\mathrm{mid}}) D(b).\end{aligned}$$

Now because $|\widehat{\Upsilon}^R| \geqslant (\frac{3}{4}|\Sigma| - |\Sigma \setminus \widehat{\Sigma}|) 2^{p-r}$ and $D(b) 2^{-e} \leqslant \frac{1}{8}$ by choice of e, it follows that

$$\begin{aligned}|\widehat{\Upsilon^R}| 2^{-p} - |\widehat{\Upsilon}^R| D(b) 2^{-q} &= |\widehat{\Upsilon^R}| 2^{-p} (1 - D(b) 2^{-e}) \\ &\geqslant |\widehat{\Upsilon^R}| 2^{-p} \tfrac{7}{8} \geqslant (\tfrac{3}{4}|\Sigma| - |\Sigma \setminus \widehat{\Sigma}|) 2^{p-r} 2^{-p} \tfrac{7}{8} \\ &= (\tfrac{3}{4}\tfrac{7}{8}|\Sigma| - \tfrac{7}{8}|\Sigma \setminus \widehat{\Sigma}|) 2^{-r} \geqslant \tfrac{5}{8}|\Sigma| 2^{-r} - |\Sigma \setminus \widehat{\Sigma}| 2^{-r}.\end{aligned}$$

Finally,

$$\begin{aligned}&\mu(G_p^{r'}(\widehat{\Sigma}\{0\}; t_0, t_{\mathrm{mid}})) \\ &\geqslant \tfrac{5}{8}|\Sigma| 2^{-r} - |\Sigma \setminus \widehat{\Sigma}| 2^{-r} + (1+\tfrac{b}{2}) a(\Sigma\{0\}, t_1) - a(\Sigma\{0\} \setminus \widehat{\Sigma}\{0\}, t_{\mathrm{mid}}) D(b).\end{aligned}$$

□

Proposition 4.5.29. *If the algorithm terminates then*

$$\mu(G_r^{r'}(\widehat{\Sigma}; t_0, t_1)) \geqslant (1 + \tfrac{b+1}{2}) a(\Sigma, t_1) - 2^{-r} D(b+1) |\Sigma \setminus \widehat{\Sigma}|.$$

Proof. Proposition 4.5.17 tells us that

$$\mu(G_r^{r'}(\widehat{\Sigma}; t_0, t_1)) \geqslant \mu(G_p^{r'}(\widehat{\Sigma}\{0\}; t_0, t_{\mathrm{mid}})) + \mu(G_r^p(\widehat{\Sigma}\{1\}; t_{\mathrm{mid}}, t_1)).$$

All we need to do now is to combine and simplify Propositions 4.5.23 and 4.5.27. We have six terms to deal with:

1. $(1 + \frac{b}{2})a(\Sigma\{1\}, t_1)$,
2. $-a(\Sigma\{1\} \setminus \widehat{\Sigma}\{1\}, t_1)D(b)$,
3. $\frac{5}{8}|\Sigma|2^{-r}$,
4. $-|\Sigma \setminus \widehat{\Sigma}|2^{-r}$,
5. $(1 + \frac{b}{2})a(\Sigma\{0\}, t_1)$, and
6. $-a(\Sigma\{0\} \setminus \widehat{\Sigma}\{0\}, t_{\mathrm{mid}})D(b)$.

Notice that

$$\begin{aligned} &a(\Sigma\{1\} \setminus \widehat{\Sigma}\{1\}, t_1)D(b) + a(\Sigma\{0\} \setminus \widehat{\Sigma}\{0\}, t_{\mathrm{mid}})D(b) \\ &\qquad = a(\Sigma \setminus \widehat{\Sigma}, t_1)D(b) < |\Sigma \setminus \widehat{\Sigma}|\tfrac{5}{4}2^{-r}D(b), \end{aligned}$$

where the last inequality follows from Proposition 4.5.21. Also,

$$\begin{aligned} &\tfrac{5}{8}|\Sigma|2^{-r} + (1 + \tfrac{b}{2})a(\Sigma\{1\}, t_1) + (1 + \tfrac{b}{2})a(\Sigma\{0\}, t_1) \\ &\quad = \tfrac{1}{2}\tfrac{5}{4}|\Sigma|2^{-r} + (1 + \tfrac{b}{2})a(\Sigma, t_1) > \tfrac{1}{2}a(\Sigma, t_1) + (1 + \tfrac{b}{2})a(\Sigma, t_1) \\ &\qquad = (1 + \tfrac{b+1}{2})a(\Sigma, t_1). \end{aligned}$$

And so, as $D(b+1) = \frac{5}{4}D(b) + 1$,

$$\begin{aligned} \mu(G_r^{r'}(\widehat{\Sigma}; t_0, t_1)) &\geqslant \mu(G_p^{r'}(\widehat{\Sigma}\{0\}; t_0, t_{\mathrm{mid}})) + \mu(G_r^p(\widehat{\Sigma}\{1\}; t_{\mathrm{mid}}, t_1)) \\ &> (1 + \tfrac{b+1}{2})a(\Sigma, t_1) - |\Sigma \setminus \widehat{\Sigma}|\tfrac{5}{4}2^{-r}D(b) - |\Sigma \setminus \widehat{\Sigma}|2^{-r} \\ &= (1 + \tfrac{b+1}{2})a(\Sigma, t_1) - 2^{-r}(\tfrac{5}{4}D(b) + 1)|\Sigma \setminus \widehat{\Sigma}| \\ &= (1 + \tfrac{b+1}{2})a(\Sigma, t_1) - 2^{-r}D(b+1)|\Sigma \setminus \widehat{\Sigma}|. \end{aligned}$$

□

Proposition 4.5.30. *If the algorithm terminates then outcome (ii) occurs.*

Proof. By Proposition 4.5.21, condition (ii) (a) holds. By Proposition 4.5.29, condition (ii) (c) holds. Thus condition (ii) (b) holds by taking $\widehat{\Sigma}$ to be Σ. □

Hence we have established the existence of an $(r, b+1, \Sigma)$-strategy. By induction we can assert the existence of an $(r, b+1, \Sigma)$-strategy for any $r, b \in \mathbb{N}$ such that $|\Sigma|\frac{5}{4}2^{-r} < 1$.

Proposition 4.5.31. *If $r \geqslant 1$ and $b2^{-r-1} \geqslant 1$, then for any σ such that $a(\sigma, t_0) = 0$, an $(r, b, \{\sigma\})$-strategy achieves outcome (i).*

Proof. Because $|\{\sigma\}|\frac{5}{4}2^{-r} < 1$, we have sufficient measure to implement such a strategy. However, if the algorithm terminates at some stage t_1, then

$$\mu(G_r^{r'}(\{\sigma\}; t_0, t_1)) \geqslant (1 + \tfrac{b}{2})a(\sigma, t_1) \geqslant (1 + \tfrac{b}{2})2^{-r}, = 2^{-r} + b2^{-r-1} > 1,$$

which is impossible. Thus outcome (i) must occur. □

We can run a countable number of winning strategies in our construction of a by dovetailing them.

Proposition 4.5.32. *There is a c.e. semimeasure a such that for all i, we have $a(0^i1) \leqslant 2^{-2i-1}$ and there exists a σ_i such that $Km(0^i1\sigma_i) > -\log(a(0^i\sigma_i))$.*

Proof. The semimeasure a can be constructed by running a $(2i+2, 2^{2i+3}, \{0^i1\})$-strategy for each i. Then for all i, we have $a(0^i1) < \frac{5}{4}2^{-2i-2} < 2^{-2i-1}$. Also, by Proposition 4.5.31, because $2^{2i+3}2^{-2i-2-1} = 1$, the strategy achieves outcome (i), and hence there is some σ_i such that $Km(0^i1\sigma_i) > -\log(a(0^i1\sigma_i))$. □

Now Theorem 4.5.1 holds by Propositions 4.5.5 and 4.5.32.

To determine a lower bound on the difference between Km and KM, we need to bound the maximum string length used by an (r, b, Σ)-strategy. We will do so by determining an upper bound for the number of bits appended to a string in Σ by the strategy. If $b = 0$, then the strategy does not use any extensions of strings in Σ, so the number of extra bits appended is 0. If $b > 0$, an upper bound is the number of bits needed to extend a string in Σ to a string in Ψ_0. Such an extension requires $1 + r_{n-1}^* - r = 1 + r' - r - S(b-1) = 1 + S(b) - S(b-1)$ many bits (the extra 1 corresponds to the use of a 0 or 1 to distinguish between the advantage and spend phases).

Now an upper bound on the maximum string length used can be obtained by taking the maximum length l of any string in Σ and adding the upper bound for the number of bits added by an (r, i, Σ) strategy for all i with $1 \leqslant i \leqslant b$. Hence, we have that the maximum possible string length is

$$l + \sum_{i=1}^{b}(1 + S(i) - S(i-1)) = l + b + S(b) - S(0) = l + b + S(b).$$

Recall that $S(b)$ can be defined inductively by $S(0) = 0$ and $S(b+1) = (8 + 2^{b+8})S(b) + b + 9$. Now we will show that for b sufficiently large, $S(b) < 2^{(b^2)}$. First note that if $b \geqslant 1$, then $S(b) \geqslant b + 9$, so

$$S(b+1) = (8 + 2^{b+8})S(b) + b + 9 \leqslant S(b)(9 + 2^{b+8}) \leqslant S(b)(2^{b+9}).$$

Now we will show by induction that if $n \geqslant 2$, then $S(n) < 2^4 \prod_{i=1}^{n-1} 2^{i+9}$. As our base case, we have $S(2) \leqslant S(1)(2^{2-1+9}) < 2^4 2^{1+9}$. Assuming that our inequality holds for n, we have

$$S(n+1) \leqslant S(n)2^{n+9} < 2^4\left(\prod_{i=1}^{n-1} 2^{i+9}\right)2^{n+9} = 2^4\prod_{i=1}^{n} 2^{i+9}.$$

So if $n \geqslant 2$, then

$$S(n) < 2^4\prod_{i=1}^{n-1} 2^{i+9} = 2^{4+9(n-1)}\prod_{i=1}^{n-1} 2^i = 2^{4+9(n-1)}2^{\frac{(n-1)n}{2}} < 2^{\frac{n^2}{2}+9n}.$$

Thus, if n is sufficiently large then $S(n) < 2^{(n^2)}$.

We will now prove the main result of this section.

Proof of Theorem 4.5.4. We need to generalize Proposition 4.5.5 a little. Fix n. We have $\sum_i 2^{-\frac{i}{n}} < \infty$, so let k_n be such that 2^{k_n} is larger than this sum. Now we can construct a semimeasure a such that $a(0^i1) \leqslant 2^{-(1+\frac{1}{n})i-k_n}$ for all i. We construct a by running a $(j(n+1)+k_n+1, 2^{j(n+1)+k_n+2}, \{0^{jn}1\})$-strategy for each j. We do not exceed the bound on the measure for a because

$$a(0^{jn}1) < \frac{5}{4}2^{-j(n+1)-k_n-1} < 2^{-j(n+1)-k_n} = 2^{-(1+\frac{1}{n})jn-k_n}.$$

Because $b2^{-r-1} = 2^{j(n+1)+k_n+2}2^{-j(n+1)-k_n-2} = 1$, each strategy achieves outcome (i). Thus, for each j there is a $\sigma_j \succcurlyeq 0^{jn}1$ such that $Km(\sigma_j) > -\log a(\sigma_j)$. We can apply the same scaling as before to a to construct a semimeasure m; i.e., for all σ, we let $m(0^i\sigma) = 2^i a(0^i\sigma)$. Again, we have

$$m(\lambda) = \sum_i m(0^i1) = \sum_i 2^i a(0^i1) \leqslant \sum_i 2^{-\frac{i}{n}-k_n} = 2^{-k_n}\sum_i 2^{-\frac{i}{n}} \leqslant 1.$$

We now have that for each j there is a $\sigma_j \succcurlyeq 0^{jn}1$ such that $Km(\sigma_j) > -\log m(\sigma_j) + jn$. By the discussion immediately preceding this proof, the maximum length of a string used by the strategy corresponding to j is at most $|0^{jn}1| + S(b) + b$, where in this case $b = 2^{j(n+1)+k_n+2}$, and if j is large enough then this number is less than $jn + 1 + 2^{(2^{j(n+1)+k_n+2})^2} + 2^{j(n+1)+k_n+2}$. Again if j is large enough, this number is less than $2^{2^{2j(n+2)}}$. Hence, for infinitely many j, we can take σ_j so that $|\sigma_j| < 2^{2^{2j(n+2)}}$, that is, $\log\log|\sigma_j| < 2j(n+2)$. As $M_{\mathcal{M}}$ majorizes all c.e. continuous semimeasures, there must be some d_n such that $Km(\sigma_j) - KM(\sigma_j) > jn - d_n$. Thus we have

$$Km(\sigma_j) - KM(\sigma_j) > jn\frac{2j(n+2)}{2j(n+2)} - d_n > \frac{n}{2(n+2)}\log\log|\sigma_j| - d_n.$$

For any $c < \frac{1}{2}$, there is an n such that $\frac{n}{2(n+2)} > c + \varepsilon$ for some $\varepsilon > 0$. Now, for sufficiently large j it must be the case that $\varepsilon \log\log|\sigma_j| > d_n$. Hence, for such j,

$$Km(\sigma_j) - KM(\sigma_j) > (c+\varepsilon)\log\log|\sigma_j| - d_n > c\log\log|\sigma_j|.$$

□

5
Effective Reals

In this chapter we study the left computably enumerable reals, and discuss some other classes of effectively approximable reals. Left computably enumerable reals occupy a similar place in the study of relative randomness to that of computably enumerable sets in the study of relative computational complexity. Most of the material in this chapter used in the rest of the book is contained in the first two sections.

Recall that all the reals we consider are in $[0,1]$, and are identified with elements of 2^ω and with subsets of $\mathbb{N}$. Recall also our convention that all reals will be irrational and hence have unique binary expansions.

5.1 Computable and left-c.e. reals

Let α be a real. By $L(\alpha)$ we mean the *left cut* of α, that is, $\{q \in \mathbb{Q} : q < \alpha\}$. It is well known that such cuts can be used to define the reals from the rationals, as can Cauchy sequences. As we will see, both of these approaches can be effectivized.

Recall that we identify a real α with the set of natural numbers A such that $\alpha = 0.A$, that is, such that the nth bit of the binary expansion of α is 1 iff $n \in A$. Thus, it is natural to define α to be a *computable real* if A is a computable set. Equivalently, α is computable if there is an algorithm that, on input n, returns the nth bit of α. (Notice that we could have used a base other than base 2 in this definition; it is easy to check that the computability of the binary expansion of α is equivalent to the computability

R.G. Downey and D. Hirschfeldt, *Algorithmic Randomness and Complexity*, Theory and Applications of Computability, DOI 10.1007/978-0-387-68441-3_5,

of the n-ary expansion of α for any $n > 1$.) Another natural definition, based on the Dedekind cut approach, is to say that α is computable if $L(\alpha)$ is computable. Fortunately, these two definitions agree.

Proposition 5.1.1. *A real α is computable iff $L(\alpha)$ is computable.*

Proof. If $L(\alpha)$ is computable then we can compute $\alpha \upharpoonright n$, since it is the lexicographically largest string $\sigma \in 2^n$ such that $0.\sigma \in L(\alpha)$. (By our convention mentioned above, we assume that α is irrational, so $\alpha \neq 0.\sigma$.)

If α is computable, then the following is an algorithm for computing $L(\alpha)$. Let $q_n = 0.(A \upharpoonright n+1)$ (i.e., q_n is the rational whose binary expansion is given by the first $n+1$ bits of the characteristic function of A). Given $q \in \mathbb{Q}$, wait until either $q \leqslant q_n$ for some n, in which case $q \in L(\alpha)$, or $q - q_n \geqslant 2^{-n}$ for some n, in which case $q \notin L(\alpha)$, since $\alpha - q_n < 2^{-n}$. It is clear that one of the two cases must occur. □

Relativizing this result, we see that a real α has the same degree as $L(\alpha)$. Soare [364] observed that (by the above proof) $\alpha \leqslant_{\mathrm{tt}} L(\alpha)$ for all α, but he also showed that there is a c.e. set A such that for $\alpha = 0.A$, we have $L(\alpha) \nleqslant_{\mathrm{tt}} \alpha$.

Turning to the Cauchy sequence approach, a natural effectivization is to consider those reals α that are limits of *computable* sequences of rationals. As we will see, though, this class is much larger than that of the computable reals, even if we insist that the sequences of rationals be monotonic. The reason is that, to fully effectivize the notion of Cauchy sequence, we should require not only that the sequence be computable, but also that it have a computable *rate of convergence*. The following result is implicit in Turing [392].

Theorem 5.1.2 (Turing [392]). *The following are equivalent.*

(i) *The real α is computable.*

(ii) *There is a computable sequence of rationals $q_0, q_1, \ldots \to \alpha$ such that $|\alpha - q_n| < 2^{-n}$ for all n.*

(iii) *There is a computable sequence of rationals $q_0, q_1, \ldots \to \alpha$ and a computable function f such that $|\alpha - q_{f(n)}| < 2^{-n}$ for all n.*

Proof. (i) ⇒ (ii) If $\alpha = 0.A$ for a computable set A then let $q_n = 0.(A \upharpoonright n+1)$. Then $q_0, q_1, \ldots \to \alpha$ and $|\alpha - q_n| < 2^{-n}$ for all n.

(ii) ⇒ (iii) Obvious.

(iii) ⇒ (i) Let $r_n = q_{f(n)}$. By our convention mentioned above, we assume α is irrational. For each k there must be an n such that the first $k+1$ bits of the binary expansions of $r_n - 2^{-n}$ and $r_n + 2^{-n}$ agree, since any convergent sequence of rationals not having this property must converge to a rational. Given k, search for an n with the above property and define $A(k)$ to be the kth bit of r_n. Since $\alpha \in (r_n - 2^{-n}, r_n + 2^{-n})$, the kth bit of α must be the same as that of the binary expansion of r_n, whence $\alpha = 0.A$. □

Of course, we can relativize the definition of computable real to any given oracle. Relativizing it to $\emptyset'$, we get the notion of a Δ^0_2 *real*. These are exactly the reals that can be approximated by a computable sequence of rationals (with a possibly noneffective rate of convergence).

Theorem 5.1.3 (Demuth [93], Ho [182]). *A real is Δ^0_2 iff there is a computable sequence of rationals converging to it.*

Proof. If A is a Δ^0_2 set, then fixing a computable sequence A_n converging to A, let $q_n = 0.(A_n \upharpoonright n)$. Then $q_0, q_1, \ldots \to 0.A$.

If $q_0, q_1, \ldots \to \alpha$ is a computable sequence of rationals, the $q \in L(\alpha)$ iff $\exists n \, \forall m > n \, (q < q_m)$ iff $\forall n \, \exists m > n \, (q < q_m)$, so $L(\alpha)$ is both Σ^0_2 and Π^0_2, and hence is Δ^0_2. □

It is well known that the computable reals (and hence, by relativization, the Δ^0_2 reals) form a real closed field (see for instance [318]). The methods used to prove this fact are along the lines of the ones used in the proof of Theorem 5.4.7 below.

Having defined computable reals, it is natural to look for a definition of computably enumerable reals. The following is the natural definition based on the Dedekind cut approach.

Definition 5.1.4. A real α is *left computably enumerable* (*left-c.e.*) if $L(\alpha)$ is c.e.

Left-c.e. reals are often referred to simply as "c.e. reals", but we wish to avoid any confusion between c.e. *reals* and c.e. *sets*. Left-c.e. reals have also been called *recursively enumerable*, *left computable*, *left semicomputable*, and *lower semicomputable*. Of course, we also have *right-c.e. reals*, which are the reals α such that $L(\alpha)$ is co-c.e. Equivalently, α is right-c.e. if $1 - \alpha$ is left-c.e.

The following is the most useful characterization of the left-c.e. reals.

Theorem 5.1.5 (Soare [363]). *The following are equivalent.*

(i) *The real α is left-c.e.*

(ii) *There is a computable sequence of rationals $q_0 < q_1 < \cdots \to \alpha$.*

(iii) *There is a computable sequence of rationals $q_0 < q_1 < \cdots \to \alpha$ such that $\{q_i : i \in \omega\}$ is computable.*[1]

(iv) *There is a computable sequence of positive rationals $r_0, r_1, \ldots$ such that $\alpha = \sum_n r_n$.*

Proof. (i) $\Rightarrow$ (iii) Suppose α is left-c.e. For $q \in \mathbb{Q}$, let $\#(q)$ be the Gödel number of q, as in Definition 2.1.1. Let $q_0 \in L(\alpha)$. Given $q_n \in L(\alpha)$, wait for

[1]Note that the difference between items (ii) and (iii) is that in (iii) we require not only that the sequence be computable, but also that its *range* be computable.

a stage s such that for $q = \max L(\alpha)[s]$, we have $q_n < q$ and $\#(q_n) < \#(q)$. Such a stage must exist because $L(\alpha)$ has no largest element. Let $q_{n+1} = q$. It is easy to see that $q_0 < q_1 < \cdots \to \alpha$. Since the q_i are increasing in Gödel number, $\{q_i : i \in \omega\}$ is computable.

(iii) $\Rightarrow$ (ii) Obvious.

(ii) $\Rightarrow$ (iv) Let $r_0 = q_0$ and $r_{n+1} = q_{n+1} - q_n$.

(iv) $\Rightarrow$ (i) $L(\alpha) = \{q \in \mathbb{Q} : \exists k\, (q < \sum_{n<k} r_n)\}$, and hence is c.e. □

It is easy to see that, in both (ii) and (iii) above, we can replace the strictly increasing sequence $q_0 < q_1 < \cdots \to \alpha$ by a nondecreasing sequence $q_0 \leqslant q_1 \leqslant \cdots \to \alpha$.

As with c.e. sets, whenever we mention a left-c.e. real α, we assume we have a fixed approximation to α in mind, that is, a sequence of rationals $\alpha_0 < \alpha_1 < \cdots$ converging to α.

If α is computable, then *every* nondecreasing approximation of α has computable range.

Proposition 5.1.6 (Folklore). *If α is computable and $q_0 \leqslant q_1 \leqslant \cdots \to \alpha$ is a computable sequence then $\{q_i : i \in \omega\}$ is computable.*

Proof. Given a rational q, if $q \notin L(\alpha)$ then $q \notin \{q_i : i \in \omega\}$. Otherwise, there must be an n such that $q \leqslant q_n$. Then $q \in \{q_i : i \in \omega\}$ iff $q = q_i$ for some $i \leqslant n$. □

It is important to note that a left-c.e. real is *not* one of the form $0.A$ for a c.e. set A. Reals of the latter form are called *strongly c.e.* It is easy to check (and will follow immediately from Theorem 5.1.7) that every strongly c.e. real is left-c.e., but as will see in Corollary 5.1.9, the converse is not true.

It is possible to characterize the sets A such that $0.A$ is left-c.e. A set A is *almost c.e.* if there is a computable approximation $\{A_s\}_{s\in\omega}$ to A such that if $A_s(n) = 1$ and $A_{s+1}(n) = 0$, then there is an $m < n$ with $A_s(m) = 0$ and $A_{s+1}(m) = 1$.

Theorem 5.1.7 (Calude, Hertling, Khoussainov, and Wang [50]). *A real α is left-c.e. iff $\alpha = 0.A$ for an almost c.e. set A.*

Proof. For strings τ and σ, it is easy to see that $0.\sigma \leqslant 0.\tau$ iff for every $n < |\sigma|$, if $\sigma(n) = 1$ and $\tau(n) = 0$, then there is an $m < n$ such that $\sigma(m) = 0$ and $\tau(m) = 1$ (where we take $\tau(k) = 0$ if $k \geqslant |\tau|$). So if α is left-c.e. then let $q_0 < q_1 < \cdots \to \alpha$ be a computable sequence of rationals and let A_s be such that $0.A_s = q_s$ for all s. Then $A = \lim_s A_s$ is almost c.e. and $\alpha = 0.A$. Conversely, if A is almost c.e. then, letting $q_s = 0.(A_s \upharpoonright s)$, we have $q_0 \leqslant q_1 \leqslant \cdots \to 0.A$. □

Almost c.e. sets do share one important property with c.e. sets: If A is almost c.e., then $A_{s+1} \neq A_s \Rightarrow \forall t > s\, (A_t \neq A_s)$. That is, once the approximation to an initial segment of A has changed, it can never return to its old value. This property is enough to carry out many constructions involving c.e. sets. Of course, c.e. sets and almost c.e. sets have the same degrees, since if A is almost c.e. then $L(0.A)$ is c.e. and has the same degree as A.

Proposition 5.1.8. *There is an almost c.e. set that is not c.e.*

Proof. We build an approximation to an almost c.e. set A. We begin with $A_0(2e) = 0$ and $A_0(2e+1) = 1$ for all e. At stage s, if $2e+1$ enters W_e then we let $A_{s+1}(2e+1) = 0$ and $A_{s+1}(2e) = 1$. (Otherwise, $A_{s+1}(2e) = A_s(2e)$ and $A_{s+1}(2e+1) = A_s(2e+1)$.) Clearly, A is almost c.e. and $A \neq W_e$ for all e. □

Corollary 5.1.9 (Soare [363]). *There is a left-c.e. real that is not strongly c.e.*

It is easy to adapt the above proof to show that there is an almost c.e. set that is not n-c.e. for any n. On the other hand, every almost c.e. set A is ω-c.e., since the approximation to $A \upharpoonright k$ can change at most 2^k many times.

Of course, not every real of the form $0.A$ for an ω-c.e. set is left-c.e. For example, if α is right-c.e. and not computable, then it cannot be left-c.e. The following is a less obvious example.

Theorem 5.1.10 (Ambos-Spies, Weihrauch, and Zheng [12]). *There is a d.c.e. set D such that $0.D$ is neither left-c.e. nor right-c.e.*

Proof. Let $A \mid_T B$ be c.e. sets. Let $D = \overline{A} \oplus B$. Assume for a contradiction that $0.D$ is left-c.e. (the right-c.e. case being analogous). Then D is almost c.e. We claim that we can compute A using B. Suppose we know $A \upharpoonright n$. Let s be such that $D_s \upharpoonright 2n = D \upharpoonright 2n$. We can find such an s using $A \upharpoonright n$ and B. Now let $t \geqslant s$ be such that either $n \in A_t$ or $D_t(2n) = 1$, which must exist by the definition of D. If $n \in A_t$ then we know that $n \in A$. If $D_t(2n) = 1$, then we must have $D(2n) = 1$, as the approximation to $D(2n)$ cannot change from 1 to 0 unless the approximation to $D \upharpoonright 2n$ changes. So in this case we know that $n \notin A$. Thus $A \leqslant_T B$, which is a contradiction. □

Four important examples of left-c.e. reals that figure prominently in the study of algorithmic randomness are the halting probabilities of prefix-free machines, the weights of c.e. prefix-free sets (where the *weight* of a prefix-free set of strings S is $\mu([\![S]\!]) = \sum_{\sigma \in S} 2^{-|\sigma|}$), the measures of Σ^0_1 classes, and the least members of Π^0_1 classes. Indeed, all of these examples exactly characterize the left-c.e. reals. The following theorem assembles the work of several researchers in the area.

Theorem 5.1.11. *The following are equivalent.*

(i) *The real α is left-c.e.*

(ii) *There is a prefix-free machine M such that $\alpha = \mu([\![\operatorname{dom} M]\!])$.*

(iii) *There is a c.e. prefix-free set* $A \subset 2^{<\omega}$ *such that* $\alpha = \sum_{\sigma \in A} 2^{-|\sigma|}$.

(iv) *There is a computable prefix-free set* $B \subset 2^{<\omega}$ *such that* $\alpha = \sum_{\sigma \in B} 2^{-|\sigma|}$.

(v) *There is a* Σ_1^0 *class* C *such that* $\alpha = \mu(C)$.

(vi) *There is a* Π_1^0 *class* P *such that* α *is the least element of* P.

(vii) *There is a computable tree* T *such that* α *is the leftmost path of* T.

Proof. (i) $\Rightarrow$ (ii) Let α be left-c.e. Then there is a computable sequence of positive rationals whose sum is α. Each rational is a sum of finitely many rationals of the form 2^{-n}, so there is computable sequence $n_0, n_1 \ldots$ such that $\sum_i 2^{-n_i} = \alpha$. Then $\{(n_i, \lambda)\}_{i \in \omega}$ is a KC set, so by the KC Theorem there is a prefix-free machine M such that $\mu([\![\operatorname{dom} M]\!]) = \alpha$.

(ii) $\Rightarrow$ (iii) Let $A = \operatorname{dom} M$.

(iii) $\Rightarrow$ (iv) Let $B = \{\tau : \exists \sigma \preccurlyeq \tau \, (\sigma \in A_{|\tau|})\}$.

(iv) $\Rightarrow$ (v) Let $C = [\![B]\!]$.

(v) $\Rightarrow$ (vi) Let R be a c.e. prefix-free set such that $C = [\![R]\!]$, and let P be the class of reals β such that $\beta \geqslant \mu(C)$. It is easy to check that $\beta \in P$ iff $0.(\beta \upharpoonright n+1) + 2^{-n} \geqslant \sum_{\sigma \in R_n} 2^{-|\sigma|}$ for all n, so P is a Π_1^0 class.

(vi) $\Rightarrow$ (vii) Let T be such that $P = [T]$.

(vii) $\Rightarrow$ (i) Let σ_s be the leftmost node at level s of T and let $q_s = 0.\sigma_s$. It is easy to check that $q_0 \leqslant q_1 \leqslant \cdots \to \alpha$. ☐

So we see that left-c.e. reals correspond to (the measures of) domains of prefix-free machines, much as c.e. sets correspond to the domains of Turing machines. This fact helps explain the importance of left-c.e. reals to the theory of algorithmic randomness.

One easy but useful fact about the class of left-c.e. reals is that it is closed under addition. Recall that we always work modulo 1, so by $\alpha + \beta$ we mean the fractional part of $\alpha + \beta$.

Proposition 5.1.12. *If* α *and* β *are left-c.e. reals, then so are* $\alpha + \beta$ *and* $\alpha\beta$.

5.2 Real-valued functions

In this section we consider effective functions from a countable domain D (such as $\mathbb{N}$, $2^{<\omega}$, or $\mathbb{Q}$) to $\mathbb{R}$. A sequence of reals is *uniformly computable* if the corresponding sequence of left cuts is uniformly computable, and *uniformly left-c.e.* if the corresponding sequence of left cuts is uniformly c.e.

Definition 5.2.1. Let $f : D \to \mathbb{R}$.

(i) The function f is *computable* if its values are uniformly computable reals.

(ii) The function f is *computably enumerable* or Σ^0_1 if its values are uniformly left-c.e. reals.

Both of these definitions can be relativized in the obvious way. It is easy to check that f is c.e. iff there are uniformly computable functions $f_s : D \to \mathbb{Q}$ such that for all s and $x \in D$, we have $f_{s+1}(x) \geqslant f_s(x)$ and $\lim_s f_s(x) = f(x)$, or, in other words, f can be approximated from below. Another characterization is that f is c.e. iff the set $\{(x,q) \in D \times \mathbb{Q} : q < f(x)\}$ is c.e., and f is computable iff this set is computable.

It is important to note that when we define a computable function $f : D \to \mathbb{Q}$, we always mean one for which there is an algorithm to determine $f(x)$ given x, *not* a computable function $f : D \to \mathbb{R}$ that happens to take values in $\mathbb{Q}$.

We also define a function $f : D \to \mathbb{R}$ to be *co-c.e.* if its values are uniformly right-c.e. reals (i.e., their left cuts are uniformly co-c.e.). Note that a function is co-c.e. iff it can be approximated from above.

5.3 Representing left-c.e. reals

As we have seen, two ways to represent a left-c.e. real α are by a computable nondecreasing sequence of rationals with limit α and by the measure of a Σ^0_1 class. In this section, we explore computability-theoretic aspects of these two ways of approximating left-c.e. reals.

5.3.1 Degrees of representations

A *representation* of a left-c.e. real α is the range of a computable sequence of rationals $q_0 \leqslant q_1 \leqslant \cdots \to \alpha$. Representations were first analyzed by Calude, Coles, Hertling, and Khoussainov [47]. By the relativized version of Proposition 5.1.6, every representation of a left-c.e. real α is computable in α, and by Theorem 5.1.5, α has a computable representation. The following result gives some more information about the possible degrees of representations of α. Recall that a c.e. splitting of a c.e. set A is a pair of disjoint c.e. sets B and C such that $A = B \cup C$.

Proposition 5.3.1 (Calude, Coles, Hertling, and Khoussainov [47]). *Let α be a left-c.e. real. Every representation of α is half of a c.e. splitting of $L(\alpha)$.*

Proof. Let $q_0 \leqslant q_1 \leqslant \cdots \to \alpha$ be a computable sequence of rationals, and let A be its range. Clearly, A is an infinite c.e. subset of $L(\alpha)$. We claim that so is $L(\alpha) \setminus A$. By our convention that α is irrational, for each n there is an $m > n$ such that $q_m > q_n$. Thus $q \in L(\alpha) \setminus A$ iff $q \in L(\alpha)$ and there is an n such that $q < q_n$ and $q \neq q_m$ for $m < n$. Thus $L(\alpha) \setminus A$ is c.e. □

If A is half of a c.e. splitting of a c.e. set B, then $A \leqslant_{\text{wtt}} B$, because to tell whether $n \in A$, we first check whether $n \in B$, and if so then we enumerate A and $B \setminus A$ until n appears in one of these sets. Thus we have the following result.

Corollary 5.3.2 (Soare [364]). *If A is a representation of α then $A \leqslant_{\text{wtt}} L(\alpha)$.*

It is not difficult to show, using a diagonalization argument, that the converse to Proposition 5.3.1 is not true. However, we do have the following partial converse.

Proposition 5.3.3 (Calude, Coles, Hertling, and Khoussainov [47]). *Let A be a representation of α. If $B \subseteq A$ is infinite, then B represents α iff B is half of a c.e. splitting of A.*

Proof. The "only if" direction has the same proof as Proposition 5.3.1. For the other direction, let $q_0 \leqslant q_1 \leqslant \cdots \to \alpha$ be a computable sequence of rationals with range A. Since B and $A \setminus B$ are both c.e., given n we can compute whether $q_n \in B$, and hence effectively produce an infinite subsequence of the q_n with range B. □

Calude, Coles, Hertling, and Khoussainov [47] also showed that every left-c.e. real α has a representation of the same degree as α. Their result follows immediately from the following exact characterization of the m-degrees of representations of a left-c.e. real.

Theorem 5.3.4 (Downey [102]). *Let α be a left-c.e. real. For every c.e. splitting $B \sqcup C$ of $L(\alpha)$, there is a representation A of α such that $A \equiv_{\text{m}} B$. Thus, the m-degrees of halves of c.e. splittings of $L(\alpha)$ and the m-degrees of representations of α coincide.*

Proof. Let $B \sqcup C = L(\alpha)$. We assume without loss of generality that B is not computable. We give the rationals Gödel numbers as in Section 2.1. We take approximations to B, C, and $L(\alpha)$ with the following properties. First, $B_s \sqcup C_s = L(\alpha)_s$ for all s. Next, each element of $L(\alpha)_s$ has Gödel number less than s. Finally, if $q \in L(\alpha)_s$ and $r < q$ has Gödel number less than s, then $r \in L(\alpha)_s$.

We build a computable sequence of rationals $a_0 < a_1 < \cdots$ and let A be its range. In our construction we will use parameters m_s, with $m_0 = 0$.

At stage s, proceed as follows. If there is no rational greater than m_s in B_s, then let $m_{s+1} = m_s$ and proceed to the next stage. Otherwise, add all elements of B_s greater than m_s to our sequence, in increasing order. (Here we mean the usual order of the rationals.) Let m_{s+1} be largest rational (again in the usual order) in $L(\alpha)_s$ and proceed to the next stage.

We claim that $\lim_s m_s = \infty$. Suppose otherwise, and let t be a stage such that $m_t = \lim_s m_t$. Let q be a rational. If $q \notin B_t$ and $q > m_t$ then $q \notin B$, since otherwise q would be added to our sequence at the stage u at which it enters B, and hence we would have $m_{u+1} \neq m_t$. If $q \leqslant m_t$ then $q \in L(\alpha)$, so by enumerating B and C until q enters one of them, we can determine whether $q \in B$. Thus B is computable, contrary to hypothesis.

It now follows from our claim that $a_0 < a_1 < \cdots$ is an infinite sequence whose limit is the same as the supremum of $L(\alpha)$, that is α. Thus A is a representation of α.

Let S be the set of all rationals q such that $q \leqslant m_s$ where s is one more than the Gödel number of q. Note that S is computable. If $q \in S$ then $q \in A$ iff $q \in A_{s+1}$, and, as above, $q \in L(\alpha)$, so by enumerating B and C until q enters one of them, we can determine whether $q \in B$. Thus $A \cap S$ and $B \cap S$ are both computable.

Now suppose that $q \notin S$. Then either $q > m_t$ for all t, in which case $q \notin A$ and $q \notin B$, or there is a least t such that $q \leqslant m_t$. In the latter case, by our assumptions on the enumerations of B, C, and $L(\alpha)$, we must have $q \in L(\alpha)_{t-1}$, and hence $q \in A$ iff $q \in B_{t-1}$ iff $q \in B$. So if $q \notin S$ then $q \in A$ iff $q \in B$. Thus $A \equiv_{\mathrm{m}} B$. □

This characterization, together with known results on c.e. splittings and wtt-degrees, yields several facts about representations, including many of the results in [47]. For instance, by Sacks' Splitting Theorem 2.12.1, every noncomputable left-c.e. real α has representations in infinitely many degrees (because Theorem 2.12.1 implies that we can split $L(\alpha)$ into Turing incomparable A_0 and A_1; but then we can also split A_0 into Turing incomparable B_0 and B_1 and have a representation of α of the same degree as B_0, and continue in this manner to obtain representations in infinitely many degrees). The following are further examples. For proofs of the corresponding theorems on splittings, see Downey and Stob [133].

Corollary 5.3.5. (i) *There is a left-c.e. real α with representations of every c.e. m-degree*

(ii) *There is a left-c.e. real β such that the set of Turing degrees of representations of β forms an atomless boolean algebra that is nowhere dense in the c.e. degrees.*

We can also obtain negative results on the existence of representations. For instance, Downey [101] showed that a c.e. degree **a** contains a set with splittings in each c.e. degree below **a** iff **a** is either (Turing) complete or low$_2$.

Corollary 5.3.6. *If a left-c.e. real α has representations in each degree below that of α, then α is either complete or low$_2$.*

It is not known whether every nonzero c.e. degree contains a left-c.e. real α that does not have representations in every c.e. degree below that of α.

5.3.2 Presentations of left-c.e. reals

Another natural way to represent left-c.e. reals is via measures.

Definition 5.3.7 (Downey and LaForte [122]). A *presentation* of a left-c.e. real α is a prefix-free c.e. set $A \subset 2^{<\omega}$ such that $\alpha = \mu([\![A]\!]) = \sum_{\sigma \in A} 2^{-|\sigma|}$.

We have seen that every left-c.e. real α has a representation of degree α. The same is not true of presentations. Downey and LaForte [122] showed that there is a noncomputable left-c.e. real all of whose presentations are computable. We will obtain this result as a corollary to Theorem 5.3.13 below. Downey and LaForte [122] also showed that such "only computably presentable" reals can be high, but that, as we will see in Theorem 5.3.16 below, they cannot be of promptly simple degree. Using a $\mathbf{0}'''$ argument (an elaboration of the infinite injury method discussed in Chapter 2), Wu [407] constructed a c.e. set A such that any A-computable, noncomputable left-c.e. real has a noncomputable presentation.[2]

Strong reducibilities often play a large role in effective mathematics, since naturally occurring reductions tend to be stronger than Turing reductions. For instance, the word problem for a finitely presented group is tt-reducible to the conjugacy problem (see [189]), algebraic closure is related to a reducibility known as Q-reducibility (see [35, 123, 257, 421]), and wtt-degrees characterize the degrees of bases of a c.e. vector space (see [131]). Here too, the classification of the degrees realized as presentations of left-c.e. reals appears to depend on a stronger reducibility than Turing reducibility. In this case, the relevant reducibility seems to be weak truth table reducibility. The following result is easy to prove.

Proposition 5.3.8 (Downey and LaForte [122]). *Let α be a left-c.e. real and let A be a presentation of α. Then $A \leqslant_{\mathrm{wtt}} \alpha$ with use function the identity.*

What is interesting is that there is a sort of converse to this result.

Theorem 5.3.9 (Downey and LaForte [122]). *If A is a presentation of a left-c.e. real α and $C \leqslant_{\mathrm{wtt}} A$ is c.e., then there is a presentation B of α with $B \equiv_{\mathrm{wtt}} C$.*

Proof. We assume that A and C are infinite, since there is nothing to prove if A is computable, and if C is finite then we can substitute it by any infinite computable set. Let Γ be a reduction with computable use γ such that $\Gamma^A = C$. As usual, we may assume that γ is increasing. We also may assume that at each stage s, exactly one element n_s enters C and $\Gamma^A(m)[s] = C_s(m)$ for all $m < s$. We choose a pairing function so that

[2] As we will see in Theorem 9.3.1, this property of always having noncomputable presentations is also true of reals whose initial segments have fairly low Kolmogorov complexity.

$\langle m,n\rangle > m,n$ for all m and n, in addition to the usual requirement that it be increasing in both arguments.

We build B by enumerating strings of certain lengths. We will ensure that $\sum_{\sigma\in B_s} 2^{-|\sigma|} = \sum_{\sigma\in A_s} 2^{-|\sigma|} \leqslant 1$ for all s, which, by the same argument as in the proof of the KC Theorem, means that we will never run out of strings. It will, of course, also ensure that B is a presentation of α.

To build B, at stage s we proceed as follows for each σ entering A at stage s. If $|\sigma| < \gamma(n_s)$ then we enumerate $2^{\langle|\sigma|,n_s\rangle-|\sigma|}$ many strings of length $\langle|\sigma|,n_s\rangle$ into B. If $|\sigma| \geqslant \gamma(n_s)$ then we enumerate $2^{\langle|\sigma|,|\sigma|+s\rangle-|\sigma|}$ many strings of length $\langle|\sigma|,|\sigma|+s\rangle$ into B.

We clearly have $\sum_{\sigma\in B_s} 2^{-|\sigma|} = \sum_{\sigma\in A_s} 2^{-|\sigma|}$ for all s, which means that, as mentioned above, we can always find available strings of the appropriate lengths, and also that $\sum_{\sigma\in B} 2^{-|\sigma|} = \sum_{\sigma\in A} 2^{-|\sigma|} = \alpha$, so B is a presentation of α.

Given n, let $s > n$ be least such that B_s agrees with B on all strings of length less than $\langle\gamma(n),n\rangle$. We claim that if $n \notin C_s$ then $n \notin C$. Assume for a contradiction that $n \in C \setminus C_s$. Then $n = n_t$ for some $t > s$. Since $\Gamma^A(n)[t-1] = C_{t-1}(n) = 0$ and $\Gamma^A(n)[t] = C_t(n) = 1$, there must be some σ with $|\sigma| < \gamma(n)$ entering A at stage t. Thus strings of length $\langle|\sigma|,n\rangle$ enter B at stage t, which is a contradiction because $\langle|\sigma|,n\rangle < \langle\gamma(n),n\rangle$. So we can compute whether $n \in C$ if we know s, which requires knowing the value of B only on strings of length less than $\langle\gamma(n),n\rangle$. Since γ is computable, $C \leqslant_{\text{wtt}} B$.

Now let $\tau \in 2^{<\omega}$. If there are no i and n such that $|\tau| = \langle i,n\rangle$ then $\tau \notin B$. Otherwise, let i and n be such that $|\tau| = \langle i,n\rangle$. If $i \geqslant \gamma(n)$, then τ can enter B at stage s only if $s = n - i$, so we can computably determine whether $\tau \in B$. Now suppose that $i < \gamma(n)$ and τ enters B at stage s. Then $n = n_s$ and $i = |\sigma|$ for some σ entering A at stage s. Thus, if $C_t \upharpoonright n+1 = C \upharpoonright n+1$ then $B(\tau) = B_t(\tau)$. Since n is computable from $|\tau|$, we have $B \leqslant_{\text{wtt}} C$. □

The Turing degree of a c.e. set A is *wtt-topped* if every c.e. set that is Turing reducible to A is wtt-reducible to A. Clearly the halting problem is such a set, but there are incomplete c.e. Turing degrees that are wtt-topped as shown by Ladner and Sasso [234, 235] and Downey and Jockusch [119]. One consequence of the above result is that if α is a strongly c.e. real whose degree is wtt-topped, then there are presentations of α in all c.e. Turing degrees less than or equal to that of α. It is an interesting fact that if a c.e. degree is wtt-topped then it is either complete or low$_2$ (see Downey and Jockusch [119]).

Proposition 5.3.8 does not hold for tt-reducibility.

Proposition 5.3.10 (Downey and Hirschfeldt [unpublished]). *There exist a strongly c.e. real α and a presentation B of α such that $B \nleqslant_{\text{tt}} \alpha$.*

Proof. Let $T_0, T_1, \ldots$ be an effective list of all truth tables. We build c.e. sets A and B and let $\alpha = 0.A$. We need to satisfy the following requirement for each e.

$$\mathcal{R}_e : \Phi_e \text{ total} \Rightarrow \exists \sigma_e\, (\sigma_e \in B \Leftrightarrow A \nvDash T_{\Phi_e(\sigma_e)}(\sigma_e)).$$

Let $D = \{0^n 1 : n \in \mathbb{N}\}$.

At stage s, begin by defining σ_s to be a fresh large string in D. Let $e \leqslant s$ be least such that $\mathcal{R}_e$ has not yet been satisfied and $\Phi_e(\sigma_e)[s]\downarrow$. (If there is no such e then proceed to the next stage.) Put $|\sigma_e|$ into A to obtain A_{s+1}. If $A_{s+1} \nvDash T_{\Phi_e(\sigma_e)}(\sigma_e)$ then put σ_e into B. Otherwise, put $\sigma_e 0$ and $\sigma_e 1$ into B. In either case, initialize all $\mathcal{R}_i$ with $i > e$ by redefining σ_i to be fresh large strings in D. All such $\mathcal{R}_i$ are now unsatisfied, while $\mathcal{R}_e$ is satisfied.

Clearly A and B are c.e., and B is prefix-free because D is prefix-free. Furthermore, $\mu(\llbracket B \rrbracket) = \mu(\llbracket A \rrbracket) = \alpha$ because we add the same measure to $\llbracket A \rrbracket$ and $\llbracket B \rrbracket$ at each stage.

Finally, assume by induction that there is a least s such that all $\mathcal{R}_i$ for $i < e$ have stopped acting by stage s. Then σ_e reaches its final value at stage s. If $\Phi_e(\sigma_e)\uparrow$ then $\mathcal{R}_e$ is satisfied and never acts after stage s. Otherwise, at the least stage $t \geqslant s$ such that $\Phi_e(\sigma_e)[t]\downarrow$, we ensure that $\sigma_e \in B \Leftrightarrow A_{t+1} \nvDash T_{\Phi_e(\sigma_e)}(\sigma_e)$. Since all $\mathcal{R}_i$ with $i > e$ are initialized at that stage, $A \vDash T_{\Phi_e(\sigma_e)}(\sigma_e)$ iff $A_{t+1} \vDash T_{\Phi_e(\sigma_e)}(\sigma_e)$, so $\mathcal{R}_e$ is permanently satisfied and never again acts. $\square$

5.3.3 Presentations and ideals

A class $I \subseteq 2^\omega$ is a *wtt-ideal* if it is closed under join and downward closed under wtt-reducibility. For a left-c.e. real α, let $\mathcal{I}(\alpha)$ be the collection of all c.e. sets C such that there is a presentation A of α with $C \equiv_{\mathrm{wtt}} A$.

Theorem 5.3.11 (Downey and LaForte [122]). *If α is a left-c.e. real then $\mathcal{I}(\alpha)$ is a Σ^0_3 wtt-ideal.*

Proof. Let A and B be presentations of α. Then $C = \{0\sigma : \sigma \in A\} \cup \{1\sigma : \sigma \in B\}$ is a presentation of α, and $C \equiv_{\mathrm{wtt}} A \oplus B$. Together with Theorem 5.3.9, this fact shows that $\mathcal{I}(\alpha)$ is a wtt-ideal.

The statement "$\mu(\llbracket W_e \rrbracket) = \alpha$" is Π^0_2 ("for all diameters ε there is a stage s such that $\mu(\llbracket W_e \rrbracket)[s]$ and $\alpha[s]$ are closer than ε"). Saying that W_e is prefix-free is Π^0_1. For a given c.e. set A, the set $\{W_e : W_e \equiv_{\mathrm{wtt}} A\}$ is Σ^0_3 (see Odifreddi [311, p. 627]; roughly, we have to say "there exists a wtt-reduction such that $\forall x\, \forall y \leqslant x\, \exists s > x$ such that at stage s the reduction gives the right answers on y").

Thus $W_e \in \mathcal{I}(\alpha)$ if and only if there exists a d such that a certain Σ^0_3 statement holds true of W_d, so $\mathcal{I}(\alpha)$ is a Σ^0_3 wtt-ideal. $\square$

To see that this result is optimal, note that if α is computable, then by Theorem 5.3.9, $\mathcal{I}(\alpha) = \{W_e : W_e \text{ computable}\}$, which is Σ^0_3-complete. $\mathcal{I}(\alpha)$ is not always Σ^0_3-complete. We have seen that there are α such that $\mathcal{I}(\alpha) = \{W_e : e \in \mathbb{N}\}$, which is trivial (as an index set). The following result, in the spirit of Rice's Theorem, says that this is in fact the *only* case in which $\mathcal{I}(\alpha)$ is not Σ^0_3-complete.

Theorem 5.3.12 (Downey and Terwijn [134]). *$\mathcal{I}(\alpha)$ is either $\{W_e : e \in \mathbb{N}\}$ or Σ^0_3-complete.*

Proof sketch. Let $\alpha = 0.A$ be a left-c.e. real. By Proposition 5.3.8 and Theorem 5.3.9, $\mathcal{I}(\alpha) = \{W_e : e \in \mathbb{N}\}$ iff A is wtt-complete. Now suppose that A is not wtt-complete. We can show that $\mathcal{I}(\alpha)$ is Σ^0_3-complete using methods of Rogers and Kallibekov (see Odifreddi [311, pp. 625-627]). Let $\mathrm{Inf} = \{e : |W_e| = \infty\}$. We use the fact that the weak jump $\{i : W_i \cap \mathrm{Inf} \neq \emptyset\}$ of Inf is Σ^0_3-complete. It suffices to build sets B_i such that if $W_i \cap \mathrm{Inf} \neq \emptyset$ then B_i is computable, and otherwise $B_i \nleqslant_{\mathrm{wtt}} A$. Then by Proposition 5.3.8 and Theorem 5.3.9, $W_i \cap \mathrm{Inf} \neq \emptyset$ iff the wtt-degree of B_i contains a presentation of α.

Let $\Gamma_0, \Gamma_1, \ldots$ be an effective listing of the wtt-functionals. For a fixed i, we have requirements

$$P_e : e \in W_i \wedge |W_e| = \infty \Rightarrow \exists n_e \, \forall n \geqslant n_e \, (\omega^{[n]} \subseteq B_i)$$

and

$$R_e : (W_i \cap \mathrm{Inf} = \emptyset \wedge \Gamma^A_e \text{ total}) \Rightarrow \exists n \, (B_i(n) \neq \Gamma^A_e(n)).$$

The constructions for different i's run independently.

The requirement P_e is handled by waiting until e enters W_i (if ever), and then enumerating $\omega^{[n]}$ into B_i for $n \geqslant n_e$ whenever an element greater than n is found to be in W_e (where n_e is a number determined by the stronger priority requirements).

The requirement R_e is handled by Sacks' coding strategy, as in Theorem 2.15.1. We maintain a length of agreement function $l(e,s)$ monitoring agreement between B_i and Γ^A_e, and code $\emptyset' \upharpoonright l(e,s)$ into $\omega^{[n]}$ for the least n such that $\omega^{[n]}$ has not been enumerated into B_i. We ensure that $n_i > n$ for weaker priority strategies P_i by redefining these n_i if necessary. Then, provided that the stronger priority requirements are finitary, R_e is also finitary (and hence satisfied), since otherwise all of $\emptyset'$ would be coded into B_i and we would have $B_i \leqslant_{\mathrm{wtt}} A$, contradicting the wtt-incompleteness of A.

If W_i contains no code for an infinite c.e. set then all P_e are finitary, and hence every R_e succeeds and $B_i \nleqslant_{\mathrm{wtt}} A$. If, on the other hand, $e \in W_i$ is least such that W_e is infinite, then all requirements stronger than P_e are finitary, so for the final value of n_e, we have $\omega^{[n]} \subseteq B_i$ for $n \geqslant n_e$, while for each $n < n_e$, either $\omega^{[n]} \subseteq B_i$ or $\omega^{[n]} \cap B_i$ is finite. Thus B_i is computable. □

We will prove the following converse to the fact that every $\mathcal{I}(\alpha)$ is a Σ^0_3 wtt-ideal.

Theorem 5.3.13 (Downey and Terwijn [134]). *Let $\mathcal{I}$ be a Σ^0_3 wtt-ideal of c.e. sets. There is a noncomputable left-c.e. real α such that $\mathcal{I}(\alpha) = \mathcal{I}$.*

The computable sets form a Σ^0_3 wtt-ideal, so we have the following result.

Corollary 5.3.14 (Downey and LaForte [122]). *There is a noncomputable left-c.e. real all of whose presentations are computable.*

The proof of Theorem 5.3.13 will make use of the following lemma, which implies that every Σ^0_3 wtt-ideal of c.e. sets can be written as a collection of uniformly c.e. sets.

Lemma 5.3.15 (Yates [409]). *Let $I \in \Sigma^0_3$ and let $\mathcal{C} = \{W_i : i \in I\}$ contain all the finite sets. There are uniformly c.e. $V_0, V_1, \ldots$ such that $\mathcal{C} = \{V_e : e \in \mathbb{N}\}$.*

Proof. Let R be a computable predicate such that

$$i \in I \text{ iff } \exists e \forall n \exists m \, R(i, e, n, m).$$

Whenever we find that $\forall n < s \exists m \, R(i, e, n, m)$ for some i, e, and s, enumerate all elements of $W_i[s]$ into $V_{\langle i,e \rangle}$. If $i \in I$ then there is an e such that $V_{\langle i,e \rangle} = W_i$. Conversely, for each i and e, either $V_{\langle i,e \rangle} = W_i$, in which case i must be in I, and so $V_{\langle i,e \rangle} \in \mathcal{C}$; or $V_{\langle i,e \rangle}$ is finite, in which case $V_{\langle i,e \rangle} \in \mathcal{C}$ by hypothesis. □

Proof of Theorem 5.3.13. We begin by outlining the main ideas of the proof. By Lemma 5.3.15, there are uniformly c.e. sets $U_0, U_1, \ldots$ such that $\mathcal{I} = \{U_0, U_1, \ldots\}$. Let $V_0, V_1, \ldots$ be an effective listing of the prefix-free c.e. sets of strings. We build α and prefix-free sets of strings $A_0, A_1, \ldots$ to satisfy the requirements

$$C_e : A_e \equiv_{\text{wtt}} U_e \wedge \mu([\![A_e]\!]) = \alpha$$

and

$$N_e : \mu([\![V_e]\!]) = \alpha \Rightarrow V_e \leqslant_{\text{wtt}} \bigoplus_{i \leqslant e} A_i.$$

The C-requirements are positive requirements, which will cause us to add certain amounts to α. To make α noncomputable, we can add requirements ensuring that $\alpha \neq 0.\overline{W_e}$. These requirements can be satisfied in the same way as the C-requirements, so for simplicity of presentation we omit them from our presentation. Adding them to the construction is straightforward.

We first describe the strategies for meeting the above requirements in isolation, and then explain how to combine them using a tree of strategies.

We attempt to ensure that $U_e \leqslant_{\text{wtt}} A_e$ by permitting. Along with A_e we define a function $\psi_e : \mathbb{N} \to 2^{<\omega}$. Whenever a number x enters U_e we put (or at least try to put) $\psi_e(x)$ into A_e.

We attempt to ensure that $A_e \leqslant_{\text{wtt}} U_e$ by allowing small strings to enter A_e only for the sake of coding U_e. Assuming that $\psi_e(x) \geqslant x$, we will then have $A_e \leqslant_{\text{wtt}} U_e$ with use the identity function.

We build α by adding rational amounts to it, thus determining a sequence of rationals $\alpha[0] \leqslant \alpha[1] \leqslant \cdots \to \alpha$. We satisfy the second part of C_e by ensuring that there are infinitely many stages s with $\alpha[s] = \mu([\![A_e]\!])[s]$.

For N_e, if $\alpha[s]$ and $\mu([\![V_e]\!])[s]$ are close, we try to make V_e computable by restraining α. We monitor how close these two values get by defining a nondecreasing, unbounded sequence of numbers $m_e[s]$. Every time we see that $|\alpha[s] - \mu([\![V_e]\!])[s]| < 2^{-m_e[s]}$, we attempt to keep α from changing on short strings by ensuring that $\alpha - \alpha[s] \leqslant 2^{-m_e[s]}$. If $\mu([\![V_e]\!]) = \alpha$ and we were to succeed completely in these attempts, then V_e would be computable, since to determine whether $\gamma \in V_e$, we could run the construction until $|\alpha[s] - \mu([\![V_e]\!])[s]| < 2^{-m_e[s]}$ with $m_e[s]$ sufficiently larger than $|\gamma|$, and then we would have $\gamma \in V_e$ iff $\gamma \in V_e[s]$.

The coding strategy for a requirement C_e can easily live with the action of stronger priority coding strategies by picking different coding locations from theirs, and, of course, the strategies for the N-requirements do not interfere with each other. We describe how the C- and N-strategies can be combined.

We first look at how N_e can deal with the strategy for a stronger priority requirement C_i. As described above, when $|\alpha[s] - \mu([\![V_e]\!])[s]| < 2^{-m_e[s]}$, the strategy for N_e attempts to restrain α and ensure that $\alpha - \alpha[s] \leqslant 2^{-m_e[s]}$. However, the coding action of C_i may spoil this attempt. Suppose that $\mu([\![V_e]\!]) = \alpha$. Although we can no longer argue that V_e is computable, we can still argue that it is computable in A_i. (We will later show that this computation is in fact a wtt-computation.) To compute whether $\gamma \in V_e$ using A_i, find an s such that $\mu([\![A_i]\!]) - \mu([\![A_i]\!])[s] \leqslant 2^{-|\gamma|-1}$ and $|\alpha[s] - \mu([\![V_e]\!])[s]| < 2^{-m_e[s]}$ with $2^{-m_e[s]} < 2^{-|\gamma|-2}$. After this stage, N_e does not change α by more than $2^{-m_e[s]}$, and C_i does not change α by more than $2^{-|\gamma|-1}$, so $\mu([\![V_e]\!])$ cannot change by more than $2^{-m_e[s]+1} + 2^{-|\gamma|-1} < 2^{-|\gamma|}$, and hence $\gamma \in V_e$ iff $\gamma \in V_e[s]$.

We now look at how C_i can deal with a stronger priority N_e. The strategy for N_e can have two outcomes. The infinitary outcome happens when there are infinitely many stages at which $\mu([\![V_e]\!])$ grows closer to α. The finitary outcome happens when, from a certain stage onwards, $\mu([\![V_e]\!])[s]$ is bounded away from $\alpha[s]$. Suppose that a number enters U_i at stage s, and C_i wants to code this event by enumerating a string δ into A_i, but $|\alpha[s] - \mu([\![V_e]\!])[s]| < 2^{-m_e[s]} < 2^{-|\delta|}$. Then C_i is not allowed to enumerate a string as short as δ into A_i, since this enumeration would cause α to change by $2^{-|\delta|}$, which is more than N_e is prepared to allow. To get around this problem, we let A_e announce that it wishes to enumerate δ, without actually doing so. We then increase α slightly, though not enough to injure N_e. If V_e does not respond with a corresponding increase, then N_e is satisfied and has finitary outcome. Otherwise, $\mu([\![V_e]\!])$ eventually grows closer to α, and we can repeat this procedure. If V_e keeps responding to the small changes we make in α, then by repeating this procedure enough times, we are eventually able to create enough space between $\mu([\![A_e]\!])$ and α for δ to enter A_e. Note that it is important that we do not allow m_e to grow during this procedure. We will refer to this strategy as the "drip-feed strategy", since we think of C_i succeeding by feeding α changes small enough to be allowed by N_e, and doing this often enough to be able to finally make its move. (In Downey [103], the analogy is drawn with a stock market trader that wants to dump a large number of shares without disrupting the market. The trader sells a small amount of shares, then waits until the price recovers before doing so again.)

The strategy for C_e becomes a little more complicated when it has to deal with the outcomes of more than one N-strategy. Suppose that C_e is below N_i, which is below N_j. Suppose that at some stage s, the strategy for C_e wants to put δ into A_e using the drip-feed strategy described above. Then C_e tries to increase α by $2^{-m_i[s]}$ a total of $2^{-|\delta|+m_i[s]}$ many times. While we are waiting for N_i to respond to the first such increase, m_j might grow, since N_j neither knows nor cares whether N_i is going to respond. When N_i finally does respond, m_j may have become so big that N_j does not allow a change of $2^{-m_i[s]}$ to α, thus frustrating C_e's drip-feed strategy. The solution to this problem is to let N_i use a drip-feed strategy of its own to get N_j to allow a change of 2^{-n} to α. If both N_i and N_j are infinitary, in the end all the changes in α requested by C_e will be allowed. After every successfully completed drip-feed strategy, the N-strategies are allowed to let their m-values grow. This idea works in general for any finite number of N-strategies above C_i, by recursively nesting the drip-feed strategies.

To handle the interactions between strategies in general, we use a tree of strategies as in Section 2.14. We use $2^{<\omega}$ as our tree, assigning both C_e and N_e to each string of length e (because only the N-strategies have interesting outcomes). The outcome 0 corresponds to N_e having infinitary outcome, while the outcome 1 corresponds to its having finitary outcome. Each σ builds its own set A_σ and tries to satisfy $C_{|\sigma|}$ by building a wtt-reduction ψ_σ from $U_{|\sigma|}$ to A_σ.

To coordinate the drip-feed strategies, we equip each node σ with a counter c_σ and let σ act only at stages at which $c_\sigma = 0$. The counter c_σ indicates how many steps a drip-feed strategy corresponding to some $\tau \succ \sigma$ still needs to perform to be successfully completed. At the start of such a strategy aiming to put a string δ into α, the counter c_σ is set to $2^{-|\delta|+n}$ for some number n determined by the longest ν with $\nu 0 \preccurlyeq \tau$ that will not allow $2^{-|\delta|}$ to be added to α immediately. Every time α is allowed to increase by 2^{-n}, the counter c_σ is decreased by 1. Every time the counter reaches 0 we allow σ to act.

To enable the actions of the various coding requirements to coexist, we equip each C-strategy at σ with a list L_σ of strings. After a drip-feed strategy is successfully completed, the top element of L_σ is removed. Each string in L_σ has to wait until it is at the top of the list before a drip-feed strategy on its behalf can be started. We also have a list R_σ of lengths of strings that strategies below σ want to put into their corresponding sets.

In addition to c_σ and the lists L_σ and R_σ, each σ has associated with it a length of agreement parameter l_σ, a parameter m_σ (corresponding to the parameter m_e discussed above), and a restraint parameter r_σ. The construction proceeds in stages. When we initialize N_σ, we empty R_σ and undefine all the parameters associated with σ. When we initialize C_σ, we empty L_σ. When we add an element to a list L_σ or R_σ, we place it at the bottom of the list.

Construction.
Stage 0. Let $\alpha[0] = 0$ and initialize all σ.

Stage $s > 0$. We define the approximation TP_s to the true path at stage s recursively. Initially, allow the strategies associated with $\sigma = \lambda$ to act. If the strategies associated with some $\sigma \in 2^s$ act at stage s, then proceed to the next stage at the end of their actions.

Action for C_σ. Let $e = |\sigma|$. We first pick suitable coding locations for the elements of U_e in A_σ. For each $n \leqslant s$, if $\psi_\sigma(n)$ is not currently defined then define it to be a fresh long string not extending any string currently in A_σ. For each n entering U_e at stage s, proceed as follows. Let ρ be the longest string such that $\rho 0 \preccurlyeq \sigma$ and $r_\rho > \psi_\sigma(n)[s]$. (That is, N_ρ is the weakest strategy requiring C_σ to use a drip-feed strategy to put $\psi_\sigma(n)[s]$ into A_σ.) Add $\psi_\sigma(n)[s]$ to L_σ and add $|\psi_\sigma(x)[s]|$ to R_ρ. If there is no such ρ then simply put $\psi_\sigma(n)[s]$ into A_σ.

If L_σ is currently nonempty, let δ be its top element. Let ρ be the longest string such that $\rho 0 \preccurlyeq \sigma$ and $r_\rho[s] > |\delta|$. (The existence of such a ρ is guaranteed by the fact that δ is on L_σ.) If $|\delta|$ is currently on R_ρ then do nothing. Otherwise, δ has been successfully processed by N_ρ, and hence, by recursion, by all relevant N-strategies above σ. Put δ into A_σ and remove it from L_σ.

In any case, ensure that the approximations to α and $\mu([\![A_\sigma]\!])$ agree by putting fresh long strings into A_σ (while keeping A_σ prefix-free) or increasing the value of α, if necessary.

Action for N_σ. Let $e = |\sigma|$. Let

$$l_\sigma[s] = \begin{cases} s & \text{if } \mu([\![V_e]\!])[s] = \alpha[s] \\ \min\{n : |\alpha[s] - \mu([\![V_e]\!])[s]| > 2^{-n}\} - 1 & \text{otherwise} \end{cases}$$

and let $m_\sigma[s] = \max\{l_\sigma[t] : t < s\}$. Note that $|\alpha[s] - \mu([\![V_e]\!])[s]| \leqslant 2^{-l_\sigma[s]}$. The stage s is *σ-expansionary* if $l_\sigma[s] > m_\sigma[s]$.

If s is not σ-expansionary, then initialize all τ-strategies with $\sigma 1 <_L \tau$ and let $\sigma 1$ be the next string to act at stage s (if $|\sigma| < s$).

If s is σ-expansionary and R_σ is currently empty then proceed as follows. Let $r_\sigma = l_\sigma[s]$. If $|\sigma| = s$ then proceed to the next stage. Otherwise, initialize all τ-strategies with $\sigma 0 <_L \tau$ and let $\sigma 0$ be the next string to act at stage s (if $|\sigma| < s$).

If s is σ-expansionary and R_σ is nonempty, then proceed as follows. Let n be number at the top of R_σ. If $c_\sigma[s-1]\uparrow$ then let $c_\sigma = 2^{-n+r_\sigma[s]}$, initialize all τ-strategies with $\sigma 0 <_{\mathrm{L}} \tau$, and let $\sigma 0$ be the next string to act at stage s (if $|\sigma| < s$). If $c_\sigma[s-1]\downarrow= 0$ then σ's drip-feed strategy for n has been successfully completed. Remove n from R_σ, initialize all τ-strategies with $\sigma 0 <_{\mathrm{L}} \tau$, and let $\sigma 0$ be the next string to act at stage s (if $|\sigma| < s$).

Finally, suppose that $c_\sigma[s-1] > 0$. Then at some previous stage t this counter was set to some number $2^{-n+r_\sigma}[t]$, and r_σ has not changed since. Let ρ be the longest string such that $\rho 0 \preccurlyeq \sigma$ and $r_\rho[s] > r_\sigma[s]$. If there is no such ρ then add $2^{-r_\sigma}[s]$ to α. If $r_\sigma[s] \in R_\rho[s]$ then do nothing. (In this case $r_\sigma[s]$ is still waiting for its turn to start a drip-feed strategy.) Otherwise, $r_\sigma[s]$ was removed from R_ρ when its counter c_ρ became 0 at some stage $u \leqslant s$. Let $c_\sigma[s] = c_\sigma[s-1] - 1$, and put $r_\sigma[s]$ on R_ρ. In any case, proceed to the next stage immediately.

End of Construction.

Because the construction is computable, α is a left-c.e. real, and each A_σ is c.e. and prefix-free. Let $\mathrm{TP} = \liminf_s \mathrm{TP}_s$ be the true path of the construction. It is easy to see that TP is infinite, because whenever the construction stops at some $\sigma \in 2^{<s}$ at stage s, the value of c_σ decreases.

We prove by induction along TP that if $\sigma \prec \mathrm{TP}$ then, letting $e = |\sigma|$, we have $A_\sigma \equiv_{\mathrm{wtt}} U_e$ and $\mu([\![A_\sigma]\!]) = \alpha$, and if $\mu([\![V_e]\!]) = \alpha$ then $V_e \leqslant_{\mathrm{wtt}} \bigoplus_{\tau \preccurlyeq \sigma} A_\tau$.

First note that $A_\sigma \leqslant_{\mathrm{wtt}} U_e$: A string δ can enter A_σ only after some $\psi_e(n)$ has been defined with $\delta = \psi_e(n)$ or $|\delta| > |\psi_e(n)|$. Since $|\psi_e(n)| > n$, if U_e does not change below n then no string of length less than n can enter A_σ. Thus $A_\sigma \leqslant_{\mathrm{wtt}} U_e$ with use the identity function.

Next note that if $\rho 0 \prec \mathrm{TP}$, then every number put on R_ρ is eventually removed from R_ρ: Since there are infinitely many stages at which $\rho 0$ acts, and $\rho 0$ can act only when R_ρ is empty or $c_\rho = 0$, infinitely often either R_ρ is empty or its top element is removed.

Let s be a stage after which C_σ is never initialized, which must exist since $\sigma \in \mathrm{TP}$. Then $\psi_\sigma(n)$ has a final value for all n. Suppose n enters U_e at a stage $t > s$. Let ρ be the longest string such that $\rho 0 \preccurlyeq \sigma$ and $r_\rho[t] > \psi_\sigma(n)$. If no such ρ exists then $\psi_\sigma(n)$ enters A_σ immediately. Otherwise, $\psi_\sigma(n)$ is added to L_σ and $|\psi_\sigma(n)|$ is added to R_ρ. As noted above, $|\psi_\sigma(n)|$ is eventually removed from R_ρ, so $\psi_\sigma(n)$ is eventually removed from L_σ and put into A_σ. Since no other strategy can put $\psi_\sigma(n)$ into A_σ for any n, and C_σ will not put $\psi_\sigma(n)$ into A_σ if $n \notin U_e$, we have $n \in U_e$ iff $\psi_\sigma(n) \in A_\sigma$.

We also have $\mu([\![A_\sigma]\!]) = \alpha$, because $\mu([\![A_\sigma]\!])[s] = \alpha[s]$ at the end of C_σ's action at every stage s at which C_σ acts. Thus C_σ is satisfied.

We finish by verifying that N_σ is satisfied. Suppose that $\mu([\![V_e]\!]) = \alpha$. Let s be a stage after which N_σ is never initialized. Let $\gamma \in 2^{<\omega}$. We compute whether $\gamma \in V_e$ as follows. Let $t \geqslant s, |\gamma| + 1$ be a stage at which σ acts such that $A_\tau[t]$ agrees with A_τ on all strings of length less than or equal to

$|\gamma|+1$ for all $\tau \preccurlyeq \sigma$, and $r_\sigma[t] = l_\sigma[t] > |\gamma|+1$. There is such a stage because $\lim_s l_\sigma[s] = \infty$ and $\sigma 0$ acts infinitely often. By the definition of l we have $|\alpha[t] - \mu([\![V_e]\!])[t]| \leqslant 2^{-l_\sigma[t]}$. Assume for a contradiction that γ enters V_e at a stage $u > t$. By the choice of t, and the definition of the functions ψ_τ, the strategies C_τ with $\tau \preccurlyeq \sigma$ cannot add more than $2^{-|\gamma|-2}$ to α after stage t, and neither can the strategies C_τ with $\tau \geqslant_{\mathrm{L}} \sigma 1$, as they are initialized at stage t. The coding strategies C_τ with $\tau \succcurlyeq \sigma 0$ may wish to change α below $r_\sigma[t]$ after stage t, but they have to use the drip-feed strategy to do so, and hence cannot ever increase the difference between α and $\mu([\![V_e]\!])$ by more than $2^{-r_\sigma[t]}$, and must wait for $\mu([\![V_e]\!])$ to grow closer to α than $2^{-r_\sigma[t]}$ before each change to α they make. Thus the enumeration of γ into V_e at stage u ensures that $|\alpha[v] - \mu([\![V_e]\!])[v]| \geqslant 2^{-|\gamma|} - 2^{-|\gamma|-1} - 2^{-r_\sigma[t]} > 2^{-r_\sigma[t]}$ for all $v \geqslant u$, contradicting the assumption that $\mu([\![V_e]\!]) = \alpha$. So $\gamma \in V_e$ iff $\gamma \in V_e[t]$, and hence we can wtt-compute V_e using A_τ for $\tau \preccurlyeq \sigma$. □

The drip-feed strategy of the above proof makes it somewhat difficult to get elements into α, but it is possible to make α high via standard highness requirements. In the next subsection, and later in Section 9.3, we will see that it is possible to say something about the degrees of left-c.e. reals realizing certain ideals.

5.3.4 Promptly simple sets and presentations of left-c.e. reals

Recall from Definition 2.22.4 that a coinfinite c.e. set A is promptly simple if there are a computable function f and an enumeration $\{A_s\}_{s\in\omega}$ of A such that for every infinite c.e. set W, there are an n and an s with $n \in W_e[s] \setminus W_e[s-1] \cap A_{f(s)}$. (The statement of Definition 2.22.4 is slightly different, but easily shown to be equivalent.) This notion was introduced by Maass [256], and general technical methods for working with it were developed by Ambos-Spies, Jockusch, Shore, and Soare [7], as we have seen in, for example, Theorem 2.22.6. In this subsection, we prove the following result.

Theorem 5.3.16 (Downey and LaForte [122]). *If a left-c.e. real computes a promptly simple set then it has a noncomputable presentation.*

Proof. Let $D = \Gamma^\alpha$, where α is left-c.e. and D is promptly simple via the computable function p. By Theorem 5.1.7, there is a computable function $\alpha(i,s)$ such that $\alpha(i) = \lim_s \alpha(i,s)$ for all i, and for all i and s, if $\alpha(i,s) = 1$ and $\alpha(i,s+1) = 0$, then there is a $j < i$ such that $\alpha(j,s) = 0$ and $\alpha(j,s+1) = 1$.

We build a prefix-free set A such that $\mu([\![A]\!]) = \alpha$ to satisfy the following requirements, where $V_0, V_1, \ldots$ is an effective listing of all c.e. sets of strings.

$$R_e : |V_e| = \infty \Rightarrow \overline{A} \neq V_e,$$

where the V_e are thought of as sets of strings. We build A using the KC Theorem, by enumerating a KC set L and taking A to be the domain of the corresponding prefix-free machine. By the effectiveness of the KC Theorem, we may assume that at each stage s, the approximation A_s corresponds exactly to L_s.

To satisfy our requirements, we need to add strings of relatively short lengths to A at various stages. The strategy for satisfying R_e will involve a finite sequence of attempts to enumerate a short string from V_e into A, at least one of which will work if V_e is infinite. Because α computes the promptly simple set D, we can enumerate numbers into c.e. sets we build and use the function p witnessing the prompt simplicity of D to search for a stage at which α changes on some relatively small value (prompted by a change in D), enabling us to enumerate a string from V_e into A. The key fact is that each search can be computably bounded by p, and if V_e is infinite then there must be some search that succeeds, by the definition of prompt simplicity.

Each requirement R_e has associated with it a c.e. set U_e we build. Let g be as in the Slowdown Lemma 2.3.3 (so $W_{g(e)} = U_e$). Each R_e will also have followers that we can enumerate into U_e to attempt to provoke D-changes and consequent α-changes. At each stage s, for the least j such that R_j is unsatisfied and there is no current follower defined for R_j at s, choose a new follower for R_j.

At stage s, let $e < s$ be least such that R_e has a current follower x for which $D(x)[s] = \Gamma^{\alpha}(x)[s] = 0$ with use m_0, and $\overline{A}[s]$ and $V_e[s]$ are equal on all strings of length less than or equal to m_0. (If there is no such e, then simply add requests to L to ensure that the weight of L_s is equal to $\alpha[s]$ and proceed to the next stage.) If α changes below this use, we would like to enumerate a diagonalizing witness of length m_0 into A. However, a change in α below 2^{-m_0} may not allow the enumeration of a string of length m_0, because the m_0th position of α may be followed by a sequence of 1's. Therefore, wait for a stage $t_0 > s$ and an $m > m_0$ to appear such that $\overline{A}[t_0]$ and $V_e[t_0]$ are equal on all strings of length less than or equal to m, and there is some j with $m_0 < j < m$ and $\alpha(j)[t_0] = 0$. There must be such t_0 and m, since otherwise α would be rational, and hence computable. Then enumerate x into $U_e = W_{g(e)}$. Let $t > t_0$ be least such that $x \in W_{g(e)}[t]$. Now freeze all action in the construction until stage $p(t)$, and then check whether $x \in D[p(t)]$. If so, then $\alpha - \alpha[t] > 2^{-m}$, so wait until a stage $u \geqslant p(t)$ such that $\alpha[u] - \alpha[t] > 2^{-m}$ and add a string of length less than or equal to m to A (by enumerating an appropriate request into L), thus satisfying R_e permanently. Otherwise, let $u = p(t)$, release A from the current attack, and declare the current attempt on R_e to have failed. In either case, add requests to L to ensure that the weight of L_u is equal to $\alpha[u]$.

Since D is coinfinite, if V_e is infinite and all our attempts at satisfying R_e end in failure, then $U_e = W_{g(e)}$ is infinite. Since D is promptly simple, for some attack on R_e as described above, there is an $x \in (W_{g(e)}[t] \setminus W_{g(e)}[t-1]) \cap D[p(t)]$. By the definition of $W_{g(e)}$, the set D must change value on x between stages t_0 and $p(t)$. But then some element of $V_e[t_0]$ is enumerated into A at stage u by the construction, satisfying R_e. Since each R_e can be satisfied after a finite number of attempts, it is a straightforward induction to show that each associated strategy freezes A only finitely often. Thus all requirements are satisfied, and clearly $\mu([\![A]\!]) = \alpha$ as required. □

As we will see in Theorem 9.3.1, there are other conditions on left-c.e. reals, including ones related to Kolmogorov complexity, that ensure the existence of noncomputable presentations.

5.4 Left-d.c.e. reals

5.4.1 Basics

There are other natural classes of effective reals between the left-c.e. reals and the Δ_2^0 reals. Several researchers have investigated hierarchies in this region. See for example Zheng [418, 419], Rettinger, Zheng, Gengler, and von Braunmühl [331], or Rettinger and Zheng [420].

The following is a particularly interesting example of such a class of reals.

Definition 5.4.1. A real α is *left-d.c.e.* if there exist left-c.e. reals β and γ such that $\alpha = \beta - \gamma$.

This terminology is a bit misleading, since left-d.c.e. reals are the differences of left-c.e. reals, not the ones whose left cuts are d.c.e. sets. However, a term such as "d.l.c.e. real" seems a little too cumbersome. If A is a d.c.e. set, then $0.A$ is a left-d.c.e. real, so by Theorem 5.1.10, there are left-d.c.e. reals that are neither left-c.e. nor right-c.e. The following is an alternate characterization of the left-d.c.e. reals.

Theorem 5.4.2 (Ambos-Spies, Weihrauch, and Zheng [12]). *A real α is left-d.c.e. iff there is a computable sequence of rationals $q_0, q_1, \ldots \to \alpha$ such that $\sum_n |q_{n+1} - q_n| < \infty$.*

Proof. If such a sequence exists, then let

$$\beta = q_0 + \sum \{q_{n+1} - q_n : q_{n+1} - q_n \geqslant 0\}$$

and

$$\gamma = \sum \{q_n - q_{n+1} : q_{n+1} - q_n < 0\}.$$

Since $\sum_n |q_{n+1} - q_n| < \infty$, both β and γ are finite, and they are both left-c.e. Clearly, $\alpha = \beta - \gamma$.

For the converse, let β and γ be left-c.e. and let $\alpha = \beta - \gamma$. Let $r_0 < r_1 < \cdots \to \beta$ and $s_0 < s_1 < \cdots \to \gamma$ be computable sequences of rationals.

Let $q_n = r_n - s_n$. Then $q_0, q_1, \ldots \to \alpha$, and

$$\sum_n |q_{n+1} - q_n| = \sum_n |r_{n+1} - s_{n+1} - (r_n - s_n)|$$
$$\leqslant \sum_n (r_{n+1} - r_n) + \sum_n (s_{n+1} - s_n) = \beta - r_0 + \gamma - s_0 < \infty.$$

□

It is easy to see that if A is an n-c.e. set for some n, then $0.A$ is a left-d.c.e. real. We can push this fact one level further using Theorem 5.4.2. We begin with a lemma.

Lemma 5.4.3 (Downey, Wu, and Zheng [136]). *Let A be ω-c.e. Let f and g be computable functions such that $A(n) = \lim_s f(n, s)$ and $|\{s : f(n, s+1) \neq f(n, s)\}| < g(n)$ for all n. If $\sum_n g(n)2^{-n} < \infty$, then $0.A$ is left-d.c.e.*

Proof. We may assume that exactly one element n_s enters or leaves A at each stage s. Then $\{0.A_s\}_{s\in\omega}$ is a computable sequence of rationals converging to $0.A$, and

$$\sum_s |0.A_s - 0.A_{s+1}| = \sum_s 2^{-n_s} = \sum_n g(n)2^{-n} < \infty.$$

By Theorem 5.4.2, $0.A$ is left-d.c.e. □

Theorem 5.4.4 (Downey, Wu, and Zheng [136]). *Every ω-c.e. degree contains a left-d.c.e. real.*

Proof. Let A be ω-c.e. By Proposition 2.7.3, there are an ω-c.e. set $B \equiv_T A$ and a computable function f satisfying conditions (i)-(iii) in that proposition. Since $\sum_n n2^{-n} < \infty$, it follows from Lemma 5.4.3 that $0.B$ is a left-d.c.e. real. □

The converse to this result does not hold. Indeed, Zheng [417] showed that there is a left-d.c.e. real whose degree is not ω-c.e.[3]

We have seen in Theorem 5.1.3 that every Δ^0_2 real is the limit of a computable sequence of rationals. It might seem reasonable to conjecture that perhaps *every* Δ^0_2 degree contains a left-d.c.e. real. However, we have the following result, whose proof we omit due to space considerations.

Theorem 5.4.5 (Downey, Wu, and Zheng [136]). *There are Δ^0_2 degrees containing no left-d.c.e. reals.*

---

[3]Zheng's proof can easily be modified to show that if $\alpha < \omega^2$ then there is a left-d.c.e. real whose degree is not α-c.e.

5.4.2 The field of left-d.c.e. reals

One of the reasons to consider left-d.c.e. reals is that they form the smallest field containing the left-c.e. reals.

Theorem 5.4.6 (Ambos-Spies, Weihrauch, and Zheng [12]). *The left-d.c.e. reals form a field.*

Proof. Rearranging terms shows closure under addition, subtraction, and multiplication (e.g., $(\alpha - \beta)(\gamma - \delta) = (\alpha\gamma + \beta\delta) - (\beta\gamma + \alpha\delta)$, and we have already mentioned that the class of left-c.e. reals is closed under addition and multiplication). We show closure under division.

Let α and $\beta \neq 0$ be left-d.c.e. reals. Let $q_0, q_1, \ldots \to \alpha$ and $r_0, r_1, \ldots \to \beta$ be computable sequences of rationals such that $\sum_n |q_{n+1} - q_n| < \infty$ and $\sum_n |r_{n+1} - r_n| < \infty$. We may assume that the r_n are bounded away from 0. Let M be larger than both the above sums, and larger than $|q_n|$ and $\frac{1}{|r_n|}$ for all n. Let $s_n = \frac{q_n}{r_n}$. Then $s_0, s_1, \ldots \to \frac{\alpha}{\beta}$ is a computable sequence of rationals, so to show that $\frac{\alpha}{\beta}$ is left-d.c.e., it is enough to show that $\sum_n |s_{n+1} - s_n| < \infty$. But this sum is equal to

$$
\begin{aligned}
\sum_n \left| \frac{q_{n+1}}{r_{n+1}} - \frac{q_n}{r_n} \right| &= \sum_n \left| \frac{r_n q_{n+1} - r_{n+1} q_n}{r_n r_{n+1}} \right| \\
&= \sum_n \left| \frac{r_n q_{n+1} - r_n q_n + r_n q_n - r_{n+1} q_n}{r_n r_{n+1}} \right| \\
&\leqslant \sum_n \left| \frac{q_{n+1} - q_n}{r_{n+1}} \right| + \sum_n \left| \frac{q_n}{r_n r_{n+1}} (r_n - r_{n+1}) \right| \\
&< M \sum_n |q_{n+1} - q_n| + M^3 \sum_n |r_n - r_{n+1}| < M^2 + M^4.
\end{aligned}
$$

□

Ng [295] and Raichev [319, 320] have shown that this field behaves well analytically. Recall that a field F is *real closed* if every polynomial of odd degree with coefficients in F has a root in F, and for each $x \in F$, there is a $y \in F$ such that $x = y^2$ or $x = -y^2$.

Theorem 5.4.7 (Ng [295], Raichev [319, 320]). *The field of left-d.c.e. reals is real closed.*

Proof. We give the proof of this result from Ng [295]. Let $\mathbb{R}_2$ denote the left-d.c.e. reals. We actually show the following stronger result (see for instance [336] for more on basic concepts of real analysis).

Proposition 5.4.8. *Let f be a real function that is analytic at some $u_0 \in \mathbb{R}_2$. Suppose that its Taylor series converges in some open interval E centered at u_0, and that there are uniformly computable sequences of* *rationals* $a_{0,n}, a_{1,n} \dots \to f^{(n)}(u_0)$ *such that* $\sup_n \sum_k |a_{k+1,n} - a_{k,n}| < \infty$. *Then every root of* $f(x)$ *in* E *is also in* $\mathbb{R}_2$.

The theorem follows from this proposition: Any polynomial $f(x) \in \mathbb{R}_2[x]$ satisfies the hypotheses of the proposition, since $f^{(m)}(0) = 0$ for all sufficiently large m, so every such odd-degree polynomial has a root in $\mathbb{R}_2$, and $\sqrt{\gamma} \in \mathbb{R}_2$ for any nonnegative $\gamma \in \mathbb{R}_2$.

From now on, we work with an f satisfying the hypotheses of Proposition 5.4.8. We assume without loss of generality that $u_0 = 0$, since we can work with the function $f(x + u_0)$ instead of f. We also fix a root $r \in E$ of $f(x)$. Let k be the multiplicity of r; that is, $f(x) = (x-r)^k g(x)$ where $g(r) \neq 0$. If $k > 1$ then instead of working with $f(x)$, we can work with $f^{(k-1)}(x)$, since $f^{(k-1)}(r) = 0$ as well, and $f^{(k-1)}(x)$ satisfies the hypotheses of Proposition 5.4.8. So we assume that $k = 1$, or, in other words, that r is a simple root. Define $f_k \in \mathbb{Q}[x]$ by $f_k(x) = a_{k,0} + a_{k,1}(x - u_0) + \dots + a_{k,k}\frac{(x-u_0)^k}{k!}$.

Lemma 5.4.9. *There are rationals* α, β, M, m, m' *such that*

(i) $[\alpha, \beta]$ *is an interval in* E *containing* r *and*

(ii) *for all* $x \in [\alpha, \beta]$, *we have* $|f''(x)| < M$ *and* $0 < m < |f'(x)| < m'$.

Proof. By our assumption that r is a simple root of $f(x)$, we have $f'(r) \neq 0$, and hence there is some interval $[r-\delta, r+\delta]$ with $\delta \in \mathbb{Q}$ such that $f'(x) \neq 0$ for all $x \in [r - \delta, r + \delta]$. Let $\alpha = r - \delta$ and $\beta = r + \delta$. Then we can clearly choose m, m', and M to satisfy the conditions of the lemma. □

From now on, we fix α, β, M, m, m' as in the lemma, and we also fix δ such that $[r - \delta, r + \delta] \subseteq [\alpha, \beta]$.

Lemma 5.4.10. *Let* $x_0, x_1, \dots$ *be a sequence of points in a closed bounded interval* $I \subseteq E$. *Then* $\sum_k |f_{k+1}(x_k) - f_k(x_k)| < \infty$.

Proof. Let $T = \sup_n \sum_k |a_{k+1,n} - a_{k,n}|$ and $U = \sup_{x\in I} |x|$. Then

$$\sum_k |f_{k+1}(x_k) - f_k(x_k)|$$

$$\leqslant \sum_k |a_{k+1,0} - a_{k,0}| + \dots + |a_{k+1,k} - a_{k,k}|\frac{|x_k|^k}{k!} + |a_{k+1,k+1}|\frac{|x_k|^{k+1}}{(k+1)!}$$

$$\leqslant \sum_k \sum_n |a_{k+1,n} - a_{k,n}|\frac{U^n}{n!} + \sum_k |a_{k,k}|\frac{U^k}{k!}.$$

By Fubini's Theorem, the latter is less than or equal to

$$T\sum_n \frac{U^n}{n!} + \sum_k |a_{k,k}|\frac{U^k}{k!}.$$

Since $|a_{k,k} - f^{(k)}(0)| \leqslant \sum_{j \geqslant k} |a_{j+1,k} - a_{j,k}| \leqslant T$ for all k, the latter is less than or equal to

$$2Te^U + \sum_k |f^{(k)}(0)| \frac{U^k}{k!}.$$

Since I is closed, it must contain U, which establishes the lemma because the power series converges absolutely on I. □

It follows that $\sum_k |f^{(n)}_{k+1}(x_k) - f^{(n)}_k(x_k)| < \infty$ for all n.

Lemma 5.4.11. *$\lim_k f_k = f$ (and, similarly, $\lim_k f'_k = f'$ and $\lim_k f''_k = f''$) uniformly on $[\alpha, \beta]$.*

Proof. Let $I \subseteq E$ be a closed bounded interval containing $[\alpha, \beta]$ and 0. Since $\sup_{x \in I} |f_{k+1}(x) - f_k(x)|$ is attainable for each k, we can let $x_0, x_1, \ldots \in I$ be such that $|f_{k+1}(x_k) - f_k(x_k)| = \max_{x \in I} |f_{k+1}(x) - f_k(x)|$. Then it follows from Lemma 5.4.10 that given any $\varepsilon > 0$, there is an N_ε such that whenever $u > v \geqslant N_\varepsilon$, we have $|f_u(x) - f_v(x)| \leqslant \sum_{k \geqslant N_\varepsilon} |f_{k+1}(x_k) - f_k(x_k)| < \varepsilon$ for all $x \in I$.

It remains to show that $f_k(x) \to f(x)$ for every $x \in E$. Let $T_n = \sum_j |a_{j+1,n} - a_{j,n}|$. Then for all k,

$$\begin{aligned}\left|\sum_{n \leqslant k+1} f^{(n)}(0)\frac{x^n}{n!} - f_{k+1}(x)\right| &\leqslant \sum_{n \leqslant k+1} |f^{(n)}(0) - a_{k+1,n}| \frac{x^n}{n!} \\ &\leqslant \sum_{n \leqslant k+1} \left(T_n - \sum_{j \leqslant k} |a_{j+1,n} - a_{j,n}|\right) \frac{x^n}{n!} \\ &\leqslant \sum_{n \leqslant k+1} T_n \frac{x^n}{n!} - \sum_{n \leqslant k+1} \sum_{j \leqslant k} |a_{j+1,n} - a_{j,n}| \frac{x^n}{n!}.\end{aligned}$$

Now, since $\sum_n T_n \frac{x^n}{n!} \leqslant \sum_n \sup_m T_m \frac{x^n}{n!} < \infty$, it follows by Fubini's Theorem that $\lim_k \sum_{n \leqslant k+1} \sum_{j \leqslant k} |a_{j+1,n} - a_{j,n}| \frac{x^n}{n!} = \sum_n T_n \frac{x^n}{n!}$. Since f is represented by its Taylor series in E, we have $\lim_k f_k(x) = f(x)$. □

Lemma 5.4.12. *There is an s_0 such that for all $s \geqslant s_0$,*

1. *$[\alpha, \beta]$ contains a simple root r_s of f_s,*
2. *$|f''_s(x)| < M$, and $0 < m < |f'_s(x)| < m'$ for all $x \in [\alpha, \beta]$.*

Proof. We may assume that $f(\alpha) < 0 < f(\beta)$. Since $\lim_s f_s(\alpha) = f(\alpha)$ and $\lim_s f_s(\beta) = f(\beta)$, there is an s_0 such that for all $s \geqslant s_0$, we have $f_s(\alpha) < 0 < f_s(\beta)$, and hence there is a (simple) root r_s of f_s in $[\alpha, \beta]$. Let $\varepsilon > 0$ be such that $\min_{x \in [\alpha,\beta]} |f'(x)| - \varepsilon > m$. Since $\lim_s f'_s = f'$ uniformly on $[\alpha, \beta]$, we may assume that s_0 is large enough so that $|f'_s(x) - f'(x)| < \varepsilon$ for all $s \geqslant s_0$ and $x \in [\alpha, \beta]$. Then $|f'(x)| - |f'_s(x)| < \varepsilon$. The cases for m' and M are similar. □

Fix such an s_0 and r_s for $s \geqslant s_0$. Note that for each $s \geqslant s_0$, we have $f_s'(x) > 0$ inside $[\alpha, \beta]$, and hence r_s is the only root of f_s' in that interval.

Lemma 5.4.13. $\lim_s r_s = r$.

Proof. Let ε be such that $0 < \varepsilon < \delta$. By pointwise convergence, we can choose N_ε such that for all $s \geqslant N_\varepsilon$, we have $f_s(r-\varepsilon)f_s(r+\varepsilon) < 0$, and hence there is a root of f_s in $[r-\varepsilon, r+\varepsilon] \subseteq [\alpha, \beta]$. Since r_s is the only root of f_s in $[\alpha, \beta]$, we have $|r_s - r| < \varepsilon$. □

Let $K = \frac{M}{2m}$ and $\eta < \min\{\frac{1}{2K}, \frac{\delta}{2}\}$. For all $s \geqslant s_0$, we also want $|r_s - r| < \frac{\eta}{2}$, so adjust s_0 to be large enough to satisfy this requirement. For simplicity, we will assume from now on that the sequence $\{f_s\}_{s\leqslant\omega}$ starts with the index s_0. Let $y_0 \in \mathbb{Q}$ be such that $|y_0 - r| < \frac{\eta}{2}$. For each s, define a computable sequence of rationals by $x_{s,0} = y_0$ and $x_{s,n+1} = x_{s,n} - \frac{f_s(x_{s,n})}{f_s'(x_{s,n})}$.

Lemma 5.4.14 (Newton's Method of Locating Roots). *For each s, if $x' \in [\alpha, \beta]$ and $x'' = x' - \frac{f_s(x')}{f_s'(x')}$, then $|x'' - r_s| \leqslant K|x' - r_s|^2$.*

Proof. By Taylor expansion of $f_s(x)$ about the point x', we have

$$-f_s(x') = f_s'(x')(r_s - x') + \frac{f_s''(c)(r_s - x')^2}{2}$$

for some c between r_s and x'. Hence,

$$x'' = x' - \frac{f_s(x')}{f_s'(x')} = r_s + \frac{f_s''(c)(r_s - x')^2}{2f_s'(x')}.$$

Since $c \in [\alpha, \beta]$,

$$|x'' - r_s| = \left| \frac{f_s''(c)(r_s - x')^2}{2f_s'(x')} \right| \leqslant K|x' - r_s|^2.$$

□

Lemma 5.4.15. *For all s and n, we have $|x_{s,n+1} - x_{s,n}| \leqslant ((K\eta)^{n+1} + (K\eta)^n)|y_0 - r_s|$.*

Proof. Fix an s. We first prove by induction that $|x_{s,n} - r_s| < \eta$ for all n. First note that $|x_{s,0} - r_s| \leqslant |x_{s,0} - r| + |r_s - r| < \eta$. Suppose that $|x_{s,n} - r_s| < \eta$. Then $|x_{s,n} - r| \leqslant |x_{s,n} - r_s| + |r_s - r| < 2\eta < \delta$, so $x_{s,n} \in [\alpha, \beta]$. Thus, by Lemma 5.4.14, $|x_{s,n+1} - r_s| \leqslant K\eta^2 < \eta$.

Next, we prove that $|x_{s,n} - r_s| \leqslant (K\eta)^n|y_0 - r_s|$, again by induction. We have $|x_{s,0} - r_s| = |y_0 - r_s|$. Now assume that the case for n holds. By Lemma 5.4.14, $|x_{s,n+1} - r_s| \leqslant K|x_{s,n} - r_s|^2 < (K\eta)|x_{s,n} - r_s| \leqslant (K\eta)^{n+1}|y_0 - r_s|$.

Now the lemma follows by the triangle inequality. □

From now on we will assume that f and f_s are all increasing on $[\alpha, \beta]$. For each s, we can construct a partition $I_0, I_1, \ldots$ of $[\alpha, \beta]$ each element of which has width $\frac{1}{2^{s+1}m'}$. Then apply the sign test to f_s using $I_0, I_1, \ldots$ and let r'_s be the right endpoint of the partition element that contains the root r_s.

Lemma 5.4.16. *For each s, we can find an N_s such that $|x_{s+1,N_s} - x_{s,N_s}| < \frac{1}{m}|f_s(r'_{s+1})|$.*

Proof. From the proof of Lemma 5.4.15, it is clear that $\lim_n x_{s,n} = r_s$. Thus, for each s, we have $\lim_n |x_{s+1,n} - x_{s,n}| = |r_{s+1} - r_s|$. However, $|r_{s+1} - r_s| = \frac{|f_s(r_{s+1})|}{f'_s(c)}$ for some $r_s \leqslant c \leqslant r_{s+1}$, so $|r_{s+1} - r_s| \leqslant \frac{|f_s(r_{s+1})|}{m} < \frac{|f_s(r'_{s+1})|}{m}$. □

Define a computable sequence $y_0, y_1, \dots$ as follows.

1. Let y_0 be as above, and set $s = 0$ and $n = 1$.
2. If $|x_{s+1,n-s} - x_{s,n-s}| \geqslant \frac{1}{m}|f_s(r'_{s+1})|$ then let $y_n = x_{s,n-s}$. In this case, increment n by 1 and repeat this step.
3. If $|x_{s+1,n-s} - x_{s,n-s}| < \frac{1}{m}|f_s(r'_{s+1})|$ (which must eventually happen, by Lemma 5.4.16), then let $y_n = x_{s,n-s}$, let $y_{n+1} = x_{s+1,n-s}$, and let $y_{n+2} = x_{s+1,n-s+1}$. Increment n by 3, increment s by 1, and return to step 2.

The idea of this definition is that we wait until $|x_{s+1,n-s} - x_{s,n-s}|$ is small enough before we jump to the next level.

Lemma 5.4.17. $\lim_n y_n = r$.

Proof. For any s and n, there is a c such that $y_c = x_{s',n'}$ with $s' > s$ and $n' > n$. Let $\varepsilon > 0$. Then there is a t_0 such that $|r_a - r| < \frac{\varepsilon}{4}$ for all $a \geqslant t_0$. Let $u_0 = \frac{\log(\frac{\varepsilon}{\eta})}{\log(k\eta)}$. Let c be obtained from t_0 and u_0 as described above. Then, for all $n \geqslant c$, we have $y_n = x_{a,b}$ for some $a > t_0$ and $b > u_0$. So

$$\begin{aligned}|y_n - r| &\leqslant |x_{a,b} - r_a| + |r_a - r| < (K\eta)^b|y_0 - r_a| + \frac{\varepsilon}{4} \\ &\leqslant (K\eta)^b|y_0 - r| + \frac{\varepsilon}{4}(K\eta)^b + \frac{\varepsilon}{4} < \frac{\eta}{2}(K\eta)^b + \frac{\varepsilon}{2} < \varepsilon.\end{aligned}$$

□

Lemma 5.4.18. $r \in \mathbb{R}_2$.

Proof. It remains to show that $\sum_i |y_{i+1} - y_i| < \infty$. By Lemma 5.4.15 and the construction of the y_i, we have

$$\sum_i |y_{i+1} - y_i| \leqslant \sum_i ((K\eta)^{i+1} + (K\eta)^i)|y_0 - r_{d(i)}| + \sum_s \frac{1}{m}|f_s(r'_{s+1})|$$

for a nondecreasing sequence $d_0, d_1, \dots$. Since $|r_{s+1} - r'_{s+1}| < \frac{1}{2^{s+1}m'}$, by the Mean Value Theorem, $\frac{1}{m}|f_{s+1}(r'_{s+1})| \leqslant m'\frac{1}{2^{s+1}m'} < \frac{1}{2^s}$. By Lemma

5.4.10,

$$\sum_i |y_{i+1} - y_i|$$
$$\leqslant \sum_i ((K\eta)^{i+1} + (K\eta)^i)2\delta + \sum_s \frac{1}{m}|f_{s+1}(r'_{s+1}) - f_s(r'_{s+1})| + \sum_s \frac{1}{2^s} < \infty.$$

□

This lemma establishes Proposition 5.4.8, and hence proves the theorem. □

Similar methods can also be used to show that the computable reals form a real closed field (see for instance [318]), and hence, by relativization, that so do the Δ^0_2 reals, a fact first explictly noted and proved directly by Raichev [319, 320].

Part II

Notions of Randomness

6

Martin-Löf Randomness

In this chapter, we will introduce three cornerstone approaches to the definition of algorithmic randomness for infinite sequences.

(i) The *computational paradigm*: Random sequences are those whose initial segments are all hard to describe, or, equivalently, hard to compress. This approach is probably the easiest one to understand in terms of the previous sections.

(ii) The *measure-theoretic paradigm*: Random sequences are those with no "effectively rare" properties. If the class of sequences satisfying a given property is an effectively null set, then a random sequence should not have this property. This approach is the same as the *stochastic paradigm*: a random sequence should pass all effective statistical tests.

(iii) The *unpredictability paradigm*: This approach stems from what is probably the most intuitive conception of randomness, namely that one should not be able to predict the next bit of a random sequence, even if one knows all preceding bits, in the same way that a coin toss is unpredictable even given the results of previous coin tosses.

We will see that all three approaches can be used to define the same notion of randomness, which is called Martin-Löf randomness or 1-randomness. This notion was the first successful attempt to capture the idea of a random infinite sequence, and is still the best known and most studied of the various definitions proposed to date, in great part because it enables us to develop a rich and appealing mathematical theory. For

R.G. Downey and D. Hirschfeldt, *Algorithmic Randomness and Complexity*, Theory and Applications of Computability, DOI 10.1007/978-0-387-68441-3_6,

the development of these approaches to randomness, and the philosophical insights behind them, see van Lambalgen [397].

6.1 The computational paradigm

In a way, the definition of algorithmic randomness is more satisfying for infinite sequences than it is for strings. One of the main reasons for this phenomenon, as we will see, is that algorithmic randomness of sequences is absolute, in that no matter which universal machine one chooses, the class of random sequences remains the same.

A natural first attempt at defining a notion of randomness for a set A would be to say that A is random if $C(A \upharpoonright n) \geqslant n - O(1)$. Unfortunately, *no* set satisfies this condition. This is a fundamental observation of Martin-Löf that we have already seen in Theorem 3.1.4. As we will see in Section 6.7, it *is* possible to give a satisfactory definition of randomness for infinite sequences using plain complexity, but this is a recent development. We can vindicate the intuition leading to the incorrect attempt at a definition of randomness for infinite sequences via plain complexity by using prefix-free complexity instead.

Definition 6.1.1 (Levin [243], Chaitin [58]). A set A is 1-*random* if $K(A \upharpoonright n) \geqslant n - O(1)$.[1] We will call a degree (Turing or otherwise) 1-random if it contains a 1-random set.[2]

The reason for the term "1-random" will become clear once we introduce the notion of n-randomness for arbitrary n in Section 6.8. Notice that, in the nomenclature of Chapter 3, a sequence is 1-random iff all its initial segments are weakly K-random. One cannot replace weak K-randomness by strong K-randomness, as we saw in Theorem 3.11.1.

Recall Chaitin's halting probability Ω, which we introduced in Definition 3.13.6:

$$\Omega = \mu([\![\mathrm{dom}\,\mathcal{U}]\!]) = \sum_{\sigma \in \mathrm{dom}\,\mathcal{U}} 2^{-|\sigma|}.$$

As we will see, Ω is 1-random. It is in fact the best known example of a 1-random real. As we discussed following Definition 3.13.6, while the

[1]As we will see in Section 6.3.2, Levin [242] and Schnorr [350] used monotone complexity and process complexity, respectively, to characterize the class of 1-random sets in much the same way, and the essential idea of prefix-free complexity is implicit in that work. The history of this subject is quite involved; see Li and Vitányi [248] and van Lambalgen [397] for detailed historical remarks.

[2]We will adopt this terminology for other notions of randomness without further comment. That is, when we define a notion of randomness R for sets, we will say that a degree is R-random if it contains an R-random set.

value of Ω depends on the choice of $\mathcal{U}$, we will see in Section 9.2 that all versions of Ω are quite closely related, and it makes sense to ignore the machine-dependence of Ω in most circumstances.

Recall also that $\Omega_s = \sum_{\mathcal{U}(\sigma)[s]\downarrow} 2^{-|\sigma|}$. The rationals Ω_s approximate Ω from below, so Ω is a left-c.e. real. One way to look at Ω is as a highly compressed version of $\emptyset'$, as the following results show.

Proposition 6.1.2 (Calude and Nies [51]). $\Omega \equiv_{\text{wtt}} \emptyset'$.

Proof. Since Ω is a left-c.e. real, it is computable in $\emptyset'$. For the other direction, let M be the prefix-free machine defined by letting $M(0^e1)\downarrow = \lambda$ whenever $\Phi_e(e)\downarrow$. Since $\mathcal{U}$ is universal, there is a ρ such that $\mathcal{U}(\rho 0^e 1)\downarrow$ iff $e \in \emptyset'$. To determine whether $e \in \emptyset'$ given Ω, wait for a stage s such that $\Omega - \Omega_s < 2^{-(|\rho|+e+1)}$. If $\mathcal{U}(\rho 0^e 1)[s]\downarrow$ then $e \in \emptyset'$. Otherwise, $\mathcal{U}(\rho 0^e 1)\uparrow$, so $e \notin \emptyset'$. □

Theorem 6.1.3 (Chaitin [58]). *Ω is 1-random.*

Proof. By Proposition 6.1.2, Ω is not rational, so for each n there is an s with $\Omega_s \upharpoonright n = \Omega \upharpoonright n$. We build a prefix-free machine M. By the recursion theorem, we may assume we know its coding constant c in $\mathcal{U}$. Whenever at a stage s we have $\mathcal{U}(\tau)[s] = \Omega_s \upharpoonright n$ for some τ such that $|\tau| < n - c$ (which means that $K(\Omega_s \upharpoonright n) < n - c$), we choose a string $\mu \notin \operatorname{rng}\mathcal{U}[s]$ and declare $M(\tau) = \mu$. Since M is coded in $\mathcal{U}$ with coding constant c, there must be a ν such that $|\nu| \leqslant |\tau| + c < n$ and $\mathcal{U}(\nu) = M(\tau) = \mu$. Since $\mu \notin \operatorname{rng}\mathcal{U}[s]$, it follows that $\nu \notin \operatorname{dom}\mathcal{U}[s]$, so $\Omega - \Omega_s \geqslant 2^{-|\nu|} > 2^{-n}$, and hence $\Omega \upharpoonright n \neq \Omega_s \upharpoonright n$. This procedure ensures that if $|\tau| < n - c$ then $\mathcal{U}(\tau) \neq \Omega \upharpoonright n$, whence $K(\Omega \upharpoonright n) \geqslant n - c$ for all n. □

It is important to note that Ω is a somewhat misleading example of 1-randomness, as it is rather computationally powerful. We will see in Section 9.2 that all 1-random left-c.e. reals behave like Ω (indeed they are all versions of Ω); in particular, they are all Turing (and even weak truth table) complete. We will also see, in Section 8.3, that 1-random sets can be arbitrarily powerful, in the sense that for every set A there is a 1-random set $R \geqslant_{\text{T}} A$. However, heuristically speaking, randomness should be antithetical to computational power, inasmuch as classes of sets with a certain given amount of computational power (such as computing $\emptyset'$, or being a PA degree) tend to have measure 0. We will see below that as we move from 1-randomness to more powerful notions of algorithmic randomness, we do indeed tend to lose computational power. But even within the class of 1-random sets, there is a qualitative distinction between those 1-random sets that compute $\emptyset'$ and those that do not.[3] As we will see below, the latter exhibit behavior much closer to what we should expect of random sets

[3]We will see in Section 7.7 that there is a test set characterization of the 1-random sets that do not compute $\emptyset'$, in the spirit of the notion of Martin-Löf test discussed in

(for instance, they cannot have PA degree; see Theorem 8.8.4).[4] Thus one should keep in mind that, while Ω is certainly the most celebrated example of 1-randomness, it is not "typically 1-random".

Chaitin [63] also defined another left-c.e. real, $\widehat{\Omega} = \sum_{\sigma \in 2^{<\omega}} 2^{-K(\sigma)}$. It is not hard to modify the above proof to show that $\widehat{\Omega}$ is 1-random.

Another example of a 1-random left-c.e. real is the output probability $Q(\sigma)$ from Definition 3.9.3. The easiest way to see that $Q(\sigma)$ is 1-random for any σ is using the methods of Chapter 9.[5]

Thus we have concrete examples of 1-random sets. As we will see in the following section, almost every set is 1-random (as we would expect). It was an interesting question of Solovay whether $\liminf_s K(\Omega \upharpoonright n) - n = \infty$. This question was eventually solved in the affirmative by Chaitin [63]. More recently, Miller and Yu [280] gave a powerful characterization of randomness that has this result as a corollary. Namely, they proved that A is 1-random iff $\sum_{n \in \mathbb{N}} 2^{n-K(A \upharpoonright n)} < \infty$. We will prove this result in Theorem 6.6.1 below.

The following result is also worth noting.

Proposition 6.1.4 (Fortnow [unpublished], Nies, Stephan, and Terwijn [308]). *If there is an infinite computable set S such that $K(A \upharpoonright n) \geqslant n + O(1)$ for all $n \in S$, then A is 1-random.*

Proof. Suppose that A is not 1-random and let $S = \{s_0 < s_1 < \cdots\}$ be computable. If $\sigma = \tau\rho$ and $|\sigma| = s_{|\tau|}$, then we can give a prefix-free description of σ by giving a prefix-free description of τ and then giving ρ itself, so $K(\sigma) \leqslant K(\tau) + |\rho| + O(1)$. So if $K(A \upharpoonright n) \leqslant n - d$, then $K(A \upharpoonright s_n) \leqslant n - d + (s_n - n) + O(1) = s_n - d + O(1)$. Since for each d there is an n with $K(A \upharpoonright n) \leqslant n - d$, the same is true if we restrict ourselves to $n \in S$. □

6.2 The measure-theoretic paradigm

The main idea behind the measure-theoretic, or stochastic, paradigm is that a random sequence should have no rare properties. In a remarkable early paper, von Mises [402] attempted to formalize this notion. He pointed

the next section, and hence we can think of this condition as a notion of randomness in its own right, rather than just a mix of randomness and computability conditions.

[4] A heuristic explanation for this phenomenon is that there are two ways to pass an ignorance test. One is to be genuinely ignorant, and the other is to be knowledgeable enough to know what answers an ignorant person would give. 1-random sets above $\emptyset'$ have this kind of knowledge, in that they can compute K, but other 1-random sets do not, and thus must rely on their own lack of wits.

[5] It is also interesting to consider output probabilities for sets of strings, where the output probability of $A \subseteq 2^{<\omega}$ is the probability that $\mathcal{U}$ outputs an element of A, which is equal to $\sum_{\sigma \in A} Q(\sigma)$. This notion has been investigated by Becher and Grigorieff [32] and Becher, Figueira, Grigorieff, and Miller [31].

out that if we flip a fair coin, then we should surely expect to see as many heads as tails in the limit. Thus a random binary sequence $a_0 a_1 \ldots$ should obey the *law of large numbers* by having the property that $\lim_n \frac{\sum_{i<n} a_i}{n} = \frac{1}{2}$. But of course this condition is not enough, because highly nonrandom sequences such as $010101\ldots$ satisfy it. We clearly need the law of large numbers to hold for *subsequences* as well. Thus von Mises proposed calling a binary sequence $a_0 a_1 \ldots$ random if for every *selection function* f with $f(0) < f(1) < \cdots$, we have $\lim_n \frac{\sum_{i<n} a_{f(i)}}{n} = \frac{1}{2}$.

This definition is not quite precise, though, because of the undefined concept of a selection function. Clearly we cannot allow f to be just any increasing function, in the modern set-theoretic sense, since if a sequence $a_0 a_1 \ldots$ contains infinitely many 0's, then there is an increasing function f such that $a_{f(i)} = 0$ for all i. On the other hand, Wald [403, 404] showed that for any *countable* collection of selection functions, there is a sequence that is random in the sense of von Mises. Church [71] proposed restricting f to computable increasing functions; we now call sequences that satisfy the law of large numbers for all computable selection functions *computably stochastic*, or *Church stochastic*. We will study this notion, as well as the related one of *von Mises-Wald-Church stochasticity*, where partial computable selection functions are allowed, in Section 7.4.1.[6]

The problem with this promising notion was pointed out by Ville [401], who showed that for any countable collection of selection functions (thus in particular Church's), there is a sequence $a_0 a_1 \ldots$ that is random in the sense of von Mises but has $\sum_{i<n} a(i) \leqslant \frac{1}{2}$ for all n. Such a sequence is clearly not random. After all, if we were to flip a supposedly fair coin many times and never at any point observed an excess of tails over heads, we would surely begin to suspect that something was amiss. We will prove Ville's Theorem in Section 6.5.

Ville suggested adding a further statistical law, the law of iterated logarithms, to von Mises' definition. However, one might well ask how we can be sure that adding this law would be enough. Why should we expect there not to be a further result like Ville's exhibiting a sequence that satisfies both the law of large numbers and the law of iterated logarithms, yet clearly fails to have some other basic property that we would naturally associate with randomness?

We could add more and more statistical laws to our collection of desiderata for random sequences, but there is no reason to believe we would ever be done, and we certainly do not want a definition of randomness that

---

[6]The selection functions considered in these notions are adaptive, in the sense that, before deciding whether to bet on the nth bit of a sequence A, they are allowed to know $A \upharpoonright n$, which is of course reasonable for a notion that attempts to model gambling on a sequence of observable events. Thus these functions are best thought of as functions from strings to {yes, no}. See Sections 6.5 and 7.4.1 for more details.

changes with time, if we can avoid it. Martin-Löf's fundamental idea in [259] was to define an abstract notion of a performable statistical test for randomness, and require that a random sequence pass *all* such tests. He did so by effectivizing the notion of a set of measure 0.

To motivate Martin-Löf's definition via a simple example, consider the class C of sequences A such that $A(2^k) = 0$ for all k. Clearly, such sequences are not random. If we are presented with a sequence A that might be in C, we can perform a test for membership of A in C to within a confidence level of 2^{-n} by considering all $k < n$. If for all such k we have $A(2^k) = 0$, then we have some reason to believe that $A \in C$. (Of course, if not, then we can be certain that $A \notin C$.) We might be wrong about our belief that $A \in C$, but the set of all A that our test indicates are in C has measure 2^{-n}, so we can have greater and greater confidence that $A \in C$ as we perform finer and finer levels of this test. Martin-Löf's idea was to abstract away from the particulars of such a test, or more interesting ones such as tests for the law of large numbers, and think of a test as a collection of reasonably simple subsets of Cantor space of smaller and smaller measure, zeroing in on a null class of sequences that have some rare property, and hence should not be considered random.

Definition 6.2.1 (Martin-Löf [259]). (i) A *Martin-Löf test* is a sequence $\{U_n\}_{n\in\omega}$ of uniformly Σ^0_1 classes such that $\mu(U_n) \leqslant 2^{-n}$ for all n.

(ii) A class $C \subset 2^\omega$ is *Martin-Löf null* if there is a Martin-Löf test $\{U_n\}_{n\in\omega}$ such that $C \subseteq \bigcap_n U_n$.

(iii) A set $A \in 2^\omega$ is *Martin-Löf random* if $\{A\}$ is not Martin-Löf null.[7]

In the above definition, we did not require that $U_0 \supseteq U_1 \supseteq \cdots$, but we could have: Given a Martin-Löf test $\{U_n\}_{n\in\omega}$, let $V_n = \bigcup_{m>n} U_m$. Then $\{V_n\}_{n\in\omega}$ is a Martin-Löf test, $V_0 \supseteq V_1 \supseteq \cdots$, and $\bigcap_n U_n = \bigcap_n V_n$.

We could also have defined a Martin-Löf test to be a sequence $\{U_n\}_{n\in\omega}$ of uniformly Σ^0_1 classes for which there is a computable function $f : \mathbb{N} \to \mathbb{Q}$ such that $\lim_n f(n) = 0$ and $\mu(U_n) \leqslant f(n)$ for all n: Given such a test, let $V_n = U_m$ for the least m such that $f(m) \leqslant 2^{-n}$. Then $\{V_n\}_{n\in\omega}$ is a Martin-Löf test and $\bigcap_n U_n = \bigcap_n V_n$.[8]

[7]Demuth [93] independently developed a test-based definition of randomness equivalent to Martin-Löf's. He was working in the style of the Russian school of constructive mathematics, and saw the potential importance of random reals in computable analysis. A brief but highly informative discussion of this work may be found in Kučera and Slaman [221, Remark 3.5].

[8]A natural variation on this definition is to require only that $\lim_n \mu(U_n) = 0$, without requiring a computable rate of convergence. Such *generalized Martin-Löf tests* are perhaps too weak to correspond to a reasonable notion of performable statistical test. That is, with a Martin-Löf test, we can compute what level of the test we need to look at to approximate the corresponding null set to within a given ε, while with a general-

We can now restate the above example: The class C of all A such that $A(2^k) = 0$ for all k is Martin-Löf null, and hence no such set is Martin-Löf random. Much more interestingly, the class of sets that do not satisfy the law of large numbers is Martin-Löf null, and similarly, for any computable selection function f, the class of sets that do not satisfy the law of large numbers for the subsequence of bits picked out by f is also Martin-Löf null. Thus, if A is Martin-Löf random then it is Church stochastic. The converse is not true, however, because we can build a Martin-Löf test containing Ville's sequence mentioned above. Further discussion and proofs (such as the proof that Martin-Löf random sets obey the law of large numbers) can be found in Section 7.4, where we examine effective notions of stochasticity in detail.

Martin-Löf randomness is equivalent to 1-randomness, which helps justify the notion of 1-randomness as a reasonable notion of algorithmic randomness. To show this fact, we begin with a lemma. We will use only its first part here, but the second part will be useful below.

Lemma 6.2.2. *Let M be a prefix-free machine, let $k \in \mathbb{N}$, and let $S = \{\sigma : K_M(\sigma) \leqslant |\sigma| - k\}$. Then $\mu([\![S]\!]) \leqslant 2^{-k}\mu([\![\operatorname{dom} M]\!])$. Furthermore, $\mu([\![S]\!])$ is computable in $\mu([\![\operatorname{dom} M]\!])$ via a procedure that is uniform in k.*

Proof. For each $\sigma \in S$ there is a string τ_σ such that $|\tau_\sigma| \leqslant |\sigma| - k$ and $M(\tau_\sigma)\downarrow = \sigma$. Thus

$$\mu([\![S]\!]) \leqslant \sum_{\sigma \in S} 2^{-|\sigma|} \leqslant \sum_{\sigma \in S} 2^{-(|\tau_\sigma|+k)} = 2^{-k} \sum_{\sigma \in S} 2^{-|\tau_\sigma|}$$
$$\leqslant 2^{-k} \sum_{\tau \in \operatorname{dom} M} 2^{-|\tau|} = 2^{-k}\mu([\![\operatorname{dom} M]\!]).$$

To compute $\mu([\![S]\!])$ to within 2^{-c} given $\mu([\![\operatorname{dom} M]\!])$, find a finite set $F \subseteq \operatorname{dom} M$ such that $\mu([\![\operatorname{dom} M]\!]) - \mu([\![F]\!]) < 2^{-c+k}$. Let N_0 be the restriction of M to F and N_1 be the restriction of M to $\operatorname{dom} M \setminus F$. Let $T_i = \{\sigma : K_{N_i}(\sigma) \leqslant |\sigma| - k\}$. Note that T_0 is finite, so we can compute its measure. Now $\mu([\![\operatorname{dom} N_1]\!]) < 2^{-c+k}$, so $\mu([\![T_1]\!]) < 2^{-c}$. Since $S = T_0 \cup T_1$, we have $\mu([\![S]\!]) - \mu([\![T_0]\!]) \leqslant \mu([\![T_1]\!]) < 2^{-c}$. □

Theorem 6.2.3 (Schnorr, see [58][9]). *A set is Martin-Löf random iff it is 1-random.*

Proof. (⇒) Let $U_k = \{X : \exists n\, K(X \upharpoonright n) \leqslant n - k\}$. The U_k are uniformly Σ^0_1, and by Lemma 6.2.2, $\mu(U_k) \leqslant 2^{-k}$, so $\{U_k\}_{k\in\omega}$ is a Martin-Löf test.

ized Martin-Löf we might have no idea. However, generalized Martin-Löf tests are quite interesting from the mathematical viewpoint, as they correspond to a fruitful notion of randomness strictly stronger than Martin-Löf randomness known as *weak 2-randomness*, as we will discuss in Section 7.2.

[9]As we will see in Theorem 6.3.10, Levin [242] and Schnorr [350] proved essentially equivalent results for monotone complexity and process complexity, respectively.

If A is Martin-Löf random then $A \notin \bigcap_k U_k$, so there is a k such that $K(A \upharpoonright n) > n - k$ for all n, and thus A is 1-random.

($\Leftarrow$) Let A be a set that is not Martin-Löf random. Let $\{U_n\}_{n\in\omega}$ be a Martin-Löf test such that $A \in \bigcap_n U_n$. Let $R_0, R_1, \ldots$ be a uniformly c.e. sequence of prefix-free sets such that $U_n = [\![R_n]\!]$ for all n. We have

$$\sum_{n\geqslant 2}\sum_{\sigma\in R_{n^2}} 2^{-(|\sigma|-n)} = \sum_{n\geqslant 2} 2^n \mu(U_{n^2}) \leqslant \sum_{n\geqslant 2} 2^{-n^2+n} < \sum_{m\geqslant 2} 2^{-m} < 1.$$

So by the minimality of K among information content measures (Theorem 3.7.8), there is a constant c such that if $\sigma \in R_{n^2}$ for some $n \geqslant 2$ then $K(\sigma) \leqslant |\sigma| - n + c$. Since $A \in U_{n^2}$ for all n, for each n there is a k such that $K(A \upharpoonright k) \leqslant k - n + c$, and hence A is not 1-random. □

The $\Leftarrow$ direction of the above proof is taken from Chaitin [63]. It is also possible to prove this direction of the theorem using the KC Theorem; see for instance [118].

One quite important property of Martin-Löf's definition is the existence of a *universal* Martin-Löf test, in the following sense.

Definition 6.2.4 (Martin-Löf [259]). A Martin-Löf test $\{U_n\}_{n\in\omega}$ is *universal* if $\bigcup_n U_n$ contains every Martin-Löf null set, in other words, for any Martin-Löf test $\{V_n\}_{n\in\omega}$, we have $\bigcap_n V_n \subseteq \bigcap_n U_n$.

In other words, there *is* a single statistical test leading to a good definition of randomness for individual sequences. (However, it is certainly not a natural one in the sense that the law of large numbers and the law of the iterated logarithms are natural.)

The Martin-Löf test built in the first part of the proof of Theorem 6.2.3 is universal. We give another construction of such a test in the following proof.

Theorem 6.2.5 (Martin-Löf [259]). *There exists a universal Martin-Löf test.*

Proof. Let $\{R_n^0\}_{n\in\omega}, \{R_n^1\}_{n\in\omega}, \ldots$ be an effective listing of all uniformly c.e. subsets of $2^{<\omega}$. Let S_n^i be the result of enumerating R_n^i and stopping the enumeration if the measure of $[\![R_n^i]\!]$ ever threatens to exceed 2^{-n}. Then $\{[\![S_n^0]\!]\}_{n\in\omega}, \{[\![S_n^1]\!]\}_{n\in\omega}, \ldots$ is an effective listing of all Martin-Löf tests. Let $U_n = \bigcup_i [\![S_{n+i+1}^i]\!]$.

The U_n are uniformly Σ_1^0 and

$$\mu(U_n) = \sum_i \mu([\![S_{n+i+1}^i]\!]) \leqslant \sum_i 2^{-(n+i+1)} = 2^{-n},$$

so $\{U_n\}_{n\in\omega}$ is a Martin-Löf test. For any Martin-Löf test $\{V_n\}_{n\in\omega}$, there is an i such that $V_n = [\![S_n^i]\!]$ for all n. Then $V_{n+i+1} \in U_n$ for all n, so $\bigcap_n V_n \in \bigcap_n U_n$. □

We will see another construction of a universal Martin-Löf test due to Kučera in Section 8.5. Note that if $\{U_n\}_{n\in\omega}$ is a universal Martin-Löf test then a set A is 1-random iff $A \notin \bigcap_n U_n$. In particular, each complement $\overline{U_n}$ is a Π^0_1 class consisting entirely of 1-random sets, a fact that will often be quite useful. (For instance, it implies that there are low 1-random sets, by the low basis theorem.) That there is no Π^0_1 class consisting exactly of the 1-random sets follows from the following result, since the only Π^0_1 class of measure 1 is 2^ω. (However, we will see in Lemma 6.10.1 that there are Π^0_1 classes consisting only of 1-random sets that contain all 1-random sets up to finite shifts.)

Corollary 6.2.6 (Martin-Löf [259]). *The class of* 1*-random sets has measure* 1.

Proof. Let $\{U_n\}_{n\in\omega}$ be a universal Martin-Löf test. The class of 1-random sets is the complement of $\bigcap_n U_n$, and $\mu(\bigcap_n U_n) = 0$. □

Solovay gave the following alternate definition of 1-randomness.

Definition 6.2.7 (Solovay [371]). A *Solovay test* is a sequence $\{S_n\}_{n\in\omega}$ of uniformly Σ^0_1 classes such that $\sum_n \mu(S_n) < \infty$. A set A is *Solovay random* if for every such test, A is in only finitely many S_n.

Equivalently, A is Solovay random if for all computable sequences $\{I_n\}_{n\in\omega}$ of intervals with rational endpoints such that $\sum_n |I_n| < \infty$, the set A is in only finitely many I_n. Thus, we also refer to such a sequence of intervals as a Solovay test.

Theorem 6.2.8 (Solovay [371]). *A set is Solovay random iff it is* 1*-random.*

Proof. A Martin-Löf test is a Solovay test, so if a set is Solovay random then it is Martin-Löf random. Now suppose that A is Martin-Löf random, and let $\{S_n\}_{n\in\omega}$ be a Solovay test. There is an m such that $\sum_{n>m} \mu(S_n) < 1$. Let $U_k = [\![\{\sigma : \exists^{\geqslant 2^k} n > m\,([\![\sigma]\!] \in S_n)\}]\!]$. The U_k are uniformly Σ^0_1, and it is not hard to see that $\mu(U_k) \leqslant 2^{-k} \sum_{n>m} \mu(S_n) < 2^{-k}$. Thus $\{U_k\}_{k\in\omega}$ is a Martin-Löf test, and hence there is a k such that $A \notin U_k$. So A is in at most $2^k + m$ many S_n. Since $\{S_n\}_{n\in\omega}$ in an arbitrary Solovay test, A is Solovay random. □

6.3 The unpredictability paradigm

6.3.1 Martingales and supermartingales

It seems reasonable to say that most people would intuitively identify randomness with unpredictability. In a random process such as repeatedly tossing a fair coin, knowledge of the first n tosses should be of no help for predicting the result of the $(n + 1)$st toss. Similarly, if we are betting on the successive bits of a random sequence, we should not expect to be able to make much money, no matter what betting strategy we apply. We can formalize the notion of a betting strategy as follows.

Definition 6.3.1 (Levy [244]). A function $d : 2^{<\omega} \to \mathbb{R}^{\geqslant 0}$ is a *martingale* if for all σ,

$$d(\sigma) = \frac{d(\sigma 0) + d(\sigma 1)}{2}.$$ [10]

It is a *supermartingale* if for all σ,

$$d(\sigma) \geqslant \frac{d(\sigma 0) + d(\sigma 1)}{2}.$$

A (super)martingale d *succeeds* on a set A if $\limsup_n d(A \upharpoonright n) = \infty$. The collection of all sets on which d succeeds is called the *success set* of d, and is denoted by $S[d]$.

The idea is that a martingale $d(\sigma)$ represents the capital that we have after betting on the bits of σ while following a particular betting strategy ($d(\lambda)$ being our starting capital). The *martingale condition* $d(\sigma) = \frac{d(\sigma 0)+d(\sigma 1)}{2}$ is a fairness condition, ensuring that the expected value of our capital after a bet is equal to our capital before the bet. (In the case of supermartingales, we are allowed to discard part of our capital, such as by buying drinks or tipping the dealer.)

Ville [401] proved that the success sets of (super)martingales correspond precisely to the sets of measure 0. (This fact can be proved in the same way as Theorem 6.3.4 below, ignoring the effectivity of the notions involved in that result.)

We note a few basic properties of (super)martingales. The two in the following proposition are easily proved directly from the definitions, and we use them below without further comment.

Proposition 6.3.2. (i) *If d is a (super)martingale and $r \in \mathbb{R}^{\geqslant 0}$, then rd is a (super)martingale.*

(ii) *If $d_0, d_1, \ldots$ are (super)martingales such that $\sum_n d_n(\lambda) < \infty$, then $\sum_n d_n$ is a (super)martingale.*

The following result is known as Kolmogorov's Inequality, but is due to Ville [401].

Theorem 6.3.3 (Kolmogorov's Inequality, Ville [401]). *Let d be a (super)martingale.*

(i) *For any string σ and any prefix-free set S of extensions of σ, we have $\sum_{\tau \in S} 2^{-|\tau|} d(\tau) \leqslant 2^{-|\sigma|} d(\sigma)$.*

[10] A more complex notion of martingale is used in probability theory. We will discuss this notion, and the connection between it and ours, in Section 6.3.4.

(ii) *Let* $R_k = \{\sigma : d(\sigma) \geqslant k\}$. *Then* $\mu([\![R_k]\!]) \leqslant \frac{d(\lambda)}{k}$.

Proof. To prove (i), it is enough to consider finite S. We proceed by induction. For the $n = 1$ case, if $\tau \succcurlyeq \sigma$ then $2^{-|\tau|}d(\tau) \leqslant 2^{-|\sigma|}d(\sigma)$ follows easily from the definition of a (super)martingale.

Suppose (i) holds for sets of at most n elements, and let S have $n+1$ many elements. Let ν be the longest string such that every element of S extends ν. For $i < 2$, let $S_i = \{\tau \in S : \nu i \preccurlyeq \tau\}$. Then for $i < 2$ we have $|S_i| \leqslant n$, so by the inductive hypothesis, $\sum_{\tau \in S_i} 2^{-|\tau|}d(\tau) \leqslant 2^{-|\nu i|}d(\nu i)$. Thus

$$\sum_{\tau \in S} 2^{-|\tau|}d(\tau) \leqslant 2^{-(|\nu|+1)}(d(\nu 0) + d(\nu 1)) \leqslant 2^{-|\nu|}d(\nu) \leqslant 2^{-|\sigma|}d(\sigma),$$

the last inequality following by the $n = 1$ case above.

To prove (ii), let $P \subseteq R_k$ be a prefix-free set such that $[\![P]\!] = [\![R_k]\!]$. By part (i) with $\sigma = \lambda$,

$$\mu([\![P]\!]) = \sum_{\tau \in P} 2^{-|\tau|} \leqslant \sum_{\tau \in P} \frac{d(\tau)}{k} 2^{-|\tau|} \leqslant \frac{d(\lambda)}{k}.$$

□

To define a notion of randomness using martingales, we have to restrict the class of martingales we consider. Schnorr [348, 349] did so by effectivizing the notion of martingale. We say that a (super)martingale d is *computably enumerable* (or Σ^0_1) if it is a c.e. function in the sense of Definition 5.2.1.[11]

Theorem 6.3.4 (Schnorr [348, 349]). *A set is 1-random iff no c.e. (super)martingale succeeds on it.*

Proof. We show that Martin-Löf tests and (super)martingales are essentially the same, thus effectivizing Ville's work mentioned above.

Let d be a c.e. (super)martingale. Let $U_n = [\![\{\sigma : d(\sigma) \geqslant 2^n\}]\!]$. The U_n are uniformly Σ^0_1 classes, and $\mu(U_n) \leqslant 2^{-n}$ by Kolmogorov's Inequality. So $\{U_n\}_{n \in \omega}$ is a Martin-Löf test. Moreover, $A \in \bigcap_n U_n$ iff $A \in S[d]$.

Conversely, let $\{U_n\}_{n \in \omega}$ be a Martin-Löf test. Let $R_0, R_1, \ldots$ be a uniformly c.e. sequence of prefix-free generators for this test. For each n, define d_n as follows. Whenever a string σ enters R_n, add 1 to the value of $d_n(\tau)$ for every $\tau \succcurlyeq \sigma$ and add $2^{k-|\sigma|}$ to $d_n(\sigma \upharpoonright k)$ for each $k < |\sigma|$. It is easy to check that the d_n are uniformly c.e. martingales and $d_n(\lambda) \leqslant 2^{-n}$. Thus $d = \sum_n d_n$ is a c.e. martingale. Moreover, $A \in S[d]$ iff $A \in \bigcap_n U_n$. □

[11]One might have expected to see *computable* martingales rather than c.e. ones as the natural effectivization of the notion of martingale. Indeed, Schnorr [348, 349] did consider computable martingales, and used them to define notions of randomness that are strictly weaker than 1-randomness. We will return to this topic in Chapter 7.

By applying the second part of the above proof to a universal Martin-Löf test, we have the following result.

Corollary 6.3.5 (Schnorr [348, 349]). *There is a* universal *c.e. martingale, that is, a c.e. martingale d such that for any c.e. martingale f, we have $S[f] \subseteq S[d]$.*

As we have seen, not only is there a universal prefix-free machine, but in fact prefix-free complexity is minimal among information content measures. Given a martingale d, if f is a constant multiple of d then $S[f] = S[d]$, and in fact d and f behave essentially the same on all sequences. Thus martingales are in a sense really specified only up to constant multiples. This observation leads to the following definition.

Definition 6.3.6. A c.e. (super)martingale d is *optimal* if for each (super)martingale f there is a constant c such that $cd(\sigma) \geqslant f(\sigma)$ for all σ.

We can strengthen Corollary 6.3.5 for supermartingales as follows.

Theorem 6.3.7 (Schnorr [348, 349], also essentially Levin, see [425]). *There is an optimal c.e. supermartingale.*

Proof. We can construct a computable enumeration $d_0, d_1, \ldots$ of all c.e. supermartingales up to multiplication by a constant as follows. First notice that we can list all c.e. functions d such that $d(\sigma) \leqslant 2^{|\sigma|}$ for all σ. Then we can modify each such function d by not allowing the approximation to $d(\sigma i)$ to increase while that increase threatens to violate the condition $d(\sigma) \geqslant \frac{d(\sigma 0)+d(\sigma 1)}{2}$. Now the supermartingale $d(\sigma) = \sum_n 2^{-n} d_n(\sigma)$ is optimal. □

We will see in Section 6.3.3 that this result does not hold for martingales in place of supermartingales.

We finish this section by noting that the use of limsup's in the definition of success for (super)martingales is not essential, as witnessed by the following result, sometimes known as the "savings trick". The name comes from the idea of waiting until we win, say, two dollars, then saving one dollar and betting the second dollar until we have three dollars, at which point we save two dollars and bet one, and so on. This idea can be turned into a formal construction, but we also give a different proof that is easier in the case of c.e. martingales.

Proposition 6.3.8 (Folklore). *Let d be a (super)martingale. From d we can effectively define a (super)martingale $\widehat{d}$ such that $S[\widehat{d}] = S[d]$ and for all A we have* $\limsup_n d(A \upharpoonright n) = \infty$ *iff* $\lim_n \widehat{d}(A \upharpoonright n) = \infty$. *If d is computable, we can make $\widehat{d}$ also be computable, and if d is c.e., we can make $\widehat{d}$ also be c.e.*

Proof. We first give a direct construction of $\widehat{d}$. We may assume that $d(\sigma) > 0$ for all σ. We define $\widehat{d}$ using an auxiliary "savings function" $s : 2^{<\omega} \to \mathbb{Q}$, whose value at any string will be less than $\widehat{d}$. Let $\widehat{d}(\lambda) = d(\lambda)$ and $s(\lambda) = 0$. Given $\widehat{d}(\sigma)$ and $s(\sigma)$, for $i = 0, 1$, let $\widehat{d}(\sigma i) = s(\sigma) + (\widehat{d}(\sigma) - s(\sigma))\frac{d(\sigma i)}{d(\sigma)}$. Intuitively, we bet $s(\sigma)$ much of our capital evenly, and copy d's bet on the rest. Now, for each $i = 0, 1$, approximate $\widehat{d}(\sigma i) - s(\sigma)$ to within $\frac{1}{4}$, and if this approximation r is greater than $\frac{3}{4}$, then let $s(\sigma i) = s(\sigma) + r - \frac{1}{4}$ (which ensures that $0 < \widehat{d}(\sigma i) - s(\sigma i) < 1$). Otherwise, let $s(\sigma i) = s(\sigma)$. (In this case, $0 < \widehat{d}(\sigma i) - s(\sigma i) \leqslant 1$.)

It is now easy to check that $\widehat{d}$ is a d-computable (super)martingale, and that $A \in S[d]$ iff $\limsup_n d(A \restriction n) = \infty$ iff $\lim_n s(A \restriction n) = \infty$ iff $\lim_n \widehat{d}(A \restriction n) = \infty$ iff $A \in S[\widehat{d}]$.

For the c.e. martingale case, we have the following easier proof. From d we can construct a Martin-Löf test as in the first part of the proof of Theorem 6.3.4. From that test we can construct a martingale $\widehat{d}$ as in the second part of that proof. Then $S[\widehat{d}] = S[d]$. But it is easy to check that if $A \in S[\widehat{d}]$ then in fact $\lim_n \widehat{d}(A \restriction n) = \infty$. □

Note that the $\widehat{d}$ built in our first construction has the property that for all σ and τ, we have $\widehat{d}(\sigma\tau) \geqslant \widehat{d}(\sigma) - 2$, since the unsaved part of our capital never reaches 2. We will refer to this feature of $\widehat{d}$ as the *savings property*.

6.3.2 Supermartingales and continuous semimeasures

Recall the notions of a continuous semimeasure and of the complexity measure KM from Section 3.16. As discussed in that section, Levin (see [425]) directly constructed an optimal c.e. continuous semimeasure, but there is a natural correspondence between continuous semimeasures and supermartingales, so his result can be interpreted as a result about supermartingales. (Figuring out the history of concepts in this area is often difficult, as several people had similar but not always exactly congruent ideas.)

More precisely, let d be a supermartingale. Then $\delta([\![\sigma]\!]) = 2^{-|\sigma|}d(\sigma)$ is a continuous semimeasure, and this process can be reversed. Thus Schnorr's optimal c.e. supermartingale is equivalent to Levin's optimal c.e. continuous semimeasure δ. The quantity $\delta([\![\sigma]\!])$ is sometimes called the *a priori probability* of $[\![\sigma]\!]$. See Li and Vitányi [248] for a discussion of the connection between optimal c.e. continuous semimeasures and Bayes' rule [30].

In particular, we see that, since $KM(\sigma)$ is defined as $-\log \delta([\![\sigma]\!])$ for a fixed optimal c.e. continuous semimeasure δ, we have $KM(\sigma) = -\log d(\sigma) + |\sigma|$, where d is the optimal c.e. supermartingale corresponding to δ. Another way of obtaining KM is the following.

Proposition 6.3.9 (Uspensky [394]). *The a priori entropy KM is (up to an additive constant) the smallest function f that is approximable from above and such that $\sum_{\sigma \in M} 2^{-f(\sigma)} \leqslant 1$ for any prefix-free set M.*

Proof. Clearly KM is approximable from above. Let d be an optimal c.e. supermartingale with $d(\lambda) = 1$. If M is prefix-free then $\sum_{\sigma \in M} 2^{-KM(\sigma)} = \sum_{\sigma \in M} 2^{-|\sigma|} d(\sigma) \leqslant 1$ by Kolmogorov's Inequality (Theorem 6.3.3).

Now let δ be our fixed optimal c.e. continuous semimeasure. If f satisfies the conditions of the proposition, then let $m([\![\sigma]\!])$ be the maximum of $\sum_{\tau \in M} 2^{-f(\sigma\tau)}$ over all prefix-free sets M. Note that $m([\![\sigma]\!]) \geqslant 2^{-f(\sigma)}$. Then m is a c.e. continuous semimeasure, so $\delta(\sigma) \geqslant O(m([\![\sigma]\!]))$, and hence $KM(\sigma) = -\log \delta([\![\sigma]\!]) \leqslant -\log m([\![\sigma]\!]) + O(1) \leqslant f(\sigma) + O(1)$. □

One easy consequence of the supermartingale characterization of KM is that A is 1-random iff $KM(A \upharpoonright n) = n \pm O(1)$. The same is true for the related notions of monotone and process complexity, which we introduced in Section 3.15.

Theorem 6.3.10 (Levin [242], Schnorr [350]). *A set A is 1-random iff $Km(A \upharpoonright n) = Km_D(A \upharpoonright n) \pm O(1) = n \pm O(1)$.*

Proof. If $Km(A \upharpoonright n) \geqslant n - O(1)$ then $K(A \upharpoonright n) \geqslant n - O(1)$, so A is 1-random. We now prove the converse. Since $Km(A \upharpoonright n) \leqslant Km_D(A \upharpoonright n) + O(1) \leqslant n + O(1)$, it is enough to assume that A is 1-random and show that $Km(A \upharpoonright n) \geqslant n - O(1)$.

Write $\mathcal{M}(\sigma)[s] = \tau$ to mean that at stage s, the machine $\mathcal{M}$ has read σ and output τ so far. Let $U_k = [\![\{\rho : \exists s\, \exists \sigma\, (|\sigma| \leqslant |\rho| - k) \wedge \rho \preccurlyeq \mathcal{M}(\sigma)[s])\}]\!]$. Note that if $Km(\rho) \leqslant |\rho| - k$, then $\rho \in U_k$. The U_k are uniformly Σ_1^0 classes. Let R be a prefix-free set of generators for U_k. For each $\rho \in R$, let σ_ρ be such that $|\sigma_\rho| \leqslant |\rho| - k$ and $\rho \preccurlyeq \mathcal{M}(\sigma_\rho)[s]$ for some s. By monotonicity, the set of σ_ρ for $\rho \in R$ is prefix-free, so

$$\mu(U_k) = \sum_{\rho \in R} 2^{-|\rho|} \leqslant \sum_{\rho \in R} 2^{-(|\sigma_\rho| + k)} = 2^{-k} \sum_{\rho \in R} 2^{-|\sigma_\rho|} \leqslant 2^{-k}.$$

Thus $\{U_k\}_{k \in \omega}$ is a Martin-Löf test, so if A is 1-random then there is a k such that $A \notin U_k$, which implies that $Km(A \upharpoonright n) > n - k$ for all n. □

One consequence of the above result is that all 1-random sets have the same initial segment complexity with respect to both monotone complexity and process complexity. Thus, if we are interested in relating initial segment complexity to levels of randomness, these complexities, like KM, are too coarse.

6.3.3 Martingales and optimality

In this section we show that Theorem 6.3.7 does not hold for martingales; that is, there is no optimal c.e. martingale. We begin by showing that the particular proof of Theorem 6.3.7 cannot work, as there is no computable enumeration of all c.e. martingales. (This result follows from Theorem 6.3.12 below, but is more easily proved directly.)

Theorem 6.3.11 (Downey, Griffiths and LaForte [110][12]). *There is no computable enumeration of all c.e. martingales.*

Proof. Suppose that $d_0, d_1, \ldots$ is a computable enumeration of all c.e. martingales. (We do not require that all approximations to each d_i appear on the list, just that for every c.e. martingale d there is an i such that $d = d_i$.) From this enumeration we can produce an enumeration $f_0, f_1, \ldots$ of all c.e. martingales that are not the constant zero function as follows. Let $S = \{i : \exists s\, d_i(\lambda)[s] > 0\}$. Since S is c.e., we can enumerate its elements $s_0, s_1, \ldots$, and let $f_i = d_{s_i}$. Note that for each i and n, since f_i is a martingale (rather than just a supermartingale), there must be a $\sigma \in 2^n$ such that $f_i(\sigma) > 0$.

We now derive a contradiction by defining a strictly positive c.e. martingale d not equal to any f_i. In fact, d will be a computable rational-valued martingale. For a string $\sigma \neq \lambda$, let $\sigma^- = \sigma \upharpoonright (|\sigma| - 1)$, that is, the string obtained by removing the last bit of σ, and let $\sigma^c = \sigma^-(1 - \sigma(|\sigma|))$, that is, the string obtained by flipping the last bit of σ.

Let s be such that $f_0(\lambda)[s] > 0$ and let $d(\lambda) = \frac{f_0(\lambda)[s]}{2}$. Having defined d on strings of length n, search for an s and a $\sigma \in 2^{n+1}$ such that $f_{n+1}(\sigma)[s] > 0$. Let $d(\sigma) = \min(d(\sigma^-), \frac{f_{n+1}(\sigma)[s]}{2})$, let $d(\sigma^c) = 2d(\sigma^-) - d(\sigma)$, and for all $\tau \in 2^{n+1}$ other than σ, let $d(\tau) = d(\tau^-)$.

It is straightforward to check that d is a strictly positive c.e. martingale, but for each n there is a $\sigma \in 2^n$ such that $d(\sigma) < f_n(\sigma)$. □

The following result may well have been known to Schnorr, Levin, and others, but it seems that the first proof in the literature was given by Downey, Griffiths, and LaForte [110].

Theorem 6.3.12 (Downey, Griffiths, and LaForte [110]). *There is no optimal c.e. martingale.*

Proof. Let d be a c.e. martingale. We build a c.e. martingale f such that for each c there is a σ with $f(\sigma) \geqslant cd(\sigma)$, which implies that d is not optimal. It is enough to build uniformly c.e. martingales $f_0, f_1, \ldots$ so that for each n we have $f_n(\lambda) = 1$ and $f_n(\sigma) \geqslant 2^{2n} d(\sigma)$ for some σ, since we can then take $f = \sum_n 2^{-n} f_n$.

Given n, we begin by letting $f_n(\lambda) = 1$. Let $\sigma_0 = \lambda$. As long as $d(\lambda)[s] < 2^{-2n}$, we define $f_n(0^{s+1}) = 2^{s+1}$ and $f_n(\tau) = 0$ for all other strings of length $s+1$. If we find an s_0 such that $d(\lambda)[s_0] \geqslant 2^{-2n}$, then we wait until a stage t_0 such that $\sum_{\tau \in 2^{s_0+1}} d(\tau)[t_0] \geqslant 2^{s_0+1-2n}$, which must occur because d is a martingale. Let $i < 2$ be such that $d(0^{s_0} i)[t_0] \leqslant d(0^{s_0}(1-i))[t_0]$, and let $\sigma_1 = 0^{s_0} i$. Let $f_n(\sigma_1) = 2^{s_0+1}$, and let $f_n(\tau) = 0$ for all other $\tau \in 2^{s_0+1}$.

[12] There are statements to the contrary in the literature, but it seems likely that this fact was known before [110]; in particular, it is implicit in Levin's work such as [242].

Note that

$$\left(\sum_{\tau\in 2^{s_0+1}} d(\tau)[t_0]\right) - d(\sigma_1)[t_0] \geqslant 2^{s_0-2n},$$

since $d(0^{s_0}(1-i))[t_0]$ is at least as big as $d(\sigma_1)[t_0]$. Thus, for any m, if $d(\sigma_1) \geqslant m2^{-2n}f_n(\sigma_1) = m2^{s_0+1-2n}$, then

$$\begin{aligned} d(\lambda) &= 2^{-(s_0+1)} \sum_{\tau\in 2^{s_0+1}} d(\tau) \\ &\geqslant 2^{-(s_0+1)}(2^{s_0-2n} + m2^{s_0+1-2n}) = (m+\tfrac{1}{2})2^{-2n}. \end{aligned}$$

We now repeat the above procedure with σ_1 in place of λ. That is, as long as $d(\sigma_1)[s] < 2^{-2n}f_n(\sigma_1)$, we define $d(\sigma_1 0^{s+1}) = 2^{|\sigma_1|+s+1}$ and $f_n(\tau) = 0$ for all other strings of length $|\sigma_1| + s + 1$. If we find an s_1 such that $d(\sigma_1)[s_1] \geqslant 2^{-2n}f_n(\sigma_1) = 2^{|\sigma_1|-2n}$, then we wait until a stage t_1 such that $\sum_{\tau\in 2^{s_1+1}} d(\sigma_1\tau)[t_1] \geqslant 2^{|\sigma_1|+s_1+1-2n}$, which must occur because d is a martingale. Let $i < 2$ be such that $d(\sigma_1 0^{s_1} i)[t_1] \leqslant d(\sigma_1 0^{s_1}(1-i))[t_1]$, and let $\sigma_2 = \sigma_1 0^{s_1} i$. Let $f_n(\sigma_2) = 2^{|\sigma_1|+s_1+1}$, and let $f_n(\tau) = 0$ for all other $\tau \in 2^{|\sigma_1|+s_1+1}$. Now, as above,

$$\left(\sum_{\tau\in 2^{s_1+1}} d(\sigma_1\tau)[t_1]\right) - d(\sigma_2)[t_1] \geqslant 2^{|\sigma_1|+s_1-2n},$$

so if $d(\sigma_2) \geqslant m2^{-2n}f_n(\sigma_2) = m2^{|\sigma_1|+s_1+1-2n}$, then

$$\begin{aligned} d(\sigma_1) &= 2^{-(s_1+1)} \sum_{\tau\in 2^{s_1+1}} d(\sigma_1\tau) \\ &\geqslant 2^{-(s_1+1)}(2^{|\sigma_1|+s_1-2n} + m2^{|\sigma_1|+s_1+1-2n}) \\ &= (m+\tfrac{1}{2})2^{|\sigma_1|-2n} = (m+\tfrac{1}{2})2^{s_0+1-2n}, \end{aligned}$$

and hence $d(\lambda) \geqslant (m+\frac{1}{2})2^{-2n}$.

We now repeat this procedure with σ_2 in place of σ_1, and so on. Each time we define σ_i, it is because $d(\sigma_{i-1}) \geqslant 2^{-2n}f_n(\sigma_{i-1})$. The latter implies that $d(\lambda) \geqslant \frac{i+1}{2}2^{-2n}$, which cannot be the case for all i. So there is an i such that σ_i is never defined, which means that $d(\sigma_{i-1}) < 2^{-2n}f_n(\sigma_{i-1})$. □

6.3.4 Martingale processes

As mentioned above, our concept of martingale is a simple special case of the original notion from probability theory, which we now discuss. Let us begin by recalling some basic notions. (We will define these in the context of the uniform measure μ on 2^ω, but they can be defined for any probability space. See for example [144] for details.) A *σ-algebra* on 2^ω is a collection of subsets of 2^ω closed under complements and countable unions. For any collection $\mathcal{C}$ of subsets of 2^ω, there is a smallest σ-algebra containing $\mathcal{C}$, which we say is the σ-algebra *generated* by $\mathcal{C}$. The σ-algebra $\mathcal{B}$ generated by the collection of basic clopen sets of 2^ω is called the *Borel σ-algebra on 2^ω*. For a σ-algebra $\mathcal{F}$, a function from 2^ω to $\mathbb{R}$ is *$\mathcal{F}$-measurable* if $f^{-1}((-\infty, r)) \in \mathcal{F}$ for all $r \in \mathbb{R}$. A *random variable* on 2^ω is a function $X : 2^\omega \to \mathbb{R}$ that is $\mathcal{B}$-measurable. The *expectation* $E[X]$ of X is its integral over 2^ω with respect to μ. For $A \subseteq 2^\omega$ such that $\mu(A) > 0$, the *conditional expectation of X given A*, denoted by $E[X \mid A]$ is $\frac{E[X \cdot \chi_A]}{\mu(A)}$, where χ_A is the characteristic function of A.

A function $d : 2^{<\omega} \to \mathbb{R}$ can be thought of as a sequence of random variables $X_0^d, X_1^d, \ldots$, where $X_n^d(\alpha) = d(\alpha \upharpoonright n)$. It is then easy to check that d is a martingale iff it is nonnegative and for each $\sigma \in 2^{<\omega}$,

$$E[X_{|\sigma|+1}^d \mid [\![\sigma]\!]] = d(\sigma). \tag{6.1}$$

However, in probability theory martingales are usually defined using a weaker condition.

Definition 6.3.13. A sequence of random variables $X_0, X_1, \ldots$ is a *martingale* if for every n we have $E[X_n] < \infty$ and for every $r_0, \ldots, r_n \in \mathbb{R}$,

$$E[X_{n+1} \mid \{\alpha : X_0(\alpha) = r_0, \ldots, X_n(\alpha) = r_n\}] = r_n. \tag{6.2}$$

In other words, a martingale is a sequence of random variables such that the expectation of each random variable conditional on the observed values of the previous ones is equal to the observed value of the immediately preceding one.

Hitchcock and Lutz [181] defined a function $d : 2^{<\omega} \to \mathbb{R}$ to be a *martingale process* if the corresponding random variables $X_0^d, X_1^d, \ldots$ form a martingale. It is easy to see that condition (6.1) implies condition (6.2), so every martingale is a martingale process. The following is an alternative definition of martingale process, also given in [181] and easily seen to be equivalent to the one above, when we restrict attention to nonnegative functions.

Definition 6.3.14 (Hitchcock and Lutz [181])**.** Let $d : 2^{<\omega} \to \mathbb{R}^{\geqslant 0}$ be a function. We write $\sigma \sim_d \tau$ if $|\sigma| = |\tau|$ and $d(\sigma \upharpoonright n) = d(\tau \upharpoonright n)$ for all $n \leqslant |\sigma|$. We write $s_d(\sigma)$ for the size of the $\sim_d$-equivalence class of σ. A function $d : 2^{<\omega} \to \mathbb{R}^{\geqslant 0}$ is a *martingale process* if for all σ,

$$s_d(\sigma)d(\sigma) = \sum_{\tau \sim_d \sigma} \frac{d(\tau 0) + d(\tau 1)}{2}.$$

As Hitchcock and Lutz [181] remarked, in the fairness condition for martingales given in Definition 6.3.1, the average is taken over all sequences with the same bit history, while in the fairness condition for martingale processes, the average is taken over all sequences with the same *capital* history.

It should be noted that there is a more general notion of martingale in probability theory that has as subcases both martingale processes and martingales in our sense. See [181] or [268] for a discussion of this fact.

As with martingales, we say that a martingale process d *succeeds* on a set A if $\limsup_n d(A \upharpoonright n) = \infty$, and the collection of all sets on which d succeeds is denoted by $S[d]$. In addition to having its source in a probability-theoretic notion of martingale, the notion of martingale process is interesting to us because it provides a computable, rather than computably enumerable, characterization of 1-randomness. (See the discussion of "Schnorr's critique" in the introduction to Chapter 7.) Putting together results of Hitchcock and Lutz [181] and Merkle, Mihailović, and Slaman [268], we now show that a set is 1-random iff no computable martingale process succeeds on it. We begin with an analog of Lemma 6.3.3, adapted from Hitchcock and Lutz [181].

Lemma 6.3.15. *Let d be a martingale process.*

(i) *Let B be a set of $\sim_d$-equivalent strings, and let S be a prefix-free set of extensions of elements of B such that S is closed under $\sim_d$. Let $\sigma \in B$. Then*

$$\sum_{\tau \in S} 2^{-|\tau|} d(\tau) \leqslant s_d(\sigma) 2^{-|\sigma|} d(\sigma), \tag{6.3}$$

where, as above, $s_d(\sigma)$ is the size of the $\sim_d$-equivalence class of σ.

(ii) *Let $R_k = \{\sigma : d(\sigma) \geqslant k\}$. Then $\mu([\![R_k]\!]) \leqslant \frac{d(\lambda)}{k}$.*

Proof. Since (6.3) holds iff it holds for all finite subsets of S, to prove (i), it is enough to consider finite S. We proceed by induction on the number n of $\sim_d$-equivalence classes in S. If $n = 1$ then all elements of S have the same length k, so if we let C be the set of all strings of length k that extend elements of B, then

$$\sum_{\tau \in S} 2^{-|\tau|} d(\tau) \leqslant 2^{-k} \sum_{\tau \in C} d(\tau) \leqslant s_d(\sigma) 2^{-|\sigma|} d(\sigma),$$

the last inequality following easily by induction on k from the definition of martingale process.

Now suppose (i) holds for sets with at most $n \geqslant 1$ many $\sim_d$-equivalence classes, and let S have $n+1$ many $\sim_d$-equivalence classes. For each k, let S_k be the set of all $\tau \in 2^k$ that have a (not necessarily proper) extension in S. Let m be the length of the shortest element of S. If S_m has only one $\sim_d$-equivalence class then $S_m \subseteq S$, since S is closed under $\sim_d$, whence $S = S_m$, since S is prefix-free. But that conclusion contradicts our choice of S. Thus there is a least k such that S_k has at least two $\sim_d$-equivalence classes, and $|\sigma| < k \leqslant m$. Partition S_k into its $\sim_d$-equivalence classes $C_0, \ldots, C_p$. For each i, let $\sigma_i \in C_i$ and let T_i be the elements of S that extend C_i. Then each T_i has at most n many $\sim_d$-equivalence classes, so by induction

$$\sum_{\tau \in T_i} 2^{-|\tau|} d(\tau) \leqslant s_d(\sigma_i) 2^{-k} d(\sigma_i).$$

But since the elements of S_{k-1} are all $\sim_d$-equivalent, for $\rho \in S_{k-1}$ the definition of martingale process implies that

$$\sum_{i \leqslant p} s_d(\sigma_i) 2^{-k} d(\sigma_i) \leqslant s_d(\rho) 2^{-(k-1)} d(\rho).$$

By the $n = 1$ case above with the $\sim_d$-equivalence class of ρ in place of S, this quantity is less than or equal to $s_d(\sigma) 2^{-|\sigma|} d(\sigma)$. Thus

$$\sum_{\tau \in S} 2^{-|\tau|} d(\tau) = \sum_i \sum_{\tau \in T_i} 2^{-|\tau|} d(\tau) \leqslant s_d(\sigma) 2^{-|\sigma|} d(\sigma).$$

To prove (ii), let $S = \{\tau : d(\tau) \geqslant k \wedge \forall \rho \prec \tau\, (d(\rho) < k)\}$. Then S is prefix-free and closed under $\sim_d$, and $[\![S]\!] = [\![R_k]\!]$. By part (i) with $B = \{\lambda\}$,

$$\mu([\![S]\!]) = \sum_{\tau \in S} 2^{-|\tau|} \leqslant \sum_{\tau \in S} \frac{d(\tau)}{k} 2^{-|\tau|} \leqslant \frac{d(\lambda)}{k}.$$

□

Theorem 6.3.16 (Hitchcock and Lutz [181]). *If A is 1-random then no computable martingale process succeeds on A.*

Proof. The proof is basically the same as that of the corresponding direction of Theorem 6.3.4: Let d be a computable martingale process. Let $U_n = [\![\{\sigma : d(\sigma) > 2^n\}]\!]$. The U_n are uniformly Σ^0_1 classes, and $\mu(U_n) \leqslant 2^{-n}$ by Lemma 6.3.15. So $\{U_n\}_{n \in \omega}$ is a Martin-Löf test. Moreover, $A \in \bigcap_n U_n$ iff $A \in S[d]$. So if A is 1-random then $A \notin S[d]$. □

We now turn to the converse of this result, beginning with an auxiliary lemma.

Lemma 6.3.17 (Merkle, Mihailović, and Slaman [268]). *Let $C \subset 2^{<\omega}$ be a computable prefix-free set such that $\mu([\![C]\!]) \leqslant \frac{1}{2}$. We can effectively define a computable martingale process d such that $d(\lambda) = 1$ and $d(\sigma) = 2$ for all $\sigma \in C$.*

Proof. Let D be the set of all extensions of elements of C. For $\sigma \in D$, let $d(\sigma) = 2$. For $\sigma \notin D$, let $b = \left|2^{|\sigma|} \setminus D\right|$, let $c = \left|C \cap 2^{|\sigma|}\right|$, and let $d(\sigma) = 1 - \frac{c}{b}$, which must be nonnegative by our assumption that $\mu([\![C]\!]) \leqslant \frac{1}{2}$. It is easy to check by induction that d is a martingale process. □

Theorem 6.3.18 (Merkle, Mihailović, and Slaman [268]). *There is a computable martingale process that succeeds on every non-1-random set.*

Proof. Let $U_0, U_1, \ldots$ be a universal Martin-Löf test. Let $V_\sigma = U_{|\sigma|+1} \cap [\![\sigma]\!]$. Let $D_\sigma \subset 2^{<\omega}$ be uniformly computable prefix-free sets such that $V_\sigma =$

$[\![\sigma D_\sigma]\!]$. Since $\mu(U_{|\sigma|+1}) \leqslant 2^{-|\sigma|-1}$, we have $\mu([\![D_\sigma]\!]) < \frac{1}{2}$, so there are uniformly computable martingale processes $\widetilde{d}_\sigma$ such that $\widetilde{d}_\sigma(\lambda) = 1$ and $\widetilde{d}_\sigma(\tau) = 2$ for all $\tau \in D_\sigma$. Let d_σ be the martingale process defined by letting $d_\sigma(\sigma\rho) = \widetilde{d}_\sigma(\rho)$ and $d_\sigma(\nu) = 1$ if $\sigma \not\preccurlyeq \nu$.

We now use the d_σ to define a computable martingale process d. It is easiest to describe the action of d along a particular sequence A. At first d copies d_λ. If there is an n_0 such that $d_\lambda(A \upharpoonright n_0) = 2$ (and hence $d(A \upharpoonright n_0) = 2$), then d begins to copy $2d_{A\upharpoonright n_0}$. If there is an n_1 such that $d_{A\upharpoonright n_0}(A \upharpoonright n_1) = 2$ (and hence $d(A \upharpoonright n_0) = 4$), then d begins to copy $4d_{A\upharpoonright n_1}$. In general, with n_k having been defined, d copies $2^{k+1}d_{A\upharpoonright n_k}$ until, if ever, there is an n_{k+1} such that $d_{A\upharpoonright n_k}(A \upharpoonright n_{k+1}) = 2$ (and hence $d(A \upharpoonright n_0) = 2^{k+2}$). Then d begins to copy $2^{k+2}d_{A\upharpoonright n_{k+1}}$.

For each $\tau \in 2^{<\omega}$, let σ_τ be such that $d(\tau)$ is defined as copying d_{σ_τ}. It is easy to see by induction on the length of strings that $\sigma \mapsto d_\sigma$ is a computable function, and that if $\tau \sim_d \tau'$ then $\sigma_\tau = \sigma_{\tau'}$. Since the d_σ are themselves computable martingale processes, we see that d is a computable martingale process. Clearly, if $A \in \bigcap_n U_n$, then d succeeds on A. □

As a final note on computable martingale processes, we mention the following useful result. For a proof, see [181].

Theorem 6.3.19 (Hitchcock and Lutz [181]). *For every computable martingale process f and every $\varepsilon > 0$, there is a martingale process $d' : 2^{<\omega} \to \mathbb{Q}^{\geqslant 0}$ that is computable as a function from strings to rationals, so that $|d(\sigma) - d'(\sigma)| < \varepsilon$ for all σ.*

6.4 Relativizing randomness

Like most computability-theoretic notions, 1-randomness can be relativized in a straightforward way. Given a set X, we say that A is *1-random relative to X* if $K^X(A \upharpoonright n) \geqslant n - O(1)$. We can also define a Martin-Löf test relative to X in the same way as we defined an unrelativized Martin-Löf test, but with classes that are Σ^0_1 relative to X. The same proof as above shows that A is 1-random relative to X iff it passes every Martin-Löf test relative to X iff no X-c.e. martingale succeeds on X.

Most other notions in the theory of algorithmic randomness can be similarly relativized, and we often do so below without further comment. There are a few situations, however, in which relativization is more problematic. See Chapter 15 for an example.

It is useful to note that the construction of a universal Martin-Löf test above can be easily adapted to produce a *universal oracle Martin-Löf test*, that is, a test $U_0^X, U_1^X, \ldots$ that is a universal Martin-Löf test relative to X for all X.

6.5 Ville's Theorem

In this section, we prove the theorem of Ville mentioned above. Our proof will be taken from Lieb, Osherson, and Weinstein [249], which is a simplified version of the proof of Uspensky, Semenov, and Shen [395].

A *selection function*, or *selection rule*, is a partial function $f : 2^{<\omega} \to \{\text{yes}, \text{no}\}$. We think of f as deciding whether or not to select the $(k+1)$st bit of a sequence based on the observed values of the first k bits. For a sequence α and a selection function f, let $s_f(\alpha, n)$ be the nth number k such that $f(\alpha \upharpoonright k) = \text{yes}$, if such a number exists. If $s_f(\alpha, n-1)$ is defined, let $S_f(\alpha, n) = \sum_{i<n} \alpha(s_f(\alpha, i))$. In other words, $S_f(\alpha, n)$ is the number of 1's among the first n many bits of α selected by f. If f is the function sending every string to yes, then we write $S(\alpha, n)$ for $S_f(\alpha, n)$. (So $S(\alpha, n)$ is the number of 1's among the first n bits of α.)

Theorem 6.5.1 (Ville's Theorem [401]). *Let E be any countable collection of selection functions. Then there is a sequence $\alpha = \alpha_0\alpha_1\dots$ such that the following hold.*

(i) $\lim_n \frac{S(\alpha,n)}{n} = \frac{1}{2}$.

(ii) *For every $f \in E$ that selects infinitely many bits of α, we have* $\lim_n \frac{S_f(\alpha,n)}{n} = \frac{1}{2}$.

(iii) *For all n, we have* $\frac{S(\alpha,n)}{n} \leqslant \frac{1}{2}$.

Before proving the full theorem, we prove a finite version. Strictly speaking, the following result is not needed for the proof of Ville's Theorem we give, but we believe that it is helpful to the comprehension of the ideas of the proof.

Proposition 6.5.2 (Finite version of Ville's Theorem). *Let E be any finite collection of selection functions. Then there is a sequence α satisfying the conclusion of Theorem 6.5.1.*

Proof. Without loss of generality, we will assume that the function sending every string to yes is in E, and hence we need to meet only conditions (ii) and (iii) of Theorem 6.5.1. We build α in stages.

Given $\alpha \upharpoonright n$, let $C(n) = \{f \in E : f(\alpha \upharpoonright n) = \text{yes}\}$ and $\alpha_n = |\{j < n : C(j) = C(n)\}| \bmod 2$. That is, we let α_n be 1 iff the subset $C(n)$ of E consisting of those functions that select the nth bit of α appears an even number of times among the $C(j)$ with $j \leqslant n$. Evidently, α satisfies (iii), since each 1 appearing in α is preceded by an occurrence of 0 that can be uniquely chosen to match it. (In other words, if $\alpha_n = 1$ then there must be an $m < n$ such that $C(m) = C(n)$, and for the largest such m we have $\alpha_m = 0$.)

As an illustration, let $E = \{h, f_1, f_2\}$, with $h(\sigma) = \text{yes}$ for all σ; and f_1 and f_2 defined so that $f_1(\sigma) = \text{yes}$ for all σ of length 0, 2, or 4, but

$f_1(\sigma) = \text{no}$ for all other σ of length less than 8; while $f_2(\sigma) = \text{yes}$ for all σ of length 0, 3, or 6, but $f_2(\sigma) = \text{no}$ for all other σ of length less than 8. Then we have the following:

$$
\begin{array}{lll}
C(0) = \{h, f_1, f_2\}, & \alpha_0 = 0 & \\
C(1) = \{h\}, & \alpha_1 = 0 & \\
C(2) = \{h, f_1\}, & \alpha_2 = 0 & \\
C(3) = \{h, f_2\}, & \alpha_3 = 0 & \\
C(4) = \{h, f_1\}, & \alpha_4 = 1 & (\text{because } C(4) = C(2)) \\
C(5) = \{h\}, & \alpha_5 = 1 & (\text{because } C(5) = C(1)) \\
C(6) = \{f, f_1, f_2\}, & \alpha_6 = 1 & (\text{because } C(6) = C(0)) \\
C(7) = \{h\}, & \alpha_7 = 0 & (\text{because } C(7) = C(1) = C(5))
\end{array}
$$

Thus $\alpha \upharpoonright 8 = 00001110$.

Now suppose that $|\{n : f(\alpha \upharpoonright n) = \text{yes}\}| = \infty$ and let $n_0 < n_1 < \cdots$ be a list of all n such that $f(\alpha \upharpoonright n) = \text{yes}$. For any $C \in E$, if we take the (possibly finite) sequence $n_{i_0} < n_{i_1} < \cdots$ of all n_i such that $C(n_i) = C$, we have $C(n_{i_j}) = 0$ for j even and $C(n_{i_j}) = 1$ for j odd, so for all n, the number of 1's among the first n many bits of α selected by f differs from the number of 0's among these bits by at most 1 for each $C \in E$. In other words, $|\frac{n}{2} - S_f(\alpha, n) \leqslant 2^{|E|}|$. Thus $\lim_n \frac{S_f(\alpha,n)}{n} = \frac{1}{2}$. □

Notice that the proof above actually shows that for every $f \in E$, we have $0 \leqslant \frac{n}{2} - S_f(\alpha, n) \leqslant 2^{|E|}$.

The method above clearly fails when we try to use it in the case that E is infinite. The problem is that (for example) each subset of E might occur only once among the $C(n)$, making $\alpha = 0^\omega$. The proof of Ville's Theorem in the general case uses the construction of a *finite* subset $C(n)$ to determine q_n, together with a combinatorial trick to decide which of the $f \in E$ are allowed to be in $C(n)$. Roughly, f_k is allowed to occur with f_{k+m+1} only if it has occurred sufficiently often by itself, or with some of $f_1, \ldots, f_{k+m}$, as made precise below.

The key to the proof of Theorem 6.5.1 is the following lemma. Let $\mathcal{A}$ denote the class of infinite sequences of subsets of $\mathbb{N}$. For $A \in \mathcal{A}$, let $I_\ell^A = \{n : \ell \in A(n)\}$. For $\alpha \in 2^\omega$ and $I = \{n_0 < n_1 < \cdots\} \subseteq \mathbb{N}$, recall that $\alpha \upharpoonright I = \alpha(n_0)\alpha(n_1)\ldots$.

Lemma 6.5.3. *To each $A \in \mathcal{A}$ we can assign a sequence α such that the value of $\alpha(n)$ depends only on $A(0), \ldots, A(n)$; for any ℓ such that I_ℓ^A is infinite, $\lim_n \frac{S(\alpha \upharpoonright I_\ell^A, n)}{n} = \frac{1}{2}$; and $\frac{S(\alpha,n)}{n} \leqslant \frac{1}{2}$ for all n.*

Assuming the lemma for now, we can prove Theorem 6.5.1 as follows.

Proof of Theorem 6.5.1 from Lemma 6.5.3. Let $f_0, f_1, \ldots$ list the elements of E. We may assume that f_0 is the function sending every string to yes, so we need to meet only conditions (ii) and (iii) of Theorem 6.5.1. Let

$A(0) = \{i : f_i(\lambda) = \text{yes}\}$ and let $\alpha(0)$ be as in the lemma. Given $\alpha \upharpoonright n$, let $A(n) = \{i : f_i(\alpha \upharpoonright n) = \text{yes}\}$ and let $\alpha(n)$ be as in the lemma.

Then condition (iii) is satisfied by the lemma, as is condition (ii), since for any f_i such that $f_i(\alpha \upharpoonright n) = \text{yes}$ for infinitely many n,

$$\lim_n \frac{S_{f_i}(\alpha, n)}{n} = \lim_n \frac{S(\alpha \upharpoonright I_i^A, n)}{n} = \frac{1}{2}.$$

□

Proof of Lemma 6.5.3. We first build a map from $\mathcal{A}$ into itself, denoting the image of A by A^*. Each coordinate of A^* will be a nonempty finite subset of the corresponding coordinate of A. In building A^*, we also define an auxiliary family of numbers $I(n)$.

Suppose that we have already defined $A^*(m)$ and $I(m)$ for all $m < n$ so that $A^*(m) = \{j \in A(m) : j \leqslant I(m)\}$. Let $I(n)$ be the least i such that there is a $j \in A(n)$ with $|\{m < n : j \in A^*(m) \wedge I(m) = i\}| \leqslant 3^i$ and let

$$A^*(n) = \{j \in A(n) : j \leqslant I(n)\}.$$

The construction of $A^*(n)$ depends only on $\{A(i) : i \leqslant n\}$. Furthermore, for each i, we have $I(n) = i$ for at most $i3^i$ many n.

From A^* we get α by letting

$$\alpha(n) = |\{j < n : A^*(j) = A^*(n)\}| \bmod 2.$$

Clearly, $\alpha \upharpoonright n$ depends only on $A(0), \dots, A(n)$. Furthermore, as with the finite construction, we can pair each i such that $\alpha(i) = 1$ with a $j < i$ such that $\alpha(j) = 0$, so $\frac{S(\alpha,n)}{n} \leqslant \frac{1}{2}$ for all n. To verify the remaining property in the lemma, fix an ℓ that occurs in infinitely many $A(n)$. We need to show that $\lim_n \frac{S(\alpha \upharpoonright I_\ell^A, n)}{n} = \frac{1}{2}$.

Let $n_0 < n_1 < \cdots$ be a listing of I_ℓ^A. Since $I(n) = \ell$ for at most finitely many n, it follows that $\ell \in A^*(n_m)$ for cofinitely many m. For each $i \geqslant \ell$, there are at least 3^i many occurrences of i in the list $I(n_0), I(n_1), \dots$ prior to the first occurrence of $i + 1$ in that list.

Let k be least such that for the least m with $I(n_m) = k$, we have $\ell < I(n_i)$ for all $i \geqslant m$. Let

$$\gamma = A^*(n_m)A^*(n_{m+1})\dots.$$

For $j \geqslant k$, let

$$\sigma(j) = A^*(n_i)A^*(n_{i+1})A^*(n_{i+2})\dots A^*(n_{i+r}),$$

where i is least such that $I(n_i) = j$ and r is least such that $I(n_{i+r+1}) = j+1$. Note that $\gamma = \sigma(k)\sigma(k+1)\dots$. Also, $A^*(i)$ is part of γ for cofinitely many i such that $\ell \in A(i)$.

For $i \geqslant k$, each of the sets appearing in $\sigma(i)$ is a subset of $\{0, \dots, i\}$, so there are at most 2^i many such sets. Therefore, since there are at least 3^i many occurrences of i in $I(n_0), I(n_1), \dots$ prior to the first occurrence of

$i+1$, we see that γ has the form $\sigma(k)\sigma(k+1)\sigma(k+2)\ldots$, where for all $m \geqslant 0$, the block $\sigma(k+m)$ has length at least 3^{k+m} and contains at most 2^{k+m} many distinct sets.

Let m be such that $\gamma(0) = A^*(n_m)$, and let $\beta = \alpha \upharpoonright (I_\ell^A \cap [n_m, \infty))$. Since β is a tail of $\alpha \upharpoonright I_\ell^A$, it is enough to show that $\lim_n \frac{S(\beta,n)}{n} = \frac{1}{2}$.

Let j be sufficiently large so that there is an $m(j)$ such that $\gamma(j)$ is within $\sigma(k+m(j)+1)$. Let $N_0(j)$ be the number of 0's in $\beta \upharpoonright j$ and $N_1(j)$ the number of 1's in $\beta \upharpoonright j$. Since the block $\sigma(k+m(j))$ has at least $3^{k+m(j)}$ many coordinates, $N_0(j)+N_1(j) \geqslant 3^{k+m(j)}$.

Let p be the length of the initial segment of $\alpha \upharpoonright I_\ell^A$ missing from β. Then $N_1(j) \leqslant N_0(j)+p$, whence

$$N_1(j) \leqslant \frac{1}{2}(N_0(j)+N_1(j)+p). \tag{6.4}$$

There are at most 2^{k+i} distinct sets in $\sigma(k+i)$, and this number bounds the number of unmatched 0's in that block. Therefore,

$$N_0(j) \leqslant N_1(j) + \sum_{i \leqslant m(j)+1} 2^{k+i} \leqslant N_1(j) + 2^{k+m(j)+2}.$$

Thus,

$$N_1(j) \geqslant \frac{1}{2}(N_0(j)+N_1(j)-2^{k+m(j)+2}). \tag{6.5}$$

We finish by evaluating $R(j) = \frac{N_1(j)}{(N_0(j)+N_1(j))}$. Clearly, if $\lim_j R(j) = \frac{1}{2}$ then $\lim_j \frac{S(\beta,n)}{n} = \frac{1}{2}$. By (6.4),

$$R(j) \leqslant \frac{N_0(j)+N_1(j)+p}{2(N_0(j)+N_1(j))},$$

which has limit $\frac{1}{2}$. For the lower bound, we use (6.5), which gives us

$$R(j) \geqslant \frac{N_0(j)+N_1(j)-2^{k+m(j)+2}}{2(N_0(j)+N_1(j))} = \frac{1}{2} - \frac{2^{k+m(j)+2}}{N_0(j)+N_1(j)},$$

which converges to $\frac{1}{2}$, as $N_0(j)+N_1(j) \geqslant 3^{k+m(j)}$. □

Lieb, Osherson, and Weinstein [249] made the following observations about their proof above.

Let h be the function sending every string to yes. Choose a selection function f_ℓ that selects infinitely many bits of α, and define the *fluctuation about the mean* to be

$$\delta_\ell(n) = S_{f_\ell}(\alpha, n) - \frac{1}{2}.$$

By the reasoning above we have seen that δ_ℓ is bounded by an ℓ-dependent constant. This property mimics the behavior of h, whose fluctuation is never positive. Furthermore, using the reasoning above, there is a number

$C_\ell \geqslant 0$ such that $\delta_\ell(n) \geqslant -C_\ell n^{\frac{\log 2}{\log 3}}$. The 3 occurs because of the use of 3^i in the proof, and an arbitrary number r could have been used instead of 3, yielding the conclusion that for each $\varepsilon > 0$, there is a constant $C_\ell(\varepsilon) \geqslant 0$ such that for every n,

$$\delta_\ell(n) \geqslant -C_\ell(\varepsilon)n^\varepsilon. \tag{6.6}$$

Lieb, Osherson, and Weinstein pointed out that this bound is remarkable, because for a random coin toss, the law of the iterated logarithm states that the fluctuations exceed $(1-\varepsilon')\frac{\sqrt{n \log\log n}}{\sqrt{2}}$ for any $\varepsilon' > 0$ infinitely often almost surely (see Feller [144]). They observed that for any slow growing function g, there is a suitably fast growing function p such that using $p(i)$ in place of 3^i will enforce a bound analogous to (6.6) with $g(n)$ in place of n^ε, and a suitable constant $C_\ell(g)$, reducing the fluctuations above the mean even further.

6.6 The Ample Excess Lemma

While the definition of a set A being 1-random requires only that $K(A \upharpoonright n) \geqslant n - O(1)$, there is a "gap phenomenon" that ensures that, in fact, the initial segment complexity of A must be quite a bit higher than this lower bound.

Theorem 6.6.1 (Ample Excess Lemma, Miller and Yu [280]). *A set A is 1-random iff $\sum_n 2^{n-K(A\upharpoonright n)} < \infty$.*

Proof. If A is not 1-random then there are infinitely many n such that $K(A \upharpoonright n) < n$, so $\sum_n 2^{n-K(A\upharpoonright n)} = \infty$.

For the other direction, note that for any m,

$$\sum_{\sigma\in 2^m}\sum_{n\leqslant m} 2^{n-K(\sigma\upharpoonright n)} = \sum_{\sigma\in 2^m}\sum_{\tau\preccurlyeq\sigma} 2^{|\tau|-K(\tau)}$$
$$= \sum_{\tau\in 2^{\leqslant m}} 2^{m-|\tau|}2^{|\tau|-K(\tau)} = 2^m \sum_{\tau\in 2^{\leqslant m}} 2^{-K(\tau)} < 2^m.$$

Therefore, for each c there are at most 2^{m-c} strings $\sigma \in 2^m$ for which $\sum_{n\leqslant m} 2^{n-K(\sigma\upharpoonright n)} \geqslant 2^c$. Thus $\mu(\{A : \sum_{n\leqslant m} 2^{n-K(A\upharpoonright n)} \geqslant 2^c\}) \leqslant 2^{-c}$, and hence $U_c = \{A : \sum_n 2^{n-K(\alpha\upharpoonright n)} \geqslant 2^c\}$ has measure at most 2^{-c}. Furthermore, the U_c are uniformly Σ^0_1, and hence form a Martin-Löf test. If A is 1-random then there is a c such that $A \notin U_c$. Then $\sum_n 2^{n-K(A\upharpoonright n)} < 2^c$. $\square$

Corollary 6.6.2 (Chaitin [63]). *A set A is 1-random iff $\lim_n K(A \upharpoonright n) - n = \infty$.*

Corollary 6.6.3 (Miller and Yu [280]). *Let A be 1-random and let f be a function such that $\sum_n 2^{-f(n)} = \infty$. Then there are infinitely many n such that $K(A \upharpoonright n) > n + f(n) - O(1)$.*[13]

Proof. If there is an m such that $K(A \upharpoonright n) \leqslant n+f(n)-O(1)$ for all $n > m$, then $\sum_n 2^{n-K(A\upharpoonright n)} \geqslant \sum_{n>m} 2^{n-K(A\upharpoonright n)} \geqslant \sum_{n>m} 2^{-(f(n)-O(1))} = \infty$, so A is not 1-random. □

Corollary 6.6.4 (Miller and Yu [280]). *If A is 1-random then $K^A(n) \leqslant K(A \upharpoonright n) - n + O(1)$.*

Proof. Let d be such that $\sum_n 2^{n-K(A\upharpoonright n)-n} < d$. Let

$$S = \{(c+d, n) : \exists s\,(K_s(A \upharpoonright n) - n < c)\}.$$

The set S is c.e. relative to A and

$$\sum_{(c+d,n)\in S} 2^{-(c+d)} \leqslant \sum_n 2^{n-K(A\upharpoonright n)-d} < 1.$$

Furthermore, for each n, we have $(K(A \upharpoonright n)-n+d+1, n) \in S$. Thus, by the relativized form of the KC Theorem, $K^A(n) \leqslant K(A \upharpoonright n) - n + O(1)$. □

Using Corollaries 3.11.3 and 6.6.2, we can prove the result mentioned in Section 3.8 that there are many strings that are weakly K-random yet highly non-C-random.

Corollary 6.6.5. *There are infinitely many strings σ such that $K(\sigma) \geqslant |\sigma|$ but $C(\sigma) \leqslant |\sigma| - \log|\sigma|$.*

Proof. Let A be 1-random. By Corollary 3.11.3, there are infinitely many n such that $C(A \upharpoonright n) \leqslant n - \log n$. By Corollary 6.6.2, for all but finitely many such n, we have $K(A \upharpoonright n) \geqslant n$. □

We finish this section with a result about the complexity of blocks, rather than just initial segments, of a 1-random set.

Theorem 6.6.6 (Merkle, see [306]). *If $A = \sigma_0\sigma_1\sigma_2\ldots$ and $K(\sigma_i) < |\sigma_i|$ for all i, then A is not 1-random.*

Proof. Let M be the prefix-free machine that, on input τ, searches for n and a partition $\tau = \rho\nu_0\ldots\nu_{n-1}$ such that $\mathcal{U}(\rho)\downarrow = n$ and $\mathcal{U}(\nu_i)\downarrow$ for all $i < n$, and if these are found, outputs $\mathcal{U}(\nu_0)\ldots\mathcal{U}(\nu_{n-1})$. Then for each n we have $M(n^*\sigma_0^*\ldots\sigma_{n-1}^*) = \sigma_0\ldots\sigma_{n-1}$, so

$$\begin{aligned} K(\sigma_0\ldots\sigma_{n-1}) &\leqslant |n^*\sigma_0^*\ldots\sigma_{n-1}^*| + O(1) \\ &= K(n) + \sum_{i<n} K(\sigma_i) \leqslant 2\log n + |\sigma_0\ldots\sigma_{n-1}| - n + O(1). \end{aligned}$$

[13]Solovay [371] proved this result for computable f.

Thus for each k there is an m such that $K(A \upharpoonright m) \leqslant m - k$, and hence A is not 1-random. □

6.7 Plain complexity and randomness

Though the characterizations of 1-random sets in terms of initial segment complexities such as monotone and prefix-free complexity are satisfying, they raise the natural question, which remained open for nearly forty years, of whether there is a plain complexity characterization of 1-randomness. (We will see in Section 6.11 that having infinitely often maximal plain complexity suffices but is not necessary.) Miller and Yu [280] have given such a characterization, which we now present, along with characterizations that mix plain and prefix-free complexity.

Definition 6.7.1 (Miller and Yu [280]). Define a computable function $G : \mathbb{N} \to \mathbb{N}$ by

$$G(n) = \begin{cases} K_{s+1}(t) & \text{if } n = 2^{\langle s,t \rangle} \text{ and } K_{s+1}(t) \neq K_s(t) \\ n & \text{otherwise.} \end{cases}$$

The function G is a variation on Solovay's Solovay function from the proof of Theorem 3.12.1. Note that

$$\sum_n 2^{-G(n)} \leqslant \sum_n 2^{-n} + \sum_t \sum_{m \geqslant K(t)} 2^{-m} = 2 + 2 \sum_t 2^{-K(t)} < \infty.$$

Furthermore, if $n = 2^{\langle s,t \rangle}$ for the least s such that $K_{s+1}(t) = K(t)$, then $G(n) = K(t) \leqslant K(n) + O(1)$. So we can think of G as an infinitely often correct computable simulation of K that grows fairly fast (cf. Theorem 3.12.1).

Theorem 6.7.2 (Miller and Yu [280], Gács [165] for (i) $\Leftrightarrow$ (ii)). *The following are equivalent.*

(i) *A is 1-random.*

(ii) $C(A \upharpoonright n \mid n) \geqslant n - K(n) - O(1)$.

(iii) $C(A \upharpoonright n) \geqslant n - K(n) - O(1)$.

(iv) $C(A \upharpoonright n) \geqslant n - g(n) - O(1)$ *for every computable function g such that* $\sum_n 2^{-g(n)} < \infty$.

(v) $C(A \upharpoonright n) \geqslant n - G(n) - O(1)$.

Proof. (i) $\Rightarrow$ (ii): Let $U_k = \{A \mid \exists n\, C(A \upharpoonright n \mid n) < n - K(n) - k\}$. Then $A \in U_k$ iff $\exists n\, \exists s\, C_s(A \upharpoonright n \mid n) + K_s(n) < n - k$, so the U_k are uniformly

Σ^0_1. Furthermore,

$$\begin{aligned}\mu(U_k) &\leqslant \sum_n \mu(\{A \mid C(A \upharpoonright n \mid n) < n - K(n) - k\}) \\ &\leqslant \sum_n 2^{-n}|\{\sigma \in 2^n \mid C(\sigma \mid n) < n - K(n) - k\}| \\ &\leqslant \sum_n 2^{-n}2^{n-K(n)-k} = 2^{-k}\sum_n 2^{-K(n)} \leqslant 2^{-k}.\end{aligned}$$

Thus $\{U_k\}_{k\in\omega}$ is a Martin-Löf test. If A is 1-random, then there is a k such that $A \notin U_k$, whence $\forall n\, C(A \upharpoonright n) \geqslant n - K(n) - k$.

(ii) ⇒ (iii): Immediate.

(iii) ⇒ (iv): Let g be a computable function such that $\sum_n 2^{-g(n)} < \infty$. By the minimality of K among information content measures (Theorem 3.7.8), we have $K(n) \leqslant g(n) + O(1)$, so if $C(A \upharpoonright n) \geqslant n - K(n) - O(1)$ then $C(A \upharpoonright n) \geqslant n - g(n) - O(1)$.

(iv) ⇒ (v): Immediate since G is computable and $\sum_n 2^{-G(n)} < \infty$.

(v) ⇒ (i): Assume that A is not 1-random. We show that (v) does not hold. By Theorem 3.7.6, there a c such that for all t and k,

$$|\{\sigma \in 2^t \mid K(\sigma) \leqslant t - k\}| \leqslant 2^{t-K(t)-k+c}.$$

We construct a (non-prefix-free) machine M that gives relatively short descriptions of $A \upharpoonright n$ when $n = 2^{\langle s,t\rangle}$ and s is least such that $K_{s+1}(t) = K(t)$.

For $s, t \in \omega$, let $n = 2^{\langle s,t\rangle}$. To $\langle s,t\rangle$ we devote the M-programs with lengths from $\frac{n}{2} + c + 1$ to $n + c$. Note that distinct pairs do not compete for elements in the domain of M.

Fix $k \in \omega$ and let $m = n - K_{s+1}(t) - k + c$. Note that $m \leqslant n + c$. If $m \geqslant \frac{n}{2} + c + 1$, then for each $\sigma \in 2^n$ such that $K(\sigma \upharpoonright t) \leqslant t - k$, we try to pick a $\tau \in 2^m$ and define $M(\tau) = \sigma$. Different k do not compete for programs, but it is still possible that there are not enough strings of length m for all such σ, so we assign programs until we run out.

If $K_{s+1}(t) = K(t)$, though, then we cannot run out, because the number of $\sigma \in 2^n$ for which $K(\sigma \upharpoonright t) \leqslant t - k$ is equal to

$$2^{n-t}|\{\rho \in 2^t \mid K(\rho) \leqslant t - k\}| \leqslant 2^{n-t}2^{t-K(t)-k+c} = 2^{n-K(t)-k+c} = 2^m.$$

The point of the definition of M is that if $K_{s+1}(t) = K(t)$ and n, k, m are as above, then as long as $m \geqslant \frac{n}{2} + c + 1$, for every $\sigma \in 2^n$ such that $K(\sigma \upharpoonright t) \leqslant t - k$, we have $C_M(\sigma) \leqslant m$.

Fix k. Since A is not 1-random, there is a t such that $K(x \upharpoonright t) \leqslant t - k$. We may assume that t is large enough so that $K(t) \leqslant 2^{t-1} - k - 1$. Let s be least such that $K_{s+1}(t) = K(t)$, let $n = 2^{\langle s,t\rangle}$, and let $m = n - K(t) - k + c$. Then $m \geqslant n - 2^{t-1} + k + 1 - k + c \geqslant \frac{n}{2} + c + 1$, because $n \geqslant 2^t$. Thus

$C_M(A \upharpoonright n) \leqslant m$. Furthermore, $G(n) = K_{s+1}(t) = K(t)$, so

$$C(A \upharpoonright n) \leqslant C_M(A \upharpoonright n) + O(1) \leqslant m + O(1) \\ = n - K(t) - k + c + O(1) \leqslant n - G(n) - k + O(1),$$

where the constant is independent of n and k. Because k is arbitrary, (v) does not hold. □

Too recently for a proof to be included in this book, Bienvenu, Merkle, and Nies [unpublished] have shown that the function G in the above result can be replaced by any Solovay function, or indeed any co-c.e. function with the same properties as a Solovay function.

Theorem 6.7.3 (Bienvenu, Merkle, and Nies [unpublished]). *The following are equivalent for a co-c.e. function g.*

(i) $\sum_n 2^{-g(n)} < \infty$ *and* $\liminf_n g(n) - K(n) < \infty$.

(ii) *A set A is 1-random iff* $C(A \upharpoonright n) \geqslant n - g(n) - O(1)$.

6.8 n-randomness

There appear to be three natural ways to extend Martin-Löf's definition to obtain a notion of n-randomness for $n > 1$. One is simply to replace the Σ^0_1 classes in his definition by Σ^0_n classes. Another is to notice the importance of the fact that the components of a Martin-Löf test are open, and hence replace them by *open* Σ^0_n classes. The third is to view Σ^0_1 classes as generated by c.e. subsets of $2^{<\omega}$, and hence replace them by classes generated by Σ^0_n subsets of $2^{<\omega}$, that is, by $\Sigma^{0,\emptyset^{(n-1)}}_1$ classes, hence equating n-randomness with 1-randomness relative to $\emptyset^{(n-1)}$. Fortunately, while these approaches may not yield the same tests, they do yield the same notion of randomness. The key to proving this fact is part (i) of Theorem 6.8.3 below. Before turning to that result, we need two lemmas. Recall the effective listings $S^n_0, S^n_1, \dots$ of the Σ^0_n classes given in Section 2.19.2.

Lemma 6.8.1 (Kurtz [228]). *For each $n > 0$, the set $C_n = \{(i, q) : q \in \mathbb{Q} \wedge \mu(S^n_i) > q\}$ is Σ^0_n. Thus, the measures $\mu(S^n_i)$ are uniformly $\emptyset^{(n)}$-computable.*

Proof. For $n = 1$ we use Proposition 2.19.7, which says that if S is a Σ^0_1 class then we can effectively obtain a c.e. set $W \subseteq 2^{<\omega}$ such that $S = [\![W]\!]$. Thus $\mu(S) > q$ iff there is an s such that $\sum_{\sigma \in W_s} 2^{-|\sigma|} > q$, which clearly implies that C_1 is c.e.

If S is a Σ^0_{n+1} class then we can find uniformly Σ^0_n classes $S^n_{i_0} \supseteq S^n_{i_1} \supseteq \cdots$ such that S is the complement of $\bigcap_k S^n_{i_k}$. Then $\mu(S) = 1 - \lim_k \mu(S^n_{i_k})$, so $\mu(S) > q$ iff there is a k and a rational $r > 0$ such that $\mu(S^n_{i_k}) \leqslant 1 - q - r$, that is, such that $(i_k, 1-q-r) \notin C_n$. By induction, C_n is Σ^0_n, so C_{n+1} is Σ^0_{n+1}. □

Lemma 6.8.2. *Let $f = \Phi^{\emptyset'}_e$ be a total function. Then $\bigcup_i S^1_{f(i)}$ is a $\Sigma^{0,\emptyset'}_1$ class, and an index for this class can be obtained effectively from e.*

Proof. We can define a $\emptyset'$-c.e. set $W \subseteq 2^{<\omega}$ (whose index we can clearly obtain from e) as follows. First find c.e. sets $R_i \subseteq 2^{<\omega}$ such that $S^1_{f(i)} = [\![R_i]\!]$ for all i. Then let $W = \bigcup_i R_i$. From W we can effectively pass to an index for $\bigcup_i S^1_{f(i)} = [\![W]\!]$ as a $\Sigma^{0,\emptyset'}_1$ class. □

Theorem 6.8.3 (Kurtz [228], Kautz [200]).

(i) *From an index of a Σ^0_n class S and $q \in \mathbb{Q}$, we can compute an index of a $\Sigma^{0,\emptyset^{(n-1)}}_1$ class $U \supseteq S$ such that $\mu(U) - \mu(S) < q$.*

(ii) *From an index of a Π^0_n class P and $q \in \mathbb{Q}$, we can compute an index of a $\Pi^{0,\emptyset^{(n-1)}}_1$ class $V \subseteq P$ such that $\mu(P) - \mu(V) < q$.*

(iii) *From an index of a Σ^0_n class S and $q \in \mathbb{Q}$, we can $\emptyset^{(n)}$-compute an index of a closed Π^0_{n-1} class $V \subseteq S$ such that $\mu(S) - \mu(V) < q$. Moreover, if $\mu(S)$ is $\emptyset^{(n-1)}$-computable then an index of V can be found $\emptyset^{(n-1)}$-computably.*

(iv) *From an index of a Π^0_n class P and $q \in \mathbb{Q}$, we can $\emptyset^{(n)}$-compute an index of an open Σ^0_{n-1} class $U \supseteq P$ such that $\mu(U) - \mu(P) < q$. Moreover, if $\mu(P)$ is $\emptyset^{(n-1)}$-computable then an index of U can be found $\emptyset^{(n-1)}$-computably.*

Proof. For $n = 1$, (i) and (ii) are obvious. For (iii), let $W \subseteq 2^{<\omega}$ be a c.e. set such that $S = [\![W]\!]$, obtained effectively from S as in Proposition 2.19.7, and let $S_s = [\![W_s]\!]$. Note that each S_s is a union of finitely many basic clopen sets, and hence is a Π^0_0 class. Each $S \setminus S_s$ is a Σ^0_1 class, so by Lemma 6.8.1, we can $\emptyset'$-computably find an s such that $\mu(S) - \mu(S_s) < q$. Let $V = S_s$. If $\mu(S)$ is computable, then s can be found computably. Now (iv) follows by taking complements.

We now turn to proving (i) and (iii) for the $n+1$ case. Items (ii) and (iv) then follow by taking complements. Let S be a Σ^0_{n+1} class and let $P_0 \subseteq P_1 \subseteq \cdots$ be uniformly Π^0_n classes such that $S = \bigcup_i P_i$.

(i) By induction, we can $\emptyset^{(n)}$-compute indices for $\Sigma^{0,\emptyset^{(n-1)}}_1$ classes $U_i \supseteq P_i$ such that $\mu(U_i) - \mu(P_i) < 2^{-(i+1)}q$. Let $U = \bigcup_i U_i$. Since U is a union of $\Sigma^{0,\emptyset^{(n-1)}}_1$ classes with $\emptyset^{(n)}$-computable indices, by the relativized form of Lemma 6.8.2, we can computably determine an index for U as a $\Sigma^{0,\emptyset^{(n)}}_1$

class. Since $S \subseteq U$, we have $U \setminus S = \bigcup_i (U_i \setminus P_i)$, so

$$\mu(U) - \mu(S) = \mu(U \setminus S) = \mu\Big(\bigcup_i (U_i \setminus P_i)\Big)$$
$$\leqslant \sum_i \mu(U_i \setminus P_i) < \sum_i 2^{-(i+1)} q = q.$$

(iii) By Lemma 6.8.1, we can $\emptyset^{(n+1)}$-computably find an i such that $\mu(P_i) \geqslant \mu(S) - \frac{q}{2}$. (While $\emptyset^{(n)}$ is enough to compute $\mu(P_i)$, we need $\emptyset^{(n+1)}$ to compute $\mu(S)$.) By induction, we can obtain an index of a $\Pi_1^{0,\emptyset^{(n-1)}}$ class $V \subseteq P_i$ such that $\mu(P_i) - \mu(V) < \frac{q}{2}$. Then $V \subseteq S$ and $\mu(S) - \mu(V) < q$. The only place we used $\emptyset^{(n+1)}$ as an oracle was to compute $\mu(S)$. Thus, if $\mu(S)$ is $\emptyset^{(n)}$-computable, then an index of V can be computed from $\emptyset^{(n)}$. □

We can now define n-randomness using the first approach mentioned above, and it will follow easily from the above result that this definition is equivalent to the ones arising from the other two approaches.

Definition 6.8.4 (Kurtz [228][14]). (i) A Σ_n^0 *(Martin-Löf) test* is a sequence $\{U_n\}_{n\in\omega}$ of uniformly Σ_n^0 classes such that $\mu(U_n) \leqslant 2^{-n}$ for all n.

(ii) A set A is *n-random* (or *Σ_n^0-random*) if for every Σ_n^0 test $\{U_n\}_{n\in\omega}$, we have $A \notin \bigcap_n U_n$.

(iii) We can similarly define Π_n^0 tests, Δ_n^0 tests, and so on, and associated notions of randomness.

(iv) A set A is *arithmetically random* if it is n-random for all n.

Notice that a Σ_1^0 test is a Martin-Löf test. As usual, we can relativize the notion of n-randomness to any oracle X by using $\Sigma_n^{0,X}$ classes in place of Σ_n^0 classes. An *open* Σ_n^0 *test* is a Σ_n^0 test whose components are open.

Corollary 6.8.5 (Kautz [200]). *The following are equivalent.*

(i) *The set A is n-random.*

(ii) *For every open Σ_n^0 test $\{U_n\}_{n\in\omega}$, we have $A \notin \bigcap_n U_n$.*

(iii) *The set A is 1-random relative to $\emptyset^{(n-1)}$.*

Proof. Obviously (i) implies (ii), and (ii) implies (iii) because every $\Sigma_1^{0,\emptyset^{(n-1)}}$ class is an open Σ_n^0 class. So it is enough to show that ¬(i) implies ¬(iii). Suppose there is a Σ_n^0 test $\{U_n\}_{n\in\omega}$ such that $A \in \bigcap_n U_n$. By Theorem 6.8.3, for each n, we can effectively obtain a $\Sigma_1^{0,\emptyset^{(n-1)}}$ class

[14] The original definition in [228] used higher-level analogs of Solovay tests. It was proved equivalent to this definition by Kautz [200].

$V_n \supseteq U_{n+1}$ such that $\mu(V_n) \leqslant \mu(U_{n+1}) + 2^{-(n+1)} \leqslant 2^{-n}$. Then $\{V_n\}_{n\in\omega}$ is a Martin-Löf test relative to $\emptyset^{(n-1)}$, and $A \in \bigcap_n V_n$. □

It is typically most useful to think of n-randomness as 1-randomness relative to $\emptyset^{(n-1)}$, as we can then apply the relativized form of results obtained for 1-randomness. For example, for each n, there are Δ^0_{n+1} sets that are n-random, while no Δ^0_{n+1} set can be $(n+1)$-random. Thus, for each n there are n-random sets that are not $(n+1)$-random. As another example, we have the following version of Schnorr's Theorems 6.2.3 and 6.3.4, where a Σ^0_n (super)martingale is one that is c.e. relative to $\emptyset^{(n-1)}$.

Corollary 6.8.6 (Kautz [200], after Schnorr [348, 349]). *The following are equivalent.*

(i) *The set A is n-random.*

(ii) $K^{\emptyset^{(n-1)}}(A \upharpoonright n) \geqslant n - O(1)$.

(iii) *No Σ^0_n (super)martingale succeeds on A.*

We can define a relativized version of Ω by letting Ω^X be the halting probability of $\mathcal{U}^X$. Then $\Omega^{\emptyset^{(n-1)}}$ is a somewhat natural example of an n-random real. Becher and Grigorieff [33] gave a number of examples of n-random reals based on output probabilities of (unrelativized) universal monotone machines.

6.9 Van Lambalgen's Theorem

In this section, we introduce a fundamental tool in the study of n-randomness. Suppose we have a random sequence. Intuitively, we would expect that if we pick out two subsequences that do not share elements, then these subsequences should be highly independent. Conversely, if we put together two sequences that are random relative to each other, we would expect the result to remain random. Van Lambalgen's Theorem confirms these intuitions for n-randomness. As we will see in Section 8.11.3, the analog of van Lambalgen's Theorem fails for other notions of effective randomness such as Schnorr, computable, and weak 1-randomness (notions of randomness introduced in Chapter 7), although, perhaps surprisingly, the "hard" direction (Theorem 6.9.2) does hold for these weaker notions of randomness. For any relativizable notion of randomness R, we say that A and B are *relatively R-random* if A is R-random relative to B and B is R-random relative to A.

Theorem 6.9.1 (van Lambalgen [398]). *If $A \oplus B$ is n-random then A and B are relatively n-random.*

Proof. We do the $n = 1$ case. The general case follows by relativizing the proof to $\emptyset^{(n-1)}$. Suppose that $A \oplus B$ is 1-random. We show that B is 1-random relative to A, the other direction being symmetric.

Suppose that B is not 1-random relative to A. Let $U_0, U_1, \ldots$ be a universal oracle Martin-Löf test. Then $B \in \bigcap_i U_i^A$. Let $V_i = \{[\![\sigma \oplus \tau]\!] : \tau \in U_{2i}^\sigma \wedge |\sigma| = i\}$. The V_i are uniformly Σ_1^0 classes and $\mu(V_i) \leqslant 2^{-i}$ because $\mu(U_{2i}^X) \leqslant 2^{-2i}$ for all X. Thus $V_0, V_1, \ldots$ is a Solovay test. But $A \oplus B \in V_i$, since there are infinitely many initial segments $\sigma \prec A$ and $\tau \prec B$ with $\sigma \oplus \tau$ in some U_{2i}. So $A \oplus B$ is not 1-random. □

Theorem 6.9.2 (van Lambalgen [398]). *If A is n-random and B is n-random relative to A, then $A \oplus B$ is n-random.*

Proof. This proof is due to Nies (see [118]). Suppose that $A \oplus B$ is not n-random. We show that either A is not n-random or B is not n-random relative to A. Let $V_0 \supseteq V_1 \supseteq \cdots$ be uniformly Σ_n^0 open sets such that $A \oplus B \in \bigcap_i V_i$ and $\mu(V_i) \leqslant 2^{-2i}$, which exist by Corollary 6.8.5. We write $[\![\sigma \oplus \tau]\!]$ for the class of sets $X = X_0 \oplus X_1$ such that $\sigma \prec X_0$ and $\tau \prec X_1$.

Let S_i be the open set generated by $\{\sigma : \mu(V_i \cap [\![\sigma \oplus \lambda]\!]) \geqslant 2^{-i-|\sigma|}\}$. Clearly, $S_{i+1} \subseteq S_i$, and the S_i are uniformly Σ_n^0 open sets. Let $\sigma_0, \sigma_1, \ldots$ be a prefix-free set of generators for S_i. Since the sets $V_i \cap [\![\sigma_j \oplus \lambda]\!]$ are pairwise disjoint and $\mu(V_i) \leqslant 2^{-2i}$, we have $\sum_j 2^{-i-|\sigma_j|} \leqslant 2^{-2i}$, and hence $\mu(S_i) \leqslant \sum_j 2^{-|\sigma_j|} \leqslant 2^{-i}$. Thus, if $A \in \bigcap_i S_i$ then A is not n-random.

Otherwise, there is a j such that $A \notin S_i$ for all $i > j$. For such i, let R_i^k be the open set generated by $\{\tau \in 2^k : [\![(A \upharpoonright k) \oplus \tau]\!] \subseteq V_i\}$. Then $\mu(R_i^k) \leqslant 2^{-i}$, since $A \notin S_i$. Moreover, since V_i is open, $R_i^k \subseteq R_i^{k+1}$. Let $R_i = \bigcup_k R_i^k$. The R_i are open and uniformly Σ_n^0 relative to A, and $\mu(R_i) = \sup_k \mu(R_i^k) \leqslant 2^{-i}$ for $i > j$. Furthermore, $B \in R_i$ for each $i > j$, so B is not n-random relative to A. □

Corollary 6.9.3 (van Lambalgen's Theorem [398]). *The following are equivalent.*

(i) *$A \oplus B$ is n-random.*

(ii) *A is n-random and B is n-random relative to A.*

(iii) *B is n-random and A is n-random relative to B.*

(iv) *A and B are relatively n-random.*

In particular, if A and B are both n-random, then A is n-random relative to B iff B is n-random relative to A.

The last part of van Lambalgen's Theorem may seem counterintuitive, as it says that if A is n-random, then there is no way to build a set B that is n-random relative to A without at the same making A be n-random relative to B. It implies for instance that if A is Δ_2^0 and 1-random, and

B is 2-random, then A is 1-random relative to B, and also that every n-random set is n-random relative to measure 1 many sets. Nevertheless, it is one of the most useful basic properties of relative randomness. We note a few consequences of van Lambalgen's Theorem here, and will use it several times below.

Corollary 6.9.4. *If $A \oplus B$ is 1-random, then $A \mid_T B$, so $A, B <_T A \oplus B$.*

Corollary 6.9.5 (Kurtz [228]). *No minimal degree is 1-random.*

Given an infinite and coinfinite set X, let $x_0 < x_1 < \cdots$ be the elements of X, let $y_0 < y_1 < \cdots$ be the elements of $\overline{X}$, and define $A \oplus_X B$ to be $\{x_n : n \in A\} \cup \{y_n : n \in B\}$. For example, for the set E of even numbers, $A \oplus_E B = A \oplus B$. The proof of van Lambalgen's Theorem clearly works for $A \oplus_X B$ in place of $A \oplus B$ for any computable X. The following is an immediate consequence.

Corollary 6.9.6. *If A is n-random then so is the ith column $A^{[i]}$ of A.*

6.10 Effective 0-1 laws

In this section, we prove effective versions of measure-theoretic 0-1 laws such as Kolmogorov's 0-1 Law (Theorem 1.2.4).

Lemma 6.10.1 (Kučera [215]). *Let P be a Π^0_1 class of positive measure. If A is 1-random then some translate of A lies in P. That is, there are $\sigma \in 2^{<\omega}$ and $B \in P$ such that $A = \sigma B$.*

Proof. Suppose that for every σ and B, if $A = \sigma B$ then $B \notin P$. Let $W \subset 2^{<\omega}$ be a prefix-free c.e. set such that $\overline{P} = [\![W]\!]$. Let $S_0 = W$ and $S_{n+1} = \{\sigma\tau : \sigma \in S_n \wedge \tau \in W\}$. Let $U_n = [\![S_n]\!]$. The U_n are uniformly Σ^0_1. Furthermore, $\mu(U_0) < 1$ and $\mu(U_{n+1}) = \mu(U_n)\mu(U_0) = \mu(U_0)^{n+2}$. Thus we can pick out a Martin-Löf test $U_{n_0}, U_{n_1}, \ldots$. Since we are assuming that if $A = \sigma B$ then $B \in \overline{P}$, we have $A \in \bigcap_n U_n$. Thus A is not 1-random. □

Theorem 6.10.2 (Kautz [200, 201]). *Let $n > 0$ and let P be a Π^0_n class of positive measure. If A is n-random then there are $\sigma \in 2^{<\omega}$ and $B \in P$ such that $A = \sigma B$. Thus, P contains a member of each n-random degree.*

Proof. By Theorem 6.8.3, there is a $\Pi^{0,\emptyset^{(n-1)}}_1$ class $V \subseteq P$ of positive measure. By the relativized form of Lemma 6.10.1, there are $\sigma \in 2^{<\omega}$ and $B \in V \subseteq P$ such that $A = \sigma B$. □

Theorem 8.21.2 below will show that this result cannot be extended to the notion of weak n-randomness introduced in the next chapter.

Corollary 6.10.3 (Kautz [200, 201]). *Let $n > 0$ and let C be a Σ^0_{n+1} or Π^0_{n+1} class that is degree invariant, or even just closed under translations. Then C contains either all n-random sets or no n-random sets.*

Proof. It is enough to prove the result for a Σ^0_{n+1} class C, since the result for a Π^0_{n+1} class then follows by taking its complement. Let A be n-random. By Kolmogorov's 0-1 Law, C has measure 0 or 1. If C has measure 1, then it is a union of Π^0_n classes, at least one of which has positive measure. By Theorem 6.10.2, this class must contain a translation of A, and hence C must contain A. If C has measure 0 then it is a union of Π^0_n classes of measure 0. For any such class P, using Theorem 6.8.3, we can $\emptyset^{(n-1)}$-computably find $\Sigma^{0,\emptyset^{(n-1)}}_1$ classes $U_0, U_1, \ldots$ such that $\mu(U_i) \leqslant 2^{-i}$ and $P \subseteq \bigcap_i U_i$. Then $U_0, U_1, \ldots$ is a Martin-Löf test relative to $\emptyset^{(n-1)}$. Thus $A \notin \bigcap_i U_i$, and hence $A \notin P$. So $A \notin C$. □

Note that this result implies that a Σ^0_{n+1} or Π^0_{n+1} class of measure 0 cannot contain any n-random sets.

We will see several important applications of 0-1 laws below, such as Theorem 8.21.8 that every 2-random set is c.e. in some set of strictly smaller degree.

6.11 Infinitely often maximally complex sets

One might wonder whether there is a plain complexity characterization of 1-randomness simpler than the ones in Theorem 6.7.2. We have seen that we cannot have $C(A \upharpoonright n) \geqslant n - O(1)$ for *all* n, so the following weakening of this condition is a natural candidate.

Definition 6.11.1. A set A is *infinitely often C-random* if there are infinitely many n such that $C(A \upharpoonright n) \geqslant n - O(1)$.

Martin-Löf [260] noted that being infinitely often C-random implies being 1-random.[15] An easy proof of this fact was found by Nies, Stephan, and Terwijn [308]: By Proposition 3.10.4, we know that $C(\sigma\tau) \leqslant K(\sigma) + C(\tau) + O(1)$, and hence $C(\sigma\tau) \leqslant K(\sigma) + |\tau| + O(1)$. If A is not 1-random, then for each d there is an n with $K(A \upharpoonright n) < n - d$. If $m > n$ then, by the above, $C(A \upharpoonright m) \leqslant K(A \upharpoonright n) + (m - n) < m - d$. Since d is arbitrary, A is not infinitely often C-random.

As we will see, the notion of being infinitely often C-random turns out to be too strong to capture 1-randomness. In fact, it is a plain complexity characterization of 2-randomness. Before proving this remarkable fact, we note the following result.

Theorem 6.11.2 (after Martin-Löf [260], see Li and Vitányi [248]). *The following are equivalent.*

(i) *The set A is infinitely often C-random.*

[15]Though Martin-Löf [260] looked at sets A such that $C(A \upharpoonright n \mid n) \geqslant n - O(1)$, which by Theorem 6.11.2 is equivalent to being infinitely often C-random.

(ii) *There are infinitely many* n *such that* $C(A \upharpoonright n \mid n) \geqslant n - O(1)$.

Proof. Obviously (ii) implies (i). Now suppose that there are infinitely many n such that $C(A \upharpoonright n) \geqslant n - O(1)$. We have

$$C(A \upharpoonright n) \leqslant C(A \upharpoonright n \mid n) + 2\log(|n - C(A \upharpoonright n \mid n)|) + O(1),$$

since the $2\log(|n - C(A \upharpoonright n \mid n)|)$ term allows room for a description of n given $C(A \upharpoonright n \mid n)$. So there are infinitely many n such that

$$n - C(A \upharpoonright n \mid n) \leqslant 2\log(|n - C(A \upharpoonright n \mid n)|) + O(1).$$

For such n, we have $n - C(A \upharpoonright n \mid n) \leqslant O(1)$. □

To show that being infinitely often C-random is equivalent to being 2-random, Nies, Stephan, and Terwijn [308] began with the following result.

Theorem 6.11.3 (Nies, Stephan, and Terwijn [308]). *If a set is infinitely often* C*-random then it is* 2*-random.*

Proof. Suppose that A is not 2-random. Then there are $n_0, n_1, \ldots$ such that $K^{\emptyset'}(A \upharpoonright n_i) < n_i - i$ for all i. Let σ_i be a minimal length $\mathcal{U}^{\emptyset'}$-program for $A \upharpoonright n_i$. Let $s_i > n_i$ be such that $\mathcal{U}^{\emptyset'}(\sigma_i)[s_i]\downarrow$ with $\emptyset'$-correct use. (That is, for the use u of this computation, $\emptyset'_{s_i} \upharpoonright u = \emptyset' \upharpoonright u$.)

Let M be a Turing machine defined as follows. On input τ, first M searches for σ and μ such that $\sigma\mu = \tau$ and $\mathcal{U}^{\emptyset'}(\sigma)[|\tau|]\downarrow$. If there is such a σ (which must then be unique), let $\nu = \mathcal{U}^{\emptyset'}(\sigma)[|\tau|]$. Then M outputs $\nu\mu$.

Fix i and let $t \geqslant s_i$. Let $\mu = A(n_i)\ldots A(t-1)$. Then $M(\sigma_i\mu)\downarrow = (A \upharpoonright n_i)\mu = A \upharpoonright t$, so $C(A \upharpoonright t) \leqslant |\sigma_i\mu| < t - i + O(1)$. Since for each i this fact holds for all sufficiently large t, we conclude that A is not infinitely often C-random. □

Let $\mathcal{V}$ be a universal Turing machine. For a function g, let $C^g(\sigma) = \min\{|\tau| : \mathcal{V}(\tau)[g(\sigma)]\downarrow = \sigma\}$. (We consider only functions that are sufficiently fast growing so that this set is not empty for any σ.) Analyzing the above proof, we see that M has quite low running time. Thus, there is a computable function g such that if there are infinitely many n with $C^g(A \upharpoonright n) \geqslant n - O(1)$, then A is 2-random. Indeed, this fact is true of all sufficiently fast growing g. By an appropriate choice of universal Turing machine, there is a constant c such that we can take $g(n) = n^2 + c$.

Miller [276] proved the converse to Theorem 6.11.3, thus establishing the equivalence between being infinitely often C-random and being 2-random. Nies, Stephan, and Terwijn [308] obtained the same result independently, with a somewhat simpler proof that we now present.

Definition 6.11.4 (Nies, Stephan, and Terwijn [308]). A *compression function* is a one-to-one function $F : 2^{<\omega} \to 2^{<\omega}$ such that $|F(\sigma)| \leqslant C(\sigma)$ for all σ.

Lemma 6.11.5 (Nies, Stephan, and Terwijn [308]). *There is a low compression function.*

Proof. Let $\mathcal{V}$ be the universal Turing machine relative to which we define C. Let P be the Π_1^0 class of graphs of partial functions extending $\mathcal{V}$. Applying the low basis theorem, let A be a low element of P and let f be the partial function determined by A. Let $F(\sigma)$ be the length-lexicographically least τ such that $f(\tau) = \sigma$. Note that such a τ always exists because f extends $\mathcal{V}$, so F is total, and F is clearly one-to-one. Furthermore, $F \leqslant_{\mathrm{T}} A$, so F is low, and $F(\sigma)$ is at least as short as the shortest $\mathcal{V}$-program for σ, so $|F(\sigma)| \leqslant C(\sigma)$ for all σ. □

Theorem 6.11.6 (Miller [276], Nies, Stephan, and Terwijn [308]). *A set is 2-random iff it is infinitely often C-random.*

Proof. By Theorem 6.11.3, it is enough to assume that A is not infinitely often C-random and show that A is not 2-random. Let F be a low compression function. By the definition of compression function, $\lim_n n - |F(A \upharpoonright n)| \geqslant \lim_n n - C(A \upharpoonright n) = \infty$. Let $P_{i,m} = \{X : \forall n \geqslant m\, (|F(X \upharpoonright n)| < n - i)\}$, and let $U_i = \bigcup_m P_{i,m}$. The U_i are uniformly Σ_2^0 relative to F. Furthermore,

$$\begin{aligned}\mu(P_{i,m}) &\leqslant \mu(\{X : |F(X \upharpoonright m)| < m - i\}) \\ &= 2^{-m}|\{\sigma \in 2^m : |F(\sigma)| < m - i\}| < 2^{-m}2^{m-i} = 2^{-i}.\end{aligned}$$

Since $P_{i,0} \subseteq P_{i,1} \subseteq \cdots$, it follows that $\mu(U_i) \leqslant 2^{-i}$. Thus $U_0, U_1, \ldots$ is a Σ_2^0 test relative to F, and $A \in \bigcap_n U_n$. Thus A is not 2-random relative to F, and hence is not 1-random relative to F'. But F is low, so A is not 1-random relative to $\emptyset'$, and hence is not 2-random. □

By the comment following the proof of Theorem 6.11.3, we also have the following result, which can be a useful tool in studying 2-randomness. (We will give an example of its application in Section 8.21.1.)

Theorem 6.11.7 (Nies, Stephan, and Terwijn [308]). *For every sufficiently fast growing computable function g, a set A is 2-random iff there are infinitely many n such that $C^g(A \upharpoonright n) \geqslant n - O(1)$. By an appropriate choice of universal Turing machine, there is a c such that we can take "sufficiently fast growing" to mean that $g(n) \geqslant n^2 + c$.*

Turning to prefix-free complexity, we have the following analog of Definition 6.11.1.

Definition 6.11.8. A set A is *infinitely often strongly K-random* if there are infinitely many n such that $K(A \upharpoonright n) \geqslant n + K(n) - O(1)$.

By Corollary 4.3.3, if a set is infinitely often strongly K-random then it is infinitely often C-random, and hence 2-random. The following result is a partial converse.

Lemma 6.11.9 (Yu, Ding, and Downey [415], after Solovay [371]). *If a set is 3-random then it is infinitely often strongly K-random.*

Proof. Let $P_{i,m} = \{A : \forall n \geqslant m\,(K(A \upharpoonright n) \leqslant n + K(n) - i)\}$ and let $U_i = \bigcup_i P_{i,m}$. Since $\emptyset'$ can compute K, the U_i are uniformly Σ^0_3 classes. Furthermore, by Theorem 3.7.6,

$$\mu(P_{i,m}) \leqslant 2^{-m}|\{\sigma \in 2^m : K(\sigma) \leqslant m + K(m) - i\}| = O(2^{-i}).$$

Since $P_{i,0} \subseteq P_{i,1} \subseteq \cdots$, it follows that $\mu(U_i) = O(2^{-i})$. Thus there is a c such that $U_c, U_{c+1}, \ldots$ is a Σ^0_3 test. If A is not infinitely often strongly K-random, then $A \in \bigcap_{i \geqslant c} U_i$, so A is not 3-random. □

It had been a very interesting open question whether being infinitely often strongly K-random is equivalent to being 2-random, to being 3-random, or to neither. This problem was solved by Miller [277], who showed that a set is 2-random iff it is infinitely often strongly K-random. It follows that a set is infinitely often C-random iff it is infinitely often strongly K-random. We will prove Miller's result as Theorem 15.6.5. We delay the proof because it relies on notions of lowness not introduced until later in the book.

It is natural to ask whether there are unrelativized complexity characterizations (using either plain or prefix-free complexity) of 3-randomness, or even of n-randomness for larger n. Such characterizations can be obtained using the results in Section 10.2.4 below. Theorem 10.2.10, which is due to Vereshchagin [399], states that $C^{\emptyset'}(\sigma) = \limsup_n C(\sigma \mid n) \pm O(1)$. Using this limit complexity result, we can iterate the plain complexity characterization of 1-randomness given in Theorem 6.7.2, in relativized form, to characterize n-randomness in terms of unrelativized plain complexity. Theorem 10.2.11, which is due to Bienvenu, Muchnik, Shen, and Vereshchagin [42] and states that $K^{\emptyset'}(\sigma) = \limsup_n K(\sigma \mid n) \pm O(1)$, can be similarly used to give an unrelativized prefix-free complexity characterization of n-randomness. Whether there are simpler unrelativized complexity characterizations of n-randomness is open.

6.12 Randomness for other measures and degree-invariance

6.12.1 Generalizing randomness to other measures

We have restricted our development so far to the context of the uniform measure μ, but it is straightforward to adapt our definitions and many results to any other probability measure ν on Cantor space. When doing so, however, we need to take into account the complexity of ν. In this context, it is best to think of probability measures as generated by premeasures.

Definition 6.12.1. A (probability) *premeasure* is a function $\rho : 2^{<\omega} \to \mathbb{R}^{\geqslant 0}$ such that $\rho(\lambda) = 1$ and $\rho(\sigma 0) + \rho(\sigma 1) = \rho(\sigma)$ for all σ.[16]

For a premeasure ρ, let the function $\mu_\rho^* : 2^\omega \to \mathbb{R}^{\geqslant 0}$ be defined by letting $\mu_\rho^*(A)$ be the infimum of $\sum_{\sigma \in U} \rho(\sigma)$ over all U such that $A \subseteq [\![U]\!]$. Then μ_ρ^* is an outer measure. Let μ_ρ be the corresponding measure. We have $\mu_\rho([\![\sigma]\!]) = \rho(\sigma)$ for all σ. For instance, if $\rho(\sigma) = 2^{-|\sigma|}$ for all σ, then $\mu_\rho = \mu$. See for instance Royden [335] for more on basic measure theory.

Definition 6.12.2. The *rational representation* of a premeasure ρ is the set $\{(\sigma, r, q) : \rho(\sigma) \in (r, q)\} \subset 2^{<\omega} \times \mathbb{Q} \times \mathbb{Q}$. We identify ρ with this representation, which allows us to talk about the degree of ρ and relativize concepts to ρ.

A measure ν on 2^ω is *computable* if $\nu = \mu_\rho$ for some computable ρ.

We can now make the following definition. Many other definitions and results can be adapted in the same way (for instance, to define n-μ_ρ-randomness).

Definition 6.12.3. Let ρ be a premeasure.

(i) A *Martin-Löf μ_ρ-test* is a sequence $\{U_n\}_{n \in \omega}$ of uniformly $\Sigma_1^{0,\rho}$ classes such that $\mu_\rho(U_n) \leqslant 2^{-n}$ for all n.

(ii) A class $C \subset 2^\omega$ is *Martin-Löf μ_ρ-null* if there is a μ_ρ-Martin-Löf test $\{U_n\}_{n \in \omega}$ such that $C \subseteq \bigcap_n U_n$.

(iii) A set $A \in 2^\omega$ is *Martin-Löf μ_ρ-random*, or *1-μ_ρ-random*, if $\{A\}$ is not Martin-Löf μ_ρ-null.[17]

When we are given a measure ν, we assume we have a particular premeasure ρ such that $\nu = \mu_\rho$, and hence write simply "1-ν-random". This notation makes particular sense when ν is computable, in which case we always assume that the corresponding ρ is computable, making the classes in the definition of Martin-Löf ν-test actual Σ_1^0 classes.

Clearly, randomness is not invariant under change of measure. For example, let ν be defined by letting $\nu([\![\sigma 0]\!]) = \frac{\nu([\![\sigma]\!])}{3}$ and $\nu([\![\sigma 1]\!]) = \frac{2\nu([\![\sigma]\!])}{3}$. Then no 1-random set is 1-ν-random. But in this book we will often be more interested in degrees than in individual sets, which leads to the natural question of whether the 1-random and 1-ν-random *degrees* are the same.

Even among computable measures, there are some that will lead to different 1-random degrees than μ. For example, we can simply concentrate

[16] These are of course related to the continuous semimeasures of Section 3.16.

[17] It seems reasonable to incorporate the complexity of ρ into the definition of 1-μ_ρ-randomness, but this approach is not without its drawbacks for noncomputable ρ. See Reimann [326] for further discussion of this issue. We will not deal with noncomputable measures except in Section 8.7.

all our measure on a computable set, for instance defining $\nu([\![0^n]\!]) = 1$ for all n and $\nu([\![\sigma]\!]) = 0$ for all other σ. Then 0^ω is a computable 1-ν-random set. To isolate this kind of example, define a measure ν to be *atomic* if $\nu(\{A\}) > 0$ for some $A \in 2^\omega$. We call such an A an *atom* of ν. A nonatomic measure is called a *continuous* measure. Our example above is an extreme example of an atomic measure. In particular, it is a *trivial* measure, which is a measure ν such that $\sum_{A \in \mathcal{A}} \nu(\{A\}) = 1$, where $\mathcal{A}$ is the collection of atoms of ν.

As it turns out, computability and continuity are enough to ensure invariance. In the following subsection, we will prove that if ν is computable and continuous, then a degree is 1-ν-random iff it is 1-random.

As this material is not central to this book, we will do no more than touch on it. Considerations arising from working with measures other than the uniform measure are more fully discussed in van Lambalgen [397], Li and Vitányi [248], and Reimann [326].

One further use we will make of this material, however, is in Section 8.6, where we will prove Demuth's remarkable theorem that if A is tt-below a 1-random set, then the wtt-degree of A contains a 1-random set, which can be seen as a kind of downwards closure of 1-randomness. We will also revisit it briefly in Section 8.7, where we will prove the result due to Reimann and Slaman [327] that if A is noncomputable then there is a ν such that A is 1-ν-random and A is not an atom of ν, and will discuss related results.

6.12.2 Computable measures and representing reals

In this subsection, we will show that if ν is computable and continuous, then a degree is 1-ν-random iff it is 1-random. This result was first proved by Levin (see [425]), but also appears in Kautz' dissertation [200], whose account we follow. The key intuition we will exploit is that the identification of 2^ω with $[0,1]$ actually depends on the measure. That is, which subsets of 2^ω we should identify with what intervals depends on the choice of measure. In the usual representation, if $A \in 2^\omega$ begins with 10, say, then the 1 corresponds to the fact that the real α identified with A is in $[\frac{1}{2}, 1]$ and the 0 to the fact that it is in $[\frac{1}{2}, \frac{3}{4}]$. That is, looking at the first n bits of A corresponds to knowing α to within 2^{-n}, by computing an interval of length 2^{-n} within which α must lie. Now suppose that ν is the measure mentioned above corresponding to the distribution where 1's are twice as likely as 0's (that is, the measure defined by $\nu([\![\sigma 0]\!]) = \frac{\nu([\![\sigma]\!])}{3}$ and $\nu([\![\sigma 1]\!]) = \frac{2\nu([\![\sigma]\!])}{3}$). Then the first bit of A being 1 indicates that the real identified with A is in $[\frac{1}{3}, 1]$, while the second bit being 0 indicates that it is in $[\frac{1}{3}, \frac{5}{9}]$. Thus we have the following definition, where from now on we fix a computable probability measure ν on 2^ω and a corresponding computable premeasure ρ.

Definition 6.12.4. For a string σ, let $L_\sigma = \{\tau : |\tau| = |\sigma| \wedge \tau <_{\mathrm{L}} \sigma\}$. The *interval determined by σ with respect to ν*, denoted by $(\sigma)_\nu$, is the interval $[l, r]$ where $l = \sum_{\tau \in L_\sigma} \nu(\llbracket \tau \rrbracket)$ and $r = l + \nu(\llbracket \sigma \rrbracket)$.

Notice that $\mu((\sigma)_\nu) = \nu(\llbracket \sigma \rrbracket)$.

We can define a computable function $(\sigma, s) \mapsto \rho_s(\sigma)$ such that $\rho_s(\sigma)$ is a dyadic rational and $|\rho(\sigma) - \rho_s(\sigma)| < 2^{-s}$ for all s and σ. Using this function, we can define a computable approximation to $(\sigma)_\nu$ as follows.

Definition 6.12.5. For $\sigma \in 2^k$, let $(\sigma)_{\nu,s}$ be the interval $[l, r]$ where $l = \sum_{\tau \in L_\sigma} \rho_{s+k+2}(\tau) - 2^{-(s+2)}$ and $r = l + \rho_{s+k+2}(\sigma) + 2^{-(s+2)}$.

Note that $(\sigma)_{\nu,s} \supseteq (\sigma)_\nu$, and the length of $(\sigma)_{\nu,s}$ exceeds that of $(\sigma)_\nu$ by at most 2^{-s}.

For a real number $\alpha \in [0, 1]$, suppose that for each n, there is a unique string σ of length n with $\alpha \in (\sigma)_\nu$. Then we define the sequence *representing α in 2^ω*, denoted by $\mathrm{seq}_\nu(\alpha)$, as the unique A such that $\alpha \in (A \upharpoonright n)_\nu$ for all n. For the uniform measure, if α is not a dyadic rational, then $\mathrm{seq}_\mu(\alpha)$ is defined, and is equal to α thought of as an element of 2^ω. Note that, since ν is computable, if α is not computable then $\mathrm{seq}_\nu(\alpha)$ is defined.

The following lemma is explicit in Kautz [200], but is also implicit in Levin's work, such as in Zvonkin and Levin [425].

Lemma 6.12.6 (Kautz [200], Levin, see [425]). *If $A = \mathrm{seq}_\nu(\alpha)$ is defined then*

(i) *$A \leqslant_{\mathrm{T}} \alpha$, and*

(ii) *if A is not an atom of ν then $\alpha \leqslant_{\mathrm{T}} A$.*

Proof. (i) For each n, we need to compute the unique string $\sigma_n \in 2^n$ such that $\alpha \in (\sigma_n)_\nu$. Suppose we have computed σ_n. Search for an $i < 2$ and an s such that $\alpha \notin (\sigma_n i)_{\nu,s}$ and let $\sigma_{n+1} = \sigma(1-i)$.

(ii) Given n, search for an s such that $\mu((A \upharpoonright s)_{\nu,s}) < 2^{-n}$, which must exist since A is not an atom of ν. Then we have an approximation of α up to 2^{-n}. □

The following lemma says that, even in the case of atomic measures, noncomputable sets are still well-behaved. This proof was communicated to us by Jan Reimann.

Lemma 6.12.7 (Kautz [200], Levin, see [425]). *If A is noncomputable then* $\lim_s \nu(\llbracket A \upharpoonright s \rrbracket) = 0$. *Hence all atoms of a computable measure are computable.*

Proof. Suppose that $\lim_s \nu(\llbracket A \upharpoonright s \rrbracket) > \varepsilon > 0$. Let $T = \{\sigma : \rho_{|\sigma|}(\sigma) > \varepsilon - 2^{-|\sigma|}\}$. Then T is a computable tree and $A \in [T]$. But if $B \in [T]$ then $\nu(\{B\}) \geqslant \varepsilon$, so $[T]$ is finite. Hence A is an isolated path in a computable tree, and hence is computable. □

If α is computable, then so is $\mathrm{seq}_\nu(\alpha)$, but if ν is atomic and α is noncomputable, it is still possible for $\mathrm{seq}_\nu(\alpha)$ to be an atom of ν and hence computable. If ν is continuous, however, then that cannot be the case, so we have the following.

Corollary 6.12.8 (Kautz [200], Levin, see [425]). *If ν is continuous and $\mathrm{seq}_\nu(\alpha)$ is defined then $\mathrm{seq}_\nu(\alpha) \equiv_{\mathrm{T}} \alpha$.*

The following is the main result of this subsection.

Theorem 6.12.9 (Levin, see [425], see also Kautz [200]).

(i) *If α is 1-random, then $\mathrm{seq}_\nu(\alpha)$ is 1-ν-random.*

(ii) *If $\mathrm{seq}_\nu(\alpha)$ is 1-ν-random and noncomputable, then α is 1-random.*

(iii) *If ν is continuous and $\mathbf{a} > \mathbf{0}$ then $\mathbf{a}$ contains a 1-random set iff $\mathbf{a}$ contains a 1-ν-random set.*

Proof. (i) Suppose that $\mathrm{seq}_\nu(\alpha)$ is not 1-ν-random. Let $\{U_i\}_{i\in\omega}$ be a Martin-Löf ν-test covering $\mathrm{seq}_\nu(\alpha)$. Let $V_0, V_1, \ldots$ be uniformly c.e. sets of generators for the U_i. We will define a Martin-Löf (μ-)test $\{\widehat{U}_i\}_{i\in\omega}$ covering α, thus showing that α is not 1-random. For each i and k, proceed as follows. Let σ be the kth string in the enumeration of V_{i+1}. Compute $\tau_0, \ldots, \tau_n$ such that $(\sigma)_{\nu,k+i+3} = \bigcup_{j\leqslant n}(\tau_j)_\mu$ (which is possible because the endpoints of $(\sigma)_{\nu,k+i+3}$ are dyadic rationals). Put each $[\![\tau_j]\!]$ into $\widehat{U}_i$. Clearly the $\widehat{U}_i$ are uniformly Σ^0_1, and

$$\mu(\widehat{U}_i) \leqslant \mu(U_{i+1}) + \sum_k 2^{-(k+i+2)} \leqslant 2^{-(i+1)} + 2^{-(i+1)} = 2^{-i}.$$

Thus the $\widehat{U}_i$ form a Martin-Löf test. For each i, there is a $\sigma \in V_{i+1}$ such that $\sigma \preccurlyeq \mathrm{seq}_\nu(\alpha)$. Say that σ is the kth string in the enumeration of V_{i+1}. Then $\alpha \in (\sigma)_\nu \subseteq (\sigma)_{\nu,k+i+2}$, so $\alpha \in \widehat{U}_i$. Thus $\alpha \in \bigcap_i \widehat{U}_i$.

(ii) Now suppose that α is not 1-random and $\mathrm{seq}_\nu(\alpha)$ is not computable. Let $\{U_i\}_{i\in\omega}$ be a Martin-Löf test covering α. Let $V_0, V_1, \ldots$ be uniformly c.e. sets of generators for the U_i. For each i and k, proceed as follows. Let σ be the kth string in the enumeration of V_{i+1}. Let p and q be such that $[p, q] = (\sigma)_\mu$, and let $I_k = [p - 2^{-(i+k+3)}, q + 2^{-(i+k+3)}]$. Let

$$\widehat{U}_i = \bigcup_k \{[\![\tau]\!] : \exists s\, ((\tau)_{\nu,s} \subseteq I_k)\}.$$

Clearly the $\widehat{U}_i$ are uniformly Σ^0_1. Since $\nu([\![\tau]\!]) = \mu((\tau)_\nu)$,

$$\nu(\widehat{U}_i) \leqslant \sum_k \mu(I_k) \leqslant \mu(U_{i+1}) + \sum_k 2^{-i+k+2} \leqslant 2^{-(i+1)} + 2^{-(i+1)} = 2^{-i}.$$

Thus the $\widehat{U}_i$ form a Martin-Löf ν-test, and we are left with showing that $\mathrm{seq}_\nu(\alpha) \in \widehat{U}_i$ for all i.

The only difficulty here is that ν may be atomic, but we can use the hypothesis that $\mathrm{seq}_\nu(\alpha)$ is not computable. Fix i and let $\sigma \in V_{i+1}$ be such that $\sigma \prec \alpha$. Suppose σ is the kth string enumerated into V_{i+1}. Since $\mathrm{seq}_\nu(\alpha)$ is not computable, it is not an atom of ν, so there is a $\tau \prec \mathrm{seq}_\nu(\alpha)$ such that $\mu((\tau)_\nu) = \nu(\llbracket\tau\rrbracket) < 2^{-(i+k+4)}$. Then there is an s such that $\mu((\tau)_{\nu,s}) < 2^{-(i+k+3)}$. Since $\alpha \in (\tau)_\nu \subseteq (\tau)_{\nu,s}$, letting I_k be as above, we have $(\tau)_{\nu,s} \subset [\alpha - 2^{-(i+k+3)}, \alpha + 2^{-(i+k+3)}] \subset I_k$, whence $\mathrm{seq}_\nu(\alpha)\llbracket\tau\rrbracket \subseteq \widehat{U}_i$.

(iii) now follows from Lemmas 6.12.6 and 6.12.7. □

For atomic measures ν, the behavior of 1-ν-random sets can be strange. For instance, Kautz [200] showed that there is a nontrivial computable measure ν such that no noncomputable Δ^0_2 set is 1-ν-random. (Recall that ν is trivial if $\sum_{A\in\mathcal{A}} \nu(\{A\}) = 1$, where $\mathcal{A}$ is the collection of atoms of ν.) However, once we get to the level of 2-randomness, such problems disappear.

Theorem 6.12.10 (Kautz [200]). *Let ν and ν' be nontrivial computable measures. Then every noncomputable degree containing a 2-ν'-random set contains a 2-ν-random set.*

Proof. Let $A >_{\mathrm{T}} \emptyset$ be 2-ν'-random. Let $B \in \bigcap_n (A \upharpoonright n)_{\nu'}$. Then $A = \mathrm{seq}_{\nu'} B$, since A is not computable. Thus, by the relativized form of Theorem 6.12.9, B is 2-random. It is enough to show that there is a 2-ν-random set $C \equiv_{\mathrm{T}} B$.

Let

$$S = \{\alpha : \mathrm{seq}_\nu(\alpha)\downarrow \wedge \forall \varepsilon > 0\, \exists n\, (\nu(\mathrm{seq}_\nu(\alpha) \upharpoonright n) < \varepsilon)\}.$$

It is easy to see that $\mu(S) > 0$, since ν is nontrivial. Let $\{U_i\}_{i\in\omega}$ be a universal Martin-Löf test. Let $P_i = \overline{U_i}$, and let k be large enough so that $\mu(P_k) > 1 - \mu(S)$. Now, P_k is a Π^0_1 class containing only 1-random sets, and if α is 1-random then α is noncomputable, and hence $\mathrm{seq}_\nu(\alpha)$ is defined. Thus

$$P_k \cap S = P_k \cap \{\alpha : \forall \varepsilon > 0\, \exists n (\nu(\mathrm{seq}_\nu(\alpha) \upharpoonright n) < \varepsilon)\},$$

which is clearly a Π^0_2 class. Since this class has positive measure, by Lemma 6.10.2 it contains an $\alpha \equiv_{\mathrm{T}} B$. Let $C = \mathrm{seq}_\nu(\alpha)$. By Theorem 6.12.9, C is 2-ν-random. Furthermore, by Lemma 6.12.6, $C \equiv_{\mathrm{T}} \alpha \equiv_{\mathrm{T}} B$, since the fact that $\alpha \in S$ implies that C is not an atom of ν. □

7

Other Notions of Algorithmic Randomness

In [348, 349], Schnorr analyzed his characterization of 1-randomness in terms of c.e. martingales (Theorem 6.3.4). He argued that this result demonstrates a failure of 1-randomness to capture the intuition behind Martin-Löf's original definition, because effective randomness should be concerned with defeating *computable* betting strategies rather than computably enumerable ones, as the latter are fundamentally asymmetric, in the same way that a c.e. set is semi-decidable rather than decidable.[1] One can make a similar argument about Martin-Löf tests being effectively null (in the sense that we know how fast their components converge to zero), but not effectively given, in the sense that the test sets themselves are not computable, but only Σ^0_1.[2]

We will begin this chapter by looking at two natural notions of effective randomness introduced by Schnorr [348, 349] with this critique in mind. We will then discuss several further notions, including weak n-randomness, introduced by Kurtz [228], and nonmonotonic randomness, which modifies the concept of betting strategies to allow for betting on the bits of a sequence out of order.

[1] In Section 6.3.4, we saw how to replace c.e. martingales by computable martingale processes. Schnorr did not have this result available, of course, and one might use it to argue against his critique, particularly in light of Theorem 6.3.19.

[2] Some confusion may have been created by the fact that every Σ^0_1 class has a computable set of generators, but there is a distinction to be made between general Σ^0_1 classes and those with computable measures. The former behave much more like c.e. objects than like computable ones.

R.G. Downey and D. Hirschfeldt, *Algorithmic Randomness and Complexity*, Theory and Applications of Computability, DOI 10.1007/978-0-387-68441-3_7,

7.1 Computable randomness and Schnorr randomness

7.1.1 Basics

As mentioned in Section 6.3.1, c.e. martingales are not the most obvious effectivization of the notion of martingale. It is natural to investigate, as Schnorr [348, 349] did, what happens if we define randomness with respect to *computable* martingales, which are those that are computable functions in the sense of Definition 5.2.1.[3]

Definition 7.1.1 (Schnorr [348, 349]). A set is *computably random* if no computable martingale succeeds on it.

In this definition, we can take our martingales to be rational-valued. (Recall that when we say that a rational-valued function f is computable, we mean that there is an algorithm to determine $f(n)$ given n, not just that f is a computable function in the sense of Definition 5.2.1 that happens to take values in $\mathbb{Q}$.)

Proposition 7.1.2 (Schnorr [348, 349]). *For each computable martingale d there is a computable martingale $f : 2^{<\omega} \to \mathbb{Q}^{\geqslant 0}$ such that $S[f] = S[d]$. In fact, $d(\sigma) < f(\sigma) < d(\sigma) + 1$ for all σ.*

Proof. Let $f(\lambda)$ be a rational strictly between $d(\lambda)$ and $d(\lambda) + 1$. Assume that we have defined $f(\sigma)$ to be a rational strictly between $d(\sigma)$ and $d(\sigma)+1$. It is easy to check that we can find rationals r_0 and r_1 such that $f(\sigma) = \frac{r_0+r_1}{2}$ and for each $i < 2$, we have $d(\sigma i) < r_i < d(\sigma i) + 1$. Let $f(\sigma i) = r_i$. Now f is a computable rational-valued martingale, and clearly $S[f] = S[d]$. □

There is also a somewhat surprising characterization of computable randomness in terms of the mere existence of limits of martingales. When we say a limit exists, we mean that it is finite.

Theorem 7.1.3 (Folklore). *A is computably random iff $\lim_n d(A \upharpoonright n)$ exists for all computable martingales d.*

Proof. If $\lim_n d(A \upharpoonright n)$ exists for all computable martingales d then clearly A is computably random.

For the nontrivial direction, suppose that A is computably random but d is a computable martingale such that $\lim_n d(A \upharpoonright n)$ fails to exist. Since $\limsup_n d(A \upharpoonright n) < \infty$, there are rationals $r < s$ such that there are

[3]Miniaturizations of the notion of computable randomness form the basis of the theory of resource-bounded measure; see for instance Ambos-Spies and Mayordomo [10] and Lutz [251].

infinitely many n with $d(A \upharpoonright n) < r$ and infinitely many n with $d(A \upharpoonright n) > s$.

We define a new computable martingale $\widehat{d}$. We begin with $\widehat{d}(\lambda) = 1$. Along a sequence B, we bet as follows. We bet evenly until (if ever) we find an n_0 such that $d(B \upharpoonright n_0) < r$, then follow d's bets until (if ever) we find an n_1 such that $d(B \upharpoonright n_1) > s$, then bet evenly until we find an n_2 such that $d(B \upharpoonright n_2) < r$, and so on.

If $B = A$ then we will find such $n_0, n_1, \ldots$. Between $A \upharpoonright n_{2i}$ and $A \upharpoonright n_{2i+1}$, we increase our capital by a factor greater than $\frac{s}{r}$, while between $A \upharpoonright n_{2i+1}$ and $A \upharpoonright n_{2i+2}$, we do not change our capital. Thus $\widehat{d}$ succeeds on A, contradicting the computable randomness of A. □

According to Schnorr, however, computable randomness is not quite effective enough, because given a set that is not computably random, we do have a computable strategy for making arbitrarily much money while betting on its bits, but we may not be able to know ahead of time how long it will take us to increase our capital to a given amount. In a way, this situation is similar to having a computable approximation to a real without necessarily having a computable modulus of convergence, which we know is a characterization of the real being Δ^0_2, rather than computable. Thus we have the following weaker notion of randomness.

Definition 7.1.4 (Schnorr [348, 349]). (i) An *order* is an unbounded nondecreasing function from $\mathbb{N}$ to $\mathbb{N}$.[4] For a (super)martingale d and an order h, let $S_h[d] = \{X : \limsup_n \frac{d(X \upharpoonright n)}{h(n)} = \infty\}$. We say that this (super)martingale *h-succeeds* on the elements of $S_h[d]$, and call $S_h[d]$ the *h-success set* of d.

(ii) A set A is *Schnorr random* if $A \notin S_h[d]$ for every computable martingale d and every computable order h.

Note that if $\limsup_n \frac{d(X \upharpoonright n)}{g(n)} > 0$ for an order g, then $X \in S_h[d]$ for any sufficiently slower growing order h.

One might wonder whether the limsup in the above definition should not be a liminf, which would mean we *really* know how fast we can increase our capital. (Indeed, in that case, for each X we could replace h by a suitable finite modification g such that if $\liminf_n \frac{d(X \upharpoonright n)}{h(n)} = \infty$ then $d(X \upharpoonright n) \geqslant g(n)$ for all n.) As it turns out, making this modification leads to a characterization of the notion of *weak 1-randomness*, as we will see in Theorem 7.2.13. This notion is strictly weaker than Schnorr randomness, and is in fact weak enough that it is questionable whether it is really a notion of randomness at all (see Section 8.20.2).

Schnorr randomness also has a pleasing characterization in terms of tests.

[4]An "Ordnungsfunktion" in Schnorr's terminology is always computable, but we prefer to leave the complexity of orders unspecified in general.

Definition 7.1.5 (Schnorr [349]). (i) A Martin-Löf test $\{U_n\}_{n\in\omega}$ is a *Schnorr test* if the measures $\mu(U_n)$ are uniformly computable.

(ii) A class $C \subset 2^\omega$ is *Schnorr null* if there is a Schnorr test $\{U_n\}_{n\in\omega}$ such that $C \subseteq \bigcap_n U_n$.

It is sometimes convenient to take an alternate definition of a Schnorr test as a Martin-Löf test $\{U_n\}_{n\in\omega}$ such that $\mu(U_n) = 2^{-n}$ for all n. As we now show, these definitions yield the same null sets, so we use them interchangeably.

Proposition 7.1.6 (Schnorr [349]). *Let $\{U_n\}_{n\in\omega}$ be a Schnorr test. There is a Schnorr test $\{V_n\}_{n\in\omega}$ such that $\mu(V_n) = 2^{-n}$ and $\bigcap_n U_n \subseteq \bigcap_n V_n$.*

Proof. For each n, proceed as follows. Let $r_0 < r_1 < \cdots < \mu(U_n)$ be a computable sequence of rationals such that $\mu(U_n) - r_i \leqslant 2^{-i}$. At stage s, first ensure that $V_n[s] \supseteq U_n[s]$. If there is an i such that $\mu(V_n[s]) < 2^{-n} - 2^{-i}$ and $\mu(U_n[s]) \geqslant r_i$, then add basic open sets to $V_n[s]$ to ensure that its measure is equal to $2^{-n} - 2^{-i}$. It is easy to check that this action ensures that $V_n \supseteq U_n$ and $\mu(V_n) = 2^{-n}$. □

Theorem 7.1.7 (Schnorr [349]). *A class $C \subset 2^\omega$ is Schnorr null iff there are a computable martingale d and a computable order h such that $C \subseteq S_h[d]$. Thus, a set A is Schnorr random iff $\{A\}$ is not Schnorr null.*

Proof. ($\Leftarrow$) Let d be a computable martingale and h a computable order. We build a Schnorr null set containing $S_h[d]$. By Proposition 7.1.2, we may assume that d is rational-valued. We may also assume that $d(\lambda) \in (0,1)$.

Let $U_i = \bigcup\{[\![\sigma]\!] : d(\sigma) > h(|\sigma|) > 2^i\}$. The U_i are uniformly Σ^0_1 classes, and $\mu(U_i) \leqslant 2^{-i}$ by Kolmogorov's Inequality (Theorem 6.3.3). To compute $\mu(U_i)$ to within 2^{-c}, let l be such that $h(l) > 2^c$. Let

$$V_i = \bigcup\{[\![\sigma]\!] : d(\sigma) > h(|\sigma|) > 2^i \wedge |\sigma| \leqslant l\}.$$

Then $U_i \setminus V_i \subseteq U_c$. Thus $\mu(U_i) - \mu(V_i) \leqslant \mu(U_c) \leqslant 2^{-c}$, so $\{U_i\}_{i\in\omega}$ is a Schnorr test.

Suppose $A \in S_h[d]$. Then $d(A \upharpoonright n) > h(n)$ for infinitely many n, so for each i there is an n such that $d(A \upharpoonright n) > h(n) > 2^i$, whence $A \in U_i$. Thus $S_h[d] \subseteq \bigcap_i U_i$.

($\Rightarrow$) Let $\{U_n\}_{n\in\omega}$ be a Schnorr test. We build a computable martingale d and a computable order h such that $\bigcap_n U_n \subseteq S_h[d]$. Let $\{R_n\}_{n\in\omega}$ be uniformly computable prefix-free sets of strings such that $U_n = [\![R_n]\!]$. Let $R_n^k = \{\sigma : \sigma \in R_n \wedge |\sigma| \geqslant k\}$.

Since the measures $\mu(U_n)$ are uniformly computable and tend to 0 effectively, there is a computable order g such that $\sum_n \mu([\![R_n^k]\!]) \leqslant 2^{-2g(k)}$ for all k. Then

$$\sum_n \sum_{\sigma\in R_n^k} 2^{g(k)-|\sigma|} = 2^{g(k)} \sum_n \sum_{\sigma\in R_n^k} 2^{-|\sigma|} = 2^{g(k)} \sum_n \mu([\![R_n^k]\!]) \leqslant 2^{-g(k)},$$

so there is a computable order f such that $\sum_n \sum_{\sigma \in R_n^{f(k)}} 2^{g(k)-|\sigma|} < 2^{-k}$.

For each n and k, define $d_{n,k}$ as follows. For each σ in $R_n^{f(k)}$, add $2^{g(k)}$ to the value of $d_{n,k}(\tau)$ for each $\tau \succcurlyeq \sigma$ and add $2^{g(k)-|\sigma|+i}$ to $d_{n,k}(\sigma \upharpoonright i)$ for each $i < |\sigma|$. This definition ensures that each $d_{n,k}$ is a martingale. Furthermore, $d_{n,k}(\lambda) = \sum_{\sigma \in R_n^{f(k)}} 2^{g(k)-|\sigma|}$, so $\sum_{k,n} d_{n,k}(\lambda) \leqslant \sum_k 2^{-k} < \infty$, whence $d = \sum_{n,k} d_{n,k}$ is a martingale.

If $A \in \bigcap_n U_n$ then for each n there is an i such that $A \upharpoonright i \in R_n$. Let n be large enough so that $i \geqslant f(0)$. Then $A \upharpoonright i \in R_n^{f(k)}$ for the largest k such that $f(k) \leqslant i$, so $d(A \upharpoonright i) \geqslant d_{n,k}(A \upharpoonright i) \geqslant 2^{g(k)}$. Let $\widehat{h}(i) = 2^{g(k)}$ for the largest k such that $f(k) \leqslant i$. Then $\limsup_i \frac{d(A \upharpoonright i)}{\widehat{h}(i)} \geqslant 1$, so for any computable order h that grows sufficiently slower than $\widehat{h}$, we have $A \in S_h[d]$. So we are left with showing that d is computable.

To compute $d(\sigma)$ to within 2^{-c}, proceed as follows. There are only finitely many n and k such that R_n^k contains a substring of σ, and we can find all of them and compute the amount q added to $d(\sigma)$ when substrings of σ enter R_n^k's. The rest of the value of each $d_{n,k}(\sigma)$ is equal to $r_{n,k} = \sum_{\tau \in R_n^{f(k)} \wedge \tau \succ \sigma} 2^{g(k)-|\tau|+|\sigma|}$. We can compute an $s_{n,k}$ such that $r_{n,k} - \sum_{\tau \in R_n^{f(k)}[s_{n,k}] \wedge \tau \succ \sigma} 2^{g(k)-|\tau|+|\sigma|} < 2^{-(c+n+k+2)}$. Then

$$d(\sigma) - \left(q + \sum_{n,k} \sum_{\substack{\tau \succ \sigma \\ \tau \in R_n^{f(k)}[s_{n,k}]}} 2^{g(k)-|\tau|+|\sigma|} \right) < \sum_{n,k} 2^{-(c+n+k+2)} = 2^{-c}.$$

□

Instead of looking at the rate of success of a martingale, we can look at the dual notion of how long it takes for that martingale to accrue a given amount of capital. Franklin and Stephan [158] observed this fact as part of a more technical result that will be useful in Section 12.2. Recall that a martingale d is said to have the savings property if $d(\sigma\tau) + 2 \geqslant d(\sigma)$ for all σ and τ.

Theorem 7.1.8 (Franklin and Stephan [158], after Schnorr [348, 349]). *The following are equivalent.*

(i) *A is not Schnorr random.*

(ii) *There is a computable martingale d and a computable function f such that $\exists^\infty n\,(d(A \upharpoonright f(n)) \geqslant n)$.*

(iii) *There is a computable martingale d' with the savings property and a computable function f' such that $\exists^\infty n\,(d'(A \upharpoonright f'(n)) \geqslant n)$.*

Proof. Clearly (iii) implies (ii). We begin by showing that (ii) implies (iii), with a version of the savings trick. By Proposition 7.1.2, we may assume that d is rational-valued.

Define computable martingales $d_0, d_1, \ldots$ as follows. Let $d_k(\lambda) = d(\lambda)$. If $d(\sigma) \leqslant 2^k$, then let $d_k(\sigma i) = d(\sigma i)$ for $i = 0, 1$. Otherwise, let $d_k(\sigma i) = d_k(\sigma)$ for $i = 0, 1$. Let $d' = \sum_k 2^{-k} d_k$. Then d' is a computable martingale. Let $f'(n) = \max\{f(m) : m \leqslant n\}$.

By (ii), there are infinitely many n such that $d(A \upharpoonright f(m)) \geqslant m$ for some $m \in [2^n, 2^{n+1})$. For any such n and m, and all $k \leqslant n$, we have $d_k(A \upharpoonright f(m)) \geqslant 2^k$, whence $d_k(A \upharpoonright f'(n)) \geqslant 2^k$, by the definition of d_k and the fact that $f'(n) \geqslant f(m)$. Thus, for any such n,

$$d'(A \upharpoonright f'(n)) \geqslant \sum_{k \leqslant n} 2^{-k} d_k(A \upharpoonright f'(n)) \geqslant \sum_{k \leqslant n} 2^{-k} 2^k \geqslant n.$$

To complete the proof that (ii) implies (iii), we need to show that d' has the savings property. Fix σ and τ and choose n maximal with $2^n \geqslant d(\sigma)$. For all $k \geqslant n$, the martingale d_k follows d at σ, whereas for $k < n$, the martingale d_k is constant above σ. Therefore the following two equations hold.

$$d'(\sigma) = \sum_{k<n} 2^{-k} d_k(\sigma) + \sum_{k \geqslant n} 2^{-k} d(\sigma)$$

and

$$d'(\sigma\tau) = \sum_{k<n} 2^{-k} d_k(\sigma) + \sum_{k \geqslant n} 2^{-k} d(\sigma\tau).$$

Now, $\sum_{k \geqslant n} 2^{-k} d(\sigma) \leqslant \sum_{k \geqslant n} 2^{-k} 2^n = 2$, so $d'(\sigma\tau) + 2 \geqslant d'(\sigma)$.

We now show that (iii) implies (i). First note that the function f' in (iii) can be chosen to be strictly increasing. To see this fact, let $\widehat{f}'(0) = f(0) + f(1) + f(2)$ and $\widehat{f}'(n+1) = f'(n+3) + \widehat{f}'(n) + 1$. There exist infinitely many n such that $d'(A \upharpoonright f'(n+2)) \geqslant n+2$, so there exist infinitely many n such that $d'(A \upharpoonright \widehat{f}'(n)) \geqslant n$, since $\widehat{f}'(n) \geqslant f'(n+2)$ and d' has the savings property. Now let $g(n)$ be the largest m such that $\widehat{f}'(m) < n$ (or 0 if there is none). There are infinitely many m such that $d'(A \upharpoonright \widehat{f}'(m)) \geqslant m$, and for each such m, letting $n = \widehat{f}'(m)$, we have $d'(A \upharpoonright n) \geqslant g(n)$. So d' and g witness the fact that A is not Schnorr random.

To complete the proof, we show that (i) implies (ii). Suppose that A is not Schnorr random, so there is a computable martingale c and a computable order g such that $c(A \upharpoonright n) \geqslant g(n)$ for infinitely many n. We can use the same construction we used to obtain d' from d above to build a new martingale c' such that $c'(\sigma\tau) \geqslant m$ for all τ whenever $c(\sigma) > 2^{m+4}$. Let $f(m) = \min\{n : g(n) > 2^{m+4}\}$. There are infinitely many m such that, for some $n \in (f(m), f(m+1)]$, we have $c(A \upharpoonright n) \geqslant g(n)$. By the properties of c', we have $c'(A \upharpoonright n\tau) \geqslant m$ for all τ and, in particular, $c'(A \upharpoonright f(m)) \geqslant m$. □

Many notions connected with 1-randomness can be adapted to Schnorr randomness if the right way to "increase the effectivity" is found. For example, the following is a characterization of Schnorr randomness analogous to

Solovay's Definition 6.2.7. (It is equivalent to a definition in terms of martingales mentioned in Wang [405].) We will see another example in Section 7.1.3.

Definition 7.1.9 (Downey and Griffiths [109]). A *total Solovay test* is a sequence $\{S_n\}_{n\in\omega}$ of uniformly Σ^0_1 classes such that $\sum_n \mu(S_n)$ is finite and a computable real. A set A *passes* this test if it is in only finitely many of the S_n.

Theorem 7.1.10 (Downey and Griffiths [109]). *A set is Schnorr random iff it passes all total Solovay tests.*

Proof. A Schnorr test is a total Solovay test, so if a set passes all total Solovay tests then it is Schnorr random. Now let A be Schnorr random and let $\{S_n\}_{n\in\omega}$ be a total Solovay test. The measures $\mu(S_n)$ are uniformly computable, since they are uniformly left-c.e. and their sum is finite and computable. There is an m such that $\sum_{n>m} \mu(S_n) < 1$. Let

$$U_k = [\![\{\sigma : \exists^{\geqslant 2^k} n > m\,([\![\sigma]\!] \in S_n)\}]\!].$$

The U_k are uniformly Σ^0_1, and it is not hard to see that $\mu(U_k) \leqslant 2^{-k}\sum_{n>m}\mu(S_n) < 2^{-k}$.

To compute $\mu(U_k)$ to within 2^{-c}, let l be such that $\sum_{n\geqslant l}\mu(S_n) < 2^{-(c+1)}$. For each $n \in (m,l)$, find a finite set $F_n \subset 2^{<\omega}$ such that $[\![F_n]\!] \subseteq S_n$ and $\mu(S_n \setminus [\![F]\!]) < 2^{-(c+n+1)}$. Let $V_k = [\![\{\sigma : \exists^{\geqslant 2^k} n > m\,(\sigma \in F_n)\}]\!]$. Then $V_k \subseteq U_k$, and

$$\mu(U_k) - \mu(V_k) \leqslant \sum_{n\geqslant l}\mu(S_n) + \sum_{m<n<l}\mu(S_n \setminus [\![F_n]\!])$$
$$< 2^{-(c+1)} + \sum_{m<n<l} 2^{-(c+n+1)} < 2^{-c}.$$

Thus $\{U_k\}_{k\in\omega}$ is a Schnorr test, and hence there is a k such that $A \notin U_k$. So A is in at most $2^k + m$ many S_n. □

Clearly, 1-randomness implies computable randomness, which in turn implies Schnorr randomness. We will show in Section 8.11.2 that neither of these implications can be reversed.

7.1.2 Limitations

Despite Schnorr's critique, 1-randomness has remained the paradigmatic notion of algorithmic randomness, and has received considerably more attention than Schnorr randomness. One reason may simply be that Martin-Löf's definition came first, and is perfectly adequate for many results. Another important reason, however, is that the mathematical theory of Schnorr randomness is not as well behaved as that of 1-randomness. For example, the existence of universal Martin-Löf tests (and corresponding universal objects such as universal c.e. martingales and prefix-free complexity) is a powerful tool in the study of 1-randomness that is not available in the case of Schnorr randomness.

Proposition 7.1.11 (Schnorr [349]). *There is no universal Schnorr test.*

Proof. Let $\{U_i\}_{i\in\omega}$ be a Schnorr test. Define a computable set $A \notin U_1$ as follows. Suppose we have defined $A \upharpoonright n$ so that

$$2^n\mu(U_1 \cap [\![A \upharpoonright n]\!]) \leqslant \sum_{1\leqslant k\leqslant n} 2^{-k}.$$

Then there is an $i < 2$ such that $2^{n+1}\mu(U_1 \cap [\![(A \upharpoonright n)i]\!]) \leqslant \sum_{1\leqslant k\leqslant n} 2^{-k}$, so by approximating $\mu(U_1)$ to within $2^{-(n+1)}$, we can determine an $i < 2$ such that $2^{n+1}\mu(U_1 \cap [\![(A \upharpoonright n)i]\!]) \leqslant \sum_{1\leqslant k\leqslant n+1} 2^{-k}$. Let $A(n) = i$. The set A is computable, and $[\![A \upharpoonright n]\!] \nsubseteq U_1$ for all n, so, since U_1 is open, $A \notin U_1$. Thus there is a computable set not contained in $\bigcap_i U_i$, and hence $\{U_i\}_{i\in\omega}$ is not universal. □

In a similar vein, the proof of Theorem 6.3.11 also establishes the following fact.

Proposition 7.1.12 (Schnorr [348, 349]). *There is no effective enumeration of all computable (super)martingales, nor is there an effective enumeration of all computable rational-valued (super)martingales.*

Another basic tool in the study of 1-randomness that is not available for either Schnorr or computable randomness is van Lambalgen's Theorem. As observed by several people, the more difficult direction of van Lambalgen's Theorem, namely Theorem 6.9.2, does hold for both Schnorr and computable randomness, with essentially the same proof. Furthermore, if $A \oplus B$ is either Schnorr or computably random, then so are A and B.

Theorem 7.1.13. (i) *If A is Schnorr random and B is Schnorr random relative to A, then $A \oplus B$ is Schnorr random.*

(ii) *If $A \oplus B$ is Schnorr random then so are A and B.*

(iii) *Items (i) and (ii) also hold for computable randomness.*

The proof is more or less the same as that of Theorem 6.9.2.

The analog of Theorem 6.9.1 fails, however. That is, there are sets A and B such that $A \oplus B$ is Schnorr random but A and B are not relatively Schnorr random, and the same is true for computable randomness. We will prove this result of Merkle, Miller, Nies, Reimann, and Stephan [269], and in a stronger form Yu [412], in Section 8.11.3.

Another reason the theory of Schnorr randomness had remained relatively undeveloped was that many of the basic questions about this notion were open. For instance, a cornerstone of Martin-Löf's version of randomness is that it can be characterized via all three basic approaches (initial segment complexity, tests, and martingales), giving us a mathematically robust notion. Some of these characterizations had been missing in the cases of Schnorr and computable randomness. However, in the following sections we will see that such characterizations do exist. Even so, in many ways the mathematical theory of 1-randomness remains considerably smoother.

7.1.3 Computable measure machines

One of the problems with the mathematical theory of Schnorr randomness had been the lack of a machine characterization analogous to the Kolmogorov complexity definition of 1-randomness. Whether such a characterization could be given was a long-standing open question (see e.g. Ambos-Spies and Kučera [9] and Ambos-Spies and Mayordomo [10]), which was solved by Downey and Griffiths [109], who gave a characterization in terms of a new class of machines.

Definition 7.1.14 (Downey and Griffiths [109]). A *computable measure machine* is a prefix-free machine M such that $\mu([\![\operatorname{dom} M]\!])$ is computable.

Theorem 7.1.15 (Downey and Griffiths [109]). *A set A is Schnorr random iff $K_M(A \upharpoonright n) \geqslant n - O(1)$ for all computable measure machines M.*

Proof. ($\Rightarrow$) Suppose that M is a computable measure machine and $\limsup_n n - K_M(A \upharpoonright n) = \infty$. Let $U_k = \{A : \exists n\, K_M(A \upharpoonright n) \leqslant n - k\}$. The U_k are uniformly Σ^0_1 classes, and by Lemma 6.2.2, $\mu(U_k) \leqslant 2^{-k}$ and the measures $\mu(U_k)$ are uniformly computable. Thus $\{U_k\}_{k\in\omega}$ is a Schnorr test. Since $A \in \bigcap_k U_k$, it follows that A is not Schnorr random.

($\Leftarrow$) Suppose that A is not Schnorr random and let $\{U_k\}_{k\in\omega}$ be a Schnorr test (with $\mu(U_k) = 2^{-k}$) such that $A \in \bigcap_k U_k$. Let $\{R_k\}_{k\in\omega}$ be uniformly c.e. prefix-free sets of strings such that $U_k = [\![R_k]\!]$ for all k. Let

$$L = \{(|\sigma| - k, \sigma) : k \geqslant 1 \wedge \sigma \in R_{2k}\}.$$

Then L is a KC set, since it is clearly c.e. and its weight is

$$\sum_{k\geqslant 1} \sum_{\sigma\in R_{2k}} 2^{-|\sigma|+k} = \sum_{k\geqslant 1} 2^k \mu(U_{2k}) = \sum_{k\geqslant 1} 2^k 2^{-2k} = 1.$$

So by the KC Theorem there is a prefix-free machine M such that if $\sigma \in R_{2k}$ for $k \geqslant 1$ then $K_M(\sigma) \leqslant |\sigma| - k$. Furthermore, $\mu([\![\operatorname{dom} M]\!])$ is equal to the weight of L, which is 1, so M is a computable measure machine. For each k there is an n such that $A \upharpoonright n \in R_{2k}$, so $\limsup_n n - K_M(A \upharpoonright n) = \infty$. □

We can obtain analogs of some basic facts about general prefix-free machines for computable measure machines. An example is the subadditivity of prefix-free complexity.

Proposition 7.1.16. *For all computable measure machines M_0 and M_1 there is a computable measure machine N such that $K_N(\sigma\tau) \leqslant K_{M_0}(\sigma) + K_{M_1}(\tau)$ for all σ and τ.*

Proof. Define N as follows. On input ρ, look for ν_0 and ν_1 such that $\rho = \nu_0\nu_1$ and $M_i(\nu_i)\downarrow$ for $i = 0, 1$. If these exist then they must be unique. In this case, output $M_0(\nu_0)M_1(\nu_1)$. Then clearly $K_N(\sigma\tau) \leqslant K_{M_0}(\sigma) + K_{M_1}(\tau)$ for all σ and τ, and N is a computable measure machine because $\mu([\![\mathrm{dom}\, N]\!]) = \mu([\![\mathrm{dom}\, M_0]\!])\mu([\![\mathrm{dom}\, M_1]\!])$. □

We also have a complexity upper bound similar to the one for prefix-free complexity.

Proposition 7.1.17 (Downey, Griffiths, and LaForte [110]). *There is a computable measure machine M such that $K_M(\sigma) \leqslant |\sigma| + 2\log|\sigma| + O(1)$.*

Proof. For a string $\tau = a_0a_1 \ldots a_m$, let $\overline{\tau} = a_0a_0a_1a_1 \ldots a_ma_m01$. That is, $\overline{\tau}$ is the result of doubling each bit of τ and adding 01 to the end. For each n, let ρ_n be the binary representation of n. For each σ, let $M(\overline{\rho_{|\sigma|}}\sigma)\downarrow= \sigma$. It is easy to see that M is prefix-free and $K_M(\sigma) = |\sigma| + 2\log|\sigma| + 2$.

Let $L = \{\overline{\rho_n} : n \in \mathbb{N}\}$. For $\tau \in L$ the domain of M contains all extensions of τ of length $|\tau| + n$ (and every element of dom M is such an extension for some $\tau \in L$). The combined measure of these extensions is $2^n 2^{-|\tau|+n} = 2^{-|\tau|}$. Thus $\mu([\![\mathrm{dom}\, M]\!]) = \sum_{\tau \in L} 2^{-|\tau|}$. There are two strings of length 4 in L (0001 and 1101). There are two strings of length 6 in L (110001 and 111101) and four strings of length 8. Generally, it is easy to check that there are 2^i many strings of length $2i + 4$ in L for each $i \geqslant 1$. Thus $\mu([\![\mathrm{dom}\, M]\!]) = 2^{-2} + \sum_i 2^i 2^{-(2i+4)} = 2^{-2} + \sum_i 2^{-(i+4)} = 2^{-2} + 2^{-3} = \frac{3}{8}$, and hence M is a computable measure machine. □

For the purposes of defining measures of complexity, we can replace computable measure machines by ones whose domains have measure 1.

Proposition 7.1.18. *For each computable measure machine M there is a prefix-free machine N such that $\mu([\![\mathrm{dom}\, N]\!]) = 1$ and $K_N(\sigma) \leqslant K_M(\sigma)$ for all σ.*

Proof. Since $\mu([\![\mathrm{dom}\, M]\!])$ is computable, we can computably determine $k_0, k_1, \ldots$ such that $\mu([\![\mathrm{dom}\, M]\!]) + \sum_n 2^{-k_n} = 1$. Let

$$L = \{(|\sigma|, M(\sigma)) : M(\sigma)\downarrow\} \cup \{(k_n, 0^n) : n \in \mathbb{N}\}.$$

Then L is a KC set, and the corresponding prefix-free machine N given by the KC Theorem has the desired properties. □

No universal prefix-free machine can be a computable measure machine, since the measure of such a machine is a version of Ω, and hence 1-random. However, we have the following result.

Proposition 7.1.19. *For each computable measure machine M there is a computable measure machine N such that* $\operatorname{rng} N = 2^{<\omega}$ *and*

$$K_N(\sigma) \leqslant \min\{|\sigma| + 2\log|\sigma|\,,\, K_M(\sigma)\} + O(1).$$

Furthermore, N can be chosen such that $\mu([\![\operatorname{dom} N]\!]) = 1$.

Proof. Let N_0 be a computable measure machine such that $K_{N_0}(\sigma) \leqslant |\sigma| + 2\log|\sigma| + O(1)$, as in Proposition 7.1.17. Define a computable measure machine N_1 by $N_1(0\sigma) = M(\sigma)$ and $N_1(1\sigma) = N_0(\sigma)$. Let N be a computable measure machine such that $\mu([\![\operatorname{dom} N]\!]) = 1$ and $K_N(\sigma) \leqslant K_{N_1}(\sigma)$ for all σ, as in Proposition 7.1.18. It is easy to check that N has the desired properties. □

7.1.4 Computable randomness and tests

In this section we present a test characterization of computable randomness.

Definition 7.1.20 (Downey, Griffiths, and LaForte [110]). A *computably graded test* is a pair consisting of a Martin-Löf test $\{V_n\}_{n\in\omega}$ and a computable function $f : 2^{<\omega} \times \omega \to \mathbb{R}$ such that, for any $n \in \omega$, any $\sigma \in 2^{<\omega}$, and any finite prefix-free set of strings $\{\sigma_i\}_{i\leqslant I}$ with $\bigcup_{i=0}^{I}[\![\sigma_i]\!] \subseteq [\![\sigma]\!]$, the following conditions are satisfied:

(i) $\mu(V_n \cap [\![\sigma]\!]) \leqslant f(\sigma, n)$,

(ii) $\sum_{i=0}^{I} f(\sigma_i, n) \leqslant 2^{-n}$, and

(iii) $\sum_{i=0}^{I} f(\sigma_i, n) \leqslant f(\sigma, n)$.

A set passes the test $(\{V_n\}_{n\in\omega}, f)$ if it passes $\{V_n\}_{n\in\omega}$.

If condition (ii) holds for any finite prefix-free set of strings then it also holds for any infinite prefix-free set of strings: the infinite sum is just the supremum of the associated finite sums, and so is also no greater than 2^{-n}. Similarly, if (iii) holds for finite prefix-free sets then it also holds for infinite prefix-free sets. If $\bigcup_{i\leqslant I}[\![\sigma_i]\!] = [\![\sigma]\!]$ then we can summarize conditions (i)–(iii) by the following: $\mu(V_n \cap [\![\sigma]\!]) \leqslant \sum_{i=0}^{I} f(\sigma_i, n) \leqslant f(\sigma, n) \leqslant 2^{-n}$.

An equivalent notion was defined by Merkle, Mihailović, and Slaman [268].

Definition 7.1.21 (Merkle, Mihailović, and Slaman [268]). (i) A *computable rational probability distribution* (or measure) is a computable function $\nu : 2^{<\omega} \to \mathbb{Q}$ such that $\nu(\lambda) = 1$ and $\nu(\sigma) = \nu(\sigma 0) + \nu(\sigma 1)$.

(ii) A *bounded Martin-Löf test* is a Martin-Löf test $\{V_n\}_{n\in\omega}$ for which there exists a computable rational probability distribution ν such that $\mu(V_n \cap [\![\sigma]\!]) \leqslant 2^{-n}\nu(\sigma)$ for all n and σ.

It is not difficult to check that $\{V_n\}_{n\in\omega}$ is a bounded Martin-Löf test iff there is an f such that $(\{V_n\}_{n\in\omega}, f)$ is a computably graded test.

We will show that computably graded tests characterize computable randomness. We first need a lemma. Recall that a real-valued function is co-c.e. if it can be effectively approximated from above.

Lemma 7.1.22 (Schnorr [348, 349]). *From a co-c.e. martingale $c : 2^{<\omega} \to \mathbb{R}$ we can effectively find a computable martingale $d : 2^{<\omega} \to \mathbb{Q}$ such that $d(\sigma) \geqslant c(\sigma)$ for all σ.*

Proof. Let $\{c_s\}_{s\in\omega}$ be an effective decreasing approximation to c. That is, the c_s are uniformly computable functions from $2^{<\omega}$ to $\mathbb{Q}$, and for all σ and s we have $c_{s+1}(\sigma) < c_s(\sigma)$ and $c(\sigma) = \lim_s c_s(\sigma)$. We inductively define a computable martingale d such that $d(\sigma) > c(\sigma) + 2^{-|\sigma|}$ for all σ.

Let $d(\lambda) = c_0(\lambda) + 1$. Now assume that $d(\sigma)$ has been defined so that $d(\sigma) > c(\sigma) + 2^{-|\sigma|}$. Let n be such that $2d(\sigma) > c_n(\sigma 0) + c_n(\sigma 1) + 2^{-|\sigma|+1}$. Let $d(\sigma 1) = c_n(\sigma 1) + 2^{-|\sigma|}$ and $d(\sigma 0) = 2d(\sigma) - d(\sigma 1)$.

By definition $d(\sigma 1) > c(\sigma 1) + 2^{-|\sigma 1|}$, and $d(\sigma 0)$ is defined explicitly to satisfy the martingale property. Furthermore,

$$\begin{aligned} d(\sigma 0) &= 2d(\sigma) - d(\sigma 1) = 2d(\sigma) - c_n(\sigma 1) - 2^{-|\sigma|} \\ &> c_n(\sigma 0) + c_n(\sigma 1) + 2^{-|\sigma|+1} - c_n(\sigma 1) - 2^{-|\sigma|} > c_n(\sigma 0) + 2^{-|\sigma 0|}. \end{aligned}$$

□

Theorem 7.1.23 (Downey, Griffiths, and LaForte [110], implicit in Merkle, Mihailović, and Slaman [268]).

(i) *From a computable martingale $d : 2^{<\omega} \to \mathbb{Q}$ we can effectively define a computably graded test $(\{V_n\}_{n\in\omega}, f)$ such that if $\limsup_n d(A \upharpoonright n) = \infty$ then $A \in \bigcap_n V_n$.*

(ii) *From a computably graded test $(\{V_n\}_{n\in\omega}, f)$ we can effectively define a computable martingale $d : 2^{<\omega} \to \mathbb{Q}$ such that if $A \in \bigcap_n V_n$ then $\limsup_n d(A \upharpoonright n) = \infty$.*

Therefore, a set is computably random iff it passes all computably graded tests iff it passes all bounded Martin-Löf tests.

Proof. (i) We may assume without loss of generality that $d(\lambda) = 1$. Let $V_n = \bigcup\{[\![\sigma]\!] : d(\sigma) \geqslant 2^n\}$ and let $f(\sigma, n) = d(\sigma)2^{-(|\sigma|+n)}$. By Kolmogorov's Inequality (Theorem 6.3.3),

$$\frac{\mu(V_n \cap [\![\sigma]\!])}{\mu([\![\sigma]\!])} \leqslant \frac{d(\sigma)}{2^n},$$

so $\mu(V_n \cap [\![\sigma]\!]) \leqslant f(\sigma, n)$. Furthermore, again using Kolmogorov's Inequality, if $\{\sigma_i\}_{i\leqslant I}$ is a prefix-free set and $\bigcup_{i\leqslant I}[\![\sigma_i]\!] \subseteq [\![\sigma]\!]$, then

$$\sum_{i\leqslant I} f(\sigma_i, n) = 2^{-n}\sum_{i\leqslant I} d(\sigma_i)\mu([\![\sigma_i]\!]) \leqslant 2^{-n}d(\sigma)\mu([\![\sigma]\!]) = f(\sigma, n) \leqslant 2^{-n}.$$

So $(\{V_n\}_{n\in\omega}, f)$ is a computably graded test. Finally, if $\limsup_n d(A \upharpoonright n) = \infty$ then $A \in \bigcap_n V_n$ by the definition of the V_n.

(ii) Without loss of generality we may assume that $V_{n+1} \subseteq V_n$ for all n. We define d via two auxiliary functions: a co-c.e. function $h : 2^{<\omega} \times \omega \to \mathbb{R}$ and a co-c.e. martingale $c : 2^{<\omega} \to \mathbb{R}$.

Let P_σ be the collection of all finite partitions of $[\![\sigma]\!]$ into a finite prefix-free set, that is, all finite prefix-free sets F such that $[\![F]\!] = [\![\sigma]\!]$ (for example, $\{\sigma 0, \sigma 1\} \in P_\sigma$). Let

$$h(\sigma, n) = 2^{|\sigma|} \inf\left\{\sum_{i\leqslant I} f(\sigma_i, n) \mid \{\sigma_i\}_{i\leqslant I} \in P_\sigma\right\}.$$

Since f satisfies conditions (i) and (ii) of Definition 7.1.20, we have $2^{|\sigma|}\mu(V_n \cap [\![\sigma]\!]) \leqslant h(\sigma, n) \leqslant 2^{|\sigma|-n}$. Thus $\sum_n h(\sigma, n) \leqslant 2^{|\sigma|}\sum_n 2^{-n} = 2^{|\sigma|+1}$, and we can define $c(\sigma) = \sum_n h(\sigma, n)$.

Fix n. By condition (iii) of Definition 7.1.20,

$$2^{|\sigma|} f(\sigma, n) \geqslant 2^{|\sigma|}(f(\sigma 0, n) + f(\sigma 1, n)) \geqslant \tfrac{1}{2}(h(\sigma 0, n) + h(\sigma 1, n)).$$

Each partition of $[\![\sigma]\!]$ into a finite prefix-free set, other than the singleton $\{\sigma\}$, is a union of a partition of $[\![\sigma 0]\!]$ and a partition of $[\![\sigma 1]\!]$, so

$$h(\sigma, n) = \min(\tfrac{1}{2}(h(\sigma 0, n) + h(\sigma 1, n)), 2^{|\sigma|} f(\sigma, n)) = \tfrac{1}{2}(h(\sigma 0, n) + h(\sigma 1, n)).$$

In other words, $\lambda\sigma.h(\sigma, n)$ is a martingale. Thus c is a martingale.

It is easy to see that h is co-c.e. Let $\{h_s\}_{s\in\omega}$ be an effective approximation of h from above. To see that c is co-c.e., let $c_s(\sigma) = \sum_{n\leqslant s} h_s(\sigma, n) + \sum_{n>s} 2^{|\sigma|-n}$. This sum is computable, since the first summand is a finite sum of computable rational numbers, while the second is simply $2^{|\sigma|-s}$. In passing from $c_s(\sigma)$ to $c_{s+1}(\sigma)$, we replace h_s values by h_{s+1} values, which are no larger, and replace $2^{|\sigma|-(s+1)}$ by $h_{s+1}(\sigma, s+1)$, which is also no larger. So $c_{s+1}(\sigma) \leqslant c_s(\sigma)$ for all σ. Also, $c(\sigma) = \lim_s c_s(\sigma)$ for all σ. Thus c is a co-c.e. martingale.

Let d be as in Lemma 7.1.22. Suppose that $A \in \bigcap_n V_n$. Given i, let $\sigma \prec A$ be such that $[\![\sigma]\!] \subseteq V_i$. Then

$$d(\sigma) \geqslant c(\sigma) \geqslant \sum_{j\leqslant i} h(\sigma, j) \geqslant 2^{|\sigma|}\sum_{j\leqslant i} \mu(V_j \cap [\![\sigma]\!]) = 2^{|\sigma|}(i+1)2^{-|\sigma|} = i + 1.$$

So $\limsup_n d(A \upharpoonright n) = \infty$. □

7.1.5 Bounded machines and computable randomness

It is also possible to obtain a machine characterization for computable randomness. If M is a prefix-free machine, let

$$S_M^n = \{\sigma : K_M(\sigma) \leqslant |\sigma| - n\}.$$

Definition 7.1.24 (Mihailović [personal communication]). A *bounded machine* is a prefix-free machine such that there is a computable rational probability distribution ν with $\mu([\![S^n_M]\!] \cap [\![\sigma]\!]) \leqslant 2^{-n}\nu(\sigma)$ for all σ and n.

Theorem 7.1.25 (Mihailović [personal communication]). *A set X is computably random iff $K_M(X \upharpoonright n) \geqslant n - O(1)$ for every bounded machine M.*

Proof. Suppose there is a bounded machine M such that $\forall c \exists n\, (K_M(X \upharpoonright n) < n - c)$. By definition $\mu([\![S^n_M]\!] \cap [\![\sigma]\!]) \leqslant 2^{-n}\nu(\sigma)$, so $[\![S^0_M]\!], [\![S^1_M]\!], \dots$ is a bounded Martin-Löf test covering X. Thus X is not computably random.

Now suppose that X is not computably random. Let $A_0, A_1, \dots$ be uniformly c.e. prefix-free sets such that the $[\![A_n]\!]$ form a bounded ML-test with associated computable distribution ν, and $X \in \bigcap_n A_n$. It is straightforward to use the KC theorem to define a prefix-free machine M such that if $\sigma \in A_{2c+2}$ then $M(\tau) = \sigma$ for some τ such that $|\tau| = |\sigma| - c$, as in the KC Theorem version of the proof of Theorem 6.2.3. For this machine, $\forall c \exists n\, (K_M(X \upharpoonright n) < n - c)$.

To complete this direction of the proof we need to show that M is bounded. Let $\tau_{n,0}, \tau_{n,1}, \dots$ list the elements of A_n. Then $S^n_M = \{\tau_{2(n+k+1),i} : k, i \in \mathbb{N}\}$, so for each σ and n,

$$[\![S^n_M]\!] \cap [\![\sigma]\!] = \bigcup_{k \geqslant 1} \bigcup_i \left([\![\tau_{2(n+k),i}]\!] \cap [\![\sigma]\!]\right).$$

Consequently,

$$\mu([\![S^n_M]\!] \cap [\![\sigma]\!]) \leqslant \sum_{k \geqslant 1} \mu\left(A_{2(n+k)} \cap [\![\sigma]\!]\right) \leqslant \sum_{k \geqslant 1} 2^{-2(n+k)}\nu(\sigma) < 2^{-n}\nu(\sigma).$$

□

7.1.6 Process complexity and computable randomness

In Section 6.3.2, we saw that process complexity can be used to characterize 1-randomness. In this section, we show that a variation on process complexity can be used to give an analogous characterization of computable randomness.

Definition 7.1.26 (Levin, see [425], Day [89]). A process machine P is a *quick process machine* if it is total and there is a computable order h such that $|P(\tau)| \geqslant h(|\tau|)$ for all τ.

For a quick process machine P, any P-description of a string σ must be among the strings τ such that $h(|\tau|)) \leqslant |\sigma|$, so the complexity $C_P(\sigma)$ of σ relative to P can be determined by computing the values of $P(\tau)$ for all such τ (which are defined, since P is total). Thus C_P is computable.

Definition 7.1.27 (Day [89]). A is *quick process random* if $C_P(A \upharpoonright n) \geqslant n - O(1)$ for all quick process machines P.

Theorem 7.1.28 (Day [89]). *A set is quick process random iff it is computably random.*

Proof. First suppose that A is not quick process random. Then there is a quick process machine P such that for all c there is an n with $C_P(A \upharpoonright n) < n - c$. Let h be the order associated with P and let $g(n) = \min\{x : h(x) \geqslant n\}$, so that if $\tau \in 2^{g(n)}$ then $|P(\tau)| \geqslant n$. As we may assume without loss of generality that $h(n) \leqslant n$, we may also assume that $g(n) \geqslant n$. We define a computable martingale d as follows. First, for each σ let $E_\sigma = \{\tau \in 2^{g(|\sigma|)} : P(\tau) \succcurlyeq \sigma\}$. Then let

$$d(\sigma) = \frac{|E_\sigma|}{2^{g(|\sigma|)-|\sigma|}}.$$

Since P is total, E_σ can be computed from σ, and hence d is computable. We now show that d is a martingale. For any σ, the sets $E_{\sigma 0}$ and $E_{\sigma 1}$ are disjoint, as P is a process machine. If $\tau \in E_{\sigma 0}$ then $\tau \upharpoonright g(|\sigma|) \in E_\sigma$, because $P(\tau \upharpoonright g(|\sigma|)) \preccurlyeq P(\tau)$ and $\sigma \preccurlyeq P(\tau)$, and $|\sigma| \leqslant |P(\tau \upharpoonright g(|\sigma|))|$. Hence $[\![E_{\sigma 0}]\!] \subseteq [\![E_\sigma]\!]$. Similarly, $[\![E_{\sigma 1}]\!] \subseteq [\![E_\sigma]\!]$. Now, if $\tau \in E_\sigma$ and $\tau' \succcurlyeq \tau$ with $|\tau'| = h(|\sigma| + 1)$, then $\tau' \in E_{\sigma 0} \cup E_{\sigma 1}$, since P is total, $P(\tau') \succcurlyeq P(\tau) \succcurlyeq \sigma$, and $|P(\tau')| \geqslant g(|\sigma| + 1)$. Thus

$$(|E_{\sigma 0}| + |E_{\sigma 1}|)2^{g(|\sigma|)-g(|\sigma+1|)} = |E_\sigma|,$$

and hence

$$\begin{aligned} d(\sigma) = \frac{|E_\sigma|}{2^{g(|\sigma|)-|\sigma|}} &= \frac{|E_{\sigma 0}| + |E_{\sigma 1}|}{2^{g(|\sigma+1|)-|\sigma|}} \\ &= \frac{1}{2}\frac{|E_{\sigma 0}| + |E_{\sigma 1}|}{2^{g(|\sigma+1|)-(|\sigma|+1)}} = \frac{1}{2}(d(\sigma 0) + d(\sigma 1)). \end{aligned}$$

Given c, let n and τ be such that $|\tau| < n - c$ and $P(\tau) = A \upharpoonright n$. Since $g(n) \geqslant n > |\tau| + c$, if $\tau' \succcurlyeq \tau$ and $|\tau'| = h(n)$, then $P(\tau') \succcurlyeq A \upharpoonright n$, and so $\tau' \in E_{A \upharpoonright n}$. Hence $|E_{A \upharpoonright n}| \geqslant 2^{c+g(n)-n}$, so $d(A \upharpoonright n) = \frac{|E_{A \upharpoonright n}|}{2^{g(n)-n}} \geqslant 2^c$. Thus $\limsup_n d(A \upharpoonright n) = \infty$, so A is not computably random.

Now suppose that A is not computably random. By Proposition 7.1.2, there is a computable rational-valued martingale d that succeeds on A. It is clear from the proof of that proposition that we may in fact assume that all values of d are dyadic rationals. We may also assume that $d(\lambda) = 1$. By the savings trick (Proposition 6.3.8), we may further assume that $\lim_n d(A \upharpoonright n) = \infty$. We will construct a quick process machine P such that for each c there is an n with $C_P(A \upharpoonright n) \leqslant n - c$.

Let f be a strictly increasing computable function such that for each σ there is a natural number a with $\frac{d(\sigma)}{2^{|\sigma|}} = a2^{-f(|\sigma|)}$.

We will define a function $l : \mathbb{N} \to \mathbb{N}$. For strings with lengths in the range of l, we will give short P-descriptions to those strings with large d-values. To describe strings of length $l(s+1)$, we will use descriptions of length between $f(l(s)) + 1$ and $f(l(s+1))$. To make our strings nonrandom, we need to make the gap between $f(l(s))$ and $l(s+1)$ increase as s increases. Thus we define l inductively by $l(0) = 0$ and $l(s+1) = f(l(s)) + s + 1$.

We will construct P in stages while ensuring that the following conditions hold.

1. $\operatorname{dom} P_s = 2^{\leqslant f(l(s))}$.

2. $|P_s(\tau)| = l(s)$ for all $\tau \in 2^{f(l(s))}$.

3. $2^{-|\sigma|}d(\sigma) = 2^{-f(l(s))}|\{\tau \in 2^{f(l(s))} : P_s(\tau) = \sigma\}|$ for all $\sigma \in 2^{l(s)}$.

At stage 0, we define $P(\sigma) = \lambda$ for all strings of length less than or equal to $f(0)$. The conditions above are clearly met.

At stage $s+1$, for every $\sigma \in 2^{l(s)}$, we proceed as follows.

For all $\upsilon \succcurlyeq \sigma$ such that $|\upsilon| = l(s+1)$ we know that $d(\upsilon)2^{-|\upsilon|} = a2^{-f(|\upsilon|)}$ for some natural number a. So there are $a_0, \ldots, a_n$ such that $d(\upsilon)2^{-|\upsilon|} = a_0 2^{-f(l(s))-1} + a_1 2^{-f(l(s))-2} + \cdots + a_n 2^{-f(l(s+1))}$, where $n = f(l(s+1)) - f(l(s)) - 1$ and $a_i \in \{0,1\}$ for $1 \leqslant i \leqslant n$. Note that a_0 may be greater than 1.

Let $U = \{\upsilon \in 2^{l(s+1)} : \upsilon \succcurlyeq \sigma\}$. Then $\sum_{\upsilon \in U} \sum_{i \leqslant n} a_i 2^{-(f(l(s))+i+1)} = \sum_{\upsilon \in U} 2^{-|\upsilon|}d(\upsilon) = 2^{-|\sigma|}d(\sigma) \leqslant 1$, so by the KC Theorem we can effectively find pairwise disjoint sets of strings T_υ for $\upsilon \in U$ such that T_υ has a_i many strings of length $f(l(s)) + i + 1$ for each $i \leqslant n$, and $T_\sigma = \bigcup_{\upsilon \in U} T_\upsilon$ is prefix-free. Furthermore, we may assume that we define this set as in the proof of the KC Theorem, always taking the leftmost string of the required length that preserves prefix-freeness.

Let $S_\sigma = \{\tau \in 2^{f(l(s))} : P_s(\tau) = \sigma\}$. By condition 3,

$$\mu([\![T_\sigma]\!]) = 2^{-|\sigma|}d(\sigma) = |S_\sigma|2^{-f((l(s))} = \mu([\![S_\sigma]\!]).$$

Let $R_\sigma = \{\rho \upharpoonright f(l(s)) : \rho \in T_\sigma\}$. Since $\mu([\![S_\sigma]\!]) = \mu([\![T_\sigma]\!])$, all the elements of T_σ have length at least $f(l(s)) + 1)$, and T_σ was defined as in the proof of the KC Theorem, we must have $|R_\sigma| = |S_\sigma|$. Hence there is a bijection $h : R_\sigma \to S_\sigma$. For $\rho \in T_\sigma$, let $g(\rho)$ be the string formed by replacing the first $f(l(s))$ many bits of ρ with the image of these bits under h. Let $\widehat{T}_\sigma$ be the image of T_σ under g.

Now we define P_{s+1} as follows. For $|\rho| \leqslant f(l(s+1))$, let

$$P_{s+1}(\rho) = \begin{cases} P_s(\rho) & |\rho| \leqslant f(l(s)) \\ P_s(\rho \upharpoonright f(l(s))) & |\rho| > f(l(s)) \wedge \rho \prec \tau \text{ for some } \tau \in \widehat{T}_\upsilon \\ \upsilon & |\rho| > f(l(s)) \wedge \rho \succcurlyeq \tau \text{ for some } \tau \in \widehat{T}_\upsilon. \end{cases}$$

We now verify that conditions 1-3 are satisfied and, assuming by induction that P_s is a process machine, so is P_{s+1}.

The nonempty sets $[\![S_\sigma]\!]$ for $\sigma \in 2^{l(s)}$ partition 2^ω, by conditions 1 and 2. Furthermore, by the above construction, the nonempty sets $[\![\widehat{T}_\upsilon]\!]$ for $\upsilon \succcurlyeq \sigma$ and $|\upsilon| = l(s+1)$ partition $[\![S_\sigma]\!]$. Thus the nonempty sets $[\![\widehat{T}_\upsilon]\!]$ for υ of length $l(s+1)$ partition 2^ω. So P_{s+1} is defined for all strings of length less than or equal to $f(l(s+1))$, meeting condition 1.

If τ has length $f(l(s+1))$, then τ extends some element of some $\widehat{T}_\upsilon$, which implies that $|P_{s+1}(\tau)| = |\upsilon| = l(s+1)$, and hence condition 2 is met.

If $\upsilon \in 2^{l(s+1)}$, then for all τ of length $f(l(s+1))$ we have $[\![\tau]\!] \subseteq [\![\widehat{T}_\upsilon]\!]$ iff $P_{s+1}(\tau) = \upsilon$. Thus, as $\mu(\widehat{T}_\upsilon) = \mu(T_\upsilon) = 2^{-|\upsilon|}d(\upsilon)$, we have

$$d(\upsilon)2^{-|\upsilon|} = \mu(\widehat{T}_\upsilon) = 2|\{\tau \in 2^{f(l(s+1))} : P_{s+1}(\tau) = \upsilon\}|2^{-f(l(s+1))},$$

so condition 3 is met.

Assuming P_s is a process machine, the first two parts of the definition of P_{s+1} preserve the process machine condition. To see that the third part also does so, it is enough to consider the case where $\tau \in \widehat{T}_\upsilon$ for some υ. By construction, $\tau \succcurlyeq \xi$ for some ξ such that $|\xi| = f(l(s))$ and $\xi \in S_\sigma$ for some $\sigma \preccurlyeq \upsilon$. Then for any ξ' with $\xi \preccurlyeq \xi' \prec \tau$, we have $P_{s+1}(\xi') = P_s(\xi) = \sigma \preccurlyeq \upsilon = P_{s+1}(\tau)$.

As P_s is a process machine for all s, we have that P is a process machine. Furthermore, it is a quick process machine: Let $k(n)$ be the largest s such that $f(l(s)) \leqslant n$. Given any σ, let $\sigma' = \sigma \upharpoonright f(l(k(|\sigma|)))$. Then $|P(\sigma)| \geqslant |P(\sigma')| = l(k(|\sigma|)) \geqslant k(|\sigma|)$.

To show that A is not quick process random, take any $c > 0$. As $\lim_n d(A \upharpoonright n) = \infty$, there must be a stage $s+1 > c$ such that $d(A \upharpoonright l(s+1)) \geqslant 2^c$. Let $\upsilon = A \upharpoonright l(s+1)$. Then $d(\upsilon)2^{-|\upsilon|} \geqslant 2^{-|\upsilon|+c} = 2^{-f(l(s))-s-1+c}$, since by definition $|\upsilon| = l(s+1) = f(l(s)) + s + 1$. Also, $d(\upsilon)2^{-|\upsilon|} = a_0 2^{-f(l(s))-1} + a_1 2^{-f(l(s))-2} + \cdots + a_n 2^{-f(l(s+1))}$ with $a_i \in \{0,1\}$ if $i > 0$. If $i > s-c$, then $i > 0$, and so $a_i \leqslant 1$. Hence, there must be some $i \leqslant s-c$ such that $a_i \neq 0$. For this i, there is some string of length $f(l(s))+i+1$ in T_υ. But $f(l(s))+i+1 \leqslant f(l(s))+s+1-c = l(s+1)-c$. It follows that there is some string ρ of length $l(s+1)-c$ in $\widehat{T}_\upsilon$, and that $P_{s+1}(\rho) = \upsilon = A \upharpoonright l(s+1)$. Thus A is not quick process random. □

7.2 Weak n-randomness

7.2.1 Basics

Kurtz [228] introduced a notion of randomness based on the idea of being contained in effective sets of measure 1 rather than avoiding effective sets of measure 0.

Definition 7.2.1 (Kurtz [228]). A set is *weakly* 1-*random*, or *Kurtz random*, if it is contained in every Σ^0_1 class of measure 1.

We will later see that the relativized notion of weak $(n+1)$-randomness is actually a strong from of n-randomness.

There is an equivalent formulation of this notion in terms of tests, established by Wang [405] but implicit in some of the proofs in Kurtz [228].

Definition 7.2.2 (Wang [405]). A *Kurtz null test* is a Martin-Löf test $\{V_n\}_{n\in\omega}$ for which there is a computable function $f : \omega \to (2^{<\omega})^{<\omega}$ such that $V_n = [\![f(n)]\!]$ for all n.

Another way to state this definition is that there are finite, uniformly computable $S_0, S_1, \ldots \subset 2^{<\omega}$ such that $V_n = [\![S_n]\!]$.

Note that if $\{V_n\}_{n\in\omega}$ is a Kurtz null test, then both $\{V_n\}_{n\in\omega}$ and $\{\overline{V_n}\}_{n\in\omega}$ are uniformly Δ^0_1 classes.

Theorem 7.2.3 (Wang [405], after Kurtz [228]). *A set is weakly* 1*-random iff it passes all Kurtz null tests.*

Proof. Suppose that A is not weakly 1-random and let U be a Σ^0_1 class of measure 1 such that $A \notin U$. To define V_n, let s be least such that $\mu(U_s) > 1 - 2^{-n}$. Let $V_n = \overline{U_s}$. It is easy to check that $\{V_n\}_{n\in\omega}$ is a Kurtz null test, and that $A \in \bigcap_n V_n$.

Conversely, suppose there is a Kurtz null test $\{V_n\}_{n\in\omega}$ such that $A \in \bigcap_n V_n$. Let $U = \bigcup_n \overline{V_n}$. Then U is a Σ^0_1 class of measure 1, and $A \notin U$, so A is not weakly 1-random. $\square$

A Kurtz null test is clearly a Schnorr test, so we see that every Schnorr random set is weakly 1-random.

Of course, we can generalize Kurtz randomness to higher levels. Thus a set is *weakly n-random*, or *Kurtz n-random*[5], if it is a member of all Σ^0_n classes of measure 1. Here the distinction between classes and open classes is important. It is not true that being a member of every Σ^0_n class of measure 1 is the same as being a member of every $\Sigma^{0,\emptyset^{(n-1)}}_1$ class of measure 1. For instance, let A be 2-generic. Then it is not hard to see that A is in every $\Sigma^{0,\emptyset'}_1$ class of measure 1, and hence is weakly 1-random relative to $\emptyset'$. (This is the relativized form of Theorem 8.11.7 below.) But as we will see in Proposition 8.11.9, A cannot be weakly 2-random (or even Schnorr random, which, as we will see in Theorem 7.2.7, is a weaker notion than weak 2-randomness).

Thus weak n-randomness is *not* the same as weak 1-randomness relative to $\emptyset^{(n-1)}$. This observation is important since many results on n-randomness rely on Theorem 6.8.5, that n-randomness is the same as 1-randomness relative to $\emptyset^{(n-1)}$. The following result says that we *can* recover a little of the spirit of that fact, though, if we allow for an extra quantifier.

[5]Some authors, however, have used "Kurtz n-random" to mean Kurtz random relative to $\emptyset^{(n-1)}$.

Lemma 7.2.4 (Kautz [200]). *Let $n \geqslant 2$.*

(i) *From the index of a Σ^0_n class C we can computably obtain the index of a $\Sigma^{0,\emptyset^{(n-2)}}_2$ class $\widehat{C} \subseteq C$ such that $\mu(\widehat{C}) = \mu(C)$.*

(ii) *From the index of a Π^0_n-class V we can uniformly and computably obtain the index of a $\Pi^{0,\emptyset^{(n-2)}}_2$ class $\widehat{V} \supseteq V$ such that $\mu(\widehat{V}) = \mu(V)$.*

Proof. Let C be a Σ^0_n class. Then C is the union of uniformly Π^0_{n-1} classes $T_0, T_1, \ldots$. By Theorem 6.8.3, we can uniformly find, for each i and j, a $\Pi^{0,\emptyset^{(n-2)}}_1$ class $\widehat{T}_{i,j} \subseteq T_i$ with $\mu(T_i) - \mu(\widehat{T}_{i,j}) \leqslant 2^{-j}$. Let $\widehat{C} = \bigcup_{i,j} \widehat{T}_{i,j}$. Then $\widehat{C} \subseteq C$ and $\mu(\widehat{C}) = \mu(C)$. The proof of (ii) is symmetric. □

Corollary 7.2.5. *Let $n \geqslant 2$. A set is weakly n-random iff it is in every $\Sigma^{0,\emptyset^{(n-2)}}_2$ class of measure 1.*

We can also have a "one jump" characterization of weak n-randomness via the analog of a Kurtz null test. We will refer to the tests in part (iii) of the following theorem as Σ^0_n *Kurtz null tests.*

Theorem 7.2.6 (Kautz [200], Wang [405], after Kurtz [228]). *The following are equivalent for $n \geqslant 2$.*

(i) *A is weakly n-random.*

(ii) *For every $\emptyset^{(n-1)}$-computable sequence of Σ^0_{n-1} classes $\{S_i\}_{i\in\omega}$ with $\mu(S_i) \leqslant 2^{-i}$, we have $A \notin \bigcap_i S_i$.*

(iii) *For every $\emptyset^{(n-1)}$-computable sequence of $\Sigma^{0,\emptyset^{(n-2)}}_1$ classes $\{S_i\}_{i\in\omega}$ with $\mu(S_i) \leqslant 2^{-i}$, we have $A \notin \bigcap_i S_i$.*

Proof. The equivalence between (ii) and (iii) follows from Theorem 6.8.3.

If $A \in \bigcap_i S_i$, where the S_i are as in (ii), then A is not weakly 1-random, since the complement of $\bigcap_i S_i$ is a Σ^0_n set of measure 1.

Finally, suppose that A is not weakly 1-random. Then it is contained in some Π^0_n null set T. Now, T is of the form $\bigcap_i U_i$, where the U_i are uniformly Σ^0_{n-1} classes. Using $\emptyset^{(n-1)}$ as an oracle, for each i we can find a k such that $\mu(\bigcap_{j\leqslant k} U_j) < 2^{-i}$ and let $S_i = \bigcap_{j\leqslant k} U_j$. Then the S_i are as in (ii), and $A \in \bigcap_i S_i$. □

Weak 2-randomness is quite a natural notion. When we introduced the notion of Martin-Löf randomness, we mentioned the possibility of relaxing the definition of a Martin-Löf test $\{U_n\}_{n\in\omega}$ to require only that $\lim_n \mu(U_n) = 0$, that is, eliminating the requirement that there be a computable bound on the rate of convergence of these measures. We called such tests *generalized Martin-Löf tests*. For such a test, $\bigcap_n U_n$ is a Π^0_2 class of measure 0, and every Π^0_2 class of measure 0 can be expressed in this way, so being weak 2-random is the same as passing all generalized Martin-Löf tests. Weak 2-randomness was first studied by Gaifman and Snir [168], in the sense that their paper is the first occurrence of this notion in print (to our knowledge). However, the notion is already present in Solovay's notes [371], which include a proof due to Martin that weakly 2-random sets are not Δ^0_2 (Corollary 7.2.9 below).

Weak n-randomness and n-randomness are related as follows.

Theorem 7.2.7 (Kurtz [228]). *Every n-random set is weakly n-random and every weakly $(n+1)$-random set is n-random.*

Proof. An n-random set passes every Σ^0_n Kurtz null test, and hence is weakly n-random.

If A is not n-random then there is a Σ^0_n Martin-Löf test $U_0, U_1, \ldots$ such that $A \in \bigcap_n U_n$. Let $V = \overline{\bigcap_n U_n}$. Then V is a Σ^0_{n+1} class of measure 1 not containing A, so A is not weakly $(n+1)$-random. □

This result, and characterizations such as the one above in terms of generalized Martin-Löf tests, have led some to argue that weak n-randomness for $n > 1$ should be called strong $(n-1)$-randomness. The traditional terminology is well-established, however.

We will see in Section 8.13 that neither of the implications in Theorem 7.2.7 can be reversed.

In some ways, weak 2-randomness is the weakest level of randomness at which "typical" random behavior happens. A good example of this phenomenon is the following result, which says that the behavior of weak 2-random sets is very unlike that of computationally powerful 1-random sets such as Ω. It will be generalized below in Theorem 8.13.1.

Theorem 7.2.8 (Downey, Nies, Weber, and Yu [130]). *Every weakly 2-random degree forms a minimal pair with $\mathbf{0}'$.*

Proof. Let A be a Δ^0_2 set and R a weakly 2-random set such that $A = \Phi^R$ for some reduction Φ. We show that A is computable. The class

$$S = \{X : \forall n\, \forall s\, \exists t > s\, (\Phi^X(n)[t]\downarrow = A_t(n))\}$$

is a Π^0_2 class containing R, and hence has positive measure. (Here, the oracle in the computation $\Phi^X(n)[t]$ is always X, of course, since X is not being approximated in any sense.)

We apply a majority vote argument. Let r be a rational such that $\frac{\mu(S)}{2} < r < \mu(S)$. Then there is a finite set $F \subset 2^{<\omega}$ such that $\mu([\![F]\!]) < \mu(S)$ and $\mu([\![F]\!] \cap S) > r$. To compute $A(n)$, we search for a finite set $G \subset 2^{<\omega}$ with $\mu([\![G]\!]) > r$ and $[\![G]\!] \subseteq [\![F]\!]$ so that for any $\sigma, \tau \in G$, we have $\Phi^\sigma(n)\downarrow = \Phi^\tau(n)\downarrow$. Such a set exists because $\mu([\![F]\!] \cap S) > r$. Then $A(n) = \Phi^\sigma(n)$, since otherwise $[\![G]\!] \in \overline{S}$, which is impossible because then $\mu([\![F]\!] \cap S) \leqslant \mu([\![F]\!] \setminus [\![G]\!]) < \mu(S) - r < r$. Thus A is computable. □

Corollary 7.2.9 (Martin, see Solovay [371]). *There is no Δ^0_2 weakly 2-random set.*

Corollary 7.2.10 (Downey, Nies, Weber, and Yu [130]). *There is no universal generalized Martin-Löf test.*

Proof. If there were such a test then, taking the complement of any of its components of measure less than 1, we would have a nonempty Π^0_1 class containing only weakly 2-random sets. But then there would be a Δ^0_2 weakly 2-random set. □

We can combine Theorem 7.2.8 with the following result to obtain a characterization of the weakly 2-random sets within the 1-random sets.

Theorem 7.2.11 (Hirschfeldt and Miller, see [130]). *For any Σ^0_3 class S of measure 0, there is a noncomputable c.e. set A such that $A \leqslant_T X$ for all 1-random $X \in S$.*[6]

Proof. Let $\{U^i_n : i, n \in \mathbb{N}\}$ be uniformly Σ^0_1 sets such that $S = \bigcup_i \bigcap_n U^i_n$ and $\lim_n \mu(U^i_n) = 0$ for all i. For each e, choose a fresh large n_e. If we ever reach a stage s such that $\mu(U^i_{n_e,s}) > 2^{-e}$ for some $i \leqslant e$, then redefine n_e to be a fresh large number and restart. If n_e ever enters W_e, then put n_e into A and stop the action of e.

Clearly, A is c.e., and each n_e reaches a final value, whence $W_e \neq \overline{A}$ for all e, so A is noncomputable. Now suppose that $X \in S$ is 1-random. Let i be such that $X \in \bigcap_n U^i_n$. Let $T = \{U^i_{n_e,s} : e \geqslant i \wedge n_e \text{ enters } A \text{ at stage } s\}$. Then the sum of the measures of the elements of T is bounded by $\sum_{e \geqslant i} 2^{-e}$, so T is a Solovay test. Thus X is in only finitely many elements of T. So for all but finitely many n, if n enters A at stage s then $X \notin U^i_{n,s}$. Let B be the set of all n such that $n \in A_s$ for the least s such that $X \in U^i_{n,s}$. Then B is X-computable and $A =^* B$, so A is X-computable. □

It is worth noting that this result cannot be substantially improved. By Corollary 8.12.2 below, no noncomputable set can be computed by positive measure many sets. By Theorem 2.19.10 applied to a Π^0_1 class of 1-random sets, for any c.e. set A, there is a Δ^0_2 (and even a low) 1-random set that does not compute A, and the Δ^0_2 sets are a Σ^0_4 class of measure 0.

Corollary 7.2.12 (Downey, Nies, Weber, and Yu [130]). *For a 1-random set A, the following are equivalent.*

(i) *A is weakly 2-random.*

(ii) *The degree of A forms a minimal pair with $\mathbf{0}'$.*

(iii) *A does not compute any noncomputable c.e. set.*

In Corollaries 8.11.8 and 8.11.10, we will see that each hyperimmune degree contains a weakly 1-random set, and indeed one that is not Schnorr

[6]We will revisit this result in Section 11.8, where we will see that it leads to a notion of randomness theoretic weakness, that of *diamond classes*, which will be of particular interest in Chapter 14.

random. On the hyperimmune-free degrees, however, weak 1-randomness implies 1-randomness, as we will see in Theorem 8.11.11. The precise classification of the weakly 1-random degrees remains open.

7.2.2 Characterizations of weak 1-randomness

There is also a martingale characterization of weak 1-randomness.

Theorem 7.2.13 (Wang [405]). *A is not weakly 1-random iff there is a computable martingale d and a computable order h such that $d(A \upharpoonright n) > h(n)$ for all n.*[7]

Proof. We follow the proof in Downey, Griffiths, and Reid [111].

Suppose that A is not weakly 1-random, as witnessed by the Kurtz null test $\{[\![S_i]\!]\}_{i\in\omega}$, where the S_i are uniformly computable, finite, and prefix-free. Let $g(i)$ be the length of the longest string in S_i. Note that g is computable, and $g(i) \geqslant i$.

Let

$$w_\sigma(\tau) = \begin{cases} 1 & \text{if } \sigma \preccurlyeq \tau \\ 2^{-(|\sigma|-|\tau|)} & \text{if } \tau \prec \sigma \\ 0 & \text{otherwise,} \end{cases}$$

and let

$$d(\tau) = \sum_n \sum_{\sigma\in S_n} w_\sigma(\tau).$$

It is straightforward to check that each w_σ is a martingale, and $\sum_{\sigma\in S_n} w_\sigma(\lambda) = \mu([\![S_n]\!]) \leqslant 2^{-n}$, so d is a martingale. Furthermore, we claim that d is computable. To see that this is the case, notice that, for any k, strings in S_k increase $d(\lambda)$ by at most $\mu([\![S_k]\!]) \leqslant 2^{-k}$, so these strings increase $d(\tau)$ by at most $2^{|\tau|-k}$. Thus, for any s, if we let $k = |\tau| + s$, then $\sum_{n\leqslant k} \sum_{\sigma\in S_n} w_\sigma(\tau)$ is within 2^{-s} of $d(\tau)$.

Let $h(n) = |\{j : g(j) \leqslant n\}|$. Since $g(j) \geqslant j$ for all j and g is computable, h is computable. Furthermore, $h(n)$ is non-decreasing and unbounded, so it is a computable order. Now fix n. Since A is in all $[\![S_i]\!]$, for any j with $g(j) \leqslant n$ there is a $\sigma_j \in S_j$ such that $\sigma_j \preccurlyeq A \upharpoonright n$. Thus

$$d(A \upharpoonright n) \geqslant \sum_{j:g(j)\leqslant n} w_{\sigma_j}(A \upharpoonright n) = \sum_{j:g(j)\leqslant n} 1 = h(n).$$

Now suppose that there are a computable martingale d and a computable order h such that $d(A \upharpoonright n) \geqslant h(n)$ for all n. By scaling d and h, we may

[7] Note that this condition is equivalent to saying that there is a computable martingale d and a computable order g such that $d(A \upharpoonright n) > g(n)$ for almost all n, since we can replace the first few values of g by 0 to obtain a new order h such that $d(A \upharpoonright n) > h(n)$ for all n.

assume that $d(\lambda) \leqslant 1$. By Proposition 7.1.2, we can take d to be rational-valued. For each k, let $g(k)$ be the least n such that $h(n) \geqslant 2^{k+1}$. Note that g is total and computable. Let $S_k = \{\sigma \in 2^{\leqslant g(k)} : d(\sigma) > 2^k\}$. The S_k are finite and uniformly computable, and $\mu([\![S_k]\!]) \leqslant 2^{-k}$, by Kolmogorov's Inequality (Theorem 6.3.3). Thus $\{[\![S_k]\!]\}_{k\in\omega}$ is a Kurtz null test. For each k, we have $d(A \upharpoonright g(k)) \geqslant h(g(k)) \geqslant 2^{k+1}$, so $A \in [\![S_k]\!]$ for all k, and hence A is not weakly 1-random. □

Downey, Griffiths, and Reid [111] gave a machine characterization of weak 1-randomness, along the lines of the one for Schnorr randomness in Theorem 7.1.15. That is, it uses initial segment complexity but measured with respect to a restricted class of machines.

Definition 7.2.14 (Downey, Griffiths, and Reid [111]). A *computably layered machine* is a prefix-free machine M for which there is a computable function $f : \omega \to (2^{<\omega})^{<\omega}$ such that

(i) $\bigcup_i f(i) = \operatorname{dom} M$.

(ii) If $\sigma \in f(i+1)$, then there is a $\tau \in f(i)$ such that $M(\tau) \preccurlyeq M(\sigma)$.

(iii) If $\sigma \in f(i)$, then $|M(\sigma)| = |\sigma| + i + 1$.

The idea of a computably layered machine is that each layer $f(i)$ of the domain provides a layer of the range, and the elements of the range become more refined as i increases. For the next theorem, recall that if σ is not in the range of a machine M, then $K_M(\sigma) = \infty$.

Theorem 7.2.15 (Downey, Griffiths, and Reid [111]). *A is weakly 1-random iff for all computably layered machines M, we have $K_M(A \upharpoonright n) \geqslant n - O(1)$.*

Proof. Suppose that A is not weakly 1-random, as witnessed by a Kurtz null test $\{[\![S_i]\!]\}_{i\in\omega}$, where the S_i are finite, prefix-free, and uniformly computable, and $[\![S_i]\!] \supseteq [\![S_{i+1}]\!]$ for all i. By replacing strings by sufficiently long extensions, we may assume that the S_i are pairwise disjoint and that for each $\tau \in S_{i+1}$ there is a $\sigma \in S_i$ such that $\sigma \prec \tau$.

We have

$$\sum_n \sum_{\sigma\in S_{2n+2}} 2^{-(|\sigma|-(n+1))} = \sum_n 2^{n+1}\mu([\![S_{2n+2}]\!]) \leqslant \sum_n 2^{n+1}2^{-2n-2} = 1,$$

so by the KC Theorem, there is a prefix-free machine M such that, for each n and $\sigma \in S_{2n+2}$, there is a τ of length $|\sigma| - (n+1)$ such that $M(\tau) = \sigma$.

Let $f(n) = \{\tau : \exists\sigma \in S_{2n+2}\,(M(\tau) = \sigma)\}$. We claim that f witnesses the fact that M is computably layered. First, f is computable, since S_{2n+2} is finite and the KC Theorem is effective, and clearly $\operatorname{dom}(M) = \bigcup_n f(n)$. By our assumptions on the S_n, for all $\tau \in f(n+1)$, there is a $\sigma \in f(n)$ such that $M(\sigma) \prec M(\tau)$. Finally, let $\tau \in f(n)$. Then it follows directly from the definition of M that $|M(\tau)| = \tau + n + 1$.

Thus M is a computably layered machine. Since A is in every $[\![S_i]\!]$, for each i there is an n such that $A \upharpoonright n \in S_i$, whence $K_M(A \upharpoonright n) = n - (i+1)$.

Now suppose there is a computably layered machine M such that for each d there is an n with $K_M(A \upharpoonright n) < n - d$. Let f be a function witnessing that M is computably layered. Let S_k be the set of all σ such that $K_M(\sigma) < |\sigma| - k$ but $K_M(\tau) \geqslant |\tau| - k$ for all $\tau \prec \sigma$. Then

$$\mu([\![S_k]\!]) = \sum_{\sigma \in S_k} 2^{-|\sigma|} \leqslant \sum_{\sigma \in S_k} 2^{-K_M(\sigma)-k} \leqslant 2^{-k}.$$

Suppose that $\tau \in f(k)$ and let $\sigma = M(\tau)$. Then $|\sigma| = |M(\tau)| = |\tau|+k+1$, so $K_M(\sigma) \leqslant |\tau| = |\sigma| - k - 1$, so $\sigma \in S_k$. Conversely, if $\sigma \in S_k$ then there is a τ such that $M(\tau) = \sigma$ and $|\tau| < |\sigma| - k$. For such a τ, we have $|M(\tau)| = |\sigma| > |\tau|+k$, so $\tau \notin f(j)$ for $j < k$. Thus $\tau \in f(j)$ for some $j \geqslant k$. By the properties of f, there is a $\rho \in f(k)$ such that $M(\rho) \preccurlyeq M(\tau) = \sigma$. But since no proper initial segment of σ is in S_k, in fact $M(\rho) = \sigma$.

So $S_k = \{M(\tau) : \tau \in f(k)\}$, and hence the S_k are finite and uniformly computable. Thus $\{[\![S_k]\!]\}_{k\in\omega}$ is a Kurtz null test. Furthermore, by the choice of M, the set A is in every element of this test, and hence is not weakly 1-random. □

In Theorem 7.1.15, we saw that Schnorr randomness can be characterized in terms of computable measure machines. It is an indication of the close relationship between Schnorr randomness and weak 1-randomness that this class of machines can also be used to characterize weak 1-randomness.

Theorem 7.2.16 (Downey, Griffiths, and Reid [111]). *A is not weakly 1-random iff there is a computable measure machine M and a computable function f such that for all n, we have $K_M(A \upharpoonright f(n)) < f(n) - n$.*

Proof. Suppose that A is not weakly 1-random, so there is a Kurtz null test $\{[\![S_n]\!]\}_{n\in\omega}$ such that $A \in \bigcap_n [\![S_n]\!]$, where the S_n are finite and uniformly computable. We may assume that for each S_n, all the strings in S_n have the same length $g(n)$, where g is computable. As shown in Theorem 7.2.15, $\sum_n \sum_{\sigma\in S_{2n+2}} 2^{-(|\sigma|-(n+1))} \leqslant 1$, so by the KC Theorem, there is a prefix-free machine M such that, for each n and $\sigma \in S_{2n+2}$, there is a τ of length $|\sigma| - (n+1)$ such that $M(\tau) = \sigma$.

Let $\alpha = \sum_{\tau \in \mathrm{dom}\, M} 2^{-|\tau|}$. Then

$$\alpha = \sum_n \sum_{\sigma \in S_{2n+2}} 2^{-(|\sigma|-(n+1))} = \sum_n 2^{n+1}\mu([\![U_{2n+2}]\!]).$$

But for any s,

$$\sum_{n>s} 2^{n+1}\mu([\![U_{2n+2}]\!]) \leqslant \sum_{n>s} 2^{n+1-2n-2} = 2^{-s-1},$$

so $\sum_{n\leqslant s} 2^{n+1}\mu([\![U_{2n+2}]\!])$ is an approximation to α to within 2^{-s}, and hence α is computable. Thus M is a computable measure machine.

Let $f(n) = g(2n+2)$. Since $A \in \bigcap_n [\![S_n]\!]$, for each n we have $A \upharpoonright g(2n+2) \in S_n$, whence

$$K_M(A \upharpoonright f(n)) = K_M(A \upharpoonright g(2n+2)) = g(2n+2) - (n+1) < f(n) - n.$$

Now suppose we have a computable measure machine M and a computable function f such that $K_M(A \upharpoonright f(n)) < f(n) - n$ for all n. Let $S_n = \{\sigma \in 2^{f(n)} : K_M(\sigma) < f(n) - n\}$. As in the proof of Theorem 7.2.15, $\mu([\![S_n]\!]) \leqslant 2^{-n}$. Furthermore, the S_n are finite and uniformly computable, since the domain of a computable measure machine is computable. Thus $\{[\![S_n]\!]\}_{n\in\omega}$ is a Kurtz null test, and by choice of M, we have $A \in \bigcap_n [\![S_n]\!]$, so A is not weakly 1-random. □

We finish this section with a Solovay-type characterization of weak 1-randomness.

Definition 7.2.17 (Downey, Griffiths, and Reid [111]). A *Kurtz-Solovay test* is a pair (f, V) consisting of a computable function f and a computable collection $V = \{V_i\}_{i\in\omega}$ of finite, uniformly computable sets of strings such that $\sum_n \mu([\![V_n]\!])$ is finite and computable. We say that A *fails* a Kurtz-Solovay test if for all n, the set A is in at least n many of $[\![V_0]\!], \dots, [\![V_{f(n)}]\!]$.

Note that given any Kurtz-Solovay test (f, V), a new Kurtz-Solovay test $(n \mapsto n, \widehat{V})$ can be defined via $\widehat{V}_k = V_{f(k)} \cup \cdots \cup V_{f(k+1)-1}$.

Theorem 7.2.18 (Downey, Griffiths, and Reid [111]). *A is weakly 1-random iff A does not fail any Kurtz-Solovay test.*

Proof. Suppose that A is not weakly 1-random, so there is a Kurtz null test $\{[\![V_n]\!]\}_{n\in\omega}$ such that $A \in \bigcap_n [\![V_n]\!]$. It is easy to check that $(n \mapsto n, \{V_n\}_{n\in\omega})$ is a Kurtz-Solovay test, and since A is in every $[\![V_n]\!]$, it fails this test.

Now suppose that A fails a Kurtz-Solovay test $(f, \{V_n\}_{n\in\omega})$. Assume without loss of generality that $\sum_n \mu([\![V_n]\!]) \leqslant 1$. Let T_k be the set of all σ for which there are at least 2^k many V_i with $i \leqslant f(2^k)$ such that σ extends an element of V_i. Let S_k be the set of all $\sigma \in T_k$ such that $\tau \notin T_k$ for $\tau \prec \sigma$. Then $\sum_n \mu([\![V_n]\!]) \geqslant 2^k \mu([\![S_k]\!])$, so $\mu([\![S_k]\!]) \leqslant 2^{-k}$. Furthermore, the S_k are finite and uniformly computable, since the V_n are, so $\{[\![S_k]\!]\}_{k\in\omega}$ is a Kurtz null test.

Since A fails the Kurtz-Solovay test $(f, \{V_n\}_{n\in\omega})$, for each k, the set A is in at least 2^k many of $[\![V_0]\!], [\![V_1]\!], \dots, [\![V_{f(2^k)}]\!]$, so there is an m for which there are at least 2^k many $i \leqslant f(2k)$ such that $A \upharpoonright m$ extends a string in V_i. Thus $A \in \bigcap_k [\![S_k]\!]$, and hence A is not weakly 1-random. □

7.2.3 Schnorr randomness via Kurtz null tests

Schnorr randomness can also be characterized in terms of Kurtz null tests.

Definition 7.2.19 (Downey, Griffiths, and Reid [111]). A *Kurtz array* is a uniform family of Kurtz null tests $\{V_j^n\}_{n,j\in\omega}$ such that $\mu(V_j^n) \leqslant 2^{-j+n+1}$ for all n and j.

The uniformity in this definition means that the V_j^n are uniformly Σ_1^0 classes and that the functions witnessing that the tests $\{V_j^n\}_{j\in\omega}$ are Kurtz null tests are uniformly computable.

Theorem 7.2.20 (Downey, Griffiths, and Reid [111]). *A set A is Schnorr random iff for all Kurtz arrays $\{V_j^n\}_{n,j\in\omega}$, there is an n such that $A \notin V_j^n$ for all j.*

Proof. Suppose that A is not Schnorr random, and let $\{U_n\}_{n\in\omega}$ be a Schnorr test with $\mu(U_n) = 2^{-n}$ such that $A \in \bigcap_n U_n$. Let s_j be the least stage s such that $\mu(U_n[s]) \geqslant 2^{-n} - 2^{-(n+j+1)}$ and let $V_j^n = U_n[s_j+1] \setminus U_n[s_j]$ for all n and j. Then

$$\mu(V_j^n) = \mu(U_n[s_j+1]) - \mu(U_n[s_j]) \leqslant 2^{-n} - (2^{-n} - 2^{-(n+j+1)}) = 2^{-(n+j+1)}.$$

It is clear that the other conditions for being a Kurtz array hold of $\{V_j^n\}_{n,j\in\omega}$, so this family is a Kurtz array. Since $A \in \bigcap_n U_n$ and $\bigcup_j V_j^n = U_n$, for each n there is a j such that $A \in V_j^n$.

Conversely, suppose we have a Kurtz array $\{V_j^n\}_{n,j\in\omega}$ such that for each n there is a j with $A \in V_j^n$. Let $U_n = \bigcup_j V_j^n$. Then the U_n are uniformly Σ_1^0 and the measures $\mu(U_n)$ are uniformly computable, since $\mu(U_n) - \mu(\bigcup_{j\leqslant c} V_j^n) \leqslant 2^{-c}$. Furthermore, $\mu(U_n) \leqslant \sum_j \mu(V_j^n) \leqslant \sum_j 2^{-n+j+1} = 2^{-n}$. Thus $\{U_n\}_{n\in\omega}$ is a Schnorr test, and clearly $A \in \bigcap_n U_n$. □

Nicholas Rupprecht noticed that the characterization above allows for another elegant characterization in terms of a variation on Kurtz null tests.

Definition 7.2.21 (Rupprecht [personal communication]). A *finite total Solovay test* is a sequence $\{S_n\}_{n\in\omega}$ of uniformly computable clopen sets (i.e., $S_n = [\![\{\sigma : \sigma \in D_{g(n)}\}]\!]$ where g is computable) such that $\sum_n \mu(S_n)$ is finite and computable. A set A *passes* this test if it is in only finitely many of the S_n.

Notice that this is the Kurtz-style analog of Downey and Griffith's notion of total Solovay test from [109] (see Definition 7.1.9). Indeed, we have avoided the term *total Kurtz-Solovay test* only to avoid confusion with the Kurtz-Solovay tests from Definition 7.2.17. The next result should be compared with Theorem 7.1.10.

Corollary 7.2.22 (Rupprecht [personal communication]). *A set is Schnorr random iff it passes all finite total Solovay tests.*

Proof. One direction is clear from Theorem 7.1.10, since every finite total Solovay test is a total Solovay test. For the other direction, suppose that A passes all finite total Solovay tests. Let $\{V_j^n\}_{n,j\in\omega}$ be a Kurtz array. This array is clearly a finite total Solovay test, so A is in only finitely many of its elements, and hence there is an n such that $A \notin V_j^n$ for all j. □

7.2.4 Weakly 1-random left-c.e. reals

There are no weakly 1-random c.e. sets. In fact, we have the following, where a set is *bi-immune* if neither it nor its complement contains an infinite c.e. set.

Theorem 7.2.23 (Jockusch, see Kurtz [228]). *If A is weakly 1-random then A is bi-immune.*

Proof. Let W be an infinite c.e. set. Let $U = \{X : \exists n\,(n \in W \wedge X(n) = 0)\}$. Then U is a Σ_1^0 class of measure 1, so every weakly 1-random set must be in U. The same argument applies to the complement of a weakly 1-random set. □

Jockusch [186] showed that there are continuum many degrees that contain no bi-immune sets, so we have the following.

Corollary 7.2.24 (Jockusch, see Kurtz [228]). *There are continuum many degrees that contain no weakly 1-random sets.*

While no c.e. set can be weakly 1-random, the same is not true of c.e. *degrees*. Of course we know that the complete c.e. degree is 1-random, and hence weakly 1-random, but in fact, as shown by Kurtz [228], every nonzero c.e. degree contains a weakly 1-random set. The following is an extension of that result. (See Theorem 8.13.3 for a relativized form of this theorem.)

Theorem 7.2.25 (Downey, Griffiths, and Reid [111]). *Every nonzero c.e. degree contains a weakly 1-random left-c.e. real.*

Proof sketch. Let B be a noncomputable c.e. set. We build a weakly 1-random left-c.e. real $\alpha \equiv_T B$. The construction combines a technique for avoiding test sets with permitting and coding. We use an enumeration of partial Kurtz null tests $U^0, U^1, \dots$ and ensure that, for each U^i that really is a Kurtz null test, α is not in the null set determined by that test. A permitting condition ensures that if $B_s \upharpoonright n = B \upharpoonright n$ then $\alpha_s \upharpoonright n = \alpha \upharpoonright n$.

We build α by defining sets $[0,1] \supseteq X_0 \supseteq X_1 \supseteq \cdots$ and letting $\alpha_s = \inf X_s$. We have two kinds of requirements:

$$\mathcal{R}_i : \text{If } U^i \text{ is a Kurtz null test then } \exists k, s\,(X_s \cap U_k^i = \emptyset)$$

and

$$\mathcal{P}_j : \exists n\, \forall i < j\,(\alpha(n-j) + i = B(i-1)).$$

The latter requirements code B into α, although it is still necessary to argue that the coding locations can be recovered from α.

Each requirement $\mathcal{R}_i$ has infinitely many strategies $R_{\langle i,j\rangle}$. The strategy R_e with $e = \langle i,j\rangle$ deals with a test set U^i_k, where k is determined during the construction to make sure the maximum possible measure of the test set is sufficiently small. The strategy for a single strategy R_e is as follows.

If τ_e is not defined, let $\tau_e = \tau_{e-1}0$ (where τ_{e-1} is a string defined by previous requirements), and choose k large enough so that $\mu(U^i_k) < 2^{-|\tau_e|-2}$. If R_e never acts and is never initialized then the entire construction takes place within $[\![\tau_e]\!]$, producing a real α extending τ_e. We have $[\![\tau_e[s]]\!] \subseteq X_s$ at each stage s, but the τ_e are not "permanent" like the X_s are, in the sense that while $X_{s+1} \subseteq X_s$ for all s, we sometimes have $\tau_e[s+1]$ not extending $\tau_e[s]$.

The strategy R_e requires attention if U^i_k becomes nonempty. Once R_e requires attention, it acts if $B_s \upharpoonright |\tau_e|$ changes, at which point R_e defines $X_{s+1} = X_s \cap \overline{U^i_k} \cap \overline{[\![\tau_e]\!]}$, causing the construction to move out of $[\![\tau_e]\!]$. For a nonempty string τ, let τ^+ be the string obtained by changing the last bit of τ from 0 to 1 or vice versa. Since $\mu(U^i_k) < 2^{-|\tau_e|-2}$, there is a $\sigma_e \succcurlyeq \tau^+_e$ such that $[\![\sigma_e]\!] \cap X_s = [\![\sigma_e]\!]$. The construction then continues within such a cone $[\![\sigma_e]\!]$.

The strategy for a single requirement $\mathcal{P}_e$ is as follows. Given τ_e, extend it by e many bits to code $B \upharpoonright e$. This action extends the string τ_e defined by R_e. When defining τ_{e+1}, the strategy R_{e+1} uses this extended version of τ_e.

In the construction we use an additional notion of satisfaction: If R_e acts, where $e = \langle i,j\rangle$, then we declare $R_{e'}$ to be satisfied for all $e' = \langle i,j'\rangle$ with $j' \in \mathbb{N}$. A strategy $R_{e'}$ remains satisfied for the rest of the construction, and hence never requires attention or acts, unless it is initialized by the action of a stronger priority strategy. When a strategy R_e is initialized, its string τ_e is canceled, as is its choice of k. When a strategy for a requirement $\mathcal{P}_e$ is initialized it simply ceases to have any impact in updating strings in the construction.

The measures of the U^i_k are chosen so that at no time can we run out of space to meet the requirements.

The construction is now a reasonably straightforward application of the finite injury priority method with permitting and coding. See [111] for details. □

7.2.5 Solovay genericity and randomness

Solovay [370] used forcing with closed sets of positive measure in his construction of a model of set theory (without the full axiom of choice but with dependent choice) in which every set of reals is Lebesgue measurable. For those familiar with the basics of set-theoretic forcing, we note that the generic extension of a ground model M obtained by Solovay forcing is of the form $M[x]$ for a *random real* x, which has the property that it is not contained in any null Borel set coded in M. (See Jech [185] for more details.) The connection between this notion and our notions of algorithmic randomness should be clear. Kautz [200] made it explicit by giving a miniaturization (i.e., an effectivization) of Solovay's notion that yields a characterization of weak n-randomness in terms of a forcing relation, in the same way that Cohen forcing is miniaturized to yield the notion of n-genericity. Thus, while there is no correlation between Cohen forcing and randomness,[8] we do have a notion of forcing related to algorithmic randomness.

Let $\mathbb{P}_n$ denote the partial ordering of Π^0_n classes of positive measure under inclusion. We work in the language of arithmetic with an additional set constant X and a membership symbol $\in$. For a sentence φ in this language and a set A, we write $A \vDash \varphi$ to mean that φ holds when X is interpreted as A and all other symbols are interpreted in the usual way.

Definition 7.2.26 (Kautz [200]). (i) For $T \in \mathbb{P}_n$, we write $T \Vdash \varphi$ if $A \vDash \varphi$ for all $A \in T$.

(ii) For a set A, we write $A \Vdash \varphi$ if there is a $T \in \mathbb{P}_n$ such that $A \in T$ and $T \Vdash \varphi$.

(iii) A set A is *Solovay n-generic* if for every Σ^0_n formula φ, either $A \Vdash \varphi$ or $A \Vdash \neg\varphi$.

Kautz [200] showed that this notion is well-behaved.

Proposition 7.2.27 (Kautz [200]).

(i) *(Monotonicity) If $T \Vdash \varphi$ then for all $\widehat{T} \subset T$ in $\mathbb{P}_n$, we have $\widehat{T} \Vdash \varphi$.*

(ii) *(Consistency) It is not the case that $T \Vdash \varphi$ and $T \Vdash \neg\varphi$.*

(iii) *(Quasi-completeness) For every Σ^0_n sentence φ and each $T \in \mathbb{P}_n$, there is an $S \subseteq T$ in $\mathbb{P}_n$ such that either $S \Vdash \varphi$ or $S \Vdash \neg\varphi$.*

(iv) *(Forcing=Truth) A is Solovay n-generic iff for each Σ^0_n or Π^0_n sentence φ, we have $A \Vdash \varphi$ iff $A \vDash \varphi$.*

Quasi-completeness is interesting to us in that it can be proved using algorithmic randomness: Let $U_0, U_1, \dots$ be a universal Martin-Löf test relative to $\emptyset^{(n-1)}$. Let P_i be the complement of U_i. Since the measures of the P_i go to 1, there must be an i such that $T \cap P_i \in \mathbb{P}_n$. Let $S = T \cap P_i$. If $A \vDash \varphi$ for all $A \in S$ we are done, since then $S \Vdash \varphi$. Otherwise the Π^0_n class $\widehat{S} = S \cap \{A : A \vDash \neg\varphi\}$ is nonempty. Since $\widehat{S}$ contains (only) n-randoms, it must be in $\mathbb{P}_n$, and $\widehat{S} \Vdash \neg\varphi$.

---

[8] We will explore the relationship between algorithmic randomness and n-genericity in Chapter 8.

Kautz [200] also showed that Solovay n-genericity exactly characterizes weak n-randomness.

Theorem 7.2.28 (Kautz [200]). *A set is Solovay n-generic iff it is weakly n-random.*

Proof. Suppose that A is not weakly n-random. Then A is in some Π^0_n class S of measure 0. Let φ be a Π^0_n formula such that $S = \{B : B \vDash \varphi\}$. Since $A \vDash \varphi$, we cannot have $A \Vdash \neg\varphi$. But since S has measure 0, there is no $T \in \mathbb{P}_n$ such that $T \Vdash \varphi$. Thus A is not Solovay n-generic.

Now suppose that A is weakly n-random and let φ be a Σ^0_n sentence. Let $S = \{B : B \vDash \varphi\}$. The class S is a union of Π^0_{n-1} classes $C_0, C_1, \ldots$. If $A \in S$, then A is in some C_i. This C_i must have positive measure, so $C_i \in \mathbb{P}_n$ and $C_i \Vdash \varphi$. Thus $A \Vdash \varphi$. If $A \notin S$ then A is in the Π^0_n class $\overline{S} = \{B : B \vDash \neg\varphi\}$. Again, $\overline{S} \in \mathbb{P}_n$, and $\overline{S} \Vdash \neg\varphi$. Thus $A \Vdash \neg\varphi$. □

7.3 Decidable machines

Bienvenu and Merkle [40] introduced a class of machines that can be used to classify most of the randomness notions we have met so far, in particular, weak 1-randomness, Schnorr randomness, and 1-randomness.

Definition 7.3.1 (Bienvenu and Merkle [40]). A machine M is *decidable* if $\mathrm{dom}(M)$ is computable.

Any computable measure machine is decidable, as is any bounded machine.

As remarked following the proof of Theorem 2.19.2, any Σ^0_1 class can be generated by a computable set of strings, so Martin-Löf tests can be thought of as determined by uniformly computable sets of strings. Then if we follow the KC Theorem version of the proof of Schnorr's Theorem 6.2.3, which converts tests to machines, it is not hard to show the following.

Theorem 7.3.2 (Bienvenu and Merkle [40]). *A set X is 1-random iff $K_M(X \upharpoonright n) \geqslant n - O(1)$ for all decidable prefix-free machines M. Moreover, there is a fixed decidable prefix-free machine N such that X is 1-random iff $K_N(X \upharpoonright n) \geqslant n - O(1)$.*[9]

Note that K_M for a decidable machine M is a particular example of a computable function f with $\sum_n 2^{-f(n)} \leqslant 1$, so the above result can be restated as follows.

---

[9] Another way to prove this result is to notice that, given a prefix-free machine M, we can define a decidable prefix-free machine N by waiting until σ enters $\mathrm{dom}(M)$ at stage s and then letting $N(\sigma\tau) = M(\sigma)\tau$ for all $\tau \in 2^s$. For any X, if $K_M(X \upharpoonright n) \leqslant n - c$ then there is an s such that $K_N(X \upharpoonright n + s) \leqslant n + s - c$.

Corollary 7.3.3. *A set X is 1-random iff for all computable functions f with $\sum_n 2^{-f(n)} < \infty$, we have $f(X \upharpoonright n) \geqslant n - O(1)$.*

For Schnorr randomness, we have the following.

Theorem 7.3.4 (Bienvenu and Merkle [40]). *A set X is Schnorr random iff for all decidable prefix-free machines M and all computable orders g, we have $K_M(X \upharpoonright n) \geqslant n - g(n) - O(1)$.*

Proof. Suppose that X is not Schnorr random. Then by Definition 7.1.4, there is a computable martingale d and a computable order h such that $d(X \upharpoonright n) \geqslant h(n)$ for infinitely many n. Let g be a computable order with $g(n) = o(h(n))$. We may assume that $d(\lambda) \leqslant 1$. Let A_k be the set of strings σ such that $d(\sigma) \geqslant 2^{k+1}g(|\sigma|)$ but $d(\tau) < 2^{k+1}g(|\tau|)$ for all $\tau \prec \sigma$. Then $X \in \bigcap_k [\![A_k]\!]$. By Kolmogorov's Inequality (Theorem 6.3.3),

$$2^{k+1} \sum_{\sigma \in A_k} 2^{-|\sigma| + \log(g(|\sigma|))} = \sum_{\sigma \in A_k} 2^{-|\sigma|+k+1+\log(g(|\sigma|))}$$
$$\leqslant \sum_{\sigma \in A_k} 2^{-|\sigma|} d(\sigma) \leqslant 1.$$

Thus

$$\sum_k \sum_{\sigma \in A_k} 2^{-|\sigma| + \log(g(|\sigma|))} \leqslant 1.$$

Therefore, we can apply the KC Theorem to get a prefix-free machine M corresponding to the requests $(|\sigma| - \log(g(|\sigma|)), \sigma)$ for all k and $\sigma \in A_k$.

Since $d(\lambda) \leqslant 1$, for all σ we have that $2^{|\sigma|} \geqslant d(\sigma)$, so if $\sigma \in A_k$ then $|\sigma| - \log(g(|\sigma|)) \geqslant k$. Thus, to check whether $\tau \in \operatorname{dom} M$, it suffices to consider A_k for $k \leqslant |\tau|$. For each such k, there are only finitely many σ with $|\sigma| - \log(g(|\sigma|)) = |\tau|$. Once we have made requests for all such σ, we know τ can no longer be added to the domain of M.

Hence M is a decidable machine, and since $K_M(\sigma) \leqslant |\sigma| - \log(g(|\sigma|))$ for all $\sigma \in A_k$, there are infinitely many k such that $K_M(X \upharpoonright k) \leqslant k - \log(g(k))$. Taking a computable order $\widehat{g}$ with $\widehat{g}(n) = o(\log g(n))$, for each c there is an n such that $K_M(X \upharpoonright n) < n - \widehat{g}(n) - c$.

For the converse, suppose we have a computable order g and a prefix-free decidable machine M such that for each k we have $K_M(X \upharpoonright n) < n - g(n) - k$ for infinitely many n. We may assume that g is $o(\log n)$ without loss of generality. For each k let A_k be the set of σ such that $K_M(\sigma) < |\sigma| - g(|\sigma|) - k$ but $K_M(\tau) \geqslant |\tau| - g(|\tau|) - k$ for all $\tau \prec \sigma$. The A_k form a uniformly computable family of prefix-free subsets of $2^{<\omega}$ such that, for all k,

$$\sum_{\sigma \in A_k} 2^{-|\sigma| + g(|\sigma|)} \leqslant \sum_{\sigma \in A_k} 2^{-K_M(\sigma) - k} \leqslant 2^{-k}.$$

We can then define a martingale d as follows.

Let d^p_σ be the martingale that doubles its capital along σ except for the first p many bits. That is, let $d^p_\sigma(\tau) = 1$ if $|\tau| \leqslant p$, let $d^p_\sigma(\tau) = 2^{\min(|\sigma|,|\tau|)}$ if $p < |\tau|$ and $\tau(p)\dots\tau(\min(|\sigma|,|\tau|)-1) = \sigma(p)\dots\sigma(\min(|\sigma|,|\tau|)-1)$, and let $d^p_\sigma(\tau) = 0$ for all other τ. Let

$$d(\tau) = \sum_k \sum_{\sigma \in A_k} 2^{-|\sigma|+g(|\sigma|)} d_\sigma^{\frac{g(|\sigma|)}{2}}(\tau).$$

Clearly, d is a martingale. Furthermore,

$$d(\lambda) = \sum_k \sum_{\sigma \in A_k} 2^{-|\sigma|+g(|\sigma|)},$$

and since $\sum_{\sigma \in A_k} 2^{-|\sigma|+g(|\sigma|)} \leqslant 2^{-k}$, we can computably approximate $d(\lambda)$, which is thus a computable real. Now we show that if we can compute $d(\tau)$ then we can compute $d(\tau i)$ for $i = 0, 1$. We have

$$d(\tau i) - d(\tau) = \sum_k \sum_{\sigma \in A_k} 2^{-|\sigma|+g(|\sigma|)} (d_\sigma^{\frac{g(|\sigma|)}{2}}(\tau i) - d_\sigma^{\frac{g(|\sigma|)}{2}}(\tau)).$$

This sum is actually a finite sum, as

$$d_\sigma^{\frac{g(|\sigma|)}{2}}(\tau) = d_\sigma^{\frac{g(|\sigma|)}{2}}(\tau i) = 1$$

for all σ with $g(|\sigma|) \geqslant 2|\tau| + 2$. Thus, by induction, d is computable.

To finish the proof, note that if $\sigma \in \bigcup_k A_k$, then

$$d(\sigma) \geqslant 2^{-|\sigma|+g(|\sigma|)} d_\sigma^{\frac{g(|\sigma|)}{2}}(\sigma) \geqslant 2^{\frac{g(|\sigma|)}{2}}.$$

But $2^{\frac{g(|\sigma|)}{2}}$ is a computable order, and there are infinitely many prefixes of X in $\bigcup_k A_k$, so X is not Schnorr random by Definition 7.1.4. □

For weak 1-randomness, we have the following.

Theorem 7.3.5 (Bienvenu and Merkle [40]). *The following are equivalent.*

(i) *X is not weakly 1-random.*

(ii) *There exists a decidable prefix-free machine M and a computable order f such that $C_M(X \upharpoonright f(n)) \leqslant f(n) - n$ for all n.*

(iii) *There exists a decidable (plain) machine M and a computable order f such that $C_M(X \upharpoonright f(n)) \leqslant f(n) - n$ for all n.*

Proof. If X is not weakly 1-random, then by Theorem 7.2.16, there is a computable measure machine M and a computable increasing function f such that $C_M(X \upharpoonright f(n)) < f(n) - n$ for all n. This machine is a decidable prefix-free machine, so we have (ii) and (iii). Since (ii) clearly implies (iii), we are left with showing that (iii) implies (i).

Assume (iii) and let

$$B_n = \{\sigma : |\sigma| = f(2n) \wedge C_M(\sigma) \leqslant |\sigma| - 2n\}.$$

Let d_σ be the martingale that doubles its capital along σ; that is, $d_\sigma(\tau) = 2^{-|\tau|}$ for $\tau \preccurlyeq \sigma$ and $d_\sigma(\tau) = 2^{-|\sigma|}$ for $\tau \succ \sigma$, with $d_\sigma(\tau) = 0$ for all other τ. Define the martingale d by

$$d(\tau) = \sum_n \sum_{\sigma \in B_n} 2^{-f(2n)+n} d_\sigma(\tau).$$

For all n,

$$\sum_{\sigma \in B_n} d_\sigma(\tau) \leqslant |B_n| 2^{|\tau|} \leqslant 2^{f(2n)-2n+|\tau|+1},$$

so

$$\sum_{\sigma \in B_n} 2^{-f(2n)+n} d_\sigma(\tau) \leqslant 2^{-n+|\tau|+1},$$

and hence d is computable.

Furthermore, $X \upharpoonright f(2n) \in B_n$ for all n, and therefore for all $m \geqslant f(2n)$, we have $d_\sigma(X \upharpoonright m) = 2^{f(2n)}$ and hence

$$d(X \upharpoonright m) \geqslant \sum_{\sigma \in B_n} 2^{-f(2n)+n} d_\sigma(X \upharpoonright m) \geqslant 2^n.$$

Thus if we let $g(m) = 2^n$ for the largest n such that $f(2n) \leqslant m$ (or $g(m) = 0$ if there is none), then, by Theorem 7.2.13, g is a computable order showing, together with d, that X is not weakly 1-random. □

Using similar methods, Bienvenu and Merkle [40] also obtained the following characterization of weak 1-randomness.

Theorem 7.3.6 (Bienvenu and Merkle [40]). *The following are equivalent.*

(i) *X is not weakly 1-random.*

(ii) *There exists a decidable prefix-free machine M and a computable order h such that $C_M(x \upharpoonright n) \leqslant n - h(n)$ for all n.*

(iii) *There exists a decidable (plain) machine M and a computable order h such that $C_M(x \upharpoonright n) \leqslant n - h(n)$ for all n.*

7.4 Selection revisited

7.4.1 Stochasticity

In this section we return to the roots of the subject, re-examining von Mises' idea of selection. As we have seen in Section 6.5, a selection function is a partial function $f : 2^{<\omega} \to \{\text{yes}, \text{no}\}$. Recall that we think of f as a rule that, given some bits of a sequence, selects the next bit to bet on.

Recall also the following notation from Section 6.5. For a sequence A and a selection function f, let $s_f(A, n)$ be the nth number k such that

$f(A \upharpoonright k) =$ yes, if such a number exists. If $s_f(A, n-1)$ is defined, let $S_f(A, n) = \sum_{i<n} A(s_f(A, i))$. In other words, $S_f(A, n)$ is the number of 1's among the first n many bits of A selected by f. If f is the function sending every string to yes, then we write $S(\alpha, n)$ for $S_f(\alpha, n)$. We call $s_0(A, n), s_1(A, n), \ldots$ the sequence of places of A *selected* by f.

Given a collection $\mathcal{C}$ of selection functions, we say that A is *stochastic for* $\mathcal{C}$ if for any $f \in \mathcal{C}$, either the sequence of places of A selected by f is finite, or $\lim_n \frac{S_f(A,n)}{n} = \frac{1}{2}$.

Definition 7.4.1. A sequence is *von Mises-Wald-Church stochastic* if it is stochastic for all partial computable selection functions.

A sequence is *Church stochastic* if it is stochastic for all computable selection functions.

There is a natural way to turn a selection function f into a (super)martingale d. For each k and $i = 0, 1$, define the martingale d_k^i as follows. Let $d_k^i(\lambda) = 1$. Given $d_k^i(\sigma)$, if $f(\sigma) =$ no, then let $d_k^i(\sigma j) = d_k^i(\sigma)$ for $j = 0, 1$. If $f(\sigma) =$ yes, then let $d_k^i(\sigma i) = (1 + 2^{-k})d_k^i(\sigma)$ and $d_k^i(\sigma(1-i)) = (1 - 2^{-k})d_k^i(\sigma)$. If $f(\sigma)\uparrow$, then let $d_k^i(\sigma j) = 0$ for $j = 0, 1$. In other words, d_k^i waits for f to select a place, then bets a part of its capital that depends on k that the next bit will be i.

Let $d(\sigma) = \sum_k 2^{-k}(d_k^0(\sigma) + d_k^1(\sigma))$. Then d is clearly a martingale, and it is also easy to see that if f is total computable then d is a computable martingale, while if f is partial computable then d is a c.e. supermartingale.

Now suppose that the sequence of places of A selected by f is infinite, and $\lim_n \frac{S_f(A,n)}{n} \neq \frac{1}{2}$. For each n, let us denote $S_f(A, n)$ by n_1 and $n - S_f(A, n)$ by n_0. In other words, n_0 and n_1 are the number of 0's and 1's, respectively, in the first n bits of A selected by f. Suppose that $\varepsilon > 0$ is such that there are infinitely many n with $n_0 > (\frac{1}{2} + \varepsilon)n$. (The case in which there are infinitely many n with $n_1 > (\frac{1}{2} + \varepsilon)n$ is of course symmetric.) For any such n, let $m = s_f(A, n) + 1$, where recall that $s_f(A, n)$ is the nth place of A selected by f. Then for any k we have

$$d_k^0(A \upharpoonright m) = (1 + 2^{-k})^{n_0}(1 - 2^{-k})^{n_1} \geqslant (1 + 2^{-k})^{(\frac{1}{2}+\varepsilon)n}(1 - 2^{-k})^{(\frac{1}{2}-\varepsilon)n}.$$

Thus

$$\log d_k^0(A \upharpoonright m) \geqslant n((\tfrac{1}{2} + \varepsilon)\log(1 + 2^{-k}) + (\tfrac{1}{2} - \varepsilon)\log(1 - 2^{-k})).$$

Now consider the function $h : \mathbb{R} \to \mathbb{R}$ defined by

$$h(x) = (\tfrac{1}{2} + \varepsilon)\log(1 + x) + (\tfrac{1}{2} - \varepsilon)\log(1 - x).$$

We have $h(0) = 0$, and the derivative of h is $h'(x) = \frac{\frac{1}{2}+\varepsilon}{1+x} - \frac{\frac{1}{2}-\varepsilon}{1-x}$, so $h'(0) = 2\varepsilon > 0$. Thus, if $x > 0$ is sufficiently small, $h(x) > 0$. So if we choose k large enough, then $\log d_k^0(A \upharpoonright m) \geqslant \delta n$ for some $\delta > 0$ independent of n. Since n can be chosen to be arbitrarily large, $A \in S[d_k]$, and hence $A \in S[d]$.

Thus we have the following facts, which are implicit in the work of Schnorr [349]. A version of the first for a stronger notion of stochasticity appears in Shen [353]. The second is proved in Wang [405].

Theorem 7.4.2 (Schnorr [349], Shen [353], Wang [405]). *If A is 1-random then A is von Mises-Wald-Church stochastic. If A is computably random then A is Church stochastic.*

So we see that computably random sets satisfy the law of large numbers with respect to computable selection functions.

We will show in Corollary 7.4.7 that computable randomness does not imply von Mises-Wald-Church stochasticity. Later, at the end of section 8.4, we will show that Schnorr randomness does not imply Church stochasticity, a result due to Wang [405].

The converse to Theorem 7.4.2 fails to hold. Indeed, for any countable collection E of selection functions, being stochastic for E is not enough to imply even weak 1-randomness. To see that this is the case, fix E and let α be as in Ville's Theorem 6.5.1. That is, α is stochastic for E, but $\frac{S(\alpha,n)}{n} \leqslant \frac{1}{2}$ for all n. Then α is not weakly 1-random, because it is contained in the Π^0_1 class $\{X : \forall n\,(\frac{S(X,n)}{n} \leqslant \frac{1}{2})\}$, which has measure 0.

7.4.2 Partial computable martingales and a threshold phenomenon for stochasticity

In defining a martingale d based on a partial computable selection function f as in the previous subsection, instead of having $d(\sigma j) = 0$ if $f(\sigma)\uparrow$, we can let $d(\sigma j)$ be undefined in that case. We can also apply the proof of Proposition 7.1.2 to make d rational-valued. This definition makes d into a *partial computable martingale.*

Definition 7.4.3. A *partial computable (super)martingale* is a partial computable function $d : 2^{<\omega} \to \mathbb{Q}^{\geqslant 0}$ such that, if $d(\sigma i)$ is defined, then so are $d(\sigma)$ and $d(\sigma(1-i))$, and d, where defined, satisfies the (super)martingale property.

A set is *partial computably random* if no partial computable martingale succeeds on it.[10]

This strengthening of the notion of computable randomness was first considered by Ambos-Spies and Wang (see Ambos-Spies [6], just before the bibliography). Partial computable martingales are also discussed in Terwijn [386], where they are attributed to Fortnow, Freivalds, Gasarch, Kummer, Kurtz, Smith, and Stephan [149]. By the comments above, if a set is partial computably random then it is von Mises-Wald-Church stochastic. It is also

[10]Note that for a partial computable martingale d to succeed on A, we must have $d(A \upharpoonright n)\downarrow$ for all n.

clear that 1-random sets are partial computably random, since a partial computable martingale d can be turned into a c.e. martingale $\widehat{d}$ by defining $\widehat{d}(\sigma)$ to be 0 while $d(\sigma)$ is undefined and then redefining $\widehat{d}(\sigma)$ to be $d(\sigma)$.

Using this notion, we can show that there are von Mises-Wald-Church stochastic sets whose initial segment complexities are quite far from those of 1-random sets. The following theorem follows a line of work including Daley [86] and Li and Vitányi [248].

Theorem 7.4.4 (Merkle [266], Lathrop and Lutz [236], Muchnik, see [289][11]).

(i) *There is a computably random A such that for all computable orders f, we have $C(A \upharpoonright n \mid n) \leqslant f(n)$ for almost all n.*

(ii) *There is a partial computably random B such that for all computable orders f, we have $C(B \upharpoonright n \mid n) \leqslant f(n) \log n$ for almost all n.*

Proof. We begin by proving part (i). Let $F_s = \{i \leqslant s : \Phi_i \text{ is an order}\}$. Let $d_0, d_1, \ldots$ be an effective enumeration of all partial computable martingales with initial capital 1, and let $D_s = \{i \leqslant s : d_i \text{ is total}\}$. Let $n_0 = 0$ and

$$n_{s+1} = \min\{n > n_s : \Phi_i(n) > 3(s+1) \text{ for all } i \in F_s\}.$$

Let $I_s = [n_s, n_{s+1})$.

We build A in stages. Let $\widehat{d}_s = \sum_{i \in D_s} 2^{-(i+n_i+1)} d_i$. Note that $\widehat{d}_s$ is a martingale. Assume we have defined $A \upharpoonright n$. Let $\sigma = A \upharpoonright n$ and let s be such that $n \in I_s$. Let $A(n) = 0$ if $\widehat{d}_s(\sigma 0) \leqslant \widehat{d}_s(\sigma)$ and $A(n) = 1$ otherwise.

We claim that for all s and $n \in I_s$, we have $\widehat{d}_s(A \upharpoonright n) < 2 - 2^{-s}$. We prove this claim by induction on n. The case $n = 0$ is clear. For the induction step, since the construction of A ensures that $\widehat{d}_s(A \upharpoonright n)$ is nonincreasing on I_s, it suffices to consider $n = n_s$. Let $\sigma = A \upharpoonright (n-1)$. Then

$$\begin{aligned}\widehat{d}_s(\sigma A(n)) \leqslant \widehat{d}_s(\sigma) &= \widehat{d}_{s-1}(\sigma) + 2^{-(s+n+1)} d_s(\sigma) \\ &< 2 - 2^{-(s-1)} + 2^{-s} = 2 - 2^{-s}.\end{aligned}$$

This fact establishes the claim. Let i be such that d_i is total. Then for $s \geqslant i$ and $n \in I_s$, we have $d_i(A \upharpoonright n) \leqslant 2^{i+n_i+1} \widehat{d}_s(A \upharpoonright n) < 2^{i+n_i+2}$, so A is computably random.

To conclude the proof, we need to show that for all computable orders f, we have $C(A \upharpoonright n \mid n) \leqslant f(n)$ for almost all n. The key observation is that the sets F_s and D_s can be coded by a string τ_s of length $2s$ and that, given these two sets, we can simulate the construction of $A \upharpoonright n_{s+1}$. Thus, for any $n \in I_s$, we have $C(A \upharpoonright n \mid n) \leqslant 2s + O(1)$. So for any computable

[11] This result was proved by Merkle in the form stated here, but he points out in [266] that the slightly weaker results of Lathrop and Lutz and of Muchnik discussed below are close to parts (i) and (ii), respectively, and were proved by essentially the same methods.

order Φ_i, if s is sufficiently large and $n \in I_s$, then

$$C(A \upharpoonright n \mid n) \leqslant 2s + O(1) < 3s < \Phi_i(n_s) \leqslant \Phi_i(n).$$

The proof of part (ii) is a modification of that of part (i). We now let D_s be all $i \leqslant s$, but in defining the sum $\widehat{d}_s(\sigma)$, we omit any d_i such that $d_i(\sigma)\uparrow$. In this case, in order to simulate the construction of $A \upharpoonright n_{s+1}$, we still need s bits to code F_s, but to decode $A \upharpoonright n$ for $n < n_{s+1}$, we now also need to know for each d_i with $i \leqslant s$, whether $d_i(A \upharpoonright n-1)$ is defined, and if not, what is the largest $m < n$ such that $d_i(A \upharpoonright m)$ is undefined. This information can be given with s many strings of $\log n$ many bits each. The result now follows as in part (i). □

Theorem 7.4.4 can be viewed as the culmination of a long sequence of results on stochastic and random sequences. Daley [86] looked at replacing some results on randomness due to Loveland by results on stochasticity. Lathrop and Lutz [236] introduced what they called *ultracompressible* sets, defined as those sets X such that for every computable order g, we have $K(X \upharpoonright n) \leqslant K(n)+g(n)$ for almost all n. They proved the following result, which follows from Theorem 7.4.4 (i) by taking, say, $f(n) = \log g(n)$, since $K(X \upharpoonright n) \leqslant K(n) + O(C(X \upharpoonright n \mid n))$.

Theorem 7.4.5 (Lathrop and Lutz [236]). *There are computably random ultracompressible sets.*[12]

Similarly, Theorem 7.4.4 (ii) shows that there are partial computably random sets X such that $K(X \upharpoonright n) \leqslant O((\log n)^2)$, say, thus establishing a strong failure of the converse to the first part of Theorem 7.4.2.

A weaker form of Theorem 7.4.4 (ii) was also established by An. A. Muchnik in [289, Theorem 9.5]. In that version, the set being constructed depends on the computable order f, rather than there being a single set that works for all computable orders.

Merkle [266] also showed that being stochastic does have *some* consequences for the initial segment complexity of a set. The following result generalizes the fact that no c.e. set can be von Mises-Wald-Church stochastic (which is obvious because every infinite c.e. set contains an infinite computable subset). Together with Theorem 7.4.4 (ii), this result establishes a kind of threshold phenomenon in the initial segment complexity behavior of von Mises-Wald-Church stochastic sequences.

[12] In Chapter 11, we will discuss the important notion of a *K-trivial set*, which is a set X such that $K(X \upharpoonright n) \leqslant K(n) + O(1)$. As we will see in that chapter, the K-trivial sets are far from random in several senses. In particular, K-trivial sets cannot be computably random, or even Schnorr random, because, as we will see, every K-trivial set is low (Theorem 11.4.1), and every low Schnorr random set is 1-random (Theorem 8.11.2). Theorem 7.4.5 shows that computably random sets can nevertheless be "nearly K-trivial".

Theorem 7.4.6 (Merkle [266]). *If there is a c such that $C(X \upharpoonright n) \leqslant c \log n$ for almost all n, then X is not von Mises-Wald-Church stochastic.*

Proof. Let $k = 2c + 2$. Choose a computable sequence $m_0, m_1, \dots$ with each m_i a multiple of $k+1$, such that for all i,

$$10(m_0 + \dots + m_{i-1}) < \frac{m_i}{k+1}.$$

Now partition $\mathbb{N}$ into blocks of consecutive integers $I_0, I_1, \dots$ with $|I_i| = m_i$, and then divide each I_i into $k+1$ many consecutive disjoint intervals $J_i^0, \dots, J_i^k$, each of length $\frac{m_i}{k+1}$. Let $\sigma_i = X \upharpoonright I_i$ and $\sigma_i^j = X \upharpoonright J_i^j$.

We begin by showing that there is an effective procedure that, given $X \upharpoonright \min J_i^t$, enumerates a set T_i^t of strings such that for some $t \leqslant k$,

(i) $\sigma_i^t \in T_i^t$ for almost all i and

(ii) $|T_i^t| \leqslant \frac{m_i}{5(k+1)}$ for infinitely many i.

Let $A_i = \{\sigma \in 2^{m_i} : C(\sigma) < k \log m_i\}$. Note that $|A_i| < 2^{k \log m_i} = m_i^k$. Since $m_0 + \dots + m_{i-1} < m_i$, for almost all i,

$$\begin{aligned} C(\sigma_i) = C(X \upharpoonright I_i) &\leqslant C\Big(X \upharpoonright \sum_{j \leqslant i} m_j\Big) + C\Big(\sum_{j<i} m_j\Big) \\ &\leqslant c \log \sum_{j \leqslant i} m_j + \log \sum_{j<i} m_j \\ &\leqslant c \log(2m_i) + \log(m_i) \leqslant (2c+1)\log m_i = (k-1)\log m_i, \end{aligned}$$

so $\sigma_i \in A_i$.

For each i, let

$$T_i^k = \{\tau : \sigma_i^0 \dots \sigma_i^{k-1} \tau \in A_i\}$$

and for $j < k$, let

$$T_i^j = \{\tau : |\tau| = |J_i^j| \text{ and there are at least } (\tfrac{m_i}{5(k+1)})^{k-j} \\ \text{many strings } \rho \text{ such that } \sigma_i^0 \dots \sigma_i^{j-1} \tau\rho \in A_i\}.$$

There is an effective procedure that, on input i, enumerates A_i, and hence there is an effective procedure that, given i, j, and $\sigma_i^0, \dots, \sigma_i^{j-1}$, enumerates T_i^j. Of course, given $X \upharpoonright \min J_i^t$, we can find i, j, and $\sigma_i^0, \dots, \sigma_i^{j-1}$, so we are left with showing that (i) and (ii) are satisfied for some t.

If $t > 0$ does not satisfy (ii) then, for almost all i, there are more than $\frac{m_i}{5(k+1)}$ many strings in T_i^t; that is, there are more than $\frac{m_i}{5(k+1)}$ many strings τ such that each τ can be extended by at least $(\frac{m_i}{5(k+1)})^{k-t}$ many strings ρ to a string $\sigma_i^0 \dots \sigma_i^{t-1} \tau\rho \in A_i$. Thus, for each such i, there are more than $(\frac{m_i}{5(k+1)})^{k-(t-1)}$ many strings $\tau\rho$ that extend $\sigma_i^0 \dots \sigma_i^{t-1}$ to a string in

A_i, which implies that $\sigma_i^{t-1} \in T_i^{t-1}$. So in this case (i) is satisfied with t replaced by $t-1$.

Condition (i) is satisfied for $t = k$, so if (ii) is satisfied for $t = k$ as well, then we are done. Otherwise, by the previous argument, we know that (i) is satisfied for $t = k-1$ and we can iterate the argument. Proceeding this way, it suffices to argue that (ii) cannot fail for $t = 0$. Assuming that it does, for almost all i, there are more than $\frac{m_i}{5(k+1)}$ many strings τ of length $|J_i^0|$ such that each such τ can be extended in at least $(\frac{m_i}{5(k+1)})^k$ many ways to strings in A_i. Thus, for almost all i, we have $|A_i| > (\frac{m_i}{5(k+1)})^{k+1} > m_i^k$, which is a contradiction, since, as noted above, $|A_i| < m_i^k$.

Now that we have a t satisfying (i) and (ii), we can define two partial computable selection functions r_0 and r_1 that demonstrate that X is not von Mises-Wald-Church stochastic. The idea is that r_j tries to select places in J_i^t such that the corresponding bit of X is j. For each i, let $\tau_i^0, \tau_i^1, \ldots, \tau_i^{|T_i^t|-1}$ be a computable enumeration of T_i^t given $X \upharpoonright \min J_i^t$. Pick i_0 so that $\sigma_i \in T_i^t$ for all $i \geqslant i_0$. Both selection functions select numbers in intervals of the form J_i^t for $i \geqslant i_0$.

On entering such an interval, r_j lets $e = 0$. It then starts scanning bits of X in the interval. It assumes that $\tau_i^e = \sigma_i^t$ and selects n iff the corresponding bit of τ_i^e is j. It proceeds in this way until either the end of the interval is reached or one of the scanned bits differs from the corresponding one of τ_i^e, and thus r_j realizes that τ_i^e is the wrong guess for σ_i^t. In the second case, r_j increments the counter e and continues the procedure. By the choice of i_0, the counter e always settles on a value such that $\tau_i^e = \sigma_i^t$.

For all $i \geqslant i_0$, every number in the interval J_i^t is selected by either r_0 or r_1. We say that a number n is *selected correctly* if it is selected by r_j and $X(n) = j$. In each J_i^t there are at most $|T_i^t| - 1$ many numbers that are selected incorrectly, since each incorrect selection causes each r_j to increment its counter. So by (ii), there are infinitely many i for which at least $\frac{4m_i}{5(k+1)}$ numbers in J_i^t are selected correctly. Hence for some j and infinitely many i, the selection function r_j selects at least $\frac{2m_i}{5(k+1)}$ of the numbers in J_i^t correctly, and at most $\frac{m_i}{5(k+1)}$ incorrectly. By the choice of the m_i, for each such i there are at most $\frac{m_i}{10(k+1)}$ many numbers that r_j could have selected before it entered the interval J_i^t. Hence, up to and including each such interval J_i^t, the selection function r_j selects at least $\frac{2m_i}{5(k+1)}$ many numbers correctly and at most $\frac{3m_i}{10(k+1)}$ incorrectly. Thus r_j witnesses that X is not von Mises-Wald-Church stochastic. □

By Theorem 7.4.4, there is a computably random X such that $C(X \upharpoonright n) \leqslant 2\log n + O(1)$, so we have the following result.

Corollary 7.4.7 (Ambos-Spies [6]). *There is a computably random set that is not von Mises-Wald-Church stochastic.*

7.4.3 A martingale characterization of stochasticity

Ambos-Spies, Mayordomo, Wang, and Zheng [11] have shown that stochasticity can be viewed as a notion of randomness for a restricted kind of martingale. These authors stated the following for a notion of time-bounded stochasticity, but their proof works for Church stochasticity as well.

Definition 7.4.8 (Ambos-Spies, Mayordomo, Wang, and Zheng [11]).

(i) A martingale d is *simple* if there is a number $q \in \mathbb{Q} \cap (0,1)$ such that for all σ and $i = 0, 1$,

$$d(\sigma i) \in \{d(\sigma), (1+q)d(\sigma), (1-q)d(\sigma)\}.$$

(ii) A martingale d is *almost simple* if there is a finite set $\{q_0, \ldots, q_m\} \subset \mathbb{Q} \cap (0,1)$ such that for all σ and $i = 0, 1$, there is a $k \leqslant m$ such that

$$d(\sigma i) \in \{d(\sigma), (1+q_k)d(\sigma), (1-q_k)d(\sigma)\}.$$

We say that a set is *(almost) simply random*[13] if no (almost) simple computable martingale succeeds on it. Actually, almost simple randomness and simple randomness coincide.

Lemma 7.4.9 (Ambos-Spies, Mayordomo, Wang, and Zheng [11]). *If d is an almost simple martingale then there are finitely many simple martingales $d_0, \ldots, d_m$ such that $S[d] \subseteq \bigcup_{k \leqslant m} S[d_k]$.*

Proof. Suppose that d is almost simple via the rationals $\{q_o, \ldots, q_m\}$. For each $i \leqslant m$, define a simple martingale d_k that copies d on all σ such that $d(\sigma i) \in \{d(\sigma), (1+q_k)d(\sigma), (1-q_k)d(\sigma)\}$ and is defined by $d_k(\sigma i) = d_k(\sigma)$ for $i = 0, 1$ otherwise. If d succeeds on A then clearly one of the d_k must also succeed on A. □

Corollary 7.4.10. *A set is almost simply random iff it is simply random.*

We can now state the following characterizations of stochasticity.

Theorem 7.4.11 (Ambos-Spies, Mayordomo, Wang, and Zheng [11]).

(i) *A set is Church stochastic iff it is simply random.*

(ii) *A set is von Mises-Wald-Church stochastic iff no partial computable (almost) simple martingale succeeds on it.*

Proof. We prove (i); the proof of (ii) is essentially the same.

Suppose there is a computable simple martingale d with rational q that succeeds on A. We define a computable selection function f by letting

$$f(X \upharpoonright n) = \begin{cases} \text{no} & \text{if } d((X \upharpoonright n-1)0) = d(X \upharpoonright n) \\ \text{yes} & \text{otherwise.} \end{cases}$$

[13] Ambos-Spies, Mayordomo, Wang, and Zheng [11] used the terminology "weakly random", which is already used in this book in relation to Kurtz randomness.

Then f is computable and succeeds on A:

$$\limsup_n \frac{|\{y < n : d((A \upharpoonright y-1)A(y)) = (1+q)d(A \upharpoonright y-1)\}|}{|\{y < n : d((A \upharpoonright y-1)A(y)) = (1-q)d(A \upharpoonright y-1)\}|} > 1,$$

so the limsup of the proportion of the bits of A selected by f that are 1 is bigger than $\frac{1}{2}$, and hence A is not Church stochastic.

For the other direction, let the martingales d^i_k be as in Section 7.4.1. Then each d^i_k is a simple martingale, and, as shown in that subsection, if A is not Church stochastic then some d^i_k succeeds on A. □

7.5 Nonmonotonic randomness

7.5.1 Nonmonotonic betting strategies

In this section we consider the effect of allowing betting strategies that can bet on the bits of a sequence out of order. This concept was introduced by Muchnik, Semenov, and Uspensky [289]. We use the notation of Merkle, Miller, Nies, Reimann, and Stephan [269].

Definition 7.5.1. A *finite assignment (f.a.)* is a sequence

$$x = (r_0, a_0), \dots, (r_n, a_n) \in (\mathbb{N} \times \{0,1\})^{<\omega}$$

such that the r_i are pairwise distinct. We call the set of r_i the *(selection) domain* and denote it by $\operatorname{dom}(x)$.

A *scan rule* is a partial function s from the set of finite assignments to $\mathbb{N}$ such that for all finite assignments x, we have $s(x) \notin \operatorname{dom}(x)$.

The idea is that the r_i are the places selected by our nonmonotonic betting strategy, and the scan rule is the function that determines the next place to bet on based on the observed values of the previously selected places, i.e., the a_i.

Definition 7.5.2 (Merkle, Miller, Nies, Reimann, and Stephan [269]). A *stake function* is a partial function from the collection of finite assignments to $[0,2]$.

A *nonmonotonic betting strategy* is a pair consisting of a scan rule and a stake function.

We can now define the analog of a martingale for a nonmonotonic betting strategy (s,q). This is called in [269] a *capital function*, d. The idea is that given a set X, we begin with $d(\lambda)$, and given a finite assignment x, the strategy picks $s(x)$ as the next place to bet on. If $q(x) < 1$, it is betting that $X(s(x)) = 1$, and staking $1 - q(x)$ much of its capital on that bet; if $q(x) > 1$, it is betting that $X(s(x)) = 0$, and staking $q(x) - 1$ much of its capital on that bet; and if $q(x) = 1$, it is betting evenly. Then, as in the case of a martingale, if $X(s(x)) = 0$, the current capital is multiplied by $q(x)$, and otherwise it is multiplied by $2 - q(x)$. (That is, if the strategy makes the correct guess then the amount it staked on that guess is doubled, and otherwise that amount is lost.)

We can consider nonmonotonic betting strategies as a game played on sequences. Let $b = (s, q)$ be a nonmonotonic betting strategy. We define the partial functional p by $p^X(0) = \lambda$ and

$$p^X(n+1) = p^X(n)^\frown\big(s(p^X(n)), q(p^X(n))\big).$$

We have $p^X(n+1)\uparrow$ if $s(p^X(n))$ is undefined. Using this functional we can formally define the payoff of our strategy as

$$c^X(n+1) = \begin{cases} qp^X(n) & \text{if } X(p^X(n)) = 0 \\ (2-q)p^X(n) & \text{if } X(p^X(n)) = 1. \end{cases}$$

Finally, we can define the *payoff function* of b, which is our notion of a nonmonotonic martingale, as

$$d_b^X(n) = d_b^X(\lambda)\prod_{i=1}^{n} c^X(i).$$

(This definition depends on a choice of $d_b^X(\lambda)$, but that choice does not affect any of the relevant properties of d_b.)

Definition 7.5.3 (Muchnik, Semenov, and Uspensky [289]). A nonmonotonic betting strategy b *succeeds* on X if

$$\limsup_{n\to\infty} d_b^X(n) = \infty.$$

We say that X is *nonmonotonically random* (or *Kolmogorov-Loveland random*) if no partial computable nonmonotonic betting strategy succeeds on it.

We say that $C \subseteq 2^\omega$ is *Kolmogorov-Loveland null* if there is a partial computable nonmonotonic betting strategy succeeding on all $X \in C$.

The use of partial computable nonmonotonic strategies in Definition 7.5.3 is not essential.

Theorem 7.5.4 (Merkle [265]). *A sequence X is nonmonotonically random iff no total computable nonmonotonic betting strategy succeeds on it.*

Proof sketch. It is enough to show that if a partial computable nonmonotonic strategy succeeds on X then there is a total computable nonmonotonic strategy that also succeeds on X. Suppose the partial computable strategy (s, q) succeeds on X. This strategy selects a sequence of places $s_0, s_1, \dots$ so that unbounded capital is gained on the sequence $A(s_0), A(s_1)\dots$. If we decompose $s_0, s_1, \dots$ into even and odd places, then the unbounded capital gain must be true of either the subsequence of even places or that of odd places. Without loss of generality, suppose it is the former.

Now the idea is to build a total computable betting strategy that emulates (s, q) on the even places, but, while it is waiting for a convergence, plays on fresh odd places, betting evenly. If the convergence ever happens, the strategy returns to emulating (s, q). □

The fundamental properties of nonmonotonic randomness were first established by Muchnik, Semenov, and Uspensky [289]. Many of these were improved in the later paper of Merkle, Miller, Nies, Reimann, and Stephan [269], which, by and large, used techniques that were elaborations of those of [289].

Theorem 7.5.5 (Muchnik, Semenov, and Uspensky [289]). *If A is 1-random then A is nonmonotonically random.*

Proof. Suppose that A is not nonmonotonically random and that b is a partial computable betting strategy that succeeds on A. We define a Martin-Löf test $\{V_n : n \in \mathbb{N}\}$ as follows. We put $[\![\sigma]\!]$ into V_n if there is a j such that $d_b^\sigma(j) \geqslant 2^n$. (Note that this notation implies that the first j places selected by b are all less than $|\sigma|$.) It is straightforward to check that Kolmogorov's Inequality (Theorem 6.3.3) holds for nonmonotonic martingales as well, and that this fact implies that $\{V_n : n \in \mathbb{N}\}$ is a Martin-Löf test. Since clearly $A \in \bigcap_n V_n$, we see that A is not 1-random. □

At the time of writing, it remains a fundamental open question whether this theorem can be reversed. It seems that most researchers in the area believe that the answer is no.

Open Question 7.5.6 (Muchnik, Semenov, and Uspensky [289]). Is every nonmonotonically random sequence 1-random?

Some partial results toward the solution of this problem will be reported here and in Section 7.9, where we discuss work by Kastermans and Lempp [199] on variations of nonmonotonic randomness called permutation and injective randomness.

Thus we know that 1-randomness implies nonmonotonic randomness, which in turn clearly implies (partial) computable randomness, since monotonic betting strategies are a special case of nonmonotonic ones. The same proof as above shows that if we looked at computably enumerable nonmonotonic betting strategies, we would have a notion equivalent to 1-randomness.

We can separate nonmonotonic randomness from computable (or even partial computable) randomness by combining the remark following Theorem 7.4.5 with the following result, which shows that nonmonotonic randomness is quite close to 1-randomness in a certain sense.

Theorem 7.5.7 (Muchnik, see [289][14]).

(i) *Let h be a computable order such that*

$$K(A \upharpoonright h(n)) \leqslant h(n) - n$$

for all n. Then A is not nonmonotonically random.

(ii) *Indeed, there are two partial computable nonmonotonic betting strategies such that any sequence satisfying the hypothesis of (i) is covered by one of them.*

(iii) *Moreover, these strategies can be converted into total computable ones.*

Proof sketch. For an interval I, let $A \upharpoonright I$ denote the restriction of A to I. Using h, we can define a computable function g such that

$$K\big(A \upharpoonright [g(n), g(n+1))\big) < g(n+1) - g(n) - n$$

for all n. (Having defined $g(n)$, we can choose a sufficiently large m that codes $g(n)$ (say by having $m = \langle g(n), i\rangle$ for some i) and let $g(n+1) = h(m)$.) Let $I_n = [g(n), g(n+1))$. We have two betting strategies, one based upon the belief that there are infinitely many e such that the approximation to $K(A \upharpoonright I_{2e})$ settles no later than that of $K(A \upharpoonright I_{2e+1})$, and the other based on the belief that there are infinitely many e such that the approximation to $K(A \upharpoonright I_{2e+1})$ settles no later than that of $K(A \upharpoonright I_{2e})$. These strategies are symmetric, so we assume that A satisfies the first hypothesis and describe the corresponding strategy.

The idea is to scan $A \upharpoonright I_{2e+1}$, betting evenly on those bits, and then wait until a stage t such that $K_t(A \upharpoonright I_{2e+1}) < g(2e+2) - g(2e+1) - 2(e+1)$. At this stage we begin to bet on the interval I_{2e}, using half of our current capital. We bet only on those strings σ of length $g(2e+1) - g(2e)$ such that $K_t(\sigma) < g(2e+1) - g(2e) - 2e$. If the hypothesis about settling times is correct for this e, then one of these strings really is $A \upharpoonright I_{2e}$. The capital is divided into equal portions and bet on all such strings. If we lose on all strings then we have lost half of the remaining capital. If the hypothesis is correct for this e, though, then a straightforward calculation shows that we increase our capital enough to make up for previous losses, so that, since the hypothesis will be correct for infinitely many e, this betting strategy succeeds on A. □

Notice that we can replace nonmonotonic randomness by 1-randomness and delete the word "computable" before h in the statement of Theorem 7.5.7 part (i).

[14]The statements (ii) and (iii) were not present in Muchnik's original result, but these stronger statements can be extracted from the proof, as pointed out in [269].

One key problem when dealing with nonmonotonic randomness is the lack of universal tests. The level to which the lack of universality hurts us can be witnessed by the following simple result.

Theorem 7.5.8 (Merkle, Miller, Nies, Reimann, and Stephan [269]). *No partial computable nonmonotonic betting strategy succeeds on all computably enumerable sets.*

Proof. Let $b = (s, q)$ be partial computable. We build a c.e. set W. We compute $x_n = (r_0, a_0), \dots, (r_{n-1}, a_{n-1})$, starting with $x_0 = \lambda$, and setting $r_{n+1} = s(x_n)$, with $a_{n+1} = 1$ if $q(x_n) \geqslant 1$ and $a_{n+1} = 0$ otherwise. We enumerate r_{n+1} into W if $a_{n+1} = 1$. Clearly, b cannot succeed on W. □

Strangely enough, it turns out that *two* nonmonotonic betting strategies are enough to succeed on all c.e. sets.

Theorem 7.5.9 (Muchnik, see [289], Merkle, Miller, Nies, Reimann, and Stephan [269]). *There exist computable nonmonotonic betting strategies b_0 and b_1 such that for each c.e. set W, at least one of b_0 or b_1 succeeds on W.*

Proof. Divide $\mathbb{N}$ into intervals $\{I_k : k \in \omega\}$ with $|I_{k+1}| = 5|I_k|$ and let $J_e = \bigcup_j I_{\langle e,j \rangle}$.

The first strategy is monotonic and extremely simple. It always bets $\frac{2}{3}$ of its current capital that the next bit is 0. This strategy succeeds on all sequences X such that there are infinitely many initial segments $X \upharpoonright n$ where fewer than $\frac{1}{4}$ of the bits are 1. In particular, it succeeds on all X such that $J_e \cap X$ is finite for some e.

The second strategy succeeds on all W_e that have infinite intersection with J_e. Fix an enumeration of all pairs $\{(e_i, z_i) : i \in \omega\}$ such that $z_i \in W_{e_i} \cap J_{e_i}$ for some e_i. The betting strategy $b = (s, q)$ splits its initial capital so that it devotes 2^{-e-1} to W_e (so the initial capital is 1). Thus the capital function d_b^X is broken into parts $d_{b,e}^X$. Given the finite assignment $x_n = (r_0, a_0), \dots, (r_{n-1}, a_{n-1})$, we let $s(x_n) = z_n$ and $q(x_n) = 1 - \frac{d_{b,e_n}^X(n)}{d_b^X(n)}$. (Here we think of $d_{b,e}^X(n)$ as the capital accrued by beginning with 2^{-e-1} and betting all our capital on 1 at stages n such that $e_n = e$.) This strategy will succeed on all W_e such that $X_e \cap J_e$ infinite, since for each number in this intersection, the capital $d_{b,e}^{W_e}$ is doubled. □

Corollary 7.5.10 (Merkle, Miller, Nies, Reimann, and Stephan [269]). *The class of Kolmogorov-Loveland null sets is not closed under finite unions.*

7.5.2 Van Lambalgen's Theorem revisited

We have seen that looking at splittings yields significant insight into randomness, as witnessed by van Lambalgen's Theorem (see Section 6.9).

For an infinite and coinfinite set Z, let $z_0 < z_1 < \cdots$ be the elements of Z, let $y_0 < y_1 < \cdots$ be the elements of $\overline{Z}$, and recall that $A_0 \oplus_Z A_1 = \{z_n : n \in A_0\} \cup \{y_n : n \in A_1\}$. That is, we use Z as a guide as to how to merge A_0 and A_1. Clearly, the proof of van Lambalgen's Theorem shows that if Z is computable then $A_0 \oplus_Z A_1$ is 1-random iff A_i is 1-random relative to A_{1-i} for $i = 0, 1$. Here is an analog of van Lambalgen's Theorem for nonmonotonic randomness.

Theorem 7.5.11 (Merkle, Miller, Nies, Reimann, and Stephan [269]). *Suppose that $A = A_0 \oplus_Z A_1$ for a computable Z. Then A is nonmonotonically random iff A_i is nonmonotonically random relative to A_{1-i} for $i = 0, 1$.*

Proof. If A not nonmonotonically random, then let b be a nonmonotonic betting strategy succeeding on A. Let b_0 and b_1 be strategies with the same scan rule as b, but such that b_0 copies b's bets on places in Z, while betting evenly on places in $\overline{Z}$, while b_1 copies b's bets on places in $\overline{Z}$, while betting evenly on places in Z. One of b_0 or b_1 must also succeed on A. Suppose it is b_0, the other case being symmetric. It is easy to transform b_0 into a strategy that is computable relative to A_1 and succeeds on A_0, whence A_0 is not nonmonotonically random relative to A_1.

For the other direction, suppose that b is an A_1-computable nonmonotonic betting strategy that succeeds on A_0, the other case being symmetric. Then we can define a computable nonmonotonic betting strategy by scanning the $\overline{Z}$ positions of A, corresponding to A_1, betting evenly on those, until we get an initial segment of A_1 that allows us to compute a new value of b. Then we place a bet on the A_0 portion of A according to this new value of b, and repeat this procedure. □

An important corollary of this result is the following.

Corollary 7.5.12 (Merkle, Miller, Nies, Reimann, and Stephan [269]). *If Z is computable and $A_0 \oplus_Z A_1$ is nonmonotonically random, then at least one of A_0 or A_1 is 1-random.*

Proof. Let $U_0, U_1, \ldots$ be a universal Martin-Löf test. Suppose that neither of the A_i is 1-random and let $f_i(n)$ be the least s such that $A_i \in U_n[s]$. Let i be such that there are infinitely many n with $f_{1-i}(n) \leqslant f_i(n)$. Let $V_n = \bigcup_{m>n} U_n[f_i(n)]$. Then $V_0, V_1, \ldots$ is a Schnorr test relative to A_i, and $A_{1-i} \in \bigcap_n V_n$. Thus A_{i-1} is not Schnorr random relative to A_i, and hence not nonmonotonically random relative to A_i. By Theorem 7.5.11, $A_0 \oplus_Z A_1$ is not nonmonotonically random. □

7.6 Demuth randomness

In this section we introduce a notion of randomness due to Demuth [94, 95], whose underlying thesis was that reasonable functions should behave well on random points.

Definition 7.6.1 (Demuth [94, 95]). A sequence of Σ^0_1 classes $\{[\![W_{g(e)}]\!]\}_{e\in\omega}$ is called a *Demuth test* if

(i) $\mu([\![W_{g(e)}]\!]) \leqslant 2^{-e}$ and

(ii) g is an ω-c.e. function; that is, there are a computable function f and a computable approximation $g(e) = \lim_s g(e,s)$ such that $|\{s : g(e,s+1) \neq g(e,s)\}| < f(e)$ for all e.

We say that a set A *passes* this Demuth test if it passes it in the Solovay test sense: $A \notin [\![W_{g(e)}]\!]$ for almost all e.

A set is *Demuth random* if it passes all Demuth tests.

The idea here is that while the levels of the test are all c.e. objects, the function picking the indices of the levels is not computable but only approximable.[15] If the function g used to define the test members is only Δ^0_2 then we get another notion of randomness, called *limit randomness*, studied by Kučera and Nies [220]. Limit randomness is implied by Schnorr randomness relative to $\emptyset'$ (a concept further studied by Barmpalias, Miller, and Nies [27]), and hence by 2-randomness. Kučera and Nies [220] also studied weak Demuth randomness, where a set is *weakly Demuth random* if it passes all Demuth tests $\{[\![W_{g(e)}]\!]\}_{e\in\omega}$ such that $[\![W_{g(0)}]\!] \supseteq [\![W_{g(1)}]\!] \supseteq \cdots$. See [220] for more on these notions.

Every Martin-Löf test is a Demuth test, and every Demuth test is a Martin-Löf test relative to $\emptyset'$, so we have the following.

Proposition 7.6.2. *2-randomness implies Demuth randomness, which in turn implies 1-randomness.*

Notice that if a set is ω-c.e. then it cannot be Demuth random, and hence Ω is not Demuth random. (Consider the finite Demuth test given by $V_e = [\![\Omega \upharpoonright e+1]\!]$ for $e \in \omega$.) Thus Demuth randomness is stronger than 1-randomness. Demuth [95] constructed a Δ^0_2 Demuth random set, showing that 2-randomness is stronger than Demuth randomness. One method to establish this result is to construct a test that serves a purpose similar to that of a universal Martin-Löf test. (There is no universal Demuth test.)

[15] Barmpalias [personal communication] has noted that a natural example of a Demuth test is the null class of all sets that compute functions not dominated by a Δ^0_2 *almost everywhere dominating function* f, that is, a function f such that for almost every $\mathbf{a}$ and almost every $g \leqslant_T \mathbf{a}$, the function f dominates g. That these sets can be captured by a Demuth test can be seen by using the natural construction of Kurtz [228] in Theorem 8.20.6 below. We will examine almost everywhere domination further in Section 10.6.

This is done by enumerating all pairs $\{(\varphi_e(\cdot,\cdot),\psi_e) : e \in \omega\}$, where φ_e and ψ_e are partial computable functions, and where we allow $\varphi_e(x,s)[t]\downarrow$ only if

1. $\varphi_e(y,s)[t]\downarrow$ for all $y \leqslant x$,
2. $\psi_e(x)[t]\downarrow$,
3. $|\{u : u \leqslant t \wedge \varphi_e(x,u+1) \neq \varphi_e(x,u)\}| \leqslant \psi_e(x)$, and
4. $\mu(W_{\varphi_e(x,s)}[t]) \leqslant 2^{-x}$.

That is, we enumerate all partial Demuth tests and then we can assemble the tails as usual to make a test universal for Demuth randomness. This test is of the form $\{[\![W_{h(e)}]\!]\}_{e\in\omega}$ with h a Δ^0_2 function (in fact an $(\omega+1)$-c.e. function). The leftmost set passing this test will be Demuth random and Δ^0_2. Thus we have the following.

Theorem 7.6.3 (Demuth [95]). *There exists a Δ^0_2 Demuth random set.*

We will show in Theorem 8.14.2 that all Demuth random sets are GL_1. It is also possible to show that no Demuth random set is of hyperimmune-free degree. (Indeed, Miller and Nies (see [306]), proved that if a set is GL_1 and DNC then it is hyperimmune. Hence no 1-random set that is GL_1 can be hyperimmune-free. But there are hyperimmune free weakly 2-random sets, as we see in the next chapter.) This result shows that weak 2-randomness and Demuth randomness are incomparable notions.

7.7 Difference randomness

Following the proof of Theorem 6.1.3, we discussed the class of 1-random sets that do not compute $\emptyset'$. Results such as Theorems 8.8.4 and 11.7.4 below will show that the sets in this class behave much more like "truly random" sets than computationally powerful 1-random sets such as Ω. In this section, we present a test set characterization of this class due to Franklin and Ng [157], which attests to its naturality as a notion of randomness.

Definition 7.7.1 (Franklin and Ng [157]). A *d.c.e. test* is a sequence $\{U_n \setminus V_n\}_{n\in\omega}$ such that the U_n and V_n are uniformly Σ^0_1 classes and $\mu(U_n \setminus V_n) \leqslant 2^{-n}$ for all n. A set A *passes* this test if $A \notin \bigcap_n U_n \setminus V_n$.
A set is *difference random* if it passes all d.c.e. tests.

This definition can be generalized in a natural way to define n-c.e. tests and n-c.e. randomness for all $n > 1$ (where 2-c.e. randomness is what we have called difference randomness). However, Franklin and Ng [157] showed that this hierarchy of randomness notions collapses; that is, for every $n > 1$, a set is n-c.e. random iff it is difference random.

Difference randomness can also be characterized in terms of a special kind of Demuth test.

Definition 7.7.2 (Franklin and Ng [157]). A Demuth test $\{[\![W_{g(n)}]\!]\}_{n\in\omega}$ is *strict* if g has an ω-c.e. approximation $g(n,s)$ such that if $g(n,s+1) \neq g(n,s)$ then $[\![W_{g(n),s+1}]\!] \cap [\![W_{g(n),t}]\!] = \emptyset$ for all $t \leqslant s$.

Lemma 7.7.3 (Franklin and Ng [157]). *A set A is difference random iff for every strict Demuth test $\{[\![W_{g(n)}]\!]\}_{e\in\omega}$, we have $A \notin \bigcap_n [\![W_{g(n)}]\!]$.*

Proof. Suppose there is a strict Demuth test $\{[\![W_{g(n)}]\!]\}_{n\in\omega}$ such that $A \in \bigcap_n [\![W_{g(n)}]\!]$. Let $U_n = \bigcup_s [\![W_{g(n,s)}]\!]$ and $V_n = \bigcup\{[\![W_{g(n,s)}]\!] : g(n,s+1) \neq g(n,s)\}$. It is easy to check that $\{U_n \setminus V_n\}_{n\in\omega}$ is a d.c.e. test that A does not pass.

Now suppose there is a d.c.e. test $\{U_n \setminus V_n\}_{n\in\omega}$ that A does not pass. We may assume without loss of generality that $\mu(U_n[s] \setminus V_n[s]) \leqslant 2^{-n}$ for all n and s. We may also assume that A is 1-random, since otherwise there is a Martin-Löf test that A does not pass, and every Martin-Löf test is a strict Demuth test. Let $\{C_{n,i} : n \in \omega,\ i \leqslant 2^n\}$ be uniformly Σ^0_1 classes defined as follows.

Let $s_{n,0} = 0$. For each n, let $C_{n,0}$ copy U_{n+1} until $\mu(C_{n,0})$ exceeds 2^{-n}. If such a stage $s_{n,1}$ is ever reached, then stop building $C_{n,0}$ and begin building $C_{n,1}$ by copying $U_{n+2} \setminus C_{n,0}$ until $\mu(C_{n,1})$ exceeds 2^{-n}. (Note that, in this case, $C_{n,0}$ is a Δ^0_1 class, so $U_{n+2} \setminus C_{n,0}$ is still a Σ^0_1 class.) Continue in this fashion, at step i building $C_{n,i}$ by copying $U_{n+i+1} \setminus (C_{n,0} \cup \cdots \cup C_{n,i-1})$ until $\mu(C_{n,i})$ exceeds 2^{-n} at some stage $s_{n,i+1}$, if ever. It is easy to see that for each n there is an $i_n \leqslant 2^n$ such that this construction enters step i_n but never leaves it.

The $C_{n,i}$ are clearly uniformly Σ^0_1, so we can define a computable function g such that for each n and s, we have $[\![W_{g(n,s)}]\!] = C_{n,i}$ for the largest i such that $s \geqslant s_{n,i}$. Let $g(n) = \lim_s g(n,s)$. It is easy to check that $\{[\![W_{g(n)}]\!]\}_{n\in\omega}$ is a strict Demuth test, and hence so is $\{[\![W_{g(n)}]\!]\}_{n\geqslant N}$ for any N. We now show that there is an N such that $A \in \bigcap_{n\geqslant N} [\![W_{g(n)}]\!]$.

Let

$$S = \{U_{n+i}[s_{n,i}] \setminus V_{n+i}[s_{n,i}] : n \in \omega \wedge 0 < i \leqslant i_n\}.$$

The sum of the measures of the elements of S is bounded $\sum_n \sum_i 2^{-n+i} < \infty$, so S is a Solovay test. By our assumption that A is 1-random, there is an N such that $A \notin U_{n+i}[s_{n,i}] \setminus V_{n+i}[s_{n,i}]$ for all $n \geqslant N$ and $0 < i \leqslant i_n$. Let $n \geqslant N$. For $0 < i \leqslant i_n$, we have $A \notin V_{n+i}$, so that $A \notin V_{n+i}[s_{n,i}]$, and hence $A \notin U_{n+i}[s_{n,i}] = C_{n,i-1}$. But $A \in U_{n+i_n+1}$, so

$$A \in U_{n+i_n+1} \setminus (C_{n,0} \cup \cdots \cup C_{n,i_n-1}) = C_{n,i_n} = [\![W_{g(n)}]\!].$$

Thus $A \in \bigcap_{n\geqslant N} [\![W_{g(n)}]\!]$. □

Using this characterization, we can show that the difference random sets are exactly the "computationally weak" 1-random sets.

Theorem 7.7.4 (Franklin and Ng [157]). *A set is difference random iff it is 1-random and does not compute $\emptyset'$.*

Proof. Suppose that A is 1-random but not difference random. Let $\{[\![W_{g(n)}]\!]\}_{n\in\omega}$ be a strict Demuth test such that $A \in \bigcap_n [\![W_{g(n)}]\!]$. Let $t(n)$ be an A-computable function such that for each n there is a k with $A \upharpoonright k \in W_{g(n)}[t(n)]$. Let $S = \{[\![W_{g(n)}[s]]\!] : n \in \emptyset'_{s+1} \setminus \emptyset'_s\}$. Then S is a Solovay test, so for almost all n, if n enters $\emptyset'$ at stage $s+1$, then $A \notin [\![W_{g(n)}[s]]\!]$, and hence $s < t(n)$. Thus $n \in \emptyset'$ iff $n \in \emptyset'_{t(n)}$ for almost all n, and hence $\emptyset' \leqslant_T t \leqslant_T A$.

For the other direction, since every difference random set is 1-random, it is enough to assume that $A \geqslant_T \emptyset'$ and build a d.c.e. test that A does not pass. We build an auxiliary c.e. set C. By the recursion theorem, we may assume we have a reduction $C = \Gamma^A$ (as explained in the proof of Theorem 2.20.1). Let

$$S_{n,i} = \{X : \forall j < i\,(\Gamma^X(\langle n,j\rangle)\downarrow = 1) \wedge \Gamma^X(\langle n,i\rangle)\downarrow = 0\}.$$

Let $C = \{\langle n,i\rangle : \mu(S_{n,i}) > 2^{-n}\}$, let $U_n = \bigcup\{S_{n,i} : \forall j < i\,(\mu(S_{n,j}) > 2^{-n})\}$, and let $V_n = \bigcup\{S_{n,i} : \mu(S_{n,i}) > 2^{-n}\}$. The $S_{n,i}$ are uniformly Σ^0_1 classes, and hence so are the U_n and the V_n. Fix n. The $S_{n,i}$ are pairwise disjoint, so there is a least i such that $\mu(S_{n,i}) \leqslant 2^{-n}$. Then $U_n \setminus V_n = S_{n,i}$, and if $\Gamma^X = C$ then $X \in S_{n,i}$, so in particular $A \in S_{n,i}$. It follows that $\{U_n \setminus V_n\}_{n\in\omega}$ is a d.c.e. test that A does not pass. □

Thus every difference random set is 1-random, and this implication is strict. Lemma 7.7.3 shows that every Demuth random set is difference random. As we will see in Theorem 8.13.1, no weakly 2-random set can compute $\emptyset'$, so weak 2-randomness also implies difference randomness. As mentioned in the previous section, Demuth randomness and weak 2-randomness are incomparable notions, so both of these implications are strict.

See [157] for a martingale characterization of difference randomness.

7.8 Finite randomness

A *finite Martin-Löf test* is a Martin-Löf test $\{[\![V_e]\!] : e \in \omega\}$ where $|V_e| < \infty$ for all e; that is, each $[\![V_e]\!]$ is clopen. A set is *finitely random* if it passes all finite Martin-Löf tests. We say that a finite Martin-Löf test is a *computably finite Martin-Löf test* if, additionally, there is a computable function f such that $|V_e| < f(e)$. A set is *computably finitely random* if it passes all computably finite Martin-Löf tests. Interestingly, for Δ^0_2 sets finite randomness and 1-randomness coincide.

Proposition 7.8.1. *If A is finitely random and Δ^0_2 then A is 1-random.*

Proof. Suppose that A is Δ^0_2 and not 1-random. Let $U_0, U_1, \ldots$ be a universal Martin-Löf test. Let $V_0, V_1, \ldots$ be the test defined by letting $V_i[s] = U_i[t]$ for the largest $t \leqslant s$ such that $A_s \in U_i[t]$, if there is one, and $t = s$ otherwise. Then $V_0, V_1, \ldots$ is a finite test, and its intersection contains A. □

Beyond the Δ_2^0 sets the notions are quite different. One could argue that notions of finite randomness are not really randomness notions (because they are not stochastic), but it might in any case be interesting to see what insight they give into computability. We do not cover these notions further here, but point out one recent theorem, which indicates that they do provide some insight. A degree is *totally ω-c.e.* if every function it computes is ω-c.e.

Theorem 7.8.2 (Brodhead, Downey, and Ng [44]). *A computably enumerable degree contains a computably finitely random set iff it is not totally ω-c.e.*

At the time of writing, little else is known about these notions.

7.9 Injective and permutation randomness

Two variations on nonmonotonic randomness were suggested by Miller and Nies [278] as possible methods of attacking Question 7.5.6. Both use the idea of restricting betting strategies to *oblivious* scan rules; that is, no matter what the input sequence A is, the places to be scanned are determined exactly by the previous *places* we have bet on, independently of the observed values of A at these places, so that the scan rule maps $\mathbb{N}^{<\omega}$ to $\mathbb{N}$. Thus, there is an f such that if we have bet on positions $n_0, \dots, n_k$, then we will bet on position $f(\langle n_0, \dots, n_k \rangle)$, where of course this value cannot be in $\{n_0, \dots, n_k\}$. A sequence is *injectively random* if it is nonmonotonically random for all computable betting strategies based on such scan rules. It is *permutation random* if it is nonmonotonically random for all computable betting strategies based on such scan rules with the additional requirement that the strategy must bet on all bits eventually. (That is, the scan rule is also surjective.)

Clearly, every nonmonotonically random set is injectively random, every injectively random set is permutation random, and every permutation random set is computably random. The following is what is known in this area. Due to space limitations, we only sketch the proof.

Theorem 7.9.1 (Kastermans and Lempp [199]). *There is an injectively random set that is not 1-random.*

Proof sketch. We need to build a c.e. martingale M and a set X such that M is unbounded along X but X is injectively random. We will think of M as an infinite sum of uniformly c.e. martingales M_i, each weighted so as to make sure that $M = \sum_i M_i$ is a martingale. Each M_i bases its procedure on a guess; in order to win, it suffices that one of the M_i be unbounded along X. This idea is familiar from Theorem 6.3.7, where we constructed an optimal supermartingale, and Corollary 7.4.7. In the following, we will restrict ourselves to dealing with just two injective computable martingales. For the general case, dealing with all such martingales, see [199].

We first sketch a construction to make X permutation random: We need to ensure that each permutation martingale is bounded on X. For a single permutation martingale d, we have our c.e. martingale M_0 guess that d is total. Consequently, M_0 will always favor the successor of a node on which d gains less. In this way, we determine a sequence A on which M_0 succeeds, but such that d is bounded on A, so if M_0's guess is correct, we can take $X = A$. It is true that d is not monotonic so d may be betting elsewhere before it bets on the next bit. However, since d is assumed to be total, we can always wait until bets have been placed on the next bit and then simply take the statistical average, thereby providing a "monotonized" version of d. We also have, for the ith node $\sigma \in 2^{<\omega}$, a c.e. martingale M_{i+1} guessing that d is not defined on σ. This martingale can simply concentrate its capital on a sequence B extending σ, and if its guess is correct, we can take $X = B$.

To defeat two permutation martingales d_0 and d_1, each with initial capital $\leqslant 1$, say, we have two cases for d_1: Under the guess that d_0 is not defined on σ, we can simply run the above strategy in the cone above σ. Under the guess that d_0 is partial, the strategy for d_1 is more complicated; we cannot simply run the above strategy since d_1 may be undefined only on nodes σ where d_0 is very large. (Strictly speaking, this is not a problem for this two-strategy case, but it would be for the general construction.) So we modify the above strategy by distinguishing the following cases:

(i) d_1 is undefined on a node σ at which d_0 is bounded by 2, say. We can then safely restrict our attention to nodes above σ and proceed as for a single permutation martingale.

(ii) d_1 is total when restricted to nodes σ at which d_0 is bounded by 2. We can then pretend that d_1 is indeed total without restrictions by modifying d_1 to a permutation martingale d_1' that behaves like d_1 but bets evenly as soon as a node σ is reached at which d_0 reaches 2. We now use a "monotonized" version of $d_0 + \frac{1}{2c}d_1'$, for some suitable c. Since our sequence X will not extend any σ at which d_0 has reached 2, it is safe to use d_1' in place of d_1.

Finally, to deal with injective martingales, we need one more ingredient. The additional difficulty is that we can no longer "monotonize" as above, since we cannot afford to wait until all bets on the next bit have been placed. Instead, for a single injective martingale, M bets only on bits for which it knows that d bets as well (i.e., an infinite computable subset of the bits on which d bets). To deal with two injective martingales d_0 and d_1, say, we distinguish cases, dealt with by separate strategies. If there are infinitely many bits on which both d_0 and d_1 bet, then we simply restrict ourselves to an infinite computable set of such bits. If there are only finitely many bits on which both d_0 and d_1 bet, say none past bit k, then past this bit k, we can run separate strategies against d_0 and d_1 on disjoint sets of bits, which will not interfere with each other. The details are a bit messy; see Kastermans and Lempp [199] for the full proof. □

There are two views on the above theorem. The first is that injective randomness is very different from nonmonotonic randomness, and the theorem says nothing about the question of whether nonmonotonic randomness and 1-randomness coincide. The second view is that perhaps the result could be generalized to solve that question. Maybe some kind of measure-theoretic generalization of the Kastermans-Lempp argument (looking at the measure of where two nonmonotonic martingales coincide) might work, but the problem seems difficult.

There seem to be a number of other potentially interesting randomness notions intermediate between computable randomness and 1-randomness. We mention two that can be motivated by thinking about the coding of tests into supermartingales in the proof of Schnorr's Theorem 6.3.4 that a set is 1-random iff no c.e. supermartingale succeeds on it. There, we start with a uniformly c.e. sequence $R_0, R_1, \ldots$ of prefix-free generators for a Martin-Löf test. We build a c.e. supermartingale d that bets evenly on $\sigma 0$ and $\sigma 1$ until it finds that, say, $\sigma 0 \in R_n$, at which point it starts to favor $\sigma 0$, to an extent determined by n. If later d finds that $\sigma 1 \in R_m$, then what it does is determined by the relationship between m and n. If $m < n$ then d still favors $\sigma 0$, though to a lesser extent than before. If $m = n$ then d again bets evenly on $\sigma 0$ and $\sigma 1$. If $m > n$ then d switches allegiance and favors $\sigma 1$. Of course, this switch can happen several times, as we find more R_i to which $\sigma 0$ or $\sigma 1$ belong.

The computable enumerability of d is essential in the above. A computable supermartingale (which we have seen we may assume is rational-valued without loss of generality) has to decide which side to favor, if any, immediately. Hitchcock has asked whether an intermediate notion, where we allow our supermartingale to be c.e. but do not allow it to switch allegiances in the way described above, is still powerful enough to capture 1-randomness. The purest version of this question was suggested by Kastermans, in discussing Hitchcock's question with Downey and Lempp. A *Kastergale*[16] is a pair consisting of a partial computable function $g : 2^{<\omega} \to \{0, 1\}$ and a c.e. supermartingale d such that $g(\sigma) \downarrow = i$ iff $\exists s\, (d_s(\sigma i) > d_s(\sigma(1-i))$ iff $d(\sigma i) > d(\sigma(1-i))$. A set is *Kastermans random* if no Kastergale succeeds on it. A *Hitchgale* is the same as a Kastergale, except that in addition the proportion $\frac{d_s(\tau j)}{d_s(\tau)}$ (where we regard $\frac{0}{0}$ as being 0) is a Σ^0_1 function, so that if we ever decide to bet some percentage of our capital on τj, then we are committed to betting at least that per-

[16]We reflect here this (so far informally adopted) practice of portmanteau naming of martingale varieties, without necessarily endorsing it. It may be worth noting that a martingale is not a martin-gale. The *Oxford English Dictionary* suggests that the word comes from the name of the French town of Martigues.

centage from that point on, even if our total capital on τ increases later. A set is *Hitchcock random* if no Hitchgale succeeds on it. It is open whether these notions differ from each other or from 1-randomness.

8
Algorithmic Randomness and Turing Reducibility

In this chapter, we look at the distribution of 1-random and n-random degrees among the Turing (and other) degrees. Among the major results we discuss are the Kučera-Gács Theorem 8.3.2 [167, 215] that every set is computable from a 1-random set; Theorem 8.8.8, due to Barmpalias, Lewis, and Ng [24], that every PA degree is the join of two 1-random degrees; and Stillwell's Theorem 8.15.1 [382] that the "almost all" theory of degrees is decidable. The latter uses Theorem 8.12.1, due to de Leeuw, Moore, Shannon, and Shapiro [92], that if a set is c.e. relative to positive measure many sets, then it is c.e. This result has as a corollary the fundamental result, first explicitly formulated by Sacks [341], that if a set is computable relative to positive measure many sets, then it is computable. Its proof will introduce a basic technique called the majority vote technique.

We also explore several other topics, such as the relationship between genericity and randomness; the computational power of n-random sets, especially with respect to n-fixed point free functions; and some important unpublished results of Kurtz [228] on properties that hold of almost all sets, in the sense of measure. These results use a technique called risking measure, which has recently found applications elsewhere, such as in Downey, Greenberg, and Miller [108].

R.G. Downey and D. Hirschfeldt, *Algorithmic Randomness and Complexity*, Theory and Applications of Computability, DOI 10.1007/978-0-387-68441-3_8,

8.1 Π_1^0 classes of 1-random sets

For each $n \geqslant 1$, relativizing Ω to $\emptyset^{(n-1)}$ shows that there are n-random sets computable in $\emptyset^{(n)}$.[1] We can get a stronger result using Π_1^0 classes. For each constant c, the class $\{A : \forall n\, K(A \upharpoonright n) \geqslant n - c\}$ is clearly a Π_1^0 class, so basic facts about Π_1^0 classes give us several interesting results about the 1-random sets, which have been noted by several authors.

Proposition 8.1.1. *The collection of* 1*-random sets is a* Σ_2^0 *class.*

Proposition 8.1.2. *There exist low* 1*-random sets.*

Proof. Apply the Low Basis Theorem 2.19.8. □

Proposition 8.1.3. *There exist* 1*-random sets of hyperimmune-free degree.*

Proof. Apply the Hyperimmune-Free Basis Theorem 2.19.11. □

Proposition 8.1.2 is obviously particular to 1-randomness, since no 2-random set can be Δ_2^0, let alone low. In Theorem 8.21.2, we will see that this is also the case for Proposition 8.1.3, since every 2-random set has hyperimmune degree. On the other hand, the above results obviously relativize, so, for instance, for all $n \geqslant 1$, there exist n-random sets with $\emptyset^{(n)}$-computable jumps.

8.2 Computably enumerable degrees

Kučera [215] completely answered the question of which c.e. degrees contain 1-random sets, by showing that the only such degree is the complete one.

Theorem 8.2.1 (Kučera [215]). *If A is* 1*-random, B is a c.e. set, and $A \leqslant_T B$, then $B \equiv_T \emptyset'$. In particular, if A is* 1*-random and has c.e. degree, then $A \equiv_T \emptyset'$.*

Proof. Kučera's original proof used Arslanov's Completeness Criterion (Theorem 2.22.3). We give a new direct proof.

Suppose that A is 1-random, B is c.e., and $\Psi^B = A$. Let c be such that $K(A \upharpoonright n) > n - c$ for all n. We will enumerate a KC set, with constant d given by the recursion theorem. Let $k = c + d + 1$. We want to ensure that if $B \upharpoonright \psi^B(n+k)[s] = B_s \upharpoonright \psi^B(n+k)[s]$, then $\emptyset'_s(n) = \emptyset'(n)$, which clearly ensures that $\emptyset' \leqslant_T B$. We may assume that our approximations are sufficiently sped-up so that $\Psi^B(n+k)[s]\downarrow$ for all s and all $n \leqslant s$.

If n enters $\emptyset'$ at some stage $s \geqslant n$, we wish to change B below $\psi^B(n+k)[s]$. We do so by forcing A to change below $n+k$. That is, we enumerate a KC

[1] It is also easy to construct an arithmetically random set computable from $\emptyset^{(\omega)}$.

request $(n+1, A_s \upharpoonright n+k)$. This request ensures that $K(A_s \upharpoonright n+k) \leqslant n+d+1 = n+k-c$, and hence that $A \upharpoonright n+k \neq A_s \upharpoonright n+k$. Thus $B \upharpoonright \psi^B(n+k)[s] \neq B_s \upharpoonright \psi^B(n+k)[s]$, as required. (Note that we enumerate at most one request, of weight $2^{-(n+1)}$, for each $n \in \mathbb{N}$, and hence our requests indeed form a KC set.) □

In the above proof, if Ψ is a wtt-reduction, then so is the reduction from B to $\emptyset'$ that we build. Hence, we have the following result.

Corollary 8.2.2. *If A is 1-random, B is a c.e. set, and $A \leqslant_{\text{wtt}} B$, then $B \equiv_{\text{wtt}} \emptyset'$. In particular, if A is 1-random and has c.e. wtt-degree, then $A \equiv_{\text{wtt}} \emptyset'$.*

8.3 The Kučera-Gács Theorem

In this section we present a basic result, proved independently by Kučera [215] and Gács [167], about the distribution of 1-random sets and the relationship between 1-randomness and Turing reducibility. Specifically, we show that every set is computable from some 1-random set. We begin with an auxiliary result.

Lemma 8.3.1 (Space Lemma, see Merkle and Mihailović [267]). *Given a rational $\delta > 1$ and integer $k > 0$, we can compute a length $l(\delta, k)$ such that, for any martingale d and any σ,*

$$|\{\tau \in 2^{l(\delta,k)} : d(\sigma\tau) \leqslant \delta d(\sigma)\}| \geqslant k.$$

Proof. By Kolmogorov's Inequality (Theorem 6.3.3), for any l and σ, the average of $d(\sigma\tau)$ over strings τ of length l is $d(\sigma)$. Thus

$$\frac{|\{\tau \in 2^l : d(\sigma\tau) > \delta d(\sigma)\}|}{2^l} < \frac{1}{\delta}.$$

Let $l(\delta, k) = \lceil \log \frac{k}{1-\delta^{-1}} \rceil$, which is well-defined since $\delta > 1$. Then

$$|\{\tau \in 2^{l(\delta,k)} : d(\sigma\tau) > \delta d(\sigma)\}| < \frac{2^{l(\delta,k)}}{\delta},$$

so

$$\begin{aligned}|\{\tau \in 2^{l(\delta,k)} : d(\sigma\tau) \leqslant \delta d(\sigma)\}| &> 2^{l(\delta,k)} - \frac{2^{l(\delta,k)}}{\delta} \\ &= 2^{l(\delta,k)}(1-\delta^{-1}) \geqslant \frac{k}{1-\delta^{-1}}(1-\delta^{-1}) = k.\end{aligned}$$

□

One should think of the Space Lemma as saying that, for any σ and any martingale d, there are at least k many extensions τ of σ of length

$|\sigma| + l(\delta, k)$ such that d cannot increase its capital at σ by more than a factor of δ while betting along τ.

We wish to show that a given set X can be coded into a 1-random set R. Clearly, unless X itself is 1-random, there is no hope of doing such a coding if the reduction allows for the recovery of X as an identifiable subsequence of R. For instance, it would be hopeless to try to ensure that $X \leqslant_{\mathrm{m}} R$. As we will show, however, we can get $X \leqslant_{\mathrm{wtt}} R$. The key idea in the proof below, which we take from Merkle and Mihailović [267], is to use the intervals provided by the Space Lemma to do the coding.

Theorem 8.3.2 (Kučera [215], Gács [167]). *Every set is wtt-reducible to a 1-random set.*

Proof. Let d be a universal c.e. martingale. We assume that we have applied the savings trick of Proposition 6.3.8 to d so that for any R, if $\liminf_n d(R \upharpoonright n) < \infty$ then R is 1-random.

Let $r_0 > r_1 > \cdots$ be a collection of positive rationals such that, letting $\beta_i = \prod_{j \leqslant i} r_j$, the sequence $\{\beta_i\}_{i \in \omega}$ converges to some value β. Let $l_s = l(r_s, 2)$ be as in the Space Lemma, which means that for any σ there are at least two strings τ of length l_s with $d(\sigma\tau) \leqslant r_s d(\sigma)$. Partition $\mathbb{N}$ into consecutive intervals $\{I_s\}_{s \in \omega}$ with $|I_s| = l_s$.

Fix a set X. We construct a 1-random set R that wtt-computes X. At stage s, we specify R on the elements of I_s. We denote the part of R specified before stage s by σ_s. (That is, $\sigma_s = R \upharpoonright \sum_{i<s} l_i$.) If $s > 0$, then we assume by induction that $d(\sigma_s) \leqslant \beta_{s-1}$. We say that a string τ of length l_s is *s-admissible* if $d(\sigma_s \tau) \leqslant \beta_s$. Since $\beta_s = r_s \beta_{s-1}$ (when $s > 0$) and $l_s = l(r_s, 2)$, there are at least two s-admissible strings. Let τ_0 and τ_1 be the lexicographically least and greatest among such strings, respectively. Let $\sigma_{s+1} = \sigma_s \tau_i$, where $i = X(s)$.

Now $\liminf_n d(R \upharpoonright n) \leqslant \beta$, so R is 1-random. We now show how to compute $X(s)$ from $\sigma_{s+1} = R \upharpoonright \sum_{i \leqslant s} l_i$. We know that σ_{s+1} is either the leftmost or the rightmost s-admissible extension of σ_s, and being s-admissible is clearly a co-c.e. property, so we wait until either all extensions of σ to the left of σ_{s+1} are seen to be not s-admissible, or all extensions of σ to the right of σ_{s+1} are seen to be not s-admissible. In the first case, $s \notin X$, while in the second case, $s \in X$. $\square$

We will refer to the kind of coding used in the above proof as *Gács coding*, as it is an adaptation by Merkle and Mihailović [267] of the original method used by Gács [167].

Merkle and Mihailović [267] also adapted the methods of Gács [167] to show that the use of the wtt-reduction in the Kučera-Gács Theorem can be quite small, on the order of $n + o(n)$. This proof is along the lines of the above, but is a bit more delicate. We will see in Theorem 9.13.2 that this bound cannot be improved to $n + O(1)$.

8.4 A "no gap" theorem for 1-randomness

The Kučera-Gács Theorem allows us to examine more deeply the characterization of 1-randomness by Miller and Yu, Theorem 6.7.2. We recall that this theorem states that a set is 1-random iff any of the following equivalent conditions holds.

(i) $C(A \upharpoonright n \mid n) \geqslant n - K(n) - O(1)$.

(ii) $C(A \upharpoonright n) \geqslant n - K(n) - O(1)$.

(iii) $C(A \upharpoonright n) \geqslant n - g(n) - O(1)$ for every computable function g such that $\sum_n 2^{-g(n)} < \infty$.

(iv) $C(A \upharpoonright n) \geqslant n - G(n) - O(1)$,

where

$$G(n) = \begin{cases} K_{s+1}(t) & \text{if } n = 2^{\langle s,t \rangle} \text{ and } K_{s+1}(t) \neq K_s(t) \\ n & \text{otherwise.} \end{cases}$$

This function is clearly a Solovay function in the sense of Definition 3.12.3, that is, a computable upper bound for K that agrees with K up to a constant infinitely often. Using the Kučera-Gács Theorem, Bienvenu and Downey [39] showed that this is not a coincidence, as *all* functions that can take the place of G in Theorem 6.7.2 are Solovay functions.

Theorem 8.4.1 (Bienvenu and Downey [39]). *Let g be a function such that A is 1-random iff $C(A \upharpoonright n) \geqslant n - g(n) - O(1)$. Then g is a Solovay function.*

To prove this result, we will show that in both characterizations of 1-randomness, $K(\alpha \upharpoonright n) \geqslant n - O(1)$ and $C(\alpha \upharpoonright n) \geqslant n - K(n) - O(1)$, the lower bound on the complexity is very sharp; that is, there is no "gap phenomenon".

In Corollary 6.6.2, we saw that A is 1-random iff $\lim_n K(A \upharpoonright n) - n = \infty$. Together with Schnorr's Theorem 6.2.3, this result gives the following dichotomy: Either A is not 1-random, in which case $K(\alpha \upharpoonright n) - n$ takes arbitrarily large negative values, or A is 1-random, in which case $K(\alpha \upharpoonright n) - n$ tends to infinity. So, for instance, there is no A such that $K(A \upharpoonright n) = n \pm O(1)$. We can ask whether this dichotomy is due to a gap phenomenon. That is, is there a function h that tends to infinity, such that for every 1-random A, we have $K(A \upharpoonright n) \geqslant n + h(n) - O(1)$? Similarly, is there a function g that tends to infinity such that for every A, if $K(A \upharpoonright n) \geqslant n - g(n) - O(1)$ then A is 1-random? We will give negative answers to both of these questions, as well as their plain complexity counterparts.

Theorem 8.4.2 (Bienvenu [37], see also Bienvenu and Downey [39]).

(i) *There is no function h that tends to infinity such that if $K(A \upharpoonright n) \geqslant n - h(n) - O(1)$ then A is 1-random.*

In fact, there is no function h that tends to infinity such that if $K(A \upharpoonright n) \geqslant n - h(n) - O(1)$ then A is Church stochastic (as defined in Definition 7.4.1).

(ii) *There is no function h such that if $C(A \upharpoonright n) \geqslant n - K(n) - h(n) - O(1)$ then A is 1-random (or even Church stochastic).*

Proof. Since we can replace h by the function $n \mapsto \min\{h(k) : k \geqslant n\}$, we may assume that h is nondecreasing. We build a single A that establishes all parts of the theorem simultaneously. Let $h^{-1}(n)$ be the least m such that $h(m) = n$.

If h is computable, then we can simply take a 1-random X and obtain A by inserting zeroes into X at a sufficiently sparse set of positions, say $h^{-1}(0), h^{-1}(1), \ldots$.[2] However, we are working with an arbitrary order h, which may grow slower than any computable order, so this direct construction may not work, since inserting zeroes at a noncomputable set of positions may not affect the randomness of the resulting set. To overcome this problem, we invoke the Kučera-Gács Theorem and choose our 1-random set X so that $h \leqslant_T X$. Intuitively, the sequence A resulting from inserting zeroes into X at positions $h^{-1}(0), h^{-1}(1), \ldots$ should not be 1-random, or even Church stochastic, since the part of A consisting of the original bits of X should be able to compute the places at which zeroes were inserted. However, the insertion of zeroes may destroy the Turing reduction Φ from X to h^{-1}. In other words, looking at A, we may not be able to distinguish the bits of X from the inserted zeroes.

We solve this problem by delaying the insertion of the zeroes to "give Φ enough time" to compute the positions of the inserted zeroes. More precisely, we insert the kth zero at position $n_k = h^{-1}(k)+t(k)$ where $t(k)$ is the time needed by Φ to compute $h^{-1}(k)$ from X. This way, n_k is computable from $X \upharpoonright n_k$ in time at most n_k. We can then construct a computable selection rule that selects precisely the inserted zeroes, witnessing the fact that A is not Church stochastic (and hence not 1-random). Moreover, since the "insertion delay" makes the inserted zeroes even more sparse, we still have $K(A \upharpoonright n) \geqslant n - h(n) - O(1)$. And similarly, since X is 1-random, by Theorem 6.7.2 we have $C(A \upharpoonright n) \geqslant n - K(n) - h(n) - O(1)$.

The details are as follows. We may assume that t is a nondecreasing function. Let A be the set obtained by inserting zeroes into X at positions $h^{-1}(n) + t(n)$. To show that A is not Church stochastic, we construct a (total) computable selection rule S that filters the inserted zeroes from A. We proceed by induction to describe the action of S on a sequence Z.

Let k_n the number of bits selected by S from $Z \upharpoonright n$ and let σ_n be the sequence obtained from $Z \upharpoonright n$ by removing all selected bits. At stage $n+1$,

[2]This approach was refined by Merkle, Miller, Nies, Reimann, and Stephan [269], who used an insertion of zeroes at a co-c.e. set of positions to construct a left-c.e. real that is not von Mises-Wald-Church stochastic, but has initial segments of high complexity.

the rule S selects the nth bit of Z iff $\Phi^{\sigma_n}(k_n)[n]\downarrow$ and for the computation time s of $\Phi^{\sigma_n}(k_n)$, we have $\Phi^{\sigma_n}(k_n) + s = n$.

Clearly, S is a total computable selection rule. We claim that, on A, the rule S selects exactly the zeroes that have been inserted into X to obtain A. Suppose that the first i many bits of A selected by S are the first i many inserted zeroes, the last of these being $A(m)$. Let $A(n)$ be the next inserted zero. Let $l \in (m, n)$ and assume by induction that no bit of A in (m, l) is selected by S. Then $\sigma_l \prec X$ and $k_l = i$, so if $\Phi^{\sigma_l}(k_l)\downarrow$ then $\Phi^{\sigma_l}(k_l) = \Phi^X(i) = h^{-1}(i)$, and the time of this computation is $t(i)$. But $\Phi^X(i) + t(i) \neq l$, since l is not an insertion place, and hence $A(l)$ is not selected by S. So, by induction, no bit of A in (m, n) is selected by S. Thus $\sigma_n \prec X$ and $k_n = i$. Furthermore, since n is the $(i + 1)$st insertion place, $n = h^{-1}(i)+t(i)$, and $\Phi^{\sigma_n}(k_n)[n]\downarrow = \Phi^X(i) = h^{-i}(i)$, so $A(n)$ is selected by S. Thus we have established our claim, which implies that A is not Church stochastic.

Now fix n and let i be the number of inserted zeroes in $A \upharpoonright n$. Then $X \upharpoonright n - i$ can be computed from $A \upharpoonright n$, so $K(A \upharpoonright n) \geqslant K(X \upharpoonright n - i) - O(1) \geqslant n - i - O(1)$. By the choice of insertion positions, $i \leqslant h(n)$, so $K(A \upharpoonright n) \geqslant n - h(n) - O(1)$. A similar calculation shows that $C(A \upharpoonright n) \geqslant n - K(n) - h(n) - O(1)$. □

The above construction can also be used to get the following dual version of Theorem 8.4.2.

Corollary 8.4.3 (Bienvenu and Downey [39]). *There is no function g that tends to infinity such that $K(A \upharpoonright n) \geqslant n + g(n) - O(1)$ for every 1-random A.*

Similarly, there is no function g that tends to infinity such that $C(A \upharpoonright n) \geqslant n - K(n) + h(n) - O(1)$ for every 1-random A.

Proof. We prove the first statement, the proof of the second being essentially identical.

Assume for a contradiction that such a g exists. We may assume that g is nondecreasing. Let h be an order that is sufficiently slow-growing so that $h(n) \leqslant g(n - h(n)) + O(1)$ and perform the construction in the proof of Theorem 8.4.2. Then, letting i be the number of inserted zeroes in $A \upharpoonright n$, we have

$$K(A \upharpoonright n) \geqslant K(X \upharpoonright n - i) - O(1) \geqslant n - i + g(n - i) - O(1)$$
$$\geqslant n - h(n) + g(n - h(n)) - O(1) \geqslant n - O(1),$$

contradicting the fact that A is not 1-random. □

Miller and Yu [279] extended the above result to any unbounded function (rather than only those that tend to infinity). We will present this result in Theorem 10.4.3. Bienvenu and Downey [39] also used the results above to give a different proof of Theorem 6.7.2. A further application of these results is to prove Theorem 8.4.1.

Proof of Theorem 8.4.1. Let g be a function such that A is 1-random iff $C(A \upharpoonright n) \geqslant n - g(n) - O(1)$. Let $h(n) = g(n) - K(n)$. Then A is 1-random iff $C(A \upharpoonright n) \geqslant n - K(n) - h(n) - O(1)$, so by Theorem 8.4.2, h cannot tend to infinity, and thus g is a Solovay function. □

The consequences of Theorem 8.4.2 go beyond its applications to Solovay functions. For example, it can be used to show that Schnorr randomness does not imply Church stochasticity, as mentioned in Section 7.4.1. By Theorem 7.3.4, if $K(A \upharpoonright n) \geqslant n - h(n) - O(1)$ for some computable order h, then A is Schnorr random. On the other hand, Theorem 8.4.2 says that this condition is not sufficient for A to be Church stochastic.

One can also adapt the proof of Theorem 8.4.2 to separate Church stochasticity from Schnorr randomness within the left-c.e. reals, as we now sketch. Let α be a 1-random left-c.e. real. Let $t(n)$ be least such that $t(n) > t(n-1)$ and $|\alpha - \alpha_{t(n)}| < 2^{-n}$. Let β be obtained from α by inserting zeroes in positions $t(0), t(1), \dots$. Since t is approximable from below, β is left-c.e., and by the same reasoning as above, it is not Church stochastic. Let $f(n)$ be the least m such that $t(m) > n$. The same kind of computation as above shows that $K(\beta \upharpoonright n) \geqslant n - f(n) - O(1)$. It is easy to show that t grows faster than any computable function, so f grows more slowly than any computable order, whence β is Schnorr random. This result improves a theorem of Merkle, Miller, Nies, Reimann, and Stephan [269], who proved an equivalent fact for a weaker notion of stochasticity. For details on that result, see Bienvenu [37].

8.5 Kučera coding

One of the most basic questions we might ask about the distribution of 1-random sets is which Turing degrees contain such sets. Kučera [215] gave the following partial answer, which was later extended by Kautz [200] to n-random sets using the jump operator, as we will see in Theorem 8.14.3.

Theorem 8.5.1 (Kučera [215]). *If* $\mathbf{a} \geqslant \mathbf{0}'$ *then* $\mathbf{a}$ *contains a* 1*-random set.*

Proof. Let $\mathbf{a} \geqslant \mathbf{0}'$ and let $X \in \mathbf{a}$. Let R be as in the proof of Theorem 8.3.2. Then $X \leqslant_{\mathrm{T}} R$. Furthermore, we can compute R if we know X and can tell which sets are s-admissible for each s. The latter question can be answered by $\emptyset'$. Since $X \geqslant_{\mathrm{T}} \emptyset'$, it follows that $R \leqslant_{\mathrm{T}} X$. Thus R is a 1-random set of degree $\mathbf{a}$. □

We now give a different proof of Theorem 8.5.1, which is of course also an alternative proof of the Kučera-Gács Theorem 8.3.2, along the lines of the original proof of Kučera [215]. This version is due to Reimann [324] (see also Reimann and Slaman [327]). Let $S_0, S_1, \dots$ be an effective list of the prefix-free c.e. subsets of $2^{<\omega}$, and let $S_{k,s}$ be the stage s approximation to S_k. We begin with Kučera's useful construction of a universal Martin-Löf test.

Kučera's universal Martin-Löf test. Fix $n \in \mathbb{N}$. For each $e > n$, enumerate all elements of $S_{\Phi_e(e)}$ (where we take $S_{\Phi_e(e)}$ to be empty if $\Phi_e(e)\uparrow$) into a set R_n as long as $\sum_{\sigma \in S_{\Phi_e(e),s}} 2^{-|\sigma|} < 2^{-e}$. (That is, if this sum ever gets to 2^{-e}, stop enumerating the elements of $S_{\Phi_e(e)}$ into R_n before it does.) Let $U_n = [\![R_n]\!]$.

The R_n are uniformly c.e. and $\sum_{\sigma \in R_n} 2^{-|\sigma|} \leqslant \sum_{e>n} 2^{-e} = 2^{-n}$. Thus $\{U_n\}_{n\in\omega}$ is a Martin-Löf test. To see that it is universal, let $\{V_n\}_{n\in\omega}$ be a Martin-Löf test. Let e be such that $V_i = [\![S_{\Phi_e(i)}]\!]$ for all i. Every computable function possesses infinitely many indices, so for each n there is an $i > n$ such that $\Phi_e = \Phi_i$. For such an i, we have $[\![S_{\Phi_i(i)}]\!] = [\![S_{\Phi_e(i)}]\!] = V_i$, which means that every element of $[\![S_{\Phi_i(i)}]\!]$ is enumerated into R_n. So $\bigcap_m V_m \subseteq U_n$. Thus $\bigcap_m V_m \subseteq \bigcap_n U_n$.

We next need a lemma similar in spirit to the Space Lemma.

Lemma 8.5.2. *Let $\{U_n\}_{n\in\mathbb{N}}$ be Kučera's universal Martin-Löf test, and let P_n be the complement of U_n. Let C be a Π^0_1 class. Then there exists a computable function $\gamma : 2^{<\omega} \times \mathbb{N} \to \mathbb{Q}^+$ such that for any $\sigma \in 2^{<\omega}$ and $n \in \mathbb{N}$,*

$$P_n \cap C \cap [\![\sigma]\!] \neq \emptyset \Rightarrow \mu(C \cap [\![\sigma]\!]) \geqslant \gamma(\sigma, n).$$

Proof. It is easy to check that if $P_n \cap C \cap [\![\sigma]\!] \neq \emptyset$ then $\mu(C \cap [\![\sigma]\!]) > 0$, but we need to show that we can give an *effective* positive lower bound for $\mu(C \cap [\![\sigma]\!])$.

Since C is a Π^0_1 class, there is an index k such that $\overline{C} = [\![S_k]\!]$. Fix σ and n, and define the partial computable function Φ as follows. On input j, search for an s such that $\mu([\![\sigma]\!] \setminus [\![S_{k,s}]\!]) < 2^{-j}$. If such an s is ever found, then let $\Phi(j)$ be such that $S_{\Phi(j)}$ is finite, $[\![S_{\Phi(j)}]\!]$ covers $[\![\sigma]\!] \setminus [\![S_{k,s}]\!]$, and $\mu([\![S_{\Phi(j)}]\!]) \leqslant 2^{-j}$. Clearly, $\{[\![S_{\Phi(j)}]\!]\}_{j\in\omega}$ is a Martin-Löf test. Let $e > n$ be an index such that $\Phi_e = \Phi$, obtained effectively from σ and n. Let $\gamma(\sigma, n) = 2^{-e}$.

Suppose that $\Phi_e(e)\downarrow$. Then $[\![S_{\Phi_e(e)}]\!] \subseteq U_n$, so there is an s such that $[\![\sigma]\!] \setminus [\![S_{k,s}]\!] \subseteq U_n$. But

$$C \cap [\![\sigma]\!] = [\![\sigma]\!] \setminus [\![S_k]\!] \subseteq [\![\sigma]\!] \setminus [\![S_{k,s}]\!],$$

so $C \cap [\![\sigma]\!] \subseteq U_n$, and hence $P_n \cap C \cap [\![\sigma]\!] = \emptyset$.

Now suppose that $\Phi_e(e)\uparrow$. Then $\mu([\![\sigma]\!] \setminus [\![S_{k,s}]\!]) \geqslant 2^{-e}$ for every s, so

$$\mu(C \cap [\![\sigma]\!]) = \mu([\![\sigma]\!] \setminus [\![S_k]\!]) = \lim_s \mu([\![\sigma]\!] \setminus [\![S_{k,s}]\!]) \geqslant 2^{-e} = \gamma(\sigma, n).$$

□

Alternate proof of Theorem 8.5.1. Let $B \geqslant_T \emptyset'$. We need to show that there is a 1-random set A such that $A \equiv_T B$. Let $\{U_n\}_{n\in\omega}$ be Kučera's universal Martin-Löf test. We describe how to code B into an element A of $\overline{U_0}$. Let T be a computable tree such that $[T] = \overline{U_0}$ and let E be the set of extendible nodes of T (i.e., those nodes extended by paths of T). Note that E is co-c.e., and hence $\emptyset'$-computable.

Let γ be as in Lemma 8.5.2 with $C = \overline{U_0}$, and let $b(\sigma) = \lceil -\log \gamma(\sigma, 0) \rceil$. Then we know that, for any σ, if $\overline{U_0} \cap [\![\sigma]\!] \neq \emptyset$, then $\mu(\overline{U_0} \cap [\![\sigma]\!]) \geqslant 2^{-b(\sigma)}$. Thus, if $\sigma \in E$ then σ has at least two extensions of length $b(\sigma)+1$ in E.

Suppose that, at stage n, we have defined $A \upharpoonright m_n$ for some m_n. Let $\sigma = A \upharpoonright m_n$. We assume by induction that $\sigma \in E$. Let τ_0 and τ_1 be the leftmost and rightmost extension of σ of length $b(\sigma)+1$ in E, respectively. As pointed out in the previous paragraph, $\tau_0 \neq \tau_1$. Let $A \upharpoonright b(\sigma) = \tau_i$, where $i = B(n)$.

Since $A \in [T] = \overline{U_0}$, we know that A is 1-random. We now show that $A \equiv_T B$.

The construction of A is computable in B and $\emptyset'$. Since we are assuming that $B \geqslant_T \emptyset'$, we have $A \leqslant_T B$. For the other direction, first note that the function $n \mapsto m_n$ is computable in A. To see that this is the case, assume that we have already computed m_n. Then $m_{n+1} = b(A \upharpoonright m_n) + 1$. Now, to compute $B(n)$ using A, let $\sigma = A \upharpoonright m_n$ and let $\tau = A \upharpoonright m_{n+1}$. We know that τ is either the leftmost or the rightmost extension of σ of length m_{n+1} in E. Since E is co-c.e., we can wait until either all extensions of σ of length m_{n+1} to the left of τ leave E, or all extensions of σ of length m_{n+1} to the right of τ leave E. In the first case, $s \notin B$, while in the second case, $s \in B$. □

We call the coding technique in the above proof *Kučera coding*.

The Kučera-Gács Theorem goes against the intuition that random sets should be highly disordered, and hence computationally weak. However, note that this result is quite specific to 1-randomness. For example, if A is 2-random then it is 1-random relative to $\emptyset'$, and hence relative to Ω, so by van Lambalgen's Theorem, Ω is 1-random relative to A, and hence $\Omega \nleqslant_T A$. Thus, no 2-random set can compute $\emptyset'$. (We will have more to say on this topic in the next section.) Furthermore, Theorem 8.5.1 can be combined with van Lambalgen's Theorem to prove the following result, which shows how randomness is in a sense inversely proportional to computational strength.

Theorem 8.5.3 (Miller and Yu [280]). *Let A be 1-random and B be n-random. If $A \leqslant_T B$ then A is n-random.*

Proof. The $n = 1$ case is trivial, so assume that $n > 1$. Let $X \equiv_T \emptyset^{(n-1)}$ be 1-random. Since B is n-random, it is 1-random relative to X. By van Lambalgen's Theorem, X is 1-random relative to B, and hence relative to

A. Again by van Lambalgen's Theorem, A is 1-random relative to X, and hence relative to $\emptyset'$. Thus A is n-random. □

8.6 Demuth's Theorem

By Theorem 8.2.1, the only 1-random c.e. degree is $\mathbf{0}'$, so the class of 1-random degrees is not closed downwards, even among the nonzero degrees. The following result shows that there is a sense in which it *is* closed downwards with respect to truth table reducibility. The proof we give is due to Kautz [200], and uses the results and notation of Section 6.12.

Theorem 8.6.1 (Demuth's Theorem [95]). *If A is 1-random and $B \leqslant_{\mathrm{tt}} A$ is not computable, then there is a 1-random $C \equiv_{\mathrm{T}} B$.*

Proof. Let e be such that $\Phi_e^A = B$ and Φ_e^X is total for all oracles X. Let

$$\rho(\sigma) = \mu\left(\bigcup\{[\![\tau]\!] : \forall n < |\sigma|\,(\Phi_e^\tau(n)\downarrow = \sigma(n))\}\right)$$

and let $\nu = \mu_\rho$. We claim that B is 1-ν-random. Suppose otherwise, and let $\{V_n\}_{n\in\omega}$ be a Martin-Löf ν-test such that $B \in \bigcap_n V_n$. Let $U_n = \{X : \Phi_e^X \in V_n\}$. It is easy to check that the U_n are uniformly Σ_1^0 classes and $\mu(U_n) = \nu(V_n) \leqslant 2^{-n}$, so the U_n form a Martin-Löf test. But $A \in \bigcap_n U_n$, contradicting the hypothesis that A is 1-random. Thus B is 1-ν-random.

Let $C \in \bigcap_s (B \upharpoonright s)_\nu$. Then $B = \mathrm{seq}_\nu C$, since B is not computable, and hence neither is C. By Theorem 6.12.9, $C \equiv_{\mathrm{T}} B$ and C is 1-random. □

Too recently for inclusion in this book, Bienvenu and Porter [private communication] gave an example of a set $B \leqslant_{\mathrm{tt}} \Omega$ such that there is no 1-random $C \equiv_{\mathrm{wtt}} B$.

Corollary 8.6.2 (Kautz [200]). *There is a 1-random degree* **a** *such that every noncomputable* $\mathbf{b} \leqslant \mathbf{a}$ *is 1-random.*

Proof. By Proposition 8.1.3, there is a 1-random set A of hyperimmune-free degree. By Proposition 2.17.7, if $B \leqslant_{\mathrm{T}} A$ then $B \leqslant_{\mathrm{tt}} A$, so the corollary follows from Demuth's Theorem. □

It is not known whether **a** can be made hyperimmune. We will extend this result to weak 2-randomness in Corollary 8.11.13.

Another nice application of Demuth's Theorem is an easy proof of an extension of the result of Calude and Nies [51] that Ω is not tt-complete.

Corollary 8.6.3. *If A is an incomplete left-c.e. real then $A \nleqslant_{\mathrm{tt}} \Omega$.*

Proof. By Theorem 8.2.1, no incomplete c.e. degree is 1-random. □

As a final corollary, pointed out by Nies, we get a short proof of a theorem of Lachlan [233] whose direct proof is considerably more difficult.

Corollary 8.6.4 (Lachlan [233]). *There is a c.e. set that is wtt-complete but not tt-complete.*

Proof. The previous corollary, combined with Proposition 6.1.2, shows that Ω is wtt-complete but not tt-complete, so it is enough to define a c.e. set $A \equiv_{tt} \Omega$. An example of such a set is the set of dyadic rationals less than Ω. □

8.7 Randomness relative to other measures

In this section, we revisit the material of Section 6.12. It is natural to ask, given a set X, whether there is a (possibly noncomputable) measure ν such that X is 1-ν-random. (This question can be thought of as asking whether X has *some* randomness content that can be extracted by an appropriate choice of ν.) Of course, every set is 1-ν-random if it is an atom of ν. If X is computable then $\{X\}$ is a Σ^0_1 class, so being an atom is the only way that X can be 1-ν-random. The following result shows that if X is noncomputable, then there is always a less trivial way to make X be 1-ν-random.

Theorem 8.7.1 (Reimann and Slaman [327]). *If A is noncomputable then there is a ν such that A is 1-ν-random and A is not an atom of ν.*

The proof of this result uses the relativized form of the following basis theorem. (In Section 15.5 we will study the special case of this basis theorem in which $X = \Omega$.)

Theorem 8.7.2 (Reimann and Slaman [327], Downey, Hirschfeldt, Miller, and Nies [115]). *For every 1-random set X and every nonempty Π^0_1 class P, there is an X-left-c.e. real $A \in P$ such that X is 1-random relative to A.*

Proof. Let

$$V_i = \bigcup \{ [\![\sigma]\!] : \exists s \, \forall A \in P_s \, \exists \tau \preccurlyeq \sigma \, (K^A(\tau) \leqslant |\tau| - i) \}.$$

It is easy to see that the V_i are uniformly Σ^0_1 classes, and that $\mu(V_i) \leqslant 2^{-i}$, since if $A \in P$ then $V_i \subseteq \{X : \exists n \, (K^A(X \upharpoonright n) \leqslant n - i)\}$. Thus $\{V_i\}_{i \in \omega}$ is a Martin-Löf test. If X is not 1-random relative to A for all $A \in P$, then, by compactness, for each i there is a $\sigma \prec X$ such that $[\![\sigma]\!] \subseteq V_i$, and hence $X \in \bigcap_i V_i$.

Thus, if X is 1-random, then there is an $A \in P$ such that X is 1-random relative to A. We must still show that A can be taken to be an X-left-c.e. real. For each i, let $S_i = \{A \in P : \forall n \, (K^A(X \upharpoonright n) > n - i)\}$. Each S_i is a $\Pi^{0,X}_1$ class. We have shown that S_i is nonempty for large enough i. For such an i, the lexicographically least element A of S_i is an X-left-c.e. real satisfying the statement of the theorem. □

We will also need the fact that we can represent the space of all probability measures on 2^ω as a Π^0_1 class $\mathcal{P}$. It is not too difficult to do so using basic methods from effective descriptive set theory; see [325, 327].

Proof of Theorem 8.7.1. It is straightforward to relativize the proof of Theorem 8.5.1 to show that for all X and Y such that $X \oplus Y \geqslant_T X'$, there is an R that is 1-random relative to X such that $X \oplus Y \equiv_T X \oplus R$. Let A be noncomputable. By Theorem 2.16.2, there is an X such that $X \oplus A \geqslant_T X'$. Fix such an X and let R be 1-random relative to X and such that $X \oplus A \equiv_T X \oplus R$.

Let Φ and Ψ be X-computable functionals such that $\Phi^R = A$ and $\Psi^A = R$. Let $p(\sigma)$ be the shortest string τ such that $\sigma \preccurlyeq \Phi^\tau$ and $\tau \preccurlyeq \Psi^\sigma$. Of course, $p(\sigma)$ may be undefined, but it will be defined if $\sigma \prec A$.

We wish to define a measure ν such that A is 1-ν-random and A is not an atom of ν. To make A be 1-ν-random, we ensure that ν dominates an image measure induced by Φ, thereby ensuring that every 1-random set in the domain of Φ is mapped by Φ to a 1-ν-random set. Thus, we restrict ourselves to measures ν such that $\mu([\![p(\sigma)]\!]) \leqslant \nu([\![\sigma]\!]) \leqslant \mu([\![\Psi^\sigma]\!])$ for all σ such that $p(\sigma)$ is defined. The first inequality ensures the required domination and the second that ν is not atomic on the domain of Ψ.

It is easy to see that the subclass M of $\mathcal{P}$ consisting of representations of those ν that satisfy the above inequalities is a $\Pi^{0,X}_1$ class, since $\mu([\![p(\sigma)]\!])$ is X-approximable from below and $\mu([\![\Psi^\sigma]\!])$ is X-approximable from above. Furthermore, M is nonempty, since the inequalities involved in its definition yield compatible nonempty intervals, and hence we can take an extension Γ of Φ to a total functional and use Γ to define a measure with a representation contained in M.

By the relativized form of Theorem 8.7.2, there is a $P \in M$ such that R is 1-random relative to $X \oplus P$. Let ν be the measure encoded by P. Since A is not an atom of ν, we are left with showing that A is not 1-ν-random. Assume for a contradiction that A is covered by the Martin-Löf ν-test $\{V_n\}_{n\in\mathbb{N}}$. Let $G_0, G_1, \ldots$ be uniformly $(X \oplus P)$-c.e. prefix-free sets of generators for the V_i. Let $U_n = \bigcup_{\sigma\in G_n} [\![p(\sigma)]\!]$. The U_n are uniformly $\Sigma^{0,X\oplus P}_1$-classes, and $\mu(U_n) \leqslant \nu(V_n)$, since for each σ we have $\mu([\![p(\sigma)]\!]) \leqslant \nu([\![\sigma]\!])$. Thus the U_n form a Martin-Löf test relative to $X \oplus P$. But for each n there is a $\sigma \prec A$ in V_n, and $p(\sigma) \prec R$ is in U_n. Thus $R \in \bigcap_n U_n$, contradicting the fact that R is 1-random relative to $X \oplus P$. □

A rather more subtle question is which sets are 1-ν-random for some *continuous* measure ν. Reimann and Slaman [327] showed that a variation on the halting problem is *never continuously random*.[3] Subsequently, Kjos-Hanssen and Montalbán (see [327]) noted the following.

[3]Their particular example was the set $\{s_n : n \in \mathbb{N}\}$ where $s_0 = 0$ and $s_{n+1} = \max(\min\{s : \emptyset'_s \upharpoonright n+1 = \emptyset' \upharpoonright n+1\}, s_n + 1)$.

Theorem 8.7.3 (Kjos-Hanssen and Montalbán, see [327]). *If P is a countable Π^0_1 class and ν is continuous, then no member of P is 1-ν-random.*

Proof. Since ν is continuous and P is countable, $\nu(P) = 0$, so there is a ν-computable function t such that $\nu(P_{t(n)}) \leqslant 2^{-n}$. Thus $\{P_{t(n)}\}_{n\in\omega}$ is a Martin-Löf ν-test covering P.[4] □

We now make some brief comments for those familiar with concepts and results from higher computability theory. For any computable ordinal α, there is a set X of degree $\mathbf{0}^\alpha$ that is a member of some countable Π^0_1 class, so there is no bound below Δ^1_1 on the complexity of the collection NCR of never continuously random sets. Reimann and Slaman [327, 329] have further explored this class and, more generally, the classes NCR_n of sets that are never n-ν-random for a continuous ν, obtaining some remarkable results. They showed that $\text{NCR} \subset \Delta^1_1$ and, using very deep methods such as Borel Determinacy, that every class NCR_n is countable. They also showed that, quite surprisingly, there is a precise sense in which metamathematical methods such as Borel Determinacy are *necessary* to prove this result. It seems strange that, although randomness-theoretic definitions such as n-randomness have relatively low complexity levels, the metamathematics of proving the countability of the classes NCR_n is so complex. See [327, 328, 329] for more on this subject.

8.8 Randomness and PA degrees

In light of earlier results in this chapter, it is natural to ask whether the collection of 1-random degrees is closed upwards. In this section we give a negative answer to this question by examining the relationship between randomness and the PA degrees introduced in Section 2.21, a connection first explored by Kučera [215].

As we saw in Section 2.21, one of the characterizations of the PA degrees (which we can take as a definition) is that $\mathbf{a}$ is PA iff each partial computable $\{0,1\}$-valued function has an $\mathbf{a}$-computable total extension. As we saw in Section 2.22, this fact implies that if $\mathbf{a}$ is PA then it computes a diagonally noncomputable (DNC) function, that is, a total function g such that $g(n) \neq \Phi_n(n)$ for all n. The same is true of 1-random degrees.

Theorem 8.8.1 (Kučera [215]). *Every 1-random set computes a DNC function.*

Proof. Let A be 1-random. Let $f(n)$ be the position of $A \upharpoonright n$ in some effective listing of finite binary strings. Since A is 1-random, $K(f(n)) =$

[4] In fact, this proof shows that no member of P is even weakly 1-ν-random.

$K(A \upharpoonright n) \pm O(1) \geqslant n - O(1)$. On the other hand, if $\Phi_n(n)\downarrow$, then $K(\Phi_n(n)) \leqslant K(n) + O(1)$, so there are only finitely many n such that $f(n) = \Phi_n(n)$. By altering f at these finitely many places, we obtain an A-computable DNC function. □

This result has the following interesting consequences, the first of which also has a direct proof using a version of the recursion theorem.

Corollary 8.8.2 (Kučera [216]). *If* $\mathbf{a}$ *is* 1*-random and c.e. then* $\mathbf{a} = \mathbf{0}'$.

Proof. Apply Arslanov's Completeness Criterion, Theorem 2.22.3 (together with Theorem 2.22.1). □

Corollary 8.8.3 (Kučera [216]). *If* A *and* B *are* 1*-random and* $A, B \leqslant_T \emptyset'$, *then the degrees of* A *and* B *do not form a minimal pair.*

Proof. By Theorem 8.8.1, each of A and B computes a DNC function, and hence computes a fixed-point free function (by Theorem 2.22.1). By Theorem 2.22.7, the degrees of A and B do not form a minimal pair. □

Corollary 8.8.3 also follows from Theorem 7.2.11, since if $A, B \leqslant_T \emptyset'$, then $\{A, B\}$ is a Σ^0_3 class (in fact, a Π^0_2 class).

Let A and B be relatively 1-random Δ^0_2 sets. Heuristically, A and B should have very little common information, and thus we might expect their degrees to form a minimal pair. Corollary 8.8.3 shows that this is not the case, however. Still, our intuition is not far off. We will see in Corollary 8.12.4 that if A and B are relatively weakly 2-random, then their degrees form a minimal pair. Furthermore, we will see in Corollary 11.7.3 that even for relatively 1-random A and B, any set computable in both A and B must be quite close to being computable, in a sense that we will discuss in Chapter 11.

A further connection between PA degrees and 1-random degrees is that, since there are Π^0_1 classes consisting entirely of 1-random sets, every PA degree computes a 1-random set (by the Scott Basis Theorem 2.21.2). On the other hand, Kučera [215] showed that the class of sets of PA degree has measure 0, and hence there are 1-random degrees that are not PA. He also showed that there are PA degrees that are not 1-random, and hence the collection of 1-random degrees is not closed upwards. The exact relationship between PA degrees and 1-random degrees was clarified by the following result of Stephan [379], which also yields Kučera's aforementioned results as corollaries.

Theorem 8.8.4 (Stephan [379]). *If a degree* $\mathbf{a}$ *is both PA and* 1*-random then* $\mathbf{a} \geqslant \mathbf{0}'$.

Proof. Let $A \not\geqslant_T \emptyset'$ have PA degree. We first construct a partial computable function f such that for each e, the class of all sets B such that Φ^B_e is a total extension of f has small measure. Then we use f to show that A is not 1-random, using the fact that, since A has PA degree, A can compute a total extension of f.

We proceed as follows for all e simultaneously. Let $I_e = [2^{e+2}, 2^{e+3} - 1]$. Within I_e, define f as follows. At stage s, let a_s be the least element of I_e such that $f(a_s)$ has not yet been defined. (We will show below that such a number always exists.) For $i = 0, 1$, let $P_{e,s,i}$ be the class of all B such that, for all $n \in I_e$,

1. $\Phi_e^B(n)[s]\downarrow$
2. if $n < a_s$ then $\Phi_e^B(n) = f(n)$, and
3. if $n = a_s$ then $\Phi_e^B(n) = i$.

Let $d_{e,s,i} = \mu(P_{e,s,i})$. By the usual use conventions, whether $B \in P_{e,s,i}$ depends only on $B \upharpoonright s$, so $P_{e,s,i}$ is a Δ_1^0 class. For the same reason, $d_{e,s,i}$ is rational and the function $(e, s, i) \mapsto d_{e,s,i}$ is computable. If $d_{e,s,0} + d_{e,s,1} > 2^{-(e+1)}$, then choose $i < 2$ such that $d_{e,s,i} \leqslant d_{e,s,1-i}$ and let $f(a_s) = i$. Otherwise, do nothing at this stage.

Clearly, f is partial computable. When $f(a_s)$ is defined at stage s, we ensure that Φ_e^B does not extend f for all $B \in P_{e,s,1-f(a_s)}$, and $\mu(P_{e,s,1-f(a_s)}) \geqslant 2^{-(e+2)}$. Furthermore, for two such stages s and t, we have $P_{e,s,1-f(a_s)} \cap P_{e,t,1-f(a_t)} = \emptyset$, so we cannot define f on all of I_e. Thus there is a stage t such that $d_{e,s,0} + d_{e,s,1} \leqslant 2^{-(e+1)}$ for all $s > t$.

Since A is PA, it can compute a total $\{0,1\}$-valued extension g of f. Let $e_0 < e_1 < \cdots$ be such that $\Phi_{e_i}^A = g$ for all i. Let $k_0, k_1, \ldots$ be a computable enumeration of $\emptyset'$ without repetitions.

Let $e(s) = e_{k_s}$ and let $r(s)$ be the first stage $t > s$ such that $d_{e(s),t,0} + d_{e(s),t,1} \leqslant 2^{-(e(s)+1)}$. Let $S = \{P_{e(s),r(s),0} \cup P_{e(s),r(s),1} : s \in \mathbb{N}\}$. Then S is a collection of uniformly Σ_1^0 classes. Furthermore, $\sum_s d_{e(s),r(s),0} + d_{e(s),r(s),1} \leqslant \sum_s 2^{-(e(s)+1)} \leqslant 1$, so S is a Solovay test.

Let $h(i)$ be the least s such that all computations $\Phi_{e_i}^A(n)$ for $n \in I_{e_i}$ have settled by stage s. Then $h \leqslant_T A$. There must be infinitely many s such that $h(k_s) < s$, since otherwise, for all but finitely many n, we would have $n \in \emptyset'$ iff $n = k_s$ for some $s \leqslant h(n)$, which would imply that $A \geqslant_T \emptyset'$, contrary to hypothesis. For each s such that $h(k_s) < s$, we also have $h(k_s) < r(s)$, and hence $A \in P_{e(s),r(s),0} \cup P_{e(s),r(s),1}$. Thus A is in infinitely many elements of S, and hence is not 1-random. □

Corollary 8.8.5 (Kučera [215]). *There are PA degrees that are not 1-random.*

Proof. Apply Theorem 8.8.4 to a low PA degree. □

Corollary 8.8.6 (Kučera [215]). *The collection of 1-random degrees is not closed upwards.*

Proof. As mentioned above, every PA degree computes a 1-random set. Now apply the previous corollary. □

Stephan [379] noted the following improvement of this result.

Corollary 8.8.7 (Stephan [379]). *Let* $\mathbf{a} \not\geqslant \mathbf{0}'$. *Then there is a degree* $\mathbf{b} \geqslant \mathbf{a}$ *that is not* 1*-random.*

Proof. Let $f(n)$ be the least s such that $\emptyset'_s \upharpoonright n = \emptyset' \upharpoonright n$. Then a set computes $\emptyset'$ iff it computes a function that majorizes f. By the relativized form of the hyperimmune-free basis theorem, there is a PA degree $\mathbf{b} \geqslant \mathbf{a}$ that is hyperimmune-free relative to $\mathbf{a}$. Since $\mathbf{a} \not\geqslant \mathbf{0}'$, there is no $\mathbf{a}$-computable function that majorizes f. Since every $\mathbf{b}$-computable function is majorized by some $\mathbf{a}$-computable function, there is no $\mathbf{b}$-computable function that majorizes f. Thus $\mathbf{b} \not\geqslant \mathbf{0}'$. Since $\mathbf{b}$ is a PA degree, it cannot be 1-random. □

As Stephan [379] put it, Theorem 8.8.4 "says that there are two types of Martin-Löf random sets: the first type are the computationally powerful sets which permit to solve the halting problem [$\emptyset'$]; the second type of random sets are computationally weak in the sense that they are not [PA]. Every set not belonging to one of these two types is not Martin-Löf random." We have already alluded to this dichotomy between the 1-random sets that compute $\emptyset'$ and the ones that do not (in the paragraph following Theorem 6.1.3), and have seen in Section 7.7 that the latter can be characterized as the difference random sets. We will see other results that point to a real qualitative difference in terms of computability-theoretic strength between these two kinds of 1-random sets. As we have already pointed out, we should expect randomness to be antithetical to computational power. Indeed, as we move from 1-randomness to 2-randomness, or even weak 2-randomness, we do lose computational power. However, Stephan's result exemplifies the fact that we do not need to go so far. If we ignore the 1-random sets above $\emptyset'$ (which, as we pointed out following Theorem 6.1.3, there are reasonable heuristic reasons to do), then phenomena such as the Kučera-Gács Theorem disappear, and we find that 1-random sets are indeed computationally weak in various ways.

We conclude this section with a further interesting connection between PA and 1-random degrees.

Theorem 8.8.8 (Barmpalias, Lewis, and Ng [24]). *Every PA degree is the join of two* 1*-random degrees.*

Thus, an incomplete PA degree is an example of a non-1-random degree that is the join of two 1-random degrees.

Note that Theorem 8.8.8 does not hold for 1-genericity, or even weak 1-genericity, in place of 1-randomness, since there are hyperimmune-free PA degrees, but by Theorem 2.24.12, every weakly 1-generic set has hyperimmune degree.

Before we prove Theorem 8.8.8, we point out a corollary. While the 1-random degrees are not closed upwards, one might wonder about weaker notions of randomness such as weak 1-randomness. After all, every hyperimmune degree is weakly 1-random. The following corollary was obtained by direct methods, before it was noticed that it could be obtained by an application of Theorems 8.8.4 and 8.8.8, together with Theorem 8.11.11 below, which states that on the hyperimmune-free degrees, 1-randomness and weak 1-randomness are equivalent.

Corollary 8.8.9 (Downey and Hirschfeldt [unpublished]). *The weakly* 1-*random degrees are not closed upwards. Indeed, there is a degree that is not weakly* 1-*random but is above a* 1-*random degree.*

Proof. Let **a** be hyperimmune-free and PA. By Theorem 8.8.4, **a** is not 1-random. By Theorem 8.11.11, **a** is not weakly 1-random. But by Theorem 8.8.8, **a** is the join of two 1-random degrees. □

Note that it follows from this result that the degrees corresponding to any notion intermediate between weak 1-randomness and 1-randomness, such as Schnorr or computable randomness, are also not closed upwards.

The idea of the proof of Theorem 8.8.8 is the following. Let C have PA degree, and let P be a Π^0_1 class consisting entirely of 1-random sets. For a perfect tree T such that $[T] \subseteq P$, we will define a method for coding C into the join of two paths A and B of T, thus ensuring that $C \leqslant_{\mathrm{T}} A \oplus B$. The coding will be done in such a way that if C can compute the tree T, then we also have $A \oplus B \leqslant_{\mathrm{T}} C$. We will then build a class of such trees defined by a Π^0_1 formula (that is, there will be a Π^0_1 class whose elements effectively represent the trees in this class). Then we can use the fact that C is of PA degree to obtain a tree in this class that is computable from C (an idea of Solovay we have met in Corollary 2.21.4). A key ingredient of the proof is the use of *indifferent sets* for the coding.

Definition 8.8.10 (Figueira, Miller, and Nies [146]). For a set I, we write $R =_I \widehat{R}$ to mean that $R(i) = \widehat{R}(i)$ for all $i \notin I$.

A set I is *indifferent* for a 1-random set R if $\widehat{R}$ is 1-random for all $\widehat{R} =_I R$.

Figueira, Miller, and Nies [146] showed that every 1-random set has an infinite indifferent set. Their proof uses a computability-theoretic notion due to Trakhtenbrot [390]. A set A is *autoreducible* if there is a Turing functional Φ such that $\Phi^{A \setminus \{n\}}(n) = A(n)$ for all n. That is, membership of n in A can be determined from A without querying A about n itself. An example of such a set is a set A coding a complete theory. There, to find out whether the code of a sentence φ is in A, we can simply ask whether the code of $\neg\varphi$ is in A.

Figueira, Miller, and Nies [146] observed that no 1-random set is autoreducible. Indeed, if A is autoreducible then it is easy to define a partial computable nonmonotonic betting strategy that succeeds on A, so A is not nonmonotonically random, and hence not 1-random, by Theorem 7.5.5. (It is also not hard to build a c.e. martingale succeeding on A directly.)

For a Π^0_1 class P and $A \in P$, say that I is *indifferent for A in P* if $\widehat{A} \in P$ for all $\widehat{A} =_I A$.

Theorem 8.8.11 (Figueira, Miller, and Nies [146]). *If P is a Π^0_1 class and $A \in P$ is not autoreducible, then there is an infinite $I \leqslant_T A'$ that is indifferent for A in P. Thus, since every 1-random set is contained in a Π^0_1 class all elements of which are 1-random, every 1-random set has an infinite indifferent set.*

Proof. First we claim that if there is no n such that $\{n\}$ is indifferent for A in P, then A is autoreducible. Indeed, in this case, we can let B_0 and B_1 be the two sets that are equal to A except possibly at n, and wait until one of these B_i leaves P, which must happen. Then $A(n) = B_{1-i}(n)$. This argument can easily be extended inductively to show that there is an infinite set $I = \{n_0, n_1 \ldots\}$ such that each finite set $\{n_0, \ldots, n_k\}$ is indifferent for A in P. Since P is closed, I is indifferent for A in P.

We can define n_k as the least $n > n_{k-1}$ such that $\{n_0, \ldots, n_{k-1}, n\}$ is indifferent for A in P, and it is easy to see that this n can be found using A', so we can choose $I \leqslant_T A'$. □

We say that a set is *indifferent* if it is indifferent for some 1-random set. We will not discuss indifferent sets further, but will mention that Figueira, Miller, and Nies [146] showed that an infinite indifferent set must be quite sparse and compute $\emptyset'$, but there are co-c.e. indifferent sets. It is an interesting open question whether there is a 1-random set X that computes a set that is indifferent for X. The concept of indifference has also been explored for genericity; see Day and Fitzgerald [91].

Proof of Theorem 8.8.8. We will be working with perfect trees, as in Section 2.17. That is, in this proof, a tree is a partial function T from $2^{<\omega}$ to $2^{<\omega}$ such that for every $\sigma \in 2^{<\omega}$ and $i \in \{0,1\}$, if $T(\sigma i)\downarrow$, then $T(\sigma)\downarrow$ and $T(\sigma(1-i))\downarrow$, and we have $T(\sigma) \prec T(\sigma i)$ and $T(\sigma(1-i)) \mid T(\sigma i)$. A tree T is perfect if $T(\sigma)\downarrow$ for all σ. A finite tree T of level n is just the restriction of a tree (as a map) to strings of length n. We write $[T]$ for the class of all B for which there is an A with $T(A \upharpoonright n) \prec B$ for all n.

As mentioned above, we want to code a set C of PA degree into 1-random sets A and B. A first idea is to use an infinite indifferent set $I = \{n_0 < n_1 < \cdots\}$ for some 1-random set X to do the coding, by letting A be the set defined by $A(n_i) = C(i)$ and $A(n) = X(n)$ for $n \notin I$, and letting B be the set defined by $B(n_i) = 1 - C(i)$ and $B(n) = X(n)$ for $n \notin I$. Then A and B are 1-random, and $I = \{n : A(n) \neq B(n)\}$, so $I \leqslant_T A \oplus B$, and hence $C \leqslant_T A \oplus B$.

The problem with this approach is that the class of perfect trees cannot be expressed as a Π^0_1 class in Cantor space, because 2^ω is compact while the space of perfect trees, with the natural topology generated by the finite trees, is not. Thus, although we can achieve $C \leqslant_{\mathrm{T}} A \oplus B$, we cannot achieve Turing equivalence through this approach. To get around this problem, we work in a compact subspace of the space of trees.

Let f be an increasing function. (For convenience we let $f(-1) = 0$.) For a set A, let $\sigma_A(0), \sigma_A(1), \dots$ be the unique sequence of strings such that $|\sigma_A(i)| = f(i) - f(i-1)$ and $A = \sigma_A(0)\sigma_A(1)\dots$. Say that A and B are *piecewise f-different from level n* if $\sigma_A(i) \neq \sigma_B(i)$ for all $i \geqslant n$.

Given A and B that are piecewise f-different from level n, define the tree $T^{f,n}_{A,B}$ as follows.

$$\begin{aligned} T^{f,n}_{A,B}(\emptyset) &= A \upharpoonright f(n-1) \\ T^{f,n}_{A,B}(\tau 0) &= T^{f,n}_{A,B}(\tau)^\frown \min\{\sigma_A(n+|\tau|), \sigma_B(n+|\tau|)\} \\ T^{f,n}_{A,B}(\tau 1) &= T^{f,n}_{A,B}(\tau)^\frown \max\{\sigma_A(n+|\tau|), \sigma_B(n+|\tau|)\}, \end{aligned}$$

where the min and max are with respect to lexicographic ordering. Let $\mathcal{T}^{f,n} = \{T^{f,n}_{A,B} \mid A \text{ and } B \text{ are piecewise } f\text{-different from level } n\}$, thought of as a subspace of the space of perfect trees. It is not hard to see that $\mathcal{T}^{f,n}$ is compact and f-computably homeomorphic to 2^ω.

Let P be a Π^0_1 class consisting entirely of 1-random sets. If f is computable, then

$$\mathcal{C}^n_f = \{A \oplus B \mid A, B \text{ are piecewise } f\text{-different from level } n \text{ and } [T^{f,n}_{A,B}] \subseteq P\}$$

is a Π^0_1 class. Of course, we do not know that it is nonempty, but if so, then we can finish the proof as follows: If C is of PA degree, then it computes some member $T^{f,n}_{A,B}$ of $\mathcal{C}^n_f$. Without loss of generality, we may assume that $A \upharpoonright f(n-1) = B \upharpoonright f(n-1)$ and that for each $i \geqslant n$ the string $\sigma_A(i)$ is lexicographically smaller than $\sigma_B(i)$ iff $C(i) = 0$. Then the sets A and B are members of $[T^{f,n}_{A,B}] \subseteq P$, and hence are 1-random. Clearly, $A \oplus B \leqslant_{\mathrm{T}} C$. Furthermore, $C(i) = 0$ iff $\sigma_A(i)$ is lexicographically smaller than $\sigma_B(i)$, so $C \leqslant_{\mathrm{T}} A \oplus B$.

Thus, we are left with showing that there is a computable increasing function f and an n such that $\mathcal{C}^n_f \neq \emptyset$.

We will need to work with finite approximations to the notion of piecewise difference, so we introduce the following terminology. Fix an increasing function f and define $\sigma_A(i)$ as above. We say that $A \in P$ can be *f-switched within* $[n, m]$ if there is a B such that $\sigma_A(i) \neq \sigma_B(i)$ for all $i \in [n, m]$ and for every sequence $X_0, X_1, \dots \in \{A, B\}^\omega$ such that $X_i = A$ for $i \notin [n, m]$, we have $\sigma_{X_0}(0)\sigma_{X_1}(1)\dots \in P$. In this case we say that B is an *f-switching partner for A within* $[n, m]$. We say that $A \in P$ can be *f-switched from n* if there is a B such that $\sigma_A(i) \neq \sigma_B(i)$ for all $i \geqslant n$ and for every sequence $X_0, X_1, \dots \in \{A, B\}^\omega$ such that $X_i = A$ for $i < n$, we have $\sigma_{X_0}(0)\sigma_{X_1}(1)\dots \in P$. In this case we say that B is an *f-switching partner for A from n*.

Let $C_{n,m}(A)$ be the class of f-switching partners for A within $[n,m]$ and C_n be the class of f-switching partners for A from n. Notice that $C_n(A) = \bigcap_m C_{n,m}(A)$ Notice also that each $C_{n,m}(A)$ is clopen and each $C_n(A)$ is closed. Let $D_{n,m}$ be the class of sets that cannot be f-switched within $[n,m]$. Notice that $D_{n,m} \subseteq D_{n,m+1}$, and the classes $D_{n,m}$ are uniformly $\Sigma_1^{0,f}$. Let D_n be the class of sets that cannot be f-switched from n. If $A \in \bigcap_m \overline{D}_{n,m}$ then, by compactness, $C_n(A) = \bigcap_m C_{n,m}(A) \neq \emptyset$, so $A \in \overline{D}_n$. But, clearly, if $A \in \overline{D}_n$ then $A \in \bigcap_m \overline{D}_{n,m}$, so in fact $\overline{D}_n = \bigcap_m \overline{D}_{n,m}$, and hence $D_n = \bigcup_m D_{n,m}$. Let $\widehat{D}_{n,m} = D_n \cap P$ and $\widehat{D}_n = D_n \cap P$.

To show that there is a computable increasing function f and an n such that $C_f^n \neq \emptyset$, we will show that there is a computable increasing function f such that if $X \in P$ is sufficiently random (weakly 2-random suffices), then for some n and some Y such that X and Y are piecewise f-different from level n, we have $[T_{X,Y}^{f,n}] \subseteq P$. It is enough to define a computable increasing function f such that $\mu(\widehat{D}_n) \leqslant O(2^{-n})$, because then $\bigcap_i \widehat{D}_i$ is a Π_2^0 class of measure 0, and hence for every weakly 2-random $X \in P$ there is some n such that $X \notin D_n$, which means that $[T_{X,Y}^{f,n}] \subseteq P$ for some Y such that X and Y are piecewise f-different from level n.

We will show that for any increasing function f, we have

$$\mu(\widehat{D}_{n,n}) \leqslant 2^{f(n-1)}2^{-f(n)}$$

and

$$\mu(\widehat{D}_{n,m+1} \setminus \widehat{D}_{n,m}) \leqslant 2^{f(m)}2^{f(m)-f(n-1)}2^{-f(m+1)}.$$

Letting $f(0) = 1$ and $f(n+1) = 2f(n) + n + 2$, we then have

$$\mu(\widehat{D}_{n,n}) \leqslant 2^{-n-1}$$

and

$$\mu(\widehat{D}_{n,m+1} \setminus \widehat{D}_{n,m}) \leqslant 2^{-n-m-2},$$

from which it follows that $\mu(\widehat{D}_n) \leqslant O(2^{-n})$.

We first show that $\mu(\widehat{D}_{n,n}) \leqslant 2^{f(n-1)}2^{-f(n)}$. Fix σ of length $f(n-1)$, and for each τ of length $f(n) - f(n-1)$, let $M_{\sigma\tau}(n,n)$ be the set of all B such that $\sigma\tau B \in \widehat{D}_{n,n}$. By the definition of $\widehat{D}_{n,n}$, we have that $M_{\sigma\tau}(n,n) \cap M_{\sigma\rho}(n,n) = \emptyset$ for all $\tau \neq \rho$ of length $f(n) - f(n-1)$. Hence $\sum_{\tau \in 2^{f(n)-f(n-1)}} \mu(M_{\sigma\tau}(n,n)) \leqslant 1$, and so $\mu(\widehat{D}_{n,n} \cap [\![\sigma]\!]) \leqslant 2^{-f(n)}$. Since there are $2^{f(n-1)}$ many such σ, we have that $\mu(\widehat{D}_{n,n}) \leqslant 2^{f(n-1)}2^{-f(n)}$.

Finally, we show that $\mu(\widehat{D}_{n,m+1} \setminus \widehat{D}_{n,m}) \leqslant 2^{f(m)}2^{f(m)-f(n-1)}2^{-f(m+1)}$. Say that a string τ of length $f(m)-f(n-1)$ is a *switching string* for $A \in P$ within $[n,m]$ if for some (or equivalently, for all) η of length $f(n-1)$ and all B, the set $\eta\tau B$ is an f-switching partner for A within $[n,m]$. For any string τ of length $f(m) - f(n-1)$, let L_τ be the set of elements of P for which τ is a switching string within $[n,m]$. Since every $A \in P \setminus \widehat{D}_{n,m}$ belongs to some L_τ, we have

$$\widehat{D}_{n,m+1} \setminus \widehat{D}_{n,m} = \bigcup\{\widehat{D}_{n,m+1} \cap L_\tau \cap [\![\sigma]\!] \mid \sigma \in 2^{f(m)} \wedge \tau \in 2^{f(m)-f(n-1)}\}.$$

Fix strings σ, τ of lengths as above and for each string ρ of length $f(m+1)-f(m)$ let $M_{\sigma\rho,\tau}(n,m+1)$ be the set of all B such that $\sigma\rho B \in \widehat{D}_{n,m+1} \cap L_\tau$. As before, we have that $M_{\sigma\rho,\tau}(n,m+1) \cap M_{\sigma\rho',\tau}(n,m+1) = \emptyset$ for any $\rho \neq \rho'$ of length $f(m+1)-f(m)$. Hence

$$\sum_{\rho \in 2^{f(m+1)-f(m)}} \mu(M_{\sigma\rho,\tau}(n,m+1)) \leqslant 1,$$

and so $\mu(\widehat{D}_{n,m+1} \cap L_\tau \cap [\![\sigma]\!]) \leqslant 2^{-f(m+1)}$. Thus $\mu(\widehat{D}_{n,m+1} \setminus \widehat{D}_{n,m}) \leqslant 2^{f(m)} 2^{f(m)-f(n-1)} 2^{-f(m+1)}$. □

8.9 Mass problems

A *mass problem* is a subset of ω^ω. We view the elements of such a class P as solutions to some problem, which we identify with P. (For instance, if $P = \{f : \forall n\, (\emptyset'_{f(n)} \upharpoonright n = \emptyset' \upharpoonright n)\}$, then we identify P with the "problem" of majorizing the settling time of $\emptyset'$.) There are two natural notions of reducing one problem to another in this context.

Definition 8.9.1 (Muchnik [286], Medvedev [263]). Let P and Q be mass problems.

(i) P is *weakly reducible* (or *Muchnik reducible*) to Q, denoted by $P \leqslant_{\mathrm{w}} Q$, if for each $f \in Q$, there is a $g \leqslant_{\mathrm{T}} f$ in P.

(ii) P is *strongly reducible* (or *Medvedev reducible*) to Q, denoted by $P \leqslant_{\mathrm{s}} Q$, if there is a functional Ψ such that $\Psi^f \in P$ for every $f \in Q$.

In other words, P is weakly reducible to Q if from each solution to Q we can effectively obtain a solution to P, and P is strongly reducible to Q if there is a single effective procedure for converting solutions to Q into solutions to P.

Note that if $X, Y \in 2^\omega$ then $\{X\} \leqslant_{\mathrm{w}} \{Y\}$ iff $\{X\} \leqslant_{\mathrm{s}} \{Y\}$ iff $X \leqslant_{\mathrm{T}} Y$, so these notions can be seen as extensions of Turing reducibility. It is interesting to note also that $\mu(P) > 0$, where $P \subseteq 2^\omega$, then P is incomparable (in terms of both weak and strong reducibility) with any of these singleton classes except the ones of the form $\{X\}$ with X computable, since the Turing lower cone of a set has measure 0 because it is countable, while the Turing upper cone of a noncomputable set has measure 0 by Corollary 8.12.2 below.

We can take equivalence classes of mass problems under these reducibilities to arrive at the notions of weak and strong degrees of mass problems. The weak and strong degrees both form lattices, with bottom element the degree of ω^ω (which consists exactly of those mass problems that have computable elements), and top element $\emptyset$. The join and meet of the degrees of mass problems P and Q (in both the strong and weak degrees) are the degrees of $\{f \oplus g : f \in P \wedge g \in Q\}$ and $\{0f : f \in P\} \cup \{1g : g \in Q\}$, respectively. (In the weak degrees, the latter is the same as the weak degree of $P \cup Q$.) Particular attention has been paid to the weak and strong degrees of Π^0_1 classes (in 2^ω). These form sublattices of the corresponding global structures, with the top degree being that of the Π^0_1 class of (codes of) completions of PA. (That this class is complete for weak reducibility follows from the Scott Basis Theorem 2.21.2; for the strong reducibility case see [359].)

Let R be the mass problem consisting of all 1-random sets. While R is not itself a Π^0_1 class, it is weakly equivalent to any nonempty Π^0_1 class P all of whose elements are 1-random, such as the complement of one of the levels of a universal Martin-Löf test. Clearly $R \leqslant_{\mathrm{w}} P$, since $P \subset R$, and $P \leqslant_{\mathrm{w}} R$ by Theorem 6.10.1. Indeed, this theorem shows that $Q \leqslant_{\mathrm{w}} R$ for any Π^0_1 class of positive measure, so the weak degree of R can be characterized as the largest weak degree of Π^0_1 classes of positive measure, as noted by Simpson [359]. Simpson and Slaman [unpublished] and Terwijn [388] have shown that there is no largest, or even maximal, strong degree of Π^0_1 classes of positive measure.

Let $\mathcal{P}_{\mathrm{w}}$ be the structure of weak degrees of Π^0_1 classes, with $\mathbf{0}$ and $\mathbf{1}$ its bottom and top degrees, respectively. We establish some further properties of the weak degree $\mathbf{r}_1$ of R, beginning with a couple of lemmas.

Lemma 8.9.2 (Simpson [359]). *Let $P, Q \subseteq 2^\omega$ be nonempty Π^0_1 classes such that $\mu(P) > 0$ and $\deg_{\mathrm{w}}(Q) < \mathbf{1}$. Then $\deg_{\mathrm{w}}(P) \wedge \deg_{\mathrm{w}}(Q) < \mathbf{1}$.*

Proof. Assume for a contradiction that $\deg_{\mathrm{w}}(P) \wedge \deg_{\mathrm{w}}(Q) = \mathbf{1}$. Let S be the Π^0_1 class of separating sets for effectively inseparable c.e. sets A and B, so that $S \in \mathbf{1}$. Let $g \in Q$. Then for every $f \in P$, there is an element of S computable in $f \oplus g$. Since there are only countably many Turing reductions, there are a functional Ψ and a class $\widehat{P} \subseteq P$ such that $\mu(\widehat{P}) > 0$ and $\Psi^{f \oplus g} \in S$ for all $f \in \widehat{P}$. By Lebesgue density, there is a σ such that $\mu(\widehat{P} \cap [\![\sigma]\!]) > \frac{3}{4}2^{-|\sigma|}$. Given n, we can g-computably find an $i < 2$ such that $\Psi^{f \oplus g}(n) = i$ for a class of $f \in [\![\sigma]\!]$ of measure at least $\frac{3}{8}2^{-|\sigma|}$ and let $h(n) = i$. If $n \in A$ then $h(n) = 1$, since otherwise there would be an $f \in \widehat{P} \cap [\![\sigma]\!]$ such that $\Psi^{f \oplus g} \notin S$. Similarly, if $n \in B$ then $h(n) = 0$. Thus h is a g-computable element of S. Since $g \in Q$ is arbitrary, we have $S \leqslant_{\mathrm{w}} Q$, contrary to hypothesis. $\square$

Lemma 8.9.3 (Simpson [359]). *Let $P, Q \subseteq 2^\omega$ be nonempty Π^0_1 classes such that $P \leqslant_{\mathrm{w}} Q$. Then there is a nonempty Π^0_1 class $\widehat{Q} \subseteq Q$ such that $P \leqslant_{\mathrm{s}} \widehat{Q}$.*

Proof. By the hyperimmune-free basis theorem, there is a hyperimmune-free $Y \in Q$. Let $X \in P$ be such that $X \leqslant_{\mathrm{T}} Y$. By Theorem 2.17.7, there is a total functional Ψ such that $\Psi^Y = X$. Let $\widehat{Q} = \{Z \in Q : \Psi^Z \in P\}$. It is easy to see that this class has the desired properties. □

In particular, if Q is weakly reducible to R then it is strongly reducible to some nonempty Π^0_1 class of 1-random sets.

Theorem 8.9.4 (Simpson [359]).

(i) $\mathbf{0} < \mathbf{r_1} < \mathbf{1}$.

(ii) *If* $\mathbf{q} \in \mathcal{P}_{\mathrm{w}}$ *is such that* $\mathbf{q} < \mathbf{1}$, *then* $\mathbf{r_1} \wedge \mathbf{q} < \mathbf{1}$. *(That is,* $\mathbf{r_1}$ *does not join to* $\mathbf{1}$.*)*

(iii) *If* $\mathbf{q_0}, \mathbf{q_1} \in \mathcal{P}_{\mathrm{w}}$ *and* $\mathbf{r_1} \geqslant \mathbf{q_0} \vee \mathbf{q_1}$, *then* $\mathbf{r_1} \geqslant \mathbf{q_0}$ *or* $\mathbf{r_1} \geqslant \mathbf{q_1}$. *(That is,* $\mathbf{r_1}$ *is* meet-irreducible.*)*

Proof. The class R has no computable elements, and it has an element that does not compute a completion of PA, by Kučera's result mentioned above Theorem 8.8.4, so we have (i). Part (ii) follows from Lemma 8.9.2.

For part (iii), suppose that $R \geqslant_{\mathrm{w}} Q_0 \cup Q_1$, where $Q_0, Q_1 \subseteq 2^\omega$ are Π^0_1 classes. Let P be a nonempty Π^0_1 subclass of R. Then $P \geqslant_{\mathrm{w}} Q_0 \cup Q_1$, so by Lemma 8.9.3, there is a nonempty Π^0_1 class $\widehat{P} \subseteq P$ such that $\widehat{P} \geqslant_{\mathrm{s}} Q_o \cup Q_1$. Thus there is a total functional Ψ such that $\Psi^f \in Q_o \cup Q_1$ for all $f \in \widehat{P}$. Let $\widehat{P}_i = \{f \in \widehat{P} : \Psi^f \in Q_i\}$. Then there is an $i < 2$ such that $\widehat{P}_i$ is nonempty. Since $\widehat{P}_i$ is a nonempty Π^0_1 class of 1-random sets, as mentioned above, it is weakly equivalent to R, so $R \equiv_{\mathrm{w}} \widehat{P}_i \geqslant_{\mathrm{s}} Q_i$. □

That R is weakly equivalent to some Π^0_1 class also follows from the following general result, known as the Embedding Lemma. (See [360] for a proof.)

Theorem 8.9.5 (Simpson [360]). *Let* $P \subseteq 2^\omega$ *be a nonempty* Π^0_1 *class and let* $S \subseteq \omega^\omega$ *be a* Σ^0_3 *class. Then there is a nonempty* Π^0_1 *class* $Q \subseteq 2^\omega$ *such that* $Q \equiv_{\mathrm{w}} P \cup S$.

Thus, in particular, if $S \subseteq 2^\omega$ is a Σ^0_3 class with a nonempty Π^0_1 subclass, then it is weakly equivalent to a Π^0_1 class. If S is a Σ^0_3 class with no nonempty Π^0_1 subclass, for example the class of 2-random sets, then the natural Π^0_1 class to take as P in the above theorem is the class of completions of PA, since in that case the weak degree of $S \cup P$ is the largest degree in $\mathcal{P}_{\mathrm{w}}$ below that of S. Simpson [360] characterized the weak degree $\mathbf{r}_2^*$ of the mass problem of sets that are either 2-random or completions of PA as follows.

Theorem 8.9.6 (Simpson [360]). *The degree* $\mathbf{r}_2^*$ *is the largest weak degree of a* Π^0_1 *subset of* 2^ω *whose upward closure in the Turing degrees has positive measure.*

Proof. Let P be a Π^0_1 class in $\mathbf{r}_2^*$. If $Q \leqslant_w P$ then every 2-random set computes an element of Q, so the upward closure of Q in the Turing degrees has measure 1. Conversely, suppose that the upward closure $\widehat{Q}$ in the Turing degrees of the Π^0_1 class $Q \subseteq 2^\omega$ has positive measure. It is straightforward to show that $\widehat{Q}$ is a Σ^0_3 class, so it has a Π^0_2 subclass of positive measure. By Theorem 6.10.2, this subclass contains translations of every 2-random set, so every 2-random set computes some element of Q. Since Q is a Π^0_1 class, every completion of PA also computes some element of Q. Thus $Q \leqslant_w P$. □

Thus $\mathbf{r_1} \leqslant \mathbf{r}_2^*$. In fact, as shown by Simpson [360], we have $\mathbf{r_1} < \mathbf{r}_2^* < \mathbf{1}$. These inequalities can be shown in several ways, for example as consequences of Theorem 8.8.4, which implies that an incomplete Δ^0_2 1-random set cannot compute a completion of PA (and can obviously also not compute a 2-random set), while no 2-random set can compute a completion of PA.

In this way, many of the classes of sets and functions we discuss in this book, such as the class of DNC functions, can be studied in the context of weak degrees of Π^0_1 classes. Indeed, the weak degree $\mathbf{d}$ of the class of DNC functions is in $\mathcal{P}_w$, since every PA degree computes a DNC function. Results such as Theorem 8.8.1, that every 1-random set computes a DNC function, can be reinterpreted as statements about degrees of mass problems (in most cases, the weak degrees being the most applicable). For instance, as noted by Simpson [360], Theorem 8.8.1 implies that $\mathbf{d} \leqslant \mathbf{r_1}$, and this inequality is in fact strict, by Theorem 8.10.3 below.

For more on mass problems, see Sorbi [373], Simpson [359, 360, 361], and Cole and Simpson [72].

8.10 DNC degrees and subsets of random sets

In this section, we prove a strong extension of Kučera's Theorem 8.8.1 that every 1-random set computes a DNC function, by characterizing the DNC degrees in terms of 1-random sets. The following lemma and variations on it can be quite useful. Let $P_0, P_1, \ldots$ be an effective listing of all Π^0_1 classes.

Lemma 8.10.1 (Kučera [215]). *If P is a Π^0_1 class of positive measure, then there is a nonempty Π^0_1 class $Q \subseteq P$ and a c such that for all e,*

$$Q \cap P_e \neq \emptyset \Rightarrow \mu(Q \cap P_e) \geqslant 2^{-e-c}.$$

Proof. Let c be such that $2^{1-c} < \mu(P)$. Let Q be the Π^0_1 subclass of P obtained by removing $P_e[s]$ whenever $\mu(P_e[s] \cap Q[s]) < 2^{-e-c}$. Then $\mu(Q) \geqslant \mu(P) - \sum_e 2^{-e-c} = \mu(P) - 2^{1-c} > 0$, so Q is nonempty. □

Theorem 8.10.2 (Kjos-Hanssen [204], Greenberg and Miller [171][5]). *The following are equivalent.*

(i) *A computes a DNC function.*

(ii) *A computes an infinite subset of a 1-random set.*

(iii) *There is a $\Pi_1^{0,A}$ class of measure 0 containing a 1-random set. (In other words, there is a 1-random set that is not weakly 1-random relative to A.)*

Proof. (i) $\Rightarrow$ (ii). Let $f \leqslant_T A$ be a DNC function. Let P be a Π_1^0 class containing only 1-random sets and let Q and c be given by Lemma 8.10.1. For any set S, let $Q_S = \{X \in Q : S \subseteq X\}$. We construct an A-computable set $S = \{n_0 < n_1 < n_2 < \cdots\}$ such that Q_S is nonempty.

Assume that we have defined $S_i = \{n_j\}_{j<i}$ and that $Q_{S_i} \neq \emptyset$. Uniformly in S_i, we can compute an e such that $P_e = Q_{S_i}$. By Lemma 8.10.1, $\mu(Q_{S_i}) \geqslant 2^{-e-c}$. Let $B = \{n : Q_{S_i \cup \{n\}} = \emptyset\}$. By compactness, B is c.e. Denote the elements of B, in the order that they are enumerated, by $b_0, b_1, \ldots$. We have $\mu(Q_{S_i}) \leqslant \mu(\{X : B \cap X = \emptyset\}) = 2^{-|B|}$, so $|B| \leqslant e + c$.

Let $\gamma_0, \gamma_1, \ldots$ be an effective listing of $\omega^{<\omega}$. Using f, we can effectively find numbers $d_0, \ldots, d_{e+c-1}$ such that $d_j \neq \gamma_{b_j}(j)$ if the latter is defined (because, for each j, we can effectively find an index k such that $\Phi_k(k) = \gamma_{b_j}(j)$). Now let n_i be such that $\gamma_{n_i} = (d_0, \ldots, d_{e+c-1}, v)$, where v is chosen so that $n_i > n_{i-1}$. For each $j < |B|$, we have ensured that $\gamma_{n_i}(j) \neq \gamma_{b_j}(j)$, so $n_i \notin B$. Therefore, $Q_{S_i \cup \{n_i\}}$ is nonempty.

By construction, $S \leqslant_T f \leqslant_T A$. Since $Q_S = \bigcap_i Q_{S_i}$ is a nested intersection of nonempty compact sets, it is nonempty. Therefore, S is a subset of some 1-random set.

(ii) $\Rightarrow$ (iii). Let X be 1-random and let $S \subseteq X$ be infinite and A-computable. Then the $\Pi_1^{0,A}$ class of all sets that contain S has measure 0 and contains X.

(iii) $\Rightarrow$ (i) For each e, let $U_0, U_1, \ldots$ be an effective listing of all clopen subsets of 2^ω. Let P be a $\Pi_1^{0,A}$ class of measure 0 containing a 1-random set. There is an A-computable function f such that $P \subseteq U_{f(e)}$ and $\mu(U_{f(e)}) \leqslant 2^{-e}$ for all e. For each n, let V_n be the union of the clopen sets $U_{\Phi_e(e)}$ such that $e > n$ and $\mu(U_{\Phi_e(e)}) \leqslant 2^{-e}$. Then $\{V_n\}_{n\in\omega}$ is a Martin-Löf test. If $f(e) = \Phi_e(e)$ infinitely often, then $P \subseteq \bigcap_n V_n$. Since P contains a 1-

[5]The precise history of Theorem 8.10.2 is the following. Kjos-Hanssen [204] proved that (iii) implies (i), by essentially the proof given here. He also proved (ii), and hence (iii), from a strong form of (i): that A computes a sufficiently slow-growing DNC function. Independently, Greenberg and Miller [171] proved that (i) implies (iii), implicitly proving (ii) from (i) at the same time. The short elementary proof that (i) implies (ii) given here is due to Miller [personal communication to Downey]. Kjos-Hanssen's proof relies on work in probability theory and, like the proof of Greenberg and Miller, is somewhat involved.

random set, this is not the case. Hence, $f(e) = \Phi_e(e)$ only finitely often, so A computes a DNC function. □

In the proof that (i) implies (ii), it is easy to code a set A into S by adding $A(i)$ into the sequence used to define n_i. Thus, the degrees of infinite subsets of 1-random sets are closed upward, and hence actually coincide with the degrees of DNC functions.

The connection between DNC degrees and 1-randomness can be clarified as follows.

Theorem 8.10.3 (Ambos-Spies, Kjos-Hanssen, Lempp, and Slaman [8], Kumabe and Lewis [225]). *There is a DNC degree that does not bound any 1-random degree.*

Kumabe and Lewis [225] showed that there is a minimal DNC degree, which, by Corollary 6.9.5, cannot be 1-random. (The proof in their paper had existed in manuscript form for several years prior to publication.) Ambos-Spies, Kjos-Hanssen, Lempp, and Slaman [8] showed that there is an ideal in the Turing degrees containing a DNC degree but no 1-random degree. Indeed, they built an ideal I in the Turing degrees such that for every $X \in I$, there is a $G \in I$ that is DNC relative to X, and such that there is no 1-random degree in I, and used this result to derive a separation between two principles in the context of reverse mathematics.

By Theorems 8.10.2 and 8.10.3, there is a subset of a 1-random set that does not compute any 1-random sets.

8.11 High degrees and separating notions of randomness

8.11.1 High degrees, Schnorr randomness, and computable randomness

We have seen in Corollary 8.8.2 that all 1-random sets of c.e. degree (and in particular all 1-random left-c.e. reals) are of Turing degree $\mathbf{0}'$. This result fails for computably random (and hence for Schnorr random) sets.

Theorem 8.11.1 (Nies, Stephan, and Terwijn [308]). *Every high c.e. degree is computably random.*

We will prove a stronger version of this result in Theorem 8.11.6 below. An earlier proof for Schnorr random sets was given by Downey, Griffiths, and LaForte [110], effectivizing arguments of Wang [405, 406].

Conversely, we have the following result.

Theorem 8.11.2 (Nies, Stephan, and Terwijn [308]). *If a nonhigh set is Schnorr random then it is 1-random.*

Proof. Suppose that A is nonhigh and not 1-random. Let $\{U_n\}_{n\in\omega}$ be a universal Martin-Löf test. Let $f(n)$ be the least s such that $A \in U_n[s]$. Then $f \leqslant_T A$, so by Theorem 2.23.7, there is a computable function g such that $g(n) \geqslant f(n)$ for infinitely many n. Let $V_n = U_n[g(n)]$. Then $\{V_n\}_{n\in\omega}$ is a total Solovay test and $A \in V_n$ for infinitely many n, so A is not Schnorr random by Theorem 7.1.10. □

Corollary 8.11.3 (Nies, Stephan, and Terwijn [308]). *Every Schnorr random set of c.e. degree is high.*

Corollary 8.11.4 (Downey and Griffiths [109]). *Every Schnorr random left-c.e. real is high.*

The following is a direct proof of this corollary.

Proof of Corollary 8.11.4. Let α be a Schnorr random left-c.e. real. Let $T = \{\langle i,j\rangle : |W_i| > j\}$. Note that T is c.e. We build a functional Γ such that for each i, we have $\Gamma^\alpha(i,k) = T(\langle i,k\rangle)$ for almost all k. Then it is easy to see that α' can decide which W_i are infinite, and hence α is high. For each i, we also build a collection Q_i of open intervals with rational endpoints forming a total Solovay test.

At each stage s, proceed as follows. For each $\langle i,k\rangle < s$ such that $\Gamma^{\alpha_s}(i,k)$ is currently undefined, let $\Gamma^{\alpha_s}(i,k) = T_s(\langle i,k\rangle)$ with use k. For each $\langle i,k\rangle$ entering T at stage s, add $(\alpha_s, \alpha_s + 2^{-k})$ to Q_i.

Each Q_i is either finite or contains an interval of length 2^{-k} for each k. In either case, Q_i is a total Solovay test. Since α can be in only finitely many intervals in Q_i, for almost all k, if $\langle i,k\rangle$ enters T at stage s, then $\alpha \upharpoonright k \neq \alpha_s \upharpoonright k$, whence $\Gamma^\alpha(i,k) = T(\langle i,k\rangle)$. □

8.11.2 Separating notions of randomness

In Section 7.1.1, we mentioned that 1-randomness, computable randomness, and Schnorr randomness are all distinct, even for left-c.e. reals. (These are results of Schnorr [348] and Wang [405, 406] for the noneffective case and Downey, Griffiths, and LaForte [110] for the left-c.e. case.) Nies, Stephan, and Terwijn [308] established a definitive result on separating these notions of randomness, by showing that the degrees within which they can be separated are exactly the high degrees. The easy direction of this result is Theorem 8.11.2. Remarkably, the converse to this theorem also holds. To prove this fact, we will need the following extension of the Space Lemma 8.3.1.

Lemma 8.11.5. *Given a rational $\delta > 1$ and integer $k > 0$, we can compute a length $l(\delta,k)$ such that, for any martingale d and any σ,*

$$|\{\tau \in 2^{l(\delta,k)} : \forall \rho \preccurlyeq \tau\, (d(\sigma\rho) \leqslant \delta d(\sigma))\}| \geqslant k.$$

Proof. As in the Space Lemma, let $l(\delta, k) = \lceil \log \frac{k}{1-\delta^{-1}} \rceil$, which is well-defined since $\delta > 1$. Let

$$S = \{\tau \in 2^{l(\delta,k)} : \exists \rho \preccurlyeq \tau\,(d(\sigma\rho) > \delta d(\sigma))\}.$$

For each $\tau \in S$, let ρ_τ be the shortest substring of τ such that $d(\sigma\rho_\tau) > \delta d(\sigma)$. Then $\{\rho_\tau : \tau \in S\}$ is prefix-free, so by Kolmogorov's Inequality (Theorem 6.3.3), $\sum_{\tau \in S} 2^{-|\rho_\tau|} d(\sigma\rho_\tau) \leqslant d(\sigma)$. Thus $d(\sigma) \geqslant \sum_{\tau \in S} 2^{-|\rho_\tau|}\delta d(\sigma)$, and hence $\mu(S) = \sum_{\tau \in S} 2^{-|\rho_\tau|} \leqslant \delta^{-1}$. So

$$|2^{l(\delta,k)} \setminus S| \geqslant 2^{l(\delta,k)}(1-\delta^{-1}) \geqslant \frac{k}{1-\delta^{-1}}(1-\delta^{-1}) = k.$$

□

Theorem 8.11.6 (Nies, Stephan, and Terwijn [308]). *The following are equivalent.*

(i) *A is high.*

(ii) *There is a $B \equiv_{\mathrm{T}} A$ that is computably random but not 1-random.*

(iii) *There is a $C \equiv_{\mathrm{T}} A$ that is Schnorr random but not computably random.*

Furthermore, the same equivalences hold if A, B, and C are restricted to left-c.e. reals.[6]

Proof. (iii) ⇒ (i) and (ii) ⇒ (i) follow by Theorem 8.11.2.

(i) ⇒ (ii) Let $M_0, M_1, \ldots$ be an effective listing of all partial computable martingales such that $M_i(\lambda) = 1$ if defined. We will first define a partial computable martingale M. There will be a perfect class P whose elements represent guesses as to which M_i converge on certain inputs. Along any such element, M will either be undefined from some point on, or its values will be bounded. Furthermore, for any $B \in P$ whose guesses are correct, M will multiplicatively dominate all computable martingales on X; that is, for each i there will be an $\varepsilon > 0$ such that $M(\sigma) \geqslant \varepsilon M_i(B \upharpoonright n)$ for all n. Thus, for any such B, no computable martingale will succeed on B. Then, given A, we will build such a B in two steps. First, we will define a set $F \equiv_{\mathrm{T}} A$ containing information about A and partial information about the behavior of computable martingales. Second, we will use M and the information in F to build a $B \equiv_{\mathrm{wtt}} F$ as above. We will also ensure that there is an infinite computable set of numbers n such that $B(n)$ is computable from $B \upharpoonright n$, from which it is easy to argue that B is not 1-random (or even partial computably random).

[6]As we saw in Corollary 8.11.4, all Schnorr random left-c.e. reals are high, so this theorem says that, among left-c.e. reals, the three notions of randomness can be separated in any degree in which they occur.

By Lemma 8.11.5, there is a computable f such that if $\sigma \in 2^n$ and M is a partial martingale defined on all $\tau \succcurlyeq \sigma$ with $\tau \in 2^{\leqslant f(n)}$, then there are at least two strings $\tau_0 <_{\mathrm{L}} \tau_1 \succcurlyeq \sigma$ with $\tau_0, \tau_1 \in 2^{f(n)}$ such that for $i = 0, 1$, if $\sigma \preccurlyeq \rho \preccurlyeq \tau_i$ then $M(\rho) \leqslant (1 + 2^{-n})M(\sigma)$. Given a particular σ and M as above, we can M-computably find τ_0 and τ_1 as above. We denote such τ_i by $\tau^M_{\sigma,i}$. Let $z_0 = 0$ and $z_{k+1} = f(z_k + 1)$. The idea behind this definition is that if $\sigma \in 2^{z_k+1}$ then $\tau^M_{\sigma,i} \in 2^{z_{k+1}}$.

For a partial martingale M, we say that $\eta \in 2^{z_k}$ is *M-poor* if for each $j < k$ there is an $a_j = 0, 1$ such that $\tau^M_{\eta \upharpoonright z_j+1, a_j} \preccurlyeq \eta$. In this case, we call $(a_0, \ldots, a_{k-1})$ the *M-sequence* of η. The perfect class P mentioned above is the class of all X such that every $X \upharpoonright 2^{z_k}$ is M-poor.

We begin by defining M as described above, together with auxiliary numbers r_σ. Let $M(\lambda) = r_\lambda = 1$. Now suppose that $M(\eta)$ and r_η are defined for an M-poor $\eta \in 2^{z_k}$. Let $(a_0, \ldots, a_{k-1})$ be the M-sequence of η. We will try to define $M(\tau)$ for all $\tau \succcurlyeq \eta$ with $|\tau| \leqslant z_{k+1}$ as follows. Let $E = \{i : \langle i, 0\rangle < k \wedge \forall j\, (\langle i, j\rangle < k \Rightarrow a_{\langle i,j\rangle} = 1)\}$. Let $D = \{\tau \succ \eta : |\tau| \leqslant z_{k+1}\}$. For all $e \in E$ and $\tau \in D$, compute $M_e(\tau)$. If all such computations terminate, then for $\tau \in D$, let

$$M(\tau) = r_\tau + \sum_{e \in E} 2^{-2z_{\langle e,0\rangle+1}-1} M_e(\tau),$$

where r_τ is defined recursively so that for all $\tau' \prec \tau$, we have $M(\tau'0) + M(\tau'1) = 2M(\tau')$ and $r_{\tau'0} = r_{\tau'1}$.

The r_τ are necessary because at every level z_k, some M_i might be dropped from the sum, and (at most) one new M_i might be added. This new martingale is added if $k = 1 + \langle i, 0\rangle$ and $a_{\langle i,0\rangle} = 1$. In this case, it is added with the factor 2^{-2z_k-1}, which guarantees that $2^{-2z_k-1}M_i(\eta)$ is at most 2^{-z_k-1} for all $\eta \in 2^{z_k}$. (Note that we have $M_i(\eta) \leqslant 2^{z_k}$ since $M_i(\lambda) = 1$.) Thus this addition increases the sum by at most 2^{-z_k-1}, and therefore can be compensated by r_τ. At every level, $r_\tau \geqslant 2^{-|\tau|}$ and at most $2^{-|\tau|-1}$ of this capital is lost to maintain the martingale property of M.

We now define $F \equiv_{\mathrm{T}} A$. The idea is to have $F(\langle i, j\rangle)$ for $i > 0$ code whether M_i is defined on all strings of length up to $z_{\langle i,j+1\rangle+1}$. Since A is high, there is an A-computable g that dominates all computable functions. Let F be defined as follows.

1. Let $F(\langle 0, 0\rangle) = 0$.

2. Let $F(\langle 0, j+1\rangle) = A(j)$ for all j.

3. For $i > 0$, let $F(\langle i, j\rangle) = 1$ if $F(\langle i, j'\rangle) = 1$ for all $j' < j$ and $M_i(\tau)$ is computed within $g(i + j)$ many steps for all $\tau \in 2^{<\omega}$ with $|\tau| \leqslant z_{\langle i+j+1, i+j+1\rangle+1}$. Otherwise let $F(\langle i, j\rangle) = 0$.

Clearly $F \equiv_{\mathrm{T}} A$.

Finally, we define B by recursion. The idea is to code $F(k)$ into $B \upharpoonright z_{k+1}$ while ensuring that $B(z_k)$ is computable from $B \upharpoonright z_k$. Suppose that $\sigma =$

$B \upharpoonright z_k$ has been defined. If $M(\sigma 0) \leqslant M(\sigma 1)$ then let $B(z_k) = 0$. Otherwise, let $B(z_k) = 1$. Let $\eta = B \upharpoonright z_k + 1$ and let $B \upharpoonright z_{k+1} = \tau^M_{\eta, F(k)}$.

Of course, this definition depends on certain values of M being defined, so we need to check that this is indeed the case. Note that the $a_{\langle i,j \rangle}$ in the construction of M always exist for $\eta \prec B$, and are just the bits $F(\langle i,j \rangle)$. Furthermore, for all $i \in E$ with $i > 0$, we have $\langle i,j \rangle \in F$ for $j \leqslant j'$ where j' is maximal such that $\langle i,j' \rangle < k$, so M_i is defined on all strings of length up to $z_{\langle i+j'+1, i+j'+1 \rangle + 1} \geqslant z_{k+1}$. Thus the computations in the definition of M all terminate, and hence M is defined on all extensions of $B \upharpoonright z_k$ of length up to z_{k+1}. It follows that B is defined up to z_{k+1} and $F(k)$ is coded into B.

Note that the coding ensures that $F \leqslant_{\mathrm{wtt}} B$. Furthermore, for each k we can compute $B \upharpoonright z_k$ using $F \upharpoonright z_k$, so in fact $B \equiv_{\mathrm{wtt}} F$. Since $A \equiv_{\mathrm{T}} F$, we have $B \equiv_{\mathrm{T}} A$.

To see that B is not 1-random, it suffices to observe that $B(z_k)$ can be computed from $B \upharpoonright z_k$. Then we can easily define a partial computable martingale (and hence a c.e. martingale, as noted in Section 7.4.2) that succeeds on B.

To see that B is computably random, note first that the values of M on B are bounded, since M's capital while betting on B is not increased at z_k, while between $z_k + 1$ and z_{k+1}, the gain in this capital is at most $1 + 2^{-z_k}$, by the choice of the z_k, and $\prod_k 1 + 2^{-z_k} < \prod_k 1 + 2^{-k} < \infty$. Now let d be a computable martingale. Since g dominates every computable function, and every computable martingale appears infinitely often in the list $M_0, M_1, \ldots$, there is an i such that $M_i = d$, and for all j, the value $g(i+j)$ is greater than the number of steps required to compute $M_i(\tau)$ for all $\tau \in 2^{\leqslant z_{\langle i+j+1, i+j+1 \rangle + 1}}$. It follows that, for all $\eta \preccurlyeq B$, we have $d(\eta) \leqslant 2^{2 z_{\langle i,0 \rangle + 1} + 1} M(\eta)$, so d does not succeed on B.

(i) $\Rightarrow$ (ii), left-c.e. case. If A is a c.e. set then we can choose the function g in the above proof to be approximable from below. This choice makes F c.e., which makes B almost c.e. (as defined in Section 5.1): $B(z_k)$ is computed from $B \upharpoonright z_k$. Then, letting $\eta = B \upharpoonright z_k + 1$, we may assume that $B \upharpoonright z_{k+1} = \tau^M_{\eta,0}$ unless k enters F, in which case we know that $B \upharpoonright z_{k+1} = \tau^M_{\eta,1}$ (and recall that $\tau^M_{\eta,0} <_{\mathrm{L}} \tau^M_{\eta,1}$).

(i) $\Rightarrow$ (iii) We adopt the notation of the previous part of the proof. The set C will equal B except on a thin set of z_k's, where we will have $C(z_k) = 0$ regardless of the value of M. These guaranteed 0's will be distributed so that they appear rarely enough that no computable martingale can succeed on C computably fast, but frequently enough that some computable martingale can succeed on C.

If $\Phi_e(x)\downarrow$ then let $\psi(e,x) = z_{\langle e,x,s \rangle + 1}$ for the least s such that $\Phi_e(x)[s]\downarrow$. Otherwise, let $\psi(e,x)\uparrow$. Note that ψ is 1-1, and $\psi(e,x) \geqslant z_{x+1} > x$ when defined. Also, for any n, we can effectively check whether $n \in \operatorname{rng} \psi$, and if so, find the unique e and x such that $\psi(e,x) = n$.

Define a function p by recursion as follows. If there is an $x < n$ and $e \leqslant \log p(x)$ such that $\psi(e,x) = n$, then let $p(n) = p(x)+1$. Otherwise, let $p(n) = n+4$. The function p is computable, unbounded, and attains each value only finitely often. Assume without loss of generality that Φ_0 is total, that g is nondecreasing, and that $g(x) \geqslant \psi(0,x)$ for all x, where g is as above. Let

$$h(x) = \max\{\psi(e,x) : \psi(e,x)\downarrow \leqslant g(x) \wedge e < \log p(x) - 1\}.$$

Note that $h \leqslant_T A$ and h is nondecreasing. Furthermore, for any computable function f, there is an e such that $\Phi_e(x) = 2^{2^{f(x)}}$. By the usual conventions on halting times, $\psi(e,x) > 2^{2^{f(x)}}$ for all x. Thus, since g dominates all computable functions, $h(\log\log x) > f(x)$ for almost all x.

Let B and z_k be as above. If $z_k = h(x)$ for some $x < z_k$, then let $C(z_k) = 0$. For all other numbers, let $C(n) = B(n)$. Since $h \leqslant_T A$, we have $C \equiv_T A$.

To show that C is Schnorr random, assume for a contradiction that there are an i and a computable f such that that $M_i(C \upharpoonright f(m)) > m$ for infinitely many m. As with B, when betting along C, the martingale M increases its capital by less than $1+2^{-k}$ between z_k and z_{k+1}. At z_k, it cannot increase its capital if $z_k \notin \operatorname{rng} h$. If $z_k \in \operatorname{rng} h$ then M can double its capital at z_k, but $h(\log\log m) > f(m)$ for almost all m. Thus $M(C \upharpoonright f(m)) \leqslant O(\log m)$, whence $M_i(C \upharpoonright f(m)) \leqslant O(\log m)$, which is a contradiction.

Finally, we describe a computable martingale d witnessing the fact that C is not computably random. Let

$$G_n = \{\psi(e,n) : \psi(e,n)\downarrow \wedge e < \log p(n) - 1\}.$$

These sets are pairwise disjoint, and G_n contains at least one z_k such that $C(z_k) = 0$ (since by assumption Φ_0 is total and $g(x) \geqslant \psi(0,x)$ for all x). We have numbers n and m, initially set to 0. We bet on 0 at strings of lengths in G_n and increase m every time our bet is wrong. Note that $|G_n| \leqslant \log p(n) - 1$, so along C, we cannot be wrong $\log p(n)$ many times. Once we bet correctly, we move to a new n and reset m to 0. Our bets are designed to ensure that we increase our capital by $\frac{1}{p(n)}$ whenever we bet correctly.

More precisely, we define d as follows. Let $d(\lambda) = 1$, let $n_\lambda = 0$, and let $m_\lambda = 0$. Given $d(\sigma)$, proceed as follows. If $|\sigma| \notin G_n$ or $m_\sigma = \log p(n)$, then for $i = 0,1$, let $d(\sigma i) = d(\sigma)$, let $n_{\sigma i} = n_\sigma$, and let $m_{\sigma i} = m_\sigma$. Otherwise, let $d(\sigma 0) = d(\sigma) + \frac{2^m}{p(n)}$ and $d(\sigma 1) = d(\sigma) - \frac{2^m}{p(n)}$. Let $n_{\sigma 0} = |\sigma|$ and $m_{\sigma 0} = 0$. Let $n_{\sigma 1} = n_\sigma$ and $m_{\sigma 1} = m_\sigma + 1$. It is easy to check by induction that $d(\sigma 0) > 1$. Note also that $p(|\sigma|) = p(n_\sigma) + 1$, by the definition of p.

When betting along C, once we reach a $\sigma 0 \prec C$ such that $\sigma \in G_0$, which must exist, we have $d(\sigma 0) = 1 + \frac{1}{p(0)} = 1 + \frac{1}{4}$. Then, when we reach a $\tau 0 \prec C$ such that $\tau \in G_{|\sigma|}$, which again must exist, we have

$d(\tau 0) = 1 + \frac{1}{p(0)} + \frac{1}{p(|\sigma|)} = 1 + \frac{1}{4} + \frac{1}{5}$. Proceeding in this fashion, we see that $\limsup_k d(C \upharpoonright k) = \limsup_i 1 + \frac{1}{4} + \frac{1}{5} + \cdots + \frac{1}{i+4} = \infty$.

(i) ⇒ (iii), left c.e. case. If A is a c.e. set, then we can take g to be approximable from below, so that h is also approximable from below. Let $h_0, h_1, \ldots$ be such an approximation. We may assume we have defined g, and hence h, so that if $h_{s+1}(n) > h_s(n)$, then $h_{s+1}(m) > z_s$ for all $m \geqslant n$.

We now describe how to give C an almost c.e. approximation $C_0, C_1, \ldots$. We define C_s as follows, beginning with $k = 0$.

1. Assume that $\sigma = C_s \upharpoonright z_k$ has been defined. If $M_s(\sigma 0)\uparrow$ then go to step 3. If there is an $x < z_k$ such that $z_k = \psi(e, x)$ for some $x < z_k$ and $e < \log(p(x)) - 1$, and $h_s(x) = z_k$, then let $C_s(z_k) = 0$. In this case, we say that k is *active for* h_s. Otherwise, if $M_s(\sigma 0) \leqslant M_s(\sigma 1)$ then let $C_s(z_k) = 0$, and otherwise, let $C_s(z_k) = 1$.

2. Let $\eta = C_s \upharpoonright z_k + 1$. If $M_s(\eta\tau)\uparrow$ for some $\tau \in 2^{z_{k+1} - z_k - 1}$ then go to step 3. Let $C_s \upharpoonright z_{k+1} = \tau_{\eta, F_s(k)}$. If $k < s$ then go to step 1 for $k+1$. Otherwise, go to step 3.

3. If the recursive definition above is terminated after defining an initial segment σ for some string σ, then let $C_s = \sigma 0^\omega$. We say that C_s was *terminated due to* σ.

It is easy to see that $C = \lim_s C_s$, so we are left with showing that $C_s \leqslant_{\mathrm{L}} C_{s+1}$ for all s. Fix s, and assume that $C_s \neq C_{s+1}$. There are three cases.

1. If C_s is terminated for σ and $\sigma \prec C_{s+1}$, then $C_s \leqslant_{\mathrm{L}} C_{s+1}$, since $C_s = \sigma 0^\omega$.

2. If the first disagreement between C_s and C_{s+1} happens in step 1 of the kth iteration of the procedure, then $k \leqslant s$ and k must be active for one of h_s or h_{s+1} but not the other. It cannot be the case that k is active for h_{s+1}, because then, for x as in step 1, we would have $h_s(x) < h_{s+1}(x)$, which would mean that $h_{s+1}(x) > z_s \geqslant z_k$, by our assumption on h. So k is active for h_s but not for h_{s+1}, which means that the disagreement between C_s and C_{s+1} happens because $C_s(z_k) = 0$ but $C_{s+1}(z_k) = 1$, and hence $C_s <_{\mathrm{L}} C_{s+1}$.

3. If the first disagreement between C_s and C_{s+1} happens in step 2 of the kth iteration of the procedure, then, for η as in that step, $\tau_{\eta, F_s(k)} \neq \tau_{\eta, F_{s+1}(k)}$. Since F is c.e., $\tau_{\eta, F_s(k)} = \tau_{\eta, 0} <_{\mathrm{L}} \tau_{\eta, 1} = \tau_{\eta, F_{s+1}(k)}$, so $C_s <_{\mathrm{L}} C_{s+1}$.

□

For separating weak 1-randomness from stronger randomness notions, the dividing line is hyperimmunity. We will show that every hyperimmune degree contains a weakly 1-random set that is not Schnorr random, but if a set of hyperimmune-free degree is weakly 1-random, then it is in fact weakly

2-random. The first result can be proved by considering the relationship between weak 1-randomness and weak 1-genericity. (We will return to the relationship between randomness and genericity in Section 8.20.)

Theorem 8.11.7 (Kurtz [228]). *Every weakly 1-generic set is weakly 1-random.*

Proof. Let G be weakly 1-generic. Let S be a Σ_1^0 class of measure 1. Let V be a c.e. set of strings generating S. Since S has measure 1, V is dense, so G meets V, and hence must be a member of S. □

By Theorem 2.24.19, we have the following.

Corollary 8.11.8 (Kurtz [228]). *Every hyperimmune degree is weakly 1-random.*

Neither Theorem 8.11.7 nor Corollary 8.11.8 can be reversed, as we have seen in Proposition 8.1.3 that there are 1-random sets of hyperimmune-free degree, and by Theorem 2.24.19, the weakly 1-generic degrees coincide with the hyperimmune degrees.

Combining Theorem 8.11.7 with the following fact also yields the separation result mentioned above.

Proposition 8.11.9. *No weakly 1-generic set is Schnorr random.*

Proof. Let A be weakly 1-generic. Let $S_n = \{\sigma 0^n : \sigma \in 2^n\}$ and $S = \bigcup_n S_n$. Then S is computable and dense, so A meets S infinitely often. In other words, $A \in [\![S_n]\!]$ for infinitely many n. But $\sum_n \mu([\![S_n]\!]) = \sum_n 2^{-n} = 2$, so $\{[\![S_n]\!]\}_{n\in\omega}$ is a total Solovay test, and hence, by Theorem 7.1.10, A is not Schnorr random. □

Corollary 8.11.10. *Every hyperimmune degree contains a weakly 1-random set that is not Schnorr random.*

However, the following result shows that outside of the hyperimmune degrees, many of our notions of randomness coincide.

Theorem 8.11.11 (Nies, Stephan, and Terwijn [308]). *If A has hyperimmune-free degree then A is weakly 1-random iff A is 1-random.*

Proof. Suppose that A has hyperimmune-free degree and is not 1-random. Let $\{V_n\}_{n\in\omega}$ be a nested Martin-Löf test such that $A \in \bigcap_n V_n$. Using A, we can compute a stage $g(n)$ such that $A \in V_n$. Since A has hyperimmune-free degree, there is a computable function f so that $f(n) \geqslant g(n)$ for all n. Let $U_n = V_n[f(n)]$. Then $\{U_n\}_{n\in\omega}$ is a Kurtz null test such that $A \in \bigcap_n U_n$, so A is not weakly 1-random. □

Actually, as observed by Yu [unpublished], we can replace the Martin-Löf test in the above proof by a generalized Martin-Löf test to show the following.

Theorem 8.11.12 (Yu [unpublished]). *If A has hyperimmune-free degree then A is weakly 1-random iff A is weakly 2-random.*

This result improves an earlier direct proof by Miller [personal communication] that there is a weakly 2-random hyperimmune-free degree. It has the following interesting corollary, which extends Corollary 8.6.2.

Corollary 8.11.13 (Downey and Hirschfeldt [unpublished]). *There is a degree* $\mathbf{a}$ *such that every nonzero degree* $\mathbf{b} \leqslant \mathbf{a}$ *is weakly 2-random.*

Proof. By Proposition 8.1.3, there is a 1-random set A of hyperimmune-free degree. Let $B \leqslant_{\mathrm{T}} A$ be noncomputable. By Proposition 2.17.7, $B \leqslant_{\mathrm{tt}} A$, so by Demuth's Theorem 8.6.1, there is a 1-random $C \equiv_{\mathrm{T}} B$. By Theorem 8.11.12, C is weakly 2-random. □

As in the 1-randomness case, it is not known whether $\mathbf{a}$ can be made hyperimmune.

8.11.3 When van Lambalgen's Theorem fails

We are now in a position to prove the result, mentioned in Section 7.1.2, that van Lambalgen's Theorem fails for Schnorr and computable randomness. This result was originally proved by Merkle, Miller, Nies, Reimann, and Stephan [269], with the following extension obtained by Yu [412].

Theorem 8.11.14 (Yu [412]). *Let $A \oplus B$ be Schnorr random and computable in an incomplete c.e. set. Then A is not Schnorr random relative to B and B is not Schnorr random relative to A. The same is true for computable randomness.*

Proof. By Theorem 7.1.13, A and B are Schnorr random. By Theorem 8.2.1, A, B, and $A \oplus B$ are not 1-random. By Theorem 8.11.2, they are high. Thus $(A \oplus B)' \equiv_{\mathrm{T}} \emptyset'' <_{\mathrm{T}} \emptyset''' \equiv_{\mathrm{T}} B''$. By Theorem 8.11.2 relativized to B, we conclude that A is not Schnorr random relative to B, since otherwise it would be 1-random relative to B, and hence 1-random. The symmetric argument shows that B is not Schnorr random relative to A.

This result holds also for computable randomness because if $A \oplus B$ is computably random then it is Schnorr random, and if A is not Schnorr random relative to B then A is not computably random relative to B. □

By Theorem 8.11.1 (and the existence of an incomplete c.e. set, shown in Section 2.14.3), there is a computably random (and hence Schnorr random) set computable in an incomplete c.e. set, so we see that van Lambalgen's Theorem fails for Schnorr and computable randomness.

Corollary 8.11.15 (Merkle, Miller, Nies, Reimann, and Stephan [269]). *There are sets A and B such that $A \oplus B$ is Schnorr random but A and B are not relatively Schnorr random. The same is true for computable randomness.*

Barmpalias, Downey, and Ng [22] have shown that this result holds also for weak 2-randomness.

8.12 Measure theory and Turing reducibility

The first applications of measure theory to computability theory were due to Spector [375], who showed that almost all pairs of hyperdegrees (a generalization of the notion of Turing degree to higher computability theory) are incomparable, and, even earlier, to de Leeuw, Moore, Shannon, and Shapiro [92]. Their result, which we now discuss, was not well known in the computability theory community until recently, and has as an immediate corollary another fundamental theorem first explicitly stated by Sacks [341]. It says that if a set is c.e. relative to positive measure many oracles, then it is in fact c.e. Its proof uses what is known as the *majority vote* technique.

Theorem 8.12.1 (de Leeuw, Moore, Shannon, and Shapiro [92]). *If $\mu(\{X : A \text{ is c.e. in } X\}) > 0$ then A is c.e.*

Proof. If $\{X : A \text{ is c.e. in } X\}$ has positive measure then there is an e such that $S = \{X : W_e^X = A\}$ has positive measure. By the Lebesgue Density Theorem 1.2.3, there is an X such that $\lim_n 2^n \mu(S \cap [\![X \upharpoonright n]\!]) = 1$. Let n be such that $2^n \mu(S \cap [\![X \upharpoonright n]\!]) > \frac{1}{2}$ and let $\sigma = X \upharpoonright n$. We can enumerate A by "taking a vote" among the sets extending σ. More precisely, $n \in A$ iff $2^n \mu(\{Y : \sigma \prec Y \wedge n \in W_e^Y\}) > \frac{1}{2}$, and the set of n for which this inequality holds is clearly c.e. □

Theorem 8.12.1 has a very interesting corollary, which was not explicitly stated in [92], but later independently formulated by Sacks [341]. For a set A, let $A^{\leqslant_T} = \{B : A \leqslant_T B\}$. It is natural to ask whether there is a noncomputable set A such that $A^{\leqslant_T}$ has positive measure. Such a set would have a good claim to being "almost computable". Furthermore, the existence of a noncomputable set A and an i such that $\mu(\{B : \Phi_i^B = A\}) = 1$ could be considered a counterexample to the Church-Turing Thesis, since a machine with access to a random source would be able to compute A. The following result lays such worries to rest.

Corollary 8.12.2 (Sacks [341]). *If $\mu(A^{\leqslant_T}) > 0$ then A is computable.*

Proof. If $\mu(A^{\leqslant_T}) > 0$ then there is an i such that $\{B : \Phi_i^B = A\}$ has positive measure. It is now easy to show that there are j and k such that $\{B : W_j^B = A\}$ and $\{B : W_k^B = \overline{A}\}$ both have positive measure. Thus A and $\overline{A}$ are both c.e. □

It is not hard to adapt the proof of Theorem 8.12.1 to show that if $\mu(\{B : A \text{ is } \Delta_2^{0,B}\}) > 0$ then A is Δ_2^0. From this result it follows that if

$\mathbf{d} > \mathbf{0}'$, then $\mu(\{B : \deg(B') \geqslant \mathbf{d}\}) = 0$. In Section 8.14 we will see that, in fact, almost all sets are GL_1.

The following is a useful consequence of Corollary 8.12.2.

Corollary 8.12.3. *If $A >_{\mathrm{T}} \emptyset$ and X is weakly 2-random relative to A, then $A \nleqslant_{\mathrm{T}} X$.*

Proof. Suppose that $\emptyset <_{\mathrm{T}} A \leqslant_{\mathrm{T}} X$. Let e be such that $\Phi_e^X = A$, and let $S = \{B : \Phi_e^B = A\}$. Then S is a $\Pi_2^{0,A}$ class, and by Corollary 8.12.2, it is null. Since $X \in S$, it follows that X is not weakly 2-random relative to A. □

We will see in Section 11.7 that this result does not hold for 1-randomness in place of weak 2-randomness, although it does come close to holding in that case. The sets A that can be computed by a set that is 1-random relative to A are called *bases for 1-randomness*, and turn out to form a class of "randomness-theoretically weak" sets with several natural characterizations. Also known as the K-trivial sets, they will be the focus of Chapter 11. (In the terminology introduced in that chapter, Corollary 8.12.3 says that there are no noncomputable bases for weak 2-randomness.)

Corollary 8.12.4 (Kautz [200]). *If two sets are relatively weakly 2-random, then their degrees form a minimal pair.*

Proof. Let B and C be relatively weakly 2-random, and let $A \leqslant_{\mathrm{T}} B, C$. Since B is weakly 2-random relative to C, it is weakly 2-random relative to A. By Corollary 8.12.3, A is computable. □

As we have seen in Corollary 8.8.3, Corollary 8.12.4 does not hold for 1-randomness, and indeed we have the following.

Corollary 8.12.5. *The class of sets of the form $A \oplus B$ such that A and B form a minimal pair has measure 1, and includes all weakly 2-random sets but not all 1-random sets.*[7]

Note that, by Kolmogorov's 0-1 Law, Theorem 1.2.4, any reasonable degree-theoretic property like being the join of a minimal pair will hold of either almost all or almost no sets. As in the previous corollary, for many properties P that hold of almost all sets, careful analysis has revealed the least n such that P holds of all n-random sets. For example, by Corollary 6.9.5 the class of all A that have nonminimal degree has measure 1, and includes every 1-random set. We will see other examples below, for instance in Theorems 8.14.1, 8.21.2, and 8.21.8.

Corollary 8.12.2 has the following generalization, whose proof is a straightforward modification of the majority vote proof of Theorem 8.12.1.

[7] That this class has measure 1 was first shown by Stillwell [382].

Theorem 8.12.6 (Stillwell [382]). *If* $\mu(\{X : A \leqslant_{\mathrm{T}} B \oplus X\}) > 0$ *then* $A \leqslant_{\mathrm{T}} B$.

An immediate corollary to this result (which we will improve in Theorem 8.15.1) is the following.

Corollary 8.12.7 (Stillwell [382]). *Let* $\mathbf{a}$ *and* $\mathbf{b}$ *be degrees. Then* $(\mathbf{a} \vee \mathbf{b}) \wedge (\mathbf{a} \vee \mathbf{c})$ *is defined and equal to* $\mathbf{a}$ *for almost all* $\mathbf{c}$.

Proof. Let $A \in \mathbf{a}$ and $B \in \mathbf{b}$. For any set D, Theorem 8.12.6 implies that $\mu(\{C : D \leqslant_{\mathrm{T}} A \oplus C \wedge D \nleqslant_{\mathrm{T}} A\}) = 0$. Since there are only countably many $D \leqslant_{\mathrm{T}} A \oplus B$,

$$\mu(\{C : \exists D \leqslant_{\mathrm{T}} A \oplus B\,(D \leqslant_{\mathrm{T}} A \oplus C \wedge D \nleqslant_{\mathrm{T}} A)\}) = 0.$$

So for almost all C, every D that is computable in both $A \oplus B$ and $A \oplus C$ is also computable in A. Since A is computable in $A \oplus B$ and $A \oplus C$, the corollary follows. □

8.13 n-randomness and weak n-randomness

In Theorem 7.2.7, we saw that every n-random set is weakly n-random, and every weakly $(n+1)$-random set is n-random. In this section, we show that neither implication can be reversed, even at the level of degrees.

An important special case of the following result was given in Theorem 7.2.8.

Theorem 8.13.1 (Downey and Hirschfeldt [unpublished]). *If* A *is weakly* $(n+1)$*-random and* $\emptyset <_{\mathrm{T}} B \leqslant_{\mathrm{T}} \emptyset^{(n)}$, *then* $A \mid_{\mathrm{T}} B$.

Proof. Clearly $A \nleqslant_{\mathrm{T}} B$, since otherwise $\{A\}$ would be a Π^0_{n+1} class of measure 0. Thus it is enough to show that A cannot compute B.

Let $P_e = \{X : \Phi^X_e \text{ is total}\}$, let $Q_e = \{X : \forall k\,(\Phi^X_e(k)\downarrow \;\Rightarrow\; \Phi^X_e(k) = B(k))\}$, and let $R_e = P_e \cap Q_e$. Then P_e is a Π^0_2 class, and Q_e is a $\Pi^{0,\emptyset^{(n)}}_1$ class, since for any string σ, if $\Phi^\sigma_e(k)\downarrow$, then the condition $\Phi^\sigma_e(k) = B(k)$ can be checked effectively in $\emptyset^{(n)}$. Since $n \geqslant 1$, we see that R_e is a Π^0_{n+1} class. If $X \in R_e$ then X computes B, so by Corollary 8.12.2, R_e has measure 0, and hence cannot contain a weakly $(n+1)$-random set. The theorem now follows, since any set computing B must be in R_e for some e. □

It follows immediately from the above theorem that no weakly $(n+1)$-random set can be $\emptyset^{(n)}$-computable, or even compute a noncomputable $\emptyset^{(n)}$-computable set. Since there are $\emptyset^{(n)}$-computable n-random sets, we have the following result.

Corollary 8.13.2 (Kurtz [228]). *For every* $n \geqslant 1$, *there is an* n*-random set that is not of weakly* $(n+1)$*-random degree, and indeed cannot be computed by any set of weakly* $(n+1)$*-random degree.*

Kurtz [228] showed that there is a weakly 1-random set that is not of 1-random degree. Kautz [200] extended this result (at the set level) to show that if $n \geqslant 1$, then there is a weakly n-random set that is not n-random (though this result was stated without proof earlier by Gaifman and Snir [168]). Kautz' proof was fairly complicated, but we will get a simpler one, which works at the level of degrees as well, using the following relativized form of Theorem 7.2.25. Note that this result does not follow immediately by relativizing the proof of Theorem 7.2.25, because weak $(n+1)$-randomness is not the same as weak 1-randomness relative to $\emptyset^{(n)}$.

Theorem 8.13.3 (Downey and Hirschfeldt [unpublished]). *If $X >_{\mathrm{T}} \emptyset^{(n-1)}$ is c.e. in $\emptyset^{(n-1)}$ then there is a weakly n-random set A such that $A \oplus \emptyset^{(n-1)} \equiv_{\mathrm{T}} X$.*

Proof. The $n = 1$ case is Theorem 7.2.25, so let $n \geqslant 2$. By Theorem 7.2.6, A is weakly n-random iff for every $\emptyset^{(n-1)}$-computable sequence of $\Sigma_1^{\emptyset^{(n-2)}}$ classes $\{U_i\}_{i \in \omega}$ such that $\mu(U_i) \leqslant 2^{-i}$, we have $A \notin \bigcap_i U_i$. We do the $n = 2$ case using this characterization. The general case then follows by a straightforward relativization.

Thus we have a Σ_2^0 set $X \geqslant_{\mathrm{T}} \emptyset'$. We build a weakly n-random A with $A \oplus \emptyset' \equiv_{\mathrm{T}} X$ via a $\emptyset'$-computable construction. Let $X_0, X_1, \ldots$ be an approximation to X as a $\emptyset'$-c.e. set. Let $S_0, S_1, \ldots$ be an effective listing of the Σ_1^0 classes. We will first discuss how to build $A \leqslant_{\mathrm{T}} X$, and later explain how to add coding to the construction to ensure that $A \oplus \emptyset^{(n-1)} \equiv_{\mathrm{T}} X$.

For simplicity of presentation, we adopt the convention that $\Phi_e^{\emptyset'}(i)\downarrow \Rightarrow \mu(S_{\Phi_e^{\emptyset'}(i)}) \leqslant 2^{-i}$ (that is, we do not allow $\Phi_e^{\emptyset'}(i)$ to converge unless $\mu(S_{\Phi_e^{\emptyset'}(i)}) \leqslant 2^{-i}$, which we can determine using $\emptyset'$). We need to satisfy the requirements

$$R_e : \Phi_e^{\emptyset'} \text{ total } \Rightarrow \exists i\, (A \notin S_{\Phi_e^{\emptyset'}(i)})$$

while making A be X-computable.

Associated with each R_e will be a number r_e, which is initially set to equal $e+1$ and may be redefined during the construction. We say that R_e requires attention at stage s if R_e is not currently satisfied and for some i, we have $\Phi_e^{\emptyset'}(r_e + i)\downarrow$ and $X_{s+1}(i) \neq X_s(i)$. When a requirement R_e is satisfied, it will be satisfied through a particular number i_e (which indicates that we have committed ourselves to keeping A out of $S_{\Phi_e^{\emptyset'}(i_e)}$). Initially each i_e is undefined.

We build A as the limit of strings $\sigma_0, \sigma_1, \ldots$ with $|\sigma_s| = s$. Let $\sigma_0 = \lambda$. At stage s, we proceed as follows.

1. Fix the least $e \leqslant s$ that requires attention. (If there is none then proceed to step 2.) Define $i_e = r_e + i$ for the least i such that $\Phi_e^{\emptyset'}(r_e + i)\downarrow$ and $X_{s+1}(i) \neq X_s(i)$. Declare R_e to be satisfied. For each $e' > e$, declare $R_{e'}$ to be unsatisfied and undefine $i_{e'}$ and $r_{e'}$.

2. Let $S = \bigcup_{i_j\downarrow} S_{\Phi_j^{\emptyset'}(i_j)}$. Let $\sigma_{s+1} \in 2^{s+1}$ be such that $\mu([\![\sigma_{s+1}]\!] \cap S) < 1$ and $\sigma_{s+1} \upharpoonright i_e = \sigma_s \upharpoonright i_e$.

3. For all e' such that $r_{e'}$ is undefined, define $r_{e'}$ to be a fresh large number, so that $\mu([\![\sigma_{s+1}]\!] \cap S) + \sum_{e'>e} 2^{-r_{e'}} < 1$.

It is easy to check by induction that the definition of σ_{s+1} at step 2 is always possible, because of how we define the $r_{e'}$ at step 3. Let A be the limit of the σ_s. It is also easy to check that A is well-defined and X-computable (since if $n < s$ then $\sigma_{s+1} \upharpoonright n = \sigma_s \upharpoonright n$ unless some number less than or equal to n enters X at stage s). Furthermore, the usual finite injury argument shows that if $\Phi_e^{\emptyset'}$ is total then R_e is eventually permanently satisfied, because once all R_j for $j < e$ have stopped requiring attention at some stage s, the fact that $X \nleqslant_{\mathrm{T}} \emptyset'$ implies that R_e eventually requires attention after stage s. The fact that the S_i are open then implies that R_e is satisfied.

Adding coding to this construction to ensure that X is computable in $A \oplus \emptyset'$ is not difficult. We have coding markers $m_n[s]$ such that $m_n = \lim_s m_n[s]$ exists. Every time we have $m_n[s+1] \neq m_n[s]$, we ensure that $A \upharpoonright m_n[s] \neq \sigma_s \upharpoonright m_n[s]$. We also ensure that if n enters X at stage s then $A \upharpoonright m_n[s] \neq \sigma_s \upharpoonright m_n[s]$. It is straightforward to add such markers to the construction, moving all markers of weaker priority whenever R_e acts. The requirements on the markers ensure that, knowing A, we can follow the construction (which we can do using $\emptyset'$) to find an s such that $A \upharpoonright m_n[s] = \sigma_s \upharpoonright m_n[s]$, at which point we know that $n \in X$ iff $n \in X_s$. □

Corollary 8.13.4 (Kurtz [228] for $n = 1$, Kautz [200] (at the set level)). *Let $n \geqslant 1$. There is a weakly n-random set that is not of n-random degree.*

Proof. Let X be c.e. in $\emptyset^{(n-1)}$ and such that $\emptyset^{(n-1)} <_{\mathrm{T}} X <_{\mathrm{T}} \emptyset^{(n)}$. By the theorem, there is a weakly n-random set S such that $S \oplus \emptyset^{(n-1)} \equiv_{\mathrm{T}} X$. By the relativized form of Corollary 8.8.2, if Y is $\emptyset^{(n-1)}$-c.e. and there is an n-random set R with $R \oplus \emptyset^{(n-1)} \equiv_{\mathrm{T}} Y$, then $Y \equiv_{\mathrm{T}} \emptyset^{(n)}$, so there is no n-random set Turing equivalent to S. □

Barmpalias, Downey, and Ng [22] have improved Theorem 8.13.3 in the $n = 2$ case as follows.

Theorem 8.13.5 (Barmpalias, Downey, and Ng [22]). *If the degree of X is hyperimmune relative to $\emptyset'$ then there is a weakly 2-random set A such that $A \oplus \emptyset' \equiv_{\mathrm{T}} A' \equiv_{\mathrm{T}} X$.*

There is no known exact characterization of the degrees that are jumps of weak 2-random sets.

8.14 Every 2-random set is GL$_1$

The fact that all 1-random left-c.e. reals are complete might lead to the false impression that randomness is a highness notion. In general, however, the reality is quite the opposite. We already saw results in this direction in Section 8.8, and will see further results (in Sections 15.5 and 15.6, for instance) showing that randomness is in fact antithetical to computational power, and in many ways, sufficiently random sets begin to resemble highly nonrandom (e.g., computable) ones. Thus randomness is in a sense a lowness notion. In this section, we prove a result that lends evidence to this claim. Recall that a set X is generalized low (GL$_1$) if $X' \equiv_T \emptyset' \oplus X$. The following result generalizes Corollary 8.12.2. We will see in Corollary 8.14.4 that the $n+1$ in its statement is optimal.

Theorem 8.14.1 (Kautz [200]). *Let $n > 0$. The class $\{X : X^{(n)} \equiv_T X \oplus \emptyset^{(n)}\}$ includes every $(n+1)$-random set, and hence has measure* 1. *In particular, every* 2*-random set is GL$_1$.*[8]

Proof. We build a functional Φ such that the classes $\{A : A^{(n)}(e) \neq \Phi^{A\oplus\emptyset^{(n)}}(e)\}$ for $e \in \omega$ form a Σ^0_{n+1}-test. It then follows that if A is $(n+1)$-random, then $A^{(n)}(e) = \Phi^{A\oplus\emptyset^{(n)}}(e)$ for almost all e, and hence $A^{(n)} \leqslant_T A \oplus \emptyset^{(n)}$. (Of course, $A^{(n)} \geqslant_T A \oplus \emptyset^{(n)}$ is automatic.)

Let $C^i_e = \{A : e \in A^{(i)}\}$ and write C_e for C^n_e. We claim that the C_e are uniformly Σ^0_n classes. To establish this claim, assume by induction that the C^{i-1}_e are uniformly Σ^0_{i-1} classes. Then the classes $D^{i-1}_\sigma = \{A : \sigma \prec A^{(n-1)}\}$ are uniformly Δ^0_i, and $C^i_e = \bigcup_{\Phi^\sigma_e(e)\downarrow} D^{i-1}_\sigma$, whence the C^i_e are uniformly Σ^0_i.

Thus, by Theorem 6.8.3, uniformly in $\emptyset^{(n)}$, we can find $\Sigma^{\emptyset^{(n-1)}}_1$ classes U_e with $C_e \subseteq U_e$ and $\mu(U_e) - \mu(C_e) \leqslant 2^{-(e+1)}$ for all e. There is an $\emptyset^{(n)}$-computable f taking natural numbers to finite sets of strings such that for each e we have $[\![f(e)]\!] \subseteq U_e$ and $\mu(U_e \setminus [\![f(e)]\!]) \leqslant 2^{-(e+1)}$. Let Ψ be a functional such that $f = \Psi^{\emptyset^{(n)}}$. Let

$$\Phi^{A\oplus B}(e) = \begin{cases} 1 & \text{if } \Psi^B(e)\downarrow \wedge A \in [\![\Psi^B(e)]\!] \\ 0 & \text{if } \Psi^B(e)\downarrow \wedge A \notin [\![\Psi^B(e)]\!] \\ \uparrow & \text{otherwise.} \end{cases}$$

Then

$$\Phi^{A\oplus\emptyset^{(n)}}(e) = \begin{cases} 1 & \text{if } A \in [\![f(e)]\!] \\ 0 & \text{otherwise.} \end{cases}$$

Let $V_e = \{A : A^{(n)}(e) \neq \Phi^{A\oplus\emptyset^{(n)}}(e)\}$. Then $A \in V_e$ iff either $A \in C_e$ and $A \notin [\![f(e)]\!]$, or $A \notin C_e$ and $A \in [\![f(e)]\!]$. Since $\mu(C_e \setminus [\![f(e)]\!]) \leqslant \mu(U_e \setminus$

[8] Kautz [200] points out that the "almost all" version of this result (that $X^{(n)} \equiv_T X \oplus \emptyset^{(n)}$ for almost every X) is due to Sacks [341] and Stillwell [382].

$[\![f(e)]\!]) \leqslant 2^{-(e+1)}$ and $\mu([\![f(e)]\!] \setminus C_e) \leqslant \mu(U_e \setminus C_e) \leqslant 2^{-(e+1)}$, we have $\mu(V_e) \leqslant 2^e$. Since the sets $[\![f(e)]\!]$ are clopen and uniformly computable in $\emptyset^{(n)}$, the V_e are uniformly Σ^0_{n+1} classes. Thus the V_e form a Σ^0_{n+1}-test, as required. □

In the $n = 1$ case of the above proof, we can take $U_e = C_e$, and it is easy to see that we can also ensure that $f \leqslant_{\mathrm{wtt}} \emptyset'$. It then follows that the V_e form a Demuth test, so we have the following result, which was first stated by Demuth [95], with a proof sketch, a full proof later appearing in Nies [306].

Theorem 8.14.2 (Demuth [95]). *All Demuth random sets are GL_1.*

Using Theorem 8.14.1, Kautz [200] generalized Theorem 8.5.1 as follows.

Theorem 8.14.3 (Kautz [200]). *If $\mathbf{a} \geqslant \mathbf{0}^{(n)}$ then there is an n-random set A with $A^{(n-1)} \in \mathbf{a}$.*

Proof. The proof of Theorem 8.5.1 relativizes. Recall that in that proof we constructed a perfect tree $T \leqslant_{\mathrm{T}} \emptyset'$ such that $[T] \subseteq \overline{U_0}$, where U_0 is the first element of Kučera's universal Martin-Löf test. To ensure the effectiveness of the coding of sets into paths of T used in the proof, we used Lemma 8.5.2, which allows us to compute effective lower bounds for the measures of nonempty sets of the form $\overline{U_0} \cap [\![\sigma]\!]$. We can relative this construction to $\emptyset^{(n-1)}$. We can construct T computably in $\emptyset^{(n)}$, now letting U_0 be the first element of Kučera's universal Martin-Löf test relativized to $\emptyset^{(n-1)}$. The necessary lower bounds given by the relativized form of Lemma 8.5.2 are now computable in $\emptyset^{(n-1)}$. We thus get an n-random A such that $A \oplus \emptyset^{(n-1)} \in \mathbf{a}$. By Theorem 8.14.1, $A^{(n-1)} \equiv_{\mathrm{T}} A \oplus \emptyset^{(n-1)}$, so $A^{(n-1)} \in \mathbf{a}$. □

Corollary 8.14.4 (Kautz [200]). *Let $n > 0$. The class $\{X : X^{(n)} \equiv_{\mathrm{T}} X \oplus \emptyset^{(n)}\}$ does not contain every n-random set.*

Proof. Let A be n-random and such that $A^{(n-1)} \equiv_{\mathrm{T}} \emptyset^{(n)}$. Then $A^{(n)} \equiv_{\mathrm{T}} \emptyset^{(n+1)}$ while $A \oplus \emptyset^{(n)} \leqslant_{\mathrm{T}} A^{(n-1)} \oplus \emptyset^{(n)} \equiv_{\mathrm{T}} \emptyset^{(n)}$. □

By relativizing Theorem 8.14.1 and Corollary 8.14.4, we get the following result, which will be useful below.

Theorem 8.14.5. *The class $\{X : (X \oplus A)^{(n)} \equiv_{\mathrm{T}} X \oplus A^{(n)}\}$ includes every set that is $(n+1)$-random relative to A, and hence has measure 1, but does not include every set that is n-random relative to A.*

8.15 Stillwell's Theorem

It is well known that the theory of the Turing degrees is undecidable, as shown by Lachlan [232] and in fact computably isomorphic to theory of second order arithmetic, as shown by Simpson [358]. On the other hand, in this section we use material from previous sections to prove Stillwell's Theorem that the "almost all" theory of the Turing degrees is decidable. Here the quantifier $\forall$ is interpreted to mean "for measure 1 many". By Fubini's Theorem (see [335]), $A \subset (2^\omega)^n$ has measure 1 iff almost all sections of A with first coordinate fixed have measure 1. This fact allows us to deal with nested quantifiers.

Theorem 8.15.1 (Stillwell [382]). *The "almost all" theory of the Turing degrees is decidable.*

Proof. Here variables $\mathbf{a}, \mathbf{b}, \mathbf{c}, \ldots$ range over degrees. Our terms are built from these variables, $\mathbf{0}$, $'$ (jump), $\vee$, and $\wedge$. An atomic formula is one of the form $t_0 \leqslant t_1$ for terms t_0, t_1, and formulas in general are built from atomic ones using the connectives & (used here for "and" to avoid confusion with the meet symbol) and $\neg$, and the quantifier $\forall$, interpreted to mean "for measure 1 many".

Corollary 8.12.7 allows us to compute the meet of any two terms of the form $\mathbf{a}_0 \vee \mathbf{a}_1 \vee \cdots \vee \mathbf{a}_k \vee \mathbf{0}^{(m)}$ and $\mathbf{b}_0 \vee \mathbf{b}_1 \vee \cdots \vee \mathbf{b}_{k'} \vee \mathbf{0}^{(n)}$ as $\mathbf{c}_0 \vee \mathbf{c}_1 \vee \cdots \vee \mathbf{c}_l \vee \mathbf{0}^{(\min\{m,n\})}$, where the $\mathbf{c}_i$ are the variables common to both terms. For example, $(\mathbf{a}_1 \vee \mathbf{a}_3 \vee \mathbf{0}^{(4)}) \wedge (\mathbf{a}_1 \vee \mathbf{a}_5 \vee \mathbf{a}_7 \vee \mathbf{0}^{(6)}) = \mathbf{a}_1 \vee \mathbf{0}^{(4)}$. Note that we also have $\mathbf{a} \wedge \mathbf{c} = \mathbf{0}$.

Now we can give a normal form for terms. By Theorem 8.14.5, $\mathbf{a}^{(n)} = \mathbf{a} \vee \mathbf{0}^{(n)}$ for almost all $\mathbf{a}$. We can use this fact to compute the jump of any term of the form $\mathbf{a}_0 \vee \mathbf{a}_1 \vee \cdots \vee \mathbf{a}_m \vee \mathbf{0}^{(l)}$. That is, as $(\mathbf{a}_0 \vee \mathbf{a}_1 \vee \mathbf{a}_m \cdots \vee \mathbf{0}^{(l)}) = (\mathbf{a}_0 \vee \mathbf{a}_1 \vee \cdots \vee \mathbf{a}_m)^{(l)}$, it follows that

$$(\mathbf{a}_0 \vee \mathbf{a}_1 \vee \cdots \vee \mathbf{a}_m \vee \mathbf{0}^{(l)})' = \mathbf{a}_0 \vee \mathbf{a}_1 \vee \cdots \vee \mathbf{a}_m \vee \mathbf{0}^{(l+1)}.$$

Hence, using the rule for $\wedge$, the jump rule, and the join rule $(\mathbf{a}_0 \vee \mathbf{a}_1 \vee \mathbf{a}_m \vee \cdots \vee \mathbf{0}^{(l)}) \vee (\mathbf{b}_0 \vee \mathbf{b}_1 \vee \mathbf{b}_n \vee \cdots \vee \mathbf{0}^{(k)}) = (\mathbf{a}_0 \vee \mathbf{a}_1 \vee \cdots \vee \mathbf{a}_m \vee \mathbf{b}_0 \vee \cdots \vee \mathbf{b}_n \vee \mathbf{0}^{(\max\{l,k\})})$, we can reduce any term t to one of the form

$$(\mathbf{a}_0 \vee \mathbf{a}_1 \vee \cdots \vee \mathbf{a}_m \vee \mathbf{0}^{(l)}).$$

The proof is completed by giving the decision procedure. We show that every formula with free variables is *effectively* 0-1-*valued*. That is, it is satisfied by a set of instances of measure 0 or 1, and we can effectively determine which is the case. We proceed by structural induction.

To see that $t_0 \leqslant t_1$ is effectively 0-1-valued, first put the terms t_i in normal form, then calculate $t_0 \wedge t_1$. If $t_0 \wedge t_1 = t_0$ then $t_0 \leqslant t_1$ for almost all instances. Otherwise, we must have $t_0 \wedge t_1 < t_0$, either because t_0 contains a variable not in t_1, or because the $\mathbf{0}^{(l)}$ term in t_0 is too big. In either case, $t_0 \leqslant t_1$ is false for almost all instances.

If ψ_0, ψ_1 are effectively 0-1-valued then clearly so are $\psi_0 \& \psi_1$ and $\neg\psi_i$. Fubini's Theorem shows that if ψ is effectively 0-1-valued, then so is $\forall a_i \psi(a_o, \ldots, a_n)$, thus completing the proof. ☐

8.16 DNC degrees and autocomplexity

Kjos-Hanssen, Merkle, and Stephan [205] extended Theorem 8.8.1 to characterize the sets that compute diagonally noncomputable functions in terms of Kolmogorov complexity. Kanovich [197, 198] formulated the following definition of complexity and autocomplexity for computably enumerable sets, and stated the result that complex c.e. sets are wtt-complete and autocomplex sets are Turing complete, as we will see below.

Definition 8.16.1 (Kjos-Hanssen, Merkle, and Stephan [205], Kanovich [197, 198]).

(i) A is *h-complex* if $C(A \upharpoonright n) \geqslant h(n)$ for all n.

(ii) A is *(order) complex*[9] if there is a computable order h such that A is h-complex.

(iii) A is *autocomplex* if there is an A-computable order h such that A is h-complex.

Notice that we could have used K in place of C in the definition above, since the two complexities differ by only a log factor. Notice too that every 1-random set is complex.

We now establish some interesting characterizations of autocomplexity and complexity.

Lemma 8.16.2 (Kjos-Hanssen, Merkle, and Stephan [205]). *The following are equivalent.*

(i) *A is autocomplex.*

(ii) *There is an A-computable h such that $C(A \upharpoonright h(n)) \geqslant n$ for all n.*

(iii) *There is an A-computable f such that $C(f(n)) \geqslant n$ for all n.*

(iv) *For every (A)-computable (order) h, there is an A-computable g such that $C(g(n)) \geqslant h(n)$ for all n.*

Proof. (i) $\Rightarrow$ (ii). Let g be an A-computable order such that $C(A \upharpoonright n) \geqslant g(n)$ for all n. Then we get (ii) by taking $h(n) = \min\{k : g(k) \geqslant n\}$.

(ii) $\Rightarrow$ (iii). Let $\widehat{f}(n)$ be the encoding of $A \upharpoonright h(n)$ as a natural number. Then $C(\widehat{f}(n)) \geqslant n - O(1)$, so we can take $f(n) = \widehat{f}(n+k)$ for a suitable k.

(iii) $\Leftrightarrow$ (iv). Clearly (iv) implies (iii). Now let h be A-computable and let f be as in (iii). Let $g(n) = f(h(n))$. Then $C(g(n)) = C(f(h(n)) \geqslant h(n)$.

(iii) $\Rightarrow$ (i). Let f be as in (iii). Let Φ be such that $\Phi^A = f$ and let g be the use function of that computation, which by the usual assumptions

[9] This notion should not be confused with that of *Kummer complex* sets, which we will meet in Chapter 16.

on the use is an A-computable order. Then for any $m \geqslant g(n)$, the value of $f(n)$ can be computed from n and $A \upharpoonright m$, so

$$n \leqslant C(f(n)) \leqslant C(A \upharpoonright m) + 2\log n + O(1).$$

Hence, for almost all n and all $m \geqslant g(n)$, we have $C(A \upharpoonright m) \geqslant \frac{n}{2}$. Therefore, a finite variation of the A-computable order $n \mapsto \frac{1}{2}\max\{m : g(m) \leqslant n\}$ witnesses the autocomplexity of A. □

Similar methods allow us to characterize the complex sets.

Theorem 8.16.3 (Kjos-Hanssen, Merkle, and Stephan [205]). *The following are equivalent.*

(i) *A is complex.*

(ii) *There is a computable function h such that $C(A \upharpoonright h(n)) \geqslant n$ for all n.*

(iii) *A tt-computes a function f such that $C(f(n)) \geqslant n$ for all n.*

(iv) *A wtt-computes a function f such that $C(f(n)) \geqslant n$ for all n.*

The following result can be viewed as the ultimate generalization of Kučera's Theorem 8.8.1 that 1-randoms have DNC degree.

Theorem 8.16.4 (Kjos-Hanssen, Merkle, and Stephan [205]). *A set is autocomplex iff it is of DNC degree.*

Proof. Let A be autocomplex and let f be as in Lemma 8.16.2 (iii). Then for almost all n,

$$C(\Phi_n(n)) \leqslant C(n) + O(1) \leqslant \log n + O(1) < n \leqslant C(f(n)),$$

so a finite variation of f is DNC.

Now suppose that A is not autocomplex. We show that no Φ_i^A is DNC. Fix i. Let U be the universal machine used to define C. For each σ let $e(\sigma)$ be such that $\Phi_{e(\sigma)}(n)$ is computed as follows. If $U(\sigma) = \tau$ for some τ, then compute $\Phi_i^\tau(n)$ and output the result if this computation halts.

Let $h(n)$ be the maximum of the uses of all computations $\Phi_i^A(e(\sigma))$ with $|\sigma| < n$. Then $h \leqslant_T A$, so by Lemma 8.16.2, there are infinitely many n such that $C(A \upharpoonright h(n)) < n$. For any such n, let $\sigma_n \in 2^{<n}$ be such that $U(\sigma_n) = A \upharpoonright h(n)$. Then

$$\Phi_{e(\sigma_n)}(e(\sigma_n)) = \Phi_i^{A \upharpoonright h(n)}(e(\sigma_n)) = \Phi_i^A(e(\sigma_n)),$$

so Φ_i^A is not DNC. □

Again, similar methods yield results for complex sets.

Theorem 8.16.5 (Kjos-Hanssen, Merkle, and Stephan [205]). *The following are equivalent.*

(i) *A is complex.*

(ii) *A tt-computes a DNC function.*

(iii) *A wtt-computes a DNC function.*

In particular, the sets that wtt-compute DNC functions and those that wtt-compute computably bounded DNC functions coincide.

By Theorems 8.10.3 and 8.16.4, there is an autocomplex set that does not compute any 1-random set. Kjos-Hanssen, Merkle, and Stephan [205] showed that the proof of Theorem 8.10.3 can be used to extend this result as follows.

Theorem 8.16.6 (Kjos-Hanssen, Merkle, and Stephan [205]). *There is a complex set that does not compute any 1-random set.*

Kjos-Hanssen, Merkle, and Stephan [205] also showed that a set is complex iff it is not wtt-reducible to any hyperimmune set. Miller [275] defined a set A to be *hyperavoidable* if there is a computable order h such that if $\Phi_e(n)\downarrow$ for all $n < e$ then $A \upharpoonright h(e) \neq \Phi_e \upharpoonright h(e)$. Miller [275] showed that these sets are exactly the ones that are not wtt-reducible to a hyperimmune set, so it turns out that a set is hyperavoidable iff it is complex. The fact that a set is complex iff it is not wtt-reducible to any hyperimmune set has also been used as a tool for proving results in computable model theory by Chisholm, Chubb, Harizanov, Hirschfeldt, Jockusch, McNicholl, and Pingrey [64].

Initial segment complexity and Turing complexity are strongly related in the presence of effective enumerations. For instance, in Theorem 9.14.6, we will show that if a left-c.e. real α is 1-random and B is a c.e. set, then there is a wtt-reduction Γ with identity use such that $\Gamma^\alpha = B$. In the present context, we have the following result, which follows from the lemmas above and Arslanov's Completeness Criterion (Theorem 2.22.3; see also the comment following the proof of that theorem and Theorem 2.22.1, which says that computing DNC functions is equivalent to computing fixed-point free functions).

Theorem 8.16.7 (Kanovich [197, 198]). *Let A be a c.e. set.*

(i) *A is complex iff A is wtt-complete.*

(ii) *A is autocomplex iff A is Turing complete.*

One of the points of [205] was to show how to avoid the use of Arslanov's Completeness Criterion in results like the above. Thus, a direct proof of Theorem 8.16.7 was given in that paper. (Kanovich [197, 198] stated the result without proof.) We could also give a direct proof based on the method of Theorem 8.2.1. That is, suppose that $C(A \upharpoonright n) \geqslant h(n)$ for a computable order h. We build a Turing machine M with coding constant c in the universal machine used to define C. For each k we can effectively find an n_k such that $h(n_k) > k+c$. If k enters $\emptyset'$ at stage s, we let $M(0^k) = A_s \upharpoonright n_k$, thus ensuring that $K(A_s \upharpoonright n_k) \leqslant k + c < h(n_k)$, whence $A \upharpoonright n_k \neq A_s \upharpoonright n_k$.

For the autocomplex case, we can proceed in the same way, except that we now approximate h, so while k is not in $\emptyset'$, the value of n_k can change. We can still recover $\emptyset'$ from A because the final value of n_k is A-computable, but this is no longer a wtt-reduction.

We finish this section with a result that will be important when we consider lowness for weak 1-randomness in Section 12.4. A set A is *weakly computably traceable* if there is a computable h such that for all $f \leqslant_T A$, there is a computable g with $|D_{g(n)}| \leqslant h(n)$ for all n and $f(n) \in D_{g(n)}$ for infinitely many n.

Theorem 8.16.8 (Kjos-Hanssen, Merkle, and Stephan [205]). *The following are equivalent.*

(i) *The degree of A is DNC or high.*

(ii) *A is autocomplex or of high degree.*

(iii) *There is a $g \leqslant_T A$ such that either g dominates all computable functions or for every partial computable h, we have $g(n) \neq h(n)$ for almost all n.*

(iv) *There is an $f \leqslant_T A$ such that for every computable h, we have $f(n) \neq h(n)$ for almost all n.*

(v) *A is not weakly computably traceable.*

Furthermore, if the degree of B is hyperimmune-free and not DNC, then for each $g \leqslant_T B$, there are computable h and $\widehat{h}$ such that

$$\forall n\, \exists m \in [n, \widehat{h}(n)]\, (h(m) = g(m)).$$

Proof. (i) $\Leftrightarrow$ (ii) by Theorem 8.16.4.

(ii) $\Rightarrow$ (v). Suppose that (v) fails but A is either autocomplex or high. Let h be a computable function witnessing the fact that A is weakly computably traceable.

If A is autocomplex, by Lemma 8.16.2, there is an A-computable function p such that $C(A \upharpoonright p(n)) > \log n + h(n)$ for all n. Let g be a computable function such that $\{D_{g(n)}\}_{n \in \omega}$ weakly traces $p(n)$ and $|D_{g(n)}| < h(n)$ for all n. We can describe $p(n)$ by giving n and the program for g, together with $\log h(n)$ many bits to say which of the elements of $D_{g(n)}$ is $p(n)$. Thus for almost all n, we have $C(p(n)) \leqslant \log n + O(\log h(n)) < \log n + h(n)$, contradicting the choice of p.

If A is high, then let $p \leqslant_T A$ dominate all computable functions. Let g be a computable function such that $\{D_{g(n)}\}_{n \in \omega}$ weakly traces $p(n)$. Then the function $n \mapsto \max D_{g(n)} + 1$ is computable, so there are infinitely many n such that $p > \max D_{g(n)}$, which is a contradiction.

(v) $\Rightarrow$ (iv). If (iv) fails then given any $f \leqslant_T A$, there is a computable function h with $f(n) = h(n)$ for infinitely many n. Then (v) fails by letting g be such that $D_{g(n)} = \{h(n)\}$.

(iv) $\Rightarrow$ (iii). If A is high then, by Theorem 8.16.4, there is an A-computable function that dominates all computable functions. So suppose that A is not high. Let $f \leqslant_T A$ be such that for every computable function h, we have $f(n) \neq h(n)$ for almost all n.

Suppose that φ is a partial computable function such that $f(n) = \varphi(n)$ for infinitely many n. Let $p \leqslant_T A$ be such that for each k there is an $n \geqslant k$ with $\varphi(n)[p(k)]\downarrow = f(n)$. Since A is not high, there is a computable function q such that $q(k) > p(k)$ for infinitely many k. We may assume that q is nondecreasing. Let $h(n) = \varphi(n)[q(n)]$ if this value is defined, and $h(n) = 0$ otherwise. Then h is total and computable. If $q(k) \geqslant p(k)$ then there is an $n \geqslant k$ such that $\varphi(n)[q(n)] = \varphi(n)[q(k)] = \varphi(n)[p(k)] = f(n)$, whence $h(n) = f(n)$. Thus there are infinitely many n such that $f(n) = h(n)$, contradicting the choice of f.

(iii) $\Rightarrow$ (i). By Theorem 2.23.7, if g dominates all computable functions then A is high. Otherwise, let $h(e) = \Phi_e(e)$. Then $g(e) \neq h(e)$ for almost all e, so a finite variation of g is DNC.

Finally, we verify the last part of the theorem. Let B be a set whose degree is hyperimmune-free and not DNC, and let $g \leqslant_T B$. Then B is not high, so there is a computable h such that $h(n) = g(n)$ infinitely often. Let $f(n)$ be the least $m \geqslant n$ such that $h(m) = g(m)$. Then $f \leqslant_T B$. Since B has hyperimmune-free degree, there is a computable function $\widehat{h}$ such that $f(n) \leqslant \widehat{h}(n)$ for all n. Then $\forall n\, \exists m \in [n, \widehat{h}(n)]\, (h(m) = g(m))$. □

8.17 Randomness and n-fixed-point freeness

Many results in this book demonstrate that randomness is antithetical to computational strength, and is in a sense a lowness property. Nevertheless, as the results of this section will show, n-random sets do have some computational power.[10]

Definition 8.17.1 (Jockusch, Lerman, Soare, and Solovay [191]). We define a relation $A \sim_n B$ as follows.

(i) $A \sim_0 B$ if $A = B$.

[10]Heuristically, we can distinguish between "hitting power" and "avoiding power". Computing the halting problem, for example, requires hitting power, while having hyperimmune degree, say, may be better characterized as an avoidance property (i.e., avoiding domination by computable functions). Of course, the real distinction is between properties that define a class of measure 0 and those that define a class of measure 1. (Most natural properties fall into one of these two cases.) The former will not hold of any sufficiently random sets, while the latter will necessarily hold of all sufficiently random sets. Obviously, a property defining a class of measure 0 is the same as the negation of a property defining a class of measure 1, but this fact does not diminish the heuristic usefulness of this observation.

(ii) $A \sim_1 B$ if $A =^* B$.

(iii) If $n \geqslant 2$ then $A \sim_n B$ if $A^{(n-2)} \equiv_T B^{(n-2)}$.

A total function f is *n-fixed-point free* (*n-FPF*) if $W_{f(x)} \not\sim_n W_x$ for all x.

Note that the 0-FPF functions are just the usual fixed-point free functions. In Theorem 8.8.1 we saw that every 1-random set computes a DNC function, and hence a fixed-point free function. We now extend this result as follows.

Theorem 8.17.2 (Kučera [218]). *Every $(n+1)$-random set computes an n-FPF function.*

Proof. We begin with the case $n = 1$, proving that each 2-random set computes a 1-FPF function. We then indicate how to modify that proof to obtain the general case.

Let $\{U_n\}_{n\in\omega}$ be Kučera's universal Martin-Löf test, as constructed in Section 8.5. We need only the first element of this test, whose definition we now recall. Let $S_0, S_1, \ldots$ be an effective list of the prefix-free c.e. subsets of $2^{<\omega}$. For each $e > 0$, enumerate all elements of $S_{\Phi_e(e)}$ (where we take $S_{\Phi_e(e)}$ to be empty if $\Phi_e(e)\uparrow$) into a set R as long as $\sum_{\sigma \in S_{\Phi_e(e),s}} 2^{-|\sigma|} < 2^{-e}$. (That is, if this sum ever gets to 2^{-e}, stop enumerating the elements of $S_{\Phi_e(e)}$ into R before it does.) Let $U_0 = [\![R]\!]$.

This construction relativizes to a given set X in the obvious way, yielding a class U_0^X. Let D^X be the complement of U_0^X. Note that D^X has positive measure.

Now let A be 2-random. Since we are interested in A only up to degree, we may assume by Theorem 6.10.2 that $A \in D^{\emptyset'}$. Let h be a computable function such that $W_{h(e)}^{\emptyset'} = \{i : W_e^{[i]} \text{ is finite}\}$. (Recall that $W_e^{[i]}$ is the ith column of W_e.) For each e and j, define the $\Sigma_1^{0,\emptyset'}$ class V_j^e as follows. If $|W_{h(e)}^{\emptyset'}| < j+1$ then let $V_j^e = \emptyset$. Otherwise, let F_j be the smallest $j+1$ many elements of $W_{h(e)}^{\emptyset'}$ and let $V_j^e = \bigcup\{[\![\tau]\!] : \forall i \in F_j\,(\tau(i) = 1)\}$. The V_j^e are uniformly $\Sigma_1^{0,\emptyset'}$ classes, and $\mu(V_j^e) < 2^{-j}$. Using the recursion theorem with parameters, let g be a computable function such that $S_{\Phi_{g(e)}(g(e))} = V_{g(e)}^e$ for all e. We may assume that $g(e) > 0$ for all e.

By the construction of $U_0^{\emptyset'}$, we have $V_{g(e)}^e \cap D^{\emptyset'} = \emptyset$ for all e. Let σ_e be the shortest initial segment of A containing $g(e)+1$ many elements. Then, for each e, either $|W_{h(e)}^{\emptyset'}| < g(e)+1$ or there is an $i < |\sigma_e|$ such that $W_{h(e)}^{\emptyset'}(i) \neq \sigma_e(i)$, since otherwise we would have $[\![\sigma_e]\!] \subseteq V_{g(e)}^e$, contradicting our assumption that $A \in D^{\emptyset'}$.

We are ready to define our 1-FPF function f. Let f be an A-computable function such that

$$W_{f(e)} = \{\langle i, n\rangle : i < |\sigma_e| \wedge \sigma_e(i) = 0 \wedge n \in \mathbb{N}\}.$$

To show that f is 1-FPF, fix e. If $|W^{\emptyset'}_{h(e)}| < g(e)+1$ then almost every column of W_e is infinite. Since only finitely many columns of $W_{f(e)}$ are nonempty, in this case $W_{f(e)} \neq^* W_e$. Otherwise, there is an $i < |\sigma_e|$ such that $W^{\emptyset'}_{h(e)}(i) \neq \sigma_e(i)$. If $i \in W^{\emptyset'}_{h(e)}$ then $W_e^{[i]}$ is finite but $W^{[i]}_{f(e)}$ is infinite; otherwise, $W_e^{[i]}$ is infinite but $W^{[i]}_{f(e)}$ is empty. In either case, $W_{f(e)} \neq^* W_e$.

We now turn to the $n \geqslant 2$ case. For a set B, let $B^{[\neq i]} = \bigoplus_{i \neq j} B^{[j]}$. As before, we assume that A is an $(n+1)$-random set in $D^{\emptyset^{(n)}}$. It is straightforward to adapt and relativize the proof of the Friedberg-Muchnik Theorem to build a set B that is c.e. relative to $\emptyset^{(n-2)}$, low relative to $\emptyset^{(n-2)}$, and such that for all i, we have $\emptyset^{(n-2)} \leqslant_T B^{[i]}$ and $B^{[i]} \mid_T B^{[\neq i]}$. Since B is low relative to $\emptyset^{(n-2)}$, given e, i, and k, we can determine whether $W_e^{(n-2)} = \Phi_k^{B^{[\neq i]}}$ using $\emptyset^{(n)}$ as an oracle. Thus, by analogy with the $n = 1$ case, we can let h be a computable function such that

$$W^{\emptyset^{(n)}}_{h(e)} = \{i : W_e^{(n-2)} \leqslant_T B^{[\neq i]}\}.$$

Define V_i^e, g, and σ_e as before, but with $W^{\emptyset^{(n)}}_{h(e)}$ in place of $W^{\emptyset'}_{h(e)}$. As before, for each e, either $|W^{\emptyset^{(n)}}_{h(e)}| < g(e)+1$ or there must be an $i < |\sigma_e|$ such that $W^{\emptyset^{(n)}}_{h(e)}(i) \neq \sigma_e(i)$.

Let $\widehat{f}$ be an A-computable function such that

$$W^{\emptyset^{(n-2)}}_{\widehat{f}(e)} = \{\langle i, n\rangle \in B : i < |\sigma_e| \wedge \sigma_e(i) = 0 \wedge n \in \mathbb{N}\}.$$

We may assume that $A(0) = 0$, so that $W^{\emptyset^{(n-2)}}_{\widehat{f}(e)} \geqslant_T B^{[0]} \geqslant_T \emptyset^{(n-2)}$. We claim that $W_e^{(n-2)} \not\equiv_T W^{\emptyset^{(n-2)}}_{\widehat{f}(e)}$ for all e.

Fix e. If $|W^{\emptyset^{(n-2)}}_{h(e)}| < g(e)+1$ then there is a $i \geqslant |\sigma_e|$ such that $i \notin W^{\emptyset^{(n)}}_{h(e)}$, which means that $W_e^{(n-2)} \nleqslant_T B^{[\neq i]}$. But $W^{\emptyset^{(n-2)}}_{\widehat{f}(e)} \leqslant_T B^{[\neq i]}$, so in this case, $W_e^{(n-2)} \not\equiv_T W^{\emptyset^{(n-2)}}_{\widehat{f}(e)}$.

Otherwise, there is a $i < |\sigma_e|$ such that $W^{\emptyset^{(n)}}_{h(e)}(i) \neq \sigma_e(i)$. If $i \in W^{\emptyset^{(n)}}_{h(e)}$ then $W_e^{(n-2)} \leqslant_T B^{[\neq i]}$ but the ith column of $W^{\emptyset^{(n-2)}}_{\widehat{f}(e)}$ is $B^{[i]}$. Since $B^{[i]} \nleqslant_T B^{[\neq i]}$, we have $W_e^{(n-2)} \not\equiv_T W^{\emptyset^{(n-2)}}_{\widehat{f}(e)}$.

Finally, if $i \notin W^{\emptyset^{(n)}}_{h(e)}$ then $W_e^{(n-2)} \nleqslant_T B^{[\neq i]}$ but the ith column of $W^{\emptyset^{(n-2)}}_{\widehat{f}(e)}$ is empty and the other columns of $W^{\emptyset^{(n-2)}}_{\widehat{f}(e)}$ are uniformly computable from $B^{[\neq i]}$. Thus $W^{\emptyset^{(n-2)}}_{\widehat{f}(e)} \leqslant_T B^{[\neq i]}$, and hence in this case also $W_e^{(n-2)} \not\equiv_T W^{\emptyset^{(n-2)}}_{\widehat{f}(e)}$.

Thus $W_e^{(n-2)} \not\equiv_T W_{\widehat{f}(e)}^{\emptyset^{(n-2)}}$ for all e. Since $W_{\widehat{f}(e)}^{\emptyset^{(n-2)}}$ is CEA($\emptyset^{(n-2)}$) for each e, and $\widehat{f}$ is A-computable, the fact that the proof of the Sacks Jump Inversion Theorem 2.16.5 is uniform implies that there is an A-computable function f such that for all e,

$$W_{f(e)}^{(n-2)} \equiv_T W_{\widehat{f}(e)}^{\emptyset^{(n-2)}}.$$

Therefore $W_{f(e)}^{(n-2)} \not\equiv_T W_e^{(n-2)}$ for all e, as required. □

8.18 Jump inversion

In this section, we show that the jump operator can be used to study the distribution of 1-random (Δ_2^0) degrees. We do this by proving a basis theorem for Π_1^0 classes of positive measure. It is of course not the case that a nontrivial Π_1^0 class must have members with all possible jumps, since we could be dealing with a countable Π_1^0 class, which might even have only one noncomputable member. However, as we recall from Theorem 2.19.18, if P is a nonempty Π_1^0 class with no computable members and $X \geqslant_T \emptyset'$, then there is an $A \in P$ such that $A' \equiv_T A \oplus \emptyset' \equiv_T X$.

Applying this result to a Π_1^0 class of 1-random sets, we have the following.

Corollary 8.18.1. *If $X \geqslant_T \emptyset'$ then there is a 1-random A such that $A' \equiv_T A \oplus \emptyset' \equiv_T X$.*

The situation for Δ_2^0 1-randoms is less clear, because there is no extension of Theorem 2.19.18 where we additionally have $A \leqslant_T \emptyset'$. In fact, Cenzer [55] observed that there are Π_1^0 classes with no computable members[11] such that every member is GL_1, and hence every Δ_2^0 member is low.

To prove jump inversion for Δ_2^0 1-randoms, we replace Theorem 2.19.18 with a similar basis theorem for *fat* Π_1^0 classes.

Theorem 8.18.2 (Kučera [217], Downey and Miller [126][12]). *Let P be a Π_1^0 class of positive measure, and let $X \geqslant_T \emptyset'$ be Σ_2^0. Then there is a Δ_2^0 set $A \in P$ such that $A' \equiv_T X$.*

Corollary 8.18.3 (Kučera [217], Downey and Miller [126]). *For every Σ_2^0 set $X \geqslant_T \emptyset'$, there is a 1-random Δ_2^0 set A such that $A' \equiv_T X$.*

The proof of Theorem 8.18.2 can be viewed as a finite injury construction relative to $\emptyset'$. In that sense, it is similar to Sacks' construction in [342] of a

[11] Specifically, what is known as a *thin* perfect class.

[12] In [217], Kučera constructed a high incomplete 1-random set, and in Remark 8 stated that similar methods allow for a proof of Theorem 8.18.2 (additionally avoiding upper cones above a given C such that $\emptyset <_T C <_T \emptyset'$). He also noted that this result gives 1-random sets at all levels of the high/low hierarchy.

minimal degree below $\mathbf{0}'$. We require two additional ideas. The first is the method of forcing with Π^0_1 classes, which was introduced by Jockusch and Soare [195] to prove the low basis theorem. This method is used to ensure that $A' \leqslant_T X$. The second is Kučera's Lemma 8.10.1, which allows us to computably bound the positions of branchings as in Kučera coding.

Even though randomness is not explicit in the statement of Kučera's Lemma, it is worth noting its implicit presence. Lemma 8.10.1 is proved using concepts from randomness and its main application has been to the study of the Turing degrees of 1-random sets.

Proof of Theorem 8.18.2. Let P be a Π^0_1 class with positive measure and let $X \geqslant_T \emptyset'$ be a Σ^0_2 set. Let Q and c be as in Lemma 8.10.1. That is, $Q \subseteq P$ is a Π^0_1 class, and for an effective listing $P_0, P_1, \ldots$ of Π^0_1 classes, if $Q \cap P_e \neq \emptyset$, then $\mu(Q \cap P_e) \geqslant 2^{-(e+c)}$. Note that $\mu(Q) > 0$ since $P_e = Q$ for some e. We will construct a Δ^0_2 set $A \in Q$ such that $A' \equiv_T X$.

Before describing the construction, we give a few preliminary definitions. For each $\sigma \in 2^{<\omega}$, define a Π^0_1 class

$$F_\sigma = \{B \in Q : \forall e < |\sigma| \, (\sigma(e) = 0 \Rightarrow \Phi^B_e(e)\uparrow)\}.$$

At each stage s of the construction, we will define a string $\sigma_s \in 2^s$, which is intended to approximate $A' \upharpoonright s$. We will tentatively restrict A to the class F_{σ_s} in order to force its jump. It is important to note that this restriction may be injured at a later stage by the enumeration of an $e < s$ into X.

Next we define a computable function f that grows fast enough to ensure that it eventually bounds the branchings between elements of F_σ for every σ. We will use f to code elements of X into A (or more precisely, into A'). Let $h : 2^{<\omega} \times 2^{<\omega} \to \omega$ be a computable function such that $P_{h(\tau,\sigma)} = [\![\tau]\!] \cap F_\sigma$ for all τ and σ. Let $f(0) = 0$ and let

$$f(s+1) = 1 + \max\{h(\tau, \sigma) + c : \tau \in 2^{f(s)} \wedge \sigma \in 2^s\}.$$

Now take $\tau \in 2^{f(t)}$ and $\sigma \in 2^s$, for $t \geqslant s$, such that $[\![\tau]\!] \cap F_\sigma \neq \emptyset$. We claim that τ has distinct finite extensions $\rho_0, \rho_1 \in 2^{f(t+1)}$ that extend to elements of F_σ. Suppose not, and let $\widehat{\sigma} = \sigma 1^{t-s}$. Then $F_{\widehat{\sigma}} = F_\sigma$, so $\mu(Q \cap P_{h(\tau,\widehat{\sigma})}) = \mu([\![\tau]\!] \cap F_\sigma) \leqslant 2^{-f(t+1)} < 2^{-(h(\tau,\widehat{\sigma})+c)}$, which contradicts the choice of Q.

Kučera used the fact that we can bound branchings in a Π^0_1 class of positive measure to code information into members of such a class. The most basic form of Kučera coding constructs a sequence by extensions, choosing the leftmost or rightmost permissible extension to encode the next bit. For our construction, we distinguish only between the rightmost extension and any other permissible extension. Recall that $\leqslant_L$ is the length-lexicographic ordering of $2^{<\omega}$. For a Π^0_1 class R and $\tau \in 2^{f(s+1)}$ for some s, let $H_f(R; \tau)$ hold iff

$$\forall \rho \in 2^{f(s+1)} \left((\rho \upharpoonright f(s) = \tau \upharpoonright f(s) \wedge \tau <_L \rho) \Rightarrow R \cap [\![\rho]\!] = \emptyset \right).$$

By compactness, $R \cap [\![\rho]\!] = \emptyset$ iff there is an s such that $R[s] \cap [\![\rho]\!] = \emptyset$, so $H_f(R;x)$ is a Σ^0_1 condition, and if $R \cap [\![\tau]\!] \neq \emptyset$, then $H_f(R;\tau)$ is true iff τ is the rightmost extension of $\tau \restriction f(s)$ of length $f(s+1)$ that can be extended to an element of R.

It will be useful to understand the interaction between f and H_f. Assume that we have $\tau \in 2^{f(t)}$ for some $t \geqslant s$, and $\sigma \in 2^s$ such that $[\![\tau]\!] \cap F_\sigma \neq \emptyset$. Let $\widehat{\tau} \in 2^{f(t+1)}$ be the leftmost extension of τ such that $[\![\widehat{\tau}]\!] \cap F_\sigma \neq \emptyset$. By the definition of f, there are multiple extensions to choose from, so $H_f(F_\sigma, \widehat{\tau})$ is false. In fact, if $\rho \preccurlyeq \sigma$, then $F_\sigma \subseteq F_\rho$, so $H_f(F_\rho, \widehat{\tau})$ is also false.

We are now ready to describe the construction. Let $\{X_s\}_{s\in\omega}$ be a $\emptyset'$-computable enumeration of the Σ^0_2 set X. We may assume that $X_0 = \emptyset$ and $|X_{s+1} \setminus X_s| = 1$ for all s. We construct A by initial segments using a $\emptyset'$ oracle. At each stage s, we find a string $\tau_s \in 2^{f(t)}$ for some $t \geqslant s$. We will let $A = \bigcup_s \tau_s$. Each stage also produces a string $\sigma_s \in 2^s$, which is an approximation to A', although not necessarily an initial segment of it. For each s, we require that the following conditions hold.

1. $[\![\tau_s]\!] \cap F_{\sigma_s} \neq \emptyset$.
2. If $\rho = \sigma_s \restriction e+1$ for $e < s$ and $B \in [\![\tau_s]\!] \cap F_\rho$, then $B'(e) = \rho(e)$.

Construction.

Stage 0. Let τ_0 and σ_0 both be the empty string. Then $[\![\tau_0]\!] \cap F_{\sigma_0} = Q \neq \emptyset$, so (1) is satisfied. Notice that (2) is vacuous.

Stage $s+1$. Assume that we have already constructed $\tau_s \in 2^{f(t)}$ for some $t \geqslant s$ and $\sigma_s \in 2^s$ satisfying (1) and (2). Let e be the unique element of $X_{s+1} \setminus X_s$.

Case 1. If $e > s$, then let $\tau_{s+1} \in 2^{f(t+1)}$ be the leftmost extension of τ_s such that $[\![\tau_{s+1}]\!] \cap F_{\sigma_s} \neq \emptyset$. Note that $\emptyset'$ can determine whether $[\![\rho]\!] \cap F_{\sigma_s} = \emptyset$, for each $\rho \in 2^{<\omega}$, so $\emptyset'$ can find τ_{s+1}. If $[\![\tau_{s+1}]\!] \cap F_{\sigma_s 0} \neq \emptyset$, then let $\sigma_{s+1} = \sigma_s 0$. Otherwise, let $\sigma_{s+1} = \sigma_s 1$. Again, this choice can be made using the $\emptyset'$ oracle. Note that (1) and (2) are satisfied by our choices of τ_{s+1} and σ_{s+1}.

Case 2. If $e \leqslant s$, then let $\rho_e = \sigma_s \restriction e$. Let m be least such that $f(\langle e,m\rangle) \geqslant |\tau_s|$. First let $\widehat{\tau}_s \in 2^{f(\langle e,m\rangle)}$ be the leftmost extension of τ_s such that $[\![\widehat{\tau}_s]\!] \cap F_{\rho_e} \neq \emptyset$. Next let $\tau_{s+1} \in 2^{f(\langle e,m\rangle+1)}$ be the rightmost extension of $\widehat{\tau}_s$ such that $[\![\tau_{s+1}]\!] \cap F_{\rho_e} \neq \emptyset$. Now inductively define ρ_k for each $e < k \leqslant s+1$. If we have already defined ρ_k, then determine whether $[\![\tau_{s+1}]\!] \cap F_{\rho_k 0} \neq \emptyset$. If so, let $\rho_{k+1} = \rho_k 0$. Otherwise, let $\rho_{k+1} = \rho_k 1$. Finally, let $\sigma_{s+1} = \rho_{s+1}$. Again, the construction is computable relative to $\emptyset'$, and we have ensured that (1) and (2) continue to hold.

End of Construction.

We turn to the verification. The construction is $\emptyset'$-computable, so A is Δ^0_2. Furthermore, (1) tells us that $[\![\tau_s]\!] \cap F_{\sigma_s} \neq \emptyset$, for each s. Because $F_{\sigma_s} \subseteq Q \subseteq P$, this fact implies that every τ_s can be extended to an element of P. But P is closed, so $A = \bigcup_s \tau_s \in P$. All that remains to verify is that $A' \equiv_T X$.

First we prove that $A' \leqslant_T X$. To determine whether $e \in A'$, use X and $\emptyset'$ to find a stage $s > e$ such that $X_s \upharpoonright e+1 = X \upharpoonright e+1$. Let $\rho = \sigma_s \upharpoonright e+1$. We claim that $\sigma_t \upharpoonright e+1 = \rho$ for all $t \geqslant s$, because the only way that $\sigma_s \upharpoonright e+1$ can be injured during the construction is in Case 2, when an element less than or equal to e is enumerated into X, which will never happen after stage s. Therefore, for all $t \geqslant s$, we have $\rho \preccurlyeq \sigma_t$ and hence $F_{\sigma_t} \subseteq F_\rho$. So $[\![\tau_t]\!] \cap F_\rho \neq \emptyset$ for all $t \geqslant s$, which implies that $A \in F_\rho$. By (2), we have $A'(e) = \rho(e)$. Thus we can uniformly decide whether $e \in A'$ using only $X \oplus \emptyset' \equiv_T X$. Therefore, $A' \leqslant_T X$.

Now we must show that $X \leqslant_T A'$. Assume by induction that we have determined $X \upharpoonright e$ for some e. Find the least $s \geqslant e$ such that $X_s \upharpoonright e = X \upharpoonright e$. Let $\rho = \sigma_s \upharpoonright e$ and note, as above, that $\rho \preccurlyeq \sigma_t$ for all $t \geqslant s$. Find the least m such that $f(\langle e, m\rangle) \geqslant |\tau_s|$. Of course, both s and m can be found by $\emptyset'$. We claim that $e \in X$ iff either $e \in X_s$ or there is an $n \geqslant m$ such that $H_f(F_\rho; A \upharpoonright f(\langle e, n\rangle + 1))$. If $e \in X \setminus X_s$, then Case 2 ensures that $H_f(F_\rho; A \upharpoonright f(\langle e, n\rangle + 1))$ holds for some $n \geqslant m$. So, assume that $e \notin X$. Then for every $n \geqslant m$, the construction chooses the leftmost extension of $A \upharpoonright f(\langle e, n\rangle)$ that is extendible in the appropriate Π^0_1 class. This class is of the form $F_{\widehat{\rho}}$, where $\widehat{\rho} \preccurlyeq \sigma_t$ for some $t \geqslant s$ and $|\widehat{\rho}| \geqslant e$. Then $\rho \preccurlyeq \widehat{\rho}$, so $F_{\widehat{\rho}} \subseteq F_\rho$. The definition of f ensures that there are distinct extensions of $A \upharpoonright f(\langle e, n\rangle)$ of length $f(\langle e, n\rangle + 1))$ that can be extended to elements of $F_{\widehat{\rho}}$. Therefore, the leftmost choice consistent with $F_{\widehat{\rho}}$ must be left of the rightmost choice consistent with F_ρ. Hence $H_f(F_\rho; A \upharpoonright f(\langle e, n\rangle + 1))$ is false. Finally, note that A' can decide whether there is an $n \geqslant m$ such that $H_f(F_\rho; A \upharpoonright f(\langle e, n\rangle + 1))$, because H_f is Σ^0_1. Therefore A' can determine whether $e \in X$, proving that $X \leqslant_T A'$. $\square$

8.19 Pseudo-jump inversion

In the same way that the construction of a low c.e. set was generalized by Jockusch and Shore [193, 194] (as we have seen in Section 2.12.2), Nies and Kučera independently realized that Theorem 8.18.2 can be extended to a similar pseudo-jump theorem. Recall that an operator of the form $V^Y = Y \oplus W^Y$ for a c.e. set W with $Y <_T V^Y$ for all oracles Y is called a nontrivial pseudo-jump operator. The following is a randomness version of Theorem 2.12.3.

Theorem 8.19.1 (Nies [306], Kučera [unpublished]). *For any nontrivial pseudo-jump operator V there is a 1-random set B with $V^B \equiv_{wtt} \emptyset'$. Indeed, if P is any Π^0_1 class of positive measure, then there is an $A \in P$ such that $V^A \equiv_{wtt} \emptyset'$.*

Nies' proof in [306] is a full approximation argument, and hence an effective construction, but we will use Kučera's oracle construction, as it is simpler. We thank George Barmpalias for telling us of this proof.

Proof of Theorem 8.19.1. The proof resembles that of the Friedberg Completeness Criterion, Theorem 2.16.1, combined with Kučera-Gács coding. Let P be a Π^0_1 class of positive measure, and let Q and c be as in Lemma 8.10.1. That is, $Q \subseteq P$ is a Π^0_1 class, and for an effective listing $P_0, P_1, \ldots$ of Π^0_1 classes, if $Q \cap P_e \neq \emptyset$, then $\mu(Q \cap P_e) \geqslant 2^{-(e+c)}$. Let $k > -\log \mu(Q)$.

We build an $A \in Q$ with $V^A \equiv_{\text{wtt}} \emptyset'$. As in the proof of the Friedberg Completeness Criterion, at even stages we force the (pseudo-)jump and at odd ones we code.

At stage 0 we consider the Π^0_1 class $M_0 = \{Y : 0 \notin V^Y\}$. Let e be such that $P_e = M_0$. If $M_0 \cap Q = \emptyset$, let $Q_0 = Q$. Otherwise, let $Q_0 = Q \cap M_0$. In either case, let $A_0 = \lambda$.

At stage 1, we want to code whether $0 \in \emptyset'$. Let e be such that $P_e = Q_0$ and let $m_0 = 2^{e+c} + 1$. Then $\mu(Q_0) > 2^{-m_0}$, so there is a split in Q_0 by level m_0. That is, there are at least two strings of length m_0 that can be extended to elements of Q_0. As with Kučera-Gács coding, if $0 \in \emptyset'$ then let A_1 be the rightmost such string, and otherwise let A_1 be the leftmost such string. Let $Q_1 = Q_0 \cap [\![A_1]\!]$.

The construction now works inductively in the obvious way. At stage $2n$ we look at $M_n = \{Y : n \notin V^Y\}$. If $M_n \cap Q_{n-1} = \emptyset$, we let $Q_n = Q_{n-1}$. Otherwise, we let $Q_n = Q_{n-1} \cap M_0$. In either case we let $A_{2n} = A_{2n-1}$. At stage $2n+1$, we let e be such that $P_e = Q_{2n}$ and let $m_n = 2^{e+c} + 1$. As before, there are at least two strings of length m_n that can be extended to elements of Q_n. If $0 \in \emptyset'$, we let A_{2n+1} be the rightmost such string, and otherwise we let A_{2n+1} be the leftmost such string. Finally, we let $Q_{2n+1} = Q_{2n} \cap [\![A_{2n+1}]\!]$.

It is easy to see that the questions we have to ask of $\emptyset'$ at each stage can be computably bounded in advance, so this construction produces an A with $V^A \equiv_{\text{wtt}} \emptyset'$. □

Other extensions along similar lines can be found in Cenzer, LaForte, and Wu [56]. For instance, using somewhat similar techniques, they showed the following.

Theorem 8.19.2 (Cenzer, LaForte, and Wu [56]). *Let V be a nontrivial pseudo-jump operator, let P be a Π^0_1 class of positive measure, and let $C \geqslant_T \emptyset'$. Then there is an $A \in P$ such that $V^A \equiv_T C$.*

It is interesting to note that, in contrast to Theorem 8.19.1, there are nontrivial pseudo-jump operators V for which there is no c.e. set A with $V^A \equiv_{\text{wtt}} \emptyset'$, as was recently proved by Ng and Wu [personal communication].

8.20 Randomness and genericity

Martin-Löf's original definition of 1-randomness arises from the classical interpretation of randomness as a notion of being *typical in terms of measure*. We can also look at sets that are typical in terms of category. These are the (Cohen) generic sets, which are members of every (suitably definable) dense open class. In the effective setting, we have the n-generic and weakly n-generic sets introduced in Section 2.24.

In this section, we look at how these two notions of being typical relate to each other. The answer, perhaps surprisingly, is that genericity and randomness are more or less orthogonal, especially when we look at higher levels of the arithmetic hierarchy of classes.

8.20.1 Similarities between randomness and genericity

Before concentrating on the differences between randomness and genericity, we note that some results we have discussed above are special cases of general results on forcing, and hence have analogs for genericity. Van Lambalgen's Theorem is an example.

Theorem 8.20.1 (Yu [411]). *The following are equivalent for any $n \geqslant 1$.*

(i) *$A \oplus B$ is n-generic.*

(ii) *A is n-generic and B is n-generic relative to A.*

(iii) *B is n-generic and A is n-generic relative to B.*

(iv) *A and B are relatively n-generic (i.e., A is n-generic relative to B and B is n-generic relative to A).*

Proof. It is enough to show that (i) and (ii) are equivalent, since the equivalence of (i) and (iii) then follows by a symmetric argument, while (iv) is just the conjunction of (ii) and (iii). We write $\sigma \oplus \tau$ for the string ρ of length $2\min(|\sigma|, |\tau|)$ such that $\rho(2n) = \sigma(n)$ and $\rho(2n+1) = \tau(n)$ for all $n \leqslant \min(|\sigma|, |\tau|)$.

Suppose that (ii) holds. Let $S \subseteq 2^{<\omega}$ be Σ^0_n and let $\widehat{S} = \{\tau : \exists \sigma \prec A\,(\sigma \oplus \tau \in S)\}$. Then $\widehat{S}$ is Σ^A_n. If there is a $\tau \prec B$ with $\tau \in \widehat{S}$ then there is a σ such that $\sigma \oplus \tau \prec A \oplus B$ and $\sigma \oplus \tau \in S$. Otherwise, since B is n-generic relative to A, there is a $\tau \prec B$ with no extension in $\widehat{S}$. Let $\sigma = A \upharpoonright |\tau|$ and let $T = \{\mu : \exists \nu\,(\sigma \oplus \tau \preccurlyeq \mu \oplus \nu \in S)\}$. Then T is Σ^0_n and no member of T is an initial segment of A, since otherwise we would have an extension of τ in $\widehat{S}$. Since A is n-generic, there is a $\sigma' \prec A$ with no extension in T. Then $(A \oplus B) \upharpoonright 2|\sigma'|$ has no extension in S. Thus $A \oplus B$ is n-generic.

Now suppose that (i) holds. First suppose that A is not n-generic. Let $T \subseteq 2^{<\omega}$ be a Σ^0_n set such that no member of T is an initial segment of A and every initial segment of A has an extension in T. Let $\widehat{T} = \{\sigma \oplus \tau : \sigma \in$

$T \wedge \tau \in 2^{<\omega}\}$. Then $\widehat{T}$ is Σ_n^0, no member of $\widehat{T}$ is an initial segment of $A \oplus B$, and every initial segment of $A \oplus B$ has an extension in $\widehat{T}$, contradicting the assumption that $A \oplus B$ is n-generic. Thus A is n-generic.

Now suppose that B is not n-generic relative to A. Let S be a Σ_n^A set such that no member of S is an initial segment of B and every initial segment of B has an extension in S. There is a Σ_n^0 relation R with $S = \{\tau : \exists n\, R(A \upharpoonright n, \tau)\}$. Let $\widehat{S} = \{\sigma \oplus \tau 0^{(|\sigma|-|\tau|)} : |\tau| \leqslant |\sigma| \wedge R(\sigma, \tau)\}$. Then $\widehat{S}$ is Σ_n^0, and for all $\sigma \oplus \tau \prec A \oplus B$, we have $\sigma \oplus \tau \notin \widehat{S}$. However, for all $\sigma \oplus \tau \prec A \oplus B$, there exists a $\sigma' \oplus \tau' \succ \sigma \oplus \tau$ with $\sigma' \oplus \tau' \in \widehat{S}$, contradicting the assumption that $A \oplus B$ is n-generic. □

Another example of a theorem about randomness that has an analog for genericity is Theorem 8.5.3.

Theorem 8.20.2 (Csima, Downey, Greenberg, Hirschfeldt, and Miller [82]). *Let B be 1-generic relative to X and let $A \leqslant_T B$ be 2-generic. Then A is 1-generic relative to X.*

Proof. Let Φ be a reduction such that $\Phi^B = A$. Let $W \subseteq 2^{<\omega}$ be c.e. in X. Suppose that no initial segment of A is in W. Let $V = \{\sigma \in 2^{<\omega} : \exists \tau \preccurlyeq \Phi^\sigma\, (\tau \in W)\}$. Then V is c.e. in X, and no initial segment of B is in V. Thus there is some $\tau \prec B$ with no extension in V. Let $U = \{\mu \in 2^{<\omega} : \neg\exists \sigma \succcurlyeq \tau\, (\mu \prec \Phi^\sigma)\}$. Then U is co-c.e. and no initial segment of A is in U, so there is some $\mu \prec A$ with no extension in U. If $\nu \succcurlyeq \mu$ then there is a $\sigma \succcurlyeq \tau$ such that $\nu \prec \Phi^\sigma$, so if $\nu \in W$ then $\sigma \in V$, contradicting the choice of τ. Thus μ is an initial segment of A with no extension in W. □

Corollary 8.20.3 (Csima, Downey, Greenberg, Hirschfeldt, and Miller [82]). *If B is n-generic and $A \leqslant_T B$ is 2-generic, then A is n-generic.*

Proof. Let $X = \emptyset^{(n-1)}$ in Theorem 8.20.2. □

It is natural to ask whether the full analog of Theorem 8.5.3 holds for genericity, that is, whether a 1-generic set below an n-generic set is automatically n-generic. The following result, whose proof can be found in [82], gives a negative answer to this question.

Theorem 8.20.4 (Csima, Downey, Greenberg, Hirschfeldt, and Miller [82]). *Every 1-generic set computes a 1-generic set that is not weakly 2-generic.*

8.20.2 n-genericity versus n-randomness

We now discuss the interplay between n-genericity and n-randomness. In general, genericity and randomness are antithetical. We already saw in Proposition 8.11.9 that 1-genericity is enough to ensure that a set is not even Schnorr random. For 1-randomness, we have the following stronger result. (As we have seen in Theorem 8.11.7, for weak 1-randomness, the situation is quite different.)

Theorem 8.20.5 (Demuth and Kučera [96]). *If A is 1-generic and $B \leqslant_T A$ then B is not 1-random.*

Proof. By Theorem 2.24.5, the degree of B is not DNC, and hence by Theorem 8.8.1, B is not 1-random. □

Since $\Omega \equiv_T \emptyset'$ and there are Δ_2^0 1-generics, this theorem works only in one direction.

Kurtz [228] showed that the upward closure of the weakly 2-generic degrees has measure 0. (We will see in Theorem 8.21.3 that this result cannot be extended to 1-genericity.) To prove this result, we need the following lemma, whose proof is fairly typical (no pun intended) of measure-theoretic arguments in computability theory.

Lemma 8.20.6 (Kurtz [228]). *There is an $f \leqslant_T \emptyset'$ such that for almost every A, the function f dominates every A-computable function.*

Proof. It is enough to build uniformly $\emptyset'$-computable functions $f_{n,k}$ such that for each n and k, for measure $1 - 2^{-(n+k+1)}$ many sets A, if Φ_k^A is total then $f_{n,k}$ majorizes Φ_k^A. We can then let $f(m) = \max_{k,n \leqslant m} f_{k,n}(m)$ and it is easy to check that f is as required, since it dominates every $f_{n,k}$.

We define $f_{n,k}(m)$ as follows. Let $S = \{A : \Phi_k^A(m)\downarrow\}$. It is easy to see that $\mu(S)$ is a left-c.e. real, so using $\emptyset'$, we can find a rational q such that $q < \mu(S)$ and $\mu(S) - q \leqslant 2^{-(n+k+m+2)}$. We can then find a prefix-free finite set F of strings such that $\sigma \in F \Rightarrow \Phi_k^\sigma(m)\downarrow$ and $\mu([\![F]\!]) > q$. Let $f_{n,k}(m) = \max\{\Phi_k^\sigma(m) : \sigma \in F\}$.

This definition ensures that, for each m, the class of all A such that $\Phi_k^A(m)\downarrow > f_{n,k}(m)$ has measure less than $2^{-(n+k+m+2)}$. Thus the class of all A such that Φ_k^A is total but not dominated by $f_{n,k}$ is less than $\sum_m 2^{-(n+k+m+2)} = 2^{-(n+k+1)}$. □

We will examine this idea of "almost everywhere domination" further in Section 10.6.

Theorem 8.20.7 (Kurtz [228]). *The upward closure of the weakly 2-generic degrees has measure 0.*

Proof. Let f be as in Lemma 8.20.6. Recall that the principal function p_G of an infinite set $G = \{a_0 < a_1 < \cdots\}$ is defined by $p_G(n) = a_n$, and that for a string σ, we let $p_\sigma(k)$ be the position of the kth 1 in σ, or undefined if there is no such position. Let S_n be the set of strings such that for at least n many k, we have $p_\sigma(k) > f(k)$. Each S_n is a Δ_2^0 dense set of strings, so if G is weakly 2-generic, then it meets each S_n, which implies that p_G is not dominated by f. So if a set computes a weakly 2-generic set, then it must be in the class of measure 0 of sets computing functions not dominated by f. □

8.21 Properties of almost all degrees

Randomness is, of course, deeply connected with "almost everywhere" behavior, since any property that holds of almost all sets holds of all sufficiently random sets. In this section, we prove several results about computability theoretic properties that hold of almost all degrees. We begin with Martin's Theorem 8.21.1 that almost all degrees are hyperimmune. We then proceed to three theorems due to Kurtz [228], with related proofs of increasing complexity: Theorem 8.21.3 that almost every degree bounds a 1-generic degree, Theorem 8.21.8 that almost every degree is CEA, and Theorem 8.21.16 that for almost every degree **a**, the 1-generic degrees are downwards dense below **a**. We will also comment on the levels of effective randomness needed to ensure that a particular set has each of these properties.

Of course, Theorem 8.21.16 implies Theorem 8.21.3 (as does Theorem 8.21.8, as we will see in Theorem 8.21.15), which in turn implies Theorem 8.21.1, since every 1-generic degree is hyperimmune, but presenting the simpler proofs of Theorems 8.21.1 and 8.21.3 will help in explaining Kurtz' method of risking measure, which is an elaboration of the method used in the proof of Martin's Theorem. (Similar ideas had even earlier been used by Paris [314], in proving Corollary 8.21.23 below.)

8.21.1 Hyperimmunity

Theorem 8.21.1 (Martin [unpublished]). *Almost every degree is hyperimmune.*

Proof. By Kolmogorov's 0-1 Law, Theorem 1.2.4, it suffices to prove that there are positive measure many sets of hyperimmune degree. To do so, we construct a functional Ξ so that for positive measure many A, we have that Ξ^A is total and not majorized by any computable function. We will meet the following requirements for positive measure many sets A.

$$R_e : \Phi_e \text{ total} \Rightarrow \Xi^A \text{ is not majorized by } \Phi_e.$$

The most naive attempt to meet R_e is to choose a witness n_e and define $\Xi^A(n_e) = \Phi_e(n_e) + 1$ for all A. The problem with this approach, of course, is that $\Phi_e(n_e)$ may not be defined, and we need to make Ξ^A be total for positive measure many sets A. Thus we begin with a small class of A's, choose a witness n_e^0, and define $\Xi^A(n_e^0) = \Phi_e(n_e^0) + 1$ for all A in our class. If $\Phi_e(n_e^0)\uparrow$, then $\Xi^A(n_e^0)\uparrow$ for all such A, but R_e is automatically met, because Φ_e is not total. If $\Phi_e(n_e^0)\downarrow$, then we eventually satisfy R_e for all A in our class, and can then move to a new class of sets, using a new witness n_e^1. This process can continue until we either cover all sets or have a final class C of sets for which we have appointed a harmful witness n_e^k such that $\Phi_e(n_e^k)\uparrow$, whence $\Xi^A(n_e^k)\uparrow$ for all $A \in C$. By ensuring that the measure of

C is at most $2^{-(e+2)}$, we can restrict the total effect of harmful witnesses in the construction to a class of measure at most $\frac{1}{2}$.

The R_e work independently. Let $\nu_i^0, \dots, \nu_i^{2^i-1}$ list 2^i in lexicographic order. Then R_e begins by working only above ν_{e+2}^0, appointing a witness n_e^0 for all extensions of ν_{e+2}^0. We ask that $\Xi^A(n_e^0)\uparrow$ for all A extending ν_{e+2}^0 unless we see that $\Phi_e(n_e^0)\downarrow$, at which point we define $\Xi^A(n_e^0) = \Phi_e(n_e^0) + 1$ for all such A. We then begin working above ν_{e+2}^1, appointing a fresh large witness n_e^1 for all extensions of ν_{e+2}^1. Again we ask that $\Xi^A(n_e^1)\uparrow$ for all A extending ν_{e+2}^1 unless we see that $\Phi_e(n_e^1)\downarrow$, at which point we define $\Xi^A(n_e^1) = \Phi_e(n_e^1) + 1$ for all such A and begin working above ν_{e+2}^2, and so on. At each stage s, if no R_e has asked that $\Xi^A(s)\uparrow$ or already defined $\Xi^A(s)$, then we define $\Xi^A(s) = 0$.

Since each R_e can get stuck on at most one cone, and that cone has measure $2^{-(e+2)}$, we see that Ξ^A fails to be total on a class of measure at most $\sum_e 2^{-(e+2)} = \frac{1}{2}$, and for all other A, each R_e is met. □

Kautz [200] noted the following feature of the above proof. The class of all A such that Ξ^A is total is a Π_2^0 class of positive measure and hence, by Theorem 6.10.2, contains elements of all 2-random degrees. Furthermore, by construction, for every A in this class, Ξ^A is not majorized by any computable function, so we have the following result.

Theorem 8.21.2 (Kautz [200]). *If* **a** *is* 2*-random, then* **a** *is hyperimmune. Thus, the class of sets of hyperimmune degree includes every* 2*-random set but not every* 1*-random set.*

We have already seen, in Theorem 8.11.12, that this result cannot be extended from 2-randomness to weak 2-randomness. Note that this fact shows that Theorem 6.10.2 cannot be extended from n-randomness to weak n-randomness.

Kurtz [228] showed that there is no single total computable operator Ψ such that for almost every A, the function Ψ^A is not majorized by any computable function.

Theorem 8.21.2 can also be obtained by the following elegant argument of Nies, Stephan, and Terwijn [308]. By Theorem 6.11.7, there is a computable g and a d such that a set A is 2-random iff $C^g(A \upharpoonright n) \geqslant n - O(1)$. Fix a 2-random set A and let d be such that $C^g(A \upharpoonright n) \geqslant n - d$ for all n. Let $f(k)$ be the least n such that there are $p_0, \dots, p_{k-1} \leqslant n$ with $C^g(A \upharpoonright p_i) \geqslant p_i - d$ for $i < k$. Then f is A-computable. We claim that f is not majorized by any computable function. Assume for a contradiction that h is computable and majorizes f. Define the Π_1^0 class

$$P = \{Z : \forall k\, \exists p_1, \dots, p_k \leqslant h(k)\, (C^g(Z \upharpoonright p_i) \geqslant p_i - d)\}.$$

Then $P \neq \emptyset$, and every member of P is 2-random. Since P must have a Δ_2^0 member and there are no Δ_2^0 sets that are 2-random, we have a contradiction.

8.21.2 Bounding 1-generics

The following result follows from Theorem 8.21.8 below, but discussing its proof will help us to understand the more difficult proofs of Theorems 8.21.8 and 8.21.16. It should be contrasted with Theorem 8.20.7.

Theorem 8.21.3 (Kurtz [228]). *Almost every set computes a 1-generic set.*

Proof Sketch. By Kolmogorov's 0-1 Law, Theorem 1.2.4, it suffices to prove that there are positive measure many sets computing 1-generic sets.

Let $V_0, V_1, \dots$ be an effective enumeration of the c.e. sets of strings. We build a functional Ξ so that for positive measure many sets A, we have that Ξ^A is total and the following requirements are met.

$$R_e : \Xi^A \text{ meets or avoids } V_e.$$

It will convenient to think of Ξ as a partial computable function from strings to strings, but we write Ξ^σ instead of $\Xi(\sigma)$. Recall from Section 2.9 that the main rule we need to observe is that for $\sigma \prec \tau$, if $\Xi^\sigma \downarrow$ and $\Xi^\tau \downarrow$, then $\Xi^\sigma \preccurlyeq \Xi^\tau$. Note that it is not necessary that if $\Xi^\tau \downarrow$ then $\Xi^\sigma \downarrow$ for all $\sigma \prec \tau$.

Let us first discuss how to meet the single requirement R_0. We would like to find some $\sigma \in V_0$ and ensure that $\Xi^A \succ \sigma$ for all A, thereby meeting R_0. However, V_0 might be empty, and we cannot wait forever to define Ξ. Thus, as in the proof of Theorem 8.21.2, we set aside a portion of 2^ω of relatively small measure where we choose not to define Ξ while waiting for some σ to occur in V_0. For R_0, we divide 2^ω into two portions, say $[\![00]\!]$ and $\overline{[\![00]\!]}$. We think of $[\![00]\!]$ as taking the role of ν_0^0 in our proof of Theorem 8.21.2. While we are waiting for some string σ to occur in V_0, we pursue a strategy based on the belief that $V_0 = \emptyset$, and hence R_0 is automatically satisfied. This strategy builds the reduction Ξ within $\overline{[\![00]\!]}$.

Thus, we will never define Ξ^A for any $A \in [\![00]\!]$ unless some σ enters V_0. Should we find such a σ at a stage s, then we define $\Xi^{00} = \sigma$; that is, we ensure that $\Xi^A \succ \sigma$ for all $A \in [\![00]\!]$, hence meeting R_0 within $[\![00]\!]$. At this point, following the model of the proof of Theorem 8.21.2, we would like to switch attention to $[\![01]\!]$, trying to satisfy R_0 within that cone. The main problem not found in the proof of Theorem 8.21.2 is that we can no longer satisfy R_0 by picking a single new witness and defining the value of Ξ^A on that witness, independent of other values on which Ξ^A may already have been defined. While we were waiting for a σ to enter V_0, other strategies might well have already defined Ξ^ν for several $\nu \in 2^{\leqslant s}$ extending 01, 10, and 11. We might have such ν_0 and ν_1 with $\Xi^{\nu_i} = \delta_i$ and $\delta_0 \mid \delta_1$. To satisfy R_0 within $[\![\nu_i]\!]$, we need to seek a $\gamma_i \succcurlyeq \delta_i$ in V_0. It might be the case that, say, there is no such γ_0 in V_0 but there is such a γ_1 in V_0. Thus we need to pursue completely separate strategies above each ν_i. In particular, we cannot work only above 01, since V_0 may contain no extensions of Ξ^{01} and yet contain extensions of Ξ^{10}, say.

The solution to this problem is to pursue independent constructions above all strings of length s in $\overline{[\![00]\!]}$, each of which is basically a copy of the original construction. To organize these multiple constructions, we will color certain strings, using four basic colors: red, blue, green, and yellow. Each of these will also have a subscript denoting what requirement the color refers to, so that red_4, say, is red for R_4.[13]

In the beginning, we give the empty string λ the color blue_0, indicating that a strategy for R_0 is being carried out above it. We also give the string 00 the color red_0, indicating that we are actively working above 00. As before, we would like to find some $\sigma \in V_0$ and define $\Xi^{00} = \sigma$, thereby meeting R_0 within the cone $[\![00]\!]$. If we actually get to meet R_0 in this way within this cone, then the color of 00 changes to green_0, indicating that we have satisfied R_0 within $[\![00]\!]$.

While we are waiting for some σ to appear in V_0, we assign the color yellow_0 to the strings of length 2 not colored red_0. The idea is that if 00 becomes green_0 then we try to deal with the yellow_0 strings (via extensions). While we are acting in this way for R_0, we assign R_1 to $[\![0100]\!]$, giving 01 the color blue_1, giving 0100 the color red_1, and giving the other length 2 extensions of 01 the color yellow_1.

As before, if no σ ever appears in V_0, we satisfy R_0 everywhere. Now suppose that there is a stage s at which 00 becomes green_0 because we see some σ enter V_0 and get to define $\Xi^{00} = \sigma$. At this stage, we deal with the yellow_0 strings (namely 01, 10, and 11). As discussed above, it may well be the case that there are extensions ν of these strings for which Ξ^{ν} has already been defined, say by the action of R_1. Each such extension has length at most s, so for convenience we can work above the strings $\nu_0, \dots, \nu_p$ of length s in $\overline{[\![01]\!]}$, first defining $\Xi^{\nu_i} = \Xi^{\sigma}$ for the longest $\sigma \preccurlyeq \nu_i$ for which Ξ has been defined.

We first remove the color yellow_0 from the length 2 strings. We then give each ν_i the color blue_0 and begin a new construction at each of them that is a clone of the basic construction. That is, we make each $\nu_i 00$ a red_0 string, and give the other length 2 extensions of the ν_i the color yellow_0.

Now the goal of R_0 via each red_0 string $\nu_i 00$ is to find a string $\sigma_i \in V_0$ with $\Xi^{\nu_i} \preccurlyeq \sigma_i$, and then make $\nu_i 00$ green_0 by defining $\Xi^{\nu_i 00} = \sigma_i$.

Of course, once R_0 is satisfied within the cone $[\![00]\!]$, we can have R_1 take the role of R_0 and satisfy it within that cone precisely as we did for R_0.

More generally, R_e will have a number of blue_e nodes ν, with all its length $e+2$ extensions colored yellow_e, save one such extension ρ that is

[13]For those familiar with the terminology, we mention that these are really e-states, and the argument to follow is a kind of full approximation argument.

colored red$_e$. This string will turn green$_0$ once we find a $\gamma \in V_e$ extending Ξ^ν and define $\Xi^\rho = \gamma$.

The key point is that each time we attempt to satisfy R_e above some string ν, either the red$_e$ extension ρ of ν never becomes green$_e$, in which case R_e is satisfied within $[\![\nu]\!]$, or it does, in which case R_e is satisfied within $[\![\rho]\!]$ and the construction can continue to try to satisfy R_e within the yellow$_e$ extensions of ν. We can then argue that the R_e are satisfied on a class of positive measure.

We will give more details of this construction and its analysis in the proof of Theorem 8.21.8. □

Kautz [200] analyzed the proof of Theorem 8.21.3 and showed the following.

Theorem 8.21.4 (Kautz [200]). *Every* 2*-random set computes a* 1*-generic set.*

In Theorem 8.21.8, we will show that every 2-random set is CEA, and in Theorem 8.21.15, that every CEA set computes a 1-generic, from which Theorem 8.21.4 will follow. We will also give a direct proof at the end of Section 8.21.3.

By Theorem 8.11.12, there are weakly 2-random sets of hyperimmune-free degree, and by Theorem 2.24.12, none of these can compute a 1-generic. Thus Theorem 8.21.4 cannot be extended from 2-randomness to weak 2-randomness .

Kurtz [228] pointed out the following corollary to the above results.

Corollary 8.21.5 (Kurtz [228]). *For almost all degrees* **a**, *and indeed for any* 2*-random degree* **a**, *the degrees below* **a** *are not densely ordered.*

Proof. Let **a** bound a 1-generic degree **b**. By Theorem 2.24.9, **b** is c.e. in some strictly lower degree. The corollary now follows by applying the relativized form of Theorem 2.18.5 that every nonzero c.e. degree bounds a minimal degree. □

Although almost every degree bounds a 1-generic degree, almost no degrees are bounded by a 1-generic degree.

Theorem 8.21.6 (Kurtz [228]). *Almost no set is computable in a* 1*-generic set.*

Proof. Suppose otherwise. Then there must be a Φ and a k for which the set of A such that $\Phi^G = A$ for some 1-generic G has measure greater than 2^{-k}. We obtain a contradiction by building a c.e. $S \subseteq 2^{<\omega}$ such that $\mu(\{A : A = \Phi^B \text{ for some } B \text{ meeting } S\}) \leqslant 2^{-k}$, and if G is 1-generic, then either G meets S or Φ^G is not total.

Let $\sigma_0, \sigma_1, \ldots$ be an effective listing of $2^{<\omega}$. Let $f(i)$ be the least n such that $\sigma_n \succcurlyeq \sigma$ and Φ^{τ_n} is defined on at least $k+i+1$ many inputs, if such an n exists, and let $f(i)$ be undefined otherwise. Let $S = \{\sigma_{f(i)} : f(i)\downarrow\}$.

Clearly, S is c.e. If $f(i)\downarrow$, then the class of all A such that $A = \Phi^B$ for some $B \succ \sigma_{f(i)}$ has measure at most $2^{-(k+i+1)}$, so $\mu(\{A : A = \Phi^B \text{ for some } B \text{ meeting } S\}) \leqslant \sum_i 2^{-(k+i+1)} = 2^{-k}$. Now let G be 1-generic. If G does not meet S then there is an i such that $\sigma_i \prec G$ and no extension of σ_i is in S, which implies that $f(i)\uparrow$, and hence Φ^G can be defined on at most $k+i$ many inputs. □

There is a local characterization of the sets computable in 1-generic ones. A c.e. $S \subseteq 2^{<\omega}$ is a Σ^0_1-*cover* of a set A if for each $\sigma \prec A$ there is a $\tau \succcurlyeq \sigma$ in S. This Σ^0_1-cover is *proper* if no element of S is an initial segment of A. It is *tight* if it is proper and for each Σ^0_1-cover $\widehat{S}$ of A, there are $\sigma \in S$ and $\tau \in \widehat{S}$ such that $\sigma \preccurlyeq \tau$.[14] One might think of a tight cover as a "simple set for covers". The following result completely classifies the sets that are computable in 1-generic ones.

Theorem 8.21.7 (Chong and Downey [69, 70]). *A set A has no tight Σ^0_1-cover iff there is a 1-generic $G \geqslant_T A$.*

The proof in [70] shows that there is a single procedure Φ such that if A is computable in a 1-generic set, then there is a 1-generic $G \leqslant_T A''$ such that $A = \Phi^G$. Notice that, by Theorems 8.21.6 and 8.21.7, almost every set has a tight Σ^0_1-cover.

8.21.3 Every 2-random set is CEA

In Theorem 2.24.9 we saw that every 1-generic set A is CEA, that is, computably enumerable relative to some $X <_T A$. In this section we prove the remarkable result of Kurtz [228] that being CEA is typical behavior for sets also in the measure-theoretic sense. That is, almost every set, and in fact every 2-random set, is CEA. Kurtz [228] showed that the particular X used in the proof of Theorem 2.24.9 will not work for this measure-theoretic version, because it is almost always A-computable, so a different and more complex approach will be needed. The proof resembles that of Theorem 8.21.3 (that almost every set computes a 1-generic set). The main ideas of the proof we present are due to Kurtz [228], but we will give the details as carefully presented by Kautz [200]. Kautz' version allows us to show that 2-randomness suffices to ensure that a set is CEA.

The following result should also be compared with Theorem 15.4.1 below, which states that every 2-random real α is equal to Ω^B for some B (and hence is left-c.e. relative to B). As we will see in Chapter 11, however, this B cannot be α-computable.

Theorem 8.21.8 (Kurtz [228], Kautz [200]). *Every 2-random set is CEA.*

[14] In Chong and Downey [69, 70], a tight Σ^0_1-cover was called Σ^0_1 *dense in* A, which would perhaps be confusing in the present context.

Proof. We construct a functional Ξ so that $\mu(\{A : \Xi^A \text{ total} \wedge \Xi^A \nleqslant_T A\}) \geqslant \frac{1}{4}$ and A is c.e. in Ξ^A whenever Ξ^A is total. By Kolmogorov's 0-1 Law, Theorem 1.2.4, the existence of such a functional is enough to conclude that almost every set is CEA. At the end of the proof we will argue that 2-randomness suffices.

To make A c.e. in Ξ^A we will ask that $n \in A$ iff $\langle n, m \rangle \in \Xi^A$ for some m. We say that a string ξ is *acceptable* for a string σ if $\xi(\langle n, m \rangle) = 1 \Rightarrow \sigma(n) = 1$. We will always require that $\Xi^\sigma[s]$ be acceptable. Of course, restricting ourselves to acceptable strings is not enough, since it does not ensure that if $n \in A$ then $\langle n, m \rangle \in \Xi^A$ for some m. We will explicitly take care of that condition during the construction (which will be easy to do since for every σ and n there is a $\tau \succcurlyeq \sigma$ with $\tau(\langle n, m \rangle) = 1$ for some m). We will also meet requirements of the form

$$R_e : A \neq \Phi_e^{\Xi^A}.$$

In the proof of Theorem 8.21.3, there are blue$_e$ strings, each of which is the base of a cone within which we are attempting to meet R_e. Above each such string, there is a tree of strings whose leaves are yellow$_e$, except for one red$_e$ leaf above which we are testing the c.e. set of strings V_e in an attempt to turn the red$_e$ node green$_e$. The method of this construction is in some ways similar, but more complex.

As before, we attempt to meet R_e in the cone above a blue$_e$ string ν. We give the color red$_e$ to $\nu 1^{e+2}$, and give the other extensions of ν of the same length the color yellow$_e$. However, the role of the red$_e$ node will be different in this construction, and there are now new players, the purple$_e$ strings. These represent cones R_e forbids us to build within during the construction, because we seem to be failing to satisfy R_e within these cones, as explained below. We cannot afford to allow the measure of such cones to become too large, so the role of the red$_e$ strings is, as Kurtz put it, to act as "safety valves" for the pressure exerted by the purple$_e$ strings. If the measure of cones corresponding to purple$_e$ strings becomes too large, the "safety valve" pops, and a backup strategy allows us to succeed. The following is the key definition.

Definition 8.21.9. At a stage s, we say that a string $\theta \in 2^{\leqslant s}$ *threatens* a requirement R_e if there are $\nu \prec \tau \preccurlyeq \theta$ such that ν is blue$_e$ and τ is yellow$_e$, and a $\xi \in 2^{\leqslant s}$ that is acceptable for θ, such that

(i) $\Xi^\tau[s] \preccurlyeq \xi$,

(ii) $\Phi_e^\xi(k)[s] = \tau(k) = 0$ for some k such that $|\nu| < k \leqslant |\tau|$, and

(iii) no initial segment of θ has color purple$_j$ for $j \leqslant e$.

In the construction, we will give any string that threatens R_e the color purple$_e$. If θ is purple$_e$, then its image under Ξ could be an initial segment of a set B such that $\Phi_e^B = A$ for some A extending θ. We hope to avoid having $\Xi^A = B$ for such A and B, so we stop building Ξ above purple$_e$ nodes.

If $A \succ \tau$ for a yellow$_e$ string τ and no initial segment of A is purple$_j$ for $j \leqslant e$, then we cannot have $A = \Phi_e^{\Xi^A}$, and hence A satisfies R_e. To see that this is the case, suppose otherwise. Then $\Phi_e^{\Xi^A}(k) = \nu(k) = 0$ for some k with $|\nu| < k \leqslant |\tau|$, since τ is not $\nu 1^{e+2}$. But then some initial segment of A extending τ will eventually threaten R_e, and hence be colored purple$_e$.

Thus, if there are not too many purple$_e$ strings, then R_e is met on a class of sufficiently large measure. Our main concern is what to do when we do have too many purple$_e$ strings.

For each purple$_e$ string θ, let θ' be the unique string of length $|\theta|$ extending the red$_e$ string $\rho \succ \nu$ with $\theta(m) = \theta'(m)$ for all $m \geqslant |\rho|$. Note that item (ii) above implies that there is a k such that $\Phi_e^{\xi}(k) = \tau(k) = 0 \neq 1 = \rho(k)$, since $\rho = \nu 1^{e+2}$. Thus, if we choose to define Ξ^A on sets $A \succ \rho$ to emulate Ξ^{ξ}, then we cannot have $\Phi_e^{\Xi^A} = A$ for such A. If the density of purple$_e$ strings above ν grows too big, then using this fact we will be able to satisfy R_e above these θ', giving them color green$_e$. (By *density* here we mean the measure of the union of the cones $[\![\sigma]\!]$ above purple$_e$ strings σ divided by the measure of $[\![\nu]\!]$.)

More precisely, when the density of purple$_e$ strings above the blue$_e$ string ν exceeds $2^{-(e+3)}$, there must be some yellow$_e$ string τ such that the density of purple$_e$ strings above τ also exceeds $2^{-(e+3)}$. Let $\theta_0, \ldots, \theta_n$ be the purple$_e$ strings above such a τ. For each θ_i, let ξ_i be a string witnessing the threat to R_e as in Definition 8.21.9. Then

(i) ξ_i is acceptable for θ_i,

(ii) $\Xi^\tau \preccurlyeq \xi_i$, and

(iii) $\Phi_e^{\xi_i}(k) = 0 = \theta_i(k)$ for some k with $\rho(k) = 1$.

The construction will be such that $\Xi^\rho[s] = \Xi^\tau[s]$.

Now we act as follows. First, any string extending ν loses its color, including ν itself. (We are considering R_e in isolation here. In the presence of other requirements, strings colored purple$_i$ for $i < e$ do not lose their colors, to respect the priority order of requirements.) Then we give each θ_i' color green$_e$. Finally, for each $i \leqslant n$, we define $\Xi^{\theta_i'} = \xi_i$, which ensures that $\Phi_e^{\Xi^{\theta_i'}}(k) \neq \theta_i'(k)$ for some k with $|\nu| < k \leqslant |\tau|$, justifying the use of the color green$_e$ for the strings θ_i'. Note that each time we are forced to pop our safety valve in this way, we are guaranteed to satisfy R_e on a set of relative measure at least $2^{-(e+5)}$ above ν. We will be able to show that this measure is sufficient for our purposes. Notice also that we are now able to replicate this construction on strings extending those that have lost their color.

We now proceed with the formal details.

Construction.

At each stage s, we let D_s be the set of strings σ on which we have defined $\Xi^\sigma[s]$. The leaves of D_s are called the *active strings* at stage $s+1$.

Stage 0. Assign λ the color blue$_0$, assign 00, 01, and 10 the color yellow$_0$, and assign 11 the color red$_0$.

Stage $s+1$. This stage consists of four substages.

Substage 1. For each $e \leqslant s$ and each $\sigma \in D_s$, if σ threatens R_e then color σ purple$_e$.

Substage 2. For each $e \leqslant s$ and each blue$_e$ string ν, if the density of purple$_e$ strings extending ν is at least $2^{-(e+3)}$, then proceed as follows. (We say that R_e *acts for* ν.)

Let ρ be the red$_e$ string extending ν, and τ a yellow$_e$ string extending ν with the highest density of purple$_e$ strings extending it. Let $\theta_0, \dots, \theta_n$ be the purple$_e$ strings extending τ, and let $\xi_0, \dots, \xi_n$ be corresponding witnesses for the θ_i's threat to R_e. For each $i \leqslant n$, let θ'_i be the string of length $|\theta_i|$ extending ρ with $\theta_i(m) = \theta'_i(m)$ for all $m \geqslant |\rho|$.

Declare that every $\sigma \succcurlyeq \nu$ loses its color unless it is colored purple$_j$ for some $j < e$. There are now two cases.

Case 1. ρ has an extension with color purple$_j$ for some $j < e$. In this case, do nothing.

Case 2. Otherwise. Then for each $i \leqslant n$, let $\Xi^{\theta'_i} = \xi_i$. Give each θ'_i color green$_e$.

Substage 3. For each active string σ that is not red$_e$ for any e and has no substring that is purple$_e$ for any e, proceed as follows. Let e be least such that σ has no substring colored green$_e$ or yellow$_e$. Let ξ be the lexicographically least string such that $\sigma(n) = 1$ iff $\xi(\langle n, m\rangle) = 1$ for some m. (Note that ξ is acceptable for σ.) Let $\Xi^{\sigma 0} = \Xi^{\sigma 1} = \xi$, and give $\sigma 0$ and $\sigma 1$ color blue$_e$.

Substage 4. For each e and each active blue$_e$ string ν, let $\Xi^{\nu\sigma} = \Xi^\nu$ for all $\sigma \in 2^{e+2}$. Give $\nu 1^{e+2}$ color red$_e$. Give the other length $e+2$ extensions of ν color yellow$_e$.

End of Construction.

Verification. We will need the following color classes.

$$B_e = \{A : \exists \sigma \prec A\, (\sigma \text{ has final color yellow}_e \text{ or green}_e)\}.$$

$$S_e = \{A : \exists \sigma \prec A\, (\sigma \text{ has final color red}_e)\}.$$

$$P_e = \{A : \exists \sigma \prec A\, (\sigma \text{ has final color purple}_e)\}.$$

Let $S = \bigcup_e S_e$ and $P = \bigcup_e P_e$.

Lemma 8.21.10. *Let $A \in \bigcap_e B_e$. Then Ξ^A is total, A is c.e. in Ξ^A, and $A \nleqslant_T \Xi^A$.*

Proof. Substages 3 and 4 of the construction ensure that Ξ^A is total and that $n \in A$ iff $\langle n, m\rangle \in \Xi^A$ for some m, whence A is c.e. in Ξ^A. Thus we are left with showing that $A \not\leqslant_T \Xi^A$. Assume for a contradiction that there is a least e such that $A = \Phi_e^{\Xi^A}$. Let $\sigma \prec A$ have final color yellow$_e$ or green$_e$.
Case 1. σ has final color green$_e$. Then, by construction, at some stage we define $\Xi^\sigma = \xi$ for some ξ with $\Phi_e^\xi(k) = 0 \neq 1 = \sigma(k) = 1$ for some k, which is a contradiction.
Case 2. σ has final color yellow$_e$. Let ρ be the associated red$_e$ string. There is a k such that $\rho(k) = 1 \neq 0 = \sigma(k)$. By our assumption, $\sigma(k) = \Phi_e^{\Xi^A}(k)$. Let ξ be an initial segment of Ξ^A such that $\Phi_e^\xi(k) = 0$. Then ξ is acceptable for σ, and thus σ threatens R_e via ξ at all sufficiently large stages. Thus σ is colored purple$_e$ unless some initial segment of it is colored purple$_j$ for some $j \leqslant e$. In any case, there is a $\tau \preccurlyeq \sigma$ that is colored purple$_j$ for some $j \leqslant e$ at some point in the construction. The string τ can never later lose its color, for if it did, then σ would also lose its yellow$_e$ color. But then the construction above τ is eventually permanently halted, contradicting the assumption that $A \in \bigcap_e B_e$. □

We will now show through a sequence of lemmas that $\mu(\bigcap_e B_e) \geqslant \frac{1}{4}$. Let $B_{-1} = 2^\omega$.

Lemma 8.21.11. $\mu(B_{e-1} \setminus (B_e \cup S \cup P)) = 0$.

Proof. We do the case $e > 0$. The $e = 0$ case is similar, using $\sigma = \lambda$.

Assume for a contradiction that $\mu(B_{e-1} \setminus (B_e \cup S \cup P)) > 0$. The class B_{e-1} is a disjoint union of clopen sets $[\![\sigma]\!]$ where σ has final color yellow$_{e-1}$ or green$_{e-1}$. For some such σ, we have $\mu([\![\sigma]\!] \setminus (B_e \cup S \cup P)) > 0$. Let s_0 be the stage at which σ receives its final color.

By the Lebesgue Density Theorem 1.2.3, there is a $\widehat{\sigma} \succcurlyeq \sigma$ such that $\mu([\![\widehat{\sigma}]\!] \setminus (B_e \cup S \cup P)) > 2^{-|\widehat{\sigma}|}(1-2^{-(2e+5)})$. In particular, $[\![\widehat{\sigma}]\!]$ is not contained in $B_e \cup S \cup P$, so no substring of $\widehat{\sigma}$ has final color red$_i$ or purple$_i$ for any i, and no substring of $\widehat{\sigma}$ has final color yellow$_e$, green$_e$, red$_e$, or purple$_e$, which implies that no substring of $\widehat{\sigma}$ has final color blue$_e$. We may assume that $\widehat{\sigma}$ is sufficiently long so that some substring τ of $\widehat{\sigma}$ is active at stage s_0.

First suppose that τ has a purple$_i$ substring γ for some i at stage s_0. We know that γ will eventually lose its color. Suppose this loss of color comes from some R_j with $j < e$ acting for a blue$_j$ node ν. Then it is easy to check from the construction that $\nu \prec \sigma$, so R_j's action also causes σ to lose its color, which is a contradiction. Thus γ's loss of color must come from some R_j with $j \geqslant e$ acting for a blue$_j$ node $\nu \preccurlyeq \tau$. Now it is easy to check from the construction that some predecessor of τ must have color blue$_e$ at some stage $s \geqslant s_0$.

Now suppose that τ has no purple$_i$ substrings for any i at stage s_0. It cannot be the case that τ is colored red$_j$ for some $j < e$, since then σ would not have its color. If τ is colored red$_j$ for some $j \geqslant e$, then it has a blue$_e$ substring. Otherwise, it becomes blue$_e$ at stage s_0.

Thus, in either case, there is some stage $s \geqslant s_0$ at which $\widehat{\sigma}$ has a blue$_e$ substring. Let ν be the longest such substring. At some stage t, the string ν loses its color. By the same argument as above, this loss of color cannot come from the action of some R_j with $j < e$, since then σ would lose its color, and it cannot come from the action of R_j for $j > e$, since ν cannot have any blue$_j$ substrings. Thus it comes from the action of R_e itself.

So the density of purple$_e$ strings above ν is at least $2^{-(e+3)}$ at stage t. At the end of stage t, there are pairwise incompatible strings $\gamma_0, \ldots, \gamma_m$ such that $[\![\nu]\!] = \bigcup_{i \leqslant m} [\![\gamma_i]\!]$ and each γ_i is either green$_e$, blue$_e$, or has a purple$_j$ substring for some $j < e$. If γ_i is green$_e$ then that is its final color, and if γ_i has a purple$_j$ substring for some $j < e$, then purple$_j$ is that substring's final color (in both cases by the same argument as above, that a loss of color would have to come from the action of some R_k with $k < e$, which would also cause σ to lose its color). In either case, $\widehat{\sigma}$ cannot extend γ_i. But if γ_i has color blue$_e$ at stage t, then again $\widehat{\sigma}$ cannot extend γ_i, by the choice of ν. Thus $\widehat{\sigma}$ does not extend any γ_i, and hence $[\![\widehat{\sigma}]\!]$ is a union of sets of the form $[\![\gamma_i]\!]$. Since we are assuming that $\mu([\![\widehat{\sigma}]\!] \setminus (B_e \cup S \cup P)) > 2^{-|\widehat{\sigma}|}(1-2^{-(2e+5)})$, there must be an i such that $\mu([\![\gamma_i]\!] \setminus (B_e \cup S \cup P)) > 2^{-|\gamma_i|}(1-2^{-(2e+5)})$.

Such a γ_i cannot have color green$_e$ or have a substring with color purple$_j$ for $j < e$, since, as noted above, in either case these colors would be final, and we would have $[\![\gamma_i]\!] \subseteq B_e \cup S \cup P$. Thus γ_i is colored blue$_e$ at stage t.

This color cannot be final, since otherwise every set extending γ_i would have an initial segment with final color red$_e$ or yellow$_e$, and hence we would have $[\![\gamma_i]\!] \subseteq B_e \cup S \cup P$. So there is a stage at which γ_i loses its color. By the same argument as above, this loss can happen only through the action of R_e, so there is a stage at which the density of purple$_e$ strings above γ_i is at least $2^{-(e+3)}$. Let $\rho = \gamma_i 1^{e+2}$ be the red$_e$ string above γ_i.

If ρ has a substring with color purple$_j$ for some $j < e$ then this substring's color is final, so $[\![\rho]\!] \subseteq P$, whence $\mu([\![\gamma_i]\!] \cap (B_e \cup S \cup P)) \geqslant 2^{-(|\gamma_i|+e+2)}$, which is a contradiction.

Otherwise, it follows from the construction that the density of green$_e$ strings above ρ is at least $2^{-(e+3)}$, and, as argued before, each of these strings has green$_e$ as its final color. Thus $\mu([\![\gamma_i]\!] \cap (B_e \cup S \cup P)) \geqslant 2^{-(|\rho|+e+3)} = 2^{-(|\gamma_i|+2e+5)}$, which again is a contradiction. □

Lemma 8.21.12. *$B_{e+1} \subseteq B_e$.*

Proof. Let $A \in B_{e+1}$, and let $\sigma \prec A$ have final color green$_{e+1}$ or yellow$_{e+1}$, with $\nu \prec \sigma$ the associated blue$_{e+1}$ string. When ν received its blue$_{e+1}$ color, there must have been some string $\tau \prec \nu$ with color green$_e$ or yellow$_e$, as otherwise ν would have been colored blue$_e$. Any action removing this color from τ would necessarily remove the color from σ as well, and hence τ's color is final. □

Lemma 8.21.13. $\mu(S \cup P) + \mu(\bigcap_e B_e) = 1$.

Proof. We again let $B_{-1} = 2^\omega$. Since

$$(B_{e-1} \setminus B_e) \cap \overline{S \cup P} = B_{e-1} \setminus (B_e \cup S \cup P),$$

it follows from Lemma 8.21.11 that $\mu((B_{e-1} \setminus B_e) \cap \overline{S \cup P}) = 0$, and hence

$$\mu\left(\bigcup_e (B_{e-1} \setminus B_e) \cap \overline{S \cup P}\right) = 0.$$

By Lemma 8.21.12, $\bigcup_e (B_{e-1} \setminus B_e) \cup \bigcap_e B_e = 2^\omega$, and it is easy to see from the construction that $(S \cup P) \cap (\bigcap_e B_e) = \emptyset$, so $S \cup P \subseteq \bigcup_e (B_{e-1} \setminus B_e)$, and hence $\mu(S \cup P) = \mu(\bigcup_e (B_{e-1} \setminus B_e))$.

Thus

$$\mu(S \cup P) + \mu\left(\bigcap_e B_e\right) = \mu\left(\bigcup_e (B_{e-1} \setminus B_e)\right) + \mu\left(\bigcap_e B_e\right) = 1.$$

□

Lemma 8.21.14. $\mu(S) \leqslant \frac{1}{2}$ *and* $\mu(P) \leqslant \frac{1}{4}$.

Proof. By construction, the set of strings ν with final color blue$_e$ is prefix-free. For any such ν, there is a single red$_e$ node τ above ν, and $\mu(\llbracket\tau\rrbracket) = 2^{-(e+2)}\mu(\llbracket\nu\rrbracket)$. Thus $\mu(S_e) \leqslant 2^{-(e+2)}$, and hence $\mu(S) \leqslant \frac{1}{2}$. Similarly, the density of purple$_e$ strings in $\llbracket\nu\rrbracket$ for any blue$_e$ string ν is bounded by $2^{-(e+3)}$, and hence $\mu(P_e) \leqslant 2^{-(e+3)}$, whence $\mu(P) \leqslant \frac{1}{4}$. □

Putting together the previous two lemmas, we have $\mu(\bigcap_e B_e) \geqslant \frac{1}{4}$, which together with Lemma 8.21.10 and Kolmogorov's 0-1 Law, shows that almost every set is CEA.

The class $\{A : \Xi^A \text{ total}\}$ is a Π^0_2 class of positive measure, and hence, by Theorem 6.10.2, for every 2-random set X, there are A and σ such that $X = \sigma A$ and Ξ^A is total. If $A \in S \cup P$ then Ξ^A is not total, and if $A \in \bigcap_e B_e$ then $\Xi^A <_T A$, so by Lemma 8.21.13, $\mu(\{A : \Xi^A \text{ total} \wedge A \leqslant_T \Xi^A\}) = 0$. This class is the union of the Π^0_2 classes $\{A : \Xi^A \text{ total} \wedge A = \Phi_e^{\Xi^A}\}$, so it cannot contain any 2-random sets. Thus for every 2-random set X, there are A and σ with $X = \sigma A$ such that Ξ^A is total (which implies that A is c.e. in Ξ^A) and $\Xi^A <_T A$, so that A is CEA, and hence so is X. □

The following result shows that Theorem 8.21.3 follows from Theorem 8.21.8. We give a proof due to Shore (see [228]).

Theorem 8.21.15 (Folklore). *If a set is CEA then it computes a* 1*-generic set.*

Proof. Let A be c.e. in $B <_T A$. We construct a 1-generic set $G \leqslant_T A$ via a finite extension argument. Let $A_0, A_1, \ldots$ be a B-c.e. approximation to A. Let $c(n)$ be the least s such that $A_s \upharpoonright n = A \upharpoonright n$. Let $V_0, V_1, \ldots$ be an effective enumeration of the c.e. sets of strings. Let $G_0 = \lambda$. At stage s, if there is a least $e \leqslant s$ such that we have never acted for e and there is a $\sigma \in V_e[c(s+1)]$ with $\sigma \succcurlyeq G_s$, then let $G_{s+1} = \sigma$. (In this case, we say we have acted for e.) Otherwise, let $G_{s+1} = G_s$.

It is easy to check that $\lim_s |G_s| = \infty$. Let $G = \lim_s G_s$. Assume for a contradiction that G is not 1-generic. We show that $c \leqslant_{\mathrm{T}} B$, which is impossible, as it implies that $A \leqslant_{\mathrm{T}} B$. Let e be such that G neither meets nor avoids V_e. Let s_0 be a stage after which we never act for a number less than e. Let $s \geqslant s_0$ and assume we know G_s. Then we can find a stage t such that some extension of G_s occurs in $V_e[t]$. (Such an extension must exist, since G does not avoid V_e.) We must have $t > c(s+1)$, since otherwise we would have acted for e at stage s. Thus we can compute $c(s+1)$ using B (as the least u such that $A_u \upharpoonright n = A_t \upharpoonright n$), from which we can compute G_{s+1}. Proceeding by induction, we can compute c from B. □

As mentioned following Theorem 8.21.4, there are weakly 2-random sets that do not compute any 1-generic sets. Thus there are weakly 2-random sets that are not CEA.

Theorems 8.21.8 and 8.21.15 together give us Kautz' Theorem 8.21.4 that every 2-random set computes a 1-generic set. The following is a direct proof, applying the analysis in the proof of Theorem 8.21.8 to the similar (but simpler) construction in the proof of Theorem 8.21.3.

Proof of Theorem 8.21.4. Let Ξ be the functional built in the proof of Theorem 8.21.3. Then $\{A : \Xi^A \text{ total}\}$ is a Π^0_2 class of positive measure, and hence, by Theorem 6.10.2, contains elements of all 2-random degrees. Thus it is enough to show that if Ξ^A is total and A is 2-random, then Ξ^A is 1-generic.

For the construction in the proof of Theorem 8.21.3, let

$$B_e = \{A : \exists \sigma \prec A\, (\sigma \text{ has final color yellow}_e \text{ or green}_e)\},$$

$$S_e = \{A : \exists \sigma \prec A\, (\sigma \text{ has final color red}_e)\},$$

and $S = \bigcup_e S_e$. (Recall that in this construction there are no purple strings.) Arguing as in the proof of Theorem 8.21.8, we can show that $\mu(S) + \mu(\bigcap_e B_e) = 1$.

Let Y_e be the class of all A such that, infinitely often, some initial segment of A receives color yellow$_e$. Then Y_e is a Π^0_2 class, and $Y_e \cap S = Y_e \cap \bigcap_e B_e = \emptyset$, so $\mu(Y_e) = 0$. Thus if A is 2-random, then $A \notin Y_e$ for all e. We will show that then $A \in \bigcap_e B_e$, which implies by construction that if Ξ^A is total then it is 1-generic, thus proving the theorem.

So we are left with showing that if $A \notin \bigcap_e B_e$ then $A \in Y_e$ for some e. Let e be least such that $A \notin B_e$. We do the argument for the case $e > 0$; the case $e = 0$ is similar.

Let s be such that for each $i < e$, some initial segment of A has received final color yellow$_i$ or green$_i$ by stage s. Let $\sigma \prec A$ have final color yellow$_{e-1}$ or green$_{e-1}$. Suppose that $\tau \prec A$ has some color$_e$ at a stage $t > s$. Recall that if τ later loses its color through the action of some R_i, then τ must have a blue$_i$ substring ν, and in this case every successor of ν loses its color. Thus τ can lose its color only through the action of R_e, since for $i > e$ no substring of τ can be blue$_i$, while for $i < e$, any blue$_i$ substring of τ is also a substring of σ, whose color is permanent.

Now assume for a contradiction that the color τ has at stage t is red$_e$. Since Ξ^A is total, this color cannot be permanent, so at some point it is removed through the action of R_e, which means that τ then receives color green$_e$, which must be permanent, since R_e never acts to remove this color, and by the argument in the previous paragraph, neither does any other R_i. But we are assuming that $A \notin B_e$, so we have a contradiction.

Thus no initial segment of A receives color red$_e$ after stage s. It is then easy to check from the construction that there must be a stage $s' > s$ at which some initial segment of A has color yellow$_e$. This color cannot be permanent, since $A \notin B_e$, so there must be a stage $s'' > s'$ at which again some initial segment of A receives color yellow$_e$, and so on. Thus $A \in Y_e$. □

8.21.4 Where 1-generic degrees are downward dense

A class C of degrees is *downward dense* below a degree $\mathbf{a}$ if for all nonzero $\mathbf{b} \leqslant \mathbf{a}$ there is a $\mathbf{c} \leqslant \mathbf{b}$ in C.

Theorem 8.21.16 (Kurtz [228]). *For almost all degrees* $\mathbf{a}$, *the class of 1-generic degrees is downward dense below* $\mathbf{a}$.[15]

Proof. The method of this proof is based on that of Theorem 8.21.3, but is considerably more complicated. Assume for a contradiction that the class of degrees below which the class of 1-generic degrees is not downward dense has positive measure. Then there is an e such that the class C of A such that Φ_e^A is total, noncomputable, and does not compute a 1-generic set is positive. By the Lebesgue Density Theorem 1.2.3, there is a σ such that $\mu(C \cap [\![\sigma]\!]) > \frac{7}{8}2^{-|\sigma|}$. Let $\Psi^A = \Phi_e^{\sigma A}$. Then the class of all A such that Ψ^A is total, noncomputable, and does not compute a 1-generic set is greater than $\frac{7}{8}$. Our contradiction will be obtained by constructing a functional Φ such that $\mu(\{A : \Phi^{\Psi^A}$ total and 1-generic$\}) > \frac{1}{8}$. To do so, we need to ensure that for measure $\frac{1}{8}$ many sets A, we have that Φ^{Ψ^A} is total and the following requirements are met, where $V_0, V_1, \ldots$ is an effective enumeration of the c.e. sets of strings.

$$R_e : \Phi^{\Psi^A} \text{ meets or avoids } V_e.$$

[15]The precise level of randomness necessary to ensure that $\mathbf{a}$ has this property is not known.

Let

$$p^*(\sigma) = \mu(\{A : \Psi^A \text{ is total, noncomputable, and extends } \sigma\}).$$

We will use the method of Theorem 8.21.3, but with $p^*(\sigma)$ replacing $2^{-|\sigma|}$ as the measure of $[\![\sigma]\!]$. Again we will have blue$_e$, red$_e$, yellow$_e$, and green$_e$ strings, but we will need much more subtlety in the way that these colors are assigned. There will also be an additional color, gray$_e$, whose role will be discussed later.

Unfortunately, we cannot actually compute p^*. If we could, then we could proceed very much as in the proof of Theorem 8.21.3. Working above a blue$_e$ string ν for the sake of R_e, we would search for a maximal finite set E_ν of pairwise incompatible extensions of ν such that for some $\rho \in E_\nu$,

$$p^*(\nu)2^{-(e+3)} \leqslant p^*(\rho) \leqslant p^*(\nu)2^{-(e+2)}.$$

By Corollary 8.12.2, $\lim_n p^*(X \upharpoonright n) = 0$ for all X, and $p^*(\sigma) = p^*(\sigma 0) + p^*(\sigma 1)$ for all σ, so such a set exists. We would then give ρ color red$_e$ and the other members of E_ν color yellow$_e$, and proceed much as before. Such a construction would give us a Φ such that

$$\mu(\{A : \Psi^A \text{ total and } \Phi^{\Psi^A} \text{ not 1-generic}\}) \leqslant \frac{1}{2},$$

which would yield our contradiction, since then

$$\begin{aligned}\mu(\{A : \Phi^{\Psi^A} &\text{ total and 1-generic}\}) \\ &\geqslant \mu(\{A : \Psi^A \text{ total}\}) - \mu(\{\Psi^A \text{ total and } \Phi^{\Psi^A} \text{ not 1-generic}\}) \\ &\geqslant \frac{7}{8} - \frac{1}{2} > \frac{1}{8}.\end{aligned}$$

Of course, we cannot compute the actual value of p^*, so we will be forced to use an approximation p to p^* defined as follows. Let $F(\sigma)$ be the longest initial segment of $\Psi^\sigma[|\sigma|]$. Let

$$p_s(\sigma) = \mu([\![\{\tau \in 2^s : \sigma \preccurlyeq F(\tau)\}]\!])$$

and let $p(\sigma) = \lim_s p_s(\sigma)$. Note that $p(\sigma) = \mu(\{A : \sigma \preccurlyeq \Psi^A\})$ (where by $\sigma \preccurlyeq \Psi^A$ we mean that $\Psi^A(n)\downarrow = \sigma(n)$ for all $n < |\sigma|$.) At a stage s of the construction, we will use p_s in place of p^*. The new ideas in this construction will allow us to overcome the difficulties that this use of approximations causes.

One obvious issue is that p_s converges to p and not to p^*. Let

$$Y = \{\sigma : \mu(\{A : \sigma \preccurlyeq \Psi^A \wedge \Psi^A \text{ is nontotal or computable}\}) > \tfrac{p(\sigma)}{2}\}.$$

We will later show that the class of sets A that meet Y has measure less than $\frac{1}{4}$. We will discuss two problems arising out of the p_s not converging to p^*. Both cause the apparent density of red$_e$ strings extending certain blue$_e$ strings to be too large. Our solution in both cases will be to argue that in such cases the relevant red$_e$ strings belong to Y, and hence the measure of the class of sets extending them is not unacceptably large.

The first difficulty arises because Ψ^A might not be total for all A, and hence it might be that $p(\sigma) \neq p(\sigma 0) + p(\sigma 1)$ for some σ. Let us for now assume we are dealing directly with p, rather than with its approximations p_s. Let ν be an active blue$_e$ string. Suppose that we use the following strategy for choosing red$_e$ and yellow$_e$ strings. Begin by giving ν color red$_e$. During later stages, if ρ is the current red$_e$ string extending ν, compute $p(\rho 0)$ and $p(\rho 1)$. If $p(\rho i) \leqslant p(\nu)2^{-(e+3)}$ for $i = 0, 1$ then do nothing. Otherwise, let i be least such that $p(\rho i) > p(\nu)2^{-(e+3)}$ and make ρi the new red$_e$ extension of ν, giving $\rho(1-i)$ color yellow$_e$.

The problem with this strategy is that we might well have $p(\rho) > p(\nu)2^{-(e+2)}$ but $p(\rho i) \leqslant p(\nu)2^{-(e+3)}$ for $i = 0, 1$. In this case, if we allow ρ to remain red$_e$, then we might lose an unacceptably large fraction of the potential domain in this attempt to meet R_e. On the other hand, if we make one of the ρi red$_e$, then we risk having insufficient density of green$_e$ strings if V_e contains an extension of ν.

The solution to this dilemma is to give one of the ρi the color red$_e$ if $p(\rho i) > p(\nu)2^{-(e+4)}$. Now, of course, it may be that $p(\rho) > p(\nu)2^{-(e+2)}$ but $p(\rho i) \leqslant p(\nu)2^{-(e+4)}$ for $i = 0, 1$, so it would appear that the same problem as before presents itself. However, in this case we have $\rho \in Y$, and hence the apparent loss of measure caused by leaving ρ with the color red$_e$ can be blamed on Y. By controlling the measure of Y, and hence the effect of strings in Y on the construction, we will ensure that this kind of loss of measure occurs only acceptably often.

The second problem we face is that Ψ^A might be computable for some A. There might be a computable set $C \succ \nu$ such that $\mu(\{A : \Psi^A = C\}) > p(\nu)2^{-(e+4)}$, and we may always choose our red$_e$ strings $\rho \succcurlyeq \nu$ so that $\rho \prec C$, which would cause us to pick a new red$_e$ string infinitely often. One apparent problem this situation causes is that our finite maximal set E_ν of pairwise incompatible extensions of ν grows each time we change our red$_e$ extension of ν, and hence can be infinite in the limit. This problem turns out to be irrelevant: whether the final set of red$_e$ and yellow$_e$ extensions of ν is finite or infinite is immaterial; the only question is whether the measures assigned to the colors are correct.

More important is the fact that, along C, we may still lose an unacceptably large amount of measure while attempting vainly to settle upon a final red$_e$ string. However, if $\mu(\{A : \Psi^A = C\}) > 0$, then for all sufficiently large n,

$$\mu(\{A : \Psi^A = C\}) > \frac{\mu(\{A : C \upharpoonright n \preccurlyeq \Psi^A\})}{2} = \frac{p(C \upharpoonright n)}{2},$$

since $\{A : \Psi^A = C\} = \bigcap_n \{A : C \upharpoonright n \preccurlyeq \Psi^A\}$. Thus $C \upharpoonright n \in Y$, and we are again saved by the fact that the measure loss due to strings in Y is controlled.

The last problem we must overcome is that we have to work with p_s instead of p. Suppose that at stage s we have a red$_e$ string ρ extending a blue$_e$ string ν with the desired condition $p_s(\nu)2^{-(e+2)} > p_s(\rho) \geqslant p_s(\nu)2^{-(e+4)}$. At a later stage t, we could have $p_t(\nu) > p_s(\nu)$ while $p_t(\rho) = p_s(\rho)$, which could mean that the ratio of $p_t(\rho)$ to $p_t(\nu)$ is unacceptably small. (Since we need to ensure only that the density of red$_e$ and green$_e$ strings above each blue$_e$ string is bounded away from zero, we can declare "unacceptably small" to mean less than $2^{-(e+6)}$, for technical reasons that will become clear later.)

It is now that the new color gray$_e$ comes in. The gray$_e$ strings will act as "traffic lights", as explained below. The red$_e$ and yellow$_e$ strings will occur as extensions of gray$_e$ strings, while the blue$_e$ strings control the placement of the gray$_e$ strings. In this construction, it will be possible for one blue$_e$ string to extend another. With this fact in mind, we say that a blue$_e$ string ν' *belongs* to a blue$_e$ string ν if ν is the longest blue$_e$ proper substring of ν'. A green$_e$ or gray$_e$ string γ belongs to ν if ν is the longest (not necessarily proper) blue$_e$ substring of γ. Finally, a red$_e$ string ρ belongs to ν if ρ extends a gray$_e$ string belonging to ν. We will ensure that if ν is a blue$_e$ string, then either no string properly extending ν has a color, or else the green$_e$, blue$_e$, and gray$_e$ strings that belong to ν form a finite maximal set of incomparable extensions of ν. When we compute the density of green$_e$ and red$_e$ strings that extend a blue$_e$ string ν, we will use only those that belong to ν.

Suppose that ν is an active blue$_e$ string at a stage s such that $p_s(\nu) > 0$. (No action will be taken for ν until $p_s(\nu) > 0$.) We begin by giving ν itself the color gray$_e$ (without removing the color blue$_e$ from ν). Suppose that at a stage $t > s$ we appoint a red$_e$ string belonging to ν, and that at a later stage u, the density of red$_e$ and green$_e$ strings belonging to ν becomes unacceptably small. That is, for the red$_e$ and green$_e$ strings $\delta_0, \ldots, \delta_n$ belonging to ν,

$$\frac{\sum_{j \leqslant n} p_u(\delta_j)}{p_u(\nu)} \leqslant 2^{-(e+6)}.$$

We then remove all colors from all strings properly extending ν, and remove the color gray$_e$ from ν. We refer to this process as a *wipe-out* above ν. Let $\alpha_0, \ldots, \alpha_m$ be the active strings extending ν at stage u. We do nothing above ν unless there is a stage $v > u$ such that $\sum_{j \leqslant m} p_v(\alpha_j) > \frac{p_v(\nu)}{2}$. The key observation is that, unless $\nu \in Y$, such a v must exist. In this case, we give each α_j the color gray$_e$, and for each $j \leqslant m$ we begin to seek red$_e$ extensions of α_j.

If at some stage $w > v$, the density of red$_e$ and green$_e$ strings belonging to ν is again unacceptably small, then we again perform a wipe-out above ν, and try to place gray$_e$ strings above ν as before. Note that wipe-outs can occur at most finitely often, since each wipe-out requires the approximation to $p(\nu)$ to at least double. After the final wipe-out, we can meet R_e above ν without any interference.

We now turn to the formal construction. Let Ψ and p_s be defined as above.

Construction.

Stage 0. The only active string is λ. Give λ the color blue$_0$ and define $\Phi^\lambda = \lambda$.

Stage $s+1$. At this stage, we work for each $e \leqslant s+1$. The stage is divided into five substages.

Substage 1. (Red action) For each red$_e$ string ρ for which there is a $\nu \in V_e[s]$ with $\Phi^\rho \preccurlyeq \nu$, proceed as follows. Let $\Phi^{\rho i} = \nu$ for $i = 0, 1$. Remove the color red$_e$ from ρ and give it the color green$_e$. For the unique gray$_e$ string $\gamma \preccurlyeq \rho$, remove the color gray$_e$ from γ, and remove the color of all yellow$_e$ strings extending γ.

Substage 2. (Gray placement, or wipe-out recovery) For each blue$_e$ and nongray$_e$ string ν such that no string properly extending ν has a color, proceed as follows. Let $\alpha_0, \ldots, \alpha_n$ be the active strings that extend ν. If $\sum_{j \leqslant n} p_s(\alpha_j) > \frac{p_s(\nu)}{2}$ then give each α_i the colors gray$_e$ and red$_e$.

Substage 3. (Red push-out) For each red$_e$ string ρ, proceed as follows. Let γ be the unique gray$_e$ substring of ρ. If $\frac{p_{s+1}(\rho i)}{p_{s+1}(\gamma)} < 2^{-(e+4)}$ for $i = 0, 1$ then do nothing. Otherwise, let i be least such that $\frac{p_{s+1}(\rho i)}{p_{s+1}(\gamma)} \geqslant 2^{-(e+4)}$. Remove the red$_e$ color from ρ. Give the color red$_e$ to ρi and the color yellow$_e$ to $\rho(1-i)$. Let $\Phi^{\rho j} = \Phi^\rho$ for $j = 0, 1$.

Substage 4. (Wipe-outs) For each blue$_e$ string ν, proceed as follows. Let $\delta_0, \ldots, \delta_n$ be the red$_e$ and green$_e$ strings belonging to ν. If $\frac{\sum_{j \leqslant n} p_{s+1}(\delta_j)}{p_{s+1}(\nu)} > 2^{-(e+6)}$ then do nothing. Otherwise, remove all colors from all proper extensions of ν; if ν has color gray$_e$ then remove this color.

Substage 5. (Blue placement) For each nonactive string σ, proceed as follows. If there is an e such that σ has a blue$_e$ and nongray$_e$ substring ν none of whose proper extensions has a color (so that we are still attempting wipe-out recovery above ν), then do nothing. Otherwise, let e be least such that σ extends neither a green$_e$ nor a yellow$_e$ string, and give σ the color blue$_e$.

End of Construction.

Verification. We will need the following classes.

$$B_e = \{X : X \text{ has an initial segment with final color green}_e \text{ or yellow}_e\}.$$

$$S_e = \{X : X \text{ has an initial segment with final color red}_e\}.$$

Let Y be as above.

Let $X \in \bigcap_e B_e$. We claim that Φ^X is total and 1-generic. To establish this claim, fix e. Since $X \in B_e$ there is a string $\sigma \prec X$ with final color green$_e$

or yellow$_e$. In green$_e$ case, there is a $\tau \preccurlyeq \Phi^X$ in V_e by the construction. In the yellow$_e$ case, there cannot be an extension of Φ^σ in V_e, since otherwise R_e would eventually act to remove the color yellow$_e$ from σ. In either case, Φ^X meets or avoids V_e. Since for each n there is an e such that $V_e = 2^{\geqslant n}$, we see that Φ^X is also total.

Thus it is enough to show that $\mu(\{A : \Psi^A \text{ total and in } \bigcap_e B_e\}) > \frac{1}{8}$. Every set is in one of the following classes, where we let $B_{-1} = 2^\omega$.

(i) $\{A : \Psi^A \text{ total and in } \bigcap_e B_e\}$,

(ii) $\{A : \Psi^A \text{ total and in } [\![Y]\!]\}$,

(iii) $\bigcup_e \{A : \Psi^A \text{ total and in } S_e \setminus [\![Y]\!]\}$,

(iv) $\bigcup_e \{A : \Psi^A \text{ total and in } B_{e-1} \setminus (B_e \cup S_e \cup [\![Y]\!])\}$,

(v) $\{A : \Psi^A \text{ not total}\}$.

The last class has measure less than $\frac{1}{8}$, so it is enough to show that the sum of the measures of the classes in items 2–4 is at most $\frac{3}{4}$. We will do so by showing that $\mu(\{A : \Psi^A \in [\![Y]\!]\}) < \frac{1}{4}$, that $\mu(\{A : \Psi^A \text{ total and in } S_e \setminus [\![Y]\!]\}) \leqslant 2^{-(e+2)}$, and that $\mu(\{A : \Psi^A \text{ total and in } B_{e-1} \setminus (B_e \cup S_e \cup [\![Y]\!])\}) = 0$.

Lemma 8.21.17. $\mu(\{A : \Psi^A \in [\![Y]\!]\}) < \frac{1}{4}$.

Proof. Let T be the set of elements of Y with no proper substring in T. Then

$$\begin{aligned}
\frac{1}{4} &\geqslant 2\mu(\{A : \Psi^A \text{ is nontotal or computable}\}) \\
&\geqslant 2\mu(\{A : \exists \sigma \in T\, (\sigma \preccurlyeq \Psi^A) \text{ and } \Psi^A \text{ is computable or nontotal}\}) \\
&= 2\sum_{\sigma \in T} \mu(\{A : \sigma \preccurlyeq \Psi^A \text{ and } \Psi^A \text{ is computable or nontotal}\}) \\
&> \sum_{\sigma \in T} p(\sigma) = \sum_{\sigma \in T} \mu(\{A : \sigma \preccurlyeq \Psi^A\}) = \mu(\{A : \Psi^A \in [\![Y]\!]\}).
\end{aligned}$$

□

Lemma 8.21.18. $\mu(\{A : \Psi^A$ *is total and in* $S_e \setminus [\![Y]\!])\}) \leqslant 2^{-(e+2)}$.

Proof. Let R be the set of strings with final color red$_e$ and G be the set of strings with final color gray$_e$. Note that the elements of G are pairwise incompatible. Each element of R has a substring in G, and each element of G has at most one extension in R.

Let $\rho \in R$ and $\gamma \in G$ be such that $\gamma \preccurlyeq \rho$. If $p(\rho) > 2^{-(e+2)} p(\gamma)$ then $p(\rho 0) + p(\rho 1) < \frac{p(\rho)}{2}$, since otherwise the color red$_e$ would be passed from

ρ to one of the pi at some stage. Thus in this case $\rho \in Y$. So

$$\begin{aligned}\mu(\{A : \Psi^A \text{ is total and in } S_e \setminus [\![Y]\!])\}) &\leqslant \sum\{p(\rho) : \rho \in R \setminus Y\} \\ &\leqslant \sum\{2^{-(e+2)} p(\gamma) : \gamma \in G\} \leqslant 2^{-(e+2)}.\end{aligned}$$

□

We finish by showing that $\mu(\{A : \Psi^A \text{ total and in } B_{e-1} \setminus (B_e \cup S_e \cup [\![Y]\!])\}) = 0$. The intuitive reason that this fact is true is that if Ψ^A is total and in $B_{e-1} \setminus (B_e \cup S_e \cup [\![Y]\!])$, then we make infinitely many attempts to satisfy R_e for A, and as we will see, the probability that we do so is 0. We begin with some auxiliary lemmas.

Lemma 8.21.19. $B_e \subseteq B_{e-1}$.

Proof. The proof is the same as that of Lemma 8.21.12. □

Lemma 8.21.20. $\mu(\{A : \Psi^A$ *is computable and not in* $[\![Y]\!]\}) = 0$.

Proof. Assume not. Then there is a computable set $C \notin [\![Y]\!]$ such that $\mu(\{A : \Psi^A = C\}) > 0$. Since $\{A : \Psi^A = C\} = \bigcap_n \{A : C \upharpoonright n \prec \Psi^A\}$, for all sufficiently large n we have

$$\mu(\{A : \Psi^A = C\}) > \frac{\mu(\{A : C \upharpoonright n \preccurlyeq \Psi^A\})}{2} = \frac{p(C \upharpoonright n)}{2},$$

whence $C \upharpoonright n \in Y$, contradicting the assumption that $C \notin [\![Y]\!]$. □

Lemma 8.21.21. *Suppose that* $\mu(\{A : \Psi^A$ *total and in* $B_{e-1} \setminus (B_e \cup S_e \cup [\![Y]\!])\}) > 0$ *and let* $\delta < 1$. *Then there is a* σ *such that* $\mu(\{A : \Psi^A$ *total and in* $[\![\sigma]\!] \setminus (B_e \cup S_e \cup [\![Y]\!])\}) > \delta 2^{-|\sigma|}$.

Proof. It will be convenient to work in 3^ω. For $\sigma \in 3^{<\omega}$, we write $[\![\sigma]\!]_3$ for the basic open set of all extensions of σ in 3^ω. To avoid confusion, for $\sigma \in 2^{<\omega}$, we write $[\![\sigma]\!]_2$ instead of $[\![\sigma]\!]$ for the set of extensions of σ in 2^ω.

Let Θ be a functional from 2^ω to 3^ω defined by letting $\Theta^A(n) = \Psi^A(n)$ if the latter is defined, and $\Theta^A(n) = 2$ otherwise. Clearly Θ is Borel. Let $q(\sigma) = \mu(\{A : \sigma \prec \Theta^A\})$ for $\sigma \in 3^{<\omega}$. Note that if $\sigma \in 2^{<\omega}$ then $q(\sigma) = p(\sigma)$. By a result of Carathéodory (see Royden [335, p. 257]), there is a unique extension of q to a measure $\overline{q}$ on the Borel sets of 3^ω. It is easy to check that $\overline{q}(U) = \mu(\{A : \Theta^A \in U\})$ for Borel U. The Lebesgue Density Theorem can be proved for $\overline{q}$, so for every Borel $U \subseteq 3^\omega$ of positive $\overline{q}$-measure, there is a $\sigma \in 3^\omega$ such that the $\overline{q}$-density of U in $[\![\sigma]\!]_3$ exceeds δ.

By the hypothesis of the lemma, $\overline{q}(B_{e-1} \setminus (B_e \cup S_e \cup [\![Y]\!]_2)) > 0$, so there is a $\sigma \in 3^\omega$ such that the $\overline{q}$-density of $[\![\tau]\!]_2 \setminus (B_e \cup S_e \cup [\![Y]\!]_2)$ in $[\![\sigma]\!]_3$ exceeds δ. Clearly $\sigma \in 2^{<\omega}$, since otherwise $[\![\sigma]\!]_3 \cap ([\![\tau]\!]_2 \setminus (B_e \cup S_e \cup [\![Y]\!]_2)) = \emptyset$, and by the definition of $\overline{q}$ we have that $\mu(\{A : \Psi^A$ total and in $[\![\sigma]\!]_2 \setminus (B_e \cup S_e \cup [\![Y]\!]_2)\}) > \delta 2^{-|\sigma|}$. □

Lemma 8.21.22. *$\mu(\{A : \Psi^A$ total and in $B_{e-1} \setminus (B_e \cup S_e \cup [\![Y]\!])\}) = 0$.*

Proof. Assume for a contradiction that the lemma fails. Let σ be as in the previous lemma for $\delta = 1 - 2^{-(e+7)}$. If $e > 0$ then, since B_{e-1} is generated by the strings with final color green$_e$ or yellow$_e$, we may assume that σ extends such a string.

If a string has final color gray$_e$ then every set extending it is either in $B_e \cup S_e$ or is the limit of a sequence of red$_e$ strings, in which case it is computable. Thus, by Lemma 8.21.20, σ cannot extend such a string. It follows that we appoint a maximal set I of pairwise incompatible extensions of σ and give each of them the color blue$_e$. There is a $\nu \in I$ such that $\mu(\{A : \Psi^A$ total and in $[\![\nu]\!] \setminus (B_e \cup S_e \cup [\![Y]\!])\}) > (1 - 2^{-(e+7)})2^{-|\nu|}$.

After ν has wiped-out for the last time at a stage s_0, we appoint a maximal set of pairwise incompatible gray$_e$ strings $\gamma_0, \ldots, \gamma_m \succcurlyeq \nu$. Let δ_i^s be the red$_e$ or green$_e$ string extending γ_i at stage $s \geqslant s_0$, or $\delta_i^s = \gamma_i$ if there is no such string. Let $C_s = [\![\{\delta_s^i : i \leqslant m\}]\!]$ and let $C = \bigcap_s C_s$. Let $X \in C$. If there is an i such that the δ_i^s come to a finite limit $\delta_i \prec X$ then δ_i is either green$_e$ or red$_e$, and hence $X \in B_e \cup S_e$. Otherwise, X is the limit of δ_i^s for some i, and hence is computable. Thus, by Lemma 8.21.20, $\mu(\{A : \Psi^A$ total and in $C\}) \leqslant \mu(\{A : \Psi^A$ total and in $B_e \cup S_e \cup [\![Y]\!]\})$.

Therefore, to obtain a contradiction, it is enough to show that $\mu(\{A : \Psi^A$ total and in $C\}) \geqslant 2^{-(e+7)}2^{-|\nu|}$. Assume not. Then, since $C_{s_0} \supseteq C_{s_0+1} \supseteq \cdots$, for all sufficiently large s, we have $\mu(\{A : \Psi^A$ total and in $C_s\}) < 2^{-(e+7)}2^{-|\nu|}$. It is then easy to see that for all sufficiently large s we have $\sum_{i \leqslant m} p_s(\delta_i^s) < 2^{-(e+7)}2^{-|\nu|} < 2^{-(e+6)}p_s(\nu)$, the last inequality holding because $p(\nu) > 2^{-|\nu|+1}$. Therefore, ν must wipe-out again after stage s_0, contradicting the choice of s_0. □

As argued above, this lemma completes the proof of the theorem. □

The original proof of the following consequence of the above result was, to the authors' knowledge, the first use of the method of risking measure.

Corollary 8.21.23 (Paris [314]). *The upward closure of the class of minimal degrees has measure* 0.

Jockusch [188] showed that the initial segment of degrees below a 1-generic degree is never a lattice, so we have the following.

Corollary 8.21.24 (Kurtz [228]). *The upward closure of the class of degrees whose initial segments form lattices has measure* 0.

Part III

Relative Randomness

9
Measures of Relative Randomness

Measures of relative complexity such as Turing reducibility, wtt-reducibility, and so on have proven to be central tools in computability theory. The resulting degree structures have been widely studied, and there has been considerable interplay between structural results and insights informing our understanding of the concept of computability and its application to such areas as effective mathematics and reverse mathematics. In this chapter, we examine reducibilities that can act as measures of relative complexity, and hence perform a similar role in the theory of algorithmic randomness.

We use the term "reducibility" loosely, to mean any transitive and reflexive preorder on 2^ω. For example, given the association between randomness and high prefix-free complexity of initial segments, it is natural to consider *K-reducibility*, where $A \leqslant_K B$ if $K(A \upharpoonright n) \leqslant K(B \upharpoonright n) + O(1)$, and think of this preorder as a reducibility measuring relative randomness, although there is no corresponding concept of reduction in this case. That is, we have no way of generating a short description for $A \upharpoonright n$ from one for $B \upharpoonright n$, just the knowledge that there is one. Before studying this important notion, we introduce some stronger reducibilities, many of which are "real" reducibilities, beginning with one defined by Solovay [371]. In Section 9.2 we will discuss Solovay's motivation for considering this notion.

R.G. Downey and D. Hirschfeldt, *Algorithmic Randomness and Complexity*, Theory and Applications of Computability, DOI 10.1007/978-0-387-68441-3_9,

9.1 Solovay reducibility

As we will see below, probably the easiest way to define Solovay reducibility on left-c.e. reals is to say that α is Solovay reducible to β if there are a constant c and a left-c.e. real γ such that $c\beta = \alpha + \gamma$. We begin, however, with Solovay's original definition, which is not restricted to left-c.e. reals (although Solovay reducibility is badly behaved outside the left-c.e. reals (see Proposition 9.6.1 below), and hence its applications to date have been restricted to the left-c.e. reals).

Definition 9.1.1 (Solovay [371]). A real α is *Solovay reducible*, or *S-reducible*, to a real β (written $\alpha \leqslant_S \beta$) if there are a constant c and a partial computable function $f : \mathbb{Q} \to \mathbb{Q}$ such that if $q \in \mathbb{Q}$ and $q < \beta$, then $f(q)\downarrow < \alpha$ and $\alpha - f(q) < c(\beta - q)$.

One way to look at this definition is that a sequence of rationals converging to β from below can be used to generate one that converges to α from below at the same rate or faster. This idea is made precise for left-c.e. reals in the following result.

Proposition 9.1.2 (Calude, Coles, Hertling, and Khoussainov [47]). *Let α and β be left-c.e. reals, and let $q_0 < q_1 < \cdots \to \alpha$ and $r_0 < r_1 < \cdots \to \beta$ be computable sequences of rationals. Then $\alpha \leqslant_S \beta$ iff there are a constant c and a computable function g such that $\alpha - q_{g(n)} < c(\beta - r_n)$ for all n.*

Proof. Suppose that $\alpha \leqslant_S \beta$, and let c and f be as in Definition 9.1.1. Given n, we have $f(r_n)\downarrow < \alpha$, so there is an m such that $f(r_n) < q_m$. Let $g(n) = m$. Then $\alpha - q_{g(n)} < \alpha - f(r_n) < c(\beta - r_n)$.

Conversely, suppose there are c and g as above. Given $s \in \mathbb{Q}$, search for an n such that $s < r_n$, and if such an n is found, then let $f(s) = q_{g(n)}$. If $s < \beta$ then n exists, and $\alpha - f(s) < c(\beta - r_n) < c(\beta - s)$. □

The connection between Solovay reducibility and relative randomness comes from the fact that Solovay reducibility implies K-reducibility (as well as *C-reducibility*, where $A \leqslant_C B$ if $C(A \upharpoonright n) \leqslant C(B \upharpoonright n) + O(1)$). To prove this fact, we begin with a lemma.

Lemma 9.1.3 (Solovay [371]). *For each k there is a constant c_k such that for all n and all $\sigma, \tau \in 2^n$, if $|0.\sigma - 0.\tau| < 2^{k-n}$, then $C(\sigma) = C(\tau) \pm c_k$ and $K(\sigma) = K(\tau) \pm c_k$.*

Proof. Fix k. Given σ of some length n, we can compute the set S of $\tau \in 2^n$ such that $|0.\sigma - 0.\tau| < 2^{k-n}$. The size of S depends only on k, and we can describe any $\tau \in S$ by giving σ and τ's position in the lexicographic ordering of S. Thus $C(\tau) \leqslant C(\sigma) + O(1)$ and $K(\tau) \leqslant K(\sigma) + O(1)$, where the constants depend only on k. The lemma follows by symmetry. □

Theorem 9.1.4 (Solovay [371]). *If $\alpha \leqslant_S \beta$ then $C(\alpha \upharpoonright n) \leqslant C(\beta \upharpoonright n) + O(1)$ and $K(\alpha \upharpoonright n) \leqslant K(\beta \upharpoonright n) + O(1)$.*

Proof. Let c and f be as in Definition 9.1.1. Let k be such that $c+2 < 2^k$. Let $\beta_n = 0.(\beta \upharpoonright n)$ and $\alpha_n = 0.(\alpha \upharpoonright n)$. Since β_n is rational and $\beta - \beta_n \leqslant 2^{-n}$, we have $\alpha - f(\beta_n) < c2^{-n}$. Let $\tau_n \in 2^n$ be such that $|0.\tau_n - f(\beta_n)| < 2^{-n}$. Then

$$|\alpha_n - 0.\tau_n| \leqslant |\alpha - \alpha_n| + \alpha - f(\beta_n) + |0.\tau_n - f(\beta_n)| < (c+2)2^{-n} < 2^{k-n}.$$

Thus, by Lemma 9.1.3, $K(\alpha \upharpoonright n) \leqslant K(\tau_n) + O(1)$. But τ_n can be obtained computably from $\beta \upharpoonright n$, so $K(\alpha \upharpoonright n) \leqslant K(\beta \upharpoonright n) + O(1)$. The proof for plain complexity is the same. □

One useful property of Solovay reducibility is that it also implies Turing reducibility (which we will see later is not the case for K-reducibility).

Proposition 9.1.5. *For any reals α and β, if $\alpha \leqslant_S \beta$ then $\alpha \leqslant_T \beta$.*

Proof. Let c and f be as in Definition 9.1.1. For each n, we can β-computably find a rational $q_n < \beta$ such that $\beta - q_n < 2^{-n}$. Then $g(q_0), g(q_1), \ldots$ is a β-computable sequence of rationals converging to α at a computably bounded rate. Thus $\alpha \leqslant_T \beta$. □

On the other hand, S-reducibility does not imply wtt-reducibility. Recall that a real is strongly c.e. if it is a c.e. set when thought of as a subset of $\mathbb{N}$.

Theorem 9.1.6 (Downey, Hirschfeldt, and LaForte [113]). *There exist left-c.e. reals $\alpha \leqslant_S \beta$ such that $\alpha \nleqslant_{wtt} \beta$. Moreover, β can be chosen to be strongly c.e.*

Proof. It will be convenient to build an almost c.e. set A and a c.e. set B and think of α and β as $0.A$ and $0.B$, respectively. We ensure that $\alpha \leqslant_S \beta$ while meeting the following requirement for each e and i.

$$\mathcal{R}_{e,i} : \forall n\, (\varphi_e^B(n)\downarrow < \Phi_i(n)\downarrow) \;\Rightarrow\; \Phi_e^B \neq A.$$

We arrange these requirements into a priority list in the usual way.

The idea for satisfying a single requirement $\mathcal{R}_{e,i}$ is simple. We choose a number n and wait until $\Phi_i(n)[s]\downarrow$. We then put n into B and put the interval $(n, s]$ into A. This action adds 2^{-n} to β and less than 2^{-n} to α. We then wait until $\Phi_e^B(n)\downarrow= 0$ with use less than $\Phi_i(n)$ (and hence less than s, by the usual use conventions). If this happens, we put n into A, remove the interval $(n, s]$ from A, and put s into B. This action adds 2^{-s} to both α and β. It also preserves $\varphi_e^B(n)$, and hence ensures that $\Phi_e^B(n) = 0 \neq A(n)$.

We now proceed to the general construction. Each requirement $\mathcal{R}_{e,i}$ begins by picking a fresh large $n_{e,i}$. Initially, we say that all requirements are in the *first phase.* At stage s, we say that $\mathcal{R}_{e,i}$ *requires attention* if either $\mathcal{R}_{e,i}$ is in the first phase and $\Phi_i(n_{e,i})[s]\downarrow$, or $\mathcal{R}_{e,i}$ is in the second phase (defined below) and $\Phi_e^B(n_{e,i})[s]\downarrow= 0$ with $\varphi_e^B(n_{e,i})[s] < \Phi_i(n_{e,i})$.

At stage s, let $\mathcal{R}_{e,i}$ be the strongest priority requirement that requires attention. (If there is no such requirement then proceed to the next stage.)

Initialize all weaker priority requirements, which means they have to pick their n's to be fresh large numbers and are all now in the first phase. If $\mathcal{R}_{e,i}$ is in its first phase, then put $n_{e,i}$ into B, put the interval $(n_{e,i}, s]$ into A, let $s_{e,i} = s$, and declare $\mathcal{R}_{e,i}$ to be in its *second phase.* Note that $n_{e,i}$ was not already in B because requirements weaker than $\mathcal{R}_{e,i}$ work beyond $n_{e,i}$, while whenever a requirement stronger than $\mathcal{R}_{e,i}$ requires attention, $n_{e,i}$ is picked to be a fresh large number. Thus, this action adds $2^{-n_{e,i}}$ to β and less than $2^{-n_{e,i}}$ to α. If $\mathcal{R}_{e,i}$ is in its second phase, then put $n_{e,i}$ into A, remove the interval $(n_{e,i}, s_{e,i}]$ from A, and put $s_{e,i}$ into B. This action adds $2^{-s_{e,i}}$ to both α and β.

This completes the construction. Clearly, A is almost c.e. and B is c.e. Furthermore, $\alpha \leqslant_S \beta$, since at each stage we add at least as much to β as to α. Assume by induction that we are at a point in the construction such that no requirement stronger than $\mathcal{R}_{e,i}$ will ever require attention, so $n_{e,i}$ has reached its final value. If $\Phi_i(n_{e,i})\downarrow$ then eventually $\mathcal{R}_{e,i}$ will require first phase attention, at a stage $s_{e,i}$. Note that $\Phi_i(n_{e,i}) \leqslant s_{e,i}$. At this point, $(n_{e,i}, s_{e,i}]$ enters A, but $n_{e,i}$ is not in A. If we never have $\Phi_e^B(n_{e,i})[t]\downarrow = 0$ with $\varphi_e^B(n_{e,i})[t] < \Phi_i(n_{e,i})$ for $t > s_{e,i}$, then $\mathcal{R}_{e,i}$ is satisfied, since we never put $n_{e,i}$ into A. Otherwise, at the first such stage t, we put $n_{e,i}$ into A but do not change B below $\varphi_e^B(n_{e,i})[t]$. From that point on, we never change B below $\varphi_e^B(n_{e,i})[t]$, and never remove $n_{e,i}$ from A. Thus $\mathcal{R}_{e,i}$ is satisfied. In any case, $\mathcal{R}_{e,i}$ eventually stops requiring attention. □

We finish this section by giving another characterization of Solovay reducibility on left-c.e. reals already mentioned above, namely that α is Solovay reducible to β iff there are a constant c and a left-c.e. real γ such that $c\beta = \alpha + \gamma$. We begin with a lemma that will also be useful below. Here and below, when we have a sequence $r_0, r_1, \ldots$, we take the expression $r_n - r_{n-1}$ to have value r_0 when $n = 0$.

Lemma 9.1.7 (Downey, Hirschfeldt, and Nies [116]). *Let α and β be left-c.e. reals and let $r_0 < r_1 < \cdots \to \beta$ be a computable sequence of rationals. Then $\alpha \leqslant_S \beta$ iff there is a computable sequence of rationals $p_0 < p_1 < \cdots \to \alpha$ such that for some constant d we have $p_s - p_{s-1} < d(r_s - r_{s-1})$ for all s.*

Proof. If there is a sequence $p_0 < p_1 < \cdots$ as in the lemma, then $\alpha - p_n = \sum_{s>n} p_s - p_{s-1} < d \sum_{s>n} r_s - r_{s-1} = d(\beta - r_n)$, so by Proposition 9.1.2, $\alpha \leqslant_S \beta$. We now prove the converse.

Let $q_0 < q_1 < \cdots \to \alpha$ be a computable sequence of rationals, let c and g be as in Proposition 9.1.2, and let $d > c$ be such that $q_{g(0)} < dr_0$. We may assume without loss of generality that g is increasing. Let $p_0 = q_{g(0)}$.

There must be an $s_0 > 0$ such that $q_{g(s_0)} - q_{g(0)} < c(r_{s_0} - r_0)$, since otherwise we would have $\alpha - q_{g(0)} = \lim_s q_{g(s)} - q_{g(0)} \geqslant \lim_s c(r_s - r_0) = c(\beta - r_0)$, contradicting our choice of c and g. We can now define $p_1, \ldots, p_{s_0}$ so that $p_0 < \cdots < p_{s_0} = q_{g(s_0)}$ and $p_s - p_{s-1} \leqslant c(r_s - r_{s-1}) < d(r_s - r_{s-1})$

for all $s \leqslant s_0$. For example, if we let μ the minimum value of $c(r_s - r_{s-1})$ for $s \leqslant s_0$ and let t be least such that $p_0 + c(r_t - r_0) > q_{g(s_0)} - 2^{-t}\mu$, then we can define

$$p_{s+1} = \begin{cases} p_s + c(r_{s+1} - r_s) & \text{if } s+1 < t \\ q_{g(s_0)} - 2^{-(s+1)}\mu & \text{if } t \leqslant s+1 < s_0 \\ q_{g(s_0)} & \text{if } s+1 = s_0. \end{cases}$$

We can repeat the procedure in the previous paragraph with s_0 in place of 0 to obtain an $s_1 > s_0$ and $p_{s_0+1}, \dots, p_{s_1}$ such that $p_{s_0} < \cdots < p_{s_1} = q_{g(s_1)}$ and $p_s - p_{s-1} < d(r_s - r_{s-1})$ for all $s_0 < s \leqslant s_1$. Proceeding by recursion in this way, we can define a computable sequence of rationals $p_0 < p_1 < \cdots$ with the desired properties. □

Theorem 9.1.8 (Downey, Hirschfeldt, and Nies [116]). *Let α and β be left-c.e. reals. The following are equivalent.*

(i) $\alpha \leqslant_S \beta$.

(ii) *For each computable sequence of nonnegative rationals $b_0, b_1, \dots$ such that $\beta = \sum_n b_n$, there are a constant d and a computable sequence of rationals $\varepsilon_0, \varepsilon_1, \dots \in [0, d]$ such that $\alpha = \sum_n \varepsilon_n b_n$.*

(iii) *There are a constant d and a left-c.e. real γ such that $d\beta = \alpha + \gamma$.*

Proof. (i) ⇒ (ii) Let $b_0, b_1, \dots$ be a computable sequence of nonnegative rationals such that $\beta = \sum_i b_i$ and let $r_n = \sum_{i \leqslant n} b_i$. Apply Lemma 9.1.7 to obtain d and $p_0, p_1, \dots$ as in that lemma. Let $\varepsilon_n = \frac{p_n - p_{n-1}}{b_n}$. Then $\sum_n \varepsilon_n b_n = \sum_n p_n - p_{n-1} = \alpha$, and $\varepsilon_n = \frac{p_n - p_{n-1}}{(r_n - r_{n-1})} \in [0, d]$ for all n.

(ii) ⇒ (iii) Let $b_0, b_1, \dots$ be a computable sequence of nonnegative rationals such that $\beta = \sum_n b_n$. Let $\varepsilon_0, \varepsilon_1, \dots$ be as in (ii), and let $\gamma = \sum_n (d - \varepsilon_n) b_n$.

(iii) ⇒ (i) Let $r_0 < r_1 < \cdots \to \alpha$ and $s_0 < s_1 < \cdots \to \gamma$ be computable sequences. Let $p_n = \frac{r_n + s_n}{d}$. Then $p_0 < p_1 < \cdots \to \beta$ and $\alpha - r_n < d(\beta - p_n)$, so by Proposition 9.1.2, $\alpha \leqslant_S \beta$. □

9.2 The Kučera-Slaman Theorem

Solovay introduced Solovay reducibility to define a class of reals with many of the properties of Ω, but with a machine-independent definition. First he noted that Ω is *Solovay complete*, in the sense that $\alpha \leqslant_S \Omega$ for all left-c.e. reals α.

Proposition 9.2.1 (Solovay [371]). *If α is a left-c.e. real then $\alpha \leqslant_S \Omega$.*

Proof. Let α be a left-c.e. real. Let M be a prefix-free machine such that $\alpha = \mu([\![\mathrm{dom}\, M]\!])$, and let τ be such that $\mathcal{U}(\tau\sigma) = M(\sigma)$ for all σ. If we can approximate Ω to within $2^{-(|\tau|+n)}$, then we can approximate α to within 2^{-n}, so $\alpha \leqslant_S \Omega$. $\square$

Furthermore, for any (not necessarily left-c.e.) real α, if $\Omega \leqslant_S \alpha$ then, by Theorem 9.1.4, α is 1-random. Solovay [371] proved that the Solovay-complete left-c.e. reals (which he called *Ω-like*) possess many of the properties of Ω. He remarked: "It seems strange that we will be able to prove so much about the behavior of $[K(\Omega \upharpoonright n)]$ when, a priori, the definition of Ω is thoroughly model dependent. What our discussion has shown is that our results hold for a class of reals (that include the value of the universal measures ...) and that the function $[K(\Omega \upharpoonright n)]$ is model independent to within $O(1)$."

Several left-c.e. reals that arise naturally in the theory of algorithmic randomness are Ω-like. For example, Kučera and Slaman [221] showed that if $\{U_n\}_{n\in\omega}$ is a universal Martin-Löf test, then $\mu(U_n)$ is Ω-like for all $n > 0$.[1] Another example are the values $Q(\sigma)$ from Definition 3.9.3.

The following two results establish that using Ω-like reals in place of Ω makes no difference in the same way that using any set of the same m-degree as the halting problem gives a version of the halting problem, by Myhill's Theorem. Thus, it turns out that Solovay's observations are not so strange after all.

The first result establishes that any Ω-like real is a halting probability.

Theorem 9.2.2 (Calude, Hertling, Khoussainov, and Wang [50]). *If α is Ω-like then there is a universal prefix-free machine $\widehat{\mathcal{U}}$ such that $\mu([\![\operatorname{dom}\widehat{\mathcal{U}}]\!]) = \alpha$.*

Proof. By Lemma 9.1.7, there are approximations to α and Ω, and a constant c such that $\Omega_{s+1} - \Omega_s < 2^c(\alpha_{s+1} - \alpha_s)$ for all s. We may assume that c is large enough so that $\alpha + 2^{-c} < 1$ and $2^{-c} < \alpha$.

Let $\beta = \alpha + 2^{-c}(1 - \Omega)$. Note that β is a left-c.e. real, since

$$\beta = \sum_s \big(\alpha_{s+1} - \alpha_s + 2^{-c}(1 - (\Omega_{s+1} - \Omega_s))\big),$$

and each summand is positive. Also, $\beta < 1$, so there is a prefix-free machine M such that $\mu([\![\operatorname{dom} M]\!]) = \beta$. Since $\beta > 2^{-c}$, we may assume that there is a $\rho \in 2^c$ such that $M(\rho)\downarrow$. Let $\widehat{\mathcal{U}}(\sigma) = M(\sigma)$ if $\sigma \not\succcurlyeq \rho$ and let $\widehat{\mathcal{U}}(\rho\tau) = \mathcal{U}(\tau)$ for all τ. Then $\widehat{\mathcal{U}}$ codes $\mathcal{U}$ and hence is universal, and $\mu([\![\operatorname{dom}\widehat{\mathcal{U}}]\!]) = \mu([\![\operatorname{dom} M]\!]) - 2^{-c} + 2^{-c}\Omega = \beta - 2^{-c}(1 - \Omega) = \alpha$. $\square$

The complete characterization of the 1-random left-c.e. reals in terms of Solovay reducibility is given by the following result.

---

[1]Kučera and Slaman [221] noted that a version of this result was proved earlier by Demuth [93].

Theorem 9.2.3 (Kučera-Slaman Theorem [221]). *If α is 1-random and left-c.e. then it is Ω-like.*

Proof. Let β be a left-c.e. real. We need to show that $\beta \leqslant_S \alpha$. Define a Martin-Löf test $\{U_n\}_{n\in\omega}$ in stages. At stage s act as follows. If $\alpha_s \in U_n[s]$ then do nothing. Otherwise let t be the last stage at which we put anything into U_n (or $t = 0$ if there is no such stage), and put the interval $(\alpha_s, \alpha_s + 2^{-n}(\beta_s - \beta_t))$ into U_n. We have $\mu(U_n) \leqslant 2^{-n}\beta$, so $\{U_n\}_{n\in\omega}$ is a Martin-Löf test. Thus there is an n such that $\alpha \notin U_n$. Let $s_0 = 0$ and let $s_1, s_2, \ldots$ be the stages at which we put something into U_n. Then for $i > 0$ we have $\alpha_{s_{i+1}} - \alpha_{s_i} > 2^{-n}(\beta_{s_i} - \beta_{s_{i-1}})$, so $\beta \leqslant_S \alpha$. □

Thus we see that for left-c.e. reals α, the following are equivalent.

(i) α is 1-random.

(ii) $\beta \leqslant_S \alpha$ for all left-c.e. reals β.

(iii) $\Omega \leqslant_S \alpha$.

(iv) $K(\beta \upharpoonright n) \leqslant K(\alpha \upharpoonright n) + O(1)$ for all left-c.e. reals β.

(v) $K(\Omega \upharpoonright n) \leqslant K(\alpha \upharpoonright n) + O(1)$.

(vi) $K(\Omega \upharpoonright n) = K(\alpha \upharpoonright n) \pm O(1)$.

(vii) α is the halting probability of some universal machine, that is, a version of Ω.

Notice in particular that if α and β are both 1-random left-c.e. reals, then $\alpha \equiv_S \beta$, and hence $K(\alpha \upharpoonright n) = K(\beta \upharpoonright n) \pm O(1)$. Since the 1-randomness of X requires only that $K(X \upharpoonright n) \geqslant n + O(1)$, but $K(X \upharpoonright n)$ can be as large as $n + K(n) \pm O(1)$, the prefix-free complexity of the initial segments of a 1-random set can oscillate quite a bit. However, this oscillation is the same for all left-c.e. reals. That is, remarkably, all 1-random left-c.e. reals have high complexity (well above n) and relatively low complexity (close to n) at the same initial segments.

These results can be seen as providing a randomness-theoretic version of Myhill's Theorem 2.4.12.

It is interesting to note that all 1-random left-d.c.e. reals are either left-c.e. or right-c.e.

Theorem 9.2.4 (Rettinger [unpublished]). *Let α be a 1-random left-d.c.e. real. Then either α or $1 - \alpha$ is a left-c.e. real.*

Proof. By the characterization of left-d.c.e. reals in Theorem 5.4.2, there is a computable sequence of rationals $q_0, q_1, \ldots$ such that $\lim_i q_i = \alpha$ and $\sum_i |q_{i+1} - q_i| < 1$. Suppose there is an n such that $q_i \leqslant \alpha$ for all $i > n$. Then we can pick out a nondecreasing subsequence of the q_i converging to α, and hence α is left-c.e. Similarly, if there is an n such that $q_i \geqslant \alpha$ for all $i > n$ then $1 - \alpha$ is left-c.e. We claim that one of these two cases must hold. Suppose otherwise, and let I_i be (q_i, q_{i+1}) if $q_i \leqslant q_{i+1}$ and (q_{i+1}, q_i) if $q_i > q_{i+1}$. Then $\alpha \in I_i$ for infinitely many i. But $\sum_i |I_i| < 1$, so the I_i form a Solovay test, contradicting the 1-randomness of α. □

9.3 Presentations of left-c.e. reals and complexity

Recall from Chapter 5 that a presentation of a left-c.e. real α is a prefix-free c.e. set $W \subset 2^{<\omega}$ such that $\alpha = \sum_{\sigma \in W} 2^{-|\sigma|}$. In Corollary 5.3.14 we saw that there are noncomputable left-c.e. reals α such that any presentation of α is computable. By Theorems 9.2.2 and 9.2.3, such reals cannot be 1-random, since the domain of a universal prefix-free machine is not computable. However, Stephan and Wu [380] showed that they must have rather high initial segment complexity, and in particular must be weakly 1-random.

Theorem 9.3.1 (Stephan and Wu [380]). *Let α be a left-c.e. real for which there is a computable f such that $K(\alpha \upharpoonright f(n)) < f(n) - n$ for all n. Then α has a noncomputable presentation.*

Proof. We may assume that f is increasing. It is easy to see that there is a computable sequence of rationals $\alpha_0 < \alpha_1 < \cdots \to \alpha$ such that, thinking of the α_s as strings, for each s we have $|\alpha_s| > f(s)$ and $K(\alpha_s \upharpoonright f(n)) < f(n) - n$ for all $n \leqslant s$. Let $r_0 = \alpha_0$ and $r_{s+1} = \alpha_{s+1} - \alpha_s$. Thinking of the r_s as strings, let $L = \{(n, 0^s) : s \in \mathbb{N} \wedge r_s(n) = 1\}$. Then $\sum_{(n,0^s) \in L} 2^{-n} = \sum_s r_s = \alpha$, so L is a KC set, and the domain P of the corresponding prefix-free machine is a presentation of L. Thus it is enough to show that P is not computable.

Assume for a contradiction that P is computable. Then for each n we know all strings of length n in P, and hence know all s such that $(n, 0^s) \in L$. Thus there is a computable g such that $s > g(n) \Rightarrow r_s < 2^{-n}$ for all n. Since α is not computable, there is an n such that $\alpha - \alpha_{g(f(n))} > 2^{-n+2}$. Since $K(\alpha_s \upharpoonright f(n)) < f(n) - n$ for all $s \geqslant g(f(n))$, we have $|\{\alpha_s \upharpoonright f(n) : s \geqslant g(f(n))\}| < 2^{f(n)-n}$. It follows that there is an $s \geqslant g(f(n))$ such that $r_{s+1} = \alpha_{s+1} - \alpha_s > 2^{-n+2} 2^{-(f(n)-n)-2} = 2^{-f(n)}$, contradicting the definition of g. □

In particular, by Theorem 7.2.16, we have the following.

Corollary 9.3.2 (Stephan and Wu [380]). *If every presentation of a left-c.e. real α is computable then α is either computable or weakly 1-random but not 1-random.*

9.4 Solovay functions and 1-randomness

Recall from Section 3.12 that Solovay proved the existence of a Solovay function, that is, a computable function f such that $\sum_n 2^{-f(n)} < \infty$, whence $K(n) \leqslant f(n) + O(1)$, and $\liminf_n f(n) - K(n) < \infty$. It turns out that, among the computable functions f such that sum $\sum_n 2^{-f(n)}$ is finite, the Solovay functions are precisely those for which this sum is a 1-random real. The proof of this result exploits the fact that the Kučera-Slaman Theorem provides a method for characterizing Solovay functions in terms of Ω.

Theorem 9.4.1 (Bienvenu and Downey [39]). *Let f be a computable function. The following are equivalent.*

(i) *f is a Solovay function.*

(ii) *$\sum_n 2^{-f(n)}$ is a 1-random real.*

Proof. (i) $\Rightarrow$ (ii). If f is a Solovay function, we already know by definition that $\alpha = \sum_n 2^{-f(n)}$ is finite. Let us now prove that α is 1-random. Suppose it is not. Then for each c there is a k such that $K(\alpha \upharpoonright k) \leqslant k - c$. Given $\alpha \upharpoonright k$, we can effectively find an s such that $\sum_{n>s} 2^{-f(n)} \leqslant 2^{-k}$. Hence, by a standard KC Theorem argument, we have $K(n \mid \alpha \upharpoonright k) \leqslant f(n) - k + O(1)$ for all $n > s$. Thus, for all $n > s$,

$$K(n) \leqslant f(n) + K(\alpha \upharpoonright k) - k + O(1)$$
$$\leqslant f(n) + (k - c) - k + O(1) \leqslant f(n) - c + O(1).$$

Since c can be taken arbitrarily large, $\lim_n f(n) - K(n) = \infty$; i.e., f is not a Solovay function.

(ii) $\Rightarrow$ (i). Suppose for a contradiction that f is not a Solovay function but $\alpha = \sum_n 2^{-f(n)}$ is 1-random. By the Kučera-Slaman Theorem 9.2.3, $\Omega \leqslant_S \alpha$. Let g be as in the definition of Solovay reducibility. That is, g is a partial computable function such that, for some d, if q is a rational less than α, then $g(q)\downarrow < \Omega$ and $\Omega - g(q) < 2^d(\alpha - q)$.

Fix c and suppose that $\alpha \upharpoonright k$ is given for some k. Since $\alpha - (\alpha \upharpoonright k) < 2^{-k}$, we have $\Omega - g(\alpha \upharpoonright k) < 2^{-k+d}$. Thus, from $\alpha \upharpoonright k$ we can compute an $s(k)$ such that $\sum_{n>s(k)} 2^{-K(n)} \leqslant 2^{-k+d}$. If k is large enough, then $n > s(k) \Rightarrow K(n) \leqslant f(n) - c - d$ (because f is not a Solovay function), whence

$$\sum_{n>s(k)} 2^{-f(n)} \leqslant 2^{-c-d} \sum_{n>s(k)} 2^{-K(n)} \leqslant 2^{-c-d}2^{-k+d} \leqslant 2^{-k-c}.$$

So for large enough k, knowing $\alpha \upharpoonright k$ suffices to effectively approximate α to within 2^{-k-c}. In other words, $\alpha \upharpoonright (k + c)$ can be computed from $\alpha \upharpoonright k$ and c. Therefore, for all large enough k,

$$K(\alpha \upharpoonright (k + c)) \leqslant K(\alpha \upharpoonright k, c) + O(1) \leqslant K(\alpha \upharpoonright k) + 2\log c + O(1).$$

The constant in that expression is independent of c, so choose c such that the expression $2\log c + O(1)$ in the above inequality is smaller than $c/2$. Then, for all large enough k,

$$K(\alpha \upharpoonright (k+c)) \leqslant K(\alpha \upharpoonright k) + \frac{c}{2}.$$

An easy induction then shows that $K(\alpha \upharpoonright k) \leqslant O\left(\frac{k}{2}\right)$, contradicting the assumption that α is 1-random. □

The following easy corollary, which says that there are *nondecreasing* computable upper bounds for K, is not at all obvious without the previous result.

Corollary 9.4.2 (Bienvenu and Downey [39]). *There exist nondecreasing Solovay functions.*

Proof. It suffices to take a computable sequence $\{r_n\}_{n\in\omega}$ of rational numbers such that every r_n is a negative power of 2, the r_n are nonincreasing, and $\sum_n r_n$ is a 1-random real. (It is easy to see that such sequences exist.) Then let $f(n) = -\log(r_n)$ for all n. The function f is computable, nondecreasing, and, by Theorem 9.4.1, is a Solovay function. □

9.5 Solovay degrees of left-c.e. reals

As with any reducibility, we can take equivalence classes of reals under S-reducibility, which we call *Solovay degrees* or *S-degrees*, and are partially ordered in the obvious way. One way to express the main result of Section 9.2 is that there is a largest S-degree of left-c.e. reals, which consists exactly of the 1-random left-c.e. reals, or, equivalently, the versions of Ω. We have seen that S-reducibility implies Turing reducibility, and it is easy to show that if α is computable then $\alpha \leqslant_S \beta$ for any left-c.e. real β. Thus there is also a least S-degree of left-c.e. reals, which consists exactly of the computable reals. As we will see, between these two extremes there is a rich structure.

It was observed by Solovay [371] and others, such as Calude, Hertling, Khoussainov, and Wang [50], that the Solovay degrees of left-c.e. reals form an uppersemilattice, with the join operation induced by addition (or multiplication). Downey, Hirschfeldt, and Nies [116] showed that this uppersemilattice is distributive, where an uppersemilattice is *distributive* if $c \leqslant a \vee b \Rightarrow \exists c_0 \leqslant a\, \exists c_1 \leqslant b\, (c = c_0 \vee c_1)$.

Theorem 9.5.1 (Solovay [371], Calude, Hertling, Khoussainov, and Wang [50], Downey, Hirschfeldt, and Nies [116]). *The Solovay degrees of left-c.e. reals form a distributive uppersemilattice, with the join operation induced by addition.*

Proof. Let α and β be left-c.e. reals. By Theorem 9.1.8, $\alpha, \beta \leqslant_S \alpha + \beta$. Now suppose that $\alpha, \beta \leqslant_S \gamma$. Let $q_0, q_1, \ldots$ be a computable sequence of nonnegative rationals such that $\gamma = \sum_n q_n$. By Theorem 9.1.8, there is a constant d and computable sequences of rationals $\varepsilon_0, \varepsilon_1, \ldots \in [0, d]$ and $\delta_0, \delta_1, \ldots \in [0, d]$ such that $\alpha = \sum_n \varepsilon_n q_n$ and $\beta = \sum_n \delta_n q_n$. Then $\varepsilon_n + \delta_n \in [0, 2d]$ for all n, and $\alpha + \beta = \sum_n (\varepsilon_n + \delta_n) q_n$. So, again by Theorem 9.1.8, $\alpha + \beta \leqslant_S \gamma$. Thus addition induces a join operation on the S-degrees of left-c.e. reals.

Now suppose that $\gamma \leqslant_S \alpha + \beta$. Let $a_0, a_1, \ldots$ and $b_0, b_1, \ldots$ be computable sequences of nonnegative rationals such that $\alpha = \sum_n a_n$ and $\beta = \sum_n b_n$. By Theorem 9.1.8, there is a constant d and a computable sequence of rationals $\varepsilon_0, \varepsilon_1, \ldots \in [0, d]$ such that $\gamma = \sum_n \varepsilon_n (a_n + b_n)$. Let $\gamma_0 = \sum_n \varepsilon_n a_n$ and $\gamma_1 = \sum_n \varepsilon_n b_n$. Then $\gamma = \gamma_0 + \gamma_1$ and, again by Theorem 9.1.8, $\gamma_0 \leqslant_S \alpha$ and $\gamma_1 \leqslant_S \beta$. Thus the uppersemilattice of the S-degrees of left-c.e. reals is distributive. □

It is straightforward to modify the above proof to show that the join operation on the S-degrees of left-c.e. reals is also induced by multiplication. On the other hand, the S-degrees of left-c.e. reals do not form a lattice.

Theorem 9.5.2 (Downey and Hirschfeldt [unpublished]). *There exist c.e. sets A and B such that the Solovay degrees of A and B have no infimum in the Solovay degrees of left-c.e. reals.*

Proof. We actually prove something stronger, namely that there exist c.e. sets A and B such that for any set $X \leqslant_T A, B$, there is a c.e. set S with $S \leqslant_S A, B$ and $S \nleqslant_T X$. The proof is a straightforward adaptation of the proof that the c.e. wtt-degrees are not a lattice, using a method introduced by Jockusch [190]. We build c.e. sets A and B and auxiliary c.e. sets $S_{i,j}$ to meet the following requirement for each i, j, k.

$$\mathcal{R}_{i,j,k} : \Phi_i^A = \Phi_j^B \text{ total} \Rightarrow S_{i,j} \leqslant_S A, B \wedge S_{i,j} \neq \Phi_k^{\Phi_i^A}.$$

The proof is a standard finite injury argument, and it will suffice to describe our action for a single $\mathcal{R}_{i,j,k}$.

At stage s, let m_s be largest such that $\Phi_i^A(m)[s]\downarrow$ for all $m < m_s$ and $\Phi_i^A[s] \upharpoonright m_s = \Phi_j^B[s] \upharpoonright m_s$. Let $\sigma = \Phi_i^A[s] \upharpoonright m_s$. Choose a fresh large n and wait for a stage s such that $\Phi_k^\sigma(n)[s]\downarrow$. Then initialize all weaker priority requirements (which means they have to pick new fresh large n's). If $\Phi_k^\sigma(n)[s] \neq 0$ then do nothing. Otherwise, proceed as follows. First put n into A. Suppose there is a stage $t > s$ such that $\Phi_i^A[t] \upharpoonright m_s = \Phi_j^B[t] \upharpoonright m_s$ (and $\mathcal{R}_{i,j,k}$ has not been initialized meanwhile). Note that $\Phi_j^B[t] \upharpoonright m_s = \Phi_j^B[s] \upharpoonright m_s = \sigma$, because requirements weaker than $\mathcal{R}_{i,j,k}$ do not put numbers into $B \upharpoonright \varphi_j^B(m_s - 1)[s]$ at stages greater than or equal to s. Now put n into B and into $S_{i,j}$.

If $\mathcal{R}_{i,j,k}$ is never initialized after stage t then no number enters $A \upharpoonright \varphi_i^A(m_s - 1)[t]$ at stages greater than or equal to t, so if $\mathcal{R}_{i,j,k}$'s hypothesis holds, then $\sigma \prec \Phi_i^A$, so $\Phi_k^{\Phi_i^A}(n) = \Phi_k^\sigma(n)[s]$. If this value is 0, we eventually put n into $S_{i,j}$, while otherwise we never put n into $S_{i,j}$. In either case, $S_{i,j}(n) \neq \Phi_k^{\Phi_i^A}(n)$.

Suppose that $\Phi_i^A = \Phi_j^B$ and fix s. Any n being controlled by some $\mathcal{R}_{i,j,k}$ at stage s will eventually enter $S_{i,j}$ unless $\mathcal{R}_{i,j,k}$ is initialized. Thus we can find a stage $g(s)$ such that if such an n ever enters $S_{i,j}$, it does so by stage $g(s)$. All numbers entering $S_{i,j}$ after stage $g(s)$ must also enter A and B after stage s. Thus, thinking of our c.e. sets as reals, $S_{i,j} - S_{i,j}[g(s)] \leqslant A - A[s]$ and $S_{i,j} - S_{i,j}[g(s)] \leqslant B - B[s]$ for all s, and hence $S_{i,j} \leqslant_S A, B$. □

Some results about the structure of the S-degrees of left-c.e. reals come for free from the fact that S-reducibility implies Turing reducibility. For instance, there are minimal pairs of S-degrees of left-c.e. reals because there are minimal pairs of c.e. Turing degrees. Other results require work, however. The question that led both authors into the study of algorithmic randomness was whether the partial order of S-degrees of left-c.e. reals is dense. This question led to the following results, which we will prove in a general context, applicable to many other reducibilities, in Section 9.8.

Theorem 9.5.3 (Downey, Hirschfeldt, and Nies [116]). *Let $\gamma <_S \alpha <_S \Omega$ be left-c.e. reals. There are left-c.e. reals β_0 and β_1 such that $\gamma <_S \beta_i <_S \alpha$ for $i = 0, 1$ and $\beta_0 + \beta_1 = \alpha$.*

In other words, in the S-degrees of left-c.e. reals, every incomplete degree splits over every lesser degree.

Theorem 9.5.4 (Downey, Hirschfeldt, and Nies [116]). *Let $\gamma <_S \Omega$ be a left-c.e. real. There is a left-c.e. real β such that $\gamma <_S \beta <_S \Omega$.*

These two theorems together establish the following result.

Corollary 9.5.5 (Downey, Hirschfeldt, and Nies [116]). *The partial order of Solovay degrees of left-c.e. reals is dense.*

The hypothesis that $\alpha <_S \Omega$ in the statement of Theorem 9.5.3 is necessary. In fact, the S-degree of Ω does not split at all in the S-degrees of left-c.e. reals, which can be seen as a structural reflection of the qualitative difference between 1-random and non-1-random left-c.e. reals. This fact will follow from a stronger result that shows that, despite the upwards density of the S-degrees of left-c.e. reals, there is a sense in which the S-degree of Ω is very much above all other S-degrees of left-c.e. reals. We begin with two lemmas, the second of which will not actually be necessary in the proof of Theorem 9.5.8 below, but will be helpful in motivating that proof, and will also be used in Section 9.8.

Lemma 9.5.6 (Downey, Hirschfeldt, and Nies [116]). *Let α and β be left-c.e. reals and let $\alpha_0 < \alpha_1 < \cdots \to \alpha$ and $\beta_0 < \beta_1 < \cdots \to \beta$ be computable sequences of rationals. Let f be an increasing computable function and let $k > 0$. If there are infinitely many s such that $k(\alpha - \alpha_s) > \beta - \beta_{f(s)}$, but* *only finitely many s such that $k(\alpha_t - \alpha_s) > \beta_{f(t)} - \beta_{f(s)}$ for all $t > s$, then $\beta \leqslant_S \alpha$.*

Proof. By taking $\beta_{f(0)}, \beta_{f(1)}, \ldots$ instead of $\beta_0, \beta_1, \ldots$ as an approximating sequence for β, we may assume that f is the identity.

By hypothesis, there is an r such that for all $s > r$ there is a $t > s$ with $k(\alpha_t - \alpha_s) \leqslant \beta_t - \beta_s$. Furthermore, there is an $s_0 > r$ such that $k(\alpha - \alpha_{s_0}) > \beta - \beta_{s_0}$. Given s_i, let s_{i+1} be the least number greater than s_i such that $k(\alpha_{s_{i+1}} - \alpha_{s_i}) \leqslant \beta_{s_{i+1}} - \beta_{s_i}$.

Assuming by induction that $k(\alpha - \alpha_{s_i}) > \beta - \beta_{s_i}$, we have

$$k(\alpha-\alpha_{s_{i+1}}) = k(\alpha-\alpha_{s_i})-k(\alpha_{s_{i+1}}-\alpha_{s_i}) > \beta-\beta_{s_i}-(\beta_{s_{i+1}}-\beta_{s_i}) = \beta-\beta_{s_{i+1}}.$$

Thus $s_0 < s_1 < \cdots$ is a computable sequence such that $k(\alpha-\alpha_{s_i}) > \beta-\beta_{s_i}$ for all i.

Now define the computable function g by letting $g(n)$ be the least s_i that is greater than or equal to n. Then $\beta - \beta_{g(n)} < k(\alpha - \alpha_{g(n)}) \leqslant k(\alpha - \alpha_n)$ for all n, and hence $\beta \leqslant_S \alpha$. □

Lemma 9.5.7 (Downey, Hirschfeldt, and Nies [116]). *Let $\beta \nleqslant_S \alpha$ be left-c.e. reals. Let f be a total computable function and $k \in \mathbb{N}$.*

(i) *For each n either*

  (a) *$\beta_t - \beta_{f(n)} < k(\alpha_t - \alpha_n)$ for all sufficiently large t or*

  (b) *$\beta_t - \beta_{f(n)} > k(\alpha_t - \alpha_n)$ for all sufficiently large t.*

(ii) *There are infinitely many n such that* (b) *holds.*

Proof. If there are infinitely many t such that $\beta_t - \beta_{f(n)} \leqslant k(\alpha_t - \alpha_n)$ and infinitely many t such that $\beta_t - \beta_{f(n)} \geqslant k(\alpha_t - \alpha_n)$ then

$$\beta - \beta_{f(n)} = \lim_t \beta_t - \beta_{f(n)} = \lim_t k(\alpha_t - \alpha_n) = k(\alpha - \alpha_n),$$

which implies that $\beta \equiv_S \alpha$.

If there are infinitely many t such that $\beta_t - \beta_{f(n)} \leqslant k(\alpha_t - \alpha_n)$ then

$$\beta - \beta_{f(n)} = \lim_t \beta_t - \beta_{f(n)} \leqslant \lim_t k(\alpha_t - \alpha_n) = k(\alpha - \alpha_n).$$

So if this happens for all but finitely many n then $\beta \leqslant_S \alpha$. (The finitely many n for which $\beta - \beta_{f(n)} > k(\alpha - \alpha_n)$ can be brought into line by increasing the constant k.) □

Theorem 9.5.8 (Downey, Hirschfeldt, and Nies [116]). *Let α and β be left-c.e. reals and let $\alpha_0 < \alpha_1 < \cdots \to \alpha$ and $\beta_0 < \beta_1 < \cdots \to \beta$ be computable sequences of rationals. Let f be an increasing computable function and let $k > 0$. If β is 1-random and there are infinitely many s such that $k(\alpha-\alpha_s) > \beta - \beta_{f(s)}$, then α is 1-random.*

Proof. As in Lemma 9.5.6, we may assume that f is the identity. If α is rational then we can replace it with an irrational computable real α' such that $\alpha' - \alpha'_s \geqslant \alpha - \alpha_s$ for all s, so we may assume that α is not rational.

We assume that α is not 1-random and there are infinitely many s such that $k(\alpha - \alpha_s) > \beta - \beta_s$, and show that β is not 1-random. The idea is to take a Solovay test $A = \{I_i\}_{i \in \mathbb{N}}$ such that $\alpha \in I_i$ for infinitely many i and use it to build a Solovay test $B = \{J_i\}_{i \in \mathbb{N}}$ such that $\beta \in J_i$ for infinitely many i.

Let $U = \{s : k(\alpha - \alpha_s) > \beta - \beta_s\}$. Since we are assuming β is 1-random but α is not, $\beta \not\leqslant_S \alpha$, so Lemma 9.5.7 guarantees that U is Δ^0_2. Thus a first attempt at building B could be to run the following procedure for all i in parallel. Look for the least t such that there is an $s < t$ with $s \in U_t$ and $\alpha_s \in I_i$. If there is more than one number s with this property then choose the least among such numbers. Begin to add the intervals

$$[\beta_s, \beta_s + k(\alpha_{s+1} - \alpha_s)], [\beta_s + k(\alpha_{s+1} - \alpha_s), \beta_s + k(\alpha_{s+2} - \alpha_s)], \ldots \quad (9.1)$$

to B, continuing to do so as long as s remains in U and the approximation of α remains in I_i. If the approximation of α leaves I_i then end the procedure. If s leaves U, say at stage u, then repeat the procedure (only considering $t \geqslant u$, of course).

If $\alpha \in I_i$ then the variable s in the above procedure eventually assumes a value in U. For this value, $k(\alpha - \alpha_s) > \beta - \beta_s$, from which it follows that $k(\alpha_u - \alpha_s) > \beta - \beta_s$ for some $u > s$, and hence that $\beta \in [\beta_s, \beta_s + k(\alpha_u - \alpha_s)]$. So β must be in one of the intervals (9.1) added to B by the above procedure.

Since α is in infinitely many of the I_i, running the above procedure for all i guarantees that β is in infinitely many of the intervals in B. The problem is that we also need the sum of the lengths of the intervals in B to be finite, and the above procedure gives no control over this sum, since it could easily be the case that we start working with some s, see it leave U at some stage u (at which point we have already added to B intervals whose lengths add up to $\alpha_{u-1} - \alpha_s$), and then find that the next s with which we have to work is much smaller than u. Since this could happen many times for each i, we would have no bound on the sum of the lengths of the intervals in B.

This problem would be solved if we had an infinite computable subset T of U. For each I_i, we could look for an $s \in T$ such that $\alpha_s \in I_i$, and then begin to add the intervals (9.1) to B, continuing to do so as long as the approximation of α remained in I_i. (Of course, in this easy setting, we could also simply add the single interval $[\beta_s, \beta_s + k\,|I_i|]$ to B.) It is not hard to check that this would guarantee that if $\alpha \in I_i$ then β is in one of the intervals added to B, while also ensuring that the sum of the lengths of these intervals is less than or equal to $k\,|I_i|$. Following this procedure for all i would give us the desired Solovay test B. Since $\beta \not\leqslant_S \alpha$, though, there is no infinite computable $T \subseteq U$, so we use Lemma 9.5.6 to obtain the next best thing.

Let

$$S = \{s : \forall t > s(k(\alpha_t - \alpha_s) > \beta_t - \beta_s)\}.$$

By Lemma 9.5.6 and the assumption that $\beta \nleqslant_S \alpha$, we may assume that S is infinite. Note that $k(\alpha - \alpha_s) \geqslant \beta - \beta_s$ for all $s \in S$. In fact, we may assume that $k(\alpha - \alpha_s) > \beta - \beta_s$ for all $s \in S$, since if $k(\alpha - \alpha_s) = \beta - \beta_s$ then $k\alpha$ and β differ by a rational amount, and hence β is not 1-random.

The set S is co-c.e. by definition, but it has an additional useful property. Let

$$S[t] = \{s : \forall u \in (s,t](k(\alpha_u - \alpha_s) > \beta_u - \beta_s)\}.$$

If $s \in S[t-1] \setminus S[t]$ then no $u \in (s,t)$ is in S, since for any such u we have

$$k(\alpha_t - \alpha_u) = k(\alpha_t - \alpha_s) - k(\alpha_u - \alpha_s) \leqslant \beta_t - \beta_s - (\beta_u - \beta_s) = \beta_t - \beta_u.$$

In other words, if s leaves S at stage t then so do all numbers in (s,t).

To construct B, we run the following procedure P_i for all i in parallel. Note that B is a multiset, so we are allowed to add more than one copy of a given interval to B.

1. Look for an s such that $\alpha_s \in I_i$.
2. Let $t = s+1$. If $\alpha_t \notin I_i$ then terminate the procedure.
3. If $s \notin S[t]$ then let $s = t$ and go to step 2. Otherwise, add the interval
$$[\beta_s + k(\alpha_{t-1} - \alpha_s), \beta_s + k(\alpha_t - \alpha_s)]$$
to B, increase t by one, and repeat step 3.

This concludes the construction of B. We now show that the sum of the lengths of the intervals in B is finite and that β is in infinitely many of the intervals in B.

For each i, let B_i be the set of intervals added to B by P_i and let l_i be the sum of the lengths of the intervals in B_i. If P_i never leaves step 1 then $B_i = \emptyset$. If P_i eventually terminates then $l_i \leqslant k(\alpha_t - \alpha_s)$ for some s, t such that $\alpha_s, \alpha_t \in I_i$, and hence $l_i \leqslant k\,|I_i|$. If P_i reaches step 3 and never terminates then $\alpha \in I_i$ and $l_i \leqslant k(\alpha - \alpha_s)$ for some s such that $\alpha_s \in I_i$, and hence again $l_i \leqslant k\,|I_i|$. Thus the sum of the lengths of the intervals in B is less than or equal to $k\sum_i |I_i| < \infty$.

To show that β is in infinitely many of the intervals in B, it is enough to show that, for each i, if $\alpha \in I_i$ then β is in one of the intervals in B_i. Fix i such that $\alpha \in I_i$. Since α is not rational, $\alpha_u \in I_i$ for all sufficiently large u, so P_i must eventually reach step 3. By the properties of S discussed above, the variable s in the procedure P_i eventually assumes a value in S. For this value, $k(\alpha - \alpha_s) > \beta - \beta_s$, from which it follows that $k(\alpha_u - \alpha_s) > \beta - \beta_s$ for some $u > s$, and hence that $\beta \in [\beta_s, \beta_s + k(\alpha_u - \alpha_s)]$. So β must be in one of the intervals (9.1), all of which are in B_i. □

The following corollary appears originally in Demuth [93], without proof, and was independently rediscovered by Downey, Hirschfeldt, and Nies [116]. We thank Antonin Kučera for bringing Demuth's paper to our attention. (A discussion of this paper may be found in [221, Remark 3.5].)

Corollary 9.5.9 (Demuth [93]). *If α_0 and α_1 are left-c.e. reals such that $\alpha_0 + \alpha_1$ is 1-random then at least one of α_0 and α_1 is 1-random.*

Proof. Let $\beta = \alpha_0 + \alpha_1$. For $i = 0, 1$, let $\alpha_{i,0} < \alpha_{i,1} < \cdots \to \alpha_i$ be a computable sequence of rationals, and let $\beta_s = \alpha_{0,s} + \alpha_{1,s}$. For each s, either $3(\alpha_0 - \alpha_{0,s}) > \beta - \beta_s$ or $3(\alpha_1 - \alpha_{1,s}) > \beta - \beta_s$, so for some $i < 2$ there are infinitely many s such that $3(\alpha_i - \alpha_{i,s}) > \beta - \beta_s$. By Theorem 9.5.8, α_i is 1-random. □

Combining Theorem 9.5.3 and Corollary 9.5.9, we have the following results, the second of which also depends on Theorem 9.2.3.

Theorem 9.5.10 (Downey, Hirschfeldt, and Nies [116]). *A left-c.e. real γ is 1-random if and only if it cannot be written as $\alpha + \beta$ for left-c.e. reals $\alpha, \beta <_S \gamma$.*

Theorem 9.5.11 (Downey, Hirschfeldt, and Nies [116]). *Let* **d** *be a Solovay degree of left-c.e. reals. The following are equivalent:*

1. **d** *is incomplete.*
2. **d** *splits.*
3. **d** *splits over any lesser Solovay degree.*

These results apply only to left-c.e. reals. For example, given $\Omega = 0.a_0a_1a_2\ldots$, let $\alpha = 0.a_00a_20\ldots$ and $\beta = 0.0a_10a_3\ldots$. Then neither α nor β is 1-random, but $\alpha + \beta = \Omega$.

We finish this section by noting that the structure of the S-degrees of left-c.e. reals is not too simple.

Theorem 9.5.12 (Downey, Hirschfeldt, and LaForte [114]). *The first-order theory of the uppersemilattice of Solovay degrees of left-c.e. reals is undecidable.*

The proof of this result uses Nies' [301] method of interpreting effectively dense boolean algebras.

9.6 cl-reducibility and rK-reducibility

Despite the success of S-reducibility in characterizing the 1-random left-c.e. reals, there are reasons to search for other measures of relative randomness. For one thing, S-reducibility is quite strong, and is rather uniform in a way that K-reducibility, for instance, is not. (That is, if $\alpha \leqslant_S \beta$ then α is quite closely tied to β in a computability-theoretic sense, while there is no reason to suppose that, whatever we mean by "A is no more random than B", this notion should imply that A is so closely tied to B.) Furthermore, S-reducibility is quite badly behaved outside the left-c.e. reals, as exemplified by the following result.

Proposition 9.6.1. *There is a right-c.e. real β that is not S-above any left-c.e. real (including the computable reals).*

Proof. It is enough to build β so that $\beta \not\geqslant_S 1$. To do so, we satisfy the requirements

$$\mathcal{R}_e : \exists q \in \mathbb{Q}\,(q < \beta \wedge (\Phi_e(q)\downarrow < 1 \Rightarrow 1 - \Phi_e(q) > e(\beta - q))),$$

where we think of $\Phi_0, \Phi_1, \ldots$ as functions from rationals to rationals. We denote the stage s approximation of β by β_s. We begin with $\beta_0 = 1$. We initially choose $q_0 < q_1 < \cdots < 1$. At stage s, we look for the least $e \leqslant s$ such that $\Phi_e(q_e)[s]\downarrow < 1$ and $1 - \Phi_e(q_e) \leqslant e(\beta_s - q_e)$. If there is no such e, we let $\beta_{s+1} = \beta_s$ and proceed to the next stage. Otherwise, we let $\beta_{s+1} \leqslant \beta_s$ be such that $q_e < \beta_{s+1}$ and $1 - \Phi_e(q_e) > e(\beta_{s+1} - q_e)$. We then redefine all q_i for $i > e$ so that $q_e < q_{e+1} < \cdots < \beta_{s+1}$. We say that $\mathcal{R}_e$ *acts* at stage s.

Assume by induction that all $\mathcal{R}_i$ with $i < e$ act only finitely often, and let t be the least stage by which all such requirements have stopped acting. Then the value of q_e at stage t is permanent. If $\Phi_e(q_e)\uparrow$ or $\Phi_e(q_e)\downarrow \geqslant 1$ then $\mathcal{R}_e$ is satisfied and never acts after stage t. Otherwise, there is a least stage $s \geqslant t$ such that $\Phi_e(q_e)[s]\downarrow$. We ensure that $1 - \Phi_e(q_e) > e(\beta_{s+1} - q_e)$. Furthermore, we have $q_e < \beta_u \leqslant \beta_{s+1}$ for all $u > s$, whence $1 - \Phi_e(q_e) > e(\beta - q_e)$. Thus $\mathcal{R}_e$ is satisfied and never acts after stage s. □

Downey, Hirschfeldt, and LaForte [113] introduced another measure of relative complexity, now often called *computable Lipschitz* or cl-reducibility. This reduction was originally called *sw-reducibility* by Downey, Hirschfeldt, and LaForte.[2]

Definition 9.6.2 (Downey, Hirschfeldt, and LaForte [113], Csima [80] and Soare [368]). A set A is *cl-reducible* to a set B (written $A \leqslant_{cl} B$ if there is a functional Γ such that $\Gamma^B = A$ and $\gamma^B(n) \leqslant n + O(1)$.

If the constant is zero, then we will call this an *ibT-reduction*, for *identity bounded Turing* reduction, and write $A \leqslant_{ibT} B$.

If $A \leqslant_{cl} B$ then we can describe $A \upharpoonright n$ using $B \upharpoonright n$ and $O(1)$ many more bits (to represent the additional bits of B below $\gamma^B(n)$). Thus $C(A \upharpoonright n) \leqslant C(B \upharpoonright n) + O(1)$ and $K(A \upharpoonright n) \leqslant K(B \upharpoonright n) + O(1)$. In other words, like S-reducibility, cl-reducibility implies both K-reducibility and C-reducibility. Obviously, cl-reducibility also implies Turing (and even wtt-) reducibility.

A strong form of ibT-reducibility has been used by Nabutovsky and Weinberger [292] for problems in differential geometry, as described in

[2] This abbreviation stands for "strong weak truth table reducibility". The authors have deservedly received a certain amount of flak over this terminology. Hence the name change, suggested by Barmpalias and Lewis [247], which reflects the fact that cl-reducibility is an effective version of a Lipschitz transformation. See [247] for more on this view of cl-reducibility.

Soare [368] and Csima and Soare [85]. For a c.e. set W_e, the *modulus function*, or *settling time function*, m_e of W_e is defined by letting $m_e(n)$ be the least s such that $W_{e,s} \upharpoonright n = W_{e,t} \upharpoonright n$ for all $t > s$. Suppose that A and B are c.e. sets. We say that B is *settling time dominated* by B if there is an enumeration W_j of B and an enumeration W_i of A such that for all computable functions f, we have $m_i(n) > f(m_j(n))$ for almost all n. One can replace the existential quantifiers in this definition by universal ones, as this notion is invariant on cl-degrees (Soare [368]). We do not pursue this notion further, but clearly there seem to be interesting connections with Kolmogorov complexity; see Csima [80], Csima and Shore [84], Csima and Soare [85], and Soare [368]. For a discussion of extensions beyond the c.e. sets, see Csima [81].

We will see in Section 9.10 that S-reducibility and cl-reducibility are different on left-c.e. reals, and indeed neither implies the other, but that they agree on c.e. *sets*. We will also see that cl-reducibility is much less well behaved than S-reducibility. For instance, there is no largest cl-degree of left-c.e. reals, and there is no join operation on the cl-degrees of left-c.e. reals.

We would like a measure of relative randomness combining the best features of S-reducibility and cl-reducibility while being less uniform and more closely tied to initial segment complexity. The following is a natural candidate, introduced by Downey, Hirschfeldt, and LaForte [113].

Definition 9.6.3 (Downey, Hirschfeldt, and LaForte [113]). A set A is *relative K-reducible* or *rK-reducible* to a set B (written $A \leqslant_{\mathrm{rK}} B$) if $K(A \upharpoonright n \mid B \upharpoonright n) \leqslant O(1)$.

Since $C(\sigma \mid \tau) \leqslant K(\sigma \mid \tau) + O(1)$ and $K(\sigma \mid \tau) \leqslant 2C(\sigma \mid \tau) + O(1)$, it would not change this definition to use plain complexity in place of prefix-free complexity (and thus there is no separate notion of "rC-reducibility"). If $A \leqslant_{\mathrm{rK}} B$ then the initial segments of A are easy to describe given the corresponding initial segments of B, and thus it makes sense to think of A as no more random than B. Clearly, rK-reducibility implies K-reducibility and C-reducibility.

We now give alternate characterizations of rK-reducibility that demonstrate how it can be seen as a less uniform version of both S-reducibility and cl-reducibility. Item (ii) below can be seen as a form of "computation with advice".

Theorem 9.6.4 (Downey, Hirschfeldt, and LaForte [113]). *The following are equivalent.*

(i) $A \leqslant_{\mathrm{rK}} B$.

(ii) *There are a partial computable function* $f : 2^{<\omega} \times \mathbb{N} \to 2^{<\omega}$ *and a constant* k *such that for each* n *there is a* $j \leqslant k$ *for which* $f(B \upharpoonright n, j)\downarrow = A \upharpoonright n$.

(iii) *There are a partial computable function* $g : 2^{<\omega} \to \mathbb{Q}$ *and a constant* c *such that for each* n *there is a* $\tau \in 2^{n+c}$ *with* $|0.B - 0.\tau| \leqslant 2^{-n}$ *for which* $g(\tau)\downarrow$ *and* $|0.A - g(\tau)| \leqslant 2^{-n}$.

Proof. (i) $\Rightarrow$ (ii) Suppose that $K(A \upharpoonright n \mid B \upharpoonright n) < c$ for all n. Let $\tau_0, \dots, \tau_k$ be the strings of length less than c and define f as follows. For a string σ and $j \leqslant k$, if $\mathcal{U}^\sigma(\tau_j)\downarrow$ then $f(\sigma, j) = \mathcal{U}^\sigma(\tau_j)$, and otherwise $f(\sigma, j)\uparrow$. For each n there must be a $j \leqslant k$ such that $\mathcal{U}^{B\upharpoonright n}(\tau_j)\downarrow= A \upharpoonright n$. For this j we have $f(B \upharpoonright n, j)\downarrow= A \upharpoonright n$.

(ii) $\Rightarrow$ (iii) Let c be such that $2^c \geqslant k$ and define the partial computable function g as follows. Given a string σ of length n, whenever $f(\sigma, j)\downarrow$ for some new $j \leqslant k$, choose a new $\tau \succcurlyeq \sigma$ of length $n + c$ and define $g(\tau) = 0.f(\sigma, j)$. Then for each n there is a $\tau \succcurlyeq B \upharpoonright n$ such that $g(\tau)\downarrow= 0.(A \upharpoonright n)$. We have $|0.B - 0.\tau| \leqslant 2^{-n}$ and $|0.A - g(\tau)| \leqslant 2^{-n}$.

(iii) $\Rightarrow$ (i) For a string $\sigma \in 2^n$, let S_σ be the set of all ν for which there is a $\tau \in 2^{n+c}$ with $|0.\sigma - 0.\tau| \leqslant 2^{-n+1}$ and $|0.\nu - g(\tau)| \leqslant 2^{-n+1}$. It is easy to check that there is a k such that $|S_\sigma| \leqslant k$ for all σ, and hence that $K(\nu \mid \sigma) \leqslant O(1)$ for all σ and $\nu \in S_\sigma$. Fix n and let $\tau \in 2^{n+c}$ be such that $|0.B - 0.\tau| \leqslant 2^{-n}$ and $|0.A - g(\tau)| \leqslant 2^{-n}$. Then $|0.(B \upharpoonright n) - 0.\tau| \leqslant 2^{-n+1}$ and $|0.(A \upharpoonright n) - g(\tau)| \leqslant 2^{-n+1}$. Thus $A \upharpoonright n \in S_{B\upharpoonright n}$, and hence $K(A \upharpoonright n \mid B \upharpoonright n) \leqslant O(1)$. □

Corollary 9.6.5 (Downey, Hirschfeldt, and LaForte [113]). *If* $A \leqslant_{\mathrm{cl}} B$ *then* $A \leqslant_{\mathrm{rK}} B$.

Proof. Suppose that $A = \Gamma^B$ and $\gamma^B(n) \leqslant n+c$ for all n. Let $\sigma_0, \dots, \sigma_{2^c-1}$ be the strings of length c. For $j < 2^c$, let $f(\tau, j) = \Gamma^{\tau\sigma_j} \upharpoonright |\tau|$ if the latter is defined. Then for each n there is a $j < 2^c$ such that $f(B \upharpoonright n, j)\downarrow= A \upharpoonright n$. Thus item (ii) in Theorem 9.6.4 holds. □

Corollary 9.6.6 (Downey, Hirschfeldt, and LaForte [113]). *If* $\alpha \leqslant_{\mathrm{S}} \beta$ *then* $\alpha \leqslant_{\mathrm{rK}} \beta$.

Proof. Let the partial computable function f and the constant k be such that if $q \in \mathbb{Q}$ and $q < \beta$, then $f(q)\downarrow< \alpha$ and $\alpha - f(q) < k(\beta - q)$. Let c be such that $2^c \geqslant k$ and let $g(\sigma) = f(0.\sigma)$ if the latter is defined. Given n, we have $\beta - 0.(\beta \upharpoonright (n + c)) \leqslant 2^{-(n+c)}$. Thus $g(\beta \upharpoonright (n + c))\downarrow< \alpha$ and $|\alpha - g(\beta \upharpoonright n + c)| \leqslant 2^{-n}$. So item (iii) in Theorem 9.6.4 holds. □

For left-c.e. reals, we have another characterization of rK-reducibility in terms of "settling times". It roughly says that if $\alpha \leqslant_{\mathrm{rK}} \beta$ then there are approximations to α and β such that $\alpha \upharpoonright n$ cannot change much after the stage at which $\beta \upharpoonright n$ settles to its true value. For a left-c.e. real α and a fixed computable approximation $\alpha_0 < \alpha_1 < \cdots \to \alpha$, let the *mind-change function* $m(\alpha, n, s, t)$ be the cardinality of $\{u \in [s, t] : \alpha_u \upharpoonright n \neq \alpha_{u+1} \upharpoonright n\}$, and let $m(\alpha, n, s) = \lim_t m(\alpha, n, s, t)$.

Theorem 9.6.7 (Downey, Hirschfeldt, and LaForte [113]). *Let α and β be left-c.e. reals. The following are equivalent.*

(i) $\alpha \leqslant_{\mathrm{rK}} \beta$.

(ii) *There are a constant k and computable approximations $\alpha_0 < \alpha_1 < \cdots \to \alpha$ and $\beta_0 < \beta_1 < \cdots \to \beta$ such that for all n and $t > s$, if $\beta_t \upharpoonright n = \beta_s \upharpoonright n$ then $m(\alpha, n, s, t) \leqslant k$.*

(iii) *There are a constant k and computable approximations $\alpha_0 < \alpha_1 < \cdots \to \alpha$ and $\beta_0 < \beta_1 < \cdots \to \beta$ such that for all n and s, if $\beta \upharpoonright n = \beta_s \upharpoonright n$ then $m(\alpha, n, s) \leqslant k$.*

Proof. (i) $\Rightarrow$ (ii) We may assume that α and β are irrational, since otherwise (ii) is easy to show. Let c be such that $K(\alpha \upharpoonright n \mid \beta \upharpoonright n) < c$ for all n. Let $\widehat{\beta}_0 < \widehat{\beta}_1 < \cdots \to \beta$ and $\widehat{\alpha}_0 < \widehat{\alpha}_1 < \cdots \to \alpha$ be computable sequences of rationals. Let $\alpha_0 = \beta_0 = 0$. Suppose we have defined α_n and β_n. Search for i and j such that $\widehat{\alpha}_i > \alpha_n$ and $\widehat{\beta}_j > \beta_n$, and for all $m \leqslant n+1$, we have $K(\widehat{\alpha}_i \upharpoonright m \mid \widehat{\beta}_j \upharpoonright m) < c$. Such i and j must exist because the approximations to α and β eventually settle on their first $n+1$ many bits. Let $\alpha_{n+1} = \widehat{\alpha}_i \upharpoonright (n+1)$ and $\beta_{n+1} = \widehat{\beta}_j \upharpoonright (n+1)$.

It is easy to see that $\alpha_0 < \alpha_1 < \cdots \to \alpha$ and $\beta_0 < \beta_1 < \cdots \to \beta$. Suppose that $\beta_t \upharpoonright n = \beta_s \upharpoonright n$. Then for all $u \in [t, s]$, we have $K(\alpha_u \upharpoonright n \mid \beta_t \upharpoonright n) < c$. Thus $\alpha_u \upharpoonright n$ assumes fewer than 2^c many values for such u, and hence $m(\alpha, n, s, t) \leqslant 2^c$.

(ii) $\Rightarrow$ (iii) Obvious.

(iii) $\Rightarrow$ (i) Define a partial computable function f as follows. Given τ and $j \leqslant k$, wait for a stage s such that $\tau = \beta_s \upharpoonright |\tau|$. If such a stage is found, then wait for a stage $t > s$ such that $m(\alpha, n, s, t) = j$. If such a stage is found, then let $f(\tau, j) = \alpha_{t+1} \upharpoonright |\tau|$. Then for each n there is a $j \leqslant k$ such that $f(\beta \upharpoonright n, j) = \alpha \upharpoonright n$. □

Despite its nonuniform nature, rK-reducibility implies Turing reducibility.

Theorem 9.6.8 (Downey, Hirschfeldt, and LaForte [113]). *If $A \leqslant_{\mathrm{rK}} B$ then $A \leqslant_{\mathrm{T}} B$.*

Proof. Let k be the least number for which there exists a partial computable function f such that for each n there is a $j \leqslant k$ with $f(B \upharpoonright n, j)\downarrow = A \upharpoonright n$. There must be infinitely many n for which $f(B \upharpoonright n, j)\downarrow$ for all $j \leqslant k$, since otherwise we could change finitely much of f to contradict the minimality of k. Let $n_0 < n_1 < \cdots$ be a B-computable sequence of such n. Let T be the B-computable subtree of $2^{<\omega}$ obtained by pruning, for each i, all the strings of length n_i except for the values of $f(B \upharpoonright n_i, j)$ for $j \leqslant k$. The tree T has bounded width, so each element of $[T]$ is B-computable. But $A \in [T]$, so $A \leqslant_{\mathrm{T}} B$. □

Since any computable set is rK-reducible to any other set, the above theorem shows that the computable sets form the least rK-degree. By the Kučera-Slaman Theorem, together with the fact that rK-reducibility implies K-reducibility and is implied by S-reducibility, the largest rK-degree of left-c.e. reals is the same as the largest S-degree of left-c.e. reals, namely the 1-random left-c.e. reals. Furthermore, like the case of S-reducibility but unlike that of cl-reducibility, the rK-degrees of left-c.e. reals are an uppersemilattice, with join induced by addition.

Theorem 9.6.9 (Downey, Hirschfeldt, and LaForte [113]). *The rK-degrees of left-c.e. reals form an uppersemilattice with least degree that of the computable sets, highest degree that of the 1-random left-c.e. reals, and join induced by addition.*

Proof. All that is left to show is that addition induces a join. Let α and β be left-c.e. reals. Since $\alpha, \beta \leqslant_S \alpha + \beta$, we have $\alpha, \beta \leqslant_{rK} \alpha + \beta$. Let $\alpha, \beta \leqslant_{rK} \gamma$. Then we can compute $(\alpha + \beta) \upharpoonright n$ given $\alpha \upharpoonright n$ and $\beta \upharpoonright n$, together with a couple of bits of information to indicate whether there are carries from further bits of α and γ. Since $K(\alpha \upharpoonright n \mid \gamma \upharpoonright n) \leqslant O(1)$ and $K(\beta \upharpoonright n \mid \gamma \upharpoonright n) \leqslant O(1)$, it follows that $K((\alpha + \beta) \upharpoonright n \mid \gamma \upharpoonright n) \leqslant O(1)$. □

Notice that in the above proof, the only use made of the fact that we were working with left-c.e. reals was in showing that $\alpha, \beta \leqslant_{rK} \alpha + \beta$. That is of course not necessarily the case in general, since, for example, $\Omega + (1 - \Omega) \nleqslant_{rK} 1$. It follows from the proof of Theorem 9.5.2 that the rK-degrees of left-c.e. reals are not a lattice.

As we will see in Section 9.8, the analogs of Theorem 9.5.3 and Corollary 9.5.5 hold for rK-reducibility. Together with Corollary 9.5.9, they give the following result.

Theorem 9.6.10 (Downey, Hirschfeldt, and LaForte [113]). *The partial order of rK-degrees of left-c.e. reals is dense. Furthermore, in the rK-degrees of left-c.e. reals, every incomplete degree splits over every lesser degree, while the complete degree does not split at all.*

Raichev [319, 320] observed that rK-lower cones are well-behaved, in the following sense.

Theorem 9.6.11 (Raichev [319, 320]). *For any A, the reals rK-reducible to A form a real closed field.*

The proof uses similar approximation methods to that of Theorem 5.4.7. See [319] for details.

Thus rK-reducibility shares many of the nice structural properties of S-reducibility on the left-c.e. reals, while still being a reasonable measure of relative randomness on all sets. There are still some basic open questions about rK-reducibility, however, such as whether the semilattice of rK-degrees of left-c.e. reals is distributive, or whether every set is rK-reducible to a 1-random set. We will see in Section 9.13 that there are sets that are not cl-reducible to any 1-random set.

9.7 K-reducibility and C-reducibility

Recall that A is K-reducible to B (written $A \leqslant_K B$) if $K(A \upharpoonright n) \leqslant K(B \upharpoonright n) + O(1)$, and A is C-reducible to B (written $A \leqslant_C B$) if $C(A \upharpoonright n) \leqslant C(B \upharpoonright n) + O(1)$. These reducibilities are the most basic measures of relative randomness based on the Kolmogorov complexity approach. If A is 1-random and $A \leqslant_K B$, then B is clearly 1-random. The same holds if $A \leqslant_C B$ by Theorem 6.7.2.

We have seen in Theorem 3.4.4 that a set A is computable iff $C(A \upharpoonright n) \leqslant C(n) + O(1)$. The following theorem extends that result.

Theorem 9.7.1 (Stephan [personal communication]). *Let α and β be left-c.e. reals. If $\alpha \leqslant_C \beta$ then $\alpha \leqslant_T \beta$.*[3]

Proof. If $\beta \equiv_T \emptyset'$, then there is nothing to prove, so we assume that $\beta <_T \emptyset'$. Let $f(n)$ be the least s such that $n \in \emptyset'_s$, if there is such an s, and $f(n)\uparrow$ otherwise. Let $g(n)$ be the least s such that $\beta \upharpoonright n = \beta_s \upharpoonright n$. Then there are infinitely many n such that $f(n)\downarrow > g(n)$, since otherwise we could compute $\emptyset'$ using g and hence using β. Thus we can find a β-computable infinite set $S \subseteq \emptyset'$ such that $f(n) > g(n)$ for all $n \in S$.

For $n \in S$, we can determine $\beta \upharpoonright n$ by computing $f(n)$, since then $\beta \upharpoonright n = \beta_{f(n)} \upharpoonright n$. Thus for all such n we have $C(\beta \upharpoonright n) \leqslant C(n) + O(1)$, and hence $C(\alpha \upharpoonright n) \leqslant C(n) + O(1)$. Since S is β-computable, the relativized form of Chaitin's Theorem 3.4.5 implies that $\alpha \leqslant_T \beta$. □

We will see in Chapter 11 that this result is not true if we replace plain complexity by prefix-free complexity. Indeed, even the analogue of Theorem 3.4.4 fails to hold in that case, because there are noncomputable sets A such that $K(A \upharpoonright n) \leqslant K(n) + O(1)$. Sets with this property (including all the computable sets) are called *K-trivial* because they form the lowest K-degree, and are of great interest in the theory of algorithmic randomness, as we will see in Chapter 11.

For left-c.e. reals, it follows from the Kučera-Slaman Theorem that the largest K-degree and the largest C-degree both consist exactly of the 1-random left-c.e. reals. Furthermore, the K-degrees and C-degrees of left-c.e. reals have basic structural properties similar to those of the S-degrees and rK-degrees of left-c.e. reals, as we now show.

[3]This result is not true in general outside the left-c.e. reals. If $C(A \upharpoonright n) \leqslant \frac{n}{2}$, say, then $A \leqslant_C \Omega$, but there are uncountably many such A.

Theorem 9.7.2 (Downey, Hirschfeldt, Nies, and Stephan [117]). *Let α and β be left-c.e. reals. Then $C((\alpha+\beta) \upharpoonright n) = \max(C(\alpha \upharpoonright n), C(\beta \upharpoonright n)) \pm O(1)$ and $K((\alpha+\beta) \upharpoonright n) = \max(K(\alpha \upharpoonright n), K(\beta \upharpoonright n)) \pm O(1)$.*

Proof. We do the proof for prefix-free complexity; the same works for plain complexity. Let $\gamma = \alpha + \beta$. Let $\alpha_0 < \alpha_1 < \cdots \to \alpha$ and $\beta_0 < \beta_1 < \cdots \to \beta$ be computable sequences of rationals and let $\gamma_s = \alpha_s + \beta_s$.

If we know $\gamma \upharpoonright n$ then we can find an s such that $\gamma_s \upharpoonright n = \gamma \upharpoonright n$. The approximation to $\alpha \upharpoonright n$ can change at most once after stage s, since if there were two such changes, we would have $\gamma - \gamma_s \geqslant \alpha - \alpha_s > 2^{-n}$, and hence $\gamma_s \upharpoonright n \neq \gamma \upharpoonright n$. Thus we can describe $\alpha \upharpoonright n$ given $\gamma \upharpoonright n$ and one more bit of information, whence $K(\alpha \upharpoonright n) \leqslant K(\gamma \upharpoonright n) + O(1)$. Similarly, $K(\beta \upharpoonright n) \leqslant K(\gamma \upharpoonright n) + O(1)$.

For the other direction, fix n. Let s be least such that $\alpha_s \upharpoonright n = \alpha \upharpoonright n$ and let t be least such that $\beta_t \upharpoonright n = \beta \upharpoonright n$. Suppose that $s \geqslant t$. Then given $\alpha \upharpoonright n$, we can compute s, which also gives us $\beta \upharpoonright n = \beta_s \upharpoonright n$. From this information plus a couple of bits to represent possible carries from further bits of α and β, we obtain $\gamma \upharpoonright n$. Thus $K(\gamma \upharpoonright n) \leqslant K(\alpha \upharpoonright n) + O(1)$. Similarly, if $t \geqslant s$ then $K(\gamma \upharpoonright n) \leqslant K(\beta \upharpoonright n) + O(1)$. □

Corollary 9.7.3 (Downey, Hirschfeldt, Nies, and Stephan [117]). *The K-degrees and C-degrees of left-c.e. reals both form uppersemilattices with join given by addition.*

We will see in Section 9.8 that the analogs of Theorem 9.5.3 and Corollary 9.5.5 hold for K-reducibility and C-reducibility. Together with Corollary 9.5.9, they give the following result.

Theorem 9.7.4 (after Downey, Hirschfeldt, Nies, and Stephan [117]). *The partial orders of K-degrees and C-degrees of left-c.e. reals are dense. Furthermore, in both the K-degrees and C-degrees of left-c.e. reals, every incomplete degree splits over every lesser degree, while the complete degree does not split at all.*

As mentioned above, the fact that S-reducibility, cl-reducibility, and rK-reducibility imply Turing reducibility allows us to transfer certain results, such as the existence of minimal pairs, from the Turing case. This tool is not available for K-reducibility. We will see in Theorem 9.15.8 that minimal pairs of K-degrees do exist, but it is not known whether there are minimal pairs of K-degrees of left-c.e. (or even Δ_2^0) reals.

In Chapter 10, we will discuss the structure of the K-degrees and C-degrees of 1-random sets.

9.8 Density and splittings

In this section, we give a unified proof of the density and splitting theorems for various reducibilities considered above (Corollary 9.5.5 and Theorems 9.5.3, 9.6.10, and 9.7.4). Indeed, we will show that analogous results hold for all reducibilities with a few basic properties given in the following definition.

Definition 9.8.1. Let $C_0, C_1, \dots$ be an effective list of all left-c.e. reals.

A reducibility r on the left-c.e. reals is Σ^0_3 if there is a total computable function Φ such that for all a, b, we have $C_a \leqslant_{\mathrm{r}} C_b$ iff $\exists k\, \forall m\, \exists n\, \Phi(a, b, k, m, n)$.

The reducibility r is *standard* if r is Σ^0_3, every computable real is r-reducible to any given left-c.e. real, addition is a join in the r-degrees of left-c.e. reals, and for any left-c.e. real α and any rational $q > 0$, we have $\alpha \equiv_{\mathrm{r}} q\alpha$.

Standard reducibilities include Solovay reducibility, rK-reducibility, K-reducibility, and C-reducibility (but not cl-reducibility, as addition is not a join in the cl-degrees of left-c.e. reals). We begin with the splitting theorem.

Theorem 9.8.2 (after Downey, Hirschfeldt, and Nies [116]). *Let r be a standard reducibility on the left-c.e. reals. Let $\gamma <_{\mathrm{r}} \alpha <_{\mathrm{S}} \Omega$ be left-c.e. reals. There are left-c.e. reals β^0 and β^1 such that $\gamma <_{\mathrm{r}} \beta^i <_{\mathrm{r}} \alpha$ for $i = 0, 1$ and $\beta^0 + \beta^1 = \alpha$.*

Proof. Let a be such that $C_a = \alpha$ and let Φ be as in Definition 9.8.1. We build left-c.e. reals β^0 and β^1. By the recursion theorem, we have b_0 and b_1 such that $\beta^i = C_{b_i}$. We want to ensure that $\gamma \leqslant_{\mathrm{r}} \beta^i \leqslant_{\mathrm{r}} \alpha$ for $i = 0, 1$ and $\beta^0 + \beta^1 = \alpha$ while satisfying the following requirement for each e and $i = 0, 1$.

$$\mathcal{R}_{i,e} : \exists n\, \forall m\, \neg\Phi(a, b^i, e, n, m).$$

These requirements ensure that $\beta^i \not\geqslant_{\mathrm{r}} \alpha$. Since $\beta^0 + \beta^1 = \alpha$ and $\gamma \not\geqslant_{\mathrm{r}} \alpha$, they also ensure that $\gamma \not\geqslant_{\mathrm{r}} \beta^i$.

By Lemma 9.1.7 and the fact that $c\gamma \equiv_{\mathrm{r}} \gamma$ for any rational c, we may assume without loss of generality that $2(\gamma_s - \gamma_{s-1}) \leqslant \alpha_s - \alpha_{s-1}$ for all s. (We adopt the convention that $\mu_0 - \mu_{-1} = \mu_0$ for any left-c.e. real μ.)

In the absence of requirements of the form $\mathcal{R}_{1-i,e}$, it is easy to satisfy simultaneously all requirements of the form $\mathcal{R}_{i,e}$: simply let $\beta^i_s = \gamma_s$ and $\beta^{1-i}_s = \alpha_s - \gamma_s$. In the presence of requirements of the form $\mathcal{R}_{1-i,e}$, however, we cannot afford to be quite so cavalier in our treatment of β^{1-i}; enough of α has to be kept out of β^{1-i} to guarantee that β^{1-i} is not r-above α.

Most of the essential features of our construction are already present in the case of two requirements $\mathcal{R}_{i,e}$ and $\mathcal{R}_{1-i,e'}$, which we now discuss. We assume that $\mathcal{R}_{i,e}$ has priority over $\mathcal{R}_{1-i,e'}$. We will think of the β^j as being built by adding amounts to them in stages. Thus β^j_s will be the total amount added to β^j by the end of stage s. At each stage s we begin by adding $\gamma_s - \gamma_{s-1}$ to the current value of each β^j; in the limit, this action ensures that $\beta^j \geqslant_r \gamma$.

We will say that $\mathcal{R}_{i,e}$ is *satisfied through* n *at stage* s if $\forall m < s \neg\Phi(a, b^i, e, n, m)$. The strategy for $\mathcal{R}_{i,e}$ is to act whenever either it is not currently satisfied or the least number through which it is satisfied changes. Whenever this happens, $\mathcal{R}_{i,e}$ initializes $\mathcal{R}_{1-i,e'}$, which means that the amount of $\alpha - 2\gamma$ that $\mathcal{R}_{1-i,e'}$ is allowed to funnel into β^i is reduced. More specifically, once $\mathcal{R}_{1-i,e'}$ has been initialized for the mth time, the total amount that it is thenceforth allowed to put into β^i is reduced to 2^{-m}.

The above strategy guarantees that if $\mathcal{R}_{1-i,e'}$ is initialized infinitely often then the amount put into β^i by $\mathcal{R}_{1-i,e'}$ (which in this case is all that is put into β^i except for the coding of γ) adds up to a computable real. In other words, $\beta^i \equiv_r \gamma <_r \alpha$. But then there is a stage s after which $\mathcal{R}_{i,e}$ is always satisfied and the least number through which it is satisfied does not change. So we conclude that $\mathcal{R}_{1-i,e'}$ is initialized only finitely often, and that $\mathcal{R}_{i,e}$ is eventually permanently satisfied.

We now have the problem of designing a strategy for $\mathcal{R}_{1-i,e'}$ that respects the strategy for $\mathcal{R}_{i,e}$. The problem is one of timing. To simplify notation, let $\widehat{\alpha} = \alpha - 2\gamma$ and $\widehat{\alpha}_s = \alpha_s - 2\gamma_s$. Since $\mathcal{R}_{1-i,e'}$ is initialized only finitely often, there is a certain amount 2^{-m} that it is allowed to put into β^i after the last time it is initialized. Thus, if $\mathcal{R}_{1-i,e'}$ waits until a stage s such that $\widehat{\alpha} - \widehat{\alpha}_s < 2^{-m}$, adding nothing to β^i until such a stage is reached, then from that point on it can put all of $\widehat{\alpha} - \widehat{\alpha}_s$ into β^i, which of course guarantees its success. The problem is that, in the general construction, a strategy working with a quota 2^{-m} cannot effectively find an s such that $\widehat{\alpha} - \widehat{\alpha}_s < 2^{-m}$. If it uses up its quota too soon, it may find itself unsatisfied and unable to do anything about it.

The key to solving this problem (and the reason for the hypothesis that $\alpha <_S \Omega$) is the observation that, since the sequence $\Omega_0, \Omega_1, \ldots$ converges much more slowly than the sequence $\widehat{\alpha}_0, \widehat{\alpha}_1, \ldots$, we can use Ω as an "investment adviser", which tells $\mathcal{R}_{1-i,e'}$ how much to put into β^i at each stage. More specifically, at a stage s, if $\mathcal{R}_{1-i,e'}$'s current quota is 2^{-m} then it puts into β^i as much of $\widehat{\alpha}_s - \widehat{\alpha}_{s-1}$ as possible, subject to the constraint that the total amount put into β^i by $\mathcal{R}_{1-i,e'}$ since the last stage at which it was initialized must not exceed $2^{-m}\Omega_s$. As we will see below, the fact that $\Omega >_S \alpha$ implies that there is a stage v after which $\mathcal{R}_{1-i,e'}$ is allowed to put all of $\widehat{\alpha} - \widehat{\alpha}_v$ into β^i.

In general, at a given stage s there will be several requirements, each with a certain amount that it wants (and is allowed) to direct into one of the β^j. We will work backwards, starting with the weakest priority requirement that we are currently considering. This requirement will be allowed to direct as much of $\widehat{\alpha}_s - \widehat{\alpha}_{s-1}$ as it wants (subject to its current quota, of course). If any of $\widehat{\alpha}_s - \widehat{\alpha}_{s-1}$ is left then the next weakest priority strategy will be allowed to act, and so on up the line.

We now proceed with the full construction. We give $\mathcal{R}_{i,e}$ stronger priority than $\mathcal{R}_{i',e'}$ if $2e + i < 2e' + i'$. Recall that we say that $\mathcal{R}_{i,e}$ is satisfied through n at stage s if $\forall m < s \neg\Phi(a, b^i, e, n, m)$. Let $n_s^{i,e}$ be the least n through which $\mathcal{R}_{i,e}$ is satisfied at stage s, if such an n exists, and let $n_s^{i,e} = \infty$ otherwise. We say that $\mathcal{R}_{i,e}$ *requires attention* at stage s if either $n_s^{i,e} = \infty$ or $n_s^{i,e} \neq n_{s-1}^{i,e}$. If $\mathcal{R}_{i,e}$ requires attention at stage s then we say that each requirement of weaker priority than $\mathcal{R}_{i,e}$ is *initialized* at stage s.

Each requirement $\mathcal{R}_{i,e}$ has associated with it a left-c.e. real $\tau^{i,e}$, which records the amount put into β^{1-i} for the sake of $\mathcal{R}_{i,e}$. We decide how to distribute $\delta = \alpha_s - \alpha_{s-1}$ between β^0 and β^1 at stage s as follows.

1. Let $j = s$ and $\varepsilon = 2(\gamma_s - \gamma_{s-1})$, and add $\gamma_s - \gamma_{s-1}$ to the current value of each β^i.

2. Let $i < 2$ and $e \in \mathbb{N}$ be such that $2e + i = j$. Let m be the number of times $\mathcal{R}_{i,e}$ has been initialized and let t be the last stage at which $\mathcal{R}_{i,e}$ was initialized (or $t = 0$ if there has been no such stage). Let
$$\zeta = \min(\delta - \varepsilon, 2^{-(j+m)}\Omega_s - (\tau_{s-1}^{i,e} - \tau_t^{i,e})).$$
Add ζ to ε and to the current values of $\tau^{i,e}$ and β^{1-i}.

3. If $\varepsilon = \delta$ or $j = 0$ then add $\delta - \varepsilon$ to the current value of β^0 and end the stage. Otherwise, decrease j by one and go to step 2.

This completes the construction. Clearly, $\gamma \leqslant_{\mathrm{r}} \beta^i \leqslant_{\mathrm{r}} \alpha$ for $i = 0, 1$ and $\beta^0 + \beta^1 = \alpha$. We now show by induction that each requirement initializes requirements of weaker priority only finitely often and is eventually satisfied.

Assume by induction that $\mathcal{R}_{i,e}$ is initialized only finitely often. Let $j = 2e + i$, let m be the number of times $\mathcal{R}_{i,e}$ is initialized, and let t be the last stage at which $\mathcal{R}_{i,e}$ is initialized. The following are clearly equivalent.

1. $\mathcal{R}_{i,e}$ is satisfied.

2. $\lim_s n_s^{i,e}$ exists and is finite.

3. $\mathcal{R}_{i,e}$ eventually stops requiring attention.

Assume for a contradiction that $\mathcal{R}_{i,e}$ requires attention infinitely often. Since $\Omega \nleqslant_{\mathrm{S}} \alpha$, part (ii) of Lemma 9.5.7 implies that there are $v > u > t$ such that for all $w > v$ we have $2^{-(j+m)}(\Omega_w - \Omega_u) > \alpha_w - \alpha_u$. Furthermore, by the way the amount ζ added to $\tau^{i,e}$ at a given stage is defined in step 2 of the construction, $\tau_u^{i,e} - \tau_t^{i,e} \leqslant 2^{-(j+m)}\Omega_u$ and $\tau_{w-1}^{i,e} - \tau_u^{i,e} \leqslant \alpha_{w-1} - \alpha_u$.

Thus for all $w > v$,

$$\begin{aligned}
\alpha_w - \alpha_{w-1} &= \alpha_w - \alpha_u - (\alpha_{w-1} - \alpha_u) \\
&< 2^{-(j+m)}(\Omega_w - \Omega_u) - (\alpha_{w-1} - \alpha_u) \\
&= 2^{-(j+m)}\Omega_w - (2^{-(j+m)}\Omega_u + \alpha_{w-1} - \alpha_u) \\
&\leqslant 2^{-(j+m)}\Omega_w - (\tau_u^{i,e} - \tau_t^{i,e} + \tau_{w-1}^{i,e} - \tau_u^{i,e}) \\
&= 2^{-(j+m)}\Omega_w - (\tau_{w-1}^{i,e} - \tau_t^{i,e}).
\end{aligned}$$

Thus, after stage v, the reverse recursion performed at each stage never gets past j, and hence everything put into β^i after stage v is put in either to code γ or for the sake of requirements of weaker priority than $\mathcal{R}_{i,e}$.

Let τ be the sum of all $\tau^{1-i,e'}$ such that $\mathcal{R}_{1-i,e'}$ has weaker priority than $\mathcal{R}_{i,e}$. Let $s_l > t$ be the lth stage at which $\mathcal{R}_{i,e}$ requires attention. If $\mathcal{R}_{1-i,e'}$ is the pth requirement on the priority list and $p > j$ then $\tau^{i',e'} - \tau^{i',e'}_{s_l} \leqslant 2^{-(p+l)}\Omega$. Thus $\tau - \tau_{s_l} \leqslant \sum_{p \geqslant 1} 2^{-(p+l)}\Omega = 2^{-l}\Omega \leqslant 2^{-l}$, and hence τ is computable.

Putting together the results of the previous two paragraphs, we see that $\beta^i \leqslant_{\mathrm{r}} \gamma$. Since $\alpha \nleqslant_{\mathrm{r}} \gamma$, we have $\alpha \nleqslant_{\mathrm{r}} \beta^i$. It now follows that there is an $n \in \omega$ such that $\mathcal{R}_{i,e}$ is eventually permanently satisfied through n, and such that $\mathcal{R}_{i,e}$ is eventually never satisfied through any $n' < n$. Thus $\lim_s n_s^{i,e}$ exists and is finite, and hence $\mathcal{R}_{i,e}$ is satisfied and eventually stops requiring attention. □

We now prove the upwards density theorem.

Theorem 9.8.3 (after Downey, Hirschfeldt, and Nies [116]). *Let r be a standard reducibility on the left-c.e. reals. Let $\gamma <_{\mathrm{r}} \Omega$ be a left-c.e. real. There is a left-c.e. real β such that $\gamma <_{\mathrm{r}} \beta <_{\mathrm{r}} \Omega$.*

Proof. Let a and c be such that $C_a = \gamma$ and $C_c = \Omega$, and let Φ be as in Definition 9.8.1. We build $\beta \geqslant_{\mathrm{r}} \gamma$ (with b such that $C_b = \beta$ given by the recursion theorem) to satisfy the following requirements for each e.

$$\begin{aligned}
\mathcal{R}_e &: \exists n\, \forall m\, \neg\Phi(b, a, e, n, m). \\
\mathcal{S}_e &: \exists n\, \forall m\, \neg\Phi(c, b, e, n, m).
\end{aligned}$$

As in the previous proof, the analysis of an appropriate two-strategy case will be enough to outline the essentials of the full construction. Let us consider the strategies $\mathcal{S}_e$ and $\mathcal{R}_{e'}$, the former having priority over the latter.

The strategy for $\mathcal{S}_e$ is basically to make β look like γ. At each point of the construction, $\mathcal{R}_{e'}$ has a certain fraction of Ω that it is allowed to put into β (in addition to the coding of γ into β, of course). We will say that $\mathcal{S}_e$ is *satisfied through n at stage s* if $\forall m < s\, \neg\Phi(c, b, e, n, m)$. Whenever either $\mathcal{S}_e$ is not currently satisfied or the least number through which it is satisfied changes, $\mathcal{S}_e$ initializes $\mathcal{R}_{e'}$, which means that the fraction of Ω that $\mathcal{R}_{e'}$ is allowed to put into β is reduced.

As in the previous proof, if $\mathcal{S}_e$ is not eventually permanently satisfied through some n then the amount put into β by $\mathcal{R}_{e'}$ is computable, and hence $\beta \equiv_r \gamma$, which, as before, implies that there is a stage after which $\mathcal{S}_e$ is permanently satisfied through some n and never again satisfied through any $n' < n$. Once this stage has been reached, $\mathcal{R}_{e'}$ is free to code a fixed fraction of Ω into β, and hence it too succeeds.

We now proceed with the full construction. For $e < e'$, we give a requirement $\mathcal{X}_e$ stronger priority than a requirement $\mathcal{Y}_{e'}$. We also give $\mathcal{R}_e$ stronger priority than $\mathcal{S}_e$. As mentioned above, we say that $\mathcal{R}_e$ is satisfied through n at stage s if $\forall m < s \, \neg\Phi(b, a, e, n, m)$. Similarly, we say that $\mathcal{S}_e$ is satisfied through n at stage s if $\forall m < s \, \neg\Phi(c, b, e, n, m)$. For a requirement $\mathcal{X}_e$, let $n_s^{\mathcal{X}_e}$ be the least n through which $\mathcal{X}_e$ is satisfied at stage s, if such an n exists, and let $n_s^{\mathcal{X}_e} = \infty$ otherwise. We say that the requirement $\mathcal{X}_e$ *requires attention* at stage s if either $n_s^{\mathcal{X}_e} = \infty$ or $n_s^{\mathcal{X}_e} \neq n_{s-1}^{\mathcal{X}_e}$.

At stage s, proceed as follows. First add $\frac{\gamma_s - \gamma_{s-1}}{2}$ to the current value of β. If no requirement requires attention at stage s then end the stage. Otherwise, let $\mathcal{X}_e$ be the strongest priority requirement requiring attention at stage s. We say that $\mathcal{X}_e$ *acts* at stage s. If $\mathcal{X} = \mathcal{S}$ then initialize all weaker priority requirements and end the stage. If $\mathcal{X} = \mathcal{R}$ then let m be the number of times that $\mathcal{R}_e$ has been initialized. If s is the first stage at which $\mathcal{R}_e$ acts after the last time it was initialized (or is the very first stage at which $\mathcal{R}_e$ acts), then let t be the last stage at which $\mathcal{R}_e$ was initialized (or let $t = 0$ if there has been no such stage), and otherwise let t be the last stage at which $\mathcal{R}_e$ acted. Add $2^{-(e+m+3)}(\Omega_s - \Omega_t)$ to the current value of β and end the stage.

This completes the construction. Since β is bounded by $\frac{\gamma}{2} + \sum_e 2^{-e+2}\Omega = \frac{\gamma+\Omega}{2}$, it is a well-defined left-c.e. real. Furthermore, $\gamma \leqslant_r \beta$.

We now show by induction that each requirement initializes requirements of weaker priority only finitely often and is eventually satisfied. Assume by induction that there is a stage u such that no requirement of stronger priority than $\mathcal{X}_e$ requires attention after stage u. The following are clearly equivalent.

1. $\mathcal{X}_e$ is satisfied.
2. $\lim_s n_s^{\mathcal{X}_e}$ exists and is finite.
3. $\mathcal{X}_e$ eventually stops requiring attention.
4. $\mathcal{X}_e$ acts only finitely often.

First suppose that $\mathcal{X} = \mathcal{R}$. Let m be the number of times that $\mathcal{R}_e$ is initialized. (Since $\mathcal{R}_e$ is not initialized at any stage after stage u, this number is finite.) Suppose that $\mathcal{R}_e$ acts infinitely often. Then the total amount added to β for the sake of $\mathcal{R}_e$ is $2^{-(e+m)}\Omega$, and hence $\beta \equiv_r \Omega \nleqslant_r \gamma$.

Thus there is an n such that $\mathcal{R}_e$ is eventually permanently satisfied through n, and such that $\mathcal{R}_e$ is eventually never satisfied through $n' < n$. Thus $\lim_s n_s^{\mathcal{R}_e}$ exists and is finite, and hence $\mathcal{R}_e$ is satisfied and eventually stops requiring attention.

Now suppose that $\mathcal{X} = \mathcal{S}$ and $\mathcal{S}_e$ acts infinitely often. If $v > u$ is the mth stage at which $\mathcal{S}_e$ acts then the total amount added to β after stage v for purposes other than coding γ is bounded by $\sum_i 2^{-(i+m+2)}\Omega < 2^{-m+1}$. It follows that $\beta \equiv_{\mathrm{r}} \gamma \not\geqslant_{\mathrm{r}} \Omega$. Thus there is an n such that $\mathcal{S}_e$ is eventually permanently satisfied through n, and such that $\mathcal{S}_e$ is eventually never satisfied through $n' < n$. So $\lim_s n_s^{\mathcal{S}_e}$ exists and is finite, and hence $\mathcal{S}_e$ is satisfied and eventually stops requiring attention. □

Combining Theorems 9.8.2 and 9.8.3, we have the following result.

Corollary 9.8.4 (after Downey, Hirschfeldt, and Nies [116]). *Let r be a standard reducibility on the left-c.e. reals that is at least as strong as Solovay reducibility. Then the r-degrees of left-c.e. reals are dense.*

9.9 Monotone degrees and density

One notable reducibility missing from the list above is monotone reducibility, introduced in Section 4.5. Certainly this is a Σ_3^0 reducibility for which the degree of Ω is the top degree among left-c.e. reals and the computable sets form the bottom degree. However, it is not known whether addition induces a join on this degree structure.

Open Question 9.9.1. Does addition induce a join on the monotone degrees of left-c.e. reals?

We conjecture that the answer is no. In spite of this lack of knowledge, there is still a downward density theorem for monotone reducibility.

Theorem 9.9.2 (Calhoun [46]). *The monotone degrees of left-c.e. reals are downward dense, meaning that if* $\mathbf{b}$ *is a nonzero Km-degree of left-c.e. reals then there is a Km-degree of left-c.e. reals* $\mathbf{a}$ *with* $\mathbf{b} > \mathbf{a} > \mathbf{0}$.

The proof uses the following useful lemma, which says that we can use simple permitting in this case.

Lemma 9.9.3 (Calhoun [46]). *Suppose that* $A = \lim_s A_s$ *and* $B = \lim_s B_s$ *are monotonic approximations to left-c.e. reals* A *and* B *and* f *is a computable function such that* $B_s \upharpoonright n = B \upharpoonright n \Rightarrow A_{f(s)} \upharpoonright n = A \upharpoonright n$ *for all* s *and* n. *Then* $A \leqslant_{Km} B$.

Proof. Let U be a universal monotone machine. We build a monotone machine M by letting $M(\sigma) = A_{f(s)} \upharpoonright n$ whenever $U(\sigma) = B_s \upharpoonright n$ and defining $M(\sigma)$ in this way does not violate the monotonicity of M. By the hypothesis of the lemma, for all n, if $U(\sigma) = B \upharpoonright n$ them $M(\sigma) = A \upharpoonright n$. □

Proof of Theorem 9.9.2. The argument is a finite injury one. We are given a noncomputable left-c.e. real $B = \lim_s B_s$ and build a noncomputable left-c.e. real $A <_{Km} B$. (In fact, A will be a c.e. set.) We keep $A \leqslant_{Km} B$ by Lemma 9.9.3 and simple permitting. We must meet the requirements

$$R_{2e} : B \nleqslant_{Km} A \text{ with constant } e$$

and

$$R_{2e+1} : \overline{A} \neq W_e.$$

The R_{2e+1} are enough to make A nontrivial, as the trivial Km-degree consists of the computable sets. Associated with the R_j are movable markers $n(j, s)$, with $n(-1, s) = 0$ for all s. We meet R_j between $n(j - 1, s)$ and $n(j, s)$. It will be clear from the construction that $\lim_s n(j, s)$ exists for all j.

To meet R_{2e}, we allow R_{2e} to assert control of various locations of A. If R_{2e} asserts control of position n at stage s, we ensure, with the appropriate priority, that $A_t(n) = A_s(n)$ for all $t > s$. At stage s, the requirement R_{2e} will have control of $A \upharpoonright [n(2e - 1, s), n(2e, s))$. At stage $s + 1$, if we see $Km_s(B_s \upharpoonright n(2e, s)) \leqslant Km_s(A_s \upharpoonright n(2e, s)) + e$, then we allow R_{2e} to assert control of the next position by setting $n(2e, s + 1) = n(2e, s) + 1$. Notice that, once R_{2e} has priority, this can happen only finitely often, lest B be computable.

Meeting R_{2e+1} we use a simple permitting argument. Once R_{2e+1} has priority, if it has control of position n, when we see that $\overline{A}_s \upharpoonright n(2e+1, s) = W_{e,s} \upharpoonright n(2e + 1, s)$ we set $n(2e + 1, s + 1) = n(2e + 1, s) + 1$, and if ever B_t permits $n(2e + 1, s)$ then we can make a disagreement in the usual way by changing $A_t(n(2e + 1, s))$. By Lemma 9.9.3, it cannot be the case that R_{2e+1} asks for permission infinitely often but never receives it, since in that case A would be computable but we would also have $B \leqslant_{Km} A$, which would make B computable. □

Open Question 9.9.4. Are the Km-degrees of left-c.e. reals dense?

9.10 Further relationships between S-, cl-, and rK-reducibilities

It follows from Theorem 9.1.6 that S-reducibility does not imply cl-reducibility on the left-c.e. reals. The following result shows that S-reducibility and cl-reducibility are in fact incomparable on the left-c.e. reals.

Theorem 9.10.1 (Downey, Hirschfeldt, and LaForte [113]). *There exist left-c.e. reals $\alpha \leqslant_{\text{cl}} \beta$ such that $\alpha \nleqslant_{\text{S}} \beta$. Moreover, α can be chosen to be strongly c.e.*

Proof. We must build α and β so that $\alpha \leqslant_{\mathrm{cl}} \beta$ and α is strongly c.e., while satisfying the following requirement for each e.

$$\mathcal{R}_e : \exists q \in \mathbb{Q}\,(q < \beta \wedge (\Phi_e(q)\downarrow < \alpha \Rightarrow e(\beta - q) < \alpha - \Phi_e(q))).$$

These requirements suffice because any partial computable function is equal to Φ_e for infinitely many e.

We discuss the strategy for a single requirement $\mathcal{R}_e$. Let k be such that $e \leqslant 2^k$. We must make the difference between β and some rational $q < \beta$ quite small while making the difference between α and $\Phi_e(q)$ relatively large. At a stage t we pick a fresh large number d. For the sake of $\mathcal{R}_e$, we will control the first $d+k+2$ many bits of β and α. We set $\beta_t(n) = 1$ for all n with $d \leqslant n \leqslant d+k+1$, while at the same time keeping $\alpha_t(n) = 0$ for all such n. We let $q = \beta_t$. Note that, since we are restraining the first $d+k+2$ bits of β, we know that, unless this restraint is lifted, $\beta - \beta_t \leqslant 2^{-(d+k+2)}$.

We now need do nothing until we come to a stage $s \geqslant t$ such that $\Phi_{e,s}(q)\downarrow < \alpha_s$ and $\alpha_s - \Phi_{e,s}(q) \leqslant 2^{-(d+2)}$. Our action then is the following. First we add $2^{-(d+k+1)}$ to β_s. Then we again restrain $\beta \upharpoonright d+k+2$. Assuming that this restraint is successful, $e(\beta - q) \leqslant 2^{-(d+2)} + 2^{-(d+1)} < 2^{-d}$.

Finally we win by our second action, which is to add 2^{-d} to α. Then $\alpha - \alpha_s \geqslant 2^{-d}$, so $\alpha - \Phi_e(q) \geqslant 2^{-d} > e(\beta - q)$, as required.

The theorem now follows by a simple application of the finite injury priority method. When we add $2^{-(d+k+1)}$ to β at stage s, since $\beta_s(n) = 1$ for all n with $d \leqslant n \leqslant d+k+1$, bit $d-1$ of β changes from 0 to 1. On the α side, when we add 2^{-d} at stage s, the only change is that bit $d-1$ of α changes from 0 to 1. Hence we keep $\alpha \leqslant_{\mathrm{cl}} \beta$ (with constant 0). It is also clear that α is strongly c.e. □

On the other hand, S-reducibility and cl-reducibility do coincide on c.e. *sets*, as the following results show.

Theorem 9.10.2 (Downey, Hirschfeldt, and LaForte [113]). *Let α be a left-c.e. real and β be a strongly c.e. real. If $\alpha \leqslant_{\mathrm{cl}} \beta$ then $\alpha \leqslant_{\mathrm{S}} \beta$.*

Proof. Let A be an almost c.e. set and B be a c.e. set such that there is a reduction $\Gamma^B = A$ with use $n + c$. Let $\alpha = 0.A$ and $\beta = 0.B$. We may assume that we have chosen approximations of A and B such that $\Gamma^B(n)[s] = A_s(n)$ for all s and $n \leqslant s$. We may also assume that if n enters A at stage s then $n \leqslant s$. If n enters A at stage s then some number less than or equal to $n + c$ must enter B at stage s. Since B is c.e., it follows that $\beta_s - \beta_{s-1} \geqslant 2^{-(n+c)}$. But n entering A corresponds to a change of at most 2^{-n} in the value of α, so $\beta_s - \beta_{s-1} \geqslant 2^{-c}(\alpha_s - \alpha_{s-1})$. Thus for all s we have $\alpha - \alpha_s \leqslant 2^c(\beta - \beta_s)$, and hence $\alpha \leqslant_{\mathrm{S}} \beta$. □

Theorem 9.10.3 (Downey, Hirschfeldt, and LaForte [113]). *Let α be a strongly c.e. real and β be a left-c.e. real. If $\alpha \leqslant_{\mathrm{S}} \beta$ then $\alpha \leqslant_{\mathrm{cl}} \beta$.*

Proof. Let α and β satisfy the hypotheses of the theorem. Let the computable function f and the constant k be such that $\alpha - \alpha_{f(s)} < 2^{k-1}(\beta - \beta_s)$ for all s. To compute $\alpha \upharpoonright n$ using $\beta \upharpoonright n+k$, find the least stage s such that $\beta_s \upharpoonright n+k = \beta \upharpoonright n+k$. Then $\beta - \beta_s < 2^{-(n+k)}$, so $\alpha - \alpha_{f(s)} < 2^{k-1}2^{-(n+k)} = 2^{-(n+1)}$. Since α is strongly c.e., we must have $\alpha \upharpoonright n = \alpha_{f(s)} \upharpoonright n$, since any change in the value of $\alpha \upharpoonright n$ adds at least $2^{-(n+1)}$ to the value of α. □

Corollary 9.10.4 (Downey, Hirschfeldt, and LaForte [113]). *For c.e. sets A and B, we have $A \leqslant_{\mathrm{S}} B$ iff $A \leqslant_{\mathrm{cl}} B$.*

Thus cl-reducibility can be a particularly useful tool in studying c.e. sets. For example, we have seen that there is a largest S-degree of left-c.e. reals, but we now show that there is no largest S-degree of c.e. *sets*.

Theorem 9.10.5 (Downey, Hirschfeldt, and LaForte [113]). *Let A be a c.e. set. There is a c.e. set that is not cl-below A, and hence is not S-below A.*

Proof. The argument is a finite injury construction, but is nonuniform, in the sense that we build two c.e. sets B and C, one of which is not cl-below A. Let Γ_e be Φ_e with use restricted to $n+e$ on input n. We satisfy the following requirements.

$$\mathcal{R}_{e,i} : \Gamma_e^A \neq B \vee \Gamma_i^A \neq C.$$

These requirements suffice because if $B \leqslant_{\mathrm{cl}} A$ then there is an e such that $\Gamma_e^A = B$, in which case the requirements of the form $\mathcal{R}_{e,i}$ ensure that $C \nleqslant_{\mathrm{cl}} A$.

The idea for satisfying a single requirement $\mathcal{R}_{e,i}$ is simple. Let

$$l(e,i,s) = \max\{n : \forall m \leqslant n\,(\Gamma_e^A(m)[s] = B_s(m) \wedge \Gamma_i^A(m)[s] = C_s(m))\}.$$

Pick a fresh large number k and let $\mathcal{R}_{e,i}$ assert control over the interval $[k, 3k]$ in both B and C, waiting until a stage s such that $l(e,i,s) > 3k$. First work with C. Put $3k$ into C, and wait for the next stage t where $l(e,i,t) > 3k$. Note that some number must enter $A_t \setminus A_s$ below $3k+i$. Now repeat with $3k-1$, then $3k-2$, and so on. In this way, $2k$ many numbers are made to enter A below $3k+i$. Now we can win using B, by repeating the process and noticing that, since k is larger than e and i, we cannot have $2k$ many numbers entering A below $3k+i$ *and* $2k$ many other numbers entering A below $3k+e$.

The theorem now follows by a standard application of the finite injury method. □

Since both S-reducibility and cl-reducibility imply rK-reducibility, it follows from Theorems 9.1.6 and 9.10.1 that rK-reducibility does not imply either of them on left-c.e. reals. We now show that this is the case even for c.e. sets.

Theorem 9.10.6 (Downey, Hirschfeldt, and LaForte [113]). *There exist c.e. sets A and B such that $A \leqslant_{\mathrm{rK}} B$ but $A \nleqslant_{\mathrm{cl}} B$.*

Proof. Let Γ_e be Φ_e with use restricted to $n+e$ on input n. We build c.e. sets $A \leqslant_{\mathrm{rK}} B$ to satisfy the following requirements.

$$\mathcal{R}_e : \Gamma_e^B \neq A.$$

The construction is a standard finite injury argument. We discuss the satisfaction of a single requirement $\mathcal{R}_e$. For the sake of this requirement, we choose a fresh large n, restrain n from entering A, and restrain $n+e$ from entering B. If we find a stage s such that $\Gamma_e^B(n)[s]\downarrow = 0$ then we put n into A, put $n+e$ into B, and restrain the initial segment of B of length $n+e$. Unless a higher priority strategy acts at a later stage, this action guarantees that $\Gamma_e^B(n) \neq A(n)$.

We ensure that the followers picked by different requirements are far enough apart that for each m there is at most one e such that $\mathcal{R}_e$ has a follower $n < m$ but $n+e \geqslant m$. Thus, if $B \upharpoonright m = B_s \upharpoonright m$ then $A \upharpoonright m$ can change at most once after stage s. By Theorem 9.6.7, $A \leqslant_{\mathrm{rK}} B$. □

One further difference between cl-reducibility and S-reducibility is that if α is a noncomputable left-c.e. real, then there is a noncomputable c.e. set cl-below α, while there may not be any noncomputable c.e. set S-below α.

Proposition 9.10.7 (Downey, Hirschfeldt, and LaForte [113]). *Let α be a left-c.e. real. Then there is a c.e. set B such that $B \leqslant_{\mathrm{cl}} \alpha$ and $\alpha \leqslant_{\mathrm{tt}} B$.*

Proof. At stage $s+1$, for each n, if $\alpha_s(n) \neq \alpha_{s+1}(n)$ then put $\langle n, i\rangle$ in B for the least i such that $\langle n, i\rangle \notin B_s$. If $\alpha_s \upharpoonright m = \alpha \upharpoonright m$ then $B_s \upharpoonright m = B \upharpoonright m$, since $\langle n, i\rangle \geqslant n$ for all n. Thus $B \leqslant_{\mathrm{cl}} \alpha$. There are at most 2^n many i such that $\langle n, i\rangle \in B$, and $\alpha(n) = 0$ iff there are an even number of such i. Thus $\alpha \leqslant_{\mathrm{tt}} B$. □

Theorem 9.10.8 (Downey, Hirschfeldt, and LaForte [113]). *There is a noncomputable left-c.e. real α such that all c.e. sets S-below α are computable.*

Proof. Recall that a prefix-free c.e. set $A \subset 2^{<\omega}$ is a presentation of α if $\sum_{\sigma \in A} 2^{-|\sigma|} = \alpha$. By Corollary 5.3.14, there is a noncomputable left-c.e. real α such that every presentation of α is computable. Let $\beta \leqslant_{\mathrm{S}} \alpha$ be strongly c.e. Then there is a positive $q \in \mathbb{Q}$ and a left-c.e. real γ such that $\alpha = q\beta + \gamma$. Let k be such that $2^{-k} \leqslant q$ and let $\delta = \gamma + (q - 2^{-k})\beta$. Then δ is a left-c.e. real such that $\alpha = 2^{-k}\beta + \delta$.

Let $b_0, b_1, \ldots$ and $d_0, d_1, \ldots$ be computable sequences of natural numbers such that $2^{-k}\beta = \sum_i 2^{-b_i}$ and $\delta = \sum_i 2^{-d_i}$. Since β is strongly c.e., so is $2^{-k}\beta$, and hence we can choose $b_0, b_1, \ldots$ to be pairwise distinct, so that the nth bit of β is 1 iff $n + k = b_i$ for some i.

By the KC Theorem, since $\sum_i 2^{-b_i} + \sum_i 2^{-d_i} = \alpha < 1$, there is a prefix-free c.e. set A with an enumeration $\sigma_0, \sigma_1, \ldots$ such that $|\sigma_{2i}| = b_i$ and $|\sigma_{2i+1}| = d_i$ for all i. Now $\sum_{\sigma \in A} 2^{-|\sigma|} = \alpha$, so A is a presentation of α, and hence is computable. Now we can compute β as follows. Given n, run through all strings of length $n+k$ in A and determine whether any of them is σ_{2i} for some i. If so, then $\beta(n) = 1$, while otherwise, $\beta(n) = 0$. □

9.11 A minimal rK-degree

In this section, we will prove the following result.

Theorem 9.11.1 (Raichev and Stephan [321]). *There is a minimal rK-degree.*

This result is interesting because rK is one of the few measures of relative randomness for which we know whether or not there is a minimal degree. The proof below uses the fact that rK is reasonably well-behaved on very sparse sets. Merkle and Stephan [270] have exploited this idea of using sparse sets to establish results about measures of relative randomness quite fruitfully, as we will see in Section 9.15.

Proof of Theorem 9.11.1. We build a Π^0_1 class $[T]$ for a computable tree T with no computable paths. The tree T will have the property that for all total functionals Φ, for all $X \in [T]$, there is a string $\sigma \prec X$ such that one of the following holds:

(i) Φ^X and Φ^Y are compatible for all $Y \in [T]$ extending σ or

(ii) Φ^Z and Φ^Y are incompatible for all $Z \neq Y$ extending σ in $[T]$.

We make the set S of splitting nodes of $[T]$ computably sparse. That is, for all computable functions g,

$$\forall^\infty \sigma \in S \, \forall \tau \in S, (\sigma \prec \tau \rightarrow g(|\sigma|) < |\tau|).$$

The proof uses movable markers. For each string ν, at each stage s the marker m_ν rests on a splitting node of T_s. At stage 0, we have $T_0 = 2^{<\omega}$ and $m_\nu = \nu$. At each stage s we will prune T_s to make T_{s+1}. The basic action is called procedure CUT(σ, τ). This procedure can be invoked for $\sigma \prec \tau$. It prunes all paths that extend $m_{\sigma'}$ for all $\sigma \preccurlyeq \sigma' \prec \tau$, but not m_τ. Then all markers are moved accordingly. That is, we move m_σ to m_τ, and $m_{\sigma\nu}$ to $m_{\tau\nu}$.

The construction at stage s works for nodes of length $\leqslant s$ and has the following actions.

(a) If there is a σ, an $i < 2$, and an $e \leqslant |\sigma|$ with $\Phi_e(x)[s] = m_{\sigma i}(x)$ for all $x \leqslant |\sigma|$, then invoke CUT$(\sigma, \sigma(1-i))$.

(b) If there are σ, δ, ν, and $e \leqslant |\sigma|$ such that $\Phi_e^{m_{\sigma 0}}[s]$ and $\Phi_e^{m_{\sigma 1}}[s]$ are compatible for all arguments $y \leqslant |\sigma|$, but $\Phi_e^{m_{\sigma 0 \delta}}[s]$ and $\Phi_e^{m_{\sigma 1 \nu}}[s]$ are incompatible at some argument $y \leqslant |\sigma|$, then invoke $\mathrm{CUT}(\sigma 0, \sigma 0 \delta)$ and $\mathrm{CUT}(\sigma 1, \sigma 1 \nu)$.

(c) Finally, if there are σ, τ, ν, and $e \leqslant |\sigma|$ with $\sigma \prec \tau \prec \nu$ and $|m_\tau| \leqslant \Phi_e(|m_\sigma|)[s] < m_\nu$, then invoke $\mathrm{CUT}(\tau, \nu)$.

It is easy to show that all the markers stop moving at some stage. Additionally, at each stage the tree T_s is perfect, and hence $\bigcap_s T_s$ is a perfect tree. By (a), $[T]$ has no computable members, and by (b) and (c), for all $X \in [T]$, there is a string $\sigma \prec X$ satisfying either (i) or (ii) above, and the splitting nodes of T are computably sparse. Now let A be a path on T of hyperimmune-free degree, obtained using the Hyperimmune-Free Basis Theorem 2.19.11. We claim that A has minimal rK-degree. Suppose that $\emptyset \neq_{\mathrm{T}} B \leqslant_{\mathrm{rK}} A$. Then $B \leqslant_{\mathrm{T}} A$ also and hence, as A is hyperimmune free, $B \leqslant_{\mathrm{tt}} A$. Let $\Phi^A = B$ be the witnessing truth table reduction with computable use φ.

We show that $A \leqslant_{\mathrm{rK}} B$. Since B is not computable, (ii) must hold for Φ. Let σ be the string mentioned in (ii). We need the following lemma.

Lemma 9.11.2. *For almost all n and almost all stages t, the tree T_t has at most two extensions of σ of length n with extensions in T_t that map to $B \restriction n$ under Φ.*

Proof. For $k > |\sigma|$ let $f(k)$ be the first stage such that for all strings ν with $A \restriction (k-1)^\frown(1 - A(k)) \prec \nu$ of length $\varphi(s)$ on T_s, there exists $x \leqslant s$ with $\Phi^\nu(x) \downarrow \neq \Phi^A(x)$. Let $f(k) = 1$ for $k \leqslant |\sigma|$. The function f is total, since otherwise there is a k such that for each s there is a string ν_s with $A \restriction (k-1)^\frown(1 - A(k)) \prec \nu_s$ of length $\varphi(s)$ on T_s and $\Phi^{\nu_s}(x) = \Phi^A(x)$ for all $x \leqslant s$. Then $Y = \liminf_s \nu_s \in [T]$ is distinct from A and $\Phi^A = \Phi^Y$. However, (ii) holds as B is noncomputable, so this is a contradiction.

Notice that f is A-computable, and hence, as A is hyperimmune free, there is a computable function g majorizing f.

Now choose n larger than $|\sigma|$, the length at which T becomes g-sparse, and the length of the first splitting node of A on T. Let τ be the last splitting node on $A \restriction n$ and $\nu \prec \tau$ any splitting node extending σ. Then by sparseness, we know that for $s = f(|\sigma|)$,

$$s \leqslant g(|\sigma|) < |\tau| \leqslant n.$$

Thus by stage s, every $\rho \in T_s$ extending $A \restriction (|\nu| - 1)^\frown(1 - A(|\nu|)) = \nu^\frown(1 - A(|\nu|)$ will have an argument $x \leqslant s$ with $\Phi^\rho(x) \neq \Phi^A(x) = B(x)$. Therefore ρ cannot map to $B \restriction n$ under Φ. As ν is an arbitrary splitting node of T below the last splitting node of $A \restriction n$, only strings extending the last splitting node of $A \restriction n$ can map to $B \restriction n$ under Φ. $\square$

To complete the proof, given $B \upharpoonright n$, run through computable approximations of T_s until a sufficiently large stage t is found where T_t has at most two extensions of σ that can map to $B \upharpoonright n$ under Φ. The stage t exists by Lemma 9.11.2. We can find these extensions effectively from $B \upharpoonright n$ as Φ is a tt-reduction. The output of the two strings being found, one will be $A \upharpoonright n$. This is an rK-reduction. □

Raichev and Stephan [321] established various facts about minimal rK-degrees. For example, they showed that there are $2^{\aleph_0}$ many of them, as the hyperimmune-free basis theorem shows that every Π^0_1 class with no computable members has $2^{\aleph_0}$ many hyperimmune-free members. Additionally, they showed that minimal rK-degrees have fairly low initial segment complexity.

Theorem 9.11.3 (Raichev and Stephan [321]). *If A has minimal rK-degree, then for any computable order g, and for Q either C or K,*

$$Q(A \upharpoonright n) \leqslant Q(n) + g(n) + O(1).$$

Proof. Given any computable strictly increasing function h, define the h-*dilution* A_h of A by $A_h(h(n)) = A(n)$ and $A_h(k) = 0$ for $k \notin \operatorname{rng} h(n)$. Notice that $A_h \leqslant_{\mathrm{S}} A \leqslant_{\mathrm{T}} A_h$ and hence $A_h \equiv_{\mathrm{rK}} A$ if A has minimal rK-degree. To describe $A_h(n) \upharpoonright n$ we need only $Q(n)$ plus k bits of information, where k is the number of elements of $\operatorname{rng} h(n)$ that are less than n. Since $A \leqslant_{\mathrm{rK}} A_h$, the same is true of A, up to a constant. Thus, given any g, it is easy to choose a fast enough growing h to make $Q(A \upharpoonright n) \leqslant Q(n) + g(n) + O(1)$. □

This result shows that if A has minimal rK-degree then it is far from random. By the Kučera-Gács Theorem 8.3.2, we know that there is a 1-random R with $A \leqslant_{\mathrm{wtt}} R$. Now choose an h growing much faster than the use of the reduction $A \leqslant_{wtt} R$. Then $A_h \leqslant_{\mathrm{S}} R$, where A_h is as in the above proof, and hence we have the following result.

Theorem 9.11.4 (Raichev and Stephan [321]). *Every real of minimal rK-degree is rK-reducible to a 1-random real.*

Raichev and Stephan also showed that there are 1-random reals with no minimal rK-degrees below them.

9.12 Initial segment complexity and completeness for left-c.e. reals

Although K-reducibility is far from implying cl-reducibility, even on left-c.e. reals, if the prefix-free complexity of the initial segments of a left-c.e. real α is much greater than that of the corresponding initial segments of a left-c.e. real β, then we do have $\beta <_{\mathrm{cl}} \alpha$.

Theorem 9.12.1 (Downey, Hirschfeldt, and LaForte [113]). *Let α and β be left-c.e. reals such that* $\lim_n K(\alpha \upharpoonright n) - K(\beta \upharpoonright n) = \infty$. *Then* $\beta <_{\mathrm{cl}} \alpha$.

Proof. Since cl-reducibility implies K-reducibility, $\alpha \nleqslant_{\mathrm{cl}} \beta$, so it is enough to show that $\beta \leqslant_{\mathrm{cl}} \alpha$.

Let $c_\alpha(n)$ be the least s such that $\alpha_s \upharpoonright n = \alpha \upharpoonright n$, and define $c_\beta(n)$ analogously. Define a prefix-free machine M as follows. For each n, s, and σ, if $\mathcal{U}(\sigma)[s]\downarrow = \beta_s \upharpoonright n$ and $M(\sigma)$ has not been defined before stage s, then let $M(\sigma) = \alpha_s \upharpoonright n$. Suppose that $c_\beta(n) \geqslant c_\alpha(n)$. If $\mathcal{U}(\sigma)\downarrow = \beta \upharpoonright n$ then $M(\sigma)\downarrow = \alpha \upharpoonright n$, so $K(\alpha \upharpoonright n) \leqslant K(\beta \upharpoonright n) + O(1)$. Thus $c_\beta(n) < c_\alpha(n)$ for almost all n, which clearly implies that $\beta \leqslant_{\mathrm{cl}} \alpha$. □

Stephan [personal communication] has shown that this result has quite limited applicability, however. Its hypothesis implies that $\lim_n K(\alpha \upharpoonright n) - K(n) = \infty$, which implies in turn that α is wtt-complete.

Theorem 9.12.2 (Stephan [personal communication]). *Let α be a left-c.e. real such that* $\lim_n K(\alpha \upharpoonright n) - K(n) = \infty$. *Then α is wtt-complete, and indeed* $\alpha \geqslant_{\mathrm{cl}} \emptyset'$.

Proof. We give a new proof of this result. For Stephan's original proof, see Downey [103]. Let $n_0, n_1, \ldots$ be an enumeration without repetitions of $\emptyset'$. Let $L = \{(K_t(n_s), \alpha_s \upharpoonright n_s) : t \geqslant s\}$. Then the weight of L is bounded by $\sum_s \sum_{\mathcal{U}(\sigma)=n_s} 2^{-|\sigma|} < 1$, so L is a KC-set. Thus $K(\alpha_s \upharpoonright n_s) \leqslant K(n_s) + O(1)$. Hence, for all but finitely many s, we have $\alpha \upharpoonright n_s \neq \alpha_s \upharpoonright n_s$. So, for all but finitely many n, we can compute $\emptyset'(n)$ using $\alpha \upharpoonright n$ by searching for a stage s such that $\alpha \upharpoonright n = \alpha_s \upharpoonright n$, and noting that $n \in \emptyset'$ iff $n = n_t$ for some $t \leqslant s$. □

Of course, we can use any c.e. set in place of $\emptyset'$ in the above proof, so we have the following result, whose second part follows by Theorem 9.10.5.

Corollary 9.12.3. *Let α be a left-c.e. real. Then either $\alpha \geqslant_{\mathrm{cl}} B$ for all c.e. sets B or there are infinitely many n such that* $K(\alpha \upharpoonright n) \leqslant K(n) + O(1)$.

Thus, if A is a c.e. set then there are infinitely many n such that $K(A \upharpoonright n) \leqslant K(n) + O(1)$.

Stephan [personal communication] also noted that the analog of Theorem 9.12.2 holds for plain complexity. He attributes this result to folklore.

Theorem 9.12.4. *Let α be a left-c.e. real such that* $\lim_n C(\alpha \upharpoonright n) - C(n) = \infty$. *Then α is wtt-complete, and indeed* $\alpha \geqslant_{\mathrm{cl}} \emptyset'$.

Proof. Let $f(n)$ be the least s such that $x \in \emptyset'_s$, if there is such an s, and $f(n) = 0$ otherwise. Let $g(n)$ be the least s such that $\alpha \upharpoonright n = \alpha_s \upharpoonright n$. If $\alpha \ngeqslant_{\mathrm{cl}} \emptyset'$ then g does not dominate f. In other words, there are infinitely many n such that $g(n) < f(n)$. For any such n, we have $\alpha \upharpoonright n = \alpha_{f(n)} \upharpoonright n$, whence $C(\alpha \upharpoonright n) \leqslant C(n) + O(1)$. □

9.13 cl-reducibility and the Kučera-Gács Theorem

Recall that the Kučera-Gács Theorem 8.3.2 states that every set is wtt-reducible to a 1-random set. In this section, we show that this wtt-reduction cannot in general be improved to a cl-reduction. In other words, the use of the reduction in the Kučera-Gács Theorem cannot be made to be $n+O(1)$. Indeed, there is a $\emptyset'$-computable set that is not cl-reducible to any complex set. (Recall that a set A is complex if there is a computable order h such that $K(A \upharpoonright n) > h(n)$ for all n.)

Lemma 9.13.1 (Downey and Hirschfeldt [unpublished]). *Let Γ be a cl-reduction with use bounded by $x+c$, let $\sigma \in 2^{<\omega}$, and let f be a computable order. There exists a $\tau \succ \sigma$ such that for every $\mu \in 2^{|\tau|+c}$, if $\Gamma^\mu = \tau$ then $K(\mu) < f(|\mu|)$. Furthermore, τ can be found $\emptyset'$-computably.*

Proof. It is enough to prove the existence of such a τ, since then we can $\emptyset'$-computably search for one. We assume the usual convention that if $\Gamma^\mu = \nu$ and $\nu' \prec \nu$ then there is a $\mu' \preccurlyeq \mu$ such that $\Gamma^{\mu'} = \nu'$.

Let $h(\nu)$ be the number of strings μ of length $2^{|\nu|+c}$ such that $\Gamma^\mu = \nu$. Then $h(\nu 0) + h(\nu 1) \leqslant 2h(\nu)$, so h is an integer-valued supermartingale. Let $\sigma' \succ \sigma$ be such that $h(\sigma')$ is minimal among all extensions of σ. Then $h(\sigma' 0) = h(\sigma')$, since $h(\sigma' 0) \geqslant h(\sigma')$ by the choice of σ', and $h(\sigma' 0) \leqslant h(\sigma')$ since otherwise $h(\sigma' 1) < h(\sigma')$. Similarly, $h(\sigma' 1) = h(\sigma)$. Proceeding this way by induction, we see that $h(\nu) = h(\sigma')$ for all $\nu \succ \sigma'$. Thus there is a k such that if $\Gamma^\mu = \nu$ for $\nu \succ \sigma'$, then $K(\mu) \leqslant K(\nu) + k$.

Let $\tau \succ \sigma'$ be such that $K(\tau) < f(|\tau|+c) - k$. It is easy to see that such a τ exists, because $K(\sigma' 0^n) \leqslant K(n) + O(1)$ and $K(n)$ has no computable lower bound, so that we can take $\tau = \sigma' 0^n$ for a sufficiently large n. Then τ has the desired properties. □

Theorem 9.13.2 (Downey and Hirschfeldt [unpublished]). *There is an $A \leqslant_{\mathrm{T}} \emptyset'$ that is not cl-reducible to any complex set.*

Proof. Let $\Gamma_0, \Gamma_1, \ldots$ be an effective listing of the cl-reductions, with the use of Γ_n bounded by $x+n$. Let $f_0, f_1, \ldots$ be a $\emptyset'$-effective listing of the computable orders. Let $\sigma_0 = \lambda$. Given $\sigma_{\langle n,e\rangle}$, by Lemma 9.13.1 we can $\emptyset'$-computably find a $\tau \succ \sigma_{\langle n,e\rangle}$ such that for every $\mu \in 2^{|\tau|+n}$, if $\Gamma_n^\mu = \tau$ then $K(\mu) < f_e(|\mu|)$. Let $\sigma_{\langle n,e\rangle+1} = \tau$. Let $A = \bigcup_i \sigma_i$. Then $A \leqslant_{\mathrm{T}} \emptyset'$. If $A \leqslant_{\mathrm{cl}} X$ then there are infinitely many n such that $\Gamma_n^X = A$. For any such n and any computable order f_e, let $k = |\sigma_{\langle n,e\rangle+1}|$. Then $K(X \upharpoonright k+n) < f(k+n)$. Thus X is not complex. □

9.14 Further properties of cl-reducibility

This section could be called "When reducibilities go bad". We will see that in spite of a number of nice features mentioned in the previous section, cl-reducibility also has some undesirable properties.

9.14.1 cl-reducibility and joins

By Theorem 9.5.2, and the note following it, the cl-degrees of left-c.e. reals do not form a lowersemilattice. That is a common feature of many reducibilities. However, the cl-degrees of left-c.e. reals also do not form an uppersemilattice; that is, there is no join operation for them. This result was first proved directly by Downey, Hirschfeldt, and LaForte in [113], but follows from the proof of the following result of Yu and Ding [414].

Theorem 9.14.1 (Yu and Ding [414]). *There is no cl-complete left-c.e. real.*

Actually, they proved something even stronger:

Theorem 9.14.2 (Yu and Ding [414]). *There are two left-c.e. reals α_0 and α_1 such that there is no left-c.e. real β with $\alpha_i \leqslant_{\mathrm{cl}} \beta$ for $i = 0, 1$.*

Proof. The proof of this theorem has gone through a number of simplifications, particularly in the induction. The first significant streamlining was due to Barmpalias and Lewis [246]. The proof we will follow is due to Barmpalias, Downey, and Greenberg [21].

The main idea of the construction is that if β is a left-c.e. real that cl-computes both α_0 and α_1, then alternatingly adding little bits to α_0 and α_1 (drip-feeding them, as it were) is sufficient to drive β to be too large. Intuitively, a real β computing another real γ with use x for every x means that as soon as γ changes at position x, the real β must change at a position less than or equal to x. That is, if γ can be computed with oracle β and use x, then β is not less than γ. So if there were a largest c.e. cl-degree β, we could select two reals α_0 and α_1 and change them alternatingly to drive β to be very large.

Furthermore, we can reserve parts of the reals for this purpose, to work independently for each requirement. In more detail, suppose that Γ_0 and Γ_1 are cl-reductions and that β is a left-c.e. real. For all such triples, we need to meet the requirement

$$R_{\Gamma_0,\Gamma_1,\beta} : \text{ Either } \Gamma_0^\beta \neq \alpha_0 \text{ or } \Gamma_1^\beta \neq \alpha_1.$$

For simplicity of presentation, we will take the reductions Γ_i to be ibT-reductions, but this assumption is inessential to the proof below; in the general case, the only change is that longer interval such as $[k, k + 2^{k+c}]$

instead of $[k, k+2^k]$ would be needed.[4] We view left-c.e. reals as both infinite binary sequences and as the corresponding elements in the Euclidean interval $[0,1]$ (via binary expansions). Addition means the usual arithmetic addition.

To meet requirement $R = R_{\Gamma_0,\Gamma_1,\beta}$, we describe a family of modules, each indexed by an interval of natural numbers. Let $a \leqslant b$. A stage s is *expansionary* for the $[a,b)$-module (for R) if for both $i = 0,1$ we have $\Gamma_i^{\beta_s}[s] \supset \alpha_{i,s} \upharpoonright b$. The instructions for the module are as follows.

> Repeat the following $2^{b-a} - 1$ many times:
>
> 1. At the next expansionary stage, add 2^{-b} to α_0.
> 2. At the next expansionary stage, add 2^{-b} to α_1.
>
> At the end, wait for the next expansionary stage and then return.

To meet the requirement R, we run the $[k, k+2^k)$-module for R for some k. We will shortly argue that this module cannot return, so it must get stuck waiting for some expansionary stage, and hence R is met. It is easy to see that assuming that we start with $\alpha_i \upharpoonright [a,b) = 0^{b-a}$, the $[a,b)$-module for any requirement makes changes only in $\alpha_i \upharpoonright [a,b)$ (for both $i = 0,1$) and so if for distinct requirements we run modules on disjoint intervals, then there is no interaction between the requirements and so we can meet them all.

The verification relies on the following lemma. For this lemma, we think of a finite binary string also as a natural number (via binary expansion).

Lemma 9.14.3. *Suppose that $\alpha_{0,t_0} \upharpoonright [a,b) = \alpha_{1,t_0} \upharpoonright [a,b) = 0^{b-a}$. Suppose that at stage t_0, an $[a,b)$-module for R begins and returns at a stage t_1. Then*

$$\beta_{t_1} \upharpoonright a - \beta_{t_0} \upharpoonright a \geqslant b - a.$$

Proof. By induction on $b - a$. If $b = a$ there is nothing to prove. Assume the lemma holds when $b - a = n$, and let $a < b$ be such that $b - a = n + 1$. The key observation is that the $[a,b)$-module consists of three parts:

1. Running the $[a+1, b)$-module.
2. Running one iteration of adding 2^{-b} to α_0 and then α_1 (and waiting for expansionary stages).
3. Running the $[a+1, b)$-module again.

[4] In fact, as observed in [21], if A and B are sets with an upper bound in the cl-degrees, then they also have one in the ibT-degrees, and similarly, if a set A is cl-reducible to a 1-random (left-c.e.) real, then it is ibT-reducible to a 1-random (left-c.e.) real.

Note also that both times we run the $[a+1, b)$-module, we start with $\alpha_i \upharpoonright [a+1, b) = 0^n$: the first time by the assumption of the lemma, and the second because when the first $[a+1, b)$-module halts we have $\alpha_i \upharpoonright [a, b) = 01^n$ for both i; we then add 2^{-b}, which makes $\alpha_i \upharpoonright [a, b) = 10^n$.

Let s_0 be the stage at which the first $[a+1, b)$-module returns, and s_1 be the stage at which the second one begins. By induction,

$$\beta_{s_0} \upharpoonright a+1 - \beta_{t_0} \upharpoonright a+1 \geqslant n$$

and

$$\beta_{t_1} \upharpoonright a+1 - \beta_{s_1} \upharpoonright a+1 \geqslant n.$$

Between s_0 and s_1 we have a change in $\alpha_0(a)$, which forces a change in $\beta \upharpoonright a+1$ by the next expansionary stage, and then a change in $\alpha_1(n)$, which forces another change in $\beta \upharpoonright a+1$. Each of these changes adds at least 1 to $\beta \upharpoonright a+1$. Thus, in total,

$$\beta_{t_1} \upharpoonright a+1 - \beta_{t_0} \upharpoonright a+1 \geqslant 2(n+1),$$

which implies that

$$\beta_{t_1} \upharpoonright a - \beta_{t_0} \upharpoonright a \geqslant n+1,$$

as required. □

This concludes the verification: the $[k, k+2^k)$-module can never return because that would force $\beta \upharpoonright k \geqslant 2^k$, which is impossible. □

The Kučera-Slaman Theorem 9.2.3 says that all 1-random left-c.e. reals are the same in terms of their complexity oscillations, and have sequences of rationals converging to them at essentially the same rates; and that from any of them, we can obtain any given left-c.e. real via a rather strong reduction. One consequence of Theorem 9.14.2, however, is that, in general, there is no efficient algorithm (in terms of the number of bits used) to obtain the *bits* of a left-c.e. real from the bits of a 1-random left-c.e. real.

9.14.2 Array noncomputability and joins

By adding multiple permitting to the argument above, Barmpalias, Downey, and Greenberg [21] were able to classify the degrees within which constructions such as the one in the proof of Theorem 9.14.2 are possible.

Theorem 9.14.4 (Barmpalias, Downey, and Greenberg [21]). *The following are equivalent for a degree* $\mathbf{d}$.

(i) *There are left-c.e. reals* α_0 *and* α_1 *in* $\mathbf{d}$ *that do not have a common upper bound in the ibT-degrees (or cl-degrees) of left-c.e. reals.*

(ii) $\mathbf{d}$ *is c.e. and array noncomputable.*

Proof. We begin by showing that we can perform the construction in the previous subsection within an array noncomputable c.e. degree. Recall from Section 2.23 that a c.e. degree $\mathbf{d}$ is array noncomputable iff for each (or some) very strong array (i.e., partition $F_0, F_1, \ldots$ of $\mathbb{N}$ of increasing size), there is a c.e. set $D \in \mathbf{d}$ such that for all c.e. sets W there are infinitely many n with $W \upharpoonright F_n = D \upharpoonright F_n$. Later, we will calculate the desired size of F_n for this proof. Assuming this has been done, fix some $D \in \mathbf{d}$ that satisfies the definition for this $F_0, F_1, \ldots$. To get sufficiently many permissions, a requirement $R = R_{\Gamma_0,\Gamma_1,\beta}$ as above enumerates an auxiliary c.e. set W_R and ties its actions to permissions from F_n.

Again, a module for requirement R will operate on some interval $[a, b)$; the notion of an expansionary stage for a module for R on an interval $[a, b)$ is defined as before. To such a module, we will assign an n such that $|F_n| > 2(2^{b-a} - 1)$. Note that we choose distinct n's for each module for R. To *request permission*, the module picks some $x \in F_n$ that is not yet in W_R and enumerates it into W_R. Permission is *received* when at a later stage, x enters D. The standard modus operandi for multiple permitting is used: if some $x \in F_n$ enters D before it is enumerated into W_R, then F_n can be made incorrect for permitting by withholding x from ever entering W_R, so we assume this never happens.

The new module follows the following instructions:

Repeat the following $2^{b-a} - 1$ many times:

1. Wait for an expansionary stage, then request permission. When permission is received, add 2^{-b} to α_0.
2. Wait for another expansionary stage, then request permission. When permission is received, add 2^{-b} to α_1.

At the end, wait for the next expansionary stage and return.

Note that the choice of n ensures that we can always request new permissions, as the module above requests at most $2(2^{b-a} - 1)$ many permissions, and so we never get $F_n \subseteq W_R$.

The overall construction is as expected. For every R we pick an infinite set of intervals of the form $[k, k + 2^k)$ and run modules on each interval separately (all of these modules together enumerate W_R, though). We ensure that these intervals are pairwise disjoint and that the intervals used by different requirements are also pairwise disjoint. Also, to code in D, we fix a computable set C disjoint from every interval used by any requirement. Let c_n be the nth element of C. For $i = 0, 1$, we declare that $\alpha_i(c_n) = 1$ iff $n \in D$. Since D is a c.e. set and all modules change α_i only on their assigned intervals, we see that both α_i are still left-c.e. reals.

To conclude the construction, we need to specify the required size of F_n so that we can assign, for every requirement R, almost every n as a permitting number for some module working for R. So after we specify the coding location set C and assign the intervals for every requirement, we define $|F_n|$ to be large enough so that for every $m \leqslant n$, for each of the first m many requirements, if $[a, b)$ is the nth interval assigned to R, then $|F_n| > 2(2^{b-a} - 1)$, so that F_n can be assigned as a permitting set for the $[a, b)$-module for R.

For the verification, we note that Lemma 9.14.3 holds for the new construction, with the same proof. Thus, for any requirement R, no $[k, k+2^k)$-module for R ever returns. The standard permitting argument now shows that it cannot be that every module for some requirement R gets stuck waiting for permission: For almost all n, the set F_n is assigned as a permitting set for some module for R, so there is some such n with $W_R \upharpoonright F_n = D \upharpoonright F_n$, whence the module to which F_n is assigned is never stuck waiting for permission. As a result, this module must get stuck waiting for an expansionary stage, and so the requirement R is met.

It is clear by coding that $D \leqslant_{\mathrm{T}} \alpha_0, \alpha_1$. To conclude the verification, we show that $\alpha_0, \alpha_1 \leqslant_{\mathrm{T}} D$. Fix $i < 2$ and x. We compute $\alpha_i(x)$ with oracle D as follows. If $x \in C$ then we can calculate the n such that $x = c_n$ and then consult D for the value of $\alpha_i(x)$. Otherwise, x belongs to some interval $[a, b)$ on which a module for some requirement R is working. This requirement is assigned some permitting set F_n. Wait for a stage s at which $D_s \upharpoonright F_n = D \upharpoonright F_n$. Then, after stage s the segment $\alpha_i \upharpoonright [a, b)$ is fixed, and so $\alpha_i(x) = \alpha_{i,s}(x)$.

We now prove the converse: If α_0 and α_1 are left-c.e. reals with array computable (Turing) degrees, then α_0 and α_1 have a common upper bound in the cl-degrees. The idea is that we can approximate α_0 and α_1 with the number of mind changes (i.e., the function taking n to $|\{s : \alpha_{i,s+1} \upharpoonright n \neq \alpha_{i,s} \upharpoonright n\}|$) bounded by a very slow growing function. This fact follows from the characterization of array computability as uniform total ω-c.e.-ness in Lemma 2.23.6: A c.e. degree $\mathbf{d}$ is array computable iff for every computable order h, every $f \leqslant_{\mathrm{T}} \mathbf{d}$ has an h-c.e. approximation. We can then use this slow bound on the number of mind changes to build a left-c.e. real β that changes somewhere on its first n digits whenever either α_0 or α_1 does so.

Again we think of these reals as elements of the interval $[0, 1]$. A request that $\beta \upharpoonright n$ change is met by adding 2^{-n} to β. If the number of requests for a $\beta \upharpoonright n$ change does not exceed a bound $g(n)$ such that

$$\sum_{n \geqslant 1} g(n) 2^{-n} < 1, \tag{9.2}$$

then we can construct a left-c.e. real that changes appropriately whenever we ask it to. In our case, a request to change $\beta \upharpoonright n$ is made whenever we see a new value for $\alpha_0 \upharpoonright n$ or $\alpha_1 \upharpoonright n$, so if the number of such new values is at most $\frac{g(n)}{2}$, then the plan will work. Thus, all we need to do is fix some computable order g that grows sufficiently slowly so that (9.2) holds, and approximate the functions $n \mapsto \alpha_i \upharpoonright n$ in a $\frac{g(n)}{2}$-c.e. way, which is possible, as mentioned above.

There is not much to add to give a formal construction. Fix a computable order g that satisfies (9.2). For $i = 0, 1$, fix computable binary functions f_i such that (writing $f_{i,s}(n)$ for $f_i(s, n)$), for all n, the value $f_{i,s}(n)$ is a binary string of length n,

$$|\{s : f_{i,s+1}(n) \neq f_{i,s}(n)\}| \leqslant \frac{g(n)}{2},$$

and

$$\lim_s f_{i,s}(n) = \alpha_i \upharpoonright n.$$

We define a left-c.e. real β: start with $\beta_0 = 0$ and let

$$\beta_{s+1} = \beta_s + \sum\{2^{-n} : f_{i,s+1}(n) \neq f_{i,s}(n)\}.$$

The fact that g satisfies (9.2) and the restriction on the number of mind-changes for the f_i imply that $\beta = \lim_s \beta_s < 1$, so β is well-defined.

Lemma 9.14.5. $\alpha_i \leqslant_{\mathrm{ibT}} \beta$.

Proof. If s is a stage such that $\beta_s \upharpoonright n = \beta \upharpoonright n$ then we never add 2^{-n} to β after stage s. This fact implies that $f_{i,t}(n) = f_{i,s}(n)$ for all $t > s$. Thus $f_{i,s}(n) = \alpha_i \upharpoonright n$. □

This concludes the proof of the theorem. □

Barmpalias, Downey, and Greenberg [21] remarked that the above proof for the array computable case does not use the fact that the α_i are left-c.e. reals. This proof works for any sets that have array computable c.e. degrees, because approximations like the f_i are available for all sets in those degrees.

9.14.3 Left-c.e. reals cl-reducible to versions of Ω

Although there is no maximal c.e. cl-degree, we can say a little about the cl-degrees of 1-random left-c.e. reals.

Theorem 9.14.6 (Downey and Hirschfeldt [unpublished]). *If A is a c.e. set and α is a 1-random left-c.e. real, then $A \leqslant_{\mathrm{ibT}} \alpha$.*

Proof. Given A and α as above, we must construct $\Gamma^\alpha = A$ with use $\gamma(x) = x$. Since α is 1-random, there is a c such that $K(\alpha \upharpoonright n) \geqslant n - c$ for all n. We enumerate a KC set L and assume by the recursion theorem that we know an e such that if $(m, \sigma) \in L$ then $K(\sigma) \leqslant m + e$.

Initially, we define $\Gamma^{\alpha_s}(n) = 0$ for all n, and maintain this definition unless n enters $A_{s+1} \setminus A_s$. As usual, at such a stage, we would like to change $\Gamma^\alpha(n)$ from 0 to 1. To do this, we need $\alpha \upharpoonright n \neq \alpha_s \upharpoonright n$. Should we see a stage $t \geqslant s$ with $\alpha_t \upharpoonright n \neq \alpha_s \upharpoonright n$ then we can simply declare that $\Gamma^{\alpha_u}(n) = 1$ for all $u \geqslant t$. For $n > e + c + 2$, we can force such a t to exist.

We simply enumerate a request $(n-c-e-1, \alpha_s \upharpoonright n)$ into L, ensuring that $K(\alpha_s \upharpoonright n) \leqslant n-c-1$, so that $\alpha \upharpoonright n \neq \alpha_s \upharpoonright n$. Note that L is indeed a KC set because we make at most one request for each $n > e+c+2$. □

Once consequence of this result is Proposition 6.1.2, that Ω is wtt-complete.

Barmpalias and Lewis [23] proved that not every left-c.e. real is cl-reducible to a 1-random left-c.e. real. (This result should be compared with Theorem 9.13.2.) As with Theorem 9.14.2, this result was also strengthened by Barmpalias, Downey, and Greenberg [21], to classify the degrees within which it holds.

Theorem 9.14.7 (Barmpalias, Downey, and Greenberg [21]). *The following are equivalent for a c.e. degree* **d**.

(i) *There is a left-c.e. real* $\alpha \leqslant_T \mathbf{d}$ *not cl-reducible to any* 1*-random left-c.e. real.*

(ii) **d** *is array noncomputable.*

Proof. Suppose that **d** is array noncomputable. As in the previous subsection, we begin with the construction of a left-c.e. real not ibT-reducible to a 1-random left-c.e. real, and later add multiple permitting.

We build a left-c.e. real α to meet the requirements

$$R_{\Gamma,\beta}: \text{ If } \Gamma^{\beta} = \alpha \text{ then } \beta \text{ is not 1-random.}$$

Here Γ ranges over all ibT-functionals and β ranges over all left-c.e. reals. To meet $R_{\Gamma,\beta}$, we run infinitely many modules, where the nth module enumerates a finite set of strings U_n with $\mu([\![U_n]\!]) \leqslant 2^{-n}$, such that if $\Gamma^{\beta} = \alpha$ then $\beta \in [\![U_n]\!]$. Thus, together, these modules enumerate a Martin-Löf test covering β, whence $R_{\Gamma,\beta}$ is satisfied.

In the previous subsection, we used the leeway we had in the play between two left-c.e. reals to drive a potential common upper bound to be too large. Here we have only one real to play with, and the role of the second real is taken by the element of the Martin-Löf test being enumerated. This construction is much more limited because the restriction on the size of the enumerated set of strings is much stricter than that on the enumeration of a left-c.e. real.

The modules are built by recursion from smaller and smaller building blocks. Consider, for example, the following module, which changes α only from the ath bit on, and makes $\beta \upharpoonright a+1 \geqslant 2$. (Here, as before, we think of a string as a natural number, so, for example, to say that $\beta \upharpoonright a+1 \geqslant 2$ is to say that $\beta \upharpoonright a+1$ is greater than or equal to $0^{a-1}10$ in the usual lexicographic ordering of strings.) We assume for now that β is playing its optimal strategy, which is adding the minimal amount necessary to match α's movements. We later remove this assumption.

1.
(i) Set $\alpha(a+1)=1$; wait for $\beta(a+1)=1$.
(ii) Set $\alpha(a+2)=1$; wait for $\beta(a+2)=1$.
$\vdots$
(mcmlxxiv) Set $\alpha(a+1974)=1$; wait for $\beta(a+1974)=1$.

2. Enumerate $0^{a+1}1^{1974}$ into the test element; wait for $\beta = 0^a10^\omega$.

3. Add $2^{-a-1975}$ to α, thus setting $\alpha = 0^a10^\omega$. Wait for $\beta = 0^{a-1}10^\omega$.

The cost, in terms of the measure of strings enumerated into the test element, is $2^{-a-1975}$; as 1975 approaches infinity, we can make the cost as low as we like.

Now this module can be iterated to make $\beta \upharpoonright a+1 \geqslant 3$:

1.
(i) Run the 2-module from point $a+1$, to get $\alpha(a+1)=1$ and $\beta(a)=1$.
(ii) Run the 2-module from point $a+2$, to get $\alpha(a+2)=1$ and $\beta(a+1)=1$.
$\vdots$
(mcmlxxx) Run the 2-module from point $a+1979$, to get $\alpha(a+1979)=1$ and $\beta(a+1978)=1$.

2. Enumerate 0^a1^{1979} into the test element; wait for $\beta = 0^{a-1}10^\omega$.

3. Set $\alpha = 0^a10^\omega$. Wait for $\beta = 0^{a-1}110^\omega$.

Again the cost can be kept down by making the number 1980 large, and then keeping the cost of every recursive call of the 2-module low as well.

We can now define a 4-module, a 5-module, and so on. Note that there is a growing distance between the last point of change in α and the end of the string of 1's in the version of β that goes into the test. This distance, according to our calculations below, is bounded by the level of the module (i.e., it is bounded by n for an n-module).

We turn to formally describing the modules and investigating their properties, without assuming anything about how β is being built.

Let $R = R_{\Gamma,\beta}$. The module $M_R(a,n,\varepsilon)$ is indexed by: a, the bit of α where it begins acting; n, the level of the module; and ε, the bound on the measure of the c.e. open set that the module enumerates.

By induction on stages, define the notion of an *expansionary stage* for requirement R: 0 is expansionary, and if s is an expansionary stage for R, and x is the largest number mentioned at stage s or before, then the next expansionary stage is the least stage t at which $\Gamma^{\beta_t} \succcurlyeq \alpha_t \upharpoonright x$.

The module $M_R(a,1,\varepsilon)$ is the following.

Wait for an expansionary stage, then add 2^{-a-1} to α. Wait for another expansionary stage, and return $\emptyset$.

For $n > 1$, the module $M_R(a, n, \varepsilon)$ is the following, where U is the set it enumerates.

Let b be the least $b > a$ such that $2^{-b} < \frac{\varepsilon}{2}$. Let $\varepsilon' = \frac{\varepsilon}{2(b+n-a)}$.

1. For $k = a+1, a+2, \ldots, b+n$, call $M_R(k, n-1, \varepsilon')$, and add the returned set to U.
2. Add the current version of $\beta \upharpoonright b$ to U, and wait for a stage at which $\beta \upharpoonright b$ changes.
3. Wait for an expansionary stage, then add 2^{-b-n-1} to α. Wait for another expansionary stage, and return U.

We verify some properties of these modules, which will lead to the full construction.

Lemma 9.14.8. *A module $M_R(a, n, \varepsilon)$ does not change $\alpha \upharpoonright a$. Indeed, there is a computable function $c(a, n, \varepsilon)$ such that for all R, a, n, and ε, if $c = c(a, n, \varepsilon)$, and a module $M = M_R(a, n, \varepsilon)$ starts at stage s with $\alpha_s \upharpoonright [a, c) = 0^{c-a}$, then throughout its run, M changes only $\alpha \upharpoonright [a, c)$, and if it returns at a stage t, then $\alpha_t \upharpoonright [a, c) = 10^{c-a-1}$.*

Proof. By induction on n. The module $M_R(a, 1, \varepsilon)$ changes $\alpha(a)$ only from 0 to 1, so we can let $c(a, 1, \varepsilon) = a + 1$. For $n > 2$, we can calculate b (and ε') as in the instructions for the module, and let

$$c(a, n, \varepsilon) = \max\{b + n, c(k, n-1, \varepsilon') : k \in [a+1, \ldots, b+n]\}.$$

Let $c = c(a, n, \varepsilon)$. Since $c \geqslant c(k, n-1, \varepsilon')$ for all $k \in [a+1, \ldots, b+n]$, if we start with $\alpha_s \upharpoonright [a, c) = 0^{c-a}$, then by induction, after m iterations of part 1 of the module $M_R(a, n, \varepsilon)$, we have $\alpha \upharpoonright [a, c) = 01^m0^{c-a-m-1}$ and so at the end of part 1 we have $\alpha \upharpoonright [a, c) = 01^{b+n-a}0^{c-b-n-1}$. At part 2 of the module, $\alpha \upharpoonright [a, c)$ does not change, and at part 3, we set $\alpha \upharpoonright [a, c) = 10^{c-a-1}$. □

Lemma 9.14.9. *The measure of the set of strings enumerated by a module $M_R(a, n, \varepsilon)$ is at most ε.*

Proof. By a straightforward induction on n. □

For the next lemma, we again think of finite binary strings as natural numbers.

Lemma 9.14.10. *Suppose that a module $M_R(a, n, \varepsilon)$ starts running at stage s (with $\alpha_s \upharpoonright [a, c) = 0^{c-a}$, where c is as above), and returns at stage t. Then $\beta_t \upharpoonright a+1 - \beta_s \upharpoonright a+1 \geqslant n$.*

Proof. By induction on n. The base case $n = 1$ is easy: if $M_R(a, 1, \varepsilon)$ starts running at stage s and $\alpha_s(a) = 0$, then the module changes $\alpha_s(a)$ to 1, and so by the next expansionary stage we get a change in $\beta \upharpoonright a+1$, which implies that $\beta_t \upharpoonright a+1 - \beta_s \upharpoonright a+1 \geqslant 1$.

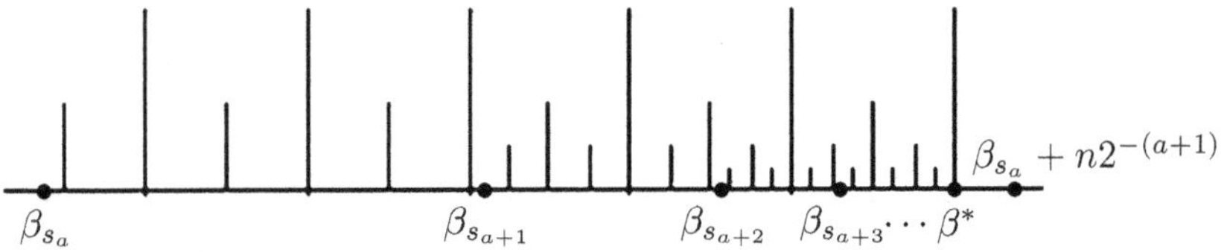

Figure 9.1. The longest lines represent elements of Q_{a+1}, the next longest lines elements of Q_{a+2}, etc. In this example, $n = 6$.

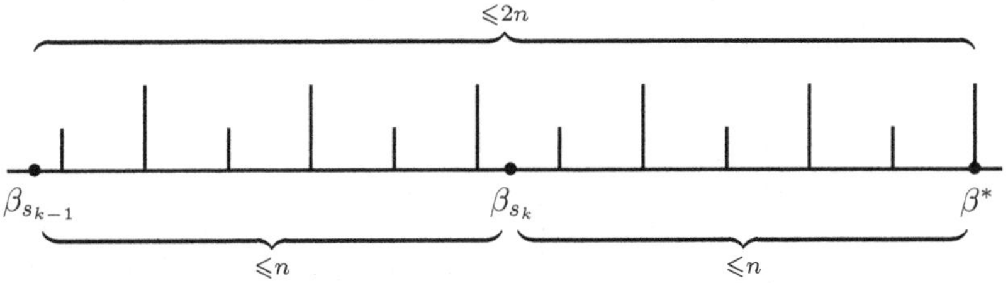

Figure 9.2. The longer lines represent elements of Q_k while the shorter lines represent elements of $Q_{k+1} \setminus Q_k$. Again in this example, $n = 6$.

Now assume that the lemma is proved for some $n \geqslant 1$. Suppose that we start running $M_R(a, n+1, \varepsilon)$ at stage s_a with $\alpha_{s_0} \upharpoonright [a, c) = 0^{c-a}$ (where $c = c(a, n+1, \varepsilon)$). Calculate the associated b and ε'. For $k = a+1, \ldots, b+n+1$, let s_k be the stage at which the recursive call of $M_R(k, n, \varepsilon')$ returns. By induction, we have, for all such k,

$$\beta_{s_k} \upharpoonright k+1 - \beta_{s_{k-1}} \upharpoonright k+1 \geqslant n.$$

For each m, let $Q_m = \{z2^{-m} : z \in \mathbb{Z}\}$. For $\gamma \in (-\infty, \infty)$, let $\llcorner\gamma\lrcorner_m$ be the greatest element of Q_m that is not greater than γ. Then for $\gamma \in 2^\omega$, again identified with an element of $[0, 1]$, we have $\gamma \upharpoonright m = 2^m \llcorner\gamma\lrcorner_m$. Also, for $\gamma < \delta$, let

$$d_m(\gamma, \delta) = 2^m \left(\llcorner\delta\lrcorner_m - \llcorner\gamma\lrcorner_m\right) = \left|\left(Q_m \cap (\gamma, \delta]\right)\right|.$$

The induction hypothesis then says that

$$d_{k+1}(\beta_{s_{k-1}}, \beta_{s_k}) \geqslant n. \tag{9.3}$$

Let $\beta^* = \llcorner\beta_{s_a}\lrcorner_{a+1} + n2^{-a-1}$, so that $\beta^* \in Q_{a+1}$. (See Figure 9.1.)

By induction on $k = a, \ldots, b+n+1$, we show that

$$d_{k+1}(\beta_{s_k}, \beta^*) \leqslant n. \tag{9.4}$$

For $k = a$ this is immediate. If $k > a$ and (9.4) is true for $k-1$, then because β^* is in Q_k, for every $x \in (Q_{k+1} \setminus Q_k) \cap (\beta_{s_{k-1}}, \beta^*]$, there is some $y > x$ in $Q_k \cap (\beta_{s_{k-1}}, \beta^*]$ and so

$$d_{k+1}(\beta_{s_{k-1}}, \beta^*) \leqslant 2n.$$

Together with (9.3), we get (9.4) for k: see Figure 9.2.

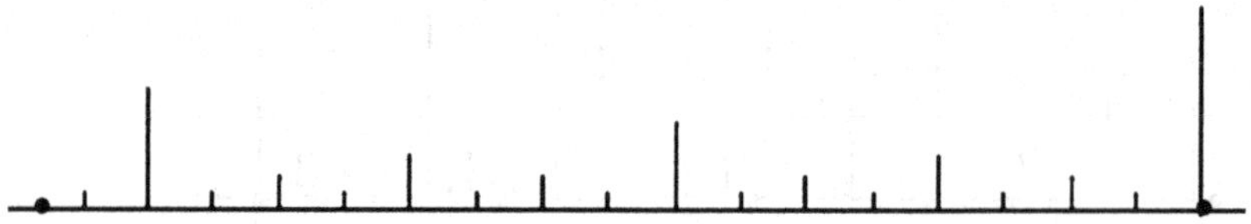

Figure 9.3. Even though $d_{b+n+2}(\beta_{s_{b+n+1}}, \beta^*)$ may be n (in this example, $n \geqslant 17$), we see that β^* is the only element of Q_{b+2} between $\beta_{s_{b+n+1}}$ and β^* itself. Again the shortest lines represent elements of Q_{b+n+2}, the next shortest ones elements of Q_{b+n+1}, etc.

At the end, we get $d_{a+b+2}(\beta_{s_{b+n+1}}, \beta^*) \leqslant n$, so $\beta^* - \beta_{s_{b+n+1}} \leqslant (n+1)2^{-b-n-2}$. Since $2^n \geqslant n+1$, we have $\beta^* - \beta_{s_{b+n+1}} \leqslant 2^{-b-2}$ (see Figure 9.3). It follows that $\beta^* \upharpoonright b = \beta_{s_{b+n+1}} \upharpoonright b$.

So at the end of step (2) of the module $M_R(a, n+1, \varepsilon)$, say at a stage t_0, we have $\beta_{t_0} > \beta^*$, so $d_{a+1}(\beta_{s_a}, \beta_{t_0}) \geqslant n$; in other words, $\beta_{t_0} \upharpoonright a+1 - \beta_{s_a} \upharpoonright a+1 \geqslant n$. At step 3 of the module, we change $\alpha(a)$, and by the next expansionary stage, we have a change in $\beta \upharpoonright a+1$, which adds at least 1 to $\beta \upharpoonright a+1$. So if the module returns at stage t_1, then

$$\beta_{t_1} \upharpoonright a+1 - \beta_{s_a} \upharpoonright a+1 \geqslant n+1,$$

as required. □

The construction is now clear: we partition $\mathbb{N}$ into disjoint intervals, all of the form $[a, c(a, 2^{a+1}, 2^{-n}))$. A requirement $R = R_{\Gamma,\beta}$ will be assigned infinitely many such intervals and run $M_R(a, 2^{a+1}, 2^{-n})$ on the nth interval assigned to it. By Lemma 9.14.10, none of these modules can return, because we cannot have $\beta \upharpoonright a+1 \geqslant 2^{a+1}$. If the hypothesis $\Gamma^\beta = \alpha$ of R holds, then the module cannot ever be stuck waiting for an expansionary stage, and so it must get stuck waiting for β to avoid the set of intervals U that it enumerates. In other words, if the nth module for R enumerates U_n, and $\Gamma^\beta = \alpha$, then $\beta \in U_n$, as required. If this is the case for all n, then β is not 1-random.

Finally, we can add multiple permitting to this construction to get the proof of this part of Theorem 9.14.7. This is done exactly as in the permitted version of Theorem 9.14.2, so we will only sketch the details. Partition $\mathbb{N}$ into an infinite computable coding set C and pairwise disjoint intervals of the form $[a, c(a, 2^{a+1}, 2^{-n}))$ (all disjoint from C). Assign to every requirement R infinitely many intervals, where the nth interval assigned to n is of the form $[a, c(a, 2^{a+1}, 2^{-n}))$. For every module $M_R(a, n, \varepsilon)$, calculate the total number $p(a, n, \varepsilon)$ of stages at which the module changes α. Now partition $\mathbb{N}$ into a very strong array $\{F_n\}_{n\in\mathbb{N}}$, where for every requirement, $|F_n| > p(a, 2^{a+1}, 2^{-n})$ for almost every n (where the nth interval for R is $[a, c)$). Let $D \in \mathbf{d}$ be $\{F_n\}$-a.n.c.

Every requirement R enumerates an auxiliary c.e. set W_R. To *request permission*, a module $M = M_R(a, 2^{a+1}, 2^{-n})$ enumerates some new $x \in$

F_n into W_R. Permission is later received when x appears in D. The new instructions for the modules are as for the original ones, except that every change in α requires permission:

The new module $M_R(a, 1, \varepsilon)$ is:

> Wait for an expansionary stage, then request permission. When permission is received, add 2^{-a-1} to α; wait for another expansionary stage, and return $\emptyset$.

For $n > 1$, the new module $M_R(a, n, \varepsilon)$ is:

> Let b be the least $b > a$ such that $2^{-b} < \frac{\varepsilon}{2}$; let $\varepsilon' = \frac{\varepsilon}{2(b+n-a)}$.
>
> 1. For $k = a + 1, a + 2, \ldots, b + n$, call $M_R(k, n - 1, \varepsilon')$, and add the returned set to U.
> 2. Add the current version of $\beta \upharpoonright b$ to U, and wait for a stage at which $\beta \upharpoonright b$ changes.
> 3. Wait for an expansionary stage, then request permission. When permission is received, add 2^{-b-n-1} to α. Wait for another expansionary stage, and return U.

For every R and n, we run $M_R(a, 2^{a+1}, 2^{-n})$ on the nth interval $[a, c)$ assigned for R. We also let $\alpha(c_n) = 1$ iff $n \in D$, where c_n is the nth element of C. That is the construction.

Lemmas 9.14.8, 9.14.9, and 9.14.10 hold for the new modules as well, so there is no interaction between the requirements. If $\Gamma^\beta = \alpha$, then the R-modules do not get stuck waiting for expansionary stages. For such R, for every n such that $W_R \upharpoonright F_n = D \upharpoonright F_n$, every request for permission by the nth module for R is granted, so the nth module for R gets stuck waiting for β to leave U_n (the open set enumerated by R). Thus for infinitely many n we have $\beta \in U_n$. By adjusting the set (letting $U'_m = \bigcup_{n>m} U_n$) we build a Martin-Löf test covering β, so β is not 1-random.

Now we turn to the other direction of the theorem: If α has array computable Turing degree, then there is some 1-random left-c.e. real $\beta \geqslant_{\text{ibT}} \alpha$.

Again the idea is to use an approximation to α which does not change too much, and build β by requesting that it change by at least 2^{-n} whenever $\alpha \upharpoonright n$ changes. On top of this, we need to ensure that β is 1-random. To accomplish this task, let U be the second element of a universal Martin-Löf test. If we ensure that $\beta \notin U$ then we will have ensured that β is 1-random.

We identify U with a prefix-free set of generators for U. Then $\sum_{\sigma \in U} 2^{-|\sigma|} \leqslant \frac{1}{2}$. To ensure that β is not in U, whenever we discover that there is some $\sigma \in U$ that is an initial segment of the current version of β, we request that this initial segment change by adding $2^{-|\sigma|}$ to β. If the approximation to α is sufficiently tight so that the total amount added to β on behalf of following α is less than $\frac{1}{2}$, this strategy will succeed.

So fix a computable order g such that $\sum_n 2^{-n} g(n) < \frac{1}{2}$ (we allow the value 0 for g for finitely many inputs; we assume that if $g(n) = 0$ then $\alpha \upharpoonright n$ is simply given to us as a parameter in the construction).

Get a computable approximation $f_s(n)$ for the function $n \mapsto \alpha \upharpoonright n$ such that for all n, we have $|\{s : f_{s+1}(n) \neq f_s(n)\}| \leqslant g(n)$. The left-c.e. real β is defined by recursion. We start with $\beta_0 = 0$ and let

$$\beta_{s+1} = \beta_s + \sum \{2^{-n} : f_{s+1}(n) \neq f_s(n)\} + \sum \{2^{-|\sigma|} : \sigma \in U_s \wedge \sigma \prec \beta_s\}.$$

Lemma 9.14.11. $\beta < 1$ *(and so is well-defined as an element of* 2^ω*).*

Proof. There are two kinds of contributions to β: following α and avoiding U. Now, g satisfies $\sum_n 2^{-n} g(n) < \frac{1}{2}$ and for all n we have $|\{s : f_{s+1}(n) \neq f_s(n)\}| \leqslant g(n)$, so the total added to β by the clause $\sum \{2^{-n} : f_{s+1}(n) \neq f_s(n)\}$ is less than $\frac{1}{2}$. Because β is a left-c.e. real, for every $\sigma \in U$, there is at most one stage s at which we have $\sigma \in U_s$ and $\sigma \prec \beta_s$, so the contribution of the clause $\sum \{2^{-|\sigma|} : \sigma \in U_s \wedge \sigma \prec \beta_s\}$ is at most $\sum_{\sigma \in U} 2^{-|\sigma|} \leqslant \frac{1}{2}$. □

Lemma 9.14.12. $\beta \notin U$.

Proof. If $\beta \in U$ then there is some $\sigma \in U$ such that $\sigma \prec \beta$. Then at a late enough stage s we have $\sigma \in U_s$ and $\sigma \prec \beta_s$, so at stage s we add $2^{-|\sigma|}$ to β and force $\sigma \not\prec \beta$ for ever. □

Finally, the first clause in the definition of β shows that $\beta \geqslant_{\mathrm{ibT}} \alpha$, as in Lemma 9.14.5. □

9.14.4 cl-degrees of versions of Ω

We have seen that the Kučera-Slaman Theorem fails for cl-reducibility. One possibility for rescuing some of the content of that result in the cl case is that at least different versions of Ω might have the same cl-degree. As we will see in this subsection, this possibility also fails.

We begin with the following definition and a result about its connection to 1-randomness.

Definition 9.14.13 (Fenner and Schaefer [145]). A set A is *k-immune* if there is no computable sequence $F_0, F_1, \ldots$ of pairwise disjoint sets, each of size at most k, such that $F_n \cap A \neq \emptyset$ for all n.

Note that every set is 0-immune, that the 1-immune sets are exactly the immune sets, and that hyperimmune sets are k-immune for all k. Fenner and Schaefer [145] showed that the classes of k-immune sets form a proper hierarchy. We now show that for 1-random sets, the situation is different.

Lemma 9.14.14. *Suppose that* $|B| = m$*, and let* $\mathcal{B}$ *be a collection of* n *pairwise disjoint subsets of* B*, each of size* k*. Then there are exactly* $2^{m-kn}(2^k - 1)^n$ *subsets of* B *that have nonempty intersection with every set in* $\mathcal{B}$*.*

Proof. Each $B' \in \mathcal{B}$ has $2^k - 1$ many nonempty subsets, so there are $(2^k - 1)^n$ many subsets of $\bigcup \mathcal{B}$ with nonempty intersection with every $B' \in \mathcal{B}$. The size of $B \setminus \bigcup \mathcal{B}$ is $m - kn$. Each subset of B with the desired property is determined by its intersections with $\bigcup \mathcal{B}$ and with $B \setminus \bigcup \mathcal{B}$, which can be chosen independently. □

Theorem 9.14.15 (Folklore). *Every* 1*-random (or even weakly* 1*-random) set is* k*-immune for all* k*, but no* 1*-random set is hyperimmune.*

Proof. Let $F_0, F_1, \ldots$ be a computable collection of pairwise disjoint sets, each of size at most k. Let $\mathcal{Q}$ be the class of sets that have nonempty intersection with every F_n. Then $\mathcal{Q}$ is a Π^0_1 class. Let $I_n = [0, \max \bigcup_{i<n} F_i]$. By Lemma 9.14.14, for each n, the number of subsets of I_n that intersect every F_i for $i < n$ is $2^{|I_n|-kn}(2^k - 1)^n$, so the measure of $\mathcal{Q}$ is bounded above by

$$2^{|I_n|-kn}(2^k - 1)^n 2^{-|I_n|} = 2^{-kn}(2^k - 1)^n = (1 - 2^{-k})^n,$$

which goes to 0 as n increases, since $1 - 2^{-k} < 1$. Thus $\mathcal{Q}$ is a null Π^0_1 class. So if A is weakly 1-random then $A \notin \mathcal{Q}$, and hence $F_0, F_1, \ldots$ witnesses the k-immunity of A.

Now let $G_0, G_1, \ldots$ be a computable sequence of pairwise disjoint sets such that $|G_n| = 2^n$. Let V_n be the class of sets A such that $G_n \cap A = \emptyset$. Then $\mu(V_n) = 2^{-n}$. So if we let $U_n = \bigcup_{m>n} V_n$ then $U_0, U_1, \ldots$ is a Martin-Löf test, and $\bigcap_n U_n$ is the collection of sets A for which there are infinitely many n with $G_n \cap A = \emptyset$, and so contains every hyperimmune set. □

We are now ready to show that not all 1-random left-c.e. reals have the same cl-degree.

Theorem 9.14.16 (Stephan, see [21]). *There exist* 1*-random left-c.e. reals of different cl-degrees.*

Proof. The following proof is from [21].

Let α be a 1-random left-c.e. real. Thinking of α as a subset of $\mathbb{N}$, we have that $\mathbb{N} \setminus \alpha$ is also 1-random, so by Theorem 9.14.15, there is a computable sequence $t_0 < t_1 < \cdots$ such that for each n, at least one bit of $\alpha \upharpoonright (t_n, t_{n+1}]$ is a 0, and the size of $(t_n, t_{n+1}]$ is increasing in n.

Let β be the real such that $\beta(x) = 1$ iff $x = t_n$ for some $n > 0$ (in other words, $\beta = \sum_{n>0} 2^{-t_n-1}$). Since β is computable, $\alpha + \beta$ is left-c.e. and 1-random.

We claim that α does not cl-compute $\alpha + \beta$. Suppose that it does. Then there is a c and a partial computable function ψ such that for all n,

$$\psi(\alpha \upharpoonright (n + c)) = (\alpha + \beta)(n).$$

For all m, the block $\alpha \upharpoonright (t_m, t_{m+1}]$ is not a string of 1's, so adding 2^{-t_m-1} to α does not create a carry before the t_mth bit of α. Thus, for every $n > 0$,

$$\alpha \upharpoonright (t_n + 1) + \beta \upharpoonright (t_n + 1) = (\alpha + \beta) \upharpoonright (t_n + 1). \tag{9.5}$$

By Theorem 9.14.15, α is not c-immune, so there are infinitely many n such that $\alpha \upharpoonright [t_n - c, t_n) = 1^c$ and $t_{n-1} < t_n - c$. By (9.5), for each such n,

$$\psi(\alpha \upharpoonright t_n) = (\alpha + \beta)(t_n - c) = 1 - \alpha(t_n).$$

We can now define a c.e. supermartingale M that succeeds on α, which is a contradiction: Begin with $M(\lambda) = 1$. If there is an n such that $|\sigma| = t_n$ and $\sigma \upharpoonright [t_n - c, t_n) = 1^c$, where $t_{n-1} < t_n - c$, then wait for $\psi(\sigma)$ to converge. If that never happens then $M(\sigma i) = 0$ for $i = 0, 1$. Otherwise, let $i = 1 - \psi(\sigma)$ and let $M(\sigma i) = 2M(\sigma)$ and $M(\sigma(1 - i)) = 0$. For all other σ, let $M(\sigma i) = M(\sigma)$ for $i = 0, 1$. □

9.15 K-degrees, C-degrees, and Turing degrees

Merkle and Stephan [270] have given simple and short but clever arguments about the structure of the C- and K-degrees, and their relationships with the Turing degrees, by using sparse sets. We will see other relationships between these measures of relative randomness and Turing degrees for *random* sets in Chapter 10.

We begin with the following result, which we state in relativized form for future reference, and which will be important in Chapter 11.

Lemma 9.15.1 (Merkle and Stephan [270], after Chaitin [61]). *If $K^X(A \upharpoonright n) \leqslant K^X(n) + O(1)$ for all n in an infinite set S then $A \leqslant_T S \oplus X'$.*

Proof. Let

$$T = \{\sigma : \forall \tau \preccurlyeq \sigma\, (|\tau| \in S \Rightarrow K^X(\tau) \leqslant K^X(|\tau|) + c)\}.$$

Then T is an $(S \oplus X')$-computable tree, $A \in [T]$, and, by the relativized form of the Counting Theorem 3.7.6, T has bounded width. Thus A is an isolated path of T, and hence is $(S \oplus X')$-computable. □

Theorem 9.15.2 (Merkle and Stephan [270]). *Let $Y \subseteq \{2^n : n \in \omega\}$ and $X \leqslant_K Y$. Then $X \leqslant_T Y \oplus \emptyset'$. Hence, if $\emptyset' \leqslant_T Y$ then $X \leqslant_K Y$ implies $X \leqslant_T Y$.*

Proof. The idea is to code Y by a certain sparse set of numbers. Let

$$g(n) = 2^n + \sum_{k<n} 2^k Y(2^{k+2}).$$

Then $g(n) \in [2^n, 2^{(n+1)} - 1]$ and we can compute $Y \upharpoonright 2^{(n+1)}$ from $g(n)$. Thus $K(Y \upharpoonright g(n)) \leqslant K(g(n)) + O(1)$, so $K(X \upharpoonright g(n)) \leqslant K(g(n)) + O(1)$. By Lemma 9.15.1, $X \leqslant_T \operatorname{rng}(g) \oplus \emptyset' \leqslant_T Y \oplus \emptyset'$. □

A similar proof establishes the following.

Theorem 9.15.3 (Merkle and Stephan [270]). *If $Y \subseteq \{2^{2^n} : n \in \omega\}$ and $X \leqslant_C Y$ then $X \leqslant_T Y$.*

Proof. Let $g(n) = 2^n + \sum_{k<n} 2^k Y\left(2^{2^{k+2}}\right)$. Given a number $m \in J_n = [2^{g(n)}, 2^{g(n)+1} - 1]$, we can determine $Y \upharpoonright m$ by knowing m and $g(n)$. Since $|J_n| = 2^{g(n)}$, we can encode m by a string σ of length $2^{g(n)}$. From σ we can also decode $g(n)$, so σ is enough to describe $Y \upharpoonright m$, whence $C(X \upharpoonright m) \leqslant C(Y \upharpoonright m) + O(1) \leqslant g(n) + O(1)$, where the constants depend on neither m nor n. Let c be the last constant in this inequality.

Now let T be the set of strings σ such that for all $\tau \preccurlyeq \sigma$, if $|\tau| \in J_n$ for some n then $C(\tau) \leqslant g(n) + c$. Then T is a Y-c.e. tree, since g is Y-computable. Furthermore, for each n, since $|J_n| = 2^{g(n)}$, there must be some $i_n \in J_n$ such that $C(i_n) \geqslant g(n)$. Then for each n we have $C(\sigma) \leqslant C(i_n) + c$ for all $\sigma \in T$ such that $|\sigma| = i_n$. By Lemma 3.4.3, T has finite width. Now we can transform T into a Y-computable tree as in the proof of Theorem 3.4.4, to conclude that X is a path in a Y-computable tree of finite width, from which it follows that $X \leqslant_T Y$. □

The following are immediate corollaries to the above result.

Corollary 9.15.4 (Merkle and Stephan [270]). *There is a minimal pair of C-degrees of computably enumerable sets.*

Proof. Choose $A, B \subseteq \{2^{2^n} : n \in \omega\}$ whose Turing degrees form a minimal pair and apply Theorem 9.15.3. □

Corollary 9.15.5 (Merkle and Stephan [270]). *A C-degree contains at most one Turing degree.*

Proof. Let $A \equiv_C B$. Let $\widehat{A} = \{2^{2^n} : n \in A\}$ and $\widehat{B} = \{2^{2^n} : n \in B\}$. Then $\widehat{A} \equiv_C \widehat{B}$, so by Theorem 9.15.3, $\widehat{A} \equiv_T \widehat{B}$, and hence $A \equiv_T B$. □

Not all C-degrees can contain entire Turing degrees. Recall that A is complex if there is a computable order h with $C(A \upharpoonright h(n)) \geqslant n$ for all n (or, equivalently, a computable order g with $K(A \upharpoonright g(n)) \geqslant n$ for all n).

Theorem 9.15.6 (Merkle and Stephan [270]). *If A is complex then neither the C-degree nor the K-degree of A contains an entire Turing degree.*

Proof. We do the proof for C, the K case being essentially the same. Fix h as above. Let $B \equiv_C A$. Let $D = \{h(4n) : n \in B\}$. Then $D \equiv_T B$, but $D \not\equiv_C A$, since $C(A \upharpoonright h(4n)) \geqslant 4n$, while $C(D \upharpoonright h(4n)) \leqslant C(B \upharpoonright n) + O(1) \leqslant n + O(1)$. □

For the K-degrees, we can apply similar methods to get minimal pairs. Recall that a set A is K-trivial if $K(A \upharpoonright n) \leqslant K(n) + O(1)$.

Lemma 9.15.7 (Merkle and Stephan [270]). *Suppose that Y is not K-trivial and $Y \leqslant_K X$. Then there is a function $f \leqslant_T Y \oplus \emptyset'$ such that, for each n, the set X has at least one element between n and $f(n)$.*

Proof. Let c be a constant with $Y \leqslant_K X$ via c. Let F_n be the collection of all sequences D such that $D(k) = 0$ for all $k > n$. Let $f(n)$ be the least number $m > n$ such that $K(D \upharpoonright m) + c < K(Y \upharpoonright m)$ for all $D \in F_n$. Such an m exists because Y is not K-trivial, and f is computable from $\emptyset'$ and Y. As $Y \leqslant_K X$ via c, for each n, the set X must differ below $f(n)$ from all $D \in F_n$, and the result follows. □

Theorem 9.15.8 (Merkle and Stephan [270]). *Suppose that A and B are $\emptyset'$-hyperimmune sets, forming a Turing minimal pair relative to $\emptyset'$. Then the K-degrees of A and B form a minimal pair. Hence there are minimal pairs of K-degrees of Σ_2^0 sets.*

Proof. Without loss of generality we may assume that $A, B \subseteq \{2^n : n \in \omega\}$. Let $Y \leqslant_K A, B$. By Theorem 9.15.2, $Y \leqslant_T A \oplus \emptyset', B \oplus \emptyset'$. Thus $Y \leqslant_T \emptyset'$, as A and B form a minimal pair above $\emptyset'$. But by Lemma 9.15.7, if Y is not K-trivial, then A and B are not hyperimmune relative to $\emptyset'$, and the result follows. □

Using similar techniques, Merkle and Stephan [270] have constructed nontrivial branching degrees in the C- and K-degrees, where a degree is *branching* if it is the infimum of two incomparable degrees.

Theorem 9.15.8 improves a basic result of Csima and Montalbán [83], who were the first to construct a minimal pair of K-degrees. Their method is interesting and informative in its own right, and will be dealt with in Section 11.12.

We finish the section with the following result.

Theorem 9.15.9 (Merkle and Stephan [270]). *There is a minimal C-degree.*

Proof. We use perfect trees whose branches are subsets of $\{2^{2^n} : n \in \omega\}$. Let T_0 be the computable tree of branches of this form. Having defined T_e, let T_{e+1} be a perfect computable subtree of T_e so that one of the following holds:

1. Φ_e^A is partial for all branches A of T_{e+1}; or
2. Φ_e^A is computable for all branches A of T_{e+1}; or
3. Φ_e^A is total for all branches A of T_{e+1} and for any two distinct branches A and B of T_{e+1}, if σ is their longest common initial segment, then there is an x such that $\Phi_e^A(x) \neq \Phi_e^B(x)$, and any branch C of T_{e+1} that extends σ coincides with either A or B up to the max of the uses of $\Phi_e^A(x)$ and $\Phi_e^B(x)$.

The usual arguments show that it is always possible to construct T_{e+1}, and that if $A \in \bigcap_e T_e$ then A is noncomputable and has minimal Turing degree. Let $B \leqslant_C A$ be noncomputable. Since $A \subset \{2^{2^n} : n \in \omega\}$, by Theorem 9.15.3, $B \leqslant_T A$. Let e be such that $\Phi_e^A = B$. Then case 3 above must hold of T_{e+1}. Given n, suppose that C and D are branches of T_{e+1} such that $\Phi_e^C(m) = B(m)$ and $\Phi_e^D(m) = B(m)$ whenever the relevant uses are less than n, but $C \upharpoonright n \neq A \upharpoonright n$ and $D \upharpoonright n \neq A \upharpoonright n$. Let σ be the longest common substring of A and C. We may assume without loss of generality that D also extends σ (since otherwise we can simply interchange the roles of C and D). But then there is an x such that $\Phi_e^C(x) \neq \Phi_e^A(x) = B(x)$ and D coincides with either A or C up to the use $\Phi_e^C(x)$. By the choice of C, this use must be greater than n. Since $C \upharpoonright n \neq A \upharpoonright n$, we conclude that $D \upharpoonright n = C \upharpoonright n$. In other words, $A \upharpoonright n$ is one of at most two strings of length n on T_{e+1} compatible with $B \upharpoonright n$, whence $C(A \upharpoonright n) \leqslant C(B \upharpoonright n) + O(1)$. □

Using more intricate methods, it is possible to prove that every c.e. C-degree bounds a minimal C-degree and a minimal rK-degree. It is unknown whether there is a minimal K-degree.

9.16 The structure of the monotone degrees

In this section we discuss results of Calhoun [46] on the structure of monotone degrees. Let $\mathcal{M}$ be our fixed universal monotone machine.

We begin with a technical lemma about the behavior of Km.

Lemma 9.16.1 (Calhoun [46]). *Let $s(\sigma, \tau)$ be the shortest initial segment of σ that is incomparable with τ if $\sigma \mid \tau$, and let $s(\sigma, \tau) = \lambda$ otherwise.*

(i) $K(s(\sigma, \tau)) \leqslant Km(\sigma) + Km(\tau) + 2 \log Km(\sigma) + 2 \log Km(\tau) + O(1)$.

(ii) $K(|\sigma|) \leqslant 3 \max\{Km(\sigma 0), Km(\sigma 1)\} + O(1)$.

(iii) $Km(\tau) \leqslant Km(\sigma\tau) + K(|\sigma|) + O(1)$.

(iv) *For each σ there is a c such that $Km(\tau) \leqslant Km(\sigma\tau) + c$ for all τ.*

(v) *For each computable set B there is a c such that $Km(\sigma^\frown(B \upharpoonright n)) \leqslant K(\sigma) + c$ for all σ and n.*

Proof. (i) Clearly $K(s(\sigma, \tau)) \leqslant K(\sigma) + K(\tau) + O(1)$, and $K(\sigma) + K(\tau) \leqslant Km(\sigma) + Km(\tau) + 2 \log Km(\sigma) + 2 \log Km(\tau) + O(1)$, by Theorem 3.15.4.

(ii) Assume that $Km(\sigma 0) \geqslant Km(\sigma 1)$, the other case being symmetric. By (i),

$$\begin{aligned} K(|\sigma|) &\leqslant K(\sigma) + O(1) \\ &\leqslant Km(\sigma 0) + 2 \log Km(\sigma 0) + Km(\sigma 1) + 2 \log Km(\sigma 1) + O(1) \\ &\leqslant 2\, Km(\sigma 0) + 4 \log Km(\sigma 0) + O(1) \leqslant 3\, Km(\sigma 0) + O(1). \end{aligned}$$

(iii) Define a monotone machine M by $M(\rho_0 \rho_1) = \nu$ if $\mathcal{U}(\rho_0) = k$ and $\mathcal{M}(\rho_1) = \mu\nu$ for some μ with $|\mu| = k$. If ρ_0 is a $\mathcal{U}$-description of $|\sigma|$ and ρ_1 is an $\mathcal{M}$-description of $\sigma\tau$, then $M(\rho_0 \rho_1) = \tau$.

(iv) follows immediately from (iii).

(v) By Theorem 3.15.7, $Km(\sigma^\frown(B \upharpoonright n)) \leqslant K(\sigma) + Km(B \upharpoonright n) + O(1)$, but since B is computable, $Km(B \upharpoonright n) \leqslant O(1)$. □

Theorem 9.16.2 (Calhoun [46]). *If A is neither* 1*-random nor computable, then there is a B such that $A \mid_{Km} B$.*

Proof. Let X be 1-random. We build B in stages by a finite extension argument.

For even s, let $B_{s+1} = B_s 0^k$ for some k such that $Km(B_s 0^k) < Km(A \upharpoonright (|B_s| + k)) - s$. Such a k exists because $Km(A \upharpoonright n)$ is unbounded, while $Km(B_s 0^k)$ is bounded, since $B_s 0^\omega$ is computable.

For odd s, let $B_{s+1} = B_s{}^\frown(X \upharpoonright k)$ for some k such that $Km(B_s{}^\frown(X \upharpoonright k)) > Km(A \upharpoonright (|B_s| + k)) + s$. Such a k exists because $B_s X$ is 1-random, and hence $Km(B_s{}^\frown(X \upharpoonright n)) = n \pm O(1)$, while A is not 1-random, and hence $Km(A \upharpoonright (|B_s| + n))$ is bounded away from n.

The even stages ensure that $Km(A \upharpoonright n) \nleqslant Km(B \upharpoonright n) + O(1)$ and the odd stages that $Km(B \upharpoonright n) \nleqslant Km(A \upharpoonright n) + O(1)$. □

It is straightforward to extend the proof of Theorem 9.16.2 to construct a perfect tree such that any two paths have incomparable Km-degrees, yielding the following.

Theorem 9.16.3 (Calhoun [46]). *There is an antichain of Km-degrees of size $2^{\aleph_0}$.*

Since $A \leqslant_{Km_D} B$ implies $A \leqslant_{Km} B$, the two previous theorems hold also of the discrete monotone degrees.

Calhoun [46] proved some further structural results about the monotone degrees, such as the following.

Theorem 9.16.4 (Calhoun [46]). *There is a minimal pair of Km-degrees.*

Proof. We construct A and B in stages. Let $A_0 = B_0 = \lambda$ and $n_0 = 0$.

At an even stage s, proceed as follows. Let c_1 be the constant from Lemma 9.16.1 (ii), and let c_2 be the constant from Lemma 9.16.1(v) applied to 0^ω. Let A_s^* be an extension of A_s with $Km(A_s^*) > Km(A_s)$. A string σ is *terminal* if there is no proper extension τ of σ with $Km(\tau) = Km(\sigma)$. Let n be large enough so that the following hold.

(i) $n \geqslant |A_s^*|$.

(ii) There is no terminal σ with $|\sigma| > n$ and $Km(\sigma) < Km(A_s^*) + c_2 + s$.

(iii) For all $m \geqslant n$, we have $K(m) \geqslant 3(K(A_s^*) + c_1 + c_2 + s)$, where c_1 is the constant from Lemma 9.16.1 (ii).

Let $B_{s+1} = B_s{}^\frown 0^{n-|B_s|}$ and $A_{s+1} = A_s^*{}^\frown 0^{n-|A_s^*|}$, and let $n_{s+1} = n$.

At an odd stage we do the same, but switching the roles of A and B.

To see that A and B form a minimal pair, suppose that $X \leqslant_{Km} A, B$ is not computable. We say that s is an *increment stage* if $Km(X \upharpoonright n_{s+1}) >$

$Km(X \upharpoonright n_s)$. There must be infinitely many increment stages, so suppose there are infinitely many even increment stages, the odd case being symmetric. For each even increment stage s, let x be such that $n_s < x \leqslant n_{s+1}$ and $Km(X \upharpoonright x-1) < Km(X \upharpoonright x)$. As $x > n_s$, if $X \upharpoonright x-1$ is terminal, then $Km(X \upharpoonright x-1) \geqslant K(A_s^*) + c_2 + s$ by condition (ii). If $X \upharpoonright x-1$ is not terminal, then

$$Km(X \upharpoonright x) = \max\{Km((X \upharpoonright x-1)^\frown 0), Km((X \upharpoonright x-1)^\frown 1)\} \geqslant \tfrac{K(x)}{3} - c_1,$$

by Lemma 9.16.1 (ii). By condition (iii), $K(x) \geqslant 3(K(A_s^*) + c_1 + c_2 + s)$. Thus, in either case, $Km(X \upharpoonright x) \geqslant K(A_s^*) + c_2 + s$. By Lemma 9.16.1(v),

$$Km(A \upharpoonright x) = Km(A_s^{*\frown} 0^{x-|A_s^*|}) \leqslant K(A_s^*) + c_2.$$

Since s is unbounded and $X \leqslant_{Km} A$, we have a contradiction. □

Calhoun [46] also showed how to construct many uncountable Km-degrees. For a set A and a strictly increasing function f, let $A \otimes f(n)$ be $A(f^{-1}(n))$ if n is in the range of f, and 0 otherwise. Similarly, $\sigma \otimes f$ is $\sigma(f^{-1}(n))$ if n is in the range of f and $f^{-1}(n) < |\sigma|$, and is 0 for all other $n < f(|\sigma|)$. Let $f^{-1}[n] = \max\{k : f(k) \leqslant n\}$.

Theorem 9.16.5 (Calhoun [46]). *If f is strictly increasing and computable, then $Km((A \otimes f) \upharpoonright n) = Km(A \upharpoonright f^{-1}[n]) \pm O(1)$. Hence, if $Km(A \upharpoonright n) = Km(B \upharpoonright n) \pm O(1)$ then $Km((A \otimes f) \upharpoonright n) = Km((B \otimes f) \upharpoonright n) \pm O(1)$.*

Proof. When specifying a monotone machine M, we issue instructions of the form $M(\sigma) \succcurlyeq \tau$. What we mean is that, on input σ, we want M to write τ on its output tape. We might also issue another instruction $M(\sigma) \succcurlyeq \tau'$. As long as τ and τ' are compatible, M is still well-defined. (Of course, to ensure that M is monotone, we have to satisfy a stricter condition: if we issue instructions $M(\sigma) \succcurlyeq \tau$ and $M(\sigma') \succcurlyeq \tau'$ and σ and σ' are compatible, then τ and τ' must be compatible.)

To show $Km((A \otimes f) \upharpoonright n) \leqslant Km(A \upharpoonright f^{-1}[n]) + O(1)$, we build a monotone machine M. Let $M(\rho) \succcurlyeq (\tau \otimes f)^\frown 0^k$ if $\mathcal{M}(\rho) \succcurlyeq \tau$ and $k < f(|\tau|+1) - f(|\tau|)$. To see that M is monotone, suppose that $M(\rho) \succcurlyeq \sigma_1$ and $M(\nu) \succcurlyeq \sigma_2$ with ρ and ν compatible. Then the corresponding τ_1 and τ_2 must also be compatible, as $\mathcal{M}$ is monotone. Assuming $\tau_1 \preccurlyeq \tau_2$, it is easy to see that $(\tau_1 \otimes f)^\frown 0^k \preccurlyeq (\tau_2 \otimes f)^\frown 0^\omega$ for any $k < f(|\tau| + 1) - f(|\tau|)$, and hence $\sigma_1 \preccurlyeq \sigma_2$. Thus M is monotone. Now, if $\sigma = (A \otimes f) \upharpoonright n$, then $M(\rho) \preccurlyeq \sigma$ where ρ is a minimal-length $\mathcal{M}$-description of $A \upharpoonright f^{-1}[n]$, and hence $Km(\sigma) \leqslant |\rho| = Km(A \upharpoonright f^{-1}[n])$.

To show $Km(A \upharpoonright f^{-1}[n]) \leqslant Km((A \otimes f) \upharpoonright n) + O(1)$, we build a monotone machine N. Let $N(\rho) \succcurlyeq \sigma$ whenever $\mathcal{M}(\rho) \succcurlyeq \sigma \otimes f$. If ρ and ν are compatible and we have made $N(\rho) \succcurlyeq \sigma$ and $N(\nu) \succcurlyeq \sigma'$, then, since $\mathcal{M}$ is monotone, $\sigma \otimes f$ and $\sigma' \otimes f$ are compatible, and we may suppose $\sigma \otimes f \preccurlyeq \sigma' \otimes f$. Then $\sigma \preccurlyeq \sigma'$ by definition of $\otimes$. Thus N is monotone. Letting $\sigma = A \upharpoonright f^{-1}[n]$, we have $\sigma \otimes f \preccurlyeq (A \otimes f) \upharpoonright n$, and hence if ρ

is a minimal length $\mathcal{M}$-description of $\sigma \otimes f$, then $Km(\sigma) \leqslant |\rho| + O(1) = Km(\sigma \otimes f) + O(1) \leqslant Km((A \otimes f) \upharpoonright n) + O(1)$. □

Corollary 9.16.6 (Calhoun [46]). *There is an order-preserving embedding from the rationals into the monotone degrees such that each degree in the image of the embedding has cardinality* $2^{\aleph_0}$.

Proof. For any rational number $r \in (0,1)$, let $f_r(n) = \lfloor \frac{n}{r} \rfloor$. Let A be 1-random. By Theorem 9.16.5, $Km(A \otimes f_r \upharpoonright n) = Km(A \upharpoonright f_r^{-1}[n]) \pm O(1) = f_r^{-1}[n] \pm O(1)$. By construction, $f_r^{-1}[n] = \max\{k : \lfloor \frac{k}{r} \rfloor \leqslant n\} = rn \pm O(1)$. Then the map $r \mapsto \deg_{KM}(A \otimes f_r)$ induces the desired embedding: If $r < s$ the $\lim_n sn - rn = \infty$, so $A \otimes f_r <_{Km} A \otimes f_s$. Furthermore, if $A \neq B$ are 1-random, then $A \otimes f_r \equiv_{Km} B \otimes f_r$ but $A \otimes f_r \neq B \otimes f_r$. Since there are continuum many 1-randoms, each degree in the range of our map has size continuum. □

9.17 Schnorr reducibility

One can define measures of relative randomness tailored to notions other than 1-randomness. We give an example in this section. Given the machine characterization of Schnorr randomness from Section 7.1.3, we can define a reducibility analogous to K-reducibility for Schnorr randomness.

Definition 9.17.1 (Downey and Griffiths [109]). A set A is *Schnorr reducible* to a set B (written $A \leqslant_{\mathrm{Sch}} B$) if for each computable measure machine M there is a computable measure machine N such that $K_N(A \upharpoonright n) \leqslant K_M(B \upharpoonright n) + O(1)$.[5]

Clearly, if A is Schnorr random and $A \leqslant_{\mathrm{Sch}} B$, then B is Schnorr random. We prove two more facts about this reducibility. The first shows that it is not implied by K-reducibility, or even by cl-reducibility.

Theorem 9.17.2 (Downey, Griffiths, and LaForte [110]). *There are c.e. sets A and B such that $A \leqslant_{\mathrm{cl}} B$ but $A \nleqslant_{\mathrm{Sch}} B$.*

Proof. By Proposition 7.1.19, we can restrict our attention to machines M such that $\mu([\![\mathrm{dom}\, M]\!]) = 1$. Let $M_0, M_1, \ldots$ be an effective list of all prefix-free machines. We build a computable measure machine M and c.e. sets $A \leqslant_{\mathrm{cl}} B$ to satisfy the requirements

$$\mathcal{R}_e : \mu([\![\mathrm{dom}\, M_e]\!]) = 1 \Rightarrow \exists n\, (K_M(B \upharpoonright n) \leqslant K_{M_e}(A \upharpoonright n) - e).$$

We build M indirectly, by enumerating a KC set L.

[5]It would be possible to define a *uniform* version of Schnorr reducibility, where an index for N must be obtained computably from an index for M, but this notion remains unexplored at the time of writing.

For each $\mathcal{R}_e$ we set aside a block $[n_e, n_e+3e+1]$, with $n_{e+1} > n_e+3e+1$. We will never allow n_e+j for $0 < j \leqslant 3e+1$ to enter B, but we may possibly put n_e into B. Thus there are 2^{e+1} many possible values for $B \upharpoonright (n_e+3e+2)$. For each e, we enumerate a request $(2e+2, \tau)$ for each of these possible values τ. These are all the requests ever put into L, so the weight of L is equal to $\sum_e 2^{e+1}2^{-(2e+2)} = \sum_e 2^{-(e+1)} = 1$. Thus there is a computable measure machine M such that $K_M(B \upharpoonright (n_e+3e+2)) = 2e+2$ for all e. So it is enough to ensure that if $\mu([\![\operatorname{dom} M_e]\!]) = 1$ then $K_{M_e}(A \upharpoonright (n_e+3e+2)) \geqslant 3e+2$.

There are fewer than 2^{3e+2} many M_e-programs of length less than $3e+2$, so there must be a string $\tau \in 2^{3e+2}$ such that if $A(n_e)\ldots A(n_e+3e+1) = \tau$, then $K_{M_e}(A \upharpoonright (n_e+3e+2)) \geqslant 3e+2$, regardless of the other values of A. So for each e we wait for a stage s such that $1 - \mu([\![\operatorname{dom} M_e[s]]\!]) < 2^{-3e+1}$. At that stage, we know $M_e(\mu)$ for all M_e-programs μ of length less than $3e+2$, and hence can determine a τ as above. We put numbers into A to ensure that $A(n_e)\ldots A(n_e+3e+1) = \tau$, and put n_e into B. The latter action ensures that $A \leqslant_{\mathrm{cl}} B$. □

It turns out that tt-reducibility is related to Schnorr reducibility much as wtt-reducibility is to K-reducibility. This is not a surprising fact, since the essential difference between a tt-reduction and a wtt-reduction is that the former has a computable domain, which is exactly what distinguishes a computable measure machine from an ordinary prefix-free machine. To obtain a version of tt-reducibility that implies Schnorr reducibility, we need to restrict the use in the same way that we did to obtain cl-reducibility from wtt-reducibility.

Definition 9.17.3 (Downey, Griffiths, and LaForte [110]). A set A is *strongly truth table reducible* to a set B (written $A \leqslant_{\mathrm{stt}} B$) if $A \leqslant_{\mathrm{tt}} B$ via a truth table reduction Γ with use $\gamma(n) \leqslant n + O(1)$.

Theorem 9.17.4 (Downey, Griffiths, and LaForte [110]). *If $A \leqslant_{\mathrm{stt}} B$ then $A \leqslant_{\mathrm{Sch}} B$.*

Proof. Let $A \leqslant_{\mathrm{stt}} B$ via a reduction Γ with use $\gamma(n) \leqslant n+c$. Let $\gamma_0, \ldots, \gamma_{2^c-1}$ be the strings of length c. Let M be a computable measure machine. Build a KC set L as follows. For every σ and τ such that $M(\sigma)\downarrow= \tau$ and every $j < 2^c$, enumerate a request $(|\sigma|+c, \Gamma^{\tau\gamma_j} \upharpoonright |\tau|)$. (Since Γ is a tt-reduction, $\Gamma^{\tau\gamma_j} \upharpoonright |\tau|$ is always defined.) For each $\sigma \in \operatorname{dom} M$, we add $2^c 2^{-(|\sigma|+c)} = 2^{-|\sigma|}$ to the weight of L, so this weight is equal to $\mu([\![\operatorname{dom} M]\!])$. Thus L is a KC set with computable weight, and hence there is a corresponding computable measure machine N given by the KC Theorem. If $M(\sigma)\downarrow= B \upharpoonright n$ then there is a string μ of length $|\sigma|+c$ such that $N(\mu)\downarrow= \Gamma^{B\upharpoonright(n+c)} \upharpoonright n = A \upharpoonright n$, so $K_N(A \upharpoonright n) \leqslant K_M(B \upharpoonright n) + O(1)$. □

10

Complexity and Relative Randomness for 1-Random Sets

In this chapter, we examine basic questions about the function K, as well as related questions about the orderings $\leqslant_C$ and $\leqslant_K$, and other measures of relative complexity. We also introduce some other natural measures of relative randomness. These measures, which include *low for 1-randomness reducibility* $\leqslant_{\mathrm{LR}}$ and *van Lambalgen reducibility* $\leqslant_{\mathrm{vL}}$, are at first sight not directly related to initial segment complexity, but can be used to naturally relate initial segment complexity to Turing reducibility and other measures of relative computational complexity. Most of the material in this chapter concerns relative initial segment complexity and relative randomness within the class of 1-random sets, where some of the stronger reducibilities considered in the previous chapter do not seem to give us much information.

10.1 Uncountable lower cones in K-reducibility and C-reducibility

We begin by establishing a relatively easy result and looking forward to some related ones we will prove later in the chapter.

One property that typical computability-theoretic reducibilities share is that, for any given set A, there are only countably many sets reducible to A. This *countable predecessor property* does not hold of $\leqslant_K$ and $\leqslant_C$.

Theorem 10.1.1 (Yu, Ding, and Downey [415]). *If A is 1-random then there are $2^{\aleph_0}$ many sets K-reducible to A, and indeed there are sets of every m-degree K-reducible to A.*

R.G. Downey and D. Hirschfeldt, *Algorithmic Randomness and Complexity*, Theory and Applications of Computability, DOI 10.1007/978-0-387-68441-3_10,

Proof. For a set B, let $\widehat{B} = \{2^m : m \in B\}$. Then $K(\widehat{B} \upharpoonright n) \leqslant K(n)+K(B \upharpoonright \log n)+O(1) \leqslant O(\log n) \leqslant n+O(1) \leqslant K(A \upharpoonright n)+O(1)$, so $\widehat{B}$ is K-reducible to A. But the map $B \mapsto \widehat{B}$ is 1-1 and m-degree preserving (except when $B = \mathbb{N}$), so the result follows. □

Essentially the same proof shows the following.

Corollary 10.1.2 (Yu, Ding, and Downey [415]). *If A is 1-random then there are $2^{\aleph_0}$ many sets C-reducible to A, and indeed there are sets of every m-degree C-reducible to A.*

Perhaps strangely, it was rather difficult to construct an uncountable K-degree. The existence of such a degree follows from work of Reimann and Stephan [330] with a little work,[1] though the original proof is an unpublished one due to Joe Miller. Space considerations preclude us from presenting this material.

One consequence of this result is that it is not obvious that there are continuum many K-degrees, since the usual argument (every degree is countable but there are continuum many sets) does not apply. However, while the cardinality of sets K-reducible to a given set A might be large, the *measure* of the class of sets K-reducible to A is always 0, as shown by Yu, Ding, and Downey [415] and proved below as Theorem 10.3.13. This result is enough to conclude that there are uncountably many K-degrees, and in fact enough to prove the result of Yu and Ding [413] that there are continuum many K-degrees, as we will discuss in Section 10.3.3.

Another route to this result is through Theorem 10.5.12 below that 1-random K-degrees are countable. Since there are continuum many 1-random sets, this result implies that there are continuum many K-degrees of 1-random sets.

In Section 10.3.4, we will see that the same facts hold of C-reducibility.

Before looking at this material, however, we will examine the initial segment complexity of Ω, and introduce other measures of relative randomness, particularly van Lambalgen reducibility, first defined by Miller and Yu [280].

[1]Referring to that paper, specifically page 9, Theorem 1 and Lemma 1, Miller points out that the construction shows (for the right choice of premeasure) that there is an X with initial segment complexity $K(X \upharpoonright n) = \frac{n}{2} \pm O(1)$. The construction is loose enough that one could code any set into X (on the bits in positions dn for some constant d), so there are continuum many sets with initial segment complexity $\frac{n}{2} \pm O(1)$.

10.2 The K-complexity of Ω and other 1-random sets

10.2.1 $K(A \upharpoonright n)$ versus $K(n)$ for 1-random sets A

We have seen a number of results, particularly those of Miller and Yu [280] in Section 6.6, establishing relatively precise bounds on the behavior of $K(A \upharpoonright n)$ for a 1-random set A. We now present results of Solovay [371] on the relationship between $K(n)$ and $K(A \upharpoonright n)$ for 1-random sets A.

Recall Corollary 6.6.3, which states that if A is 1-random and $\sum_n 2^{-f(n)} = \infty$, then there are infinitely many n such that $K(A \upharpoonright n) > n + f(n) - O(1)$. As mentioned in Section 6.6, Solovay [371] had earlier proved this result for computable f. Note that, since $K(A \upharpoonright m) \leqslant m + K(m) + O(1)$ for all m, the n such that $K(A \upharpoonright n) > n + f(n) - O(1)$ must be fairly complex, in the sense that $K(n) \geqslant f(n) - O(1)$ for all such n. Solovay [371] showed that, for computable f, there must also be such complex n for which the complexity of $A \upharpoonright n$ is not too high.

Theorem 10.2.1 (Solovay [371]). *Let A be 1-random. Let f be a computable function such that $\sum_n 2^{-f(n)} = \infty$, and let h be a computable order.*[2] *Then there exist infinitely many n such that $K(n) \geqslant f(n) - O(1)$ and $K(A \upharpoonright n) \leqslant n + h(n) + O(1)$.*[3]

Proof. Let $\widehat{f}(n) = \min\{f(n), 2\log n\}$. Since $\sum_{f(n) \geqslant 2\log n} 2^{-f(n)} < \infty$, we have $\sum_n 2^{-\widehat{f}(n)} = \infty$. It is enough to prove the theorem with $\widehat{f}$ in place of f, since then the fact that $K(n) < 2\log n$ for almost all n implies that $\widehat{f}(n) = f(n)$ for almost all of the infinitely many n mentioned in the theorem.

We claim there is a computable function $g \geqslant \widehat{f}$ such that $\sum_n 2^{-g(n)} = \infty$ and $K(n) \leqslant g(n) + h(n) + O(1)$. Assuming the claim for now, we argue as follows. Since $g \geqslant \widehat{f}$, it is enough to prove the theorem for g in place of f. By Theorem 3.11.4, $K(A \upharpoonright n) \leqslant n + K(n) - g(n) + O(1)$ for infinitely many n. For each such n,

$$K(n) \geqslant K(A \upharpoonright n) - n + g(n) - O(1) \geqslant g(n) - O(1),$$

since A is 1-random, and

$$\begin{aligned} K(A \upharpoonright n) &\leqslant n + K(n) - g(n) + O(1) \\ &\leqslant n + g(n) + h(n) - g(n) + O(1) = n + h(n) + O(1). \end{aligned}$$

Thus it remains to establish our claim. To show that $K(n) \leqslant g(n) + h(n) + O(1)$ it is enough to show that $\sum_n 2^{-g(n)-h(n)} < \infty$. We define g in

[2] The prototypes here are $f(n) = \log n$ and $h(n) = \log\log n$.

[3] It is not hard to see that this result would not hold in general without the computability hypothesis on f and h.

stages so that for each n, we have $g(n)$ equal to either $\widehat{f}(n)$ or $2\log n$. At the beginning of stage i, we have defined $g(n)$ for $n < m_i$ for some m_i. Let m_{i+1} be least such that

$$1 \leqslant \sum_{\substack{m_i \leqslant n < m_{i+1} \\ h(n) \geqslant i}} 2^{-\widehat{f}(n)} \leqslant 2,$$

which exists because $\sum_n 2^{-\widehat{f}(n)} = \infty$ and $\lim_n h(n) = \infty$. For $n \in [m_i, m_{i+1})$, let $g(n) = 2\log n$ if $h(n) < i$ and let $g(n) = \widehat{f}(n)$ otherwise. Then

$$\sum_n 2^{-g(n)} \geqslant \sum_i \sum_{\substack{m_i \leqslant n < m_{i+1} \\ h(n) \geqslant i}} 2^{-\widehat{f}(n)} \geqslant \sum_i 1 = \infty$$

and

$$\sum_n 2^{-g(n)-h(n)} \leqslant \sum_i \Bigg(\sum_{\substack{m_i \leqslant n < m_{i+1} \\ h(n) \geqslant i}} 2^{-\widehat{f}(n)-h(n)} + \sum_{\substack{m_i \leqslant n < m_{i+1} \\ h(n) < i}} 2^{-2\log n - h(n)} \Bigg)$$

$$\leqslant \sum_i 2^{-i} \sum_{\substack{m_i \leqslant n < m_{i+1} \\ h(n) \geqslant i}} 2^{-\widehat{f}(n)} + \sum_n 2^{-2\log n} \leqslant \sum_i 2^{-i+1} + \sum_n 2^{-2\log n} < \infty.$$

□

10.2.2 The rate of convergence of Ω and the α function

The following definition provides a kind of "monotone approximation" to K.

Definition 10.2.2 (Chaitin, see [371]). Let $\alpha(n) = \min\{K(m) : m \geqslant n\}$.

Note that if $n > m$ then $\alpha(n) \geqslant \alpha(m)$. We can similarly define α^X using K^X for any set X.

The function α grows slower than any computable order.

Proposition 10.2.3 (Chaitin, see [371]). *If g is a computable order then $\alpha(n) < g(n)$ for almost all n.*

Proof. Let $h(k)$ be the least n such that $g(n) > k$. Then $K(h(k)) \leqslant K(k) + O(1) \leqslant O(\log k)$. Since $h(g(n)) > n$ for all n, we have $\alpha(n) \leqslant K(h(g(n)) \leqslant O(\log g(n))$, which means that $\alpha(n) < g(n)$ for all sufficiently large n. □

We now consider the rate of convergence of Ω as a series, in the version defined as $\sum_n 2^{-K(n)}$. Let

$$s(n) = -\log \sum_{j \geqslant n} 2^{-K(j)}.$$

Notice that $s(n)$ goes to infinity with n.

Theorem 10.2.4 (Solovay [371]). $\alpha(n) - O(\log \alpha(n)) \leqslant s(n) \leqslant \alpha(n)$.

Proof. By definition, there is an $m \geqslant n$ such that $K(m) = \alpha(n)$, so $\sum_{j \geqslant n} 2^{-K(j)} \geqslant 2^{-K(m)} = 2^{-\alpha(n)}$. Taking logs, we see that $s(n) \leqslant \alpha(n)$.

For the other inequality, we will show how to compute from $\Omega \upharpoonright n$ an integer t_n so that

(i) $K(t_n \mid \Omega \upharpoonright n) = O(1)$ and

(ii) $s(t_n) > n$.

Assuming we have such integers, let $k = s(n)$. Then $s(t_k) > s(n)$, so $t_k > n$. Together with (i), this fact implies that

$$\alpha(n) \leqslant K(t_k) \leqslant K(\Omega \upharpoonright k) + O(1) \leqslant k + K(k) + O(1) = s(n) + O(\log s(n)).$$

Since $s(n) \leqslant \alpha(n)$, we have $\alpha(n) = s(n) \pm O(\log s(n))$, so $\alpha(n)$ is asymptotically equal to $s(n)$, and hence $O(\log \alpha(n)) = O(\log s(n))$, giving the desired inequality.

We finish by defining integers t_n satisfying (i) and (ii). Our result uses Theorem 3.13.2, which we now recall. Let

$$p(n) = |(\{\sigma \in 2^n : \mathcal{U}(\sigma)\downarrow\})|.$$

Then Theorem 3.13.2 states that $p(n) \sim 2^{n-K(n)}$.

As usual, let $\Omega_s = \sum_{\mathcal{U}(\sigma)[s]\downarrow} 2^{-|\sigma|}$, where we may assume that at each stage s exactly one new string σ_s enters the domain of $\mathcal{U}$. Given $\Omega \upharpoonright n$, compute the least k_n such that $\Omega_{k_n} \upharpoonright n = \Omega \upharpoonright n$. Let t'_n be the least integer greater than $|\sigma_i|$ for all $i \leqslant k_n$. Then there is a c such that

$$\begin{aligned} 2^{-n} > \Omega - \Omega \upharpoonright n \geqslant \sum \{2^{-|\sigma|} : |\sigma| \geqslant t'_n \wedge \mathcal{U}(\sigma)\downarrow\} \\ = \sum_{j \geqslant t'_n} 2^{-j} p(j) \geqslant c \sum_{j \geqslant t'_n} 2^{-j} 2^{j-K(j)} = c 2^{-s(t'_n)}. \end{aligned}$$

Taking logs, we see that $s(t'_n) \geqslant n + O(1)$. Thus, for a suitable choice of k, independent of n, if we let $t_n = t'_{n+k}$ then $s(t_n) > n$. Furthermore,

$$K(t_n \mid \Omega \upharpoonright n) \leqslant K(t_n \mid \Omega \upharpoonright n + k) + K(\Omega \upharpoonright n + k \mid \Omega \upharpoonright n).$$

The first term is $O(1)$ by the explicit description of t'_n from $\Omega \upharpoonright n$. The second is evidently $O(1)$ since k is fixed independently of n. □

10.2.3 Comparing initial segment complexities of 1-random sets

The first person to study (implicitly) the K-degrees of 1-random sets was Solovay [371]. He used the relativized version of the α function of the previous subsection to show that no 2-random set is K-reducible to Ω.[4] Of course, we already know that this is the case. Indeed, Theorem 15.6.5 (which we discussed in Section 6.11) implies that if A is 2-random and $A \leqslant_K B$, then B is 2-random. (We will extend this result to n-randomness in Corollary 10.3.11.) However, Solovay's methods are of independent interest, so we give his original proof here. We begin with the following result.

Theorem 10.2.5 (Solovay [371]). *There are infinitely many m such that $K(\Omega \upharpoonright m) \leqslant k + \alpha^{\emptyset'}(m) + O(\log \alpha^{\emptyset'}(m))$.*[5]

Proof. We work with α^{Ω}, which is equal to $\alpha^{\emptyset'}$ up to an additive constant.

Let $\mathcal{U}$ be our fixed universal prefix-free oracle machine, and adopt the convention that if $\mathcal{U}^X(\tau)\downarrow = \rho$, then the use of this computation is at least $|\rho|$. Let M be the prefix-free machine defined as follows. The machine M tries to write its input as $\sigma\tau\nu$ such that $\mathcal{U}(\sigma) = |\tau|$ and $\mathcal{U}^{\nu}(\tau)\downarrow$ with use exactly $|\nu|$. If that is possible then M outputs ν.

Let p_n be the least i such that $\alpha^{\Omega}(i) \geqslant n$. It is easy to see that $K^{\Omega}(p_n) \leqslant n + O(1)$. Let τ be a minimal-length $\mathcal{U}^{\Omega}$-program for p_n. Let σ be a minimal-length $\mathcal{U}$-program for τ. Let m_n be least such that $\mathcal{U}^{\Omega\upharpoonright m_n}(\tau)\downarrow$.

Then $M(\sigma\tau(\Omega \upharpoonright m_n))\downarrow = \Omega \upharpoonright m_n$. We have $|\tau| = n + O(1)$, whence $|\sigma| \leqslant O(\log n)$. Furthermore, $m_n \geqslant p_n$, so $\alpha^{\Omega}(m_n) \geqslant n$. Thus

$$\begin{aligned} K(\Omega \upharpoonright m_n) &\leqslant |\sigma| + |\tau| + |\Omega \upharpoonright m_n| + O(1) \\ &\leqslant m_n + n + O(\log n) \leqslant m_n + \alpha^{\Omega}(m_n) + O(\log \alpha^{\Omega}(m_n)). \end{aligned}$$

□

As we will now see, Solovay [371] also showed that if X is 2-random then $K(X \upharpoonright n) \geqslant n + \alpha(n) - O(\log \alpha(n))$. Since $\alpha^{\emptyset'}$ grows more slowly than any $\emptyset'$-computable function, this result, together with the theorem above, shows that no 2-random set is K-reducible to Ω. We begin with a lemma.

Lemma 10.2.6 (Solovay [371]). $K^{\emptyset'}(n) \leqslant K(n) - \alpha(n) + O(\log \alpha(n))$.

Proof. Let $s(n) = -\log \sum_{j \geqslant n} 2^{-K(j)}$. By Theorem 10.2.4, there is a c such that $s(n) \geqslant \alpha(n) - c \log \alpha(n)$. Let m_k be the least n such that $\alpha(n) = k$. (The sums below are taken over only those k such that m_k is defined.) Let

$$S = \{(K(n) - \alpha(n) + (c+2)\log \alpha(n), n) : n \in \mathbb{N}\}.$$

[4] Solovay actually stated his results in terms of arithmetic randomness, but the strengthening to 2-randomness can be extracted from his proofs.

[5] We will see in the proof of Theorem 10.2.9 that in fact there are infinitely many m such that $K(\Omega \upharpoonright m) \leqslant k + \alpha^{\emptyset'}(m) + O(1)$.

Then S is $\emptyset'$-computable. Furthermore,

$$\sum_n 2^{-K(n)+\alpha(n)-(c+2)\log\alpha(n)} = \sum_k \sum_{\alpha(n)=k} 2^{-K(n)+k-(c+2)\log k}$$
$$\leqslant \sum_k 2^{k-(c+2)\log k} \sum_{n\geqslant m_k} 2^{-K(n)} = \sum_k 2^{k-(c+2)\log k} 2^{-s(m_k)}$$
$$\leqslant \sum_k 2^{k-(c+2)\log k} 2^{-\alpha(m_k)+c\log\alpha(m_k)} = \sum_k 2^{k-(c+2)\log k} 2^{-k+c\log k}$$
$$= \sum_k 2^{-2\log k} < \infty.$$

Thus, by the KC Theorem relativized to $\emptyset'$, we have $K^{\emptyset'}(n) \leqslant K(n) - \alpha(n) + (c+2)\log\alpha(n) + O(1)$. □

Theorem 10.2.7 (Solovay [371]). *If X is 2-random then $K(X \upharpoonright n) \geqslant n + \alpha(n) - O(\log\alpha(n))$.*

Proof. Let p_n be the position of $X \upharpoonright n$ in the length-lexicographic listing of $2^{<\omega}$. Note that $p_n \geqslant n$. If X is 2-random then $K^{\emptyset'}(X \upharpoonright n) \geqslant n - O(1)$. By Lemma 10.2.6, we have

$$K(X \upharpoonright n) = K(p_n) \geqslant K^{\emptyset'}(p_n) + \alpha(p_n) - O(\log\alpha(p_n))$$
$$\geqslant K^{\emptyset'}(K \upharpoonright n) + \alpha(p_n) - O(\log\alpha(p_n)) \geqslant n + \alpha(p_n) - O(\log\alpha(p_n))$$
$$\geqslant n + \alpha(n) - O(\log\alpha(n)),$$

the last inequality following by the monotonicity of α. □

We will return to the connections between 2-randomness and the α and s functions at the end of Section 10.4.

Corollary 10.2.8 (Solovay [371]). *If X is 2-random then $X \nleqslant_K \Omega$.*

There is no obvious way to extend Solovay's methods beyond 2-randomness. However, we will introduce methods below that allow us to show in Corollary 10.3.11 that indeed $\Omega^{\emptyset^{(m)}} \mid_K \Omega^{\emptyset^{(m)}}$ (and, in fact, the K-degrees of $\Omega^{\emptyset(n)}$ and $\Omega^{\emptyset(m)}$ have no upper bound) for all $m \neq n$.

We finish this subsection with the following result, which shows that $K(\Omega \upharpoonright n)$ is sometimes very close to n.

Theorem 10.2.9 (Solovay [371]). *There is an infinite sequence of pairs of numbers m_n^0, m_n^1 such that for $i = 0, 1$,*

(i) $\alpha^{\emptyset'}(m_n^i) = n \pm O(1)$,

(ii) $K(\Omega \upharpoonright m_n^i) \leqslant m_n^i + n + O(1)$,

(iii) $K(m_n^0) = \alpha(m_n^0) \pm O(1)$, *and*

(iv) $K(m_n^1) = \log m_n^1 + K(\log m_n^1) \pm O(1)$.

Proof. As in the proof of Theorem 10.2.5, we work with α^{Ω} in place of $\alpha^{\emptyset'}$. We begin by building $m_0, m_1, \dots$ satisfying (i) and (ii). That is, $\alpha^{\emptyset'}(m_n) = n \pm O(1)$ and $K(\Omega \upharpoonright m_n) \leqslant m_n + n + O(1)$.

At a first pass, we could use the proof of Theorem 10.2.5. Let p_n and m_n be as in that proof. Then $\alpha^{\Omega}(m_n) \geqslant n$. But $K^{\Omega}(p_n) \leqslant n + O(1)$ and m_n can be obtained Ω-computably from p_n, so in fact $\alpha^{\Omega}(m_n) = n \pm O(1)$, as required. Furthermore, as shown in the proof of Theorem 10.2.5, $K(\Omega \upharpoonright m_n) \leqslant m_n + n + O(\log n)$.

To remove the $O(\log n)$ term, we modify the machine M from the proof of Theorem 10.2.5 to a new prefix-free machine N. The idea is to interlace the oracle and input information to eliminate the need to provide the length of the input as additional information. Thus N attempts to write its input as $x_0 y_0 x_1 y_1 \dots x_n y_n \sigma$ (where the x_i are bits and σ is a string) so that letting $\tau = x_0 \dots x_n$ and $\nu = y_0 \dots y_n \sigma$, we have $\mathcal{U}^{\nu}(\tau)\downarrow$. (We adopt the convention that if $\mathcal{U}^{\nu}(\tau)\downarrow$ then $|\nu| \geqslant |\tau|$.) If that is possible, then N outputs ν. It is easy to check that N is prefix-free and that, with m_n as above and by a similar argument as before, N witnesses the fact that $K(\Omega \upharpoonright m_n) \leqslant m_n + n + O(1)$.

Now we obtain m_n^0 and m_n^1 from m_n. Let d be such that for every m there is an $m \in [n, 4n]$ with $K(m) \geqslant \log m + K(\log m) - d$. Let m_n^0 be the least number greater than or equal to m_n such that $K(m_n^0) = \alpha(m_n)$ and let m_n^1 be the least number greater than or equal to m_n such that $K(m_n^1) \geqslant \log m_n^1 + K(\log m_n^1) - d$. Then (iii) and (iv) are satisfied.

By monotonicity, $\alpha^{\emptyset'}(m_n^i) \geqslant \alpha^{\emptyset'}(m_n) = n \pm O(1)$. But the m_n^i can be obtained $\emptyset'$-computably from m_n, so

$$\alpha^{\emptyset'}(m_n^i) \leqslant K^{\emptyset'}(m_n^i) \leqslant K^{\emptyset'}(m_n) + O(1) \leqslant n + O(1),$$

the last inequality following because the m_n can be obtained $\emptyset'$-computably from the p_n, and we have already seen that $K^{\emptyset'}(p_n) \leqslant n + O(1)$. Thus (i) is satisfied.

Finally, it is easy to check that each m_n^i is computable from $\Omega \upharpoonright m_n$, so we can describe $\Omega \upharpoonright m_n^i$ in a prefix-free way by giving a prefix-free description of $\Omega \upharpoonright m_n$, and, since that description provides us with m_n and m_n^i, a plain description of $\Omega \upharpoonright [m_n, m_n^i)$. Thus

$$\begin{aligned} K(\Omega \upharpoonright m_n^i) &\leqslant K(\Omega \upharpoonright m_n) + C(\Omega \upharpoonright [m_n, m_n^i)) + O(1) \\ &\leqslant m_n + n + m_n^i - m_n + O(1) = m_n^i + n + O(1), \end{aligned}$$

so (ii) is satisfied. □

10.2.4 Limit complexities and relativized complexities

There are echoes of Solovay's work in more recent results of Bienvenu, Muchnik, Shen, and Vereshchagin [42, 399].

Theorem 10.2.10 (Vereschagin [399]). $C^{\emptyset'}(\sigma) = \limsup_n C(\sigma \mid n) \pm O(1)$.

Proof. Let $\mathcal{V}$ be our fixed universal plain machine. Let $M(\tau, n) = \mathcal{V}^{\emptyset'}(\tau)[n]$ (where both the oracle and the universal machine are being approximated). If n is large enough and τ is a minimal-length $\mathcal{V}^{\emptyset'}$-program for σ, then $M(\tau, n) = \sigma$, whence $C(\sigma \mid n) \leqslant |\tau| + O(1) = C^{\emptyset'}(\sigma) + O(1)$. Thus $\limsup_n C(\sigma \mid n) \leqslant C^{\emptyset'}(\sigma) + O(1)$.

For the other direction, let $k = \limsup_n C(\sigma \mid n) + 1$. Let $V_n = \{\sigma : C(\sigma \mid n) < k\}$. We have $|V_n| < 2^k$ for all n. Let $B = \{\tau : \exists m \, \forall n \geqslant m \, (|V_n \cup \{\tau\}| < 2^k)\}$. Then B is $\emptyset'$-c.e. (uniformly in k), $\sigma \in B$, and $|B| < 2^k$. Since we can describe σ from $\emptyset'$ by giving its position in the enumeration of B as a string of length k, we have $C^{\emptyset'}(\sigma) \leqslant k + O(1) = \limsup_n C(\sigma \mid n) + O(1)$. ☐

Theorem 10.2.11 (Bienvenu, Muchnik, Shen, and Vereschagin [42]). $K^{\emptyset'}(\sigma) = \limsup_n K(\sigma \mid n) \pm O(1)$.

Proof. The argument that $\limsup_n K(\sigma \mid n) \leqslant K^{\emptyset'}(\sigma) + O(1)$ is the same as in the previous proof, with $\mathcal{U}$ in place of $\mathcal{V}$, since then M is prefix-free for any fixed n.

Let $(\sigma_0, m_0, k_0), (\sigma_1, m_1, k_1), \ldots$ be an effective enumeration of $2^{<\omega} \times \mathbb{N} \times \mathbb{N}$. Let $K_0 = K$. Given K_s, let J be the result of altering K_s so that $J(\sigma_s \mid n) = \min\{k_s, K(\sigma_s \mid n)\}$ for all $n \geqslant m_s$, leaving all other values of K_s unchanged. If J is an information content measure, in the sense of Definition 3.7.7, then let $K_{s+1} = J$ and say that k is good for σ_s. Otherwise let $K_{s+1} = K_s$.

Let $I(\sigma)$ be the least k that is good for σ. Checking whether a given J as above is an i.c.m. can be done $\emptyset'$-computably, so $I(\sigma)$ is $\emptyset'$-approximable from above. For each s, let $I_s(\sigma)$ be the least k that has been verified to be good for σ by stage s (or ∞ if there has been none). It is then easy to verify by induction that $\sum_\sigma 2^{-I_s(\sigma)} \leqslant 1$ for all s, so that $\sum_\sigma 2^{-I(\sigma)} \leqslant 1$. Thus I is an i.c.m. relative to $\emptyset'$, and hence $K^{\emptyset'}(\sigma) \leqslant I(\sigma) + O(1)$.

Let $k = \limsup_n K(\sigma \mid n)$, let m be such that $K(\sigma \mid n) \leqslant k$ for all $n \geqslant m$, and let s be such that $(\sigma_s, m_s, k_s) = (\sigma, m, k)$. Then the J defined at stage s of the above construction equals K_s, whence k is good for σ. Thus $I(\sigma) \leqslant k$, and hence $K^{\emptyset'}(\sigma) \leqslant k + O(1) = \limsup_n K(\sigma \mid n) + O(1)$. ☐

It is straightforward to translate the above proof into the language of discrete semimeasures, and indeed that is how the proof is presented in [42]. The *limit frequency* of a partial function f is the function $q_f(k) = \liminf_n \frac{|\{i<n : f(i)=k\}|}{n}$. Using the translation of the construction above, we have the following. (See [42] for details.)

Theorem 10.2.12 (Muchnik [287]). *Every $\emptyset'$-c.e. discrete semimeasure is equal to q_f for some total computable function f.*

Theorem 10.2.13 (Bienvenu, Muchnik, Shen, and Vereshchagin [42]). *For every partial computable function f, the function q_f is bounded above by a $\emptyset'$-c.e. discrete semimeasure.*

Using almost the same proof we can show the following.

Theorem 10.2.14 (Bienvenu, Muchnik, Shen, and Vereshchagin [42]). $KM^{\emptyset'}(\sigma) = \limsup_n KM(\sigma \mid n) \pm O(1)$.

Bienvenu, Muchnik, Shen, and Vereshchagin [42] remarked that it is unknown whether the analogous result holds for monotone complexity Km.

10.3 Van Lambalgen reducibility

In this section we introduce a measure of relative randomness that is interesting not only for its own sake, but also as a tool for the analysis of K- and C-reducibility and their interactions with Turing reducibility. The following definition is based on van Lambalgen's Theorem, which recall states that $X \oplus Y$ is 1-random iff X is 1-random and Y is 1-random relative to X.

Definition 10.3.1 (Miller and Yu [280]). We say that X is *van Lambalgen reducible to* Y, or simply *vL-reducible* to X, and write $X \leqslant_{\mathrm{vL}} Y$, if for all Z, if $X \oplus Z$ is 1-random, then $Y \oplus Z$ is 1-random.

As usual, we call the equivalence classes induced by this reducibility the van Lambalgen degrees (vL-degrees).

Nies [302] defined the following closely related notion.

Definition 10.3.2 (Nies [302]). We say that Y is *low for 1-randomness reducible* to X, or simply *LR-reducible* to X, and write $Y \leqslant_{\mathrm{LR}} X$, if for all Z, if Z is 1-random relative to X then Z is 1-random relative to Y.[6]

By van Lambalgen's Theorem, if X and Y are both 1-random, then $Y \leqslant_{\mathrm{LR}} X$ iff $X \leqslant_{\mathrm{vL}} Y$. Notice that if X is not 1-random, then $X \leqslant_{\mathrm{vL}} Y$ for all Y, so vL-reducibility is interesting only on 1-random sets.

Another related reducibility is *extended monotone reducibility*, defined by writing $X \leqslant_{Km^{\oplus}} Y$ if $X \oplus Z \leqslant_{Km} Y \oplus Z$ for all Z. Since all 1-random sets have the same Km-degree, by Theorem 6.3.10, $\leqslant_{Km^{\oplus}}$ implies $\leqslant_{\mathrm{vL}}$, but $\leqslant_{Km^{\oplus}}$ also makes sense on non-1-random sets.

We will concentrate on studying van Lambalgen reducibility, although, of course, since we will be looking only at 1-random sets, all of the results below could be phrased in terms of LR-reducibility.

[6]The name of this reducibility comes from the concept of lowness for 1-randomness, which will be discussed in Section 11.2. In the present notation, a set Y is *low for 1-randomness* if $Y \leqslant_{\mathrm{LR}} \emptyset$. As we will see in Chapter 11, the class of such sets is a natural and highly interesting one, with several characterizations in terms of notions of randomness-theoretic weakness.

The vL-degrees turn out to be a weak measure of degree of randomness. We will see in Corollaries 10.3.10 and 10.3.17 that both $\leqslant_K$ and $\leqslant_C$ refine $\leqslant_{\mathrm{vL}}$. This is the key fact that allowed Miller and Yu [280] to transfer facts about the vL-degrees to the K- and C-degrees. This method is useful because many basic properties of the vL-degrees are easy to prove from known results.

10.3.1 Basic properties of the van Lambalgen degrees

In establishing the basic properties of the van Lambalgen degrees, we use van Lambalgen's Theorem, Kučera's Theorem 8.5.1 that every degree that computes $\emptyset'$ is 1-random, and Corollary 11.2.7, due to Kučera and Terwijn, that for every X there is a $Y >_{\mathrm{T}} X$ such that every set that is 1-random relative to X is also 1-random relative to Y. Although we prove Corollary 11.2.7 only in Chapter 11, since the relevant techniques are more properly presented there, we use it here as a black box.

Theorem 10.3.3 (Miller and Yu [280]).

(i) *The least vL-degree is* $\mathbf{0}_{\mathrm{vL}} = \{X : X \text{ is not } 1\text{-random}\}$.

(ii) *If* $X \leqslant_{\mathrm{vL}} Y$ *and* X *is* n*-random, then* Y *is* n*-random.*

(iii) *If* $X \oplus Y$ *is* 1*-random, then* X *and* Y *have no upper bound in the vL-degrees, so there is no join in the vL-degrees.*

(iv) *If* $Y \leqslant_{\mathrm{T}} X$ *and* Y *is* 1*-random, then* $X \leqslant_{\mathrm{vL}} Y$.

(v) *There are* 1*-random sets* $X \equiv_{\mathrm{vL}} Y$ *such that* $X <_{\mathrm{T}} Y$.

(vi) *If* $X \oplus Y$ *is* 1*-random, then* $X \oplus Y <_{\mathrm{vL}} X, Y$ *and* $X \mid_{\mathrm{vL}} Y$.

(vii) *There is no maximal vL-degree.*

(viii) *There is no minimal* 1*-random vL-degree.*

(ix) *The* Σ^0_1 *theory of* $(R, \leqslant_{\mathrm{vL}})$ *is decidable, where* R *denotes the collection of vL-degrees of* 1*-random sets.*

Proof. (i) Immediate from the definition, since if X is not 1-random then $X \oplus Z$ is not 1-random for any Z.

(ii) The $n = 1$ case follows by (i), so let $n > 1$. By Kučera's Theorem, there is a 1-random $Z \equiv_{\mathrm{T}} \emptyset^{(n-1)}$. Then X is 1-random relative to Z, so $X \oplus Z$ is 1-random. Thus, $Y \oplus Z$ is 1-random, so Y is 1-random relative to Z, and hence Y is n-random.

(iii) Assume for a contradiction that $X, Y \leqslant_{\mathrm{vL}} Z$. Because $X \leqslant_{\mathrm{vL}} Z$ and $X \oplus Y$ is 1-random, $Z \oplus Y$ is also 1-random. Therefore, $Y \oplus Z$ is 1-random. But $Y \leqslant_{\mathrm{vL}} Z$, so $Z \oplus Z$ must also be 1-random, which is a contradiction.

(iv) Let Z be such that $X \oplus Z$ is 1-random. Then Z is 1-random relative to X, and hence Z is 1-random relative to Y, which implies that $Y \oplus Z$ is 1-random. Thus $X \leqslant_{\mathrm{vL}} Y$.

(v) Let $X = \Omega$. By Corollary 11.2.7, there is a $W >_{\mathrm{T}} X$ such that every set that is 1-random relative to X is 1-random relative to W. By Kučera's Theorem, there is a 1-random $Y \equiv_{\mathrm{T}} W$. Then $X <_{\mathrm{T}} Y$. Furthermore, $Z \oplus X$ is 1-random iff Z is 1-random relative to X iff Z is 1-random relative to W iff Z is 1-random relative to Y iff $Z \oplus Y$ is 1-random. Thus $X \equiv_{\mathrm{vL}} Y$.

(vi) By (iii), $X \mid_{\mathrm{vL}} Y$. By (iv), $X \oplus Y \leqslant_{\mathrm{vL}} X, Y$. Therefore, $X \oplus Y <_{\mathrm{vL}} X, Y$.

(vii) If $X = X_1 \oplus X_2$ is 1-random, then $X <_{\mathrm{vL}} X_1, X_2$ by (vi).

(viii) Let X be 1-random and Y be 1-random relative to X. Then $X \oplus Y$ is 1-random, so by (i) and (vi), $\emptyset <_{\mathrm{vL}} X \oplus Y <_{\mathrm{vL}} X$.

(ix) As in Lerman [240], it suffices to prove that every finite poset can be embedded into $(R, \leqslant_{\mathrm{vL}})$. Suppose $\mathbb{P} = (P, \leqslant)$ and $P = \{p_i\}_{i<n}$. Pick a 1-random $X = \bigoplus_{i<n} X_i$. For any $k < n$, define $F(k) = \{i : p_k \leqslant p_i\}$ and let $Y_k = \bigoplus_{i \in F(k)} X_i$. Let $g : P \to R$ be defined by $g(p_k) = Y_k$. It suffices to prove that $p_j \leqslant p_k \Leftrightarrow Y_j \leqslant_{\mathrm{vL}} Y_k$. If $p_j \leqslant p_k$, then $F(k) \subseteq F(j)$, so $Y_j \leqslant_{\mathrm{vL}} Y_k$. If $p_j \nleqslant p_k$, then $k \notin F(j)$, so $X_k \oplus Y_j$ is 1-random. But $X_k \oplus Y_k$ is not 1-random, since $k \in F(k)$. So $Y_j \nleqslant_{\mathrm{vL}} Y_k$. □

The following corollary improves an earlier result of Yu, Ding, and Downey [415] that $\Omega^{\emptyset^{(m)}} \nleqslant_K \Omega^{\emptyset^{(n)}}$ for all $n > m$. It follows immediately from part (iii) of Theorem 10.3.3, since if $m \neq n$ then $\Omega^{\emptyset^{(m)}} \oplus \Omega^{\emptyset^{(n)}}$ is 1-random.

Corollary 10.3.4 (Miller and Yu [280]). *If $m \neq n$, then $\Omega^{\emptyset^{(m)}}$ and $\Omega^{\emptyset^{(n)}}$ have no upper bound in the vL-degrees.*

It is also clear that Ω is the least Δ^0_2 1-random set in the vL-degrees, and that no 2-random set can be vL-above a Δ^0_2 1-random set.

Notice that parts (ii) and (iv) of Theorem 10.3.3 immediately imply Theorem 8.5.3, which states that if X is n-random and $Y \leqslant_{\mathrm{T}} X$ is 1-random, then Y is n-random.

Kučera's Theorem 8.5.1 says that every degree above $\mathbf{0}'$ is 1-random, but no such degree can be n-random for any $n > 1$. Thus we have the following.

Proposition 10.3.5. *For every n-random degree* $\mathbf{a}$ *there is a* 1*-random degree* $\mathbf{b} > \mathbf{a}$ *that is not* 2*-random.*

10.3.2 Relativized randomness and Turing reducibility

In this subsection we prove the following strong extension of Theorem 8.5.3.

Theorem 10.3.6 (Miller and Yu [280]). *Let $X \leqslant_{\mathrm{T}} Y$ and let X be* 1*-random. For every Z, if Y is* 1*-random relative to Z, then X is also* 1*-random relative to Z.*

To prove this result, we use the following lemma.

Lemma 10.3.7 (Miller and Yu [280]). *If X is 1-random then*

$$\forall e \exists c \forall n\, [\mu(\{A : \Phi_e^A \upharpoonright n = X \upharpoonright n\}) \leqslant 2^{-n+c}].$$

Proof. Let $C_\sigma = \{A : \Phi_e^A \upharpoonright n = \sigma\}$. Note that if $\sigma \mid \tau$ then $C_\sigma \cap C_\tau = \emptyset$. Now let $F_i = \{\sigma : \mu(C_\sigma) > 2^{-|\sigma|+i}\}$ and let $Q_i = [\![F_i]\!]$. The Q_i form a sequence of uniformly Σ_1^0 classes. We claim that $\mu(Q_i) \leqslant 2^{-i}$. Suppose not. Then there is some prefix-free $D \subseteq F_i$ with $\mu([\![D]\!]) > 2^{-i}$. We now have

$$\mu(\{A : \Phi_e^A \upharpoonright |\sigma| = \sigma \text{ for some } \sigma \in D\}) = \sum_{\sigma \in D} \mu(C_\sigma)$$
$$\geqslant \sum_{\sigma \in D} 2^{-|\sigma|+i} = 2^i \sum_{\sigma \in D} 2^{-|\sigma|} = 2^i \mu([\![D]\!]) > 2^i 2^{-i} = 1,$$

which is a contradiction. So the Q_i form a Martin-Löf test. Since X is 1-random, $X \notin Q_c$ for some c, and the result follows. □

Proof of Theorem 10.3.6. Let X, Y, and Z be as in the theorem. Let Φ be such that $\Phi^Y = X$, and let c be the constant for this Φ and X given by Lemma 10.3.7. For each σ, enumerate a set F_σ as follows. If $\Phi^\tau \upharpoonright |\sigma|$ has use exactly τ, then add τ to F_σ provided that doing so preserves the condition $\sum_{\rho \in F_\sigma} 2^{-|\rho|} \leqslant 2^{-|\sigma|+c}$. Since each F_σ is prefix-free, we have $\mu([\![F_\sigma]\!]) = \sum_{\tau \in F_\sigma} 2^{-|\tau|}$. Moreover, $[\![F_{X \upharpoonright n}]\!] = \{A : \Phi^A \upharpoonright n = X \upharpoonright n\}$ for all n, since the choice of c means that we are not prevented from adding any strings to $F_{X \upharpoonright n}$.

Now suppose that X is not 1-random relative to Z. For each i, define the $\Sigma_1^{0,Z}$ class $Q_i = \bigcup_{K^Z(\sigma) \leqslant |\sigma|-c-i} [\![F_\sigma]\!]$. Then

$$\mu(Q_i) \leqslant \sum_{K^Z(\sigma) \leqslant |\sigma|-c-i} \mu([\![F_\sigma]\!])$$
$$\leqslant \sum_{K^Z(\sigma) \leqslant |\sigma|-c-i} 2^{-|\sigma|+c} \leqslant \sum_{\sigma} 2^{-K^Z(\sigma)-i} \leqslant 2^{-i}.$$

Hence the Q_i form a Martin-Löf test relative to Z. Since X is not 1-random relative to Z, for each i there is an n with $K^Z(X \upharpoonright n) \leqslant n - c - i$, which implies that $Y \in \{A : \Phi^A \upharpoonright n = X \upharpoonright n\} \subseteq Q_i$, contradicting the assumption that Y is 1-random relative to Z. □

10.3.3 vL-reducibility, K-reducibility, and joins

The key ingredient in connecting $\leqslant_K$ to $\leqslant_{\mathrm{vL}}$ was the realization by Miller and Yu [280] that the initial segment complexity of X determines, for any Z, whether $X \oplus Z$ is 1-random. This idea then allowed them to prove the important result that $X \leqslant_K Y$ implies $X \leqslant_{\mathrm{vL}} Y$, which means that the results of the previous section have consequences for the K-degrees.

Recall that strings of length n can be thought of as representing the numbers between $2^n - 1$ and $2^{n+1} - 2$. We also need some additional notation for the proofs below.

Definition 10.3.8 (Miller and Yu [280]). Given $X = x_0x_1\dots$ and $Z = z_0z_1\dots$, let $X \mathbin{\widehat{\oplus}} Z$ be

$$z_0\, x_0\, x_1\, z_1\, x_2\, x_3\, x_4\, x_5\, z_2\, \dots\, z_n\, x_{2^n-2}\, \dots\, x_{2^{n+1}-3}\, z_{n+1}\, \dots$$

Clearly, $X \mathbin{\widehat{\oplus}} Z$ is 1-random iff $X \oplus Z$ is 1-random. In fact, $X \mathbin{\widehat{\oplus}} Z \equiv_{\text{vL}} X \oplus Z$. We can also define $\sigma \mathbin{\widehat{\oplus}} \tau$ for strings $\sigma, \tau \in 2^{<\omega}$, provided that $2^{|\tau|-1} - 2 \leqslant |\sigma| \leqslant 2^{|\tau|} - 2$.

Theorem 10.3.9 (Miller and Yu [280]). *$X \oplus Z$ is 1-random iff*

$$K(X \upharpoonright (Z \upharpoonright n)) \geqslant (Z \upharpoonright n) + n - O(1).$$

Proof. First, assume that $X \oplus Z$ is 1-random. Then $X \mathbin{\widehat{\oplus}} Z$ is also 1-random. Let $\sigma = Z \upharpoonright n$ and $\sigma' = Z \upharpoonright (n+1)$. Then $K(X \upharpoonright \sigma) = K((X \upharpoonright \sigma) \mathbin{\widehat{\oplus}} \sigma') \pm O(1)$. (We use σ' here to make the $\widehat{\oplus}$-join defined.) But $(X \upharpoonright \sigma) \mathbin{\widehat{\oplus}} \sigma' = (X \mathbin{\widehat{\oplus}} Z) \upharpoonright (\sigma + n + 1)$, so

$$K(X \upharpoonright \sigma') = K((X \mathbin{\widehat{\oplus}} Z) \upharpoonright (\sigma + n + 1)) \pm O(1) \geqslant \sigma + n - O(1).$$

For the other direction, define a prefix-free machine M as follows. To compute $M(\tau)$, look for τ_1, τ_2, η_1, and η_2 such that $\tau = \tau_1\tau_2$, for the universal prefix-free machine $\mathcal{U}$ we have $\mathcal{U}(\tau_1) = \eta_1 \mathbin{\widehat{\oplus}} \eta_2$, and $|\eta_1\tau_2| = \eta_2$. If these are found, define $M(\tau) = \eta_1\tau_2$.

Assume that $X \oplus Z$ is not 1-random. Then for each k, there is an m such that $K((X \mathbin{\widehat{\oplus}} Z) \upharpoonright m) \leqslant m - k$. Take strings η_1 and η_2 such that $\eta_1 \mathbin{\widehat{\oplus}} \eta_2 = (X \mathbin{\widehat{\oplus}} Z) \upharpoonright m$ and let τ_1 be a minimal $\mathcal{U}$-program for $\eta_1 \mathbin{\widehat{\oplus}} \eta_2$. Let $n = |\eta_2|$. Then $|\eta_1| \leqslant 2^n - 2$ and $\eta_2 \geqslant 2^n - 1$, so there is a string τ_2 such that $\eta_1\tau_2 = X \upharpoonright \eta_2$. Then $M(\tau_1\tau_2) = X \upharpoonright \eta_2$. Therefore,

$$\begin{aligned}
K(X \upharpoonright (Z \upharpoonright n)) &\leqslant K(X \upharpoonright \eta_2) \leqslant K_M(X \upharpoonright \eta_2) + O(1)\\
&\leqslant |\tau_1\tau_2| + O(1) \leqslant K(\eta_1 \mathbin{\widehat{\oplus}} \eta_2) + |\tau_2| + O(1)\\
&\leqslant |\eta_1\eta_2| - k + |\tau_2| + O(1) = |\eta_1\tau_2| + |\eta_2| - k + O(1)\\
&= \eta_2 + |\eta_2| - k + O(1) = Z \upharpoonright n + n - k + O(1),
\end{aligned}$$

where the constant depends only on M. Because k was arbitrary, $K(X \upharpoonright (Z \upharpoonright n)) - (Z \upharpoonright n) - n$ is not bounded below. □

Corollary 10.3.10 (Miller and Yu [280]). *If $X \leqslant_K Y$ then $X \leqslant_{\text{vL}} Y$.*

Combined with Theorem 10.3.3, this corollary has the following important consequence for the structure of the K-degrees.

Corollary 10.3.11 (Miller and Yu [280]).

(i) *If $X \leqslant_K Y$ and X is n-random, then Y is n-random.*

(ii) *If* $X \oplus Y$ *is* 1*-random, then* $X \mid_K Y$*, and* X *and* Y *have no upper bound in the* K*-degrees. Therefore, there is no join in the* K*-degrees.*

(iii) *If* $n \neq m$ *then the* K*-degrees of* $\Omega^{\emptyset^{(n)}}$ *and* $\Omega^{\emptyset^{(m)}}$ *have no upper bound.*

The following is another attractive corollary, which follows from Theorem 10.3.9 because X is 2-random iff $X \oplus \Omega$ is 1-random.

Corollary 10.3.12 (Miller and Yu [280]). *X is 2-random iff X is 1-random and* $K(X \upharpoonright (\Omega \upharpoonright n)) \geqslant \Omega \upharpoonright n + n - O(1)$.

Another important consequence of Corollary 10.3.10 is the following fundamental result, which shows that, while the cardinality of a K-lower cone might be big, its measure is always small. It was originally proved by direct and more complex methods.

Theorem 10.3.13 (Yu, Ding, and Downey [415]). *For any* Y*, we have* $\mu(\{X : X \leqslant_K Y\}) = 0$.

Proof. If X is 1-random relative to Y, then $X \nleqslant_{\mathrm{vL}} Y$, so by Corollary 10.3.10, $X \nleqslant_K Y$. Since there are measure 1 many X that are 1-random relative to Y, the result follows. □

Similar methods also show that the cardinality of the K-degrees of 1-random sets is as large as it can be. (Actually, since $\leqslant_K$ is Borel, the following result follows from Theorem 10.3.13 and Silver's Theorem[7] [357] that if a Borel (or even just coanalytic) equivalence relation has uncountably many classes, then it has continuum many classes.)

Theorem 10.3.14 (Yu and Ding [413]). *There are* $2^{\aleph_0}$ *many* K*-degrees of* 1*-random sets.*

Theorem 10.3.14 has a direct proof, but it follows from another theorem from classical measure theory, as observed by Miller and Yu.

Theorem 10.3.15 (Mycielski [290]). *For any relation* $E \subseteq 2^\omega \times 2^\omega$ *such that* E *includes the diagonal and* $\mu(E) = 0$*, there is a perfect set* $P \subseteq 2^\omega$ *such that* $\forall X, Y \in P\, (X \neq Y \Rightarrow (X, Y) \in \overline{E})$.

We can get Theorem 10.3.14 from Theorem 10.3.15 by considering the relation $E = \{(X, Y) : X \equiv_K Y \vee X \text{ not 1-random} \vee Y \text{ not 1-random}\}$.

10.3.4 vL-reducibility and C-reducibility

In this section we prove analogs of the results of the previous section for initial segment plain complexity. Our main result is the following.

[7]The original proof of Silver's Theorem was very complex. Silver's Theorem is sometimes called the Harrington-Silver Theorem because Harrington gave a much simpler proof using Gandy forcing, as reported in Harrington, Marker, and Shelah [175].

Theorem 10.3.16 (Miller and Yu [280]). *Let Z be 1-random. The following are equivalent.*

(i) *X is 1-random relative to Z.*

(ii) $C(X \upharpoonright n) \geqslant n - K^Z(n) - O(1)$.

(iii) $C(X \upharpoonright n) + K(Z \upharpoonright n) \geqslant 2n - O(1)$.

Proof. Suppose that Z is 1-random and X is 1-random relative to Z. Then, relativizing Theorem 6.7.2,

$$C(X \upharpoonright n) \geqslant C^Z(X \upharpoonright n) - O(1) \geqslant n - K^Z(n) - O(1),$$

so (i) implies (ii).

Now assume (ii). Since Z is 1-random, by the Ample Excess Lemma, Theorem 6.6.1, $K^Z(n) \leqslant K(Z \upharpoonright n) - n + O(1)$, and hence

$$C(X \upharpoonright n) \geqslant n - K^Z(n) - O(1) \geqslant 2n - K(Z \upharpoonright n) - O(1),$$

so (ii) implies (iii)

Finally, assume (iii). It is straightforward to check that (for any X) we have $C(X \upharpoonright (X \upharpoonright n)) \leqslant (X \upharpoonright n) - n + O(1)$. Thus

$$\begin{aligned} K(Z \upharpoonright (X \upharpoonright n)) &\geqslant 2(X \upharpoonright n) - C(X \upharpoonright (X \upharpoonright n)) - O(1) \\ &\geqslant 2(X \upharpoonright n) - (X \upharpoonright n) + n - O(1) = (X \upharpoonright n) + n - O(1). \end{aligned}$$

Hence, $Z \oplus X$ is 1-random by Theorem 10.3.9. Thus, by van Lambalgen's Theorem, X is 1-random relative to Z, so (iii) implies (i). □

The following corollary is more or less immediate.

Corollary 10.3.17 (Miller and Yu [280]).

(i) *$X \oplus Z$ is 1-random iff $C(X \upharpoonright n) + K(Z \upharpoonright n) \geqslant 2n - O(1)$.*

(ii) *$X \leqslant_C Y$ implies $X \leqslant_{\text{vL}} Y$.*

(iii) *Let $X \leqslant_C Y$. If X is n-random then Y is n-random.*

(iv) *If $X \oplus Y$ is 1-random then the C-degrees of Y and X have no upper bound, and hence there is no join in the C-degrees.*

(v) *If $n \neq m$ then the C-degrees of $\Omega^{\emptyset^{(n)}}$ and $\Omega^{\emptyset^{(m)}}$ have no upper bound.*

It follows, by the same arguments as in the previous section, that the measure of the class of sets C-reducible to a given set is always 0, and there are continuum many C-degrees of 1-random sets.

10.3.5 Contrasting vL-reducibility and K-reducibility

One might hope that K-reducibility and vL-reducibility coincide on the 1-random sets. However, the following result implies that they differ even for Δ^0_2 1-random sets. A slight modification of its proof shows that C-reducibility and vL-reducibility also do not coincide on the 1-random sets.

Theorem 10.3.18 (Miller and Yu [280]). *For any* 1*-random set* X*, there is a* 1*-random set* $Y \leqslant_{\mathrm{T}} X \oplus \emptyset'$ *such that* $X \mid_K Y$.

As noted above, Ω is vL-below every Δ^0_2 1-random set. On the other hand, Theorem 10.3.18 implies that there is a Δ^0_2 1-random $Y \mid_K \Omega$. Therefore, $\leqslant_{\mathrm{vL}}$ does not, in general, imply $\leqslant_K$ on the Δ^0_2 1-random sets.

The difficulty in proving Theorem 10.3.18 is getting the precise degree bound. Easier methods construct a $Y \leqslant_{\mathrm{T}} X'$ (in fact even with $Y' \leqslant_{\mathrm{T}} X'$) such that $X \mid_K Y$: Take a $\Pi^{0,X}_1$ class P of sets that are 1-random relative to X, then use the low basis theorem to get a member of P that is low relative to X. Then, by van Lambalgen's Theorem, $X \oplus Y$ is 1-random, and hence $X \mid_K Y$, by Corollary 10.3.11. This method would suffice to construct an infinite K-antichain in the Δ^0_2 degrees starting with a low 1-random set.

Proof of Theorem 10.3.18. Let $R = \{Z : \forall n\,(K(Z \upharpoonright n) \geqslant n)\}$ and note that $\mu(R) > 0$. We define two predicates:

$$\begin{aligned} A(\tau,p) &\iff \mu(\{Z \succ \tau : Z \notin R\}) > p \\ \text{and } B(\sigma,s) &\iff \exists n < |\sigma|\,(K(\sigma \upharpoonright n) > K(X \upharpoonright n) + s) \\ &\qquad \wedge \exists m < |\sigma|\,(K(\sigma \upharpoonright m) < K(X \upharpoonright m) - s), \end{aligned}$$

where $\sigma, \tau \in 2^{<\omega}$, $p \in \mathbb{Q}$, and $s \in \mathbb{N}$. Clearly, we can compute whether $B(\sigma, s)$ holds given $X \oplus \emptyset'$. To see that we can compute whether $A(\tau,p)$ holds given $\emptyset'$, note that $A(\tau,p)$ is equivalent to

$$\exists s\,(\mu(\{Z \succ \tau : (\exists n \leqslant s)\ K_s(Z \upharpoonright n) < n\}) > p).$$

We construct $Y = \bigcup_s \sigma_s$ by finite initial segments $\sigma_s \in 2^{<\omega}$ such that $B(\sigma_{s+1}, s)$ holds, which guarantees that $X \mid_K Y$. We also require the inductive assumption that $\mu(\{Z : Z \succ \sigma_s\} \cap R\}) > 0$, which ensures that $Y \in R$, because R is closed, and hence that Y is 1-random. Finally, the construction is done relative to the oracle $X \oplus \emptyset'$, so $Y \leqslant_{\mathrm{T}} X \oplus \emptyset'$.

Stage $s = 0$: Let $\sigma_0 = \lambda$. Note that $\mu(\{Z : Z \succ \sigma_0\} \cap R\}) = \mu(R) > 0$, so the inductive assumption holds for the base case.

Stage $s + 1$: We have defined σ_s so that $\mu(\{Z : Z \succ \sigma_s\} \cap R\}) > 0$. Using the oracle $X \oplus \emptyset'$, search for $\tau \succ \sigma_s$ and $p < 2^{-|\tau|}$ such that $B(\tau, s)$ and $\neg A(\tau,p)$. If these are found, then let $\sigma_{s+1} = \tau$ and note that it satisfies our requirements. In particular, $\mu(\{Z : Z \succ \sigma_{s+1}\} \cap R\}) \geqslant 2^{-|\sigma_{s+1}|} - p > 0$.

All that remains is to verify that the search succeeds. We know by Corollary 10.3.11 (ii) that $\mu(\{Z : Z \mid_K X\}) = 1$. Therefore, $\mu(\{Z \succ \sigma_s : Z \mid_K X\} \cap R) > 0$. So there is a $\tau \succ \sigma_s$ such that $B(\tau, s)$ and $\mu(\{Z : Z \succ \tau\} \cap R) > 0$, which implies that there is a $p \in \mathbb{Q}$ such that $p < 2^{-|\tau|}$ and $\neg A(\tau,p)$. ☐

A similar proof gives the following result.

Theorem 10.3.19 (Miller and Yu [280]). *For any finite collection $X_0, \ldots, X_n$ of 1-random sets, there is a 1-random $Y \leqslant_T X_0 \oplus \cdots \oplus X_n \oplus \emptyset'$ such that, for every $i \leqslant n$, the sets Y and X_i have no upper bound in the K-degrees.*

10.4 Upward oscillations and $\leqslant_K$-comparable 1-random sets

The main result of this section is a characterization by Miller and Yu [279] of the functions g for which $K(X \upharpoonright n)$ infinitely often exceeds $n + g(n)$ for every 1-random X. As we will see, these are exactly the functions such that $\sum_n 2^{-g(n)}$ diverges. We will then use this result to show that there are comparable K-degrees of 1-random sets. One direction of the Miller-Yu characterization follows from the Ample Excess Lemma (Theorem 6.6.1). For the harder direction, we prove the following.

Theorem 10.4.1 (Miller and Yu [279]). *If $\sum_n 2^{-f(n)} < \infty$, then there is a 1-random X such that $K(X \upharpoonright n) \leqslant n + f(n) + O(1)$. Furthermore, we can ensure that $X \leqslant_T f \oplus \emptyset'$.*

The proof of this result is broken up into two parts. The first part is essentially technical. We would like to be able to code f into a 1-random set in a compact way, but this may not be possible. Instead, we construct a function g such that $g(n) \leqslant f(n)$ for all n and g *can* be coded compactly, meaning that we can use Gács coding to produce a 1-random X such that $g(n)$ is computable from the first n bits of X, for all n. Furthermore, we ensure that $\sum_n 2^{-g(n)} < \infty$. The second part of the proof is verifying that X is the desired 1-random set, which is the content of the following result.

Lemma 10.4.2 (Bounding Lemma, Miller and Yu [279]). *If $\sum_n 2^{-g(n)} < \infty$ and $g \leqslant_T X$ with use the identity function, then $K(X \upharpoonright n) \leqslant n + g(n) + O(1)$.*

Proof. Because $\sum_n 2^{-g(n)} < \infty$, using the KC Theorem, we can ensure that $K^g(\sigma) \leqslant |\sigma| + g(|\sigma|) + O(1)$ for all σ. Furthermore, it is easy to see from the proof of the KC Theorem that we can arrange things so that, for $\sigma \in 2^n$, the only part of the oracle that is needed is $g \upharpoonright n+1$. Since $g \upharpoonright n+1$ is computable from $X \upharpoonright n$, we have a hope of removing the dependence on the oracle of the short description τ of $X \upharpoonright n$ given by the KC Theorem. However, it would appear that we need $X \upharpoonright n$ to tell us how to decode τ. As Miller and Yu put it, "it is as if we have encrypted the decryption key along with our message. We would know how to read the message if only we knew what the message said. The heart of the proof is resolving this circularity."

By the KC Theorem, there is a prefix-free oracle machine M and $\tau_0, \tau_1, \ldots$ such that $|\tau_n| \leqslant g(n)+O(1)$ and $M^X(\tau_n) = X \upharpoonright n$ for all n. We may assume that $M^X(\tau_n)$ has use exactly n and $M^X(\tau_n)$ reads exactly τ_n before halting.

We think of M as having one-way, read-only input and oracle tapes, such that reading a bit moves the corresponding head one position (so that we cannot look at the same position of either tape twice). In addition, we think of M as having work tapes, which it can use to store the bits of the input and oracle that it reads, which is why our assumptions do not limit the power of M.

The key step of the proof is to transform M into a machine M° with no oracle. We do this by routing any reading requests that M makes to either its input or oracle tape to the input tape of M°. We identify M° with the partial computable function that converges on τ with output ρ iff M° halts after reading exactly τ on its input tape and writing ρ on its output tape. In other words, we treat M° as a self-delimiting machine, which ensures that M° has prefix-free domain.

Now suppose that $M^X(\tau)\downarrow= \rho$ with use exactly n, and that M reads exactly all of the bits of τ from the input tape. At certain stages of the computation, M asks for the next bit of the input or the next bit of the oracle, and by our assumptions, it cannot ask for the same bit of either tape more than once. Now merge the bits of τ and $X \upharpoonright n$ together in exactly the order that they are requested by M, and call the resulting string σ. Then $M^\circ(\sigma)\downarrow= \rho$, because the computation of M° on σ is indistinguishable from the computation of M^X on τ. Therefore, $K_{M^\circ}(\rho) \leqslant |\sigma| = n+|\tau|$. Applying this observation to the τ_n shows that

$$K(X \upharpoonright n) \leqslant K_{M^\circ}(X \upharpoonright n) + O(1) \leqslant n + |\tau_n| + O(1) \leqslant n + g(n) + O(1).$$

□

Proof of Theorem 10.4.1. Let f be such that $\sum_n 2^{-f(n)} < \infty$. We want to construct a function g such that $g(n) \leqslant f(n)$ for all n and $\sum_n 2^{-g(n)} < \infty$, and furthermore g can be coded in a compact way. In particular, we require that

1. $g(n) \leqslant f(n)$ for all n,
2. $\sum_n 2^{-g(n)} < \infty$,
3. $g(0) = 0$,
4. if $n \not\equiv 3 \bmod 4$, then $g(n) = g(n+1)$, and
5. $|g(n+1) - g(n)| \leqslant 1$ for all n.

We want to define g to be (point-wise) maximal among the functions satisfying 1–5. That is, g satisfies 1–5 and if g' satisfies 1–5 then $g(n) \geqslant g'(n)$ for all n.

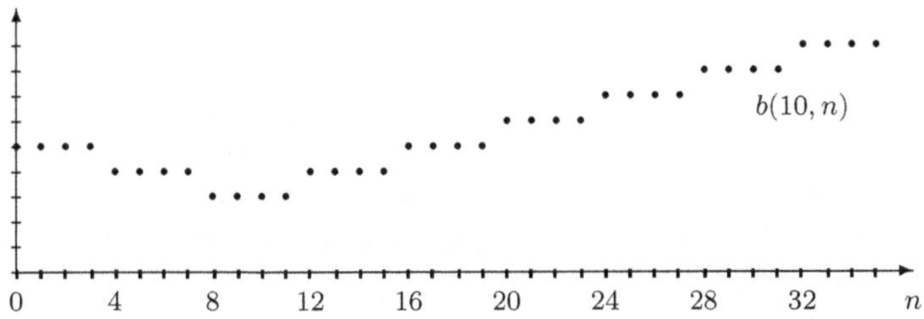

Figure 10.1. Here $f(10) = 3$ and the function $b(10, n)$ is the upper bound on the values of $g(n)$ imposed by that fact.

Any function g satisfying 3, 4, and 5 will have $g(n) \leqslant \lfloor \frac{n}{4} \rfloor$. Furthermore, because g is forced to change at a slow rate, the value of $f(n)$ not only bounds the value of $g(n)$, but also places bounds on all values of g. For example, if $f(10) = 3$, then g is at most 3 on $[8, 11]$, at most 4 on $[4, 7]$ and $[12, 15]$, and so on. Let $b(i, n)$ be the upper bound placed on $g(n)$ by the value of $f(i)$ (see Figure 10.1). Putting together all of the restrictions on $g(n)$, we define

$$g(n) = \min\{\lfloor \tfrac{n}{4} \rfloor, \min_i b(i, n)\}. \qquad (10.1)$$

Clearly g satisfies 1, 3, 4, and 5, and is point-wise maximal among functions that do so. To verify that $\sum_n 2^{-g(n)} < \infty$, note that for any i,

$$\sum_n 2^{-b(i,n)} \leqslant 4 \cdot 2^{-f(i)} + 8 \sum_{n>0} 2^{-f(i)-n} = 12 \cdot 2^{-f(i)}.$$

Therefore,

$$\sum_n 2^{-g(n)} \leqslant \sum_n \left(2^{-\lfloor \frac{n}{4} \rfloor} + \sum_i 2^{-b(i,n)} \right)$$
$$= \sum_n 2^{-\lfloor \frac{n}{4} \rfloor} + \sum_i \sum_n 2^{-b(i,n)} \leqslant 8 + \sum_i 12 \cdot 2^{-f(i)} < \infty.$$

Next we prove that $g \leqslant_{\mathrm{T}} f$. Clearly, $b \leqslant_{\mathrm{T}} f$. Although (10.1) expresses $g(n)$ as the minimum of an infinite f-computable sequence, it is not hard to see that we can ignore all but finitely many terms. In particular, if $i \geqslant 2n$, then $b(i, n) \geqslant \lfloor \frac{n}{4} \rfloor$, so

$$g(n) = \min\{\lfloor \tfrac{n}{4} \rfloor, \min_{i<2n} b(i, n)\}.$$

Thus $g \leqslant_{\mathrm{T}} f$.

The restrictions placed on g allow us to code it compactly into a set C. It is of course necessary only to record the value of $g(n+1) - g(n)$ for all $n \equiv 3 \pmod 4$. Two bits are sufficient to code $g(n+1) - g(n)$ because there are only three possible values. Thus we use the first two bits of C to record $g(4) - g(3)$, the next two for $g(8) - g(7)$, and so on. Note that $g(n)$

can be computed from $C \upharpoonright \lfloor \frac{n}{2} \rfloor$ (or more precisely, $C \upharpoonright (2\lfloor \frac{n}{4} \rfloor)$). Of course, $C \leqslant_T g \leqslant_T f$.

By the Kučera-Gács Theorem 8.3.2, there is a 1-random X such that $C \leqslant_T X$ and $X \leqslant_T C \oplus \emptyset' \leqslant_T f \oplus \emptyset'$. (The upper bound on the complexity of X is clear from the construction in the proof of Theorem 8.3.2, and made more explicit in Theorem 8.5.1.) As was mentioned following the proof of Theorem 8.3.2, the Gács version of that result produces an X that computes C with use $2n$,[8] meaning that only the first $2n$ bits of X are used to compute $C \upharpoonright n$. Therefore, $g(n)$ is computable from $X \upharpoonright n$, for all n. Hence the Bounding Lemma 10.4.2 implies that $K(X \upharpoonright n) \leqslant n + g(n) + O(1) \leqslant n + f(n) + O(1)$. □

The following corollary improves an earlier result by Bienvenu and Downey [39] (Corollary 8.4.3). Their result was the same, but assuming that the function h tends to infinity rather than just being unbounded.

Corollary 10.4.3 (Miller and Yu [279]). *If h is unbounded, then there is a 1-random X such that $K(X \upharpoonright n) < n + h(n)$ for infinitely many n.*

Proof. Choose a sequence of distinct natural numbers $\{n_i\}_{i \in \omega}$ such that $h(n_i) \geqslant 2i$. Let

$$f(n) = \begin{cases} i & \text{if } n = n_i \\ n & \text{otherwise.} \end{cases}$$

We can apply Theorem 10.4.1 because $\sum_n 2^{-f(n)} \leqslant \sum_i 2^{-i} + \sum_n 2^{-n} = 4$, so there is a 1-random X such that $K(X \upharpoonright n) \leqslant n + f(n) + O(1)$. Therefore,

$$K(X \upharpoonright n_i) \leqslant n_i + f(n_i) + O(1) = n_i + i + O(1) \leqslant n_i + h(n_i) - i + O(1).$$

When i is sufficiently large, $K(X \upharpoonright n_i) \leqslant n_i + h(n_i)$. □

To construct comparable 1-random K-degrees, we need a stronger form of Theorem 10.4.1. It is clear that we can modify the proof of that result to require that $g(n) = g(n+1)$ whenever $n \not\equiv 7 \pmod 8$. Then g can be coded into C so that $g \leqslant_T C$ with use $\lfloor n/4 \rfloor$. By Gács coding, there is a 1-random $X \leqslant_T f \oplus \emptyset'$ such that g is computable from X with use $\lfloor \frac{n}{2} \rfloor$. So for any Z, we have $g \leqslant_T X \oplus Z$ with use n. Applying the Bounding Lemma 10.4.2 gives the following result.

Theorem 10.4.4 (Miller and Yu [279]). *If $\sum_n 2^{-f(n)} < \infty$ then there is a 1-random $X \leqslant_T f \oplus \emptyset'$ such that $K((X \oplus Z) \upharpoonright n) \leqslant n + f(n) + O(1)$ for every Z.*

---

[8] Indeed, as mentioned there, Merkle and Mihailović [267] adapted the construction in Gács [167] to show that the use of the wtt-reduction in the Kučera-Gács Theorem can be on the order of $n + o(n)$.

We can now give the desired classification of functions coding the upward oscillations of initial segment complexities of 1-random sets. First we need a relatively straightforward lemma.

Lemma 10.4.5 (Miller and Yu [279]). *Assume that* $\sum_n 2^{-g(n)} < \infty$.

(i) *There is a function* $f \leqslant_T g$ *with* $f(n) \leqslant g(n)$ *for all* n *and* $\limsup_n g(n) - f(n) = \infty$ *such that* $\sum_n 2^{-f(n)} < \infty$.

(ii) *There is a function* $f \leqslant_T g'$ *such that* $\lim_n g(n) - f(n) = \infty$ *and* $\sum_n 2^{-f(n)} < \infty$.

Proof. (i) For each m, let $n_m = \min\{n : g(n) \geqslant 2m\}$ and let $f(n_m) = \lfloor g(n_m)/2 \rfloor$. Let $f(n) = g(n)$ for all other values of n. Then

$$\sum_n 2^{-f(n)} \leqslant \sum_n 2^{-g(n)} + \sum_m 2^{-m} < \infty.$$

Clearly, $f(n) \leqslant g(n)$ for all n. Furthermore, $f \leqslant_T g$ and $\limsup_n g(n) - f(n) = \infty$.

(ii) Let $c \geqslant \sum_n 2^{-g(n)}$. Then g' computes an increasing sequence $\{n_i\}_{i\in\omega}$ such that $\sum_{n \geqslant n_i} 2^{-g(n)} \leqslant \frac{c}{2^i}$ for all i. We may assume that $n_0 = 0$. Let $f(n) = g(n) - \lfloor \log |\{i : c_i \leqslant n\}| \rfloor$ (or $f(n) = 0$ if this value is negative). Then

$$\sum_n 2^{-f(n)} \leqslant \sum_n |\{i : n_i \leqslant n\}|\, 2^{-g(n)}$$
$$= \sum_i \sum_{n \geqslant n_i} 2^{-g(n)} \leqslant \sum_i \frac{c}{2^i} = 2c < \infty.$$

Furthermore, $f \leqslant_T g'$ and $\lim_n g(n) - f(n) = \infty$. □

Theorem 10.4.6 (Miller and Yu [279]). *The following are equivalent.*

(i) $\sum_n 2^{-g(n)} = \infty$.

(ii) *For every* 1*-random* X*, there are infinitely many* n *such that* $K(X \upharpoonright n) > n + g(n)$.

Proof. (i) $\Rightarrow$ (ii) We prove the contrapositive. Assume that X is 1-random and there is an m such that $\forall n \geqslant m\,(K(X \upharpoonright n) \leqslant n + g(n))$. Then $\sum_{n \geqslant m} 2^{n-K(X\upharpoonright n)} \geqslant \sum_{n\geqslant m} 2^{-g(n)}$. The first sum is finite by the Ample Excess Lemma, Theorem 6.6.1, so $\sum_n 2^{-g(n)}$ converges.

(ii) $\Rightarrow$ (i) Again we prove the contrapositive. Assume that $\sum_n 2^{-g(n)}$ converges. By Lemma 10.4.5 (ii), there is a function f such that $\lim_n g(n) - f(n) = \infty$ and $\sum_n 2^{-f(n)} < \infty$. Hence, by Theorem 10.4.1, there is a 1-random X such that $K(X \upharpoonright n) \leqslant n + f(n) + O(1)$. This inequality, together with the fact that $\lim_n g(n) - f(n) = \infty$, implies that $K(X \upharpoonright n) \leqslant n + g(n)$ for almost all n. □

We are now ready to prove that there are comparable 1-random K-degrees. It seems surprising that this result relies on such difficult methods, whereas obtaining incomparable 1-random K-degrees (as in Corollary 10.3.11) is relatively straightforward.

Theorem 10.4.7 (Miller and Yu [279]). *For every 1-random A, there is a 1-random $B \leqslant_{\mathrm{T}} A \oplus \emptyset'$ such that $B <_K A$.*

Proof. Let $g(n) = K(A \upharpoonright n) - n$ and note that $g \leqslant_{\mathrm{T}} A \oplus \emptyset'$. By Lemma 10.4.5 (i), there is a function f majorized by g such that $\sum_n 2^{-f(n)} < \infty$ and $\limsup_n g(n) - f(n) = \infty$. Furthermore, $f \leqslant_{\mathrm{T}} g \leqslant_{\mathrm{T}} A \oplus \emptyset'$. Applying Theorem 10.4.1 to f produces a 1-random $B \leqslant_{\mathrm{T}} f \oplus \emptyset' \leqslant_{\mathrm{T}} A \oplus \emptyset'$ such that $K(B \upharpoonright n) \leqslant n + f(n) + O(1)$. But then

$$K(B \upharpoonright n) \leqslant n + f(n) + O(1) \leqslant n + g(n) + O(1) = K(A \upharpoonright n) + O(1),$$

so $B \leqslant_K A$. Furthermore,

$$\begin{aligned}\limsup_n K(A \upharpoonright n) - K(B \upharpoonright n) &\geqslant \limsup_n K(A \upharpoonright n) - n - f(n) - O(1) \\ &\geqslant \limsup_n g(n) - f(n) - O(1) = \infty,\end{aligned}$$

so $A \nleqslant_K B$. □

Corollary 10.4.8 (Miller and Yu [279]). *For every Δ^0_2 1-random A, there is a Δ^0_2 1-random B such that $B <_K A$.*

Miller and Yu [279] observed that by weakening the complexity restriction on B in Theorem 10.4.7, we can replace $<_K$ with what appears to be a stronger relation.

Definition 10.4.9 (Miller and Yu [279]). We say that B is *strongly K-below* A, and write $B \ll_K A$, if $\lim_n K(A \upharpoonright n) - K(B \upharpoonright n) = \infty$.

Clearly $B \ll_K A$ implies $B <_K A$, but the converse is open.

Theorem 10.4.10 (Miller and Yu [279]). *For every 1-random A, there is a 1-random $B \leqslant_{\mathrm{T}} A'$ such that $B \ll_K A$.*

Proof. First, we wish to find a function g such that $\sum_n 2^{-g(n)}$ converges and $g(n) \leqslant K(A \upharpoonright n) - n$ for all n. To control the complexity of B, we also require g to be low relative to A (otherwise, we could simply let $g(n) = K(A \upharpoonright n) - n$). By the Ample Excess Lemma, Theorem 6.6.1, there is a c such that $\sum_n 2^{n-K(A \upharpoonright n)} \leqslant c$. Define a $\Pi^{0,A}_1$ class $S \subseteq \omega^\omega$ by

$$S = \Big\{ g \in \omega^\omega : \sum_n 2^{-g(n)} \leqslant c \text{ and } \forall n\, (g(n) \leqslant K(A \upharpoonright n) - n) \Big\}.$$

Note that S is computably bounded (meaning that there is a computable function that majorizes every element of S), because $K(A \upharpoonright n) - n \leqslant K(n) +$

$O(1) \leqslant 2\log n + O(1)$.[9] Therefore, by the low basis theorem relativized to A, there is a function $g \in S$ such that $g' \leqslant_T A'$.

By Lemma 10.4.5 (ii), there is an f such that $\sum_n 2^{-f(n)} < \infty$ and $\lim_n g(n) - f(n) = \infty$, and furthermore, $f \leqslant_T g' \leqslant_T A'$. Apply Theorem 10.4.1 to f to produce a 1-random $B \leqslant_T f \oplus \emptyset' \leqslant_T A' \oplus \emptyset' \leqslant_T A'$ such that $K(B \upharpoonright n) \leqslant n + f(n) + O(1)$. Then

$$\begin{aligned}\lim_n K(A \upharpoonright n) - K(B \upharpoonright n) &\geqslant \lim_n K(A \upharpoonright n) - n - f(n) - O(1) \\ &\geqslant \lim_n g(n) - f(n) - O(1) = \infty.\end{aligned}$$

□

Taking A in the previous corollary to be low, we have the following.

Corollary 10.4.11 (Miller and Yu [279]). *There are Δ^0_2 1-random sets A and B such that $B \ll_K A$.*

We finish this section with an application of the Bounding Lemma (and other results of Miller and Yu) to extend work of Solovay described earlier in this chapter. Recall Theorem 8.4.3, which states that there is no function g that tends to infinity such that $K(A \upharpoonright n) \geqslant n + g(n) - O(1)$ for every 1-random A. As we have seen in Corollary 10.3.17, Miller and Yu [280] showed that if Z is 1-random, then X and Z are relatively 1-random iff $K(X \upharpoonright n) + C(Z \upharpoonright n) \geqslant 2n - O(1)$. Taking $Z = \Omega$, we see that a 1-random set X is 2-random iff $K(X \upharpoonright n) \geqslant n + f(n) + O(1)$, where $f(n) = n - C(\Omega \upharpoonright n)$, which tends to infinity because Ω is not infinitely often C-random (see Theorem 6.11.3). Thus we have a "single gap characterization" of 2-randomness (which can be extended to n-randomness for $n > 2$ by replacing Ω by a 1-random set Turing equivalent to $\emptyset^{(n-1)}$), and hence Theorem 8.4.3 does not hold for 2-randomness. Miller [unpublished] has shown that there is a characterization of 2-randomness via a single gap given by a function f that is not just unbounded, but also nondecreasing (i.e., an order). In fact, f can be taken to be Solovay's function $s(n) = -\log \sum_{j \geqslant n} 2^{-K(j)}$ defined in Section 10.2.2.

It will be convenient to use a different characterization of s. We take $\Omega = \sum_m 2^{-K(m)}$ (which is a 1-random left-c.e. real and hence a version of Ω) and $\Omega_n = \sum_{m<n} 2^{-K_n(m)}$. Let $\gamma(n) = -\log(\Omega - \Omega_n)$. (It is not hard to show that γ is independent up to an additive constant of the choice of version of Ω and corresponding approximation.)

Lemma 10.4.12 (Miller [unpublished]). $\gamma(n) = s(n) \pm O(1)$.

Proof. We have $\Omega - \Omega_n \geqslant \sum_{m \geqslant n} 2^{-K(m)}$, so $\gamma(n) \leqslant s(n) + O(1)$. For the other direction, let $f(n) = -\log(\Omega_{n+1} - \Omega_n)$. Then $\sum_n 2^{-f(n)} = \Omega < \infty$.

[9] See footnote 11 on page 73 for a comment on computably bounded Π^0_1 classes in ω^ω.

Since f is computable, we have $K(m) \leqslant f(m) + O(1)$, so

$$s(n) = -\log \sum_{m \geqslant n} 2^{-K(m)} \leqslant -\log \sum_{m \geqslant n} 2^{-f(m)} + O(1)$$

$$= -\log \sum_{m \geqslant n} (\Omega_{m+1} - \Omega_m) + O(1) = -\log(\Omega - \Omega_n) + O(1) = \gamma(n) + O(1).$$

□

Let $\widehat{\gamma}(n) = \max\{k : \Omega_n \upharpoonright k = \Omega \upharpoonright k\}$. Since $\Omega - \Omega_n \leqslant 2^{-\widehat{\gamma}(n)}$, we have $\widehat{\gamma}(n) \leqslant \gamma(n) + O(1)$. (Miller asked whether $\widehat{\gamma}$ is independent up to a constant of the choice of Ω and $\{\Omega_n\}_{n \in \omega}$, and whether in fact $\widehat{\gamma}(n) = \gamma(n) \pm O(1)$.)

Theorem 10.4.13 (Miller [unpublished]). *The following are equivalent.*

(i) *A is 2-random.*

(ii) $K(A \upharpoonright n) \geqslant n + \gamma(n) - O(1)$.

(iii) $\lim_n K(A \upharpoonright n) - n - \gamma(n) = \infty$.

The same equivalences hold with γ replaced by $\widehat{\gamma}$.

Proof. It is clear that (iii) implies (ii). Since $\widehat{\gamma}(n) \leqslant \gamma(n) + O(1)$, each of (ii) and (iii) for γ implies the respective condition for $\widehat{\gamma}$. So it is enough to show that (i) implies (iii) for γ and (ii) for $\widehat{\gamma}$ implies (i). We assume that A is 1-random, since otherwise none of the conditions hold.

We first assume that (iii) does not hold and conclude that A is not 2-random. By Corollary 6.6.4, $K^A(n) \leqslant K(A \upharpoonright n) - n + O(1)$, so there is a c such that $S = \{n : K^A(n) \leqslant \gamma(n) + c\}$ is infinite. Define a prefix-free machine M^A as follows. If $\mathcal{U}^A(\sigma)\downarrow = n$, then let $M^A(\sigma 0) = \Omega_n \upharpoonright (|\sigma| - c)$ and $M^A(\sigma 1) = (\Omega_n + 2^{-|\sigma|+c}) \upharpoonright (|\sigma| - c)$. Fix $n \in S$ and let σ be a minimal length $\mathcal{U}^A$-program for n. Then $|\sigma| - c = K^A(n) - c \leqslant \gamma(n)$, so $\Omega - \Omega_n \leqslant 2^{-|\sigma|+c}$. Thus one of $M^A(\sigma 0)$ and $M^A(\sigma 1)$ is equal to $\Omega \upharpoonright (|\sigma| - c)$. Therefore, $K^A(\Omega \upharpoonright (|\sigma| - c)) \leqslant |\sigma| + O(1)$ for infinitely many σ. But then Ω is not 1-random relative to A, by the relativized version of Corollary 6.6.2, and hence, by van Lambalgen's Theorem, A is not 1-random relative to Ω. In other words, A is not 2-random.

We now assume that A is not 2-random and conclude that (ii) does not hold for $\widehat{\gamma}$. Define a function g by recursion on n as follows. To define $g(n)$, look for the length-lexicographically least σ such that $\mathcal{U}_n^{A \upharpoonright n}(\sigma) \prec \Omega_n$. If there is no such σ then let $g(n) = n$. Otherwise, let $g(n) = |\sigma|$ and mark σ as used. Note that $g(n)$ can be computed from $A \upharpoonright n$, and that $\sum_n 2^{-g(n)} \leqslant \sum_{\sigma \in \mathrm{dom}(\mathcal{U}^A)} 2^{-|\sigma|} + \sum_n 2^{-n} < \infty$. Thus, by the Bounding Lemma, Theorem 10.4.2, $K(A \upharpoonright n) \leqslant n + g(n) + O(1)$.

By van Lambalgen's Theorem, Ω is not 1-random relative to A. Fix c and let m be such that $K^A(\Omega \upharpoonright m) \leqslant m - c$. Let σ be the length-lexicographically least $\mathcal{U}^A$-program for $\Omega \upharpoonright m$. For all sufficiently large n, we have $\mathcal{U}_n^{A \upharpoonright n}(\sigma)\downarrow$ and $\Omega_n \upharpoonright m = \Omega \upharpoonright m$. Therefore, σ is eventually used in the definition of g for some n, and we have $g(n) = |\sigma| \leqslant m - c$. But $\Omega_n \upharpoonright m = \Omega \upharpoonright m$, so $\widehat{\gamma}(n) \geqslant m$. Thus

$$K(A \upharpoonright n) \leqslant n + g(n) + O(1) \leqslant n + m - c + O(1) \leqslant n + \widehat{\gamma}(n) - c + O(1).$$

Since c is arbitrary, (ii) does not hold for $\widehat{\gamma}$. □

Miller [unpublished] also showed that there is no A such that $K(A \upharpoonright n) \geqslant n + \alpha(n) - O(1)$.

10.5 LR-reducibility

On the 1-random sets, vL- and LR-reducibility coincide, but LR-reducibility is also quite interesting and important on non-1-random sets. Many questions in randomness can be construed as ones about the structure of the LR-degrees. The following basic result provides a tool for investigating LR-reducibility.

Theorem 10.5.1 (Kjos-Hanssen [203]). *The following are equivalent.*

(i) $A \leqslant_{\mathrm{LR}} B$.

(ii) *For every $\Sigma_1^{0,A}$ class T^A of measure less than 1, there is a $\Sigma_1^{0,B}$ class V^B such that $\mu(V^B) < 1$ and $T^A \subseteq V^B$.*

(iii) *For some member U^A of a universal Martin-Löf test relative to A, there is a $\Sigma_1^{0,B}$ class V^B such that $\mu(V^B) < 1$ and $U^A \subseteq V^B$.*

Consequently, $A \leqslant_{\mathrm{LR}} B$ iff every $\Pi_1^{0,A}$ class of positive measure has a $\Pi_1^{0,B}$ subclass of positive measure.

We will give a proof due to Barmpalias, Lewis, and Soskova [25], which is conceptually simpler than Kjos-Hanssen's original proof, but along similar lines.[10] We begin with three lemmas.

The first concerns oracle Martin-Löf tests. We can think of such a test as a uniformly c.e. sequence $\{U_n\}_{n\in\omega}$ of sets of axioms of the form (τ, σ), letting $U_n^\beta = [\![\{\sigma : \exists\tau \preccurlyeq \beta\,[(\tau,\sigma) \in U_n]\}]\!]$, where $\beta \in 2^\omega$ or $\beta \in 2^{<\omega}$. It is easy to see that any oracle Martin-Löf test can be represented in this way, and that the following holds.

Lemma 10.5.2 (Barmpalias, Lewis, and Soskova [25]). *There is a universal oracle Martin-Löf test $\{U_n\}_{n\in\omega}$ with the following properties.*

(i) *From a c.e. index for an oracle Martin-Löf test $\{V_n\}_{n\in\omega}$, we can compute a k such that for all $A \in 2^\omega$ and all n, we have $V_{n+k}^A \subseteq U_n^A$.*

[10] That (iii) implies (i) in the $B = \emptyset$ case was noted by Kučera and Terwijn [223] and formed an important tool in their proof that there is a noncomputable c.e. set $A \leqslant_{\mathrm{LR}} \emptyset$, Corollary 11.2.6 below.

(ii) *If* $(\tau_1, \sigma_1), (\tau_2, \sigma_2) \in U_n$ *and* $\tau_1 \prec \tau_2$, *then* $\sigma_1 \mid \sigma_2$.

(iii) *If* $(\tau, \sigma) \in U_n$ *then* $|\tau| = |\sigma|$ *and* $(\tau, \sigma) \in U_{n,|\tau|} \setminus U_{n,|\tau|-1}$.

For sets of strings U and V, let $UV = \{\sigma\tau : \sigma \in U \wedge \tau \in V\}$. Let $U^0 = 2^{<\omega}$ and $U^{n+1} = U^n U$. (So $U^1 = U$ and $U^2 = UU$, for instance.)

Lemma 10.5.3 (Kjos-Hanssen [203]). *Let* $[\![U_0]\!], [\![U_1]\!]$ *be open sets and* S *a* $\Sigma_1^{0,B}$ *class of measure less than* 1 *such that* $[\![U_0 U_1]\!] \subseteq S$. *Then there is a* $\Sigma_1^{0,B}$ *class* R *of measure less than* 1 *such that* $[\![U_i]\!] \subseteq R$ *for at least one* $i = 0, 1$.

Hence, by iteration, if $[\![U]\!]$ *is an open set and* S *is a* $\Sigma_1^{0,B}$ *class of measure less than* 1 *such that* $[\![U^n]\!] \subseteq S$ *for some* $n > 0$, *then there is a* $\Sigma_1^{0,B}$ *class* R *of measure less than* 1 *such that* $[\![U]\!] \subseteq R$.

Proof. It suffices to prove the first part of the lemma, since the second one then follows by induction.

First suppose that there is a $\sigma \in U_0$ such that $\mu([\![\sigma]\!] \setminus S) > 0$. Then we can let $R = [\![\{\tau : [\![\sigma\tau]\!] \subseteq S\}]\!]$ and note that $\mu(R) < 1$ and $[\![U_1]\!] \subseteq R$.

Otherwise, let q be a rational such that $\mu(S) < 1 - q$ and let $R = [\![\{\sigma : \mu([\![\sigma]\!] \setminus S) < q2^{-|\sigma|}\}]\!]$. Then $[\![U_0]\!] \subseteq R$ and $(1 - q)\mu(R) \leqslant \mu(S)$, whence $\mu(R) < 1$. □

Lemma 10.5.4 (Barmpalias, Lewis, and Soskova [25]). *Let* $\{U_n\}_{n\in\omega}$ *be a universal oracle Martin-Löf test. If* $A \leqslant_{\text{LR}} B$ *then there are* σ *and* $e > 0$ *such that* $[\![\sigma]\!] \not\subseteq U_1^B$ *and* $U_e^A \cap [\![\sigma]\!] \subseteq U_1^B \cap [\![\sigma]\!]$.

Proof. Suppose otherwise. Let $\sigma_0 = \lambda$. Given σ_n such that $[\![\sigma_n]\!] \not\subseteq U_1^B$, let $\sigma_{n+1} \succ \sigma_n$ be such that $[\![\sigma_{n+1}]\!] \subseteq U_n^A$ and $[\![\sigma_{n+1}]\!] \not\subseteq U_1^B$, which must exist because $U_n^A \cap [\![\sigma_n]\!] \not\subseteq U_1^B \cap [\![\sigma_n]\!]$. Let $X = \lim_n \sigma_n$. Then $X \in U_n^A$ for all n, so X is not 1-random relative to A, but $X \notin U_1^B$, so X is 1-random relative to B, which is a contradiction. □

Proof of Theorem 10.5.1. First suppose that $A \leqslant_{\text{LR}} B$. Let $\{U_n\}_{n\in\omega}$ be the test of Lemma 10.5.2. Let σ and e be as in Lemma 10.5.4. Let $W^B = \overline{[\![\sigma]\!]} \cup (U_1^B \cap [\![\sigma]\!])$. Then W^B is a $\Sigma_1^{0,B}$ class, and $U_e^A \subseteq W^B$, by the choice of σ and e. Since $[\![\sigma]\!] \not\subseteq U_1^B$, we have $\overline{W^B} \neq \emptyset$. But $\overline{W^B}$ is a $\Pi_1^{0,B}$ class, and every element of $\overline{W^B}$ is in $\overline{U_1^B}$, and hence is 1-random relative to B. Thus $\mu(\overline{W^B}) > 0$, and hence $\mu(W^B) < 1$, so we have (iii).

Now consider a $\Sigma_1^{0,A}$ class T^A of measure less than 1, thought of as a prefix-free set of strings. Then some subsequence of $\{(T^A)^k\}_{k\in\omega}$ is a Martin-Löf test relative to A. By the properties of $\{U_n\}_{n\in\omega}$, there is a k such that $(T^A)^k \subseteq U_e^A$. Hence $(T^A)^k \subseteq W^B$ and by Lemma 10.5.3 we have (ii).

Finally, assume (iii). That is, assume there exist $V^A \subseteq T^B$ such that V^A is a member of a universal Martin-Löf test relative to A, the class T^B is $\Sigma_1^{0,B}$, and $\mu(T^B) < 1$. Let X be 1-random relative to B. By the relativized form of Theorem 6.10.2, there are Y and σ such that $X = \sigma Y$

and $Y \in \overline{T^B} \subseteq \overline{V^A}$. Then Y is 1-random relative to A, and hence so is X. Thus $A \leqslant_{\mathrm{LR}} B$. □

Space considerations preclude us from giving too many details about the structure of the LR-degrees, but here are some known facts. Additional results may be found in, for example, [18, 19, 24, 25, 26]. We will meet LR-reducibility again in Section 11.9, in the context of studying lowness for weak 2-randomness.

Theorem 10.5.5 (Barmpalias, Lewis, and Soskova [25]). *Every non-GL_2 set has uncountably many LR-predecessors.*

Theorem 10.5.6 (Barmpalias, Lewis, and Stephan [26]). *Let A be noncomputable. Then there are $B \mid_{\mathrm{T}} A$ and $C >_{\mathrm{T}} A$ in the LR-degree of A.*

Theorem 10.5.7 (Barmpalias [18]). *There is no minimal pair of Δ^0_2 LR-degrees.*

Theorem 10.5.8 (Barmpalias [18]). *Every Δ^0_2 LR-degree bounds a nonzero c.e. LR-degree.*

As a representative example, we sketch the proof of Theorem 10.5.8. (The proof of Theorem 10.5.7 is similar.) We select this theorem because its proof involves a technique that is particular to the LR-degrees and relies heavily on Theorem 10.5.1.

Proof sketch of Theorem 10.5.8. Let $X \nleqslant_{\mathrm{LR}} \emptyset$ be Δ^0_2. We build a c.e. set A such that $\emptyset <_{\mathrm{LR}} A \leqslant_{\mathrm{LR}} X$. Let $\{U_n\}_{n\in\omega}$ be a universal oracle Martin-Löf test, and write U for U_4 (so that $\mu(U^Z) < \frac{1}{8}$ for all Z). By Theorem 10.5.1, to ensure that $A \leqslant_{\mathrm{LR}} X$, it is enough to build a $\Sigma^{0,X}_1$ class S^X such that $\mu(S^X) < 1$ and $U^A \subseteq S^X$.

Let $V_0, V_1, \ldots$ be an effective enumeration of all Σ^0_1 classes with $\mu(V_e) < 1 - 2^{-e}$ for all e. By Theorem 10.5.1, to ensure that $A \nleqslant_{\mathrm{LR}} \emptyset$, it is enough to build a $\Sigma^{0,A}_1$ class Q^A such that $\mu(Q^A) < 1$ and the requirements

$$R_e : Q^A \nsubseteq V_e$$

are satisfied. For the sake of these requirements, we will build auxiliary Σ^0_1 classes E_e, and use the fact that, again by Theorem 10.5.1, for each i, either $U^X_i \nsubseteq E_e$ or $\mu(E_e) = 1$, since $X \nleqslant_{\mathrm{LR}} \emptyset$.

We identify our oracle Σ^0_1 classes with their sets of generators, so that we can say, for instance, that $[\![\sigma]\!] \in U^A[s]$ with a certain use u.

Whenever we have $[\![\sigma]\!] \in (U^A \setminus S^X)[s]$, we let $a(\sigma, s)$ be the use with which $[\![\sigma]\!] \in U^A[s]$ and add $[\![\sigma]\!]$ to $S^X[s+1]$ with use $a(\sigma, s)$. Of course, $X \upharpoonright a(\sigma, s)$ may change several times, requiring us to keep putting $[\![\sigma]\!]$ back into S^X, but since X is Δ^0_2, if $a(\sigma, t) = a(\sigma, s)$ for all $t > s$, then eventually we will have $[\![\sigma]\!] \in S^X$ permanently.

This method clearly ensures that $U^A \subseteq S^X$, but since A will not be computable, $A \upharpoonright a(\sigma, s)$ may well change after stage s, at a point at which we have already put $[\![\sigma]\!]$ into S^X with an X-correct use. We have then added an interval to S^X that may not be in U^A, which is a threat to our requirement that $\mu(S^X) < 1$. Thus we estimate the *cost*[11] $c(n, s)$ of enumerating n into A at stage s to be $\mu(\{Z : Z \in U^A[s]$ with use greater than $n\})$.

To describe how these costs stack up, and how we can deal with the above problem using the fact that $X \not\leqslant_{\mathrm{LR}} \emptyset$, we discuss how we meet the R_e, which are the sources of the A-changes. The basic plan is simple. We choose a finite set of strings Δ_e such that $[\![\Delta_e]\!]$ is currently disjoint from V_e, and put $[\![\Delta_e]\!]$ into Q^A with some large use $n+1$. We then wait for $[\![\Delta_e]\!]$ to enter V_e, and remove $[\![\Delta_e]\!]$ from Q^A by enumerating n into A. We then repeat this procedure enough times to ensure that, since $\mu(V_e) < 1 - 2^{-e}$, eventually one of our $[\![\Delta_e]\!]$ never enters V_e, so that $Q^A \not\subseteq V_e$.

Unfortunately, every time we put a number n into A, we may incur a cost, as explained above. When we put $[\![\Delta_e]\!]$ into Q^A, the opponent can also put $[\![\Delta_e]\!]$ into U^A with the same use, forcing us to put $[\![\Delta_e]\!]$ into S^X. The cost incurred when we put n into A and remove $[\![\Delta_e]\!]$ from Q^A causes a problem unless we can ensure that $X \upharpoonright n+1$ is different from all the values $X[s] \upharpoonright n+1$ for which we have declared that $[\![\Delta_e]\!] \subseteq S^{X[s]\upharpoonright n+1}$. Thus, we need a method of forcing enough X-changes to avoid these problems.

To do so, we will have to be careful in how we select the $[\![\Delta_e]\!]$'s, and will use our auxiliary class E_e. We will keep $\mu(E_e) \leqslant \mu(V_e) < 1$ and, as long as V_e seems to be covering Q^A, we will attempt to make E_e cover $U^X_{b_e}$ for some $b_e > e$, chosen dynamically during the construction. (The larger b_e is, the smaller the measure of $U^X_{b_e}$ is, so being able to change b_e as we go along will allow us to deal with injuries to R_e.) Since $X \not\leqslant_{\mathrm{LR}} \emptyset$, we cannot succeed in making E_e cover $U^X_{b_e}$ for the final value of b_e. We will be able to arrange things so that the X-changes that prevent us from doing so are exactly the ones needed to ensure that the costs described above do not hurt us too much.

We now describe the basic module for satisfying R_e, using parameters a_e and b_e determined by the construction. Let $k_e[s]$ be the least k such that $U^{X[s]\upharpoonright k}_{b_e} \setminus E_e[s] \neq \emptyset$, let $C_e[s] = U^{X[s]\upharpoonright k_e[s]}_{b_e} \setminus E_e[s]$, and let $m_e[s] = \mu(C_e[s])$. The module also has a parameter r_e, initially set to 0. At a stage s_0 at which we wish to launch an attack on R_e, the module proceeds as follows.

1. Let $p_e[s_0] = 2^{-r_e[s_0]-e-6} m_e[s_0]$. Let Δ_e be a finite set of strings such that $\mu([\![\Delta_e]\!]) = p_e[s_0]$ and $[\![\Delta_e]\!] \cap V_e[s_0] = \emptyset$. Put $[\![\Delta_e]\!]$ into Q^A with a fresh large use n_e.

2. Wait for a stage $s_1 > s_0$ such that $[\![\Delta_e]\!] \subseteq V_e[s_1]$.

[11]The idea of *cost functions* will play an important role in Chapters 11 and 14.

(a) Suppose that, while we are waiting, $X \upharpoonright k_e[s_0]$ change before s_1 is found. Then increase r_e by one, declare that $[\![\Delta_e]\!]$ is *trash*, and return to step 1.

(b) Suppose that we find s_1.

i. If $c(n_e, s_0) \geqslant a_e p_e[s_0]$, then restrain $A \upharpoonright s_1$ and return to step 1.

ii. Otherwise, proceed as follows. Put n_e into A, thus removing $[\![\Delta_e]\!]$ from Q^A. Put a subset of $C_e[s_0]$ of measure $p_e[s_0]$ into E_e and return to step 1.

We first analyze this module assuming that step 2(a) does not happen. Indeed, for simplicity, let us first assume that $p_e[s_0] = m_e[s_0]$. We clearly have $\mu(E_e) \leqslant \mu(V_e)$, since we add measure to E_e only after a corresponding amount is added to V_e. Thus m_e must be bounded away from 0, as otherwise E_e would cover $U^X_{b_e}$, which cannot happen since $X \not\leqslant_{\mathrm{LR}} \emptyset$. Therefore, p_e is bounded away from 0. Since each time an attack on R_e is launched at stage s_0 and ends, the measure of V_e increases by $p_e[s_0]$, only finitely many such attacks can end, and eventually there is an attack that does not reach step 2, so R_e is satisfied.

If an attack reaches step 2(b)ii, then it removes all the measure it put into Q^A. If it reaches step 2(b)i, then the restraint imposed on A ensures that the $a_e p_e[s_0] = a_e \mu([\![\Delta_e]\!])$ much measure that must be in U^A to cause $c(n_e, s_0) \geqslant a_e p_e[s_0]$ is permanently in U^A. Since n_e is redefined to be a fresh large number each time an attack is launched, the measures permanently added to U^A each time step 2(b)i is reached come from disjoint subsets of U^A. Thus we see that each time an attack on R_e is launched, if the attack ends, then $\mu(Q^A)$ increases by at most $\frac{1}{a_e}$ as much as $\mu(U^A)$. The last attack launched on R_e may never end, so if t is the stage at which this last attack is launched, then $\mu(Q^A) \leqslant \frac{\mu(U^A)}{a_e} + p_e[t]$, which is less than 1 if a_e is at least 2.

Finally, we must argue that $\mu(S^X) < 1$. Our claim is that $\mu(S^X) \leqslant \mu(U^A) + a_e \mu(U^X_{b_e})$, which suffices if b_e is chosen to be large enough. When some elements enters U^A, the same elements are added to S^X. These elements may later leave U^A, but this event can happen only when we reach step 2(b)ii of the module and have $X \upharpoonright k_e = X[s_0] \upharpoonright k_e$. The measure of the class of elements in question is then at most $c(n_e, s_0) < a_e p_e[s_0]$. We then put $p_e[s_0]$ much measure of $C_e[s_0]$ into E_e. Since $X \upharpoonright k_e = X[s_0] \upharpoonright k_e$, all of this measure is in $U^X_{b_e}$. Such enumerations into E_e correspond to disjoint classes of elements of $U^X_{b_e}$, so $\mu(S^X \setminus U^A)$ is at most $a_e \mu(U^X_{b_e})$, as claimed.

It is straightforward to check that dropping the assumption that $p_e[s_0] = m_e[s_0]$ for the actual value $p_e[s_0] = 2^{-r_e[s_0]-e-6} m_e[s_0]$ (while still assuming that step 2(a) does not occur, and hence r_e cannot change) causes no real problems.

We now briefly discuss removing our assumption that step 2(a) does not occur. Each time this step occurs, the current attack on R_e is canceled, and the set $[\![\Delta_e]\!]$ that we put into Q^A becomes trash. However, the measure of this set is $2^{-r_e[s_0]-e-6}m_e[s_0]$, and each time step 2(a) occurs, we increase r_e by one. Thus the total measure of our trash is bounded by 2^{-e-5}. Using the fact that X is Δ^0_2, we can argue that $k_e[s]$ must reach a limit and hence so must r_e, so that eventually step 2(a) stops occurring, and R_e can be satisfied as argued above.

The remaining details of the proof are relatively straightforward, and involve choosing the parameters of the construction appropriately and applying the finite injury priority method. Each time a requirement acts, it initializes all weaker priority ones, forcing them to increase their parameters. The formal details are in [18]. □

We finish this section by showing that LR-reducibility, which can be seen as a way to compare the relative derandomization power of sets, can also be characterized in terms of relative compression power. We say that A is *low for K reducible* to B, or simply *LK-reducible* to B, and write $A \leqslant_{\mathrm{LK}} B$, if $K^B(\sigma) \leqslant K^A(\sigma) + O(1)$.[12] Clearly, if $A \leqslant_{\mathrm{LK}} B$ then $A \leqslant_{\mathrm{LR}} B$. The following result shows that these reducibilities are in fact equivalent.

Theorem 10.5.9 (Kjos-Hanssen, Miller, and Solomon [206]). *If $A \leqslant_{\mathrm{LR}} B$ then $A \leqslant_{\mathrm{LK}} B$.*

To prove this result, we need the following easy lemma from basic analysis.

Lemma 10.5.10. *Let $a_0, a_1, \ldots \in [0,1)$ be real numbers. Then $\prod_i(1-a_i) > 0$ iff $\sum_i a_i < \infty$.*

Proof of Theorem 10.5.9. Let $A \leqslant_{\mathrm{LR}} B$. Define finite sets $V_0, V_1, \ldots$ as follows. Suppose that V_t has been defined for all $t < s$. Let n and τ be such that $s = \langle n, \tau\rangle$ (where we identify τ with a natural number as usual). Let m be the length of the longest string in $\bigcup_{t<s} V_t$ (or $m = 0$ if $s = 0$), and let $V_s = \{\sigma 0^n : \sigma \in 2^m\}$. Note that for any $I \subseteq \mathbb{N}$, we have $\mu(\bigcap_{s\in I} \overline{[\![V_s]\!]}) = \prod_{\langle n,\tau\rangle \in I}(1-2^{-n})$.

Let $I = \{\langle |\sigma|, \tau\rangle : \mathcal{U}^A(\sigma) = \tau\}$. Then I is A-c.e., and hence $P = \bigcap_{s\in I} \overline{[\![V_s]\!]}$ is a $\Pi^{0,A}_1$ class. Furthermore,

$$\sum_{\langle n,\tau\rangle\in I} 2^{-n} \leqslant \sum_{\sigma\in\mathrm{dom}(\mathcal{U}^A)} 2^{-|\sigma|} < 1.$$

[12] As with LR-reducibility, this reducibility comes from a notion of lowness that will be discussed in Section 11.2.

Thus, $\langle 0, \tau\rangle \notin I$ for every τ, and hence $\mu(P) = \prod_{\langle n,\tau\rangle \in I}(1 - 2^{-n}) > 0$, by Lemma 10.5.10. Therefore, by Theorem 10.5.1, there is a $\Pi^{0,B}_1$ class $Q \subseteq P$ with $\mu(Q) > 0$.

Let $J = \{\langle n, \tau\rangle : [\![V_{\langle n,\tau\rangle}]\!] \cap Q = \emptyset\}$. Then J is B-c.e., and

$$\prod_{\langle n,\tau\rangle \in J} (1 - 2^{-n}) = \mu\Big(\bigcap_{s\in J} \overline{[\![V_s]\!]}\Big) \geqslant \mu(Q) > 0.$$

Thus, by Lemma 10.5.10, there is a c such that $\sum_{\langle n,\tau\rangle \in J} 2^{-n} < 2^c$. Let $S = \{(n + c, \tau) : \langle n, \tau\rangle \in J\}$. Then S is a KC set relative to B, so if $\langle n, \tau\rangle \in J$ then $K^B(\tau) \leqslant n + O(1)$. Since $Q \subseteq P$, we have $I \subseteq J$, and hence $\langle K^A(\tau), \tau\rangle \in J$ for each τ. Thus $K^B(\tau) \leqslant K^A(\tau) + O(1)$, and hence $A \leqslant_{\mathrm{LK}} B$. ☐

This result has several important consequences. One of them is that if A is 1-random, then the K-degree of A is countable. (We will see another one in Theorem 11.2.4.) Recall that, by Theorem 9.15.1, if $K^X(A \restriction n) \leqslant K^X(n) + O(1)$ then $A \leqslant_{\mathrm{T}} X'$.

Corollary 10.5.11. *If $A \equiv_{\mathrm{LR}} X$ then $A \leqslant_{\mathrm{T}} X'$.*

Proof. If $A \equiv_{\mathrm{LR}} X$ then $A \equiv_{\mathrm{LK}} X$, so $K^X(A \restriction n) = K^A(A \restriction n) \pm O(1) = K^A(n) \pm O(1) = K^X(n) \pm O(1)$, so Theorem 9.15.1 applies. ☐

Corollary 10.5.12 (Miller [unpublished][13]). *If X is 1-random then the K-degree of X is countable.*

Proof. Suppose that $A \equiv_K X$. By Corollary 10.3.10, $A \equiv_{\mathrm{vL}} X$. Since X and A are both 1-random, $A \equiv_{\mathrm{LR}} X$. By Corollary 10.5.11, $A \leqslant_{\mathrm{T}} X'$. Thus every element of the K-degree of X is computable in X', and hence the K-degree of X is countable. ☐

10.6 Almost everywhere domination

Motivated by a question in the reverse mathematics of measure theory, Dobrinen and Simpson [98] introduced the following concepts.

Definition 10.6.1 (Dobrinen and Simpson [98]).

(i) A set A is *almost everywhere dominating* if for almost all X (in the sense of measure), for each $g \leqslant_{\mathrm{T}} X$ there is an $f \leqslant_{\mathrm{T}} A$ that dominates g.

[13] Miller originally proved this result by other methods, before Theorem 10.5.9 was known.

(ii) A set A is *uniformly almost everywhere dominating* if there is an $f \leqslant_{\mathrm{T}} A$ such that for almost all X, the function f dominates all functions $g \leqslant_{\mathrm{T}} X$.

As we have seen in Lemma 8.20.6, Kurtz [228] showed that $\emptyset'$ (and hence any set computing $\emptyset'$) is uniformly almost everywhere dominating. Cholak, Greenberg, and Miller [67] showed that there are uniformly almost everywhere dominating sets that do not compute $\emptyset'$. On the other hand, it follows from Martin's Theorem 2.23.7 that every uniformly almost everywhere dominating set is high. It was natural to ask for a characterization of the (uniformly) almost everywhere dominating sets. One has now been found in terms of LR-reducibility. We will show through a sequence of results that the following are equivalent:

(i) A is almost everywhere dominating.

(ii) A is uniformly almost everywhere dominating.

(iii) $\emptyset' \leqslant_{\mathrm{LR}} A$.

In other words, a set A is (uniformly) almost everywhere dominating iff every set that is 1-random relative to A is 2-random. In Section 11.2, we will show that there are incomplete c.e. sets with this property, but not all high c.e. sets have it, so randomness-theoretic notions are essential in answering this question.

We begin with the following characterizations of (uniform) almost everywhere domination.

Theorem 10.6.2 (Dobrinen and Simpson [98]).

(i) *A set A is uniformly almost everywhere dominating iff for each Π^0_2 class P there is a $\Sigma^{0,A}_2$ class $Q \subseteq P$ such that $\mu(Q) = \mu(P)$.*

(ii) *A set A is almost everywhere dominating iff for each Π^0_2 class P and each $\varepsilon > 0$, there is a $\Pi^{0,A}_1$ class $Q \subseteq P$ such that $\mu(Q) \geqslant \mu(P) - \varepsilon$.*

Proof. (i) First suppose that A is uniformly almost everywhere dominating, as witnessed by the function $f \leqslant_{\mathrm{T}} A$. Let P be a Π^0_2 class. It is easy to define a functional Φ such that $P = \{X : \Phi^X \text{ total}\}$. Let $g^X(n)$ be the least s such that $\Phi^X(n)[s]\downarrow$. Then f dominates g for almost all $X \in P$, so we can take $Q = \{X : \exists c \forall n\, (\Phi^X(n)[f(n)+c]\downarrow)\}$.

Now suppose that the second half of (i) holds. Let $P = \{0^e 1 X : \Phi^X_e \text{ total}\}$ and let $Q \subseteq P$ be a $\Sigma^{0,A}_2$ class such that $\mu(Q) = \mu(P)$. Write Q as an effective union of $\Pi^{0,A}_1$ classes $Q_0, Q_1, \ldots$. By compactness, for each i, e, and n, the set $S_{e,i,n} = \{\Phi^X_e(n) : 0^e 1 X \in Q_i\}$ is finite. These sets are uniformly A-computable. Let $f(n) = \max \bigcup_{e,i<n} S_{e,i,n}$. Then for each e, the function f dominates Φ^X_e for almost all X for which Φ^X_e is total, from which it follows that for almost all X, the function f dominates all total Φ^X_e.

(ii) is just a nonuniform version of the above. First suppose that A is almost everywhere dominating. Let P be a Π^0_2 class, and let g^X be as above. For almost all $X \in P$, there is an $f \leqslant_T A$ that majorizes g^X. Since there are only countably many A-computable functions, given $\varepsilon > 0$ there are $f_0, \dots, f_k \leqslant_T A$ such that for all but measure ε many $X \in P$, some f_i with $i \leqslant k$ majorizes g^X. Let $f(n) = \max_{i \leqslant k} f_i(n)$. Then we can take $Q = \{X : \forall n\, (\Phi^X(n)[f(n)]\downarrow)\}$.

Now suppose that the second half of (ii) holds. Fix e and $\varepsilon > 0$. Let $P = \{X : \Phi^X_e \text{ total}\}$ and let $Q \subseteq P$ be a $\Pi^{0,A}_1$ class such that $\mu(Q) \geqslant \mu(P) - \varepsilon$. Arguing by compactness as above, there is an $f \leqslant_T A$ such that f majorizes Φ^X_e for every X in Q. Since ε is arbitrary, we see that for almost all X, there is an A-computable function that majorizes Φ^A_e. Since there are only countably many e, it follows that A is almost everywhere dominating. □

Theorem 10.6.3 (Binns, Kjos-Hanssen, Lerman, and Solomon [43]). *If A is almost everywhere dominating then $\emptyset' \leqslant_{LR} A$.*

Proof. Let $U_0, U_1, \dots$ be a universal Martin-Löf test relative to $\emptyset'$ and let $P = \overline{U_1}$. Then P is a Π^0_2 class of positive measure all of whose elements are 2-random. By Theorem 10.6.2, there is a $\Pi^{0,A}_1$ class $Q \subseteq P$ of positive measure. Let X be 1-random relative to A. By Theorem 6.10.2, there are $Y \in Q$ and σ such that $X = \sigma Y$. Then Y is 2-random, and hence so is X. □

The other direction of our equivalence relies on the following result, which will also be important in Section 11.9.

Theorem 10.6.4 (Kjos-Hanssen, Miller, and Solomon [206]). *The following are equivalent.*

(i) *$A \leqslant_T B'$ and $A \leqslant_{LR} B$.*

(ii) *Every $\Pi^{0,A}_1$ class has a $\Sigma^{0,B}_2$ subclass of the same measure.*

(iii) *Every $\Sigma^{0,A}_2$ class has a $\Sigma^{0,B}_2$ subclass of the same measure.*

Proof. (i) ⇒ (ii) This part of the proof is similar to the proof of Theorem 10.5.9. Extend the length-lexicographic ordering of strings $\leqslant_L$ to pairs of strings. We define sets of strings $V_{(\sigma,\tau)}$ inductively. Suppose that we have defined $V_{(\sigma',\tau')}$ for all $(\sigma',\tau') \leqslant_L (\sigma,\tau)$ and let k be the maximum of the lengths of strings in $\bigcup_{(\sigma',\tau') \leqslant_L (\sigma,\tau)} V_{(\sigma',\tau')}$. Let $V_{(\sigma,\tau)} = \{\nu 0^{|\tau|} : \nu \in 2^k\}$. It is easy to see that if $I \subseteq 2^{<\omega} \times 2^{<\omega}$, then

$$\mu\Bigg(\bigcap_{(\sigma,\tau)\in I} \overline{[\![V_{(\sigma,\tau)}]\!]}\Bigg) = \prod_{(\sigma,\tau)\in I} (1 - 2^{-|\tau|}).$$

Now let S be a nonempty $\Pi^{0,A}_1$ class. Let W^A be a A-c.e. prefix-free set of generators for $\overline{S}$, and let $I = \{(\sigma,\tau) : \tau \in W^A \text{ with use exactly } \sigma\}$.

Let $P = \bigcap_{(\sigma,\tau)\in I} \overline{[\![V_{(\sigma,\tau)}]\!]}$. Note that P is a $\Pi_1^{0,A}$ class. Recall the fact from Lemma 10.5.10 that if $a_0, a_1, \ldots \in [0,1]$ then $\prod_i(1-a_i) > 0$ iff $\sum_i a_i < \infty$. Now, $\sum_{(\sigma,\tau)\in I} 2^{-|\tau|} = \sum_{\tau\in W^A} 2^{-|\tau|} \leqslant 1$, since W^A is prefix-free, so $\mu(P) = \prod_{(\sigma,\tau)\in I}(1-2^{-|\tau|}) > 0$. Thus, by Theorem 10.5.1, there is a $\Pi_1^{0,B}$ class $Q \subseteq P$ with $\mu(Q) > 0$.

Let $J = \{(\sigma,\tau) : [\![V_{\sigma,\tau}]\!] \cap Q = \emptyset\}$. Note that J is B-c.e., and $\prod_{(\sigma,\tau)\in J}(1-2^{-|\tau|}) = \mu(\bigcap_{(\sigma,\tau)\in J} \overline{[\![V_{(\sigma,\tau)}]\!]}) > 0$, so $\sum_{(\sigma,\tau)\in J} 2^{-|\tau|} < \infty$. Since $A \leqslant_T B'$, there is a B-computable approximation $A_0, A_1, \ldots$ to A. Let

$$T_s = \{(\sigma,\tau) \in J : \exists t \geqslant s\, (\tau \in W^{A_t}[t] \text{ with use exactly } \sigma)\}$$

and

$$U_s = \{\tau : \exists \sigma\, ((\sigma,\tau) \in T_s)\}.$$

Then $\{T_s\}_{s\in\omega}$ and $\{U_s\}_{s\in\omega}$ are sequences of uniformly B-c.e. sets. Let $R = \bigcup_s \overline{[\![U_s]\!]}$. We claim that R is the desired $\Sigma_2^{0,B}$ subclass of S.

First notice that $W^A \subseteq U_s$ for all s, and hence $R \subseteq S$. Now, for each $(\sigma,\tau) \in T_0 \setminus I$, there is a final stage t such that σ is a prefix of A_t, as otherwise $(\sigma,\tau) \in I$. Then for any stage $s > t$, we have $(\sigma,\tau) \notin T_s$. Fix $\varepsilon > 0$ and choose n sufficiently large so that

$$\sum\{2^{-|\tau|} : (\sigma,\tau) \in J \wedge |\sigma|, |\tau| > n\} < \varepsilon.$$

Choose s large enough so that if $(\sigma,\tau) \in T_0 \setminus I$ and $|\sigma|, |\tau| \leqslant n$ then $(\sigma,\tau) \notin T_s$. Then

$$\mu(S \setminus \overline{[\![U_s]\!]}) \leqslant \sum_{\tau\in U_s\setminus W^A} 2^{-|\tau|} \leqslant \sum_{(\sigma,\tau)\in T_s\setminus I} 2^{-|\tau|}$$
$$\leqslant \sum\{2^{-|\tau|} : (\sigma,\tau) \in J \wedge |\sigma|, |\tau| > n\} < \varepsilon.$$

Since $\varepsilon > 0$ is arbitrary, $\mu(R) = \mu(S)$.

(ii) $\Rightarrow$ (iii) Let S be a $\Sigma_2^{0,A}$ class and let $P_0, P_1, \ldots$ be uniformly $\Pi_1^{0,A}$ classes such that $S = \bigcup_i P_i$. Let $P = \{0^i 1\alpha : \exists i\, (\alpha \in X_i)\}$. Then P is a $\Pi_1^{0,A}$ class, so by (ii) it has a $\Sigma_2^{0,B}$ subclass Q of the same measure. For each i, let $Q_i = \{\alpha : 0^i 1\alpha \in Q\}$. Then the Q_i are uniformly $\Sigma_2^{0,B}$ classes with $Q_i \subseteq P_i$ for all i. If $\mu(Y_i) < \mu(X_i)$ for some i, then $\mu(Q) = \sum_i 2^{i+1}\mu(Q_i) < \sum_i 2^{i+1}\mu(P_i) = \mu(P)$, contradicting the choice of Q, so $\mu(X_i) = \mu(Y_i)$ for all i. Now let $R = \bigcup_i Q_i$. Then R is a $\Sigma_2^{0,B}$ subclass of P, and $\mu(P \setminus R) \leqslant \sum_i \mu(P_i - Q_i) = 0$, so $\mu(R) = \mu(P)$.

(iii) $\Rightarrow$ (i) If P is a $\Pi_1^{0,A}$ class of positive measure then by (ii) (which is clearly implied by (iii)), P has a $\Sigma_2^{0,B}$ subclass S of the same measure. Now, S is a countable union of $\Pi_2^{0,B}$ classes, so one of these classes has positive measure. Thus P has a $\Pi_1^{0,B}$ subclass of positive measure, so by Theorem 10.5.1, $A \leqslant_{\mathrm{LR}} B$.

Next, we show that $A \leqslant_{\mathrm{T}} B'$. Let $\sigma_n = 0^n1$ and let $U = \bigcup_{n\in A}[\![\sigma_n]\!]$. Since U is a $\Sigma_1^{0,A}$ class (and hence a $\Pi_2^{0,A}$ class), by (iii) there is a $\Pi_2^{0,B}$ class Q such that $U \subseteq Q$ and $\mu(Q) = \mu(U) = \sum_{n\in A} 2^{-(n+1)}$. We claim that $n \in A$ iff $[\![\sigma_n]\!] \subseteq Q$. If $n \in A$, then $[\![\sigma_n]\!] \subseteq U \subseteq Q$. On the other hand, if $n \notin A$ and $[\![\sigma_n]\!] \subseteq Q$, then $\mu(Q) \geqslant \sum_{i\in A} 2^{-(i+1)} + 2^{-n} > \mu(U)$, which is a contradiction.

Let $Q_0, Q_1, \ldots$ be uniformly $\Sigma_1^{0,B}$ classes such that $Q = \bigcap_k Q_k$. Then $n \in A$ iff $[\![\sigma_n]\!] \subseteq Q$ iff $[\![\sigma_n]\!] \subseteq Q_k$ for all k. Since $[\![\sigma_n]\!] \subseteq Q_k$ is a $\Sigma_1^{0,B}$ relation, these equivalences show that A is $\Pi_2^{0,B}$. The same argument applied to the $\Sigma_1^{0,A}$ class $\bigcup_{n\notin A}[\![\sigma_n]\!]$ shows that $\overline{A}$ is $\Pi_2^{0,B}$ as well, and hence $A \leqslant_{\mathrm{T}} B'$.[14] □

Note that $A \leqslant_{\mathrm{LR}} B$ does not imply $A \leqslant_{\mathrm{T}} B'$ because there is a B with uncountably many $A \leqslant_{\mathrm{LR}} B$ (see Barmpalias, Lewis, and Soskova [25]).

Theorem 10.6.5 (Kjos-Hanssen, Miller, and Solomon [206]). *If $\emptyset' \leqslant_{\mathrm{LR}} A$ then A is uniformly almost everywhere dominating.*

Proof. Suppose that $\emptyset' \leqslant_{\mathrm{LR}} A$. Let P be a Π_2^0 class. By Theorem 6.8.3, there are uniformly $\Pi_1^{0,\emptyset'}$ classes $R_0, R_1, \ldots \subseteq P$ such that $\mu(P) - \mu(R_n) < 2^{-n}$ for all n. Let $R = \bigcup_n R_n$. Then R is a $\Sigma_2^{0,\emptyset'}$ class such that $R \subseteq P$ and $\mu(R) = \mu(P)$. Since $\emptyset' \leqslant_{\mathrm{T}} A'$, it follows from Theorem 10.6.4 that there is a $\Sigma_2^{0,A}$ class $Q \subseteq R \subseteq P$ such that $\mu(Q) = \mu(R) = \mu(P)$. The theorem now follows from Theorem 10.6.2. □

See [206] for more on almost everywhere domination and related concepts, including a discussion of the reverse mathematical questions that originally motivated the study of this notion.

[14] This proof can be used to show more, namely that $A' \leqslant_{\mathrm{T}} B'$. Applying the proof to the $\Sigma_1^{0,A}$ class $\bigcup_{n\in A'}[\![\sigma_n]\!]$, we see that A' is $\Pi_2^{0,B}$. But since $A \leqslant_{\mathrm{T}} B'$, we have that A' is $\Sigma_2^{0,B}$, so in fact $A' \leqslant_{\mathrm{T}} B'$. It follows that if $A \leqslant_{\mathrm{T}} B'$ and $A \leqslant_{\mathrm{LR}} B$, then $A' \leqslant_{\mathrm{T}} B'$.

11
Randomness-Theoretic Weakness

In this chapter, we introduce an important class of "randomness-theoretically weak" sets, the K-trivial sets. As we will see, this class has several natural characterizations, can be used to answer several questions in the theory of algorithmic randomness, and is also of great interest to computability theory.

11.1 K-triviality

Recall Chaitin's Theorem 3.4.4, which states that $C(A \upharpoonright n) \leqslant C(n) + O(1)$ iff A is computable. Chaitin asked whether the analogous result holds for K in place of C. He was able to show the following, which is Theorem 9.15.1 for the case $X = S = \emptyset$.

Theorem 11.1.1 (Chaitin [61]). *If $K(A \upharpoonright n) \leqslant K(n) + O(1)$ then A is Δ^0_2.*

Merkle and Stephan [270] noted that essentially the same proof establishes the following result, which we have already encountered in Section 9.15.

Theorem 11.1.2 (Merkle and Stephan [270]). *If $K(A \upharpoonright n) \leqslant K(n) + O(1)$ for all n in an infinite set S then $A \leqslant_{\mathrm{T}} S \oplus \emptyset'$.*

The Counting Theorem in fact shows that the width of the tree T in the proof of Theorem 11.1.1 is $O(2^c)$, so we have the following result.

R.G. Downey and D. Hirschfeldt, *Algorithmic Randomness and Complexity*, Theory and Applications of Computability, DOI 10.1007/978-0-387-68441-3_11,

Theorem 11.1.3 (Zambella [416]). *For each c there are $O(2^c)$ many sets A such that $K(A \upharpoonright n) \leqslant K(n) + c$ for all n.*

Of course, if A is computable then $K(A \upharpoonright n) \leqslant K(n) + O(1)$, but as we will see in the next subsection, the converse is not true. In other words, even though A may look identical to $\emptyset$ as far as prefix-free initial segment complexity goes, it does not follow that A is computable, even for c.e. sets A. Thus we are led to the concept of K-triviality.

Recall that a set A is K-trivial if $K(A \upharpoonright n) \leqslant K(n) + O(1)$. Equivalently, A is K-trivial if $A \leqslant_K \emptyset$. It makes no difference in the above definition if we restrict our attention to an infinite computable set of n's.

Proposition 11.1.4. *If $K(A \upharpoonright n) \leqslant K(n) + O(1)$ for all n in an infinite computable set S then A is K-trivial.*

Proof. Let $h(n)$ be the nth element of S, in natural order. For any n, we have $K(n) = K(h(n)) \pm O(1)$. Furthermore, from a description of $A \upharpoonright h(n)$, we can recover n and thus obtain $A \upharpoonright n$, so $K(A \upharpoonright n) \leqslant K(A \upharpoonright h(n)) + O(1)$. Thus $K(A \upharpoonright n) \leqslant K(n) + O(1)$ for all n. □

11.1.1 The basic K-triviality construction

Solovay [371] was the first to construct a noncomputable K-trivial set. His method was adapted by Zambella [416] to construct a noncomputable K-trivial c.e. set (see also Calude and Coles [49]). Downey, Hirschfeldt, Nies, and Stephan [117] gave a new construction of a K-trivial c.e. set, which we present below. (A similar construction had been produced independently by Kummer in unpublished work.) As we will later see, this construction gives a priority-free, and even a requirement-free, solution to Post's Problem.

Before presenting the construction from [117], we make a remark. While the proof below is easy, it is slightly hard to see why it works. So, by way of motivation, suppose that we were to asked to "prove" that $\emptyset$ has the same initial segment complexity as $\mathbb{N}$. A complicated way to do so is to build our own prefix-free machine M whose only job is to compute initial segments of $\emptyset$. If $\mathcal{U}(\sigma)\downarrow= 1^n$ then we want $M(\sigma)\downarrow= 0^n$. We can build M *implicitly*, using the KC Theorem, by enumerating the request $(|\sigma|, 0^n)$ every time $\mathcal{U}(\sigma)\downarrow= 1^n$. We are guaranteed that $\sum_{\tau \in \operatorname{dom} M} 2^{-|\tau|} \leqslant \sum_{\sigma \in \operatorname{dom} \mathcal{U}} 2^{-|\sigma|} \leqslant 1$, and hence the KC Theorem applies. Note also that we could, for convenience and as we do in the construction below, use a string of length $|\sigma| + 1$, in which case we would ensure that $\sum_{\tau \in \operatorname{dom} M} 2^{-|\tau|} < \frac{1}{2}$.

Theorem 11.1.5 (Zambella [416], after Solovay [371]). *There is a noncomputable K-trivial c.e. set.*

Proof. We define a noncomputable c.e. set A and a KC set L. As in the remark above, we follow $\mathcal{U}$ on n, in the sense that, when at a stage s we see a shorter σ with $\mathcal{U}(\sigma) = n$ than we have previously seen, we enumerate a request $(|\sigma|+1, A_s \upharpoonright n)$ into L. To make A noncomputable, we sometimes need to make $A_{s+1}(n) \neq A_s(n)$. Then for each j with $n < j \leqslant s$, for the currently shortest $\mathcal{U}$-program σ_j for j, we also enumerate a request $(|\sigma_j|, A_{s+1} \upharpoonright j)$. The construction works by making this extra measure added to the weight of L small.

Let

$$A = \left\{n : \exists e \, \exists s \left(W_{e,s} \cap A_s = \emptyset \wedge n > 2e \wedge n \in W_{e,s} \right.\right.$$
$$\left.\left. \wedge \sum_{n<j\leqslant s} 2^{-K_s(j)} \leqslant 2^{-(e+2)}\right)\right\},$$

and let L be as described above. Clearly A is c.e. Since $\sum_{j\geqslant m} 2^{-K(j)}$ goes to zero as m increases, if W_e is infinite then $A \cap W_e \neq \emptyset$. Since A is also clearly coinfinite, it follows that A is noncomputable. Finally, the extra weight of L, beyond one half of the measure of $\operatorname{dom}\mathcal{U}$, is bounded by $\sum_e 2^{-(e+2)}$ (corresponding to at most one initial segment change for each e), whence the weight of L is bounded by

$$\sum_{\sigma\in\operatorname{dom}\mathcal{U}} 2^{-(|\sigma|+1)} + \sum_e 2^{-(e+2)} \leqslant \frac{1}{2} + \frac{1}{2} = 1.$$

So the KC Theorem applies, and hence, since $(K(n), A \upharpoonright n) \in L$ for all n, we have $K(A \upharpoonright n) \leqslant K(n) + O(1)$. □

A useful way to think of this proof is in terms of *cost functions*. The function $c(n,s) = \sum_{n<j\leqslant s} 2^{-K_s(j)}$ represents the cost of enumerating n into A at stage s. To ensure that A is K-trivial, we need to ensure that $\sum\{c(n,s) : \mu n \in A_{s+1} \setminus A_s\}$ is finite. We will see another example of a cost function construction in the proof of Theorem 11.2.5, and will discuss this idea further below.

The above proof admits several variations. For instance, we can make A promptly simple, or below any nonzero c.e. degree. We cannot control the jump or make A Turing complete, since, as we will see below, all K-trivial sets are low.

11.1.2 The requirement-free version

As we will see in Section 11.3, the construction above automatically yields a Turing incomplete c.e. set. It is thus an *injury-free* solution to Post's Problem. It is not, however, *priority-free*, in that the construction depends on an ordering of the simplicity requirements, with stronger requirements allowed to add more to the weight of L. We can do methodologically better by giving a priority-free solution to Post's Problem, in the sense that no explicit diagonalization (such as that of W_e above) occurs in the construction of the incomplete c.e. set, and therefore the construction of this set (as opposed to the verification that it is noncomputable) does not depend on an ordering of requirements. We now sketch this method, which is due to Downey, Hirschfeldt, Nies, and Stephan [117], and is rather more like that of Solovay's original proof of the existence of a noncomputable K-trivial set.

Let us reconsider the key idea in the proof of Theorem 11.1.5. At certain stages we wish to change an initial segment of A for the sake of diagonalization. Our method is to make sure that the total measure added to the weight of our KC set L (which proves the K-triviality of A) due to such changes is bounded by 1. Suppose, on the other hand, that we were fortunate enough to have $\mathcal{U}$ itself "cover" the measure needed for these changes. That is, suppose we were at a stage s where we desired to put n into $A_{s+1} \setminus A_s$ and at that very stage $K_s(j)$ changed for all $j \in (n, s]$. Then *in any case* we would need to enumerate new requests describing $A_{s+1} \upharpoonright j$ for all $j \in (n, s]$, whether or not these initial segments change. Thus, at that very stage, we could also change $A_s \upharpoonright j$ for all $j \in (n, s]$ at no extra cost.

Notice that we would not need to copy $\mathcal{U}$ at every stage. We could enumerate a collection of stages $t_0, t_1 \dots$ and only update L at stages t_i. Thus, for the lucky situation outlined above to occur, we would need the approximation to $K(j)$ to change for all $j \in (n, t_s]$ only at some stage u with $t_s \leqslant u \leqslant t_{s+1}$. This observation would seem to allow a greater possibility for this lucky situation to occur, since many more stages can occur between t_s and t_{s+1}.

The key point in this discussion is the following. Let $t_0, t_1, \dots$ be a computable collection of stages. Suppose that we construct a set $A = \bigcup_s A_{t_s}$ so that for $n \leqslant t_s$, if $A_{t_{s+1}} \upharpoonright n \neq A_{t_s} \upharpoonright n$ then $K_{t_s}(j) > K_{t_{s+1}}(j)$ for all j with $n \leqslant j \leqslant t_s$. Then A is K-trivial. We are now ready to define such an A in a priority-free way.

Let $t_0, t_1, \dots$ be a collection of stages such that t_i as a function of i dominates all primitive recursive functions. (Actually, we do not need $i \mapsto t_i$ to be quite this fast growing; see below for more details.) At each stage u, let $\{a_{i,u} : i \in \mathbb{N}\}$ list $\overline{A}_u$. Let $A_{t_{s+1}} = A_{t_s} \cup [a_{n,t_s}, t_s]$, where n is the least number less than or equal to t_s such that $K_{t_{s+1}}(j) < K_{t_s}(j)$ for all $j \in (n, t_s]$. (Naturally, if no such n exists, $A_{t_{s+1}} = A_{t_s}$.) Requiring the complexity change for all $j \in (n, t_s]$, rather than just $j \in (a_{n,t_s}, t_s]$, ensures that A is coinfinite, since for each n there are only finitely many s such that $K_{t_{s+1}}(n) < K_{t_s}(n)$.

Note that there is no priority used in the definition of A. It is like the Dekker deficiency set or the so-called "dump set" (see Soare [366, Theorem V.2.5]).

It remains to prove that A is noncomputable. By the recursion theorem, we can build a prefix-free machine M and know the coding constant c of M in $\mathcal{U}$. That is, if we declare $M(\sigma) = j$ then we will have $\mathcal{U}(\tau) = j$ for some τ such that $|\tau| \leqslant |\sigma| + c$. Note further that if we put σ into the domain of M

at stage t_s, then τ will be in the domain of $\mathcal{U}$ by stage $t_{s+1}-1$. (This is why we required $i \mapsto t_i$ to dominate the primitive recursive functions. In fact, we only need this function to dominate the overhead of the recursion theorem; that is, we only need the property that if σ enters the domain of M at stage t_s, then there is a τ such that $|\tau| \leqslant |\sigma| + c$ and $\mathcal{U}_{t_{s+1}-1}(\tau)\downarrow = M(\sigma)$. The use of a fast growing sequence of stages was the key insight in Solovay's original construction.)

Now the proof looks like that of Theorem 11.1.5. We devote $2^{-(e+1)}$ of the domain of our machine M to ensuring that A satisfies the eth simplicity requirement. When we see a_{n,t_s} occur in W_{e,t_s}, where $\sum_{n<j\leqslant t_s} 2^{-K_{t_s}(j)} \leqslant 2^{-(e+c+2)}$, we provide shorter M_{t_s} descriptions of all j with $n < j \leqslant t_s$ so that $K_{t_{s+1}}(j) < K_{t_s}(j)$ for all such j. The cost of this change is bounded by $2^{-(e+1)}$, and a_{n,t_s} will enter $A_{t_{s+1}}$, as required.

As observed by Downey, Hirschfeldt, Nies, and Stephan [117], and later formally written out by Nies [303, 306], many of the usual computability-theoretic variations work for this construction. Thus, for example, there are minimal pairs of degrees containing K-trivial sets, and the following holds (though the proof is a bit tricky; see [303] for details).

Theorem 11.1.6 (Downey, Hirschfeldt, and Nies, see [303]). *If B is a low c.e. set, then there is a K-trivial c.e. set $A \nleqslant_{\mathrm{T}} B$. Indeed, if $B_0, B_1, \ldots$ is a uniformly c.e. sequence of uniformly low sets, then there is a K-trivial c.e. set A such that $A \nleqslant_{\mathrm{T}} B_i$ for all i.*

11.1.3 Solovay functions and K-triviality

Recall from Definition 3.12.3 that a Solovay function is a computable function such that $\sum_n 2^{-f(n)} < \infty$ and $f(n) \leqslant K(n) + O(1)$ for infinitely many n. In this subsection we point out an attractive connection between K-trivials and Solovay functions.

We begin with an analog of Chaitin's Theorem 3.4.4 that all C-trivials are computable (where A is *C-trivial* if $C(A \upharpoonright n) \leqslant C(n) + O(1)$).

Proposition 11.1.7 (Bienvenu and Downey [39]). *Suppose that for each computable function f with $\sum_n 2^{-f(n)} < \infty$, there exists a computable function g with $\sum_\sigma 2^{-g(\sigma)} < \infty$ such that $g(A \upharpoonright n) \leqslant f(n) + O(1)$. Then A is computable.*

Proof. Let A satisfy the hypothesis of the proposition, and let f be a Solovay function. Let g be a computable function such that $\sum_\sigma 2^{-g(\sigma)} < \infty$ and there is a c with $g(A \upharpoonright n) \leqslant f(n) + c$ for all n. Let d be such that $K(\sigma) \leqslant g(\sigma) + d$ for all σ. Since f is a Solovay function, there is an e such that $f(n) \leqslant K(n) + e$ for infinitely many n. For any such n,

$$\begin{aligned}&|\{\tau \in 2^n : g(\tau) \leqslant f(n) + c\}| \\ &\qquad \leqslant |\{\tau \in 2^n : K(\tau) \leqslant K(n) + c + d + e\}| \leqslant 2^{c+d+e+O(1)},\end{aligned}$$

where the last inequality comes from the Counting Theorem 3.7.6. So the Π^0_1 class $\{X \in 2^\omega : \forall n\,(g(X \upharpoonright n) \leqslant f(n)+c)\}$, to which A belongs, has only finitely many elements (at most $2^{c+d+e+O(1)}$ many), and hence all these elements are computable. □

We can use Solovay functions to characterize K-triviality.

Theorem 11.1.8 (Bienvenu and Downey [39]). *A set A is K-trivial iff for all computable functions f such that $\sum_n 2^{-f(n)} < \infty$, we have $K(A \upharpoonright n) \leqslant f(n)+O(1)$. Moreover, there exists a single such computable function g such that*

$$A \textit{ is } K\textit{-trivial} \Leftrightarrow K(A \upharpoonright n) \leqslant g(n) + O(1). \tag{11.1}$$

Proof. We give a simple proof due to Wolfgang Merkle.

By Lemma 3.12.2, any K-trivial A satisfies $K(A \upharpoonright n) \leqslant f(n) + O(1)$ for all computable f with $\sum_n 2^{-f(n)} < \infty$. Thus, it is enough to find such a function g so that the $\Leftarrow$ direction of (11.1) holds. In fact, we can take g to be Solovay's Solovay function, the function constructed in the proof of Theorem 3.12.1.

Let A be a set such that $K(A \upharpoonright n) \leqslant g(n)+O(1)$. Given n, let s be least such that $K_s(n) = K(n)$, and let $m = \langle n, s\rangle$. Then $g(m) \leqslant K(n)+O(1)$, as explained in the proof of Theorem 3.12.1. Since n can be computed from m, we have

$$K(A \upharpoonright n) \leqslant K(A \upharpoonright m) + O(1) \leqslant g(m) + O(1) \leqslant K(n) \pm O(1),$$

so A is K-trivial. □

Too recently for a proof to be included in this book, Bienvenu, Merkle, and Nies [unpublished] have shown that a computable function g satisfies (11.1) iff it is a Solovay function.

Theorem 11.1.9 (Bienvenu, Merkle, and Nies [unpublished]). *The following are equivalent for a computable function g.*

(i) *The function g is a Solovay function.*

(ii) *A set A is K-trivial iff $K(A \upharpoonright n) \leqslant g(n) + O(1)$.*

Bienvenu, Merkle, and Nies [unpublished] also showed that the above result still holds for co-c.e. functions g (where we remove the condition that g be computable from the definition of a Solovay function).

11.1.4 Counting the K-trivial sets

Zambella's Theorem 11.1.3 leads one to ask *exactly* how many K-trivials there are for a given constant of K-triviality, and how complicated it is to enumerate them. This question has been investigated by Downey, Miller, and Yu [127]. Let $\mathrm{KT}(c) = \{A : \forall n\,(K(A \upharpoonright n) \leqslant K(n) + c)\}$ and let

$G(c) = |\mathrm{KT}(c)|$. The function G appears to be a strangely complicated object. We calculate some bounds on its complexity. To do so, we begin with a combinatorial analysis. Let $\mathrm{KT}(c,n) = \{\sigma \in 2^n : K(\sigma) \leqslant K(n)+c\}$ and $G(c,n) = |\mathrm{KT}(c,n)|$.

Theorem 11.1.10 (Downey, Miller, and Yu [127]). $\lim_c \frac{G(c)}{2^c} = 0$. *Indeed,* $\sum_c \frac{G(c)}{2^c} < \infty$.

Proof. Let n be large enough so that if A and B are distinct elements of $\mathrm{KT}(c)$ then $A \upharpoonright n \neq B \upharpoonright n$. Then for any $m \geqslant n$, we have $G(c) \leqslant G(c,m)$. Thus for any d we have $\sum_{c<d} \frac{G(c)}{2^c} \leqslant \liminf_n \sum_{c<d} \frac{G(c,n)}{2^c}$, and hence $\sum_c \frac{G(c)}{2^c} \leqslant \liminf_n \sum_c \frac{G(c,n)}{2^c}$. But $\sum_c \frac{G(c,n)}{2^c} \leqslant O(1)$, since for all n,

$$\sum_c G(c,n)2^{-K(n)-c} \leqslant \sum_{\sigma\in 2^n} \sum_{d\geqslant 0} 2^{-K(\sigma)-d} = 2\sum_{\sigma \in 2^n} 2^{-K(\sigma)} \leqslant 2^{-K(n)+O(1)},$$

where the last inequality follows by Corollary 3.7.9. □

The above result is relatively sharp, in the following sense.

Theorem 11.1.11 (Downey, Miller, and Yu [127]). *There is an* $\varepsilon > 0$ *such that* $G(c) > \varepsilon \frac{2^c}{c^2}$ *for all large enough* c.

Proof. For any σ,

$$\begin{aligned} K(\sigma 0^r) &\leqslant K(\sigma) + K(0^r) + O(1) \\ &\leqslant K(\sigma) + K(0^{|\sigma|+r}) + O(1) \leqslant |\sigma 0^r| + K(\sigma) + O(1). \end{aligned}$$

So there is a d such that $\sigma 0^\omega \in \mathrm{KT}(K(\sigma)+d)$ for all σ. If $|\sigma| = (c-d) - 2\log(c-d)$, then $K(\sigma) \leqslant c-d$, so $\sigma 0^\omega \in \mathrm{KT}(c)$. But there are $\frac{2^{c-d}}{(c-d)^2}$ many such σ, so the theorem follows. □

We now consider the complexity of G.

Theorem 11.1.12 (Downey, Miller, and Yu [127]). $G \nleqslant_{\mathrm{T}} \emptyset'$.

Proof. Suppose that $G \leqslant_{\mathrm{T}} \emptyset'$. Let k be such that $0^\omega \in \mathrm{KT}(k)$. Using the KC Theorem, we build a machine M with coding constant d, which we know in advance by the recursion theorem. Let $c \geqslant k, 2^d$ be least such that $\frac{G(c)}{2^c} < 2^{-d}$. Such a c exists by Theorem 11.1.10, and we can approximate c as the limit of a computable sequence $c_0, c_1, \ldots$. We may assume that $c_s \geqslant d$ for all s. We build M to ensure that $\mathrm{KT}(c)$ has at least 2^{c-d} many elements, yielding a contradiction.

At stage s, proceed as follows. If $s = 0$, then let $S_0 = \{\lambda\}$. If $s > 0$ and $c_s = c_{s-1}$, then let S_s be a set of strings of length s extending the strings in S_{s-1} such that $|S_s| = \min(2^{c_s-d}, 2|S_{s-1}|)$. If $s > 0$ and $c_s \neq c_{s-1}$, then let $S_s = \{0^s\}$. In any case, promise to give each string in S_s an M-description of length $K(s) + c_s - d$, which is clearly possible because $2^{c_s-d}2^{-(K(s)+c_s-d)} = 2^{-K(s)}$.

Let t be least such that $c_s = c$ for all $s \geqslant t$. Then $S_t = \{0^t\}$, and from stage t on, $|S_s|$ grows until it reaches 2^{c-d}. Thus there are 2^{c-d} many sequences $\alpha \succ 0^t$ such that $\alpha \upharpoonright s \in S_s$ for all $s \geqslant t$. For any such α, we have $K(\alpha \upharpoonright s) \leqslant K_M(\alpha \upharpoonright s) + d \leqslant K(s) + c$ for all $s \geqslant t$, and $K(\alpha \upharpoonright s) \leqslant K(s) + k \leqslant K(s) + c$ for all $s < t$. Thus every such α is in $\mathrm{KT}(c)$, and hence $G(c) \geqslant 2^{c-d}$, for the desired contradiction. □

A crude upper bound on the complexity of G is that $G \leqslant_{\mathrm{T}} \emptyset'''$. It is unknown whether $G \leqslant_{\mathrm{T}} \emptyset''$, or even whether the answer to this question is machine dependent.

11.2 Lowness

In computability theory, a set A is called low if its jump has the same Turing degree as the jump of $\emptyset$. The idea is that, in relation to the jump operator, A has no more power as an oracle than $\emptyset$. Another way to look at this concept is that A is low iff the class of sets that are Δ_2^0 relative to A is the same as the unrelativized class of Δ_2^0 sets. We can generalize this notion to any relativizable class $\mathcal{C}$, and say that A is *low for* $\mathcal{C}$ if $\mathcal{C}^A = \mathcal{C}$. For example, we have the following important concept.

Definition 11.2.1. Let R be a relativizable notion of randomness. A set A is *low for R-randomness* if every R-random set is R-random relative to A.

So A is low for R-randomness if it has no derandomization power with respect to R-randomness. Of course, here R can be any of the notions we have previously studied, such as 1-randomness, Schnorr randomness, etc. For notions of randomness R with a test definition, we also have the following notion.

Definition 11.2.2. A set A is *low for R-tests* if every R-test relative to A is covered by an unrelativized R-test, that is, for every R-test $\{U_n\}_{n\in\omega}$ relative to A, there is an R-test $\{V_n\}_{n\in\omega}$ such that $\bigcap_n V_n \supseteq \bigcap_n U_n$.

If A is low for R-tests, then it is low for R-randomness, but the converse is not necessarily true. For any notion of randomness with universal tests, however, the two notions clearly coincide. Thus, for instance, a set is low for Martin-Löf tests iff it is low for 1-randomness.

We can also further generalize the idea of lowness to other notions, such as in the following concept due to An. A. Muchnik [unpublished].

Definition 11.2.3 (Muchnik [unpublished]). A set A is *low for K* if $K(\sigma) \leqslant K^A(\sigma) + O(1)$.

Suppose that A is low for K. Then $K(A \upharpoonright n) \leqslant K^A(A \upharpoonright n) + O(1) \leqslant K(n) + O(1)$, so A is K-trivial. Also, if X is 1-random then $K^A(X \upharpoonright n) \geqslant K(X \upharpoonright n) - O(1) \geqslant n - O(1)$, so A is low for 1-randomness.

A set A is low for 1-randomness iff $A \leqslant_{\mathrm{LR}} \emptyset$, and low for K iff $A \leqslant_{\mathrm{LK}} \emptyset$, so Theorem 10.5.9 gives us the following result, originally proved by Nies [302].

Corollary 11.2.4 (Nies [302]). *A set is low for* 1*-randomness iff it is low for* K.

Lowness for 1-randomness was first studied by Kučera and Terwijn [223], who answered a question of van Lambalgen and Zambella, first published in [416], by showing that there is a noncomputable c.e. set that is low for 1-randomness. Their result was an early example of a cost function construction (as Kučera [private communication] has put it, the strategy of such a construction is "do what is cheap"), a topic we will return to in Section 11.5. It follows from the following more recent theorem, which also gives another proof of the existence of noncomputable K-trivial c.e. sets.

Theorem 11.2.5 (Muchnik [unpublished]). *There is a noncomputable c.e. set that is low for* K.

Proof. We build a c.e. set A to be low for K while satisfying the usual simplicity requirements

$$\mathcal{R}_e : W_e \neq \overline{A}.$$

We use a cost function as in the proof of Theorem 11.1.5. Let

$$c(n, s) = \sum \{2^{-|\tau|} : \mathcal{U}^A[s](\tau)\downarrow \text{ with use greater than } n\}.$$

We think of $c(n, s)$ as the cost of enumerating n into A at stage s.

Initially, let $n_{e,0} = 2e$ for all e. Unless explicitly defined otherwise, $n_{e,s+1} = n_{e,s}$ for all e and s.

At stage s, say that $\mathcal{R}_e$ *requires attention* if $W_{e,s} \cap A_s = \emptyset$ and $n_{e,s} \in W_{e,s}$. If no $\mathcal{R}_e$ with $e \leqslant s$ requires attention, then proceed to the next stage. Otherwise, let e be least such that $\mathcal{R}_e$ requires attention. If $c(n_{e,s}, s) < 2^{-(e+2)}$ then put $n_{e,s}$ into A. Otherwise, for all $i \geqslant e$, let $n_{i,s+1}$ be fresh large numbers with $n_{i,s+1} > 2i$. In either case, we say that $\mathcal{R}_e$ *acts* at stage s.

Clearly A is c.e. and coinfinite. Assume for a contradiction that A is computable. Let e be least such that $W_e = \overline{A}$. If $i < e$ then either $W_i \cap A \neq \emptyset$ or W_i is finite. In either case, $\mathcal{R}_i$ eventually stops requiring attention. Let s be a stage by which all such $\mathcal{R}_i$ have stopped requiring attention. If there were no stage $s_0 \geqslant s$ at which $\mathcal{R}_e$ acts, then we would have $n_{e,t} = n_{e,s}$ for all $t > s$ and $n_{e,s} \notin A$. But then $n_{e,s} \in W_e$, so $\mathcal{R}_e$ would act at the least $t \geqslant s$ such that $n_{e,s} \in W_{e,t}$. So there must be such a stage s_0. At that stage, we must have $c(n_{e,s_0}, s_0) \geqslant 2^{-(e+2)}$, since otherwise we would have $n_{e,s_0} \in W_e \cap A$. Now all n_{i,s_0+1} for $i \geqslant e$ get defined to be fresh large numbers, so the $\mathcal{U}^A$-computations contributing to $c(n_{e,s_0}, s_0)$ are permanent. Thus $\mu([\![\operatorname{dom}\mathcal{U}^A]\!]) \geqslant 2^{-(e+2)}$.

But now, arguing as before, there is a stage $s_1 > s_0$ at which $\mathcal{R}_e$ acts, and $c(n_{e,s_1}, s_1) \geqslant 2^{-(e+2)}$. Again, the $\mathcal{U}^A$-computations contributing to $c(n_{e,s_1}, s_1)$ are permanent, and furthermore, they are all different from the ones that contributed to $c(n_{e,s_0}, s_0)$, since their use must be greater than n_{e,s_0+1}, which was defined to be greater than the use of computations contributing to $c(n_{e,s_0}, s_0)$. Thus $\mu([\![\operatorname{dom}\mathcal{U}^A]\!]) \geqslant 2^{-(e+1)}$. We can now repeat this argument to show that $\mu([\![\operatorname{dom}\mathcal{U}^A]\!]) \geqslant 2^{-e}$ and so on. Eventually we conclude that $\mu([\![\operatorname{dom}\mathcal{U}^A]\!]) \geqslant 2$, which is a contradiction.

It remains to show that A is low for K. Let

$$L = \{(|\tau| + 1, \sigma) : \exists s\, (\mathcal{U}^A(\tau)[s] = \sigma)\}.$$

The weight of L is bounded by

$$\frac{1}{2}\left(\mu([\![\operatorname{dom}\mathcal{U}^A]\!]) + \sum_s \mu([\![\operatorname{dom}\mathcal{U}^A[s] \setminus \operatorname{dom}\mathcal{U}^A[s+1]]\!])\right).$$

But if $\sigma \in \operatorname{dom}\mathcal{U}^A[s] \setminus \operatorname{dom}\mathcal{U}^A[s+1]$ then there must be an n entering A below the use of $\mathcal{U}^A(\sigma)[s]$ at stage s. Thus $\mu([\![\operatorname{dom}\mathcal{U}^A[s]\setminus\operatorname{dom}\mathcal{U}^A[s+1]]\!]) \leqslant c(n, s)$ for the unique n entering A at stage s. (If there is no such n, then $\operatorname{dom}\mathcal{U}^A[s] \setminus \operatorname{dom}\mathcal{U}^A[s+1] = \emptyset$.) So the weight of L is bounded by

$$\frac{1}{2}(\mu([\![\operatorname{dom}\mathcal{U}^A]\!]) + \sum\{c(n, s) : n \in A_{s+1} \setminus A_s\})$$
$$\leqslant \frac{1}{2}\left(\mu([\![\operatorname{dom}\mathcal{U}^A]\!]) + \sum_e 2^{-(e+2)}\right) = 1.$$

Thus L is a KC set. Furthermore, for each σ, the request $(K^A(\sigma) + 1, \sigma)$ is in L, so $K(\sigma) \leqslant K^A(\sigma) + O(1)$, as required. □

Corollary 11.2.6 (Kučera and Terwijn [223]). *There is a noncomputable c.e. set that is low for* 1*-randomness.*

We have already seen in Chapter 10 that the following relativized form of this result is quite useful.

Corollary 11.2.7 (Kučera and Terwijn [223]). *For every X there is a $Y >_{\mathrm{T}} X$ such that every set that is* 1*-random relative to X is* 1*-random relative to Y (i.e., $Y \leqslant_{\mathrm{LR}} X$).*

Here is another application of (the proof of) this result. The construction in the proof of Theorem 11.2.5 gives us a way to define a nontrivial pseudo-jump operator taking any set X to a set $Y \leqslant_{\mathrm{LR}} X$. By Theorem 2.12.3, there is an incomplete c.e. set X such that $\emptyset' \leqslant_{\mathrm{LR}} X$. As we have seen in Section 10.6, the latter condition is equivalent to being (uniformly) almost everywhere dominating. On the other hand, it is not difficult to build a low c.e. set A that is not K-trivial, and hence not low for K, by combining lowness requirements with requirements of the form $\exists n\,(K(A \upharpoonright n) > K(n) + c)$. (In Theorem 11.4.1, we will see that all K-trivial sets are superlow, and hence array computable (by the remark following the proof of Theorem 2.23.9). Thus the proof of Theorem 2.23.9 is another way to build such an A.) Again, we can use this construction to define a nontrivial pseudo-jump operator taking any set X to a low set $Y \not\leqslant_{\mathrm{LR}} X$. By Theorem 2.12.3, there is a high c.e. set X such that $\emptyset' \not\leqslant_{\mathrm{LR}} X$. Thus the collection of (uniformly) almost everywhere dominating sets contains incomplete c.e. sets, but does not contain all high c.e. sets.

The proof of Theorem 11.2.5 is quite similar to the direct proofs of the existence of noncomputable K-trivial sets in the previous section. It is natural to wonder whether the notions of K-triviality, lowness for 1-randomness, and lowness for K might coincide. (We have already seen that the latter two do coincide, and imply K-triviality.) When this question was first considered, there was some evidence that this should not be the case. For instance, it was known that the K-trivial sets are all Δ^0_2, and that the join of two K-trivial sets is K-trivial, but it was open whether the analogous facts hold for lowness for 1-randomness. In the other direction, it was known that the sets that are low for 1-randomness are GL_1, and that, trivially, if a set A is low for 1-randomness, then so is every A-computable set, but it was open whether the analogous facts hold for K-triviality. As we will see below, however, Nies has developed a powerful method that shows, among other things, that these three notions do in fact coincide, and hence define the same natural class of randomness-theoretically weak sets.

We finish this section by proving a useful characterization of lowness for 1-randomness (and hence of K-triviality). The "if" direction of this result is similar to a lemma Kučera and Terwijn [223] used in proving Theorem 11.2.6.

Theorem 11.2.8 (Nies and Stephan, see [299]). *A is low for 1-randomness iff there are a Σ^0_1 class R and a c such that $\mu(R) < 1$ and $K^A(\sigma) \leqslant |\sigma| - c \Rightarrow [\![\sigma]\!] \subseteq R$ for all σ.*

Proof. Suppose such a class R exists. Let X be 1-random. By Theorem 6.10.2, there are σ and $Y \in \overline{R}$ such that $X = \sigma Y$. We have $K^A(Y \upharpoonright n) > n - c$ for all n, so Y is 1-random relative to A, and hence so is X. Thus A is low for 1-randomness.

Now suppose that A is low for 1-randomness. Let V be a Σ^0_1 class such that $\mu(V) < 1$ and V contains all sets that are not 1-random. We claim that there are σ and k such that $[\![\sigma]\!] \nsubseteq V$ and $\forall \tau \succcurlyeq \sigma\,(K^A(\tau) \leqslant |\tau| - k \Rightarrow [\![\tau]\!] \subseteq V)$. Suppose that this is not the case. Then we can construct a set X as follows. Let $\tau_0 = \lambda$, and let τ_{n+1} be a proper extension of τ_n with $[\![\tau_{n+1}]\!] \nsubseteq V$ and $K^A(\tau_{n+1}) \leqslant |\tau| - n$. Let $X = \lim_n \tau_n$. Then X is not 1-random relative to A. But $X \notin V$, so X is 1-random, which contradicts the assumption that A is low for 1-randomness.

Thus we can fix σ and k as above and let $R = [\![\{\tau : [\![\sigma\tau]\!] \subseteq V\}]\!]$. Then $\overline{R}$ is a Π^0_1 class of 1-random sets, and hence cannot be null, so $\mu(R) < 1$. Furthermore, there is a c such that

$$K^A(\tau) \leqslant |\tau| - c \Rightarrow K^A(\sigma\tau) \leqslant |\sigma\tau| - k \Rightarrow [\![\sigma\tau]\!] \subseteq V \Rightarrow [\![\sigma]\!] \subseteq R.$$

□

11.3 Degrees of K-trivial sets

The technique introduced in this section, which has been called the *decanter method*, or, in its full-fledged form, the *golden run method*, is a fundamental one in the study of K-triviality. In this section we will look only at the basic method, leaving the more difficult nonuniform applications to the following section. It is not difficult to show that K-trivial sets are wtt-incomplete. The following stronger result shows that the noncomputable c.e. K-trivial sets provide a more or less natural solution to Post's Problem.

Theorem 11.3.1 (Downey, Hirschfeldt, Nies, and Stephan [117]). *Every K-trivial set is Turing incomplete.*

The decanter method evolved from attempted proofs of the negation of this result, the failures of which were eventually turned around into a proof of the theorem, in the time-honored symmetry of computability theory. Subsequently, the removal of artifacts of the original proof, and the use of a treelike structure by Nies, led to a very powerful and general technique, and, as we will see in the following section, to vast improvements of Theorem 11.3.1. The account below is similar to the one in [104].

11.3.1 A first approximation: wtt-incompleteness

The fundamental tool used in all of these proofs is what can be described as "amplification". Suppose that A is K-trivial with constant of triviality b, and we are using the KC Theorem to build a prefix-free machine M whose coding constant within the universal prefix-free machine $\mathcal{U}$ is known to be d. Then if we enumerate the request (p, n), meaning that we make M describe n by a string of length p, then $\mathcal{U}$ must describe n by a string of length at most $p + d$, and hence there must eventually also be a stage s at which $\mathcal{U}$ provides a description of $A_s \upharpoonright n$ of length at most $p + b + d$. Thinking of an opponent who provides $\mathcal{U}$-descriptions, we notice that the existence of the constants b and d means that we have to spend more measure describing n than the opponent does describing $A_s \upharpoonright n$. (That is, our description increases $\mu([\![\operatorname{dom} M]\!])$ more than the opponent's increases $\mu([\![\operatorname{dom} \mathcal{U}]\!])$.)

If we are trying to claim that A is *not* K-trivial, then we want to force the opponent to waste more measure trying to make A be K-trivial than we do in playing our strategy. The most basic idea is to force the opponent to give short descriptions of many different strings of the same length (i.e., versions of $A_s \upharpoonright n$ for different s but the same n). The easiest illustration of this method is to show that no K-trivial is wtt-complete.

Proposition 11.3.2. *If A is K-trivial then A is wtt-incomplete.*

Proof. Suppose that A is K-trivial and wtt-complete. We know that A is Δ^0_2, so we fix an approximation of A. Let b be a constant of K-triviality for A. We build a c.e. set B, and a prefix-free machine M via the KC Theorem. By the recursion theorem, we may assume we know a coding constant d of M in $\mathcal{U}$, and also a wtt-reduction $\Gamma^A = B$ with computable use γ (as explained in the proof of Theorem 2.20.1).

Let $\ell(s)$ be the length of agreement of $\Gamma^{A_s}[s]$ and B_s. We pick $k = 2^{b+d+1}$ many followers $m_0 > \cdots > m_{k-1}$ targeted for B and wait for a stage s such that $\ell(s) > m_0$.

At this stage we choose a fresh large $n > \gamma(m_0)$ (and hence greater than $\gamma(m_i)$ for all $i < k$), and enumerate a KC request $(0, n)$. At some stage s_0 we must get a $\mathcal{U}$-description of $A_{s_0} \upharpoonright n$ of length $b + d$ or less. That is, at least $2^{-(b+d)}$ must be added to the measure of the domain of $\mathcal{U}$.

At the first such stage s_0, we put m_0 into B, ensuring that $A \upharpoonright n \neq A_{s_0} \upharpoonright n$, since $n > \gamma(m_0)$. (In this case we could use any of the m_i's, but later it will be important that the m_i's enter in reverse order of size.) Now there must be a stage $s_1 > s_0$ with $\ell(s_1) > m_0$ such that $A_{s_1} \upharpoonright n \neq A_{s_0} \upharpoonright n$ and $A_{s_1} \upharpoonright n$ *also* has a $\mathcal{U}$-description of length at most $b+d$. Thus we now know that $\mu([\![\mathrm{dom}\,\mathcal{U}]\!])$ is at least $2 \cdot 2^{-(b+d)}$.

We now put m_1 into B, which leads once again to a stage $s_2 > s_1$ with $\ell(s_2) > m_0$ such that $A_{s_2} \upharpoonright n \neq A_{s_i} \upharpoonright n$ for $i = 0, 1$ and $A_{s_2} \upharpoonright n$ has a $\mathcal{U}$-description of length at most $b + d$. We now know that $\mu([\![\mathrm{dom}\,\mathcal{U}]\!])$ is at least $3 \cdot 2^{-(b+d)}$.

If we repeat this process one time for each m_i, we eventually conclude that $\mu([\![\mathrm{dom}\,\mathcal{U}]\!]) \geqslant k \cdot 2^{-(b+d)} = 2^{b+d+1}2^{-(b+d)} = 2$, which is impossible. $\square$

11.3.2 A second approximation: impossible constants

The argument above is fine for weak truth table reducibility, since the use does not change once defined, but there clearly are problems when Γ is a *Turing* reduction. That is, suppose that our new goal is to show that no K-trivial is Turing complete. The problem with the above construction is now the following.

When we play our M-description of n, we use all the measure of dom M to describe a single number. Now it is in the opponent's power to move the use $\gamma(m_0, s)$ (or even $\gamma(m_{k-1}, s)$) to some value bigger than n before matching our description of n with a description of $A_t \upharpoonright n$ for some t. Thus it costs the opponent very little to match our M-description of n: the opponent changes $A \upharpoonright \gamma(m_{k-1}, s)$, makes $\gamma(m_{k-1}, s+1)$ larger than n, then describes $A_{s+1} \upharpoonright n$, and we can no longer cause *any* changes of A below n, as all the Γ-uses we control are too big.

It is at this point that we realize it is pretty dumb of us to try to describe n in one go. All that really matters is that we load lots of measure beyond some point where the opponent will be forced to match it many times. For instance, in the wtt case, we certainly could have used many n's beyond $\gamma(m_0)$, giving each a description of length e for some large e, and attacking the opponent by putting markers into B only once we have amassed the requisite measure of descriptions of numbers beyond $\gamma(m_0)$. This is the idea behind our second approximation to the proof of Theorem 11.3.1.

In this case, we assume we are given a Turing reduction $\Gamma^A = B$ and make the following *impossible assumption*: We assume that the constants b and d, defined as in the proof of Proposition 11.3.2, are both 0.

Hence, when we enumerate a request (p, n) for M, the opponent will eventually enumerate a $\mathcal{U}$-description of $A_s \upharpoonright n$ of length at most p. (Notice that, with this assumption, in the wtt case we would need only one follower.)

With Γ a Turing reduction, we still have the problem outlined above, even with our impossible assumption. That is, if we use the dumb strategy of the wtt case, then the opponent can move Γ-uses before describing initial segments of A, thus describing each such segment only once.

To get around this problem, we use a drip-feed strategy for loading measure, as discussed above. To make our terminology more precise, when we issue a request (p, n) for M, we say that we have *loaded* 2^{-p} much measure at n. We pick a follower m and attempt to load a large amount of measure, say $\frac{3}{4}$, at n's greater than $\gamma(m)$ (we write $\gamma(m)$ instead of $\gamma(m, s)$, thinking of $\gamma(m)$ as a movable marker with value $\gamma(m, s)$ at stage s). Suppose we succeed, and the opponent provides corresponding short descriptions of initial segments of the current approximation to A, which amounts to adding $\frac{3}{4}$ to the domain of $\mathcal{U}$. Then we can force $A \upharpoonright \gamma(m)$ to change, and the opponent will not have another measure $\frac{3}{4}$ many short descriptions for the initial segments of the new version of A.

To deal with the possibility of $A \upharpoonright \gamma(m)$ changing before we are ready to force it to change ourselves, we establish a *trash quota*, say $\frac{1}{8}$. We want to make sure that the total measure corresponding to descriptions we waste (that is, descriptions that do not force the opponent to issue two corresponding descriptions of initial segments of approximations to A) does not exceed this quota. Thus, we begin by loading measure in chunks of size $\frac{1}{16}$. That is, we pick an $n_0 > \gamma(m)$ and issue the request $(4, n_0)$.

The opponent now has two options. One is to change $A \upharpoonright \gamma(m)$ and move $\gamma(m)$. In this case, we have wasted $\frac{1}{16}$ much measure. Then we restart our loading procedure, but in chunks of size $\frac{1}{32}$. The opponent's other option is to issue a description of length 4 of the current approximation to $A \upharpoonright n_0$. If that happens then we pick a new large number n_1 and load another $\frac{1}{16}$ much measure at n_1. Again we wait for the opponent's reaction.

If the opponent issues a description of length 4 of the current approximation to $A \upharpoonright n_1$, then we pick a new large number n_2 and load yet another $\frac{1}{16}$ much measure at n_2. However, if instead the opponent moves $\gamma(m)$, we make the following crucial observation: The $\frac{1}{16}$ much measure we loaded at n_1 is wasted, but the $\frac{1}{16}$ much measure we loaded at n_0 is not, because the opponent has already issued a description of length 4 of a version of $A \upharpoonright n$. By changing $A \upharpoonright \gamma(m)$, the opponent is now committed to issuing a second description of length 4, for the new approximation to $A \upharpoonright n$ (since $n > \gamma(m)$, and hence $A \upharpoonright n$ also changes). So we can move on to loading measure in chunks of $\frac{1}{32}$ while having added only $\frac{1}{16}$ to our total wasted measure.

In general, every time the opponent moves $\gamma(m)$ and forces us to go from loading measure in chunks of size 2^{-k} to loading it in chunks of size $2^{-(k+1)}$, we add only 2^{-k} to our total wasted measure, since only the very last chunk of measure of size 2^{-k} we loaded is wasted. Thus our total wasted measure never exceeds our trash quota $\frac{1}{8}$. If indeed $\Gamma^B = A$, then the opponent can move $\gamma(m)$ only finitely often, so we eventually reach a final level at which we are loading measure in chunks of some fixed size 2^{-k}. Once the total measure we have loaded, not counting the wasted amount, reaches our goal of $\frac{3}{4}$, we force $A \upharpoonright \gamma(m)$ to change ourselves, and win as before.

We think of the above strategy as a procedure $P(\frac{3}{4}, \frac{1}{8})$ designed to load $\frac{3}{4}$ much measure beyond $\gamma(m)$ and then change $A \upharpoonright \gamma(m)$, while wasting at most $\frac{1}{8}$ much measure. We call the set of n such that we give n a short description and then force the opponent to give two corresponding descriptions of versions of $A \upharpoonright n$ a *2-set*, and we call the sum of the measure we loaded at these n the *weight* of this set.

In this simplified construction, building a 2-set of weight $\frac{3}{4}$ (or any weight greater than $\frac{1}{2}$) is all we need to do, so running the single procedure $P(\frac{3}{4}, \frac{1}{8})$ suffices. In the next subsection, we introduce the general concept of a k-*set*, and use it to prove that K-trivials cannot be Turing complete.

11.3.3 The less impossible case

We now remove the simplifying assumption of the previous section. A k-*set* is a set of numbers n such that we give n a short description and then force the opponent to give at least k many corresponding descriptions of versions of $A \upharpoonright n$. As before, the *weight* of such a set is the sum of the measure we load at these n. In the previous section, by a "corresponding description", we meant one of the same length as the one we gave. But without the simplifying assumption of that section, when we give n a description of length m, all we know is that the opponent will eventually have to give $A \upharpoonright n$ a description of length at most $m+b+d$, where b and d are as in the proof of Proposition 11.3.2. So it is no longer enough to force the opponent to provide two descriptions to each one of ours. We now need the opponent to provide at least 2^{b+d+1} many descriptions to each one of ours. In other words, where in the previous section we built a 2-set of weight greater than $\frac{1}{2}$, we now need to build a 2^{b+d+1}-set of weight greater than $\frac{1}{2}$. To do so, we take the key idea from the wtt case, in which the use is fixed but the coding constants are nontrivial, namely, that we can use multiple followers to build a k-set for any k we want.

To simplify our discussion for now, suppose that $b+d = 1$. Emulating the wtt-case, we work with $k = 2^{1+1} = 4$ and try to build a 4-set of sufficient weight. We break this task into the construction of a 2-set, which is turned into a 3-set, which is finally turned into the desired 4-set. We view these constructions as procedures P_j for $2 \leqslant j \leqslant 4$, which are called in reverse order as follows.

Our overall construction begins with, say, $P_4(\frac{3}{4}, \frac{1}{8})$, whose task is to build a 4-set C_4 of weight $\frac{3}{4}$ while wasting at most $\frac{1}{8}$ much measure.

To do this, $P_4(\frac{3}{4}, \frac{1}{8})$ calls procedures of the form $P_3(g, q)$, which build a 3-set C_3 by calling procedures of the form $P_2(g', q')$. The latter build a 2-set C_2 and enumerate a KC set L.

Each procedure P_j has rational parameters $g, q \in [0, 1]$. The *goal* g is the weight the procedure wants C_j to reach, and the *trash quota* q is how much measure it is allowed to waste.

The main idea is that procedures P_j will ask that procedures P_i for $i < j$ do the work for them, with P_2 eventually really doing the work. The goals of the P_i are determined inductively by the trash quotas of the P_j for $j > i$, in such a way as to ensure that if the procedures are canceled before completing their tasks, then the amount of measure wasted is acceptably small.

We begin the construction by starting $P_4(\frac{3}{4}, \frac{1}{8})$. Its action is first to choose a follower m_4 and wait until $\Gamma^A(m_4)\downarrow$. Then P_4 calls $P_3(2^{-4}, 2^{-5})$. The idea here is that, instead of directly loading measure in chunks of size $\frac{1}{16}$ beyond $\gamma(m_4)$ as in the previous section, P_4 delegates that task to P_3. (The precise numbers being used here are immaterial, of course, except that we need to keep the total wasted measure below P_4's trash quota of $\frac{1}{8}$.)

While we are waiting for P_3 to return, if $\gamma(m_4)$ moves, then we restart, this time calling $P_3(2^{-4}, 2^{-6})$. Otherwise, the following occurs.

The procedure $P_3(2^{-4}, 2^{-5})$ picks a follower $m_3 > m_4$, waits until $\Gamma^A(m_3)\downarrow$, and then calls $P_2(2^{-5}, 2^{-6})$. That procedure picks its own follower $m_2 > m_3$ and waits until $\Gamma^A(m_2)\downarrow$. At this point, P_2 begins to try to load 2^{-5} much measure beyond $\gamma(m_2)$, in chunks of size 2^{-7}, just as in the previous section. (That is, P_2 uses L to give descriptions of length 7 to n's bigger than $\gamma(m_2)$.)

While all of this action is occurring, many things can happen. The simplest case is that nothing happens to the uses, and hence, as with the wtt case, P_2 successfully loads its goal amount 2^{-5} beyond $\gamma(m_2, s)$. Should this happen then P_2 enumerates m_2 into B, forcing $A \upharpoonright \gamma(m_2, s)$ to change and hence creating a 2-set C_2 of weight 2^{-5}. Then P_2 returns.

Now P_3 sees that it has 2^{-5} much measure loaded beyond $\gamma(m_3)$, but it would like another chunk to be loaded there, so it again calls $P_2(2^{-5}, 2^{-6})$ (which now chooses a new follower m_2). If P_2 again returns successfully, then we have a 2-set of weight 2^{-4} consisting of numbers greater than $\gamma(m_3)$ (which we are assuming has not moved). Now P_3 enumerates m_3 into B, causing this 2-set to become a 3-set of weight 2^{-4}, and returns.

Now, of course, P_4 needs to call P_3 again, which will cause further calls to P_2. One can think of this construction as "wheels within wheels within wheels", spinning ever faster.

Of course, our difficulties all come about because uses can change, but the construction in the previous section gave us a technique to deal with that issue. For example, if only $\gamma(m_2)$ moves then, as before, only the last amount of measure loaded by P_2 is wasted. So, again as before, P_2 starts loading measure in chunks that are half the size of the ones it had been previously using. Since we are assuming that $\Gamma^A = B$, and hence all uses stabilize, this problem will eventually stop occurring for any particular run of P_2.

In general, the inductive procedures work similarly. For example, if $\gamma(m_3)$ moves during a run of P_3, then P_3 cancels the current run of $P_2(g, q)$ and calls $P_2(g, \frac{q}{2})$ instead. Any measure that this run of $P_2(g, q)$ had loaded is wasted, but what previous calls to P_2 had accomplished is not. In the end, we can argue by induction that all tasks are completed.

We now turn to the formal details of the construction.

Proof of Theorem 11.3.1. Suppose that A is K-trivial and Turing complete. We know that A is Δ^0_2, so we fix an approximation of A. Let b be a constant of K-triviality for A. We build a c.e. set B, and a prefix-free machine M via the KC Theorem. By the recursion theorem, we may assume we know a coding constant d of M in $\mathcal{U}$, and also a reduction $\Gamma^A = B$. As above, we will think of the use $\gamma^A(n)$ as a marker whose value might change during the construction. Let $k = 2^{b+d+1}$.

We assume we have sped up our enumeration of stages enough so that $K_s(A_s \upharpoonright n) \leqslant K_s(n) + b$ for all s and all n mentioned in the construction by stage s.

As in the wtt case, our construction will build a k-set C_k of weight greater than $\frac{1}{2}$ to reach a contradiction. The procedure P_j for $2 \leqslant j \leqslant k$ enumerates a j-set C_j. As explained above, the construction begins by calling P_k, which calls P_{k-1} several times, and so on down to P_2, which enumerates L (and C_2). Each call of a procedure P_j has parameters $g = 2^{-x}$ and $q = 2^{-y}$ with $q < g$, again as explained above.

We now describe the procedure $P_j(g, q)$.

1. Choose m_j large.

2. Wait until $\Gamma^A(m_j)\downarrow = 0$.

3. Let v be the number of times this procedure has gone through step 2.

$j = 2$: Pick a large number n. Put (r, n) into L, where $2^{-r} = 2^{-v}q$. Wait for a stage t such that $K_t(n) \leqslant r + d$, and put n into C_1.

$j > 2$: Let w be the number of P_{j-1} procedures called so far. Call $P_{j-1}(2^{-v}q, 2^{j-k-w-1}q)$.

4. If the weight of C_{j-1} is less than g then repeat step 3.

5. Put m_j into B. This action forces A to change below $\gamma^A(m_j) < \min(C_{j-1})$, and hence makes C_{j-1} into a j-set (if we assume inductively that C_{j-1} is a $(j-1)$-set). So put C_{j-1} into C_j, declare $C_{j-1} = \emptyset$, and return.

If $\gamma^A(m_j)$ changes during the execution of the loop at step 3, then cancel the runs of all subprocedures, and go to step 2. Despite the cancellations, C_{j-1} is now a j-set because of this very change. (This is an important point, as it ensures that the measure associated with numbers already in C_{j-1} is not wasted.) So put C_{j-1} into C_j and declare $C_{j-1} = \emptyset$.

This completes the description of the procedures. The construction consists of calling $P_k(\frac{3}{4}, \frac{1}{8})$, say. It is straightforward to argue that since trash quotas are inductively halved each time they are injured by a use change, their sum is bounded by $\frac{1}{4}$, and that therefore L is a KC set. Furthermore C_k is a k-set of weight $\frac{3}{4}$, which is a contradiction since then the measure of $\mathcal{U}$ exceeds 1, as in the proof of Proposition 11.3.2. □

The following description is taken from [118]. (We have changed some variable names in this quote to match the ones we use.) "We can visualize this construction by thinking of a machine similar to Lerman's pinball machine (see [366, Chapter VIII.5]). However, since we enumerate rational quantities instead of single objects, we replace the balls in Lerman's machine by amounts of a precious liquid, say 1955 Biondi-Santi Brunello. Our machine consists of decanters $C_k, C_{k-1}, \ldots, C_0$. At any stage C_j is a j-set. We put C_{j-1} above C_j so that C_{j-1} can be emptied into C_j. The height of a decanter is changeable. The procedure $P_j(g, q)$ wants to add weight g to C_j, by filling C_{j-1} up to g and then emptying it into C_j. The emptying corresponds to adding one more A-change.

"The emptying device is a hook (the $\gamma^A(m)$-marker), which besides being used on purpose may go off finitely often by itself. When C_{j-1} is emptied into C_j then $C_{j-2}, \ldots, C_0$ are spilled on the floor, since the new hooks emptying $C_{j-1}, \ldots, C_0$ may be much longer (the $\gamma^A(m)$-marker may move to a much bigger position), and so we cannot use them any more to empty those decanters in their old positions.

"We first pour wine into the highest decanter C_0, representing the left domain of L, in portions corresponding to the weight of requests entering L. We want to ensure that at least half the wine we put into C_0 reaches C_k.

Recall that the parameter β is the amount of garbage $P_j(g,q)$ allows. If v is the number of times the emptying device has gone off by itself, then P_j lets P_{j-1} fill C_{j-1} in portions of size $2^{-v}q$. Then when C_{j-1} is emptied into C_j, at most $2^{-v}q$ much liquid can be lost because of being in higher decanters $C_{j-2},\ldots,C_0$. The procedure $P_2(g,q)$ is special but limits the garbage in the same way: it puts requests (r_n,n) into L where $2^{-r_n}=2^{-v}q$. Once it sees the corresponding $A\restriction n$ description, it empties C_0 into C_1 (but C_0 may be spilled on the floor before that because of a lower decanter being emptied)."

11.4 K-triviality and lowness

At first glance, it may seem unclear whether the K-trivial sets are merely an artifact of the definition of prefix-free complexity. (Recall from Theorem 3.4.4 that all C-trivial sets are computable.) However, work of several researchers has shown that the class of K-trivial sets is remarkably robust, in that it has a host of natural characterizations via other notions of randomness theoretic weakness. This phenomenon is similar to what we saw for 1-randomness, where various approaches yield the same notion, but in this case the equivalence proofs are often rather involved. These alternate definitions also have significant degree-theoretic implications. For example, all K-trivial sets are superlow, and the class of K-trivial sets is closed downward under Turing reducibility, and in fact is an ideal (i.e., is also closed under join). In this section, we prove Nies' result from [302] that every K-trivial set is low for 1-randomness, and hence low for K. We have already seen that the latter two notions are equivalent, and lowness for K clearly implies K-triviality, so all three notions coincide.

We begin with a proof that all K-trivial sets are superlow, and then describe how to modify this proof to obtain lowness for 1-randomness. The method we introduce here, called the *golden run* method, has proved to be one of the major tools in the study of K-triviality and related notions.

Theorem 11.4.1 (Nies [302]). *Every K-trivial set is superlow.*

Proof. We build on the terminology and notation of the previous section, and introduce an improved version of the decanter method.

Let A be K-trivial. In approximating A', when we see a convergent computation $\Phi_e^{A_s}(e)$, we need to decide whether to believe this computation. If we make only finitely many mistakes for each e, then we ensure that A is low, while if we can keep the number of mistakes below a computable bound, then we ensure that A is superlow. There is no claim to uniformity in the theorem, so we can have infinitely many guessing procedures, as long as one them is successful.

As before, we exploit the fact that changes to the approximation of a K-trivial set come at a certain cost, in terms of additional short descriptions of initial segments. By loading measure beyond the use of a convergent computation $\Phi_e^{A_s}(e)$, we ensure that any violation of this use will come at a relatively large cost. Only once we have loaded sufficient measure will we believe this computation. This procedure ensures that the number of times we believe an incorrect computation of this form for a given e is computably bounded. (If the cost to the opponent of violating the use of a computation is made to be 2^{-k}, say, then we know we will believe no more than 2^k many incorrect computations.) Thus we can approximate A' in an ω-c.e. manner, whence A is superlow.

In the proof of Theorem 11.3.1, we built a c.e. set B and assumed we had a reduction $\Gamma^A = B$. Whenever we wanted to change A at a stage s to transform a $(j-1)$-set C_{j-1} into a j-set, we could do so simply by enumerating some number m_j into B, since we arranged things so that an A-change below $\gamma^A(m_j)[s]$ was sufficient to make C_{j-1} into a j-set, and such a change was guaranteed to happen once m_j entered B. What caused us problems was that A could change *before* we wanted it to, but we had no trouble ensuring that A would change once we wanted it to. When showing that A is superlow, rather than merely incomplete, we no longer have quite so much power. If the opponent is to prevent A from being superlow, it has to change A reasonably often, but we cannot force such changes to occur every time we would like them to.

We get around this problem by further distributing our measure-loading strategy among subprocedures. In the proof of Theorem 11.3.1, a procedure P_j called a P_{j-1} procedure several times, thus obtaining several $(j-1)$-sets. When it had enough such sets, it then promoted them to j-sets by forcing appropriate changes in A. The analogous procedure in this proof will run several subprocedures simultaneously. Each subprocedure will be associated with some index e. Each $(j-1)$-set C produced by such a subprocedure will have its corresponding measure loaded beyond some number n, so that a change of the approximation to $A \upharpoonright n$ to a hitherto unseen string will cause C to become a j-set. Our level j procedure will assume that such changes do not occur and, under that assumption, will guess at values of A'. That is, when it has an m such that a change in $A \upharpoonright m$ would allow it to transform a $(j-1)$-set C of sufficient weight given to it by a subprocedure associated with e into a j-set, and it sees that $\Phi_e^{A_s}(e)\downarrow$ with use below m, then it will believe that computation. If it is wrong, then C will be promoted. If it is wrong sufficiently often for subprocedures associated with some e, then it will build up a j-set with weight equal to its goal, and hence will return. If not, then it will be able to bound the number of wrong guesses it makes about the value of each $A'(e)$, and hence ensure that A is superlow.

We envision the construction as happening on an infinitely branching tree of finite depth k (where k is as in the proof of Theorem 11.3.1), with each procedure on the tree having infinitely many subprocedures below it. As in the proof of Theorem 11.3.1, the top procedure will attempt to produce a k-set of inconsistently large measure, and hence will never return. Thus, at some point in the construction, we will start a run of some procedure that neither returns nor is canceled, but such that all the subprocedures it ever calls either return or are canceled. As outlined above, this run will succeed in guessing A' with sufficiently few mistakes to ensure that A is superlow. We call such a run a *golden run*.

It will be convenient to have two kinds of procedures. The procedure P_j calls subprocedures $Q_{j-1,e,u}$, corresponding to potential uses u of convergent computations $\Phi_e^{A_s}(e)$, which in turn call procedure P_{j-1} (except for the procedures $Q_{1,e,u}$, which are the ones that actually perform the measure loading by enumerating requests into a KC set L). Each call to a procedure comes with two parameters, as in the proof of Theorem 11.3.1, a goal g and a trash quota q. As in that proof, a run of a procedure may be canceled due to a premature A-change, in which case it will generate a certain amount of "wasted measure". Again as in that proof, the trash quota will bound that amount. We choose our trash quotas to ensure that the total amount of wasted measure produced over the entire construction is small, and choose the goals of calls to subprocedures made by a particular run of a procedure to be small enough that the measure wasted by their potential cancelations adds up to no more than the trash quota of that run.

We now proceed with the formal details of the description of the procedures and the construction. The approximation to A' showing that A is superlow will not happen during the construction, but will be built after the fact, in the verification. Let b be a constant of K-triviality for A. We assume we have sped up our stages sufficiently so that $K_s(A \upharpoonright n) \leqslant K_s(n)+b$ for all s. Let d be a coding constant, given by the recursion theorem, for the machine corresponding to the KC set L we build. Let $k = 2^{b+d+1}$.

Procedure $P_i(g,q)$, where $1 < i \leqslant k$ and $g = 2^{-l} \geqslant q = 2^{-r}$ for some l and r. This procedure enumerates a set C, initially empty. At stage s, declare s to be *available*. (Availability is a local notion, applicable only to this particular run of this procedure.) For each $e \leqslant s$, proceed as follows.

1. If e is available and $\Phi_e^A(e)[s]\downarrow$, then let u be the use of this computation and call $Q_{i-1,e,u}(2^{-(e+1)}g, \min(2^{-(e+1)}g, 2^{-(2i+n)}))$, where n is the number of runs of Q_{i-1}-procedures that have been started by this point. Declare e to be unavailable.

2. If e is unavailable due to a run of $Q_{i-1,e,u}(g',q')$ and $A_s \upharpoonright u \neq A_{s-1} \upharpoonright u$, then declare e to be available, say that this run of $Q_{i-1,e,u}(g',q')$ is *released* and proceed as follows, where D is the set being built by the run of $Q_{i-1,e,u}(g',q')$.

   (a) If the weight of $C \cup D$ (defined as in the proof of Theorem 11.3.1) is less than g then put D into C and proceed to step 2(b). Otherwise, let $\widehat{D} \subseteq D$ be such that the weight of $C \cup \widehat{D}$ is g and put $\widehat{D}$ into C. (It will be easy to see that $\widehat{D}$ exists from the way D is defined below, because g is of the form 2^{-l} for some l smaller than all p such that we put (p, n) into L for $n \in D$.) Cancel all runs of subprocedures, and end this run of P_i, returning C.

(b) If the run of $Q_{i-1,e,u}(g', q')$ has not yet returned, then cancel it and all runs of subprocedures it has called.

Procedure $Q_{j,e,u}(g, q)$, *where* $1 < j < k$ *and* $g = 2^{-l} \geqslant q = 2^{-r}$ *for some* l *and* r. This procedure enumerates a set D, initially empty. Call $P_j(q, 2^{-(2j+3+n)})$, where n is the number of runs of P_j procedures started so far. If this procedure returns a set C, then put C into D. If the weight of D is less than g then repeat this process, calling a new run of P_j. Otherwise, end the procedure, returning D. (It is easy to see that in this case the weight of D is equal to g.)

Procedure $Q_{1,e,u}(g, q)$, *where* $g = 2^{-l} \geqslant q = 2^{-r}$ *for some* l *and* r. Choose a fresh large number n and put (r, n) into L. Wait for a stage $t > n$ such that $K_t(n) \leqslant r + d$ and then put n into D. If the weight of D is less than g then repeat this process. Otherwise, end the procedure, returning D. (Again, in this case the weight of D is equal to g.)

The construction begins by calling $P_{k,0}(1, 2^{-3})$. At each stage we perform one more cycle of each procedure that is currently running, descending through the levels and working in some effective order within each level.

We now verify that this construction works as intended. Let D_j be the union of the sets enumerated by Q_j-procedures. For $j > 1$, let C_j the union of the sets enumerated by P_j-procedures, and let $C_1 = \{n : \exists r\ ((r, n) \in L)\}$.

Lemma 11.4.2. *Each* C_i *is an* i*-set.*

Proof. For each $n \in D_1$, let s_n be the stage at which n enters D_1, and let r_n be the unique number such that $(r_n, n) \in L$. By construction, we have $K_{s_n}(A_{s_n} \upharpoonright n) \leqslant r_n + b + d$. Let $i \in [2, k]$ and assume by induction that for every $n \in D_{i-1}$, if n enters D_i at stage t then there are at least $i - 1$ many distinct strings σ of the form $K_v \upharpoonright n$ for $v \in [s_n, t]$ such that $K(\sigma) \leqslant r+b+d$. We show that C_i also has this property, which clearly implies that it is an i-set, and that D_i also has the property if $i < k$, so that the induction may continue. Suppose that n enters C_i at stage t. This enumeration happens at step 2(a) in the action of a run of some P_i-procedure for some e, and corresponds to the release of some run of a subprocedure $Q_{i-1,e,u}(g', q')$. By the inductive hypothesis, there are $i-1$ distinct strings σ of the form $A_v \upharpoonright n$ for $v \in [s_n, t)$ such that $K_v(\sigma) \leqslant r+b+d$. Furthermore, the approximation to $A \upharpoonright u$ cannot have changed between stages s_n and $t - 1$, since such a change would have caused the run of $Q_{i-1,e,u}(g', q')$ to have been released sooner. Since $A_t \upharpoonright u \neq A_{t-1} \upharpoonright u$, there is a new string $\tau = A_t \upharpoonright n$, not equal to any of these σ, such that $K_t(\tau) \leqslant r+b+d$. Since n is an arbitrary element of C_i, we see that C_i has the desired property, an in particular is an i-set. $\square$

The next lemma shows that trash quotas are respected.

Lemma 11.4.3. (i) *For $j \in [1, k)$, the weight of the set of numbers in $C_j \setminus D_j$ corresponding to a run of $Q_{j,e,u}(g, q)$ is at most q.*

(ii) *For $i \in (1, k]$, the weight of the set of numbers in $D_{i-1} \setminus C_i$ corresponding to a run of $P_i(g, q)$ is at most q.*

Proof. (i) There is at most one n corresponding to a run of $Q_{1,e,u}(g, q)$ in $C_1 \setminus D_1$, since no number is put into C_1 by this run until the previous number it put into C_1 enters D_1. For such an n, the unique $(r, n) \in L$ is such that $2^{-r} = q$. Thus the weight of n is q.

If $j > 1$, then all numbers in $C_j \setminus D_j$ corresponding to a run of $Q_{j,e,u}(g, q)$ correspond to a single run of $P_j(q, q')$, because each time such a run returns, its numbers enter D_j. Thus this number never returns, and hence the weight of the set of numbers corresponding to it is at most q.

(ii) Let n be one of the numbers corresponding to a run of $P_i(g, q)$ that is in D_{i-1} by a stage t but never enters C_i. Then n is put in D_{i-1} by a run of a subprocedure $Q_{i-1,e,u}(2^{-(e+1)}q, q')$ called by this run of $P_i(g, q)$. We claim that this run of $P_i(g, q)$ never calls a subprocedure $Q_{i-1,e,u'}$ after stage t. To verify this claim, first suppose that $A_s \restriction u \neq A_{s-1} \restriction u$ for some $s > t$. Since n does not enter C_i at stage s, it must be the case that the run of $P_i(g, q)$ returns at that stage, and n is not needed for that run to reach its goal. Now suppose that there is no such s. Then the run of $Q_{i-1,e,u}$ that put n into D_{i-1} is never released, and e is never available after stage t. In either case, the claim holds.

Thus, for each e there is at most one run of a subprocedure of the form $Q_{i-1,e,u}(2^{-(e+1)}q, q')$ called by our run of $P_i(g, q)$ that leaves numbers in $D_{i-1} \setminus C_i$. Thus the sum of the weights of these numbers over all such e is at most $\sum_e 2^{-(e+1)}q = q$. $\square$

Lemma 11.4.4. *L is a KC set.*

Proof. Since C_k is a k-set and $k = 2^{b+d+1}$, the weight of C_k is at most $\frac{1}{2}$, while the weight of $C_1 \setminus C_k$ is less than or equal to $\sum_{1 \leqslant j < k} C_j \setminus D_j + \sum_{1 < i \leqslant k} D_{i-1} \setminus C_i$, which by the previous lemma is bounded by the sum of the trash quotas of all procedures. These quotas were chosen so that this sum is at most $\frac{1}{2}$, so the weight of C_1 is at most 1. But the weight of L is equal to the weight of C_1, so L is a KC set. $\square$

There cannot be a k-set of weight 1, so the top procedure started at the beginning of the construction can never return, and of course it is never canceled. Since there are only finitely many levels of procedures, there must be some run of some procedure that neither returns nor is canceled, but such that all the subprocedures it calls either return or are canceled. In other words, there is a golden run of some procedure. This procedure cannot be a Q-procedure, since each run of a Q-procedure calls P-subprocedures with the same goal, and never cancels any of them itself, so that if it is never canceled, then it eventually fulfills its goal and returns. Thus the golden run is of some procedure P_i. We now show how to guess at A' in an ω-c.e. way.

Fix e. We begin by guessing that $e \notin A'$. Every time the golden run sees that $\Phi_e^A(e)[s]\downarrow$, it starts a run of a subprocedure $Q_{i-1,e,u}$, where u is the use of this computation. This run returns unless this use is violated before it can do so. If the subprocedure returns, we guess that $e \in A'$. If the use u is later violated, then we go back to guessing that $e \notin A'$. Every time a run of a subprocedure $Q_{i-1,e,u}$ returns, it adds $2^{-(e+1)}g$ to the weight of the set C associated with the golden run. Hence, we cannot guess wrongly at whether e is in A' more than 2^e many times, lest the golden run reach its goal and return. Thus A is superlow. □

Corollary 11.4.5 (Nies [302]). *Every K-trivial set is ω-c.e.*

The above proof also shows that the K-trivial sets have the following property, which will be relevant when we discuss strong jump traceability in Chapter 14. We write J^A for the jump of A thought of as a partial function. That is, $J^A(e) = \Phi_e^A(e)$.

Definition 11.4.6 (Nies [303]). A set A is *h-jump traceable* for a computable order h if there are uniformly c.e. sets $T_0, T_1, \ldots$ such that $|T_n| \leqslant h(n)$ and $J^A(n)\downarrow \;\Rightarrow J^A(n) \in T_n$ for all n.

A set A is *jump traceable* if it is h-jump traceable for some computable order h.

It is easy to see that there is a computable function f such that $J^A(f(e,n)) = \Phi_e^A(n)$ for all e and n, so A is jump traceable iff every A-partial computable function has a trace with some computable bound. Nies [303] showed the following.

Theorem 11.4.7 (Nies [303]). *A c.e. set is jump traceable iff it is superlow.*

On the other hand, Nies [303] also showed that there is a perfect Π_1^0 class of jump traceable sets (see Theorem 14.5.3 below), and that even within the ω-c.e. sets, jump traceability and superlowness are incomparable notions. For more on jump traceability, see Chapter 14, Nies [303], and Figueira, Nies, and Stephan [147].

It is easy to see that the proof of Theorem 11.4.1 also yields the following result, because instead of guessing at whether e is in A' with at most 2^e many mistakes for each e, we could just as easily trace the value of $J^A(e)$ for each e with at most 2^e many mistakes.

Theorem 11.4.8 (Nies [302]). *Every K-trivial set is jump traceable.*[1]

The proof of Theorem 11.4.1 can be modified to prove the following.

Theorem 11.4.9 (Nies and Hirschfeldt, see Nies [302]). *If a set is K-trivial then it is low for K.*

Proof. The proof is essentially the same as that of Theorem 11.4.1, except that the "triggering condition" for having a P-strategy launch a Q-substrategy changes. Thus we limit ourselves to giving the description of the procedures (which will be quite similar to the ones in the proof of Theorem 11.4.1) and the necessary changes to the verification.

Procedure $P_i(g, q)$, where $1 < i \leqslant k$ and $g = 2^{-l} \geqslant q = 2^{-r}$ for some l and r. This procedure enumerates a set C, initially empty. At stage s, declare each $\sigma \in 2^s$ to be *available.* For each $\sigma \in 2^{\leqslant s}$, proceed as follows.

1. If σ is available and $\mathcal{U}^A(\sigma)[s]\downarrow = \tau$ for some τ, then let u be the use of this computation and call $Q_{i-1,\sigma,\tau,u}(2^{-|\sigma|}g, \min(2^{-|\sigma|}g, 2^{-(2i+n)}))$, where n is the number of runs of Q_{i-1}-procedures that have been started by this point. Declare σ to be unavailable.

2. If σ is unavailable due to a run of $Q_{i-1,\sigma,\tau,u}(g', q')$ and $A_s \upharpoonright u \neq A_{s-1} \upharpoonright u$, then declare σ to be available, say that this run of $Q_{i-1,\sigma,\tau,u}(g', q')$ is *released* and proceed as follows, where D is the set being built by the run of $Q_{i-1,\sigma,\tau,u}(g', q')$.

   (a) If the weight of $C \cup D$ is less than g then put D into C and proceed to step 2(b). Otherwise, let $\widehat{D} \subseteq D$ be such that the weight of $C \cup \widehat{D}$ is g and put $\widehat{D}$ into C. Cancel all runs of subprocedures, and end this run of P_i, returning C.

   (b) If the run of $Q_{i-1,\sigma,\tau}(g', q')$ has not yet returned, then cancel it and all runs of subprocedures it has called.

Procedure $Q_{j,\sigma,\tau,u}(g, q)$, where $1 < j < k$ and $g = 2^{-l} \geqslant q = 2^{-r}$ for some l and r. This procedure enumerates a set D, initially empty. Call $P_j(q, 2^{-(2j+3+n)})$, where n is the number of runs of P_j procedures started so far. If this procedure returns a set C, then put C into D. If the weight of D is less than g then repeat this process, calling a new run of P_j. Otherwise, end the procedure, returning D.

Procedure $Q_{1,\sigma,\tau,u}(g, q)$, where $g = 2^{-l} \geqslant q = 2^{-r}$ for some l and r. Choose a fresh large number n and put (r, n) into L. Wait for a stage $t > n$ such that $K_t(n) \leqslant r + d$ and then put n into D. If the weight of D is less than g then repeat this process. Otherwise, end the procedure, returning D.

---

[1]Zambella had earlier observed that if a set is low for 1-randomness then it is jump traceable. See Kučera and Terwijn [223].

The construction runs as before. The verification that there is a golden run is also essentially as before, except for the last paragraph of the proof of Lemma 11.4.3. In this case, the same argument as in that proof shows that for each σ, there is at most one run of a subprocedure of the form $Q_{i-1,\sigma,\tau,u}(2^{-|\sigma|}q, q')$ called by our run of $P_i(g, q)$ that leaves numbers in $D_{i-1} \setminus C_i$. Furthermore, either none of these subprocedures are ever released, in which case all of the corresponding σ's are in $\operatorname{dom} \mathcal{U}^A$, or the run of $P_i(g, q)$ terminates at a stage s such that none of these subprocedures terminate before stage s, in which case all of the corresponding σ's are in $\operatorname{dom} \mathcal{U}^{A_{s-1}}$. Thus the sum of the weights of these numbers over all such σ is bounded by either $\Omega^A q$ or $\Omega^A_{s-1} q$, and in either case is less than q.

Thus, all that is left to do is to take a golden run of some $P_i(g, q)$ and use it to show that A is low for K. To do so, we build a KC set W. Let $c = \log \frac{g}{q}$. Whenever a run of $Q_{i-1,\sigma,\tau,u}(2^{-|\sigma|}q, q')$ called by the golden run returns, put $(|\sigma| + c + 1, \tau)$ into W. We first show that W is a KC set.

Suppose that $(|\sigma| + c + 1, \tau)$ enters W at stage s because a run of $Q_{i-1,\sigma,\tau,u}(2^{-|\sigma|}q, q')$ returns, and $A_t \upharpoonright u = A_s \upharpoonright u$ for all $t > s$. Then $\sigma \in \operatorname{dom} \mathcal{U}^A$, so the weight contributed by all such requests is bounded by $2^{-(c+1)}\Omega^A < \frac{1}{2}$.

Now suppose that $(|\sigma| + c + 1, \tau)$ enters W at stage s because a run of $Q_{i-1,\sigma,\tau,u}(2^{-|\sigma|}q, q')$ returns, and there is a $t > s$ such that $A_t \upharpoonright u \neq A_s \upharpoonright u$. Then the set D returned by this run has weight $2^{-|\sigma|}q$ and enters the set C built by the golden run. Thus the weight contributed by all such requests is bounded by $\frac{2^{-(c+1)}}{q}$ times the weight of C. Since $\frac{2^{-(c+1)}}{q} = \frac{1}{2g}$ and the weight of C is bounded by g, the weight contributed by all such requests is bounded by $\frac{1}{2}$.

Now fix τ and let s be the least stage such that for some σ of length $K^A(\tau)$, we have $\mathcal{U}^A(\sigma) \downarrow [s] = \tau$ with use u and $A_t \upharpoonright u = A_s \upharpoonright u$ for all $t > s$. It follows easily from the minimality of s that σ must be available at s. Thus a run of $Q_{i-1,\sigma,\tau,u}$ is launched. This run is never canceled, and thus must return, by the definition of golden run. So $(|\sigma| + c + 1, \tau) \in W$, and hence $K(\tau) \leqslant K^A(\tau) + O(1)$, where the constant does not depend on τ. Since τ is arbitrary, A is low for K. □

The following corollary is immediate.

Corollary 11.4.10 (Nies [302]). *The class of K-trivial sets is closed downward under Turing reducibility.*

Theorems 11.2.4 and 11.4.9, together with the fact that lowness for K implies K-triviality, give us the following result, which speaks to the naturality of K-triviality as a notion of randomness-theoretic weakness.

Theorem 11.4.11 (Nies [302]). *The following are equivalent.*

(i) *A is K-trivial.*

(ii) *A is low for 1-randomness.*

(iii) *A is low for K.*

Thus we see that a set has trivial information content iff it has no derandomization power iff it has no compression power.

11.5 Cost functions

The idea of a cost function probably first explicitly appeared in Downey, Hirschfeldt, Nies, and Stephan [117], but is certainly implicit in earlier work such as Kučera and Terwijn [223], and arguably even in the first works on priority arguments. The following definition encompasses many important examples.

Definition 11.5.1 (Nies [306], Greenberg and Nies [172]).

(i) A *cost function* is a computable function $c : \mathbb{N} \times \mathbb{N} \to \mathbb{Q}^{\geqslant 0}$. It satisfies the *limit condition* if $\lim_n \sup_s c(n,s) = 0$. It is *monotone* if for each n, the sequence $c(n,0), c(n,1), \dots$ is nondecreasing and tends to a limit (which we denote by $c(n)$), and for each s, the sequence $c(0,s), c(1,s), \dots$ is nonincreasing. (Note that in this case, the limit condition can be expressed as $\lim_n c(n) = 0$.) We think of c as determining the *cost* $c(n,s)$ of changing the approximation to $A(n)$ at stage s for some Δ^0_2 set A being constructed.

(ii) Let $A_0, A_1, \dots$ be a computable approximation to a Δ^0_2 set A, and let n_s be the least n such that $A_{s+1}(n) \neq A_s(n)$. This approximation *obeys* the cost function c if $\sum_s c(n_s, s) < \infty$. A Δ^0_2 set A obeys c if it has some computable approximation that obeys c. When A is c.e., we assume this approximation $A_0, A_1, \dots$ is an approximation in the c.e. sense (i.e., $A_0 \subseteq A_1 \subseteq \cdots$).

We have already seen two examples of cost functions: the *standard cost function* for K-triviality, $c(n,s) = \sum_{n<i\leqslant s} 2^{-K_s(i)}$ and the cost function for lowness for K in the proof of Theorem 11.2.5, $c(n,s) = \sum\{2^{-|\tau|} : \mathcal{U}^A[s](\tau)\downarrow$ with use greater than $n\}$. Both satisfy the limit condition (as do all cost functions in which we are interested), but the latter is not monotone. It is straightforward to modify the proof of Theorem 11.1.5 to show that for any cost function c that satisfies the limit condition, there is a noncomputable (indeed, promptly simple) c.e. set that obeys c.

In the study of randomness-theoretic weakness, there are several constructions that can be cast in terms of cost functions. For example, in Theorem 14.4.5 we will see that for each Δ^0_2 1-random set Y, there is a cost function c such that every c.e. set that obeys c is computable from Y. In Section 14.4, we will further exploit the connections between cost functions and lowness notions.

One outgrowth of Nies' golden run method was the realization that not only can cost functions be used to build K-trivials sets, but they can in fact be used to *characterize* K-triviality.

Lemma 11.5.2 (Nies [302]). *Let A be K-trivial. There is a computable sequence of stages $v(0) < v(1) < \cdots$ such that, letting n_s be the least n such that $A_{v(s+1)}(n) \neq A_{v(s+2)}(n)$, and $\widehat{c}(n,s) = \sum_{n<i\leqslant v(s)} 2^{-K_{v(s+1)}(i)}$, we have $\sum_s \widehat{c}(n_s,s) < \infty$.*

Proof. Run the construction in the proof of Theorem 11.4.9, but with $\mathcal{U}^A$ replaced by M^A for a machine M such that for any σ and X, we have $M^X(\sigma) = \mathcal{U}(\sigma)$, and if this computation converges then the use of $M^X(\sigma)$ is $\mathcal{U}(\sigma)+1$ (where we identify numbers with strings as usual).

Choose a golden run of some procedure $P_i(g,q)$, and let C be the set it builds. For each e, since the approximation to $A \upharpoonright e+1$ eventually settles, there must be a run of $Q_{i-1,\sigma,e,e+1}(2^{-|\sigma|}q, q')$ started by our golden run with σ a minimal length $\mathcal{U}$-description of e, such that this run of $Q_{i-1,\sigma,e,e+1}(2^{-|\sigma|}q, q')$ returns but is never released. Thus we can let $v(0) = 0$ and let $v(s+1)$ be the first stage such that for all $e \leqslant v(s)$, a run of $Q_{i-1,\sigma_e,e,e+1}(2^{-|\sigma_e|}q, q')$ called by our golden run has returned and not yet been released, where σ_e is a minimal length $\mathcal{U}_{v(s+1)}$-description of e. Then, letting n_s be as above, every one of these runs corresponding to an $i \in (n_s, v(s)]$ is released by stage $v(s+2)$. Each such release contributes at least $2^{-|\sigma_e|}q = 2^{-K_{v(s+1)}(i)}q$ to the weight of C, so together they contribute at least $\widehat{c}(n_s,s)q$ to the weight of C. Since the weight of C is less than g, we have $\sum_s \widehat{c}(n_s,s) < \frac{g}{q} < \infty$. □

Theorem 11.5.3 (Nies [302]). *A set is K-trivial iff it obeys the standard cost function.*

Proof. Let A be K-trivial. Let c be the standard cost function, and let $\widehat{c}$, $v(s)$, and n_s be as in Lemma 11.5.2. Let s_0 be such that $\sum_{s\geqslant s_0} \widehat{c}(n_s,s) < 1$. Let $\widehat{A}_t = A_{v(s_0+t+1)}$. Then letting m_t be the least n such that $\widehat{A}_{t+1}(n) \neq \widehat{A}_t(n)$ (so that $m_t = n_{s_0+t}$), we have

$$\sum_t c(m_t,t) = \sum_t \sum_{m_t<i\leqslant t} 2^{-K_t(i)}$$
$$\leqslant \sum_t \sum_{m_t<i\leqslant v(s_0+t)} 2^{-K_{v(s_0+t+1)}(i)} \leqslant \sum_{s\geqslant s_0} \widehat{c}(n_s,s) < 1.$$

Thus $\widehat{A}_0, \widehat{A}_1, \ldots$ is an approximation witnessing the fact that A obeys the standard cost function. □

One consequence of this result is that K-triviality is basically a computably enumerable phenomenon.

Corollary 11.5.4 (Nies [302]). *Every K-trivial set is tt-computable from some c.e. K-trivial set.*

Proof. Let A be K-trivial and let $A_0, A_1, \ldots$ be an approximation to A witnessing the fact that A obeys the standard cost function. We may assume that $A_0 = \emptyset$. By Corollary 11.4.5 and the proof of Theorem 11.5.3, which shows that we can take the A_i to be a subsequence of any given approximation to A, we may also assume that we have a computable function f such that $|\{s : A_{s+1}(n) \neq A_s(n)\}| \leqslant f(n)$ for all n. Let $B_0 = \emptyset$. Let B_{s+1} be obtained from B_s as follows. First put all of B_s into B_{s+1}. Then, for each n such that $A_{s+1}(n) \neq A_s(n)$, let k be least such that $\langle n, k \rangle \notin B_s$ and add $\langle n, k \rangle$ to B_{s+1}. The B_i form an enumeration of a c.e. set B. It is easy to see that the B_i obey the standard cost function, whence B is K-trivial. Furthermore, $A(n)$ is equal to the parity of the largest $m \leqslant f(n)$ such that $\langle n, k \rangle \in B$ for all $k < m$, which is clearly a tt-reduction. □

The following lemma, noted by Downey, Hirschfeldt, Miller, and Nies [115], will be useful in Section 15.8. Its proof is similar to that of Lemma 11.5.2.

Lemma 11.5.5 (Downey, Hirschfeldt, Miller, and Nies [115]). *Let M be a prefix-free oracle machine and let A be K-trivial. There is a computable sequence of stages $v(0) < v(1) < \cdots$ such that, letting n_s be the least n such that $A_{v(s+1)}(n) \neq A_{v(s+2)}(n)$ and*

$$\widehat{c}(n, s) = \sum \{2^{-|\sigma|} : M^A(\sigma)[v(s+1)]\downarrow \\ \wedge\ n < \mathrm{use}(M^A(\sigma)[v(s+1)]) \leqslant v(s)\},$$

we have $\sum_s \widehat{c}(n_s, s) < \infty$.

There are of course many possible variations on the idea of a cost function. Nies [298] has begun a program he calls the *calculus of cost functions*, which seeks to gain insight into notions related to algorithmic randomness by abstracting the idea of a cost function. As a by-product of this work, he obtained an interesting characterization of K-triviality that does not seem to involve randomness notions directly, although it does involve left-c.e. reals, and its proof uses halting probabilities. (In Miller's Theorem 15.9.2 we will see another such characterization of K-triviality, involving left-d.c.e. reals.)

Nies began by associating a cost function to the approximation of a left-c.e. real α, namely $c_\alpha(n, s) = \alpha_s - \alpha_n$. His characterization of K-triviality is then as follows.

Theorem 11.5.6 (Nies [298]). *A set is K-trivial iff it obeys c_α for every left-c.e. real α.*

Proof. Any left-c.e. real α is the halting probability of some prefix-free machine N. We may assume that $\alpha_s = \mu(\mathrm{dom}\, N[s])$. We may also assume that exactly one string τ_s enters $\operatorname{dom} N$ at each stage s. We use an idea from the proof of Theorem 3.12.1. Let M be a prefix-free machine such that $M(\tau_s)\downarrow = s$ for each s, and $M(\sigma)\uparrow$ for all other strings σ. We may assume that we have sped up our stages sufficiently so that $M(\tau_s)[s]\downarrow = s$ for all s.

Let c_M be defined in the same way as the standard cost function, but with K_M in place of K. That is, writing $K_M[s]$ for the stage s approximation to K_M, we have $c_M(n,s) = \sum_{n<t\leqslant s} 2^{-K_M[s](t)}$. Then

$$c_\alpha(n,s) = \sum_{n<t\leqslant s} 2^{-|\tau_t|} = \sum_{n<t\leqslant s} 2^{-K_M[s](t)} = c_M(n,s),$$

so the proof of Theorem 11.5.3 shows that every K-trivial set obeys c_α, and if we take $\alpha = \Omega$, so that c_M is the standard cost function, then every set obeying c_α is K-trivial. □

11.6 The ideal of K-trivial degrees

Recall that a collection of degrees is an ideal if it is closed downward and under join. By Theorem 9.7.2, the left-c.e. K-trivial reals are closed under addition. Let A and B be K-trivial c.e. sets. Then $\alpha = A \oplus \emptyset$ and $\beta = \emptyset \oplus B$ are also K-trivial, so $A \oplus B = \alpha + \beta$ is K-trivial. In Corollary 11.4.10, we have seen that the K-trivials are closed downward under Turing reducibility, so we have the following result.

Theorem 11.6.1 (Nies [302]). *The K-trivial c.e. degrees form a Σ^0_3 ideal in the c.e. degrees.*

Proof. It remains to show that being K-trivial is a Σ^0_3 property. But A is K-trivial iff there is a c such that for all n and $m \leqslant n$, there is a stage s with $K_s(A_s \upharpoonright m) \leqslant K_s(m) + c$, which is clearly a Σ^0_3 definition. □

There are not many known natural ideals in the c.e. degrees, and the K-trivials form the first nontrivial example whose complexity is this low.

It turns out that closure under addition and join is a more general fact about K-triviality.

Theorem 11.6.2 (Downey, Hirschfeldt, Nies, and Stephan [117]). *If α and β are K-trivial then so is $\alpha + \beta$.*

Proof. Let α and β be K-trivial. We may assume that $\alpha + \beta$ is not computable, since otherwise we are done. Let c be such that $K(\alpha \upharpoonright n)$ and $K(\beta \upharpoonright n)$ are both below $K(n) + c$ for every n. By the Counting Theorem 3.7.6, there is a d such that for each n there are at most d many strings $\tau \in 2^n$ satisfying $K(\tau) \leqslant K(n) + c$. Let W_n be the set of such strings, and note that the W_n are uniformly c.e.

We can describe $(\alpha+\beta) \upharpoonright n$ by giving a description of n, the positions i and j of $\alpha \upharpoonright n$ and $\beta \upharpoonright n$ in the enumeration of W_n, and the carry bit from bit $n+1$ to bit n when adding α and β, which is well defined since we are assuming that $\alpha+\beta$ is not computable, and hence in particular not rational. Since $i, j \leqslant d$ for all n, we have that $K((\alpha+\beta) \upharpoonright n) \leqslant K(n)+O(1)$. □

Corollary 11.6.3 (Downey, Hirschfeldt, Nies, and Stephan [117]). *The class of K-trivial sets is closed under join.*

Proof. As above, if A and B are K-trivial then so are $\alpha = A \oplus \emptyset$ and $\beta = \emptyset \oplus B$, so $A \oplus B = \alpha + \beta$ is K-trivial. □

One consequence of this result is that not every superlow set is K-trivial. A proof of the following result appears in Nies [303], and in essence in Downey, Jockusch, and Stob [120]. (The original proof was in an unpublished manuscript.)

Theorem 11.6.4 (Bickford and Mills [36]). *There exist superlow c.e. sets A and B such that $A \oplus B \equiv_T \emptyset'$.*

Proof sketch. We build a c.e. trace $V_0, V_1, \ldots$ such that $|V_e| \leqslant 3^{e+1}$, to satisfy requirements of the forms $\Phi_e^A(e) \in V_e$ and $\Phi_e^B(e) \in V_e$. We code $\emptyset'$ into $A \oplus B$ using coding markers $\gamma(n,s)$. If n enters $\emptyset'$ at stage n then we put $\gamma(n,s)$ into whichever set does the least overall damage (in terms of injury to requirements). We also move markers to build our trace. The idea is that if we see that $\Phi_e^A(e)[s]\downarrow$, say, then we can put $\Phi_e^A(e)[s]$ into $V_{e,s+1}$ and move the markers $\gamma(n,s)$ for $n \geqslant e$ to fresh large values, while also putting them into B to preserve the coding. Then the $\Phi_e^A(e)[s]$ computation can be injured only by computations corresponding to stronger priority requirements and by coding of markers corresponding to $n < e$. □

Corollary 11.6.5 (Nies [302]). *The K-trivial sets form a proper subclass of the superlow sets.*

By work of Bickford and Mills [36] and Downey, Jockusch, and Stob [120], we cannot replace $\equiv_T$ by $\equiv_{wtt}$ in Theorem 11.6.4. Indeed, Downey, Jockusch, and Stob [120] proved that the wtt-degrees of c.e. array computable sets form an ideal in the c.e. wtt-degrees, and as mentioned following the proof of Theorem 2.23.9, all superlow sets are array computable.

From Corollary 11.6.3, Downey, Hirschfeldt, Nies, and Stephan [117] concluded that the wtt-degrees of K-trivials form an ideal. However, by Corollary 11.4.10, we have the following stronger result. (An ideal I is *generated* by $S \subseteq I$ if it is the smallest ideal containing S.)

Theorem 11.6.6 (Nies [302]). *The K-trivial degrees form an ideal generated by the class of c.e. K-trivial degrees.*

An ideal is *principal* if it has a greatest element (in other words, if it is of the form $\{X : X \leqslant_T A\}$ for some A). By Theorems 11.1.6 and 11.4.8, there is no greatest K-trivial degree, so the ideal of K-trivial degrees is not principal.

11.7 Bases for 1-randomness

The following notion of randomness-theoretic weakness is due to Kučera [219].

Definition 11.7.1 (Kučera [219]). Let R be a relativizable notion of randomness. A set A is a *base for R-randomness* if there is a set $X \geqslant_T A$ such that X is R-random relative to A.

In this section we focus on bases for 1-randomness. Recall Sacks' Theorem (Corollary 8.12.2), which states that if A is not computable then $\mu(\{X : X \geqslant_T A\}) = 0$. In other words, the Turing upper cone above any noncomputable set is null. However, by the Kučera-Gács Theorem 8.3.2, such upper cones are *never* Martin-Löf null. Thus we could say that Sacks' Theorem cannot be effectivized. On the other hand, it seems too much to expect to effectivize Sacks' Theorem for the upper cone above A without reference to A itself. Thus it is more reasonable to ask: When is the upper cone above A Martin-Löf null *relative to* A? It follows easily from the existence of universal Martin-Löf tests that the upper cone above A is Martin-Löf null relative to A iff A is not a base for 1-randomness.

We have seen in Corollary 8.12.3 that there are no bases for weak 2-randomness other than the computable sets. Kučera [219] showed that all bases for 1-randomness are GL_1. He also observed that if A is low for 1-randomness, then it is a base for 1-randomness, since then the 1-random $X \geqslant_T A$ whose existence is guaranteed by the Kučera-Gács Theorem 8.3.2 is also 1-random relative to A. Thus every K-trivial set is a base for 1-randomness.[2] The following result shows that the converse is also true, and thus we have yet another characterization of the K-trivial sets in terms of a notion of randomness-theoretic weakness. Its proof is known as the "hungry sets construction".

Theorem 11.7.2 (Hirschfeldt, Nies, and Stephan [178]). *A set is K-trivial iff it is a base for* 1*-randomness.*

[2]Kučera's [219] original construction of a base for 1-randomness was different: Take a low 1-random set A and use the relativized low basis theorem to get a low set B that is 1-random relative to A. Then use Corollary 8.8.3 to get a noncomputable set $X \leqslant_T A, B$. Such an X is a base for 1-randomness, because $X \leqslant_T B$ and B is 1-random relative to X, as it is 1-random relative to A and $X \leqslant_T A$.

Proof. As remarked above, it is enough to let A be a base for 1-randomness and show that A is K-trivial. Fix a set $X \geqslant_T A$ that is 1-random relative to A and a reduction $\Phi^X = A$. We will enumerate KC sets L_d for $d \in \mathbb{N}$ so that there is a d for which L_d contains $(K(|\tau|) + d + 2, \tau)$ for each $\tau \prec A$, thus ensuring that A is K-trivial.

To define the L_d, we will build uniformly Σ_1^0 classes C_d^τ so that the following hold.

1. For each d, the C_d^τ are pairwise disjoint.

2. $\mu(C_d^\tau) \leqslant 2^{-K(|\tau|)-d}$.

3. If $X \notin \bigcup_{\tau \prec A} C_d^\tau$, then $\mu(C_d^\tau) = 2^{-K(|\tau|)-d}$ for all $\tau \prec A$.

Suppose we can build such classes, and let $U_d = \bigcup_{\tau \prec A} C_d^\tau$. The U_d are uniformly Σ_1^0 relative to A, and $\mu(U_d) = \sum_{\tau \prec A} \mu(C_d^\tau) \leqslant \sum_{\tau \prec A} 2^{-K(|\tau|)-d} \leqslant 2^{-d}$, so $\{U_d\}_{d \in \omega}$ is a Martin-Löf test relative to A.

We now define

$$L_d = \{(K_s(|\tau|) + d + 2, \tau) : \mu(C_d^\tau[s]) \geqslant 2^{-K_s(|\tau|)-d-1}\}.$$

For a fixed τ, the requests $(r, \tau) \in L_d$ contribute to the weight of L_d at most twice the weight of the one with the smallest r. Thus the weight of L_d is bounded by $\sum_\tau \mu(C_d^\tau)$, which is less than or equal to 1 since the C_d^τ are pairwise disjoint. So the L_d are KC sets.

Since X is 1-random relative to A, we have $X \notin U_d$ for some d, and hence $\mu(C_d^\tau) = 2^{-K(|\tau|)-d}$ for all $\tau \prec A$, which implies that $(K(|\tau|)+d+2, \tau) \in L_d$ for all $\tau \prec A$, as desired. So it is enough to build the C_d^τ with the above properties.

To do so, as long as $\mu(C_d^\tau) < 2^{-K_s(|\tau|)-d}$, we look for strings σ such that $\tau \preccurlyeq \Phi^\sigma$ and $\mu(C_d^\tau) + 2^{-|\sigma|} \leqslant 2^{-K_s(|\tau|)-d}$, and put $[\![\sigma]\!]$ into C_d^τ. To keep our sets pairwise disjoint, we then ensure that no $[\![\sigma']\!]$ such that σ' is compatible with σ is later put into any C_d^ν. If $X \notin U_d$, then no $[\![\sigma]\!]$ with $\sigma \prec X$ is ever put into any C_d^τ, so if $\tau \prec A = \Phi^X$ then $\mu(C_d^\tau) = 2^{-K(|\tau|)-d}$.

We now give the details of the construction. We have a separate procedure for each $d \in \mathbb{N}$. Initially, all strings are *unused.* Each stage s has 2^s many substages, one for each $\sigma \in 2^s$. Let $C_{d,\sigma}^\tau$ denote the approximation to C_d^τ at the beginning of the substage corresponding to σ. For each $\sigma \in 2^s$ in turn, if σ is not used then look for the shortest $\tau \preccurlyeq \Phi^\sigma[s]$ such that $\mu(C_{d,\sigma}^\tau) + 2^{-s} \leqslant 2^{-K_s(|\tau|)-d}$. If there is such a τ, then put $[\![\sigma]\!]$ in C_d^τ and declare every extension of σ to be *used.*

Note that, for a fixed d, the C_d^τ are pairwise disjoint, as we only enumerate unused strings of length s at stage s. Furthermore, it is clear from the construction that $\mu(C_d^\tau) \leqslant 2^{-K(|\tau|)-d}$ for all d and τ. Thus we are left with verifying property 3 above.

Suppose that $X \notin \bigcup_{\tau \prec A} C_d^\tau$. Assume for a contradiction that $\mu(C_d^\tau) < 2^{-K(|\tau|)-d}$ for some $\tau \prec A$. Let s be a stage such that

1. $K(|\tau|) = K_s(|\tau|)$,
2. $\mu(C_d^\tau) + 2^{-s} \leqslant 2^{-K(|\tau|)-d}$, and
3. $\Phi^X \upharpoonright (|\tau|+1)[s]\downarrow$.

Then $[\![X \upharpoonright (s+1)]\!]$ must enter C_d^τ at the substage corresponding to $X \upharpoonright (s+1)$ unless it enters some other $C_d^{\tau'}$ or is already used. In any case, there is a ν and an n such that $[\![X \upharpoonright n]\!]$ is in C_d^ν. But then $\nu \preccurlyeq \Phi^{X\upharpoonright n} \prec \Phi^X = A$, so $X \in [\![X \upharpoonright n]\!] \subseteq \bigcup_{\tau \prec A} C_d^\tau$, contrary to hypothesis. Thus $\mu(C_d^\tau) = 2^{-K(|\tau|)-d}$ for all $\tau \prec A$. □

It is not difficult to adapt the above proof to show directly that every base for 1-randomness is low for K. The details are in Nies [306]. (Note, however, that this fact does not give us a new proof that every K-trivial is low for K, since the fact that every K-trivial is a base for 1-randomness still comes from the golden run proof that every K-trivial is low for 1-randomness.)

As mentioned above, it follows from the Kučera-Gács Theorem that every set that is low for 1-randomness is a base for 1-randomness. Thus, the above result also provides an alternate proof that every set that is low for 1-randomness is K-trivial (and even low for K, using the version in [306] mentioned above). It also helps restore the intuition that relatively 1-random sets should have little common information, which was apparently contradicted by Kučera's result that there are relatively 1-random sets whose degrees do not form a minimal pair (Corollary 8.8.3).[3]

Corollary 11.7.3 (Hirschfeldt, Nies, and Stephan [178]). *If A and B are relatively 1-random then any $X \leqslant_T A, B$ is K-trivial.*

Proof. Since A is 1-random relative to B, it is 1-random relative to X. Thus X is a base for 1-randomness, and hence is K-trivial. □

The following is another interesting application of Theorem 11.7.2.

Corollary 11.7.4 (Hirschfeldt, Nies, and Stephan [178]). *Let A be c.e., and let Z be 1-random and such that $\emptyset' \nleqslant_T A \oplus Z$. Then Z is 1-random relative to A.*

Consequently, if A is c.e. and $A \leqslant_T Z$ for some 1-random $Z \ngeqslant_T \emptyset'$ (i.e., a difference random set Z, as defined in Section 7.7), then A is K-trivial.

Proof. It is enough to prove the first statement, as the second one then follows by Theorem 11.7.2.

Let $U_0^A, U_1^A, \ldots$ be a universal Martin-Löf test relative to A. Suppose that $Z \in \bigcap_n U_n^A$ but $\emptyset' \nleqslant_T A \oplus Z$. We may assume that $\mu(U_n^{A_s}[s]) \leqslant 2^{-n}$ for all n and s. Let the function $f \leqslant_T A \oplus Z$ be defined by letting $f(n)$ be the least s for which there is a k such that $Z \upharpoonright k \in U_n^{A_s}[s]$ with use u and

[3]See Kučera's original construction of a base for 1-randomness mentioned in the previous footnote.

$A_s \upharpoonright u = A \upharpoonright u$. For such s and k, we have $Z \upharpoonright k \in U_n^{A_t}[t]$ for all $t \geqslant s$. Now let $m(n)$ be the least s such that $n \in \emptyset'_s$ if there is such an s, and let $m(n)$ be undefined otherwise. Then $\exists^\infty n\ (m(n)\downarrow \geqslant f(n))$, as otherwise we could compute $\emptyset'$ from $A \oplus Z$ because, for almost all n, we would have $n \in \emptyset'$ iff $n \in \emptyset'_{f(n)}$.

Let $S_n = \bigcup_{x>n, x\in\emptyset'} U_x^{A_{m(x)}}[m(x)]$. The classes $\{S_n\}_{n\in\omega}$ are uniformly Σ_1^0, and $\mu(S_n) \leqslant 2^{-n}$. Moreover, $Z \in \bigcap_n S_n$, since $f(x) < m(x)$ for infinitely many x. Thus Z is not 1-random. □

Hirschfeldt, Nies, and Stephan [178] also studied bases for computable randomness. They showed that these include every Δ_2^0 set that is not DNC, but no set of PA degree. Jockusch, Lerman, Soare, and Solovay [191] showed that if an n-c.e. set is DNC, then it is Turing complete. Since $\mathbf{0}'$ is a PA degree, it follows that an n-c.e. set is a base for computable randomness iff it is Turing incomplete. Franklin, Stephan, and Yu [159] showed that a set is a base for Schnorr randomness iff it does not compute $\emptyset'$.

11.8 ML-covering, ML-cupping, and related notions

Corollary 11.7.4 suggests the following definition.

Definition 11.8.1. A c.e. set A is *Martin-Löf coverable* if there exists a 1-random $Z \not\geqslant_T \emptyset'$ (i.e., a difference random Z) such that $A \leqslant_T Z$.

The Martin-Löf coverable sets form a subclass of the class of K-trivial c.e. sets. It is an open question whether they form a *proper* subclass.

Open Question 11.8.2. Is every c.e. K-trivial set Martin-Löf coverable?

The following are two other notions of randomness-theoretic weakness arising from results, such as Corollary 11.7.4, that indicate that there is a qualitative difference between those 1-random sets that compute $\emptyset'$ and those that do not.

Definition 11.8.3 (Kučera, see Nies [304]). A set A is *weakly Martin-Löf cuppable* if there is a 1-random $Z \not\geqslant_T \emptyset'$ (i.e., a difference random Z) such that $\emptyset' \leqslant_T A \oplus Z$. It is *Martin-Löf cuppable* if Z can be chosen to be strictly below $\emptyset'$.

For any A, we have $A' \leqslant_T A \oplus \Omega^A$. By Theorem 11.7.2, if A is not K-trivial then $A \nleqslant_T \Omega^A$, so if A is Δ_2^0 and not K-trivial then it is weakly Martin-Löf cuppable. Similarly, if A is low and K-trivial then it is Martin-Löf cuppable (since lowness implies that $\Omega^A \leqslant_T \emptyset'$). In fact, this argument shows that if A computes a set that is low and not K-trivial, then it is Martin-Löf cuppable. Sacks [342] showed that if A is c.e. then it can be written as the disjoint union of two low c.e. sets. By the same argument as in the proof of Corollary 11.6.3 below, if A is not K-trivial, then at least one of these sets must be non-K-trivial. Thus, if a c.e. set is not K-trivial, then it is Martin-Löf cuppable, and hence the c.e. sets that are not Martin-Löf cuppable form a subclass of the K-trivials. As we will prove below, Nies [304] showed that this subclass contains more than just the computable sets.

Theorem 11.8.4 (Nies [304]). *There is a noncomputable c.e. set that is not weakly Martin-Löf cuppable.*

Again, proper containment is an open question.

Open Question 11.8.5. Is every K-trivial (c.e.) set not (weakly) Martin-Löf cuppable?

Franklin and Ng [157] have shown that a c.e. set is Martin-Löf coverable iff it is a base for difference randomness, and not weakly Martin-Löf cuppable iff it is low for difference randomness.

Recall from Theorem 7.2.11 that Hirschfeldt and Miller (see [130]) showed that for any Σ^0_3 class S of measure 0, there is a noncomputable c.e. set A such that $A \leqslant_T X$ for all 1-random $X \in S$. Inspired by this result, Nies [306] suggested the following definition.

Definition 11.8.6 (Nies [306], after Hirschfeldt and Miller (see [130])). For a class $S \subseteq 2^\omega$, let $S^\diamond$ be the collection of c.e. sets computable from every 1-random element of S. We call classes of the form $S^\diamond$ *diamond classes*.

Of course, $S^\diamond$ always contains the computable sets, and by Corollary 8.12.2, if $\mu(S) > 0$ then $S^\diamond$ consists exactly of the computable sets. Theorem 7.2.11 can be rephrased by saying that if S is a Σ^0_3 class of measure 0, then $S^\diamond$ contains noncomputable sets. (We have already remarked, following the proof of Theorem 7.2.11, that this fact cannot be extended much beyond Σ^0_3 classes.)

A set X is *Y-trivializing* if Y is K-trivial relative to X (that is, $K^X(Y \upharpoonright n) \leqslant K^X(n) + O(1)$). Let S be the class of $\emptyset'$-trivializing sets.[4] It is not hard to check that S is Σ^0_3. The following also holds.

Lemma 11.8.7. $\mu(S) = 0$.

Proof. Relativizing the fact that every K-trivial set is low, we see that every set in S is high. By Theorem 8.14.1, for all but measure 0 many high sets, $X \oplus \emptyset' \geqslant_T X' \geqslant_T \emptyset''$. By the relativized version of Corollary 8.12.2, the class of sets X such that $X \oplus \emptyset' \geqslant_T \emptyset''$ has measure 0. Thus the class of high sets has measure 0. □

[4]Note that if X is Y-trivializing then $X \oplus Y$ is K-trivial relative to X, so by the relativized form of Theorem 11.4.11, $X \oplus Y \leqslant_{LR} X$, whence $Y \leqslant_{LR} X$. In particular, by Theorem 10.6.5, every $\emptyset'$-trivializing set is (uniformly) almost everywhere dominating.

Thus $S^\diamond$ contains noncomputable sets. We can use the basic construction of a noncomputable K-trivial c.e. set to define a nontrivial pseudo-jump operator taking any set X to a set that is K-trivial relative to X. Then Theorem 8.19.1 shows that there is a 1-random set $X <_T \emptyset'$ in S. Thus every set in $S^\diamond$ is Martin-Löf coverable. More surprisingly, every set in $S^\diamond$ is also not weakly Martin-Löf cuppable.

Theorem 11.8.8 (Hirschfeldt and Nies, see [305]). *Let A be K-trivial and X be 1-random. If $A \oplus X \geqslant_T \emptyset'$ then X is $\emptyset'$-trivializing.*

Proof. We show that $\emptyset' \oplus X$ is low for 1-randomness relative to X, which implies that $\emptyset' \oplus X$ is K-trivial relative to X (by the relativized version of the equivalence between K-triviality and lowness for 1-randomness), and hence that $\emptyset'$ is K-trivial relative to X.

Let Z be 1-random relative to X. By van Lambalgen's Theorem, $Z \oplus X$ is 1-random, and hence $Z \oplus X$ is 1-random relative to A. By the relativized version of van Lambalgen's Theorem, Z is 1-random relative to $A \oplus X$. Since $A \oplus X \geqslant_T \emptyset' \oplus X$, it follows that Z is 1-random relative to $\emptyset' \oplus X$. □

Thus, if $A \in S^\diamond$ and $A \oplus X \geqslant_T \emptyset'$, then $A \leqslant_T X$, so that $X \geqslant_T \emptyset'$. Hence, every set in $S^\diamond$ is not weakly Martin-Löf cuppable. In particular, since $S^\diamond$ contains noncomputable sets, we have Theorem 11.8.4.

Thus $S^\diamond$ is a particularly good candidate for a class with a randomness-theoretic definition that is a proper subclass of the K-trivials and contains a noncomputable set. (In Chapter 14 we will see such a proper subclass with a more combinatorial definition.) However, the following question is still open.

Open Question 11.8.9. Let S be the class of $\emptyset'$-trivializing sets. Is every K-trivial c.e. set in $S^\diamond$?

We will return to diamond classes in Section 14.4.

Nies' original proof of Theorem 11.8.4 was a cost function construction showing that if $Y <_T \emptyset'$ is 1-random, then there is a promptly simple set A such that for all 1-random sets Z, if $Y \leqslant_T A \oplus Z$ then $Y \leqslant_T Z$. Barmpalias [17] extended this result as follows.

Theorem 11.8.10 (Barmpalias [17]). *Let $0 <_T Y <_T \emptyset'$. There is a promptly simple set A such that for every 1-random set Z, if $Y \leqslant_T A \oplus Z$ then $Y \leqslant_T Z$.*

A simplified proof of this result, using Theorem 7.2.11, appears in [24].

11.9 Lowness for weak 2-randomness

There have been several further characterizations of the K-trivials. We now discuss one that came as something of a surprise. Recall that a generalized Martin-Löf test (relative to A) is a sequence of uniformly Σ^0_1 ($\Sigma^{0,A}_1$) classes $\{U_n\}_{n\in\omega}$ such that $\lim_n \mu(U_n) = 0$. Applying Definition 11.2.2 to this notion, we have the following definition: a set A is low for generalized Martin-Löf tests if for each generalized Martin-Löf test $\{U_n\}_{n\in\omega}$ relative to A, there is an unrelativized generalized Martin-Löf test $\{V_n\}_{n\in\omega}$ such that $\bigcap_n U_n \subseteq \bigcap_n V_n$.

If A is low for generalized Martin-Löf tests, then every weakly 2-random set is weakly 2-random relative to A, so A is low for weak 2-randomness. The null classes determined by generalized Martin-Löf tests (i.e., those of the form $\bigcap_n U_n$ for a generalized ML-test $\{U_n\}_{n\in\omega}$) are exactly the Π^0_2 classes of measure 0. Thus, A is low for generalized ML-tests iff every $\Pi^{0,A}_2$ class of measure 0 is contained in a Π^0_2 class of measure 0 iff every $\Sigma^{0,A}_2$ class of measure 1 has a Σ^0_2 subclass of measure 1.

Downey, Nies, Weber, and Yu [130] showed that there are noncomputable c.e. sets that are low for generalized Martin-Löf tests, and hence low for weak 2-randomness. They also proved the following result.

Theorem 11.9.1 (Downey, Nies, Weber, and Yu [130]). *If A is low for weak 2-randomness then A is K-trivial.*

In the proof of this result, we will use the following notation.

Definition 11.9.2 (Kjos-Hanssen, Nies, and Stephan [207]). Let $\mathcal{C}$ and $\mathcal{D}$ be classes of sets given by relativizable definitions, and let $\mathcal{D}^A$ be the relativization of $\mathcal{D}$ to A. A set A is in $\mathrm{Low}(\mathcal{C},\mathcal{D})$ if $\mathcal{C} \subseteq \mathcal{D}^A$.[5]

If $\mathcal{C} = \mathcal{D}$, we write simply $\mathrm{Low}(\mathcal{C})$.

For example, letting MLR be the class of 1-random sets, $A \in \mathrm{Low}(\mathsf{MLR}) = \mathrm{Low}(\mathsf{MLR},\mathsf{MLR})$ means exactly that A is low for 1-randomness.

Relativizing a class $\mathcal{D}$ determined by a notion of randomness usually makes it smaller, of course, so if A is powerful enough, we would expect that $\mathcal{C} \not\subseteq \mathcal{D}^A$ even if $\mathcal{C} \subseteq \mathcal{D}$. The sets in $\mathrm{Low}(\mathcal{C},\mathcal{D})$ are the ones that are not powerful enough for this situation to obtain.

Let $\mathsf{W2R}$ be the class of weakly 2-random sets. Theorem 11.9.1 follows immediately from the following result, since every Martin-Löf test is a generalized Martin-Löf test, and hence $\mathsf{W2R}^A \subseteq \mathsf{MLR}^A$ for any A.

Theorem 11.9.3 (Downey, Nies, Weber, and Yu [130]). *We have* $\mathrm{Low}(\mathsf{W2R},\mathsf{MLR}) = \mathrm{Low}(\mathsf{MLR})$. *In other words, if every weakly 2-random set is 1-random relative to A, then A is in fact low for 1-randomness, and hence K-trivial.*

Proof. This presentation of the proof is due to Joe Miller.

---

[5] We will say a little more about this notion in Section 12.6.

Suppose that A is not low for 1-randomness. We show that $\mathsf{W2R} \not\subseteq \mathsf{MLR}^A$ by building a set $Z \in \mathsf{W2R}$ that is not 1-random relative to A. We define a sequence of nonempty Π^0_1 classes $V_0 \supseteq V_1 \supseteq V_2 \supseteq \cdots$ and let Z be an element of $\bigcap_n V_n$ (which is nonempty, by compactness). Let V_0 be a nonempty Π^0_1 class containing only 1-random sets. Let $\{U_{e,n}\}_{e,n\in\omega}$ be a (noneffective) enumeration of all generalized Martin-Löf tests and let $\{U^A_n\}_{n\in\omega}$ be a universal Martin-Löf test relative to A.

Assume that we have defined V_e. We claim that there is an $X \in V_e$ that is not 1-random relative to A. To see that this is the case, let $\widehat{X}$ be any set that is 1-random but not 1-random relative to A. Since V_e contains a 1-random element, it must have positive measure. Hence, by Lemma 6.10.1, there is an $X =^* \widehat{X}$ such that $X \in V_e$. This X is not 1-random relative to A. Take $\tau_e \prec X$ such that $[\![\tau_e]\!] \subseteq U^A_e$. It will follow from the construction that $\tau_e \prec Z$ for each e, and hence Z is not 1-random relative to A.

Now choose m large enough that $\mu(U_{e,m}) < \mu([\![\tau]\!] \cap V_e)$ and let $V_{e+1} = ([\![\tau]\!] \cap V_e) \setminus U_{e,m}$. So V_{e+1} is a nonempty Π^0_1 subclass of V_e, and no element of V_{e+1} is in $\bigcap_n U_{e,n}$. Since we ensure that this is the case for all e, it follows that Z is weakly 2-random. □

It had been strongly suspected that the class of sets that are low for weak 2-randomness is a proper subclass of the K-trivials. The reason for this suspicion was that the cost function used in the proof of the existence of a noncomputable set that is low for weak 2-randomness seems to decrease much more slowly than the one used in the proof of the existence of a noncomputable K-trivial. This conjecture was surprisingly disproved, independently by Nies [306] and Kjos-Hanssen, Miller, and Solomon [206]. The original proofs of the following result used the golden run method, but there is a more informative proof using LR-reducibility.

Theorem 11.9.4 (Nies [306], Kjos-Hanssen, Miller, and Solomon [206]). *If A is K-trivial then A is low for generalized Martin-Löf tests. Therefore, K-triviality, lowness for generalized Martin-Löf tests, and lowness for weak 2-randomness are all equivalent.*

Proof. If A is K-trivial then $A \leqslant_{\mathrm{T}} \emptyset'$ and $A \leqslant_{\mathrm{LR}} \emptyset$, so by Theorem 10.6.4, every $\Sigma^{0,A}_2$ class of measure 1 has a Σ^0_2 subclass of measure 1, which we have already observed is equivalent to A being low for generalized Martin-Löf tests. □

11.10 Listing the K-trivial sets

In this section we prove a result about the presentation of the class $\mathcal{K}$ of K-trivial sets. As is true for every class that contains the finite sets and has a Σ^0_3 index set, there is a uniformly c.e. listing of the c.e. sets in $\mathcal{K}$.

(See the proof of Theorem 11.11.1 below.) We will use the following lemma to show that there is in fact a listing that includes the witnesses of the Σ^0_3 statement, namely the constants via which the sets are K-trivial, and that this fact is true even in the general Δ^0_2 case. We say that A is K-trivial *via* c if $K(A \upharpoonright n) \leqslant K(n) + c$ for all n.

Lemma 11.10.1 (Downey, Hirschfeldt, Nies, and Stephan [117]). *There is an effective list $\{(B_{e,s}\}_{s\in\omega}, b_e, Q_e)$ of Δ^0_2-approximations, constants, and computable sets of stages with the following properties, where $Q_e = \{v_e(0) < v_e(1) < \cdots\}$ (which may be a finite set).*

1. *For each e, the limit $\lim_s B_{e,s}$ exists and is K-trivial.*
2. *Every K-trivial set is $\lim_s B_{e,s}$ for some e.*
3. *$B_{e,s}(x) \neq B_{e,s-1}(x) \Rightarrow s = v_e(r)$ for some $r \geqslant 2$.*
4. *Let n_s be the least number n (if any) such that $B_{e,s}(n) \neq B_{e,s-1}(n)$. If $v_e(s+1)$ is defined, then let $\widehat{c}(n,s) = \sum_{n<x\leqslant v_e(s)} 2^{-K_{v_e(s+1)}(x)}$. Then*

$$\sum_{n_{v_e(s+2)}\downarrow} \widehat{c}(n_{v_e(s+2)}, s) < 2^{b_e}.$$

Proof. We use Lemma 11.5.2 and its proof. By Lemma 5.3.15, there is a uniformly c.e. listing of the K-trivial c.e. sets. By Theorem 11.5.4, this listing can be used to obtain a uniformly ω-c.e. listing of all K-trivial sets $A^0, A^1, \ldots$.

We think of the number e as a tuple $\langle m, c, i, n, b\rangle$ and let $b_e = b$. The idea is that m is the index for an A^m that we hope is K-trivial via c, the number i is the level at which we hope to have a golden run for the construction in the proof of Lemma 11.5.2, and n stands for the nth run of P_i in that construction, which we hope is a golden run $P_i(g,q)$ with $2^b = 2\frac{g}{q}$. For each e, we run the construction in Lemma 11.5.2 with the K-trivial set A^m and c as the purported constant of K-triviality. We wait until the nth run of P_i is launched, with some parameters g and q. If $2^b \neq 2\frac{g}{q}$ then $Q_e = \emptyset$ and $B_e = \emptyset$. Otherwise, we start computing the numbers $v(0) < v(1) < \cdots$ as in the proof Lemma 11.5.2, letting Q_e consist of these numbers. (Note that we know at stage s whether s is in Q_e, which makes $Q_0, Q_1, \ldots$ uniformly computable.) Of course, if we have the wrong guess for c, i, or n, then Q_e might be finite.

Let $B_s = \emptyset$ for all $s < v(2)$, or all s if $v(2)$ is never defined. For $r \geqslant 2$, let $B_s = A^m_{v(r)}$ for all $s \in [v(r), v(r+1))$, or all $s \geqslant v(r)$ if $v(r+1)$ is never defined. It is easy to check from the proof of Lemma 11.5.2 that property 4 of the lemma holds whether or not our guesses are correct. (In that proof, we showed that the relevant sum of costs is less than $\frac{g}{q}$. The extra factor of 2 in the requirement that $2^b = 2\frac{g}{q}$ is simply to take care of the cost associated with the initial change in approximation from $B_{v(2)-1}$ to $B_{v(2)}$.)

Property 1 holds because every B_e is either some A^m or finite, while property 3 holds by construction. If c is a correct constant of K-triviality for A^m, then the construction will have a golden run. If the nth run of P_i is a golden run and $2^b = 2\frac{g}{q}$, then $B_e = A^m$ for $e = \langle m, c, i, n, b\rangle$. Thus property 2 also holds. □

Theorem 11.10.2 (Downey, Hirschfeldt, Nies, and Stephan [117]). *There are uniformly computable approximations $B_{e,s}$ and a computable sequence of constants d_e such that for every e, the set $B_e = \lim_s B_{e,s}$ exists and is K-trivial via d_e; and every K-trivial set is B_e for some e.*

Proof. Let $B_{e,s}$, b_e, Q_e, and v_e be as in Lemma 11.10.1. Uniformly in e, we define KC sets V_e such that $(K(n)+b_e+3, B_e \upharpoonright n) \in V_e$ for all n. Then we obtain d_e by adding to b_e+3 the coding constant of a prefix-free machine uniformly obtained from V_e.

At stage s, for each $e, n \leqslant s$, put $(K_s(n)+b_e+3, B_{e,s} \upharpoonright n)$ into V_e if

(i) $n = s$, or

(ii) $n < s$ and $K_s(n) < K_{s-1}(n)$, or

(iii) $B_{e,s-1} \upharpoonright n \neq B_{e,s} \upharpoonright n$.

Clearly, $(K(n)+b_e+3, B_e \upharpoonright n) \in V_e$ for each e and n. It remains to show that each V_e is a KC set. The weight contributed by requests added for reasons (i) and (ii) is at most $2^{-(b_e+3)} 2 \sum_n 2^{-K(n)} < 2^{-(b_e+2)} \leqslant \frac{1}{4}$.

Now consider the requests added for reason (iii). Since B_e changes only at stages in Q_e, for each n there are at most two enumerations at a stage $s = v_e(r+2)$ such that $n > v_e(r)$. The weight contributed by all n at such stages is at most $\frac{\Omega}{4}$. Now suppose that (iii) occurs for $s = v_e(r+2)$ and $n \leqslant v_e(r)$.

First we consider the case $K_{v_e(r+1)}(n) > K_s(n)$. This case occurs at most once for each value $K_s(n)$ for $s \in Q_e$. Since each value corresponds to a new description of n, the overall contribution to the weight of V_e of enumerations made when this case occurs, over all n, is at most $\frac{\Omega}{8}$.

Now we consider the case $K_{v_e(r+1)}(n) = K_s(n)$. Since the approximation to $B_e(x)$ changes for some least $x < n$ at stage s, the term $2^{-K_s(n)}$ occurs in the sum $\widehat{c}(x,r)$ from Lemma 11.10.1. Since the sum of all such costs is bounded by 2^{b_e}, the overall contribution to the weight of V_e of enumerations made when this case occurs, over all n, is at most $\frac{1}{8}$. □

Using a c.e. version of Lemma 11.10.1, we can obtain a c.e. version of the above result with the same proof.

Theorem 11.10.3 (Downey, Hirschfeldt, Nies, and Stephan [117]). *There are uniformly c.e. sets $A_0, A_1, \ldots$ and a computable sequence of constants d_e such that A_e is K-trivial via d_e for each e, and every c.e. K-trivial set is A_e for some e.*

Let C be an index set such that if $W_e = W_i$ then $e \in C$ iff $i \in C$. We say that C is *uniformly* Σ^0_3 if there is a Π^0_2 relation P such that $e \in C$ iff $\exists n\,(P(e,n))$, and there is an effective sequence $\{(e_n, b_n)\}_{n\in\omega}$ such that $P(e_n, b_n)$ for all n and for each $e \in C$ there is an n with $W_e = W_{e_n}$. We have proved that $\mathcal{K}$ is uniformly Σ^0_3. It would be interesting to know which other properly Σ^0_3 index sets have that property, for instance the class of computable sets.

In Theorem 11.4.9, we saw that every K-trivial set is low for K. However, the constant c in the definition of being low for K was not obtained in a uniform way from the constant of K-triviality. The following result shows that this nonuniformity is necessary. We say that A is low for K via c if $\forall \sigma\,(K(\sigma) \leqslant K^A(\sigma) + c)$.

Lemma 11.10.4. *From an index for a c.e. set A and a c such that A is low for K via c, we can effectively compute a lowness index for A.*

Proof. Let $f(e)$ be the least s such that $\Phi_e^{A_s}(e)[s]\downarrow$ with an A-correct computation, if there is such an s, and let $f(e)$ be undefined otherwise. Then $f \leqslant_{\mathrm{T}} A$, and indeed there is a uniform procedure for computing f given A. Thus there is a d, independent of A, such that whenever $f(e)\downarrow$, we have $K(f(e)) \leqslant K^A(f(e)) + c \leqslant e + c + d$. To compute whether $e \in A'$ using $\emptyset'$, we find the largest s such that $K(s) \leqslant e + c + d$. Then $e \in A'$ iff $\Phi_e^{A_s}(e)[s]\downarrow$ with an A-correct computation. It is clear that an index for this procedure can be found effectively from a c.e. index for A and c. ☐

Corollary 11.10.5 (Downey, Hirschfeldt, Nies, and Stephan [117]). *There is no effective way to obtain from a pair (A, b), where A is a c.e. set that is K-trivial via b, a constant c such that A is low for K via c.*

Proof. Suppose otherwise. Then, by Theorem 11.10.3 we can obtain a uniformly c.e. listing $A_0, A_1, \ldots$ of the sets that are low for K, along with a computable sequence $c_0, c_1, \ldots$ such that each A_n is low for K via c_n. By the lemma, the A_n are uniformly low, contradicting Theorem 11.1.6. ☐

11.11 Upper bounds for the K-trivial sets

We have mentioned in Theorem 11.1.6 that given any low c.e. set B we can construct a K-trivial $A \not\leqslant_{\mathrm{T}} B$. The following result shows that we cannot replace low by low$_2$. It is a good example of a purely computability-theoretic result that has significant consequences for the study of the interactions between computability and randomness.

Theorem 11.11.1 (Barmpalias and Nies [28]). *Let I be a nontrivial Σ^0_3 ideal in the c.e. Turing degrees. There is a low$_2$ c.e. set A such that $W \leqslant_{\mathrm{T}} A$ for all $W \in I$.*

By Corollary 11.5.4 and Theorem 11.6.1, we have the following.

Corollary 11.11.2 (Barmpalias and Nies [28]). *There is a low$_2$ c.e. set A such that $X \leqslant_T A$ for all K-trivial sets X.*

Downey, Hirschfeldt, Nies, and Stephan [117] had earlier shown that there is an incomplete c.e. set A such that $X \leqslant_T A$ for all K-trivial sets X. This simpler result can be proved as follows. Since the collection of K-trivial c.e. sets is Σ^0_3 and contains the finite sets, by Lemma 5.3.15, there is a c.e. set A such that every K-trivial c.e. set is a column of A, and every column of A is K-trivial. Since the K-trivials are closed under join, $A^{[<n]}$ is incomplete for all n, so the result follows from the Strong Thickness Lemma, Theorem 2.14.13.

We now turn to the proof of Theorem 11.11.1. The method of proof below is called the Δ^0_3 method, and is slightly more difficult than the Π^0_2 method we first encountered in the proof of the Minimal Pair Theorem 2.14.1.

Proof of Theorem 11.11.1. Our method of proof is similar to that of Theorem 5.3.13. By Lemma 5.3.15, we can suppose that I is given to us as uniformly c.e. sets $U_0, U_1, U_2, \ldots$. By replacing U_e with $\bigoplus_{j \leqslant e} U_j$, we may assume that $U_i \leqslant_T U_{i+1}$ via a uniform reduction. It will also be important to know that the U_i are uniformly low$_2$, which follows purely from the fact that I is nontrivial and Σ^0_3, as we now see.

Lemma 11.11.3 (Nies, see [28]). *Uniformly in the index of a c.e. set U, we can define a uniformly c.e. sequence $V_0, V_1, \ldots$ such that if Φ^U_e is total then $V_e \leqslant_T U$, while otherwise $V_e =^* \emptyset'$.*

Proof. Let $f(e,s)$ be the least n such that either $\Phi^U_e(n)[s] \uparrow$ or the computation of $\Phi^U_e(n)$ has changed between stages $s-1$ and s. If $n \in \emptyset'_s$ and $n > f(e,s)$ then put n into V_e. If Φ^U_e is total then, given n, we can use U to compute an s_n such that $f(e,t) > n$ for all $t \geqslant s_n$. If $n \notin V_e[s_n]$, then $n \notin V_e$, so $V_e \leqslant_T U$. If Φ^U_e is not total then $f(e,s)$ has a finite liminf, so $V_e =^* \emptyset'$. □

Corollary 11.11.4 (Nies, see [28]). *The U_i are uniformly low$_2$.*

Proof. By the lemma, we have a computable function f such that if $\Phi^{U_i}_e$ is total then $W_{f(e,i)} \leqslant_T U_i$, while otherwise $W_{f(e,i)} =^* \emptyset'$. Then $\Phi^{U_i}_e$ is total iff $W_{f(e,i)} \in I$. Thus the question of whether $\Phi^{U_i}_e$ is total is Σ^0_3. But it is easy to see that it is also Π^0_3, since the U_i are uniformly c.e. Thus this question can be answered by $\emptyset''$, and hence (since the totality question relative to an oracle U is Π^0_2-complete relative to U), the U_i are uniformly low$_2$. □

We will satisfy each coding requirement

$$C_e : U_e \leqslant_T A$$

by building a reduction $\Gamma^A_e = U_e$. (In truth, we will have several strategies for meeting C_e. The one on the true path of the construction will build the correct reduction Γ_e.) We will define Γ_e in stages. As usual, if x enters U_e

after stage s, then we will change $A_s \upharpoonright \gamma_e^A(x)[s]$. As we will see, there will be other reasons we might want to change A below this use, but as long as the use does not go to infinity, we will still succeed in building Γ_e.

To make A low$_2$, we will satisfy the following requirements.

$$N_i : \limsup_s \ell(\tau, s) = \infty \Rightarrow \Phi_i^A \text{ total},$$

where $\ell(\tau, s)$ is the length of convergence $\max\{x : \forall y \leqslant x\,(\Phi_i^A(y)[s]\downarrow)\}$,

measured at the stages at which the node τ on the true path devoted to N_i has its true outcome, in a sense that will be made clear below. As usual for an infinite injury argument, the true path will be $\emptyset''$-computable, so these requirements ensure that $\emptyset''$ can tell which Φ_i^A are total, thus making A low$_2$. Each requirement N_i has subrequirements

$$N_{i,j} : \limsup_s \ell(\tau, s) = \infty \Rightarrow \Phi_i^A(j)\downarrow.$$

The priority tree will have 3 types of nodes:

- β nodes, which work for C-requirements and have a single outcome ∞. We denote the e such that β works for C_e by $e(\beta)$.
- τ nodes, which work for N-requirements and, as a first approximation to the actual construction, have outcomes $\infty <_{\mathrm{L}} f$ (these outcomes will be modified later, when we incorporate the concept of "τ-correctness" into the construction).
- α nodes below the ∞ outcome of a τ node, working for subrequirements of the requirement associated with τ, with outcomes $\cdots <_{\mathrm{L}} 3 <_{\mathrm{L}} 2 <_{\mathrm{L}} 1 <_{\mathrm{L}} 0$. (If α works for $N_{i,j}$, then the outcome n is meant to represent that $\Phi_i^A(j)\downarrow$ with use n.) The unique τ node associated with α will be denoted by $\tau(\alpha)$. We will refer to α as a *subnode* (of τ) and to τ as α's *main node.*

The action of a β node is as described above. When we visit β, we define more of a reduction $\Gamma_\beta^A = U_{e(\beta)}$ by defining more uses $\gamma_\beta^A(x)[s]$ and enumerating $\gamma_\beta^A(x)[s] - 1$, if defined, into A should x have entered $U_{e(\beta)}$ since the previous time we visited β. In the construction to follow, the $\gamma_\beta^A(x)[s]$ will possibly be moved by weaker priority α nodes. However, any such action will be controlled by a $\tau(\alpha)$ of stronger priority than β, and we will ensure that if β is on the true path then $\lim_s \gamma_\beta^A(x)[s]$ exists.

Below the infinite outcome of a τ node, where the limsup of the relevant length of convergence looks infinite, there will be a tree of α subnodes of τ, each devoted to some subrequirement of the requirement associated with τ. These will be able to tolerate some amount of "finite noise from above", but will essentially act like lowness requirements. The basic idea is that as the length of convergence rises, and hence $\tau^\frown\infty$ looks increasingly correct, we want to preserve more and more of A to try to force Φ_i^A to be total if infinitely often it looks total. This preservation is implemented by the tree of subnodes below the main node τ.

Now, there are two quite different issues that τ must deal with. One is the presence of β nodes above τ, whose coding action is more or less out of control as far as τ is concerned. As much as τ might wish to preserve a computation $\Phi_i^A(j)\downarrow$, it cannot stop such a β from encoding $U_{e(\beta)}$ into A, even if that encoding destroys the computation. The situation is similar to that in the proof of the Thickness Lemma, where a negative requirement must deal with encodings above it that it cannot control, but there is a notion of a node τ's computations being "correct", which implies that no injury from above can occur to a given computation.

We will develop an analogue to this notion of correctness using the fact that here the injury from above will be uniformly low$_2$, because the U_e are uniformly low$_2$. The general idea is that above τ will be a finite number of β nodes, coding sets U_i for a finite number of i's, and we have thus a uniformly low$_2$ amount of "noise" in the τ-computations. Before we say exactly how we will deal with this noise, we discuss the other issue that τ must confront: the impact of coding nodes of weaker priority than τ.

So assume that τ is able to guess the behavior of stronger priority β nodes and uses only the τ-correct computations alluded to above. Let N_i be the requirement assigned to τ. If $\limsup_s \ell(\tau,s)=\infty$ then we need to ensure that Φ^A is total. As mentioned above, for a given j, we have nodes α below $\beta^\frown\infty$ dedicated to ensuring that $\Phi^A(j)\downarrow$. For such an α, we need to deal with potential injuries to computations from β nodes between $\tau^\frown\infty$ and α (of course, β nodes below α will be restrained by α, and we are working under the assumption that τ can deal with β nodes above it). The point, of course, is that such β nodes are trying to put infinitely many elements into A while α is trying to preserve computations with oracle A.

The node α deals with a β node between τ and it as follows. Suppose that α is at a stage s at which it wants to preserve a τ-correct computation $\Phi_i^A(j)[s]\downarrow$. (Note that, since α is below $\tau^\frown\infty$, for α to be relevant at stage s, this stage must be one at which we believe the ∞ outcome of τ is plausible. That is, it must be *τ-expansionary*, which means that the length of convergence $\ell(\tau,s)$ must be larger than the longest length of convergence previously seen.) The node α cannot really stop β from putting its numbers (which may well be below the use $\varphi_i^A(j)[s]$) into A. Instead, α tries to lift the relevant Γ_β-uses above $\varphi_i(j)[s]$. If α almost always succeeds, then the computation it is trying to preserve eventually becomes not only τ-correct, but α-correct, and hence α can eventually preserve this computation forever. If, on the other hand, α fails infinitely often, then we must arrange things so that the ∞ outcome of τ is not in fact the true one, that is, that $\limsup_s \ell(\tau,s)<\infty$. The trick is to destroy certain computations ourselves rather than try to preserve them, as we now explain.

Suppose that $\gamma_\beta^A(x)[s] < \varphi_i^A(j)[s]$ for $x > j$. What α does (or more accurately, what τ does, blaming α) is put some $z < \gamma_\beta^A(x)[s]$ into A and lift $\gamma_\beta^A(y)$ above s for all $y > x$.

The entry of z into A will kill the computation α wanted to preserve, and hence it is now reasonable to not believe that s is τ-expansionary after all (i.e., that the increase in the length of convergence $\ell(\tau, s)$ that caused us to consider taking the ∞ outcome of τ at stage s was not real). So at stage s, we take the f outcome of τ instead of the ∞ outcome. Let s' be the next potential $(\tau^\frown\infty)$-stage. The number z has entered A below the use of the $\Phi_i^A(j)[s]\downarrow$ computation, and we have reset $\gamma_\beta^A(x)[s]$. At stage s', we check whether we now have $\gamma_\beta^A(x)[s'] \geqslant \varphi_i^A(j)[s']$ for all $x > j$, or whether we are in the same bad situation as at stage s. (Note that s' being a potential $(\tau^\frown\infty)$-stage means that s' is τ-expansionary, so that $\ell(\tau, s') > \ell(\tau, s)$, and hence $\Phi_i^A(j)[s']\downarrow$.) In the former case, we no longer have to worry about β. (It is true that we might have $\gamma_\beta^A(x)[s'] < \varphi_i^A(j)[s']$ for some $x \leqslant j$, but since there are only finitely many such x, this situation can cause β to injure α only finitely often, which is fine, since α needs to preserve its computation only in the limit.) Otherwise, we repeat what we did at s, enumerating some number less than $\gamma_\beta^A(x)[s']$ into A, once again destroying the computation $\Phi_i^A(j)[s']\downarrow$ rather than preserving it, and once again taking the finitary outcome f of τ.

Now, if this cycle repeats itself infinitely often, then there are only finitely many $\tau^\frown\infty$ stages and, indeed, Φ_i^A is not total.

Suppose on the other hand that we hit τ at some τ-correct stage t and all of the offending γ_β-uses for β between τ and α have cleared $\varphi_i^A(j)[t]$. At such a stage, we allow α to impose restraint, initializing weaker priority requirements. Modulo the notion of a τ-correct computation, α can now be injured only by $\gamma_\beta^A(x)[s]$ where β is between τ and α and $x \leqslant j$. As mentioned above, these produce only finite injury. Thus, still depending on the notion of τ-correctness, if $\tau^\frown\infty$ is on the true path, then Φ_i^A will indeed be total. Once α asserts control at some τ-correct stage, after some finite injury noise, α's restraint will be successful and preserve the $\Phi_i^A(k)[t]\downarrow$ computation forever.

We now turn to discussing the notion of τ-correctness. We have seen that β nodes above τ can also affect things, but it is not within τ's power to clear γ_β-markers associated with such stronger priority β. That is, suppose that we reach a stage t that appears to be τ-expansionary. Let M be the maximum of the uses of the computations witnessing that t is τ-expansionary. We do not know whether to believe that t is in fact τ-expansionary because there may be γ_β-markers for β above τ that are less than or equal to M. Action for the sake of these markers can injure the computations witnessing that t is τ-expansionary. If infinitely often we have such "fake" expansionary stages at which τ believes computations that are later injured, then τ will not succeed in satisfying its requirement. So what is τ to do?

It is now that we use the fact that the U_e are uniformly low$_2$. Let B be the collection of β nodes above τ and let $U_\tau = \bigoplus_{\beta \in B} U_{e(\beta)}$. We write k_β for the position of U_τ corresponding to the kth position of $U_{e(\beta)}$. We build a reduction $\Xi_\tau^{U_\tau}$. By the recursion theorem, we know which questions to ask $\emptyset''$ to find out whether this reduction is total. So we have a uniformly Δ_3^0 way to decide whether $\Xi_\tau^{U_\tau}$ is total. For now, let us think that we are getting "$\emptyset''$-certifications" as to the totality of $\Xi_\tau^{U_\tau}$. (One way to think of these certifications is to pretend for now that our decision procedure is Π_2^0 rather than Δ_3^0. Then there is a computable process that infinitely often certifies that our reduction is total iff it is in fact total.)

When we are ready to believe that a stage t is τ-expansionary, we declare that $\Xi_\tau^{U_\tau}(n)[t]\downarrow$ for the least n for which $\Xi_\tau^{U_\tau}(n)$ was undefined, with use $\max\{k_\beta : \beta \in B \wedge \gamma_\beta^A(k)[t] \leqslant M\} + 1$, where M is as above. We then do the same for the next n for which $\Xi_\tau^{U_\tau}(n)$ was undefined, and keep doing it for larger and larger n until one of the following occurs.

1. For some β above τ and some n, we see that U_τ changes below the use of the computation $\Xi_\tau^{U_\tau}(n)$.

2. We get a new $\emptyset''$-certification that $\Xi_\tau^{U_\tau}$ is total.

One of these two possibilities must happen, since otherwise we would make $\Xi_\tau^{U_\tau}$ total but would not get this totality certified. In the first case, we know that our original belief that t is τ-expansionary is wrong, so we can take the f outcome of τ. In the second case, we have some endorsement of our original belief, and can take the ∞ outcome after all. Notice that, if the second case happens infinitely often, then $\Xi_\tau^{U_\tau}$ is indeed total, so almost all stages that we believe to be τ-expansionary in fact are so, and the ∞ outcome is the correct one.

However, the above description proceeded under the simplifying assumption that our approximation to the totality of $\Xi_\tau^{U_\tau}$ is Π_2^0. In truth, it is Δ_3^0, which means that we have a Σ_3^0 approximation for totality and also a Σ_3^0 approximation for nontotality. We can think of a Σ_3^0 approximation as infinitely many Π_2^0 processes, such that the condition being approximated holds iff one of these processes provides infinitely many certifications. (It is easy to see that we may assume that at most one process provides infinitely many certifications.) So we replace the two outcomes of τ by infinitely many outcomes $(0,\infty) <_{\mathrm{L}} (0,f) <_{\mathrm{L}} (1,\infty) <_{\mathrm{L}} (1,\infty) <_{\mathrm{L}} \cdots$. The outcomes (i,∞) represent the Σ_3^0 outcomes for totality, and the outcomes (i,f) represent the Σ_3^0 outcomes for nontotality. By the parenthetical remark above, we may assume that exactly one of these is correct infinitely often.

As a final remark before turning to the construction, we note that one might worry about the action of a node τ' above τ working for a requirement $N_{i'}$, since such a node also moves γ_β-markers for $\beta \prec \tau$. However, this is the case only if $\tau'^\frown(k,\infty) \prec \tau$ for some k, which means that if τ is on the true path then $\Phi_{i'}^A$ is total, and hence we can ensure that, by the time τ gets to act, all markers that could be moved by τ' have already been moved. We do so by moving $\gamma_\beta^A(x)[s]$ not only when it is less than $\varphi_{i'}^A(j)[s]$ for some $j < x$, but also preventively when $\Phi_{i'}^A(j)[s]\uparrow$ for such a j, since we know that, if τ' has infinitary outcome, then $\Phi_{i'}^A(j)$ will eventually converge and would then possibly cause us to move $\gamma_\beta^A(x)[s]$.

We now turn to the formal details. Define the priority tree as follows. Let λ be on the priority tree. Suppose that ν is on the priority tree. There are three cases.

1. If $|\nu| = 0 \bmod 3$ then let e be least such that C_e is not assigned to any $\rho \prec \nu$. The node ν is a β node devoted to C_e. Put $\nu^\frown\infty$ on the priority tree and let $e(\nu) = e$.

2. If $|\nu| = 3i+1$ then ν is a τ node devoted to N_i. Put $\nu^\frown(k,\infty)$ and $\nu^\frown(k,f)$ on the priority tree for all $k \in \mathbb{N}$, with the ordering $\nu^\frown(0,\infty) <_{\mathrm{L}} \nu^\frown(0,f) <_{\mathrm{L}} \nu^\frown(1,\infty) <_{\mathrm{L}} \nu^\frown(1,f) <_{\mathrm{L}} \cdots$. Let $i(\nu) = i$.

3. Otherwise, let (i,j) be the least pair such that N_i is assigned to some ρ with $\rho^\frown(k,\infty) \preccurlyeq \nu$ for some k, and $N_{i,j}$ is not assigned to any $\eta \prec \nu$. If there is no such pair (because there are no ρ and k such that $\rho^\frown(k,\infty) \preccurlyeq \nu$), then proceed as in case 1 (assigning some C_e to ν). Otherwise, ν is an α node devoted to $N_{i,j}$. Put $\nu^\frown k$ on the priority tree for each $k \in \mathbb{N}$, with the ordering $\nu^\frown(k+1) <_{\mathrm{L}} \nu^\frown k$. Let $i(\nu) = i$, let $j(\nu) = j$, and let $\tau(\nu) = \rho$.

Construction.

Associated to each β node ν is a reduction $\Gamma_\nu^A(n)$. Associated to each τ node ν is a reduction $\Xi_\nu^{U_\nu}$ as described above, with its corresponding Δ_3^0 approximation T_ν to totality. We think of this approximation as providing values $T_\nu(0), T_\nu(1), \ldots$, which are of the form (n,f) or (n,∞), with $\Xi_\nu^{U_\nu}$ being total iff there is an n such that the value (n,∞) is seen infinitely often iff there is no n such that the value (n,f) is seen infinitely often. Also associated to each τ mode ν are functions $\ell(\nu,s)$ and $m(\nu,s)$, defined for all stages s at which ν is accessible (which will be called *ν-stages*). The length of convergence function ℓ has been discussed above. The function m represents the maximum ν-correct length of convergence seen so far. Initially, $m(\nu,0) = 0$.

At stage s of the construction, we approximate the true path TP as follows. Begin at λ and say that s is a λ-stage. Suppose that s is a ν-stage. If $|\nu| = s$ then let $\mathrm{TP}_s = \nu$, initialize all nodes γ such that $\gamma \not\leqslant_{\mathrm{L}} \nu$ (which means that all objects associated with them are now undefined), and proceed to the next stage. Otherwise, let t be the last ν-stage before s, or 0 if there have been no such stages. There are now three cases.

Case 1. ν is a β node. For each $n \leqslant s$, proceed as follows. If $\Gamma_\nu^A(n)[s]$ is not defined then define it to be $U_{e(\nu)}(n)[s]$ with the use $\gamma_\nu^A(n)[s]$ a fresh, large number (ensuring as usual that such uses are increasing in n). If

$\Gamma^A_\nu(n)[s]\downarrow\neq U_{e(\nu)}(n)[s]$ then put $\gamma^A_\nu(n)[s]-1$ into A. In this case, if $\rho\succ\nu$ is an α node such that $\tau(\rho)\prec\nu$ and $j(\nu)\geqslant n$, then initialize ρ.

Case 2. ν is a τ node. Let $i=i(\nu)$. For each j, each β node $\rho\succcurlyeq\nu^\frown(j,\infty)$, each n, and each $k\leqslant n$ such that $\gamma^A_\rho(n)[s]\downarrow$ and either $\Phi^A_i(k)[s]\uparrow$ or $\gamma^A_\rho(n)[s]\leqslant\varphi^A_i(k)[s]$, enumerate $\gamma^A_\rho(n)[s]-1$ into A, declaring $\Gamma^A_\rho(m)$ to be undefined for all $m\geqslant n$. (Note that at this point we do not redefine $\Gamma^A_\rho(m)$, and hence do not redefine the use $\gamma^A_\rho(m)$. Such redefinitions will occur the next time we visit ρ.) Let $\ell(\nu,s)=\max\{x:\forall y\leqslant x\,(\Phi^A_i(y)[s]\downarrow)\}$, where these computations take into account the values just enumerated into A (and so do not converge if a number was put into A below the old use $\varphi^A_i(y)[s]$).

If $\ell(\nu,s)\leqslant m(\nu,t)$, then let u be the last stage before s at which ν had outcome (k,f) for some k, or 0 if there has been no such stage. Look for the least $v>u$ such that $T_\nu(v)=(j,f)$ for some j, which must exist since we are not defining any new values of $\Xi^{U_\nu}_\nu$, and declare that s is a $(\nu^\frown(j,f))$-stage. Let $m(\nu,s)=m(\nu,t)$, and call $\ell(\nu,s)$ the ν-correct length of convergence at stage s.

If $\ell(\nu,s)>m(\nu,t)$, then proceed as follows. let u be the last stage before s at which ν had outcome (k,∞) for some k, or 0 if there has been no such stage. Let B_ν be the collection of β nodes above ν and start to define $\Xi^{U_\nu}_\nu(n)$ for larger and larger n, all with use

$$\max\{k_\rho:\rho\in B_\nu\wedge\gamma^A_\rho(k)[s]\leqslant\min(\varphi^A_i(n)[s],\varphi^A_i(m(\nu,t)+1)[s])\},$$

where k_ρ is, as above, the position of U_ν corresponding to position k of $U_{e(\rho)}$, until one of the following occurs.

1. Some use $\xi^{U_\nu}_\nu(n)$ is violated.
2. For some least $v>u$ and some j, we have $T_\nu(v)=(j,\infty)$.

In the former case, let u be the last stage before s at which ν had outcome (k,f) for some k, or 0 if there has been no such stage. Look for the least $v>u$ such that $T_\nu(v)=(j,f)$ for some j, which must exist since we are not defining any new values of $\Xi^{U_\nu}_\nu$, and declare that s is a $(\nu^\frown(j,f))$-stage, setting $m(\nu,s)=m(\nu,t)$. Let n be the largest number such that the computation $\Xi^{U_\nu}_\nu(n)$ is still valid (or 0 if there is no such number). Call $\max(n,m(\nu,t))$ the ν-correct length of convergence at stage s.

In the latter case, declare that s is a $\nu^\frown(j,\infty)$-stage, let $m(\nu,s)=m(\nu,t)+1$, and call this value the ν-correct length of convergence at stage s.

Case 3. ν is an α node. If $\Phi^A_{i(\nu)}(j(\nu))[s]\downarrow$ then declare that s is a $(\nu^\frown\varphi^A_{i(\nu)}(j(\nu))[s])$-stage. Otherwise, declare that s is a $(\nu^\frown 0)$-stage.
End of Construction.

To finish the proof, we verify the following by simultaneous induction on $\nu\subset\mathrm{TP}$ (in the process showing in particular that TP is well-defined).

(i) If ν is a β node then $\Gamma_\nu^A = U_{e(\nu)}$, whence $C_{i(\nu)}$ is satisfied. In particular, $\lim_s \gamma_\nu(n)[s]$ exists for all n.

(ii) If ν is a τ node, then the following hold.

(a) There is a j such that either $\nu^\frown(j,f) \prec \mathrm{TP}$ or $\nu^\frown(j,\infty) \prec \mathrm{TP}$.
(b) If $\nu^\frown(j,f) \prec \mathrm{TP}$, then ν has only finite effect on the nodes extending $\nu^\frown(j,f)$, and the limit of the ν-correct length of convergence at $(\nu^\frown(j,f))$-stages is finite.
(c) If $\nu^\frown(j,\infty) \prec \mathrm{TP}$ then the limit of the ν-correct length of convergence at $(\nu^\frown(j,\infty))$-stages is infinite, and for each k, the node ν takes no action for k at almost all $(\nu^\frown(j,\infty))$-stages.
(d) $\exists j\,(\nu^\frown(j,\infty) \prec \mathrm{TP})$ iff $\Phi_{i(\nu)}^A$ is total, whence $N_{i(\nu)}$ is satisfied.

(iii) If ν is an α node then the following hold.

(a) The node ν is initialized only finitely often.
(b) There is a k such that ν has outcome k almost always.

We assume (i)–(v) for all $\sigma \prec \nu$. There are three cases to consider.

Case 1. ν is a β node. Then there is a stage s_0 after which ν is never again initialized. Since ν gets to act infinitely often, we will have $\Gamma_\nu^A(n)\downarrow = U_{e(\nu)}(n)$ provided that $\lim_s \gamma_\nu^A(n)[s]$ exists. After stage s_0, there are only two ways we can have $\gamma_\nu^A(n)[s]$ change. One is for n to enter $U_{e(\nu)}$, which can happen only once. The other is for some τ node above ν to take action for a number less than or equal to n, which by our inductive hypothesis can happen only finitely often.

Case 2. ν is a τ node. Let $i = i(\nu)$. First suppose that there is a least n such that $\Xi_\nu^{U_\nu}(n)\uparrow$. Then there is a unique j such that $T_\nu(u) = (j,f)$ for infinitely many u. Furthermore, either $\Xi_\nu^{U_\nu}(n)$ is defined only finitely often, or it is defined infinitely often but its use is violated each time it is defined. In the former case, we must have $\ell(\nu,s) \leqslant m(\nu,t)$ for almost all ν-stages s, where t is as in the construction. In particular, Φ_i^A is not total. In the latter case, because of the way the use $\xi_\nu^{U_\nu}(n)[s]$ is defined, there is an $m \leqslant n$ such that the use of $\Phi_i^A(m)$ is violated infinitely often, whence Φ_i^A is not total. In either case, $\nu^\frown(j,f) \prec TP$, the limit of the ν-correct length of convergence at $(\nu^\frown(j,f))$-stages is finite, and clearly ν has only finite effect on the nodes extending $\nu^\frown(j,f)$.

Now suppose that $\Xi_\nu^{U_\nu}(n)$ is total. Then there is a unique j such that $T_\nu(u) = (j,\infty)$ for infinitely many u. Furthermore, we must have $\lim_s m(\nu,s) = \infty$, since if this limit were a finite number m, then there would be infinitely many ν-stages s at which $\xi_\nu^{U_\nu}(m+1)[s]$ is violated. It follows that $\nu^\frown(j,\infty) \prec TP$ (since ν has an infinitary outcome each time $m(\nu,s)$ increases). We are left with showing that Φ_i^A is total, which implies that the limit of the ν-correct length of convergence at $(\nu^\frown(j,\infty))$-stages is infinite, and hence that for each k, the node ν takes no action for k at almost all $(\nu^\frown(j,\infty))$-stages.

Every $(\nu^\frown(j,\infty))$-stage is expansionary, so for each sufficiently large $(\nu^\frown(j,\infty))$-stage s, we have $\ell(\nu,s) \geqslant k$. For such an s, we have $\Phi_i^A(k)[s]\downarrow$. Assuming that s is large enough that ν is not initialized after stage s, there are only two ways a number can enter A below $\varphi_i^A(k)[s]$. One is through some $n < k$ entering $U_{e(\rho)}$ for some β node ρ such that ρ is between $\nu^\frown(j,\infty)$ and some α node working for $N_{i,k}$. Since there are only finitely many such n and $e(\rho)$, if s is large enough then no number will enter A below $\varphi_i^A(k)[s]$ for this reason. The other way a number may enter A below $\varphi_i^A(k)[s]$ is through the action of a β node above ν. But for any large enough n, if such a number enters A, then the use $\xi_\nu^{U_\nu}(n)[s]$ is violated. Thus, since $\Xi_\nu^{U_\nu}$ is total, if s is large enough then no number will enter A below $\varphi_i^A(k)[s]$ for this reason either. Thus there is an s such that $\Phi_i^A(k)[s]\downarrow$ and no number enters A below $\varphi_i^A(k)[s]$ during or after stage s, whence $\Phi_i^A(k)\downarrow$.

Case 3. ν is an α-node. That ν is initialized only finitely often is clear from the description of the action of the β nodes above ν. Since $\tau(\nu)^\frown(k,\infty) \preccurlyeq \nu$ for some k, we know that $\Phi_{i(\nu)}^A$ is total, so in particular $\Phi_{i(\nu)}^A(j(\nu))\downarrow$, and ν has outcome $\varphi_{i(\nu)}^A(j(\nu))$ almost always. □

We have seen that there is a low$_2$ c.e. degree above all K-trivials, but no such low c.e. degree. What happens if the computable enumerability condition is removed? The following is a general theorem of Kučera and Slaman [222] about ideals in the Δ_2^0 degrees, which implies that the K-trivials have a low upper bound.

Theorem 11.11.5 (Kučera and Slaman [222]). *The following are equivalent for an ideal I in the Δ_2^0 degrees.*

(i) *I has a low upper bound.*

(ii) *I is contained in an ideal generated by uniformly Δ_2^0 sets $A_0, A_1, \ldots$, and there is a Δ_2^0 function that dominates every partial function computable by a set in I.*

The method of proof is a forcing one akin to the forcing proof of the low basis theorem with coding steps interleaved; see [222]. A remaining open question is whether the low upper bound for the K-trivials can be made 1-random. (Indeed, it is not even known whether there is a 1-random set that computes all K-trivials but does not compute $\emptyset'$ (i.e., a difference random set that computes all K-trivials); the existence of such a set would answer Question 11.8.2.)

11.12 A gap phenomenon for K-triviality

In Theorem 9.15.8, we saw that there is a minimal pair of K-degrees, that is, a pair of non-K-trivial sets A and B such that for all X, if $X \leqslant_K A, B$ then

X is K-trivial. In this section, we give the original proof of this result, which is due to Csima and Montalbán [83] and involves a lemma of significant independent interest.

A reasonable strategy for building such a pair of sets would be to ensure that, for some constant c and all n,

$$K(A \upharpoonright n) \leqslant K(n) + c \quad \text{or} \quad K(B \upharpoonright n) \leqslant K(n) + c, \tag{11.2}$$

while preventing A and B from being K-trivial. For any string σ, we know that $\sigma 0^\omega$ is K-trivial, so we could try to do the following. We start building A and B (thought of as sequences that we build up over time) by making A look random and adding 0's to B. Then, once we have ensured that A has an initial segment of fairly high K-complexity, we start adding 0's to A to bring down the K-complexity of its initial segments, while still adding 0's to B. Once we have reached an m such that $K(A \upharpoonright m)$ is sufficiently low, we start making B look random while adding 0's to A. Once we have ensured that B has an initial segment of fairly high K-complexity, we start adding 0's to B to bring down the K-complexity of its initial segments, while still adding 0's to A. Once we have reached an n such that $K(B \upharpoonright n)$ is sufficiently low, we go back to the beginning, making A look random while adding 0's to B.

The problem with such a construction is that, although $\sigma 0^\omega$ is indeed K-trivial for any σ, *the constant of K-triviality depends on σ*. Thus, while adding 0's to a previously defined initial segment of A might bring the complexity of longer initial segments down quite a bit, it may never result in an n such that $K(A \upharpoonright n) \leqslant K(n) + c$ for a given c fixed ahead of time.

The clever solution to this problem, found by Csima and Montalbán [83], is to prove the following surprising "gap result", which shows that we can replace c in (11.2) by a sufficiently slow-growing function of n. Recall that $\mathrm{KT}(c)$ denotes the class of sets that are K-trivial via c.

Theorem 11.12.1 (Csima and Montalbán [83]). *There is an order f such that a set X is K-trivial iff $K(X \upharpoonright n) \leqslant K(n) + f(n)$ for almost all n.*[6]

Proof. The "only if" direction is obvious. For the other direction, for each $e > 0$ we build an unbounded nondecreasing function f_e such that $f_e(0) = e - 1$ and if $K(X \upharpoonright n) \leqslant K(n) + f_e(n)$ for all n, then $X \in \mathrm{KT}(e)$. Given such functions, let $f(n) = \min\{f_{2e}(n) - e : e > 0\}$. It is easy to check that f is nondecreasing and unbounded. Furthermore, if $K(X \upharpoonright n) \leqslant K(n) + f(n)$ for almost all n then there is an $e > 0$ such that $K(X \upharpoonright n) \leqslant K(n) + f(n) + e$ for all n, which means that $K(X \upharpoonright n) \leqslant K(n) + f_{2e}$ for all n, and hence $X \in \mathrm{KT}(2e)$.

Fix $e > 0$. We want to define a sequence $0 = n_0 < n_1 < \cdots$ and let $f_e(k) = e + i - 1$ whenever $k \in [n_i, n_{i+1})$. First let $n_0 = 0$. Let n_1 be

[6] One may compare this result with Theorem 11.1.8, but note that in that result, the function $g(n) - K(n)$ is not an order.

such that for any set $Y \in \mathrm{KT}(e+1) \setminus \mathrm{KT}(e)$, there is an $m < n_1$ with $K(Y \upharpoonright m) > K(m) + e$. Such a number must exist because, by Theorem 11.1.3, $\mathrm{KT}(e+1)$ is finite.

We similarly choose n_2 so that for any set $Y \in \mathrm{KT}(e+2) \setminus \mathrm{KT}(e)$, there is an $m < n_2$ such that $K(Y \upharpoonright m) > K(m) + e$.

We now come to the heart of this argument. We choose n_3 so that for any set $Y \in \mathrm{KT}(e+3) \setminus \mathrm{KT}(e)$, there is an $m < n_3$ such that $K(Y \upharpoonright m) > K(m)+e$, but we also impose an extra condition on n_3. Let Z be a set such that the least m with $K(Z \upharpoonright m) > K(m) + e$ is in $[n_1, n_2)$. Then Z cannot be in $\mathrm{KT}(e+1)$ by the choice of n_1, so we can require that n_3 be such that for each such Z there is an $l < n_3$ such that $K(Z \upharpoonright l) > K(l) + e + 1$.

It is important to consider more carefully why such an n_3 exists. Suppose it did not. Then for each l there would be a string σ of length l such that the least m with $K(\sigma \upharpoonright m) > K(m)+e$ is in $[n_1, n_2)$ and yet $K(\sigma) \leqslant K(l)+e+1$. Thus, by König's Lemma (that every infinite, finitely branching tree has an infinite path), there would be a set Z such that the least m with $K(Z \upharpoonright m) > K(m)+e$ is in $[n_1, n_2)$ and yet $K(Z \upharpoonright l) \leqslant K(l)+e+1$ for all l. Such a Z would be in $\mathrm{KT}(e+1)$, contradicting the choice of n_1.

The definition of n_i for $i > 3$ is analogous. That is, we choose n_i so that

1. for any set $Y \in \mathrm{KT}(e+i) \setminus \mathrm{KT}(e)$, there is an $m < n_i$ such that $K(Y \upharpoonright m) > K(m) + e$, and
2. for any Z such that the least m with $K(Z \upharpoonright m) > K(m) + e$ is in $[n_{i-2}, n_{i-1})$, there is an $l < n_i$ such that $K(Z \upharpoonright l) > K(l) + e + i - 2$.

The same argument as in the $i = 3$ case shows that such an n_i exists.

As mentioned above, we let $f_e(k) = e + i - 1$ whenever $k \in [n_i, n_{i+1})$. Suppose that $K(X \upharpoonright n) \leqslant K(n) + f_e(n)$ for all n. We need to show that $X \in \mathrm{KT}(e)$. Suppose not, and let i be least such that there is an $m \in [n_i, n_{i+1})$ with $K(X \upharpoonright m) > K(m) + e$. Then, by the choice of n_{i+2}, there is an $l < n_{i+2}$ such that $K(X \upharpoonright l) > K(l) + e + i$. On the other hand, $K(X \upharpoonright l) \leqslant K(l) + f_e(l) \leqslant K(l) + e + i$, which is a contradiction. □

Corollary 11.12.2 (Csima and Montalbán [83]). *There is a minimal pair of K-degrees.*

Proof. Let f be as in Theorem 11.12.1. We build A and B by finite extensions. Let $A_0 = B_0 = \lambda$. At stage $e+1$ with e even, first define $\widetilde{A}_{e+1} \succ A_e$ so that $K(\widetilde{A}_{e+1}) > K(|\widetilde{A}_{e+1}|) + e$. Let $m_e = |\widetilde{A}_{e+1}| - |A_e|$. Now let c_e be such that $\widetilde{A}_{e+1}0^\omega \in \mathrm{KT}(c_e)$, and let n_e be such that $f(n_e) > c_e$. Let $A_{e+1} = \widetilde{A}_{e+1}0^{n_e}$ and $B_{e+1} = B_e 0^{m_e+n_e}$.

At stage $e+1$ with e odd, do the same with the roles of A and B interchanged.

It is straightforward to check that this construction ensures that A and B are not K-trivial, and that $\min(K(A \upharpoonright n), K(B \upharpoonright n)) \leqslant K(n) + f(n)$ for all n, which implies that if $X \leqslant_K A, B$ then X is K-trivial. □

Analysis of the above proofs shows that f can be chosen to be Δ^0_4, and hence so can A and B. It is unknown whether there is a minimal pair of K-degrees of Δ^0_2 sets. (By Theorem 9.15.8, there is a minimal pair of K-degrees of Σ^0_2 sets.) More interestingly, it is also unknown whether there is a minimal pair of K-degrees of left-c.e. reals.

12

Lowness and Triviality for Other Randomness Notions

12.1 Schnorr lowness

We now turn to lowness notions for other notions of randomness. We begin with Schnorr randomness. Since there is no universal Schnorr test, it is not clear that the notions of a set A being *low for Schnorr randomness* (i.e., every Schnorr random set is Schnorr random relative to A) and being *low for Schnorr tests* (i.e., every Schnorr test relative to A can be covered by an unrelativized Schnorr test[1]) should be the same. In fact, this was an open question in Ambos-Spies and Kučera [9]. As we will see, it was solved by Kjos-Hanssen, Nies, and Stephan [207].

12.1.1 Lowness for Schnorr tests

In such cases, it is usually easiest to begin with the test set version. A complete characterization of lowness for Schnorr tests was obtained by Terwijn and Zambella [389], using the notion of computable traceability introduced in Definition 2.23.15. Recall from that definition that a degree $\mathbf{a}$ is computably traceable if there is a computable function h such that, for each function $f \leqslant_{\mathrm{T}} \mathbf{a}$, there is a computable function g satisfying, for all n,

(i) $|D_{g(n)}| \leqslant h(n)$ and

[1] Another way of thinking of this notion is as lowness for Schnorr null sets: every set that is Schnorr null relative to A is Schnorr null.

R.G. Downey and D. Hirschfeldt, *Algorithmic Randomness and Complexity*, Theory and Applications of Computability, DOI 10.1007/978-0-387-68441-3_12,

(ii) $f(n) \in D_{g(n)}$.

Computable traces are often represented by a single computable set $T = \{\langle y, n\rangle : y \in D_{g(n)}\}$. We will sometimes use this method, and write $T^{[n]}$ for $\{y : \langle y, n\rangle \in T\}$.

The following lemma is an analog of Proposition 2.23.12.

Lemma 12.1.1 (Terwijn and Zambella [389]). *Let A be computably traceable and let h be a computable order such that $h(0) > 0$. Then A is computably traceable with bound h.*

Proof. We show how to arbitrarily slow down the tracing process. Suppose that A is computably traceable with bound $\widehat{h}$, and fix $f \leqslant_T A$. Let q be a computable function such that, if we let i_k be the least number such that $q(i_k) > k$, then $\widehat{h}(i_k) \leqslant h(k)$ for all k.

Let $\{T_n\}_{n\in\omega}$ be a computable trace with bound $\widehat{h}$ for the function taking i to $\langle f(0), \ldots, f(q(i) - 1)\rangle$. Let S_k be the set of all a_k for which T_{i_k} has an element of the form $\langle a_0, \ldots a_{q(i)-1}\rangle$. Clearly, $\{S_n\}_{n\in\omega}$ is a computable trace for f, and it is bounded by $\widehat{h}(i_k) \leqslant h(k)$. □

It is worth noting that sometimes the exact growth rate of orders does matter, as we will see in Chapter 14.

The notion of computable traceability was inspired by arguments from set theory, particularly Raisonnier's proof in [322] of Shelah's result that the inaccessible cardinal cannot be removed from Solovay's construction in [370] of a model of set theory (without the full axiom of choice but with dependent choice) in which every set of reals is Lebesgue measurable.

As we noted in Section 2.23, Terwijn and Zambella [389] observed that the hyperimmune-free degree constructed by Miller and Martin (Theorem 2.17.3) is computably traceable, and that if a degree is computably traceable then it is hyperimmune-free, since computable traceability is actually a uniform version of hyperimmune-freeness. The difference between being hyperimmune-free and being computably traceable for a degree **a** is that for the latter there is a single computable bound h that works for all $f \leqslant_T \mathbf{a}$, whereas for the former, for each $f \leqslant_T \mathbf{a}$ there is a separate computable function bounding f. This difference can be turned around into a proof that the concepts are different. We can derive this result most easily using Theorem 12.1.2 below, though, so we will return to it after we have proved the theorem.

Since all computably traceable degrees are hyperimmune-free, no computably traceable degree is Δ^0_2. In particular, if a set is low for 1-randomness then it is not computably traceable. This fact is particularly interesting in view of the following result.

Theorem 12.1.2 (Terwijn and Zambella [389]). *A degree is low for Schnorr tests iff it is computably traceable.*

Proof. For the "if" direction, let A be computably traceable. Let $\{[\![U_n]\!]\}_{n\in\omega}$ be a Schnorr test relative to A, with $\mu([\![U_n]\!]) = 2^{-n}$. We need to build an unrelativized Schnorr test $\{[\![V_n]\!]\}_{n\in\omega}$ with $\bigcap_n [\![V_n]\!] \supseteq \bigcap_n [\![U_n]\!]$. It will be convenient to build the V_n so that $\mu([\![V_n]\!])$ is less than or equal to 2^{-n} and computable (rather than equal to 2^{-n}).

Identifying finite strings with their codes as usual, we have a computable trace T for the finite A-approximations $U_{n,s}$. (So $U_{n,s} \in T^{[\langle n,s\rangle]}$ for all n and s.) By Lemma 12.1.1, we may assume that T is bounded by a sufficiently slow growing bound h, to be specified below. We will use T to enumerate the V_n. The crucial idea is to make sure that the bulk of U_n is enumerated before we trace it, so the approximation generated by T is a good one. Thus we speed up the A-enumeration of the U_n so that $\mu([\![U_{n,s}]\!]) > 2^{-n}(1-2^{-s})$.

Given T, we define a new trace $\widehat{T}$ as follows. Let $\widehat{T}^{[\langle n,s\rangle]}$ be the set of those $D \in T^{[\langle n,s\rangle]}$ such that

1. D is a finite subset of $2^{<\omega}$ (again identifying finite sets with their codes);
2. $2^{-n}(1-2^{-s}) \leqslant \mu([\![D]\!]) \leqslant 2^{-n}$; and
3. $C \subseteq D$ for some $C \in \widehat{T}^{[\langle n,s-1\rangle]}$ (if $s > 0$).

Here we have pruned those members of T that are not possible values of $U_{n,s}$. Note that $\widehat{T}$ is still a computable trace that captures the $U_{n,s}$. We are now ready to define our Schnorr test.

Let $V_{n,r} = \bigcup_{s<r} \widehat{T}^{[\langle 2n,s\rangle]}$ and $V_n = \bigcup_r V_{n,r}$. Then

$$\mu([\![V_n]\!]) \leqslant 2^{-2n}|\widehat{T}^{[\langle 2n,0\rangle]}| + \sum_s 2^{-2n-s}|\widehat{T}^{[\langle 2n,s\rangle]}|.$$

Using Lemma 12.1.1, we can choose h so that $|\widehat{T}^{[\langle 2n,s\rangle]}|$ is small enough to ensure that $\mu([\![V_n]\!]) \leqslant 2^{-n}$. Furthermore,

$$\mu\left(\left[\!\!\left[\bigcup_{s>r} \widehat{T}^{[\langle 2n,s\rangle]}\right]\!\!\right]\right) \leqslant \sum_{s\leqslant r} 2^{-2n-s}|\widehat{T}^{[\langle 2n,s\rangle]}|,$$

so again using Lemma 12.1.1, we can choose h to be sufficiently slow growing so that $\mu([\![V_{n,r}]\!])$ converges computably to $\mu([\![V_n]\!])$.

The other direction is more difficult. Let A be low for Schnorr tests. Let

$$B_{k,i} = [\![\{\tau 1^k : \tau \in 2^i\}]\!].$$

Note that $\mu(B_{k,i}) = 2^{-k}$. The idea is to use these clopen sets to code an arbitrary function $g \leqslant_T A$. To do this, fix such a function and let

$$U_n = \bigcup_{k>n} B_{k,g(k)}.$$

Clearly, $\{U_n\}_{n\in\omega}$ is a Schnorr test relative to A, and hence is covered by an unrelativized Schnorr test. We will need only one of the levels of that test, say the fourth one, which is a Σ^0_1 class V of measure $\frac{1}{8}$ containing the intersection of the U_n.

For technical reasons that will become clear below, we want to ensure that $\mu(B_{k,i} \setminus V) \neq 2^{-(i+3)}$ for all k and i. We can do this by adding elements to V while still keeping V a Σ^0_1 class with computable measure less than $\frac{1}{4}$, so we assume we have done so. (The idea is that if we see the difference between $B_{k,i}$ and V_s getting close $2^{-(i+3)}$, then we add enough of $B_{k,l}$ to V to ensure that equality will not happen; we can certainly do this in such a way as to keep the measure computable and below $\frac{1}{4}$.)

We first make the simplifying assumption that $\mu(U_n \setminus V) = 0$ for some n, eliminating this assumption later. Let T be defined by

$$T^{[k]} = \{i : \mu(B_{k,i} \setminus V) < 2^{-(i+3)}\}.$$

Clearly $g(k) \in T^{[k]}$ for all $k > n$, since $\mu(U_n \setminus V) = 0$, so a finite modification of T traces g. We now must show that there is a computable function h such that $T^{[k]} = D_{h(k)}$ for all k and that $|T^{[k]}|$ is bounded by a computable function that does not depend on g. To achieve the first goal, it is enough to show that each $T^{[k]}$ is finite and that both T and the function $k \mapsto |T^{[k]}|$ are computable. Note that the computability of this function does give us a computable bound on $|T^{[k]}|$ (and hence is enough to show that A has hyperimmune-free degree), but this bound depends on g, so we will still have to provide a computable bound independent of g.

We begin by showing that T is computable. It is easy to see that T is c.e., so to show that it is computable, it is enough to describe how to enumerate its complement. Suppose $i \notin T^{[k]}$. Let $s_0 = 0$. Having defined s_j, let $\varepsilon_j = \mu(B_{k,i} \setminus V_{s_j}) - 2^{-(i+3)}$. Note that $\varepsilon_j > 0$, since $i \notin T^{[k]}$ and we have built V so that $\mu(B_{k,i} \setminus V) \neq 2^{-(i+3)}$. Let s_{j+1} be such that $\mu(V_{s_{j+1}}) > \mu(V) - \frac{\varepsilon_j}{2}$.

Clearly, the ε_j converge to a limit ε and $\varepsilon > 0$, again by the assumption that $\mu(B_{k,i} \setminus V) \neq 2^{-(i+3)}$. So there is a j such that $\frac{\varepsilon_j}{2} < \varepsilon_{j+1}$. If we enumerate V up to stage s_{j+1}, we know for sure that $i \notin T^{[k]}$, since then

$$\begin{aligned}\mu(B_{k,i} \setminus V) &\geqslant \mu(B_{k,i} \setminus V_{s_{j+1}}) - \mu(V) + \mu(V_{s_{j+1}}) \\ &> \varepsilon_{j+1} + 2^{-(i+3)} - \frac{\varepsilon_j}{2} > 2^{-(i+3)}.\end{aligned}$$

Thus we can enumerate the complement of T, and hence T is computable.

We now show that each $T^{[k]}$ is finite and we can compute $|T^{[k]}|$ given k. It suffices to show that we can effectively find an i_k such that $i \notin T^{[k]}$ for all $i > i_k$. Find a stage s such that $\mu(V_s) > \mu(V) - 2^{-(k+2)}$. Let G be a finite set of generators for V_s and let i_k be larger than k and the length of all strings in G. Let $i > i_k$. It is easy to check that $\mu(B_{k,i} \setminus V_s) = 2^{-k}(1 - \mu(V_s))$, so

$$\mu(B_{k,i} \setminus V) \geqslant \mu(B_{k,i} \setminus V_s) + \mu(V_s) - \mu(V) > 2^{-k}(1 - \mu(V_s)) - 2^{-(k+2)}$$
$$\geqslant 2^{-k}(1 - \frac{1}{4}) - 2^{-(k+2)} > 2^{-(k+2)} > 2^{-(i+3)},$$

whence $i \notin T^{[k]}$.

It remains to show that $|T^{[k]}|$ is bounded by a computable function that does not depend on g. We claim that $|T^{[k]}| < 2^k k$. Suppose not. Then we can find $i_0 < \cdots < i_{2^k-1} \in T^{[k]}$ such that $i_{j+1} - i_j \geqslant k$. Recall that $\mu(B_i) = 2^{-k}$ for all i. It is also easy to see that if $j > l$ then $\mu(B_{i_j} \cap B_{i_l}) = 2^{-2k}$, whence $\mu(B_{i_j} \setminus \bigcup_{l<j} B_{i_l}) \geqslant 2^{-k} - j2^{-2k}$. So

$$\mu(\bigcup_{i \in T^{[k]}} B_{k,i}) \geqslant \mu(\bigcup_{j<2^k} B_{k,i_j}) \geqslant \sum_{j<2^k} 2^{-k} - j2^{-2k}$$
$$> \sum_{j<2^{k-1}} 2^{-k} - 2^{k-1}2^{-2k} = \sum_{j<2^{k-1}} 2^{-k-1} = 1,$$

which is impossible.

We now show that we can remove the hypothesis that $\mu(U_n \setminus V) = 0$, weakening it to the hypothesis that $\mu_\sigma(V) < \frac{1}{4}$ and $\mu_\sigma(U_n \setminus V) = 0$ for some σ and n, where $\mu_\sigma(W) = \frac{\mu(W \cap [\![\sigma]\!])}{\mu([\![\sigma]\!])}$. First we show that the proof still works with this weaker hypothesis, and then we show that this hypothesis always holds.

Suppose that $\mu_\sigma(V) < \frac{1}{4}$ and $\mu_\sigma(U_n \setminus V) = 0$. For a class W, let $W^\sigma = [\![\{\tau : [\![\sigma\tau]\!] \subseteq W\}]\!]$.

We may assume that $g(k) > k$ for every k because a trace for $g(k) + k$ immediately yields a trace for g. Clearly we may also assume that $n > |\sigma|$. Let $\tilde{V} = V^\sigma$ and $\tilde{g}$ be the translation of g defined by $\tilde{g}(k) = \max(g(k) - |\sigma|, 0)$. Let $\tilde{U}_n$ be defined as U_n, but with $\tilde{g}$ in place of g. We claim that $\mu(\tilde{U}_n \setminus \tilde{V}) = 0$. If $i > |\sigma|$ then $B^\sigma_{k,i} = B_{k,i-|\sigma|}$. Since $g(k) > k$ and $n > |\sigma|$, we have $U^\sigma_n = \tilde{U}_n$, so $\mu(\tilde{U}_n \setminus \tilde{V}) = \mu_\sigma(U_n \setminus V) = 0$. This proves the claim. Now, it is clear that $\mu(\tilde{V})$ is less than $\frac{1}{4}$ and computable. So the proof given above is valid when $\tilde{V}$ and $\tilde{g}$ are substituted for V and g, and ensures the existence of a computable trace for $\tilde{g}$. But from a trace of $\tilde{g}$ we immediately obtain a trace for g.

Finally, suppose that there are no σ and n such that $\mu_\sigma(U_n \setminus V) = 0$ and $\mu_\sigma(V) < \frac{1}{4}$. We obtain a contradiction by constructing a set in $\bigcap_n U_n \setminus V$. Let σ_0 be the empty string and assume we have defined σ_n so that $\mu_{\sigma_n}(V) < \frac{1}{4}$. By hypothesis, $\mu_{\sigma_n}(U_n \setminus V) > 0$, so there is a $[\![\tau]\!] \subseteq U_n$ such that $\mu_{\sigma_n}([\![\tau]\!] \setminus V) > 0$. In particular, $\tau \succcurlyeq \sigma_n$ and $\mu_\tau(V) < 1$. By the Lebesgue Density Theorem 1.2.3, applied to the complement of V, there is a $\sigma_{n+1} \succ \tau$ such that $\mu_{\sigma_{n+1}}(V) < \frac{1}{4}$. Let $\alpha = \bigcup_n \sigma_n$. Since $[\sigma_{n+1}] \subseteq U_n$ for all n, we have $\alpha \in \bigcap_n U_n$. But $[\sigma_n] \nsubseteq V$ for every n, so, since V is open, $\alpha \notin V$. This contradiction completes the proof. □

As mentioned above, the following result has an easy proof as an application of the above theorem.

Theorem 12.1.3 (Terwijn and Zambella [389]). *There are continuum many degrees that are hyperimmune-free but not computably traceable.*

Proof. As noted in Proposition 8.1.3, it follows from the hyperimmune-free basis theorem that there are 1-random (and hence Schnorr random) sets of hyperimmune-free degree. As observed after the proof of Theorem 2.19.11, it is not hard to adjust the construction in that proof to show that a Π^0_1 class with no computable members has continuum many members of hyperimmune-free degree, so there are in fact continuum many 1-random sets of hyperimmune-free degree. Let A be such a set. We can A-computably construct a Schnorr test covering A, but that test cannot be covered by an unrelativized Schnorr test. Thus A is not low for Schnorr tests, and hence is not computably traceable. □

12.1.2 Lowness for Schnorr randomness

We now turn to the apparently weaker notion of lowness for Schnorr randomness. It is clear that if A is low for Schnorr tests then A is low for Schnorr randomness. Kjos-Hanssen, Nies, and Stephan [207] showed that the converse also holds, via some intermediate results of independent interest.

Theorem 12.1.4 (Kjos-Hanssen, Nies, and Stephan [207]). *A set A is c.e. traceable iff every Schnorr null set relative to A is Martin-Löf null.*

Proof. First suppose that every Schnorr null set relative to A is Martin-Löf null. Follow the proof of Theorem 12.1.2 until the definition of V. Now we still have a Σ^0_1 class V such that $\bigcap_n U_n \subseteq V$ and $\mu(V) < \frac{1}{4}$, but the measure of V is no longer computable. We can now continue to follow the proof of Theorem 12.1.2, with straightforward modifications.

For the other direction, suppose that A is c.e. traceable. Let $\{U_n\}_{n\in\omega}$ be a Schnorr test relative to A with $\mu(U_n) = 2^{-n}$. We may assume that $U_0 \supset U_1 \supset \cdots$.

Let $D_0, D_1, \ldots$ be a canonical listing of the finite sets of strings. Let $f \leqslant_T A$ be such that $[\![\bigcup_s D_{f(\langle n,s\rangle)}]\!] = U_n$ for all n, and for all n and s, we have $\mu([\![D_{f(\langle n,s\rangle)}]\!]) > 2^{-n}(1-2^{-s})$ and $[\![D_{f(\langle n,s+1\rangle)}]\!] \supseteq [\![D_{f(\langle n,s\rangle)}]\!]$. By Lemma 2.23.12, f has a c.e. trace $T_0, T_1, \ldots$ such that $|T_i| \leqslant i$ for all $i > 0$. We may also assume that if $e \in T_{\langle n,s\rangle}$ then $2^{-n}(1-2^{-s}) < \mu([\![D_e]\!]) \leqslant 2^{-n}$ and, if $s > 0$, then $[\![D_e]\!] \supseteq [\![D_i]\!]$ for some $i \in T_{\langle n,s-1\rangle}$.

Let

$$\widehat{V}_n = \bigcup\{[\![D_e]\!] : \exists s\,(e \in T_{\langle n,s\rangle})\}.$$

Then it is easy to see that $\mu(\widehat{V}_n) \leqslant 2^{-n}|T_{\langle n,0\rangle}| + \sum_s 2^{-s-n}|T_{\langle n,s\rangle}|$. By the bound on the sizes of the $T_{\langle n,s\rangle}$, it follows that we can compute a function

g such that $\mu(\widehat{V}_{g(n)}) \leqslant 2^{-n}$ for all n. Let $V_n = \widehat{V}_{g(n)}$. Then the V_n form a Martin-Löf test, and clearly $\bigcap_i U_i \subseteq \bigcap_i V_i$. □

Lemma 12.1.5 (Kjos-Hanssen, Nies, and Stephan [207]). *If A is of hyperimmune-free degree and c.e. traceable, then A is computably traceable.*

Proof. Let T be the c.e. trace of some function $g \leqslant_{\mathrm{T}} A$. Let $f(n) = \mu s\,(g(n) \in T^{[n]}[s])$. Then $f \leqslant_{\mathrm{T}} A$, so f is majorized by some computable function h. Let $\widetilde{T}^{[n]} = T^{[n]}[h(n)]$. Then $\widetilde{T}$ is a computable trace for g with the same bound as T. □

So to show that lowness for Schnorr tests coincides with lowness for Schnorr randomness, it is enough to show that every set that is low for Schnorr randomness has hyperimmune-free degree. This final step was actually the first result proved about lowness for Schnorr randomness, and is due to Bedregal and Nies [34].

Theorem 12.1.6 (Bedregal and Nies [34]). *If A is either low for computable randomness or low for Schnorr randomness, then A is of hyperimmune-free degree.*

Proof. Suppose that A is of hyperimmune degree, so that there is a function $g \leqslant_{\mathrm{T}} A$ such that, for any computable function h, we have $h(x) < g(x)$ for infinitely many x. We build a computably random set R and an A-computable martingale F that succeeds on R in the Schnorr sense.

Let M_e be the eth partial computable martingale (as defined in Definition 7.4.3). Let $T = \{e : M_e \text{ is total}\}$. For certain finite sets D, we will define strings σ_D such that if $D \subset E$ then $\sigma_D \prec \sigma_E$. We will ensure that for each $e \in T$ there is a c such that if $e \in D \subset E$ then $M_e(\sigma) < c$ for all σ such that $\sigma_D \preccurlyeq \sigma \preccurlyeq \sigma_E$. We will also ensure that σ_D is defined for all finite $D \subset T$. These two conditions ensure that $R = \bigcup_{D \subset T} \sigma_D$ is computably random. We will also ensure that A can know enough about this construction to compute a martingale F that succeeds quickly on R. To help us with that part of the construction, we will impose a lower bound on the length of σ_D, the reason for which will become clear in the construction of F.

We define the σ_D by induction, along with auxiliary constants p_D and partial computable martingales M_D. We ensure that if σ_D is defined then $M_D(\sigma_D)\!\downarrow < 2$, and that this convergence happens in at most $g(|\sigma_D|)$ many steps. We begin with $\sigma_\emptyset = \lambda$. Suppose that σ_E has been defined to have the above properties, and that $D = E \cup \{i\}$, where $i > \max E$. Let $p_D = 2^{-|\sigma_E|-1}(2 - M_E(\sigma_E))$ and $M_D = M_E + p_D M_e$. Since M_e is a martingale on its domain, $M_e(\tau) < 2^{|\tau|}$ for all τ, so $M_D(\sigma_E) < 2$ if it is defined.

Let e be the index of D in the canonical listing of finite sets. Look for $\sigma \succ \sigma_E$ with $|\sigma| > 4e$ such that M_D does not increase between σ_E and σ, and $M_D(\sigma)\!\downarrow$ in at most $g(|\sigma|)$ many steps. If such a string is found, then let $\sigma_D = \sigma$.

We claim that if $D \subset T$ then such a σ must exist. Let $f(m) = \mu s \forall \tau \in 2^m (M_D(\tau)[s]\downarrow)$. Then f is a total computable function, and hence there is an $m > |\sigma_E|, 4e$ such that $g(m) > f(m)$. Clearly, there is a $\sigma \in 2^m$ such that M_D does not increase between σ_E and σ, and by the choice of m, we have that $M_D(\sigma)\downarrow$ in at most $g(|\sigma|)$ many steps. Thus σ_D is defined.

So we can define $R = \bigcup_{D \subset T} \sigma_D$. To see that R is computably random, let M_e be total and let $D = T \cap [0, e]$. Suppose that $D \subseteq E$ and $E' = E \cup \{i\} \subset T$, where $i > \max E$. If $\sigma_E \prec \sigma \prec \sigma_{E'}$, then $p_D M_e(\sigma) \leqslant M_E(\sigma) \leqslant M_E(\sigma_E) < 2$. Thus $M_e(\sigma) < \frac{2}{p_D}$ for all sufficiently long $\sigma \prec R$.

Thus we are left with showing that R is not Schnorr random relative to A. We build a martingale $F \leqslant_T A$ for which there are infinitely many $\sigma \prec R$ with $F(\sigma) > 2^{\frac{|\sigma|}{4}}$.

For each finite set D, define a martingale F_D as follows. Let e be the index of D in the canonical listing of finite sets. If σ_D is undefined then let $F_D(\tau) = 2^{-e}$ for all τ. Otherwise, let $\sigma = \sigma_D \upharpoonright \lfloor \frac{|\sigma_D|}{2} \rfloor$ and define

$$F_D(\tau) = \begin{cases} 2^{-e} & \text{if } \tau \nsucc \sigma \\ 2^{-e+|\tau|-|\sigma|} & \text{if } \sigma \prec \tau \preccurlyeq \sigma_D \\ 2^{-e+|\sigma_D|-|\sigma|} & \text{if } \tau \succ \sigma_D \\ 0 & \text{if } \tau \succ \sigma \wedge \tau \mid \sigma_D. \end{cases}$$

That is, F_D bets evenly except following σ, where it concentrates its capital along σ_D.

Let $F = \sum_D F_D$. Clearly $F(\lambda)$ is finite, and hence F is a martingale. For each $D \subseteq T$ with canonical index e, we have $F(\sigma_D) \geqslant F_D(\sigma_D) = 2^{-e+|\sigma_D|-|\sigma|} > 2^{-\frac{|\sigma_D|}{4}+|\sigma_D|-\frac{|\sigma_D|}{2}} = 2^{\frac{|\sigma_D|}{4}}$.

Thus we are left with showing that $F \leqslant_T A$. It is clearly enough to show that the F_D are uniformly A-computable. Given τ and D, we can run through the inductive definition of σ_D to check whether $|\sigma_D| \leqslant 2|\tau|$. (That is, while we cannot know whether σ_D is defined, we can check whether some σ of length at most $2|\tau|$ is defined to be σ_D.) If not, then $F_D(\tau) = 2^{-e}$, where e is the canonical index of D. Otherwise, we can determine the value of F_D from the definitions of σ_D and F_D. □

As discussed above, we now have the following.

Corollary 12.1.7 (Kjos-Hanssen, Nies, and Stephan [207]). *A is low for Schnorr randomness iff A is computably traceable iff A is low for Schnorr tests.*

12.1.3 Lowness for computable measure machines

Recall the characterization of Schnorr randomness in terms of computable measure machines presented in Section 7.1.3: A prefix-free machine is a computable measure machine if the measure of its domain is computable, and Downey and Griffiths [109] showed that A is Schnorr random iff for every computable measure machine M we have $K_M(A \upharpoonright n) \geqslant n - O(1)$. We can relativize this notion, and say that a prefix-free oracle machine with oracle A is an *A-computable measure machine* if the measure of its domain is A-computable.

There is a potential worry here, namely the distinction between prefix-free oracle machines M such that $\mu(\llbracket \operatorname{dom} M^A \rrbracket)$ is A-computable and those such that $\mu(\llbracket \operatorname{dom} M^X \rrbracket)$ is X-computable for all oracles X. However, we need not worry about this distinction, because given a prefix-free oracle machine M such that $\mu(\llbracket \operatorname{dom} M^A \rrbracket)$ is A-computable, we can define a prefix-free oracle machine N such that $N^A = M^A$ and $\mu(\llbracket \operatorname{dom} N^X \rrbracket)$ is X-computable for all oracles X. To define N, let e be such that, thinking of Φ_e^A as a function from $\mathbb{N}$ to $\mathbb{Q}$, we have $\Phi_e^A(s) = \mu(\llbracket \operatorname{dom} M^A[s] \rrbracket)$. On oracle X, the machine N^X is defined as follows. At stage s, let $q = \Phi_e^X(t)[s]$ for the largest $t \leqslant s$ such that $\Phi_e^X(t)[s]\downarrow$. (If there is no such t then proceed to the next stage.) Search for a stage u such that $\mu(\llbracket \operatorname{dom} M^X[u] \rrbracket) = q$ and ensure that N^X agrees with M^X on $\operatorname{dom} M^X[u]$. If there is no such u, then the definition of N^X never leaves stage s. If at any later stage v we find that $\mu(\llbracket \operatorname{dom} M^X[v] \rrbracket) > q + 2^{-t}$, then immediately stop defining N^X on new strings. It is easy to check that for all X, either $\operatorname{dom} N^X$ is finite, or Φ_e^X is total and $0 \leqslant \mu(\llbracket \operatorname{dom} N^X \rrbracket) - \Phi_e^X(t) \leqslant 2^{-t}$, whence $\operatorname{dom} N^X$ is X-computable. It is also easy to check that $N^A = M^A$.

We can define an analog of lowness for K for computable measure machines.

Definition 12.1.8 (Downey, Greenberg, Mihailović, and Nies [107]). A set A is *low for computable measure machines* if for each A-computable measure machine M there is a computable measure machine N such that $K_N(\sigma) \leqslant K_M(\sigma) + O(1)$.

In Chapter 11 we saw that lowness for 1-randomness and lowness for K coincide. It is natural to ask whether the same is true for Schnorr randomness. That is, are lowness for Schnorr randomness and lowness for computable measure machines the same?

Downey, Greenberg, Mihailović, and Nies [107] have given a positive answer to this question. By the relativized version of Theorem 7.1.15, a set X is Schnorr random relative to A iff $K_M(X \upharpoonright n) \geqslant n - O(1)$ for all A-computable measure machines M. Thus, if a set is low for computable measure machines then it is low for Schnorr randomness. The converse follows from the following result, together with Corollary 12.1.7.

Theorem 12.1.9 (Downey, Greenberg, Mihailović, and Nies [107]). *A set is low for computable measure machines iff it is computably traceable.*

Proof. The "only if" direction follows from the fact that lowness for computable measure machines implies lowness for Schnorr randomness, together with Corollary 12.1.7. Now let A be computably traceable and let

M be an A-computable measure machine. We need to define a computable measure machine N such that $K_N(\sigma) \leqslant K_M(\sigma) + O(1)$.

Let $D_0, D_1, \ldots$ be a canonical list of the finite subsets of $2^{<\omega} \times 2^{<\omega}$. Recall that the domain of D_i is the set of all σ such that $(\sigma, \tau) \in D_i$ for some τ. Let t_n be the least t such that $\mu([\![\text{dom}\, M - \text{dom}\, M[t]]\!]) < 2^{-2n}$. Let G_s be the graph of $M[s]$, that is, the set of all (σ, τ) such that $M(\sigma)[s] = \tau$. Let c_n be such that $D_{c_0} = G_{t_0}$ and $D_{c_{n+1}} = G_{t_{n+1}} \setminus G_{t_n}$. Note that $\mu([\![\text{dom}\, D_{c_{n+1}}]\!]) < 2^{-2n}$. Let $F_0, F_1, \ldots$ be a computable sequence of finite sets such that for each n we have $|F_n| \leqslant 2^n$ and $c_n \in F_n$. Such a sequence exists because the function $n \mapsto c_n$ is A-computable and A is computably traceable. By removing elements if necessary, we may assume that for each $c \in F_{n+1}$, the domain of D_c is prefix-free and $\mu([\![\text{dom}\, D_c]\!]) < 2^{-2n}$.

Let $L = \{(|\tau| + 1, \sigma) : \exists n\, \exists c \in F_n\, ((\tau, \sigma) \in D_c)\}$. This set is c.e., and its weight is

$$\sum_n \sum_{c \in F_n} \frac{\mu([\![\text{dom}\, D_c]\!])}{2} < \sum_n |F_n| 2^{-(2n+1)} \leqslant \sum_n 2^n 2^{-(2n+1)} = 1.$$

Thus L is a KC set. Furthermore, the weight of L is computable, since we can approximate it to within 2^{-m} by $\sum_{n \leqslant m} \sum_{c \in F_n} \frac{\mu([\![\text{dom}\, D_c]\!])}{2}$. Now the KC Theorem gives us a prefix-free machine N such that for each request (d, σ) in L, there is a $\nu \in 2^d$ such that $N(\nu) = \tau$. In particular, if $M(\sigma) = \tau$ then $(\sigma, \tau) \in D_{c_n}$ for some n, and hence there is a ν such that $|\nu| = |\sigma| + 1$ and $N(\nu) = \tau$. Furthermore, $\mu([\![\text{dom}\, N]\!])$ is equal to the weight of L, and hence is computable. So N is a computable measure machine and $K_N(\sigma) \leqslant K_M(\sigma) + O(1)$. □

Corollary 12.1.10 (Downey, Greenberg, Mihailović, and Nies [107]). *A set is low for computable measure machines iff it is low for Schnorr randomness.*

Nies [private communication to Downey] has observed that essentially the same proof yields the following.

Corollary 12.1.11 (Nies [private communication]). *A is c.e. traceable iff for all A-computable measure machines M and all σ, we have $K_M(\sigma) \geqslant K(\sigma) - O(1)$.*

Proof Sketch. If A is c.e. traceable, then A-computable functions such as K_M for an A-computable measure machine M can be traced arbitrarily slowly, so that we have few enough possibilities and hence can enumerate possible values of $K(\sigma)$ based on apparent $K_M(\sigma)$.

Conversely, if $K_M(\sigma) \geqslant K(\sigma) - O(1)$ for all A-computable measure machines M, then given an A-computable function f, we can look at the particular A-computable measure machine M defined by $M(1^n 0) = f(n)$. Since $K_M(\sigma) \geqslant K(\sigma) - O(1)$, for each n we can compute a weak index for $T_n = \{\sigma : K(\sigma) \leqslant 2n\}$, and $f(n) \in T_n$ for almost all n. □

12.2 Schnorr triviality

In Section 9.17, we defined the notion of Schnorr reducibility: $A \leqslant_{\mathrm{Sch}} B$ if for each computable measure machine M there is a computable measure machine N such that $K_N(A \upharpoonright n) \leqslant K_M(B \upharpoonright n) + O(1)$. Naturally, this notion gives rise to a notion of triviality.

Definition 12.2.1 (Downey and Griffiths [109]). A is *Schnorr trivial* if $A \leqslant_{\mathrm{Sch}} \emptyset$.

The first construction of a noncomputable Schnorr trivial set was by Downey and Griffiths [109]. As we will see, Schnorr trivial sets behave quite differently from both K-trivial sets and sets that are low for Schnorr randomness. However, one implication does hold.

Theorem 12.2.2 (Franklin [151, 153]). *If A is low for Schnorr randomness then A is Schnorr trivial.*

Proof. This proof is from Downey, Greenberg, Mihailović, and Nies [107]. Let A be low for Schnorr randomness. Then A is low for computable measure machines, by Theorem 12.1.10. Let M be a computable measure machine. Let L be the A-computable measure machine defined by letting $L(\sigma) = A \upharpoonright n$ whenever $M(\sigma) = 0^n$. Then there is a computable measure machine N such that $K_N(A \upharpoonright n) \leqslant K_L(A \upharpoonright n)+O(1) \leqslant K_N(0^n)+O(1)$. □

12.2.1 Degrees of Schnorr trivial sets

Downey, Griffiths, and LaForte [110] and Franklin [151, 152, 153] began systematic investigations of the concept of Schnorr triviality. Downey, Griffiths, and LaForte proved the following result, which clearly highlights the differences between Schnorr triviality on the one hand and K-triviality or lowness for Schnorr randomness on the other.

Theorem 12.2.3 (Downey, Griffiths, and LaForte [110]). *There is a Turing complete Schnorr trivial c.e. set.*

We do not give the proof of Theorem 12.2.3 here, as it will follow from Corollary 12.2.16 below.

The following result shows that Schnorr trivials behave rather strangely with respect to Turing reducibility. Later we will explore the question of whether Turing reducibility is the correct notion to study in this context.

Theorem 12.2.4 (Franklin [151, 153]). *Every high degree contains a Schnorr trivial set. In other words, if $\mathbf{a}' \geqslant \mathbf{0}''$ then $\mathbf{a}$ contains a Schnorr trivial set.*[2]

[2]Using a forcing construction, Franklin [155] showed that, in fact, every Turing degree greater than or equal to $\mathbf{a}$ contains a Schnorr trivial set iff $\mathbf{a}' \geqslant \mathbf{0}''$.

Because both computable and complete Schnorr trivial c.e. sets exist, one might wonder whether every c.e. degree contains a Schnorr trivial set. The following theorem yields a negative answer to this question.

Theorem 12.2.5 (Downey, Griffiths, and LaForte [110]). *There is a c.e. degree* $\mathbf{b}$ *such that for each* $B \in \mathbf{b}$ *there is a computable measure machine* N *with* $\forall c\, \exists n\, (K(B \upharpoonright n) > K_n(n) + c)$. *Hence* $\mathbf{b}$ *contains neither Schnorr trivial nor* K*-trivial sets.*

Proof. We build a c.e. set A and for each pair of functionals Φ and Ψ a computable measure machine $N_{\Phi,\Psi}$, defined using the KC Theorem, to satisfy the following requirements.

$$R_{\Phi,\Psi} : \Psi^{\Phi^A} = A \Rightarrow \forall c\, \exists n\, (K(\Phi^A \upharpoonright n) > K_{N_{\Phi,\Psi}}(n) + c).$$

Each such requirement has subrequirements

$$S_{\Phi,\Psi,i} : \Psi^{\Phi^A} = A \Rightarrow \exists n\, (K(\Phi^A \upharpoonright n) > K_{N_{\Phi,\Psi}}(n) + i).$$

The strategy for $R_{\Phi,\Psi}$ has substrategies for its subrequirements $S_{\Phi,\Psi,i}$, which are allowed to act only on a sequence of stages at which $\Psi^{\Phi^A} = A$ appears more and more likely to be the case. Each such substrategy has a large number 2^k associated with it and picks a sequence of witnesses $x_0, \ldots, x_{2^k-1}$ such that $\psi^{\Phi^A}(x_i) < x_{i+1}$ for every $i < 2^k - 1$ (where, as usual, ψ is the use of Ψ). (Of course, what we really mean here is that $\psi^{\Phi^A}(x_i)[s] < x_{i+1}$ at the stage s at which we pick our witnesses, but since we control A, when thinking of a single strategy in isolation, we may assume that these uses do not change unless the strategy itself causes them to change.) Once these witnesses have been chosen, the strategy enumerates $(k - i - 1, \psi^{\Phi^A}(x_{k-1}))$ into our KC set for $N_{\Phi,\Psi}$. If there are a later stage s and a $\sigma \in 2^{<k}$ such that $\mathcal{U}(\sigma)[s] = \Phi^A \upharpoonright \psi^{\Phi^A}(x_{k-1})[s]$, the strategy enumerates the greatest $x_j \notin A[s]$ into A. If $\Psi^{\Phi^A} = A$, then Φ^A must change below $\psi^{\Phi^A}(x_j)$, so if this case were to occur for all the x_i then $\mathcal{U}$ would be forced to converge on at least 2^k many different strings of length less than k, which is not possible.

The priority organization of the requirements requires interleaving these strategies. We use the tree of strategies $2^{<\omega}$ to control the construction, and we adopt the convention that all uses with c.e. oracles are nondecreasing in the stage and increasing in the argument. Assign requirements to nodes in $2^{<\omega}$ so that the following conditions are satisfied for any $f \in 2^\omega$.[3]

[3] It is not difficult to build an assignment satisfying these conditions. We can use a list function L, defined recursively on the nodes in $2^{<\omega}$ and the natural numbers. Let $L(\lambda, \langle e, i\rangle) = R_{\Phi_e,\Phi_i}$. For each σ and n, if $L(\sigma, 0) = R_{\Phi,\Psi}$ then let $L(\sigma 1, n) = L(\sigma, n+1)$, let $L(\sigma 0, 2n) = L(\sigma, n+1)$, and let $L(\sigma 0, 2n+1) = S_{\Phi,\Psi,n}$. Otherwise, let $L(\sigma 0, n) = L(\sigma 1, n) = L(\sigma, n+1)$. Each σ has requirement $L(\sigma, 0)$ assigned to it.

1. Each requirement of the form $R_{\Phi,\Psi}$ is assigned to a unique node in f.

2. If $R_{\Phi,\Psi}$ is assigned to a node β and $\beta 0 \prec f$, then for each i there is a unique α such that $\beta 0 \preccurlyeq \alpha \prec f$ and $S_{\Phi,\Psi,i}$ is assigned to α. We say that β is α's *coordinator.*

3. If α is assigned some $S_{\Phi,\Psi,i}$, then α has a coordinator. (In other words, there is a unique β such that $\beta 0 \preccurlyeq \alpha$ and β is assigned $R_{\Phi,\Psi}$.)

The S-strategies have no outcomes, so we will arbitrarily give them outcome 0 at all stages.

A node is initialized by having all its associated parameters undefined and all its associated sets set to $\emptyset$. A node α with a requirement $R_{\Phi,\Psi}$ assigned to it has a machine N_α assigned to it that is built by enumerating a KC set L_α. A node α with a requirement $S_{\Phi,\Psi,i}$ assigned to it has associated with it a parameter $k_\alpha[s]$ and witnesses $x_\alpha(0)[s], \ldots, x_\alpha(2^{k_\alpha+i})[s]$.

Construction.
Stage 0. Initialize all nodes in $2^{<\omega}$.

Stage $s+1$. We define an approximation to the true path $f[s]$, of length at most s, and allow each node $\alpha \preccurlyeq f[s]$ to act. For such an α, we call s an *α-stage.* Let $n = |\alpha|$. Let s^- be the most recent α-stage or the most recent stage at which α was initialized, whichever is greater.
Case 1. Suppose α has $R_{\Phi,\Psi}$ assigned to it. Define the length-of-agreement function

$$l^\alpha[s] = \{n : \forall m < n\,(\Psi^{\Phi^A}(m)[s] = A(m)[s])\}.$$

Let s_0 be the stage at which α was last initialized. A stage s is *α-expansionary* if $l^\alpha[s] > \max\{l^\alpha[t] : s_0 < t < s \text{ and } t \text{ is an } \alpha\text{-stage}\}$.

For each $\gamma \succ \alpha$ with a requirement $S_{\Phi,\Psi,i}$ assigned to it, if $x_\gamma(j)[s]\downarrow$ for all $j \leqslant 2^{k_\gamma[s]+i}$ and $l_\beta[s] > x_\gamma(2^{k_\gamma+i})[s]$ but $l_\beta[s^-] \leqslant x_\gamma(2^{k_\gamma+i})[s]$, then enumerate $(k_\gamma[s], \psi^{\Phi^A}(x_\gamma(2^{k_\gamma+i}))[s])$ into L_β.

If s is not α-expansionary, then let $f(n)[s] = 1$, so that $\alpha 1$ is accessible at stage $s+1$, and initialize all nodes β such that $\alpha 1 <_{\mathrm{L}} \beta$. If s is α-expansionary, then let $f(n)[s] = 0$, so that $\alpha 0$ is accessible at stage $s+1$, and initialize all nodes β such that $\alpha 0 <_{\mathrm{L}} \beta$.
Case 2. Suppose α has $S_{\Phi,\Psi,i}$ assigned to it. Let β be α's coordinator.

1. If $x_\alpha(0)[s]\uparrow$, then let $k_\alpha[s]$ and $x_\alpha(0)[s]$ be fresh large numbers.

2. If there is a least $j \leqslant 2^{k_\alpha[s]+i}$ such that $x_\alpha(j)[s]\uparrow$ and $x_\alpha(j-1)[s]\downarrow < l_\beta$, then let $x_\alpha(j)[s]$ be a fresh large number.

3. If there is a $\sigma \in 2^{<k_\alpha[s]+i}$ such that $\mathcal{U}_s(\sigma) = \Phi^A \upharpoonright \psi^{\Phi^A}(x_\alpha(2^{k_\alpha+i}))[s]$, and there is a greatest j such that $x_\alpha(j)[s] \notin A[s]$, then enumerate $x_\alpha(j)[s]$ into A.

If any of these cases obtains, immediately end stage $s+1$ and initialize all $\gamma >_{\mathrm{L}} \alpha$. Otherwise, let $f(n)[s] = 0$, so that $\alpha 0$ is accessible at stage $s+1$, and initialize all nodes β such that $\alpha 0 <_{\mathrm{L}} \beta$.

End of Construction.

Let the *true path* f be $\liminf_s f[s]$. Once a node chooses a sequence of witnesses and is never again initialized, it acts to change A or initialize other nodes only a finite number of times. It follows by a straightforward induction that each $\alpha \prec f$ is initialized only finitely often.

Lemma 12.2.6. *Let $\alpha \prec f$ have $S_{\Phi,\Psi,i}$ assigned to it. Let β be α's coordinator. Then $k_\alpha[s]$ has a final value k_α, for each $j \leqslant 2^{k_\alpha+i+1}$, the witness $x_\alpha(j)[s]$ has a final value $x_\alpha(j)$, and $(k_\alpha, \psi^{\Phi^A}(x_\alpha(2^{k_\alpha+i+1}))) \in L_\beta$.*

Proof. By induction, for every $\alpha' \prec \alpha$ with an S-strategy assigned to it, there is a stage after which the construction never stops at α'. Thus, there is a stage after which α is never initialized, and there are infinitely many α-stages. Since $\beta 0 \preccurlyeq \alpha$, it must be the case that $\limsup_s l_\beta[s] = \infty$. Thus the $S_{\Phi,\Psi,i}$ strategy at α succeeds in permanently defining its witnesses, after which point β eventually enumerates a request on α's behalf into L_β. □

The above lemma shows that f is infinite. Suppose $\beta \prec f$ has requirement $R_{\Phi,\Psi}$ assigned to it. Assume that $\Psi^{\Phi^A} = A$, as otherwise there is nothing to prove. In this case, $\beta 0 \prec f$, and hence each subrequirement $S_{\Phi,\Psi,i}$ is assigned to some node in f. The following lemmas verify that $R_{\Phi,\Psi}$ is satisfied.

Lemma 12.2.7. *The set L_β is a KC set with computable weight, so N_β is a computable measure machine.*

Proof. Every time an α-strategy for some requirement $\S_{\Phi,\Psi,i}$ chooses a value for $k_\alpha[s]$, it chooses it to be a fresh large number. Since $\limsup_s l_\beta[s] = \infty$, once $x_\alpha(2^{k_\gamma+i})[s]$ becomes defined, either α is later initialized or β eventually enumerates $(k_\alpha[s], \psi^{\Phi^A}(x_\alpha(2^{k_\gamma+i}))[s])$ into L_β. It follows easily that the weight of L_β is less than 1 and is computable. □

Lemma 12.2.8. *For each i there is an n with $K(\Phi^A \upharpoonright n) \geqslant K_{N_\beta}(k) + i$.*

Proof. Let $\alpha \succ \beta 0$ be the unique node in f with $S_{\Phi,\Psi,i}$ assigned to it. Suppose we have passed the stage after which α is last initialized, so that the only S-strategies that can act are ones extending α and ones to its right. Then none of the uses relevant to α can be violated by numbers entering A except when α itself puts numbers into A. By Lemma 12.2.6, final values k_α and $x_\alpha(j)$ for $j \leqslant 2^{k_\alpha+i+1}$ are eventually chosen. Let $n = \psi^{\Phi^A}(x_\alpha(2^{k_\alpha+i}))[s]$, where s is the stage at which $x_\alpha(2^{k_\alpha+i})$ becomes defined. Assume for a contradiction that $K(\Phi^A \upharpoonright n) < K_{N_\beta}(k)+i$. The request (k_α, n) is put into L_β, so $K(\Phi^A \upharpoonright n) < k_\alpha + i$. Thus, eventually, case 3 of the action of the description of the action of the α-strategy will obtain, and $x_\alpha(2^{k_\alpha+i})$ will be put into A. This action forces $\Phi^A \upharpoonright n$ to change, without violating any of the other uses relevant to α, since $x_\alpha(2^{k_\alpha+i})$ was chosen to be a fresh large number. Now, eventually, case 3 will obtain again, but now for a different σ, and $x_\alpha(2^{k_\alpha+i}-1)$ will be put into A. This situation will continue to occur until all witnesses have entered A. At that point, there will be at least $2^{k_\alpha+i}$ many $\mathcal{U}$-programs of length less than $k_\alpha + i$, which is a contradiction. □

The last two lemmas establish the theorem. □

12.2.2 Schnorr triviality and strong reducibilities

In contrast to Theorem 12.2.3, we have the following result. Downey, Griffiths, and LaForte [110] stated it for left-c.e. reals, but the proof works more generally.

Theorem 12.2.9 (Downey, Griffiths, and LaForte [110]). *If A is Δ^0_2 and Schnorr trivial then it is wtt-incomplete.*

Proof. The proof is similar to that of Theorem 11.3.2. Let A be Δ^0_2 and wtt-complete. We construct a c.e. set B that forces the approximation to A to change too often for A to be Schnorr trivial. As in the proof of Theorem 11.3.2, by the recursion theorem, we may assume that a wtt-reduction $\Gamma^A = B$ is given in advance. We also build a computable measure machine M using the KC Theorem to satisfy the requirements

$$R_e : \exists n\, (K(A \upharpoonright n) \geqslant K_M(n) + e).$$

These requirements clearly suffice, since if A is Schnorr trivial and M is a computable measure machine, then $K(A \upharpoonright n) \leqslant K_M(n) + O(1)$. The main difference between this proof and that of Theorem 11.3.2 is that here we need to work for all e, rather than for a single one given by the recursion theorem, because even if A is Schnorr trivial, there need be no effective way to pass from a computable measure machine M to a computable measure machine N and a constant c such that $K_N(A \upharpoonright n) \leqslant K_M(n) + c$ for all n.

The basic strategy for satisfying a single R_e is the same as in the proof of Theorem 11.3.2 (except that of course we can no longer use the request $(0, n)$ as in that proof, but must use some more modest request, which we can compensate for by increasing the number of followers k). We put together the strategies for different R_e using a finite injury construction.

Associated with each R_e will be followers $m_0, \ldots, m_{k_e}$ and a number n_e greater than $\gamma(m^e_j)$ for all $j \leqslant k_e$. Initially these parameters are undefined. We assume we have sped up our stages so that at stage s, we have $\Gamma^{A_s}(x)[s]\downarrow = B_s(x)$ for all numbers x mentioned in the construction so far.

At stage s, proceed as follows. First, choose the least e (if any) such that k_e is defined, $K_s(A_s \upharpoonright n_e) < \log k_e$, and there is a least j such that m^e_j is not yet in B. Put m^e_j into B and undefine all parameters associated with

R_i for $i > e$. Next, let e be least such that k_e is not defined. Let k_e be a fresh large number. Let $m_0^e, \ldots, m_{k_e}^e$ be fresh large numbers and let n_e be larger than $\gamma(m_j^e)$ for all $j \leqslant k_e$. Enumerate a KC request $((\log k_e) - e, n_e)$ for M.

Notice first that M is a computable measure machine, since if a request of the form $((\log k_e) - e, n_e)$ is made at a stage s then $(\log k_e) - e > s$.

To show that R_e is satisfied, let s be a stage by which all R_i for $i < e$ have stopped changing B and M, and such that k_e becomes defined at stage s. This value of k_e is the final one, and associated with it are final values of $m_0^e, \ldots, m_{k_e}^e$ and n_e. The construction ensures that $K_M(n_e) \leqslant (\log k_e) - e$.

Assume for a contradiction that $K(A \upharpoonright n_e) < K_M(n_e) + e \leqslant \log k_e$. Then there are stages $s < s_0 < \cdots < s_{k_e}$ such that $K_{s_j}(A_{s_j} \upharpoonright n_e) < \log k_e$. At stage s_j, we put m_j^e into B. By the choice of n_e, it must therefore be the case that $A_{s_j} \upharpoonright n_e \neq A_{s_i} \upharpoonright n_e$ for $i \neq j$. Thus there are more than k_e many strings with K-complexity less than $\log k_e$, which is impossible. So we have a contradiction, and hence R_e is satisfied. □

In Chapter 7, we saw that Schnorr reducibility is naturally related to truth table reducibility. This relationship extends to Schnorr triviality.

Theorem 12.2.10 (Downey, Griffiths, and LaForte [110]). *If A is Schnorr trivial and $B \leqslant_{\mathrm{tt}} A$, then B is Schnorr trivial.*

Proof. Let $B = \Gamma^A$ be a tt-reduction with use bounded by the strictly increasing computable function γ. Let M be a computable measure machine. We must build a computable measure machine N such that $K_N(B \upharpoonright n) \leqslant K_M(n) + O(1)$.

It is easy to define a computable measure machine $\widehat{M}$ such that $K_{\widehat{M}}(\gamma(n)) \leqslant K_M(n)$ for all n. Since A is Schnorr trivial, there is a computable measure machine M_A such that $K_{M_A}(A \upharpoonright \gamma(n)) \leqslant K_{\widehat{M}}(\gamma(n)) + O(1) \leqslant K_M(n) + O(1)$.

If $M_A(\sigma) = \tau$, then let $N(\sigma) = \Gamma^{\tau \upharpoonright \gamma(j)} \upharpoonright j$ for the largest j such that $\gamma(j) \leqslant |\tau|$. Then, if $M_A(\sigma) = A \upharpoonright \gamma(n)$, we have $N(\sigma) = \Gamma^{A \upharpoonright \gamma(n)} \upharpoonright n = B \upharpoonright n$, so $K_N(B \upharpoonright n) \leqslant K_{M_A}(A \upharpoonright \gamma(n)) \leqslant K_M(n) + O(1)$. Since Γ is total on all oracles, $\mu(\operatorname{dom} N) = \mu(\operatorname{dom} M_A)$, so N is a computable measure machine. □

Given the above result, to show that the Schnorr trivials form an ideal in the tt-degrees it is enough to show that the join of two Schnorr trivial sets is still Schnorr trivial. We show that this is the case in the following section, where we obtain a natural characterization of Schnorr triviality in terms of initial segment complexity.

12.2.3 Characterizing Schnorr triviality

As we saw in Section 12.1, a set is low for Schnorr randomness iff it is computably traceable, and hence all such sets have hyperimmune-free degree.

Thus, results such as Theorem 12.2.3 show that the beautiful coincidence between K-triviality and lowness for 1-randomness, which is one of the arguments for the naturality of the notion of K-triviality, do not hold in the case of Schnorr randomness. However, Franklin and Stephan [158] obtained a rather satisfying characterization of Schnorr triviality in terms of relativized truth tables and initial segment complexity, which argues for the naturality of this notion. Their key realization is that to relativize weak notions of randomness like Schnorr or computable randomness, Turing reducibility may not be the correct notion, and should be replaced by truth table reducibility. That is, while we have no hope of showing that Schnorr triviality coincides with lowness for Schnorr randomness, as we did for K-triviality, there is some hope for a characterization along such lines if we restrict what we mean by relativization.

We begin by recalling Theorem 7.1.8, which states that the following are equivalent.

(i) X is not Schnorr random.

(ii) There is a computable martingale d and a computable function f such that $\exists^\infty n\,(d(X \upharpoonright f(n)) \geqslant n)$.

(iii) There is a computable martingale d with the savings property and a computable function f such that $\exists^\infty n\,(d(X \upharpoonright f(n)) \geqslant n)$.

Armed with this characterization, Franklin and Stephan [158] suggested the following restricted notion of relativization.

Definition 12.2.11 (Franklin and Stephan [158]). A set X is *truth table Schnorr random relative to A* if there are no martingale $d \leqslant_{\mathrm{tt}} A$ and no function $g \leqslant_{\mathrm{tt}} A$ such that $\exists^\infty n\,(d(X \upharpoonright g(n)) \geqslant n)$.[4]

A set A is *truth table low for Schnorr randomness* if every Schnorr random set is tt-Schnorr random relative to A.

We can simplify the definition above by considering only computable g, rather than all $g \leqslant_{\mathrm{tt}} A$.

Lemma 12.2.12 (Franklin and Stephan [158]). *A set X is tt-Schnorr random relative to A iff there are no martingale $d \leqslant_{\mathrm{tt}} A$ and no computable function g such that $\exists^\infty n\,(d(X \upharpoonright g(n)) \geqslant n)$.*

Proof. Suppose there is a martingale $d \leqslant_{\mathrm{tt}} A$ and a function $h \leqslant_{\mathrm{tt}} A$ such that $\exists^\infty n\,(d(X \upharpoonright h(n)) \geqslant n)$. It is easy to check from the proof of (ii) implies (iii) in Theorem 7.1.8 that we may assume that d has the savings property. We may also assume that h is nondecreasing. Since $h \leqslant_{\mathrm{tt}} A$, given n, we can compute all possible values of $h(n)$, so there is a computable g such that $g(n) \geqslant h(4n+4)$ for all n. For infinitely many n, there is an

[4] See [158] for an explanation of why relativizing the usual martingale definition of Schnorr randomness will not work in this case.

$m \in [4n, 4n+3]$ such that $d(X \upharpoonright h(m)) \geqslant m$. For all such n, we have $d(X \upharpoonright g(n)) \geqslant n$. □

We will show that a set is Schnorr trivial iff it is tt-low for Schnorr randomness. We begin with the following lemma. We will then show that condition (ii) in this result is equivalent to Schnorr triviality.

Lemma 12.2.13 (Franklin and Stephan [158]). *For each A, at least one of the following conditions holds.*

(i) *There is a computably random set that is not tt-Schnorr random relative to A.*

(ii) *There is a computable function h such that, for every computable function u, there are uniformly computable finite sets of strings $T_0, T_1, \ldots$ with $|T_n| \leqslant h(n)$ and $A \upharpoonright u(n) \in T_n$ for all n.*

Proof. Clearly, in (ii) we can restrict attention to strictly increasing functions u. Let $d_0, d_1, \ldots$ be a (noneffective) listing of all computable positive-valued martingales. We build a set X and a (noneffective) martingale d.

Fix a computable strictly increasing function u. Let $J_n = 2^{u(n)}$ and partition $\mathbb{N}$ into intervals I_σ for $\sigma \in \bigcup_n J_n$ so that I_σ has $2n$ elements for each $\sigma \in J_n$.

We define X and d in stages. Let $d(\lambda) = 1$. At stage n, we work with the nth interval I_σ in natural number order. Let n be such that $\sigma \in J_n$. Let k be the largest index among the martingales mentioned before this stage. Let $m = \min(I_\sigma)$. Before this stage, we will have defined $X \upharpoonright m$ and numbers $c_0, \ldots, c_k \leqslant m$ so that for all $\tau \in 2^m$ we have

$$d(\tau) = 2^{-k} + \sum_{i \leqslant k} 2^{-i} \frac{d_i(\tau)}{d_i(\tau \upharpoonright c_i)}. \tag{12.1}$$

Extend d to all τ with length between $m+1$ and $m+2n$, preserving (12.1).

Now check which of the following cases holds.

1. $\sigma \neq A \upharpoonright u(n)$.
2. $\sigma = A \upharpoonright u(n)$ and $d((X \upharpoonright m)^\frown 1^{2n}) \leqslant d(X \upharpoonright m) + 2^{-n}$.
3. Otherwise.

In cases 1 and 3, define X on I_σ so that $d(X \upharpoonright (m+2n))$ is as small as possible. In case 1, we have $d(X \upharpoonright (m+2n)) \leqslant d(X \upharpoonright m)$. In case 3, the gain of 2^{-n} on the sequence 1^{2n} implies a loss of at least 8^{-n} on at least one of the $4^n - 1$ other possible extensions of X on I_σ, so $d(X \upharpoonright (m+2n)) \leqslant (X \upharpoonright m) - 8^{-n}$. In both these cases, we do not incorporate any new martingales into d at this stage.

In case 2, let $X \upharpoonright (m+2n) = (X \upharpoonright m)^\frown 1^{2n}$. Let $c_{k+1} = m+2n$. Note that for $\tau \in 2^{m+2n}$, (12.1) and the fact that $\frac{d_{k+1}(\tau)}{d_{k+1}(\tau \upharpoonright c_{k+1})} = 1$ imply that

$$d(\tau) = 2^{-k-1} + \sum_{i \leqslant k+1} 2^{-i} \frac{d_i(\tau)}{d_i(\tau \upharpoonright c_i)}.$$

In other words, (12.1) continues to hold at level $m+2n$ with k replaced by $k+1$, as needed for the construction to proceed.

We have completed the definitions of X and d. There are now two cases.

First suppose that case 2 occurs infinitely often. By the savings trick, to show that X is not computably random, it is enough to show that no d_k succeeds strongly on X. Each d_k is incorporated into d from some point on, so if d_k succeeds strongly on X then so does d. But d gains no capital along X in cases 1 or 3, and gains at most 2^{-n} in case 2, which occurs only once for each n. Thus d does not succeed strongly on X, whence no d_k succeeds strongly on X, and X is computably random. On the other hand, there are infinitely many n with $I_{A \upharpoonright u(n)} \subseteq X$. We can build a martingale $d \leqslant_{\text{tt}} A$ that splits its capital into pieces of size 2^{-n-1} and uses each piece to make the $2n$ many bets that all members of $I_{A \upharpoonright u(n)}$ are in X. It is easy to check that this martingale witnesses the fact that X is not tt-Schnorr random relative to A.

Now suppose that case 2 occurs only finitely often. Then for almost all n, at the stage in which $\sigma = A \upharpoonright u(n)$, case 3 obtains, and hence d loses 8^{-n} along X. For such n, let T_n be the set of all strings in J_n such that case 3 obtains at the stage corresponding to σ. (For the finitely many other n, let $T_n = \{A \upharpoonright u(n)\}$.) Then $A \upharpoonright u(n) \in T_n$ for all n. When case 1 obtains, d gains no capital along X, so the capital reached by d on X at the end of the stages of the construction has a maximum value r. Thus $|T_n| \leqslant r8^n$ for all n. Since we eventually stop incorporating d_k's into d, the martingale d and the set X are both computable, so the T_n are uniformly computable. □

Theorem 12.2.14 (Franklin and Stephan [158]). *The following are equivalent.*

(i) *A is Schnorr trivial.*

(ii) *There is a computable function h such that, for every computable function u, there are uniformly computable finite sets of strings $T_0, T_1, \ldots$ with $|T_n| \leqslant h(n)$ and $A \upharpoonright u(n) \in T_n$ for all n.*

(iii) *The tt-degree of A is computably traceable. That is, there is a computable function g such that for each $f \leqslant_{\text{tt}} A$, there are uniformly computable finite sets $S_0, S_1, \ldots$ with $|S_n| \leqslant g(n)$ and $f(n) \in S_n$ for all n.*

(iv) *For each computable order g with $g(0) > 0$ and each $f \leqslant_{\text{tt}} A$, there are uniformly computable finite sets $S_0, S_1, \ldots$ with $|S_n| \leqslant g(n)$ and $f(n) \in S_n$ for all n.*

(v) *A is tt-low for Schnorr randomness.*

Proof. (i) implies (ii). Let A be Schnorr trivial. Let $h(n) = 2^{2n}$. Let u be a computable function, which we may assume is strictly increasing. Let $M(1^n0) = u(n)$ for all n and let M be undefined on all other inputs. Then M is a computable measure machine, so there is a computable measure machine N such that $K_N(A \upharpoonright u(n)) \leqslant K_M(u(n)) + O(1) = n + O(1)$. For each n, we can wait until $\mu(\operatorname{dom} N) - \mu(\operatorname{dom} N[s]) < 2^{-2n}$, and we will then know the set T_n of all σ such that $K_N(\sigma) < 2n$. By modifying finitely many T_n if necessary, we have $|T_n| \leqslant h(n)$ and $A \upharpoonright u(n) \in T_n$ for all n.

(ii) implies (iii). Let h be as in (ii). Let $f \leqslant_{\text{tt}} A$ via a tt-reduction Γ with use u. Let $T_0, T_1, \ldots$ be as in (ii). We may assume that $T_n \subseteq 2^{u(n)}$ for all n. Let $S_n = \{\Gamma^\sigma(n) : \sigma \in T_n\}$. Since Γ is a tt-reduction, $S_0, S_1, \ldots$ are uniformly computable. Furthermore, $|S_n| \leqslant |T_n| \leqslant h(n)$ and $f(n) \in S_n$ for all n.

(iii) implies (iv). Let g be as in (iii). We may assume that $g(0) = 1$. Let $\widehat{g}$ be a computable order and let $f \leqslant_{\text{tt}} A$ via a tt-reduction Γ with nondecreasing use function γ. Let $p(n)$ be a computable order such that $g(p(n)) \leqslant \widehat{g}(n)$ for all n and let m_i be the least n such that $p(n) > i$. Let $\widehat{f}(i) = \langle f(0), \ldots, f(m_i) \rangle$. Let $S_0, S_1, \ldots$ be as in (iii). Let $\widehat{S}_n = \{k : k \text{ is the } n\text{th element of a sequence in } S_{p(n)}\}$. Then the $\widehat{S}_n$ are uniformly computable, and $|\widehat{S}_n| \leqslant |S_{p(n)}| \leqslant g(p(n)) \leqslant \widehat{g}(n)$ and $f(n) \in \widehat{S}_n$ for all n.

(iv) implies (i). Suppose (iv) holds. Let M be a computable measure machine. We may assume that $n \in \operatorname{rng} M$ for all n, whence we can compute $K_M(n)$ for all n. Since $\sum_n 2^{-K_M(n)-1}$ is less than 1 and computable, there is a computable order g such that $\sum_n g(n)2^{-K_M(n)-1}$ is still less than 1 and computable. We use the KC Theorem to build a computable measure machine N with $K_N(A \upharpoonright n) \leqslant K_M(n) + O(1)$.

Let $\sigma_0, \sigma_1, \ldots$ be the length-lexicographic ordering of $2^{<\omega}$. Let f be such that $\sigma_{f(n)} = A \upharpoonright n$. Note that $f \leqslant_{\text{tt}} A$. By (iv), there are uniformly computable $S_0, S_1, \ldots$ such that $|S_n| \leqslant g(n)$ and $f(n) \in S_n$ for all n. Let $L = \{(K_M(n) + 1, \sigma_m) : m \in S_n\}$. Then the weight of L is $\sum_n |S_n| 2^{-K_M(n)-1} \leqslant \sum_n g(n) 2^{-K_M(n)-1} < 1$, so L is a KC-set, determining a prefix-free machine N, and $K_N(A \upharpoonright n) \leqslant K_M(n) + 1$ for all n. Since $\sum_n g(n)2^{-K_M(n)-1}$ is computable and $\sum_{n>m} |S_n| 2^{-K_M(n)-1} \leqslant \sum_{n>m} g(n) 2^{-K_M(n)-1}$ for all m, we have that $\sum_n |S_n| 2^{-K_M(n)-1}$ is also computable. Thus N is a computable measure machine.

(v) implies (ii) follows from Lemma 12.2.13.

(iv) implies (v). Suppose (iv) holds and let X be a set for which there are a computable function q and a martingale $d \leqslant_{\text{tt}} A$ such that $d(X \upharpoonright q(n)) \geqslant n$ for infinitely many n. We show that X is not Schnorr random. The basic idea is to use a trace of d with small bound to define a computable martingale $\widehat{d}$ that succeeds fast on X.

Let $m_0, m_1, \ldots$ be an effective listing of all initial segments of rational valued martingales (i.e., each m_i is a function from $2^{\leqslant n}$ to $\mathbb{Q}^{\geqslant 0}$ for some n, satisfying the martingale condition). Let g and h be computable orders such that $g(0) > 0$ and if n_k is the least n with $k \leqslant h(n)$, then $\sum_{i \leqslant n_k} g(i) \leqslant \log\log k + O(1)$.

Let $r(n) = \max_{i \leqslant h(n)} q(i)$. Let f be such that $m_{f(n)} = d \upharpoonright 2^{\leqslant r(n)}$ for all n. Note that $f \leqslant_{\mathrm{tt}} A$. Let $S_0, S_1, \ldots$ be as in (iv).

Define martingales $d_0, d_1, \ldots$ as follows. Initially, $d_j[0] = \emptyset$ for all j. At each stage n, for each $i \in S_n$ in turn, find the least j such that $m_{f(i)}$ extends the current approximation $d_j[n]$ (one must exist because only finitely many $d_j[n]$ will be different from $\emptyset$), and let $d_j[n+1] = m_{f(n)}$. For each j such that $d_j[n] \neq \emptyset$ and $d_j[n]$ has not been extended, extend $d_j[n]$ to $d_j[n+1]$ arbitrarily, taking care only to preserve the martingale property. Note that the number of j's such that $d_j[n+1] \neq \emptyset$ is bounded by $\sum_{i \leqslant n} g(i)$.

Let $\widehat{d} = \sum_j 2^{-j} d_j$. It is easy to see that $\widehat{d}$ is a computable martingale. Suppose that $d(X \upharpoonright q(k)) \geqslant k$. Let n be least such that $k \leqslant h(n)$. Then there is a $j \leqslant \sum_{i \leqslant n} g(i)$ such that $d_j(X \upharpoonright q(k)) = d(X \upharpoonright q(k)) \geqslant k$, whence $\widehat{d}(X \upharpoonright q(k)) \geqslant 2^{-j} k \geqslant 2^{-\sum_{i \leqslant n} g(i)} k \geqslant \frac{k}{c \log k}$ for some c.

Let $p(n) = \min_{q(k) \geqslant n} \frac{k}{c \log k}$. Then p is a computable order, and there are infinitely many k such that $\widehat{d}(X \upharpoonright q(k)) \geqslant \frac{k}{c \log k} \geqslant p(q(k))$, whence $\limsup_n \frac{\widehat{d}(X \upharpoonright n)}{p(n)} \geqslant 1$. Thus X is not Schnorr random. □

The above characterization can be used to show that the Schnorr trivials form an ideal in the tt-degrees.

Corollary 12.2.15 (Franklin and Stephan [158]). *Let A and B be Schnorr trivial. Then $A \oplus B$ is Schnorr trivial. Thus the Schnorr trivial sets form an ideal in the tt-degrees.*

Proof. By Theorem 12.2.14, there are computable functions g and h such that, for every computable function u, there are uniformly computable finite sets of strings $S_0, S_1, \ldots$ and $T_0, T_1, \ldots$ with $|S_n|, |T_n| \leqslant h(n)$, and $A \upharpoonright u(n) \in S_n$ and $B \upharpoonright u(n) \in T_n$, for all n. Let $f(2n) = g(n)h(n)$ and $f(2n+1) = g(n+1)h(n)$.

Let u be a computable function, and let $S_0, S_1, \ldots$ and $T_0, T_1, \ldots$ be as above. Let $U_{2n} = \{\sigma \oplus \tau : \sigma \in S_n \wedge \tau \in T_n\}$ and $U_{2n+1} = \{\sigma \oplus \tau : \sigma \in S_{n+1} \wedge \tau \in T_n\}$. Then $|U_n| \leqslant f(n)$ and $(A \oplus B) \upharpoonright n \in U_n$ for all n. So by Theorem 12.2.14, $A \oplus B$ is Schnorr trivial. □

Franklin and Stephan [158] observed that their characterization cannot be extended to weak truth table reducibility. They also provided a number of relatively natural examples of Schnorr trivial sets, such as the following. A c.e. set is *dense simple* if the principal function of its complement is dominant (i.e., dominates all computable functions).

Corollary 12.2.16 (Franklin and Stephan [158]). *If a c.e. set A is dense simple and $B \supseteq A$, then B is Schnorr trivial.*

Proof. Let u be computable. Then there is an m such that $\big|[0, u(n))\setminus A\big| < n$ for all $n \geqslant m$. For $n < m$, let $T_n = \{A \upharpoonright n\}$. For $n \geqslant m$, find an s such that $\big|[0, u(n)) \setminus A_s\big| < n$ and let T_n be the 2^n many strings σ of length $u(n)$ for which $i \in A_s \Rightarrow \sigma(i) = 1$ for all $i < u(n)$. Then $|T_n| \leqslant 2^n$ and $B \upharpoonright u(n) \in T_n$ for all n, so B is Schnorr trivial. □

We can combine this result with the following theorem due to Martin [258] to conclude that every high c.e. degree contains a Schnorr trivial c.e. set.

Theorem 12.2.17 (Martin [258]). *Every high c.e. degree contains a dense simple c.e. set.*

Proof. Let A be a high c.e. set. By Martin's Theorem 2.23.7, there is a dominant function $f \leqslant_{\mathrm{T}} A$. We may assume that f also dominates the modulus function of A (i.e., that $A_{f(n)}(n) = A(n)$ for all n). Let Φ be such that $f = \Phi^A$. Let $g(n)$ be the least s such that for all $m \leqslant n$, we have $\Phi^A(m)[s]\downarrow$ via an A-correct computation. Clearly $g \leqslant_{\mathrm{T}} A$, and, by the usual convention on approximations, $g(n) \geqslant f(n)$ for all n, so g also dominates the modulus function of A, and hence in fact $g \equiv_{\mathrm{T}} A$. Let $G = \{\langle n, g(n)\rangle : n \in \mathbb{N}\}$, where our pairing function is chosen so that $\langle x, y\rangle \geqslant y$ for all y. Then it is easy to see that G is co-c.e. and that $G \equiv_{\mathrm{T}} g \equiv_{\mathrm{T}} A$. Furthermore, if $m \geqslant n$ then $\langle m, g(m)\rangle \geqslant g(m) \geqslant g(n) \geqslant f(n)$, so there are at most n many elements of G that are less than $f(n)$, which means that the principal function of G majorizes f, and hence is dominant. Thus the complement of G is a dense simple c.e. set of the same degree as A. □

Corollary 12.2.18 (Franklin [151]). *Every high c.e. degree contains a Schnorr trivial c.e. set.*

We can apply the same argument to the Π^0_1 class of separating sets of a Sacks splitting of a maximal set (which is dense simple) to show the following. (See [151, 152] for details.)

Corollary 12.2.19 (Franklin [151, 152]). *There is a perfect Π^0_1 class of Schnorr trivial sets.*

Franklin and Stephan [158] also considered possible analogs to the fact that a set is K-trivial iff it is a base for 1-randomness. The obvious analog would be that A is Schnorr trivial iff there is a $B \geqslant_{\mathrm{tt}} A$ that is Schnorr random relative to A. Franklin and Stephan [158] observed that this result fails, but showed that one direction does hold: if $A \leqslant_{\mathrm{tt}} B$ and B is Schnorr random relative to A, then A is Schnorr trivial. They also considered extensions to stronger reducibilities. See [158] for more details.

12.3 Tracing weak truth table degrees

12.3.1 Basics

In Theorem 12.2.14 we saw that Schnorr triviality corresponds to a very natural tracing notion when we view the world through strong reducibilities. Specifically, we saw that A is Schnorr trivial iff the truth table degree of A is computably traceable. In this section we will look at the situation for weak truth table reducibility and establish a deep connection between the complexity of a set and tracing properties of its weak truth table degree.

Recall that a set A is complex if there is a computable order h such that $C(A \upharpoonright h(n)) \geqslant n$ for all n. As we saw in Theorem 8.16.3, Kjos-Hanssen, Merkle, and Stephan [205] showed that A is complex iff there is a function $f \leqslant_{\mathrm{wtt}} A$ such that $C(f(n)) \geqslant n$ for all n. Motivated by this result, we make the following definition.

Definition 12.3.1 (Franklin, Greenberg, Stephan, and Wu [156]). A set A is *anti-complex* if for every computable order f, we have $C(A \upharpoonright f(n)) \leqslant n$ for almost all n.

The intuition here is that anti-complex sets are highly compressible.

Theorem 12.3.2 (Franklin, Greenberg, Stephan, and Wu [156]). *The following are equivalent for a set A.*

(i) *A is anti-complex.*

(ii) *The wtt-degree of A is c.e. traceable.*

(iii) *A is wtt-reducible to a Schnorr trivial set.*

Here, of course, a weak truth table degree $\mathbf{a}$ is c.e. traceable if there is a computable order h such that for every function $f \leqslant_{\mathrm{wtt}} \mathbf{a}$, there is a computable collection $\{W_{g(x)} : x \in \omega\}$ with $|W_{g(x)}| \leqslant h(x)$ and $f(x) \in W_{g(x)}$ for all x. The argument of Lemma 12.1.1 shows that we can replace h by any computable order.

We devote the rest of this section to proving Theorem 12.3.2.

An interesting consequence of Theorems 12.2.14 and 12.3.2 is that a weak truth table degree $\mathbf{a}$ is c.e. traceable iff there is a weak truth table degree $\mathbf{b} \geqslant \mathbf{a}$ that contains a set whose truth table degree is computably traceable.

12.3.2 Reducibilities with tiny uses

To prove Theorem 12.3.2, Franklin, Greenberg, Stephan, and Wu [156] introduced yet another variation on weak truth table reducibility.

Definition 12.3.3 (Franklin, Greenberg, Stephan, and Wu [156]). Let $A, B \in 2^{\omega}$.

(i) We say that A is *uniformly reducible to B with tiny use*, and write $A \leqslant_{\mathrm{uT(tu)}} B$, if there is a Turing reduction $\Phi^B = A$ whose use function is dominated by every computable order.

(ii) We say that A is *reducible to B with tiny use*, and write $A \leqslant_{\mathrm{T(tu)}} B$, if for every computable order h, there is a Turing reduction of A to B whose use function is bounded by h.

Some of the basic properties of these reducibilities are easy to obtain. For instance, if $A \leqslant_{\mathrm{uT(tu)}} B$ then $A \leqslant_{\mathrm{T(tu)}} B$, and if $A \leqslant_{\mathrm{T(tu)}} B$ then $A \leqslant_{\mathrm{wtt}} B$. It is also easy to see that if $A \leqslant_{\mathrm{wtt}} C \leqslant_{\mathrm{T(tu)}} B$ then $A \leqslant_{\mathrm{T(tu)}} B$, and if $A \leqslant_{\mathrm{T(tu)}} C \leqslant_{\mathrm{wtt}} B$ then $A \leqslant_{\mathrm{T(tu)}} B$. Thus, the relation $\leqslant_{\mathrm{T(tu)}}$ is invariant on weak truth table degrees (and is preserved by increasing the degree on the range or decreasing the degree on the domain). The same holds for $\leqslant_{\mathrm{uT(tu)}}$. Moreover, for a fixed B, the classes $\{A : A \leqslant_{\mathrm{T(tu)}} B\}$ and $\{A : A \leqslant_{\mathrm{uT(tu)}} B\}$ are wtt-ideals.

Franklin, Greenberg, Stephan, and Wu [156] gave another formulation of these notions using not the use functions but their discrete inverses. If $\Phi^B = A$ is a Turing reduction, then let $\Phi(B \upharpoonright n)$ be the longest initial segment of A that is computed by Φ^B querying the oracle B only on numbers smaller than n. Recall that a function is dominant if it dominates every computable function. The following is easy to show.

Lemma 12.3.4 (Franklin, Greenberg, Stephan, and Wu [156]). *Let $A, B \in 2^\omega$.*

(i) *$A \leqslant_{\mathrm{T(tu)}} B$ iff, for every computable order g, there is a Turing reduction $\Phi^B = A$ such that the map $n \mapsto |\Phi(B \upharpoonright n)|$ bounds g.*

(ii) *$A \leqslant_{\mathrm{uT(tu)}} B$ iff there is a Turing reduction $\Phi^B = A$ such that the map $n \mapsto |\Phi(B \upharpoonright n)|$ is dominant.*

We begin our analysis of these reducibilities with some further easy observations.

Lemma 12.3.5. (i) *If $A \leqslant_{\mathrm{T(tu)}} A$ then A is computable.*

(ii) *If A is computable then $A \leqslant_{\mathrm{uT(tu)}} B$ for all B.*

Proof. Let $f(n) = n + 1$. If $\Phi^A = A$ and for all n we have $\Phi(A \upharpoonright n) \succcurlyeq A \upharpoonright n+1$ then we can recursively compute $A(n)$ by applying Φ to $A \upharpoonright n$, which we previously computed. For the second part, use a reduction $\Phi^B = A$ whose use function is the constant function 0. □

Corollary 12.3.6. *If $A \leqslant_{\mathrm{T(tu)}} B$ and A is noncomputable, then $A <_{\mathrm{wtt}} B$.*

Proof. If $B \leqslant_{\mathrm{wtt}} A \leqslant_{\mathrm{T(tu)}} B$ then B is computable, and hence so is A. □

Thus, for instance, if $\deg_{\mathrm{wtt}}(B)$ is minimal, then every $A \leqslant_{\mathrm{T(tu)}} B$ is computable. In fact, something stronger is true.

Theorem 12.3.7 (Franklin, Greenberg, Stephan, and Wu [156]). *If there is a noncomputable A such that $A \leqslant_{\mathrm{uT(tu)}} B$, then B is high.*

Proof. For any Turing reduction Φ, if Φ^B is total, then the map $n \mapsto |\Phi(B \upharpoonright n)|$ is computable in B (indeed, weak truth table reducible to B). For a Φ that witnesses that $A \leqslant_{\mathrm{uT(tu)}} B$, this map dominates every computable function. By Martin's Theorem 2.23.7, B is high. □

See [156] for more on the degrees of sets that tiny use bound noncomputable sets.

12.3.3 Anti-complex sets and tiny uses

The following straightforward result shows that anti-complexity is invariant for wtt-degrees.

Lemma 12.3.8 (Franklin, Greenberg, Stephan, and Wu [156]). *A set A is anti-complex iff $C(f(n)) \leqslant n + O(1)$ for every $f \leqslant_{\mathrm{wtt}} A$.*

We now come to our first characterization of anti-complexity.

Theorem 12.3.9 (Franklin, Greenberg, Stephan, and Wu [156]). *A set is anti-complex iff its wtt-degree is c.e. traceable.*

Proof. Suppose that A is anti-complex, and let $f \leqslant_{\mathrm{wtt}} A$. By Lemma 12.3.8, there is a c such that $C(f(n)) \leqslant n + c$ for all n. Let $T_n = \{x : C(x) \leqslant n + c\}$. Then $\{T_n\}_{n\in\omega}$ is a c.e. trace for f, and $|T_n| \leqslant 2^{n+c+1}$ for all n. By altering finitely many T_n, we can get a c.e. trace for f with bound 2^{2n}. Thus $\deg_{\mathrm{wtt}}(A)$ is c.e. traceable.

For the other direction, suppose that $\deg_{\mathrm{wtt}}(A)$ is c.e. traceable, and let $f \leqslant_{\mathrm{wtt}} A$. By Lemma 12.1.1, let $\{T_n\}_{n\in\omega}$ be a c.e. trace for f bounded by the order $h(n) = n$. Let U be our universal machine. We can construct a machine M that on input σ, first computes $U(\sigma)$, then, if this computation converges, interprets the result as a pair (n, m), and if $m < n$, outputs the mth element enumerated into T_n. If $f(n)$ is the mth element enumerated into T_n, then $C(f(n)) \leqslant C_M(f(N)) + O(1) \leqslant C(n, m) + O(1) \leqslant 2C(n) + O(1) \leqslant 2\log n + O(1)$, so the condition of Lemma 12.3.8 holds. □

For the next characterization, we need a kind of monotone approximation to the function $n \mapsto C(A \upharpoonright n)$. Let $g_A(k)$ be the least n such that $C(A \upharpoonright m) > k$ for all $m \geqslant n$. Clearly $g_A \leqslant_{\mathrm{T}} A'$. Let $\mathcal{V}$ be our fixed universal (plain) machine. Recall that σ_C^* is the first τ of length $C(\sigma)$ for which we see that $\mathcal{V}(\tau) = \sigma$. Let

$$A^* = \left\{ (A \upharpoonright g^A(k))_C^* : k \in \mathbb{N} \right\}.$$

Clearly $A^* \leqslant_{\mathrm{T}} A'$.

Lemma 12.3.10 (Franklin, Greenberg, Stephan, and Wu [156]). *For every A, the map $k \mapsto (A \upharpoonright g_A(k))^*_C$ is bounded by some computable function, where we identify a string with its position in the length-lexicographic ordering of $2^{<\omega}$.*

Proof. Clearly there is a constant c such that $C(\tau 0), C(\tau 1) \leqslant C(\tau)+c$ for all τ. For any k, let τ_k be a binary string and $i < 2$ be such that $A \upharpoonright g_a(k) = \tau_k i$. By definition of $g_A(k)$, we have $C(\tau_k) \leqslant k$, and so $C(A \upharpoonright g_A(k)) \leqslant k + c$. Hence $(A \upharpoonright g_A(k))^*_C < 2^{k+c+1}$. □

Theorem 12.3.11 (Franklin, Greenberg, Stephan, and Wu [156]). *The following are equivalent.*

(i) *There is some set B such that $A \leqslant_{\mathrm{T(tu)}} B$.*

(ii) *A is anti-complex.*

(iii) *g_A is dominant.*

(iv) *$A \leqslant_{\mathrm{uT(tu)}} A^*$.*

Proof. (i) implies (ii): Assume that $A \leqslant_{\mathrm{T(tu)}} B$. Suppose that $f \leqslant_{\mathrm{wtt}} A$, so there is a functional Γ such that $\Gamma^A = f$ and the use of this computation is bounded by a computable function g. We can find a Φ such that $\Phi^B = A$ and $\Phi(B \upharpoonright n)$ is longer than $A \upharpoonright g(n)$ for all n. Then $C(f(n)) \leqslant C(\Phi(B \upharpoonright n)) + O(1) \leqslant C(B \upharpoonright n) + O(1) \leqslant n + O(1)$. By Lemma 12.3.8, A is anti-complex.

(ii) implies (iii): Suppose that A is anti-complex. Let f be an increasing computable function. By definition, $C(A \upharpoonright f(n)) \leqslant n$ for almost all n. Hence, $g_A(n) > f(n)$ for almost all n. It follows that g_A dominates every computable function.

(iii) implies (iv): For every A we have $A \leqslant_{\mathrm{T}} A^*$, because for our universal machine $\mathcal{V}$, we have $A = \bigcup\{\mathcal{V}(\sigma) : \sigma \in A^*\}$ (in other words, $A(x) = \mathcal{V}(\sigma)(x)$ for any $\sigma \in A^*$ such that $x < |\mathcal{V}(\sigma)|$, and for every x there is indeed some $\sigma \in A^*$ such that $|\mathcal{V}(\sigma)| > x$). But if g_A is dominant then this reduction witnesses that $A \leqslant_{\mathrm{uT(tu)}} A^*$. To see this, let Φ be this reduction, and let f be an increasing computable function. We need to show that $n \mapsto |\Phi(A^* \upharpoonright n)|$ dominates f.

Let g be a computable function that dominates $k \mapsto (A \upharpoonright g_A(k))^*_C$, which exists by Lemma 12.3.10. Since g_A is dominant, $g_A(k) \geqslant f(g(k+1))$ for almost all k. Suppose that k is large enough and that $(A \upharpoonright g_A(k))^*_C < n \leqslant (A \upharpoonright g_A(k+1))^*_C$. Then $n \leqslant g(k+1)$ and so $g_A(k) \geqslant f(n)$. But $|\Phi(A^* \upharpoonright n)| \geqslant g_A(k)$, since $(A \upharpoonright g_A(k))^*_C < n$, and from $(A \upharpoonright g_A(k))^*_C$ we can compute $A \upharpoonright g_A(k)$. Thus $|\Phi(A^* \upharpoonright n)| \geqslant f(n)$ as required. □

12.3.4 Anti-complex sets and Schnorr triviality

We have seen that Schnorr triviality is not invariant in the weak truth table degrees. However, Theorem 12.3.2 concerns the downward closure of the wtt-degrees containing Schnorr trivial sets.

Proposition 12.3.12 (Franklin, Greenberg, Stephan, and Wu [156]). *Every Schnorr trivial set is anti-complex.*

Proof. Let A be Schnorr trivial. Fix a computable order h. Let Φ be a wtt-functional with computable bound g on its use function. The map $n \mapsto A \upharpoonright g(n)$ is tt-reducible to A, so by Theorem 12.2.14, there is a computable trace $\{T_n\}_{n\in\omega}$ for this map that is bounded by h. If $f = \Phi^A$ is total then we can enumerate a trace $\{S_n\}_{n\in\omega}$ for f (with bound h) by putting $\Phi^\sigma(n)$ into S_n for those $\sigma \in T_n$ for which Φ^σ converges with domain greater than n. Hence $\deg_{\mathrm{wtt}}(A)$ is c.e. traceable. By Lemma 12.3.9, A is anti-complex. □

Combining this result with Lemma 12.3.8, which shows that the class of anti-complex sets is closed downwards under wtt-reducibility, we see that if A is wtt-reducible to a Schnorr trivial set, then it is anti-complex. Combined with Lemma 12.3.11, the following result establishes the converse, and hence completes the proof of Theorem 12.3.2.

Theorem 12.3.13 (Franklin, Greenberg, Stephan, and Wu [156]). *If g_A is dominant then A is wtt-reducible to some Schnorr trivial set.*

Proof. Let $f_0, f_1, \dots$ be a sequence of total computable functions such that

1. each f_i is strictly increasing;
2. the range of f_{i+1} is contained in the range of f_i; and
3. every computable function is bounded by some f_i.

By Lemma 12.3.10, let g be a computable function that bounds the function $k \mapsto (A \upharpoonright g_A(k))^*_C$. For each $k > 0$, let $q_k = \langle (A \upharpoonright g_A(k))^*_C, f_i(k)\rangle$, where i is greatest such that $\langle g(k), f_i(k)\rangle \leqslant g_A(k-1)$. Note that $q_k \leqslant g_A(k-1)$ for all $k > 0$. Let $B = \{q_k : k > 0\}$. We claim that $A \leqslant_{\mathrm{wtt}} B$ and B is Schnorr trivial.

For a fixed n, let k be greatest such that $g_A(k) \leqslant n$. Then $q_{k+1} \leqslant g_A(k) \leqslant n$ and $A \upharpoonright g_A(k+1)$ can be effectively obtained from q_{k+1}. This procedure allows us to generate $A \upharpoonright n$ effectively from $B \upharpoonright n+1$, so $A \leqslant_{\mathrm{wtt}} B$.

To see that B is Schnorr trivial, we appeal to Theorem 12.2.14. Here is where we use the fact that g_A is dominant. The point is that, for every i, all but finitely many elements of B are pairs whose second coordinates are contained in the range of f_i, which follows from the fact that the map $k \mapsto \langle g(k), f_i(k)\rangle$ is computable, and so dominated by g_A: for all but finitely many k, we have $q_k = \langle (A \upharpoonright g_A(k))^*_C, f_{i'}(k)\rangle$ for some $i' \geqslant i$, and the range of $f_{i'}$ is contained in the range of f_i.

So let Ψ be a truth table functional. There is some i such that f_i bounds the use function of Ψ. After specifying a fixed initial segment of B (specifying those $q_{k'}$ whose second coordinates are not in the range of f_i), there are at most $2^{kg(k)}$ many possibilities for $B \upharpoonright f_i(k)$, because apart from the finitely many fixed numbers, there are only $kg(k)$ many numbers below $f_i(k)$ that can be elements of B, as they all have the form $\langle p, f_i(m)\rangle$ for some $p < g(k)$ and $m < k$. After applying Ψ, we get a computable trace for Ψ^B whose kth element has size at most $2^{kg(k)}$. So $\deg_{\text{tt}}(B)$ is computably traceable, and hence, by Theorem 12.2.14, B is Schnorr trivial. □

12.4 Lowness for weak genericity and randomness

As in other cases, when considering weak 1-randomness, there are two reasonable notions: lowness for weak 1-randomness and the possibly stronger notion of lowness for Kurtz null tests. We begin with a result that sandwiches both notions of lowness between the hyperimmune-free sets and the computably traceable ones.

Theorem 12.4.1 (Downey, Griffiths, and Reid [111]).

(i) *If a set is computably traceable then it is low for Kurtz null tests.*

(ii) *If a set is low for weak* 1*-randomness then it has hyperimmune-free degree.*

Proof. (i) Let A be computably traceable. Let $\{U_n\}_{n\in\omega}$ be a Kurtz null test relative to A. Then there is an A-computable function $f : \omega \to (2^{<\omega})^{<\omega}$ such that $V_n = [\![f(n)]\!]$. Let T be a computable trace for f with bound $n \mapsto n+1$. We can think of $T^{[n]}$ as a set of finite sets of strings. Let $g(n) = \bigcup\{D \in T^{[n+1]} : \mu([\![D]\!]) \leqslant 2^{-n}\}$ and $V_n = [\![g(n)]\!]$. Then $\mu(V_n) \leqslant (n+2)2^{-(n+1)} \leqslant 2^{-n}$, so the V_n form a Kurtz null test, and clearly $\bigcap_n V_n \supseteq \bigcap_n U_n$.

(ii) In Corollary 8.11.8, we proved that every hyperimmune degree is weakly 1-random, and clearly no weakly 1-random degree can be low for weak 1-randomness. □

We will now work toward showing that lowness for weak 1-randomness and lowness for Kurtz null tests coincide, and that the sets that are low for weak 1-randomness can be completely characterized as those whose degrees are hyperimmune-free and not DNC. As we will see, these are also the sets that are *low for weak 1-genericity*, i.e., the sets A such that if a set meets every dense Σ^0_1 class, then it meets every dense $\Sigma^{0,A}_1$ class.

Recall that a degree $\mathbf{a}$ is DNC if there is a function $f \leqslant_{\text{T}} \mathbf{a}$ such that $f(e) \neq \Phi_e(e)$ for all e. Recall also from Theorem 8.16.8 that Kjos-Hanssen, Merkle, and Stephan [205] showed that if the degree of B is hyperimmune-free and not DNC, then for each $g \leqslant_{\text{T}} B$, there are computable h and $\widehat{h}$

such that $\forall n \, \exists m \in [n, \widehat{h}(n)] \, (h(m) = g(m))$. This result can be used to establish the following theorem.

Theorem 12.4.2 (Stephan and Yu [381]). *Suppose the degree of A is hyperimmune-free and not DNC.*

(i) *Every $\Sigma_1^{0,A}$ class of measure 1 has a Σ_1^0 subclass of measure 1.*

(ii) *Every dense $\Sigma_1^{0,A}$ class has a dense Σ_1^0 subclass.*

Proof. Let S be a $\Sigma_1^{0,A}$ class of measure 1. Note that S is necessarily dense. We build a Σ_1^0 subclass of S that has measure 1 and is dense. This construction establishes (i), and (ii) follows by the same proof with all measure considerations removed.

Define a function $f \leqslant_T A$ as follows. Given n, search for an $m > n$ such that every $\sigma \in 2^n$ is extended by some $\tau \in 2^m$ with $[\![\tau]\!] \in S$. (Note that every $m' > m$ will also have this property.) Then search for a $k \geqslant m$ such that $\mu(\bigcup\{[\![\sigma]\!] : \sigma \in 2^k \wedge [\![\sigma]\!] \subseteq S\}) \geqslant 1 - 2^{-n}$. Let $f(n) = k$. Since X has hyperimmune-free degree, there is a computable function p such that $p(n) \geqslant f(n)$ for all n. Let $q(0) = 0$ and $q(n+1) = p(q(n))$.

Let $g : \mathbb{N} \to (2^{<\omega})^{<\omega}$ be an A-computable function such that for all n,

1. $g(n) \subseteq 2^{q(n+1)}$,
2. $[\![g(n)]\!] \subseteq S$,
3. for each $\sigma \in 2^{q(n)}$ there is a $\tau \in g(n)$ extending σ, and
4. $\mu([\![g(n)]\!]) \geqslant 1 - 2^{-n}$.

By Theorem 8.16.8, there are computable functions $h : \mathbb{N} \to (2^{<\omega})^{<\omega}$ and $\widehat{h} : \mathbb{N} \to \mathbb{N}$ such that for all n,

1. $h(n) \subseteq 2^{q(n+1)}$,
2. for each $\sigma \in 2^{q(n)}$ there is a $\tau \in h(n)$ extending σ,
3. $\mu([\![h(n)]\!]) \geqslant 1 - 2^{-n}$, and
4. there is an $m \in [n, \widehat{h}(n)]$ such that $h(m) = g(m)$.

Let

$$T = \{X : \exists n \, \forall m \in [n, \widehat{h}(n)] \, (X \upharpoonright q(m+1) \in h(m))\}.$$

Then T is a Σ_1^0 class. Furthermore, for each $X \in T$, there is an n and $m \in [n, \widehat{h}(n)]$ such that $g(m) = h(m)$. Then $X \in [\![h(m)]\!] = [\![g(m)]\!]$, and therefore $T \subseteq S$.

The measure of T is 1 because for all n,

$$\begin{aligned}\mu(\{X : \forall m \in [n, \widehat{h}(n)]\,(X \upharpoonright m \in h(m))\}) \\ = 1 - \mu\Big(\bigcup_{m \in [n,\widehat{h}(n)]} \overline{[\![h(m)]\!]}\Big) \geqslant 1 - \sum_{m\in[n,\widehat{h}(n)]} 2^{-m} > 1 - 2^{-n+1}.\end{aligned}$$

Finally, T is dense because given $\sigma \in 2^n$, there is an extension σ' of σ in $2^{q(n)}$. But then there is an extension τ_0 of σ' in $h(n)$. Since $h(n) \subseteq 2^{q(n+1)}$, there is an extension τ_1 of τ_0 in $h(n+1)$. Continuing in this way, we get a sequence $\sigma \prec \sigma' \prec \tau_0 \prec \tau_1 \prec \cdots$ such that $\tau_i \in h(n+i)$. Then $\bigcup_i \tau_i$ is an element of T extending σ. □

Corollary 12.4.3 (Stephan and Yu [381]). *If a degree is hyperimmune-free and not DNC then is is low for Kurtz null tests and low for weak 1-genericity.*

Stephan and Yu [381] also completely characterized the sets that are low for weak 1-genericity.

Theorem 12.4.4 (Stephan and Yu [381]). *The following are equivalent.*

(i) *Every dense $\Sigma_1^{0,A}$ class has a dense Σ_1^0 subclass.*

(ii) *A is low for weak 1-genericity.*

(iii) *The degree of A is hyperimmune-free and every 1-generic is weakly 1-generic relative to A.*

(iv) *The degree of A is hyperimmune-free and not DNC.*

Proof. Clearly (i) implies (ii), and (ii) implies (iii) by the $n = 0$ case of Theorem 2.24.14, which implies that every hyperimmune degree contains a weakly 1-generic set. Also, (iv) implies (i) by Theorem 12.4.2. To finish the proof, we show that if every 1-generic is weakly 1-generic relative to A then the degree of A is not DNC.

Suppose that A is DNC and each 1-generic set is also weakly 1-generic relative to A. By Theorem 8.16.4, A is autocomplex, so there is an A-computable function f such that $K(A \upharpoonright m) \geqslant n$ for all $m \geqslant f(n)$. By replacing f with the use function of its computation from A, we may assume that $f(n)$ can be computed from $A \upharpoonright f(n)$. Let

$$S = \{\sigma^\frown(A \upharpoonright f(|\sigma|)) : \sigma \in 2^{<\omega}\}.$$

Then S is dense. By Theorem 2.24.2, each noncomputable c.e. set computes a 1-generic, so we can choose B to be low for K and 1-generic. By hypothesis, B is weakly 1-generic relative to A, so B meets S infinitely often, and hence there are infinitely many n with $(B \upharpoonright n)^\frown(A \upharpoonright f(n)) \prec B$. For such an n, we can compute $A \upharpoonright f(n)$ from $B \upharpoonright n + f(n)$ and n. Furthermore, with B as an oracle, we can compute $f(n)$ from n. Thus, for such n,

$$n \leqslant K(A \upharpoonright f(n)) \leqslant K(B \upharpoonright n + f(n), n) + O(1) \leqslant K^B(B \upharpoonright n + f(n), n) + O(1) \leqslant K^B(n) + O(1).$$

So there are infinitely many n with $K^B(n) \geqslant n - O(1)$, which is a contradiction. □

It may not be surprising that lowness for weak 1-randomness and lowness for weak 1-genericity are related, since both weak 1-randoms and weak 1-generics occur in each hyperimmune degree (as shown in Theorems 2.24.19 and 8.11.8). The following result shows that these notions of lowness in fact coincide. The original proof of this result was rather complex and used "svelte trees", but subsequently the simple proof we present was discovered by Miller (in giving a simple proof of Theorem 8.10.2).

Theorem 12.4.5 (Greenberg and Miller [171]). *A is low for weak 1-randomness iff A is low for Kurtz null tests iff A is low for weak 1-genericity. Thus, A is low for weak 1-randomness iff A is hyperimmune free and not DNC.*

Proof. If the degree of A is hyperimmune-free and not DNC, then, by Theorem 12.4.3, A is both low for Kurtz null tests and low for weak 1-randomness.

By Theorems 12.4.1 and 12.4.4, if A has hyperimmune degree then it is neither low for weak 1-randomness nor low weak 1-genericity.

If A has DNC degree, then, by Theorem 12.4.4, A is not low weak 1-genericity, while by Theorem 8.10.2, there is a 1-random set that is not weakly 1-random relative to A, so A is also not low for weak 1-randomness. □

One consequence of this characterization (which already follows from Corollary 12.4.3) is that lowness for weak 1-randomness and lowness for Schnorr randomness are different.

Theorem 12.4.6 (Stephan and Yu [381]). *There is a perfect Π^0_1 class of sets that are neither of DNC degree nor c.e. traceable.*

Applying the hyperimmune-free basis theorem to this result (and keeping in mind that a c.e. traceable set of hyperimmune-free degree is computably traceable), we have the following.

Corollary 12.4.7 (Stephan and Yu [381]). *There are sets that are not computably traceable but are low for Kurtz null tests.*

Proof of Theorem 12.4.6. We construct a Π^0_1 class $[P]$ in stages. For each e, we have the following requirements for all $A \in [P]$:

$$R_e : \exists n\, (\Phi^A_e(n) = \Phi_n(n))$$

(which ensure that A does not compute a fixed-point free function, and hence does not have DNC degree, by Theorem 2.22.1) and

$$Q_e : \Phi_e \text{ total and an order} \Rightarrow A \text{ is not c.e. traceable with order } \Phi_e.$$

For the R-requirements, we use the recursion theorem with parameters to find a computable function g such that we can control $\Phi_{g(n)}(g(n))$ for all n. We will define $\Phi_{g(n)}(g(n))$ for infinitely many n to ensure that for each e and each $A \in [P]$ with Φ_e^A total, there is some n such that $\Phi_e^A(g(n)) = \Phi_{g(n)}(g(n))$.

The strategy for R_e is as follows. At a stage s at which R_e begins acting, we have pairwise incompatible strings $\sigma_0^s, \ldots, \sigma_m^s$ with $P_s = \bigcup_{i \leqslant m} [\![\sigma_i^s]\!]$. For each $i \leqslant m$ in parallel, we proceed as follows. Working in $[\![\sigma_i^s]\!]$, we pick a large number $d = g(n)$ for some n, and wait until there is some $\tau \succcurlyeq \sigma_i^s$ with $\Phi_e^\tau(d)\downarrow$. Should this never happen then Φ_e^A is not total for all $A \in [\![\sigma_i^s]\!]$. If τ is found then we let $\Phi_d(d) = \Phi_e^\tau(d)$, and prune P so that $P \cap [\![\sigma_i^s]\!] \subseteq [\![\tau]\!]$, initializing all weaker priority requirements. Now R_e is met within $P \cap [\![\sigma_i^s]\!]$.

The strategy for Q_e is as follows. We define a function Ψ such that Ψ^A is total for all $A \in [P]$ if Φ_e is total and an order. We break Q_e into subrequirements $Q_{e,i}$. Each such subrequirement works to ensure that W_i does not trace Ψ^A with order Φ_e for $A \in [P]$. Working within a cone $[\![\sigma_l^s]\!]$ as above, we pick a large number n and wait until $\Phi_e(n)\downarrow$. If this convergence ever happens, we choose a $\tau \succcurlyeq \sigma_l^s$ such that $[\![\tau]\!]$ is currently a subset of P and prune P by removing all elements of $[\![\sigma_l^s]\!] \setminus [\![\tau]\!]$. Let $m > |\tau|$ be such that $2^m > \Phi_e(n)$, and let $\tau_0, \ldots, \tau_{2^m-1}$ be the extensions of τ of length m. We ensure that no weaker priority strategy makes $[P] \cap [\![\tau_j]\!] = \emptyset$. For each $j < 2^m$, we let $\Psi_e^{\tau_j}(k) = 0$ for all $k < n$ for which $\Psi_e^{\tau_j}(k)$ is not yet defined, and let $\Psi_e^{\tau_j}(n) = j$. We also initialize all weaker priority requirements.

From this point on, as long as $|W_i^{[n]}| \leqslant \Phi_e(n)$, whenever $j < 2^m$ enters $W_i^{[n]}$, we prune P to remove all of $[\![\tau_j]\!]$ from $[P]$ and initialize all weaker priority requirements. This action never removes all of $[\![\tau]\!]$ from $[P]$, and ensures that $Q_{e,i}$ is satisfied within $[\![\sigma_l^s]\!]$, since it guarantees that if W_i is a trace with order Φ_e and $A \in [P] \cap [\![\sigma_l^s]\!]$, then $A \in [\![\tau_j]\!]$ for some $j \notin W_i^{[n]}$, whence $\Psi_e^A(n) = j \notin W_i^{[n]}$.

The remainder of the proof is a straightforward application of the finite injury method. □

The above proof is rather different from the original method of Stephan and Yu [381], who proved the following.

Theorem 12.4.8 (Stephan and Yu [381]). *There is a partial computable 0-1 valued function ψ with coinfinite domain such that every set whose characteristic function extends ψ is neither autocomplex nor c.e. traceable.*

We end this section by noting that there are no noncomputable sets that are low for 1-genericity. (Lowness for 1-genericity and for weak 1-genericity were first investigated by Nitzpon [309], who showed that if X is low for weak 1-genericity then X has hyperimmune-free degree.)

Theorem 12.4.9 (Greenberg and Miller [unpublished], Yu [411]). *If X is low for 1-genericity then X is computable.*

Proof. Suppose that X is noncomputable and low for 1-genericity. By Theorem 2.24.4, there is a 1-generic A such that $A \oplus X \equiv_T X'$. Then A is 1-generic relative to X, so by the relativized form of Theorem 2.24.3, $X'' \equiv_T (A \oplus X)' \equiv_T A \oplus X' \equiv_T X'$, which is a contradiction. □

12.5 Lowness for computable randomness

As we saw in Theorems 12.1.6 and 12.4.1, if a set is low for either Schnorr randomness or weak 1-randomness, then it is of hyperimmune-free degree. This fact may not be too surprising, since Schnorr randomness and weak 1-randomness are both related to total computable functions, as reflected in tests with uniformly computable measures. Martin-Löf randomness is concerned with c.e. objects, or partial computable functions, which may help explain why the corresponding lowness notion is more closely related to jump traceability than traceability.

What of computable randomness? Here the graded tests are *somewhat* computable, but the overall measure is not. As it turns out, the situation for computable randomness is dramatically different from either of the above cases. We already saw in Theorem 12.1.6 that sets that are low for computable randomness are of hyperimmune-free degree. In this section, we prove the following remarkable result of Nies [302], which verifies a conjecture of Downey.

Theorem 12.5.1 (Nies [302]). *If a set is low for computable randomness then it is computable.*

We present a different proof from the one given by Nies in [302, 306]. This proof is also due to Nies [300], and is included here with his permission. We will assume that all martingales in this section are rational-valued, which we have already seen in Proposition 7.1.2 we can do with no loss of generality for computable, or more generally A-computable, martingales.

The following lemma is obvious but quite useful. Following Nies, we call it the "nonascending path trick".

Lemma 12.5.2. *Let M be a computable martingale. For each σ and each $n > |\sigma|$, we can compute a string $\tau \succ \sigma$ such that $|\tau| = n$ and $M(\tau \upharpoonright k+1) \leqslant M(\tau \upharpoonright k)$ for each k with $|\sigma| \leqslant k < n-1$.*

Recall that we say that a martingale M has the savings property if

$$\tau \succ \sigma \Rightarrow M(\tau) \geqslant M(\sigma) - 2.$$

We saw in the comments following Proposition 6.3.8 that we may assume without loss of generality that our martingales have the savings property.

A *martingale operator* is a Turing functional L such that L^X is a martingale for each oracle X. To prove Theorem 12.5.1, we will define a martingale operator L. Given a set A that is low for computable randomness, we will apply the following purely combinatorial lemma to $N = L^A$ and the (non-effectively listed) family $B_0, B_1, \ldots$ of computable martingales with the savings property.

Lemma 12.5.3. *Let N be a martingale with $N(\lambda) \leqslant 1$. Let $B_0, B_1, \ldots$ be martingales with the savings property such that $S[N] \subseteq \bigcup_i S[B_i]$. Then there are σ, d, and a martingale $M = \sum_{i \leqslant n} q_i B_i$, with each $q_i \in \mathbb{Q}^{>0}$, such that $M(\sigma) < 2$ and $\forall \tau \succ \sigma\, (N(\tau) \geqslant 2^d \Rightarrow M(\tau) \geqslant 2)$.*

Proof. Assume for a contradiction that no such M exists. We define a sequence of strings $\sigma_0 \prec \sigma_1 \prec \cdots$ and positive rationals $q_0, q_1, \ldots$ such that for all n, we have $N(\sigma_n) \geqslant 2^n - 1$ and $\sum_{i \leqslant n} q_i B_i(\sigma_n) < 2$.

Let $\sigma_0 = \lambda$ and $q_0 = \frac{1}{B_0(\lambda)}$. Suppose we are given $\sigma_0, \ldots, \sigma_{n-1}$ and $q_0, \ldots, q_{n-1}$ with the required properties. Since $\sum_{i<n} q_i B_i(\sigma_{n-1}) < 2$, we can choose q_n to be sufficiently small so that $\sum_{i \leqslant n} q_i B_i(\sigma_{n-1}) < 2$. Let $M = \sum_{i \leqslant n} q_i B_i$. Since we are assuming that the lemma does not hold, there is a $\tau \succ \sigma$ such that $N(\tau) \geqslant 2^n$ and $M(\tau) < 2$. Let $\sigma_n = \tau$.

Now let $X = \bigcup_n \sigma_n$. Then N succeeds on X (though, interestingly, not necessarily in the effective sense of Schnorr). On the other hand, for each i and $n \geqslant i$, we have $q_i B_i(\sigma_n) < 2$. Since B_i has the savings property, $\limsup_n B_i(X \upharpoonright n) < \infty$, so B_i does not succeed on X. Thus $X \in S[N] \setminus \bigcup_i S[B_i]$, contrary to hypothesis. □

We are now ready to prove that every set that is low for computable randomness is computable. Let $M_0, M_1, \ldots$ be an effective listing of all partial computable martingales (as defined in Definition 7.4.3).

Proof of Theorem 12.5.1. Let A be low for computable randomness. Let $B_0, B_1, \ldots$ be the family of all (total) computable martingales with the savings property. (Note that this listing is not effective.) Fix an effective listing $\{\eta_m\}_{m \geqslant 1}$ of all triples (e, σ, d) with $\sigma \in 2^{<\omega}$ and $e, d \in \mathbb{N}$. We think of e as the index of a partial computable martingale M_e and think of η_m as a potential witness (with $M = M_e$) to the truth of Lemma 12.5.3 for a martingale N that we will build.

We will build, independently but uniformly, rational valued martingale operators L_m for each $m \geqslant 1$, with $L_m^X(\sigma) = 2^{-m}$ for all X and all $\sigma \in 2^{\leqslant m}$, and let $L^X = \sum_{m \geqslant 1} L_m^X$. For each σ, the contributions of $L_m^X(\sigma)$ for $m > |\sigma|$ will add up to $2^{-|\sigma|}$, so L will be a rational valued martingale operator. We will then let $N = L^A$. Our goal is to use the fact that $S[N] \subseteq \bigcup_i S[B_i]$ (which follows from the fact that A is low for computable randomness) to compute A. The computation procedure for A will be based on a witness

$\eta_m = (e, \sigma, d)$ given by Lemma 12.5.3. Since we cannot determine this witness effectively, to make L a martingale operator we need to consider all η_m, including those for which the corresponding M_e is partial.

The idea behind our procedure for computing A is the following. Once L is defined, if $\eta_m = (e, \sigma, d)$ is a witness to the truth of Lemma 12.5.3 for $N = L^A$, then let $M = M_e$ and consider the tree

$$T_m = \{\gamma : \forall \tau \succ \sigma\, (L_m^{\gamma}(\tau)\downarrow \geqslant 2^d \Rightarrow M(\tau) \geqslant 2)\}.$$

By the choice of η_m and the fact that $L^A \geqslant L_m^A$, we see that A is a path of T_m. Let $k = 2^{d+m}$, and let E_k be the collection of k-element sets of strings of equal length. Let α range over elements of E_k. We write α_r for the rth element of α in lexicographic order, and identify α with the string $\alpha_0\alpha_1 \ldots \alpha_{k-1}$. For each α, we will ensure that $\alpha \not\subseteq T_m$ in an effective way. That is, given α, we will be able to find an $s < k$ such that $\alpha_s \notin T_m$. This fact will allow us to define a computable tree $R \supseteq T_m$ of width less than k. Since every path of a tree of finite width is computable and A is a path of $T_m \subseteq R$, this fact will imply that A is computable.

Let $\sigma_0, \ldots, \sigma_{k-1}$ be the strings of length $d+m$ in lexicographic order. We describe in more detail the strategy that, given α, produces an s such that $\alpha_s \notin T_m$. Suppose that $\rho \succcurlyeq \sigma$ is a string such that $M(\rho) < 2$, and no value $L_m^{\gamma}(\rho')$ has been defined for any $\rho' \preccurlyeq \rho$ (we call ρ an *α-destroyer*). In this case we may define $L_m(\rho) = 2^{-m}$ regardless of the oracle. For each $s < k$, we ensure that $L_m^{\alpha_s}(\rho\sigma_s) = 2^d$, by betting all our capital along $\rho\sigma_s$ from ρ on. Since $M(\rho) < 2$, by the nonascending path trick (Lemma 12.5.2) we can compute an s such that $M(\rho\sigma_s) < 2$. Then $\rho\sigma_s$ witnesses that $\alpha_s \notin T_m$.

We want to carry out this strategy independently for different α, so we assign to each α a string ν_α. Given $\eta_m = (e, \sigma, d)$, let $M = M_e$ and let

$$\widehat{M}(\nu) = \max\{M(\nu') : \sigma \preccurlyeq \nu' \preccurlyeq \nu\}.$$

The assignment function $G_m : E_k \to 2^{<\omega}$ mapping α to ν_α will satisfy the following conditions.

1. The range of G_m is an antichain of strings ν such that $\widehat{M}(\nu) < 2$.
2. The functions G_m and G_m^{-1} are uniformly partial computable over all m.
3. If $M_e(\sigma) < 2$ and M is total, then G_m is total.

We cannot quite apply the strategy above with $\rho = \nu_\alpha$, since we cannot tell whether G_m is total, but if we find out the value of ν_α at stage s, then we can use the nonascending path trick to find a $\rho \succ \nu_\alpha$ of length s such that $\widehat{M}(\rho) < 2$. This ρ will be our α-destroyer.

The choice of G_m is irrelevant as long as the above properties hold, so we defer defining G_m.

We define L_m by declaring axioms of the form $L_m^{\gamma}(\rho) = p$, in such a way that

(a) $|\gamma| \leqslant |\rho|$, and given γ and ρ we can determine computably whether we ever declare an axiom $L^{\gamma}(\rho) = p$ for some p; and

(b) whenever distinct axioms $L^{\gamma}(\rho) = p$ and $L^{\delta}(\rho) = q$ are declared then γ and δ are incompatible.

If some axiom $L^{\gamma}_m(\rho) = p$ has been declared for $\gamma \prec X$ (which can be determined computably, by (a)), then we let $L^X_m(\rho) = p$. Otherwise, we let $L^X_m(\rho)$ be the "default value" 2^{-m}.

Given a string ρ, we check whether there is a $\nu \preccurlyeq \rho$ such that $G_m^{-1}(\nu)\downarrow$ in exactly $|\rho|$ many steps. If so, then let $\alpha = G_m^{-1}(\nu)$. (We assume the usual convention that it takes at least $\max(|\nu|, |\alpha|)$ many steps for $G_m^{-1}(\nu)$ to converge.) In this case, we declare axioms as follows (implementing the strategy outlined above): For each $\tau = \rho\upsilon$ and each $s < k$, let $L^{\alpha_s}_m(\tau) = 0$ unless υ is compatible with σ_s. In that case, let $L^{\alpha_s}_m(\tau) = 2^{-m+|\upsilon|}$ if $\upsilon \preccurlyeq \sigma_s$, and $L^{\alpha_s}_m(\tau) = 2^d$ if $\sigma_s \preccurlyeq \upsilon$.

We have concluded the construction of L_m. Clearly (a) holds. Furthermore, (b) holds because the strings ν_α form an antichain, we declare axioms $L^{\gamma}_m(\tau) = p$ with $\nu_\alpha \preccurlyeq \tau$ only if $\gamma \in \alpha$, and the elements of α are pairwise incompatible. Finally, L^X is clearly a martingale for each oracle X.

Recall that $B_0, B_1, \ldots$ are the (total) computable martingales with the savings property. If A is low for computable randomness, then $S[L^A] \subseteq \bigcup_i S[B_i]$. The linear combination M obtained in Lemma 12.5.3 is computable. So the following lemma suffices to compute A, since, as explained above, the existence of the tree R implies that A is computable.

Lemma 12.5.4. *Suppose $\eta_m = (e, \sigma, d)$, where $M = M_e$ is total and M, σ, d witness the truth of Lemma 12.5.3 with $N = L^A$. Then there is a computable tree $R \supseteq T_m$ of width less than k.*

Proof. We define the levels $R^{(j)}$ of R recursively. Let $R^{(0)} = \{\lambda\}$. Let $j > 0$ and suppose we have determined $R^{(j-1)}$. Carry out the following procedure to determine $R^{(j)}$.

1. Let F be the set of strings of length j that extend strings in $R^{(j-1)}$ (so $|F| = 2|R^{(j-1)}|$).

2. If $|F| \geqslant k$, then let α consist of the k leftmost strings of F.

   (a) Compute $\nu_\alpha = G_m(\alpha)$, and let s be the stage at which $G_m(\alpha)\downarrow$.

   (b) By the nonascending path trick, find $\rho \succ \nu_\alpha$ of length s such that $\widehat{M}(\rho) < 2$.

   (c) Search for $r < k$ such that $\widehat{M}(\rho\sigma_r) < 2$. Remove α_r from F and repeat step 2.

3. Once $|F| < k$, let $R^{(j)} = F$.

Clearly R is computable and has width less than k. By the definition of L_m, for r as above we have $L_m^{\alpha_r}(\rho\sigma_r) = 2^{-d}$, whence $\alpha_r \notin T_m$. Thus $R \supseteq T_m$. $\square$

To conclude the proof it remains to define G_m. Recall that $\widehat{M}(\nu) = \max\{M(\nu') : \sigma \preccurlyeq \nu' \preccurlyeq \nu\}$. We first prove a lemma using the following instance of Kolmogorov's Inequality: If $M(\tau) < b$ then

$$\mu_\tau(\{\nu \succcurlyeq \tau : \widehat{M}(\nu) \geqslant b\}) \leqslant \frac{M(\tau)}{b},$$

where $\mu_\tau(X) = 2^{|\tau|}\mu(X \cap [\![\tau]\!])$.

Lemma 12.5.5. *Given η_m, suppose that $M(\tau) < b$ for $b \in \mathbb{Q}$. Let*

$$P = \{\nu \succcurlyeq \tau : \widehat{M}(\nu) < b\}$$

and let r be such that $2^{-r} \leqslant 1 - \frac{M_e(\tau)}{b}$. Then given i we can compute $\nu^{(i)}$ of length $i+r+1$ such that $\nu^{(i)} \in P$ and the strings $\nu^{(i)}$ form an antichain. If M is partial, then we can compute $\nu^{(i)}$ for each i such that M is defined for strings of length up to $i+r+1$.

Proof. Suppose inductively that $\nu^{(q)}$ has been computed for $q < i$. Since $\sum_{q<i} 2^{-|\nu^{(q)}|} = 2^{-r}(1-2^{-i})$ and $2^{-r} \leqslant \mu_\tau(P)$, by Kolmogorov's Inequality, we can compute $\nu \in P$ such that $|\nu| = i+r+1$ and $\nu_q \not\preccurlyeq \nu$ for all $q < i$. Let $\nu_i = \nu$. $\square$

To obtain G_m, let $b = 2$, and let n_α be a number greater than the length of each string in α, assigned to α in an effective 1-1 way. Let $G_m(\alpha) = \nu^{(n_\alpha)}$, as given by the lemma with $\tau = \sigma$. Clearly the required properties hold. $\square$

Extending these techniques, Nies [300] proved similar results about lowness for partial computable martingales.

Theorem 12.5.6 (Nies [300]). *If every partial computably random set is computably random relative to A, then A is computable.*

Space considerations preclude us from including proofs of this and related results.

Another notion of randomness whose corresponding lowness notion sits somewhere between computability and hyperimmune-freeness is Demuth randomness. Downey and Ng [128] showed that if a set is low for Demuth randomness then it is hyperimmune-free, and they conjecture that such a set must in fact be computable.

12.6 Lowness for pairs of randomness notions

Recall from Definition 11.9.2 that for classes $\mathcal{C}$ and $\mathcal{D}$ given by relativizable definitions, $\mathrm{Low}(\mathcal{C}, \mathcal{D})$ is the class of sets A such that $\mathcal{C} \subseteq \mathcal{D}^A$. We saw in

	weak 2-	1-	comp.	Schnorr	weak 1-
weak 2-	K-triv.	K-triv.	K-triv.	c.e. trac.	?
1-	X	K-triv.	K-triv.	c.e. trac.	$\neg$DNC
comp.	X	X	comp.	comp. trac.	$\neg$DNC nonhigh
Schnorr	X	X	X	comp. trac.	$\neg$DNC nonhigh
weak 1-	X	X	X	X	$\neg$DNC hyp.-fr.

Table 12.1. Lowness for pairs of randomness notions

Theorem 11.9.3 that Low($\mathsf{W2R}$, MLR) is exactly the class of K-trivial sets, where MLR is the class of 1-random sets and $\mathsf{W2R}$ is the class of weakly 2-random sets. We also saw in Section 10.6 that, writing $\mathsf{ML2R}$ for the class of 2-random sets, Low($\mathsf{ML2R}$, MLR) is the class of (uniformly) almost everywhere dominating sets. There has been considerable work on characterizing lowness for other pairs of randomness notions. In this brief section, we state some results in that direction and summarize them, together with Theorems 11.4.11, 11.9.1, 11.9.3, 12.4.5, and 12.5.1 and Corollary 12.1.7, in Table 12.1. We write CompR, SchR, and $\mathsf{W1R}$ for the classes of sets that are computably random, Schnorr random, and weakly 1-random, respectively.

Theorem 12.6.1 (Nies [302]). *A set is in* Low(MLR, CompR) *iff it is K-trivial.*

Theorem 12.6.2 (Kjos-Hanssen, Nies, and Stephan [207]). *A set is in* Low(MLR, SchR) *iff it is c.e. traceable, and in* Low(CompR, SchR) *iff it is computably traceable.*

Note that the first part of the above result is Theorem 12.1.4 (given Corollary 12.1.7).

Theorem 12.6.3 (Nies [306]). *A set is in* Low($\mathsf{W2R}$, CompR) *iff it is K-trivial.*

Theorem 12.6.4 (Greenberg and Miller [171]). *A set is contained in* Low(MLR, $\mathsf{W1R}$) *iff its degree is not DNC, and in* Low(CompR, $\mathsf{W1R}$) = Low(SchR, $\mathsf{W1R}$) *iff its degree is not DNC and not high.*

Note that the first part of the above result is part of Theorem 8.10.2.

Theorem 12.6.5 (Bienvenu and Miller [41]). *A set is in* Low($\mathsf{W2R}$, SchR) *iff it is c.e. traceable.*

At the time of writing, there is no known exact characterization of Low($\mathsf{W2R}$, $\mathsf{W1R}$).

There has also been work on highness for randomness notions, a concept introduced by Franklin, Stephan, and Yu [159]. Space considerations preclude us from going further into this material. A survey of lowness and highness for randomness notions may be found in Franklin [154].

13 Algorithmic Dimension

Not all classes of measure 0 are created equal, and the classical theory of dimension provides a method for classifying them. Likewise, some nonrandom sets are more random than others. In this chapter, we look at effectivizations of Hausdorff dimension and other notions of dimension, and explore their relationships with calibrating randomness.

13.1 Classical Hausdorff dimension

The study of measure as a way of specifying the size of sets began with work of Borel and others in the late 19th century. In his famous thesis [237], Lebesgue introduced the measure that is now called Lebesgue measure. In 1914, Carathéodory [54] gave a more general construction that included Lebesgue measure as a special case. For $\mathbb{R}$, Carathéodory's definition yields the s-dimensional measure $\mu^s(A) = \inf\{\sum_i |I_i|^s : A \subseteq \bigcup_i I_i\}$, where each I_i is an interval. In 1919, Hausdorff [177] used s-dimensional measure to generalize the notion of dimension to non-integer values.

This idea of changing the way we measure open sets by an additional factor in the exponent is realized in Cantor space as follows. For $0 \leqslant s \leqslant 1$, the *$s$-measure* of a clopen set $[\![\sigma]\!]$ is $\mu_s([\![\sigma]\!]) = 2^{-s|\sigma|}$. Notice that the 1-measure is the same as the uniform measure.

Definition 13.1.1. (i) A set of strings D is an *n-cover* of $R \subseteq 2^\omega$ if $R \subseteq [\![D]\!]$ and $D \subseteq 2^{\geqslant n}$.

(ii) Let $H_n^s(R) = \inf\{\sum_{\sigma \in D} \mu_s([\![\sigma]\!]) : D$ is an n-cover of $R\}$.

R.G. Downey and D. Hirschfeldt, *Algorithmic Randomness and Complexity*, Theory and Applications of Computability, DOI 10.1007/978-0-387-68441-3_13,

(iii) The *s-dimensional outer Hausdorff measure* of R is $H^s(R) = \lim_n H^s_n(R)$.

This notion has been widely studied. The fundamental result is the following.

Theorem 13.1.2. *For each $R \subseteq 2^\omega$ there is an $s \in [0,1]$ such that*

(i) *$H^t(R) = 0$ for all $t > s$ and*

(ii) *$H^u(R) = \infty$ for all $0 \leqslant u < s$.*

Proof. For all $s, r \in [0,1]$, and $n \in \mathbb{N}$,

$$H^{s+r}_n(R) = \inf\left\{\sum_{\sigma \in D} 2^{-s|\sigma|}2^{-r|\sigma|} : D \text{ is an } n\text{-cover of } R\right\} \leqslant 2^{-rn}H^s_n(R).$$

So if $H^s(R) = 0$ then $H^{s+r}_n(R) = 0$, while if $H^{s+r}_n(R) = \infty$ then $H^s(R) = \infty$.

To complete the proof, notice that if $t > 1$ then $\lim_n H^t_n(R) \leqslant \lim_n \sum_{\sigma \in 2^n} 2^{-t|\sigma|} = \lim_n 2^n 2^{-tn} = 0$. □

Theorem 13.1.2 means that the following definition makes sense.

Definition 13.1.3. For $R \subseteq 2^\omega$, the *Hausdorff dimension* of R is $\dim_{\mathrm{H}}(R) = \inf\{s : H^s(R) = 0\}$.

Hausdorff dimension has a number of important basic properties.

Proposition 13.1.4. (i) *If $\mu(X) > 0$ then $\dim_{\mathrm{H}}(X) = 1$.*

(ii) *(monotonicity) If $X \subseteq Y$ then $\dim_{\mathrm{H}}(X) \leqslant \dim_{\mathrm{H}}(Y)$.*

(iii) *(countable stability) If P is a countable collection of subsets of 2^ω, then $\dim_{\mathrm{H}}(\bigcup_{X \in P} X) = \sup_{X \in P} \dim_{\mathrm{H}}(X)$. In particular, $\dim_{\mathrm{H}}(X \cup Y)$ is $\max\{\dim_{\mathrm{H}}(X), \dim_{\mathrm{H}}(Y)\}$.*

Proof sketch. This proposition is well known, but its proof is worth sketching. We begin with a lemma.

Lemma 13.1.5. *If X is measurable then $H^1(X) = \mu(X)$.*

Proof. By definition, $\mu(X)$ is the infimum of $\sum_{\sigma \in U} 2^{-\sigma}$ over all covers U of X. For any cover U of X, we can replace any $\sigma \in U$ such that $|\sigma| < n$ by all its extensions of length n to obtain an n-cover V of X such that $\sum_{\sigma \in V} 2^{-\sigma} = \sum_{\sigma \in U} 2^{-\sigma}$, so $H^1_n(X) = \mu(X)$ for all n. □

Part (i) of Proposition 13.1.4 follows immediately from the lemma. To see that part (ii) holds, take any $s > \dim_{\mathrm{H}}(Y)$. Then since any n-cover of Y is an n-cover of X, we have $H^s_n(X) \leqslant H^s_n(Y)$ for all n, so $H^s(X) = 0$. Part (iii) is proved by a similar manipulation of covers. □

13.2 Hausdorff dimension via gales

The first person to effectivize Hausdorff dimension explicitly was Lutz [252, 253, 254]. To do so, he used a generalization of the notion of (super)martingale. This idea was, however, in a sense implicit in the work of Schnorr [348, 349], who used orders to calibrate the rates of success of martingales, as we have seen in Chapter 7, in much the same way that the s factor calibrates the growth rate of the measure of covers. Recall that, for a (super)martingale d and an order h, the h-success set of d is $S_h[d] = \{A : \limsup_n \frac{d(A\restriction n)}{h(n)} = \infty\}$. As we will see, the theory of Hausdorff dimension can be developed in terms of orders on martingales, but Lutz [252, 254] originally used the following notions.

Definition 13.2.1 (Lutz [252, 254]). An *s-gale* is a function $d : 2^{<\omega} \to \mathbb{R}^{\geqslant 0}$ such that $d(\sigma) = 2^{-s}(d(\sigma 0) + d(\sigma 1))$ for all σ.

An *s-supergale* is a function $d : 2^{<\omega} \to \mathbb{R}^{\geqslant 0}$ such that $d(\sigma) \geqslant 2^{-s}(d(\sigma 0) + d(\sigma 1))$ for all σ.

We define the success set $S[d]$ of an s-(super)gale in the same way as for martingales.

A 1-(super)gale is the same as a (super)martingale. For $s < 1$, we can think of an s-gale as capturing the idea of betting in an inflationary environment, in which not betting costs us money. In the case of martingales, if we are not prepared to favor one side or the other in our bet following σ, we just make $d(\sigma i) = d(\sigma)$ for $i = 0, 1$, and are assured of retaining our current capital. In the case of an s-gale with $s < 1$, we are no longer able to do so. If we want to have $d(\sigma 0) = d(\sigma 1)$, then we will have $d(\sigma i) < d(\sigma)$ for $i = 0, 1$, and hence will necessarily lose money.

It is quite easy to go between s-gales and rates of success of martingales.

Lemma 13.2.2. *For each (super)martingale d there is an s-(super)gale $\widehat{d}$ such that $S[\widehat{d}] = S_{2^{(1-s)n}}[d]$. Conversely, for each s-(super)gale $\widehat{d}$ there is a (super)martingale d such that $S[\widehat{d}] = S_{2^{(1-s)n}}[d]$.*

Proof. For a (super)martingale d, let $\widehat{d}$ be defined by $\widehat{d}(\sigma) = 2^{(s-1)|\sigma|}d(\sigma)$. It is easy to check that $\widehat{d}$ is an s-(super)gale. For each k, we have $\frac{d(A\restriction n)}{2^{(1-s)n}} > k$ iff $\widehat{d}(A \restriction n) = 2^{(s-1)n}d(A \restriction n) > 2^{(1-s)n}2^{(s-1)n}k = k$, so $S[\widehat{d}] = S_{2^{(1-s)n}}[d]$. The converse is symmetric. ☐

Note that, in the above proof, if s is rational then we can pass effectively from d to $\widehat{d}$ or vice versa, so, for instance, d is c.e. iff $\widehat{d}$ is c.e.

Lutz' key insight was that Hausdorff dimension can be quite naturally characterized using either s-gales or growth rates of martingales.

Theorem 13.2.3 (Lutz [252, 254]). *For a class $X \subseteq 2^{\omega}$ the following are equivalent.*

(i) $\dim_{\mathrm{H}}(X) = r$.

(ii) $r = \inf\{s \in \mathbb{Q} : X \subseteq S[d]$ *for some s-(super)gale d*$\}$.

(iii) $r = \inf\{s \in \mathbb{Q} : X \subseteq S_{2^{(1-s)n}}[d]$ *for some (super)martingale d*$\}$.

Proof. By Lemma 13.2.2, (ii) and (iii) are equivalent.

We first prove that $\dim_{\mathrm{H}}(X) \geqslant \inf\{s \in \mathbb{Q} : X \subseteq S_{2^{(1-s)n}}[d]$ for some (super)martingale $d\}$. We first consider the supermartingale formulation.

Let $s > \dim_{\mathrm{H}}(X)$ and let $\{U_k\}_{k \in \omega}$ witness that X is H^s-null. That is, for all k we have $X \subseteq [\![U_k]\!]$ and $\sum_{\sigma \in U_k} 2^{s|\sigma|} \leqslant 2^{-k}$. We may assume that the U_k are prefix-free. For each σ and k, let $U_k^\sigma = \{\tau \in U_k : \sigma \preccurlyeq \tau\}$. For each k, let

$$d_k(\sigma) = 2^{|\sigma|} \sum_{\tau \in U_k^\sigma} 2^{-s|\tau|},$$

and let

$$d(\sigma) = \sum_k d_k(\sigma).$$

If $\sigma \in U_k$, then $U_k^{\sigma i} = \emptyset$ for $i = 0, 1$, so $d_k(\sigma 0) + d_k(\sigma 1) = 0 \leqslant 2d_k(\sigma)$. If $\sigma \notin U_k$, then $U_k^\sigma = U_k^{\sigma 0} \cup U_k^{\sigma 1}$, so

$$\begin{aligned} d_k(\sigma 0) + d_k(\sigma 1) &= 2^{|\sigma|+1}\Bigg(\sum_{\tau \in U_k^{\sigma 0}} 2^{-s|\tau|} + \sum_{\tau \in U_k^{\sigma 1}} 2^{-s|\tau|}\Bigg) \\ &= 2 \cdot 2^{|\sigma|}\Bigg(\sum_{\tau \in U_k^\sigma} 2^{-s|\tau|}\Bigg) = 2d_k(\sigma). \end{aligned}$$

Thus each d_k is a supermartingale. Furthermore, $d_k(\lambda) = \sum_{\sigma \in U_k} 2^{s|\sigma|} \leqslant 2^{-k}$, so d is a supermartingale.

Now suppose that $A \in \bigcap_k [\![U_k]\!]$. Then for each k there is an n_k such that $A \upharpoonright n_k \in U_k$. Let $t > s$. Then

$$\frac{d(A \upharpoonright n_k)}{2^{(1-t)n_k}} \geqslant \frac{d_k(A \upharpoonright n_k)}{2^{(1-t)n_k}} = \frac{2^{(1-s)n_k}}{2^{(1-t)n_k}} = 2^{(t-s)n_k},$$

so $\limsup_n \frac{d(A \upharpoonright n)}{2^{(1-t)n}} = \infty$, and hence $A \in S_{2^{(1-t)n}}[d]$. Since $t > s > \dim_{\mathrm{H}}(X)$ are arbitrary, $\dim_{\mathrm{H}}(X) \geqslant \inf\{s \in \mathbb{Q} : X \subseteq S_{2^{(1-s)n}}[d]$ for some supermartingale $d\}$.

To get the same result for martingales,[1] we slightly change the definition of d_k to

$$d_k(\sigma) = \begin{cases} 2^{|\sigma|} \sum_{\tau \in U_k^\sigma} 2^{-s|\tau|} & \text{if } U_k^\sigma \neq \emptyset \\ 2^{(1-s)m} & \text{if } \sigma \upharpoonright m \in U_k \text{ for } m < |\sigma| \\ 0 & \text{otherwise.} \end{cases}$$

We now prove that $\dim_{\mathrm{H}}(X) \leqslant \inf\{s \in \mathbb{Q} : X \subseteq S_{2^{(1-s)n}}[d]$ for some supermartingale $d\}$. Suppose that d is a supermartingale and $X \subseteq S_{2^{(1-s)n}}[d]$. We may assume that $d(\lambda) \leqslant 1$. Let

$$V_k = \left\{\sigma : \frac{d(\sigma)}{2^{(1-s)|\sigma|}} \geqslant 2^k\right\}.$$

Let U_k be the set of $\sigma \in V_k$ such that $\tau \notin V_k$ for $\tau \prec \sigma$. Then the U_k are prefix-free and cover X. Furthermore,

$$\sum_{\sigma \in U_k} 2^{-s|\sigma|} \leqslant \sum_{\sigma \in U_k} 2^{-s|\sigma|} \frac{d(\sigma)}{2^{(1-s)|\sigma|}} 2^{-k} = 2^{-k} \sum_{\sigma \in U_k} 2^{-|\sigma|} d(\sigma) \leqslant 2^{-k},$$

the last inequality following by Kolmogorov's Inequality (Theorem 6.3.3). Thus $\{U_k\}_{k \in \omega}$ witnesses the fact that X is H^s-null. □

Lutz [255] made the following remarks about the above characterization: "Informally speaking, the above theorem says that the dimension of a set is the *most hostile environment* (i.e., the most unfavorable payoff schedule, i.e., the infimum s) in which a single betting strategy can *achieve infinite winnings* on every element of the set."

13.3 Effective Hausdorff dimension

Using the martingale characterization of Hausdorff dimension, we can effectivize that notion as follows.

Definition 13.3.1 (Lutz [252, 253, 254]). For a complexity class $\mathcal{C}$ of real-valued functions, the $\mathcal{C}$ *(Hausdorff) dimension* of $R \subseteq 2^\omega$ is

$$\inf\{s \in \mathbb{Q} : R \subseteq S_{2^{(1-s)n}}[d] \text{ for some martingale } d \in \mathcal{C}\}.$$

For $A \in 2^\omega$, the $\mathcal{C}$ dimension of A is the $\mathcal{C}$ dimension of $\{A\}$.

Note that this infimum is equivalent to

$$\inf\{s \in \mathbb{Q} : R \subseteq S[d] \text{ for some } s\text{-gale } d \in \mathcal{C}\}.$$

[1] In the effective setting, we will discuss the issue of passing from supergales to gales when we prove Theorem 13.3.2.

We will be particularly interested in the case $\mathcal{C} = \Sigma_1^0$. The Σ_1^0 Hausdorff dimension of R is sometimes called the *constructive (Hausdorff) dimension* of R, but we will refer to is as the *effective Hausdorff dimension*, or simply the *effective dimension*, of R, and denote it by $\dim(R)$.

In Lutz' original paper [252], he defined $\mathcal{C}$ dimension using gales, but in the journal version [254], he used supergales. The issue here is one of multiplicative optimality versus universality. Let us consider the Σ_1^0 case. By Theorem 6.3.5, there is a universal c.e. martingale, but while there is an optimal c.e. supermartingale (Theorem 6.3.7), there is no optimal c.e. *martingale* (Corollary 6.3.12). As noted by Hitchcock, Lutz, and others, it is not known whether there is always a c.e. r-gale that is universal for the class of all c.e. r-supergales. However, we have the following result, which shows that if $r < t$ then there is a t-gale that is optimal for the class of all r-supergales. Thus gales suffice for defining effective dimension, and Lutz' original formulation of effective dimension in terms of gales is equivalent to the one in terms of supergales.

Theorem 13.3.2 (Hitchcock [179]). *Let $0 \leqslant r < t$ be rationals. There is a c.e. t-gale d^* such that for all c.e. r-supergales d, we have $S[d] \subseteq S[d^*]$.*

Proof. Let d be a multiplicatively optimal c.e. r-supergale with $d(\lambda) < 1$ (constructed as in the proof of Theorem 6.3.7). It is enough to build d^* so that $S[d] \subseteq S[d^*]$.

Let $A = \{\sigma : d(\sigma) > 1\}$ and let $A^{[n]} = A \cap 2^n$. By Kolmogorov's Inequality (Theorem 6.3.3), $|A^{[n]}| \leqslant 2^{rn}$ for all n. Let d_n^* be defined by

$$d_n^*(\sigma) = \begin{cases} 2^{-t(n-|\sigma|)}|\{\tau \in A^{[n]} : \sigma \preccurlyeq \tau\}| & \text{if } |\sigma| \leqslant n \\ 2^{(t-1)(|\sigma|-n)} d_n^*(\sigma \upharpoonright (n-1)) & \text{if } |\sigma| > n. \end{cases}$$

Then it is easy to check that each d_n^* is a t-gale and $d_n^*(\sigma) = 1$ for all $\sigma \in A^{[n]}$.

Now let $s \in (r, t)$ be rational and let

$$d^* = \sum_n 2^{(s-r)n} d_n^*.$$

Then $d^*(\lambda) = \sum_n 2^{(s-r)n} 2^{-tn} |A^{[n]}| \leqslant \sum_n 2^{(s-t)n} < \infty$, so d^* is well-defined, and hence is a t-gale. Furthermore, it is c.e., since A is c.e.

Let $X \in S[d]$. Then $X \upharpoonright (n-1) \in A$ for infinitely many A. For such n,

$$d^*(X \upharpoonright (n-1)) \geqslant 2^{(s-r)n} d_n^*(X \upharpoonright (n-1)) = 2^{(s-r)n}.$$

Hence $X \in S[d^*]$. ∎

Of course, this result translates into the language of martingales. Say that a (super)martingale d *s-succeeds* on A if $\limsup_n \frac{d(A\upharpoonright n)}{2^{(1-s)n}} = \infty$. We can build a c.e. martingale that $(s+\varepsilon)$-succeeds on every set A for which there is a c.e. supermartingale that s-succeeds on A. However, we do not know whether for each such A there necessarily is a martingale that s-succeeds on A.

In any case, $\dim(R)$ is equal to $\inf\{s \in \mathbb{Q} : R \subseteq S_{2^{(1-s)n}}[d]\}$, where d is an optimal c.e. supermartingale. It follows immediately that $\dim(R) = \sup\{\dim(A) : A \in R\}$ and, more generally, the effective dimension of an arbitrary union of classes is the supremum of the effective dimensions of the individual classes. (Notice that for classical Hausdorff dimension, the corresponding fact is true only for countable unions.)

We can also effectivize Definition 13.1.1 directly. For Σ^0_1 dimension, we have the following.

Definition 13.3.3. (i) A set of strings D is an *effective n-cover* if it is an n-cover and c.e.

(ii) Let $\widehat{H}^s_n(R) = \inf\{\sum_{\sigma \in D} \mu_s([\![\sigma]\!]) : D \text{ is an effective } n\text{-cover of } R\}$.

(iii) The *effective s-dimensional outer Hausdorff measure* of R is $\widehat{H}^s(R) = \lim_n \widehat{H}^s_n(R)$.

(iv) The *effective Hausdorff dimension* of R is the unique $s \in [0,1]$ such that $\widehat{H}^t(R) = 0$ for all $t > s$ and $\widehat{H}^u(R) = \infty$ for all $0 \leqslant u < s$.

It is straightforward to effectivize our earlier work and show that the effective analog of Theorem 13.2.3 holds. That is, the above definition agrees with our earlier definition of effective Hausdorff dimension. A similar comment holds for other suitable complexity classes.

There is another fundamental characterization of effective Hausdorff dimension, in terms of initial segment complexity.

Theorem 13.3.4 (Mayordomo [262]). *For $A \in 2^\omega$, we have*

$$\dim(A) = \liminf_n \frac{K(A \upharpoonright n)}{n} = \liminf_n \frac{C(A \upharpoonright n)}{n}.[2]$$

Proof. The second equation is immediate, since C and K agree up to a log factor. We prove the first equation.

First suppose that $\dim(A) < s$. Let d be a universal c.e. supermartingale. Then $\limsup_n \frac{d(A\upharpoonright n)}{2^{(1-s)n}} = \infty$. Now, as noted in Section 6.3.2, $d(A \upharpoonright n) = 2^{n-KM(A\upharpoonright n)\pm O(1)}$, so $\limsup_n 2^{sn-KM(A\upharpoonright n)} = \infty$. But by Theorem 3.15.4, $K(A \upharpoonright n) \leqslant KM(A \upharpoonright n) + O(\log n)$, so $\limsup_n 2^{sn-K(A\upharpoonright n)+O(\log n)} = \infty$. Thus there are infinitely many n such that $K(A \upharpoonright n) < sn + O(\log n)$, and hence $\liminf_n \frac{K(A\upharpoonright n)}{n} \leqslant s$.

[2]Staiger [378] showed that Theorem 13.3.4 can be obtained from results of Levin in [425]. There were also a number of earlier results indicating the deep relationship between effective Hausdorff dimension and Kolmogorov complexity, such as those of Cai and Hartmanis [45], Ryabko [338, 339, 340], and Staiger [376, 377]. These results are discussed in Lutz [254] (Section 6, in particular) and Staiger [378].

Now suppose that $\liminf_n \frac{K(A\upharpoonright n)}{n} < r < s$ for rationals r and s. Let $D = \{\sigma : K(\sigma) < r|\sigma|\}$. Then S is c.e., and by Theorem 3.7.6, $|D \cap 2^n| \leqslant O(2^{rn-K(n)})$. Let

$$d(\sigma) = 2^{(s-r)|\sigma|}\left(\sum_{\sigma\tau\in D} 2^{-r|\tau|} + \sum_{\nu\in D \wedge \nu\prec\sigma} 2^{(r-1)(|\sigma|-|\nu|)}\right).$$

Then $d(\lambda) \leqslant \sum_{\tau\in D} 2^{-r|\tau|} \leqslant O(\sum_n 2^{rn-K(n)}2^{-rn}) = O(\sum_n 2^{-K(n)}) < \infty$, and a straightforward calculation shows that d is an s-gale. Since D is c.e., so is d. There are infinitely many n such that $A \upharpoonright n \in D$. For any such n, we have $d(A \upharpoonright n) \geqslant 2^{(s-r)n}$, so d succeeds on A, and hence $\dim(A) \leqslant s$.[3] □

One consequence of this characterization is that if A has positive effective Hausdorff dimension, then A is complex, since if $\dim(A) > r > 0$, then $C(A \upharpoonright n) > rn$ for almost all n.

The Kolmogorov complexity characterization of effective dimension also allows us to easily produce sets with fractional effective dimension. Let A be 1-random. Then $B = A \oplus 0^\omega$ has effective dimension $\frac{1}{2}$, since $K(B \upharpoonright n) = K(A \upharpoonright \lfloor \frac{n}{2} \rfloor) \pm O(1)$, and hence $\liminf_n \frac{K(B\upharpoonright n)}{n} = \liminf_n \frac{K(A\upharpoonright \lfloor \frac{n}{2} \rfloor)}{n} = \frac{1}{2}$. Recall the following definition. Given an infinite and coinfinite set X, let $x_0 < x_1 < \cdots$ be the elements of X, let $y_0 < y_1 < \cdots$ be the elements of $\overline{X}$, and define $C \oplus_X D$ to be $\{x_n : n \in C\} \cup \{y_n : n \in D\}$. For a computable real $r \in [0, 1]$, we can find a computable X such that $\lim_n \frac{|X\cap[0,n)|}{n} = r$. Then it is easy to check that $A \oplus_X 0^\omega$ has effective dimension r. Thus we have the following result.

Theorem 13.3.5 (Lutz [252, 254]). *For every computable real s, there is a set of effective Hausdorff dimension s.*

Clearly, every 1-random set has effective dimension 1, but if we take $r = 1$ in the above construction, then we have an example of a set of effective dimension 1 that is not 1-random.

Schnorr [349] considered exponential orders on martingales, and hence was in a sense implicitly studying dimension. We thank Sebastiaan Terwijn for the following comments on Schnorr's work. There is no explicit reference in Schnorr's book to Hausdorff dimension. After introducing orders of growth of martingales, he places special emphasis on exponential orders. It is interesting to ask why he did this, and whether he might have been inspired by the theory of dimension, but when asked at a recent meeting, he said he was not so motivated, so it is unclear why he gave such emphasis to exponential orders. Chapter 17 of [349] is titled "Die Zufallsgesetze von exponentieller Ordnung" ("The statistical laws of exponential

---

[3] Using the characterization in Definition 13.3.3, we can give a slightly cleaner proof. Let $D_n = \{\sigma \in 2^{\geqslant n} : K(\sigma) < r|\sigma|\}$. Then there are infinitely many n such that D_n is an effective n-cover of A, and for all n, we have $\sum_{\sigma\in D_n} 2^{-r|\sigma|} \leqslant \sum_{\sigma\in D_n} 2^{-K(\sigma)} < 1$. Thus $\dim(A) \leqslant r$.

order") and it starts as follows: "Nach unserer Vorstellung entsprechen den wichtigsten Zufallsgesetzen Nullmengen mit schnell wachsenden Ordnungsfunktionen. Die exponentiell wachsenden Ordnungsfunktionen sind hierbei von besonderer Bedeutung."[4]

Satz 17.1 then says that for any measure 0 set A the following are equivalent.

1. There are a computable martingale d and an $a > 1$ such that A is contained in $\{X : \limsup_n \frac{d(X\upharpoonright n)}{a^n} > 0\}$.
2. There are a Schnorr test $\{[\![U_n]\!]\}_{n\in\omega}$ and a $b > 0$ such that A is contained in $\{X : \limsup_n m_U(X \upharpoonright n) - bn > 0\}$, where m_U is a "Niveaufunktion" from strings to numbers defined by $m_U(\sigma) = \min\{n : \sigma \in U_n\}$.

This result is a test characterization saying something about the speed at which a set is covered, and resembles characterizations of effective Hausdorff dimension.

In this chapter we will focus on the Σ^0_1 notion of effective dimension, but as with notions of algorithmic randomness, there are many possible variations. For instance, we can vary arithmetic complexity of the gales used in the definition of dimension. In Section 13.15, we will examine the effect of replacing Σ^0_1 gales by computable ones, to yield a notion of computable dimension. We can also take the test set approach and study variations on that, for instance Schnorr dimension, which turns out to be equivalent to computable dimension, as we will see in Section 13.15. Some known relationships between notions of randomness and dimension are summarized in the following diagram from [118]. Here Δ^0_2 randomness is the relativization of computable randomness to $\emptyset'$ (so not the same as 2-randomness), and similarly for Schnorr Δ^0_2 randomness and Δ^0_2 dimension.

$$
\begin{array}{ccc}
\Delta^0_2 \text{ random} & & \\
\Downarrow & & \\
\text{Schnorr } \Delta^0_2 \text{ random} & \Longrightarrow & \Delta^0_2 \text{ dimension } 1 \\
\Downarrow & & \Downarrow \\
\text{1-random} & \Longrightarrow & \text{effective dimension } 1 \\
\Downarrow & & \\
\text{computably random} & & \Downarrow \\
\Downarrow & & \\
\text{Schnorr random} & \Longrightarrow & \text{computable dimension } 1
\end{array}
$$

No other implications hold than the ones indicated.

[4] "In our opinion, the important statistical laws correspond to null sets with fast growing orders. Here the exponentially growing orders are of special significance."

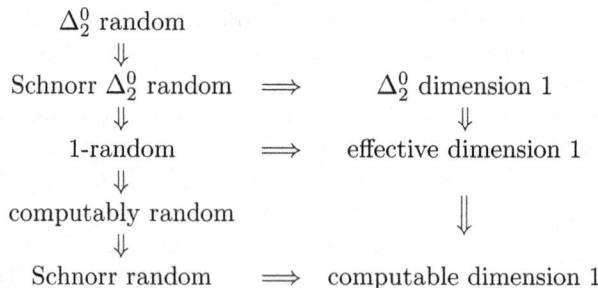

13.4 Shift complex sets

Not every set of high effective Hausdorff dimension is a "watered down" version of a 1-random set.

Definition 13.4.1. Let $0 < d < 1$. A set A is *d-shift complex* if for every $m < n$, we have $K(A \upharpoonright [m,n]) \geqslant d(n-m) - O(1)$.

If A is d-shift complex then $K(A \upharpoonright n) \geqslant dn - O(1)$, so the effective Hausdorff dimension of A is at least d. On the other hand, a 1-random set cannot be d-shift complex for any $d > 0$, since it must contain arbitrarily long sequences of 0's. Thus Theorem 13.4.3 below, which states that d-shift complex sets exist for every $d \in (0,1)$, shows that sets of high effective dimension can be quite different from 1-random sets. (Note that any 1-shift complex set would be 1-random, and hence no such sets exist.) We give a proof due to Miller [274], though the original proof in Durand, Levin, and Shen [138] is also not complicated.

We say that a set A *avoids* a string σ if there are no $m < n$ such that $\sigma = A \upharpoonright [m,n]$. Theorem 13.4.3 also follows from a stronger result due to Rumyantsev and Ushakov [337], who showed that if $c < 1$ and for each n, we have a set $F_n \subset 2^n$ with $|F_n| \leqslant 2^{cn}$, then there is an A such that for all sufficiently large n, the set A avoids every element of F_n.

Lemma 13.4.2 (Miller [274]). *Let $S \subseteq 2^{<\omega}$ and $c \in (\frac{1}{2}, 1)$ be such that $\sum_{\tau \in S} c^{|\tau|} \leqslant 2c - 1$. Then there is an A that avoids every element of S.*

Proof. Let $p = \sum_{\tau \in S} c^{|\tau|}$. Since $p < 1$, we have $\lambda \notin S$. Let

$$w(\sigma) = \sum \{c^{|\rho|} : \exists \tau \in S\, (|\rho| < |\tau| \wedge \sigma\rho \text{ ends in } \tau)\}.$$

We think of $w(\sigma)$ as measuring the threat that an extension of σ ends in an element of S. Note in particular that if σ itself ends in some $\tau \in S$ then $w(\sigma) \geqslant c^{|\lambda|} = 1$, so it is enough to build A so that $w(A \upharpoonright n) < 1$ for all n. We have $w(\lambda) = 0$. Now suppose that we have defined $A \upharpoonright n = \sigma$ so that $w(\sigma) < 1$. It is easy to check that $c(w(\sigma 0) + w(\sigma 1)) = w(\sigma) + p < 2c$, so there is an $i < 2$ such that $w(\sigma i) < 1$, and we can let $A(n) = i$. □

Theorem 13.4.3 (Durand, Levin, and Shen [138]). *Let $0 < d < 1$. There is a d-shift complex set.*

Proof. Let $b = -\log(1-d) + 1$, let $c = 2^{-d}$, and let $S = \{\tau \in 2^{<\omega} : K(\tau) \leqslant d|\tau| - b\}$. We have

$$\sum_{\tau \in S} c^{|\tau|} = \sum_{\tau \in S} 2^{-d|\tau|} \leqslant \sum_{\tau \in S} 2^{-K(\tau)-b} \leqslant 2^{-b} \sum_{\tau \in S} 2^{-K(\tau)}$$
$$\leqslant 2^{-b} = \frac{1-d}{2} < 2^{1-d} - 1 = 2c - 1,$$

where the last inequality is easy to show using the fact that $d \in (0,1)$. Thus, by the lemma, there is an A that avoids every element of S. This A is clearly d-shift complex. □

13.5 Partial randomness

Results such as Theorem 13.3.4 show that effective dimension can be thought of as a notion of "partial randomness". Indeed, as we saw above, a set such as $A \oplus 0$ for a 1-random A, which one would intuitively think of as "$\frac{1}{2}$-random", does indeed have effective dimension $\frac{1}{2}$. In this section, we look at a different, though closely related, approach to defining a notion of s-randomness for $s \in [0,1]$.

We begin with the measure-theoretic approach. We will see that there are at least two reasonable ways to define the concept of s-Martin-Löf randomness. The first is a straightforward generalization of the original definition.

Definition 13.5.1 (Tadaki [385]). Let $s \in [0,1]$.

(i) A *test for weak s-Martin-Löf randomness*[5] is a sequence of uniformly c.e. sets of strings $\{V_k\}_{k\in\omega}$ such that $\sum_{\sigma\in V_k} 2^{-s|\sigma|} \leqslant 2^{-k}$ for all k.

(ii) A is *weakly s-Martin-Löf random* if $A \notin \bigcap_k [\![V_k]\!]$ for all tests for weak s-Martin-Löf randomness $\{V_k\}_{k\in\omega}$.

We can also define A to be *weakly s-random* if $K(A \upharpoonright n) \geqslant sn - O(1)$. The analog of Schnorr's Theorem that 1-randomness is the same as Martin-Löf randomness is straightforward.

Theorem 13.5.2 (Tadaki [385]). *Let $s \in [0,1]$ be a computable real. A set A is weakly s-Martin-Löf random iff A is weakly s-random.*

Proof. This proof directly mimics the one of Theorem 6.2.3. We give it here as an example. For other similar results whose proofs are straightforward modifications of the $s = 1$ case, we simply mention that fact.

Suppose that A is weakly s-Martin-Löf random. Let $V_k = \{\sigma : K(\sigma) \leqslant s|\sigma| - k\}$. Then $\sum_{\sigma\in V_k} 2^{-s|\sigma|} \leqslant \sum_{\sigma\in V_k} 2^{-K(\sigma)-k} \leqslant 2^{-k}$, so the V_k form a test for weak s-Martin-Löf randomness, and hence $A \notin \bigcap_k [\![V_k]\!]$. Thus there is a k such that $K(A \upharpoonright n) \geqslant sn - k$.

[5] Below, we will define the notion of tests for strong s-Martin-Löf randomness. Since they will determine a stronger notion of s-randomness, these tests will be weaker than the ones we define here. The terminology adopted here is meant to avoid the confusion of talking about weak tests in connection with strong randomness and strong tests in connection with weak randomness, or the equally confusing possibility of having objects called "weak tests" that are actually stronger than ones called "strong tests".

Conversely, suppose that A is not weakly s-Martin-Löf random. Let $\{V_k\}_{k\in\omega}$ be a test for weak s-Martin-Löf randomness such that $A \in \bigcap_k [\![V_k]\!]$. Then it is easy to check that $\{(s|\sigma| - k, \sigma) : \sigma \in V_{k^2},\ k > 2\}$ is a KC set, so for each c there is an n such that $K(A \upharpoonright n) < sn - c$. □

Of course, weak s-randomness is closely related to effective dimension.

Proposition 13.5.3. *For all A, we have* $\dim(A) = \sup\{s : A$ *is weakly* s*-random*$\}$.

Proof. If A is weakly s-random then $\liminf_n \frac{K(A\upharpoonright n)}{n} \geqslant s$, so $\dim(A) \geqslant s$. Conversely, if A is not weakly s-random and $r < s$, then $\liminf_n \frac{K(A\upharpoonright n)}{n} \leqslant s < r$, so $\dim(A) < r$. Since $r < s$ is arbitrary, $\dim(A) \leqslant s$. □

Whether A is $\dim(A)$-random depends on A, of course. We have seen that there are sets of effective dimension 1 that are not 1-random, and it is easy to construct similar examples for $s < 1$. On the other hand, the examples we gave in connection with Theorem 13.3.5 have effective dimension s and are weakly s-random, so we have the following extension of that result.

Theorem 13.5.4 (Lutz [252, 254])**.** *For every computable real $s \in [0, 1]$, there is a set of effective Hausdorff dimension s that is weakly s-random.*

The discussion above tells us that the concept of s-randomness does give us some information beyond what we can get from effective dimension alone.

Using Theorem 13.5.2, we can emulate the proof that Ω is 1-random to show the following.

Theorem 13.5.5 (Tadaki [385])**.** *Let $s \in (0, 1]$ and let*

$$\Omega^s = \sum_{\mathcal{U}(\sigma)\downarrow} 2^{-\frac{|\sigma|}{s}}.$$

Then Ω^s is weakly s-random.

Similarly, we can construct a universal test for weak s-Martin-Löf randomness and develop other tools of the theory of 1-randomness. For example, it is useful to have an analog of Solovay tests for s-randomness.

Definition 13.5.6. Let $s \in [0, 1]$. A *Solovay s-test* is a c.e. set $S \subseteq 2^{<\omega}$ such that $\sum_{\sigma\in S} 2^{-s|\sigma|} < \infty$. A set A is *covered* by this test if $A \in [\![\sigma]\!]$ for infinitely many $\sigma \in S$.

The following result can be proved in much the same way as the $s = 1$ case. Although one direction is slightly weaker than in the $s = 1$ case, this result is enough to establish that for all A, we have $\dim(A) = \inf\{s :$ A is covered by some Solovay s-test$\}$.

Theorem 13.5.7 (Reimann [324]). *If A is weakly s-random then A is not covered by any Solovay s-test. If A is covered by some Solovay s-test then A is not weakly t-random for any $t > s$.*

The following variant will be useful in the proof of Theorem 13.8.1 below.

Definition 13.5.8. An *interval Solovay s-test* is a c.e. set T of intervals in $[0, 1]$ with dyadic rational endpoints such that $\sum_{I \in T} |I|^s < \infty$ (where $|I|$ is the length of I).

It is easy to transform an interval Solovay s-test T into a Solovay s-test S as follows. For each $[q, q + r] \in T$, first let n be largest such that $[q, q + r] \subseteq [q, q + 2^{-n}]$. Note that $2^{-n} < 2r$. Let σ_0 and σ_1 be such that $0.\sigma_0 = q$ and $0.\sigma_1 = q + 2^{-n}$. Let $\tau_i = (\sigma_i 0^\omega) \upharpoonright n$. Put τ_0 and τ_1 into S. It is easy to check that if $A \in I$ for infinitely many $I \in T$ then $A \in [\![\tau]\!]$ for infinitely many $\tau \in S$, and $\sum_{\tau \in S} 2^{-s|\tau|} \leqslant 2 \sum_{I \in T} (2|I|)^s < \infty$. Thus, we can use interval Solovay s-tests in place of Solovay s-tests in bounding the dimension of a real.

Turning now to the martingale approach to randomness, we run into some trouble. The following definitions are natural.

Definition 13.5.9. Let $s \in [0, 1]$.

(i) A is *martingale s-random* if for all c.e. martingales d, we have $A \notin S_{2^{(1-s)n}}[d]$.

(ii) A is *supermartingale s-random* if for all c.e. supermartingales d, we have $A \notin S_{2^{(1-s)n}}[d]$.

It is currently unknown whether these notions are the same, for the kind of reasons we mentioned when discussing Theorem 13.3.2.

We would like to show that at least one of these notions of martingale s-randomness coincides with weak s-randomness, but one direction of the equivalence does not work. Consider Schnorr's proof that if a set is Martin-Löf random then no c.e. (super)martingale can succeed on it. We are given a c.e. (super)martingale d, and when we see $d(\sigma) > 2^k$, we put $[\![\sigma]\!]$ into a test set U_k. Now imagine we follow the same proof for the $s < 1$ case. Here our test sets V_k are sets of strings. We might see that $d_s(\sigma 0) > 2^k$ and put $\sigma 0$ into V_k. Since d is only c.e., at some later stage $t > s$ we might see that $d_t(\sigma) > 2^k$. We would like to have $[\![\sigma]\!] \subseteq [\![V_k]\!]$, but of course putting σ into V_k is a waste, since $\sigma 0$ is already there, and indeed the measure calculation in Schnorr's proof is unlikely to work if V_k is not prefix-free. If we were to follow Schnorr's proof, we would simply put $\sigma 1$ into V_k. Unfortunately, $2(2^{-s(|\sigma|+1)}) > 2^{-s|\sigma|}$, so the simple measure calculation that allowed Schnorr's proof to succeed is no longer available.

This problem was overcome by the following definition of Calude, Staiger, and Terwijn [52].

Definition 13.5.10 (Calude, Staiger, and Terwijn [52]). Let $s \in [0, 1]$.

(i) A *test for strong s-Martin-Löf randomness* is a sequence of uniformly c.e. sets of strings $\{V_k\}_{k\in\omega}$ such that for every k and every prefix-free $\widehat{V}_k \subseteq V_k$, we have $\sum_{\sigma\in\widehat{V}_k} 2^{-s|\sigma|} \leqslant 2^{-k}$.

(ii) A is *strongly s-Martin-Löf random* if $A \notin \bigcap_k [\![V_k]\!]$ for all tests for strong s-Martin-Löf randomness $\{V_k\}_{k\in\omega}$.

Now the following result can be proved by a straightforward modification of Schnorr's proof mentioned above. The point is that when we notice that $d(\sigma) > 2^k$, we can put σ into V_k even if, say, $\sigma 0$ is already there, because any prefix-free subset of V_k will contain at most one of σ and $\sigma 0$.

Theorem 13.5.11 (Calude, Staiger, and Terwijn [52]). *Let $s \in (0,1]$ be a computable real. A set A is strongly s-Martin-Löf random iff it is supermartingale s-random.*

Reimann and Stephan [330] showed that weak and strong s-randomness are indeed distinct. The proof is technical and basically involves careful KC calculations, and we omit it due to space considerations.

Theorem 13.5.12 (Reimann and Stephan [330]). *For all computable $s \in (0,1)$, there is a set that is weakly s-random but not strongly Martin-Löf s-random.*

On the other hand, we do have the following.

Theorem 13.5.13 (Reimann [324]). *If $t < s$ and A is weakly s-random, then A is strongly Martin-Löf t-random.*

Proof. Suppose that A is not strongly Martin-Löf t-random, so there is a test for strong t-Martin-Löf randomness $\{U_n\}_{n\in\omega}$ such that $A \in \bigcap_n U_n$. For each n,

$$\sum_{\sigma\in U_n} 2^{-s|\sigma|} = \sum_k \sum_{\sigma\in U_n\cap 2^k} 2^{-sk}$$
$$= \sum_k 2^{(t-s)k} \sum_{\sigma\in U_n\cap 2^k} 2^{-tk} \leqslant \sum_k 2^{(t-s)k} 2^{-n},$$

where the last inequality holds because each $U_n \cap 2^k$ is prefix-free. Now, $\sum_k 2^{(t-s)k} < \infty$, so if we let m be such that $\sum_k 2^{(t-s)k-m} \leqslant 1$, then $\{U_n\}_{n\geqslant m}$ is a test for weak s-Martin Löf randomness witnessing the fact that A is not weakly s-random. □

As pointed out by Calude, Staiger, and Terwijn [52], Theorem 13.5.11 implies that strong s-randomness can be characterized in terms of KM since, as noted in Section 6.3.2, $KM(\sigma) = -\log d(\sigma) + |\sigma| \pm O(1)$ for an optimal c.e. supermartingale d. But we would still want to have a machine-based characterization of strong s-randomness. The following definition provides one.

Definition 13.5.14 (Downey and Reid, see [323]). Let $f : 2^{<\omega} \to 2^{<\omega}$ be a partial computable function computed by a Turing machine M, and let $Q \subseteq \operatorname{rng} f$. The *$M$-pullback* of Q is the unique subset Q^* of $\operatorname{dom} f$ satisfying the following conditions.[6]

(i) $f(Q^*) = Q$.

(ii) If $\sigma \in Q^*$ and $f(\tau) = f(\sigma)$, then $|\tau| \geqslant |\sigma|$.

(iii) If $\sigma \in Q^*$ and $f(\tau) = f(\sigma)$ with $|\tau| = |\sigma|$ then σ is enumerated into $\operatorname{dom} M$ before τ is. (We assume that elements enter $\operatorname{dom} M$ one at a time.)

A machine M is *s-measurable* if for all $Q \subseteq \operatorname{rng} M$, we have $\sum_{\sigma \in Q^*} 2^{-s|\sigma|} \leqslant 1$.

Theorem 13.5.15 (Downey, Reid, and Terwijn, see [323]). *Let $s \in (0,1]$ be a computable real. A set A is strongly s-Martin-Löf random iff $K_M(A \upharpoonright n) \geqslant n - O(1)$ for all s-measurable machines M.*

We know of no characterization of strong s-randomness in terms of initial segment prefix-free or plain complexity.

Before we prove Theorem 13.5.15, we need a lemma, which takes the role of the KC Theorem in this setting.

Lemma 13.5.16 (Downey, Reid, and Terwijn, see [323]). *Let $s \in (0,1]$. Let $\{U_k\}_{k \in \omega}$ be a test for strong s-Martin-Löf randomness. There is an s-measurable machine M such that for each k and $\sigma \in U_{2k+2}$, there is a τ of length $|\sigma| - (k+1)$ with $M(\tau) = \sigma$.*

Proof. If $\sigma \in U_{2k+2}$ then $2^{-|\sigma|} \leqslant 2^{-s|\sigma|} \leqslant 2^{-(2k+2)}$, so $|\sigma| \geqslant 2k+2$, whence $|\sigma| - (k+1) > 0$. So for a single such σ, requiring that there be a τ of length $|\sigma| - (k+1)$ with $M(\tau) = \sigma$ does not cause a problem.

We define M in the most obvious way: Whenever we see σ enter U_{2k+2}, we find the leftmost τ of length $|\sigma| - (k+1)$ and let $M(\tau) = \sigma$. We must show that there is always such a τ available, that is, that for each n there are at most 2^n many strings of length n needed for the definition of M.

As argued above, if $\sigma \in U_{2k+2}$ then $|\sigma| \geqslant 2k+2$, so if $k > n-1$ then $|\sigma| - (k+1) > n$. Thus we need to worry about only those U_{2k+2} with $k \leqslant n-1$. Note that strings $\sigma \in U_{2k+2}$ that require a domain element τ of length n must have length $n+k+1$.

For a set S of strings, let $\#(S,n)$ denote the number of strings of length n in S. As the set of all strings in U_{2k+2} of length $n+k+1$ is prefix-free,

$$\sum \{2^{-s(n+k+1)} : \sigma \in U_{2k+2} \wedge |\sigma| = n+k+1\} \leqslant 2^{-(2k+2)}.$$

[6]Roughly speaking, this definition is an approximation to the notion of σ^* for Kolmogorov complexity introduced in Chapter 3.

Thus

$$\#(U_{2k+2}, n+k+1)2^{-s(n+k+1)} \leqslant 2^{-(2k+2)},$$

so

$$\#(U_{2k+2}, n+k+1) \leqslant 2^{s(n+k+1)-(2k+2)} \leqslant 2^{(n+k+1)-(2k+2)} \leqslant 2^{-n-k-1}.$$

Therefore,

$$\sum_{k<n} \#(U_{2k+2}, n+k+1) = \sum_{k<n} 2^{n-k-1} \leqslant 2^{n-1} \sum_{k<n} 2^{-k} < 2^n.$$

Finally, we need to show that M is an s-measurable machine. Let $Q \subseteq \operatorname{rng} M$ be prefix-free. Then $Q \subseteq \bigcup_k U_{2k+2}$, so let $Q_k = U_{2k+2} \cap Q$, which is a prefix free subset of U_{2k+2}. Then

$$\sum_{\sigma \in Q_k} 2^{-s|\sigma|} 2^{s(k+1)} = 2^{s(k+1)} \sum_{\sigma \in Q_k} 2^{-s|\sigma|} \leqslant 2^{s(k+1)} 2^{-(2k+2)} \leqslant 2^{-k-1}.$$

Since Q_k is prefix-free and $s \leqslant 1$, it follows that

$$\sum_{\sigma \in Q^*} 2^{-s|\sigma|} \leqslant \sum_k \sum_{\sigma \in Q_k^*} 2^{-s|\sigma|} \leqslant \sum_k 2^{-k-1} = 1,$$

where Q^* is as in Definition 13.5.14. □

Proof of Theorem 13.5.15. First suppose we have an s-measurable machine M such that for each c there is an n with $K_M(A \upharpoonright n) < n - c$. Let $U_k = \{\sigma : K_M(\sigma) < |\sigma| - \frac{k}{s}\}$. The U_k are uniformly c.e., and $A \in [\![U_k]\!]$ for all k. Now we need a calculation to show that the U_k form a test for strong s-Martin-Löf randomness. Let $Q \subseteq U_k$ be prefix-free. Then

$$\sum_{\sigma \in Q} 2^{-s|\sigma|} \leqslant \sum_{\sigma \in Q} 2^{-s(K_M(\sigma)+\frac{k}{s})}$$
$$\leqslant \sum_{\sigma \in Q} 2^{-k} 2^{-sK_M(\sigma)} \leqslant 2^{-k} \sum_{\tau \in Q^*} 2^{-s|\tau|} \leqslant 2^{-k},$$

where Q^* is as in Definition 13.5.14.

Now suppose that A is not strongly s-random. Then there is a test for strong s-Martin-Löf randomness with $A \in \bigcap_k [\![U_k]\!]$. Let M be as in Lemma 13.5.16. Then for each c there is an n such that $K_M(A \upharpoonright n) < n - c$. □

13.6 A correspondence principle for effective dimension

Hausdorff dimension and its effective counterpart are of course quite different in general. However, there are situations in which they coincide. We have seen that many important subsets of Cantor space are Π^0_1 classes.

Hitchcock [180] showed that for such classes, and in fact even for arbitrary countable unions of Π^0_1 classes, the classical Hausdorff dimension of a class is equal to its effective Hausdorff dimension, and hence to the supremum of the Hausdorff dimensions of its elements. Thus, for such classes, we can think of classical Hausdorff dimension, which at a first look seems clearly to be a global property of a class, as a pointwise phenomenon.

Theorem 13.6.1 (Hitchcock [180]). *Let P be a countable union of Π^0_1 classes. Then* $\dim_{\mathrm{H}} P = \dim P$.

Proof. It is enough to prove the result for the case in which P is a single Π^0_1 class, since the Hausdorff dimension of a countable union of classes is the supremum of the Hausdorff dimension of the individual classes, and similarly for effective dimension.

It is enough to show that $\dim P \leqslant \dim_{\mathrm{H}} P$, so let $s > \dim_{\mathrm{H}} P$. Then for each n there is a set of strings U_n such that $\sum_{\sigma \in U_n} 2^{-s|\sigma|} \leqslant 2^{-n}$ and $P \subseteq [\![U_n]\!]$. Because P is closed and 2^ω is compact, P is compact, so the U_n can be taken to be finite.

Given n, we can search for a finite set of strings V_n and a stage s such that $\sum_{\sigma \in V_n} 2^{-s|\sigma|} \leqslant 2^{-n}$ and $P_s \subseteq [\![V_n]\!]$, where P_s is as usual the stage s approximation to P. We have seen that such a V_n must exist, and we can recognize when we have found one. Then the V_n form a test for weak s-Martin-Löf randomness, and $P \subseteq \bigcap_n [\![V_n]\!]$, so no element of P is weakly s-Martin-Löf random, and hence $\dim(A) < s$ for all $A \in P$.

Thus $\dim P < s$. Since $s > \dim_{\mathrm{H}} P$ is arbitrary, $\dim P \leqslant \dim_{\mathrm{H}} P$. □

Hitchcock [180] also showed that if P is a Σ^0_2 class (i.e., a union of uniformly Π^0_1 classes), then the Hausdorff dimension of P is equal to its computable Hausdorff dimension (that is, the dimension defined using computable, rather than c.e., martingales, which is equivalent to the concept of Schnorr Hausdorff dimension defined below).

Note that, as observed by Hitchcock [180], Theorem 13.6.1 cannot be extended even to a single Π^0_2 class, since $\{\Omega\}$ is a Π^0_2 class.

13.7 Hausdorff dimension and complexity extraction

There have been several results about the dimensions of classes of sets defined in computability-theoretic terms. One important theme is the following: given a set of positive effective dimension, to what extent is it possible to extract a greater level of complexity/randomness from that set? As we will see, there are several ways to formalize this question. (Note that we have already seen in Theorem 8.16.6 that there are sets of reasonably high initial segment complexity that do not compute 1-random sets.)

We begin by pointing out a fundamental difference between the degrees of 1-random sets and those of sets of high effective Hausdorff dimension.

Lemma 13.7.1 (Folklore). *Let $A \leqslant_{\mathrm{m}} B$. There is a $C \equiv_{\mathrm{m}} B$ such that A and C have the same effective Hausdorff dimension. The same result holds for any weaker reducibility, such as Turing reducibility.*

Proof. Let f be a fast-growing computable function, such as Ackermann's function (though a much slower-growing function than that will do for this argument). For each n, replace $A(f(n))$ by $B(n)$. Call the resulting set C. Then $C \equiv_{\mathrm{m}} B$, and A and C have the same effective Hausdorff dimension because $K(A \upharpoonright m)$ and $K(C \upharpoonright m)$ are very close for all m. The same procedure works for any weaker reducibility. □

As we saw in Corollary 8.8.6, Kučera [215] proved that the Turing degrees of 1-random sets are not closed upwards. This fact is true even in the Δ^0_2 degrees, for instance by Theorem 8.8.4. Hence, we have the following.

Corollary 13.7.2 (Folklore). *There are Δ^0_2 degrees of effective Hausdorff dimension* 1 *containing no* 1*-random sets.*

Proof. Choose $\mathbf{a} < \mathbf{b} < \mathbf{0}'$ such that $\mathbf{a}$ is 1-random but $\mathbf{b}$ is not. By Lemma 13.7.1, $\mathbf{b}$ contains a set of effective Hausdorff dimension 1. □

Since $\Omega \leqslant_{\mathrm{tt}} \emptyset'$, the method above also gives the following result.

Corollary 13.7.3 (Reimann [324]). *The tt-degree of $\emptyset'$ has effective Hausdorff dimension* 1.

The only way we have seen to make a set of effective Hausdorff dimension 1 that is not 1-random is to take a 1-random set and "mess it up" by a process such as inserting 0's at a sparse set of locations. It is natural to ask whether this is in some sense the only way we can produce such a set. One way to formalize this question is by asking whether it is always possible to extract randomness from a source of effective Hausdorff dimension 1.

Question 13.7.4 (Reimann). Let A have effective Hausdorff dimension 1. Is there necessarily a 1-random $B \leqslant_{\mathrm{T}} A$?

We will give a negative answer to this question due to Greenberg and Miller [170] in Section 13.9, where we will present their construction of a set of effective Hausdorff dimension 1 and minimal Turing degree. We saw in Corollary 6.9.5 that no minimal degree is 1-random.

Similarly, one of the only methods we have seen for making a set of fractional effective Hausdorff dimension is to take a set of higher effective Hausdorff dimension and "thin it out" (the other method being the construction of shift complex sets in Section 13.4). Again we are led to ask whether, given a set A of fractional effective Hausdorff dimension, it is always possible to find a set $B \leqslant_{\mathrm{T}} A$ of higher effective Hausdorff dimension, or even of effective Hausdorff dimension 1, or even a 1-random $B \leqslant_{\mathrm{T}} A$. By

Lemma 13.7.1, these questions remain the same if we replace $\leqslant_T$ by $\equiv_T$, so we can think of them as questions about the relationship between the effective Hausdorff dimension of A and that of its degree. Thus we can ask the following question.

Question 13.7.5 (Reimann, Terwijn). Is there a Turing degree **a** of effective Hausdorff dimension strictly between 0 and 1? If so, can **a** be Δ_2^0?

Question 13.7.5 is known as the *broken dimension question*. In Section 13.8, we will give a positive answer to it due to Miller [273]. Before doing so, we mention some earlier attempts to solve this question that are interesting and insightful in their own right.

We have seen in Theorem 8.8.1 that 1-random sets can always compute DNC functions. Terwijn [387] proved that this is also the case for sets of nonzero effective Hausdorff dimension. We can easily extract this result from our results on autocomplex sets and DNC functions: As mentioned following Theorem 13.3.4, if A has positive effective Hausdorff dimension, then A is complex, so by Theorem 8.16.4, A computes a DNC function. However, Terwijn's original proof is instructive and short, so we give it below.

Theorem 13.7.6 (Terwijn [387]). *If* $\dim(A) > 0$ *then* A *can compute a DNC function.*

Proof. By Theorem 2.22.1, it is enough to show that A can compute a fixed-point free function.

Let s be such that $\dim(A) > s > 0$ and $\frac{1}{s} \in \mathbb{N}$. For each e, let e_0 and e_1 be indices chosen in some canonical way so that $W_e = W_{e_0} \oplus W_{e_1}$. For a string σ, let $\widehat{\sigma}$ be the string of length $|\sigma|$ such that $\widehat{\sigma}(n) = 1 - \sigma(n)$. Let

$$B_{e,n} = \{\sigma \in 2^{\frac{n}{s}} : \exists t\, (W_{e_0,t} \upharpoonright \tfrac{n}{s} = \sigma \wedge W_{e_1,t} \upharpoonright \tfrac{n}{s} = \widehat{\sigma})\}.$$

If there is a σ such that $W_{e_0} \upharpoonright \frac{n}{s} = \sigma$ and $W_{e_1,t} \upharpoonright \frac{n}{s} = \widehat{\sigma}$, then $\sigma \in B_{e,n}$, but no other string is in $B_{e,n}$. Otherwise, $B_{e,n}$ is empty. In either case, $|B_{e,n}| \leqslant 1$, so $\sum_{\sigma \in B_{e,n}} 2^{-s|\sigma|} \leqslant 2^{-s\frac{n}{s}} = 2^{-n}$, and hence the $B_{e,n}$ form a test for weak s-Martin-Löf randomness for each e. We can effectively find indices $g(e)$ for each such test. (That is, $W_{\Phi_{g(e)}(n)}$ enumerates $B_{e,n}$ for each e and n.)

The usual construction of a universal test applied to tests for weak s-Martin Löf randomness produces a universal test for weak s-Martin-Löf randomness $\{U_n\}_{n\in\omega}$ such that for each index i, for the ith test for weak s-Martin-Löf randomness $\{V_n\}_{n\in\omega}$, we have $V_{n+i+1} \in U_n$ for all n. Since $\dim(A) > s$, there is an n such that $A \notin [\![U_n]\!]$, so $A \notin [\![B_{e,n+g(e)+1}]\!]$ for all e.

To construct the fixed-point free function $h \leqslant_T A$, given e, let $h(e)$ be an index so that $W_{h(e)_0} \upharpoonright f(n+g(e)+1) = A \upharpoonright f(n+g(e)+1)$ and $W_{h(e)_1} \upharpoonright f(n+g(e)+1) = \overline{A} \upharpoonright f(n+g(e)+1)$. If $W_{h(e)} = W_e$, then

$A \upharpoonright f(n+g(e)+1) \in B_{e,n+g(e)+1}$, which is not the case, so $W_{h(e)} \neq W_e$ for all e. □

Corollary 13.7.7 (Terwijn [387]). *If $A <_T \emptyset'$ is c.e. then $\{B : B \leqslant_T A\}$ has effective Hausdorff dimension* 0.

Proof. If not, then A computes a set of positive effective Hausdorff dimension, and hence computes a fixed-point free function. But then A is Turing complete, by Arslanov's Completeness Criterion, Theorem 2.22.3. □

Note that the proofs above give weak truth table reductions, so we also obtain the following corollary for free.

Corollary 13.7.8. *If $A <_{\mathrm{wtt}} \emptyset'$ is c.e. then $\{B : B \leqslant_{\mathrm{wtt}} A\}$ has effective Hausdorff dimension* 0.

One consequence of Corollary 13.7.7 is that if A has positive effective Hausdorff dimension, then, by Theorem 8.10.2, A computes an infinite subset of a 1-random set. Thus, if such an A cannot compute a 1-random set then something fairly subtle must be going on.

The results above also suggest an approach to the basic questions mentioned above. If we could show that being strong enough to compute a DNC function implies being strong enough to compute a 1-random, then we would be able to answer all those questions. However, we have already seen in Theorem 8.10.3 that this is not the case.

Reimann and Terwijn (see [324]) showed that Question 13.7.5 has a positive answer for m-reducibility, even for Δ_2^0 sets, by showing that there is a Δ_2^0 set A such that $\{B : B \leqslant_m A\}$ has fractional effective Hausdorff dimension. (An example is the set A defined by starting with a Δ_2^0 1-random set X and letting $A(n) = X(n) \cdot X(n+1)$, where $\cdot$ denotes multiplication.) Before Miller's solution to the broken dimension problem, the best partial result was the following one by Nies and Reimann [307]. We will not prove it here, as it is a consequence of Miller's result presented in the next section. It is worth noting, though, that the method of proof in [307] is rather different than that used for Miller's result.

Theorem 13.7.9 (Nies and Reimann [307]). *For any computable real α with $0 < \alpha < 1$ there is a Δ_2^0 set A such that the effective Hausdorff dimension of $\{B : B \leqslant_{\mathrm{wtt}} A\}$ is α.*

13.8 A Turing degree of nonintegral Hausdorff dimension

In this section, we present Miller's proof of the following result, whose significance was discussed in the previous section.

Theorem 13.8.1 (Miller [273]). *Let $\alpha \in (0,1)$ be a left-c.e. real. There is a Δ^0_2 set A of effective Hausdorff dimension α such that if $B \leqslant_T A$ then the effective Hausdorff dimension of B is at most α.*

Proof. To simplify the presentation, we take $\alpha = \frac{1}{2}$. It should be clear how to modify the proof to work for any rational α, and not too difficult to see how to handle the general case.

We will build A as the intersection of a sequence of nested Π^0_1 classes of positive measure. We will begin with a class all of whose members have effective dimension at least $\frac{1}{2}$, thus ensuring that $\dim(A) \geqslant \frac{1}{2}$. At each stage we will satisfy a requirement of the form Ψ^A_e total $\Rightarrow \exists k > n\,(K(\Psi^A_e \upharpoonright k) \leqslant (\frac{1}{2} + 2^{-n})k)$. To do so, we will want to wait until a large set of oracles that appear to be in our current Π^0_1 class P compute the same string via Ψ_e, and then compress that string. A key to showing that we can do this will be to use the dimension of the measure of P. Thus we will work with Π^0_1 classes such that $\dim(\mu(P)) \leqslant \frac{1}{2}$.

We begin by introducing some concepts that will be needed in the proof.

Definition 13.8.2. Let $S \subseteq 2^{<\omega}$. The *direct weight* of S is $\mathrm{DW}(S) = \sum_{\sigma \in S} 2^{-\frac{|\sigma|}{2}}$. The *weight* of S is $W(S) = \inf\{\mathrm{DW}(V) : [\![S]\!] \subseteq [\![V]\!]\}$.

Note that $W(S) \leqslant 1$ because $[\![S]\!] \subseteq [\![\{\lambda\}]\!]$ and $\mathrm{DW}(\{\lambda\}) = 1$. The weight of S is essentially the minimum cost of compressing some initial segment of each set in $[\![S]\!]$ by a factor of 2 (although programs cannot have fractional length, so the cost of compressing a string of length 5 by a factor of 2 is actually 2^{-2}, not $2^{-2.5}$). Of course, there is no reason to think that this compression can be realized effectively. In other words, even if S is c.e., there may not be a prefix-free machine M compressing some initial segment of each set in $[\![S]\!]$ by a factor of 2 so that the measure of the domain of M is close to $W(S)$.

Suppose that S is finite and let V be such that $[\![S]\!] \subseteq [\![V]\!]$. It is suboptimal for V to contain any string incomparable with every $\sigma \in S$ or to contain a proper extension of some $\sigma \in S$. In other words, it is always possible to find a $\widehat{V}$ with $[\![S]\!] \subseteq [\![\widehat{V}]\!]$ and $\mathrm{DW}(\widehat{V}) \leqslant \mathrm{DW}(V)$, so that every string in V has an extension in S. Therefore, there are only finitely many V that need to be considered in computing the infimum in the definition of $W(S)$. Hence this infimum is achieved, justifying the following definition when S is finite.

Definition 13.8.3. An *optimal cover* of $S \subseteq 2^{<\omega}$ is a set $S^{oc} \subseteq 2^{<\omega}$ such that $[\![S]\!] \subseteq [\![S^{oc}]\!]$ and $\mathrm{DW}(S^{oc}) = W(S)$. For the sake of uniqueness, we also require $[\![S^{oc}]\!]$ to have the minimum measure among all possible contenders.

It is not hard to see that optimal covers, if they exist, are unique and prefix-free. The analysis above shows that when S is finite, we can compute both the optimal cover of S and $W(S)$.

Now consider an infinite S. Let $\{S_t\}_{t\in\omega}$ be an enumeration of S, i.e., a sequence of finite sets $S_0 \subset S_1 \subset \cdots$ such that $S = \bigcup_t S_t$. If $\sigma \in S_t^{oc}$, then the only way for σ to not be in S_{t+1}^{oc} is for some $\tau \prec \sigma$ to be in S_{t+1}^{oc}. This fact has some nice consequences. First, it implies a *nesting property*: $[\![S_t^{oc}]\!] \subseteq [\![S_{t+1}^{oc}]\!]$ for all t. Second, it proves that the S_t^{oc} have a pointwise limit V. It is not hard to see that $V = S^{oc}$, demonstrating that the definition above is valid for any $S \subseteq 2^{<\omega}$.

If S is c.e., the above construction applied to an effective enumeration shows that the optimal cover S^{oc} is Δ_2^0. More importantly, the nesting property implies that $[\![S^{oc}]\!]$ is a Σ_1^0 class. There will not generally be a c.e. set $V \subseteq 2^{<\omega}$ such that $[\![S^{oc}]\!] = [\![V]\!]$ and $\mathrm{DW}(V) = W(S)$, or even such that the direct weight of V is finite. However, we can find such a V for which the direct weight of any prefix-free subset is bounded by $W(S)$. Here and below, we write $\tau 2^{<\omega}$ for $\{\tau\sigma : \sigma \in 2^{<\omega}\}$.

Lemma 13.8.4. *For any c.e. set $S \subseteq 2^{<\omega}$, we can effectively find a c.e. $V \subseteq 2^{<\omega}$ such that $[\![V]\!] = [\![S^{oc}]\!]$ and if $P \subseteq V$ is prefix-free, then* $\mathrm{DW}(P) \leqslant W(S)$.

Proof. Let $\{S_t\}_{t\in\omega}$ be an effective enumeration of S. Let $V = \bigcup_t S_t^{oc}$. Then V is c.e. and $[\![V]\!] = [\![S^{oc}]\!]$. If there is an infinite prefix-free $P \subseteq V$ such that $\mathrm{DW}(P) > W(S)$, then there is a finite $P' \subset P$ with the same property. So assume that $P \subseteq V$ is finite and prefix-free. We will prove that if $\tau \in V$, then $\mathrm{DW}(P \cap \tau 2^{<\omega}) \leqslant \mathrm{DW}(\{\tau\})$, by induction on the distance k from τ to its longest extension in P (the claim being trivial if $P \cap \tau 2^{<\omega}$ is empty). The case $k = 0$ is immediate. Now take $\tau \in V \setminus P$. There is a unique t such that $\tau \in S_{t+1}^{oc} \setminus S_t^{oc}$. Then $\mathrm{DW}(S_t^{oc} \cap \tau 2^{<\omega}) \leqslant \mathrm{DW}(\{\tau\})$, as otherwise $\tau \in S_t^{oc}$. The nesting property implies that $[\![S_t^{oc}]\!] \cap [\![\tau]\!]$ covers $[\![P]\!] \cap [\![\tau]\!]$, since every element of $P \cap \tau 2^{<\omega}$ must have entered V by stage t. Hence, applying the inductive hypothesis to the elements of $S_t^{oc} \cap \tau 2^{<\omega}$, we have $\mathrm{DW}(P \cap \tau 2^{<\omega}) \leqslant \mathrm{DW}(S_t^{oc} \cap \tau 2^{<\omega})$. Of course, $[\![S^{oc}]\!]$ covers $[\![P]\!]$, so $\mathrm{DW}(P) \leqslant \mathrm{DW}(S^{oc}) = W(S)$. □

We will build a set A by approximations. As usual, the type of approximation—or in terminology borrowed from set theory, the type of *forcing condition*—determines the nature of the requirements that we can satisfy during the construction. Our conditions will be pairs (σ, S) with $\sigma \in 2^{<\omega}$ and $S \subseteq \sigma 2^{<\omega}$ c.e. and such that $\sigma \notin S^{oc}$. A condition describes a restriction on the set A that is being constructed. Specifically, the class of all sets consistent with a condition (σ, S) is the Π_1^0 class $P_{(\sigma,S)} = [\![\sigma]\!] \setminus [\![S^{oc}]\!]$. Our definition of condition guarantees that $P_{(\sigma,S)}$ is nonempty. We say that a condition (τ, T) *extends* (σ, S) and write

$(\tau, T) \preccurlyeq (\sigma, S)$ if $P_{(\tau,T)} \subseteq P_{(\sigma,S)}$.[7] Extending a condition corresponds, of course, to further restricting the possibilities for A.

We now establish some basic lemmas about these forcing conditions. The first shows that there is an S such that every element of $P_{(\lambda,S)}$ has effective dimension at least $\frac{1}{2}$.

Lemma 13.8.5. *Let $S = \{\sigma : K(\sigma) \leqslant \frac{|\sigma|}{2}\}$. Then (λ, S) is a forcing condition.*

Proof. All that needs to be shown is that $\lambda \notin S^{oc}$. If $\lambda \in S^{oc}$, then $\mathrm{DW}(S) \geqslant W(S) = 1$. But $\mathrm{DW}(S) = \sum_{\sigma \in S} 2^{-\frac{|\sigma|}{2}} \leqslant \sum_{\sigma \in S} 2^{-K(\sigma)} \leqslant \Omega < 1$. □

The next two lemmas show that each Π^0_1 class corresponding to a condition has positive measure, and that the effective Hausdorff dimension of its measure is at most $\frac{1}{2}$.

Lemma 13.8.6. *Let $S \subseteq \sigma 2^{<\omega}$. If $[\![\sigma]\!] \setminus [\![S^{oc}]\!]$ is nonempty, then it has positive measure.*

Proof. Let $n = |\sigma|$. The fact that $[\![S]\!] \subseteq [\![\sigma]\!]$ implies that $W(S) \leqslant 2^{-\frac{n}{2}}$. Because $[\![\sigma]\!] \setminus [\![S^{oc}]\!]$ is nonempty, we know that $\sigma \notin S^{oc}$. Hence $\tau \in S^{oc}$ implies that $|\tau| > n$. By these observations,

$$\mu([\![S^{oc}]\!]) = \sum_{\tau \in S^{oc}} 2^{-|\tau|} < \sum_{\tau \in S^{oc}} 2^{-\frac{|\tau|+n}{2}} = 2^{-\frac{n}{2}} \sum_{\tau \in S^{oc}} 2^{-\frac{|\tau|}{2}}$$
$$= 2^{-\frac{n}{2}} \mathrm{DW}(S^{oc}) = 2^{-\frac{n}{2}} W(S) \leqslant 2^{-n}.$$

Therefore, $\mu([\![\sigma]\!] \setminus [\![S^{oc}]\!]) > 0$. □

Lemma 13.8.7. *Let (σ, S) be a condition. Then* $\dim(\mu(P_{(\sigma,S)})) \leqslant \frac{1}{2}$.

Proof. We prove that $\dim(\mu([\![S^{oc}]\!])) \leqslant \frac{1}{2}$, which is sufficient because $\mu(P_{(\sigma,S)}) = 2^{-|\sigma|} - \mu([\![S^{oc}]\!])$. We may assume, without loss of generality, that S^{oc} is infinite, since otherwise $\mu([\![S^{oc}]\!])$ is rational. Let $w = W(S)$. Let $V \subseteq 2^{<\omega}$ be the c.e. set guaranteed by Lemma 13.8.4. That is, $[\![V]\!] = [\![S^{oc}]\!]$ and $\mathrm{DW}(P) \leqslant w$ whenever $P \subseteq V$ is prefix-free. Note that V must be infinite. Let $\{V_t\}_{t \in \omega}$ be an effective enumeration of V such that $V_0 = \emptyset$.

Let $s > 1/2$. We produce an interval Solovay s-test T covering $\mu([\![V]\!])$. (See Definition 13.5.8.) It consists of two parts, T_0 and T_1.

1. If $\tau \in V_{t+1} \setminus V_t$, then put $[\mu([\![V_{t+1}]\!]), \mu([\![V_{t+1}]\!]) + 2^{-|\tau|}]$ into T_0.

[7] It might seem that the $\preccurlyeq$ symbol goes in the wrong direction, but this usage is consistent with what is often done in set theory, and derives from the identification of a condition with the class of sets consistent with it.

2. If $\mu([\![V_t \cap 2^{>n}]\!]) \leqslant k2^{-n}$ and $\mu([\![V_{t+1} \cap 2^{>n}]\!]) > k2^{-n}$ for some n and k, then put $[\mu([\![V_{t+1}]\!]), \mu([\![V_{t+1}]\!]) + 2^{-n}]$ into T_1.

Let $T = T_0 \cup T_1$. Notice that T does not actually depend on s. Using the fact that $V \cap 2^n$ is prefix-free, we have

$$\begin{aligned}\sum_{I \in T_0} |I|^s &= \sum_{\tau \in V} 2^{-s|\tau|} = \sum_n 2^{-sn}|V \cap 2^n| = \sum_n 2^{\left(\frac{1}{2}-s\right)n} 2^{-\frac{n}{2}} |V \cap 2^n| \\ &= \sum_n 2^{\left(\frac{1}{2}-s\right)n} \operatorname{DW}(V \cap 2^n) \leqslant \sum_n 2^{\left(\frac{1}{2}-s\right)n} w = \frac{w}{1-2^{\frac{1}{2}-s}} < \infty.\end{aligned}$$

Now fix n and let k be the number of intervals of length 2^{-n} added to T_1. By construction, $2^{-n}k < \mu([\![V \cap 2^{>n}]\!])$. Let $P \subseteq V \cap 2^{>n}$ be a prefix-free set such that $[\![P]\!] = [\![V \cap 2^{>n}]\!]$. Then by the same argument as in the previous lemma, $\mu([\![P]\!]) < 2^{-\frac{n}{2}} \operatorname{DW}(P)$. Putting these facts together we have $2^{-n}k < 2^{-\frac{n}{2}} \operatorname{DW}(P) \leqslant 2^{-\frac{n}{2}} w$, so $k < 2^{\frac{n}{2}} w$. Thus

$$\sum_{I \in T_1} |I|^s < \sum_n 2^{\frac{n}{2}} w (2^{-n})^s = \sum_n 2^{\left(\frac{1}{2}-s\right)n} w < \infty,$$

which proves that T is an interval Solovay s-test.

Next we prove that T covers $\mu([\![V]\!])$. Call $\tau \in V_{t+1} \setminus V_t$ *timely* if $V_{t+1} \cap 2^{\leqslant n} = V \cap 2^{\leqslant n}$, in other words, if only strings longer than τ enter V after τ. Because V is infinite, there are infinitely many timely $\tau \in V$. Fix one. Let $t+1$ be the stage at which τ enters V and let $n = |\tau|$. We claim that there is an interval of length 2^{-n} in T that contains $\mu([\![V]\!])$. Note that if $u > t$, then $\mu([\![V]\!]) - \mu([\![V_u]\!]) \leqslant \mu([\![V \cap 2^{>n}]\!]) - \mu([\![V_u \cap 2^{>n}]\!])$. In response to τ entering V, we put the interval $[\mu([\![V_{t+1}]\!]), \mu([\![V_{t+1}]\!]) + 2^{-n}]$ into $T_0 \subseteq T$ at stage $t+1$. Let $I = [\mu([\![V_u]\!]), \mu([\![V_u]\!]) + 2^{-n}]$ be the last interval of length 2^{-n} added to T. If $\mu([\![V]\!]) \notin I$, then $\mu([\![V]\!]) > \mu([\![V_u]\!]) + 2^{-n}$. Since $u > t$, we have $\mu([\![V \cap 2^{>n}]\!]) > \mu([\![V_u \cap 2^{>n}]\!]) + 2^{-n}$, so another interval of length 2^{-n} is added to $T_1 \subseteq T$ after stage u, which is a contradiction. Thus $\mu([\![V]\!]) \in I$. We have proved that for any n that is the length of a timely element of V, there is an interval of length 2^{-n} in T that contains $\mu([\![V]\!])$. Since there are infinitely many timely strings, $\mu([\![V]\!])$ is covered by T.

Since T is an interval Solovay s-test for every $s > \frac{1}{2}$, it follows that $\dim(\mu([\![S^{oc}]\!])) = \dim(\mu([\![V]\!])) \leqslant \frac{1}{2}$. □

Miller [273] noted that, by applying the method of the main part of this proof (presented after the next lemma) to the identity functional, we can show that if (σ, S) extends the condition from Lemma 13.8.5, then $\dim(\mu(P_{(\sigma,S)})) \geqslant \frac{1}{2}$. Hence, Lemma 13.8.7 is tight.

Our final lemma gives a simple hypothesis on a collection of conditions that guarantees that they have a common extension.

Lemma 13.8.8. *Let* $(\sigma_0, S_0), \dots, (\sigma_n, S_n)$ *be conditions such that* $P_{(\sigma_0,S_0)} \cap \dots \cap P_{(\sigma_n,S_n)}$ *has positive measure. Then there is a condition* (τ, T) *such that* $(\tau, T) \preccurlyeq (\sigma_i, S_i)$ *for each* $i \leqslant n$.

Proof. The σ_i are comparable by hypothesis, so let $\sigma = \sigma_0 \cup \dots \cup \sigma_n$. Let $P = P_{(\sigma_0,S_0)} \cap \dots \cap P_{(\sigma_n,S_n)} = [\![\sigma]\!] \setminus [\![S_0^{oc} \cup \dots \cup S_n^{oc}]\!]$. In particular, $P \subseteq [\![\sigma]\!]$. Let b be such that $\mu(P) \geqslant 2^{-b}$. For each $m \geqslant b$, let

$$D_m = \{\tau \succcurlyeq \sigma : |\tau| = m \text{ and no prefix of } \tau \text{ is in } S_i^{oc} \text{ for any } i \leqslant n\}.$$

Now $\mu(P) \leqslant |D_m| 2^{-m}$, because if $\tau \in 2^m$ is not in D_m, then $[\![\tau]\!]$ is disjoint from $[\![P]\!]$. Hence $|D_m| \geqslant 2^{m-b}$.

Let $\tau \in D_m$ and let $T_\tau = \tau 2^{<\omega} \cap (S_0^{oc} \cup \dots \cup S_n^{oc})$. If $\tau \notin T_\tau^{oc}$, then (τ, T_τ) is the condition required by the lemma. On the other hand, $\tau \in T_\tau^{oc}$ implies that $\mathrm{DW}(T_\tau) \geqslant W(T_\tau) = 2^{-\frac{m}{2}}$. So assuming that the lemma fails, we have

$$n + 1 \geqslant \sum_{i \leqslant n} W(S_i) = \sum_{i \leqslant n} \mathrm{DW}(S_i^{oc}) \geqslant \mathrm{DW}(S_0^{oc} \cup \dots \cup S_n^{oc})$$

$$\geqslant \sum_{\tau \in D_m} \mathrm{DW}(T_\tau) \geqslant \sum_{\tau \in D_m} 2^{-\frac{m}{2}} \geqslant 2^{m-b} 2^{-\frac{m}{2}} = 2^{\frac{m}{2} - b}.$$

For large enough m, we have a contradiction. □

Note that $\emptyset'$ can find the common extension guaranteed by the lemma.

We are now ready to build A. We build a sequence of conditions $(\sigma_0, S_0) \succcurlyeq (\sigma_1, S_1) \succcurlyeq (\sigma_2, S_2) \succcurlyeq \cdots$ and take $A = \bigcup_t \sigma_t$, which will be total. Equivalently, A will be the unique element of $\bigcap_t P_{(\sigma_t,S_t)}$. The construction will be carried out with a $\emptyset'$ oracle, so that $A \leqslant_T \emptyset'$. We begin by letting (σ_0, S_0) be the condition from Lemma 13.8.5, which ensures that $\dim(A) \geqslant \frac{1}{2}$.

For each e and n, we will meet the requirement

$$R_{e,n} : \Psi_e^A \text{ total} \Rightarrow \exists k > n\, (K(\Psi_e^A \upharpoonright k) \leqslant (\tfrac{1}{2} + 2^{-n})k).$$

These requirements guarantee that if $B \leqslant_T A$, then $\dim(B) \leqslant \frac{1}{2}$, and in particular, that $\dim(A) = \frac{1}{2}$.

Suppose we have defined (σ_t, S_t). We now show how to define (σ_{t+1}, S_{t+1}) to satisfy $R_{e,n}$, where $t = \langle e, n \rangle$. Let b be such that $2^{-b} < \mu(P_{(\sigma_t,S_t)})$. Note that b exists by Lemma 13.8.6, and can be found using $\emptyset'$. We define a prefix-free machine M. The idea is that M will wait for a large set of oracles that appear to be in $P_{(\sigma_t,S_t)}$ to compute the same sufficiently long initial segment via Ψ_e, and then will compress that initial segment.

For each ρ, define $M(\rho)$ as follows. First, wait until $\mathcal{U}(\rho)\downarrow$. If that ever happens, then let $\sigma = \mathcal{U}(\rho)$ and $m = |\sigma|$. If σ is not an initial segment of the binary expansion of $\mu(P_{(\sigma_t,S_t)})$, then let $M(\rho)\uparrow$. Otherwise, proceed as follows. For each τ, let $T_\tau = \{\nu \succcurlyeq \sigma_t : \tau \preccurlyeq \Psi_e^\nu\}$. Search for a $\tau \in 2^{m-b}$ such that $\mu(P_{(\sigma_t, S_t \cup T_\tau)}) < 0.\sigma$. This condition is Σ_1^0, so $\emptyset'$ can find such a τ if there is one. If there is such a τ, then let $M(\rho) = \tau$. Note that the domain of M is a subset of the domain of $\mathcal{U}$, and hence is prefix-free.

We can effectively find a c such that $\forall \tau\, (K(\tau) \leqslant K_M(\tau) + c)$. Using $\emptyset'$, we can search for a σ that is an initial segment of the binary expansion of $\mu(P_{(\sigma_t, S_t)})$ of length $m > n+b$, and such that $K(\sigma)+c \leqslant (\frac{1}{2}+2^{-n})(m-b)$. Such a σ must exist by Lemma 13.8.7. Let ρ be a minimal length $\mathcal{U}$-program for σ. The construction now breaks into two cases, depending on whether or not $M(\rho)\downarrow$ (which $\emptyset'$ can determine, of course).

Case 1. $M(\rho)\downarrow = \tau$. In this case, we know that $\mu(P_{(\sigma_t, S_t \cup T_\tau)}) < 0.\sigma$ and $\mu(P_{(\sigma_t, S_t)}) \geqslant 0.\sigma$. Thus $P_{(\sigma_t, S_t)} \setminus P_{(\sigma_t, S_t \cup T_\tau)} = [\![(S_t \cup T_\tau)^{oc}]\!] \setminus [\![S_t^{oc}]\!]$ is nonempty. So there is a $\sigma_{t+1} \in T_\tau$ such that $[\![\sigma_{t+1}]\!] \not\subseteq [\![S_t^{oc}]\!]$, since otherwise S_t^{oc} would be the optimal cover of $[\![(S_t \cup T_\tau)^{oc}]\!]$. Note that $\emptyset'$ can find such a σ_{t+1}. By definition, $\sigma_{t+1} \succcurlyeq \sigma_t$. Because T_τ is closed under extensions, we may additionally require that σ_{t+1} properly extend σ_t. Let $S_{t+1} = \sigma_{t+1}2^{<\omega} \cap S_t$. Since no prefix of σ_{t+1} is in S_t^{oc}, we have $S_{t+1}^{oc} = \sigma_{t+1}2^{<\omega} \cap S_t^{oc}$, which implies that $P_{(\sigma_{t+1}, S_{t+1})} = [\![\sigma_{t+1}]\!] \cap [\![P_{(\sigma_t, S_t)}]\!] \neq \emptyset$. Thus (σ_{t+1}, S_{t+1}) is a valid condition and $P_{(\sigma_{t+1}, S_{t+1})} \subseteq P_{(\sigma_t, S_t)}$, so $(\sigma_{t+1}, S_{t+1}) \preccurlyeq (\sigma_t, S_t)$.

To verify that $R_{e,n}$ has been satisfied, take $A \in P_{(\sigma_{t+1}, S_{t+1})}$. Since $\sigma_{t+1} \preccurlyeq A$ and $\sigma_{t+1} \in T_\tau$, we see that $\tau \preccurlyeq \Psi_e^A$. Let $k = |\tau| = m - b$, which is larger than n by our choice of σ. Then

$$
\begin{aligned}
K(\Psi_e^A \upharpoonright k) = K(\tau) \leqslant K_M(\tau) + c \leqslant |\rho| + c = K(\sigma) + c& \\
\leqslant (\tfrac{1}{2} + 2^{-n})(m-b) = (\tfrac{1}{2} + 2^{-n})k.&
\end{aligned}
$$

Case 2. $M(\rho)\uparrow$. In this case, $\mu(P_{(\sigma_t, S_t \cup T_\tau)}) \geqslant 0.\sigma$ for each $\tau \in 2^{m-b}$. Thus, for each such τ, we have that $(\sigma_t, S_t \cup T_\tau)$ is a valid condition extending (σ_t, S_t). Furthermore, since $P_{(\sigma_t, S_t \cup T_\tau)} \subseteq P_{(\sigma_t, S_t)}$ and $\mu(P_{(\sigma_t, S_t)}) \leqslant 0.\sigma + 2^{-m}$, we have $\mu(P_{(\sigma_t, S_t)} \setminus P_{(\sigma_t, S_t \cup T_\tau)}) \leqslant 2^{-m}$. So

$$
\begin{aligned}
&\mu\Big(\bigcap_{\tau \in 2^{m-b}} P_{(\sigma_t, S_t \cup T_\tau)}\Big) = \mu\Big(P_{(\sigma_t, S_t)} \setminus \bigcup_{\tau \in 2^{m-b}} (P_{(\sigma_t, S_t)} \setminus P_{(\sigma_t, S_t \cup T_\tau)})\Big) \\
&\geqslant \mu(P_{(\sigma_t, S_t)}) - \sum_{\tau \in 2^{m-b}} \mu(P_{(\sigma_t, S_t)} \setminus P_{(\sigma_t, S_t \cup T_\tau)}) > 2^{-b} - 2^{m-b}2^{-m} = 0.
\end{aligned}
$$

Thus by Lemma 13.8.8, there is a condition (σ_{t+1}, S_{t+1}) that extends $(\sigma_t, S_t \cup T_\tau)$ for every $\tau \in 2^{m-b}$. Then $(\sigma_{t+1}, S_{t+1}) \preccurlyeq (\sigma_t, S_t)$. Furthermore, $\emptyset'$ can find (σ_{t+1}, S_{t+1}), and we may assume without loss of generality that σ_{t+1} properly extends σ_t.

To verify that $R_{e,n}$ is satisfied in this case as well, assume that Ψ_e^A is total and let $\tau = \Psi_e^A \upharpoonright (m-b)$. Since $\sigma_t \preccurlyeq A$, some $\rho \preccurlyeq A$ is in T_τ. Therefore, $A \in [\![(S_t \cup T_\tau)^{oc}]\!]$ and hence $A \notin P_{(\sigma_t, S_t \cup T_\tau)} \supseteq P_{(\sigma_{t+1}, S_{t+1})}$.

We have completed the construction. Let $A = \bigcup_t \sigma_t$, which is total because we ensured that σ_{t+1} properly extends σ_t for every t. The construction was done relative to $\emptyset'$, so A is Δ^0_2. The remainder of the verification was given above. □

13.9 DNC functions and effective Hausdorff dimension

In this section we present work of Greenberg and Miller [170] connecting the growth rates of DNC functions with effective Hausdorff dimension. In particular, we describe their construction of a set of effective Hausdorff dimension 1 and minimal Turing degree. (As mentioned above, by Corollary 6.9.5, such a set cannot compute a 1-random set, and hence this result answers Question 13.7.4.) This theorem extends earlier work of Downey and Greenberg [106], who showed that there is a set of minimal Turing degree and effective packing dimension 1 (a concept defined below in Section 13.11.3), as described in Section 13.13.

Greenberg and Miller [170] generalized effective Hausdorff dimension to a class of spaces similar to Cantor space. Let $h : \mathbb{N} \to \mathbb{N} \setminus \{0, 1\}$ be computable. Let h^ω be the product space $\prod_n \{0, 1, \ldots, h(n) - 1\}$. That is, the elements of h^ω are infinite sequences of natural numbers such that the nth element of the sequence is less than $h(n)$. Let $h^n = \prod_{m<n}\{0, 1, \ldots, h(m) - 1\}$ and $h^{<\omega} = \bigcup_n h^n$. We give h^ω a topology similar to that of Cantor space, with the basic open sets being $[\![\sigma]\!] = \{\alpha \in h^\omega : \sigma \prec \alpha\}$ for $\sigma \in h^{<\omega}$. As for Cantor space, for $A \subseteq h^{<\omega}$, we write $[\![A]\!]$ for $\bigcup_{\sigma \in A}[\![\sigma]\!]$.

The space h^ω is a compact Polish space. An analogue of the uniform measure for h^ω is obtained by dividing mass equitably: for $\sigma \in h^{<\omega}$, let

$$\mu^h([\![\sigma]\!]) = \frac{1}{|h^{|\sigma|}|} = \frac{1}{h(0) \cdots h(|\sigma| - 1)}.$$

Then μ^h can be extended to a measure on all of h^ω. When h is fixed, we write simply μ for μ^h.

For a computable function $h : \mathbb{N} \to \mathbb{N} \setminus \{0, 1\}$, let DNC_h be the set of all DNC functions in h^ω. Let DNC_n be the set of all DNC functions in n^ω. Greenberg and Miller's proof uses work of Kumabe and Lewis [225], who built a DNC function of minimal degree. We will not include the fairly long proof of this result here. An analysis of the construction in [225], which can be found in [170], shows that the following holds.

Theorem 13.9.1 (Kumabe and Lewis [225]). *For any computable order $h : \mathbb{N} \to \mathbb{N} \setminus \{0, 1\}$, there is an $f \in \mathrm{DNC}_h$ whose Turing degree is minimal.*

Thus, to show that there is a set of effective Hausdorff dimension 1 and minimal degree, it will be enough to show that there is a computable order $h : \mathbb{N} \to \mathbb{N} \setminus \{0, 1\}$ such that every $f \in \mathrm{DNC}_h$ computes a set of effective Hausdorff dimension 1. We do so in the rest of this section.

13.9.1 Dimension in h-spaces

Greenberg and Miller [170] generalized many notions we have seen in this chapter to h-spaces. The following is the natural generalization of the notions of weak and strong s-Martin-Löf randomness to h^ω.

Definition 13.9.2. Let $s \in [0,1]$.

(i) A *test for weak s-Martin-Löf randomness* is a uniformly c.e. sequence $\{V_k\}_{k\in\omega}$ of subsets of $h^{<\omega}$ such that $\sum_{\sigma\in V_K} \mu(\llbracket\sigma\rrbracket)^s \leqslant 2^{-k}$ for all k.

(ii) A *test for strong s-Martin-Löf randomness* is a uniformly c.e. sequence $\{V_k\}_{k\in\omega}$ of subsets of $h^{<\omega}$ such that for every k and every prefix-free $\widehat{V}_k \subseteq V_k$, we have $\sum_{\sigma\in\widehat{V}_k} \mu(\llbracket\sigma\rrbracket)^s \leqslant 2^{-k}$.

(iii) $A \in h^\omega$ is *weakly s-Martin-Löf random* if $A \notin \bigcap_k \llbracket V_k \rrbracket$ for all tests for weak s-Martin-Löf randomness $\{V_k\}_{k\in\omega}$.

(iv) $A \in h^\omega$ is *strongly s-Martin-Löf random* if $A \notin \bigcap_k \llbracket V_k \rrbracket$ for all tests for strong s-Martin-Löf randomness $\{V_k\}_{k\in\omega}$.

Many results proved in Section 13.5 still hold for h^ω, such as Theorem 13.5.13, which says that if $t < s$ and A is weakly s-random, then A is strongly t-random. Thus, for $A \in h^\omega$, the supremum of all s for which A is weakly s-random equals the supremum of all s for which A is strongly s-random, and, by analogy with the 2^ω case, can be called the *effective (Hausdorff) dimension of A*, denoted by $\dim^h(A)$.

We can also generalize the notion of a Solovay s-test.

Definition 13.9.3. Let $s \in [0,1]$. A *Solovay s-test* is a c.e. set $S \subseteq h^{<\omega}$ such that $\sum_{\sigma\in S} \mu(\llbracket\sigma\rrbracket)^s < \infty$. A set A is *covered* by this test if $A \in \llbracket\sigma\rrbracket$ for infinitely many $\sigma \in S$.

Theorem 13.5.7 still holds: If A is weakly s-random then A is not covered by any Solovay s-test. If A is covered by some Solovay s-test then A is not weakly t-random for any $t > s$.

We can also define martingales for h-spaces.

Definition 13.9.4. A *supermartingale* (for h) is a function $d : h^{<\omega} \to \mathbb{R}^{\geqslant 0}$ such that for all $\sigma \in h^{<\omega}$,

$$\sum_{i<h(|\sigma|)} d(\sigma i) \leqslant h(|\sigma|)d(\sigma).^{8}$$

If $s \in [0,1]$, we say that a supermartingale d *s-succeeds* on $A \in h^\omega$ if $\limsup_n d(A \upharpoonright n)\mu(\llbracket A \upharpoonright n\rrbracket)^{1-s} = \infty$.

[8]Note that this condition is equivalent to $\sum d(\tau)\mu(\llbracket\tau\rrbracket) \leqslant d(\sigma)\mu(\llbracket\sigma\rrbracket)$, where the sum is taken over all immediate successors τ of σ.

As in the 2^ω case, $A \in h^\omega$ is strongly s-Martin-Löf random iff there is no c.e. supermartingale that s-succeeds on A. The proofs are as before, using in particular the fact that Kolmogorov's Inequality holds in h^ω: For a supermartingale d and a prefix-free set $C \subset h^{<\omega}$, we have $\sum_{\sigma \in C} d(\sigma)\mu(\sigma) \leqslant d(\lambda)$. The easiest way to see that this is the case is to think of $d(\sigma)\mu(\sigma)$ as inducing a semimeasure on h^ω.

It is also worth noting that there is an optimal c.e. supermartingale for h, constructed as usual.

Our goal is to use h-spaces to construct an element of 2^ω of minimal degree with effective dimension 1. To do so, we will need to be able to translate between h^ω and 2^ω in a dimension-preserving way. If h is very well-behaved then there is no problem. For example, if $X \in 4^\omega$ and we let $Y(2n) = \lfloor \frac{X(n)}{2} \rfloor$ and $Y(2n+1) = X(n) \bmod 2$, then $Y \equiv_{\mathrm{T}} X$, and it is easy to check that $\dim(Y) = \dim^h(X)$. To handle more complicated h-spaces, it is convenient to work through Euclidean space rather than going directly from h^ω to 2^ω.

There is a natural measure-preserving surjection of h^ω onto the Euclidean interval $[0,1]$. First map strings to closed intervals: Let $\pi^h(\lambda) = [0,1]$. Once $\pi^h(\sigma) = I$ is defined, divide I into $h(|\sigma|)$ many intervals $I_0, I_1, \ldots, I_{h(|\sigma|)-1}$ of equal length and let $\pi^h(\sigma k) = I_k$ for $k < h(|\sigma|)$. Note that indeed $\mu^h(\sigma) = \mu(\pi^h(\sigma))$ for all σ. Now extend π^h continuously to h^ω by letting $\pi^h(X)$ be the unique element of $\bigcap_n \pi^h(X \restriction n)$. (The fact that $h(n) \geqslant 2$ for all n ensures that this intersection is indeed a singleton.) The mapping π^h is not quite 1-1, but it is 1-1 if we ignore the (countably many) sequences that are eventually constant. Note that for all $X \in h^\omega$, we have $X \equiv_{\mathrm{T}} \pi^h(X)$.

The theory of effective dimension can also be developed in the space $[0,1]$. We do not have martingales, but we can still, for example, define Solovay tests, as we saw in Definition 13.5.8. Let $\dim^{[0,1]}(X)$ be the infimum of all s such that there is an interval Solovay s-test that covers X (that is, such that X is in infinitely many elements of the test).

Proposition 13.9.5 (Greenberg and Miller [170]). *For all h and $X \in h^\omega$, we have* $\dim^{[0,1]}(\pi^h(X)) \leqslant \dim^h(X)$.

Proof. Let $s > \dim^h(X)$ and let S be a Solovay s-test for h that covers X. Since π^h is measure-preserving, the image of S under π^h is an interval Solovay test covering $\pi^h(X)$. □

Equality of these dimensions does not hold in general, but we will see that we do get equality if h does not grow too quickly or irregularly. Suppose that S is an interval Solovay s-test covering some $\pi^h(X)$. We would like to cover X by something like $(\pi^h)^{-1}(S)$. The problem, of course, is that the basic sets (closed intervals with rational endpoints) in $[0,1]$ are finer than the basic sets in h^ω; not every closed interval is in the range of π^h. We thus need to refine S by replacing every $I \in S$ by finitely many intervals in the range of π^h. While we can control the Lebesgue measure of such a collection, if the exponent s is smaller than 1 then the process of replacing large intervals by a collection of smaller ones may increase the s-weighted sum of the lengths of the intervals significantly. We show that if h does not grow too irregularly and we increase the exponent s slightly, then this sum remains finite.

Let $\mathcal{I}_n = \pi^h(h^n)$ and let $\mathcal{I} = \bigcup_n \mathcal{I}_n = \pi^h(h^{<\omega})$. Let $\gamma_n = \frac{1}{|h^n|}$. Then $\mathcal{I}_n$ consists of $|h^n|$ many closed intervals, each of length γ_n.

For a closed interval $I \subseteq [0,1]$, let n_I be the unique n such that $\gamma_n \geqslant |I| > \gamma_{n+1}$. Let k_I be the largest natural number such that $|I| > k\gamma_{n+1}$. Then there is an $\widehat{I} \subseteq \mathcal{I}_{n_I+1}$ of size $k_I + 1$ with $I \subseteq \bigcup \widehat{I}$.

For a set S of closed subintervals of $[0,1]$ with rational endpoints, let $\widehat{S} = \bigcup_{I\in S} \widehat{I}$. Thus $\widehat{S} \subseteq \mathcal{I}$, and if $x = \pi^h(X)$ and x is covered by S then X is covered by $(\pi^h)^{-1}(\widehat{S})$. If S is c.e. then so are $\widehat{S}$ and $(\pi^h)^{-1}(\widehat{S})$. Furthermore, $\sum_{I\in\widehat{S}} |I|^t = \sum_{\sigma\in(\pi^h)^{-1}(\widehat{S})} \mu(\sigma)^t$.

We express the regularity of h via the following condition for h and $t > s \geqslant 0$:

$$\sum_n \frac{h(n)^{1-s}}{(h(0)\cdots h(n))^{t-s}} < \infty. \tag{13.1}$$

Lemma 13.9.6 (Greenberg and Miller [170]). *Suppose that (13.1) holds for t, s, and h, and that S is a set of closed intervals in $[0,1]$ such that $\sum_{I\in S} |I|^s$ is finite. Then $\sum_{I\in\widehat{S}} |I|^t$ is also finite.*

Proof. Let I be any closed interval in $[0,1]$. Let $n = n_I$ and $k = k_I$. Since $\frac{|I|}{\gamma_{n+1}} > k$ and $k \leqslant h(n)$,

$$|I|^t = (k+1)\gamma_{n+1}^t \leqslant 2k\gamma_{n+1}^{t-s}\gamma_{n+1}^s = 2k\frac{\gamma_{n+1}^s}{|I|^s}\gamma_{n+1}^{t-s}|I|^s$$
$$< 2k^{1-s}\gamma_{n+1}^{t-s}|I|^s \leqslant \frac{2h(n)^{1-s}}{(h(0)\dots h(n))^{t-s}}|I|^s.$$

Thus if we let $S_n = \{I \in S : n_I = n\}$, then

$$\sum_{I\in\widehat{S}} |I|^t = \sum_n \sum_{I\in S_n} |I|^t \leqslant \sum_n \sum_{I\in S_n} \frac{2h(n)^{1-s}}{(h(0)\dots h(n))^{t-s}}|I|^s$$
$$\leqslant 2\sum_{I\in S} |I|^s \sum_n \frac{h(n)^{1-s}}{(h(0)\dots h(n))^{t-s}},$$

which by assumption is finite. □

Thus for all $X \in h^\omega$, if (13.1) holds for t, s, and h, and $\dim^{[0,1]}(\pi^h(X)) < s$, then $\dim^h(X) \leqslant t$. So if (13.1) holds for all $t > s \geqslant 0$, then $\dim^{[0,1]}(\pi^h(X)) = \dim^h(X)$ for all $X \in h^\omega$.

For example, (13.1) holds for all $t > s \geqslant 0$ for the constant function $h(n) = 2$. Thus, as discussed above, dimension in $[0,1]$ is the same as dimension in 2^ω. However, this condition holds for some unbounded functions h as well (for example $h(n) = 2^n$).

The following is a sufficient condition for (13.1) to hold for all $t > s \geqslant 0$.

Lemma 13.9.7 (Greenberg and Miller [170]). *If*

$$\lim_n \frac{\log h(n)}{\sum_{m \leqslant n} \log h(m)} = 0$$

then (13.1) holds for all $t > s \geqslant 0$, and so $\dim^h(X) = \dim^{[0,1]}(\pi^h(X))$ for all $X \in h^\omega$.

Proof. Let $f(n) = \log h(n)$. Let $t > s \geqslant 0$ and let $\varepsilon < \frac{t-s}{1-s}$. For sufficiently large n, we have $f(n) < \varepsilon \sum_{m \leqslant n} f(m)$. Let $g(n) = h(0) \cdots h(n)$ and let $\delta = \varepsilon(1-s) - (t-s) < 0$. For sufficiently large n, we have $h(n) < g(n)^\varepsilon$, and hence $\frac{h(n)^{1-s}}{g(n)^{t-s}} < g(n)^\delta$. Thus there is an N such that

$$\sum_{n \geqslant N} \frac{h(n)^{1-s}}{(h(0) \ldots h(n))^{t-s}} < \sum_n g(n)^\delta = \sum_n \left(2^\delta\right)^{\log g(n)},$$

which is finite because $2^\delta < 1$ and $\log g(n) \geqslant n$ (since $h(n) \geqslant 2$). ☐

The regularity condition of Lemma 13.9.7 is not, strictly speaking, a slowness condition, because, for example, $h(n) = 2^{n^2}$ satisfies this condition, yet there is a monotone function that is dominated by h but does not satisfy the condition. However, the condition does hold for all sufficiently slow monotone functions.

Lemma 13.9.8 (Greenberg and Miller [170]). *If h is nondecreasing and dominated by 2^{kn} for some k, then*

$$\lim_n \frac{\log h(n)}{\sum_{m \leqslant n} \log h(m)} = 0,$$

and so $\dim^h(X) = \dim^{[0,1]}(\pi^h(X))$ for all $X \in h^\omega$.

Proof. If h is bounded then it is eventually constant, and the condition is easily verified, so assume that h is unbounded. Fix $c > 0$. There is an N_c such that $\log h(n) > c$ for all $n \geqslant N_c$. For $n > N_c$,

$$\frac{\log h(n)}{\sum_{m \leqslant n} \log h(m)} \leqslant \frac{kn}{\sum_{N_c}^{n} \log h(m)} \leqslant \frac{kn}{c(n - N_c)}.$$

Since $\lim_n \frac{kn}{c(n-N_c)} = \frac{k}{c}$,

$$\lim_n \frac{\log h(n)}{\sum_{m \leqslant n} \log h(m)} \leqslant \frac{k}{c}.$$

Since c is arbitrary, this limit is 0. ☐

Finally, we get the result we will need to translate between h^ω and 2^ω.

Corollary 13.9.9 (Greenberg and Miller [170]). *If h is nondecreasing and dominated by 2^{kn} for some k, then every $X \in h^\omega$ computes a $Y \in 2^\omega$ such that* $\dim^h(X) = \dim(Y)$.

13.9.2 Slow-growing DNC functions and sets of high effective dimension

For natural numbers $a > b > 0$, let Q_a^b be the collection of functions f such that for all n,

1. $f(n) \subseteq \{0, \dots, a-1\}$,
2. $|f(n)| = b$, and
3. if $\Phi_n(n)\downarrow$ then $\Phi_n(n) \notin f(n)$.

By standard coding, Q_a^b can be seen as a computably bounded Π_1^0 subclass of ω^ω. Note that Q_a^1 is essentially the same as DNC_a.

To connect these sets for different values of a and b, we will use the concept of strong reducibility of mass problems from Definition 8.9.1. Recall that $P \subseteq \omega^\omega$ is strongly reducible to $R \subseteq \omega^\omega$ if there is a Turing functional Ψ such that $\Psi^f \in P$ for all $f \in R$. If P is a Π_1^0 class, then we may assume that the Ψ in the above definition is total, and hence the reduction is a truth table reduction, since we can always define $\Psi^X(n) = 0$ if there is an s such that $X \notin P[s]$ and $\Psi^X(n)[s]\uparrow$.

Lemma 13.9.10 (Greenberg and Miller [170]). *If $a > b > 0$ then $Q_{a+1}^{b+1} \leqslant_s Q_a^b$, uniformly in a and b. (Uniformity here means that an index for the reduction functional Ψ can be obtained effectively from a and b.)*

Proof. From n and $y < a$ we can compute an $m_{n,y}$ such that

1. for all $x < a$ such that $x \neq y$, we have $\Phi_{m_{n,y}}(m_{n,y})\downarrow= x$ iff $\Phi_n(n)\downarrow= x$; and
2. $\Phi_{m_{n,y}}(m_{n,y})\downarrow= y$ iff either $\Phi_n(n)\downarrow= y$ or $\Phi_n(n)\downarrow= a$.

Let $f \in Q_a^b$. Let $\widehat{f}(n) = \bigcup_{y<a} f(m_{n,y})$. Fix n. For all $y < a$, if $\Phi_n(n)\downarrow$ then $\Phi_n(n) \notin f(m_{n,y})$, so $\Phi_n(n) \notin \widehat{f}(n)$. Furthermore, if there is some $y < a$ such that $y \in f(m_{n,y})$, then $\Phi_n(n) \neq a$, so $\Phi_n(n) \notin \widehat{f}(n) \cup \{a\}$. Finally, if $|\widehat{f}(n)| = b$ then $f(m_{n,y})$ is in fact constant for all $y < a$, so that $y \in f(m_{n,y})$ for all $y \in \widehat{f}(n)$. Thus we can define Ψ as follows:

$$\Psi^f(n) = \begin{cases} \text{some subset of } \widehat{f}(n) \text{ of size } b+1 & \text{if } |\widehat{f}(n)| > b \\ \widehat{f}(n) \cup \{a\} & \text{if } |\widehat{f}(n)| = b. \end{cases}$$

□

Corollary 13.9.11 (Greenberg and Miller [170]). *If $a \geqslant 2$ then $Q^{b+1}_{a+b} \leqslant_s \mathrm{DNC}_a$, uniformly in a and b.*

For $a \geqslant 2$ and $c > 0$, let P^c_a be the collection of functions $f \in a^\omega$ such that for all n and all $x < c$, if $\Phi_{\langle n,x\rangle}(\langle n,x\rangle)\downarrow$ then $\Phi_{\langle n,x\rangle}(\langle n,x\rangle) \neq f(n)$. Note that $P^1_a \equiv_s \mathrm{DNC}_a$.

Lemma 13.9.12 (Greenberg and Miller [170]). *For all $a > b > 0$ and $c > 0$, if $c(a-b) < a$ then $P^c_a \leqslant_s Q^b_a$, uniformly in a, b, and c.*

Proof. Fix $f \in Q^b_a$ and n. For all $x < c$, if $\Phi_{\langle n,x\rangle}(\langle n,x\rangle)\downarrow$ then

$$\Phi_{\langle n,x\rangle}(\langle n,x\rangle) \in [0,a) \setminus \bigcup_{y<c} f(\langle n,y\rangle).$$

The set on the right has size at most $c(a-b)$, so if $c(a-b) < a$ then we can choose some $x < a$ not in that set and define $\Psi^f(n) = x$. ☐

Corollary 13.9.13 (Greenberg and Miller [170]). *If $a \geqslant 2$ and $c > 0$ then $P^c_{ca} \leqslant_s \mathrm{DNC}_a$, uniformly in a and c.*

Proof. Let $b = c(a-1) - a + 1$. Then $Q^{b+1}_{a+b} \leqslant_s \mathrm{DNC}_a$ and

$$c((a+b) - (b+1)) = c(a-1) < a+b,$$

so $P^c_{c(a-1)+1} = P^c_{a+b} \leqslant_s Q^{b+1}_{a+b}$. Since $c > 0$, we have $c(a-1)+1 \leqslant ca$, so $P^c_{c(a-1)+1} \subseteq P^c_{ca}$, and hence $P^c_{ca} \leqslant_s P^c_{c(a-1)+1}$. All these reductions are uniform. ☐

Greenberg and Miller [170] used the classes P^c_{ca} to construct sequences of positive effective dimension.

Theorem 13.9.14 (Greenberg and Miller [170]). *Let $a \geqslant 2$ and $\varepsilon > 0$. Every $f \in \mathrm{DNC}_a$ computes a set of effective Hausdorff dimension greater than $1 - \varepsilon$, via a reduction that is uniform in a and ε.*[9]

Proof. Fix $c > 1$. We work in the space $(ca)^\omega$. Let d be the universal c.e. supermartingale for this space. By scaling we may assume that $d(\lambda) < 1$.

For $\sigma \in (ca)^{<\omega}$, let S_σ be the set of $k < c$ such that $d(\sigma k) \geqslant a^{|\sigma|+1}$. Note that these sets are uniformly c.e. From σ, we can compute an m_σ such that for each $x < c$, we have $\Phi_{\langle m_\sigma,x\rangle}(\langle m_\sigma,x\rangle)\downarrow = k$ if k is the xth element to be enumerated into S_σ, and $\Phi_{\langle m_\sigma,x\rangle}(\langle m_\sigma,x\rangle)\uparrow$ if $|S_\sigma| < x$.

The idea here is that if $d(\sigma) \leqslant a^{|\sigma|}$ then $|S_\sigma| \leqslant c$, by the supermartingale condition, so all elements of S_σ are "captured" by the map $e \mapsto \Phi_e(e)$. We can thus use a function $g \in P^c_{ca}$ to avoid all such extensions: given such g, inductively define $X \in (ca)^{<\omega}$ by letting the $(n+1)$st digit of X be $g(m_{X\restriction n})$. Then, by induction, $d(X \restriction n) \leqslant a^n$ for all n.

---

[9]That each $f \in \mathrm{DNC}_a$ computes such a set is of course not a new fact, since the Turing degree of a bounded DNC function is PA and so computes a 1-random set. The extra information is the uniformity.

Now let $s \geqslant 0$ and suppose that d s-succeeds on X, that is, that $d(X \upharpoonright n)\mu^{ca}(X \upharpoonright n)^{1-s}$ is unbounded. Since $\mu^{ca}(X \upharpoonright n) = (ca)^{-n}$,

$$d(X \upharpoonright n)\mu^{ca}(X \upharpoonright n)^{1-s} \leqslant a^n (ca)^{-n(1-s)} = \left(c^{s-1}a^s\right)^n.$$

Thus, if d s-succeeds on X then $c^{s-1}a^s > 1$, so $a^s > c^{1-s}$. Taking the logarithm of both sides, we have $\frac{s}{\log_a c} > 1 - s$, so $s > 1 - \frac{1}{1+\log_a c}$. Thus $\dim^{ca}(X) \geqslant 1 - \frac{1}{1+\log_a c}$. Since $\lim_c \log_a c = \infty$, given ε we can find some c and X such that $\dim^{ca}(X) > 1 - \varepsilon$. By Corollary 13.9.9, X computes a $Y \in 2^\omega$ such that $\dim Y > 1 - \varepsilon$. □

Theorem 13.9.15 (Greenberg and Miller [170]). *Let $a \geqslant 2$. Every $f \in \mathrm{DNC}_a$ computes a set of effective Hausdorff dimension 1, via a reduction that is uniform in a.*

Proof. We combine the constructions of sets of effective dimensions closer and closer to 1 into one construction. Let $h(n) = (n+1)a$. Let d be the universal c.e. supermartingale for h^ω. Given $f \in \mathrm{DNC}_a$, obtain $g_n \in P^n_{na}$ for all $n > 0$ uniformly from f.

For $\sigma \in h^n$, let S_σ be the set of $k \leqslant n$ such that $d(\sigma k) \geqslant a^{|\sigma|+1}$ and compute an m_σ such that for each $x \leqslant n$, we have $\Phi_{\langle m_\sigma, x\rangle}(\langle m_\sigma, x\rangle)\downarrow = k$ if k is the xth element to be enumerated into S_σ, and $\Phi_{\langle m_\sigma, x\rangle}(\langle m_\sigma, x\rangle)\uparrow$ if $|S_\sigma| < x$. As in the previous proof, we can define $X(n) = g_{n+1}(m_{X\upharpoonright n})$ and inductively prove that $d(X \upharpoonright n) \leqslant a^n$ for all n.

Now, $\mu^h(X \upharpoonright n) = \frac{a^{-n}}{n!}$, so for $s \geqslant 0$,

$$d(X \upharpoonright n)\mu^h(X \upharpoonright n)^{1-s} \leqslant \frac{a^{sn}}{(n!)^{1-s}}.$$

Let $s < 1$. Let k be such that $k^{s-1}a^{2s-1} < 1$. For almost all n we have $n! > (ka)^n$, so for almost all n we have

$$\frac{a^{sn}}{(n!)^{1-s}} \leqslant \frac{a^{sn}}{(ka)^{n(1-s)}} = (k^{s-1}a^{2s-1})^n < 1,$$

and hence d cannot s-succeed on X. Thus $\dim^h(X) = 1$, so by Corollary 13.9.9, X computes a $Y \in 2^\omega$ of effective dimension 1. □

Finally, we can paste together these constructions for all $a \geqslant 2$ to get the desired result.

Theorem 13.9.16 (Greenberg and Miller [170]). *There is a computable order $\tilde{h} : \mathbb{N} \to \mathbb{N} \setminus \{0, 1\}$ such that every $f \in \mathrm{DNC}_{\tilde{h}}$ computes a set of effective Hausdorff dimension 1.*

Proof. Let $h(n) = (n+1)2^n$, and let d be the universal c.e. supermartingale for h. For $\sigma \in h^n$, let S_σ be the set of $k < 2^n$ such that $d(\sigma k) \geqslant (n+1)!$ and compute an m_σ such that for each $x < 2^n$, we have $\Phi_{\langle m_\sigma, x\rangle}(\langle m_\sigma, x\rangle)\downarrow = k$ if k is the xth element to be enumerated into S_σ, and $\Phi_{\langle m_\sigma, x\rangle}(\langle m_\sigma, x\rangle)\uparrow$ if $|S_\sigma| < x$.

For $n > 0$, we have $P^{2^n}_{h(n)} \leqslant \mathrm{DNC}_{n+1}$ uniformly in n, so there is an effective list of truth table functionals Ψ_n such that $\Psi^f_n \in P^{2^n}_{h(n)}$ for all $f \in \mathrm{DNC}_{n+1}$. Let ψ_n be a computable bound on the use function of Ψ_n. Let

$$m^*_n = 1 + \sup\{\langle m_\sigma, x\rangle : \sigma \in h^n \wedge x < 2^n\}$$

and let $u_n = \psi_n(m^*_n)$. Let $u_0 = 0$.

For all $n > 0$, if ρ is a sequence of length u_n that is a DNC_{n+1}-string (that is, $\rho \in (n+1)^{u_n}$ and for all $y < u_n$ such that $\Phi_y(y)\downarrow$, we have $\Phi_y(y) \neq \rho(y)$; or equivalently, ρ is an initial segment of a sequence in DNC_{n+1}) then $\Psi_n(\rho)$ is a $P^{2^n}_{h(n)}$-string (an initial segment of a sequence in $P^{2^n}_{h(n)}$) of length at least m^*_n. By increasing ψ_n we may assume that $u_n < u_{n+1}$ for all $n > 0$. Let $\tilde{h}(k) = n + 1$ for $k \in [u_{n-1}, u_n)$.

If $f \in \mathrm{DNC}_{\tilde{h}}$ then $f \upharpoonright u_n$ is a DNC_{n+1}-string for all $n > 0$, so combining the reductions Ψ_n, we can define a $g \leqslant_\mathrm{T} f$ such that for all n and all $\sigma \in h^n$,

1. $g(m_\sigma) < h(|\sigma|)$ and
2. for all $x < 2^n$, if $\Phi_{\langle m_\sigma, x\rangle}(\langle m_\sigma, x\rangle)\downarrow$ then $g(m_\sigma) \neq \Phi_{\langle m_\sigma, x\rangle}(\langle m_\sigma, x\rangle)$.

We can now use g to define $X \in h^\omega$ as in the last two constructions, by letting $X(n) = g(m_{X\upharpoonright n})$. By induction on n, we can show that $d(X \upharpoonright n) \leqslant n!$. As before, we can do so because if $\sigma \in h^n$ and $d(\sigma) \leqslant n!$, then there are at most 2^n many immediate successors τ of σ such that $d(\tau) \geqslant (n+1)!$, and so they are all captured by the function $e \mapsto \Phi_e(e)$ and avoided by g.

Finally, we show that $\dim^h(X) = 1$, which by Corollary 13.9.9 implies that X computes a $Y \in 2^\omega$ of effective dimension 1.

Let $s < 1$. For any $\sigma \in h^n$,

$$\mu^h(\sigma) = \frac{1}{2^0 2^1 \cdots 2^{(n-1)} n!} = \frac{1}{2^{\binom{n}{2}} n!}.$$

Thus for all n,

$$d(X \upharpoonright n)\mu^h(X \upharpoonright n)^{1-s} \leqslant \frac{(n!)^s}{2^{(1-s)\binom{n}{2}}} \leqslant \frac{(n!)}{2^{(1-s)\binom{n}{2}}},$$

which is bounded (and indeed tends to 0). Thus d does not s-succeed on X. □

Thus, by Theorem 13.9.1, we have the following.

Theorem 13.9.17 (Greenberg and Miller [170]). *There is a minimal degree of effective Hausdorff dimension* 1.

13.10 C-independence and Zimand's Theorem

By Miller's Theorem 13.8.1, we cannot always extract a sequence of arbitrarily high effective Hausdorff dimension from one of nonzero effective Hausdorff dimension. In this section we prove Zimand's theorem that such extraction *is* possible from *two* sufficiently independent sources of positive effective Hausdorff dimension.

We begin by briefly discussing the notion of independence of sources. This notion dates back at least to Chaitin [62], who suggested that objects x and y should be independent in terms of their information if $I(x)-I(x \mid y)$ and $I(y) - I(y \mid x)$ are small, where I is some kind of information content measure in the wide sense, such as C or K. For 1-random sets A and B, we could regard A and B as being independent iff they are mutually 1-random.

But what about nonrandom sets? For example, suppose that A and B have positive effective Hausdorff dimension but are not 1-random. What would it mean to say that A and B are independent? The theory here is largely undeveloped, but the following notions of independence are useful for our purposes. In this section, we will regard log factors as being small. We will say a little more about this convention below.[10]

Definition 13.10.1 (Zimand [424], Calude and Zimand [53]).

(i) X and Y are *C-independent*[11] if

$$C((X \upharpoonright m)^\frown(Y \upharpoonright n)) \geqslant C(X \upharpoonright m) + C(Y \upharpoonright n) - O(\log m + \log n).$$

(ii) X and Y are *globally independent* if

$$C^X(Y \upharpoonright n) \geqslant C(Y \upharpoonright n) - O(\log n)$$

and

$$C^Y(X \upharpoonright n) \geqslant C(X \upharpoonright n) - O(\log n).$$

Since C and K are within an $O(\log)$ factor of each other, both definitions remain the same if we replace C by K. Note also that $C((X \upharpoonright m)^\frown(Y \upharpoonright n))$ and $C((Y \upharpoonright n)^\frown(X \upharpoonright m))$ are the same up to an $O(\log m + \log n)$ factor, so the first definition does not depend on the order of X and Y.

As pointed out by Calude and Zimand [53], other notions of smallness are possible. For example, in (i) we could have $O(C(m)+C(n))$ in place of $O(\log m + \log n)$, in which case the definition might be different for C and

[10] In general, working up to $O(\log n)$ instead of $O(1)$ smooths out many issues, eliding the difference between various versions of Kolmogorov complexity, for example. The price one pays is losing the many important phenomena hiding in those log factors, such as K-triviality, the unrelativized complexity characterizations of 2-randomness, and so on.

[11] Calude and Zimand [53] called this notion *finitarily independent*. We choose what we feel is a more descriptive name.

for K. These modified concepts remain to be explored. We will stick to log factors, as they give enough independence for the results of this section.

Clearly, if X and Y are mutually 1-random, then they are globally independent, so global independence can be seen as an extension of the notion of mutual randomness. If X is K-trivial, then X and Y are globally independent for all Y, since $K(X \upharpoonright n) \leqslant O(\log n)$ and X is low for K, so $K^X(Y \upharpoonright n) = K(Y \upharpoonright n) \pm O(1)$. Using Lemma 13.10.2 (ii) below, this observation can be extended to show that if $C(X \upharpoonright m) \leqslant O(\log m)$, as is the case for an n-c.e. set, for instance, then X and Y are globally independent for all Y.

The following result is an easy application of symmetry of information (see Section 3.3).

Lemma 13.10.2 (Zimand [424], Calude and Zimand [53]). *The following are equivalent.*

(i) *X and Y are C-independent.*

(ii) $C(X \upharpoonright m \mid Y \upharpoonright n) \geqslant C(X \upharpoonright m) - O(\log m + \log n)$.

(iii) $C((X \upharpoonright n)^\frown(Y \upharpoonright n)) \geqslant C(X \upharpoonright n) + C(Y \upharpoonright n) - O(\log n)$.

(iv) $C(X \upharpoonright n \mid Y \upharpoonright n) \geqslant C(X \upharpoonright n) - O(\log n)$.

The same holds for K in place of C.

Theorem 13.10.3 (Calude and Zimand [53]). *If X and Y are globally independent, then X and Y are C-independent.*

Proof. If we have Y as an oracle, we can describe $X \upharpoonright n$ by giving n and a description of $X \upharpoonright n$ from $Y \upharpoonright n$, so $C^Y(X \upharpoonright n) \leqslant C(X \upharpoonright n \mid Y \upharpoonright n) + O(\log n)$. So if X and Y are globally independent, then $C(X \upharpoonright n \mid Y \upharpoonright n) \geqslant C^Y(X \upharpoonright n) - O(\log n) \geqslant C(X \upharpoonright n) - O(\log n)$, and hence item (iv) of Lemma 13.10.2 holds □

Stephan (see [53]) showed that the converse fails: there are C-independent X and Y that are not globally independent. He also showed the following.

Theorem 13.10.4 (Stephan, see [53]). *If X and Y are left-c.e. reals of positive effective Hausdorff dimension, then X and Y are not C-independent.*

Proof. Without loss of generality, there are infinitely many n such that, for the least s for which $Y_s \upharpoonright n = Y \upharpoonright n$, we also have $X_s \upharpoonright n = X \upharpoonright n$. For all such n, we have $C(X \upharpoonright n \mid Y \upharpoonright n) = O(1)$. But then, since $\dim(X) > 0$, item (iv) of Lemma 13.10.2 cannot hold. □

Theorem 13.10.5 (Calude and Zimand [53]). *If Y is 1-random relative to X, then X and Y are C-independent.*

Proof. By the same argument as in the proof of Theorem 13.10.3, $K^X(Y \upharpoonright n) \leqslant K(Y \upharpoonright n \mid X \upharpoonright n) + 2\log n + O(1)$. If X and Y are not C-independent then there are infinitely many n with $K(Y \upharpoonright n \mid X \upharpoonright n) < K(Y \upharpoonright n) - 5\log n < n - 3\log n$. For such n, we have $K^X(Y \upharpoonright n) \leqslant n - \log n + O(1)$, contradicting the fact that Y is 1-random relative to X. □

We now turn to the task of amplifying the complexity of two C-independent sources.

Theorem 13.10.6 (Zimand [424]). *For any rational $q > 0$, there is a truth table reduction Ψ such that if X and Y are C-independent and have effective Hausdorff dimension greater than q, then* $\dim(\Psi^{X \oplus Y}) = 1$. *Moreover, an index for Ψ can be determined computably from q.*

The idea of the proof will be to chop X and Y into suitable bits and reassemble them. A technical combinatorial lemma (Lemma 13.10.14) will be at the heart of the proof. It will use a well-known tool from probability theory, Chernoff bounds, which can be found in any standard probability textbook, such as Feller [144].

We give a brief introduction to the main ideas of the proof, following Zimand [424]. Suppose that we have two independent strings σ and τ of length n with $C(\sigma)$ and $C(\tau)$ both equal to qn for a positive rational q. (The independence here means that $C(\sigma\tau)$ is approximately $C(\sigma)+C(\tau) = 2qn$.) Suppose further that we can construct a function $E : 2^n \times 2^n \to 2^m$ for some suitable m, such that E is *regular*, in the sense that for each sufficiently large rectangle $B_1 \times B_2 \subseteq 2^n \times 2^n$, the function E maps about the same number of pairs in $B_1 \times B_2$ to each $\tau \in 2^m$. Then for a sufficiently large $B \times B \subseteq 2^{qn} \times 2^{qn}$, any $\tau \in 2^m$ has about $\frac{|B \times B|}{2^m}$ many preimages, and any $A \subseteq 2^m$ has about $\frac{|B \times B|}{2^m}|A|$ many preimages.

We claim that if $\rho = E(\sigma, \tau)$ then the C-complexity of ρ must be large. Assume for a contradiction that $C(\rho) < (1-\varepsilon)m$ for a fairly large ε. We have the following facts.

(i) The set $B = \{\sigma \in 2^n : C(\sigma) = qn\}$ has size approximately 2^{qn}.

(ii) The set $A = \{\tau \in 2^m : C(\tau) < (1-\varepsilon)m\}$ has size less than $2^{(1-\varepsilon)m}$.

(iii) $(\sigma, \tau) \in E^{-1}(A) \cap B \times B$.

Thus $|E^{-1}(A) \cap B \times B| \leqslant \frac{(2^{qn})^2}{2^{\varepsilon m}}$, approximately. If we effectively enumerate $E^{-1}(A) \cap B \times B$, then each pair of strings in that set can be described by its position in that enumeration, so $C(\sigma, \tau) \leqslant 2qn - \varepsilon m$, approximately, which violates the independence hypothesis on σ and τ.

Now the above argument is not quite true, as a function E with the necessary properties may not exist, but in Lemma 13.10.14 we will construct a function that makes the above argument "true enough" to prove the theorem.

Proof of Theorem 13.10.6. Note that, by hypothesis, $C(X \upharpoonright n) > qn$ and $C(Y \upharpoonright n) > qn$ for all sufficiently large n.

Lemma 13.10.7. *Let r be a rational such that $0 < r < q$. For any sufficiently large n_0, we can compute an $n_1 > n_0$ such that*

$$C(X \upharpoonright (n_0, n_1) \mid X \upharpoonright n_0) > r(n_1 - n_0).$$

Proof. Let $0 < r' < q - r$ and let $n_1 = \lceil \frac{1-r}{r'} \rceil n_0$. Suppose that $C(X \upharpoonright (n_0, n_1) \mid X \upharpoonright n_0) \leqslant r(n_1 - n_0)$. The string $X \upharpoonright n_1$ can be described by giving a description of $X \upharpoonright n_0$ and a description of $X \upharpoonright (n_0, n_1)$ given $X \upharpoonright n_0$. Thus, for sufficiently large n_0, we have

$$\begin{aligned} C(X \upharpoonright n_1) &\leqslant n_0 + O(\log n_0) + r(n_1 - n_0) \\ &\leqslant rn_1 + (1-r)n_0 + O(\log n_0) \leqslant rn_1 + r'n_1 + O(\log n_0) < qn_1. \end{aligned}$$

□

We use Lemma 13.10.7 to split up X and Y into blocks $X_1X_2\ldots$ and $Y_1Y_2\ldots$, respectively. Each X_i is chosen based on the conditional complexity given the previous blocks, and similarly for the Y_i.

Let a be a number such that Lemma 13.10.7 holds for all $n_0 \geqslant a$. Let b be the constant $\lceil \frac{1-r}{r'} \rceil$ in the proof of Lemma 13.10.7. Let $t_0 = 0$, let $t_i = a$, and let $t_{i+1} = b(t_0 + \cdots + t_i)$ for $i > 0$. For $i \geqslant 1$, let $X_i = X \upharpoonright [t_{i-1}, t_i)$ and $Y_i = Y \upharpoonright [t_{i-1}, t_i)$. Let $\vec{X}_i = X_1 \ldots X_i$ and $\vec{Y}_i = Y_1 \ldots Y_i$. Note that $t_i = ab(1+b)^{i-2}$ for $i \geqslant 2$ and $|X_i| = |Y_i| = ab^2(1+b)^{i-3}$ for $i \geqslant 3$.

The following lemma follows immediately from the definitions and Lemma 13.10.7.

Lemma 13.10.8. *The following hold for all i.*

(i) $C(X_i \mid \vec{X}_{i-1}) > r|X_i|$.

(ii) $\log |X_i| \sim i$ *and* $\log |\vec{X}_i| \sim i$.

The same holds for the Y_i.

The following inequalities follow easily by symmetry of information.

Lemma 13.10.9. *For all σ and τ,*

(i) $C(\sigma\tau) \leqslant C(\sigma) + C(\tau) + O(\log C(\sigma) + \log C(\tau))$,

(ii) $C(\tau\sigma) \geqslant C(\sigma) + C(\tau \mid \sigma) - O(\log C(\sigma) + \log C(\tau))$, *and*

(iii) $|C(\sigma \mid \tau) - (C(\sigma\tau) - C(\tau))| < O(\log |\sigma| + \log |\tau|)$.

Now we assemble some facts about the X_i and Y_i.

Lemma 13.10.10. *For all i and j,*

(i) $|C(\vec{Y}_i\vec{X}_j) - (C(\vec{Y}_i) + C(\vec{X}_j))| \leqslant O(i + j)$,

(ii) $|C(\vec{X}_i\vec{Y}_j) - (C(\vec{X}_i) + C(\vec{Y}_j))| \leqslant O(i+j)$,

(iii) $|C(X_i \mid \vec{X}_{i-1}\vec{Y}_j) - C(X_i \mid \vec{X}_{i-1})| \leqslant O(i+j)$, *and*

(iv) $|C(Y_i \mid \vec{X}_j\vec{Y}_{i-1}) - C(Y_i \mid \vec{Y}_{i-1}))| \leqslant O(i+j)$.

Proof. By Lemmas 13.10.9 and 13.10.8,

$$C(\vec{Y}_i\vec{X}_j) \leqslant C(\vec{Y}_i) + C(\vec{X}_j) + O(\log C(\vec{Y}_i) + \log C(\vec{X}_j)) \leqslant C(\vec{Y}_i) + C(\vec{X}_j) + O(i+j)$$

and

$$C(\vec{Y}_i\vec{X}_j) \geqslant C(\vec{Y}_i) + C(\vec{X}_j) - O(\log C(\vec{Y}_i) + \log C(\vec{X}_j)) \geqslant C(\vec{Y}_i) + C(\vec{X}_j) - O(i+j).$$

Putting these two inequalities together gives (i), and (ii) is similar.

Now for (iii), by Lemma 13.10.9 (iii),

$$|C(X_i \mid \vec{X}_{i-1}\vec{Y}_j) - (C(X_i\vec{X}_{i-1}\vec{Y}_j) - (C(\vec{X}_{i-1}\vec{Y}_j)))| \leqslant O(i+j).$$

Now, $C(X_i\vec{X}_{i-1}\vec{Y}_j) = C(\vec{X}_{i-1}X_i\vec{Y}_j) \pm O(i)$, and hence

$$|C(X_i \mid \vec{X}_{i-1}\vec{Y}_j) - (C(\vec{X}_i\vec{Y}_j) - (C(\vec{X}_{i-1}\vec{Y}_j)))| \leqslant O(i+j). \tag{13.2}$$

By Lemma 13.10.10 (i) and (ii), $|C(\vec{X}_i\vec{Y}_j) - (C(\vec{X}_i) + C(\vec{Y}_j))| \leqslant O(i+j)$ and $|C(\vec{X}_{i-1}\vec{Y}_j) - (C(\vec{X}_{i-1}) + C(\vec{Y}_j))| \leqslant O(i+j)$. Combining these facts with (13.2), we have

$$|C(X_i \mid \vec{X}_{i-1}\vec{Y}_j) - (C(\vec{X}_i) - C(\vec{X}_{i-1}))| \leqslant O(i+j). \tag{13.3}$$

By Lemma 13.10.9 (iii), $|C(X_i \mid \vec{X}_{i-1}) - (C(X_i\vec{X}_{i-1}) - C(\vec{X}_{i-1}))| \leqslant O(i+j)$. Thus, since $|C(X_i\vec{X}_{i-1}) - C(\vec{X}_{i-1}X_i)| \leqslant O(1)$, we have

$$|C(X_i \mid \vec{X}_{i-1}) - (C(\vec{X}_i) - C(\vec{X}_{i-1}))| \leqslant O(i+j),$$

and the result now follows by combining this inequality with (13.3). The argument for (iv) is analogous. □

The final preparatory lemma is the following.

Lemma 13.10.11. *For all* i,

$$C(X_iY_i \mid \vec{X}_{i-1}\vec{Y}_{i-1}) \geqslant C(X_i \mid \vec{X}_{i-1}\vec{Y}_{i-1}) + C(Y_i \mid \vec{X}_{i-1}\vec{Y}_{i-1}) - O(i).$$

Proof. Since $C(X_i) \leqslant |X_i| + O(1)$ and similarly for Y_i, if we apply Lemma 13.10.9 (ii) in conditional form, we get

$$C(X_iY_i \mid \vec{X}_{i-1}\vec{Y}_{i-1}) \geqslant C(X_i \mid \vec{X}_{i-1}\vec{Y}_{i-1}) + C(Y_i \mid X_i\vec{X}_{i-1}\vec{Y}_{i-1}) - O(i).$$

Since $C(Y_i \mid X_i\vec{X}_{i-1}\vec{Y}_{i-1}) = C(Y_i \mid \vec{X}_i\vec{Y}_{i-1}) \pm O(1)$, we have

$$C(X_iY_i \mid \vec{X}_{i-1}\vec{Y}_{i-1}) \geqslant C(X_i \mid \vec{X}_{i-1}\vec{Y}_{i-1}) + C(Y_i \mid \vec{X}_i\vec{Y}_{i-1}) - O(i).$$

But $C(Y_i \mid \vec{X}_i\vec{Y}_{i-1}) \geqslant C(Y_i \mid \vec{Y}_{i-1}) - O(i) \geqslant C(Y_i \mid \vec{X}_{i-1}\vec{Y}_{i-1}) - O(i)$, by Lemma 13.10.10 (iv). □

We now come to the combinatorial heart of the proof. Let $n_i = |X_i| = |Y_i|$. We will define a sequence of uniformly computable functions E_i and numbers m_i, with $E_i : 2^{n_i} \times 2^{n_i} \to 2^{m_i}$. We will then let $Z_i = E(X_i, Y_i)$. The pair (E_i, m_i) will be chosen so that $C(Z_i \mid \vec{X}_{i-1}\vec{Y}_{i-1}) > (1-\varepsilon)m_i$, which will imply that $C(Z_i \mid \vec{Z}_{i-1})$ is also close to m_i. We will then be able to show that if we define $Z = Z_1 Z_2 \ldots$, then $C(Z \upharpoonright k)$ is sufficiently close to k for all k.

The exact method of choosing E_i and m_i comes from the theory of randomness extractors and hashing. The proof below uses what is known as the probabilistic method.

Definition 13.10.12. A function $E : 2^n \times 2^n \to 2^m$ is *r-regular* if for every $B_1, B_2 \subseteq 2^n$ with $|B_i| \geqslant rn$ for $i = 1, 2$ and every $\sigma \in 2^m$,

$$|E^{-1}(\sigma) \cap (B_1 \times B_2)| \leqslant 2^{-m+1}|B_1 \times B_2|.$$

The function E is *weakly r-regular* if it obeys the above definition when we consider only B_i with $|B_1| = |B_2| = \lceil rn \rceil$.

Lemma 13.10.13. *If $E : 2^n \times 2^n \to 2^m$ is weakly r-regular then E is regular.*

Proof. Let $k = \lceil rn \rceil$ and suppose that for all B_1, B_2 with $|B_i| = 2^k$ and all $\sigma \in 2^m$, we have $|E^{-1}(\sigma) \cap (B_1 \times B_2)| \leqslant 2^{-m+1}|B_1 \times B_2| = 2^{-m+1+2k}$. Let $k_1, k_2 \geqslant k$ and let $\widehat{B}_1$ and $\widehat{B}_2$ be such that $|\widehat{B}_i| = 2^{k_i}$. Partition each $\widehat{B}_i$ into pairwise disjoint sets $A_0^i, A_1^i, \ldots, A_{2^{k_i-k}-1}^i$ of size 2^k. Then

$$|E^{-1}(\sigma) \cap (\widehat{B}_1 \times \widehat{B}_2)| = \sum_{i,j \leqslant s_i} |E^{-1}(\sigma) \cap (A_i^1 \times A_j^2)|$$
$$\leqslant 2^{k_1+k_2-2k}2^{-m+1+2k} = 2^{-m+1}2^{k_1+k_2} = 2^{-m+1}|\widehat{B}_1 \times \widehat{B}_2|.$$

□

Lemma 13.10.14. *For each $r > 0$, if $2^m < r2^{.99n}$ then with positive probability, a randomly chosen function $E : 2^n \times 2^n \to 2^m$ will be r-regular. In particular, an r-regular $E : 2^n \times 2^n \to 2^m$ exists (and hence can be found effectively by searching).*

Proof. By the previous lemma, it is enough to show that E is weakly r-regular. Let $N = 2^n$ and $M = 2^m$ (as numbers).

Choose $B_1, B_2 \subseteq 2^n$ with $|B_i| = N^r$ (ignoring rounding for simplicity). Let $j_1 \in B_1 \times B_2$ and $j_2 \in 2^m$. We think of $2^n \times 2^n$ as a table with N rows and N columns, of 2^m as colors, and of E as specifying a coloring. Then $B_1 \times B_2$ is a rectangle in this table, j_1 is a cell in this rectangle, and j_2 is one of M possible colors for this cell. Clearly $\text{Prob}(E(j_1) = j_2) = \frac{1}{M}$.

Let C_{j_2} be the number of j_2-colored cells in $B_1 \times B_2$. If there is no rectangle $B_1 \times B_2$ and j_2 such that $\frac{C_{j_2}}{N^{2r}} - \frac{1}{M} > \frac{1}{M}$, then E is weakly r-regular, so it is enough to show that this event has positive probability.

Applying the Chernoff bounds mentioned above, we have

$$\mathrm{Prob}\left(\frac{C_{j_2}}{N^{2r}} - \frac{1}{M} > \frac{1}{M}\right) < e^{-\frac{N^{2r}}{3M}}.$$

The probability that $\frac{C_{j_2}}{N^{2r}} - \frac{1}{M} > \frac{1}{M}$ for some $j_2 \in 2^m$ is less than or equal to the sum over all $j_2 \in 2^m$ of the above probability, and hence less than $Me^{-\frac{N^{2r}}{3M}}$.

The number of rectangles $B_1 \times B_2$ is

$$\binom{N}{N^r}^2 \leqslant \left(\left(\frac{eN}{N^r}\right)^{N^r}\right)^2 = e^{2N^r} e^{2N^r(1-r)\ln N}.$$

Thus, to argue that there is no rectangle $B_1 \times B_2$ and j_2 such that $\frac{C_{j_2}}{N^{2r}} - \frac{1}{M} > \frac{1}{M}$, and hence E is weakly r-regular, it is enough to show that

$$Me^{-\frac{N^{2r}}{3M}} e^{2N^r} e^{2N^r(1-r)\ln N} < 1.$$

Straightforward manipulation shows that this task is the same as showing that $\frac{N^{2r}}{3M} - \ln M > 2N^r + 2N^r(1-r)\ln N$, which holds when $M < N^{.99r}$. $\square$

We are finally ready to build Z. We proceed as follows.

1. Split $X = X_1X_2\ldots$ and $Y = Y_1Y_2\ldots$ as above, using the parameters $r = \frac{q}{2}$ and $r' = \frac{q}{4}$ to define a and b. Note that for each i, we have $C(X_i \mid \vec{X}_{i-1}) > rn_i$ and $C(Y_i \mid \vec{Y}_{i-1}) > rn_i$.

2. For the parameters $n_i = |X_i| = |Y_i|$ and $m_i = i^2$, find an $\frac{r}{2}$-regular function E_i. Let $Z_i = E_i(X_i, Y_i)$.

3. Let $Z = Z_1Z_2\ldots$.

Lemma 13.10.15. *For all $\varepsilon > 0$ and all sufficiently large i, we have $C(Z_i \mid \vec{X}_{i-1}\vec{Y}_{i-1}) \geqslant (1-\varepsilon)m_i$.*

Proof. If $C(Z_i \mid \vec{X}_{i-1}\vec{Y}_{i-1}) < (1-\varepsilon)m_i$, let

$$A = \{\sigma \in 2^{m_i} \mid C(\sigma \mid \vec{X}_{i-1}\vec{Y}_{i-1}) < (1-\varepsilon)m_i\}.$$

Then $|A| < 2^{(1-\varepsilon)m_i}$. Let $t_1 = C(X_i \mid \vec{X}_{i-1}\vec{Y}_{i-1})$ and $t_2 = C(Y_i \mid \vec{X}_{i-1}\vec{Y}_{i-1})$. For $j = 1, 2$, let $B_j = \{\sigma \in 2^{n_i} \mid C(\sigma \mid \vec{X}_{i-1}\vec{Y}_{i-1}) \leqslant t_j\}$. By Lemma 13.10.9 (iii) and (iv), if i is sufficiently large then $t_j > rn_i - O(i) > \frac{r}{2}n_i$ for $j = 1, 2$, since $C(X_i \mid \vec{X}_{i-1}) > rn_i$ and $C(Y_i \mid \vec{Y}_{i-1}) > rn_i$.

Now, $|B_j| \leqslant 2^{t_j+1}$, so we can choose $B_j' \supseteq B_j$ of size 2^{t_j+1}. The bounds on the t_j imply that the B_j' are large enough to allow us to invoke the bounds for the regularity of E_i. Therefore, for any $\sigma \in 2^{m_i}$,

$$|E^{-1}(\sigma) \cap (B_1' \times B_2')| \leqslant 2^{-m_i+1}|B_1' \times B_2'|.$$

Thus

$$\begin{aligned}|E^{-1}(A) \cap (B_1 \times B_2)| &\leqslant |E^{-1}(A) \cap (B_1' \times B_2')| \\ &\leqslant \sum_{\sigma \in A} |E^{-1}(\sigma) \cap (B_1' \times B_2')| \leqslant 2^{t_1+t_2-\varepsilon m_i+3}.\end{aligned}$$

Since $E^{-1}(A) \cap (B_1 \times B_2)$ can be effectively listed given the parameters $\vec{X}_{i-1}, \vec{Y}_{i-1}, (1-\varepsilon)m_i, t_1, t_2$, for any $(\sigma, \tau) \in E^{-1}(A) \cap (B_1 \times B_2)$, we have

$$C(\sigma\tau \mid \vec{X}_{i-1}\vec{Y}_{i-1}) \leqslant t_1 + t_2 - \varepsilon m_i + 2(\log(1-\varepsilon)m_i + \log t_1 + \log t_2) + O(1).$$

Using the facts that $m_i = i^2$ and $\log t_i = O(i)$, we see that there is a $\delta > 0$ such that $C(\sigma\tau \mid \vec{X}_{i-1}\vec{Y}_{i-1}) \leqslant t_1 + t_2 - \delta i^2$ for all sufficiently large i. In particular,

$$C(X_iY_i \mid \vec{X}_{i-1}\vec{Y}_{i-1}) \leqslant t_1 + t_2 - \delta(i^2)$$

for all sufficiently large i. However, by Lemma 13.10.11,

$$\begin{aligned}C(X_iY_i \mid \vec{X}_{i-1}\vec{Y}_{i-1}) &\geqslant C(X_i \mid \vec{X}_{i-1}\vec{Y}_{i-1}) + C(Y_i \mid \vec{X}_{i-1}\vec{Y}_{i-1}) - O(i) \\ &= t_1 + t_2 - O(i).\end{aligned}$$

For sufficiently large i, we have a contradiction. □

Lemma 13.10.16. *For any $\delta > 0$ and n, we have $C(Z \upharpoonright n) \geqslant (1-\delta)n - O(1)$. Hence Z has effective Hausdorff dimension* 1.

Proof. Let $\varepsilon = \frac{\delta}{4}$. By Lemma 13.10.15, $C(Z_i \mid \vec{X}_{i-1}\vec{Y}_{i-1}) \geqslant (1-\varepsilon)m_i$ for almost all i. Thus $(Z_i \mid \vec{Z}_{i-1}) \geqslant (1-\varepsilon)m_i - O(1)$, since we can compute $\vec{Z}_{i-1}$ from $\vec{X}_{i-1}\vec{Y}_{i-1}$. A straightforward induction shows that $C(\vec{Z}_i) \geqslant (1-3\varepsilon)(m_1 + \cdots + m_i)$ for sufficiently large i.

Now take $\sigma = Z \upharpoonright n$ between $\vec{Z}_{i-1}$ and $\vec{Z}_i$, and assume for a contradiction that $C(\sigma) \leqslant (1-\delta)|\sigma|$. Then we can describe $\vec{Z}_{i-1}$ by giving a description of σ, which takes $(1-4\varepsilon)|\sigma| < (1-4\varepsilon)(m_1+\cdots+m_i)$ many bits, the string τ such that $\sigma = \vec{Z}_{i-1}\tau$, which takes a further $|\sigma| - |\vec{Z}_{i-1}| \leqslant m_i$ many bits, and $O(\log m_i)$ many further bits to separate the descriptions of σ and τ. Therefore, for sufficiently large i,

$$\begin{aligned}C(\vec{Z}_{i-1}) &\leqslant (1-4\varepsilon)(m_1 + \cdots + m_i) + m_i + O(\log m_i) \\ &= (1-4\varepsilon)(m_1 + \cdots + m_{i-1}) + (2-4\varepsilon)m_i + O(\log m_i) \\ &< (1-3\varepsilon)(m_1 + \cdots + m_{i-1}),\end{aligned}$$

the last inequality holding because $\lim_i \frac{m_i}{m_1+\cdots+m_{i-1}} = 0$. Thus we have a contradiction, and hence $C(Z \upharpoonright n) > (1-\delta)n$ for almost all n. □

This lemma completes the proof of the theorem. □

Note that the above result implies that Miller's degree of effective Hausdorff dimension $\frac{1}{2}$ cannot compute two C-independent sources of positive effective Hausdorff dimension. This fact likely has interesting consequences for the computational power of such degrees.

Zimand [424] examined the extent to which the hypotheses on X and Y can be weakened. He stated that similar techniques can be used to show that for any $\delta > 0$, there is a c such that, given sequences X and Y that are C-independent and such that $C(X \upharpoonright n) > c \log n$ and $C(Y \upharpoonright n) > c \log n$ for every n, a Z can be produced from X and Y with $C(Z \upharpoonright n) > (1-\delta)n$ for infinitely many n.

In a more recent paper, Zimand [422] showed that even for pairs of sets of *limited dependence* (as defined in that paper), it is still possible to extract a Z of high initial segment complexity. The methods are similar to those described here, but more delicate. Also, using similar and equally delicate methods, Zimand [423] showed that from two partially random but independent *strings* (as defined in that paper), it is possible to construct polynomially many pairwise independent random strings, and if the two original strings are themselves random, then this construction can be done in polynomial time. See [53, 424, 422, 423] for more on this fascinating topic.

13.11 Other notions of dimension

Hausdorff's extension of Carathéodory's s-dimensional measure is certainly not the only generalization of the notion of dimension to non-integer values in geometric measure theory and fractal geometry, and it is also not the only one to have been effectivized. In this section, we will briefly look at a couple of further dimension concepts and their effectivizations. Further details about the classical notions may be found in Federer [142].

13.11.1 Box counting dimension

For $C \subseteq 2^\omega$, let $C \upharpoonright n = \{\sigma \in 2^n : \exists \alpha \in C\,(\sigma \prec \alpha)\}$ and define the *upper* and *lower box counting dimensions* of C as

$$\overline{\dim}_{\mathrm{B}}(C) = \limsup_n \frac{\log(|C \upharpoonright n|)}{n} \quad \text{and} \quad \underline{\dim}_{\mathrm{B}}(C) = \liminf_n \frac{\log(|C \upharpoonright n|)}{n},$$

respectively. If $\overline{\dim}_{\mathrm{B}}$ and $\underline{\dim}_{\mathrm{B}}$ coincide, then this value is called the *box counting dimension*, or *Minkowski dimension*, of C. The name "box counting" comes from the fact that, for each level n, one simply counts the number of boxes of size 2^{-n} needed to cover C. The following is clear.

Lemma 13.11.1. *For any* $C \subseteq 2^\omega$, *we have* $\dim_{\mathrm{H}}(C) \leqslant \underline{\dim}_{\mathrm{B}}(C) \leqslant \overline{\dim}_{\mathrm{B}}(C)$.

(Lower) box counting dimension gives an easy upper bound on Hausdorff dimension, although this estimate may not be very precise. For instance, let C be the class of all sequences that are 0 from some point on. Then we have $\dim_{\mathrm{H}}(C) = 0$ but $\underline{\dim}_{\mathrm{B}}(C) = 1$. (In fact, $\underline{\dim}_{\mathrm{B}}(D) = 1$ for any dense $D \subseteq 2^\omega$.) This observation shows that, in general, box counting dimension is not a stable concept of dimension, since a countable union of classes of box counting dimension 0 such as C can have box counting dimension 1. Staiger [377, 378] has investigated some conditions under which Hausdorff and box counting dimension coincide. Probably the most famous example of such a set is the Mandelbrot set.

One can modify box counting dimension to obtain a countably stable notion, yielding the concept of *modified box counting dimension*, defined as follows. The *lower modified box counting dimension* of $C \subseteq 2^\omega$ is

$$\underline{\dim}_{\mathrm{MB}}(C) = \inf\left\{\sup_i \underline{\dim}_{\mathrm{B}}(X_i) : C \subseteq \bigcup_i X_i\right\}.$$

The *upper modified box counting dimension* of $C \subseteq 2^\omega$ is

$$\overline{\dim}_{\mathrm{MB}}(C) = \inf\left\{\sup_i \overline{\dim}_{\mathrm{B}}(X_i) : C \subseteq \bigcup_i X_i\right\}.$$

If these values coincide, then they define the *modified box counting dimension* $\dim_{\mathrm{MB}}(C)$ of C. (That is, we split up a set into countably many parts and look at the dimension of the "most complicated" part. Then we optimize this value by looking for the partition with the lowest such dimension.)

The modified box counting dimensions behave more stably than their original counterparts; in particular, all countable classes have modified box counting dimension 0. However, these dimensions are usually hard to calculate, due to the extra inf / sup process involved in their definitions.

13.11.2 Effective box counting dimension

The effectivization of box counting dimension is due to Reimann [324]. An equivalent formulation of effective upper box counting dimension was also given by Athreya, Hitchcock, Lutz, and Mayordomo [15]. This concept turns out to coincide with effective packing dimension, which we discuss below.

We will be concerned only with the dimension of individual sets, and hence will not look at the modified versions of box counting dimension needed for countable stability. It is of course possible to effectivize the definition of, for example, $\overline{\dim}_{\mathrm{MB}}\, X$ as we do for box counting dimension below.

Definition 13.11.2 (Reimann [324]). A c.e. set $C \subseteq 2^{<\omega}$ is an *effective box cover* of $B \in 2^\omega$ if $B \upharpoonright n \in C$ for almost all n.

Effective box counting dimension measures how efficiently the initial segments of a set can be "enwrapped" in a c.e. set of strings. For $D \subseteq 2^{<\omega}$, let $D^{[n]} = D \cap 2^n$.

Definition 13.11.3 (Reimann [324]). Let $B \in 2^\omega$. The *effective lower box counting dimension* of B is

$$\underline{\dim}^1_{\mathrm{B}}(B) = \inf\left\{\liminf_n \frac{\log |C^{[n]}|}{n} : C \text{ is an effective box cover of } B\right\},$$

The *effective upper box counting dimension* of B is

$$\overline{\dim}^1_{\mathrm{B}}(B) = \inf\left\{\limsup_n \frac{\log |C^{[n]}|}{n} : C \text{ is an effective box cover of } B\right\}.$$

Effective upper box counting dimension is the same as a concept analyzed by Athreya, Hitchcock, Lutz, and Mayordomo [15] and Hitchcock [180], building on work of Staiger [377].

Definition 13.11.4 (Staiger [377], Athreya, Hitchcock, Lutz, and Mayordomo [15]). For $A \subseteq 2^{<\omega}$, the *entropy rate* of A is

$$H_A = \limsup_n \frac{\log |A^{[n]}|}{n}.$$

For $A \subseteq 2^{<\omega}$, let $A^{\text{i.o.}} = \{\beta \in 2^\omega : \exists^\infty n\, (\beta \upharpoonright n \in A)\}$ and $A^{\text{a.e.}} = \{\beta \in 2^\omega : \forall^\infty n\, (\beta \upharpoonright n \in A)\}$. For $C \subseteq 2^\omega$, let

$$\mathcal{H}_1(C) = \inf\{H_A : C \subseteq A^{\text{i.o.}} \wedge A \in \Sigma^0_1\}$$

and

$$\mathcal{H}^{\text{str}}_1(C) = \inf\{H_A : C \subseteq A^{\text{a.e.}} \wedge A \in \Sigma^0_1\}.$$

For $B \in 2^\omega$, let $\mathcal{H}_1(B) = \mathcal{H}_1(\{B\})$ and $\mathcal{H}^{\text{str}}_1(B) = \mathcal{H}^{\text{str}}_1(\{B\})$.

It is not hard to see that for any $B \in 2^\omega$, we have $\overline{\dim}^1_{\mathrm{B}}(B) = \mathcal{H}^{\text{str}}_1(B)$ and $\dim(B) = \mathcal{H}_1(B)$.

It is a trivial observation that, as in the classical case, effective box counting dimension always bounds effective Hausdorff dimension from above; in particular, $\dim(B) \leqslant \underline{\dim}^1_{\mathrm{B}}(B)$ for any $B \in 2^\omega$.

There is clearly a connection between effective box counting and Kolmogorov complexity, as indicated by the following observation of Kolmogorov [211], which we met in Theorem 3.2.2 (ii).

Proposition 13.11.5 (Kolmogorov [211]). *Let $A \subseteq \mathbb{N} \times 2^{<\omega}$ be computably enumerable and such that $A_m = \{x : (m, x) \in A\}$ is finite for all m. Then $C(x \mid m) \leqslant \log |A_m| + O(1)$ for all m and $x \in A_m$.*

Indeed, it is possible to give an elegant characterization of effective upper box counting dimension in terms of Kolmogorov complexity.

Theorem 13.11.6 (Reimann [324], Athreya, Hitchcock, Lutz, and Mayordomo [15]). *For any $B \in 2^\omega$,*

$$\overline{\dim^1_{\mathrm{B}}}(B) = \limsup_n \frac{K(B \upharpoonright n)}{n} = \limsup_n \frac{C(B \upharpoonright n)}{n}.$$

Proof. The second equation is immediate, since C and K agree up to a log factor.

($\leqslant$) If $\overline{\dim^1_{\mathrm{B}}}(B) < s$ then it follows immediately from Proposition 13.11.5 that $\limsup_n \frac{K(B\upharpoonright n)}{n} \leqslant s$.

($\geqslant$) Suppose that $\limsup_n \frac{K(B\upharpoonright n)}{n} < s$ for a rational s. Let $D = \{\sigma \in 2^{<\omega} : C(\sigma) < s|\sigma|\}$. Then D is an effective box cover of B. Clearly, $D^{[n]} \leqslant 2^{sn}$, so $\overline{\dim^1_{\mathrm{B}}}(B) \leqslant \limsup_n \frac{|D^{[n]}|}{n} \leqslant s$. □

13.11.3 Packing dimension

Packing dimension is another classically important fractional dimension. The effectivization of this notion was first considered by Athreya, Hitchcock, Lutz, and Mayordomo [15], but we will follow the treatment of Reimann [324], who noted the connections with the effective box counting dimension of the previous section.

Packing dimension can be seen as a dual to Hausdorff dimension. Hausdorff dimension is defined in terms of economical coverings, that is, enclosing a class from the outside; packing measures approximate from the inside, by packing a class economically with disjoint sets of small size.

A prefix-free set $P \subset 2^{<\omega}$ is a *packing* in $C \subseteq 2^\omega$ if every $\sigma \in P$ has an extension in C. If $|\sigma| \geqslant n$ for all $\sigma \in P$, then we call P an *n-packing* in C.

One can try to find a packing that is as "dense" as possible. Given $s \geqslant 0$ and n, let

$$\mathcal{P}^s_n(C) = \sup\left\{\sum_{\sigma\in P} 2^{-s|\sigma|} : P \text{ is an } n\text{-packing in } C\right\}.$$

Clearly $\mathcal{P}^s_n(X)$ is nonincreasing with n, so the limit

$$\mathcal{P}^s_\infty(C) = \lim_n \mathcal{P}^s_n(C)$$

exists. However, this definition leads to the same problems we encountered with box counting dimension. Taking for instance the class C of all sequences that are 0 from some point on, we can find denser and denser packings in C, so that for every $0 \leqslant s < 1$, we have $\mathcal{P}^s_\infty(C) = \infty$. Hence $\mathcal{P}^s_\infty$ lacks countable additivity, and in particular is not a measure. This problem can be overcome by applying a Carathéodory process to $\mathcal{P}^s_n$. Let

$$\mathcal{P}^s(C) = \inf\left\{\sum_i \mathcal{P}^s_\infty(X_i) : C \subseteq \bigcup_i X_i\right\}.$$

(The infimum is taken over arbitrary countable covers of C.) Then $\mathcal{P}^s$ is an outer measure on 2^ω, and is Borel regular (see e.g. [335] for a definition).[12] The measure $\mathcal{P}^s$ is called the *s-dimensional packing measure* on 2^ω. Packing measures were introduced by Tricot [391] and Sullivan [384]. They can be seen as dual concepts to Hausdorff measures, and behave in many ways similarly to them. In particular, one may define packing dimension in the same way as Hausdorff dimension.

Definition 13.11.7. The *packing dimension* of $C \subseteq 2^\omega$ is

$$\dim_{\mathrm{P}}(C) = \inf\{s : \mathcal{P}^s(C) = 0\} = \sup\{s : \mathcal{P}^s(C) = \infty\}.$$

Packing dimension has stability properties similar to Hausdorff dimension, such as countable stability. With some effort, one can show that it coincides with $\overline{\dim}_{\mathrm{MB}}$ (see Chapter 3 of Falconer [141]). Generally, the following relations between the different dimension concepts hold: $\dim_{\mathrm{H}}(C) \leqslant \underline{\dim}_{\mathrm{MB}}(C) \leqslant \overline{\dim}_{\mathrm{MB}}(C) = \dim_{\mathrm{P}}(C) \leqslant \overline{\dim}_{\mathrm{B}}(C)$.

Although the traditional definition of packing dimension is rather complicated, due to the additional decomposition / optimization step, there is a simple martingale characterization of this notion. This characterization was discovered by Athreya, Hitchcock, Lutz, and Mayordomo [15], and demonstrates the dual nature of Hausdorff dimension and packing dimension much more clearly. It came as a surprise to workers in the area, who had thought packing dimension was too complex to have such a simple characterization.

Definition 13.11.8. For $0 < s \leqslant 1$, a martingale d *s-succeeds strongly* on A if $\liminf_n \frac{d(A\upharpoonright n)}{2^{(1-s)n}} = \infty$.

Obviously, this condition is equivalent to $\lim_n \frac{d(\alpha\upharpoonright n)}{2^{(1-s)n}} = \infty$. From a gambling perspective, succeeding strongly means not only accumulating arbitrary high levels of capital, but also being able to guarantee that the capital stays above arbitrarily high levels from a certain time on.

Theorem 13.11.9 (Athreya, Hitchcock, Lutz, and Mayordomo [15]). *For any* $C \subseteq 2^\omega$,

$$\dim_{\mathrm{P}}(C) = \inf\{s : \textit{some martingale } s\textit{-succeeds strongly on all } A \in C\}.$$

Proof. We actually prove this result for $\overline{\dim}_{\mathrm{MB}}(C)$ in place of $\dim_{\mathrm{P}}(C)$, and rely on the fact mentioned above that $\dim_{\mathrm{P}}(C) = \overline{\dim}_{\mathrm{MB}}(C)$.

[12] This need no longer be the case if the dimension function $h(x) = x^s$ is replaced by more irregular functions not satisfying even weak continuity requirements.

($\leqslant$) Let d be a martingale that s-succeeds strongly on all $A \in C$. We show that $\overline{\dim}_{\mathrm{MB}}(C) \leqslant s$. Without loss of generality, assume that $d(\lambda) \leqslant 1$. Let

$$D_n = \{\sigma \in 2^n : d(\sigma) > 2^{(1-s)n}\}.$$

Every $A \in C$ is contained in all but finitely many $[\![D_n]\!]$, so

$$C \subseteq \bigcup_i \bigcap_{j \geqslant i} [\![D_j]\!].$$

Letting $X_i = \bigcap_{j \geqslant i} [\![D_j]\!]$, it is enough to show that $\overline{\dim}_{\mathrm{B}}(X_i) \leqslant s$ for all i.

Recall that for $X \subseteq 2^\omega$, we write $X \upharpoonright n$ for the set of strings of length n that have extensions in X. We have $X_i \subseteq [\![D_n]\!]$ for all $n \leqslant i$, so $|X_i \upharpoonright n| \leqslant |D_n|$. By Kolmogorov's Inequality (Theorem 6.3.3), $|D_n| \leqslant 2^{ns}$, so

$$\overline{\dim}_{\mathrm{B}}(X_i) = \limsup_n \frac{\log |X_i \upharpoonright n|}{n} \leqslant \limsup_n \frac{\log |D_n|}{n} \leqslant s.$$

($\geqslant$) We may assume that $\overline{\dim}_{\mathrm{MB}}(X) < 1$. Let s, t, u be such that $\overline{\dim}_{\mathrm{MB}}(C) < s < t < u < 1$. By the definition of modified box counting dimension, there are $X_0, X_1, \ldots$ such that $C \subseteq \bigcup_i X_i$ and $\overline{\dim}_{\mathrm{B}}(X_i) < s$ for all i. It is enough to show that for each i there is a martingale that t-succeeds strongly on elements of X_i, since we can then use the additivity of martingales to combine these into a single martingale that u-succeeds strongly on all elements of C.

So we assume that $X \subset 2^\omega$ is such that $\overline{\dim}_{\mathrm{B}}(X) < s' < s < t$ and show that there exists a martingale d that t-succeeds strongly on all $A \in X$.

Let $X_n = X \upharpoonright n$, and for $\sigma \in 2^{\leqslant n}$, let $X_n^\sigma = \{\tau \in X_n : \sigma \preccurlyeq \tau\}$. There is an N such that $\frac{\log |X_n|}{n} < s'$ for all $n \geqslant N$. For each $n \geqslant N$, define a martingale d_n (inductively) as follows:

$$d_n(\sigma) = \begin{cases} 2^{|\sigma| - sn} |X_n^\sigma| & \text{if } |\sigma| \leqslant n, \\ d_n(\sigma \upharpoonright n) & \text{if } |\sigma| > n. \end{cases}$$

It is easy to check that d_n is a martingale, and for $\sigma \in X_n$, we have $d_n(\sigma) = 2^{(1-s)n}$. Let $d = \sum_{n \geqslant N} d_n$. The finiteness of d follows from

$$d(\lambda) = \sum_{n \geqslant N} d_n(\lambda) = \sum_{n \geqslant N} 2^{-sn} |X_n| < \sum_{n \geqslant N} 2^{(s'-s)n} < \infty.$$

If $A \in X$, then $A \upharpoonright n \in X_n$ for all n, so for $n \geqslant N$,

$$\frac{d(A \upharpoonright n)}{2^{(1-t)n}} \geqslant \frac{d_n(A \upharpoonright n)}{2^{(1-t)n}} \geqslant \frac{2^{(1-s)n}}{2^{(1-t)n}} = 2^{(t-s)n}.$$

As $t > s$, we see that d t-succeeds strongly on all $A \in X$. □

13.11.4 Effective packing dimension

The somewhat involved definition of packing measures renders a direct Martin-Löf-style effectivization in terms of computably enumerable covers difficult. This obstacle can be overcome by using the martingale characterization provided by Theorem 13.11.9.

Definition 13.11.10 (Athreya, Hitchcock, Lutz, and Mayordomo [15]). The *effective packing dimension* of $C \subseteq 2^\omega$ is

$$\mathrm{Dim}(C) = \inf\{s : \text{there is a c.e. martingale that } s\text{-succeeds strongly on all } A \in C\}.$$

In Section 13.11.3 we stated the fact that packing dimension equals upper modified box counting dimension. For individual sets, the modifications to box counting dimension leading to countable stability can be disregarded. A careful effectivization of the proof of Theorem 13.11.9 yields the following.

Theorem 13.11.11 (Reimann [324]). *For every* $A \in 2^\omega$, *we have* $\mathrm{Dim}(A) = \overline{\dim}^1_{\mathrm{B}}(A)$.

Combining this result with Theorem 13.11.6 allows us to characterize effective packing dimension in terms of initial segment complexity.

Corollary 13.11.12 (Athreya, Hitchcock, Lutz, and Mayordomo [15]). *For every* $A \in 2^\omega$, *we have* $\mathrm{Dim}(A) = \limsup_n \frac{K(A\upharpoonright n)}{n} = \limsup_n \frac{C(A\upharpoonright n)}{n}$.

A direct proof of this statement can be obtained by a simple modification of the proof of Theorem 13.3.4 (changing liminf's to limsup's, "there are infinitely many" to "for almost all", etc.).

Notice that this characterization makes it clear that a sufficiently generic set (say a 2-generic set) has high effective packing dimension, since the set of strings of high Kolmogorov complexity is dense. Thus packing dimension is a common ground between category and measure.

This characterization also makes it easy to build sets of specified effective packing dimension, as we saw for effective Hausdorff dimension. Indeed, it is not hard to use it to build, say, a set A such that $\dim(A) = p$ and $\mathrm{Dim}(A) = q$ for any rationals p and q such that $0 \leqslant p \leqslant q \leqslant 1$. In particular, we have the following.

Corollary 13.11.13 (Athreya, Hitchcock, Lutz, and Mayordomo [15]). *There is a set of effective packing dimension* 1 *and effective Hausdorff dimension* 0.

13.12 Packing dimension and complexity extraction

Many of the questions we have investigated for Hausdorff dimension can also be examined for packing dimension. Some of the results for effective Hausdorff dimension immediately imply the same results for effective packing dimension, such as Greenberg and Miller's construction in [170] of a minimal Turing degree of effective Hausdorff dimension 1 (Theorem 13.9.17), which implies the theorem of Downey and Greenberg [106] that there is a minimal degree of effective packing dimension 1 (Theorem 13.13.1). In other ways, however, the two notions of effective dimension are quite different. For instance, we will see in Section 13.14 that there is no correspondence principle for effective packing dimension analogous to Theorem 13.6.1. Another example is Miller's Theorem 13.8.1 that there is a Turing degree of effective Hausdorff dimension $\frac{1}{2}$, which has no analog for packing dimension.

Theorem 13.12.1 (Fortnow, Hitchcock, Pavan, Vinochandran, and Wang [150]). *Let* $\varepsilon > 0$. *If* $\mathrm{Dim}(A) > 0$ *then there is a* $B \equiv_{\mathrm{wtt}} A$ *such that* $\mathrm{Dim}(B) > 1 - \varepsilon$.

Thus we conclude that there is a 0-1 law for packing dimension for weak truth table, and hence Turing, degrees. Too recently for a proof to be included in this book, Conidis [74] has shown that there is a set of positive effective packing dimension that does not compute any sets of effective packing dimension 1, and hence there is a Turing degree of effective packing dimension 1 with no element of effective packing dimension 1.

We give a new proof of Theorem 13.12.1 due to Laurent Bienvenu. It is rather simple and relies on the relationship between complexities at endpoints of intervals and their oscillations within these intervals. It is fair to say that it is along the same lines as the original, but it does not rely on the difficult result on extractors due to Barak, Impagliazzo, and Wigderson [16][13] used in the original proof.

Proof of Theorem 13.12.1. Let A be such that $\mathrm{Dim}(A) > 0$. Let $t > 0$ be a rational such that $C(A \upharpoonright n) \geqslant tn$ for infinitely many n. Let m be a fixed large integer.

[13] The original proof in [150] gave the stronger result that the set B has the same polynomial time Turing degree as A, and hence that there are 0-1 laws for low level complexity classes. However, the extractor result used in that proof (as a black box) is very complex and does not allow for a reasonable presentation in this book (its proof being over 30 pages long). The version we give here suffices for our purposes, as we do not need the result for complexity classes. Like the proof we present, the original proof is nonuniform, but in a different way, using a kind of binary search that identifies chunks of intervals of high complexity infinitely often. The closest we have in this book to this procedure is found in Section 13.10.

We claim that there exists a rational $t' > 0$ such that $C(A \upharpoonright m^k) \geqslant t'm^k$ for infinitely many k. To see this, choose any n such that $C(A \upharpoonright n) \geqslant tn$. Let k be such that $n \in [m^{k-1}, m^k)$. Then

$$\begin{aligned} C(\alpha \upharpoonright m^k) \geqslant C(\alpha \upharpoonright n) - O(\log n) \geqslant tn - O(\log n) \\ \geqslant tm^{k-1} - O(\log n) \geqslant \frac{t}{m} m^k - O(\log m^k). \end{aligned}$$

Thus, for any $t' < \frac{t}{m}$, we have $C(\alpha \upharpoonright m^k) \geqslant t'm^k$ for infinitely many k.

Now let $\sigma_k = \alpha \upharpoonright m^k$ and let $s = \limsup_k \frac{C(\sigma_k)}{|\sigma_k|}$. By the above claim we know that $s > 0$. Let s_1 and s_2 be rationals such that $0 < s_1 < s < s_2$. By the definition of s, we have $C(\sigma_k) \leqslant s_2|\sigma_k|$ for almost all k (for simplicity, we may restrict our attention to large enough k and hence assume that this condition is true for all k) and for any d, we have $C(\sigma_k) \geqslant s_1|\sigma_k| + d$ for infinitely many k.

Let $\mathcal{V}$ be our universal machine. Given A as an oracle, we can compute $\sigma_0, \sigma_1, \ldots$ and, for each k, effectively find a τ_k such that $\mathcal{V}(\tau_k) = \sigma_k$ and $|\tau_k| \leqslant s_2|\sigma_k|$. Let D be the sequence given by $\tau_0\tau_1\tau_2\ldots$. It is easy to see that $D \leqslant_{\text{wtt}} A$. If we replace a sparse set of bits of D by the bits of A (for instance, replacing each $D(2^n)$ by $A(n)$) to get B, we clearly have $B \equiv_{\text{wtt}} A$ and $\text{Dim}(B) = \text{Dim}(D)$.

So let us evaluate $\text{Dim}(D)$. For all k, we have $C(\tau_k) \geqslant C(\sigma_k) - O(1)$, as σ_k can be computed from τ_k. Thus, for infinitely many k, we have $C(\tau_k) \geqslant s_1|\sigma_k| = s_1 m^k$. Now,

$$\text{Dim}(D) \geqslant \limsup_k \frac{C(\tau_0 \ldots \tau_k)}{|\tau_0 \ldots \tau_k|}.$$

On the one hand, we have $C(\tau_0 \ldots \tau_k) \geqslant C(\tau_k) - O(\log k)$, and thus $C(\tau_0 \ldots \tau_k) \geqslant s_1 m^k - O(\log k)$ for infinitely many k. On the other hand, we have $|\tau_k| \leqslant s_2 m^k$ for all k. Therefore,

$$\limsup_k \frac{C(\tau_0 \ldots \tau_k)}{|\tau_0 \ldots \tau_k|} \geqslant \limsup_k \frac{s_1 m^k - O(\log k)}{s_2(1 + m + \ldots + m^k)} \geqslant \frac{s_1}{s_2}\left(1 - \frac{1}{m}\right).$$

Thus $\text{Dim}(B) = \text{Dim}(D) \geqslant \frac{s_1}{s_2}\left(1 - \frac{1}{m}\right)$. Since s_1 and s_2 can be taken arbitrarily close to each other and m arbitrarily large, the theorem is proved. □

On the other hand, packing dimension does have an effect on the complexity extraction question for Hausdorff dimension. The following result implies that if A is a set of positive effective Hausdorff dimension that does not compute any set of higher effective Hausdorff dimension, then A must have effective packing dimension 1.

Theorem 13.12.2 (Bienvenu, Doty, and Stephan [38]). *If* $\text{Dim}(A) > 0$ *then for each* $\varepsilon > 0$ *there is a* $B \leqslant_{\text{T}} A$ *such that* $\dim(B) \geqslant \frac{\dim(A)}{\text{Dim}(A)} - \varepsilon$.

Proof. We may assume that $\dim(A) > 0$. Let s_1, s_2, s_3, and t be rationals such that $0 < s_1 < \dim(A) < s_2 < s_3$ and $\mathrm{Dim}(A) < t$, and $\frac{s_1}{t+s_3-s_1} \geqslant \frac{\dim(A)}{\mathrm{Dim}(A)} - \varepsilon$. Let $\sigma_n \in 2^n$ be such that $A = \sigma_1\sigma_2\ldots$. The idea of the proof is to split A effectively into blocks $\nu = \sigma_n \ldots \sigma_{n+k}$ such that $K(\nu)$ is relatively small and use these to find sufficiently incompressible short prefix-free descriptions τ_i for the σ_i. We then let $B = \tau_1\tau_2\ldots$.

We will make several uses of the fact that

$$K(\sigma\tau) = K(\sigma) + K(\sigma \mid \tau) \pm O(\log|\sigma| + \log|\tau|),$$

and more generally

$$K(\rho_0 \ldots \rho_n) = \sum_{j \leqslant n} K(\rho_j \mid \rho_0 \ldots \rho_{j-1}) \pm O\Big(\sum_{j \leqslant n} \log|\rho_j|\Big).$$

These facts follow easily from the symmetry of information results proved in Section 3.3. (These results are proved for plain complexity, but as pointed out in Section 3.10, also hold for prefix-free complexity because K and C agree up to a log factor.)

Suppose that we have already defined $\eta = \tau_1 \ldots \tau_{n-1}$ for $\rho = \sigma_1 \ldots \sigma_{n-1}$ so that $|\eta| \leqslant s_3|\rho|$. By the choice of s_2, there are infinitely many k such that for $\nu = \sigma_n \ldots \sigma_{n+k}$, we have $K(\nu \mid \rho) \leqslant s_2|\nu|$. Fix such a k. For $j \leqslant k$, let $\nu_j = \sigma_n \ldots \sigma_{n+j}$.

If k is large enough (so that quantities such as $(s_3 - s_2)|\nu|$ overwhelm the relevant log terms), then, by symmetry of information,

$$\sum_{i \leqslant k} K(\sigma_{n+i} \mid \rho\nu_{i-1}) \leqslant s_3|\nu|,$$

and for all $j \leqslant k$, by symmetry of information,

$$K(\nu_j \mid \rho) \leqslant K(\rho\nu_j) - K(\rho) + O(\log|\rho| + \log|\nu_j|) \leqslant t(|\rho| + |\nu_j|) - s_1|\rho|,$$

so that, again by symmetry of information,

$$\sum_{i \leqslant j} K(\sigma_{n+i} \mid \rho\nu_{i-i}) \leqslant (t - s_1)|\rho| + t|\nu_j|.$$

Given the existence of such k, we can effectively find k and $\tau_n, \ldots, \tau_{n+k}$ such that, letting ν and ν_j be as above, each τ_{n+i} is a $\mathcal{U}$-description of σ_{n+i} given $\rho\nu_{i-1}$, and we have $\sum_{i \leqslant k} |\tau_{n+i}| \leqslant s_3|\nu|$ and $\sum_{i \leqslant j} |\tau_{n+i}| \leqslant (t - s_1)|\rho| + t|\nu_j|$ for all $j \leqslant k$. We have $|\eta\tau_n \ldots \tau_{n+k}| \leqslant s_3|\rho\nu|$, so the recursive definition can continue.

Let $B = \tau_1\tau_2\ldots$. Clearly $B \leqslant_{\mathrm{T}} A$, so we are left with showing that $\dim(B) \geqslant \frac{\dim(A)}{\mathrm{Dim}(A)} - \varepsilon$.

Fix m. Let n, k, etc. be as above so that $n \leqslant m \leqslant n + k$. Let $j = m - n$. The choice of the τ_i as appropriate $\mathcal{U}$-descriptions ensures that $K(\sigma_1 \ldots \sigma_m) \leqslant K(\tau_1 \ldots \tau_m) + O(1)$, so $K(\tau_1 \ldots \tau_m) \geqslant s_1|\sigma_1, \ldots, \sigma_m| -$

$O(1)$. Furthermore,

$$|\tau_1 \dots \tau_m| \leqslant |\eta| + |\tau_n \dots \tau_{n+j}| \leqslant s_3|\rho| + (t - s_1)|\rho| + t|\nu_j| \leqslant (t + s_3 - s_1)|\sigma_1 \dots \sigma_m|.$$

Thus

$$\liminf_m \frac{K(\tau_1 \dots \tau_m)}{|\tau_1 \dots \tau_m|} \geqslant \frac{s_1}{t + s_3 - s_1} \geqslant \frac{\dim(A)}{\mathrm{Dim}(A)} - \varepsilon.$$

Given l, let m be least such that $B \upharpoonright l \preccurlyeq \tau_1 \dots \tau_m$. Then $|\tau_1 \dots \tau_m| - l \leqslant m$, so $K(\tau_1 \dots \tau_m) \leqslant K(B \upharpoonright l) + O(m)$. Since m is sublinear in $|\tau_1 \dots \tau_m|$, it follows that

$$\dim(B) = \liminf_l \frac{K(B \upharpoonright l)}{l} \geqslant \liminf_m \frac{K(\tau_1 \dots \tau_m)}{|\tau_1 \dots \tau_m|} \geqslant \frac{\dim(A)}{\mathrm{Dim}(A)} - \varepsilon.$$

□

13.13 Clumpy trees and minimal degrees

In this section we introduce the useful notion of *clumpy trees*, using them to show that there is a minimal degree of effective packing dimension 1. This result follows from Theorem 13.9.17, of course, but can be proved using an easier method.

Theorem 13.13.1 (Downey and Greenberg [106]). *There is a set of minimal Turing degree and effective packing dimension* 1.

Proof. We give a notion of forcing $\mathbb{P}$ such that a sufficiently generic filter $G \subset \mathbb{P}$ yields a set $X_G \in 2^\omega$ with effective packing dimension 1 and minimal Turing degree.[14] This notion is a modification of the standard notion of forcing with computable perfect trees due to Sacks [345]. We need to restrict the kind of perfect trees we use so that we can always choose strings that are sufficiently complicated (i.e., not easily compressed), to be initial segments of the set we build. The problem, of course, is that we cannot determine effectively which strings are sufficiently incompressible, but our conditions, the trees, have to be computable. The solution to this problem relies on the following lemma.

[14] A *notion of forcing* is just a partial order $\mathcal{P}$, whose elements are called *conditions*, and whose ordering is called *extension*. A *filter* on $\mathcal{P}$ is a subset F of $\mathcal{P}$ such that if $p, q \in F$ then p, q have a common extension in $\mathcal{P}$, and if $p \in F$ and p extends q, then $q \in F$. A subset D of $\mathcal{P}$ is *dense* if for every $p \in \mathcal{P}$ there is a $q \in D$ extending p. The filter F is *generic* for a collection of dense sets if it contains an element of each set in the collection. By *sufficiently generic* we mean that F is generic for a countable collection of dense sets $D_0, D_1, \dots$ that will be specified in the proof below. Such an F necessarily exists, because we can let $p_0 \in D_0$ and let $p_{i+1} \in D_{i+1}$ extend p_i, and then define $F = \{q \in \mathcal{P} : \exists i\, (p_i \text{ extends } q)\}$.

Lemma 13.13.2. *For each $\sigma \in 2^{<\omega}$ and $\varepsilon \in \mathbb{Q}^{>0}$ we can computably find an n such that $\frac{K(\sigma\tau)}{|\sigma\tau|} \geqslant 1-\varepsilon$ for some $\tau \in 2^n$.*

Proof. Let $d = |\sigma|+1$ and let $S = \{\nu : K(\nu) \leqslant |\nu| - d\}$. Since $\mu(S) \leqslant 2^{-d}$, we have $[\![\sigma]\!] \not\subseteq S$. So letting $m > \frac{d}{\varepsilon}$, we see that there is some $\nu \succ \sigma$ of length m such that $K(\nu) \geqslant m - d$. Then $\frac{K(\nu)}{m} \geqslant 1 - \frac{d}{m} > 1 - \varepsilon$, so we can let $n = m - |\sigma|$. □

We denote the n corresponding to σ and ε in the above lemma by $n_\varepsilon(\sigma)$.

A *perfect function tree* is a map $T : 2^{<\omega} \to 2^{<\omega}$ that preserves extension and incompatibility. We write $[T]$ for the class of all B for which there is an A with $T(A \upharpoonright n) \prec B$ for all n. Let T be a perfect function tree, $\sigma \in \operatorname{rng} T$, and $\varepsilon \in \mathbb{Q}^{>0}$. Let $\rho = T^{-1}(\sigma)$. We say that T *contains an ε-clump above σ* if $\sigma\tau \preccurlyeq T(\rho\tau)$ for all $\tau \in 2^{n_\varepsilon(\sigma)}$. (Note that this condition implies that $T(\rho\tau) = \sigma\tau$ for all $\tau \in 2^{<n_\varepsilon(\sigma)}$.) The idea is that, by the above lemma, such a clump allows us to find extensions of σ on T that are fairly incompressible.

Given a perfect function tree T and a positive rational ε, we recursively define a labeling of part of the image of T as follows.

1. Label $T(\lambda)$ by ε.
2. If σ is labeled by a rational number δ, and T contains a δ-clump above σ, then for all binary strings τ of length $n_\delta(\sigma)$, label $T(\rho\tau)$ by $\frac{\delta}{2}$, where $\rho = T^{-1}(\sigma)$.
3. If T does not contain such a clump, stop the labeling process.

The tree T is called *ε-clumpy* if this labeling process never halts; that is, the δ-clumps required at step 2 are always present.

Let $\mathbb{P}$ be the collection of pairs (T, ε) where T is an ε-clumpy, computable tree. Note that $\mathbb{P} \neq \emptyset$, since the identity function is an ε-clumpy tree for all ε.

A perfect function tree S *extends* a perfect function tree T if there is some perfect function tree R such that $S = T \circ R$ (where $\circ$ denotes composition). If $(T, \varepsilon), (S, \delta) \in \mathbb{P}$ then we say that (S, δ) *extends* (T, ε) if S extends T and δ is the label of $S(\lambda)$ on (T, ε) (in particular, we require that $S(\lambda)$ be labeled on (T, ε)).

A standard example is that of *full* subtrees: If T is a perfect function tree and $\sigma \in \operatorname{rng} T$, let $\operatorname{Ext}_\sigma(T) = T \circ \{\tau \mapsto \rho\tau\}$, where $\rho = T^{-1}(\sigma)$. If $(T, \varepsilon) \in \mathbb{P}$ and $\sigma \in \operatorname{rng} T$ is labeled by δ, then $(\operatorname{Ext}_\sigma(T), \delta)$ is in $\mathbb{P}$ and extends (T, ε).

For $G \subset \mathbb{P}$, if $\bigcap_{(T,\varepsilon)\in G} [T]$ is a singleton, then let X_G be its unique element.

Lemma 13.13.3. *If $G \subset \mathbb{P}$ is a sufficiently generic filter, then X_G is well-defined and* $\operatorname{Dim}(X_G) = 1$. *(In particular, X_G is not computable.)*

Proof. Since G is a filter, $\bigcap_{(T,\varepsilon)\in G}[T]$ is nonempty. By considering full subtrees, we see that for each n, the set $\{(T,\varepsilon) \in G : |T(\lambda)| > n\}$ is dense in $\mathbb{P}$, so $\bigcap_{(T,\varepsilon)\in G}[T]$ is a singleton, and hence X_G is well-defined.

Let $q < 1$ and let $(T,\varepsilon) \in \mathbb{P}$. There is some ρ such that on (T,ε), the string $\sigma = T(\rho)$ is labeled by a δ with $1-\delta > q$. Let $n = n_\delta(\sigma)$. There is some τ of length n such that $\frac{K(\sigma\tau)}{|\sigma\tau|} > 1-\delta > q$. Then $T(\rho\tau)$ is labeled by $\frac{\delta}{2}$ on (T,ε) and $(\mathrm{Ext}_{T(\rho\tau)}(T), \frac{\delta}{2}) \in \mathbb{P}$ extends (T,ε). If that condition is in G then $\sigma\tau \preccurlyeq T(\rho\tau) \prec X_G$. Thus the set of conditions that force there to be a $\nu \prec X_G$ such that $\frac{K(\nu)}{|\nu|} > q$ is dense in $\mathbb{P}$. ☐

We finish by showing that if G is sufficiently generic then X_G has minimal Turing degree. Let Φ be a Turing functional. As usual in Sacks forcing, let

$$\mathrm{Div}_\Phi = \{(T,\varepsilon) \in \mathbb{P} : \exists x\, \forall \sigma \in \operatorname{rng} T\, (\Phi^\sigma(x)\uparrow)\}$$

and

$$\mathrm{Tot}_\Phi = \{(T,\varepsilon) \in \mathbb{P} : \forall x\, \forall \sigma \in \operatorname{rng} T\, \exists \sigma' \in \operatorname{rng} T\, (\sigma' \succcurlyeq \sigma \wedge \Phi^{\sigma'}(x)\downarrow)\}.$$

Let $(T,\varepsilon) \in \mathbb{P}$. If $(T,\varepsilon) \notin \mathrm{Tot}_\Phi$ then there is a $\sigma \in \operatorname{rng} T$ and an x such that for all $\sigma' \in \operatorname{rng} T$, if $\sigma' \succ \sigma$ then $\Phi^{\sigma'}(x)\uparrow$. So $(\mathrm{Ext}_\sigma(T), \delta) \in \mathrm{Div}_\Phi$ for the label δ of σ on (T,ε). Thus $\mathrm{Tot}_\Phi \cup \mathrm{Div}_\Phi$ is dense in $\mathbb{P}$.

Let Comp_Φ be the collection of conditions $(T,\varepsilon) \in \mathrm{Tot}_\Phi$ such that for all $\sigma, \sigma' \in \operatorname{rng} T$, the strings Φ^σ and $\Phi^{\sigma'}$ are compatible. If $(T,\varepsilon) \in \mathrm{Comp}_\Phi$ and $(T,\varepsilon) \in G$ then Φ^{X_G} is computable, since to determine $\Phi^{X_G}(x)$ we need only look for $\sigma \in \operatorname{rng} T$ such that $\Phi^\sigma(x)\downarrow$, which must exist and have $\Phi^\sigma(x) = \Phi^{X_G}(x)$.

Let Sp_Φ be the collection of conditions $(T,\varepsilon) \in \mathrm{Tot}_\Phi$ such that for all incompatible labeled $\sigma, \sigma' \in \operatorname{rng} T$, the strings Φ^σ and $\Phi^{\sigma'}$ are incompatible. Let $(T,\varepsilon) \in G \cap \mathrm{Sp}_\Phi$. We claim that $X_G \leqslant_{\mathrm{T}} \Phi^{X_G}$. Suppose that we have determined an initial segment σ of X_G. It is easy to check that the labeled nodes are dense in $\operatorname{rng} T$, so we can find a labeled $\sigma' \succ \sigma$ in $\operatorname{rng} T$ such that $\Phi^{\sigma'} \prec \Phi^{X_G}$. Then we must have $\sigma' \prec X_G$.

Thus if we can show that $\mathrm{Tot}_\Phi \cup \mathrm{Comp}_\Phi \cup \mathrm{Sp}_\Phi$ is dense in $\mathbb{P}$, we will have shown that either Φ^{X_G} is not total, or Φ^{X_G} is computable, or Φ^{X_G} computes X_G. Since Φ is arbitrary and we have already shown that X_G is not computable, we can then conclude that X_G has minimal degree.

Since we have already seen that $\mathrm{Tot}_\Phi \cup \mathrm{Div}_\Phi$ is dense in $\mathbb{P}$, it is enough to show that $\mathrm{Sp}_\Phi \cup \mathrm{Comp}_\Phi$ is *dense below* Tot_Φ in $\mathbb{P}$. That is, every condition in Tot_Φ is extended by one in $\mathrm{Sp}_\Phi \cup \mathrm{Comp}_\Phi$.

Lemma 13.13.4. $\mathrm{Sp}_\Phi \cup \mathrm{Comp}_\Phi$ *is dense below* Tot_Φ *in* $\mathbb{P}$.

Proof. Suppose that $(T,\varepsilon) \in \mathrm{Tot}_\Phi$ has no extension in Comp_Φ. Then for all $\sigma \in \operatorname{rng} T$, there are $\sigma_0, \sigma_1 \in \operatorname{rng} T$ extending σ such that Φ^{σ_0} and Φ^{σ_1} are incompatible.

By recursion, we define an extension (S, ε) of (T, ε) in Sp_Φ. We start by letting $S(\lambda) = T(\lambda)$ and labeling this string by ε on (S, ε). Suppose that we have defined $\sigma = S(\rho') = T(\rho)$ where σ is labeled by δ on (T, ε) and by γ on (S, ε). Assume that we have carried out the construction so far so that $n_\gamma(\sigma) \leqslant n_\delta(\sigma)$. For every τ of length strictly shorter than $n_\gamma(\sigma)$, we can let $S(\rho'\tau) = T(\rho\tau) = \sigma\tau$ (and leave it unlabeled on (S, ε)).

Let $\tau_0, \ldots, \tau_{2^n-1}$ be the strings of length $n = n_\gamma(\sigma)$. Enumerate the pairs of numbers $i < j < 2^n$ as $(i_0, j_0), \ldots, (i_m, j_m)$. For each $i \leqslant 2^n$ and $k \leqslant m$, define strings ν_k^i such that $\sigma\tau_i \prec \nu_0^i \prec \cdots \prec \nu_m^i$ and such that every ν_k^i is in the image of T. At step k, define $\nu_k^{i_k} \succ \nu_{k-1}^{i_k}$ and $\nu_k^{j_k} \succ \nu_{k-1}^{j_k}$ such that $\Phi^{\nu_k^{i_k}}$ and $\Phi^{\nu_k^{j_k}}$ are incompatible, which is possible because (T, ε) has no extension in Comp_Φ. Define $S(\rho'\tau_i)$ to be some string $\eta_i \in \operatorname{rng} T$ extending ν_m^i that is labeled by some δ_i such that $n_{\delta_i}(\eta_i) \geqslant n_{\frac{\gamma}{2}}(\eta_i)$. We can then label η_i by $\frac{\gamma}{2}$ on (S, ε). Note that the inductive hypothesis assumed above is preserved, and so the construction can continue. □

This lemma completes the proof of Theorem 13.13.1. □

13.14 Building sets of high packing dimension

One way in which effective packing dimension differs from effective Hausdorff dimension is in the absence of a correspondence principle analogous to Theorem 13.6.1. Conidis [75] built a countable Π_1^0 class P of effective packing dimension 1. (In fact, he built P to have a unique element of rank 1, so that all other elements of P are computable. See Section 2.19.1 for the definition of the rank of an element of a Π_1^0 class.) Since P is countable, its classical packing dimension is 0. Note also that, by Theorem 13.6.1, the effective Hausdorff dimension of P is 0.

Theorem 13.14.1 (Conidis [75]). *There is a countable Π_1^0 class of effective packing dimension* 1.

Proof. By Lemma 13.13.2, there is a computable sequence $0 = n_0 < n_1 < \cdots$ such that for every $\sigma \in 2^{n_k}$, there is a $\tau \in 2^{n_{k+1}}$ with $\sigma \prec \tau$ and $K(\tau) \geqslant (1 - 2^{-k})n_{k+1}$. We build finite trees $T_s \subseteq 2^{\leqslant n_s}$ such that $T_0 \subset T_1 \subset \cdots$ and let our class be $[\bigcup_s T_s]$. We will have strings σ_k whose values will change throughout the construction, but will have limit values such that $\sigma_0 \prec \sigma_1 \prec \cdots$ and $\bigcup_k \sigma_k$ is the unique rank 1 point of $[\bigcup_s T_s]$.

Construction.

Stage 0. Let $\sigma_0 = \lambda$ and $T_0 = \{\lambda\}$.

Stage $s+1$. If there is a least $k \leqslant s$ such that $K_s(\sigma_k) < (1 - 2^{-k})|\sigma_k|$ then redefine σ_k to be the leftmost extension $\tau \in 2^{|\sigma_k|}$ of σ_{k-1} on T_s such that $K_s(\tau) \geqslant (1 - 2^{-k})|\tau|$ (which we will argue below must exist). In this case, undefine all σ_j for $j > k$.

Let k be largest such that σ_k is still defined and let τ be the leftmost leaf of T_s that extends σ_k (so that $|\tau| = n_s$). Define T_{s+1} as follows. Begin by adding all extensions of τ of length n_{s+1}. For every leaf $\rho \neq \tau$ of T_s, add $\rho 0^{n_{s+1}-n_s}$ to T_{s+1}. Finally, close downwards to obtain a subtree of $2^{\leqslant n_{s+1}}$. Let $\sigma_{k+1} = \tau 0^{n_{s+1}-n_s}$.

End of Construction.

Every time σ_k is defined at a stage s to extend some $\tau \in 2^{n_s}$, every extension of τ of the same length as σ_k is added to T_{s+1}. Thus, by the choice of the n_s, if we ever find that $K_s(\sigma_k) < (1 - 2^{-k})|\sigma_k|$ then we can redefine σ_k as in the construction. Thus the construction never gets stuck, and it follows by induction that every σ_k has a final value, which we will refer to simply as σ_k, such that $\sigma_0 \prec \sigma_1 \prec \cdots$ and $K(\sigma_k) \geqslant (1 - 2^{-k})|\sigma_k|$ for all k.

Let $P = [\bigcup_s T_s]$ and $X = \bigcup_k \sigma_k$. Then $X \in P$ and $\mathrm{Dim}(X) = 1$, so $\mathrm{Dim}(P) = 1$. It is easy to see from the construction that if $\rho \neq \sigma_k$ and $|\rho| = |\sigma_k|$, then every extension of ρ on P is eventually 0. Thus every element of P other than X is eventually 0, and hence P is countable. □

Note that, in the above proof, the σ_k never move to the left, so the unique noncomputable element X of P is a left-c.e. real.

This result suggests that it is easier (from a computability-theoretic perspective) to build sets of high effective packing dimension than ones of high effective Hausdorff dimension. (Theorem 13.12.1 can also be seen as evidence for this claim.) Downey and Greenberg [106] have extended Theorem 13.14.1 as follows.

Theorem 13.14.2 (Downey and Greenberg [106]). *Every set A of array noncomputable degree computes a set B of effective packing dimension 1. If A is c.e. then B can be taken to be a left-c.e. real that is the unique rank 1 element of a Π^0_1 class.*

Before proving this result, we make a few comments. The following result shows that c.e. traceable sets have packing dimension 0.

Theorem 13.14.3 (Essentially Kummer [226], see Downey and Greenberg [106]). *If A is c.e. traceable, then for every computable order h, we have $C(A \upharpoonright n) \leqslant \log n + h(n) + O(1)$.*

Proof. Let A be c.e. traceable and fix a computable order h. (We may assume that $h(0) > 0$.) By Proposition 2.23.12, A is c.e. traceable with bound h. Let $T_0, T_1, \ldots$ be a c.e. trace with bound h for the function $n \mapsto A \upharpoonright n$. We can describe $A \upharpoonright n$ by describing n and the position of $A \upharpoonright n$ in the enumeration of T_n, so $C(A \upharpoonright n) \leqslant \log n + h(n) + O(1)$. □

Since we can choose h to be slow growing, and $\log n$ is bounded away from n, we have the following.

Corollary 13.14.4. *If A is c.e. traceable then* $\mathrm{Dim}(A) = 0$.

Combining this result with Theorem 13.14.2 and the fact that a c.e. degree is array computable iff it is c.e. traceable (Theorem 2.23.13), we have the following.

Corollary 13.14.5 (Downey and Greenberg [106]). *The following are equivalent for a c.e. set A.*

(i) *A computes a set of positive effective packing dimension.*

(ii) *A computes a set of effective packing dimension* 1.

(iii) *The degree of A is array noncomputable.*

Corollary 13.14.4, together with the existence of minimal degrees of packing dimension 1 (Theorem 13.9.17), implies Shore's unpublished result that there is a minimal degree that is not c.e. traceable. As discussed in Section 2.23, Ishmukhametov [184] showed that if a degree is c.e. traceable then it has a strong minimal cover in the Turing degrees. Yates had earlier asked the still open question of whether every minimal degree has a strong minimal cover. It follows that c.e. traceability is not enough to answer this question.

Downey and Ng [129] have further sorted out the connections between high effective packing dimension and notions such as array computability.

Theorem 13.14.6 (Downey and Ng [129]). (i) *There is a degree that is not c.e. traceable but has effective packing dimension* 0.

(ii) *There is a degree that is array computable but has effective packing dimension* 1.

Part (ii) follows by taking a hyperimmune-free 1-random degree and applying Proposition 2.23.10. For a proof of part (i), see [129]. The degrees in the above result can also be Δ^0_2, and hence there seems to be no way to relate the degrees of packing dimension 1 with any known lowness class.

We now proceed with the proof of Theorem 13.14.2.

Proof of Theorem 13.14.2. We begin with the non-c.e. case. Recall that $f \leqslant_{\mathrm{pb}} C$ means that f can be computed from oracle C by a reduction procedure with a primitive recursive bound on the use function, and that $f \leqslant_{\mathrm{pb}} \emptyset'$ iff there is a computable function $\widehat{f}(n,s)$ and a primitive recursive function p such that $\lim_s \widehat{f}(n,s) = f(n)$ and $|\{s : \widehat{f}(n,s) \neq \widehat{f}(n,s+1)\}| \leqslant p(n)$. Recall further that a set of strings S is pb-dense if there is a function $f \leqslant_{\mathrm{pb}} \emptyset'$ such that $f(\sigma) \succcurlyeq \sigma$ and $f(\sigma) \in S$ for all σ, and that a set is pb-generic if it meets every pb-dense set of strings. Finally, recall that Theorem 2.24.22 states that if $\mathbf{a}$ is array noncomputable, then there is a pb-generic set $B \leqslant_{\mathrm{T}} \mathbf{a}$. Thus, it is enough to show that if B is pb-generic then $\mathrm{Dim}(B) = 1$, which we now do.

It is easy to check that the map given by Lemma 13.13.2, which takes $\sigma \in 2^{<\omega}$ and $\varepsilon \in \mathbb{Q}^{>0}$ to an $n_\varepsilon(\sigma)$ such that $\frac{K(\sigma\tau)}{|\sigma\tau|} \geqslant 1-\varepsilon$ for some $\tau \in$

$2^{n_\varepsilon(\sigma)}$, is primitive recursive. For $k > 0$, let $S_k = \{\nu \in 2^{\geqslant k} : \frac{K(\nu)}{|\nu|} > 1 - \frac{1}{k}\}$. To see that S_k is pb-dense, first note that it is co-c.e. Let $\widehat{f}(\sigma, s)$ be the leftmost extension of σ of length $m = |\sigma 0^k| + n_{\frac{1}{k}}(\sigma 0^k)$ in $S_k[s]$. Then $\widehat{f}$ is computable, $|\{s : \widehat{f}(\sigma, s) \neq \widehat{f}(\sigma, s+1)\}| < 2^m$, which is a primitive recursive bound, and $\lim_s \widehat{f}(\sigma, s) \in S_k$. So if B is pb-generic then it meets all the S_k, which implies that $\mathrm{Dim}(B) = 1$.

We now turn to the c.e. case. Here, if we wish only to make B left-c.e. (without making it be the unique rank 1 element of a Π^0_1 class), there is a fairly simple permitting argument.[15] Let A be a c.e. set of a.n.c. degree. We have requirements

$$R_k : \exists \nu \in 2^{\geqslant k} \left(\nu \prec B \wedge \frac{K(\nu)}{|\nu|} \geqslant 1 - \frac{1}{k} \right)$$

for $k > 0$. It is enough to satisfy infinitely many of these requirements.

As noted in the proof of Theorem 13.14.1, there is a computable sequence $0 = n_0 < n_1 < \cdots$ such that for every $\sigma \in 2^{n_k}$, there is a $\tau \in 2^{n_{k+1}}$ with $\sigma \prec \tau$ and $K(\tau) \geqslant (1 - 2^{-k})n_{k+1}$. Partition $\mathbb{N}$ into consecutive intervals $I_0, I_1, \ldots$ such that $|I_k| = 2^{n_k}$. By Theorem 2.23.4, there is a $D \equiv_{\mathrm{T}} A$ such that for every c.e. set W there are infinitely many m with $D \cap I_m = W \cap I_m$.

We define B as the limit of strings $\sigma_0 \prec \sigma_1 \prec \cdots$, which can change value during the construction. We begin with $\sigma_k = 0^{n_k}$ for all k. We also build a c.e. set W, into which we enumerate requests for D-permission. Let $u_k = |I_0| + |I_1| + \cdots + |I_k|$.

At stage s, say that R_k requires attention if $D_s \cap I_k \subseteq W_s \cap I_k \neq I_k$ and $K_s(\sigma_k) < (1 - 2^{-k})|\sigma_k|$, and either

1. this is the first stage at which this inequality obtains for the current value of σ_k or

2. $D_{s+1} \upharpoonright u_k \neq D_s \upharpoonright u_k$.

If there is a least $k \leqslant s$ such that R_k requires attention then proceed as follows. If 1 holds then put the least $n \in I_k \setminus W$ into W. If 2 holds then redefine σ_k to be the leftmost extension $\tau \in 2^{n_k}$ of σ_{k-1} such that $K_s(\tau) \geqslant (1 - 2^{-k})|\tau|$ and redefine σ_j for $j > k$ to be $\sigma_k 0^{n_j - n_k}$.

[15]There is also a simple proof, due to Miller [personal communication], using material from Chapter 16: In Theorem 16.1.6 we will see that every a.n.c. c.e. degree contains a set X such that $C(X \upharpoonright n) \geqslant 2\log n - O(1)$ for infinitely many n. So let A be a c.e. set of a.n.c. degree, and let $X \equiv_{\mathrm{T}} A$ be as above. Let $B = \sum_{n \in X} \frac{1}{n \log^2 n}$. This sum converges, so B is a left-c.e. real, and $B \equiv_{\mathrm{T}} A$. Assume for a contradiction that B does not have packing dimension 1. Let $q < 1$ be such that $K(B \upharpoonright n) \leqslant qn$ for all sufficiently large n. We have $B - B \upharpoonright \lceil \log n + 2\log\log n \rceil \leqslant \frac{1}{n \log^2 n}$, so if we know $B \upharpoonright \lceil \log n + 2\log\log n \rceil$, then we can determine whether k is in X for all $k < n$. Thus

$$C(X \upharpoonright n) \leqslant K(B \upharpoonright \lceil \log n + 2\log\log n \rceil) + K(n) + O(1) \leqslant (1+q)\log n + O(\log\log(n)),$$

contradicting our choice of X.

Clearly, each σ_k has a final value. For these final values, let $B = \bigcup_k \sigma_k$. Since the σ_k move only to the right, B is a left-c.e. real. Since σ_k cannot change unless D changes below u_k, we also have $B \leqslant_{\text{wtt}} D \leqslant_{\text{T}} A$.

Now suppose that $D \cap I_k = W \cap I_k$. Let t be the least stage by which all R_j for $j < k$ have stopped requiring attention, which must exist because each R_j can require attention at most twice for each string in 2^{n_j}. It can never be the case that $D_s \cap I_k \setminus W_s \cap I_k \neq \emptyset$, since then we would never again put a number into $W \cap I_k$, ensuring that $D \cap I_k \neq W \cap I_k$. Every time we put a number into $W \cap I_k$, we move σ_k. Since $|I_k| = 2^{n_k}$ and σ_k always has length k, we never have $W_s \cap I_k = I_k$. Thus, if there is an $s \geqslant t$ such that $K_s(\sigma_k) < (1 - 2^{-k})|\sigma_k|$, then R_k requires attention at stage s, and so a number enters $W \cap I_k$. This number will later enter D, at which point R_k will again require attention, and σ_k will be redefined. Thus, for the final value of σ_k, we must have $K(\sigma_k) \geqslant (1 - 2^{-k})|\sigma_k|$, and hence R_k is satisfied.

Since there are infinitely many k such that $D \cap I_k = W \cap I_k$, infinitely many requirements are satisfied, and hence $\text{Dim}(B) = 1$.

For the full result, we combine this permitting argument with the proof of Theorem 13.14.1. We have the same requirements as above. Let D, n_k, and I_k be as above (except that it is convenient to have $|I_k| = 2^{n_k+1}$ now).

We will have strings σ_k as above, but now their lengths may change during the construction, as in the proof of Theorem 13.14.1. As in that proof, we will build a tree via approximations T_s. While we work above a particular value of σ_k, we extend all other strings of the same length by 0's. Thus, when we redefine σ_k, we must move σ_{k+1} above $\sigma_k 0^n$ for some large n. This redefinition means that we now must associate some large I_j with σ_{k+1}, since we may need many permissions to ensure that $K(\sigma_{k+1}) < (1 - 2^{-(k+1)})|\sigma_{k+1}|$ for the final value of σ_{k+1}. The main idea of the construction is that, instead of having a fixed use u_k for permitting changes to σ_k, we will now have a varying use u_k (so we will no longer have a wtt-reduction from D). When we redefine σ_k, we also redefine u_k to be $|I_0| + |I_1| + \cdots + |I_{j-1}|$, where I_j is the interval now associated with R_{k+1}. When we seek a permission to change σ_k, we do so by putting numbers into every $I_m \subseteq [u_{k-1}, u_k)$. This action will allow us to argue that each I_m such that $D \cap I_m = W \cap I_m$ gives us enough permissions to satisfy *some* requirement, and hence infinitely many requirements are satisfied.

We say that I_k is *active* at stage $s+1$ if $D_s \cap I_k \subseteq W_s \cap I_k \neq I_k$.

Construction.

Stage 0. Let $\sigma_0 = \lambda$, let $T_0 = \{\lambda\}$, and let $u_0 = 0$.

Stage $s+1$. Say that R_k requires attention if $K_s(\sigma_k) < (1 - 2^{-k})|\sigma_k|$ and either

1. this is the first stage at which this inequality obtains for the current value of σ_k or

2. $D_{s+1} \upharpoonright u_k \neq D_s \upharpoonright u_k$.

If there is a least $k \leqslant s$ such that R_k requires attention then proceed as follows. If 1 holds then for each active $I_m \subseteq [u_{k-1}, u_k)$, put the least $n \in I_m \setminus W$ into W. If 2 holds then redefine σ_k to be the leftmost extension $\tau \in 2^{|\sigma_k|}$ of σ_{k-1} on T_s such that $K_s(\tau) \geqslant (1 - 2^{-k})|\tau|$ (which must exist by the same reasoning as in the proof of Theorem 13.14.1), redefine u_k to be $|I_0| + |I_1| + \cdots + |I_s|$, and undefine all σ_j and u_j for $j > k$.

Now let k be largest such that σ_k is still defined and let τ be the leftmost leaf of T_s that extends σ_k (so that $|\tau| = n_s$). Define T_{s+1} as follows. Begin by adding all extensions of τ of length n_{s+1}. For every leaf $\rho \neq \tau$ of T_s, add $\rho 0^{n_{s+1}-n_s}$ to T_{s+1}. Finally, close downwards to obtain a subtree of $2^{\leqslant n_{s+1}}$. Let $\sigma_{k+1} = \tau 0^{n_{s+1}-n_s}$ and $u_{k+1} = |I_0| + |I_1| + \cdots + |I_{s+1}|$.

End of Construction.

Let $P = [\bigcup_s T_s]$. It is easy to check by induction that each σ_k has a final value (since, after σ_{k-1} has settled, the length of σ_k cannot change). For these final values, let $B = \bigcup_k \sigma_k$. As in the proof of Theorem 13.14.1, B is a left-c.e. real, and is the unique rank 1 element of P.

Neither σ_k nor u_k can change unless some number less than u_k enters D. Since each u_k has a final value, D can compute the final value of each σ_k, and hence can compute B.

Now suppose that $D \cap I_k = W \cap I_k$. It can never be the case that $D_s \cap I_k \setminus W_s \cap I_k \neq \emptyset$, since then I_k would become inactive, and we would never again put a number into $W \cap I_k$, ensuring that $D \cap I_k \neq W \cap I_k$. Furthermore, each time a number enters $W \cap I_k$, it does so because some string σ_k becomes redefined. It is easy to see from the construction that in that case $|\sigma_k| \leqslant n_k$, and the strings corresponding to different numbers entering $W \cap I_k$ must be different. Since $|I_k| = 2^{n_k+1}$, we never put all of I_k into W. Thus I_k is permanently active.

Let j be such that, for the final value of u_{j-1} and u_j, we have $I_k \subseteq [u_{j-1}, u_j)$, and let s_0 be a stage by which these final values are reached. Then all R_i for $i < j$ must eventually stop requiring attention (since each time such a requirement redefines σ_i, it undefines u_j), say by stage $s_1 > s_0$. If at any stage $s > s_1$ we have $K_s(\sigma_j) < (1 - 2^{-j})|\sigma_j|$, then R_j will require attention. It will then put a number into $W \cap I_k$. This number must later enter D, which will cause u_j to change. By the choice of s_0, this situation cannot happen, so in fact $K_s(\sigma_j) \geqslant (1 - 2^{-j})|\sigma_j|$ for all $s > s_1$, and hence $K(\sigma_j) \geqslant (1 - 2^{-j})|\sigma_j|$, which means that R_j is satisfied.

Since there are infinitely many k such that $D \cap I_k = W \cap I_k$ and only finitely many can have $I_k \subseteq [u_{j-1}, u_j)$ for a given j, infinitely many requirements are satisfied, and hence $\mathrm{Dim}(B) = 1$. □

13.15 Computable dimension and Schnorr dimension

13.15.1 Basics

It is natural to consider notions of dimension obtained by replacing c.e. gales by computable ones. Recall that a martingale d s-succeeds on A if $\limsup_n \frac{d(A\upharpoonright n)}{2^{(1-s)n}} = \infty$ and s-succeeds strongly on A if $\lim_n \frac{d(A\upharpoonright n)}{2^{(1-s)n}} = \infty$. As discussed in Section 13.3, the following definitions were in a sense implicit in the work of Schnorr [349].

Definition 13.15.1 (Lutz [252, 254], Athreya, Hitchcock, Lutz, and Mayordomo [15]). The *computable Hausdorff dimension* of $C \subseteq 2^\omega$ is

$$\dim_{\text{comp}}(C) = \inf\{s : \text{there is a computable martingale that } s\text{-succeeds on all } A \in C\}.$$

The *computable packing dimension* of $C \subseteq 2^\omega$ is

$$\text{Dim}_{\text{comp}}(C) = \inf\{s : \text{there is a computable martingale that } s\text{-succeeds strongly on all } A \in C\}.$$

For $A \in 2^\omega$, we write $\dim_{\text{comp}}(A)$ for $\dim_{\text{comp}}(\{A\})$ and refer to it as the computable Hausdorff dimension of A, and similarly for packing dimension.

A different approach to passing from Σ_1^0 objects to computable ones in the definition of algorithmic dimension is to consider test sets that are computable in the sense of Schnorr.

Definition 13.15.2. Let $s \geqslant 0$ be rational.

A *Schnorr s-test* is a uniformly c.e. sequence $\{S_n\}_{n\in\omega}$ of sets of strings such that $\sum_{\sigma\in S_n} 2^{-s|\sigma|} \leqslant 2^{-n}$ for all n and the reals $\sum_{\sigma\in S_n} 2^{-s|\sigma|}$ are uniformly computable.

A class $C \subseteq 2^\omega$ is *Schnorr s-null* if there exists a Schnorr s-test $\{S_n\}_{n\in\omega}$ such that $C \in \bigcap_n [\![S_n]\!]$.

The Schnorr 1-null sets are just the Schnorr null sets. As with Schnorr tests, in the above definition we could require that $\sum_{\sigma\in S_n} 2^{-s|\sigma|} = 2^{-n}$ and have the same notion of Schnorr s-null sets. The sets S_n in a Schnorr s-test are actually uniformly computable, since to determine whether $\sigma \in S_n$ it suffices to enumerate S_n until the accumulated sum given by $\sum_{\tau\in S_n} 2^{-s|\tau|}$ exceeds $2^{-n} - 2^{s|\sigma|}$ (assuming the measure of the nth level of the test is in fact 2^{-n}). If σ has not been enumerated so far, it cannot be in S_n. But of course the converse does not hold: there are computable sets of strings generating open sets with noncomputable measures. Indeed, we have mentioned before that every Σ_1^0 class can be generated by a computable set of strings.

We can adapt Definition 13.5.6 to get an s-analog of the concept of total Solovay test introduced in Definition 7.1.9. A Solovay s-test D is *total* if $\sum_{\sigma \in D} 2^{-s|\sigma|}$ is computable.

As we saw in Section 13.5, the correspondence between tests for s-Martin-Löf randomness and Solovay s-tests is close but not quite exact. In the Schnorr case, however, we do get an exact correspondence.

Theorem 13.15.3 (Downey, Merkle, and Reimann [125]). *For any rational $s \geqslant 0$, a class $C \subseteq 2^\omega$ is Schnorr s-null if and only if there is a total Solovay s-test that covers every element of C.*

Proof. Let $\{S_n\}_{n \in \omega}$ be a Schnorr s-test. Let $S = \bigcup_n S_n$. Clearly, S is a Solovay s-test that covers all of $\bigcap_n S_n$, so it is enough to show that $\sum_{\sigma \in S} 2^{-s|\sigma|}$ is computable. It is easy to see that to compute this sum to within 2^{-n}, it is enough to compute $\sum_{\sigma \in S_i} 2^{-s|\sigma|}$ to within 2^{-2n-3} for each $i \leqslant n+1$.

For the converse, let S be a total Solovay s-test Given n, compute $c = \sum_{\sigma \in S} 2^{-s|\sigma|}$ to within 2^{-n-2}. Effectively find a finite $F \subseteq S$ such that

$$c - 2^{-n-1} \leqslant \sum_{\sigma \in F} 2^{-s|\sigma|} \leqslant c - 2^{-n-2}.$$

Let $S_n = S \setminus F$. Then S_n covers every set that S covers, and $\sum_{\sigma \in S_n} 2^{-s|\sigma|} < 2^{-n}$. Furthermore, this sum is uniformly computable over all n. Thus the S_n form a Schnorr s-test whose intersection contains all sets covered by S. □

We have the following effective version of Theorem 13.1.2.

Proposition 13.15.4 (Downey, Merkle, and Reimann [125]). *For any rationals $t \geqslant s \geqslant 0$, if C is Schnorr s-null then it is also Schnorr t-null.*

Proof. It suffices to show that if $s \leqslant t$, then every Schnorr s-test is also a Schnorr t-test. Obviously, the only issue is checking the computability of the relevant sum.

Let $\{S_n\}_{n \in \omega}$ be a Schnorr s-test. Given any rational $r \geqslant 0$ and any n and k, let

$$m_n(r) = \sum_{\sigma \in S_n} 2^{-r|\sigma|}$$

and

$$m_n^k(r) = \sum_{\sigma \in S_n \cap 2^{\leqslant k}} 2^{-r|\sigma|}.$$

It is easy to check that $m_n^k(t) \leqslant m_n(t) \leqslant m_n^k(t) + 2^{(s-t)k} m_n(s)$.

Now, $m_n(s)$ is computable, and $2^{(s-t)k}$ goes to zero as k gets larger. Therefore, we can effectively approximate $m_n(t)$ to any desired degree of precision. □

Thus the following definition makes sense.

Definition 13.15.5 (Downey, Merkle, and Reimann [125]). The *Schnorr Hausdorff dimension* of $C \subseteq 2^\omega$ is

$$\dim_{\mathrm{S}}(C) = \inf\{s \geqslant 0 : C \text{ is Schnorr } s\text{-null}\}.$$

For $A \in 2^\omega$, we write $\dim_{\mathrm{S}}(A)$ for $\dim_{\mathrm{S}}(\{A\})$ and refer to it as the Schnorr Hausdorff dimension of A.

Note that the Schnorr Hausdorff dimension of any class is at most 1, since for any $\varepsilon > 0$ we can choose a computable sequence $k_0, k_1, \ldots$ such that the sets 2^{k_n} form a Schnorr $1+\varepsilon$ test covering all of 2^ω.

We saw in Section 8.11.2 that the concepts of computable randomness and Schnorr randomness do not coincide. That is, there are Schnorr random sets on which some computable martingale succeeds. However, the differences vanish when it comes to Hausdorff dimension.

Theorem 13.15.6 (Downey, Merkle, and Reimann [125]). *For any $B \in 2^\omega$, we have $\dim_{\mathrm{S}}(B) = \dim_{\mathrm{comp}}(B)$.*

Proof. ($\leqslant$) Suppose that a computable martingale d s-succeeds on B. By Theorem 7.1.2, we may assume that d is rational-valued. We may also assume that $s < 1$, since the case $s = 1$ is trivial. It suffices to show that for any $t \in (s,1)$, we can find a Schnorr t-test that covers B. Fix such a t.

Let

$$U_k = \{\sigma : 2^{-(1-t)|\sigma|} d(\sigma) \geqslant 2^k\}.$$

It is easy to see that the $\{U_k\}_{k\in\omega}$ are uniformly computable (since d is rational-valued and computable) and cover B, so we are left with showing that the reals $\sum_{\sigma\in U_k} 2^{-s|\sigma|}$ are uniformly computable.

To approximate $\sum_{\sigma\in U_k} 2^{-s|\sigma|}$ to within 2^{-r}, we first effectively find an n such that $2^{(1-t)n} \geqslant 2^r d(\lambda)$. Let $V = U_k \cap 2^{\leqslant n}$. If $\tau \in U_k \setminus V$ then $d(\tau) \geqslant 2^{(1-t)n} 2^k \geqslant 2^{r+k} d(\lambda)$. So by Kolmogorov's Inequality (Theorem 6.3.3), $\mu(U_k) - \mu(V) \leqslant 2^{-(r+k)}$.

($\geqslant$) Suppose $\dim_{\mathrm{S}}(B) < s < 1$. (Again the case $s = 1$ is trivial.) We show that there is a computable martingale d that s-succeeds on B.

Let $\{V_k\}_{k\in\omega}$ be a Schnorr s-test that covers B. Let

$$d_k(\sigma) = \begin{cases} 2^{(1-s)|\tau|} & \text{if } \tau \preccurlyeq \sigma \text{ for some } \tau \in V_k \\ \sum_{\sigma\tau\in V_k} 2^{-|\tau|+(1-s)(|\sigma|+|\tau|)} & \text{otherwise.} \end{cases}$$

We verify that d_k is a martingale. Given σ, if there is a $\tau \in V_k$ such that $\tau \preccurlyeq \sigma$, then clearly $d_k(\sigma 0) + d_k(\sigma 1) = 2d_k(\sigma)$. Otherwise,

$$\begin{aligned} d_k(\sigma 0) &+ d_k(\sigma 1) \\ &= \sum_{\sigma 0\tau \in V_k} 2^{-|\tau|+(1-s)(|\sigma|+|\tau|+1)} + \sum_{\sigma 1\tau \in V_k} 2^{-|\tau|+(1-s)(|\sigma|+|\tau|+1)} \\ &= \sum_{\sigma\rho \in V_k} 2^{(-|\rho|+1)+(1-s)(|\sigma|+|\rho|)} = 2d_k(\sigma). \end{aligned}$$

Furthermore, $d_k(\lambda) = \sum_{\tau \in V_k} 2^{-|\tau|+(1-s)|\tau|} = \sum_{\tau \in V_k} 2^{-s|\tau|} \leqslant 2^{-k}$, so $d = \sum_k d_k$ is also a martingale. It is straightforward to use the fact that $\{V_k\}_{k\in\omega}$ is a Schnorr s-test to show that the d_k are uniformly computable, and hence d is computable.

Finally, note that, for $\sigma \in V_k$, we have $d(\sigma) \geqslant d_k(\sigma) = 2^{(1-s)|\sigma|}$, so if $B \in \bigcap_k [\![V_k]\!]$, then $d(B \upharpoonright n) \geqslant 2^{(1-s)n}$ infinitely often, which means that d s-succeeds on B. □

Thus, in contrast to randomness, the approaches to dimension via Schnorr tests and via computable martingales yield the same concept. Because of the potential confusion between the terms "effective dimension" (which we have used to mean our primary notion of Σ^0_1 dimension) and "computable dimension", we will use the term "Schnorr Hausdorff dimension" and the notation $\dim_S$. For uniformity, we will also refer to computable packing dimension as *Schnorr packing dimension* and use the notation Dim_S in place of $\mathrm{Dim}_{\mathrm{comp}}$.

It follows from the definitions that $\dim_S(A) \leqslant \mathrm{Dim}_S(A)$ for any A. We call sets for which Schnorr Hausdorff and Schnorr packing dimension coincide *Schnorr regular*, following [391] and [15]. It is easy to construct a non-Schnorr regular sequence; in Section 13.15.4, we will see that such sequences occur even among the c.e. sets.

13.15.2 Examples of Schnorr dimension

The easiest way to construct examples of sequences of non-integral Schnorr Hausdorff dimension is by inserting zeroes into a sequence of Schnorr Hausdorff dimension 1. Note that it easily follows from the definitions that every Schnorr random set has Schnorr Hausdorff dimension 1. On the other hand, it is not hard to show that not every set of Schnorr Hausdorff dimension 1 is Schnorr random.

A second class of examples is based on the fact that Schnorr random sets satisfy the law of large numbers, not only with respect to the uniform measure, but also with respect to other computable Bernoulli distributions. For a sequence $\vec{p} = (p_0, p_1, \dots)$ of elements of $(0,1)$, the *Bernoulli measure* $\mu_{\vec{p}}$ is defined by $\mu_{\vec{p}}([\![\sigma]\!]) = \prod_{\sigma(i)=1} p_i \prod_{\sigma(i)=0} (1 - p_i)$. It is straightforward to modify the definition of Schnorr test to obtain Schnorr randomness notions for arbitrary computable measures, as we did for Martin-Löf randomness in Section 6.12.

Theorem 13.15.7 (Downey, Merkle, and Reimann [125]).

(i) *Let S be Schnorr random and let Z be a computable, infinite, co-infinite set such that* $\delta_Z = \lim_n \frac{|\{0,\ldots,n-1\}\cap Z|}{n}$ *exists. Let* $S_Z = S \oplus_Z \emptyset$, *where* $\oplus_Z$ *is as defined in Section 6.9. Then* $\dim_s(S_Z) = \delta_Z$.

(ii) *Let* $\vec{p} = (p_0, p_1, \ldots)$ *be a sequence of uniformly computable reals in* $(0,1)$ *such that* $p = \lim_n p_n$ *exists. Then for any Schnorr* $\mu_{\vec{p}}$*-random set* B, *we have* $\dim_s(B) = -(p \log p + (1-p)\log(1-p))$.

Part 1 of the theorem is straightforward (using for instance the martingale characterization of Schnorr Hausdorff dimension); part 2 is an easy adaption of the corresponding theorem for effective dimension (as for example in Section 13.5). Lutz [254] proved part 2 for Martin-Löf $\mu_{\vec{p}}$-randomness and effective Hausdorff dimension.

It is not hard to see that for the examples given in Theorem 13.15.7, the Schnorr Hausdorff dimension and the Schnorr packing dimension coincide, so these examples describe Schnorr regular sets. In Section 13.15.4, we will see that there are highly irregular c.e. sets: While all c.e. sets have Schnorr Hausdorff dimension 0, there are c.e. sets of Schnorr packing dimension 1.

Downey and Kach [unpublished] have noted that the method in the proof of Theorem 8.11.2 can be used to show that if a set is nonhigh, then its Schnorr Hausdorff dimension equals its effective Hausdorff dimension. We will see in Section 13.15.4 that this correspondence fails for packing dimension.

13.15.3 A machine characterization of Schnorr dimension

One of the fundamental aspects of the theory of 1-randomness is the characterization of that notion in terms of initial segment Kolmogorov complexity. There is an equally important correspondence between effective Hausdorff and packing dimensions and Kolmogorov complexity, as we saw in Theorem 13.3.4 and Corollary 13.11.12. A comparably elegant initial segment complexity characterization is not possible for Schnorr randomness, because such a characterization should be relativizable, and would therefore imply that lowness for K implies lowness for Schnorr randomness, which we saw was not the case in Section 12.1.

As we saw in Section 7.1.3, however, it is possible to obtain a machine characterization of Schnorr randomness by restricting ourselves to computable measure machines, that is, prefix-free machines whose domains have computable measures. We now see that we can use such machines to characterize Schnorr dimension as well.

Recall from Theorem 7.1.15 that Downey and Griffiths [109] showed that A is Schnorr random iff $K_M(A \upharpoonright n) \geqslant n - O(1)$ for every computable measure machine M. Building on this characterization, we can describe Schnorr dimension as asymptotic initial segment complexity with respect to computable measure machines.

Theorem 13.15.8 (Downey, Merkle, and Reimann [125]). *The Schnorr Hausdorff dimension of A is the infimum over all computable measure machines M of* $\liminf_n \frac{K_M(A\upharpoonright n)}{n}$.

Proof. ($\geqslant$) Let $s > \dim_S(A)$ be rational. We build a computable measure machine M such that $\liminf_n \frac{K_M(A\upharpoonright n)}{n} < s$.

Let $\{U_i\}_{i\in\omega}$ be a Schnorr s-test covering A. The KC Theorem is applicable to the set of requests $(\lfloor s|\sigma|\rfloor, \sigma)$ for $\sigma \in \bigcup_{i>1} U_i$, so there is a prefix-free machine M such that $K_M(\sigma) \leqslant \lfloor s|\sigma|\rfloor$ for all such σ. Furthermore, M is a computable measure machine because $\sum_{i>1}\sum_{\sigma\in U_i} 2^{-\lfloor s|\sigma|\rfloor}$ is computable.

We know that for each i there is an n_i such that $A \upharpoonright n_i \in U_n$, and clearly these n_i go to infinity. So there are infinitely many n such that $K_M(A \upharpoonright n) \leqslant \lfloor sn\rfloor \leqslant sn$, which implies that $\liminf_n \frac{K_M(A\upharpoonright n)}{n} \leqslant s$.

($\leqslant$) Suppose there is a computable measure machine M such that $\liminf_n \frac{K_M(A\upharpoonright n)}{n} < s$, where s is rational. Let $S_M = \{\sigma : K_M(\sigma) < s|\sigma|\}$.

We claim that S_M is a total Solovay s-test covering A. There are infinitely many initial segments of A in S_M, so it remains to show that $\sum_{\sigma\in S_M} 2^{-s|\sigma|}$ is finite and computable. Finiteness follows from the fact that

$$\sum_{\sigma\in S_M} 2^{-s|\sigma|} < \sum_{\sigma\in S_M} 2^{-K_M(\sigma)} \leqslant 1.$$

To show computability, given ε, compute an s such that $\mu([\![\mathrm{dom}(M) \setminus \mathrm{dom}(M_s)]\!]) < \varepsilon$, and let $S_{M_s} = \{\sigma : K_{M_s}(\sigma) < s|\sigma|\}$. Then

$$\sum_{\sigma\in S_{M_s}} 2^{-s|\sigma|} \leqslant \sum_{\sigma\in S_M} 2^{-s|\sigma|} \leqslant \sum_{\sigma\in S_{M_s}} 2^{-s|\sigma|} + \varepsilon,$$

since for any $\sigma \in S_M \setminus S_{M_s}$, we have $2^{-s|\sigma|} < 2^{-K_M(\sigma)}$, and any minimal length M-description of σ must be in $\mathrm{dom}(M)\setminus\mathrm{dom}(M_s)$, whence the sum of $2^{-s|\sigma|}$ over all such σ is bounded by $\mu([\![\mathrm{dom}(M) \setminus \mathrm{dom}(M_s)]\!]) < \varepsilon$. □

An analogous argument, using the correspondence between martingales and tests shown in Theorem 13.15.6, allows us to obtain a machine characterization of Schnorr packing dimension.

Theorem 13.15.9 (Downey, Merkle, and Reimann [125]). *The Schnorr packing dimension of A is the infimum over all computable measure machines M of* $\limsup_n \frac{K_M(A\upharpoonright n)}{n}$.

13.15.4 Schnorr dimension and computable enumerability

For left-c.e. reals, having high effective dimension has similar computability-theoretic consequences to being 1-random. For instance, as we have seen, every left-c.e. real of positive effective dimension is Turing complete. For Schnorr dimension, a straightforward generalization of Corollary 8.11.4 shows that if A is left-c.e. and $\dim_S(A) > 0$, then A is high.

Computably enumerable sets are usually of marginal interest in the context of algorithmic randomness, one reason being that they cannot be random relative to most notions of randomness. For instance, we have the following.

Proposition 13.15.10 (Folklore). *No c.e. set is Schnorr random.*

Proof. Let A be c.e. We may assume that A is infinite, and hence contains an infinite computable subset $\{b_0 < b_1 < \cdots\}$. Let $G_n = \{\sigma \in 2^{b_n} : \forall i < n\,(\sigma(b_i) = 1)\}$ and let $U_n = [\![G_n]\!]$. Then $\mu(U_n) = 2^{-n}$, so the U_n form a Schnorr test, and $A \in \bigcap_n U_n$. □

This proof does not immediately extend to showing that a c.e. set A must have Schnorr Hausdorff dimension 0. Defining coverings from the enumeration of A directly might not work either, since the dimension factor leads longer strings to be weighted more, so, depending on the enumeration, we might not get a Schnorr s-covering. However, we can exploit the somewhat predictable nature of A to define for each $s > 0$ a computable martingale that s-succeeds on A.

Theorem 13.15.11 (Downey, Merkle, and Reimann [125]). *Every c.e. set has Schnorr Hausdorff dimension* 0.

Proof. Let $s \in \mathbb{Q}^{>0}$. Let $\gamma > 2^{1-s} - 1$ be rational. Partition $\mathbb{N}$ into consecutive disjoint intervals $I_0, I_1, \ldots$ so that there is an $\varepsilon > 0$ for which, letting $i_n = |I_n|$ and $j_n = i_0 + i_1 + \cdots + i_n$, we have

$$\lim_n \frac{(1+\gamma)^{i_n}\left(\frac{1-\gamma}{1+\gamma}\right)^{\varepsilon i_n}}{2^{(1-s)j_n}} = \infty.$$

To have this hold, it is enough to have I_n be much larger than I_{n-1}, for example by letting $|I_n| = 2^{|I_0|+\cdots+|I_{n-1}|}$.

Let $\delta = \limsup_n \frac{|A \cap I_n|}{i_n}$. By replacing A with its complement if needed, we may assume that $\delta > 0$. Let $q < r \in \mathbb{Q}$ be such that $\delta \in (q, r)$ and $r - q < \varepsilon$. There is a computable sequence $n_0 < n_1 < \cdots$ such that $qi_{n_k} < |A \cap I_{n_k}| < ri_{n_k}$ for all k.

Let d be defined as follows. let $d(\lambda) = 1$. If $|\sigma| \notin I_{n_k}$ for all k, then let $d(\sigma 0) = d(\sigma 1) = d(\sigma)$. If $|\sigma| \in I_k$, then wait for an s such that $|A_s \cap I_{n_k}| > qi_{n_k}$. If $|\sigma| \in A_s$, then let $d(\sigma 0) = 0$ and $d(\sigma 1) = 2d(\sigma)$. Otherwise, let $d(\sigma 0) = (1+\gamma)d(\sigma)$ and $d(\sigma 1) = (1-\gamma)d(\sigma)$.

When betting along A, the number of times we are in the last case of the definition of d and yet $|\sigma| \in A$ is less than $(r-q)i_{n_k} < \varepsilon i_{n_k}$, so

$$d(A \upharpoonright j_{n_k}) > d(A \upharpoonright j_{n_{k-1}})(1+\gamma)^{i_{n_k}-\varepsilon i_{n_k}}(1-\gamma)^{\varepsilon i_{n_k}}$$
$$= d(A \upharpoonright j_{n_{k-1}})(1+\gamma)^{i_{n_k}}\left(\frac{1-\gamma}{1+\gamma}\right)^{\varepsilon i_{n_k}}.$$

By our choice of ε, we see that d s-succeeds on A. □

We have seen that effective Hausdorff dimension is stable; that is, the effective Hausdorff dimension of a class is the supremum of the effective Hausdorff dimensions of its elements. It is not hard to see that for every Schnorr 1-test there is a c.e. (and even a computable) set that is not covered by it. Thus the class of all c.e. sets has Schnorr Hausdorff dimension 1, and hence Schnorr Hausdorff dimension is not stable, even for countable classes.

Perhaps surprisingly, there do exist c.e. sets with Schnorr packing dimension 1. This result contrasts with the case of effective packing dimension, since as we will see in Theorem 16.1.1, if A is c.e. then $C(A \upharpoonright n) \leqslant 2\log n + O(1)$. It can be generalized to show that every hyperimmune degree contains a set of Schnorr packing dimension 1. Downey, Merkle, and Reimann [125] remarked that a straightforward forcing construction shows the existence of degrees that do not contain any set of high Schnorr packing dimension.

Theorem 13.15.12 (Downey, Merkle, and Reimann [125]). *If B has hyperimmune degree then there is an $A \equiv_T B$ with Schnorr packing dimension 1. If B is c.e. then A can be chosen to be c.e.*

Proof. We begin with the non-c.e. case. It is enough to build $C \leqslant_T B$ with Schnorr packing dimension 1, since we can then let $A = B \oplus_X C$ for a sufficiently sparse computable set X (where $\oplus_X$ is as defined in Section 6.9), say $X = \{2^n : n \in \mathbb{N}\}$.

Let $g \leqslant_T B$ be such that for any computable function f, we have $f(n) < g(n)$ for infinitely many n. Effectively partition $\mathbb{N}$ into disjoint consecutive intervals $I_0, I_1, \ldots$ such that $|I_{n+1}|$ is much greater than $|I_0| + \cdots + |I_n|$. For instance, we can choose the I_n so that $|I_{n+1}| = 2^{|I_0|+\cdots+|I_n|}$. Let $i_n = |I_n|$. Let $M_0, M_1, \ldots$ be an effective enumeration of all prefix-free machines.

If $\sum_{M_e[g(n)](\sigma)\downarrow} 2^{-|\sigma|} \leqslant 1 - 2^{-i_{\langle e,n\rangle}}$ then let $C \cap I_{\langle e,n\rangle} = \emptyset$. Otherwise, let $\sigma \in 2^{i_{\langle e,n\rangle}}$ be such that $K_{M_e[g(n)]}(\sigma) \geqslant i_{\langle e,n\rangle}$. (If such a σ does not exist, then the domain of M_e consists exactly of the finitely many strings of length $i_{\langle e,n\rangle}$, so we do not have to worry about M_e; in this case, let $C \cap I_{\langle e,n\rangle} = \emptyset$.) Note that $K_{M_e}(\sigma) \geqslant i_{\langle e,n\rangle}$. Let $C \upharpoonright I_{\langle e,n\rangle} = \sigma$. We have $C \leqslant_T g \leqslant_T B$.

Assume for a contradiction that $\mathrm{Dim}_S(C) < 1$. Then there exists a computable measure machine M and an $\varepsilon > 0$ such that $K_M(C \upharpoonright n) \leqslant (1-\varepsilon)n$ for almost all n. By Proposition 7.1.18, we may assume that $\mu([\![\mathrm{dom}\, M]\!]) =$

1. We define a machine $\widetilde{M}$ with the same domain as M. If $M(x)\downarrow$ then check whether $|M(x)| = i_0 + i_1 + \cdots + i_k$ for some k. If so, then let $\widetilde{M}(x)$ be the last i_k many bits of $M(x)$. Otherwise, let $\widetilde{M}(x) = 0$. Let e be such that $M_e = \widetilde{M}$.

Let $f(n)$ be the least stage s such that $\sum_{M_e[s](\sigma)\downarrow} 2^{-|\sigma|} > 1 - 2^{-i_{\langle e,n\rangle}}$. Since $\mu([\![\operatorname{dom} M_e]\!]) = 1$, the function f is total and computable, so there are infinitely many n such that $f(n) < g(n)$. For each such n, we have $K_{M_e}(C \upharpoonright I_{\langle e,n\rangle}) \geqslant i_{\langle e,n\rangle}$. On the other hand, for almost all n,

$$K_{M_e}(C \upharpoonright I_{\langle e,n\rangle}) \leqslant K_M(C \upharpoonright I_{\langle e,0\rangle} \cup \ldots \cup I_{\langle e,n\rangle})$$
$$\leqslant (1-\varepsilon)\Big(\sum_{j\leqslant n} i_{\langle e,j\rangle}\Big) \leqslant \Big(1 - \frac{\varepsilon}{2}\Big) i_{\langle e,n\rangle},$$

so we have a contradiction.

If B is c.e., then it is easy to see that we can let the function g above be defined by letting $g(n)$ be the least stage s such that $B_s(n) = B(n)$. If we build C as above using this g, then C is c.e., since if $n \notin B$ then $C \upharpoonright I_{\langle e,n\rangle} = \emptyset$, while otherwise we can wait until the stage $g(n)$ at which n enters B, and compute $C \upharpoonright I_{\langle e,n\rangle}$ from $g(n)$, enumerating all its elements into C at stage $g(n)$. □

As mentioned in Section 13.15.2, this result, combined with Theorem 13.14.5 (or Theorem 16.1.1 below, which implies that all c.e. sets have effective packing dimension 0), shows that, as opposed to the case of Hausdorff dimension, there are nonhigh sets with Schnorr packing dimension 1 but effective packing dimension 0.

13.16 Kolmogorov complexity and the dimensions of individual strings

In this section, we look at work of Lutz [254] on assigning dimensions to individual *strings*, and a new characterization of prefix-free complexity using such dimensions.

We have seen that the effective dimension of a set can be characterized in terms of initial segment complexity and in terms of c.e. (super)gales. To discretize the latter characterization, Lutz replaced supergales by *termgales*, which can deal with the fact that strings terminate; this change is made by first defining s-termgales, and then defining termgales, which are uniform families of s-termgales. Next, he replaced "tending to infinity" by "exceeding a finite threshold". Finally, he replaced an optimal s-supergale by an optimal termgale.

The basic idea is to introduce a new termination symbol $\square$ to mark the end of a string. A *terminated binary string* is $\sigma\square$ with $\sigma \in 2^{<\omega}$. Let T be the collection of terminated binary strings.

Definition 13.16.1 (Lutz [254]). For $s \geqslant 0$, an *s-termgale* is a function $d : 2^{<\omega} \cup T \to \mathbb{R}^{\geqslant 0}$ such that $d(\lambda) \leqslant 1$ and for all $\sigma \in 2^{<\omega}$,

$$d(\sigma) \geqslant 2^{-s}(d(\sigma 0) + d(\sigma 1) + d(\sigma\square)).$$

For $s = 1$, the s-termgale condition is akin to the usual supermartingale condition, but as noted by Lutz, if each of $0, 1, \square$ is equally likely, independently of previous bits, then the conditional expected capital after betting on the bit to follow σ is $\frac{d(\sigma 0)+d(\sigma 1)+d(\sigma\square)}{3} = \frac{2}{3}d(\sigma)$. However, the definition of s-termgales is based on the assumption that the termination symbol $\square$ should actually be regarded as having vanishingly small probability. In other words, the 1-termgale payoff condition is the same as the corresponding supermartingale condition, except that the 1-termgale must divert some of its capital to the possibility of $\square$ occurring, and this diversion is without compensation, but $\square$ can occur at most once, and we can make the impact of this diversion of capital small.

Lutz [254] provided the following example. Let $d(\lambda) = 1$. Given $d(\sigma)$, let $d(\sigma 0) = \frac{3}{2}d(\sigma)$ and $d(\sigma 1) = d(\sigma\square) = \frac{1}{4}d(\sigma)$. Then d is a 1-termgale and if σ is a string with n_0 many 0's and n_1 many 1's, then

$$d(\sigma\square) = (\frac{3}{2})^{n_0}(\frac{1}{4})^{n_1+1} = 2^{n_0(1+\log 3)-2(n_1+1)}.$$

Thus if $n_0 \gg \frac{2}{1+\log 3}(n_0 + n_1 + 1)$, then $d(\sigma\square)$ is significantly greater than $d(\lambda)$ even though d loses three quarters of its capital when $\square$ occurs.

The following facts are straightforward.

Lemma 13.16.2. *Let $d, d' : 2^{<\omega} \cup T \to \mathbb{R}^{\geqslant 0}$ be such that $2^{-s|\sigma|}d(\sigma) = 2^{-s'|\sigma|}d'(\sigma)$ for all $\sigma \in 2^{<\omega} \cup T$. Then d is an s-termgale iff d' is an s'-termgale.*

In particular, if d is a 0-termgale and $d'(\sigma) = 2^{s|\sigma|}d(\sigma)$ for all $\sigma \in 2^{<\omega} \cup T$, then d' is an s-termgale, and each s-termgale can be obtained in this way from a 0-termgale.

We need the following technical lemma.

Lemma 13.16.3 (Lutz [254]). *Let d be an s-termgale and $\tau \in 2^{<\omega}$. Then $\sum_{\sigma \in 2^{<\omega}} 2^{-s|\sigma|}d(\tau\sigma\square) \leqslant 2^s d(\tau)$.*

Proof. First suppose that $s = 0$. It is straightforward to show by induction that for all m,

$$\sum_{\sigma \in 2^{<m}} d(\tau\sigma\square) + \sum_{\sigma \in 2^m} d(\tau\sigma) \leqslant d(\tau).$$

Thus $\sum_{\sigma \in 2^{\leqslant m}} d(\tau\sigma\square) \leqslant d(\tau)$ for all m, and hence $\sum_{\sigma \in 2^{<\omega}} d(\tau\sigma\square) \leqslant d(\tau)$.

For the general case, let $d'(\sigma) = 2^{-s|\sigma|}d(\sigma)$ for all $\sigma \in 2^{<\omega} \cup T$. Then d' is a 0-termgale, and hence

$$\sum_{\sigma \in 2^{<\omega}} 2^{-s|\sigma|}d(\tau\sigma\square) = \sum_{\sigma \in 2^{<\omega}} 2^{s(|\tau|+1)}d'(\tau\sigma\square) \leqslant 2^{s(|\tau|+1)}d'(\tau) = 2^s d(\tau).$$

□

We are now ready to define (optimal) termgales.

Definition 13.16.4 (Lutz [254]). (i) A *termgale* is a family $d = \{d^s : s \geqslant 0\}$ of s-termgales such that $2^{-s|\sigma|}d^s(\sigma) = 2^{-s'|\sigma|}d^{s'}(\sigma)$ for all s, s', and $\sigma \in 2^{<\omega} \cup T$.

(ii) A termgale is Σ^0_1, or *constructive*, if d^0 is a Σ^0_1 function.

(iii) A Σ^0_1 termgale $\tilde{d}$ is *optimal* if for each Σ^0_1 termgale d there is a $c > 0$ such that for all s and $\sigma \in 2^{<\omega}$, we have $\tilde{d}^s(\sigma\square) \geqslant cd^s(\sigma\square)$.

In the same way that we connected continuous semimeasures with martingales, we can define the *termgale induced by* a c.e. discrete semimeasure m via $d[m]^s(\tau) = 2^{s|\sigma|}\sum_{\tau \preccurlyeq \sigma\square} m(\sigma)$. (See Section 3.9 for more on discrete semimeasures.)

Theorem 13.16.5 (Lutz [254]). *If m is a maximal c.e. discrete semimeasure then $d[m]$ is an optimal Σ^0_1 termgale. Thus there is an optimal Σ^0_1 termgale.*

Proof. It is easy to check that $d[m]$ is a termgale. Let $d = \{d^s : s \geqslant 0\}$ be a termgale. Let $\widehat{m}(\sigma) = d^0(\sigma\square)$. By Lemma 13.16.3, $\widehat{m}$ is a c.e. discrete semimeasure. Since m is multiplicatively optimal, for some c we have $m(\sigma) \geqslant c\widehat{m}(\sigma)$ for all $\sigma \in 2^{<\omega}$. Hence

$$d[m]^s(\sigma\square) = 2^{s|\sigma\square|}m(\sigma) \geqslant 2^{s|\sigma\square|}c\widehat{m}(\sigma) = cd^s(\sigma\square).$$

□

Definition 13.16.6 (Lutz [254]). If d is a termgale, $n > 0$, and $\sigma \in 2^{<\omega}$, then the *dimension of σ relative to d at significance level n* is

$$\dim^n_d(\sigma) = \inf\{s \geqslant 0 : d^s(\sigma\square) > n\}.$$

We can characterize this dimension in terms of an optimal termgale.

Theorem 13.16.7 (Lutz [254]). *Let $\tilde{d}$ be an optimal Σ^0_1 termgale, and let d be a Σ^0_1 termgale. Then for each $n > 0$ there is a $c > 0$ such that, for all $\sigma \in 2^{<\omega}$,*

$$\dim^n_{\tilde{d}}(\sigma) \leqslant \dim^1_d(\sigma) + \frac{c}{1 + |\sigma|}.$$

Hence, if $\tilde{d}_1$ and $\tilde{d}_2$ are both optimal Σ^0_1 termgales and $n_1, n_2 > 0$, then there is a $c > 0$ such that for all $\sigma \in 2^{<\omega}$,

$$\dim^{n_1}_{\tilde{d}_1}(\sigma) - \dim^{n_2}_{\tilde{d}_2}(\sigma) \leqslant \frac{c}{1+|\sigma|}.$$

Proof. By the optimality of $\tilde{d}$, there is a constant $b \in (0,1)$ such that for all s, we have $\tilde{d}^s(\sigma\Box) \geqslant bd^s(\sigma\Box)$. Given n, let $c = \log n - \log b$, and notice that $c > 0$. Let $s > \dim^1_d(\sigma) + \frac{c}{1+|\sigma|}$ and let $s_1 = s - \frac{c}{1+|\sigma|}$. Then $s_1 > \dim^1_d(\sigma)$, so

$$\tilde{d}^s(\sigma\Box) \geqslant bd^s(\sigma\Box) = b2^{(s-s_1)|\sigma\Box|}d^{s_1}(\sigma\Box)) = b2^c d^{s_1}(\sigma\Box) > b2^c = n.$$

□

Theorem 13.16.7 is the key to Lutz' definition of the dimension of a string, since it says that if we base our definition on a particular optimal Σ^0_1 termgale $\tilde{d}$ and significance level n, then this choice will have little effect on the dimension of a given string, particularly for longer strings. Therefore we fix an optimal Σ^0_1 termgale $d_\Box$ and make the following definition.

Definition 13.16.8 (Lutz [254]). $\dim(\sigma) = \dim^1_{d_\Box}(\sigma)$ for every $\sigma \in 2^{<\omega}$.

In this context, we lose some of the finer points of Hausdorff dimension. For example, it is no longer true that the effective dimension is bounded above by 1. But we do have the following analog.

Theorem 13.16.9 (Lutz [254]). *There is a $b > 0$ such that* $\dim(\sigma) \leqslant b$ *for all $\sigma \in 2^{<\omega}$.*

Proof. For each σ and s, let $d^s(\sigma) = 2^{(s-2)|\sigma|}$ and $d^s(\sigma\Box) = 2^{(s-2)|\sigma|+1}$. Then it is easy to check that $d = \{d^s : s \geqslant 0\}$ is a termgale, and $d^2(\sigma\Box) = 2$ for all σ. Thus, by Theorem 13.16.7, there is a c such that $\dim(\sigma) \leqslant 2 + \frac{c}{1+|\sigma|} \leqslant 2 + c$, so we can take $b = 2 + c$. □

Finally, we have an analog of the Kolmogorov complexity characterization of effective Hausdorff dimension.

Theorem 13.16.10 (Lutz [254]). $K(\sigma) = |\sigma|\dim(\sigma) \pm O(1)$.

Proof. Let m be a maximal c.e. semimeasure, as given in Theorem 3.9.2, and let $d[m]$ be the termgale induced by m. For all $\sigma \in 2^{<\omega}$ and $s > 0$, we have

$$d[m]^s(\sigma\Box) > 1 \text{ iff } 2^{s|\sigma\Box|}m(\sigma) > 1 \text{ iff } s > \frac{-\log m(\sigma)}{1+|\sigma|},$$

so $(1+|\sigma|)\dim^1_{d[m]}(\sigma) = -\log m(\sigma)$.

Thus, by Theorem 13.16.7, $(1+|\sigma|)\dim(\sigma) = -\log m(\sigma) \pm O(1)$, so by Theorem 13.16.9, $|\sigma|\dim(\sigma) = -\log m(\sigma) \pm O(1)$. But by the Coding Theorem 3.9.4, $K(\sigma) = -\log m(\sigma) \pm O(1)$, so $|\sigma|\dim(\sigma) = K(\sigma) \pm O(1)$. □

Theorem 13.16.10 implies that for any $A \in 2^\omega$, we have $\lim_n |\frac{K(A\upharpoonright n)}{n} - \dim(A \upharpoonright n)| = 0$. Thus the Kolmogorov complexity characterizations of effective Hausdorff and packing dimensions imply the following.

Corollary 13.16.11 (Lutz [254]). *For* $A \in 2^\omega$, *we have* $\dim(A) = \liminf_n \dim(A \upharpoonright n)$ *and* $\mathrm{Dim}(A) = \limsup_n \dim(A \upharpoonright n)$.

In [254], Lutz also proved several other facts about the dimensions of finite strings. Space considerations preclude us from including this material.

Part IV

Further Topics

14
Strong Jump Traceability

As we have seen, the K-trivial sets form a class of "extremely low" sets, properly contained within the class of superlow sets and closed under join. The study of K-triviality has led to an increased interest in notions of computability-theoretic weakness. In particular, various forms of traceability have played important roles. In this chapter we study the notion of *strong jump traceability* introduced by Figueira, Nies, and Stephan [147] and later studied by Cholak, Downey, and Greenberg [65], among others, and explore its connections with K-triviality and other randomness-theoretic notions. In the computably enumerable case, we will show that the strongly jump traceable c.e. sets form a proper subideal of the K-trivial c.e. sets, and can be characterized as those c.e. sets that are computable from every ω-c.e. (or every superlow) 1-random set. We will also discuss the general case in the last section. In particular, we will show that *every* s.j.t. set is K-trivial, a result of Downey and Greenberg [105].

14.1 Basics

Recall that we denote $\Phi_n^A(n)$ by $J^A(n)$, and that a set A is h-jump traceable for a computable order h if there are uniformly c.e. sets $T_0, T_1, \ldots$ such that $|T_n| \leqslant h(n)$ and $J^A(n)\downarrow \;\Rightarrow J^A(n) \in T_n$ for all n. (That is, there is a c.e. trace for J^A with bound h.) In this chapter we assume that all orders h have $h(0) > 0$.

R.G. Downey and D. Hirschfeldt, *Algorithmic Randomness and Complexity*, Theory and Applications of Computability, DOI 10.1007/978-0-387-68441-3_14,

Definition 14.1.1 (Figueira, Nies, and Stephan [147]). A set A is *strongly jump traceable (s.j.t.)* if it is h-jump traceable for every computable order h.

It follows easily from the fact that there is a computable function f such that $J^A(f(e,n)) = \Phi_e^A(n)$ for all e and n that if A is s.j.t. then for each computable order h and each partial A-computable function ψ, there is a c.e. trace for ψ with bound h. Indeed, we have the following useful fact.

Lemma 14.1.2 (essentially Cholak, Downey, and Greenberg [65], see also Nies [306]). *Let $h_0, h_1, \ldots$ be uniformly computable orders such that $h_n(0) \geqslant n$ for all n. From indices for the sequence $h_0, h_1, \ldots$ and for a sequence of uniformly computable functionals $\Psi_0, \Psi_1, \ldots$, we can effectively determine a computable order g such that for all A, if J^A has a c.e. trace $\{T_i\}_{i\in\omega}$ with bound g, then each Ψ_n^A has a c.e. trace with bound h_n, and these can be obtained effectively from an index for $\{T_i\}_{i\in\omega}$.*

It is not obvious that noncomputable s.j.t. sets exist, but the following result shows that they in fact do. We give a sketch of its proof from [65].

Theorem 14.1.3 (Figueira, Nies, and Stephan [147]). *There is a promptly simple s.j.t. c.e. set.*

Proof sketch. Suppose that we wish to construct a noncomputable c.e. set A that is h-jump traceable for a single given computable order h. Let P_e be the eth noncomputability requirement, $\overline{A} \neq W_e$, and let N_e be the requirement stating that if $J^A(e)\downarrow$ then $J^A(e) \in T_e$, for a c.e. trace $T_0, T_1, \ldots$ with bound h that we build.

We order the requirements in the following way:

$$\underbrace{N_0\, N_1\, N_2 \ldots N_e \ldots}_{h(e)=1}\; P_0\; \underbrace{\ldots N_e \ldots}_{h(e)=2}\; P_1\; \underbrace{\ldots N_e \ldots}_{h(e)=3}\; P_2 \ldots$$

The construction is straightforward: Each P_e is appointed a follower x. If x enters W_e at a stage s at which P_e is not yet satisfied, then we put x into A, satisfying P_e. If a new computation $J^A(e)$ appears at a stage s, then N_e puts its value into T_e and initializes all weaker P-requirements, which are then appointed new, large followers (in particular larger than the use of the computation $J^A(e)[s]$). It is easy to see that the arrangement of strategies ensures that $|T_e| \leqslant h(e)$.

The key to the success of this construction is that each requirement P_e acts at most once, and does not need to act again even if it is later initialized. It may be instructive to think of the priority ordering as dynamic: when P_e acts, it is removed from the list of requirements and is never troubled (nor influences other requirements) again.

To make A be h-jump traceable for all computable orders h, a further dynamic element needs to be introduced to the priority ordering. The property of a partial computable function being an order is Π_2^0, and we approximate it in this fashion. Say that a stage is *e-expansionary* if at this stage we have further evidence that the eth partial computable function Φ_e is an order. If s is e-expansionary then the positive requirements are pushed down the ordering so that for every n such that $\Phi_e(n)[s]\downarrow$, there are at most $\Phi_e(n)$ many positive requirements stronger than $N_{e,n}$, the requirement that traces $J^A(e)$ with at most $\Phi_e(n)$ many values. To protect the positive requirements from being moved down infinitely often, we stipulate that a positive requirement $P_{e'}$ cannot be moved by Φ_e if $e' < e$; these positive requirements are ignored when we count the number of positive requirements that appear before some $N_{e,n}$. If $P_{e'}$ acts then we initialize every $N_{e,n}$ and start a new trace. □

This proof admits the usual sorts of variations. For instance, Cholak, Downey, and Greenberg [65] showed that for every low c.e. set B, there is an s.j.t. c.e. set $A \not\leqslant_T B$.

Since $A \leqslant_T B$ implies that J^A is uniformly coded into J^B, we have the following.

Theorem 14.1.4 (Figueira, Nies, and Stephan [147]). *The class of strongly jump traceable sets is closed downward under Turing reducibility.*

Figueira, Nies, and Stephan [147] also studied the relationship between strong jump traceability and other kinds of approximations to the jump.

Definition 14.1.5 (Figueira, Nies, and Stephan [147]). A set D is *well-approximable* if for each computable order h there is a computable g such that for all n, we have $|\{s : g(n, s+1) \neq g(n, s)\}| \leqslant h(n)$ and $D(n) = \lim_s g(n, s)$.

Figueira, Nies, and Stephan [147] studied sets A such that A' is well-approximable. As with strong jump traceability, it is easy to see that the class of such *jump well-approximable* well sets is closed downward under Turing reducibility. We can also study the J^A version of this definition: Downey and Greenberg [unpublished] defined A to be *strongly jump well-approximable* if J^A is well-approximable. Downey and Greenberg conjectured that jump well-approximability, strong jump well-approximability, and strong jump traceability are equivalent, but this is not known to be the case in general. In the c.e. case, it is not hard to show that these notions are indeed the same.

Theorem 14.1.6 (essentially Figueira, Nies, and Stephan [147]). *The following are equivalent for a c.e. set A.*

(i) *A is strongly jump traceable.*

(ii) *A is jump well-approximable.*

(iii) *A is strongly jump well-approximable.*

Relatively weak computability-theoretic lowness properties do not imply randomness-theoretic lowness. For instance, there are 1-random sets that are low, or even superlow. However, the same is not true of very strong computability-theoretic lowness notions. For instance, we have the following plain complexity characterization of strong jump traceability.

Theorem 14.1.7 (Figueira, Nies, and Stephan [147]). *A set A is s.j.t. iff for every computable order h, we have $C(\sigma) \leqslant C^A(\sigma) + h(C^A(\sigma))$ for almost all σ.*

Proof. Let A be s.j.t. and let h be a computable order. Let $g(n) = \log h(n)$. It clearly suffices to show that $C(\sigma) \leqslant C^A(\sigma) + g(C^A(\sigma)) + O(1)$. Since $\mathcal{U}^A$ is a partial A-computable function, there is a c.e. trace $\{T_\tau\}_{\tau \in 2^{<\omega}}$ for $\mathcal{U}^A$ with bound $g(|\tau|)$. Let τ be a minimal-length $\mathcal{U}^A$-description of σ. Since $\sigma \in T_\tau$, we can describe σ by giving τ and a number less than or equal to $g(|\sigma|)$ denoting σ's position in the enumeration of T_τ. Thus $C(\sigma) \leqslant |\tau| + g(|\tau|) + O(1) = C^A(\sigma) + g(C^A(\sigma)) + O(1)$.

Conversely, suppose that for every computable order h, we have $C(\sigma) \leqslant C^A(\sigma) + h(C^A(\sigma))$ for almost all σ. If $J^A(e)\downarrow$ and $\log n = e$ then $C^A(n, J^A(e)) \leqslant C^A(n) + O(1) \leqslant e + O(1)$. Let c be this final $O(1)$ constant. Let h be a computable order. Let g be a computable order such that $3^{g(e+c)} \leqslant h(e)$ for all e. If $J^A(e)\downarrow$ and $\log n = e$ then $C(n, J^A(e)) \leqslant C^A(n, J^A(e)) + g(C^A(n, J^A(e))) \leqslant e + g(e + c) + c$. Let

$$T_e = \{m : \forall n\, (\log n = e \Rightarrow C(n, m) \leqslant e + g(e + c) + c)\}.$$

Then for almost all e, if $J^A(e)\downarrow$, then $J^A(e) \in T^{(e)}$, since for any n with $\log n = e$, we have $C(n, J^A(e)) \leqslant e + g(e + c) + c$. So it is enough to show that $|T_e| \leqslant h(e)$ for almost all e. Let n be such that $\log n = e$ and $C(n) \geqslant e$. Then for all $m \in T_e$, we have $C(n, m) \leqslant e + g(e+c) + c \leqslant C(n) + g(e+c) + c$, so by Theorem 3.4.6, for almost all e, we have $|T_e| \leqslant 3^{g(e+c)} \leqslant h(e)$. □

One consequence of the above result is that jump well-approximability implies strong jump traceability in general.

Theorem 14.1.8 (Figueira, Nies, and Stephan [147]). *If A' is well approximable, then for every computable order h, we have $C(\sigma) \leqslant C^A(\sigma) + h(C^A(\sigma))$ for almost all σ. Thus every jump well-approximable set is s.j.t.*

Proof. Let h be a computable order. Let $n_\sigma = C(\sigma \mid \sigma_A^*)$. (Recall that σ_A^* is a minimal length $\mathcal{U}^A$-description of σ.) We have $C(\sigma) \leqslant C^A(\sigma) + 2n_\sigma$ for almost all σ, so it is enough to show that $n_\sigma \leqslant \frac{h(C^A(\sigma))}{2}$ for almost all σ. In fact, we will show that $n_\sigma \leqslant 2 \log h(C^A(\sigma)) + O(1)$.

Define a partial A-computable function $\Psi(m, n, \rho)$ as follows. Wait until $\sigma = \mathcal{U}^A(\rho)$, if ever. Then search for a $\tau \in 2^n$ such that $\mathcal{U}^\rho(\tau) = \sigma$. If such a τ is found, $m < n$, and the mth bit of τ is 1, then let $\Psi(m, n, \rho)\downarrow$ (the actual value of $\Psi(m, n, \rho)$ is irrelevant). The important part of this definition is that there is some $\tau_\sigma \in 2^{n_\sigma}$ such that $\mathcal{U}^{\sigma_A^*}(\tau_\sigma) = \sigma$ and for $m < n_\sigma$, we have $\Psi(m, n_\sigma, \sigma_A^*)\downarrow$ iff $\tau_\sigma(m) = 1$.

Let f be a computable function such that $A'(f(m,n,\rho)) = 1$ iff $\Psi(m,n,\rho)\downarrow$. Let b be a computable order such that $b(f(m,n,\rho)) \leqslant mnh(|\rho|)$ for all m, n, and ρ. By definition, there is a way to approximate A' so that $A'(k)$ is approximated with at most $b(k)$ many mind changes. Thus, since $\tau_\sigma(m) = 1$ iff $A'(f(m, n_\sigma, \sigma_A^*)) = 1$, we can describe τ_σ from σ_A^* by giving n_σ and the exact number of times our approximation to $A'(f(0, n_\sigma, \sigma_A^*)), \ldots, A'(f(n_\sigma - 1, n_\sigma, \sigma_A^*))$ changes, which is bounded by $n_\sigma^2 h(|\sigma_A^*|) = n_\sigma^2 h(C^A(\sigma))$. But we can also compute σ from τ_σ and σ_A^*, so

$$\begin{aligned} n_\sigma = C(\sigma \mid \sigma_A^*) &\leqslant C(\tau_\sigma \mid \sigma_A^*) + O(1) \\ &\leqslant 2\log n_\sigma + \log(n_\sigma^2 h(C^A(\sigma))) + O(1) \\ &\leqslant 4\log n_\sigma + \log h(C^A(\sigma)) + O(1) \leqslant \frac{n_\sigma}{2} + \log h(C^A(\sigma)) + O(1), \end{aligned}$$

so $n_\sigma \leqslant 2\log h(C^A(\sigma)) + O(1)$. □

Ng [296] has shown that the index set of c.e. s.j.t. sets is Π_4^0-complete. His proof builds on the method of separating K-triviality and strong jump traceability from Theorem 14.3.7 below.

Ng has also studied relativized versions of strong jump traceability and related notions. For example, a set A is *ultra jump traceable* if A is strongly jump traceable relative to all c.e. sets X. That is, for every c.e. set X and every X-computable order h, there is an X-c.e. trace for J^A with bound h. Note that this definition is a "partial" relativization, in that we trace only J^A, not $J^{X \oplus A}$. Ng [297, 294] has shown that noncomputable ultra jump traceable sets exist, but no noncomputable set is jump traceable relative to all Δ_2^0 sets in this partial sense. He has also shown that the ultra jump traceable sets form a proper subclass of the s.j.t. sets, and that they cannot be promptly simple. They thus form the first known class defined by a cost function construction that has noncomputable elements but no promptly simple ones. This class is not yet well understood.

14.2 The ideal of strongly jump traceable c.e. sets

By Theorem 14.1.4, the class of strongly jump traceable sets is closed downward under Turing reducibility. In this section we show that the join of two s.j.t. c.e. sets is also s.j.t., and so the c.e. s.j.t. sets form an ideal in the c.e. degrees. In fact, we show that for every computable order h there is another computable order g such that if A_0 and A_1 are c.e. and g-jump traceable, then $A \oplus B$ is h-jump traceable. This result should be contrasted with Theorem 11.6.4 that there exist superlow c.e. sets A and B such that $A \oplus B \equiv_T \emptyset'$.

The following theorem improves an earlier unpublished result of Ng, who built a nontrivial class of c.e. sets $\mathcal{C}$ such that for all $A \in \mathcal{C}$ and all s.j.t. sets B, the join $A \oplus B$ is strongly jump traceable.

Theorem 14.2.1 (Cholak, Downey, and Greenberg [65]). *Let g be a computable order. There is a computable order h such that if A and B are h-jump traceable c.e. sets, then $A \oplus B$ is g-jump traceable. In particular, if A and B are s.j.t. c.e. sets then so is $A \oplus B$.*

Proof. This proof is a relatively simple example of the *box promotion* (or *box amplification*) method, so we wish to describe the motivation behind it.

Suppose that we wanted to prove the theorem wrong, that is, to construct s.j.t. c.e. sets A_0 and A_1 such that $A_0 \oplus A_1$ is not s.j.t. We could attempt to combine the construction of a promptly simple s.j.t. c.e. set in the proof of Theorem 14.1.3 to build A_0 and A_1 with a strategy to diagonalize against possible traces for $J^{A_0 \oplus A_1}$ by changing values of this computation sufficiently often.

Recall that in the proof of Theorem 14.1.3, after some requirement P_e acts, it is removed from the list of requirements, and the blocks of N-requirements to its left and right are merged. This action "promotes" the block of N-requirements to the right of P_e, in a sense increasing their priority, which means that the number of times they can be injured decreases by one.

In our attempted construction, suppose we start with the same ordering of requirements, except that there are two kinds of negative requirements, one for A_0 and one for A_1, and the positive requirements are the ones forcing us to change A_0 or A_1 to diagonalize against possible traces for $J^{A_0 \oplus A_1}$. The difference now is that the positive requirements need to act multiple times. Each time a positive requirement P_e acts, enumerating a number into some A_i, it must be demoted down the list and placed after all the negative requirements it has just injured. Since these requirements may later impose new restraints, a new follower for P_e may be needed each time such a requirement decides to impose restraint. Since some of the negative requirements are also promoted by positive requirements weaker than P_e, we cannot put any computable bound in advance on the last place P_e will occupy on the list, and hence on the number of followers it will need. Thus we cannot define the computable bound that we mean to defeat, and the construction fails. This failure is turned around in the following proof.

We are given strongly jump traceable c.e. sets A_0 and A_1, and a computable order g, and wish to trace $J^{A_0 \oplus A_1}$ with bound g. (We will later see that we can replace strong jump traceability by h-jump traceability for an order h that depends only on g.) The strategies for tracing the various values of $J^{A_0 \oplus A_1}$ act completely independently, so fix an input e. We define functionals Ψ_0 and Ψ_1. When at some stage s of the construction we discover that $J^{A_0 \oplus A_1}(e)[s]\downarrow$, before we trace the value of this computation, we want to receive some confirmation that this value is genuine. Say that the computation has use $\sigma_0 \oplus \sigma_1$, where $\sigma_i \prec A_i[s]$. We define $\Psi_i^{\sigma_i}(x) = \sigma_i$ for some x. If indeed $\sigma_i \prec A_i$ then σ_i must appear in a trace T_x^i for $\Psi_i^{A_i}$, which we may assume we are given, by the universality of J^{A_i} and the recursion theorem. Thus we can wait until both strings σ_i appear in the relevant "boxes" T_x^i, and only then believe the computation $J^{A_0 \oplus A_1}(e)[s]$. Of course, it is possible that both σ_i appear in T_x^i but neither σ_i is really an initial segment of A_i, in which case we will have traced the wrong values. In this case, however, both boxes T_x^i have been promoted, in the sense that they each contain an element that we know is not the real value of $\Psi_i^{A_i}(x)$, and $\Psi_i^{A_i}(x)$ becomes undefined (when we notice that A_i has moved to the right of σ_i) and is therefore useful to us for testing another potential value of $J^{A_0 \oplus A_1}(e)$ that may appear later. If the bound on the size of T_x^i (which we prescribe in advance, but has to eventually increase with x) is k, then we originally think of T_x^i as a "k-box", a box that may contain up to k many values. After σ_i appears in T_x^i and is shown to be wrong, we can think of the promoted box as a $(k-1)$-box. Eventually, if T_x^i is promoted $k-1$ many times, then it becomes a 1-box. If a string σ_i appears in a 1-box then we know it must be a true initial segment of A_i. In this way we can limit the number of false $J^{A_0 \oplus A_1}(e)$ computations that we trace. Since all requirements act independently, this strategy allows us to trace $J^{A_0 \oplus A_1}$ to any computable degree of precision we wish.

The above is the main idea of all "box promotion" constructions. Each such construction has particular combinatorial aspects designed to counter difficulties that arise during the construction (difficulties that we may think of as possible plays of an opponent, out to foil us). These combinatorics determine how slowly we want the size of our traces to grow, and which boxes should be used in the tests we perform. In this construction, the difficulty is the following. In the previous scenario, it is possible that, say, σ_0 is indeed a true initial segment of A_0, but σ_1 is not an initial segment of A_1, and to make matters worse, the latter fact may be discovered even before σ_1 turns up in T_x^1. However, we have already defined $\Psi_0^{A_0}(x) = \sigma_0$ with an A_0-correct use, which means that the input x will not be available later for a new definition. The box T_x^0 must be discarded, and we have received no compensation—no other box has been promoted. The mechanics of the construction detailed below tell us which boxes to pick so that this problem can be countered. The main idea (which again appears in all box promotion constructions) is to use clusters of boxes (or "meta-boxes") rather than individual boxes. Instead of testing σ_i on a single T_x^i, we bunch together a finite collection M_i of inputs x, and define $\Psi_i^{\sigma_i}(x) = \sigma_i$ for all $x \in M_i$. We believe the computation $J^{A_0 \oplus A_1}(e)[s]$ only if σ_i has appeared in T_x^i for all $x \in M_i$. If this computation is believed and later discovered to be false, then all the boxes corresponding to elements of M_i are promoted. We can then break M_i up into smaller meta-boxes and use each separately. Thus we magnify the promotion, to compensate for any losses that may occur as explained above.

We now turn to the formal details of the proof. We fix a number e and show how to trace $J^{A_0 \oplus A_1}(e)$, limiting our errors to a prescribed number m. Given m, our strategy will ask for an infinite collection of boxes and describe precisely how many k-boxes it requires for each k. As m grows, the least k for which k-boxes are required will grow as well. In our construction, we will have $k = \lfloor \frac{m}{2} \rfloor$. For m and $k \geqslant \lfloor \frac{m}{2} \rfloor$, we will let $r(k,m)$ be the number of k-boxes required to limit the size of the trace for $J^{A_0 \oplus A_1}(e)$ to m. Recall that what we mean here is that the strategy will define functionals $\Psi_{e,i}$ for $i < 2$ and expect to get traces $\{T_n^{e,i}\}_{n \in \mathbb{N}}$ for $\Psi_{e,i}^{A_i}$ such that for all $k \geqslant \lfloor \frac{m}{2} \rfloor$, the collection of n such that $|T_n^{e,i}| \leqslant k$ has size at least $r(k,m)$.

Suppose that we can show that all our strategies succeed if their expectations are met. Then, given a computable order g, we can define a computable order h such that if A_0 and A_1 are h-jump traceable, then $A_0 \oplus A_1$ is g-jump traceable. We do so as follows. For each $c > 0$, partition $\mathbb{N}$ into consecutive intervals $\{I_k^c\}_{k \geqslant c}$ such that $|I_k^c| = \sum_{e : \lfloor \frac{g(e)}{2} \rfloor \leqslant k} r(k, g(e))$, and define a function h_c by letting $h_c(n) = k$ if $n \in I_k^c$. Note that, since g is an order, for each k there are only finitely many e such that $\lfloor \frac{g(e)}{2} \rfloor \leqslant k$, so the intervals I_k^c are well-defined. Clearly, the h_c are uniformly computable orders, and $h_c(0) \geqslant c$. By Lemma 14.1.2, we can obtain a computable order h such that if A_0 and A_1 are h-jump traceable, then we can compute, uniformly in c, traces $\{S_n^{c,i}\}_{n \in \mathbb{N}}$ for $\Phi_c^{A_i}$ with bound h_c.

For each c and $k \geqslant c$, let $\{N_{k,e}^c\}_{\lfloor \frac{g(e)}{2} \rfloor \leqslant k}$ be a partition of I_k^c such that $|N_{k,e}^c| = r(k, g(e))$. For each c, we run our construction for all e such that $\lfloor \frac{g(e)}{2} \rfloor \geqslant c$ simultaneously, with the eth requirement defining $\Psi_{e,0}$ and $\Psi_{e,1}$ with domain contained in $\bigcup_{k \geqslant \lfloor \frac{g(e)}{2} \rfloor} N_{k,e}^c$, using the $\{S_n^{c,i}\}_{n \in \mathbb{N}}$ as traces. Using Posner's trick (see p. 48), we can effectively obtain an index c' such that for $i = 0, 1$, we have $\Phi_{c'}^{A_i} = \bigcup_{\lfloor \frac{g(e)}{2} \rfloor \geqslant c} \Psi_{e,i}^{A_i}$. By the recursion theorem, there is a c such that $\Phi_c = \Phi_{c'}$, and so if A_0 and A_1 are h-jump traceable, then the $\{S_n^{c,i}\}_{n \in \mathbb{N}}$ are indeed traces for $\Phi_{c'}^{A_i}$, so that for each e such that $\lfloor \frac{g(e)}{2} \rfloor \geqslant c$, our strategy for e can succeed, and hence trace $J^{A_0 \oplus A_1}(e)$ with bound $g(e)$. (The e such that $\lfloor \frac{g(e)}{2} \rfloor < c$ present no problem, of course, since there are only finitely many such e.)

With the above in the background, we fix e and m and show how to define $r(k,m)$ and the functionals $\Psi_{e,i}^{A_i}$. We also describe how, given traces $\{T_n^{e,i}\}_{n \in \mathbb{N}}$ for the $\Psi_{e,i}^{A_i}$ such that for all $k \geqslant \lfloor \frac{m}{2} \rfloor$, the collection of n with $|T_n^{e,i}| \leqslant k$ has size at least $r(k,m)$, we can trace $J^{A_0 \oplus A_1}(e)$ with fewer than m many mistakes. From now on we drop the e from all subscripts and superscripts, writing Ψ_i for $\Psi_{e,i}$, writing T_x^i for $T_x^{e,i}$, and so on.

Construction. For each n, define a *meta*$_0^n$*-box* to be any singleton $\{x\}$ and a *meta*$_{k+1}^n$*-box* to be a collection of $n+2$ many meta$_k^n$-boxes. We often ignore the distinction between a meta^n_k-box and the set of numbers appearing in its meta$^n_0$-sub-boxes. In this sense, the size of a meta^n_k-box is $(n+2)^k$. At the start of the construction, a meta-box M is an l-box (for both A_0 and A_1) if $f(x) \leqslant l$ for all $x \in M$, for an order f that we will soon define. At a later stage s, a meta-box M is an l-box for A_i if $f(x) - |T^{e,i}_x[s]| \leqslant l$ for all $x \in M$.

At the start of the construction, for each $k \geqslant \lfloor \frac{m}{2} \rfloor$ we wish to have two meta$^k_{k+1}$-boxes that are k-boxes. We thus let $r(k,m) = 2(k+2)^{k+1}$. Denote these two meta-boxes by N_k and N'_k. Let f be a computable order such that for all $k \geqslant \lfloor \frac{m}{2} \rfloor$, the set of all n with $f(n) = k$ has size at least $r(k,m)$.

We write $\frac{\mathbb{N}}{2}$ for the set of all numbers of the form $\frac{n}{2}$ with $n \in \mathbb{N}$. The construction begins at stage $\lfloor \frac{m}{2} \rfloor$. At the beginning of stage s of the construction, we have two numbers $k^*_0[s]$ and $k^*_1[s]$. (We start with $k^*_i[0] = \lfloor \frac{m}{2} \rfloor$.) For $i < 2$, each $k \in [k^*_i[s], s)$ has some *priority* $p_i(k)[s] \in \frac{\mathbb{N}}{2}$. For such k we have finitely many meta$^{\lfloor p_i(k)[s] \rfloor}_k$-boxes $M^i_0(k)[s], \dots, M^i_{d_i(k)-1}(k)[s]$, each of which is *free*, in the sense that $\Psi^{A_i}_i(x)[s]\uparrow$ for all x in any of these boxes.

At stage $s \geqslant \lfloor \frac{m}{2} \rfloor$, for $i = 0, 1$, let $M^i_0(s), \dots, M^i_{s+1}(s)$ be the meta^s_s-sub-boxes of N_s. (Recall that these are all s-boxes.) Let $p_i(s) = s$.

Suppose now that we are given a computation $J^{A_0 \oplus A_1}(e)[s]$ with use $\sigma_0 \oplus \sigma_1$, which we want to test. This test is done in steps of increasing priority (i.e., decreasing argument in $\frac{\mathbb{N}}{2}$), beginning with step s. The instructions for testing $\sigma_0 \oplus \sigma_1$ at step $n \in \frac{\mathbb{N}}{2}$ are as follows.

For $i = 0, 1$, if there is some k such that $p_i(k)[s] = n$ (there will be at most one such k for each i), then take the last meta-box $M = M^i_{d_i(k)[s]-1}(k)[s]$ and test σ_i on M by defining $\Psi^{\sigma_i}_i(x) = \sigma_i$ for all $x \in M$. Run the enumeration of the trace $\{T^i_x\}_{x \in \mathbb{N}}$ and of A_i until either σ_i appears in T^i_x for all $x \in M$, in which case we say that the test *returns*, or σ_i is found not to be an initial segment of A_i, in which case we say that the test *fails*. One of these possibilities must occur, since $\{T^i_x\}_{x \in \mathbb{N}}$ is a trace for $\Psi^{A_i}_i$.

If all tests that are started (none, one test for a single σ_i, or two tests, one for each σ_i) return, then move to test step $n - \frac{1}{2}$, unless $n = 1$, in which case the tests at all levels have returned, so we believe the computation $J^{A_0 \oplus A_1}(e)[s]$ and trace it. In the latter case, from this point on we monitor this belief. We keep defining $p_i(t)$ and $M^i_j(t)$ at later stages t as above. If at such a stage t we discover that one of the σ_i is not in fact an initial segment of A_i, we update priorities as described in the following paragraph and go back to following the instructions above. Also, if some test at step n fails, then we stop the testing at stage s and update priorities as follows, with $t = s$.

For each n such that a test of σ_i at step n returns, but at stage $t \geqslant s$, we discover that $\sigma_i \not\prec A_i$, proceed as follows. Let k be the level such that $p_i(k)[s] = n$. If $k = k^*_i[s]$ then redefine k^*_i to be $k - 1$. Redefine $p_i(k-1)$ to be n and $d_i(k-1)$ to be $\lfloor n \rfloor + 2$, and let $M^i_0(k-1)[t+1], \dots, M^i_{\lfloor n \rfloor + 1}(k -$

$1)[t+1]$ be the collection of meta$^{\lfloor n \rfloor}_{k-1}$-sub-boxes of $M^i_{d_i(k)[s]-1}$ (which was the meta$^{\lfloor n \rfloor}_{k}$-box used for the testing of σ_i at step n of stage s). If $k = s$ then redefine $p_i(k)$ to be $s + \frac{1}{2}$, redefine $d_i(s)$ to be $s+2$, and let $M^i_0(s)[t+1], \ldots, M^i_{s+1}(s)[t+1]$ be the meta^s_s-sub-boxes of N'_s. (Note that these boxes are untouched so far.)

On the other side, if a test of σ_{1-i} at step n of stage s started and returned, and $\sigma_{1-i} \prec A_{1-i}[t]$, then discard the meta-box $M^{1-i}_{d_{1-i}(k)[s]-1}(k)[s]$ and redefine $d_{1-i}(k)$ to be $d_{1-i}(k)[s] - 1$. Perform these redefinitions also if $t = s$, the step s test of σ_{1-i} at stage s returns, and the step s test of σ_i at stage s fails.

End of Construction.

Lemma 14.2.2. *Let $i < 2$, let $s \geqslant \lfloor \frac{m}{2} \rfloor$, let $k \in [k^*_i[s], s)$, let $j < d_i(k)[s]$, and let $n = p_i(k)[s]$. The meta$^{\lfloor n \rfloor}_{k}$-box $M^i_j(k)[s]$ is a k-box. Indeed, for each $x \in M^i_j(k)[s]$, there are at least $\lfloor n \rfloor - k = f(x) - k$ many strings in $T^i_x[s]$ lexicographically to the left of $A_i[s]$.*

Proof. Let s be the least such that we define $p_i(k)[s] = n$ for some k. Then $k = \lfloor n \rfloor$ and there are two possibilities.

If $n \in \mathbb{N}$ then $s = n$, the definition is made at the beginning of stage s, and we define $M^i_0(s)[s], \ldots, M^i_{s+1}(s)[s]$ to be sub-boxes of N_s, which is an s-box.

If $n \notin \mathbb{N}$ then a test was conducted at stage $\lfloor n \rfloor \leqslant s - 1$, and returned on the σ_i side, and now $\sigma_i \not\prec A_i[s]$. We then define $p_i(\lfloor n \rfloor)[s] = n$ and define $M^i_0(\lfloor n \rfloor)[s], \ldots, M^i_{\lfloor n \rfloor+1}(\lfloor n \rfloor)[s]$ to be sub-boxes of $N'_{\lfloor n \rfloor}$, which is an $\lfloor n \rfloor$-box.

In either case, the $M^i_j(\lfloor n \rfloor)[s]$ are $\lfloor n \rfloor$-boxes, so for each x in these meta-boxes, $f(x) = \lfloor n \rfloor$, and hence, vacuously, T^i_x contains at least $f(x) - \lfloor n \rfloor$ many strings.

By induction, if $n = p_i(k)[t]$ at a later stage t, then for all j, we have that $M^i_j(k)[t]$ is a sub-box of some $M^i_{j'}(\lfloor n \rfloor)[s]$, and so for all $x \in M^i_j(k)[t]$ we have $f(x) = \lfloor n \rfloor$.

Suppose that at stage t we redefine $p_i(k-1)[t+1] = n$ and redefine $M^i_j(k-1)[t+1]$. Then at some stage $u \leqslant t$, for all $x \in M^i_{d_i(k)[u]-1}[u]$, we defined $\Psi^{\sigma_i}_i(x) = \sigma_i$, where $\sigma_i \prec A_i[u]$ but $\sigma_i \not\prec A_i[t+1]$. By induction, at stage u there were at least $\lfloor n \rfloor - k$ many strings in $T^i_x[u]$ to the left of $A_i[u]$. These strings must all be distinct from σ_i. The test at stage u returned, so $\sigma_i \in T^i_x[u+1]$. Thus $T^i_x[t+1]$ contains at least $\lfloor n \rfloor - (k-1)$ many strings to the left of $A_i[t+1]$. □

Lemma 14.2.3. *The sequence $k^*_i[0], k^*_i[1], \ldots$ is nonincreasing, and all its terms are positive.*

Proof. The fact that this sequence is nonincreasing is immediate from the construction. By Lemma 14.2.2, for all $j < d_i(k_i^*)[s]$ and $x \in M_j^i(k_i^*)[s]$, we have $|T_x^i[s]| \geqslant f(x) - k_i^*[s]$. As $|T_x^i| < f(x)$, we have $k_i^*[s] > 0$. □

Lemma 14.2.4. *For each t, the sequence $p_i(0)[t], p_i(1)[t], \ldots$ is strictly increasing.*

Proof. Assume the lemma holds at the beginning of stage t. We first define $p_i(t)$ to be t at stage t, and all numbers used prior to this stage were below t, so the lemma continues to hold.

Now suppose that at stage t we update priorities because a test that returned at some stage $s \leqslant t$ is found to be incorrect. The induction hypothesis for s, and the instructions for testing, ensure that the collection of levels k for which a test returned at stage s is an interval $[k_0, s]$. Priorities then shift one step downward to the interval $[k_0 - 1, s - 1]$. (That is, for $k \in [k_0, s]$, we have $p(k-1)[t+1] = p(k)[s]$.) Hence the sequence of priorities is still increasing for $k < s$. Finally, a new priority $s + \frac{1}{2}$ is given to level s. This priority is greater than the priorities for levels $k < s$ (which have priority at most s), but smaller than the priority k given to each level $k \in (s, t]$. □

Also note that we always have $p_i(k)[s] \geqslant k$ because we start with $p_i(k)[k] = k$ and never decrease the value of $p_i(k)$.

The following key calculation ensures that we never run out of boxes at any level, on either side, so the construction never gets stuck. It ties losses of boxes on one side to gains on the other. For any $k \in [k_i^*[s], s]$, let $l_i(k)[s]$ be the least level l such that $p_{1-i}(l)[s] \geqslant p_i(k)[s]$. Such a level must exist because at the beginning of stage s we let $p_{1-i}(s)[s] = s$, which is greater than or equal to $p_i(k)[s]$ for all $k \leqslant s$. Note that $l_i(k)[s] \geqslant 1$.

Lemma 14.2.5. *At each stage s, for $i < 2$ and $k \in [k_i^*[s], s]$, the number $d_i(k)[s]$ of meta-k-boxes is at least $l_i(k)[s]$ if $p_{1-i}(l_i(k))[s] > p_i(k)[s]$, and at least $l_i(k)[s] + 1$ if $p_{1-i}(l_i(k))[s] = p_i(k)[s]$.*

Proof. We proceed by induction on stages. Suppose the lemma holds at the end of stage $t-1$. At stage t, we first define $p_i(t) = p_{1-i}(t) = t$. Thus $l_i(t)[t] = t$, while $d_i(t)[t] = t + 2$. Suppose that a test that began at stage $s \leqslant t$ is resolved at stage t, and priorities are updated. (Otherwise, there is nothing to show.)

First suppose that $\sigma_i \not\prec A_i[t+1]$ and $d_i(k)[t+1] \neq d_i(k)[t]$. If $k < s$, then a test at level $k+1$ returned at stage s. Then $d_i(k)[t+1] = \lfloor n \rfloor + 2$, where $n = p_i(k)[t+1] = p_i(k+1)[s]$. Since $p_{1-i}(\lfloor n \rfloor)[t+1] \geqslant \lfloor n \rfloor$, we have $l_i(k)[t+1] \leqslant \lfloor n \rfloor + 1$, and hence $d_i(s)[t+1] \geqslant l_i(k)[t+1] + 1$. For the $k = s$ case, we have $d_i(s)[t+1] = s + 2$ and $p_i(s)[t+1] = s + \frac{1}{2}$. Since $p_{1-i}(s+1)[t+1] \geqslant s + 1$, we have $l_i(s)[t+1] \leqslant s + 1$, so $d_i(s)[t+1] \geqslant l_i(s)[t+1] + 1$.

Now suppose that $\sigma_i \prec A_i[t+1]$. We may have lost some meta-boxes on this side, but changing priorities on the other side gives us compensation. Let $k \in [k_i^*[t], t]$. If $k > s$ then $d_i(k)[t+1] = k+2$ and $l_i(k)[t+1] = k$. If $k = s$, then $d_i(k)[t+1] = d_i(k)[s] - 1 = s+1$ and $l_i(k)[t+1] \leqslant s$, so we may assume that $k < s$.

Let $n = p_i(k)[t+1] = p_i(k)[s]$. If there is no k' such that $p_{1-i}(k')[s] = n$, then there is no k' such that $p_{1-i}(k')[t+1] = n$, because the only priority we may add at stage t (after the initial part of the stage) is $s+\frac{1}{2}$, and $n < s$. Thus, if $p_{1-i}(l_i(k))[s] > n$ then $p_{1-i}(l_i(k))[t+1] > n$. Let $k' = l_i(k)[s]$, and note that $k' < s$. Let $n' = p_{1-i}(l_i(k))[s]$. There are three possibilities.

1. A step n' test of σ_{1-i} at stage s returns. In this case, $l_i(k)[t+1] = k'-1$ and $p_{1-i}(l_i(k))[t+1] = n'$.

2. A step n' test of σ_{1-i} at stage s does not return, but a step $n'+1$ test of σ_{1-i} at stage s does return. In this case the priority n' is removed on the $1-i$ side at stage t. We redefine $p_{1-i}(k')[t+1] = p_{1-i}(k'+1)[s] > n'$. However, we still have $l_i(k)[t+1] = k'$ because (if $k' > k_{1-i}^*[s]$) we have $p_{1-i}(k'-1)[t+1] = p_{1-i}(k'-1)[s] < n$.

3. A step $n'+1$ test of σ_{1-i} at stage s is not started or does not return. In this case there is no change at level k' and $k'-1$. We have $l_i(k)[t+1] = k'$ and $p_{1-i}(k')[t+1] = n'$.

In any case, we see that $l_i(k)$ cannot increase from stage s to stage $t+1$, and we cannot have $p_{1-i}(l_i(k))[s] > n$ but $p_{1-i}(l_i(k))[t+1] = n$. Thus the required number of k-meta-boxes does not increase from stage s to stage $t+1$, and we need only check what happens if $d_i(k)[t+1] = d_i(k)[s] - 1$. Assume this is the case.

In case 1 above, the number of required boxes has decreased by one, which exactly compensates the loss. Case 3 is not possible if a k-box is lost, because a step n' test is started only after a step $p_{1-i}(k'+1)[s]$ test has returned.

The same argument shows that if case 2 holds and we lost a k-box, then necessarily $n' = n$. But then $d_i(k)[s] \geqslant k'+1$, and the fact that now $p_{1-i}(k')[t+1] > n$ implies that the number of required boxes has just decreased by one, to k', so that again our loss is compensated. □

We are now ready to finish the proof. If $J^{A_0 \oplus A_1}(e)\downarrow$ then at some point the correct computation appears and is tested. Of course, the relevant tests must return, so the correct value is traced.

If, on the other hand, a value $J^{A_0 \oplus A_1}(e)[s]$ is traced at stage s because all tests return, but at a later stage t we discover that this computation is incorrect, because $\sigma_i \not\prec A_i[t+1]$ for some $i < 2$, then $k_i^*[t+1] < k_i^*[t]$. As we always have $k_i^*[u] \geqslant 1$, this event happens fewer than $2\lfloor \frac{m}{2} \rfloor \leqslant m$ many times. It follows that the total number of values traced is at most m, as required. □

It is not known at the time of writing whether the join of two (not necessarily c.e.) s.j.t. sets must be s.j.t. (and hence whether the s.j.t. sets form an ideal), though this would follow from Conjecture 14.5.1 below.

14.3 Strong jump traceability and K-triviality: the c.e. case

In this section, we show that the s.j.t. c.e. sets form a proper subideal of the K-trivial c.e. sets. We begin with the following result.

Theorem 14.3.1 (Cholak, Downey, and Greenberg [65]). *There is a computable order h such that if A is c.e. and h-jump traceable then A is low for K, and hence K-trivial.*

In Theorem 14.5.2, we will see that in fact *every* s.j.t. set is K-trivial. (We will also obtain Theorem 14.3.1 as a corollary to Theorem 14.4.2.) However, we include the following proof of Theorem 14.3.1 here, as it is of technical interest (and proves that every s.j.t. c.e. set is low for K directly, without appealing to the equivalence between lowness for K and K-triviality).

Proof of Theorem 14.3.1. To show that A is low for K we use the KC Theorem. That is, we build a KC set L such that if $\mathcal{U}^A(\sigma) = \tau$ then $(|\sigma|, \tau) \in L$, so that $K(\tau) \leqslant |\sigma| + O(1)$. We enumerate A and thus approximate $\mathcal{U}^A$. When a string σ enters the domain of $\mathcal{U}^A$ at a stage s, we need to decide whether to believe the A_s-computation that put σ in $\operatorname{dom}\mathcal{U}^{A_s}$. We do so by testing the use $\rho \prec A_s$ of this computation. A first approximation to our strategy for doing so is to build a functional Ψ, and look at a trace $T_0, T_1, \dots$ for Ψ^A. Given ρ, we choose an n and define $\Psi^\rho(n) = \rho$. We then wait to see whether ρ ever enters T_n. If so, then we believe that $\rho \prec A$, and hence that $\sigma \in \operatorname{dom}\mathcal{U}^A$, so we enumerate $(|\sigma|, \mathcal{U}^A(\sigma))$ into L.

The problem, of course, is ensuring that the weight of L is bounded. If we believed only correct computations (that is, if we had $|T_n| = 1$ for all n), then the weight of L would be $\mu([\![\operatorname{dom}\mathcal{U}^A]\!]) < 1$. But, of course, the T_n grow with n, so we will believe some incorrect uses ρ. We need to make sure that the T_n grow slowly enough that these mistakes do not prevent L from being a KC set.

To help us do so, rather than treat each string σ individually, we deal with strings in batches. When we have a set of strings $C \subseteq \operatorname{dom}\mathcal{U}^{A_s}$ of weight 2^{-k} (i.e., such that $\sum_{\sigma \in C} 2^{-|\sigma|} = 2^{-k}$), we will verify A up to a use that puts them all in $\operatorname{dom}\mathcal{U}^{A_s}$. The greater 2^{-k} is, the more stringent the test will be (ideally, in the sense that the size of the corresponding T_n is smaller). We will put a bound m_k on the number of times that a set of strings of weight 2^{-k} can be believed and yet be incorrect. The argument will succeed as long as $\sum_k m_k 2^{-k}$ is finite.

Once we use an input n to verify the A-correctness of a use, it cannot be used again for any testing, so following this strategy, we might need 2^k many inputs for testing sets of weight 2^{-k}. Even a single error on each n (and there will be more, as $|T_n|$ goes to infinity) means that $m_k \geqslant 2^k$, which is too large. Thus we need a combinatorial strategy to assign inputs in such a way as to keep the m_k small. This strategy has two ingredients.

First, note that two sets of weight 2^{-k} can be combined into a single set of weight $2^{-(k-1)}$. So if we are testing one such set, and another one with compatible use appears, then we can let the testing machinery for $2^{-(k-1)}$ take over. Thus, even though we still need several testing locations for 2^{-k}, at any stage, the testing at level 2^{-k} is responsible for at most one set of weight 2^{-k}.

It might appear that it is now sufficient to let the size of each T_n used to test sets of weight 2^{-k} be something like k. However, sets of large weight can be built gradually. We might first see k many sets of weight 2^{-k} (with incompatible uses), each of which requires us to use the input n devoted to the first set of weight 2^{-k}, because at each stage we believe only one of these k many sets. Once T_n gets to its maximum size, we see a set of weight 2^{-k} with a correct use. Then the same sequence of events happens again. We make k mistakes on each n used for level 2^{-k} testing, and end up using about 2^k many such n's, which we have already seen we cannot do.

The solution is to make every mistake count in our favor in all future tests of sets of weight 2^{-k}. In other words, what we need to do is to maximize the benefit that is given by a single mistake. We make sure that a mistake on *some* set means one less possible mistake on *every* other set. Rather than testing a set on a single input n, we test it simultaneously on a large set of inputs and believe it is correct only if the relevant use shows up in the trace of every input tested. If our set is eventually believed but is in fact a mistake, then we have a large collection of inputs n for which the number of possible errors is reduced. We can then break up this collection into smaller collections and keep working with such subcollections.

This idea can be geometrically visualized as follows. We have an m_k-dimensional cube of inputs, each side of which has length 2^k. In the beginning we test each set on one hyperplane. If the testing on some hyperplane is believed and later found to be incorrect, then from then on we work in that hyperplane, which becomes the new cube for testing pieces of size 2^{-k}, and we test on hyperplanes of this new cube. If the size of T_n for each n in the cube is at most m_k, then we never "run out of dimensions".

We now proceed with the formal details of the construction. For $c > 1$, we partition $\mathbb{N}$ into consecutive intervals $M_0^c, M_1^c, \ldots$ such that $|M_k^c| = 2^{k(k+c)}$. For $n \in M_k^c$, let $h_c(n) = k + c - 1$. By Lemma 14.1.2, we can determine a computable order $\tilde{h}$ such that, from a trace for J^A with bound $\tilde{h}$, we can compute, uniformly in c, a trace for Φ_c^A with bound h_c.

We will define a functional Ψ. By the recursion theorem, we know some c such that $\Psi^X = \Phi_c^X$ for all $X \in 2^\omega$. Let $M_k[0] = M_k^c$ and let $\{T_n\}_{n\in\mathbb{N}}$ be a trace for Ψ^A with bound $h = h_c$. The definitions of Ψ that we make will all be of the form $\Psi^\rho(n) = \rho$. We will make such a definition at stage s only when $\rho \prec A[s]$.

Let $R_k = \{m2^{-k} : m \leqslant 2^k\}$ and let $R_k^+ = R_k \setminus \{0\}$. We can label the elements of $M_k[0]$ so that $M_k[0] = \{x_f : f : (k+c) \to R_k^+\}$. We can think of $M_k[0]$ as a $(k+c)$-dimensional cube with sides of length 2^k.

At each stage s, for each k we will have a number $d_k[s] < k+c$ and a function $g_k[s] : d_k[s] \to R_k^+$, which will determine the current value of M_k via the definition $M_k[s] = \{x_f \in M_k[0] : g_k[s] \subset f\}$. (Thus $d_k[0] = 0$ and $g_k[0]$ is the empty function.) We can think of $M_k[s]$ as a $(k+c-d_k)$-dimensional cube. For $q \in R_k^+$, let $N_k(q)[s] = \{x_f \in M_k[s] : f(d_k[s]) = q\}$, the $q2^k$th hyperplane of $M_k[s]$.

Recall that $\Omega^\rho = \mu(\mathrm{dom}\,\mathcal{U}^\rho)$, the measure of the domain of the universal machine with oracle ρ. Note that if $\rho \prec \nu$ then $\Omega^\rho \leqslant \Omega^\nu$. We adopt the convention that the running time of any computation with oracle ρ is at most $|\rho|$, so the maps $\rho \mapsto \mathcal{U}^\rho$ and $\rho \mapsto \Omega^\rho$ are computable, and $|\sigma| \leqslant |\rho|$ for all $\sigma \in \mathrm{dom}\,\mathcal{U}^\rho$. It follows that Ω^ρ is a multiple of $2^{-|\rho|}$, and hence is an element of $R_{|\rho|}$. Also note that $\Omega^\lambda = 0$.

Let $q \in \mathbb{Q}$. For ν such that $\Omega^\nu \geqslant q$, let $\varrho^\nu(q)$ be the shortest $\rho \preccurlyeq \nu$ such that $\Omega^\rho \geqslant q$. Note that if $q < q' \leqslant \Omega^\nu$ then $\varrho^\nu(q) \preccurlyeq \varrho^\nu(q')$.

Let $A[s]$ denote the approximation to A at the beginning of stage s. At the beginning of stage s, the cubes M_k will be in the following *standard configuration* for the stage: Let $k \leqslant s$ and $q \in R_k^+$. If $q \leqslant \Omega^{A[s]\upharpoonright s}$ then $\Psi^{\varrho^{A[s]\upharpoonright s}(q)}(x)[s]\downarrow = \varrho^{A[s]\upharpoonright s}(q)$ for all $x \in N_k(q)[s]$. Otherwise, $\Psi^{A[s]}(x)[s]\uparrow$ for all $x \in N_k(q)[s]$. Furthermore, for all $k > s$ and $x \in M_k[s]$, no definition of $\Psi(x)$ for any oracle has been made before stage s.

Let $\rho \preccurlyeq A[s] \upharpoonright s$. We say that ρ is *semiconfirmed* at some point during stage s if for all x such that $\Psi^\rho(x)\downarrow = \rho$ at stage s, we have $\rho \in T_x$ at that given point (which may be the beginning of the stage or later). We say that ρ is *confirmed* if every $\rho' \preccurlyeq \rho$ is semiconfirmed. Note that λ is confirmed at every stage, because $\Omega^\lambda = 0$, so we never have $\varrho^{A[s]\upharpoonright s}(q) = \lambda$ for any s and $q > 0$, and hence never define $\Psi^\lambda(x)$ for any x.

Construction. At stage s, proceed as follows. Speed up the enumeration of A and of the T_n (to get $A[s+1]$ and $T_n[s+1]$) so that for all $\rho \preccurlyeq A[s] \upharpoonright s$, either ρ is confirmed or $\rho \not\prec A[s+1]$. One of the two must happen because $\{T_n\}_{n\in\mathbb{N}}$ traces Ψ^A.

For each $k \leqslant s$, look for some $q \in R_k^+$ such that $q \leqslant \Omega^{A[s]\upharpoonright s}$ and $\varrho^{A[s]\upharpoonright s}(q)$ was confirmed at the beginning of the stage but $\varrho^{A[s]\upharpoonright s}(q) \not\prec A[s+1]$. If there is such a q then extend g_k by letting $g_k(d_k) = q$, so that $d_k[s+1] = d_k[s]+1$ and $M_k[s+1] = N_k(q)[s]$.

Finally, define Ψ as necessary so that the standard configuration holds at the beginning of stage $s+1$.

End of Construction.

Justification. We need to explain why the construction never gets stuck. There are two issues: why we can always increase d_k when asked to (since d_k must remain below $k+c$), and why we can always return to the standard configuration. To address the first issue, we prove the following.

Lemma 14.3.2. *For each s and $x \in M_k[s+1]$, there are at least $d_k[s]$ many strings in T_x, so $d_k[s] \leqslant |T_x| \leqslant h(x) = k+c-1$.*

Proof. Suppose that at stage s, we increase d_k by one. This action is witnessed by some $q \in R_k^+$ such that $\rho = \varrho^{A[s]\restriction s}(q)$ was confirmed at the beginning of the stage, and we let $M_k[s+1] = N_k(q)[s]$. The confirmation of ρ implies that $\rho \in T_x$ for all $x \in N_k(q)[s]$. But we also have that $\rho \prec A[s]$ and $\rho \nprec A[s+1]$. As A is c.e., $A[s+1]$ is to the right of ρ. If we increase d_k at stages $s_0 < s_1$ (witnessed by strings ρ_0 and ρ_1) then ρ_0 is to the left of $A[s_0+1]$, while $\rho_1 \prec A[s_1]$ (which is not to the left of $A[s_1+1]$). Thus ρ_0 is to the left of ρ_1, and, in particular, they are distinct. □

To address the second issue mentioned above, we assume that the standard configuration holds at the beginning of stage s and show that we can return to the standard configuration after stage s. Fix $k \leqslant s$ (as there is no problem with $k = s+1$).

If $M_k[s+1] \neq M_k[s]$, witnessed by some $q \in R_k^+$ and $\rho = \varrho^{A[s]\restriction s}(q)$, then $\Psi^\rho(x)\downarrow = \rho$ for all $x \in M_k[s+1]$, so if $\rho' \prec \rho$ then $\Psi^{\rho'}(x)[s]\uparrow$. As $\rho \nprec A[s+1]$ and no definitions for oracles to the right of $A[s]$ are made before stage s, we must have $\Psi^{A[s+1]}(x)[s]\uparrow$, so we are free to make the definitions needed for the standard configuration to hold at the beginning of stage $s+1$.

If $M_k[s+1] = M_k[s]$, then let $q \in R_k^+$ be such that $q \leqslant \Omega^{A[s+1]\restriction s+1}$, and let $x \in N_k(q)[s+1] = N_k(q)[s]$. We want to define $\Psi^\rho(x)\downarrow = \rho$ for $\rho = \varrho^{A[s+1]\restriction s+1}(q)$.

If $\rho \nprec A[s]$ then ρ is to the right of $A[s]$, so $\Psi^\rho(x)[s]\uparrow$ for all $x \in M_k[s]$. If $\rho \prec A[s]$, then there are two possibilities.

If $|\rho| \leqslant s$ then $\rho = \varrho^{A[s]\restriction s}(q)$, so we already have $\Psi^\rho(x)\downarrow = \rho$ for all $x \in N_k(q)[s]$.

If $|\rho| = s+1$ then, since $q > \Omega^{\rho'}$ for all $\rho' \prec \rho$, we have $q > \Omega^{A[s]\restriction s}$. Since the standard configuration holds at the beginning of stage s, we have $\Psi^{A[s]}(x)\uparrow$ for all $x \in N_k(q)$ at the beginning of stage s. Thus we are free to define $\Psi^\rho(x)$ as we wish.

Verification. Let $\rho^*[s]$ be the longest string (of length at most s) that is a common initial segment of both $A[s]$ and $A[s+1]$. Thus $\rho^*[s]$ is the longest string that is confirmed at the beginning of stage $s+1$. Let

$$L = \{(\sigma,\tau) : \mathcal{U}^{\rho^*[s]}(\sigma) = \tau \wedge s \in \mathbb{N}\}.$$

Suppose that $\mathcal{U}^A(\sigma) = \tau$, and let $\rho \prec A$ be such that $\mathcal{U}^\rho(\sigma) = \tau$. Let $s > |\rho|$ be such that $\rho \prec A[s], A[s+1]$. Then $\rho \preccurlyeq \rho^*[s]$, so $(\sigma, \tau) \in L$. Thus $\{(\sigma, \tau) : \mathcal{U}^A(\sigma) = \tau\} \subseteq L$. Since L is c.e., we are left with showing that $\sum_{(\sigma,\tau)\in L} 2^{-|\sigma|} < \infty$, from which it follows that L is a KC set witnessing the fact that A is low for K. Since $\mu(\mathrm{dom}\,\mathcal{U}^A) < 1$, it is enough to show that $\sum_{(\sigma,\tau)\in L\setminus\mathcal{U}^A} 2^{-|\sigma|} < \infty$.

For $k \leqslant s$, let $q_k[s]$ be the greatest element of R_k not greater than $\Omega^{\rho^*[s]}$. If $k < k' \leqslant s$ then $q_k[s] \leqslant q_{k'}[s]$, because $R_k \subseteq R_{k'}$. Note that $|\rho^*[s]| \leqslant s$, so $\Omega^{\rho^*[s]}$ is an integer multiple of 2^{-s}. It follows that $q_s[s] = \Omega^{\rho^*[s]}$. Furthermore, since $\Omega^\rho < 1$ for all ρ, we must have $q_0[s] = 0$.

Let $\nu_k[s] = \varrho^{\rho^*[s]}(q_k[s])$. By the monotonicity of $q_k[s]$, if $k < k' \leqslant s$ then $\nu_k[s] \preccurlyeq \nu_{k'}[s]$, and so $\Omega^{\nu_k[s]} \leqslant \Omega^{\nu_{k'}[s]}$. Furthermore, $\nu_0[s] = \lambda$, and $\Omega^{\nu_s[s]} = \Omega^{\rho^*[s]}$, whence $\mathcal{U}^{\nu_s[s]} = \mathcal{U}^{\rho^*[s]}$.

Since $q_{k-1}[s] \leqslant \Omega^{\nu_{k-1}[s]} \leqslant \Omega^{\nu_k[s]} \leqslant \Omega^{\rho^*[s]} \leqslant q_{k-1}[s] + 2^{-(k-1)}$, we have the following key fact.

Lemma 14.3.3. *Let* $1 \leqslant k \leqslant s$. *Then* $\Omega^{\nu_k[s]} - \Omega^{\nu_{k-1}[s]} \leqslant 2^{-k+1}$.

We now show that we can define sets $L_{k,t}$ of relatively small weight such that if $(\sigma, \tau) \in L \setminus \mathcal{U}^A$, then we can "charge" the mistake of adding (σ, τ) to L against some $L_{k,t}$. Formally, we define sets $L_{k,t}$ with the following properties.

1. For each k and t, we have $\sum_{(\sigma,\tau)\in L_{k,t}} 2^{-|\sigma|} \leqslant 2^{-k+1}$.
2. $L \setminus \mathcal{U}^A \subseteq \bigcup_{k,t} L_{k,t}$.
3. For each k, there are at most $k+c$ many t such that $L_{k,t}$ is nonempty.

Given these properties, we have

$$\sum_{(\sigma,\tau)\in L\setminus\mathcal{U}^A} 2^{-|\sigma|} \leqslant \sum_{k,t} \sum_{(\sigma,\tau)\in L_{k,t}} 2^{-|\sigma|} \leqslant \sum_k (k+c)2^{-k+1} < \infty,$$

as required.

If $1 \leqslant k \leqslant t$ and $\nu_k[t] \not\prec A[t+2]$ then let

$$L_{k,t} = \{(\sigma, \tau) : \mathcal{U}^{\nu_k[t]}(\sigma) = \tau \wedge \mathcal{U}^{\nu_{k-1}[t]}(\sigma)\uparrow\},$$

and otherwise let $L_{k,t} = \emptyset$. We show that properties 1–3 above hold.

Property 1 follows from Lemma 14.3.3:

$$\sum_{(\sigma,\tau)\in L_{k,t}} 2^{-|\sigma|} = \mu(\mathrm{dom}(\mathcal{U}^{\nu_k[t]} \setminus \mathcal{U}^{\nu_{k-1}[t]})) = \Omega^{\nu_k[t]} - \Omega^{\nu_{k-1}[t]} \leqslant 2^{-k+1}.$$

Lemma 14.3.4. $L \setminus \mathcal{U}^A \subseteq \bigcup_{k,t} L_{k,t}$.

Proof. Let $(\sigma, \tau) \in L \setminus \mathcal{U}^A$. Let ρ be a minimal length string such that $(\sigma, \tau) \in \mathcal{U}^\rho$ and $\rho \preccurlyeq \rho^*[s]$ for some s. Since $\rho \prec A[s], A[s+1]$ but $\rho \not\prec A$, there is a $t \geqslant s$ such that $\rho \prec A[t], A[t+1]$ but $\rho \not\prec A[t+2]$.

Since $\rho \preccurlyeq \rho^*[t]$ and $\mathcal{U}^{\rho^*[t]} = \mathcal{U}^{\nu_t[t]}$, by the minimality of ρ we have $\rho \preccurlyeq \nu_t[t]$. Since $\nu_0[t] = \lambda$, there is a $k \in [1,t]$ such that $\nu_{k-1}[t] \prec \rho \preccurlyeq \nu_k[t]$.

Since $\rho \preccurlyeq \nu_k[t]$, we have $(\sigma,\tau) \in \mathcal{U}^{\nu_k[t]}$. Since $\nu_{k-1}[t] \prec \rho^*[t]$, the minimality of ρ implies that $(\sigma,\tau) \notin \mathcal{U}^{\nu_{k-1}[t]}$. Finally, $\rho \not\prec A[t+2]$, so $\nu_k[t] \not\prec A[t+2]$. Thus $(\sigma,\tau) \in L_{k,t}$. □

Lemma 14.3.5. *If $L_{k,t} \neq \emptyset$ then $M_k[t+1] \neq M_k[t+2]$.*

Proof. Suppose that $L_{k,t} \neq \emptyset$, so that $\nu_k[t] \not\prec A[t+2]$. Let $q = q_k[t]$. Then $\nu_k[t] = \varrho^{\rho^*[t]}(q) = \varrho^{A[t]\upharpoonright t}(q)$. Now, $\nu_k[t] \preccurlyeq \rho^*[t]$, so $\nu_k[t]$ is confirmed at the beginning of stage $t+1$. Furthermore, $q > 0$, as otherwise $\nu_k[t] = \lambda \prec A[t+2]$. Thus all the conditions for redefining M_k at stage $t+1$ are fulfilled. □

Thus properties 1–3 above hold, and L is a KC set witnessing the fact that A is low for K. □

Using more intricate combinatorics it is also possible to establish the following result, where Martin-Löf cuppability is as defined in Definition 11.8.3.

Theorem 14.3.6 (Cholak, Downey, and Greenberg [65]). *There is a computable order h such that if A is c.e. and h-jump traceable then A is not Martin-Löf cuppable.*

The relationship between strong jump traceability and K-triviality in the computably enumerable case was clarified by Cholak, Downey, and Greenberg [65], who showed that the s.j.t. c.e. sets form a *proper* subclass of the K-trivial c.e. sets.

Theorem 14.3.7 (Cholak, Downey, and Greenberg [65]). *There are a K-trivial c.e. set A and a computable order h such that A is not h-jump traceable.*

Proof. The construction of a K-trivial set that is not strongly jump traceable came out of a construction of a K-trivial set that is not n-c.e. for any n. The existence of such sets can be shown using the fact the class of K-trivial sets is closed downwards under Turing reducibility, but let us consider a direct cost function construction of such a set.

The basic construction of a K-trivial promptly simple c.e. set can be described as follows. The eth requirement wishes to show that the set A we construct is not equal to $\overline{W_e}$. The requirement is given a capital of 2^{-e}. It appoints a follower x_0, and waits for its realization, that is, for x_0 to enter W_e. If, upon realization, the cost of changing $A(x_0)$ is greater than 2^{-e}, the follower is abandoned, a new one x_1 is picked, and the process repeats itself.

Suppose now that we want to ensure that A is not 2-c.e. The eth requirement wants to ensure that A is not 2-c.e. via the eth 2-c.e. approximation $Y_e \setminus Z_e$ (where both Y_e and Z_e are c.e.). Again the requirement is provided with 2^{-e} much capital to spend. A naive strategy would be the following. Appoint a follower x_0 and wait for first realization, that is, for x to enter X_e (and not Y_e, for now.) Provided the price is not too high, extract x_0 from A (we begin with $A = \mathbb{N}$) and wait for second realization, that is, for x to enter Y_e. At this point put x_0 back into A. The problem, of course, is that we cannot put x_0 into A unless the cost of changing $A(x_0)$ has remained small. For this strategy to succeed, the follower x_0 needs two "permissions" from the cost function, and the danger is that we spend some capital on the first action (the extraction), but the second action is too expensive and the follower has to be abandoned. The amount we spend on extraction is nonrefundable, though, so this strategy soon runs into trouble.

A better strategy is the following. From the initial sum 2^{-e}, we set aside a part (say $2^{-(e+1)}$), which is kept for the re-enumeration of a follower and will not be used for extraction. Of the remaining $2^{-(e+1)}$, we apportion some amount (say $2^{-(e+2)}$) for the sake of extraction of the first follower x_0. If the cost of extraction of x_0 is higher, we then abandon x_0 (at no cost to us) and allot the same amount $2^{-(e+2)}$ for the extraction of the next follower x_1. Suppose, for example, that we do indeed extract x_1, but when it is realized again and we are ready to re-enumerate it into A, the cost of doing so has risen beyond the amount $2^{-(e+1)}$ we set aside for this task. We have to abandon x_1, appoint a new follower x_2, and start from the beginning. We did lose an uncompensated $2^{-(e+2)}$, though, so we reduce the sum that we may spend on extracting x_2 to $2^{-(e+3)}$, and keep going.

Between extractions, the sum we may spend on the next extraction is kept constant, so the usual argument shows that some follower eventually gets extracted (assuming that all followers are realized, of course). Furthermore, abandoning followers upon second realization can happen only finitely often, because the cost threshold $2^{-(e+1)}$ for re-enumeration does not change. Each follower is appointed only after the previous one is canceled, and is chosen to be large, so the costs associated with attempts at re-enumeration of different followers are due to completely different parts of the domain of the universal machine having measure at least $2^{-(e+1)}$. Thus there cannot be more than 2^{e+1} many failed attempts at re-enumeration.

Note that the same reasoning may be applied to the extraction steps. When we abandon a follower at first realization, the next follower is chosen to be large. The acceptable cost 2^{-m} is not changed at that point, so this kind of abandonment cannot happen more than 2^m many times (until we have an abandonment at second realization and decrease the acceptable cost to $2^{-(m+1)}$). Putting together this argument with the previous one allows us to compute a bound on the total number of possible abandonments, which will be relevant below.

It is straightforward to modify this strategy to satisfy a requirement working toward ensuring that A is not n-c.e. for a given n. Instead of two levels of realization, we will have n many, but the basic idea remains the same. To make A not strongly jump traceable, rather than not n-c.e., we need to change $J^A(x)$ on some x more than $h(x)$ many times, where h is some computable order we specify in advance (and x is an number for which we can control $J^A(x)$). To change $J^A(x)$ we change A below the use of the computation that gives the current value of $J^A(x)$. Each time we do so, we can use a different element of A, so A can be made c.e. However, the main feature of the argument outlined above, that the same x receives attention several times, remains, so a similar strategy to the one we discussed will work here.

We will define a computable order h shortly. We may assume that $|W_e^{[n]}| \leqslant h(n)$ for all n (by stopping elements from entering W_e if their enumeration would cause this condition to be violated). We enumerate a set A and define a partial function $p = \Phi^A$. The requirement R_e is that $\{W_e^{[n]}\}_{n\in\omega}$ is not a trace for p. The requirements act independently of each other. Let us discuss the action of a single requirement R_e.

Let T_e be the set of all sequences $(k_0, k_1, \ldots, k_i)$ with $i < e+2$ and $k_j < 2^{(e+2)2^j}$ for each $j \leqslant i$. We think of T_e as a tree. An element $\sigma \in T_e$ is a *leaf* of T_e if it has length $e+2$. Let $\varepsilon_\sigma = 2^{-(e+2)2^{|\sigma|}}$.

Each leaf $\sigma \in T_e$ will correspond to an attempt at meeting R_e. If $i < e+2$ then $\varepsilon_{\sigma\restriction i}$ is the amount that we are willing to spend on the $(e+2-i)$th attack with the follower corresponding to σ, in the sense of the standard (K-triviality) cost function.

The tree T_e and the rationals ε_σ were chosen so that

1. $\varepsilon_\lambda = 2^{-(e+2)}$;

2. if $\sigma \in T_e$ is not a leaf, then it has exactly $\frac{1}{\varepsilon_\sigma}$ many immediate successors on T_e; and

3. if $\sigma \in T_e$ is not a leaf, then ε_σ is the sum of ε_τ over the immediate successors τ of σ on T_e.

Using these facts, we can show by reverse induction on $|\sigma|$ that for each $\sigma \in T_e$ that is not a leaf, the sum of ε_τ as τ ranges over all extensions of σ on T_e that are not leaves is $(e+2-|\sigma|)\varepsilon_\sigma$. Thus the sum of ε_τ as τ ranges over all elements of T_e that are not leaves is $(e+2)2^{-(e+2)}$. This quantity is the total amount we will allow R_e to spend, so the construction will obey the standard cost function, as $\sum_e (e+2)2^{-(e+2)}$ is finite.

We can now define h. Partition $\mathbb{N}$ into intervals I_e so that $\max I_e + 1 = \min I_{e+1}$, letting the size of I_e be the number of leaves of T_e. Index the elements of I_e as x_σ for leaves σ of T_e. Let $h(n) = e+1$ for all $n \in I_e$.

If not yet satisfied at a stage s, the requirement R_e will have a pointer σ pointing at some leaf of T_e, and will be conducting an attack via x_{σ_e}. This attack will have a level $i < e+2$, which decreases with time, until the attack either is abandoned or fully succeeds when we get to the root.

In the beginning, let $\sigma = 0^{e+2}$, the leftmost leaf of T_e, and begin an attack with x_σ at level $e+1$.

The following are the instructions for an attack at level $i < e+2$, at a stage s. Let $\sigma = \sigma[s]$. Recall that the cost of enumerating a number x into A at stage s is $c(x,s) = \sum_{x<n\leqslant s} 2^{-K_s(n)}$.

1. Define $p(x_\sigma) = \Phi^{A_s}(x_\sigma) = s$ with use $s+1$. Wait for s to enter $W_e^{[x_\sigma]}$. While waiting, if some other requirement puts a number $y \leqslant s$ into A, hence making $p(x_\sigma)$ undefined, redefine $p(x_\sigma)$, again with value s and use $s+1$.

2. Suppose s enters $W_e^{[x_\sigma]}$ at stage t.

   (a) If $c(s,t) \leqslant \varepsilon_{\sigma\restriction i}$, then put s into A (making $p(x_\sigma)$ undefined). Leave σ unchanged and attack with it at level $i-1$ if $i>0$. If $i=0$ then cease all action for R_e.

   (b) If $c(s,t) > \varepsilon_{\sigma\restriction i}$, then abandon x_σ. Move one step to the right of $\sigma \restriction i+1$. That is, if $\sigma = (k_0,\dots,k_{e-1})$ then let $\sigma[t+1] = (k_0,\dots,k_{i-1},k_i+1,0,\dots,0)$. Begin an attack with this new σ at level $e+1$.

We must argue that when we redefine σ in step 2(b), we remain within T_e, which amounts to showing that $k_i + 1 < \frac{1}{\varepsilon_{\sigma\restriction i}}$. Let $\sigma^* = (k_0,\dots,k_{i-1})$. We know that for all $k \leqslant k_i$, some attack was made with some string extending $\sigma^{*\frown}(k)$. Let τ_k be the rightmost string extending $\sigma^{*\frown}(k)$ that was ever used for an attack (so that $\tau_{k_i} = \sigma$). We know that we attacked with τ_k at level i and this attack was abandoned. Let s_k be the stage at which the attack with τ_k at level i began, and let $t_k > s_k$ be the stage at which this attack was abandoned (so that $t_{k_i} = t$).

Since $t_{k-1} \leqslant s_k$, the intervals $(s_k, t_k]$ are disjoint. At stage t_k, the attack with τ_k was abandoned because $c(s_k,t_k) > \varepsilon_{\sigma^*}$, so

$$1 > \sum_{k\leqslant k_i} \sum_{s_k<n\leqslant t_k} 2^{-K(n)} \geqslant \sum_{k\leqslant k_i} \sum_{s_k<n\leqslant t_k} 2^{-K_{t_k}(n)}$$

$$= \sum_{k\leqslant k_i} c(s_k,t_k) > (k_i+1)\varepsilon_{\sigma^*},$$

whence $k_i + 1 < \frac{1}{\varepsilon_{\sigma^*}}$ as required.

We now verify that the above construction works as intended. For each e and each $\tau \in T_e$ that is not a leaf, there is at most one s enumerated into A because of a successful attack with some $\sigma \succ \tau$ at level $|\tau|$. Thus the total cost due to R_e does not exceed $(e+2)2^{-(e+2)}$, and so the construction obeys the necessary cost function, which ensures that A is K-trivial.

Fix e. It cannot be the case that an attack with some x_σ at level 0 succeeds, since then we would have $|W_e^{[x_\sigma]}| > e+1 = h(x_\sigma)$. Thus there is some stage s at which we begin an attack with $x_{\sigma[s]}$ at some level, but s never enters $W_e^{[x_\sigma]}$. Then $p(x_\sigma) = s \notin W_e^{[x_\sigma]}$, so R_e is satisfied. □

These results suggest a question: Can K-triviality be characterized via h-jump traceability for some class of orders h? In investigating this question, it is most natural to take the alternate definition that a set A is h-jump traceable if every partial A-computable function has a c.e. trace with bound h. One suggestion was to consider the class of computable orders h such that $\sum_n \frac{1}{h(n)} < \infty$. Using the golden run method of Nies discussed in Chapter 11, it is not difficult to show that if a c.e. set A is K-trivial then A is h-jump traceable for all such h. However, work of Ng [296] and Barmpalias, Downey, and Greenberg [20] has shown that there are c.e. sets that are h-jump traceable for all such h but are not K-trivial. It remains open whether some other reasonably natural class of orders may capture K-triviality exactly. One possibility would be the class of all computable orders h such that $\sum 2^{-h(n)} < \infty$.

Hölzl, Kräling, and Merkle [183] have shown that A is K-trivial iff A is $O(g(n) - K(n))$-jump traceable for all Solovay functions g, and that, moreover, there is a single Solovay function f such that A is K-trivial iff A is $O(f(n) - K(n))$-jump traceable. However, the presence of K in this result might strike some as unsatisfying.

14.4 Strong jump traceability and diamond classes

Recall that for a class $S \subseteq 2^\omega$, we define $S^\diamond$ to be the collection of c.e. sets computable from every 1-random element of S. In this section, we prove theorems of Greenberg and Nies [172] and Greenberg, Hirschfeldt, and Nies [169] that show that the class of strongly jump traceable c.e. sets coincides with both $(\omega\text{-c.e.})^\diamond$ and superlow$^\diamond$. This result lends evidence to the claim that strong jump traceability is a natural notion to study in the context of algorithmic randomness, and further demonstrates the usefulness of the notion of diamond classes. As we will see, it also provides a useful tool for the study of superlowness.

It is worth noting that, by Theorem 2.19.10 applied to a Π^0_1 class of 1-random sets, for every c.e. set A, there is a low 1-random set that does not compute A, so low$^\diamond$ (and hence $(\Delta^0_2)^\diamond$) contains only the computable sets.

We will use a characterization of strong jump traceability in terms of certain special cost functions. Recall the general notion of a cost function from Definition 11.5.1. Theorems 11.5.3 and 11.10.2 say that K-trivial sets have special approximations that change only a few times, and hence have low cost. Greenberg and Nies [172] began with these results as a starting point and studied the cost functions associated with s.j.t. sets. The following definition isolates an important property of the standard cost function $c(n, s) = \sum_{n<i\leqslant s} 2^{-K_s(i)}$.

Definition 14.4.1 (Greenberg and Nies [172]). A monotone cost function c is *benign* if there is a computable function $g : \mathbb{Q}^{>0} \to \mathbb{N}$ such that for each positive rational q, if I is a set of pairwise disjoint intervals of natural numbers such that $c(n,s) \geqslant q$ for all $[n,s) \in I$, then $|I| \leqslant g(q)$.[1]

Note that benign cost functions always satisfy the limit condition.

For example, the standard cost function c is benign: If I is as in the above definition, then $|I| \leqslant \frac{1}{q}$, since

$$q|I| \leqslant \sum_{[n,s)\in I} c(n,s) \leqslant \sum_{[n,s)\in I} \sum_{n<i\leqslant s} 2^{-K(i)} \leqslant \sum_i 2^{-K(i)} \leqslant 1.$$

Thus the following result implies Theorem 14.3.1 that every s.j.t. c.e. set is K-trivial.

Theorem 14.4.2 (Greenberg and Nies [172]). *A c.e. set is strongly jump traceable iff it obeys all benign cost functions.*

One direction of this theorem follows from the following lemma, since if a c.e. set obeys all benign cost functions then it is K-trivial, and hence jump traceable, by Theorem 11.4.8.

Lemma 14.4.3 (Greenberg and Nies [172]). *Let A be a jump traceable c.e. set and let h be a computable order with $h(0) > 0$. There is a benign cost function c such that if A obeys c, then J^A has a c.e. trace bounded by h.*[2]

Proof. Let $\widehat{h}(n) = h(n) - 1$ if $h(n) > 1$, and let $\widehat{h}(n) = 1$ otherwise.

Let $\psi(n)$ be the least stage at which $J^A(n)$ converges with an A-correct computation, if there is such a stage. Since A is c.e., tracing $J^A(n)$ is equivalent to tracing the partial function ψ. Since A is jump traceable, there is a c.e. trace $S_0, S_1, \ldots$ for ψ bounded by some computable order g.

If $J^A(n)[s]\downarrow$ with use k, then we say that this computation is *certified* if there is some $t < s$ such that $A_s \upharpoonright k = A_t \upharpoonright k$ and $t \in S_n[s]$. We want to ensure that the cost of all $x < k$ at stage s is at least $\frac{1}{\widehat{h}(n)}$, so let $c(x,s)$ be the maximum of all $\frac{1}{\widehat{h}(n)}$ such that there is some $u \leqslant s$ at which a computation $J^A(n)[u]$ with use greater than x is certified (where this maximum is 0 if there is no such n). Note that c is indeed a monotone cost function.

We argue that c is benign. Let $q > 0$ be a rational and let I be a set of pairwise disjoint intervals of natural numbers such that $c(x,s) \geqslant q$ for all $[x,s) \in I$. Let n^* be such that $\widehat{h}(n^*) > \frac{1}{q}$. Let $[x,s) \in I$. Then there is

[1]Greenberg and Nies [172] suggested the following way to understand this concept. Let $q > 0$. Let $y_0^q = 0$, and if y_k^q is defined and there is some s such that $c(y_k^q, s) \geqslant q$, then let y_{k+1}^q be the least such s. If c satisfies the limit condition $\lim_n c(n) = 0$, then this process has to halt after finitely many iterations. Then c is benign iff there is a computable bound on the number of iterations of this process given q.

[2]Greenberg and Nies [172] remarked that this lemma can be uniformized to show that for each computable order h, there is a benign cost function c such that for all c.e. sets A obeying c, there is a trace for J^A bounded by h.

some $n < n^*$ and $u \leqslant s$ such that $J^A(n)[u]$ with use $k > x$ is certified. Let $t < u$ witness this certification. Then $t \in (x, s)$, since $x < k < t < u \leqslant s$, and so, since the intervals in I are pairwise disjoint and $t \in S_n$, we have $|I| \leqslant \sum_{n<n^*} |S_n| \leqslant \sum_{n<n^*} g(n)$. Since n^* is obtained effectively from q, and g is computable, this bound on $|I|$ is computable.

Now suppose that A obeys c. It is easy to see that there is a computable enumeration $\widehat{A}_0, \widehat{A}_1, \ldots$ of A such that, letting n_s be the least number in $\widehat{A}_{s+1} \setminus \widehat{A}_s$, we have $\sum_s c(n_s, s) < 1$. Enumerate a trace $T_0, T_1, \ldots$ for J^A as follows. Enumerate $J^{\widehat{A}_s}(n)$ into T_n if there is some $u < s$ such that $\widehat{A}_u \upharpoonright k = \widehat{A}_s \upharpoonright k$, where k is the use of the computation $J^{\widehat{A}_s}(n)$, and this computation is certified at stage u.

Fix n and let $s_0 < s_1 < \cdots < s_{|T_n|-1}$ be the stages at which we enumerate numbers into T_n. Say that the computation $J^{\widehat{A}_{s_i}}(n)$ gets certified at stage $u_i < s_i$. Let k_i be the use of that computation. For each $i < |T_n| - 1$, there is some stage $v_i \in [u_i, u_{i+1})$ such that $\widehat{A}_{v_i} \upharpoonright k_i \neq \widehat{A}_{v_i+1} \upharpoonright k_i$, since by stage s_{i+1}, the computation $J^{\widehat{A}_{s_i}}(n)$ is injured by some number below k_i entering A. Since $c(k_i - 1, v_i) \geqslant c(k_i - 1, s_i) \geqslant \frac{1}{\widehat{h}(n)}$, we have $|T_n| - 1 \leqslant \widehat{h}(n)$. Thus, by altering finitely many T_n if necessary, we have $|T_n| \leqslant h(n)$ for all n. □

The more difficult direction of Theorem 14.4.2 is the following lemma, whose proof we only sketch, since the methodology is quite similar to that of the proof of Theorem 14.3.1 that every s.j.t. c.e. set is K-trivial.

Lemma 14.4.4 (Greenberg and Nies [172]). *For each benign cost function c, there is a computable order h with $h(0) > 0$ such that for any c.e. set A, if J^A has a c.e. trace bounded by h then A obeys c.*

Proof sketch. We define an A-partial computable function Ψ^A. Using the recursion theorem (or universal traces, as in [172]), we may assume we have a trace $T_0, T_1, \ldots$ with a bound h that is sufficiently slow growing to make the following box promotion construction work, such that $T_0, T_1, \ldots$ traces Ψ^A for all but finitely many values.

As we have seen, the idea of a box promotion construction is to attempt to certify certain approximations to initial segments of A. For example, in the proof Theorem 14.3.1, we used certification to decide whether to believe a computation of the form $\mathcal{U}^A(\sigma)[s]\downarrow$. Here we use certification to obtain an enumeration of A that obeys c. To attempt to certify $A_s \upharpoonright u$, we define $\Psi^{A_s}(n)[s] = s$ with use u for various n's. Certification happens at a later stage t if $A_t \upharpoonright u = A_s \upharpoonright u$ and $s \in T_n[t]$ for all such n. The degree of certainty that this certification provides us depends on the bound $h(n)$ on the size of the T_n. We know that we cannot make more than $h(n) - 1$ many mistakes. If $h(n) = 1$ and $A_s \upharpoonright u$ is certified at stage t, then we know that in fact $A \upharpoonright u = A_s \upharpoonright u$, but of course $h(n) > 1$ for almost all n, so we need to develop combinatorial strategies to deal with our mistakes.

To build our enumeration $\widehat{A}_0, \widehat{A}_1, \ldots$ of A that obeys c, we speed up our given enumeration $A_0, A_1, \ldots$ and accept only sufficiently certified approximations. If $x \in \widehat{A}_{s+1} \setminus \widehat{A}_s$ and $c(x,s) \geqslant 2^{-k}$, we want $\widehat{A}_s \upharpoonright x+1$ to have been certified via some n with $h(n) \leqslant k$. Since certification through such an n cannot happen more than k many times, letting x_s be the least number in $A_{s+1} \setminus A_s$, we will then have $\sum_s c(x_s, s) < \sum_k k2^{-k+1} < \infty$.

The part of the construction dealing with those x's for which $c(x,s) \geqslant 2^{-k}$, call it requirement R_k, may ignore those x's for which $c(x,s) \geqslant 2^{-(k-1)}$, as these need to be certified by even stronger "boxes" T_n. All of these certification processes must work in concert. At a stage s, we have $u_1 < u_2 < u_3 < \cdots < u_m$ such that $A_s \upharpoonright u_1$ has to be certified with strength 2^{-1} by R_1, while $A_s \upharpoonright u_2$ has to be certified with strength 2^{-2} by R_2, and so on. The problem is that $\Psi^A(n)$ may not be traced by T_n for all n; there may be finitely many exceptions. Hence, for each $d \in \mathbb{N}$, we have a version of the construction indexed by d, which guesses that $\Psi^A(n)$ is traced by T_n for each n such that $h(n) \geqslant d$. Almost all versions will be successful. To keep the various versions from interacting, each version controls its own infinite collection of boxes T_n. That is, for each n, only one version of the construction may attempt to define $\Psi^A(n)$.

As we have seen, a common feature of all box promotion constructions is that each certification takes place along a whole block of boxes T_n, which together form a meta-box. To ensure that R_k certifies only $k-1$ many wrong guesses at initial segments of A, we need each failure to correspond to an enumeration into the same T_n. On the other hand, if a correct initial segment is tested on some T_n, then this n is never again available for testing other, longer initial segments of A. The idea is that if a meta-box B used by R_k is promoted (by some s that is in T_n for all $n \in B$ being found to correspond to an incorrect guess at an initial segment of A, which means that each T_n can now be thought of as a smaller box), then we break B up into several sub-boxes, as in previous constructions. The fact that c is benign, witnessed by a computable bound function g, allows us to set in advance the size of the necessary meta-boxes, thus making h computable. A meta-box for R_k can be broken up at most k many times, so the necessary size for an original R_k meta-box is $g(2^{-k})^{k+1}$.

The details of the construction are quite similar to those in the proof of Theorem 14.3.1, and may be found in [172]. □

Establishing a relationship between diamond classes and s.j.t. c.e. sets begins with the following basic result.

Theorem 14.4.5 (Greenberg and Nies [172]). *Let Y be a Δ^0_2 1-random set. Then there is a monotone cost function c satisfying the limit condition such that every c.e. set that obeys c is computable from Y. If Y is ω-c.e., then c can be chosen to be benign.*

Proof. Let $c(n,0) = 2^{-n}$ for all n. For $s > 0$, let k_s be the least k such that $Y_s \upharpoonright k \neq Y_{s-1} \upharpoonright k$ (which we may assume always exists). Let $c(n,s) = \max(c(n,s-1), 2^{-k_s})$ for all $n < s$ and let $c(n,s) = c(n,s-1)$ for all $n \geqslant s$. It is easy to check that c is a monotone cost function satisfying the limit condition. If there is a computable function g such that $|\{s : Y_s(m) \neq Y_{s-1}(m)\}| < g(m)$ for all k, and I is a set of pairwise disjoint intervals of natural numbers such that $c(n,s) \geqslant 2^{-k}$ for all $[n,s) \in I$, then for each $[n,s) \in I$ with $n > k$, there is a $t \in (n,s]$ such that $Y_t \upharpoonright k \neq Y_{t-1} \upharpoonright k$, and hence $|I| \leqslant (k+1) + \sum_{m<k} g(m)$. Thus, if our approximation to Y is ω-c.e. then c is benign.

Suppose that the c.e. set A obeys c, as witnessed by the approximation $A_0, A_1, \ldots$. For each n and $t \geqslant n$, let $s_n(t)$ be the least $s \leqslant t$ such that $Y_r \upharpoonright n = Y_t \upharpoonright n$ for all $r \in [s,t]$. Without loss of generality, we may assume that $s_n(t) \geqslant n$ for all $t \geqslant n$. At each stage t, if n is least such that $A_t \upharpoonright s_n(t) \neq A_{t-1} \upharpoonright s_n(t)$, then enumerate $[\![Y_t \upharpoonright n-1]\!]$ into a Solovay test G. It is easy to check that the fact that $A_0, A_1, \ldots$ obeys c implies that $\sum_{[\![\sigma]\!] \in G} 2^{-|\sigma|} < \infty$.

Since Y is 1-random, only finitely many initial segments of Y are enumerated into G. Let v be such that no such initial segment is enumerated after stage v. We claim that if $t > v, n$ and $Y \upharpoonright n-1 = Y_t \upharpoonright n-1$, then $A \upharpoonright n = A_t \upharpoonright n$, which implies that $A \leqslant_T Y$. Assume otherwise, and let $u > t$ be such that $A_u \upharpoonright n \neq A_{u-1} \upharpoonright n$. Then $A_u \upharpoonright s_n(u) \neq A_{u-1} \upharpoonright s_n(u)$. Let m be the least such that $A_u \upharpoonright s_m(u) \neq A_{u-1} \upharpoonright s_m(u)$. Then $m \leqslant n$, and we enumerate $[\![Y_u \upharpoonright m-1]\!]$ into G. Since $u > v$, we have $Y_t \upharpoonright m-1 = Y \upharpoonright m-1 \neq Y_u \upharpoonright m-1$. But then $s_u(m-1) > t > n$, so $A_u \upharpoonright s_{m-1}(u) \neq A_{u-1} \upharpoonright s_{m-1}(u)$, contradicting the minimality of m. □

Combining this result with Theorem 14.4.2, we have the following result. (Note that $(\omega\text{-c.e.})^\diamond \subseteq \text{superlow}^\diamond$, since every superlow set is ω-c.e.)

Corollary 14.4.6 (Greenberg and Nies [172]). *Every strongly jump traceable c.e. set is in $(\omega\text{-c.e.})^\diamond$, and hence in superlow$^\diamond$.*

This result has some powerful computability-theoretic consequences. It can be used to prove results of Ng [297] and Diamondstone [97] whose direct proofs are rather intricate. (These results answer natural questions about superlowness stemming from well-known results on lowness. See [97, 297] for further discussion.) We need the following version of Corollary 2.19.9, whose proof is similar.

Lemma 14.4.7 (Greenberg and Nies [172]). *Let P be a nonempty Π^0_1 class. For each B there is a $Y \in P$ such that $(Y \oplus B)' \leqslant_{tt} B'$.*

We also use the easily proved fact that if $C \leqslant_T D$ then $C' \leqslant_{tt} D'$.

Theorem 14.4.8 (Ng [297]). *There is a c.e. set A such that for every superlow c.e. set B, the join $A \oplus B$ is also superlow.*

Proof. Let A be an s.j.t. c.e. set. If B is superlow, then applying Lemma 14.4.7 to a nonempty Π^0_1 class of 1-random sets, we see that there is a 1-random set Y such that $Y' \leqslant_{tt} (Y \oplus B)' \leqslant_{tt} B' \leqslant_{tt} \emptyset'$. Then Y is superlow, so by Corollary 14.4.6, $A \leqslant_T Y$, and hence $(A \oplus B)' \leqslant_{tt} (Y \oplus B)' \leqslant_{tt} \emptyset'$. □

Note that the above proof in fact proves the stronger result that if A is any s.j.t. c.e. set and B is any (not necessarily c.e.) superlow set, then $A \oplus B$ is also superlow. Taking A to be a promptly simple s.j.t. c.e. set (as given by Theorem 14.1.3), we have the following result.

Theorem 14.4.9 (Diamondstone [97]). *There is a promptly simple c.e. set A such that for every superlow c.e. set B, we have $A \oplus B <_T \emptyset'$.*

As it turns out, Corollary 14.4.6 has a strong converse, which does not require the hypothesis of computable enumerability. (It remains open whether Corollary 14.4.6 holds beyond the c.e. sets.)

Theorem 14.4.10 (Greenberg, Hirschfeldt, and Nies [169]). *If a set is computable in every superlow 1-random set, then it is strongly jump traceable.*

Note that it is not difficult to prove that if a set A is computable in every superlow 1-random set then it is K-trivial: Let X be a superlow 1-random set. By the superlow basis theorem relative to X, there is a superlow set Y that is 1-random relative to X. By van Lambalgen's Theorem, X and Y are relatively 1-random, so by Corollary 11.7.3, A is K-trivial.

We will prove Theorem 14.4.10 below. Since $(\omega\text{-c.e.})^\diamond \subseteq \text{superlow}^\diamond$, combining Corollary 14.4.6 and Theorem 14.4.10, we have the following result.

Corollary 14.4.11. *The following are equivalent for a c.e. set A.*

(i) *A is strongly jump traceable.*

(ii) *$A \in (\omega\text{-c.e.})^\diamond$.*

(iii) *$A \in \textit{superlow}^\diamond$.*

This result implies Theorem 14.2.1, that the s.j.t. c.e. sets are closed under joins, because every diamond class is obviously closed under joins.

Recall that a set X is superhigh if $\emptyset'' \leqslant_{tt} X'$. Greenberg, Hirschfeldt, and Nies [169] showed that strong jump traceability of c.e. sets is also equivalent to being in superhigh$^\diamond$.

The proof of Theorem 14.4.10 does not make special use of 1-randomness, and in fact establishes the following stronger result.

Theorem 14.4.12 (Greenberg, Hirschfeldt, and Nies [169]). *Let P be a nonempty Π^0_1 class, and let A be a jump traceable set computable from every superlow member of P. Then A is strongly jump traceable.*

By Corollary 2.19.9, every nonempty Π^0_1 class has a superlow member, so if A satisfies the hypothesis of Theorem 14.4.12 then it is superlow. Thus, by Theorem 11.4.7, the extra hypothesis that A be jump traceable is not needed if A is c.e.

Theorem 14.4.10 follows from Theorem 14.4.12 as follows. Let $A \in \text{superlow}^{\diamond}$. Let $X \oplus Y$ be superlow and 1-random. Then both X and Y are superlow and 1-random, so $A \leqslant_{\mathrm{T}} X, Y$. But Y is 1-random relative to X, and hence relative to A, so A is a base for 1-randomness, and hence K-trivial. By Theorem 11.4.8, A is jump traceable, so applying Theorem 14.4.12 to a nonempty Π^0_1 class P all of whose elements are 1-random shows that A is s.j.t.

Another corollary to Theorem 14.4.12 comes from the Scott Basis Theorem 2.21.2, which implies that every completion of PA computes a 1-random set. The reduction in the proof of that theorem is clearly a wtt-reduction, so it is also the case that every ω-c.e. completion of PA computes an ω-c.e. 1-random set. Thus we have the following result.

Theorem 14.4.13 (Greenberg, Hirschfeldt, and Nies [169]). *A c.e. set A is strongly jump traceable iff it is computable from every superlow (or equivalently, every ω-c.e.) completion of PA.*

To prove Theorem 14.4.12, we will not use the jump traceability of A directly, but instead will use the existence of certain nice approximations to A-partial computable functions.

We think of a functional Ψ as a partial computable function $p : 2^{<\omega} \times \mathbb{N} \to \mathbb{N}$ such that for each n, the set of all σ such that $(\sigma, n) \in \operatorname{dom} p$ is prefix-free. We have $\Psi^A(n) = m$ iff $p(\sigma, n) = m$ for some $\sigma \prec A$, in which case the use $\psi^A(n)$ equals $|\sigma|$. An enumeration $\Psi_0, \Psi_1, \ldots$ of Ψ is then simply a sequence of functionals corresponding to uniformly partial computable functions $p_0 \subseteq p_1 \subseteq \cdots$ such that $\operatorname{dom} p_s \subset 2^{\leqslant s} \times [0, s]$ and $p = \bigcup_s p_s$.

Definition 14.4.14 (Greenberg, Hirschfeldt, and Nies [169]). Let $(A_s)_{s \in \omega}$ be a computable approximation to a Δ^0_2 set A, and let $(\Psi_s)_{s \in \omega}$ be an enumeration of a functional Ψ. We say that the pair $((A_s)_{s \in \omega}, (\Psi_s)_{s \in \omega})$ is a *restrained A-approximation* of Ψ^A if there is a computable function g such that for each n, the number of stages s such that $\Psi^{A_s}_s(n)\downarrow$ and $A_{s+1} \upharpoonright \psi^{A_s}_s(n) \neq A_s \upharpoonright \psi^{A_s}_s(n)$ is bounded by $g(n)$.

Theorem 14.4.15 (Greenberg, Hirschfeldt, and Nies [169]). *The following are equivalent.*

(i) *A is superlow and jump traceable.*

(ii) *Each A-partial computable function has a restrained A-approximation.*

Given this fact, Theorem 14.4.12 follows from the following result.

Theorem 14.4.16 (Greenberg, Hirschfeldt, and Nies [169]). *Let P be a nonempty Π^0_1 class, and let A be a set such that every A-partial computable* *function has a restrained A-approximation. If A is computable from every superlow element of P then A is strongly jump traceable.*

Rather than prove Theorem 14.4.15 here, we will show that we can obtain Theorem 14.4.10 from Theorem 14.4.16 without it. (See [169] for a proof of Theorem 14.4.16, which uses a characterization of sets that are both superlow and jump traceable due to Cole and Simpson [72].)

Lemma 14.4.17. *If B is a jump traceable c.e. set, then every B-partial computable function has a restrained B-approximation.*

Proof. Let $\theta = \Phi^B$ be a B-partial computable function. Let $T_0, T_1, \ldots$ be a c.e. trace for $n \mapsto B \upharpoonright \varphi^B(n)$ with a computable bound h. Define an enumeration of a functional Ψ by letting $\Psi_s^\tau(n) = \Phi_s^\tau(n)$ if $\tau \prec B_s$ and $\tau \in T_n[s]$. It is easy to verify that $\Psi^B = \theta$, and there are at most $h(n)$ many stages s such that $\Psi_s^{B_s}(y)\downarrow$ and $B_{s+1} \upharpoonright \psi_s^{B_s}(y) \neq B_s \upharpoonright \psi_s^{B_s}(y)$. ☐

Lemma 14.4.18. *If A is computable from every superlow 1-random set, then every A-partial computable function has a restrained A-approximation.*

Proof. Let A be computable from every superlow 1-random set. As noted following Theorem 14.4.10, A is K-trivial. By Theorem 11.5.4, A is computable from some c.e. K-trivial set B. By Theorem 11.4.8, B is jump traceable, so by Lemma 14.4.17, every B-partial computable function has a restrained B-approximation, from which it follows easily that every A-partial computable function has a restrained A-approximation. ☐

Thus Theorem 14.4.10 follows from Theorem 14.4.16, which we now prove.

Proof of Theorem 14.4.16. Let P be a nonempty Π_1^0 class and let A be computable from every superlow element of P and such that every A-partial computable function has a restrained A-approximation. Fix a computable order h and an A-partial computable function θ. We show that θ has a c.e. trace bounded by $n \mapsto 2^{h(n)}$, which is enough to establish strong jump traceability, since h is arbitrary. (Of course, it is enough to do this for the single case $\theta = J^A$.) Fix a restrained A-approximation $((A_s)_{s\in\omega}, (\Psi_s)_{s\in\omega})$ to θ.

The key concept in this proof is that of a *golden pair*. Recall that in the proof of the (super)low basis theorem, we build a sequence of Π_1^0 classes $Q_0 \supseteq Q_1 \supseteq \cdots$ by letting $Q_{n+1} = Q_n$ if $n \in X'$ for all $X \in Q_n$ and otherwise letting $Q_{n+1} = \{X \in Q_n : n \notin X'\}$. Then $\bigcap_n Q_n$ contains a single element Z, which is superlow, because to compute $Z'(n)$, we need only computably approximate which case of the definition of Q_{n+1} obtains, which we can do recursively, going through at most 2^k many versions of each Q_k.

We can start this construction by letting $Q_0 = Q$ for any nonempty Π_1^0 class Q. Let $Q_{n,s}$ be the stage s guess at Q_n, which is defined as follows.

First, let $Q_{0,s} = Q$. If at stage s we see that $n \in X'$ for all $X \in Q_{n,s}[s]$, then let $Q_{n+1,s} = Q_{n,s}$. Otherwise, let $Q_{n+1,s} = \{X \in Q_{n,s} : n \notin X'\}$. As mentioned above, the guess $Q_{n,s}$ changes at most 2^n many times. Thus, if we can guess at $\theta(n)$ in such a way that we make at most one guess per version of $Q_{n,s}$, we can build a trace for θ with the appropriate bound. The existence of a golden pair is what will allow us to do so.

Definition 14.4.19 (Greenberg, Hirschfeldt, and Nies [169]). A pair (Q, Φ), consisting of a nonempty Π^0_1 class Q and a functional Φ, is a *golden pair* (for Ψ and h) if for almost all n such that $\Psi^A(n)\downarrow$ and all $X \in Q_{h(n)}$, we have $\Phi^X \succcurlyeq A \upharpoonright \psi^A(n)$.

Lemma 14.4.20. *If there is a golden pair then θ has a c.e. trace bounded by $n \mapsto 2^{h(n)}$.*

Proof of Lemma 14.4.20. Let Q, Φ be a golden pair. We enumerate $T_0, T_1, \ldots$ as follows. If at stage s there is a σ such that $\Psi^\sigma_s(n)\downarrow= k$ and $\sigma \preccurlyeq \Phi^X$ for every $X \in Q_{h(n),s}[s]$, then put k into T_n.

The T_n are uniformly c.e. For each different guess $Q_{h(n),s}$, at most one number k gets enumerated into T_n, so $|T_n| \leqslant 2^{h(n)}$. By the definition of golden pair, for almost all $n \in \operatorname{dom}\theta$, we have $A \upharpoonright \psi^A(n) \preccurlyeq \Phi^X$ for all $X \in Q_{h(n)}$, which implies that if s is sufficiently large, then $A \upharpoonright \psi^A(n) \preccurlyeq \Phi^X$ for all $X \in Q_{h(n),s}[s]$, so $\theta = \Psi^{A \upharpoonright \psi^A(n)}(n) \in T_n$. Thus we can make finitely many changes to the T_n to obtain a c.e. trace for θ with bound $n \mapsto 2^{h(n)}$. $\square$

So we are left with showing that a golden pair exists. We can think of a golden pair as arising from a failed attempt at building a superlow set $Z \in P$ that does not compute A. Such an attempt can be made, starting with any $Q \subseteq P$, by interspersing the superlowness classes Q_n with ones attempting to diagonalize against computations yielding A, that is, classes of the form $\{X \in Q_m : \Phi^X_e \not\succcurlyeq \tau\}$ for some $\tau \prec A$. For each e and n we have a strategy S^e_n that monitors whether this class is empty for $\tau = A \upharpoonright \psi^A(n)$ and $m = h(n)$. As long as the class looks nonempty, so that it appears that S^e_n has succeeded in ensuring that $\Phi^Z_e \neq A$, we start a new superlow basis construction with this class, but at level $e + 1$ now. (We think of the procedures at this new level as being called by the procedure S^e_n.) It cannot be the case that strategies at all levels succeed, since otherwise Z would be a superlow element of P not computing A. The failure at some level gives us a golden pair. We will have to be careful in showing that Z is in fact superlow, since the superlowness requirements will be distributed among constructions corresponding to different levels e. Each S^e_n works with $A \upharpoonright \psi^A(n)$, the value of which can change since A is not computable. When this value changes, the strategies at level $e + 1$ called by S^e_n must be canceled. This action causes the bound witnessing superlowness to be more difficult to compute, but we will be able to show there is one by using the fact that $((A_s)_{s\in\omega}, (\Psi_s)_{s\in\omega})$ is a restrained approximation.

The construction is a nonuniform argument in the spirit of the golden run method, but with a procedure calling structure of unbounded depth, as in box promotion arguments.

For each e, we will have a procedure R^e, provided with some Π^0_1 subclass P^e of P as input, which attempts to show that (P^e, Φ_e) is a golden pair. For each n such that $\Psi^A(n)\downarrow$, we will have a subprocedure S^e_n, which attempts to show that the golden pair condition holds at n, that is, that $\Phi^X_e \not\succcurlyeq A \upharpoonright \psi^A(n)$ for all $X \in P^e_{h(n)}$. Failing that, S^e_n will try to give permanent control to the next level $e+1$.

Construction. We describe the instructions for our procedures.

A run of the procedure R_e has an input P^e and a parameter m. If it has control at stage s, it looks for the least n such that

1. $h(n) > m$,
2. $\Psi^A_s(n)\downarrow$, and
3. it is not the case that a previous run of S^e_n with input $A_s \upharpoonright \psi^A_s(n)$ has returned and not been subsequently canceled, as defined below.

If there is such an n, then R_e calls S^e_n with input $A_s \upharpoonright \psi^A_s(n)$, transferring control to S^e_n.

A run of the procedure S^e_n is provided with a string τ such that $\Psi^\tau(n)\downarrow$. It acts as follows. First it calls R^{e+1} with input $P^{e+1} = \{X \in P^e_{h(n)} : \Phi^X_e \not\succcurlyeq \tau\}$ and parameter $h(n)$. As long as P_{e+1} appears to be nonempty, it halts all activity at level e, allowing R^{e+1} to act. If P_{e+1} is ever found to be empty, it cancels the run of R^{e+1} and any subprocedures that run may have called and returns control to R^e.

A run of S^e_n with input τ believes that $\tau \prec A$ and that the current guess at $P^e_{h(n)}$ is correct. So if at any stage after the beginning of this run we find that one of these conditions is not true, then this run, and the run of R^{e+1} it called, are canceled and, if S^e_n had not yet returned, control is returned to R^e.

The construction is started by calling R^0 with input $P^0 = P$ and parameter 0.

End of Construction.

A *golden run* is a run of some R^e that is never canceled and such that every S^e_n called by that run eventually returns or is canceled.

Lemma 14.4.21. *If there is a golden run of R_e with input Q, then (Q, Φ_e) is a golden pair.*

Proof. Let m be the parameter with which the golden run is called. We claim that if $h(n) > m$ then there is a final call of S^e_n that is never canceled and hence returns. To see that this is the case, assume by induction that there is a stage t such that no runs of S_k^e for $k < n$ are ever active after stage t, our guess at $Q_{h(n)}$ has stabilized by stage t, and so has the approximation to $A \upharpoonright \psi^A(n)$. Any run of S_k^e for $k > n$ that may be active at stage t will eventually return or be canceled, so eventually a run of S_n^e that is never canceled will start, and hence return, after which point no further calls to S_n^e will be made. Since this run returns, the golden pair condition for n holds of (Q, Φ_e). Since $h(n) > m$ for almost all n, we see that (Q, Φ_e) is a golden pair. □

Thus it remains to show that there is a golden run of some R^e. We first need to do some counting to establish a computable bound on the number of times procedures can be called. Let g be the function witnessing the fact that $((A_s)_{s\in\omega}, (\Psi_s)_{s\in\omega})$ is a restrained approximation.

Lemma 14.4.22. *For each e, each run of R^e calls at most $g(n)+2^{h(n)}+1$ many runs of S_n^e.*

Proof. Fix a run of R_e with input P^e. Suppose that a run of S_n^e with input τ called by this run is canceled at stage s, but the run of R_e is not. Then either $P^e_{h(n),s} \neq P^e_{h(n),s-1}$ or $\tau \prec A_{s-1}$ but $\tau \not\prec A_s$. The first possibility can occur at most $2^{h(n)}$ many times, and the second can occur at most $g(n)$ many times, because each time it occurs, our restrained approximation to $\Psi^A(n)$ changes. A new run of S_n^e cannot be started until the previous run is canceled, so the lemma follows. □

Lemma 14.4.23. *There is a computable bound $N(n)$ on the number of times procedures S_n^e are called (over all e).*

Proof. We calculate by recursion on e and n a bound $M(e,n)$ on the number of times any R^e calls a run of S_n^e. By Lemma 14.4.22, we can let $M(e,n)$ be the product of $g(n)+2^{h(n)}+1$ with a bound on the number of runs of R^e that are called by some S_m^{e-1} with parameter $h(m) < h(n)$. Since h is monotone, the number of runs of R^e with parameter less than $h(n)$ is bounded by $\sum_{m<n} M(e-1,m)$, which completes the inductive definition of M. By induction on e we can show that the parameter of any run of R^e is at least e, so we can let $N(n) = \sum_{e<h(n)} M(e,n)$. □

Now suppose there is no golden run, so every run of every R^e is either eventually canceled, or calls a run of some S_n^e that is never canceled but never returns. By induction on e, we can see that for each e there is a run of R^e that is never canceled, with a final version of P^e. For these final versions, we have $P^0 \supseteq P^1 \supseteq \cdots$, so there is a $Z \in \bigcap_e P^e$. We will show in the next lemma that we can use approximations to the P^e and the computable bound of the previous lemma to approximate Z' in an ω-c.e. way, whence Z is superlow. By our hypothesis on A, there is some e such that $\Phi_e^Z = A$. Consider the run of some S_n^e that is neither canceled nor returns, which defines the last version of P^{e+1}. It defines this class as

$\{X \in P^e_{h(n)} : \Phi^X_e \nprec \tau\}$ for a $\tau \prec A$ (since S^e_n is never canceled). This definition contradicts the fact that $Z \in P^{e+1}$.

Lemma 14.4.24. *Z is superlow.*

Proof. Let $n > 0$, and let e be the least number such that the permanent run of R^e is started with a parameter greater than n. As mentioned in the proof of Lemma 14.4.23, the parameter of any run of R^e is at least e, so such an e exists.

Whether $n \in Z'$ depends only on P^{e-1}_{n+1}, so we can approximate an answer to the question of whether $n \in Z'$ by tracking, at each stage, the guess at P^d_{n+1} at that stage, where d is the greatest number such that the current run of R^d has parameter no greater than n.

The guess at P^d_{n+1} can change because of a call to S^e_m where $h(m) \leqslant n$ or because of the approximation inherent in the superlow basis theorem strategy. Thus the number of times this guess can change is at most $2^{n+1} \sum_{h(m) \leqslant n} N(m)$, which is a computable bound, and hence we have an ω-c.e. approximation to Z'. ☐

As argued above, this lemma completes the proof of the theorem. ☐

14.5 Strong jump traceability and K-triviality: the general case

In general, s.j.t. sets are not as well understood as the special case of c.e. s.j.t. sets. It would be quite helpful if the following analog to Corollary 11.5.4 were to be established.

Conjecture 14.5.1 (Downey and Greenberg). Every s.j.t. set is computable from some c.e. s.j.t. set.

Downey and Greenberg [105] showed that all s.j.t. sets are Δ^0_2, and have recently improved this result considerably by showing that all s.j.t. sets are K-trivial. This result extends Theorem 14.3.1, but its proof is perhaps simpler.

Theorem 14.5.2 (Downey and Greenberg [105]). *There is a computable order h such that every h-jump traceable set is K-trivial.*

Before proving this result, we note that not all orders h suffice.

Theorem 14.5.3 (Nies [303]). *There are continuum many 2^{2n+1}-jump traceable sets.*

Proof. We build a trace $T_0, T_1, \ldots$ and a sequence of uniformly computable functions $f_s : 2^{<\omega} \to 2^{<\omega}$ such that $f = \lim_s f_s$ exists. Let $f_0(\sigma) = \sigma$ for all σ. At stage $s+1$, look for the length-lexicographically least ν such that

$J^{f_s(\tau)}(|\nu|)\downarrow \notin T_{e,s}$ for some $\tau \succcurlyeq \nu$ with $\tau \in 2^{\leqslant s+1}$. If no such ν exists then let $f_{s+1}(\sigma) = f_s(\sigma)$ for all σ and proceed to the next stage. Otherwise, for every ρ, let $f_{s+1}(\nu\rho) = \tau\rho$. For every $\sigma \not\succcurlyeq \nu$, let $f_{s+1}(\sigma) = f_s(\sigma)$. Enumerate $J^{f_s(\tau)}(|\nu|)$ into T_e.

It is easy to see that for every $\sigma \in 2^e$, the value of $f_s(\sigma)$ changes at most $2^{e+1} - 1$ many times, and causes at most that many elements to be put into T_e, whence $|T_e| < 2^{2e+1}$. Moreover, the image of 2^ω under f has size continuum, and for every member A of this image, we have $J^A(e)\downarrow \Rightarrow J^A(e) \in T_e$ for all e. □

It is not hard to check that, as shown in [303], the above proof can be used to define a perfect Π^0_1 class of 2^{2n+1}-jump traceable sets. It would be interesting to improve the bounds on the levels of jump traceability that hold of continuum many sets, given by this result on the one hand, and the proof of Theorem 14.5.2 below on the other. This question is of course connected with the one mentioned at the end of Section 14.3, as well as with the question of what level of jump traceability is needed to ensure Δ^0_2-ness.

Proof of Theorem 14.5.2. We build a computable trace $\tilde{h}$ such that if J^A is $\tilde{h}$-traceable then A is K-trivial. By Theorem 11.1.8, there is a computable function g such that $\sum_n 2^{-g(n)} < 1$ and if $K(X \upharpoonright n) \leqslant g(n) + O(1)$, then X is K-trivial. We wish to build a KC set to ensure that $K(A \upharpoonright n) \leqslant g(n) + O(1)$. We have no direct access to A, so for each n, we will need to include $(g(n), \sigma)$ in our KC set for several $\sigma \in 2^n$. To keep the weight of our set finite, we need to limit the number of such σ. As in previous constructions in this chapter, we use a functional Ψ as a tester. By not believing that a given σ is a possible initial segment of A until it has been sufficiently tested, we will be able to limit the number of σ's we consider.

Suppose that $\sum_n 2^{-g(n)}$ were computable. Then there would be a computable order h such that $\sum_n h(n)2^{-g(n)} < 1$. We could then let $\Psi^\sigma(|\sigma|) = \sigma$ for all σ (thus testing every σ), take a trace $\{T_n\}_{n\in\mathbb{N}}$ for Ψ^A with bound h, and let our KC set be $\{(g(n), \sigma) : \sigma \in T_n\}$. It is easy to check that this definition would ensure that $K(A \upharpoonright n) \leqslant g(n) + O(1)$. Since $\sum_n 2^{-g(n)}$ is merely left-c.e., we will need to deal with approximations to this sum, and have a more complicated testing procedure.

Partition $\mathbb{N}$ into consecutive intervals $I_1, I_2, \ldots$ such that $|I_k| = 2^{2^{2k}}$. For $e > 1$ and $n \in I_k$, let $h_e(n) = k + e$. By Lemma 14.1.2, we can determine a computable order $\tilde{h}$ such that, for any A, from a trace for J^A with bound $\tilde{h}$, we can compute, uniformly in e, a trace for Φ^A_e with bound h_e. Let J^A be $\tilde{h}$-traceable. We show that A is K-trivial.

We will define a functional Ψ. By the recursion theorem, we know some e such that $\Psi^X = \Phi^X_e$ for all X. Let $\{T_n\}_{n\in\mathbb{N}}$ be a trace for Ψ^A with bound $h = h_e$, computed from e as described above.

Let b be such that $|I_k| \geqslant 2^{(k+e)2^k} + 2^k$ for all $k \geqslant b$. Our testing procedures will happen at levels $k \geqslant b$. For each $k \geqslant b$, let $t_0^k, \ldots, t_{2^k-1}^k$ be the first 2^k many numbers in I_k, and let M^k be the next $2^{(k+e)2^k}$ many numbers in I_k. The set M^k is split into 2^{k+e} many subsets, which are further split into 2^{k+e} many subsets, and so on for 2^k many levels. We index these subsets as follows. Let $M^k(\lambda) = M^k$. If ν is a sequence of subsets of $[0, k+e)$ of length less than or equal to 2^k and $M^k(\nu)$ is defined, then split $M^k(\nu)$ evenly into 2^{k+e} many subsets $M^k(\nu B)$ for $B \subseteq [0, k+e)$. We will use both the t_m^k and the elements of M^k as test inputs.

If $m2^{-k} < \sum_l 2^{-g(l)}$, then let n_m^k be the least n such that $m2^{-k} \leqslant \sum_{l \leqslant n} 2^{-g(l)}$. Note that the set of all k and m for which n_m^k is defined is c.e. For each $k \geqslant b$ and $m < 2^k$, if we find that n_m^k is defined, then we test every string of length n_m^k using the "initial test input" t_m^k. That is, for each $\sigma \in 2^{n_m^k}$, we let $\Psi^\sigma(t_m^k) = \sigma$. This step allows us to forget about all but at most $|T_{t_m^k}| \leqslant h(t_m^k) = k + e$ many strings of length n_m^k.

We now proceed by recursion on $k \geqslant b$, and on $m < 2^k$ within each level k, to define which strings of length n_m^k are (k,m)-*approved*, and how our testing at level m of M^k is conducted. It will be clear from the construction that the collection of (k,m)-approved strings is c.e., uniformly in k and m.

A string $\sigma \in 2^{n_m^k}$ is (k,m)-*preapproved* if for every $l \in [b,k]$ and $j < 2^l$ such that either $j2^{-l} < m2^{-k}$ or both $l < k$ and $j2^{-l} = m2^{-k}$, the string $\sigma \restriction 2^{n_j^l}$ is (l,j)-approved.

By induction, the collection of (k,m)-preapproved strings is c.e., uniformly in k and m. Let $\sigma_0(k,m), \sigma_1(k,m), \ldots$ be an effective list of the (k,m)-preapproved strings in $T_{t_m^k}$. This list has length at most $k+e$, since $|T_{t_m^k}| \leqslant h(t_m^k) = k + e$.

For a sequence $\nu = (C_0, \ldots, C_m)$ of subsets of $[0, k+e)$, a number i is ν-*appropriate* if

(i) $\sigma_i(k,m)$ is defined,

(ii) $i \in C_m$, and

(iii) for all $m' < m$, if $\sigma_j(k,m') \preccurlyeq \sigma_i(k,m)$, then $j \notin C_{m'}$.

For all sequences ν as above and all ν-appropriate i, let $\Psi^{\sigma_i(k,m)}(n) = \sigma_i(k,m)$ for all $n \in M^k(\nu)$. The idea here is that we test $\sigma_i(k,m)$ on all inputs in M^k except for those where we already tested a substring of $\sigma_i(k,m)$. It is easy to see that the above definition does in fact ensure that for all $n \in M^k$, the set of all σ for which we define $\Psi^\sigma(n) = \sigma$ is prefix-free, as it needs to be.

We say that $\sigma_i(k,m)$ is (k,m)-*approved* if for every n for which we define $\Psi^{\sigma_i(k,m)}(n) = \sigma_i(k,m)$, we have $\sigma_i(k,m) \in T_n$.

We now define our KC set G. For $k \geqslant b$, let S_k be the set of all (k,m)-approved strings, over all $m < 2^k$. For $k > b$ and $\sigma \in S_k$, let σ_k^- be the longest initial segment of σ of length n_l^{k-1} for some l such that n_l^{k-1} is defined. For $\sigma \in S_b$, let $\sigma_b^- = \lambda$. For $k \geqslant b$ and $\sigma \in S_k$, let

$$G_k(\sigma) = \{(g(|\tau|), \tau) : \sigma_k^- \prec \tau \preccurlyeq \sigma\}.$$

Let $G_k = \bigcup_{\sigma \in S_k} G_k(\sigma)$ and $G = \bigcup_{k \geqslant b} G_k$. Then G is c.e. We show that the weight of G is bounded.

To do so, we redefine G in terms of certain subsets of the G_k. For $k \geqslant b$, let L_k be the set of maximal elements of S_k (that is, elements of S_k with no proper extensions in S_k). Let $A_b = S_b$. For $k > b$, let $A_k = L_k \setminus S_{k-1}$. The following lemma shows that the A_k are small, and hence can be used in bounding the weight of G.

Lemma 14.5.4. *$|A_k| \leqslant k + e$ for all $k \geqslant b$.*

Proof. For $m < 2^k$, let $C_m = \{i : \sigma_i(k,m) \in A_k \cap 2^{n_m^k}\}$. Let $\nu = (C_0, \ldots, C_{2^k-1})$. It is easy to check that, since A_k is an antichain, we test every $\sigma \in A_k$ on the inputs in $M^k(\nu)$. Thus, for every $\sigma \in A_k$ and $n \in M^k(\nu)$, we define $\Psi^\sigma(n) = \sigma$. But then $\sigma \in T_n$, since otherwise σ would not be in S_k. Since $|T_n| \leqslant h(n) = k + e$ for all such n, we have $|A_k| \leqslant k + e$. □

The next two lemmas will allow us to express G in terms of the A_k.

Lemma 14.5.5. *Let $k > b$ and let $\sigma \in S_k \setminus L_k$. Then there are a $j \in [b, k)$ and a $\rho \in S_j$ such that $G_k(\sigma) \subseteq G_j(\rho)$.*

Proof. Let τ be a proper extension of σ in S_k. Let m be such that $|\sigma| = n_m^k$. Then $|\tau| \geqslant n_{m+1}^k$. Let $j = \lfloor \frac{m+1}{2} \rfloor$. Then $m2^{-k} < j2^{-(k-1)} \leqslant (m+1)2^{-k}$, so $\tau \upharpoonright n_j^{k-1} \in S_{k-1}$ and $\sigma \preccurlyeq \tau \upharpoonright n_j^{k-1}$. Let ρ be the shortest extension of σ in S_{k-1}, and let $j \geqslant b$ be least such that $\rho \in S_j$.

Then $\rho_j^- \prec \rho$. Since $\rho \in S_{k-1}$, we have $\rho_j^- \in S_{k-1}$ (as otherwise ρ would not have been preapproved at the $k-1$ level). By the definition of ρ, we have $\rho_j^- \prec \sigma$, so $\rho_j^- \preccurlyeq \sigma_k^-$.

Thus $\rho_j^- \preccurlyeq \sigma_k^- \preccurlyeq \sigma \preccurlyeq \rho$, from which it follows that $G_k(\sigma) \subseteq G_j(\rho)$. □

Lemma 14.5.6. *Let $k \geqslant b$ and $\sigma \in S_k$. Then there are a $j \in [b, k]$ and a $\rho \in A_j$ such that $G_k(\sigma) \subseteq G_j(\rho)$.*

Proof. We define sequences of strings and numbers by recursion. Let $\sigma_0 = \sigma$ and k_0 be least such that $\sigma \in S_{k_0}$. Suppose we have defined σ_i and k_i so that k_i is least such that $\sigma_i \in S_{k_i}$. If $\sigma_i \in A_{k_i}$ then stop the recursion. Otherwise, by the definition of A_{k_i}, we have $k_i > b$ and $\sigma_i \notin L_{k_i}$. Thus,by Lemma 14.5.5, there are a $j < k_i$ and a $\sigma_{i+1} \in S_j$ such that $G_{k_i}(\sigma_i) \subseteq G_j(\sigma_{i+1})$. Let k_{i+1} be least such that $\sigma_{i+1} \in S_{k_{i+1}}$. It is easy to see that $G_j(\sigma_{i+1}) \subseteq G_{k_{i+1}}(\sigma_{i+1})$, so $G_{k_i}(\sigma_i) \subseteq G_{k_{i+1}}(\sigma_{i+1})$.

Let i be largest such that σ_i is defined. Then $\sigma_i \in A_{k_i}$ and, by induction, $G_k(\sigma) \subseteq G_{k_i}(\sigma_i)$. □

Let $H_k = \bigcup_{\sigma \in A_k} G_k(\sigma)$ and $H = \bigcup_{k \geqslant b} H_k$. Clearly $H \subseteq G$, and it follows from Lemma 14.5.6 that $G \subseteq H$, so in fact $G = H$. We now use this fact to bound the weight of G.

Lemma 14.5.7. *If $\sigma \in A_k$ then $2^{-g(|\sigma|)} < 2^{-(k-1)}$.*

Proof. Suppose that $2^{-g(|\sigma|)} \geqslant 2^{-(k-1)}$. Then there is an m such that $|\sigma| = n_m^{k-1}$. By the definition of the approval process, $\sigma \in S_{k-1}$, contradicting the definition of A_k. □

Lemma 14.5.8. *Let $k > b$ and $\sigma \in A_k$. Then the weight of $G_k(\sigma)$ is bounded by $2^{-(k-2)}$.*

Proof. Let m be such that $n_m^k = |\sigma|$. Then $\sum_{n<|\sigma|} < m2^{-k}$. Let $l = \lfloor \frac{m}{2} \rfloor$. Since $\sigma \notin S_{k-1}$, we must have $n_i^{k-1} > n_m^k$ for all $i > l$, so $|\sigma_k^-| = n_l^{k-1}$. Thus $\sum_{n \leqslant |\sigma_k^-|} 2^{-g(n)} \geqslant l2^{-(k-1)}$. By the previous lemma, $2^{-g(|\sigma|)} < 2^{-(k-1)}$. So the weight of $G_k(\sigma)$ is

$$\sum_{|\sigma_k^-|<n\leqslant|\sigma|} 2^{-g(n)} = \left(\sum_{n<|\sigma|} 2^{-g(n)}\right) + 2^{-g(|\sigma|)} - \sum_{n\leqslant|\sigma_k^-|} 2^{-g(n)}$$
$$< m2^{-k} + 2^{-(k-1)} - l2^{-(k-1)} \leqslant 2^{-(k-2)}.$$

□

Thus weight of $G = H$ is bounded by the weight of G_b plus

$$\sum_{k>b} |A_k| 2^{-(k-2)} \leqslant \sum_{k>b} (k+e) 2^{-(k-2)} < \infty.$$

So G is a KC set, and hence, if $\sigma_k^- \prec \tau \preccurlyeq \sigma$ for σ in some S_k, then $K(\tau) \leqslant g(|\tau|) + O(1)$.

Finally, for $k \geqslant b$, let m_k be the greatest $m < 2^k$ such that $m2^{-k} < \sum_l 2^{-g(l)}$. Let $\sigma(b-1) = 0$. For $k \geqslant b$, let $\sigma(k) = A \upharpoonright n_{m_k}^k$. It is easy to see that for each $k \geqslant b$, we have $\sigma(k) \in S_k$ and $\sigma(k)_k^- = \sigma(k-1)$. Thus $K(A \upharpoonright n) \leqslant g(n) + O(1)$, and hence A is K-trivial. □

15
Ω as an Operator

15.1 Introduction

We have already seen that Chaitin's Ω is a natural example of a 1-random real. We have also seen that, in algorithmic randomness, prefix-free machines are the analogs of partial computable functions, and the measures of the domains of prefix-free machines, that is, left computably enumerable reals, take the role of the computably enumerable sets. In more detail, we have the following:

1. The domains of partial computable functions are exactly the c.e. sets, while the measures of the domains of prefix-free machines are exactly the left-c.e. reals.

2. The canonical example of a noncomputable set is the halting problem $\emptyset'$, i.e., the domain of a universal partial computable function. The canonical example of a 1-random real is Ω, the halting probability of a universal prefix-free machine.

3. $\emptyset'$ is well-defined up to computable permutation, while Ω is well-defined up to Solovay equivalence.

So far in this book we have dodged the "machine-dependence bullet" by choosing a fixed standard universal machine when looking at relativized halting probabilities and studying properties that do not depend on that choice. In this chapter we will look at results of Downey, Hirschfeldt, Miller,

R.G. Downey and D. Hirschfeldt, *Algorithmic Randomness and Complexity*, Theory and Applications of Computability, DOI 10.1007/978-0-387-68441-3_15,

and Nies [115] that grapple with versions of Ω as operators. Most of the results and proofs in this chapter are taken from that paper.

Relativizing the definition of $\emptyset'$ gives the jump operator. If $A \in 2^\omega$, then A' is the domain of a universal machine relative to A. Myhill's Theorem 2.4.12 relativizes, so A' is well-defined up to computable permutation. Furthermore, if $A \equiv_T B$, then A' and B' differ by a computable permutation. In particular, the jump is well-defined on the Turing degrees. The jump operator plays an important role in computability theory; it gives a natural, uniform, and degree invariant way to produce, for each A, a c.e. set A' with Turing degree strictly above that of A.

What happens when the definition of Ω is relativized, by defining it relative to a particular universal prefix-free oracle machine U? We will see that the Kučera-Slaman Theorem 9.2.3 and Theorem 9.2.2 of Calude, Hertling, Khoussainov, and Wang both relativize (with some care, as we see below). However, if we wish to look at Ω as an analog of the jump, then we might hope that Ω_U^A is well-defined, not just up to Solovay equivalence relative to A, but even up to Turing degree. Similarly, we might hope for Ω_U to be a degree invariant operator; that is, if $A \equiv_T B$ then $\Omega_U^A \equiv_T \Omega_U^B$. Were this the case, Ω_U would provide a counterexample to a long-standing conjecture of Martin: it would induce an operator on the Turing degrees that is neither increasing nor constant on any cone. But as we show in Theorem 15.7.7, there are oracles $A =^* B$ (i.e., A and B agree except on a finite set) such that Ω_U^A and Ω_U^B are not only Turing incomparable, but even relatively random. In particular, by choosing these A and B appropriately, we can ensure that Ω_U^A is a left-c.e. real while making Ω_U^B as random as we like. It follows easily that the Turing degree of Ω_U^A generally depends on the choice of U, and in fact, that the degree of randomness of Ω_U^A can vary drastically with this choice.

If U is a universal prefix-free oracle machine, then we call the map taking A to Ω_U^A an *Omega operator*. In spite of their failure to be Turing degree invariant, it turns out that Omega operators are rather interesting, and provide the first natural example of interesting c.e. operators that are not CEA. For example, in Section 15.4, we show that the range of an Omega operator has positive measure, and that every 2-random real is in the range of some Omega operator. (This fact is not true of every 1-random real.) In Section 15.5, we prove that A is mapped to a left-c.e. real by some Omega operator iff Ω is 1-random relative to A. (Such A's are called *low for* Ω.)

In the final section of this chapter, we consider the analytic behavior of Omega operators. We prove that Omega operators are lower semicontinuous but not continuous, and moreover, that they are continuous exactly at the 1-generic reals. We also produce an Omega operator that does not have a closed range. On the other hand, we prove that every non-2-random that is in the closure of the range of an Omega operator is actually in that range. As a consequence, for each U there is an A such that $\Omega_U^A = \sup(\operatorname{rng} \Omega_U)$.

In several proofs below, we think of a binary string σ as the rational $0.\sigma$.

15.2 Omega operators

Let us begin by recalling that a prefix-free oracle machine U is universal if for every prefix-free oracle machine M there is a prefix $\rho_M \in 2^{<\omega}$, called a coding string of M in U, such that

$$\forall A \in 2^\omega \, \forall \sigma \in 2^{<\omega} \, (U^A(\rho_M \sigma) = M^A(\sigma)).$$

Note that this condition is stronger than the requirement that U^A be a universal A-computable prefix-free machine for all A. The fixed standard machine we have been using in this book is of course an example of a universal prefix-free oracle machine. For a prefix-free oracle machine M, let Ω_M^A be the halting probability of M^A. Formally, $\Omega_M^A = \sum_{M^A(\sigma)\downarrow} 2^{-|\sigma|}$. This definition gives rise to an operator $\Omega_M \colon 2^\omega \to [0,1]$. As mentioned above, if U is a universal prefix-free oracle machine, then we call Ω_U an *Omega operator.*

It is of course a straightforward relativization of the fact that Ω is 1-random that if Ω_U is an Omega operator then Ω_U^A is 1-random relative to A. The following is a strengthening of this fact.

Theorem 15.2.1 (Downey, Hirschfeldt, Miller, and Nies [115]). *Let Ω_U be an Omega operator. There is a b such that, for each A, the real Ω_U^A is 1-random relative to A with constant b; that is, $\forall n \, (K^A(\Omega_U^A \upharpoonright n) \geqslant n - b)$.*

Proof. We define a prefix-free oracle machine M as follows. We identify a string τ with the rational $0.\tau$. For any $A \in 2^\omega$ and $\sigma \in 2^{<\omega}$, first calculate $\tau = U^A(\sigma)$. Then wait for a stage s such that $\Omega_U^A[s] \geqslant \tau - 2^{-|\tau|}$. If such an s is found, then let $M^A(\sigma) = s+1$. Because $M^A(\sigma) > s$, the convergence of $M^A(\sigma)$ cannot already be taken into account in the calculation of $\Omega_U^A[s]$ (by the usual assumption on the stage by stage approximation to U), so, letting ρ be a coding string of M in U, in this case $\Omega_U^A[s] \geqslant \Omega_U^A[s] + 2^{-|\rho\sigma|}$. Thus, either

$$\Omega_U^A < \tau - 2^{-|\tau|}$$

or

$$\Omega_U^A \geqslant \Omega_U^A[s] + 2^{-|\rho\sigma|} \geqslant \tau - 2^{-|\tau|} + 2^{-|\rho\sigma|}.$$

Assume for a contradiction that there is an A and an n such that $K^A(\Omega_U^A \upharpoonright n) < n - |\rho| - 1$. Letting σ be a minimal length program for $\Omega_U^A \upharpoonright n$, we have shown that either

$$\Omega_U^A - (\Omega_U^A \upharpoonright n) < -2^{-n}$$

or

$$\Omega_U^A - (\Omega_U^A \upharpoonright n) \geqslant -2^{-n} + 2^{-|\rho\sigma|} > -2^{-n} + 2^{-n+1} = 2^{-n}.$$

Neither of these possibilities can happen, so we have a contradiction. Hence, for every A we have $\forall n\,(K^A(\Omega_U^A \upharpoonright n) \geqslant n - |\rho| - 1)$, so we can take $b = |\rho| + 1$. □

Let U and b be as in the theorem. It is clear that if we define K^A using U, then there is a c such that $\forall A \in 2^\omega\, \forall \sigma \in 2^{<\omega}\,(K(\sigma) \geqslant K^A(\sigma) - c)$, so all reals in the range of Ω_U are 1-random with constant $b+c$. In other words, the range of Ω_U is contained in the closed set $\{X : \forall n\,(K(X \upharpoonright n) \geqslant n - b - c)\}$. In particular, every real in the closure of the range of Ω_U is 1-random. We will discuss the range of Ω_U and its closure in more depth in Section 15.10.

Of course, Ω_U^A is an A-left-c.e. real, and every A-left-c.e. real is computable from A', hence $\Omega_U^A \leqslant_T A'$. It is not usually the case that $\Omega_U^A \equiv_T A'$. Indeed, by Theorem 11.7.2, this cannot be the case unless A is K-trivial.[1] On the other hand, the fact that $\Omega \equiv_T \emptyset'$ has a natural relativization in the following simple result.

Proposition 15.2.2. $\Omega_U^A \oplus A \equiv_T A'$.

Proof. It is clear that $\Omega_U^A \oplus A \leqslant_T A'$. For the other direction, define a prefix-free oracle machine M such that $M^A(0^n1)\downarrow$ iff $n \in A'$, for all $A \in 2^\omega$ and $n \in \omega$. Assume that U simulates M by the prefix $\tau \in 2^{<\omega}$. To determine whether $n \in A'$, search for a stage s such that $\Omega_U^A - \Omega_U^A[s] < 2^{-(|\tau|+n+1)}$. This search can be done computably in $\Omega_U^A \oplus A$. Note that U^A cannot converge on a string of length $|\tau| + n + 1$ after stage s, so $n \in A'$ iff $M^A(0^n1)\downarrow$ iff $U^A(\tau 0^n 1)\downarrow$ iff $U^A(\tau 0^n 1)[s]\downarrow$. Therefore, $A' \leqslant_T \Omega_U^A \oplus A$. □

Recall that $B \in 2^\omega$ is generalized low (GL_1) if $B' \leqslant_T B \oplus \emptyset'$.

Theorem 15.2.3 (Nies and Stephan, see [115]). *If a Δ_2^0 set A is 1-random relative to B, then B is GL_1.*

Proof. Let $f(n) = \mu s\, \forall t \geqslant s\,(A_t \upharpoonright n = A_s \upharpoonright n)$, and note that $f \leqslant_T \emptyset'$. If $\Phi_e^B(e)\downarrow$ then let $V_e = [\![A_s \upharpoonright e+1]\!]$ for the least s such that $\Phi_e^B(e)[s]$. Otherwise, let $V_e = \emptyset$. Let $U_n = \bigcup_{e \geqslant n} V_e$. It is easy to see that $\{U_n\}_{n\in\omega}$ is a Martin-Löf test relative to B. Thus $A \notin \bigcap_n U_n$, so A is in only finitely many V_e's. So for almost all e such that $\Phi_e^B(e)\downarrow$, we must have $f(e) \geqslant (\mu s)\, \Phi_e^B(e)[s]\downarrow$. Hence $B' \leqslant_T B \oplus \emptyset'$. □

Theorem 15.2.3 implies that the class of low 1-random reals is closed under the action of any Omega operator.

Corollary 15.2.4. *For each Δ_2^0 1-random A, the real Ω_U^A is GL_1. If A is also low, then Ω_U^A is low.*

---

[1]The following is a simpler argument: Let A be 1-random. By van Lambalgen's Theorem, A is 1-random relative to Ω_U^A, so $A \not\leqslant_T \Omega_U^A$.

Proof. Let $B = \Omega_U^A$. Clearly B is 1-random relative to A, so by van Lambalgen's Theorem, A is 1-random relative to B, and Theorem 15.2.3 applies. If A is low, then Ω_U^A is also Δ_2^0, and hence low. □

15.3 A-1-random A-left-c.e. reals

We can relativize Solovay reducibility as follows. For $A, X, Y \in 2^\omega$, we write $Y \leqslant_S^A X$ to mean that there are a c and a partial A-computable $\varphi : 2^{<\omega} \to 2^{<\omega}$ such that if $q < X$, then $\varphi(q)\downarrow < Y$ and $Y - \varphi(q) < c(X - q)$. We say that an A-left-c.e. real X is *A-Solovay complete* if $Y \leqslant_S^A X$ for every A-left-c.e. real Y.

Some basic facts about Solovay reducibility relativize easily, with essentially the same proofs as before. For example:

Theorem 15.3.1. *If Y is 1-random relative to A and $Y \leqslant_S^A X$, then X is also 1-random relative to A.*

The relativization of the Kučera-Slaman Theorem is equally straightforward.

Theorem 15.3.2. *If an A-left-c.e. real X is 1-random relative to A then X is A-Solovay complete.*

On the other hand, a satisfactory relativization of Theorem 9.2.2, which states that each 1-random left-c.e. real is a halting probability, presents some difficulty. The direct relativization states that if X is an A-left-c.e. real and is A-Solovay complete, then there is an oracle prefix-free machine M such that M^A is universal for A-computable prefix-free machines and $X = \Omega_M^A$. It is by no means clear, though, that we should be able to relativize Theorem 9.2.2 to build a machine that is universal in our strong sense. Nevertheless, the relativized theorem is true.

Theorem 15.3.3 (Downey, Hirschfeldt, Miller, and Nies [115]). *Let X be an A-left-c.e. real that is A-Solovay complete. Then there is a universal prefix-free oracle machine U such that $X = \Omega_U^A$.*

Proof. Let V be a universal prefix-free oracle machine. Because Ω_V^A is an A-left-c.e. real, we have $\Omega_V^A \leqslant_S^A X$. Choose n and a functional φ taking strings to strings such that 2^n and φ^A witness this Solovay reduction. In other words, if $q < \Omega_V^A$ is a string, thought of as a rational by equating q with $0.q$, then $\varphi^A(q)\downarrow < \Omega_V^A$ and

$$\Omega_V^A - \varphi^A(q) < 2^n(X - q). \tag{15.1}$$

We also require n to be large enough that $2^{-n} \leqslant X \leqslant 1 - 2^{-n}$. (Clearly, no computable real can be A-Solovay complete, so $X \neq 0, 1$.)

We now define another universal prefix-free oracle machine U. To make U universal, let $U^B(0^n\sigma) = V^B(\sigma)$, for all $\sigma \in 2^{<\omega}$ and oracles $B \in 2^\omega$.

For convenience, we preserve the stage of convergence; i.e., $U^B(0^n\sigma)[t]\downarrow$ iff $V^B(\sigma)[t]\downarrow$. The other strings in the domain of U are used to ensure that $\Omega_U^A = X$. Let ψ be a functional taking numbers to strings (again thought of as rationals) such that $\{\psi^A(s)\}_{s\in\omega}$ is a nondecreasing sequence with limit X. Fix an oracle B. We add strings not extending 0^n to the domain of U in stages. For each s:

1. Compute $q_s = \psi^B(s)$.
2. Compute $r_s = \varphi^B(q_s)$.
3. Search for a t_s such that $\Omega_V^B[t_s] \geqslant r_s$.
4. If possible, add enough strings (not extending 0^n) to the domain of U at stage t_s to make $\Omega_U^B[t_s] = q_s$.

Note that (if $B \neq A$) this procedure may get stuck in any of the first three steps. In this case, U^B will converge on only finitely many strings not extending 0^n. This completes the construction of U, which is clearly a universal prefix-free oracle machine.

It remains to verify that $\Omega_U^A = X$. By the definition of ψ, we have $q_s = \psi^A(s)\downarrow< X$ for each s. Therefore, $r_s = \varphi^A(q_s)\downarrow< \Omega_V^A$. So there is a stage t_s such that $\Omega_V^A[t_s] \geqslant r_s$. Because $q_s < X \leqslant 1-2^{-n}$, there are enough strings available in step (iv) to ensure that $\Omega_U^A[t_s] \geqslant q_s$. But $\lim_s q_s = X$, so $\Omega_U^A \geqslant X$.

Now assume for a contradiction that $\Omega_U^A > X$. Because the strings extending 0^n add at most $2^{-n} \leqslant X$ to Ω_U^A, there must be some s that causes too many strings to be added to the domain of U in step (iv). In other words, there is an s such that $\Omega_U^A[t_s] = q_s$ and

$$\Omega_U^A[t_s] + 2^{-n}(\Omega_V^A - \Omega_V^A[t_s]) > X.$$

So $\Omega_V^A - \Omega_V^A[t_s] > 2^n(X - q_s)$. But in step (iii), we ensured that $\Omega_V^A[t_s] \geqslant r_s = \varphi^A(q_s)$. Therefore, $\Omega_V^A - \varphi^A(q_s) > 2^n(X - q_s)$, contradicting (15.1). Thus $\Omega_U^A = X$. □

Combining Theorems 15.2.1, 15.3.1, 15.3.2, and 15.3.3, we have the following corollary.

Corollary 15.3.4 (Downey, Hirschfeldt, Miller, and Nies [115]). *For $A, X \in 2^\omega$, the following are equivalent.*

(i) *X is an A-left-c.e. real and 1-random relative to A.*

(ii) *X is an A-left-c.e. real and A-Solovay complete.*

(iii) *$X = \Omega_U^A$ for some universal prefix-free oracle machine U.*

15.4 Reals in the range of some Omega operator

We proved in the last section that X is in the range of some Omega operator iff there is an A such that X is both 1-random relative to A and an A-left-c.e. real. What restrictions does this place on X?

The impression we have is that Ω is a very special 1-random real, and results such as Stephan's Theorem 8.8.4 that most 1-random reals are computationally feeble suggest that most 1-random reals do not resemble Ω at all. However, we will see that this impression is not true in relativized form. In this section, we show that every 2-random real is 1-random relative to A and an A-left-c.e. real for some A, but that not every 1-random real has this property. Furthermore, we prove that the range of every Omega operator has positive measure. The following theorem should be compared with Theorem 8.21.8, that every 2-random set is CEA.

Theorem 15.4.1 (Downey, Hirschfeldt, Miller, and Nies [115]). *If X is 2-random, then there is an A such that X is 1-random relative to A and an A-left-c.e. real.*

Proof. Let $A = \frac{(1-X+\Omega)}{2}$. Then $X = 1 - 2A + \Omega$ is an A-left-c.e. real. Because X is 2-random, X is 1-random relative to Ω, so by van Lambalgen's Theorem, Ω is 1-random relative to X. But then A is 1-random relative to X (because clearly, $\Omega \equiv_S^X \frac{(1-X+\Omega)}{2}$). Therefore, applying van Lambalgen's theorem again, X is 1-random relative to A. □

As was mentioned above, the previous theorem cannot be proved if X is assumed only to be 1-random.

Example 15.4.2 (Downey, Hirschfeldt, Miller, and Nies [115]). $1 - \Omega$ is not in the range of any Omega operator.

Proof. The 1-random real $X = 1 - \Omega$ is a right-c.e. real, i.e., the limit of a decreasing computable sequence of rationals. Assume that X is an A-left-c.e. real for some A. Then A computes sequences limiting to X from both sides, and hence $X \leqslant_T A$. Therefore, X is not 1-random relative to A. □

It would not be difficult to prove that $1 - \Omega$ cannot even be in the closure of the range of an Omega operator, but a direct proof is unnecessary because this fact follows from Theorem 15.10.4 below.

We now consider a fixed Omega operator. Let U be an arbitrary universal prefix-free oracle machine. We will use the theorem of Lusin that analytic sets (i.e., projections of Borel sets) are measurable. See Sacks [346] for details.[2] We will also use the fact that the image of an analytic set under

[2]Sacks actually proves that Σ_1^1 classes are measurable. However, every analytic subset of 2^ω is a Σ_1^1 class relative to some oracle, so Lusin's theorem follows by relativization.

any Borel operator—for example, Ω_U—is also analytic. For a class $S \subseteq 2^\omega$, we write $\Omega_U[S]$ for the image of S under the operator Ω_U.

Theorem 15.4.3 (Downey, Hirschfeldt, Miller, and Nies [115]). *The range of Ω_U has positive measure. In fact, if $S \subseteq 2^\omega$ is any analytic set whose downward closure under $\leqslant_T$ is all of 2^ω, then $\mu(\Omega_U[S]) > 0$.*

Proof. Let $R = \Omega_U[S]$. Note that R is an analytic subset of 2^ω and hence is measurable. Assume for a contradiction that $\mu(R) = 0$. In particular, the outer measure of R is zero, which means that there is a nested sequence $U_0 \supseteq U_1 \supseteq U_2 \supseteq \cdots$ of open subsets of 2^ω such that for each n we have $R \subseteq U_n$ and $\mu(U_n) \leqslant 2^{-n}$. Take a set $B \in S$ that codes $\{U_n\}_{n\in\omega}$ in some effective way. Then $\{U_n\}_{n\in\omega}$ is a Martin-Löf test relative to B, which implies that $\Omega_U^B \notin \bigcap_n U_n$. But $R \subseteq \bigcap_n U_n$, so $\Omega_U^B \notin R = \Omega_U[S]$, which is a contradiction. Thus $\mu(R) > 0$. □

This theorem implies that many null classes have Ω_U-images with positive measure, for example $\{A : \forall n\,(2n \notin A)\}$.

We finish this section with a simple consequence of Theorem 15.4.3.

Corollary 15.4.4 (Downey, Hirschfeldt, Miller, and Nies [115]). *For almost every X, there is an A such that $X =^* \Omega_U^A$.*

Proof. Let $S = \{X : \exists A\,(X =^* \Omega_U^A)\}$. Then S is a Σ_1^1 class, and hence measurable by Lusin's theorem mentioned above, and is closed under $=^*$. But $\mu(S) \geqslant \mu(\operatorname{rng}\Omega_U) > 0$. It follows from Kolmogorov's 0-1 Law that $\mu(S) = 1$. □

15.5 Lowness for Ω

We begin this section with the following question: For which oracles A is there a universal prefix-free oracle machine U such that Ω_U^A is a left-c.e. real? We will see that this property holds for almost every A.

Definition 15.5.1 (Nies, Stephan, and Terwijn [308], Downey, Hirschfeldt, Miller, and Nies [115]). A set A is *low for Ω* if Ω is 1-random relative to A.

It clearly does not matter in this definition which version of Ω we take, since all versions are Solovay equivalent.

Theorem 15.5.2 (Downey, Hirschfeldt, Miller, and Nies [115]). *$A \in 2^\omega$ is low for Ω iff there is a universal prefix-free oracle machine U such that Ω_U^A is a left-c.e. real.*

Proof. First assume that there is a universal prefix-free oracle machine U such that $X = \Omega_U^A$ is a left-c.e. real. Every 1-random left-c.e. real is Solovay equivalent to Ω, so $X \leqslant_S \Omega$, which means that $X \leqslant_S^A \Omega$. Both X and Ω are left-c.e. reals, and hence they are A-left-c.e. reals. Applying Theorem 15.3.1, we see that since X is 1-random relative to A, so is Ω.

For the other direction, assume that A is low for Ω. Then Ω is 1-random relative to A and an A-left-c.e. real, so by Corollary 15.3.4, $\Omega = \Omega_U^A$ for some universal prefix-free oracle machine U. □

It follows from the above proof and Proposition 15.2.2 that if A is low for Ω, then $\Omega \oplus A \equiv_T A'$. Therefore, $A' \equiv_T \emptyset' \oplus A$; that is, A is GL_1, a fact which also follows from Theorem 15.2.3.

We now show that almost every set is low for Ω.

Theorem 15.5.3 (Nies, Stephan, and Terwijn [308]). *A 1-random set A is low for Ω iff A is 2-random.*

Proof. Assume that A is 1-random. Since $\Omega \equiv_T \emptyset'$, we have that A is 2-random iff A is 1-random relative to Ω iff Ω is 1-random relative to A, where the last equivalence follows from van Lambalgen's Theorem. □

More evidence for the ubiquity of low for Ω sets is the following low for Ω basis theorem, which we already met as Theorem 8.7.2, and is an immediate corollary of Theorem 15.5.2 and Theorem 15.7.1 below.

Theorem 15.5.4 (Downey, Hirschfeldt, Miller, and Nies [115], Reimann and Slaman [327]). *Every nonempty Π_1^0 class contains a $\emptyset'$-left-c.e. real that is low for Ω.*

Every K-trivial set is low for 1-randomness, and hence low for Ω. However, by the previous result applied to the Π_1^0 class of completions of Peano Arithmetic, there are also sets that are low for Ω but neither 1-random nor K-trivial. (Suppose that A is low for Ω and has PA degree. By Theorem 8.8.4 and the fact that no 2-random set can compute $\emptyset'$, as argued for instance in the paragraph above Theorem 8.5.3, A cannot be 2-random, and hence, by Theorem 15.5.3, A cannot be 1-random. As mentioned above Theorem 8.8.4, A computes a 1-random set, so by Corollary 11.4.10, A cannot be K-trivial.)

15.6 Weak lowness for K

In this section we introduce the concept of weak lowness for K, and find surprising connections with the previous sections and with 2-randomness, culminating in a proof of two results of Miller: that having infinitely often maximal K-complexity and being 2-random coincide, and that 2-random sets are infinitely often quite trivial as oracles with respect to prefix-free complexity.

Definition 15.6.1 (Miller [277]). We say that A is *weakly low for K* if there are infinitely many n such that $K(n) \leqslant K^A(n) + O(1)$.

15.6.1 Weak lowness for K and lowness for Ω

Like their stronger analogs, lowness for K and lowness for 1-randomness, weak lowness for K and lowness for Ω coincide.

Theorem 15.6.2 (Miller [277]). *A is weakly low for K iff A is low for Ω.*

Proof. We first prove that if A is weakly low for K then A is low for Ω. This part of the proof follows Miller [277].

We prove the contrapositive. First, we define families of uniformly c.e. sets $\{W_\sigma\}_{\sigma\in 2^{<\omega}}$ and $\{D_\sigma\}_{\sigma\in 2^{<\omega}}$. Fix $\sigma \in 2^{<\omega}$. Search for the least stage s such that $\sigma \prec \Omega_s$. If no such stage is found, then let W_σ and D_σ be empty. Otherwise, for any τ such that $U(\tau)$ converges for the first time after stage s, enumerate $(|\tau|, U(\tau))$ into D_σ. Also enumerate $(|\tau|, U(\tau))$ into W_σ as long as such enumeration preserves the condition that $\sum_{(d,n)\in W_\sigma} 2^{-d} \leqslant 2^{-|\sigma|}$. Note that if $K_s(n) \neq K(n)$, then $(K(n), n) \in D_\sigma$.

We claim that if $\sigma \prec \Omega$, then $W_\sigma = D_\sigma$. It follows from our definition that $\sum_{(d,n)\in D_\sigma} 2^{-d} \leqslant \Omega - \Omega_s$. But if $\sigma \prec \Omega$ then $\Omega - \Omega_s \leqslant 2^{-|\sigma|}$, so in this case $\sum_{(d,n)\in D_\sigma} 2^{-d} \leqslant 2^{-|\sigma|}$, and hence $W_\sigma = D_\sigma$. The idea is that we have used an approximation of Ω to efficiently approximate all but finitely many values of $K(n)$.

Next, consider the A-c.e. set

$$W = \{(d + |\tau| - |\sigma|, n) : U^A(\tau) = \sigma \text{ and } (d,n) \in W_\sigma\}.$$

By the construction of $\{W_\sigma\}_{\sigma\in 2^{<\omega}}$,

$$\sum_{(e,n)\in W} 2^{-e} = \sum_{U^A(\tau)\downarrow=\sigma} \sum_{(d,n)\in W_\sigma} 2^{-d-|\tau|+|\sigma|} \leqslant \sum_{U^A(\tau)\downarrow} 2^{-|\tau|} \leqslant 1.$$

Thus W is a KC set relative to A, so $K^A(n) \leqslant e + O(1)$ for all $(e,n) \in W$.

Now, assume that Ω is not 1-random relative to A. Then for any c, there are τ and σ such that $U^A(\tau) = \sigma$, with $|\sigma| - |\tau| \geqslant c$ and $\sigma \prec \Omega$. Let s be the least stage such that $\sigma \prec \Omega_s$. There is an N such that if $n \geqslant N$, then $K_s(n) \neq K(n)$ (by the usual conventions on stages, $N = s+1$ is sufficient). For all $n \geqslant N$, we have $(K(n), n) \in W_\sigma$, and hence $(K(n)+|\tau|-|\sigma|, n) \in W$. But this means that $K^A(n) \leqslant K(n) + |\tau| - |\sigma| + O(1) \leqslant K(n) - c + O(1)$, for all but finitely many n. But c is arbitrary, so A is not weakly low for K.

The other half of Miller's proof is much more difficult, but Bienvenu [personal communication to Downey] observed that it can be replaced with an argument based on the results of Bienvenu and Downey [39] on Solovay functions.

Recall that a Solovay function is a computable function f such that $\sum_n 2^{-f(n)} < \infty$, whence $K(n) \leqslant f(n) + O(1)$, and $\liminf_n f(n) - K(n) < \infty$. Recall also the Bienvenu-Downey characterization of Solovay functions, Theorem 9.4.1: A computable function is a Solovay function iff $\sum_n 2^{-f(n)}$ is 1-random. We apply this result. Suppose that A is not weakly low for K.

Then $\lim_n K(n) - K^A(n) = \infty$. Let f be computable and such that $\Omega = \sum_n 2^{-f(n)}$. Then $f(n) \geqslant K(n) - O(1)$, and hence $\lim_n f(n) - K^A(n) = \infty$. Therefore, f is not an A-Solovay function, and so Theorem 9.4.1 relativized to A implies that $\Omega = \sum_n 2^{-f(n)}$ is not 1-random relative to A. □

As a consequence, we have the following weakly low for K basis theorem.

Corollary 15.6.3 (Miller [277]). *Every nonempty Π^0_1 class has a member that is weakly low for K.*

Proof. Given the above theorem, this result follows from Theorem 15.5.4. □

The following corollary improves an earlier unpublished result of Miller that 3-random sets are weakly low for K. It follows from Theorems 15.5.3 and 15.6.2.

Corollary 15.6.4 (Nies, Stephan, and Terwijn [308], Miller [277]). *A 1-random set is weakly low for K iff it is 2-random.*

This is one of several results we have encountered that exhibit various ways in which highly random sets are relatively computationally powerless. These results point to an interesting phenomenon: in many aspects, highly random sets resemble highly nonrandom ones.[3] One way to look at this phenomenon is that while highly random sets have high information, in the sense of initial segment complexity, this is "useless information". It would be of great potential interest to develop precise ways to define usefulness of information in the context of algorithmic randomness.

15.6.2 Infinitely often strongly K-random sets

We recall from Section 6.11 that A is infinitely often strongly K-random if $K(A \upharpoonright n) \geqslant n + K(n) - O(1)$ for infinitely many n, and infinitely often C-random if $C(A \upharpoonright n) \geqslant n - O(1)$ for infinitely many n. In that section, we saw that every 3-random set is infinitely often strongly K-random, that every infinitely often strongly K-random set is infinitely often C-random, and that being infinitely often C-random is the same as being 2-random. Thus it was a fundamental question whether being infinitely often C-random and being infinitely often strongly K-random are equivalent. Miller [277] answered this question in the affirmative, using results discussed above. Notice that the coincidence of these notions is in contrast with Solovay's result, Corollary 4.3.8, that there are C-random strings that are not strongly K-random.

[3]This phenomenon is not limited to mathematical objects: in music, for example, it is often quite hard to distinguish pieces that make extensive use of chance methods from ones written following highly predetermined rules, as in total serialism.

Theorem 15.6.5 (Miller [277]). *If A is 2-random then it is infinitely often strongly K-random.*

Proof. Assume that A is 2-random. By Theorems 15.5.3 and 15.6.2, A is weakly low for K. By Corollary 6.6.4, $K^A(n) \leqslant K(A \upharpoonright n) - n + O(1)$, so $K(A \upharpoonright n) \geqslant n + K^A(n) - O(1)$. Because A is weakly low for K, there are infinitely many n such that $K^A(n) \geqslant K(n) - O(1)$. For such n, we have $K(A \upharpoonright n) \geqslant n+K(n)-O(1)$, so A is infinitely often strongly K-random. $\square$

15.7 When Ω^A is a left-c.e. real

In this section, we consider sets A for which Ω_U^A is a left-c.e. real. Far from being a rare property, we will show that $\mu\{A : \Omega_U^A \text{ is a left-c.e. real}\} > 0$ for any fixed universal prefix-free oracle machine U. On the other hand, we will see that only a left-c.e. real can have an Ω_U-preimage with positive measure. So left-c.e. reals clearly play an important role in understanding Ω_U. Their main application here is in our proof that no Omega operator is degree invariant. Recall from the introduction to this chapter that we want to obtain reals $A =^* B$ such that Ω_U^A is a left-c.e. real while Ω_U^B is 1-random relative to a given (arbitrarily complex) Z. We show that each of these outcomes occurs with positive measure, in Theorems 15.7.4 and 15.7.5, respectively. Theorem 15.7.5 has no obvious connection to left-c.e. reals, but in fact, Theorem 15.7.4—applied to a modification of the universal machine U—is used to prove it.

Theorem 15.7.1 (Downey, Hirschfeldt, Miller, and Nies [115]). *Let M be a prefix-free oracle machine. If $P \subseteq 2^\omega$ is a nonempty Π_1^0 class, then there is a $\emptyset'$-left-c.e. real $A \in P$ such that $\Omega_M^A = \inf\{\Omega_M^X : X \in P\}$, which is a left-c.e. real.*

Proof. Let $P \subseteq 2^\omega$ be a nonempty Π_1^0 class and let $X = \inf\{\Omega_M^A : A \in P\}$. Note that X is a left-c.e. real because it is the limit of the nondecreasing computable sequence $X_s = \inf\{\Omega_M^A[s] : A \in P_s\}$. We will prove that there is an $A \in P$ such that $\Omega_M^A = X$. Choose a sequence $\{B_n\}_{n\in\omega}$ such that $B_n \in P$ and $\Omega_M^{B_n} - X \leqslant 2^{-n}$ for each n. By compactness, $\{B_n\}_{n\in\omega}$ has a convergent subsequence $\{A_n\}_{n\in\omega}$. Note that $\Omega_M^{A_n} - X \leqslant 2^{-n}$. Let $A = \lim_n A_n$. Because P is closed, $A \in P$. Therefore, $\Omega_M^A \geqslant X$. Assume for a contradiction that Ω_M^A is strictly greater than X. Let m be such that $\Omega_M^A - X > 2^{-m}$. For some s, we have $\Omega_M^A[s] - X > 2^{-m}$. Let k be the use of $\Omega_M^A[s]$ (under the usual assumptions on the use of computations, we can take $k = s$). In particular, if $B \upharpoonright k = A \upharpoonright k$, then $\Omega_M^A[s] = \Omega_M^B[s]$. Now take $n > m$ large enough so that $A_n \upharpoonright k = A \upharpoonright k$. Then

$$2^{-n} \geqslant \Omega_M^{A_n} - X \geqslant \Omega_M^{A_n}[s] - X = \Omega_M^A[s] - X > 2^{-m} \geqslant 2^{-n},$$

which is a contradiction, proving that $\Omega_M^A = X$.

Finally, we must prove that A can be a $\emptyset'$-left-c.e. real. Let $S = \{A \in P : \Omega_M^A = X\}$. Note that $S = \{A : \forall s\,(A \in P_s \wedge \Omega_M^A[s] \leqslant X)\}$. The fact that $X \leqslant_{\mathrm{T}} \emptyset'$ makes S a $\Pi_1^{0,\emptyset'}$ class. We proved above that S is nonempty, so $A = \min(S)$ is a $\emptyset'$-left-c.e. real satisfying the theorem. □

We now consider sets X such that $\Omega_U^{-1}(X)$ has positive measure.

Lemma 15.7.2 (Downey, Hirschfeldt, Miller, and Nies [115]). *Let M be a prefix-free oracle machine. If $\mu\{A : \Omega_M^A = X\} > 0$ then X is a left-c.e. real.*

Proof. By the Lebesgue Density Theorem, there is a σ such that $\mu\{A \succ \sigma : \Omega_M^A = X\} > 2^{-|\sigma|-1}$. In other words, Ω_M maps more than half of the extensions of σ to X. So X is the limit of the nondecreasing computable sequence $\{X_s\}_{s\in\omega}$, where for each s, we let X_s be the largest rational such that $\mu\{A \succ \sigma : \Omega_M^A[s] \geqslant X_s\} > 2^{-|\sigma|-1}$. □

For $X \in 2^\omega$, let $m_U(X) = \mu(\{A : \Omega_U^A = X\})$. Define the *spectrum* of Ω_U to be $\mathrm{Spec}(\Omega_U) = \{X : m_U(X) > 0\}$. By the lemma, the spectrum is a set of 1-random left-c.e. reals. We prove that it is nonempty. We use the fact that every 2-random set is weakly 2-random, and hence cannot be contained in a null Π_2^0 class.

Lemma 15.7.3 (Downey, Hirschfeldt, Miller, and Nies [115]). *$m_U(X) > 0$ iff there is a 1-random A such that $\Omega_U^A = X$.*

Proof. If $m_U(X) > 0$, then there is clearly a 1-random A such that $\Omega_U^A = X$, as there are measure 1 many 1-randoms. For the other direction, assume that A is 1-random and $\Omega_U^A = X$. By van Lambalgen's Theorem, the fact that X is 1-random relative to A implies that A is 1-random relative to X. But $X \equiv_{\mathrm{T}} \emptyset'$, because X is a 1-random left-c.e. real, so A is 2-random. But $\{B : \Omega_U^B = X\}$ is a Π_2^0 class containing this 2-random set, and hence cannot be null. Thus $m_U(X) > 0$. □

Theorem 15.7.4 (Downey, Hirschfeldt, Miller, and Nies [115]). $\mathrm{Spec}(\Omega_U)$ *is nonempty.*

Proof. Apply Theorem 15.7.1 to a nonempty Π_1^0 class containing only 1-random sets to obtain a 1-random A such that $X = \Omega_U^A$ is a left-c.e. real. By Lemma 15.7.3, $X \in \mathrm{Spec}(\Omega_U)$. □

We have proved that Ω_U maps a set of positive measure to the left-c.e. reals. One might speculate that almost every set is mapped to a left-c.e. real. We now prove that this is not the case (although we have seen that almost every set (in particular, every 2-random set), can be mapped to a left-c.e. real by *some* Omega operator).

Theorem 15.7.5 (Downey, Hirschfeldt, Miller, and Nies [115]). *There is an $\varepsilon > 0$ such that $\mu(\{B : \Omega_U^B$ is 1-random relative to $Z\}) \geqslant \varepsilon$ for all Z.*

Proof. It is easy to define a prefix-free oracle machine M such that $\Omega_M^B = B$ for every B. Define a universal prefix-free oracle machine V by $V^B(0\sigma) = U^B(\sigma)$ and $V^B(1\sigma) = M^B(\sigma)$ for all σ. Then $\Omega_V^B = \frac{\Omega_U^B + B}{2}$. Apply Theorem 15.7.4 to V to get a left-c.e. real X such that $S = \{B : \Omega_V^B = X\}$ has positive measure. Let $\varepsilon = \mu(S)$.

Now fix Z. We may assume without loss of generality that $Z \geqslant_T \emptyset'$. Let $B \in S$ be 1-random relative to Z. Then $\Omega_U^B = 2\Omega_V^B - B = 2X - B$ must also be 1-random relative to X, because $X \leqslant_T Z$. Therefore,

$$\mu(\{B \in S : \Omega_U^B \text{ is 1-random relative to } Z\})$$
$$\geqslant \mu(\{B \in S : B \text{ is 1-random relative to } Z\}) = \mu(S) = \varepsilon,$$

since there are measure 1 many sets that are 1-random relative to Z.[4] □

These results tell us that the Σ_3^0 class of sets A such that Ω_U^A is left-c.e. has intermediate measure.

Corollary 15.7.6 (Downey, Hirschfeldt, Miller, and Nies [115]). $0 < \mu(\{A : \Omega_U^A$ *is a left-c.e. real*$\}) < 1$.

The most important consequence of the work in this section is the following resoundingly negative answer to the question of whether Ω_U is degree invariant.

Theorem 15.7.7 (Downey, Hirschfeldt, Miller, and Nies [115]).

(i) *For all Z, there are $A =^* B$ such that Ω_U^A is a left-c.e. real and Ω_U^B is 1-random relative to Z.*

(ii) *There are $A =^* B$ such that $\Omega_U^A \mid_T \Omega_U^B$ (and, in fact, Ω_U^A and Ω_U^B are 1-random relative to each other).*

Proof. (i) Let $S = \{A : \Omega_U^A \text{ is a left-c.e. real}\}$ and $R = \{B : \Omega_U^B \text{ is 1-random relative to } Z\}$. By Theorems 15.7.4 and 15.7.5, respectively, both classes have positive measure. Let $\widehat{R} = \{A : \exists B \in R\,(A =^* B)\}$. By Kolmogorov's 0-1 Law, $\mu(\widehat{R}) = 1$. Hence, there is an $A \in S \cap \widehat{R}$.

(ii) By part (i), there are $A =^* B$ such that Ω_U^A is a left-c.e. real and Ω_U^B is 2-random. Then Ω_U^B is 1-random relative to Ω_U^A and, by van Lambalgen's Theorem, Ω_U^A is 1-random relative to Ω_U^B. Thus $\Omega_U^A \mid_T \Omega_U^B$. □

The following is another corollary of Theorem 15.7.1.

Corollary 15.7.8 (Downey, Hirschfeldt, Miller, and Nies [115]). *There is a properly Σ_2^0 set A such that Ω_U^A is a left-c.e. real.*

---

[4]This simple construction shows more. Because $\Omega_U^B = 2X - B$ for $B \in S$, we know that $\mu(\{\Omega_U^B : B \in S\}) = \mu(\{2X - B : B \in S\}) = \mu(S) > 0$. Therefore, the range of Ω_U has a subset with positive measure. While this fact follows from the most basic case of Theorem 15.4.3, this new proof does not resort to Lusin's theorem on the measurability of analytic sets.

We close the section with two further observations on the spectrum.

Proposition 15.7.9 (Downey, Hirschfeldt, Miller, and Nies [115]). *We have* $\sup(\operatorname{rng}\Omega_U) = \sup\{\Omega_U^A : A \text{ is 1-random}\} = \sup(\operatorname{Spec}(\Omega_U))$.

Proof. Let $X = \sup(\operatorname{rng}\Omega_U)$. Given a rational $q < X$, choose σ such that $\Omega_U^\sigma \geqslant q$. By the same proof as Theorem 15.7.4, there is a 1-random $A \succ \sigma$ such that Ω_U^A is a left-c.e. real. □

Proposition 15.7.10 (Downey, Hirschfeldt, Miller, and Nies [115]). *If* $p < q$ *are rationals and* $C = \{A : \Omega_U^A \in [p, q]\}$ *has positive measure, then* $\operatorname{Spec}(\Omega_U) \cap [p, q] \neq \emptyset$.

Proof. Note that C is the countable union of $[\![\sigma]\!] \cap C$ over all σ such that $\Omega^\sigma \geqslant p$. Because $\mu(C) > 0$, for some such σ we have $\mu([\![\sigma]\!] \cap C) > 0$. But $[\![\sigma]\!] \cap C = \{A \succ \sigma : \Omega^A \leqslant q\}$ is a Π_1^0 class. Let $R \subset 2^\omega$ be a Π_1^0 class containing only 1-randoms with $\mu(R) > 1 - \mu([\![\sigma]\!] \cap C)$. Then $R \cap [\![\sigma]\!] \cap C$ is a nonempty Π_1^0 class containing only 1-randoms. Applying Theorem 15.7.1 to this class, there is a 1-random $A \in C$ such that $X = \Omega_U^A$ is a left-c.e. real. Then $X \in \operatorname{Spec}(\Omega_U) \cap [p, q]$, by Lemma 15.7.3 and the definition of C. □

15.8 Ω^A for K-trivial A

In previous sections, we considered sets that can be mapped to left-c.e. reals by *some* Omega operator. We now look at sets A such that Ω_U^A is a left-c.e. real for *every* universal prefix-free oracle machine U. We will see that these are exactly the K-trivials.

Recall Lemma 11.5.5, which states that if A is K-trivial and M is a prefix-free oracle machine, then there is a computable sequence of stages $v(0) < v(1) < \cdots$ such that

$$\sum\{\widehat{c}(x, r) : x \text{ is minimal s.t. } A_{v(r+1)}(x) \neq A_{v(r+2)}(x)\} < \infty, \qquad (15.2)$$

where

$$\widehat{c}(z, r) = \sum\{2^{-|\sigma|} : M^A(\sigma)[v(r+1)]\downarrow \\ \wedge\ z < \operatorname{use}(M^A(\sigma)[v(r+1)]) \leqslant v(r)\}.$$

Informally, $\widehat{c}(x, r)$ is the maximum amount that $\Omega_M^A[v(r+1)]$ can decrease because of an $A(x)$ change after stage $v(r+1)$, provided we count only the $M^A(\sigma)$ computations with use $\leqslant v(r)$.

Theorem 15.8.1 (Downey, Hirschfeldt, Miller, and Nies [115]). *Let U be a universal prefix-free oracle machine. The following are equivalent.*

(i) *A is K-trivial.*

(ii) *A is Δ^0_2 and Ω^A_U is a left-c.e. real.*

(iii) $A \leqslant_T \Omega^A_U$.

(iv) $A' \equiv_T \Omega^A_U$.

Proof. (ii) $\Rightarrow$ (iii) follows from the fact that each 1-random left-c.e. real is Turing complete. (iii) $\Rightarrow$ (i) follows from Theorem 11.7.2, since (iii) implies that A is a base for 1-randomness. (iii) $\Leftrightarrow$ (iv) by Proposition 15.2.2. So we are left with showing that (i) $\Rightarrow$ (ii).

Let A be K-trivial. By Theorem 11.1.1, A is Δ^0_2. We show that there is an $r_0 \in \mathbb{N}$ and an effective sequence $\{q_r\}_{r\in\omega}$ of rationals such that $\Omega^A_U = \sup_{r\geqslant r_0} q_r$, and hence Ω^A_U is a left-c.e. real.

Applying Lemma 11.5.5 to U, we obtain a computable sequence of stages $v(0) < v(1) < \cdots$ such that (15.2) holds. The desired sequence of rationals is defined by letting

$$q_r = \sum\{2^{-|\sigma|} : U^A(\sigma)[v(r+1)]\downarrow \wedge \operatorname{use}(U^A(\sigma)[v(r+1)]) \leqslant v(r)\}.$$

Thus q_r measures the computations existing at stage $v(r+1)$ whose use is at most $v(r)$. We define r_0 below; first we verify that $\Omega^A_U \leqslant \sup_{r\geqslant r_0} q_r$ for any r_0. Given $\sigma_0, \ldots, \sigma_m \in \operatorname{dom}(U^A)$, choose r_1 so that each computation $U^A(\sigma_i)$ has settled by stage $v(r_1)$, with use $\leqslant v(r_1)$. If $r \geqslant r_1$, then $q_r \geqslant \sum_{i\leqslant m} 2^{-|\sigma_i|}$. Therefore, $\Omega^A_U \leqslant \limsup_r q_r \leqslant \sup_{r\geqslant r_0} q_r$.

Now define a Solovay test $\{I_r\}_{r\in\omega}$ as follows: if x is minimal such that $A_{v(r+1)}(x) \neq A_{v(r+2)}(x)$, then let

$$I_r = [q_r - \widehat{c}(x,r), q_r].$$

Then $\sum_r |I_r|$ is finite by (15.2), so $\{I_r\}_{r\in\omega}$ is indeed a Solovay test. Also note that, by the comment after the lemma, $\min I_r \leqslant \max I_{r+1}$ for each r.

Since Ω^A_U is 1-random, there is an r_0 such that $\Omega^A_U \notin I_r$ for all $r \geqslant r_0$. We show that $q_r \leqslant \Omega^A_U$ for each $r \geqslant r_0$. Fix $r \geqslant r_0$. Let $t \geqslant r$ be the first non-deficiency stage for the enumeration $t \mapsto A_{v(t+1)}$. That is, if x is minimal such that $A_{v(t+1)}(x) \neq A_{v(t+2)}(x)$, then

$$\forall t' \geqslant t\, \forall y < x\, (A_{v(t'+1)}(y) = A_{v(t+1)}(y)).$$

The quantity $q_t - \widehat{c}(x,t)$ measures the computations $U^A(\sigma)[v(t+1)]$ with use $\leqslant x$. These computations are stable from $v(t+1)$ on, so $\Omega^A_U \geqslant \min I_t$. Now $\Omega^A_U \notin I_u$ for $u \geqslant r_0$ and $\min I_u \leqslant \max I_{u+1}$ for any u. Applying this fact to $u = t-1, \ldots, u = r$, we see that $\Omega^A_U \geqslant \max I_r = q_r$. Therefore, $\Omega^A_U \geqslant \sup_{r\geqslant r_0} q_r$. ☐

One consequence of this theorem is that all Omega operators are degree invariant on the K-trivials. The next example shows that they need not be degree invariant anywhere else.

Example 15.8.2 (Downey, Hirschfeldt, Miller, and Nies [115]). There is an Omega operator that is degree invariant only on K-trivials.

Proof. Let M be a prefix-free oracle machine such that

$$\Omega_M^A = \begin{cases} A & \text{if } A(0) = 0 \\ 0 & \text{if } A(0) = 1. \end{cases}$$

For any A, define $\widehat{A}$ by $\widehat{A}(n) = A(n)$ iff $n \neq 0$. Define a universal prefix-free oracle machine V as follows. For all σ, let $V^A(00\sigma) = U^A(\sigma)$, let $V^A(01\sigma) = U^{\widehat{A}}(\sigma)$, and let $V^A(1\sigma) = M^A(\sigma)$. Then $|\Omega_V^A - \Omega_V^{\widehat{A}}| = \frac{A}{2}$ for all A. Assume that $\Omega_V^{\widehat{A}} \leqslant_T \Omega_V^A$. Then $A \leqslant_T \Omega_V^A$, so A is a base for 1-randomness and hence K-trivial by Theorem 11.7.2. If $\Omega_V^A \leqslant_T \Omega_V^{\widehat{A}}$, then again A is K-trivial. Therefore, if A is not K-trivial, then $\Omega_V^A \mid_T \Omega_V^{\widehat{A}}$. □

The following corollary summarizes Theorem 15.8.1 and Example 15.8.2.

Corollary 15.8.3 (Downey, Hirschfeldt, Miller, and Nies [115]). *The following are equivalent.*

(i) *A is K-trivial.*

(ii) *Every Omega operator takes A to a left-c.e. real.*

(iii) *Every Omega operator is degree invariant on the Turing degree of A.*

We have seen in Theorem 15.7.7 that no Omega operator is degree invariant. We have also seen that if A is not K-trivial, then there are Omega operators that are not invariant on the Turing degree of A. Can these two results be combined?

Open Question 15.8.4 (Downey, Hirschfeldt, Miller, and Nies [115]). For a universal prefix-free oracle machine U and an A that is not K-trivial, is there necessarily a $B \equiv_T A$ such that $\Omega_U^B \not\equiv_T \Omega_U^A$?

Finally, the following is a simple but interesting consequence of Example 15.8.2.

Corollary 15.8.5 (Downey, Hirschfeldt, Miller, and Nies [115]). *Every K-trivial is a left-d.c.e. real.*

Proof. Let V be the machine from the example. Assume that A is K-trivial and let $\widehat{A}$ be as in the example. Then Ω_V^A and $\Omega_V^{\widehat{A}}$ are both left-c.e. reals by Theorem 15.8.1. Therefore, $A = 2|\Omega_V^A - \Omega_V^{\widehat{A}}|$ is a left-d.c.e. real. □

By Theorem 5.4.7, the left-d.c.e. reals form a real closed field. The corollary gives us a nontrivial real closed subfield: the K-trivial reals. To see this, recall that in Chapter 11 we have seen that the K-trivials form an ideal in the Turing degrees. Because a zero of an odd degree polynomial can be computed relative to its coefficients, the K-trivial reals also form a real closed field.

15.9 K-triviality and left-d.c.e. reals

Having mentioned left-d.c.e. reals in the previous section, we now show that they can be used to give a rather surprising characterization of K-triviality, which does not mention randomness or initial segment complexity in any obvious way.

Definition 15.9.1. A is *low for left-d.c.e. reals* if the class of reals that are left-d.c.e. relative to A coincides with the class of left-d.c.e. reals.

Theorem 15.9.2 (Miller [unpublished]). *A is K-trivial iff A is low for left-d.c.e. reals.*

Proof. First suppose that A is low for left-d.c.e. reals. Then Ω^A is left-d.c.e. and 1-random, so by Rettinger's Theorem 9.2.4, either Ω^A or $1-\Omega^A$ is a left-c.e. real. But $1-\Omega^A$ cannot be a left-c.e. real, since that would imply Ω^A is A-computable. So Ω^A is a left-c.e. real, and hence $\Omega^A \equiv_T \emptyset'$. But A must be a left-d.c.e. real, since it is low for left-d.c.e. reals and of course is a left-d.c.e. real relative to itself. So A is Δ^0_2, and hence $A \leqslant_T \Omega^A$. By Theorem 15.8.1, A is K-trivial.

Now suppose that A is K-trivial. Let α be a left-c.e. real relative to A. Then $\Omega^A+\alpha$ is a left-c.e. real relative to A and is 1-random, so it is a version of Ω relative to A. Thus, by Theorem 15.8.1, $\Omega^A+\alpha$ is an unrelativized version of Ω, and so is a left-c.e. real. Now let $\delta=\alpha-\beta$ be a left-d.c.e. real relative to A. Then $\delta=(\Omega^A+\alpha)-(\Omega^A+\beta)$, and hence δ is a left-d.c.e. real. □

15.10 Analytic behavior of Omega operators

In this section, we examine Omega operators from the perspective of analysis. Given a universal prefix-free oracle machine U, we consider two questions:

1. To what extent is Ω_U continuous?
2. How complex is the range of Ω_U?

To answer the first question, we show that Ω_U is lower semicontinuous but not continuous. Furthermore, we prove that it is continuous exactly at 1-generic reals. Together with the semicontinuity, this fact implies that Ω_U can achieve its supremum only at a 1-generic. But must Ω_U actually achieve its supremum? This question relates to the second question above. We write S^c for the closure of S. Theorem 15.10.4 states that any real in $\operatorname{rng}(\Omega_U)^c \setminus \operatorname{rng}(\Omega_U)$ must be 2-random. Because $X=\sup(\operatorname{rng}\Omega_U)$ is a left-c.e. real, and hence not 2-random, there is an A such that $\Omega_U^A = X$.

It is natural to ask whether $\operatorname{rng}(\Omega_U)$ is closed. In other words, is Theorem 15.10.4 vacuous? Example 15.10.6 demonstrates that for *some* choice of U, the range of Ω_U is not closed, and indeed, $\mu(\mathrm{rng}(\Omega_U)) < \mu(\mathrm{rng}(\Omega_U)^c)$. Whether this is the case for *all* universal prefix-free oracle machines is open. Furthermore, we know of no nontrivial upper bound on the complexity of $\mathrm{rng}(\Omega_U)$, but we do show below that $\mathrm{rng}(\Omega_U)^c$ is a Π^0_3 class.

A function $f : \mathbb{R} \to \mathbb{R}$ is *lower semicontinuous* if $\{x : f(x) > a\}$ is open for every $a \in \mathbb{R}$. We show that for any prefix-free oracle machine M, the function Ω_M is lower semicontinuous. Note that for any A,

$$\forall \delta > 0\, \exists m\, (\Omega^A_M - \Omega^{A \upharpoonright m}_M \leqslant \delta), \tag{15.3}$$

and hence $\forall X \succ A \upharpoonright m\, (\Omega^A_M - \Omega^X_M \leqslant \delta)$.

Proposition 15.10.1 (Downey, Hirschfeldt, Miller, and Nies [115]). *Ω_M is lower semicontinuous for every prefix-free oracle machine M.*

Proof. Let $a \in \mathbb{R}$ and let A be such that $\Omega^A_M > a$. Choose a real $\delta > 0$ such that $\Omega^A_M - \delta > a$. By the observation above, there is an m such that $X \succ A \upharpoonright m$ implies that $\Omega^A_M - \Omega^X_M \leqslant \delta$. Therefore, $\Omega^X_M \geqslant \Omega^A_M - \delta > a$, so $[\![A \upharpoonright m]\!]$ is an open neighborhood of A contained in $\{X : \Omega^X_M > a\}$. But A is an arbitrary element of $\{X : \Omega^X_M > a\}$, proving that this set is open. □

We next prove that Omega operators are not continuous, and characterize their points of continuity. An open set $S \subseteq 2^\omega$ is *dense along A* if each initial segment of A has an extension in S. It is easy to see that A is 1-generic iff A is in every Σ^0_1 class that is dense along A. We prove that Ω_U is continuous exactly on the 1-generics, for any universal prefix-free oracle machine U.

Theorem 15.10.2 (Downey, Hirschfeldt, Miller, and Nies [115]). *The following are equivalent.*

(i) *A is 1-generic.*

(ii) *If M is a prefix-free oracle machine, then Ω_M is continuous at A.*

(iii) *There is a universal prefix-free oracle machine U such that Ω_U is continuous at A.*

Proof. (i) $\Rightarrow$ (ii). Let M be any prefix-free oracle machine. By (15.3), it suffices to show that

$$\forall \varepsilon\, \exists n\, \forall X \succ A \upharpoonright n\, (\Omega^X_M \leqslant \Omega^A_M + \varepsilon).$$

Suppose this condition fails for a rational ε. Take a rational $r < \Omega^A_M$ such that $\Omega^A_M - r < \varepsilon$. The following Σ^0_1 class is dense along A:

$$S = \{B : \exists n\, (\Omega^B_M[n] \geqslant r + \varepsilon)\}.$$

Thus $A \in S$. But then $\Omega^A_M \geqslant r + \varepsilon > \Omega^A_M$, which is a contradiction.

(ii) $\Rightarrow$ (iii) is trivial.

(iii) $\Rightarrow$ (i). Fix a universal prefix-free oracle machine U. We assume that A is not 1-generic and show that there is an $\varepsilon > 0$ such that

$$\forall n\, \exists B \succ A \upharpoonright n\, (\Omega_U^B \geqslant \Omega_U^A + \varepsilon). \tag{15.4}$$

Take a Σ_1^0 class S that is dense along A but such that $A \notin S$. Define a prefix-free oracle machine L^X as follows. When (some initial segment of) X enters S, then L^X converges on the empty string. Thus L^A is nowhere defined. Let c be the length of a coding string for L in U. We prove that $\varepsilon = 2^{-(c+1)}$ satisfies (15.4).

Choose m as in (15.3) for the given universal machine, where $\delta = 2^{-(c+1)}$. For each $n \geqslant m$, choose $B \succ A \upharpoonright n$ such that $B \in S$. Since L^B converges on the empty string, $\Omega_U^B \geqslant \Omega_U^A - 2^{-(c+1)} + 2^c = \Omega_U^A + \varepsilon$. ☐

Let U be a universal prefix-free oracle machine.

Corollary 15.10.3 (Downey, Hirschfeldt, Miller, and Nies [115]). *If* $\Omega_U^A = \sup(\operatorname{rng} \Omega_U)$, *then* A *is* 1*-generic.*

Proof. By the previous theorem, it suffices to prove that Ω_U is continuous at A. But note that the lower semicontinuity of Ω_U implies that

$$\{X : |\Omega_U^A - \Omega_U^X| < \varepsilon\} = \{X : \Omega_U^X > \Omega_U^A - \varepsilon\}$$

is open for every $\varepsilon > 0$, so Ω_U is continuous at A. ☐

The above corollary does not guarantee that the supremum is achieved. Surprisingly, it is. In fact, we can prove quite a bit more. One way to view the proof of the following theorem is that we are trying to prevent any real that is not 2-random from being in the closure of the range of Ω_U. If we fail for some X, then it will turn out that $X \in \operatorname{rng}(\Omega_U)$. Note that this fact is a consequence of universality; it is easy to construct a prefix-free oracle machine M such that Ω_M does not achieve its supremum.

Theorem 15.10.4 (Downey, Hirschfeldt, Miller, and Nies [115]). *If* $X \in \operatorname{rng}(\Omega_U)^{\mathrm{c}} \setminus \operatorname{rng}(\Omega_U)$, *then* X *is* 2*-random.*

Proof. Assume that $X \in \operatorname{rng}(\Omega_U)^{\mathrm{c}}$ is not 2-random and let $R_X = \Omega_U^{-1}[X] = \{A : \Omega_U^A = X\}$. For each rational $p \in [0,1]$, define $C_p = \{A : \Omega_U^A \leqslant p\}$. Note that every C_p is closed (in fact, a Π_1^0 class). For every rational $q \in [0,1]$ such that $q < X$, we will define a closed set $B_q \subseteq 2^\omega$ such that

$$R_X = \bigcap_{q<X} B_q \cap \bigcap_{p>X} C_p, \tag{15.5}$$

where q and p range over the rationals. Furthermore, we will prove that every finite intersection of sets from $\{B_q : q < X\}$ and $\{C_p : p > X\}$ is nonempty. By compactness, this property ensures that R_X is nonempty, and therefore, that $X \in \operatorname{rng}(\Omega_U)$.

We would like to define B_q to be $\{A : \Omega_U^A \geqslant q\}$, which would obviously satisfy (15.5). The problem is that $\{A : \Omega_U^A \geqslant q\}$ is a Σ_1^0 class; B_q must be closed if we are to use compactness. The solution is to let $B_q = \{A : \Omega_U^A[k] \geqslant q\}$ for some k. Then B_q is closed (in fact, clopen) and, by choosing k appropriately, we will guarantee that Ω_U^A is bounded away from X for every $A \notin B_q$.

For each rational $q \in [0,1]$, we build a prefix-free oracle machine M_q. For $A \in 2^\omega$ and $\sigma \in 2^{<\omega}$, define $M_q^A(\sigma)$ as follows.

1. Wait for a stage s such that $\Omega_U^A[s] \geqslant q$.

2. Compute $\tau = U^{\emptyset'_s}(\sigma)$.

3. Wait for a stage $t \geqslant s$ such that $\Omega_U^A[t] \geqslant \tau$.

The computation may get stuck in any one of the three steps, in which case $M_q^A(\sigma)\uparrow$. Otherwise, let $M_q^A(\sigma) = t+1$. The value to which $M_q^A(\sigma)$ converges is relevant only because it ensures that a U-simulation of M_q cannot converge before stage $t+1$.

We are ready to define $B_q \subseteq 2^\omega$ for a rational $q \in [0,1]$ such that $q < X$. Assume that U simulates M_q by the prefix ρ. Choose σ such that $U^{\emptyset'}(\sigma) = \tau \prec X$ and $|\tau| > |\rho\sigma|$. Such a σ exists because X is not 2-random. Choose k_q large enough that $U^{\emptyset'_s}(\sigma) = \tau$, for all $s \geqslant k_q$. Let $B_q = \{A : \Omega_U^A[k_q] \geqslant q\}$.

We claim that the definition of B_q ensures that Ω_U^A is bounded away from X for any $A \notin B_q$. Let $l_q = \min\{q, \tau\}$ and $r_q = \tau + 2^{-|\rho\sigma|}$. Clearly $l_q < X$. To see that $r_q > X$, note that $X - \tau \leqslant 2^{-|\tau|} < 2^{-|\rho\sigma|}$. Now assume that $A \notin B_q$ and that $\Omega_U^A \geqslant l_q$. Thus $\Omega_U^A \geqslant q$ but $\Omega_U^A[k_q] < q$, which implies that the s found in step 1 of the definition of M_q is greater than k_q. Therefore, $U^{\emptyset'_s}(\sigma) = \tau$. But $\Omega_U^A \geqslant \tau$, so step 3 eventually produces a $t \geqslant s$ such that $\Omega_U^A[t] \geqslant \tau$. Thus $M_q^A(\sigma)\downarrow = t+1$, so $U^A(\rho\sigma)\downarrow$ some time after stage t, which implies that $\Omega_U^A \geqslant \Omega_U^A[t] + 2^{-|\rho\sigma|} \geqslant \tau + 2^{-|\rho\sigma|} = r_q$. We have proved that

$$\Omega_U^A \in [l_q, r_q) \Rightarrow A \in B_q. \tag{15.6}$$

Next we verify (15.5). Assume that $A \in R_X$. We have just proved that $A \in B_q$ for all rationals $q < X$. Also, it is clear that $A \in C_p$ for all rationals $p > X$. Therefore, $R_X \subseteq \bigcap_{q<X} B_q \cap \bigcap_{p>X} C_p$. For the other direction, assume that $A \in \bigcap_{q<X} B_q \cap \bigcap_{p>X} C_p$. Then $q < X$ implies that $\Omega_U^A \geqslant \Omega_U^A[k_q] \geqslant q$, so $\Omega_U^A \geqslant X$. On the other hand, if $p > X$, then $\Omega_U^A \leqslant p$. This fact implies that $\Omega_U^A \leqslant X$, and so $\Omega_U^A = X$. Therefore, $A \in R_X$, which proves (15.5).

It remains to prove that R_X is nonempty. Let Q be a finite set of rationals less than X and P a finite set of rationals greater than X. Define $l = \max\{l_q : q \in Q\}$ and $r = \min(P \cup \{r_q : q \in Q\})$. Note that $X \in (l, r)$. Because $X \in \operatorname{rng}(\Omega_U)^c$, there is an A such that $\Omega_U^A \in (l, r)$. From (15.6) it follows that $A \in B_q$ for all $q \in Q$. Clearly, $A \in C_p$ for every $p \in P$. Hence $\bigcap_{q \in Q} B_q \cap \bigcap_{p \in P} C_p$ is nonempty. By compactness, R_X is nonempty. $\square$

If $X \in \operatorname{rng}(\Omega_U)$ is not 2-random, then an examination of the above construction gives an upper bound on the complexity of $\Omega_U^{-1}[X]$. The Π^0_1 classes C_p can be computed uniformly. The B_q are also Π^0_1 classes and can be found uniformly in $X \oplus \emptyset'$. Therefore, $\Omega_U^{-1}[X] = \bigcap_{q<X} B_q \cap \bigcap_{p>X} C_p$ is a nonempty $\Pi_1^{0,X\oplus\emptyset'}$ class.

The following corollary gives an interesting special case of Theorem 15.10.4. It is not hard to prove that there is an A such that $\Omega_U^A = \inf(\operatorname{rng}\Omega_U)$ (see Theorem 15.7.1). It is much less obvious that Ω_U achieves its supremum.

Corollary 15.10.5 (Downey, Hirschfeldt, Miller, and Nies [115]). *There is an A such that $\Omega_U^A = \sup(\operatorname{rng}\Omega_U)$.*

Proof. Since $\sup(\operatorname{rng}\Omega_U)$ is a left-c.e. real, it is not 2-random, so the corollary is immediate from Theorem 15.10.4. $\square$

By Proposition 8.11.9, no 1-generic is 1-random, so $\mu(\{A : \Omega_U^A = \sup(\operatorname{rng}\Omega_U)\}) = 0$. Therefore, $\sup(\operatorname{rng}\Omega_U)$ is an example of a left-c.e. real in the range of Ω_U that is not in $\operatorname{Spec}(\Omega_U)$.

One might ask whether Theorem 15.10.4 is vacuous. In other words, is the range of Ω_U actually closed? We can construct a specific universal prefix-free oracle machine such that it is not. The construction is somewhat similar to the proof of Theorem 15.4.3. In that case, we avoided a measure zero set by using an oracle that codes a relativized Martin-Löf test covering that set. Now we will avoid a measure zero *closed* set by using a natural number to code a finite open cover with sufficiently small measure.

Example 15.10.6 (Downey, Hirschfeldt, Miller, and Nies [115]). There is a universal prefix-free oracle machine V such that

$$\mu(\operatorname{rng}(\Omega_V)) < \mu(\operatorname{rng}(\Omega_V)^c).$$

Proof. Let U be a universal prefix-free oracle machine. Let M be a prefix-free oracle machine such that

$$\Omega_M^A = \begin{cases} 1 & \text{if } |A| > 1 \\ 0 & \text{otherwise.} \end{cases}$$

Define a universal prefix-free oracle machine V by $V^A(0\sigma) = U^A(\sigma)$ and $V^A(1\sigma) = M^A(\sigma)$ for all σ. This definition ensures that $\Omega_V^A \leqslant \frac{1}{2}$ iff $|A| \leqslant 1$. Therefore, $\mu(\operatorname{rng}(\Omega_V) \cap [0, \frac{1}{2}]) = 0$. We will prove that $\mu(\operatorname{rng}(\Omega_V)^c \cap [0, \frac{1}{2}]) > 0$.

Let $\{I_i\}_{i\in\omega}$ be an effective enumeration of all finite unions of open intervals with dyadic rational endpoints. We construct a prefix-free oracle machine N. By the recursion theorem, we may assume that we know a coding string ρ of N in V. Given an oracle A, find the least n such that

$A(n) = 1$. Intuitively, N^A tries to prevent Ω_V^A from being in I_n. Whenever a stage s occurs such that $\Omega_V^A[s] \in I_n$ and $\forall\sigma\,(V^A(\rho\sigma)[s] = N^A(\sigma)[s])$, then N^A acts as follows. Let ε be the least number such that $\Omega_V^A[s]+\varepsilon \notin I_n$ and note that ε is necessarily a dyadic rational. If possible, N^A converges on additional strings with total measure $2^{|\rho|}\varepsilon$, which ensures that $\Omega_V^A \geqslant \Omega_V^A[s]+\varepsilon$. If $\mu(I_n) \leqslant 2^{-|\rho|}$, then N^A cannot run out of room in its domain, and we have $\Omega_V^A \notin I_n$.

Assume for the sake of contradiction that $\mu(\mathrm{rng}(\Omega_V)^{\mathrm{c}} \cap [0, \frac{1}{2}]) = 0$. Then there is an open cover of $\mathrm{rng}(\Omega_V)^{\mathrm{c}} \cap [0, \frac{1}{2}]$ with measure less than $2^{-|\rho|}$. We may assume that all intervals in this cover have dyadic rational endpoints. Because $\mathrm{rng}(\Omega_V)^{\mathrm{c}} \cap [0, \frac{1}{2}]$ is compact, there is a finite subcover I_n. But $\mu(I_n) < 2^{-|\rho|}$ implies that $\Omega_V^{0^n10^\omega} \notin I_n$, which is a contradiction. Thus $\mu(\mathrm{rng}(\Omega_V)^{\mathrm{c}} \cap [0, \frac{1}{2}]) > 0$. □

Note that the proof above shows that if U is a universal prefix-free oracle machine and $S = \{\Omega_U^{0^n10^\omega} : n \in \mathbb{N}\}$, then S^{c} has positive measure and $S^{\mathrm{c}} \setminus S$ contains only 2-randoms.

Proposition 15.10.7 (Downey, Hirschfeldt, Miller, and Nies [115]). *$\mathrm{rng}(\Omega_U)^{\mathrm{c}}$ is a Π_3^0 class.*

Proof. It is easy to verify that $a \in \mathrm{rng}(\Omega_U)^{\mathrm{c}}$ iff

$$\forall\varepsilon > 0\,\exists\sigma \in 2^{<\omega}\,\big(\Omega_U^\sigma[|\sigma|] > a - \varepsilon \\ \wedge\ \forall n \geqslant |\sigma|\,\exists\tau \succ \sigma\,(|\tau| = n \wedge \Omega_U^\tau[n] < a + \varepsilon)\big),$$

where ε ranges over rational numbers. This definition is Π_3^0 because the final existential quantifier is bounded. □

16

Complexity of Computably Enumerable Sets

16.1 Barzdins' Lemma and Kummer complex sets

In this section, we look at the initial segment complexity of c.e. sets, including a fascinating gap phenomenon uncovered by Kummer [226]. We begin with an old result of Barzdins [29].

Theorem 16.1.1 (Barzdins' Lemma [29]). *If A is a c.e. set then $C(A \upharpoonright n \mid n) \leqslant \log n + O(1)$ and $C(A \upharpoonright n) \leqslant 2\log n + O(1)$.*

Proof. To describe $A \upharpoonright n$ given n, it suffices to supply the number k_n of elements in $A \upharpoonright n$ and an e such that $A = W_e$, since we can recover $A \upharpoonright n$ from this information by running the enumeration of W_e until k_n many elements appear in $W_e \upharpoonright n$. Such a description can be given in $\log n + O(1)$ many bits.

For the second part of the lemma, we can encode k_n and n as two strings σ and τ, respectively, each of length $\log n$. We can recover σ and τ from $\sigma\tau$ because we know the length of each of these two strings is exactly half the length of $\sigma\tau$. Thus we can describe $A \upharpoonright n$ in $2\log n + O(1)$ many bits. □

Barzdins also constructed an example of a c.e. set A with $C(A \upharpoonright n) \geqslant \log n$ for all n. If $C(A \upharpoonright n) \leqslant \log n + O(1)$ for all n then, by the proof of Theorem 3.4.4, A is computable. A long-standing open question was whether the $2\log n$ is optimal in the second part of Theorem 16.1.1. The best we could hope for is a c.e. set A such that $C(A \upharpoonright n) \geqslant 2\log n - O(1)$ infinitely often, since the following is known.

R.G. Downey and D. Hirschfeldt, *Algorithmic Randomness and Complexity*, Theory and Applications of Computability, DOI 10.1007/978-0-387-68441-3_16,

Theorem 16.1.2 (Solovay [unpublished]). *There is no c.e. set A such that $C(A \upharpoonright n \mid n) \geqslant \log n - O(1)$ for all n. Similarly, there is no c.e. set A such that $C(A \upharpoonright n) \geqslant 2\log n - O(1)$ for all n.*

More recently, a simple proof of a result stronger than Solovay's was discovered.

Theorem 16.1.3 (Hölzl, Kräling, and Merkle [183]). *For any c.e. set A there exist infinitely many m such that $C(A \upharpoonright m \mid m) = O(1)$ and $C(A \upharpoonright m) \leqslant C(m) + O(1)$.*

Proof. We may assume that A is infinite. Let m be such that m enters A at stage s and no number less than m enters A after stage s. There must be infinitely many such m, and the theorem clearly holds for any of them. □

Solovay [unpublished] explicitly asked whether there is a c.e. set A such that $C(A \upharpoonright n) \geqslant 2\log n - O(1)$ infinitely often. As we will see the answer is yes, and there is a precise characterization of the degrees that contain such sets.

Definition 16.1.4. A c.e. set A is *Kummer complex* if for each d there are infinitely many n such that $C(A \upharpoonright n) \geqslant 2\log n - d$.

Theorem 16.1.5 (Kummer [226]). *There is a Kummer complex c.e. set.*

Proof. Let $t_0 = 0$ and $t_{k+1} = 2^{t_k}$. Let $I_k = (t_k, t_{k+1}]$ and

$$f(k) = \sum_{i=t_k+1}^{t_{k+1}} (i - t_k + 1).$$

Note that $f(k)$ asymptotically approaches $\frac{t_{k+1}^2}{2}$, and hence $\log f(k) > 2\log t_{k+1} - 2$ for sufficiently large k. So it is enough to build a c.e. set A such that for each k there is an $n \in I_k$ with $C(A \upharpoonright n) \geqslant \log f(k)$.

Enumerate A as follows. At stage $s+1$, for each $k \leqslant s$, if $C_s(A_s \upharpoonright n) < \log f(k)$ for all $n \in I_k$ and $I_k \nsubseteq A_s$, then put the smallest element of $\overline{A_s} \cap I_k$ into A_{s+1}.

Now suppose that $C(A \upharpoonright n) < \log f(k)$ for all $n \in I_k$. Then there must be a stage s such that $A_s \upharpoonright n = A \upharpoonright n$ and $C_s(A_s \upharpoonright n) < \log f(k)$. We must have $I_k \nsubseteq A_s$, since otherwise the smallest element of $\overline{A_s} \cap I_k$ would enter A, contradicting the assumption that $A_s \upharpoonright n = A \upharpoonright n$. Thus, all of I_k is eventually put into A. So for each $n \in I_k$ there are stages $s_0 < s_1 < \cdots < s_{n-t_k}$ such that $A_{s_{i+1}} \upharpoonright n \neq A_{s_i} \upharpoonright n$ and $C_{s_i}(A_{s_i}) < \log f(k)$, and hence there are at least $n - t_k + 1$ many strings σ with $|\sigma| = n$ and $C(\sigma) < \log f(k)$. Thus, there are at least $f(k)$ many strings σ such that $C(\sigma) < \log f(k)$, which is a contradiction. □

Kummer also gave an exact characterization of the degrees containing Kummer complex c.e. sets, using the notion of array noncomputability discussed in Section 2.23.

Theorem 16.1.6 (Kummer's Gap Theorem [226]).

(i) *A c.e. degree contains a Kummer complex set iff it is array noncomputable.*

(ii) *In addition, if A is c.e. and of array computable degree, then for every computable order f,*

$$C(A \upharpoonright n) \leqslant \log n + f(n) + O(1).$$

(iii) *Hence the c.e. degrees exhibit the following gap phenomenon: for each c.e. degree* **a**, *either*

(a) *there is a c.e. set $A \in \mathbf{a}$ such that $C(A \upharpoonright n) \geqslant 2 \log n - O(1)$ for infinitely many n, or*

(b) *there is no c.e. set $A \in \mathbf{a}$ and $\varepsilon > 0$ such that $C(A \upharpoonright n) \geqslant (1 + \varepsilon) \log n - O(1)$ for infinitely many n.*

Proof. Part (iii) follows immediately from parts (i) and (ii), so we prove the latter.

Part (i): To make A Kummer complex, all we need is to have the construction from Theorem 16.1.5 work for infinitely many intervals. Let I_k and $f(k)$ be as in the proof of that theorem, and let $\mathcal{I}$ be the very strong array $\{I_k\}_{k \in \mathbb{N}}$. Let A be an $\mathcal{I}$-a.n.c. c.e. set.

Define a c.e. set W as follows. At stage $s+1$, for each $k \leqslant s$, if $C_s(A_s \upharpoonright n) < \log f(k)$ for all $n \in I_k$ and $I_k \not\subseteq A_s$, then put the smallest element of $\overline{A_s} \cap I_k$ into W.

Since A is $\mathcal{I}$-a.n.c., there are infinitely many k such that $A \cap I_k = W \cap I_k$. A similar argument to that in the proof of Theorem 16.1.5 now shows that, for any such k, if $C(A \upharpoonright n) < \log f(k)$ for all $n \in I_k$ then $I_k \subset A$, and hence that for each $n \in I_k$, there are at least $n - t_k + 1$ many strings σ with $|\sigma| = n$ and $C(\sigma) < \log f(k)$, which leads to the same contradiction as before. Thus A is Kummer complex.

By Theorem 2.23.4, each array noncomputable c.e. degree contains an $\mathcal{I}$-a.n.c. set, so each such degree contains a Kummer complex set.

Part (ii): Let A be c.e. and of array computable degree, and let f be a computable order. Let $m(n) = \max\{i : f(i) < n\}$. Note that m is a computable order, and is defined for almost all n. Let $g(n) = A \upharpoonright m(n)$. (If $m(n)$ is undefined then let $g(n) = 0$.) Since g is computable in A, Proposition 2.23.6 implies that there is a total computable approximation $\{g_s\}_{s \in \mathbb{N}}$ such that $\lim_s g_s(n) = g(n)$ and $|\{s : g_s(n) \neq g_{s+1}(n)\}| \leqslant n$ for all n. (Recall that this cardinality is known as the number of mind changes of g at n.)

Suppose that we are given n and, for $k_n = \min\{i : m(i) \geqslant n\}$, we are also given the exact number p_n of mind changes of g at k_n. Then we can compute $g(k_n) = A \upharpoonright m(k_n)$, and hence also compute $A \upharpoonright n$, since $m(k_n) \geqslant n$. In other words, we can describe $A \upharpoonright n$ given n and p_n, so

$$C(A \upharpoonright n) \leqslant \log n + 2 \log p_n + O(1).$$

By the definition of k_n, we have $m(k_n - 1) < n$, so by the definition of m, we have $k_n - 1 \leqslant f(n)$. Furthermore, $p_n \leqslant k_n$, so

$$C(A \upharpoonright n) \leqslant \log n + 2\log f(n) + O(1) \leqslant \log n + f(n) + O(1),$$

as desired. □

Kummer's Gap Theorem should be compared with results such as Downey and Greenberg's Theorem 13.14.2 on packing dimension and the Barmpalias, Downey, and Greenberg result on cl-degrees, Theorem 9.14.4, which also concern array computability.

It is natural to ask whether there is a classification of, say, all jump classes in terms of initial segment complexity.

16.2 The entropy of computably enumerable sets

In this section we consider Chaitin's notion from [59] of the *entropy* of a computably enumerable set, in the spirit of the Coding Theorem 3.9.4, and its relationship with the following notion, also taken from [59]. By a *c.e. operator* we mean a function W taking sets X to W_e^X for some e. We denote the value of W on X by W^A. For a c.e. operator W, the *enumeration probability* $P_W(A)$ of a set A relative to W is the measure of the class of all X such that $W^X = A$. This probability depends on W, of course, but there are *optimal* c.e. operators V such that for each c.e. operator W there is an $\varepsilon > 0$ for which $P_V(A) \geqslant \varepsilon P_W(A)$ for all A. For example, we can list the c.e. operators $W_0, W_1, \ldots$ and let V be a c.e. operator such that $V^{0^e1X} = W_e^X$, where 0^e1X is the sequence $0^e1X(0)X(1)\ldots$. We fix such a V and write $P(A)$ for $P_V(A)$. More generally, for a class $C \subseteq 2^\omega$, we let $P(C) = \mu(\{X : V^X \in C\})$.

If A is c.e., then clearly $P(A) > 0$. Recall that Theorem 8.12.1 says that the converse is also true: If $P(A) > 0$ then A is c.e. Recall also that the proof of Theorem 8.12.1 is the classic use of the "majority vote" technique, which uses the Lebesgue Density Theorem to find some string σ such that $n \in A$ iff a majority (in the sense of measure) of the strings extending σ believe that $n \in A$. Thus a c.e. index for A is determined by a nonuniform argument based on the Lebesgue Density Theorem. Since the application of the Lebesgue Density Theorem is to find a σ such that the measure of the class of $X \succ \sigma$ such that $V^X = A$ is large, it is not unreasonable to imagine that c.e. sets with bigger enumeration probabilities should be easier to describe. Thus, the question we address in this section is the following: What effect does the enumeration probability of a c.e. set have on the difficulty of describing a c.e. index for it? This question leads us to the following definitions.

Definition 16.2.1 (Chaitin [59]). For a c.e. set A, let $H(A) = \lceil -\log P(A) \rceil$ and $I(A) = \min\{K(j) : A = W_j\}$.[1]

Chaitin [59] established some of the basic properties of these and related notions, while Solovay [371, 372] showed that there is indeed a deep relationship between them.

Theorem 16.2.2 (Solovay [371, 372]). $I(A) \leqslant 3H(A) + 2\log H(A) + O(1)$.

It is not known to what extent Solovay's bound may be improved, but Vereshchagin [400] showed that a tighter bound can be extracted from Solovay's proof when A is finite.

Theorem 16.2.3 (Vereshchagin [400]). *If A is finite then $I(A) \leqslant 2H(A) + 2\log H(A) + O(1)$.*

We will prove both of these results in this section. Our account of Solovay's proof will be along the lines of the one given by Vereshchagin [400]. The proof relies on a combinatorial result of Martin (see [371, 372]), so we begin by presenting that result.

Martin's game is defined as follows. The game has parameters K and N. A *configuration* of the game is an N-tuple $(S_0, \dots, S_{N-1})$ of clopen subsets of 2^ω. The initial configuration is $(2^\omega, \dots, 2^\omega)$. There are two players. On its turn, player I plays a clopen set $Y \subset 2^\omega$ with $\mu(Y) > \frac{1}{K+1}$. If Y is disjoint from $S_0, \dots, S_{N-1}$ then player I wins. If not, then player II's move is to pick an $i < N$ with $S_i \cap Y \neq \emptyset$ and replace S_i by Y. Player II wins if it can prevent player I from ever winning.

Theorem 16.2.4 (Martin, see Solovay [371, 372]). *In the game above, player II has a computable winning strategy if $N = \frac{K(K+1)}{2}$.*[2]

Proof. This proof follows Solovay [372]. It uses a property of configurations called *property M*. This property is computably checkable, the initial configuration has it, and if a configuration has property M, then for any move by player I, player II has a move that results in a configuration that also has property M. Given such a property, the computable strategy for player II is simply to pick the least i so that $S_i \cap Y \neq \emptyset$ and the resulting configuration has property M.

Suppose that $N = \frac{K(K+1)}{2}$. Let $T = \{(j, i) : i \leqslant j < K\}$. Then $|T| = N$. Given a bijection $h : T \to N$ and a configuration $(Y_0, \dots, Y_{N-1})$, we

[1]We assume that our listing of c.e. sets is given by a reasonable enumeration of Turing machines, so that if we have another such listing $\widehat{W}_0, \widehat{W}_1, \dots$, then for each i we can effectively find a j such that $\widehat{W}_j = W_i$ and vice versa. It is then easy to check that $\min\{K(j) : A = W_j\} = \min\{K(j) : A = \widehat{W}_j\} \pm O(1)$, so the definition of $I(A)$ is listing-independent up to an additive constant.

[2]Ageev [1] has shown that N has to be at least on the order of εK^2 (for some $\varepsilon > 0$) for player II to win Martin's game.

write $Z_{j,i}$ for $Y_{h(j,i)}$. We think of this bijection as arranging the Y_k into a triangular array

$$\begin{array}{llll} Z_{0,0} & & & \\ Z_{1,0} & Z_{1,1} & & \\ \vdots & & & \\ Z_{K-1,0} & Z_{K-1,1} & \dots & Z_{K-1,K-1}. \end{array}$$

We say that $(Y_0, \dots, Y_{N-1})$ has *property M* if for some bijection $h : T \to N$, the resulting triangular array has the following property: For all $j < K$, if $i_0 \leqslant i_1 \leqslant \dots \leqslant i_{d-1} \leqslant j$, then $\mu(\bigcup_{k<d} Z_{j,i_k}) > \frac{d}{K+1}$.

Clearly, the initial configuration has property M, and we can effectively check whether a given configuration has property M. (Since a configuration is a finite sequence of clopen sets, it can be specified as a finite sequence of finite sets of generators.) To complete the proof, we show the following, which we state as a separate lemma for future reference.

Lemma 16.2.5. *Let $(Y_0, \dots, Y_{N-1})$ be a configuration with property M. Let Y be a clopen subset of 2^ω with $\mu(Y) > \frac{1}{K+1}$. Then there is an $i < N$ with $Y_i \cap Y \neq \emptyset$ such that the configuration obtained by replacing Y_i by Y still has property M.*

Proof. Let $h : T \to N$ be a bijection witnessing the fact that $(Y_0, \dots, Y_{N-1})$ has property M, and let $Z_{j,i}$ for $(j, i) \in T$ be the corresponding triangular array. Then $\mu(\bigcup_{i<N} Z_{K-1,i}) > \frac{K}{K+1}$, so some $Z_{K-1,i}$ has nonempty intersection with Y. Let j be least such that $Z_{j,i} \cap Y \neq \emptyset$ for some i. Permuting the jth row if necessary, we may assume that $Z_{j,j} \cap Y \neq \emptyset$. We prove that if we replace $Y_{h(j,j)}$ by Y, the resulting configuration has property M.

If $j = 1$ then there is nothing to prove, so suppose that $j > 1$. We build a new array by replacing $Z_{j,j}$ by Y and then swapping the rest of the jth row with the $(j-1)$st row. That is, let $Z'_{j,j} = Y$, let $Z'_{j-1,i} = Z_{j,i}$ and $Z'_{j,i} = Z_{j-1,i}$ for $i \leqslant j-1$, and for all other k and i, let $Z'_{k,i} = Z_{k,i}$. We claim that this new array witnesses the fact that $(Y_0, \dots, Y_{h(j,j)-1}, Y, Y_{h(j,j)+1}, \dots, Y_{N-1})$ has property M.

Since property M works on a row-by-row basis, we do not need to worry about any rows other than the $(j-1)$st and the jth. The $(j-1)$st row is the same as the jth row of the original array, so we do not need to worry about it either. So we need to show only that if if $i_0 \leqslant \dots \leqslant i_{d-1} \leqslant j$ then $\mu(\bigcup_{k<d} Z'_{j,i_k}) > \frac{d}{K+1}$. If $i_{d-1} < j$ then all elements involved in the union are taken from the $(j-1)$st row of the original array, so we are done. Thus, we may assume that $i_{d-1} = j$, so that $Z'_{j,i_{d-1}} = Y$. By our choice of j, we know that $Y \cap Z_{j-1,i} = \emptyset$ for all $i \leqslant j-1$. Thus $\mu(\bigcup_{k<d} Z'_{j,i_k}) = \mu(\bigcup_{k<d-1} Z_{j-1,i_k}) + \mu(Y) > \frac{d-1}{K+1} + \frac{1}{K+1} = \frac{d}{K+1}$, as required. □

As explained above, this lemma completes the proof of the theorem. □

We are now ready to prove Theorem 16.2.2.

Proof of Theorem 16.2.2. We will show that, for each k, we can enumerate $O(2^{2k})$ many c.e. sets such that every set A with $P(A) \geqslant 2^{-k}$ is among them. If this enumeration were uniform in k, then, taking $k = H(A)$, we could describe an index for A simply by giving k and the position of A in our enumeration, which would require fewer than $2H(A) + 2\log H(A)$ many bits. The enumeration will not be uniform in k, however, but there will be nonuniformly given strings $\rho_k \in 2^k$ such that the enumeration for k can be done on input ρ_{k+1}. The extra bits needed to describe ρ_{k+1} are what will drive our bound to $3H(A) + 2\log H(A)$.

Fix k. For a string σ, let F_σ be the finite set determined by σ, that is, $F_\sigma = \{n < |\sigma| : \sigma(n) = 1\}$. Let $S_t(\sigma) = \{X : V^X[t] \in [\![\sigma]\!]\}$. The following lemma is immediate.

Lemma 16.2.6. $P(A) = \lim_n P([\![A \upharpoonright n]\!])$.

We will also need the following lemma.

Lemma 16.2.7. $P([\![\sigma]\!]) = \lim_t \mu(S_t(\sigma))$.

Proof. Let S^1_t be the class of all X such $V^X[t] \supseteq F_\sigma$ and S^2_t be the class of all $X \in S^1_t$ such that $V^X[t] \upharpoonright |\sigma| \supsetneq F_\sigma$. Let $S^1 = \bigcup_t S^1_t$ and $S^2 = \bigcup_t S^2_t$. Then $P([\![\sigma]\!]) = \mu(S^1 \setminus S^2) = \mu(S^1) - \mu(S^2) = \lim_t(\mu(S^1_t) - \mu(S^2_t)) = \lim_t \mu(S_t(\sigma))$. □

It thus makes sense to define $P_t([\![\sigma]\!]) = \mu(S_t(\sigma))$.

An *approximating sequence* for a set A is a sequence $\sigma_0, \sigma_1, \ldots$ such that $F_{\sigma_0} \subseteq F_{\sigma_1} \subseteq \cdots$ and $\bigcup_i F_{\sigma_i} = A$.

We say that the pair (t, n) is *good for* σ if $|\sigma| = n$ and $P_t([\![\sigma]\!]) \geqslant 2^{-k-1}$. We say that a sequence of pairs $(t_0, n_0), (t_1, n_1), \ldots$ is *good for* A if there is an approximating sequence $\sigma_0, \sigma_1, \ldots$ for A and $j_0 < j_1 < \cdots$ such that (t_{j_i}, n_{j_i}) is good for σ_i for each i.

The proof now boils down to the following two lemmas.

Lemma 16.2.8. *There are strings $\rho_k \in 2^k$ and an algorithm that, on input ρ_{k+1}, computes a sequence of pairs $(t_0, n_0), (t_1, n_1), \ldots$ that is good for all A such that $P(A) \geqslant 2^{-k}$.*

Lemma 16.2.9. *There is an algorithm that, when given a sequence of pairs as in Lemma 16.2.8 as an oracle, enumerates $O(2^{2k})$ many sets $C_0, \ldots, C_{N-1}$ such that every set A for which the sequence is good coincides with some C_i.*

Given these lemmas, the theorem follows easily: Let $k = H(A)$, so that $P(A) \geqslant 2^{-k}$. Let ρ_{k+1} be as in Lemma 16.2.8, and let $C_0, \ldots, C_{N-1}$ be as in Lemma 16.2.9 when the oracle is the sequence computed from ρ_{k+1}. Then there is an $i < N$ such that $A = C_i$. Given ρ_{k+1} and i, we can determine an index j such that $A = W_j$. We can determine k from ρ_{k+1}, so

$$I(A) \leqslant K(\rho_{k+1}) + K(i \mid k) \leqslant k + 2\log k + 2k + O(1)$$
$$= 3H(A) + 2\log H(A) + O(1).$$

So to finish the proof, we need only to establish the two lemmas. We begin with the latter.

Proof of Lemma 16.2.9. Let $K = 2^{k+1}$ and $N = \frac{K(K+1)}{2}$. We are given a sequence of pairs $(t_0, n_0), (t_1, n_1), \ldots$ that is good for all A such that $P(A) \geqslant 2^{-k}$. We will enumerate sets $C_0, \ldots, C_{N-1}$ using Martin's game. We begin by letting $(X_0[0], \ldots, X_{N-1}[0])$ be the initial configuration and $C_0[0], \ldots, C_{N-1}[0]$ all be empty.

At the end of stage j of the algorithm, we have a configuration $(X_0[j], \ldots, X_{N-1}[j])$ and finite sets $C_0[j], \ldots, C_{N-1}[j]$ with the following properties.

(i) $C_i[j] \subseteq [0, n_j)$.

(ii) For every σ for which (t_j, n_j) is good, $C_i[j] = F_\sigma$ for some $i < N$.

(iii) $C_i[j] \subseteq V^X[t_j]$ for all $X \in X_i[j]$.

At stage $j+1$, we proceed as follows. Let $\sigma_0, \ldots, \sigma_l$ be the strings for which (t_{j+1}, n_{j+1}) is good. Play $Y = S_t(\sigma_0)$ for player I. Since $\mu(S_t(\sigma_0)) = P_t([\![\sigma_0]\!]) \geqslant 2^{-k-1} > \frac{1}{K+1}$, this move is legal. Let $X_i[j]$ be the set that the winning strategy for player II replaces by Y and let $X_i[j+1] = Y$.

Since $X_i[j] \cap Y \neq \emptyset$, there is some $X \in X_i[j]$ with $V^X[t_{j+1}] \in [\![\sigma_0]\!]$. By condition (iii), $C_i[j] \subseteq V^X[t_j] \subseteq V^X[t_{j+1}]$, so by condition (i), $C_i[j] \subseteq V^X[t_{j+1}] \cap [0, n_{j+1}) = F_{\sigma_0}$. So we can let $C_i[j+1] = F_{\sigma_0}$. Note that now $C_i[j+1] \subseteq V^X[t_{j+1}]$ for all $X \in X_i[j+1]$, and hence (iii) remains true for this i.

Now repeat this procedure for $\sigma_1, \ldots, \sigma_l$ in turn. By definition, the sets $S_t(\sigma_0), \ldots, S_t(\sigma_l)$ are pairwise disjoint, so the strategy for player II always picks a new $X_i[j]$ to replace. For all i such that $X_i[j]$ is not picked, let $C_i[j+1] = C_i[j]$ and $X_i[j+1] = X_i[j]$. Note that (iii) is true for all such i, since $V^X[t_{j+1}] \supseteq V^X[t_j]$ for all X.

Let $C_i = \bigcup_j C_i[j]$. To see that the algorithm works, and hence complete the proof of Lemma 16.2.9, assume that there is an approximating sequence $\tau_0, \tau_1, \ldots$ for A and $j_0 < j_1 < \cdots$ such that (t_{j_l}, n_{j_l}) is good for τ_l. Then for each l there is an $i < N$ such that $C_i[j_l] = F_{\tau_l}$. So for some $i < N$, there are infinitely many l such that $C_i[j_l] = F_{\tau_l}$. Then $A = C_i$. □

We finish by proving Lemma 16.2.8.

Proof of Lemma 16.2.8. Let $A_0, \ldots, A_r$ list all the sets A with $P(A) \geqslant 2^{-k}$, let $\rho = \sum_{i \leqslant r} P(A_i)$, and let $\rho_{k+1} = \rho \upharpoonright k+1$.

We say that (t, m, n) is *opportune* if $m \geqslant 2^{k+1}$ and for the list $\sigma_0, \ldots, \sigma_s$ of all strings in 2^n such that $P_t([\![\sigma]\!]) \geqslant 2^{-k} - \frac{1}{m}$, we have $\sum_{i \leqslant s} P_t([\![\sigma]\!]) \geqslant \rho_{k+1} - 2^{-k-1}$. Note that the first condition implies that $P_t([\![\sigma]\!]) \geqslant 2^{-k-1}$ for all $i \leqslant s$, and hence, since the $[\![\sigma]\!]$ are disjoint, $s \leqslant 2^{k+1}$.

First we will show that for each c there is an opportune triple (t, m, n) with $t, m, n > c$. Since the property of being an opportune triple is computable given ρ_{k+1}, we can then define, computably in ρ_{k+1}, a sequence of opportune triples $(t_0, m_0, n_0), (t_1, m_1, n_1), \ldots$ that is increasing in each component. Then we will show that, for such a sequence and any A such that $P(A) \geqslant 2^{-k}$, there is an approximating sequence $\tau_0, \tau_1, \ldots$ for A and $j_0 < j_1 < \cdots$ such that $P_{t_{j_i}}([\![\sigma_i]\!]) \geqslant 2^{-k} - \frac{1}{m_j} \geqslant 2^{-k-1}$ for all i. Thus $(t_0, n_0), (t_1, n_1), \ldots$ is the desired sequence that is computable from ρ_{k+1} and good for all A such that $P(A) \geqslant 2^{-k}$.

We begin by showing that for each c there is an opportune triple (t, m, n) with $t, m, n > c$.

Fix c. Let $m > c, 2^{k+1}$. Let $n' > c$ be such that the sets $A_i \cap [0, n')$ for $i = 0, \ldots, r$ are pairwise distinct. By Lemma 16.2.6, $P(A_i) = \lim_n P([\![A_i \upharpoonright n]\!])$, so there is an $n > n'$ with $P([\![A_i \upharpoonright n]\!]) > P(A_i) - \frac{1}{2m(r+1)}$ for all $i \leqslant r$.

By Lemma 16.2.7, there is a $t > c$ such that $P_t([\![A_i \upharpoonright n]\!]) > P(A_i) - \frac{1}{2m(r+1)} \geqslant 2^{-k} - \frac{1}{m}$ for all $i \leqslant r$ and $\sum_{i \leqslant r} P_t([\![A_i \upharpoonright n]\!]) > \rho - \frac{1}{2m} \geqslant \rho_{k+1} - 2^{-k-1}$. It now follows from the definition of opportune triple that (t, m, n) is such a triple.

As mentioned above, we now have a sequence of opportune triples $(t_0, m_0, n_0), (t_1, m_1, n_1), \ldots$ that is increasing in each component, and we can finish the proof by taking an A such that $P(A) \geqslant 2^{-k}$ and showing that there is an approximating sequence $\tau_0, \tau_1, \ldots$ for A and $j_0 < j_1 < \cdots$ such that $P_{t_{j_i}}([\![\sigma_i]\!]) \geqslant 2^{-k} - \frac{1}{m_j}$ for all i.[3]

Without loss of generality, by passing to a subsequence if necessary, we may assume that the number $s + 1$ of strings $\sigma \in 2^{n_j}$ with $P_{t_j}([\![\sigma]\!]) \geqslant 2^{-k} - \frac{1}{m_j}$ does not depend on j. Let $\sigma_0^j, \ldots, \sigma_s^j$ list these strings.

Let $\mathcal{B}$ be the class of all B for which there are $j_0 < j_1 < \cdots$ and $i_0, i_1, \ldots \leqslant s$ such that $\sigma_{i_0}^{j_0}, \sigma_{i_1}^{j_1}, \ldots$ is an approximating sequence for B. We want to show that $A \in \mathcal{B}$. We do so by showing that $P(B) \geqslant 2^{-k}$ for all $B \in \mathcal{B}$ and $P(\mathcal{B}) \geqslant \rho_{k+1} - 2^{-k-1}$. These facts imply that $A \in \mathcal{B}$, as otherwise the sum of $P(X)$ over all X with $P(X) \geqslant 2^{-k}$ would be greater than ρ.

We first show that $P(B) \geqslant 2^{-k}$ for all $B \in \mathcal{B}$. Suppose not. Let m be such that $P(B) < 2^{-k} - \frac{1}{m}$. By Lemma 16.2.6, there is an n such

[3]Note that, although we showed the existence of an opportune triple by finding (t, m, n) such that $P_t([\![A_i \upharpoonright n]\!]) > 2^{-k} - \frac{1}{m}$ for all $i \leqslant r$, there is no guarantee that the particular computable sequence of opportune triples $(t_0, m_0, n_0), (t_1, m_1, n_1), \ldots$ has that property.

that $P([\![B \upharpoonright n]\!]) < 2^{-k} - \frac{1}{m}$. By Lemma 16.2.7, there is a t' such that $P_t([\![B \upharpoonright n]\!]) < 2^{-k} - \frac{1}{m}$ for all $t \geqslant t'$. Let j and i be such that $\sigma_i^j \upharpoonright n \prec B$ and $t_j > t'$, and also $m_j > m$ and $n_j > n$. Then

$$P_{t_j}([\![\sigma_i^j]\!]) \leqslant P_{t_j}([\![\sigma_i^j \upharpoonright n]\!]) = P_{t_j}([\![B \upharpoonright n]\!]) < 2^{-k} - \frac{1}{m} < 2^{-k} - \frac{1}{m_j},$$

contradicting the choice of σ_i^j.

We now show that $P(\mathcal{B}) \geqslant \rho_{k+1} - 2^{-k-1}$. We first need an auxiliary fact. Suppose there is an n such that for all j with $n_j > n$, there is an $i \leqslant s$ such that $\sigma_i^j \upharpoonright n \not\prec B$ for all $B \in \mathcal{B}$. Then we can form a sequence $j_0 < j_1 < \cdots$ such that for each j_l there is a $\sigma_{i_l}^{j_l}$ such that $F_{\sigma_{i_l}^{j_l}} \not\subseteq F_{\sigma_{i_{l'}}^{j_{l'}}}$ for all $l' > l$. But then $P_{t_{j_l}}([\![\sigma_{i_l}^{j_l}, n_{j_l})]\!]) \geqslant 2^{-k-1}$ for all l, and any X that contributes to this probability for l cannot contribute to it for $l' > l$, which is a contradiction. So for each n there is a j with $n_j > n$ such that for each $i \leqslant s$, we have $\sigma_i^j \upharpoonright n \prec B$ for some $B \in \mathcal{B}$.

Since $P(B) \geqslant 2^{-k}$ for all $B \in \mathcal{B}$, we know that B is finite. Let $B_0, \dots, B_l$ be its elements. By Lemma 16.2.6, and the fact that if n is large enough then the sets $[\![B_i \upharpoonright n]\!]$ are pairwise disjoint,

$$P(\mathcal{B}) = \lim_n \sum_{i \leqslant l} P([\![B_i \upharpoonright n]\!]).$$

By Lemma 16.2.7,

$$\sum_{i \leqslant l} P([\![B_i \upharpoonright n]\!]) = \lim_t \sum_{i \leqslant l} P_t([\![B_i \upharpoonright n]\!]).$$

Let j be such that $n_j > n$ and for each $i \leqslant s$ we have $\sigma_i^j \upharpoonright n \prec B_p$ for some $p \leqslant l$. Then

$$\begin{aligned}\sum_{i \leqslant l} P_t([\![B_i \upharpoonright n]\!]) &= P_t([\![B_0 \upharpoonright n]\!] \cup \cdots \cup [\![B_l \upharpoonright n]\!]) \\ &\geqslant P_t([\![\sigma_0^j]\!] \cup \cdots \cup [\![\sigma_s^j]\!]) = \sum_{i \leqslant s} P_t([\![\sigma_i^j]\!]) \geqslant \rho_{k+1} - 2^{-k-1},\end{aligned}$$

by the definition of opportune triple. Thus $\sum_{i \leqslant l} P([\![B_i \upharpoonright n]\!]) \geqslant \rho_{k+1} - 2^{-k-1}$ for all n, and hence $P(\mathcal{B}) \geqslant \rho_{k+1} - 2^{-k-1}$. □

As discussed above, the above lemma finishes the proof of Theorem 16.2.2. □

Finally, we prove Vereshchagin's Theorem 16.2.3.

Proof of Theorem 16.2.3. For a finite set B, let $S_t(B) = \{X : V^X[t] = B\}$ and $P_t(B) = \mu(S_t(B))$.

Lemma 16.2.10. *For all finite sets B, we have $P(B) = \lim_t P_t(B)$.*

Proof. Let S^1_t be the class of all X such $V^X[t] \supseteq B$ and S^2_t be the class of all $X \in S^1_t$ such that $V^X[t] \neq B$. Now the proof is as in Lemma 16.2.7. □

Given k, we will enumerate $O(2^{2k})$ many finite sets $C_0, \ldots, C_{N-1}$ so that at the end of step t of the enumeration, every finite set B with $P_t(B) \geqslant 2^{-k-1}$ coincides with $C_i[t]$ for some $i < N$. Suppose we can do so. If B is finite and $P(B) \geqslant 2^{-k}$, then by Lemma 16.2.10, $P_t(B) \geqslant 2^{-k-1}$ for almost all t, so for some i and infinitely many t, we have $C_i[t] = B$. Then $B = C_i$. So to describe B we need to provide only k and i, which requires fewer than $2H(A) + 2 \log H(A)$ many bits.

We perform our enumeration using Martin's game with $K = 2^k$ so that at the end of each step t, the following two conditions hold, where $(X_0[t], \ldots, X_{N-1}[t])$ is the configuration of the game at the end of step t.

(i) If $P_t(B) \geqslant 2^{-k-1}$ then $C_i[t] = B$ for some $i < N$.

(ii) For all $i < N$, we have $C_i[t] \subseteq V^X[t]$ for all $X \in X_i[t]$.

As before, we begin with $C_i[0] = \emptyset$ and $X_i[0] = 2^\omega$. At step $t+1$ we let $B_0, \ldots, B_s$ be all sets B such that $P_{t+1}(B) \geqslant 2^{-k-1}$ and play $Y = S_{t+1}(B_0)$ for player I in Martin's game. As before, let i be such that the computable winning strategy for player II replaces $X_i[t]$ by Y. Let $X_i[t+1] = Y$. Since $X_i[t] \cap Y \neq \emptyset$, there is an $X \in X_i[t]$ with $B_0 = V^X[t+1]$. By condition (ii), we have $C_i[t] \subseteq V^X[t] \subseteq V^X[t+1] = B_0$, so we can let $C_i[t+1] = B_0$. As before, we repeat this procedure for each $B_1, \ldots, B_s$ in turn, and at the end, for any i such that $X_i[t]$ is not replaced, let $X_i[t+1] = X_i[t]$ and $C_i[t+1] = C_i[t]$. This algorithm clearly has the necessary properties. □

16.3 The collection of nonrandom strings

16.3.1 The plain and conditional cases

Probably the most natural computably enumerable set associated with randomness is

$$\overline{R}_C = \{\sigma : C(\sigma) < |\sigma|\},^4$$

the collection of strings that are nonrandom relative to plain complexity. This set has been extensively studied by Kummer, Muchnik, Positselsky, Allender, and others. We have already seen in Chapter 3 that $\overline{R}_C$ is a simple c.e. set, and hence is not m-complete. On the other hand, it is easily seen to be Turing complete. (This is Exercise 2.63 in Li and Vitányi [248].) In this section we will prove the remarkable fact, due to Kummer [227],

[4]Strictly speaking, we should be studying $\{\sigma : C(\sigma) < |\sigma| + d\}$ where d is largest such that this set is co-infinite. For ease of notation, we will suppress this constant. This simplification does not alter the results we discuss in this section.

that $\overline{R}_C$ is in fact truth table complete, which is by no means obvious. In fact, the reduction built in Kummer's proof is a *conjunctive* tt-reduction. (A *conjunctive tt-reduction* from A to B is a computable function f such that for all n, we have $n \in A$ iff $D_{f(n)} \in B$.)

The problem with proving this result, roughly speaking, is as follows. Suppose that we are attempting to define a reduction from the halting problem $\emptyset'$ to $\overline{R}_C$ to show that $\emptyset' \leqslant_{\mathrm{tt}} \overline{R}_C$.

The most natural idea is to have a collection of strings F_n for each n and attempt to ensure that $F_n \subset \overline{R}_C$ iff $n \in \emptyset'$. If we choose F_n appropriately, if n enters $\emptyset'$ then we can lower the complexity of all elements of F_n and force them into $\overline{R}_C$. However, it can also happen that these complexities decrease without us doing anything, forcing all of F_n into $\overline{R}_C$ even though $n \notin \emptyset'$. This possibility is particularly hard to overcome because we need to specify the sets F_n ahead of time, since we are trying to build a tt-reduction. Furthermore, we cannot make the F_n too large. For example, we cannot take F_n to be *all* the strings of length n, since we cannot force them all into $\overline{R}_C$ if n enters $\emptyset'$. As we will see, Kummer used nonuniformity and a clever counting method to overcome this difficulty. His idea is the basis for other arguments such as Muchnik's Theorem 16.3.1 below.

In fact, we will begin with Muchnik's result, since the argument is simpler and the crucial use of nonuniformity more readily apparent, which should help make the ideas underlying Kummer's proof more transparent. We consider the *overgraph*

$$O_Q = \{(\sigma, \tau, n) : Q(\sigma \mid \tau) < n\}$$

for Q equal to K, Km, or C (or other similar complexity measures).

Theorem 16.3.1 (Muchnik, see [288]). *For any choice of Q, the overgraph O_Q is m-complete.*

Proof. We fix Q as C, but the proof works with easy modifications for other complexities. Let $O = O_C$, and let $O_s = \{(\sigma, \tau, n) : C_s(\sigma \mid \tau) < n\}$.

In the course of our construction, we will build a partial computable function f. By the recursion theorem, we assume we know a constant d such that if $f(\tau) = \sigma$ then $C(\sigma \mid \tau) < d$.

We will build partial functions $g_i : \mathbb{N} \to 2^{<\omega} \times 2^{<\omega} \times \mathbb{N}$ for $i < 2^d$. For the largest i such that $g_i(n)$ is defined for infinitely many n, we will be able to argue that, for all sufficiently large n, we can find a stage s such that either $n \in \emptyset'_s$, or $n \in \emptyset'$ iff $g_i(n) \in O$. Let i_0 be this i.

Let $\sigma_0, \ldots, \sigma_{2^d-1}$ be pairwise distinct strings. The values of g_i will be of the form (σ_i, τ, d). The basic idea is that we will be able to ensure for i_0 that, from some stage on, and for almost all n, the following occurs. First, we can find a stage s such that either $n \in \emptyset'_s$ or $g_{i_0}(n)$ is permanently defined at stage s as (σ_{i_0}, τ, d) for some τ. Next, if the latter case occurs and n enters $\emptyset'$ later on, then $f(\tau) = \sigma_{i_0}$, so $g_{i_0}(n) \in O$ by the choice of d. Finally, if n never enters $\emptyset'$, then $g_{i_0}(n) \notin O$. To ensure this last condition, we design the construction so that, if $g_{i_0}(n)$ enters O without n entering $\emptyset'$, then we define $g_j(m) = (\sigma_j, \tau, d)$ for some $j > i_0$, which cannot happen more than finitely often by the choice of i_0.

We now proceed with the construction.

Construction.

Initially, all strings are active. At stage s, proceed as follows.

For each active τ with $|\tau| \leqslant s$, find the least $i < 2^d$ such that $(\sigma_i, \tau, d) \notin O_s$, which must exist since $\{\sigma : (\sigma, \tau, d) \in O\} < 2^d$. For the least $n \notin \emptyset'_s$ such that g_i is not defined, let $g_i(n) = (\sigma_i, \tau, d)$. Undefine $g_j(m)$ for all $j < i$ and all m such that $g_j(m) = (\sigma_j, \tau, d)$. We say that i *acts* at stage s.

If n enters $\emptyset'$ at stage s, then for the largest i such that $g_i(n)$ is defined (if any), let τ be such that $g_i(n) = (\sigma_i, \tau, d)$, declare τ to be inactive, and let $f(\tau) = \sigma_i$.

End of Construction.

Let $i < 2^d$ be largest such that i acts at infinitely many stages. Let s_0 be a stage after which no $j > i$ ever acts. We describe an m-reduction from $\emptyset'$ to O.

Let n be large enough so that $g_i(n)$ is not defined at the end of stage s_0 and $g_j(n)$ is never defined for $j > i$. Search for a stage $s > s_0$ such that either $n \in \emptyset'_s$ or $g_i(n)$ becomes defined at stage s. It is clear from the construction that one of these events must occur. If it is the former, then we know that $n \in \emptyset'$. Otherwise, we claim that $g_i(n) \in O$ iff $n \in \emptyset'$.

If $n \in \emptyset'$, then n enters $\emptyset'$ at some stage $t > s$. At that stage, i is largest such that $g_i(n)$ is defined, so $f(\tau) = \sigma_i$, and hence $C(\sigma_i \mid \tau) < d$, which means that $g_i(n) = (\sigma_i, \tau, d) \in O$.

Conversely, suppose that $g_i(n) = (\sigma_i, \tau, d) \in O$. Assume for a contradiction that $n \notin \emptyset'$. At stage s, we cancel all $g_j(m)$ such that $j < i$ and $g_j(m) = (\sigma_j, \tau, d)$, and no $g_j(m)$ ever gets defined as (σ_j, τ, d) after that stage, so τ is permanently active. Let $t > s_0$ be such that $(\sigma_i, \tau, d) \in O_t$. We must have $(\sigma_j, \tau, d) \in O$ for $j < i$, since otherwise $g_i(n)$ would not have been defined as (σ_i, τ, d). But by the choice of s_0 and t, there cannot be a $j > i$ such that $(\sigma_j, \tau, d) \notin O_t$, since then the least such j would be active at t. So in fact $(\sigma_j, \tau, d) \in O$ for all $j < 2^d$, which is not possible. □

We now prove Kummer's Theorem. The construction has a finite set of parameters (the $i < 2^{d+1}$ below). We will build our tt-reduction based on the largest parameter selected infinitely often during the construction. The necessity of knowing this parameter to define the reduction is the source of the nonuniformity in the proof.

Theorem 16.3.2 (Kummer [227]). *$\overline{R}_C$ is truth table complete.*

Proof. We will define a plain machine Φ with constant d given by the recursion theorem. To do so, we will build uniformly c.e. sets of strings $E_0, E_1, \ldots$ such that for each n we have $E_n \subseteq 2^n$ and $|E_n| \leqslant 2^{n-d-1}$. Then for each n, if $\sigma \in E_n$ we can ensure that $\Phi(\tau) = \sigma$ for some $\tau \in 2^{n-d-1}$.

By doing so, we will ensure that for each n and $\sigma \in E_n$, we have $C(\sigma) \leqslant C_\Phi(\sigma) + d < n$, or, in other words, that $\bigcup_n E_n \in \overline{R}_C$.

To obtain our tt-reduction, for each $i < 2^{d-1}$, we will define a possibly infinite sequence of finite sets of strings $S_{i,0}, S_{i,1} \dots$. At the end of the proof we will argue that there is a largest i such that the corresponding sequence is infinite, and such that for almost all x, we have $x \in \emptyset'$ iff $S_{i,x} \subseteq \overline{R}_C$. Hence, we will have a tt-reduction (indeed, a conjunctive tt-reduction) from $\emptyset'$ to $\overline{R}_C$.

The definition of the $S_{i,x}$ has stronger priority than that of the $S_{j,y}$ for $j < i$. If $S_{j,y}$ is defined then all of its elements will have the same length, denoted by $m_{j,y}$. At a later stage, some stronger priority $S_{i,x}$ may assert control and occupy this length, in which case we will undefine $m_{j,y}$. (The idea here is that, for this situation to occur, the opponent will have had to make more strings of this length be nonrandom, and hence the new choice $S_{i,x}$ will be more likely to succeed. See condition (iii) in the construction below.) Finally, if $m_{i,x}$ is defined and x enters $\emptyset'$, then we will let $E_{m_{i,x}} = S_{i,x}$, ensuring that $S_{i,x} \subseteq \overline{R}_C$, since $\bigcup_n E_n \in \overline{R}_C$. We will then declare the value of $m_{i,x}$ to be *used*, and hence unavailable for future use.

We will also have to argue that if x never enters $\emptyset'$, then $S_{i,x} \nsubseteq \overline{R}_C$. The basic idea here is that we work with the largest i such that all $S_{i,x}$ are defined. We set up our conditions so that if $S_{i,x} \subseteq \overline{R}_C$, then this increase in the number of nonrandom strings of a particular length allows some $j > i$ to define a new $S_{j,y}$. So if this situation happens infinitely often, then we contradict the maximality of i.

We now proceed with the formal construction. Let $O_{n,s} = \{\sigma \in 2^n : C_s(\sigma) < n\}$.

Construction. Fix a parameter d.

Stage 0. Let $\ell(i) = 0$ for all i.

Stage $s+1$. Check whether there is an $i < 2^{d+1}$ and an $n \leqslant s$ such that

(i) n is unused and $n \geqslant d+1$,

(ii) $n \neq m_{j,x}$ for all $j \geqslant i$ and all x, and

(iii) $i2^{n-d-1} \leqslant |O_{n,s}|$.

If so, then choose the largest such i, and for this i the least such n, and then perform the following actions.

1. Declare $m_{j,x}$ to be undefined for all j and x such that $m_{j,x} = n$.
2. Let $S_{i,\ell(i)}$ be the set of the least k elements in $2^n \setminus O_{n,s}$, where $k = \min(2^n - |O_{n,s}|, 2^{n-d-1})$.
3. Let $m_{i,\ell(i)} = n$.
4. Increment $\ell(i)$ by 1.

For all j and x such that $x \in \emptyset'_{s+1}$ and $m_{j,x}$ is defined and unused, let $E_{m_{j,x}} = S_{j,x}$ and declare that $m_{j,x}$ is used.
End of Construction.

Clearly, the E_n are uniformly c.e. Furthermore, at any stage $s+1$, if $m_{j,x}$ is defined then $|S_{j,x}| \leqslant 2^{m_{j,x}-d-1}$, so $|E_n| \leqslant 2^{n-d-1}$ for all n. Thus we can define a plain machine Φ such that, for each n, if $\sigma \in E_n$ then $\Phi(\tau) = \sigma$ for some $\tau \in 2^{n-d-1}$. By the recursion theorem, we may assume that d is a coding constant of Φ, so that for each n and $\sigma \in E_n$, we have $C(\sigma) \leqslant C_\Phi(\sigma) + d < n$. In other words, $\bigcup_n E_n \in \overline{R}_C$.

Conditions (i)–(iii) in the construction always hold for $i = 0$ and $n = s$ (once $s \geqslant d+1$). So at every large enough stage some i is chosen. Since there are only 2^{d+1} many relevant i, there is a largest i such that i is chosen infinitely often. Let i_0 be this i. Let s_0 be such that no $j > i$ is ever chosen at a stage after s_0. Notice that $S_{i_0,x}$ is defined for all x, and if $x \neq y$ then the strings in $S_{i_0,x}$ and $S_{i_0,y}$ are of different lengths. Furthermore, once $m_{i_0,x}$ is defined at a stage after s_0, which must happen, then $m_{i_0,x}$ is never later undefined. So there is an x_0 such that for all $x \geqslant x_0$, once $m_{i_0,x}$ is defined, it is never later undefined.

Lemma 16.3.3. *Let $x \geqslant x_0$. If $x \in \emptyset'$, then $E_{m_{i_0,x}} = S_{i_0,x}$, while if $x \notin \emptyset'$, then $E_{m_{i_0,x}} = \emptyset$.*

Proof. Let s be the stage at which $m_{i_0,x}$ first becomes defined as a value n. Then n is unused at the beginning of stage s, whence $E_n = \emptyset$ at the beginning of that stage. Since $m_{i_0,x} = n$ at all later stages, E_n remains empty at all later stages unless x enters $\emptyset'$, in which case it is defined to be $S_{i_0,x}$. □

Corollary 16.3.4. *For every $x \geqslant x_0$, we have $x \in \emptyset'$ iff $S_{i_0,x} \subseteq \overline{R}_C$.*

Proof. As argued above, $\bigcup_n E_n \in \overline{R}_C$, so by the lemma, if $x \geqslant x_0$ and $x \in \emptyset'$, then $S_{i_0,x} \subseteq \overline{R}_C$.

For the other direction, assume for a contradiction that there is an $x \geqslant x_0$ such that $x \notin \emptyset'$ but $S_{i_0,x} \subseteq \overline{R}_C$. Let $s+1$ be the stage at which $m_{i_0,x}$ becomes defined. By construction, we have $|O_{n,s}| \geqslant i_0 2^{n-d-1}$ and $S_{i_0,x} \cap O_{n,s} = \emptyset$. By hypothesis, there is a stage $t > \max(s_0, s)$ such that $S_{i_0,x} \subseteq O_{n,t}$. Now, $|S_{i_0,x}|$ is either $2^n - |O_{n,s}|$ or 2^{n-d-1}. It cannot be the former, since then we would have $O_{n,t} = 2^n$, which is clearly impossible. So $|S_{i_0,x}| = 2^{n-d-1}$, and hence $|O_{n,t}| \geqslant (i_0+1)2^{n-d-1}$. Since $|O_{n,t}| < 2^n$, we have $i_0 + 1 < 2^{d+1}$. Thus conditions (i)–(iii) in the construction are satisfied at stage $t+1$ for $i = i_0 + 1$ and $n = t+1$, and hence the i chosen at stage $t+1$ is greater than i_0, contradicting the fact that $t > s_0$. □

It follows immediately from the corollary that $\emptyset' \leqslant_{tt} \overline{R}_C$. □

With a relatively straightforward modification of the previous proof (using suitable sets of strings L_n in place of 2^n), Kummer proved the following result, which applies to sets like $\{\sigma : C(\sigma) \leqslant \log|\sigma|\}$.

Theorem 16.3.5 (Kummer [227]). *Let f be computable, with $f(\sigma) \leqslant |\sigma|$ and $\lim_{|\sigma|} f(\sigma) = \infty$. Then the set $\{\sigma : C(\sigma) < f(\sigma)\}$ is conjunctive tt-complete.*

There has been some exciting work on efficient reductions to $\overline{R}_C$, such as that of Allender, Buhrman, Koucký, van Melkebeek, and Ronneburger, (see e.g. [4]), among others. These authors observed that the Kummer reduction, while having computable use, has exponential growth in the number of queries used. (It is known that, for instance, a polynomial number of queries cannot be achieved.) They asked what sets can be, say, polynomial time reduced to $\overline{R}_C$, as well as other time- and space-bounded variants of this question. Amazingly, these questions seem to have bearing on basic separation problems between complexity classes. For instance, PSPACE $\subseteq \mathrm{P}^{\overline{R}_C}$. The methods used in this work are highly nontrivial, and beyond the scope of this book.

16.3.2 The prefix-free case

As in defining a notion of randomness for strings using prefix-free complexity (see Section 3.8), we have two reasonable analogs of $\overline{R}_C$ in the prefix-free case. Let

$$\overline{R}_K^{\mathrm{str}} = \{\sigma : K(\sigma) < |\sigma| + K(|\sigma|)\}$$

(the set of non-strongly K-random strings) and

$$\overline{R}_K = \{\sigma : K(\sigma) < |\sigma|\}$$

(the set of non-weakly K-random strings).

Clearly $\overline{R}_K$ is c.e., but it had been a long-standing open question, going back to Solovay [371], whether $\overline{R}_K^{\mathrm{str}}$ is c.e. This question was answered by Miller [271].

Theorem 16.3.6 (Miller [271]). *Fix $c \geqslant 0$ and let $B = \{\sigma : K(\sigma) < |\sigma| + K(|\sigma|) - c\}$. Let $A \supseteq B$ be such that $|A \cap 2^n| \leqslant 2^{n-1}$ for all n. Then A is not c.e.*

Before proving this theorem, we point out two consequences. The first one, which follows immediately from the theorem, answers Solovay's question.

Corollary 16.3.7. *For all $c \geqslant 0$, the set $\{\sigma : K(\sigma) < |\sigma| + K(|\sigma|) - c\}$ is not c.e.*

Miller [271] pointed out that Theorem 16.3.6 also gives a weak form of Solovay's theorem that there are strings that are C-random but not strongly K-random, Corollary 4.3.8. While the following result is weaker than Solovay's, its proof is much easier.

Corollary 16.3.8. *Let $c \geqslant 0$ and $d > 0$. There is a string that is C-random with constant d but not strongly K-random with constant c.*

Proof. If this is not the case, then the set B in Theorem 16.3.6 is contained in $A = \{\sigma : C(\sigma) < |\sigma| - d\}$. But A is c.e. and $|A \cap 2^n| < 2^{n-d}$ for all n, contradicting the theorem. □

Proof of Theorem 16.3.6. Assume for a contradiction that A is c.e. We build a KC set L to define a prefix-free machine M, with coding constant k given by the recursion theorem. For any s and n such that $K_s(n) < K_{s-1}(n)$, find $2^{n-k-c-2}$ many strings of length n that are not in A_s, which exist by hypothesis, and for each such string τ, enumerate $(n + K_s(n) - k - c - 1, \tau)$ into L. It is easy to check that L is indeed a KC set.

If $K_{s-1}(n) \neq K(n)$, then our definition of M ensures that at least $2^{n-k-c-2}$ many strings of length n that are not in A_s are each compressed by at least $c + 1$ many bits. These strings must then eventually be added to B, and hence to A, so $|A \cap 2^n| \geqslant |A_s \cap 2^n| + 2^{n-k-c-2}$.

Let b be greatest such that $|A \cap 2^n| \geqslant b2^{n-k-c-2}$ for infinitely many n. Define a partial computable function f as follows. If $|A_s \cap 2^n| \geqslant b2^{n-k-c-2}$, then let $f(n) = K_s(n)$. By the argument above and the choice of b, for almost all n, if $f(n)$ is defined then $f(n) = K(n)$. Furthermore, the choice of b guarantees that f has infinite domain. Thus, by changing finitely many values of f, we have a partial computable function with infinite domain that is equal to $K(n)$ wherever is it is defined, contradicting Proposition 3.5.5. □

Let us now turn to $\overline{R}_K$. This set is c.e., and it is also clearly Turing complete. But is it tt-complete? An. A. Muchnik (see [288]) showed that the answer may be negative, depending on the choice of universal machine. (We will see later that the answer may also be positive for other choices of universal machine.) Thus we will consider the set $\overline{R}_K^U$ for a particular universal prefix-free machine U, which is $\overline{R}_K$ when K is defined using U. Muchnik also considered the *overgraph* of K, that is, the set

$$O_K^U = \{(\sigma, n) : K(\sigma) < n\},$$

where K is defined using U. Of course, Kummer's Theorem 16.3.2 implies that the overgraph of C, that is, the set $O_C = \{(\sigma, n) : C(\sigma) < n\}$, is tt-complete independent of the choice of universal machine, but Muchnik showed that the situation is different for K. Part (ii) of the proof below has a number of interesting new ideas, especially casting complexity considerations in the context of games on finite directed graphs.

Theorem 16.3.9 (Muchnik, see [288]). *There exist universal prefix-free machines*[5] *V and U such that*

(i) *O_K^V is tt-complete but*

(ii) *O_K^U (and hence $\overline{R}_K^U$) is not tt-complete.*

Proof. (i) We define V using our fixed universal prefix-free machine $\mathcal{U}$. Let $g(k) = k$ if k is even and $g(k) = k+1$ is k is odd. Let

$$L = \{(g(k)+3, \sigma) : K_{\mathcal{U}}(\sigma) \leqslant k\} \cup \{(g(k)+2, 0^n) : K_{\mathcal{U}}(0^n) \leqslant k \wedge n \in \emptyset'\}.$$

Then L is clearly a KC set. Let V be the prefix-free machine corresponding to L. Then V is universal, and $n \in \emptyset'$ iff $K_V(0^n)$ is even. If c is such that $K_V(0^n) \leqslant \log n + c$ for all n, then $K_V(0^n)$ can be determined by querying O_K^V on $(k, 0^n)$ for $k \leqslant \log n + c$, and hence $\emptyset' \leqslant_{\text{tt}} O_K^V$.

(ii) This argument is much more difficult. We will follow Muchnik's proof, which uses strategies for finite games. It may well be possible to remove this feature of the proof, but it is an interesting technique in its own right.

The kind of game we will consider here is determined by

1. a finite set of positions (vertices),
2. a set of allowable moves for each of the two players,
3. two complementary subsets of the positions, S_1 and S_2, and
4. an initial position d_0.

The set of moves will allow players to stay in the same position, but will not allow a position to be returned to once it is left.

The game begins at position d_0, and the two players play in turns, making allowable moves from one position to another. Since positions cannot be returned to once left, the game must stabilize at some stage, and if that stable position is in S_i, then player i wins.

Clearly this game is determined, and we can effectively find a winning strategy for one of the players.[6]

[5] A minor issue here is that, as built in the following proof, V and U will not necessarily be universal by adjunction, as defined in Section 3.1. Fortunately, it is easy to get around this problem. Suppose that M is a universal prefix-free machine and c is such that $K_M(\sigma) \leqslant K(\sigma) + c$ for all σ, where K is defined using the standard prefix-free machine $\mathcal{U}$. Let τ be such that $[\![\tau]\!] \cap \operatorname{dom} M = \emptyset$ and $|\tau| > c$. Let M' be defined by letting $M'(\tau\rho) = \mathcal{U}(\rho)$ and $M'(\nu) = M(\nu)$ for all other ν. Then M' is universal by adjunction and $O_K^{M'} = O_K^M$.

[6] One procedure for doing so is to consider the set of all positions $d \neq d_0$ such that (d_0, d) is an allowable move by player 1, then for each such d consider a separate game defined like the original one but starting from d, and with the order of the players reversed. We can then continue to define residual games of this kind with fewer and fewer positions, and finally work backwards to construct a winning strategy for one of

We will construct a Σ_1^0 function F and define $H(\sigma) = \min\{K(\sigma) + 2, F(\sigma)\}$. We will show that $\sum_\sigma 2^{-H(\sigma)} \leqslant 1$, and hence we can use the KC Theorem to build a corresponding prefix-free machine U, which will clearly be universal. We will also construct a computably enumerable set W such that $W \not\leqslant_{tt} O_K^U$. Let Γ_n denote the nth partial truth table reduction. We will construct the diagonalizing set W as a set of triples $\langle n, i, j\rangle$, using those with first coordinate n to diagonalize against Γ_n.

In the construction, we will have numbers i_n and j_n and a finite game G_n associated with n. Each time n is considered, we can either let one of the players play the current game G_n, or we can change both G_n and the numbers i_n and j_n. The positions of a game G_n will be determined by a finite set of strings A_n, a set of functions $A_n \to \mathbb{N}$, and a set of pairs of rational numbers.

The idea is the following. We wait until Γ_n provides us with a truth table for the input $\langle n, i_n, j_n\rangle$. This truth table will query O_K^U for certain (σ, k). We let A_n be the set of all such σ, except for those already in A_m for $m < n$. We now define the game G_n to consist of positions (h, q, p) where the $h : A_n \to \mathbb{N}$ are potential values of H on A_n, and q and p are rationals encoding how much making H equal to such an h on A_n would cost in terms of the change to $\sum_\sigma 2^{-H(\sigma)}$. Each h, and hence each position, can be used to provide a guess as to the values of O_K^U queried by Γ_n on input $\langle n, i_n, j_n\rangle$, by assuming that H equals h on A_n. (More precisely, we need to take h together with values corresponding to strings in A_m for $m < n$. We assume these values are fixed. If that is not the case, then we will eventually cancel our game and start a new one). Thus we can divide such positions into sets X_0 and X_1 such that X_i consists of those positions that guess that $\Gamma_n^{O_K^U}(\langle n, i_n, j_n\rangle) = i$. Either player 1 has a winning strategy to eventually stabilize the game in a position in X_0, or player 2 has a winning strategy to eventually stabilize the game in a position in X_1. But in the latter case, player 1 can stay in position d_0 in its first move, and then emulate player 2's winning strategy. So for some $i = 0, 1$, player 1 has a winning strategy to eventually stabilize the game in a position in X_i. Player 1 adopts that strategy for its moves in G_n. If $i = 0$, then we put $\langle n, i_n, j_n\rangle$ into W. If $i = 1$, then we keep $\langle n, i_n, j_n\rangle$ out of W. This action will ensure that, if player 1 can carry out its strategy, then $\Gamma_n^{O_K^U}(\langle n, i_n, j_n\rangle) \neq W(\langle n, i_n, j_n\rangle)$, because in that case F will be defined to ensure that H is actually equal to h on A_n for the value of h such that G_n stabilizes on some (h, q, p).

Player 1's moves will determine the value of F (or, more precisely, the approximation F_s to F) on A_n, and hence will have to be carefully bounded to ensure that $\sum_\sigma 2^{-H(\sigma)} \leqslant 1$. Player 2's moves will be determined by the value of K_s on A_n. The rational q will code how much has been spent

---

the players. See for instance Khoussainov and Nerode [202] for more details on finite games.

on changing F, and the rational p will code how much of the measure of the standard universal prefix-free machine has been spent by player 2 in changing K_s at strings in A_n. We place a bound on p and q. If stronger priority strategies (those working for Γ_m with $m < n$) do not intervene, then either player 1 will be able to complete its strategy, or the approximation to the values of K on string in A_n will change so much that player 2 will want to violate the rules of the game (by moving to an (h, q, p) where p is above our bound). In that case we cancel the game and start a new one. This situation will occur only finitely often, since each time it does, it causes a large change in the values of K on A_n.

We begin with $i_n = j_n = 0$. Each time we reconsider n, we increase the value of i_n by 1 if there is a number $m < n$ such that either the position of G_m changed or G_m itself changed since the last time we considered n. If a change in the estimate of K_s violates the rules of G_n, as explained below, we increase the value of j_n by 1. The bound on p and q decreases every time i_n changes, but not when j_n changes.

Construction. Initially, $F_0(\sigma) = \infty$ for all σ and all games G_n and sets A_n are undefined.

Stage $s = \langle n, e\rangle$. If $e = 0$, let $i_n = j_n = 0$. Otherwise, check whether there is an $m < n$ such that either the position of G_m has changed since stage $\langle n, e-1\rangle$ or G_m has been redefined since that stage. If so, then undefine G_n and increase i_n by 1.

Case 1. G_n is not defined. Run s many steps in the computation of the table $\gamma_n(\langle n, i_n, j_n\rangle)$ for the reduction Γ_n with argument $\langle n, i_n, j_n\rangle$. If no table is produced, then G_n is undefined and we end the stage, with $F_{s+1}(\sigma) = F_s(\sigma)$ for all σ.

Otherwise, we define the game G_n. The queries made by $\gamma_n(\langle n, i_n, j_n\rangle)$ will be of the form (σ, k). Let B_n be the set of first coordinates of such queries. Let $A_n = B_n \setminus \bigcup_{m<n} A_m$, where we take $A_m = \emptyset$ if A_m is undefined.

Let $h_0(\sigma) = \min\{K_s(\sigma) + 2, F_s(\sigma)\}$ for $\sigma \in A_n$ and let $q_0 = \sum_{\sigma\in A_n} 2^{-h_0(\sigma)}$. Let S_n be the set of all functions $h : A_n \to \mathbb{N}$ such that $h(\sigma) \leqslant h_0(\sigma)$ for all $\sigma \in A_n$ and $(\sum_{\sigma\in A_n} 2^{-h(\sigma)}) - q_0 < 2^{-(n+i_n+3)}$. Note that S_n is nonempty and finite. Let R_n be the set of all rationals of the form $(\sum_{\sigma\in A_n} 2^{-h(\sigma)}) - q_0$ for $h \in S_n$. The set of positions of G_n is $S_n \times R_n \times R_n$. The initial position d_0 is $(h, 0, 0)$.

The rules of play are that player 1 can move from position (h, q, p) to position (h', q', p) if $h'(\sigma) \leqslant h(\sigma)$ for all $\sigma \in A_n$, and $q' - q = \sum_{\sigma\in A_n} 2^{-h'(\sigma)} - \sum_{\sigma\in A_n} 2^{-h(\sigma)}$ (so a move by player 1 cannot change the third coordinate) and player 2 can move from position (h, q, p) to position (h', q', p) if $h'(\sigma) \leqslant h(\sigma)$ for all $\sigma \in A_n$, and $p' - p = \sum_{\sigma\in A_n} 2^{-h'(\sigma)} - \sum_{\sigma\in A_n} 2^{-h(\sigma)}$ (so a move by player 1 cannot change the second coordinate).

Now we split the positions of G_n into two sets X_0 and X_1. Let $h \in S_n$. For $\sigma \in B_n \setminus A_n$, let $h(\sigma) = \min\{K_s(\sigma)+2, F_s(\sigma)\}$. Let $Q = \{(\sigma, k) : h(\sigma) < k\}$. Now compute $i = \Gamma^Q(\langle n, i_n, j_n\rangle)$ and put all positions (h, q, p) into X_i. As discussed above, for some $i = 0, 1$, player 1 has a winning strategy to eventually stabilize the game in a position in X_i. Player 1 adopts that strategy for its moves in G_n. If $i = 0$, then we put $\langle n, i_n, j_n \rangle$ into W. If $i = 1$, then we keep $\langle n, i_n, j_n \rangle$ out of W.

We have now defined G_n, and we end the stage, with $F_{s+1}(\sigma) = F_s(\sigma)$ for all σ.

Case 2. G_n is defined. Then first let player 1 make a move according to its strategy. This move will be from a position (h, q, p) to a position (h', q', p). If $h'(\sigma) < h(\sigma)$, then let $F_{s+1}(\sigma) = h'(\sigma)$. For all other σ, let $F_{s+1}(\sigma) = F_s(\sigma)$.

Now let player 2 move as follows. Let (h', q', p) be the current position. Let $h'' = \min\{K_s(\sigma) + 2, F_{s+1}(\sigma)\}$ for $\sigma \in A_n$. If there is a position (h'', q', p'') that player 2 can move to, then do so. Otherwise, player 2 has violated the rules of the game, so undefine G_n and A_n. In either case, end the stage.

End of Construction.

Let $H_s(\sigma) = \min\{K_s(\sigma) + 2, F_s(\sigma)\}$ and let $H(\sigma) = \lim_s H_s(\sigma)$. Let $O = \{(\sigma, k) : H(\sigma) < k\}$.

Assume by induction that there is a least stage $t = \langle n, e \rangle$ such that i_n is never incremented after stage t, and that for all A_m with $m < n$ defined at stage t (which by the first hypothesis are all the A_m that will ever be defined from that stage on), we have $H_s(\sigma) = H(\sigma)$ for all $\sigma \in A_m$.

Suppose that a version of G_n is first defined at stage $s \geqslant t$. If player 2 never violates the rules of that game, then the game will eventually stabilize in a position (h, q, p), say by stage $u = \langle n, e' \rangle$. By construction, for all $\sigma \in A_n$, we have $H(\sigma) = H_u(\sigma) = h(\sigma)$, since any change in such an H-value at stage u or later would correspond to a move by at least one of the players in G_n, or cause the game to become undefined. So if we let X_0 and X_1 be as defined in the construction at stage u and let i be such that $(h, q, p) \in X_i$, then $\Gamma^O(\langle n, i_n, j_n \rangle) = i$. Since in this case we ensured that $W(\langle n, i_n, j_n \rangle) = 1 - i$, we have $\Gamma^O \neq W$.

Let h_0 and q_0 be as in the construction at the stage s at which G_n was defined. Suppose that at stage $v = \langle n, k \rangle \geqslant s$ we reach position (h, q, p) by the end of the stage, and then at stage $v' = \langle n, k+1 \rangle$ we reach position (h', q', p'). Then it is easy to check from the construction that $p' \leqslant \sum_{\sigma \in A_n} 2^{-K_{v'}(\sigma)-2} - \sum_{\sigma \in A_n} 2^{-K_v(\sigma)-2}$. Thus, if player 2 ever violates the rules of G_n at stage w, then $\sum_{\sigma \in A_n} 2^{-K_w(\sigma)-2} - \sum_{\sigma \in A_n} 2^{-K_s(\sigma)-2} \geqslant 2^{-(n+i_n+3)}$. So this situation can occur only finitely often.

Thus, either from some point on G_n is permanently undefined, in which case Γ is not total and the inductive hypotheses clearly hold of n, or there is a final version of G_n which, as explained above, eventually stabilizes and ensures that $\Gamma^O \neq W$. In either case, the induction can continue.

Thus, all that is left to prove is that $\sum_\sigma 2^{-H(\sigma)} \leqslant 1$. Then, using the KC Theorem, we get a prefix-free machine U corresponding to H, which is clearly universal by the definition of H. For this U, we have $O = O_K^U$, whence O_K^U is not tt-complete.

Since $\sum_\sigma 2^{-(K(\sigma)+2)} < \frac{1}{4}$, it is enough to show that $r = \sum_\sigma 2^{-F(\sigma)} \leqslant \frac{3}{4}$.

Suppose that $\sigma \in A_n$ at some stage. Then for the current version of G_n, one of three things happens. Either

1. G_n is eventually canceled by i_n being increased, or
2. G_n is eventually canceled by player 2 violating its rules, or
3. G_n is permanently defined.

Let s_0 be the stage at which the current version of G_n was defined. It is easy to see by construction that until G_n is canceled (if ever), $2^{-F_s(\sigma)} - 2^{-F_{s_0}(\sigma)} < 2^{-(n+i_n+3)}$. Thus the amount added to r in cases 1 and 2 is at most $2^{-(n+i_n+3)}$ (and note that these cases cannot occur more than once for the same value of i_n). Furthermore, if case 2 happens at stage s then we must have $2^{-F_s(\sigma)} - 2^{-F_{s_0}(\sigma)} < 2^{-(n+i_n+3)} \leqslant \sum_{\tau \in A_n} 2^{-K_s(\tau)-2} - \sum_{\tau \in A_m} 2^{-K_{s_0}(\tau)-2}$. Since no string can be in two different A_m's at the same stage, we see that the sum of $2^{-F_s(\sigma)} - 2^{-F_{s_0}(\sigma)}$ over all situations in which case 2 occurs is bounded by $\sum_\tau 2^{-K(\tau)-2}$. Thus we have

$$\sum_\sigma 2^{-F(\sigma)} \leqslant \sum_n \sum_i 2^{-(n+i+3)} + \sum_\tau 2^{-K(\tau)-2} < \frac{1}{2} + \frac{1}{4} = \frac{3}{4}.$$

□

One of the original uses Muchnik made of the construction above was to show that for each d there are strings σ and τ such that $K(\sigma) > K(\tau) + d$ and $C(\tau) > C(\sigma) + d$, Theorem 4.4.1. A particularly interesting feature of this approach is that it uses a construction that depends on the choice of a particular universal machine to prove a fact that is independent of any such choice.

Allender, Buhrman, and Koucký [3] built a universal machine that makes the collection of non-C-random strings tt-complete. They noted that their proof technique can also be used for prefix-free machines, and indeed it is generalizable to other kinds of machines as well. We give a proof due to Day [personal communication], though the original proof contained similar ideas. This proof covers at once the cases of prefix-free machines, process machines (normal and strict), and monotone machines (for Km and for KM).

Theorem 16.3.10 (Allender, Buhrman, and Koucký [3], also Day [personal communication]). *Let Q be any of the following complexity measures: C, K, Km, KM, Km_D, or Km_S. There is a universal machine U for Q such that set of nonrandom strings $\overline{R}_Q^U$ is tt-complete.*

Proof. We will do the proof for the case $Q = Km$, and note at the end that it works in the other cases as well.

For a monotone machine M, let $Km_M = \min\{|\tau| : \sigma \preccurlyeq M(\tau)\downarrow\}$ and $\overline{R}_i^M = \{\sigma : Km_M(\sigma) \leqslant |\sigma| - i\}$. We will use the following lemma.

Lemma 16.3.11. *If M is a monotone machine then $\mu([\![\overline{R}_i^M]\!]) \leqslant 2^{-i}$ for all i.*

Proof. Let M be a monotone machine and fix i. Let $A \subseteq \overline{R}_i^M$ be the set of minimal elements of $\overline{R}_i^M$ under the $\preccurlyeq$ relation. For each $\sigma \in A$ let σ' be a minimal-length string such that $\sigma \preccurlyeq M(\sigma')$. Since A is prefix-free, so is $A' = \{\sigma' : \sigma \in A\}$. Thus $\mu([\![\overline{R}_i^M]\!]) = \mu([\![A]\!]) = \sum_{\sigma\in A} 2^{-|\sigma|} \leqslant \sum_{\sigma\in A} 2^{-Km_M(\sigma)-i} = 2^{-i}\sum_{\sigma\in A} 2^{-|\sigma'|} \leqslant 2^{-i}$. □

The idea behind this proof is to construct a universal machine V that describes strings symmetrically; that is to say, if σ has a description of length n, then $\overline{\sigma}$ has a description of length n as well (where $\overline{\sigma}$ is the string of length $|\sigma|$ defined by $\overline{\sigma}(n) = 1 - \sigma(n)$). Then given V, we will build another universal machine U but break the symmetry of the set of nonrandom strings in U in order to encode $\emptyset'$.

Given a universal monotone machine $\mathcal{M}$, first construct another universal machine V as follows. Each time a pair (τ, σ) enters $\mathcal{M}$, add $(0\tau, \sigma)$ and $(1\tau, \overline{\sigma})$ to V. This symmetrical construction means that the machine V has the property that $\tau \in \overline{R}_i^V$ if and only if $\overline{\tau} \in \overline{R}_i^V$, for all i.

We will construct another universal machine U from V and a prefix-free machine M as follows. We will let $U(00\sigma) = V(\sigma)$ for all σ. We will also define M and let $U(1\sigma) = M(\sigma)$ for all σ. The job of the machine M is to break the symmetry of U in certain places to encode $\emptyset'$ into $\overline{R}_{Km}^U$. To do so, we will make use of a computable sequence of natural numbers D and the KC Theorem.

At stage 0, let $M_0 = \emptyset$, and let D be the empty sequence.

At stage $2s+1$, ensure that for all (τ, σ) in V_s, we have $(00\tau, \sigma) \in U_{2s+1}$.

At stage $2s+2$, let

$$X_s = \emptyset'_s \cap \{x : |2^{x+4} \cap \overline{R}_1^{U_{2s+1}}| \text{ is even}\}.$$

Let $x_0, \ldots, x_n$ be the elements of X_s. Let l be the current length of the sequence D. For each $i \leqslant n$, extend the sequence D by letting $d_{l+i} = x_i + 2$. For each i, use the KC Theorem to find a string σ_{l+i} such that we can define $M(\sigma_{l+i}) = 11\sigma_{l+1}$ while keeping M prefix-free. We will argue below that we do not run out of room for such strings. Enumerate $(1\sigma_{l+i}, 11\sigma_{l+i})$ into U, which ensures that $11\sigma_{l+i}$ is nonrandom with respect to U. Note that $|11\sigma_{l+i}| = 2 + |\sigma_{l+i}| = 2 + d_{l+i} = x_i + 4$. The idea here is to attempt to make $|2^{x_i+4} \cap \overline{R}_1^{U_{2s+2}}|$ odd by adding a new string to $\overline{R}_1^{U_{2s+2}}$ of length $x_i + 4$.

To verify that this construction succeeds, we will show in the following lemma that each KC request we make can be honored. This lemma is the essence of the proof. The following is the basic reason it holds. Given any

x, assume we request some string σ of length $x+2$. We need to request another string of length $x+2$ only if $\overline{11\sigma}$ becomes nonrandom. However, this situation must be caused by a description coming from V of length no greater than $|11\sigma|-3$ (because of how V is coded into U), and we can bound the measure of all such descriptions.

Lemma 16.3.12. $\sum_i 2^{-d_i} \leqslant 1$.

Proof. Let $d_0, \dots, d_n$ be any initial segment of the sequence D. Let I be the set of numbers that occur in $d_0, \dots, d_n$. Note that the elements of I are all greater than or equal to 2. For each $i \in I$, let k_i be the index of the last occurrence of i in the sequence. Let $K = \{k_i : i \in I\}$. As $0, 1 \notin I$, we have $\sum_{i \in K} 2^{-d_i} < \frac{1}{2}$.

Let $J = \{0, \dots, n\} \setminus K$. If $j \in J$, then $d_k = d_j$ for some $k > j$. So at some stage after d_j is defined, $|2^{d_j+2} \cap \overline{R}_1^{U_s}|$ is even again. Taking $\sigma = 11\sigma_j$, this situation can happen only if $\overline{\sigma}$ enters $\overline{R}_1^U$. Thus, $\overline{\sigma} \in \overline{R}_3^V$ and so $\sigma \in \overline{R}_3^V$. Thus $\{11\sigma_j : j \in J\} \subseteq \overline{R}_3^V$. Now, because $\{11\sigma_j : j \in J\}$ is a prefix-free set,

$$\sum_{i \in J} 2^{-d_i-2} = \sum_{i \in J} 2^{-|11\sigma_i|} = \mu([\![\{11\sigma_i : i \in J\}]\!]) \leqslant \mu(\overline{R}_3^V) \leqslant \frac{1}{8}.$$

Thus $\sum_{i \in J} 2^{-d_i} \leqslant \frac{1}{2}$ and so $\sum_{i \leqslant n} 2^{-d_i} = \sum_{i \in K} 2^{-d_i} + \sum_{i \in J} 2^{-d_i} < \frac{1}{2} + \frac{1}{2} = 1$. Hence $\sum_i 2^{-|d_i|} = \lim_n \sum_{i \leqslant n} 2^{-|d_i|} \leqslant 1$. □

Lemma 16.3.13. *$x \in \emptyset'$ iff $|2^{x+4} \cap \overline{R}^U|$ is odd.*

Proof. If $x \notin \emptyset'$ then $x \notin X_s$ for all s, so if σ is any string of length $x+4$ in $\overline{R}_1^U$, then $\sigma \in \overline{R}_3^V$, and hence $\overline{\sigma} \in \overline{R}_3^V$ and $\overline{\sigma} \in \overline{R}_1^U$. Thus $|2^{x+4} \cap \overline{R}^U|$ is even.

If $x \in \emptyset'$, then let $I = \{s : x \in X_s\}$. The set I is finite because $\sum_i 2^{-d_i}$ converges, so let $s_0 = \max(I)$. If $t > 2s_0 + 2$, then $|2^{x+4} \cap \overline{R}_1^{U_t}|$ is odd, and thus $|2^{x+4} \cap \overline{R}^U|$ is odd. □

Lemma 16.3.11 will still hold if Km is replaced by KM. It will also hold if a universal prefix-free machine, a universal strict process machine, or a universal process machine is used instead of a universal monotone machine (with K, Km_S, or Km_D as the respective complexity measures), since prefix-free machines, process machines, and strict process machines are all monotone machines. As the machine M built in the above proof is a prefix-free machine (and so also a (strict) process machine), the same construction can be used to prove all the cases in the statement of the theorem. □

16.3.3 The overgraphs of universal monotone machines

In this section, we present results of Day [88] on the overgraph relation for monotone and process complexity. The first result answers a question posed by Muchnik and Positselsky [288]. As above, for a monotone machine M, let $Km_M = \min\{|\tau| : \sigma \preccurlyeq M(\tau)\downarrow\}$ and define the overgraph O^M_{Km} to be $\{(\sigma, k) : Km_M(\sigma) < k\}$. Recall from Theorem 3.16.2 that for a universal monotone machine U, the function M_U defined by $M_U(\sigma) = \mu([\![\{\tau : \exists \sigma' \succcurlyeq \sigma\,((\tau, \sigma') \in U)\}]\!])$ is an optimal c.e. continuous semimeasure.

Theorem 16.3.14 (Day [88]). *For any universal monotone machine U, the overgraph O^U_{Km} is tt-complete.*

Proof. We will construct a monotone machine M whose index d in U is known by the recursion theorem. To give this proof the widest possible applicability, we will make M a strict process machine (which recall means that if $\tau \in \mathrm{dom}(M)$ and $\tau' \preccurlyeq \tau$, then $\tau' \in \mathrm{dom}(M)$ and $M(\tau') \preccurlyeq M(\tau)$). In addition to M, we need to build a truth table reduction Γ. For this proof, we will omit the Km subscript and write O^M for O^M_{Km}. This notation allows us to use the subscript position as follows: For a monotone machine M, let $O^M_k = \{\sigma : (\sigma, k) \in O^M\}$.

Our truth table reduction will work as follows. For each x, a set of strings S_x will be specified. The reduction will determine which strings are in O^U_{d+x} and make a decision as to whether or not $x \in \emptyset'$ based on this information.

The simplest thing to do would be to try to encode the fact that x enters $\emptyset'$ by adding all of S_x to O^U_{d+x}. However, we run against the same problem as in proving Kummer's Theorem 16.3.2, that the opponent could wait until S_x is defined, then add all of it to O^U_{d+x} and withhold x from $\emptyset'$. In fact, given any truth table reduction Γ, the opponent can choose an x, wait until the truth table used by $\Gamma(x)$ is defined, and then adopt a winning strategy to ensure either that $\Gamma^{O^U}(x) = 0$ or that $\Gamma^{O^U}(x) = 1$. By adding x to $\emptyset'$ in the first case and keeping it out in the second case, the opponent could ensure $\Gamma^{O^U}(x) \neq \emptyset'(x)$.

We overcome this problem as in the proof of Theorem 16.3.2 by making the reduction nonuniform. In this case, we will allow it to be wrong on some initial segment of $\emptyset'$. The reduction will be constructed in such a way that the cost to the opponent of making the reduction incorrect for any x is so significant that the reduction can be incorrect only a finite number of times.

The strict process machine M we use for adding pairs to the overgraph will be constructed as follows. For each $\tau \in 2^x$ we will choose some σ_τ, so that $\{\sigma_\tau : \tau \in 2^x\}$ is a prefix-free set. The pairs (τ, σ_τ) will be candidates for addition to our machine. We will make sure that if $\tau' \prec \tau$, then either $\sigma_{\tau'} \preccurlyeq \sigma_\tau$ or $(\tau', \sigma_{\tau'})$ is never added to M. If we decide to add (τ, σ_τ) to M, then $Km(\sigma_\tau) \leqslant |\tau| + d = x + d$, and hence $\sigma_\tau \in O^U_{d+x}$.

Now, the opponent has the ability to add σ_τ to O^U_{d+x} as well. If the opponent does this, then it must have increased the measure on σ_τ, i.e., set $M_U(\llbracket\sigma_\tau\rrbracket)$ to at least 2^{-d-x}. Provided we have not described any extension of σ_τ with M, we can now bypass this measure spent by the universal machine. Bypassing the measure allows us to ensure the reduction works on almost all inputs. We wait until an appropriate stage s when we have some lower bound on the measure that we can bypass. When we define S_s, we ensure that σ_υ does not extend σ_τ for all $\upsilon \in 2^s$. Instead we will let such σ_υ extend some ρ_τ incompatible with σ_τ.

However, the opponent still has one last trick up its sleeve. Before it adds some string σ_τ to $O^U_{d+|\tau|}$, it can try to force us to enumerate some $(\tau', \sigma_{\tau'})$ into M with $\sigma_\tau \preccurlyeq \sigma_{\tau'}$. Doing so would prevent us from bypassing the measure the opponent spends on σ_τ, because if $\tau' \prec \upsilon$, then we must have $\sigma_\tau \prec \sigma_{\tau'} \prec \sigma_\upsilon$. The following reduction Γ is designed to minimize the problem this situation causes.

The reduction Γ will be defined as follows. First $\Gamma(0) = 0$. If $x \neq 0$, then at stage x in the construction, a set S_x will be defined. This set will have 2^x many elements and will be indexed by 2^x so that for each $\tau \in 2^x$ there is a unique string $\sigma_\tau \in S_x$. Let $\overline{\tau}$ be the string of length $|\tau|$ defined by $\overline{\tau}(k) = 1 - \tau(k)$. To determine whether $x \in \emptyset'$, the reduction Γ runs the construction until S_x is defined and then determines which elements of the set S_x are in O^U_{d+x}. If $S_x \subseteq O^U_{d+x}$, then $\Gamma(x) = 0$. Otherwise Γ finds the leftmost $\tau \in 2^x$ such that either

1. exactly one of σ_τ and $\sigma_{\overline{\tau}}$ are in O^U_{d+x}, in which case $\Gamma(x) = 1$; or
2. neither σ_τ nor $\sigma_{\overline{\tau}}$ are in O^U_{d+x}, in which case $\Gamma(x) = 0$.

This reduction can be thought of as checking pairs of strings in a certain order. For example, consider S_3. First the reduction checks whether σ_{000} and σ_{111} are in O^U_{d+3}. If they are not both in then the reduction can give an answer immediately. If they are both in, then the reduction checks whether σ_{001} and σ_{110} are in, and so on. This process can be described simply by looking at the indices of the σ's involved, e.g., first 000 and 111, then 001 and 110, then 010 and 101, and finally 011 and 100.

Let us see now how we can act to ensure that this reduction is correct. Again consider S_3 and assume that $3 \notin \emptyset'_0$. Now suppose that at some stage s_0, the opponent enumerates σ_{000} into $O^{U_{s_0}}_{d+3}$. This enumeration will cause $\Gamma^{O^{U_{s_0}}} = 1$. So we add $(111, \sigma_{111})$ to M at the following stage. If a corresponding description appears in the universal machine at stage s_1, then $\Gamma^{O^{U_{s_1}}} = 0$. If at a later stage s_3, we have $3 \in \emptyset'_{s_3}$, then we add $(001, \sigma_{001})$ to M. If at any later stage the opponent adds σ_{110} to O^U_{d+x} then we respond by adding $(010, \sigma_{010})$ to M, and so on.

Note that for a given x, the value of the reduction $\Gamma(x)$ can be changed by adding a single element of S_x to O^U_{d+x} (provided $S_x \nsubseteq O^U_{d+x}$). If at some stage s of the construction $\Gamma^{O^{U_s}}(x) = 0$, then there are two possible choices of string for changing the reduction to 1, while if $\Gamma^{O^{U_s}}(x) = 1$ then there is only one possible string that can enumerated into the overgraph to change $\Gamma(x)$ to 0. Also note that if (τ, σ_τ) is enumerated into M, then the only reason to enumerate $(\overline{\tau}, \sigma_{\overline{\tau}})$ into M is to keep M a strict process machine.

Now, if we get to a stage s where for some x, we have $S_x \subseteq O^{U_s}_{d+x}$ and $x \in \emptyset'_s$, then we no longer have any ability to change the reduction. At this point we give up making the reduction work on x, and in fact we go further and give up trying to make the reduction work on any value below $s+2$. We will have a marker that points to a value after which the reduction works. We move the marker to point to $s+1$ and call $s+1$ a *marker move stage*. The reason that the marker cannot be moved infinitely often is that now when we define S_{s+1}, we can do it in such a way as to avoid extending some of the strings that have been enumerated into the universal machine by the opponent.

In looking for strings that have measure we can bypass, we do not consider just those strings in S_x. We consider all strings σ_τ, where τ can have any length, such that for any ρ that occurs no later than τ in the search order of Γ, we have $\sigma_\rho \in O^{U_s}_{d+|\tau|}$ (e.g., 000, 111, 001, 110 all occur no later than 110 in the search order). Given this set of strings S, we let T be the set of indices describing the strings in S. We use T instead of S because it is easier to deal with. As $S_x \subseteq O^{U_s}_{d+|x|}$, it follows that $\mu([\![T]\!]) = 1$. Let $\widehat{T}$ be the prefix-free set formed by taking those strings in T that are maximal with respect to the $\preccurlyeq$ ordering. The way we choose our σ_τ during the construction will allow us to find a lower bound on $\mu([\![\widehat{T}]\!])$.

Let B be the set of strings in $\widehat{T}$ that index strings enumerated into the overgraph by the opponent and whose corresponding measures we can bypass. We will be able to show that we can find a lower bound on $\mu([\![B]\!])$ because nearly half the strings in $\widehat{T}$ must be in B. The reason for this fact is a little complicated and will be detailed in the proof. Basically, though, it is twofold. First, we will show that if $\tau \in \widehat{T}$, then $\overline{\tau} \in \widehat{T}$. Second, we are unlikely to add both (τ, σ_τ) and $(\overline{\tau}, \sigma_{\overline{\tau}})$ to M. The only reason we would do so would be to ensure that M is a strict process machine. Say we add (τ, σ_τ) to M to keep it a strict process machine. Then there is some $\tau' \succ \tau$ with $\tau' \in \mathrm{dom}(M)$. Since $\tau' \notin T$, as otherwise τ would not be in $\widehat{T}$, it must be that we add $(\tau', \sigma_{\tau'})$ to M to encode some x entering $\emptyset'$. However, this scenario can affect only a certain number of elements of $\widehat{T}$. This fact is what we will use to find a lower bound for $\mu([\![B]\!])$.

For the verification of the proof, it is useful to formalize the order that the reduction uses the strings in S_x, which is done by defining a relation on 2^k as follows: $\tau_1 \preccurlyeq_\Gamma \tau_2$ if $\min(\tau_1, \overline{\tau_1}) \leqslant_{\mathrm{L}} \min(\tau_2, \overline{\tau_2})$ where the minimum is with respect to the lexicographic ordering. While $\preccurlyeq_\Gamma$ is reflexive and transitive, it is not an ordering, as antisymmetry fails. However, if $\tau \preccurlyeq_\Gamma \rho$ and $\rho \preccurlyeq_\Gamma \tau$, then either $\rho = \tau$ or $\rho = \overline{\tau}$. The relation $\preccurlyeq_\Gamma$ is total in the sense that for all $\tau, \rho \in 2^k$, either $\tau \preccurlyeq_\Gamma \rho$ or $\rho \preccurlyeq_\Gamma \tau$. Note that this fact implies that if $\tau \not\preccurlyeq_\Gamma \rho$ then $\rho \prec_\Gamma \tau$.

Lemma 16.3.15. *Let $\tau_1, \tau_2, \upsilon_1, \upsilon_2$ with $|\tau_1| = |\tau_2| < |\upsilon_1| = |\upsilon_2|$ be such that $\tau_1 \prec \upsilon_1$ and $\tau_2 \prec \upsilon_2$. Then $\tau_1 \prec_\Gamma \tau_2$ implies $\upsilon_1 \prec_\Gamma \upsilon_2$.*

Proof. If $\tau_1 \prec_\Gamma \tau_2$, then $\tau_1 \neq \lambda$ so $\tau_1 \neq \overline{\tau_1}$. Assume that $\tau_1 <_{\mathrm{L}} \overline{\tau_1}$, the other case being symmetric. If $\tau_1 \prec_\Gamma \tau_2$, then $\tau_1 <_{\mathrm{L}} \tau_2$ and $\tau_1 <_{\mathrm{L}} \overline{\tau_2}$. Now, as $\tau_1 \prec \upsilon_1$ and $\tau_2 \prec \upsilon_2$, it follows that $\upsilon_1 <_{\mathrm{L}} \upsilon_2$ and $\upsilon_1 <_{\mathrm{L}} \overline{\upsilon_2}$. Hence, $\min(\upsilon_1, \overline{\upsilon_1}) <_{\mathrm{L}} \min(\upsilon_2, \overline{\upsilon_2})$, and so $\upsilon_1 \prec_\Gamma \upsilon_2$. □

In the construction and verification that follow, we will assume that we have sped up our stages sufficiently so that when we enumerate descriptions into our machine M, corresponding descriptions appear immediately in U. This assumption simplifies notation, as it implies that $O_k^{M_s} \subseteq O_{d+k}^{U_s}$ and $\{(\sigma, d+n) : (\sigma, n) \in O^{M_s}\} \subseteq O^{U_s}$.

Construction.

Stage 0. Let $\sigma_\lambda = 0$ and $S_0 = \{\sigma_\lambda\}$. The set S_0 is used only to start the construction and will not be used by Γ. Let $M_0 = \{(\lambda, \sigma_\lambda)\}$. Let $R_0 = \{0\}$. The set R_s is used to determine the position of the marker at stage s.

Stage $s+1$. We assume that M_s is a strict process machine. Let the marker c_s be the largest element in R_s. First we need to define S_{s+1}. If $s+1 \neq c_s$, then $s+1$ is not a marker move stage. In this case, for all $\tau \in 2^s$, choose four extensions $\sigma_{\tau 0}, \sigma_{\tau 1}, \rho_{\tau 0}, \rho_{\tau 1}$ of σ_τ that are pairwise incompatible and not in $O_{d+s+1}^{U_s}$, which is possible because $O_{d+s+1}^{U_s}$ is finite. Let $S_{s+1} = \{\sigma_\tau : \tau \in 2^{s+1}\}$.

If $c_s = s+1$ then $s+1$ is a marker move stage. The construction of S_{s+1} will be done in such a way as to avoid extending some strings σ_τ that have been added to $O_{d+|\tau|}^{U_s}$. The procedure for finding the σ_τ to avoid is as follows.

For all k with $1 \leqslant k \leqslant s$, let

$$T_k^{s+1} = \{\tau \in 2^k : \forall \tau' \in 2^k (\tau' \preccurlyeq_\Gamma \tau \Rightarrow \sigma_{\tau'} \in O_{d+k}^{U_s})\}.$$

The set T_k^{s+1} is defined this way because this is the order in which the reduction Γ examines the strings in S_k. Let $T^{s+1} = \bigcup_{1 \leqslant k \leqslant s} T_k^{s+1}$.

We want to work with a prefix free set, so let $\widehat{T}^{s+1} = \{\tau \in T^{s+1} : \forall \tau' \succ \tau\, (\tau' \notin T^{s+1})\}$. Note that this set consists of the maximal elements of T^{s+1}, while prefix-free sets are usually constructed using minimal elements.

To gather together those strings whose descriptions we can bypass, let $B^{s+1} = \{\tau \in \widehat{T}^{s+1} : \forall \tau' \succcurlyeq \tau\, (\tau' \notin \mathrm{dom}(M_s))\}$. For all $\upsilon \in B^{s+1}$, let $\{\upsilon_0, \ldots, \upsilon_n\}$ be the set of extensions of υ of length $s+1$. Choose $\sigma_{\upsilon_0}, \rho_{\upsilon_0}, \ldots, \sigma_{\upsilon_n}, \rho_{\upsilon_n}$ that are pairwise incompatible, not in $O_{d+s+1}^{U_s}$, and extend ρ_υ. For all $\tau \in 2^{s+1}$ that do not extend some $\upsilon \in B^{s+1}$, choose a σ_τ and a ρ_τ that are incompatible, not in $O_{d+s+1}^{U_s}$, and extend $\sigma_{\tau'}$, where $\tau' = \tau \restriction (|\tau| - 1)$. Again let $S_{s+1} = \{\sigma_\tau : \tau \in 2^{s+1}\}$.

Second, we need to determine which descriptions to commit to our machine M. Let $X_{s+1} = \{x : c_s < x < s \wedge \Gamma^{O^{U_s}}(x) \neq \emptyset'_s(x)\}$. If $X_{s+1} = \emptyset$, then let $M_{s+1} = M_s$ and $R_{s+1} = R_s$ and proceed to the next stage. Otherwise, if for any $x \in X_s$ we have $S_x \subseteq O^{U_s}_{d+x}$, then let $M_{s+1} = M_s$ and $R_{s+1} = R_s \cup \{s+2\}$, which will cause the marker to be moved at the next stage. In this case, proceed to the next stage.

Otherwise, let x_s be the least element of X_s, and choose $\tau \in 2^{x_s}$ such that $\sigma_\tau \notin O^{U_s}_{d+x_s}$ and $\sigma_{\tau'} \in O^{U_s}_{d+x_s}$ for all $\tau' \prec_{\Gamma} \tau$. We are going to add (τ, σ_τ) to M_{s+1}. However, we want to make M a strict process machine, so we need to ensure that $\mathrm{dom}(M_{s+1})$ is closed under substrings.

Let υ be the longest initial segment of τ such that $\upsilon \in \mathrm{dom}(M_s)$. Consider any $\tau' \prec \tau$. If $\tau' \preccurlyeq \upsilon$, then $\tau' \in \mathrm{dom}(M_s)$ by our assumption that M_s is a strict process machine. Now suppose that $\upsilon \prec \tau' \preccurlyeq \tau$. If $|\tau'| \leqslant c_s$, then we want to have $M_{s+1}(\tau') = M_s(\upsilon)$. Otherwise, we want to have $M_{s+1}(\tau') = \sigma_{\tau'}$. Thus, let

$$M_{s+1} = M_s \cup \{(\tau', M_s(\upsilon)) : \upsilon \prec \tau' \preccurlyeq \tau \wedge |\tau'| \leqslant c_s\} \cup \{(\tau', \sigma_{\tau'}) : \upsilon \prec \tau' \preccurlyeq \tau \wedge |\tau'| > c_s\}.$$

Finally, let $R_{s+1} = R_s$.
End of Construction.

First we will show that M is a strict process machine. To do so, we need the following lemma.

Lemma 16.3.16. *If $\tau_1 \prec \tau_2$ and $\sigma_{\tau_1} \not\prec \sigma_{\tau_2}$, then $M(\tau_1) \neq \sigma_{\tau_1}$.*

Proof. If $\tau_1 \prec \tau_2$ and $\sigma_{\tau_1} \not\prec \sigma_{\tau_2}$, then there must be some marker move stage s with $|\tau_1| < s \leqslant |\tau_2|$ and $\rho_{\tau_0} \prec \sigma_{\tau_2}$ for some $\tau_0 \in B^s$ with $\tau_0 \preccurlyeq \tau_1$. Thus, $\tau_1 \notin \mathrm{dom}(M_s)$, by the definition of B^s. However, then for all stages $t > s$, we have $M_t(\tau_1) \neq \sigma_{\tau_1}$, because once the marker has moved, if τ_1 is added to the domain of M_t, then $M_t(\tau_1) = \sigma_\upsilon$ for some $\upsilon \prec \tau_1$. □

Lemma 16.3.17. *M is a strict process machine.*

Proof. We proceed by induction on the stages of the construction. Clearly M_0 is a strict process machine. If M_s is a strict process machine then the construction ensures that M_{s+1} is at least a function whose domain is closed under initial segments, because if $M_{s+1} \neq M_s$, then M_{s+1} is formed by taking some $\tau \notin \mathrm{dom}(M_s)$ and finding the longest $\upsilon \prec \tau$ such that $\upsilon \in \mathrm{dom}(M_s)$. The strings that we add to the domain of M_{s+1} are exactly those strings τ' such that $\upsilon \prec \tau' \preccurlyeq \tau$.

We also need to show that M_{s+1} is a process. In the construction, M_{s+1} is defined to be $M_s \cup \{(\tau', M_s(\upsilon)) : \upsilon \prec \tau' \preccurlyeq \tau \wedge |\tau'| \leqslant c_s\} \cup \{(\tau', \sigma_{\tau'}) : \upsilon \prec \tau' \preccurlyeq \tau \wedge |\tau'| > c_s\}$.

First we show that $\widehat{M}_{s+1} = M_s \cup \{(\tau', M_s(\upsilon)) : \upsilon \prec \tau' \preccurlyeq \tau \wedge |\tau'| \leqslant c_s\}$ is a process. Take any $\tau_1, \tau_2 \in \mathrm{dom}(\widehat{M}_{s+1})$ with $\tau_1 \prec \tau_2$. If $\tau_2 \in M_s$ then

$\tau_1 \in M_s$, so $\widehat{M}_{s+1}(\tau_1) = M_s(\tau_1) \preccurlyeq M_s(\tau_2) = \widehat{M}_{s+1}(\tau_2)$. If $\tau_2 \notin M_s$ and $\tau_1 \in M_s$, then $\tau_1 \preccurlyeq \upsilon$, so $\widehat{M}_{s+1}(\tau_1) \preccurlyeq \widehat{M}_{s+1}(\upsilon) = \widehat{M}_{s+1}(\tau_2)$. Finally, if neither τ_1 nor τ_2 are in M_s then $\widehat{M}_{s+1}(\upsilon) = \widehat{M}_{s+1}(\tau_1) = \widehat{M}_{s+1}(\tau_2)$.

The set $\{(\tau', \sigma_{\tau'}) : \upsilon \prec \tau' \preccurlyeq \tau \wedge |\tau'| > c_s\}$ is also a process: For any $\tau_1 \prec \tau_2$ in this set, $\sigma_{\tau_1} \prec \sigma_{\tau_2}$ because the marker is not moved between the definitions of σ_{τ_1} and σ_{τ_2}.

To show that the union of these two processes is a process, consider $M_{s+1}(\upsilon)$. By construction it must be that $M_{s+1}(\upsilon) = M_{s+1}(\upsilon') = \sigma_{\upsilon'}$ for some $\upsilon' \preccurlyeq \upsilon$. From the previous lemma, this fact implies that $\sigma_{\upsilon'} \preccurlyeq \sigma_\tau$, and so $M_{s+1}(\upsilon) \preccurlyeq M_{s+1}(\tau)$.

Now for any $\tau_1 \prec \tau_2$ with τ_1 in the domain of the first process and τ_2 in the domain of the second process, $M_{s+1}(\tau_1) \preccurlyeq M_{s+1}(\upsilon)$ and $M_{s+1}(\tau_2) \preccurlyeq M_{s+1}(\tau)$. As $M_{s+1}(\upsilon) \preccurlyeq M_{s+1}(\tau)$, it follows that $M_{s+1}(\tau_1) \preccurlyeq M_{s+1}(\tau_2)$.

Therefore M_{s+1} is a strict process machine. It follows that $M = \bigcup_s M_s$ is also a strict process machine. ☐

Lemma 16.3.18. *If there are only a finite number of marker move stages, then* $\Gamma^{O^U}(x) = \emptyset'(x)$ *for almost all* x.

Proof. Let s_0 be the last marker move stage and assume for a contradiction that there is a least $x_0 > s_0$ such that $\Gamma^{O^U}(x_0) \neq \emptyset'(x_0)$. Let $s_1 > x_0$ be a stage such that $\emptyset'_{s_1} \upharpoonright (x_0+1) = \emptyset' \upharpoonright (x_0+1)$ and $S_x \cap O^U_{d+x} = S_x \cap O^{U_{s_1}}_{d+x}$ for all $x \leqslant x_0$. The latter condition implies that $\Gamma^{O^{U_{s_1}}}(x) = \Gamma^{O^U}(x)$ for all $x \leqslant x_0$.

If $x_0 \in X_{s_1}$, then it must be the least element of X_{s_1}. Because there are no more marker move stages, it must be that $S_{x_0} \not\subseteq O^{U_{s_1}}_{d+x_0}$. But there is a (τ, σ_τ) with $\tau \in 2^{x_0}$ and $\sigma_\tau \notin O^{U_{s_1}}_{d+x_0}$ added to M_{s_1+1}. This enumeration adds σ_τ to $O^U_{d+x_0}$, which is not possible because $S_{x_0} \cap O^U_{d+x_0} = S_{x_0} \cap O^{U_{s_1}}_{d+x_0}$. Hence $x_0 \notin X_s$, and so $\Gamma^{O^U}(x_0) = \Gamma^{O^{U_{s_1}}}(x_0) = \emptyset'_s(x_0) = \emptyset'(x_0)$, which is a contradiction. ☐

Now we need to show that there are only a finite number of marker move stages. We will be able to do so because each time the marker is moved, a portion of the measure that the universal machine has spent is bypassed by the construction, and can no longer be used to affect Γ. By showing that there is a lower bound on the amount of measure that is bypassed each time the marker is moved, we will show that the marker can be moved only a finite number of times, since the domain of the universal machine eventually runs out of measure. For any x there is a direct relation between the indices of the strings in S_x and the measure required to be allocated to these strings to add them to O^U_{d+x}. Hence, to determine a lower bound on the amount of measure bypassed, it is useful to find a lower bound on $\mu([\![B^s]\!])$. The first step toward achieving this bound will be to find a lower bound on $\mu([\![\widehat{T}^s]\!])$.

For the rest of the verification, fix s to be a particular marker move stage. As s is fixed, T_k will be used for T_k^s.

Lemma 16.3.19. *Let $\tau, \rho \in 2^k$ with $1 \leqslant k < s$. If $\tau \in T_k$ and $\rho \preccurlyeq_\Gamma \tau$, then $\rho \in T_k$.*

Proof. If $\rho \notin T_k$ then for some $\upsilon \in 2^k$ such that $\upsilon \preccurlyeq_\Gamma \rho$, we have $\sigma_\upsilon \notin O_{d+k}^{U_s}$. However, by the transitivity of the $\preccurlyeq_\Gamma$ relation, $\upsilon \preccurlyeq_\Gamma \tau$, and so $\tau \notin T_k$. □

Note that this lemma implies that if $\tau \in T_k$, then $\overline{\tau} \in T_k$ as well.

Lemma 16.3.20. *If $1 \leqslant k < j < s$ then either $[\![T_k]\!] \subset [\![T_j]\!]$ or $[\![T_j]\!] \subset [\![T_k]\!]$.*

Proof. If $[\![T_j]\!] \not\subset [\![T_k]\!]$, then there is some $\upsilon \in T_j$ such that if $\tau = \upsilon \upharpoonright k$, then $\tau \notin T_k$. If $\tau' \in T_k$ then $\tau' \prec_\Gamma \tau$ (because the relation $\prec_\Gamma$ is total and if $\tau \preccurlyeq_\Gamma \tau'$ then by definition $\tau' \notin T_k$). Now let υ' be any extension of τ' such that $|\upsilon'| = j$. By Lemma 16.3.15, $\upsilon' \prec_\Gamma \upsilon$, and hence $\upsilon' \in T_j$ by Lemma 16.3.19. Thus $[\![T_k]\!] \subset [\![T_j]\!]$. □

Let x be greatest such that $S_x \subseteq O_{d+x}^{U_s}$. Since s is a marker move stage, such an x exists. Additionally, x is greater than the previous marker move stage. By the previous lemma, there are $j(0) < j(1) < \cdots < j(n)$ with $j(0) = x$ and $j(n) = s - 1$, such that $[\![T_{j(0)}]\!] \supsetneq \cdots \supsetneq [\![T_{j(n)}]\!]$ and $[\![T_l]\!] \subseteq [\![T_{j(i+1)}]\!]$ whenever $j(i) < l \leqslant j(i+1)$.

For $i < n$, let $\widehat{T}_j(i) = \{\tau \in T_{j(i)} : \forall \tau' \in T_{j(i+1)} \, (\tau \not\prec \tau')\}$. Let $\widehat{T}_{j(n)} = T_{j(n)}$.

Lemma 16.3.21. *For all $i < n$, we have $\mu([\![\widehat{T}_{j(i)}]\!]) \geqslant \mu([\![T_{j(i)}]\!] \setminus [\![T_{j(i+1)}]\!]) - 2^{-j(i)+1}$.*

Proof. We have $[\![T_{j(i)}]\!] \supsetneq [\![T_{j(i+1)}]\!]$, so let τ be an element of $T_{j(i)}$ for which there is some $\tau \prec \upsilon$ such that $|\upsilon| = j(i+1)$ and $\upsilon \notin T_{j(i+1)}$, but for all $\tau' \preccurlyeq_\Gamma \tau$ and all υ' with $\tau' \prec \upsilon'$ and $|\upsilon'| = j(i+1)$, we have $\upsilon' \in T_{j(i+1)}$.

Now take any $\tau' \in T_{j(i)}$ such that $\tau \prec_\Gamma \tau'$. For any υ' of length $j(i+1)$ such that $\tau' \prec \upsilon'$, it follows by Lemma 16.3.15 that $\upsilon \prec_\Gamma \upsilon'$ and hence $\upsilon' \notin T_{j(i+1)}$, whence $\tau' \in \widehat{T}_{j(i)}$.

Thus for all $\tau' \in T_{j(i)}$, if $\tau' \prec_\Gamma \tau$ then $[\![\tau']\!] \subseteq [\![T_{j(i+1)}]\!]$. If $\tau \prec_\Gamma \tau'$ then $[\![\tau']\!] \subseteq [\![\widehat{T}_{j(i)}]\!]$. If neither $\tau' \prec_\Gamma \tau$ nor $\tau \prec_\Gamma \tau'$, then τ' must be one of τ or $\overline{\tau}$.

Thus $[\![\widehat{T}_{j(i)}]\!] \supseteq ([\![T_{j(i)}]\!] \setminus [\![T_{j(i+1)}]\!]) \setminus [\![\{\tau, \overline{\tau}\}]\!]$. The lemma follows, as $\mu([\![\{\tau, \overline{\tau}\}]\!]) = 2^{-j(i)+1}$. □

The following lemma shows that the $\widehat{T}^s$ defined in the construction (now referred to as $\widehat{T}$ because s is fixed) is equal to $\bigcup_{i \leqslant n} \widehat{T}_{j(i)}$.

Lemma 16.3.22. $\widehat{T} = \bigcup_{i \leqslant n} \widehat{T}_{j(i)}$.

Proof. If $\tau \in \widehat{T}$, then by definition, $\tau \not\preccurlyeq \tau'$ for all $\tau' \in T$. Hence $\tau \in T_{j(i)}$ for some i and $\tau' \notin T_{j(i+1)}$ for all $\tau \prec \tau'$. Thus $\tau \in \widehat{T}_{j(i)}$, so $\widehat{T} \subseteq \bigcup_{i \leqslant n} \widehat{T}_{j(i)}$.

For the other direction, first note that $\widehat{T}_{j(n)} = T_{s-1} \subseteq \widehat{T}$, because any maximal-length element must be a maximal element under $\preccurlyeq$. If $\tau \in \widehat{T}_{j(i)}$ for some $i < n$, then $\tau \not\preccurlyeq \tau'$ for all $\tau' \in T_{j(i+1)}$. Now, $[\![T_l]\!] \subseteq [\![T_{j(i+1)}]\!]$ for all $l > j(i)$, so $\tau \not\preccurlyeq \tau'$ for all $\tau' \in T_l$, and hence $\tau \in \widehat{T}$. Thus $\bigcup_{i \leqslant n} \widehat{T}_{j(i)} \subseteq \widehat{T}$. □

As $j(0) = x$ and $S_x \subseteq O^{U_s}_{d+x}$, we have $\mu[\![T_{j(0)}]\!] = 1$. We may assume that $x \geqslant 4$ because x is greater than any previous marker move stage, so this assumption will be true after at most 3 marker move stages. Then

$$\begin{aligned}\mu([\![\widehat{T}]\!]) &= \sum_{i \leqslant n} \mu([\![\widehat{T}_{j(i)}]\!]) \\ &\geqslant \sum_{i<n} (\mu([\![T_{j(i)}]\!] \setminus [\![T_{j(i+1)}]\!]) - 2^{-j(i)+1}) + \mu([\![T_{j(n)}]\!]) \\ &= \mu([\![T_{j(0)}]\!]) - \sum_{i<n} 2^{-j(i)+1} > \frac{3}{4}.\end{aligned}$$

Now we have achieved the first step discussed above by finding a lower bound on $\mu([\![\widehat{T}]\!])$. The next step is to find a lower bound on $\mu([\![B^s]\!])$. Recall that B^s was defined in the construction to be $\{\tau \in \widehat{T} : \forall \tau \preccurlyeq \tau' \, (\tau' \notin \operatorname{dom}(M_{s-1}))\}$.

Lemma 16.3.23. *If $\tau \in \widehat{T}$ then $\overline{\tau} \in \widehat{T}$.*

Proof. If $\tau \in \widehat{T}$, then $\tau \in \widehat{T}_{j(i)}$ for some i. So $\tau \in T_{j(i)}$, and thus $\overline{\tau} \in T_{j(i)}$. If $\overline{\tau} \prec \overline{\upsilon}$ and $|\overline{\upsilon}| = j(i+1)$, then $\tau \prec \upsilon$, and hence $\upsilon \notin T_{j(i+1)}$ (as $\tau \in \widehat{T}_{j(i)}$). Thus $\overline{\upsilon} \notin T_{j(i+1)}$, and so $\overline{\tau} \in \widehat{T}_{j(i)}$. □

Lemma 16.3.24. *If $\tau \in \widehat{T}$ and $\tau, \overline{\tau} \notin B^s$, then there exists $\upsilon \in \operatorname{dom}(M_{s-1})$ such that either $\tau \prec \upsilon$ or $\overline{\tau} \prec \upsilon$.*

Proof. This lemma follows from the fact that we add descriptions to M for only two reasons. The first is to change the reduction and the second is to ensure that the domain is closed under substrings. Assume that there is no $\upsilon \in \operatorname{dom}(M_{s-1})$ such that either $\tau \prec \upsilon$ or $\overline{\tau} \prec \upsilon$. In this case there is no need to add τ or $\overline{\tau}$ to the domain of M_{s-1} to close it under substrings. So if $\tau \notin B^s$, then it must be that $\tau \in \operatorname{dom}(M_{s-1})$. Furthermore, we must have added τ to the domain of M_{s-1} to change the reduction Γ. In this case there is no reason why we should add $\overline{\tau}$ to change the reduction as well. Hence $\overline{\tau} \notin \operatorname{dom}(M_{s-1})$, so $\overline{\tau} \in B^s$. □

Lemma 16.3.25. *If $\tau_1, \tau_2 \in \widehat{T}$ are such that $|\tau_1| = |\tau_2|$ and $\tau_1 \prec_\Gamma \tau_2$, then at least one of τ_2 and $\overline{\tau}_2$ is in B^s.*

Proof. First we know by Lemma 16.3.23 that $\overline{\tau}_1, \overline{\tau}_2 \in \widehat{T}$. Assume for a contradiction that $\tau_2, \overline{\tau}_2 \notin B^s$.

By the previous lemma, if $\tau_2, \overline{\tau}_2 \notin B^s$, then there must be some $\upsilon_2 \in \mathrm{dom}(M_{s-1})$ such that either $\tau_2 \prec \upsilon_2$ or $\overline{\tau_2} \prec \upsilon_2$. We will assume without loss of generality that $\tau_2 \prec \upsilon_2$.

Let $k = |\upsilon_2|$. Note that $k < s$. As $\upsilon_2 \in \mathrm{dom}(M_{s-1})$, for all $\upsilon \prec_\Gamma \upsilon_2$, we have $\sigma_\upsilon \in O^{U_s}_{d+k}$, by the way the construction chooses pairs to add to M. Hence $\upsilon \in T_k$. Take any υ_1 extending τ_1 with $|\upsilon_1| = k$. As $\tau_1 \prec_\Gamma \tau_2$, by Lemma 16.3.15, $\upsilon_1 \prec_\Gamma \upsilon_2$, and thus $\upsilon_1 \in T_k$ by Lemma 16.3.19. Thus $[\![\tau_1]\!] \subseteq T_k$ and so $\tau_1 \notin \widehat{T}$, which contradicts our initial assumption. □

We can use this last lemma to put a lower bound on the measure of B^s.

Lemma 16.3.26. *If s is a marker move stage then $\mu([\![B^s]\!]) \geqslant \frac{1}{4}$.*

Proof. The previous lemma tells us that for any given length l, there is at most a single $\tau \in \widehat{T}$ of length l such that neither τ nor $\overline{\tau}$ is in B^s. For any string υ of length l such that $\upsilon \neq \tau$ and $\upsilon \neq \overline{\tau}$, either υ or $\overline{\upsilon}$ is in B^s. Thus

$$\mu([\![B^s]\!]) \geqslant \frac{1}{2}\left(\mu([\![\widehat{T}^s]\!]) - \sum_{i \leqslant m} 2 \cdot 2^{-j(i)}\right) > \frac{1}{2}\left(\frac{3}{4} - \frac{1}{4}\right) = \frac{1}{4}.$$

□

Now for all $\tau \in B^s$, we have $\sigma_\tau \in O^{U_s}_{d+|\tau|}$ and so $Km(\sigma_\tau) \leqslant d + |\tau|$. Additionally, by construction, as B^s is a prefix-free set, so is $\{\sigma_\tau : \tau \in B^s\}$. Hence it follows that

$$M_U([\![\{\sigma_\tau : \tau \in B^s\}]\!]) = \sum_{\tau \in B^s} M_U([\![\sigma_\tau]\!]) \geqslant \sum_{\tau \in B} 2^{-d-|\tau|}$$
$$= 2^{-d} \sum_{\tau \in B} \mu([\![\tau]\!]) \geqslant 2^{-d}\mu([\![B^s]\!]) \geqslant 2^{-d-2}.$$

Lemma 16.3.27. *If s_1 and s_2 are both marker move stages and $s_1 \neq s_2$, then the sets $[\![\{\sigma_\tau : \tau \in B^{s_1}\}]\!]$ and $[\![\{\sigma_\tau : \tau \in B^{s_2}\}]\!]$ are disjoint.*

Proof. Take any $\tau \in B^{s_1}$ and $\upsilon \in B^{s_2}$. By construction, $|\tau| < s_1$, and the length of υ is larger than any previous marker move stage, so in particular $|\upsilon| > s_1 > |\tau|$. Now, if $\tau \not\prec \upsilon$, then the construction ensures that σ_υ and σ_τ are incompatible. If $\tau \prec \upsilon$, then again by construction $\rho_\tau \prec \sigma_\upsilon$ and hence σ_υ and σ_τ are incompatible. □

We can now finish the proof of the theorem. By Lemma 16.3.17, M is a monotone machine. By Lemma 16.3.18, if there are a finite number of marker moves then $\Gamma^{O^{U_s}}(x) = \emptyset'(x)$ for all but finitely many x. But there can be only a finite number of marker move stages because if R is the set of all marker move stages, then by the previous lemma

$$M_U([\![\lambda]\!]) \geqslant \sum_{s \in R} M_U([\![\{\sigma_\tau : \tau \in B^s\}]\!]) \geqslant |R| 2^{-d-2}.$$

Hence $|R| \leqslant 2^{d+2}$, and in particular R is finite. $\square$

The proof above still works if O^U_{Km} is replaced by $O^U_{KM} = \{(\sigma, k) : -\log(M_U(\sigma)) < k\}$: During the verification of the construction, it is only the measure that the universal machine places on elements of S_x that is considered, and not the length of their shortest descriptions. Additionally, if the construction enumerates some pair (σ, n) into M, this enumeration adds $(\sigma, n+d)$ to O^U_{KM} as well as O^U_{Km}, because $O^U_{Km} \subseteq O^U_{KM}$. Thus we have the following.

Corollary 16.3.28 (Day [88]). *For any universal monotone machine U the overgraph O^U_{KM} is truth table complete.*

Also, a universal process machine is a monotone machine. Hence the limitations of a universal monotone machine exploited in the proof also apply to a universal process machine. Furthermore, the machine M constructed in the proof is a strict process machine, so we have the following.

Corollary 16.3.29 (Day [88]). *For any universal process machine U, or any universal strict process machine V, the overgraphs $O^U_{Km_D}$ and $O^V_{Km_S}$ are truth table complete.*

An interesting point about the above construction is that $\emptyset'$ can determine the correct tt-reduction, because R is finite and enumerated during the construction, and hence $\emptyset'$ can determine its size. The construction used in the proof of Kummer's Theorem 16.3.2 is different. It uses a finite set of sequences $S_1, \ldots, S_n$, and the key to unraveling the construction is determining the maximum i such that S_i is infinite, which cannot be done using a $\emptyset'$ oracle.

16.3.4 The strict process complexity case

This section presents Day's proof from [88] that there are universal strict process machines whose set of nonrandom strings is not tt-complete. It is open whether this result holds for the case where "strict" is removed. In this section, we write $\overline{R}^M$ for $\overline{R}^M_{Km_S}$.

First we show that it is possible to construct a universal strict process machine whose set of nonrandom strings is closed under extensions.

Theorem 16.3.30 (Day [88]). *There exists a universal strict process machine V such that $\overline{R}^V$ is closed under extensions; i.e., if $\sigma \in \overline{R}^V$ and $\sigma' \succ \sigma$, then $\sigma' \in \overline{R}^V$.*

Proof. We build V from a standard universal strict process machine U. Let $V(\lambda) = \lambda$ and let $V(0\tau) = U(\tau)$ for all τ. This definition ensures the universality of V. We use strings in the domain of V starting with 1 to get the desired closure property. We can effectively enumerate the set S of strings τ such that $U(\tau)\downarrow = \sigma$ for some σ such that $|\tau| \leqslant |\sigma| - 2$. If $\tau \in S$, we know that $U(\rho)\downarrow$ for all $\rho \prec \tau$, so we can also effectively enumerate the prefix-free set T of strings $\tau \in S$ such that $\rho \notin S$ for all $\rho \prec \tau$. For each $\tau \in T$, let $V(1\tau\nu) = U(\tau)\nu$ for all ν and let $V(1\rho) = \lambda$ for all $\rho \prec \tau$.

This definition clearly makes V a universal strict process machine. We now verify that $\overline{R}^V$ is closed under extensions. Let $\sigma \in \overline{R}^V$, and let ν witness that fact. That is, $V(\nu) = \sigma$ and $|\nu| < |\sigma|$.

If ν is of the form 0τ, then $U(\tau) = \sigma$ and $|\tau| \leqslant |\sigma| - 2$, so $\tau \in S$. Let $\tau' \preccurlyeq \tau$ be in T and let $\sigma' = U(\tau')$. Note that $\sigma' \preccurlyeq \sigma$. If ν is of the form 1τ, then, since $\sigma \neq \lambda$, there must be a $\tau' \in T$ such that $\tau' \preccurlyeq \tau$. Let $\sigma' = V(1\tau')$, and again note that $\sigma' \preccurlyeq \sigma$.

In either case, for every ρ, we have $V(1\tau'\rho) = \sigma'\rho$, and $|1\tau'\rho| < |\sigma'\rho|$, so $\sigma'\rho \in \overline{R}^V$. In particular, every extension of σ is in $\overline{R}^V$. □

The argument used in the previous proof does not generalize to process machines. Day [88] gave the following example. Let U be a universal process machine. Suppose that we see that $U(00) = 0000$ and $U(10) = 0001$, and so far $U(\lambda)$ has not converged. If we try to follow the above construction, we set $V(100) = 0000$ and $V(110) = 0001$. If now $U(\lambda)$ converges to 00, then we would like to set $V(1) = 00$, and somehow use extensions of 1 to make all extensions of 00 nonrandom. However, consider 001. It is not possible to set $V(10) = 001$ or $V(11) = 001$ and keep V a process machine.

The definition of V in the proof of Theorem 16.3.30 can be carried out in a stage-by-stage manner. That is, whenever $U_s(\tau)\downarrow = \sigma$ and $|\tau| \leqslant |\sigma| - 2$, we can determine the unique $\tau' \preccurlyeq \tau$ such that $\tau' \in T$, and immediately define $V(1\tau'\nu) = U(\tau)\nu$ for all ν and $V(1\rho) = \lambda$ for all $\rho \prec \tau'$. This action ensures that $\overline{R}^{V_s}$ is closed under extensions for all s.

We use this idea to help build a universal strict process machine whose set of nonrandom strings is not tt-complete. This proof is an adaptation of Muchnik's proof of Theorem 16.3.9 (ii), where he constructed a universal prefix-free machine whose overgraph is not tt-complete. Recall that that proof uses the fact that the outcome of a finite game can be computably determined.

In the proof that follows there will be three roles: the champion, the opponent, and the arbitrator. The champion and the opponent will be players in the game. They will move by adding strings to $\overline{R}^V$. The arbitrator will make sure that the set of all nonrandom strings is closed under extensions. The opponent represents a fixed universal strict process machine. The index of the opponent in the proof is 000, and the index of the champion is 01. We give the champion a shorter index because it will need more measure (measure replacing money in these games). The index of the arbitrator will be 1. The arbitrator follows the strategy of the proof of Theorem 16.3.30. Because the actions of the arbitrator can be determined, both players know that once a string σ is in $\overline{R}^V$, all extensions of σ will also be in that set.

Hence, when we consider $\overline{R}^{V_s}$, we will assume that this set is closed under extensions.

Theorem 16.3.31 (Day [88]). *There exists a universal strict process machine V such that $\overline{R}^V$ is not tt-complete.*

Proof. To prove this theorem we build a universal strict process machine V and a c.e. set $A \not\leq_{\text{tt}} \overline{R}^V$. As discussed above, we assume that the arbitrator acts behind the scenes and that $\overline{R}^{V_s}$ is closed under extensions for all s. Let $\Gamma_0, \Gamma_1, \ldots$ be an enumeration of all truth table reductions.

Let U be a universal strict process machine. Let $D_s = \{\tau : U_s(\tau)\downarrow \wedge |\tau| < |U_s(\tau)| - 3\}$. The construction will ensure that if $\tau \in D_s$, then $U_s(\tau) \in \overline{R}^V$. We will use D_s to determine how much the opponent spends in the games. We will show that if the opponent plays a move in a game between stages s_0 and s_1, then we can determine a lower bound for $\mu([\![D_{s_1}]\!]) - \mu([\![D_{s_0}]\!])$.

We want to satisfy the following requirements for all n.

$$R_n : \exists i, j \left(A(\langle n, i, j\rangle) \neq \Gamma_n^{\overline{R}^V}(\langle n, i, j\rangle)\right).$$

The triples $\langle n, i, j\rangle$ will be used as follows. The number n represents the reduction to be diagonalized against. The number i is incremented every time the requirement is injured by a stronger priority requirement. It also provides an upper bound on the measure that can be used by the players in the game. The number j provides us with a series of games for each diagonalization. It will be incremented if our opponent ever "breaks the rules" of the game by using too much measure.

Construction.

Stage 0. Let $V(\lambda) = V(0) = V(00) = \lambda$. Let $A_0 = \emptyset$.

Stage $2s+1$. For all $n < s$, if R_n does not have a witness, assign $\langle n, 0, 0\rangle$ to R_n. For $n < s$, let $\langle n, i_n, j_n\rangle$ be the current witness for R_n. If R_n does not have a game assigned, run $\Gamma_n(\langle n, i_n, j_n\rangle)$ for s many steps to see whether it returns a truth table. If it does, let $X_n = \{\sigma_0, \ldots, \sigma_k\}$ be the set of strings used as variables by this truth table. For the purpose of this game, we will assume that stronger priority requirements have stopped acting, i.e., that the associated games are finished. We do not want to interrupt any earlier games, so let $Y_n = \{\sigma \in X_n : \forall \tau \in \bigcup_{i<n} X_i\, (\sigma \not\preccurlyeq \tau \vee \tau \in \overline{R}^{V_{2s}})\}$. Notice that $\sigma \in X_n \setminus Y_n$ iff adding σ to $\overline{R}^{V_{2s+1}}$ would change some variable used by a higher priority game (as $\overline{R}^{V_{2s+1}}$ is closed under extensions).

The game $G_{\langle n, i_n, j_n\rangle}$ is defined as follows. We will assume that the strings in $X_n \setminus Y_n$ do not change. The vertices in the game correspond to possible truth assignments to the variables in Y_n. The vertices are labeled with the value of the corresponding line in the truth table (assuming those variables in $X_n \setminus Y_n$ retain their current values). An edge exists from vertex v_1 to vertex v_2 if it possible to go from the row associated with v_1 to the row associated with v_2 by changing some of the truth table variables from 0 to 1. If going from vertex v_1 to vertex v_2 requires changing exactly the variables in $\Sigma \subseteq Y_n$, then the cost associated with the edge is $\mu([\![\Sigma]\!])$. The amount of measure each player has to expend on the game is 2^{-n-i_n-6}. The game $G_{\langle n,i_n,j_n\rangle}$, though defined, is said to be uninitialized.

We allow the opponent to move by letting $V(000\tau) = \sigma$ for all τ and σ such that $U_s(\tau) = \sigma$.

Stage $2s+2$. We determine whether there is any game that the champion needs to attend to. We find all games assigned to requirements that are uninitialized or where the opponent has made a move. The opponent is considered to have made a move if some new strings used by the truth table reduction have been enumerated into $\overline{R}^{V_{2s+1}} \setminus \overline{R}^{V_{2s}}$. If such games exist, let $G_{\langle n,i_n,j_n\rangle}$ be the strongest priority game (i.e., the game with the smallest n) that needs attention. First we reset all weaker priority games: For all p such that $n < p \leqslant s$, let $\langle n_p, i_p, j_p\rangle$ be the current witness assigned to R_p. Remove this witness and the associated game and let $\langle n_p, i_p+1, 0\rangle$ be the new witness.

If $G_{\langle n,i_n,j_n\rangle}$ is uninitialized, then we set the start position for the game to be the vertex that corresponds to assigning σ_i a truth value of 1 iff $\sigma_i \in \overline{R}^{V_{2s+2}}$. The champion decides whether to take a winning strategy to ensure that $\Gamma_n(\langle n, i_n, j_n\rangle) = 0$ or one to ensure that $\Gamma_n(\langle n, i_n, j_n\rangle) = 1$. Of course, one of these must exist. In the first case we add $\langle n, i_n, j_n\rangle$ to A_s; in the second case we leave it out. Let Σ be the set of strings that the champion needs to enumerate into $\overline{R}^{V_{2s+2}}$ for the first step of this strategy. We now say that the game $G_{\langle n,i_n,j_n\rangle}$ has been initialized.

If $G_{\langle n,i_n,j_n\rangle}$ is a game in which the opponent has made a move, then let $2s_0$ be the stage at which this game was initialized. If $\mu([\![D_s]\!]) - \mu([\![D_{s_0}]\!]) \geqslant 2^{-n-i_n-6}$, then the opponent has exceeded the allocated measure for the game $G_{\langle n,i_n,j_n\rangle}$. In this case, remove $\langle n, i_n, j_n\rangle$ as a witness for R_n and also remove the game. Let $\langle n, i_n, j_n+1\rangle$ be the new witness. Let $\Sigma = \emptyset$. If the opponent has not exceeded the allocated measure, then let Σ be the set of strings that the champion needs to enumerate into $\overline{R}^{V_{2s+2}}$ for the next move in the predetermined winning strategy.

Now we need to add Σ to $\overline{R}^{V_{2s+2}}$ in order to make the champion's next move. We know that the arbitrator will ensure that $\overline{R}^{V_{2s+2}}$ is closed under extensions. So if we take $\widehat{\Sigma} = \{\sigma_0, \ldots, \sigma_k\}$ to be a prefix-free set formed by taking the $\preccurlyeq$-minimal elements of Σ, then the champion needs only to enumerate $\widehat{\Sigma}$ into $\overline{R}^{V_{2s+2}}$. We will use the KC Theorem to find descriptions for these strings.

We use the KC Theorem to request a string τ_i of length $|\sigma_i| - 3$ for each $i \leqslant k$. For each such i, let $V(01\tau_i) = \sigma_i$ and $V(01\tau) = \lambda$ for all $\tau \prec \tau_i$.

Note that the champion decreases the measure available for future requests by $2^3\mu([\![\Sigma]\!])$. However, by scaling, we can regard the champion as having $\frac{1}{8}$ much measure to spend, and this move as costing it $\mu([\![\Sigma]\!])$.
End of Construction.

The first step in verifying this construction is to show that if the opponent makes a move then it must pay the cost of that move.

Lemma 16.3.32. *If the opponent enumerates a set of strings Σ into $\overline{R}^{V_{2s_1}} \setminus \overline{R}^{V_{2s_0}}$, then $\mu([\![D_{s_1}]\!]) - \mu([\![D_{s_0}]\!]) \geqslant 2^4\mu([\![\Sigma]\!])$.*

Proof. Form a prefix-free set $\widehat{\Sigma} = \{\sigma_0, \dots \sigma_k\}$ from the set of minimal elements of Σ under the $\preccurlyeq$ relation. For all $i \leqslant k$, there exists some τ_i with $U_{s_1}(\tau_i) \preccurlyeq \sigma_i$ such that $|\tau_i| \leqslant |U_{s_1}(\tau_i)| - 4$ and $\tau_i \notin \text{dom}(U_{s_0})$. Let $C = \{U_{s_1}(\tau_i) : i \leqslant k\}$. Now, $[\![C]\!] \supseteq [\![\Sigma]\!]$, so we can let $\widehat{C}$ be a minimal subset of C such that $[\![\widehat{C}]\!] \supseteq [\![\Sigma]\!]$. Then $\mu([\![\widehat{C}]\!]) \geqslant \mu([\![\Sigma]\!])$. For all $\upsilon \in \widehat{C}$, choose an i such that $U(\tau_i) = \upsilon$ and let I be the set of all such i. The set $\{\tau_i : i \in I\}$ is prefix-free, because its image under U is prefix-free and U is a strict process machine. It follows that

$$\mu([\![\{\tau_i : i \in I\}]\!]) = \sum_{i \in I} 2^{-|\tau_i|} \geqslant \sum_{i \in I} 2^{4-|U_{s_1}(\tau_i)|} = 2^4\mu([\![\widehat{C}]\!]) \geqslant 2^4\mu([\![\Sigma]\!]).$$

Finally, take any $i \leqslant k$. If $\tau_i \prec \tau$, then $\tau \notin \text{dom}(U_{s_0})$, as the domain of a strict process machine is closed under substrings. So $\tau \notin D_{s_0}$. If $\tau \prec \tau_i$ and $\tau \in D_{s_0}$, then $U_{s_0}(\tau) \in \overline{R}^{V_{s_0}}$. Since $U_{s_0}(\tau) \preccurlyeq U_{s_1}(\tau_i) \preccurlyeq \sigma_i$, it follows that $\sigma_i \in \overline{R}^{V_{s_0}}$. But we assumed that $\sigma_i \notin \overline{R}^{V_{s_0}}$, and hence $[\![\{\tau_i : i \leqslant k\}]\!] \cap [\![D_{s_0}]\!] = \emptyset$. The result follows, since $D_{s_0} \subseteq D_{s_1}$. ☐

Again by scaling, we can regard the opponent as having $\frac{1}{16}$ much measure to spend, and the cost of the move as being $\mu([\![\Sigma]\!])$.

Lemma 16.3.33. *V is a strict process machine.*

Proof. U is by assumption a strict process machine, so to check that V is a strict process machine, we need to check only the strings enumerated into V by the champion. As the champion is effectively a prefix-free machine, we need to show only that the champion does not run out of measure.

We divide the games into two sorts, those games $G_{\langle n,i,j\rangle}$ with $j = 0$, and all other games. We know the champion always keeps within the rules of the game. Let C be the cost to the champion of playing those games with $j = 0$. Then C is less than the sum of the measures allocated to each game. Hence, $C \leqslant \sum_n \sum_i 2^{-n-i-6} = \sum_n 2^{-n-5} = \frac{1}{16}$.

Now, j is incremented only if the opponent exceeds the amount of measure allocated to a game. Hence the measure the champion spends on these games is always less than the measure the opponent spends overall. As the opponent has only $\frac{1}{16}$ to spend, it follows that the champion spends less than

$C + \frac{1}{16} = \frac{1}{8}$, the amount of measure available to it. Hence the champion is a prefix-free machine and thus V is a strict process machine. □

Lemma 16.3.34. *All requirements are met.*

Proof. Take any requirement R_n. Assume that at some stage s_0 all higher priority requirements have stopped acting. Let $\langle n, i, j \rangle$ be the witness assigned to R_n at stage s_0. Because all higher priority requirements have stopped acting, i is never incremented again. So if the witness is changed, it must be because j is increased. This event must in turn be caused by the opponent exceeding its allocated measure of 2^{-n-i-6} in the previous game, which can happen only finitely often, since otherwise the opponent would run out of measure.

So there is some final witness $\langle n, i_n, j_n \rangle$ assigned to R_n. If $\Gamma_n(\langle n, i_n, j_n \rangle)$ never halts then the requirement is met. If $\Gamma_n(\langle n, i_n, j_n \rangle)$ does halt then the champion will adopt a winning strategy for the game $G_{\langle n, i_n, j_n \rangle}$, and so in either case $\Gamma_n^{\overline{R}^V}(\langle n, i_n, j_n \rangle) \neq A(\langle n, i_n, j_n \rangle)$. □

Together, the previous two lemmas complete the proof of the theorem. □

References

[1] M. Ageev. Martin's game: a lower bound for the number of sets. *Theoretical Computer Science*, 289:871–876, 2002. [732]

[2] AIM/ARCC Workshop in Effective Randomness, August 7–11, 2006, Open problem list. `http://www.math.dartmouth.edu/~frg/aimRandQsLive.pdf`. [xiii]

[3] E. Allender, H. Buhrman, and M. Koucký. What can be efficiently reduced to the Kolmogorov-random strings? *Annals of Pure and Applied Logic*, 138:2–19, 2006. [749]

[4] E. Allender, H. Buhrman, M. Koucký, D. van Melkebeek, and D. Ronneburger. Power from random strings. *SIAM Journal on Computing*, 35:1467–1493, 2006. [743]

[5] K. Ambos-Spies. Anti-mitotic recursively enumerable sets. *Mathematical Logic Quarterly*, 31:461–477, 1985. [53]

[6] K. Ambos-Spies. Algorithmic randomness revisited. In B. McGuinness, editor, *Language, Logic and Formalization of Knowledge. Coimbra Lecture and Proceedings of a Symposium held in Siena in September 1997*, pages 33–52. Bibliotheca, 1998. [303, 307]

[7] K. Ambos-Spies, C. G. Jockusch, Jr., R. A. Shore, and R. I. Soare. An algebraic decomposition of the recursively enumerable degrees and the coincidence of several degree classes with the promptly simple degrees. *Transactions of the American Mathematical Society*, 281:1089–1104, 1984. [15, 91, 92, 215]

Numbers in brackets after each entry indicate the pages on which the entry is cited.

R.G. Downey and D. Hirschfeldt, *Algorithmic Randomness and Complexity*, Theory and Applications of Computability, DOI 10.1007/978-0-387-68441-3,

[8] K. Ambos-Spies, B. Kjos-Hanssen, S. Lempp, and T. A. Slaman. Comparing DNR and WWKL. *The Journal of Symbolic Logic*, 69:102–143, 2004. [349]

[9] K. Ambos-Spies and A. Kučera. Randomness in computability theory. In P. A. Cholak, S. Lempp, M. Lerman, and R. A. Shore, editors, *Computability Theory and its Applications. Proceedings of the AMS-IMS-SIAM Joint Summer Research Conference held at the University of Colorado, Boulder, CO, June 13–17, 1999*, volume 257 of *Contemporary Mathematics*, pages 1–14. American Mathematical Society, Providence, RI, 2000. [277, 554]

[10] K. Ambos-Spies and E. Mayordomo. Resource-bounded measure and randomness. In A. Sorbi, editor, *Complexity, Logic, and Recursion Theory*, volume 187 of *Lecture Notes in Pure and Applied Mathematics*, pages 1–47. Marcel Dekker, Inc., New York, 1997. [16, 270, 277]

[11] K. Ambos-Spies, E. Mayordomo, Y. Wang, and X. Zheng. Resource-bounded balanced genericity, stochasticity and weak randomness. In C. Puech and R. Reischuk, editors, *STACS '96. Proceedings of the 13th Annual Symposium on Theoretical Aspects of Computer Science held in Grenoble, February 22–24, 1996*, volume 1046 of *Lecture Notes in Computer Science*, pages 63–74. Springer-Verlag, Berlin, 1996. [308]

[12] K. Ambos-Spies, K. Weihrauch, and X. Zheng. Weakly computable real numbers. *Journal of Complexity*, 16:676–690, 2000. [201, 217, 219]

[13] M. M. Arslanov. On some generalizations of the fixed-point theorem. *Soviet Mathematics*, 25:1–10, 1981. Translated from *Izvestiya Vysshikh Uchebnykh Zavedeniĭ. Matematika*. [89]

[14] M. M. Arslanov. Degree structures in local degree theory. In A. Sorbi, editor, *Complexity, Logic, and Recursion Theory*, volume 187 of *Lecture Notes in Pure and Applied Mathematics*, pages 49–74. Marcel Dekker Inc., New York, 1997. [27, 89]

[15] K. B. Athreya, J. M. Hitchcock, J. H. Lutz, and E. Mayordomo. Effective strong dimension in algorithmic information and computational complexity. *SIAM Journal on Computing*, 37:671–705, 2007. [636, 637, 638, 639, 641, 654, 657]

[16] B. Barak, R. Impagliazzo, and A. Wigderson. Extracting randomness using few independent sources. *SIAM Journal on Computing*, 36:1095–1118, 2006. [642]

[17] G. Barmpalias. Random non-cupping revisited. *Journal of Complexity*, 22:850–857, 2006. [536]

[18] G. Barmpalias. Elementary differences between the degrees of unsolvability and degrees of compressibility. *Annals of Pure and Applied Logic*, 161:923–934, 2010. [491, 494]

[19] G. Barmpalias. Relative randomness and cardinality. *Notre Dame Journal of Formal Logic*, 51:195–205, 2010. [491]

[20] G. Barmpalias, R. G. Downey, and N. Greenberg. K-trivial degrees and the jump traceability hierarchy. *Proceedings of the American Mathematical Society*, 137:2099–2109, 2009. [689]

[21] G. Barmpalias, R. G. Downey, and N. Greenberg. Working with strong reducibilities above totally ω-c.e. and array computable degrees. *Transac-*

tions of the American Mathematical Society, 362:777–813, 2010. [442, 443, 444, 447, 448, 455]

[22] G. Barmpalias, R. G. Downey, and K. M. Ng. Jump inversions inside effectively closed sets and applications to randomness. To appear in the *Journal of Symbolic Logic*. [358, 362]

[23] G. Barmpalias and A. E. M. Lewis. A c.e. real that cannot be sw-computed by any Ω-number. *Notre Dame Journal of Formal Logic*, 47:197–209, 2006. [448]

[24] G. Barmpalias, A. E. M. Lewis, and K. M. Ng. The importance of Π^0_1 classes in effective randomness. *The Journal of Symbolic Logic*, 75:387–400, 2010. [323, 339, 491, 536]

[25] G. Barmpalias, A. E. M. Lewis, and M. Soskova. Randomness, lowness and degrees. *The Journal of Symbolic Logic*, 73:559–577, 2008. [489, 490, 491, 499]

[26] G. Barmpalias, A. E. M. Lewis, and F. Stephan. Π^0_1 classes, LR degrees and Turing degrees. *Annals of Pure and Applied Logic*, 156:21–38, 2008. [491]

[27] G. Barmpalias, J. S. Miller, and A. Nies. Randomness notions and partial relativization. To appear. [315]

[28] G. Barmpalias and A. Nies. Upper bounds on ideals in the Turing degrees. To appear. [541, 542]

[29] J. Barzdins. Complexity of programs to determine whether natural numbers not greater than n belong to a recursively enumerable set. *Soviet Mathematics Doklady*, 9:1251–1254, 1968. [122, 728]

[30] T. Bayes. An essay towards solving a problem in the doctrine of chances, by the late Rev. Mr. Bayes, F. R. S. communicated by Mr. Price, in a letter to John Canton, A. M., F. R. S. *Philosophical Transactions of the Royal Society of London*, 53:370–418, 1763. [238]

[31] V. Becher, S. Figueira, S. Grigorieff, and J. S. Miller. Randomness and halting probabilities. *The Journal of Symbolic Logic*, 71:1411–1430, 2006. [229]

[32] V. Becher and S. Grigorieff. Random reals and possibly infinite computations. I. Randomness in $\emptyset'$. *The Journal of Symbolic Logic*, 70:891–913, 2005. [229]

[33] V. Becher and S. Grigorieff. From index sets to randomness in $\emptyset^n$: random reals and possibly infinite computations. II. *The Journal of Symbolic Logic*, 74:124–156, 2009. [257]

[34] B. R. C. Bedregal and A. Nies. Lowness properties of reals and hyperimmunity. In R. de Queiroz, E. Pimentel, and L. Figueiredo, editors, *WoLLiC '2003. 10th Workshop on Logic, Language, Information, and Computation, Ouro Preto, Minas Gerais, Brazil, 29 July–01 August 2003*, volume 84 of *Electronic Notes in Theoretical Computer Science*, pages 73–79 (electronic). Elsevier, Amsterdam, 2003. [560]

[35] O. V. Belegradek. On algebraically closed groups. *Algebra and Logic*, 13:135–143, 1974. [206]

[36] M. Bickford and C. Mills. Lowness properties of r.e. sets. Unpublished manuscript, 1982, University of Wisconsin–Madison. [530]

[37] L. Bienvenu. *Game-theoretic Characterizations of Randomness: Unpredictability and Stochasticity.* Ph.D. dissertation, University of Provence, 2008. [327, 330]

[38] L. Bienvenu, D. Doty, and F. Stephan. Constructive dimension and Turing degrees. *Theory of Computing Systems*, 45:740–755, 2009. [643]

[39] L. Bienvenu and R. G. Downey. Kolmogorov complexity and Solovay functions. In S. Albers and J.-Y. Marion, editors, *26th International Symposium on Theoretical Aspects of Computer Science. STACS 2009, February 26–28, 2009, Freiburg, Germany*, volume 3 of *Leibniz International Proceedings in Informatics*, pages 147–158 (electronic). Schloss Dagstuhl–Leibniz Center for Informatics, Dagstuhl, Germany, 2009. [138, 327, 329, 412, 413, 484, 504, 505, 714]

[40] L. Bienvenu and W. Merkle. Reconciling data compression and Kolmogorov complexity. In L. Arge, C. Cachin, T. Jurdziński, and A. Tarlecki, editors, *Automata, Languages and Programming. 34th International Colloquium, ICALP 2007, Wrocław, Poland, July 9–13, 2007. Proceedings*, volume 4596 of *Lecture Notes in Computer Science*, pages 643–654. Springer, Berlin, 2007. Extended version at `http://www.math.uni-heidelberg.de/logic/merkle/ps/icalp-2007.pdf`. [138, 139, 298, 299, 300, 301]

[41] L. Bienvenu and J. S. Miller. Randomness and lowness notions via open covers. To appear in the *Annals of Pure and Applied Logic.* [591]

[42] L. Bienvenu, An. A. Muchnik, A. Shen, and N. Vereshchagin. Limit complexities revisited. In S. Albers and P. Weil, editors, *25th International Symposium on Theoretical Aspects of Computer Science. STACS 2008, February 21–23, 2008, Bordeaux, France*, volume 1 of *Leibniz International Proceedings in Informatics*, pages 73–84 (electronic). Schloss Dagstuhl–Leibniz Center for Informatics, Dagstuhl, Germany, 2008. [263, 471, 472, 473]

[43] S. Binns, B. Kjos-Hanssen, M. Lerman, and R. Solomon. On a conjecture of Dobrinen and Simpson concerning almost everywhere domination. *The Journal of Symbolic Logic*, 71:119–136, 2006. [497]

[44] P. Brodhead, R. G. Downey, and K. M. Ng. Bounded variations of randomness. In preparation. [319]

[45] J.-Y. Cai and J. Hartmanis. On Hausdorff and topological dimensions of the Kolmogorov complexity of the real line. *Journal of Computer and System Sciences*, 49:605–619, 1994. [598]

[46] W. C. Calhoun. Degrees of monotone complexity. *The Journal of Symbolic Logic*, 71:1327–1341, 2006. [147, 432, 459, 460, 461, 462]

[47] C. Calude, R. J. Coles, P. H. Hertling, and B. Khoussainov. Degree-theoretic aspects of computably enumerable reals. In S. B. Cooper and J. K. Truss, editors, *Models and Computability. Invited Papers from Logic Colloquium '97 - European Meeting of the Association for Symbolic Logic, Leeds, July 1997*, volume 259 of *London Mathematical Society Lecture Note Series.* Cambridge University Press, Cambridge, 1999. [203, 204, 205, 405]

[48] C. S. Calude and G. J. Chaitin. What is a halting probability? *Notices of the American Mathematical Society*, 57:236–237, 2010. [12, 142]

[49] C. S. Calude and R. J. Coles. Program-size complexity of initial segments and domination relation reducibility. In J. Karhumäki, H. Mauer, G. Păun, and G. Rozenberg, editors, *Jewels are Forever*, pages 225–237. Springer-Verlag, Berlin, 1999. [501]

[50] C. S. Calude, P. H. Hertling, B. Khoussainov, and Y. Wang. Recursively enumerable reals and Chaitin Ω numbers. In M. Morvan, C. Meinel, and D. Krob, editors, *STACS 98. 15th Annual Symposium on Theoretical Aspects of Computer Science. Paris, France, February 25–27, 1998. Proceedings*, volume 1373 of *Lecture Notes in Computer Science*, pages 596–606. Springer, Berlin, 1998. [200, 409, 413]

[51] C. S. Calude and A. Nies. Chaitin Ω numbers and strong reducibilities. *Journal of Universal Computer Science*, 3:1162–1166 (electronic), 1997. [228, 333]

[52] C. S. Calude, L. Staiger, and S. A. Terwijn. On partial randomness. *Annals of Pure and Applied Logic*, 138:20–30, 2006. [604, 605]

[53] C. S. Calude and M. Zimand. Algorithmically independent sequences. In M. Ito and M. Toyama, editors, *Developments in Language Theory. 12th International Conference, DLT 2008. Kyoto, Japan, September 16–19, 2008. Proceedings*, volume 5257 of *Lecture Notes in Computer Science*, pages 183–195. Springer, Berlin, 2008. [627, 628, 635]

[54] C. Carathéodory. Über das lineare Mass von Punktmengen, eine Verallgemeinerung des Längenbegriffs. *Nachrichten von der Gesellschaft der Wissenschaften zu Göttingen, Mathematisch-Physikalische Klasse*, pages 404–426, 1914. [592]

[55] D. Cenzer. Π^0_1 classes in computability theory. In E. R. Griffor, editor, *Handbook of Computability Theory*, volume 140 of *Studies in Logic and the Foundations of Mathematics*, pages 37–85. North-Holland, Amsterdam, 1999. [74, 373]

[56] D. Cenzer, G. LaForte, and G. Wu. Pseudojumps and Π^0_1 classes. *Journal of Logic and Computation*, 19:77–87, 2009. [377]

[57] D. Cenzer and J. B. Remmel. *Effectively Closed Sets*. To be published in *Lecture Notes in Logic*. [74]

[58] G. J. Chaitin. A theory of program size formally identical to information theory. *Journal of the Association for Computing Machinery*, 22:329–340, 1975. [xiii, 121, 125, 128, 129, 133, 134, 142, 227, 228, 232]

[59] G. J. Chaitin. Algorithmic entropy of sets. *Computers & Mathematics with Applications*, 2:233–245, 1976. [731, 732]

[60] G. J. Chaitin. Information-theoretical characterizations of recursive infinite strings. *Theoretical Computer Science*, 2:45–48, 1976. [118, 119, 120]

[61] G. J. Chaitin. Nonrecursive infinite strings with simple initial segments. *IBM Journal of Research and Development*, 21:350–359, 496, 1977. [456, 500]

[62] G. J. Chaitin. Gödel's theorem and information. *International Journal of Theoretical Physics*, 21:941–954, 1982. [627]

[63] G. J. Chaitin. Incompleteness theorems for random reals. *Advances in Applied Mathematics*, 8:119–146, 1987. [129, 130, 131, 229, 233, 250]

[64] J. Chisholm, J. Chubb, V. S. Harizanov, D. R. Hirschfeldt, C. G. Jockusch, Jr., T. McNicholl, and S. Pingrey. Π^0_1 classes and strong degree spectra of relations. *The Journal of Symbolic Logic*, 72:1003–1018, 2007. [368]

[65] P. A. Cholak, R. G. Downey, and N. Greenberg. Strong-jump traceablilty. I. The computably enumerable case. *Advances in Mathematics*, 217:2045–2074, 2008. [668, 669, 670, 673, 680, 685]

[66] P. A. Cholak, R. G. Downey, and M. Stob. Automorphisms of the lattice of recursively enumerable sets: promptly simple sets. *Transactions of the American Mathematical Society*, 332:555–570, 1992. [83]

[67] P. A. Cholak, N. Greenberg, and J. S. Miller. Uniform almost everywhere domination. *The Journal of Symbolic Logic*, 71:1057–1072, 2006. [496]

[68] P. A. Cholak and L. A. Harrington. Definable encodings in the computably enumerable sets. *The Bulletin of Symbolic Logic*, 6:185–196, 2000. [83]

[69] C. T. Chong and R. G. Downey. Degrees bounding minimal degrees. *Mathematical Proceedings of the Cambridge Philosophical Society*, 105:211–222, 1989. [386]

[70] C. T. Chong and R. G. Downey. Minimal degrees recursive in 1-generic degrees. *Annals of Pure and Applied Logic*, 48:215–225, 1990. [386]

[71] A. Church. On the concept of a random sequence. *Bulletin of the American Mathematical Society*, 46:130–135, 1940. [xviii, 230]

[72] J. A. Cole and S. G. Simpson. Mass problems and hyperarithmeticity. *Journal of Mathematical Logic*, 7:125–143, 2007. [347, 696]

[73] R. J. Coles, R. G. Downey, C. G. Jockusch, Jr., and G. LaForte. Completing pseudojump operators. *Annals of Pure and Applied Logic*, 136:297–333, 2005. [42]

[74] C. J. Conidis. A real of strictly positive effective packing dimension that does not compute a real of effective packing dimension one. To appear. [642]

[75] C. J. Conidis. Effective packing dimension of Π^0_1-classes. *Proceedings of the American Mathematical Society*, 136:3655–3662, 2008. [648]

[76] S. B. Cooper. Degrees of unsolvability complementary between recursively enumerable degrees. *Annals of Mathematical Logic*, 4:31–73, 1972. [72]

[77] S. B. Cooper. Minimal degrees and the jump operator. *The Journal of Symbolic Logic*, 38:249–271, 1973. [72]

[78] S. B. Cooper. A characterisation of the jumps of minimal degrees below $0'$. In S. B. Cooper, T. A. Slaman, and S. S. Wainer, editors, *Computability, Enumerability, Unsolvability. Directions in Recursion Theory*, volume 224 of *London Mathematical Society Lecture Note Series*, pages 81–92. Cambridge University Press, Cambridge, 1996. [72]

[79] S. B. Cooper. *Computability Theory.* Chapman & Hall/CRC, Boca Raton, FL, 2004. [xiii, 8]

[80] B. F. Csima. *Applications of Computability Theory to Prime Models and Differential Geometry.* Ph.D. dissertation, The University of Chicago, 2003. [420, 421]

[81] B. F. Csima. The settling time reducibility ordering and Δ_2^0 sets. *Journal of Logic and Computation*, 19:145–150, 2009. [421]

[82] B. F. Csima, R. G. Downey, N. Greenberg, D. R. Hirschfeldt, and J. S. Miller. Every 1-generic computes a properly 1-generic. *The Journal of Symbolic Logic*, 71:1385–1393, 2006. [379]

[83] B. F. Csima and A. Montalbán. A minimal pair of K-degrees. *Proceedings of the American Mathematical Society*, 134:1499–1502, 2006. [458, 551, 552]

[84] B. F. Csima and R. A. Shore. The settling-time reducibility ordering. *The Journal of Symbolic Logic*, 72:1055–1071, 2007. [421]

[85] B. F. Csima and R. I. Soare. Computability results used in differential geometry. *The Journal of Symbolic Logic*, 71:1394–1410, 2006. [421]

[86] R. P. Daley. Minimal-program complexity of pseudo-recursive and pseudo-random sequences. *Mathematical Systems Theory*, 9:83–94, 1975. [304, 305]

[87] A. R. Day. Increasing the gap between descriptional complexity and algorithmic probability. To appear in the *Transactions of the American Mathematical Society.* [151, 153, 169, 170]

[88] A. R. Day. On the computational power of random strings. *Annals of Pure and Applied Logic*, 160:214–228, 2009. [147, 752, 761, 762, 763]

[89] A. R. Day. Process complexity and computable randomness. Manuscript, June 2009. [282, 283]

[90] A. R. Day. On process complexity. *Chicago Journal of Theoretical Computer Science*, 2010. Paper number 4 (electronic). [149]

[91] A. R. Day and A. Fitzgerald. Indifferent sets for 1-generics. In preparation. [341]

[92] K. de Leeuw, E. F. Moore, C. E. Shannon, and N. Shapiro. Computability by probabilistic machines. In C. E. Shannon and J. McCarthy, editors, *Automata Studies*, volume 34 of *Annals of Mathematics Studies*, pages 183–212. Princeton University Press, Princeton, NJ, 1956. [323, 358]

[93] O. Demuth. On constructive pseudonumbers. *Commentationes Mathematicae Universitatis Carolinae*, 16:315–331, 1975. In Russian. [199, 231, 409, 418, 419]

[94] O. Demuth. On some classes of arithmetical real numbers. *Commentationes Mathematicae Universitatis Carolinae*, 23:453–465, 1982. In Russian. [315]

[95] O. Demuth. Remarks on the structure of *tt*-degrees based on constructive measure theory. *Commentationes Mathematicae Universitatis Carolinae*, 29:233–247, 1988. [315, 316, 333, 364]

[96] O. Demuth and A. Kučera. Remarks on 1-genericity, semigenericity, and related concepts. *Commentationes Mathematicae Universitatis Carolinae*, 28:85–94, 1987. [103, 380]

[97] D. Diamondstone. Promptness does not imply superlow cuppability. *The Journal of Symbolic Logic*, 74:1264–1272, 2009. [693, 694]

[98] N. L. Dobrinen and S. G. Simpson. Almost everywhere domination. *The Journal of Symbolic Logic*, 69:914–922, 2004. [495, 496]

[99] R. G. Downey. Δ_2^0 degrees and transfer theorems. *Illinois Journal of Mathematics*, 31:419–427, 1987. [70]

[100] R. G. Downey. Subsets of hypersimple sets. *Pacific Journal of Mathematics*, 127:299–319, 1987. [83]

[101] R. G. Downey. On the universal splitting property. *Mathematical Logic Quarterly*, 43:311–320, 1997. [205]

[102] R. G. Downey. Computability, definability, and algebraic structures. In R. G. Downey, D. Ding, S. P. Tung, Y. H. Qiu, and M. Yasugi, editors, *Proceedings of the 7th and 8th Asian Logic Conferences. Held in Hsi-Tou, June 6–10, 1999 and Chongqing, August 29–September 2, 2002*, pages 63–102. Singapore University Press and World Scientific, Singapore, 2003. [204]

[103] R. G. Downey. Some computability-theoretical aspects of reals and randomness. In P. A. Cholak, editor, *The Notre Dame Lectures*, volume 18 of *Lecture Notes in Logic*, pages 97–148. Association for Symbolic Logic and A K Peters, Ltd., Urbana, IL and Wellesley, MA, 2005. [212, 440]

[104] R. G. Downey. The sixth lecture on algorithmic randomness. In S. B. Cooper, H. Geuvers, A. Pillay, and J. Väänänen, editors, *Logic Colloquium 2006. Proceedings of the Annual European Conference on Logic of the Association for Symbolic Logic held at the Radboud University, Nijmegen, July 27–August 2, 2006*, volume 32 of *Lecture Notes in Logic*, pages 103–134. Association for Symbolic Logic and Cambridge University Press, Chicago and Cambridge, 2009. [511]

[105] R. G. Downey and N. Greenberg. Strong jump traceability II: K-triviality. To appear. [668, 700]

[106] R. G. Downey and N. Greenberg. Turing degrees of reals of positive effective packing dimension. *Information Processing Letters*, 108:298–303, 2008. [618, 642, 645, 649, 650]

[107] R. G. Downey, N. Greenberg, N. Mihailović, and A. Nies. Lowness for computable machines. In C. T. Chong, Q. Feng, T. A. Slaman, W. H. Woodin, and Y. Yang, editors, *Computational Prospects of Infinity: Part II. Presented Talks, Lectures from the Workshop Held at the National University of Singapore, Singapore, June 20–August 15, 2005*, volume 15 of *Lecture Notes Series. Institute for Mathematical Sciences. National University of Singapore*, pages 79–86. World Scientific Publishing Company, Singapore, 2008. [562, 563, 564]

[108] R. G. Downey, N. Greenberg, and J. S. Miller. The upward closure of a perfect thin class. *Annals of Pure and Applied Logic*, 165:51–58, 2008. [323]

[109] R. G. Downey and E. J. Griffiths. Schnorr randomness. *The Journal of Symbolic Logic*, 69:533–554, 2004. [275, 277, 294, 350, 462, 562, 564, 658]

[110] R. G. Downey, E. J. Griffiths, and G. LaForte. On Schnorr and computable randomness, martingales, and machines. *Mathematical Logic Quarterly*, 50:613–627, 2004. [240, 278, 279, 280, 349, 350, 462, 463, 564, 565, 568, 569]

[111] R. G. Downey, E. J. Griffiths, and S. Reid. On Kurtz randomness. *Theoretical Computer Science*, 321:249–270, 2004. [290, 291, 292, 293, 294, 295, 296, 581]

[112] R. G. Downey and D. R. Hirschfeldt, editors. *Aspects of Complexity (Short Courses in Complexity from the New Zealand Mathematical Research Institute Summer 2000 Meeting, Kaikoura)*, volume 4 of *De Gruyter Series in Logic and its Applications*. Walter de Gruyter & Co., Berlin, 2001. [xi]

[113] R. G. Downey, D. R. Hirschfeldt, and G. LaForte. Randomness and reducibility. *Journal of Computer and System Sciences*, 68:96–114, 2004. [406, 420, 421, 422, 423, 424, 433, 434, 435, 436, 440, 442]

[114] R. G. Downey, D. R. Hirschfeldt, and G. LaForte. Undecidability of the structure of the Solovay degrees of c.e. reals. *Journal of Computer and System Sciences*, 73:769–787, 2007. [419]

[115] R. G. Downey, D. R. Hirschfeldt, J. S. Miller, and A. Nies. Relativizing Chaitin's halting probability. *Journal of Mathematical Logic*, 5:167–192, 2005. [334, 528, 706, 707, 708, 709, 710, 711, 712, 713, 716, 717, 718, 719, 720, 721, 723, 724, 726, 727]

[116] R. G. Downey, D. R. Hirschfeldt, and A. Nies. Randomness, computability and density. *SIAM Journal on Computing*, 31:1169–1183, 2002. [xi, 407, 408, 413, 415, 416, 418, 419, 427, 430, 432]

[117] R. G. Downey, D. R. Hirschfeldt, A. Nies, and F. Stephan. Trivial reals. In R. G. Downey, D. Ding, S. P. Tung, Y. H. Qiu, and M. Yasugi, editors, *Proceedings of the 7th and 8th Asian Logic Conferences. Held in Hsi-Tou, June 6–10, 1999 and Chongqing, August 29–September 2, 2002*, pages 103–131. Singapore University Press and World Scientific, Singapore, 2003. [426, 501, 503, 504, 511, 526, 529, 530, 539, 540, 541, 542]

[118] R. G. Downey, D. R. Hirschfeldt, A. Nies, and S. A. Terwijn. Calibrating randomness. *The Bulletin of Symbolic Logic*, 12:411–491, 2006. [233, 258, 517, 600]

[119] R. G. Downey and C. G. Jockusch, Jr. T-degrees, jump classes, and strong reducibilities. *Transactions of the American Mathematical Society*, 301:103–136, 1987. [82, 207]

[120] R. G. Downey, C. G. Jockusch, Jr., and M. Stob. Array nonrecursive sets and multiple permitting arguments. In K. Ambos-Spies, G. H. Müller, and G. E. Sacks, editors, *Recursion Theory Week. Proceedings of the Conference Held at the Mathematisches Forschungsinstitut, Oberwolfach, March 19–25, 1989*, volume 1432 of *Lecture Notes in Mathematics*, pages 141–174. Springer, Berlin, 1990. [93, 94, 95, 96, 98, 530]

[121] R. G. Downey, C. G. Jockusch, Jr., and M. Stob. Array nonrecursive degrees and genericity. In S. B. Cooper, T. A. Slaman, and S. S. Wainer, editors, *Computability, Enumerability, Unsolvability. Directions in Recursion Theory*, volume 224 of *London Mathematical Society Lecture Notes Series*, pages 93–104. Cambridge University Press, Cambridge, 1996. [93, 94, 95, 96, 97, 107, 108, 109]

[122] R. G. Downey and G. LaForte. Presentations of computably enumerable reals. *Theoretical Computer Science*, 284:539–555, 2002. [206, 208, 210, 215]

[123] R. G. Downey, G. LaForte, and A. Nies. Computably enumerable sets and quasi-reducibility. *Annals of Pure and Applied Logic*, 95:1–35, 1998. [206]

[124] R. G. Downey, S. Lempp, and R. A. Shore. Jumps of minimal degrees below $\mathbf{0}'$. *Journal of the London Mathematical Society. Second Series*, 54:417–439, 1996. [72]

[125] R. G. Downey, W. Merkle, and J. Reimann. Schnorr dimension. *Mathematical Structures in Computer Science*, 16:789–811, 2006. [655, 656, 658, 659, 660, 661]

[126] R. G. Downey and J. S. Miller. A basis theorem for Π^0_1 classes of positive measure and jump inversion for random reals. *Proceedings of the American Mathematical Society*, 134:283–288, 2006. [373]

[127] R. G. Downey, J. S. Miller, and L. Yu. On the quantity of K-trivial reals. In preparation. [505, 506]

[128] R. G. Downey and K. M. Ng. Lowness for Demuth randomness. In K. Ambos-Spies, B. Löwe, and W. Merkle, editors, *Mathematical Theory and Computational Practice. 5th Conference on Computability in Europe, CiE 2009. Heidelberg, Germany, July 19–24, 2009. Proceedings*, volume 5635 of *Lecture Notes in Computer Science*, pages 154–166. Springer, Berlin, 2009. [590]

[129] R. G. Downey and K. M. Ng. Effective packing dimension and traceability. *Notre Dame Journal of Formal Logic*, 51:279–290, 2010. [650]

[130] R. G. Downey, A. Nies, R. Weber, and L. Yu. Lowness and Π^0_2 nullsets. *The Journal of Symbolic Logic*, 71:1044–1052, 2006. [288, 289, 535, 537]

[131] R. G. Downey and J. B. Remmel. Classification of degree classes associated with r.e. subspaces. *Annals of Pure and Applied Logic*, 42:105–124, 1989. [206]

[132] R. G. Downey and R. A. Shore. There is no degree invariant half-jump. *Proceedings of the American Mathematical Society*, 125:3033–3037, 1997. [42]

[133] R. G. Downey and M. Stob. Splitting theorems in recursion theory. *Annals of Pure and Applied Logic*, 65:1–106, 1993. [205]

[134] R. G. Downey and S. A. Terwijn. Computably enumerable reals and uniformly presentable ideals. *Mathematical Logic Quarterly*, 48:29–40, 2002. [209]

[135] R. G. Downey and L. V. Welch. Splitting properties of r.e. sets and degrees. *The Journal of Symbolic Logic*, 51:88–109, 1986. [53]

[136] R. G. Downey, G. Wu, and X. Zheng. Degrees of d.c.e. reals. *Mathematical Logic Quarterly*, 50:345–350, 2004. [218]

[137] R. G. Downey and L. Yu. Arithmetical Sacks forcing. *Archive for Mathematical Logic*, 45:715–720, 2006. [103]

[138] B. Durand, L. A. Levin, and A. Shen. Complex tilings. *The Journal of Symbolic Logic*, 73:593–613, 2008. [601]

[139] H. B. Enderton. *A Mathematical Introduction to Logic.* Harcourt/Academic Press, Burlington, MA, second edition, 2001. [73, 84]

[140] R. L. Epstein, R. Haas, and R. L. Kramer. Hierarchies of sets and degrees below $\mathbf{0}'$. In M. Lerman, J. H. Schmerl, and R. I. Soare, editors, *Logic Year 1979–1980, Proceedings of Seminars and of the Conference on Mathematical Logic Held at the University of Connecticut, Storrs, Conn., November 11–13, 1979*, volume 859 of *Lecture Notes in Mathematics*, pages 32–48. Springer, Berlin, 1981. [28]

[141] K. Falconer. *Fractal Geometry. Mathematical Foundations and Applications.* John Wiley & Sons, Ltd., Chichester, 1990. [639]

[142] H. Federer. *Geometric Measure Theory*, volume 153 of *Die Grundlehren der Mathematischen Wissenschaften.* Springer-Verlag, New York, 1969. [635]

[143] S. Feferman. Some applications of the notions of forcing and generic sets. *Fundamenta Mathematicae*, 56:325–345, 1964/1965. [100]

[144] W. Feller. *An Introduction to Probability Theory and its Applications*, volume I. John Wiley & Sons, Inc., New York, 1950. [241, 250, 629]

[145] S. Fenner and M. Schaefer. A note on a variant of btt-reducibility, immunity and minimal programs. *Mathematical Logic Quarterly*, 45:3–21, 1999. [454]

[146] S. Figueira, J. S. Miller, and A. Nies. Indifferent sets. *Journal of Logic and Computation*, 19:425–443, 2009. [340, 341]

[147] S. Figueira, A. Nies, and F. Stephan. Lowness properties and approximations of the jump. In R. de Queiroz, A. Macintyre, and G. Bittencourt, editors, *Proceedings of the 12th Workshop of Logic, Language, Information and Computation (WoLLIC 2005). Held in Florianópolis, July 19–22, 2005*, volume 143 of *Electronic Notes in Theoretical Computer Science*, pages 45–57. Elsevier Science B.V., Amsterdam, 2006. [120, 523, 668, 669, 670, 671]

[148] L. Fortnow. Kolmogorov complexity. In R. G. Downey and D. R. Hirschfeldt, editors, *Aspects of Complexity (Short Courses in Complexity from the New Zealand Mathematical Research Institute Summer 2000 Meeting, Kaikoura)*, volume 4 of *De Gruyter Series in Logic and its Applications*, pages 73–86. Walter de Gruyter & Co., Berlin, 2001. [xi, 132]

[149] L. Fortnow, R. Freivalds, W. I. Gasarch, M. Kummer, S. A. Kurtz, C. H. Smith, and F. Stephan. On the relative sizes of learnable sets. *Theoretical Computer Science*, 197:139–156, 1998. [303]

[150] L. Fortnow, J. M. Hitchcock, A. Pavan, V. Vinochandran, and F. Wang. Extracting Kolmogorov complexity with applications to dimension zero-one laws. In M. Bugliesi, B. Preneel, V. Sassone, and I. Wegener, editors, *Automata, Languages and Programming. 33rd International Colloquium, ICALP 2006. Venice, Italy, July 10–14, 2006. Proceedings, Part I*, volume 4051 of *Lecture Notes in Computer Science*, pages 335–345. Springer, Berlin, 2006. [642]

[151] J. N. Y. Franklin. *Aspects of Schnorr Randomness.* Ph.D. dissertation, University of California, Berkeley, 2007. [564, 575]

[152] J. N. Y. Franklin. Hyperimmune-free degrees and Schnorr triviality. *The Journal of Symbolic Logic*, 73:999–1008, 2008. [564, 575]

[153] J. N. Y. Franklin. Schnorr trivial reals: a construction. *Archive for Mathematical Logic*, 46:665–678, 2008. [564]

[154] J. N. Y. Franklin. Lowness and highness properties for randomness notions. In T. Arai, J. Brendle, H. Kikyo, C. T. Chong, R. G. Downey, Q. Feng, and H. Ono, editors, *Proceedings of the 10th Asian Logic Conference. Kobe, Japan, 1–6 September 2008*, pages 124–151. World Scientific, Singapore, 2010. [591]

[155] J. N. Y. Franklin. Schnorr triviality and genericity. *The Journal of Symbolic Logic*, 75:191–207, 2010. [564]

[156] J. N. Y. Franklin, N. Greenberg, F. Stephan, and G. Wu. Anti-complexity, lowness and highness notions and reducibilities with tiny uses. In preparation. [576, 577, 578, 579, 580]

[157] J. N. Y. Franklin and K. M. Ng. Difference randomness. To appear in the *Proceedings of the American Mathematical Society*. [316, 317, 318, 535]

[158] J. N. Y. Franklin and F. Stephan. Schnorr trivial sets and truth-table reducibility. *The Journal of Symbolic Logic*, 75:501–521, 2010. [273, 570, 571, 572, 574, 575]

[159] J. N. Y. Franklin, F. Stephan, and L. Yu. Relativizations of randomness and genericity notions. To appear. [534, 591]

[160] R. M. Friedberg. A criterion for completeness of degrees of unsolvability. *The Journal of Symbolic Logic*, 22:159–160, 1957. [64]

[161] R. M. Friedberg. Two recursively enumerable sets of incomparable degrees of unsolvability. *Proceedings of the National Academy of Sciences of the United States of America*, 43:236–238, 1957. [32, 34, 36]

[162] R. M. Friedberg and H. Rogers, Jr. Reducibility and completeness for sets of integers. *Zeitschrift für Mathematische Logik und Grundlagen der Mathematik*, 5:117–125, 1959. [82]

[163] P. Gács. Lecture notes on descriptional complexity and randomness. Boston University, 1993–2005, available at `http://www.cs.bu.edu/faculty/gacs/recent-publ.html`. [138]

[164] P. Gács. On the symmetry of algorithmic information. *Soviet Mathematics Doklady*, 15:1477–1480, 1974. [133, 134, 143, 144]

[165] P. Gács. Exact expressions for some randomness tests. *Zeitschrift für Mathematische Logik und Grundlagen der Mathematik*, 26:385–394, 1980. [154, 252]

[166] P. Gács. On the relation between descriptional complexity and algorithmic probability. *Theoretical Computer Science*, 22:71–93, 1983. [147, 153, 169, 170]

[167] P. Gács. Every set is reducible to a random one. *Information and Control*, 70:186–192, 1986. [323, 325, 326, 484]

[168] H. Gaifmann and M. Snir. Probabilities over rich languages, testing and randomness. *The Journal of Symbolic Logic*, 47:495–548, 1982. [287, 361]

[169] N. Greenberg, D. R. Hirschfeldt, and A. Nies. Characterizing the strongly jump traceable sets via randomness. To appear. [689, 694, 695, 696, 697]

[170] N. Greenberg and J. S. Miller. Diagonally non-recursive functions and effective Hausdorff dimension. To appear in the *Bulletin of the London Mathematical Society*. [609, 618, 619, 620, 621, 622, 623, 624, 625, 626, 642]

[171] N. Greenberg and J. S. Miller. Lowness for Kurtz randomness. *The Journal of Symbolic Logic*, 74:665–678, 2009. [348, 584, 591]

[172] N. Greenberg and A. Nies. Benign cost functions and lowness properties. To appear in the *Journal of Symbolic Logic*. [526, 689, 690, 691, 692, 693]

[173] M. J. Groszek and T. A. Slaman. Π^0_1 classes and minimal degrees. *Annals of Pure and Applied Logic*, 87:117–144, 1997. [79]

[174] W. P. Hanf. The Boolean algebra of logic. *Bulletin of the American Mathematical Society*, 81:587–589, 1975. [84]

[175] L. A. Harrington, D. Marker, and S. Shelah. Borel orderings. *Transactions of the American Mathematical Society*, 310:293–302, 1988. [478]

[176] L. A. Harrington and R. I. Soare. Post's program and incomplete recursively enumerable sets. *Proceedings of the National Academy of Sciences of the United States of America*, 88:10242–10246, 1991. [83]

[177] F. Hausdorff. Dimension und äußeres Maß. *Mathematische Annalen*, 79:157–179, 1919. [592]

[178] D. R. Hirschfeldt, A. Nies, and F. Stephan. Using random sets as oracles. *Journal of the London Mathematical Society. Second Series*, 75:610–622, 2007. [531, 533, 534]

[179] J. M. Hitchcock. Gales suffice for constructive dimension. *Information Processing Letters*, 86:9–12, 2003. [597]

[180] J. M. Hitchcock. Correspondence principles for effective dimensions. *Theory of Computing Systems*, 38:559–571, 2005. [608, 637]

[181] J. M. Hitchcock and J. H. Lutz. Why computational complexity requires stricter martingales. *Theory of Computing Systems*, 39:277–296, 2006. [242, 243, 244, 245]

[182] C.-K. Ho. Relatively recursive reals and real functions. *Theoretical Computer Science*, 210:99–120, 1999. [199]

[183] R. Hölzl, T. Kräling, and W. Merkle. Time bounded Kolmogorov complexity and Solovay functions. In R. Královič and D. Niwiński, editors, *Mathematical Foundations of Computer Science 2009. 34th International Symposium, MFCS 2009. Novy Smokovec, High Tatras, Slovakia, August 24–28, 2009. Proceedings*, volume 5734 of *Lecture Notes in Computer Science*, pages 392–402. Springer, Berlin, 2009. [139, 689, 729]

[184] S. Ishmukhametov. Weak recursive degrees and a problem of Spector. In M. M. Arslanov and S. Lempp, editors, *Recursion Theory and Complexity. Proceedings of the International Workshop on Recursion Theory and Complexity Theory (WORCT'97) held at Kazan State University, Kazan, July 14–19, 1997*, volume 2 of *De Gruyter Series in Logic and its Applications*, pages 81–88. Walter de Gruyter & Co., Berlin, 1999. [98, 99, 100, 650]

[185] T. Jech. *Set Theory*. Springer Monographs in Mathematics. Springer-Verlag, Berlin, third millennium edition, 2003. [297]

[186] C. G. Jockusch, Jr. The degrees of bi-immune sets. *Zeitschrift für Mathematische Logik und Grundlagen der Mathematik*, 15:135–140, 1969. [295]

[187] C. G. Jockusch, Jr. Relationships between reducibilities. *Transactions of the American Mathematical Society*, 142:229–237, 1969. [70]

[188] C. G. Jockusch, Jr. Degrees of generic sets. In F. R. Drake and S. S. Wainer, editors, *Recursion Theory: its Generalisations and Applications*, volume 45 of *London Mathematical Society Lecture Note Series*, pages 110–139. Cambridge University Press, Cambridge, 1980. [101, 102, 104, 401]

[189] C. G. Jockusch, Jr. Fine degrees of word problems in cancellation semigroups. *Zeitschrift für Mathematische Logik und Grundlagen der Mathematik*, 26:93–95, 1980. [206]

[190] C. G. Jockusch, Jr. Three easy constructions of recursively enumerable sets. In M. Lerman, J. H. Schmerl, and R. I. Soare, editors, *Logic Year 1979–1980, Proceedings of Seminars and of the Conference on Mathematical Logic Held at the University of Connecticut, Storrs, Conn., November 11–13, 1979*, volume 859 of *Lecture Notes in Mathematics*, pages 83–91. Springer, Berlin, 1981. [414]

[191] C. G. Jockusch, Jr., M. Lerman, R. I. Soare, and R. M. Solovay. Recursively enumerable sets modulo iterated jumps and extensions of Arslanov's completeness criterion. *The Journal of Symbolic Logic*, 54:1288–1323, 1989. [87, 370, 534]

[192] C. G. Jockusch, Jr. and D. Posner. Double jumps of minimal degrees. *The Journal of Symbolic Logic*, 43:715–724, 1978. [72]

[193] C. G. Jockusch, Jr. and R. A. Shore. Pseudojump operators I: The r.e. case. *Transactions of the American Mathematical Society*, 275:599–609, 1983. [41, 42, 376]

[194] C. G. Jockusch, Jr. and R. A. Shore. Pseudojump operators II: Transfinite iterations, hierarchies, and minimal covers. *The Journal of Symbolic Logic*, 49:1205–1236, 1984. [42, 64, 376]

[195] C. G. Jockusch, Jr. and R. I. Soare. Degrees of members of Π^0_1 classes. *Pacific Journal of Mathematics*, 40:605–616, 1972. [77, 81, 84, 87, 89, 374]

[196] C. G. Jockusch, Jr. and R. I. Soare. Π^0_1 classes and degrees of theories. *Transactions of the American Mathematical Society*, 173:33–56, 1972. [77, 78, 79, 81, 82, 84, 86, 87]

[197] M. I. Kanovich. On the decision complexity of algorithms. *Soviet Mathematics Doklady*, 10:700–701, 1969. [366, 368]

[198] M. I. Kanovich. On the decision and enumeration complexity of predicates. *Soviet Mathematics Doklady*, 11:17–20, 1970. [366, 368]

[199] B. Kastermans and S. Lempp. Comparing notions of randomness. *Theoretical Computer Science*, 411:602–616, 2010. [311, 319, 320, 321]

[200] S. M. Kautz. *Degrees of Random Sets*. Ph.D. dissertation, Cornell University, 1991. [xiii, 79, 255, 256, 257, 259, 265, 266, 267, 268, 287, 297, 298, 330, 333, 359, 361, 362, 363, 364, 382, 385, 386]

[201] S. M. Kautz. An improved zero-one law for algorithmically random sequences. *Theoretical Computer Science*, 191:185–192, 1998. [259]

[202] B. Khoussainov and A. Nerode. *Automata Theory and Its Applications.* Progress in Computer Science and Applied Logic, 21. Birkhäuser Boston, Inc., Boston, 2001. [746]

[203] B. Kjos-Hanssen. Low for random reals and positive-measure domination. *Proceedings of the American Mathematical Society*, 135:3703–3709, 2007. [489, 490]

[204] B. Kjos-Hanssen. Infinite subsets of random sets of integers. *Mathematics Research Letters*, 16:103–110, 2009. [348]

[205] B. Kjos-Hanssen, W. Merkle, and F. Stephan. Kolmogorov complexity and the recursion theorem. In B. Durand and W. Thomas, editors, *STACS 2006. Proceedings of the 23rd Annual Symposium on Theoretical Aspects of Computer Science, Marseille, France, February 23–25, 2006*, volume 3884 of *Lecture Notes in Computer Science*, pages 149–161. Springer-Verlag, Berlin, 2006. [366, 367, 368, 369, 576, 581]

[206] B. Kjos-Hanssen, J. S. Miller, and R. Solomon. Lowness notions, measure and domination. To appear. [494, 497, 499, 538]

[207] B. Kjos-Hanssen, A. Nies, and F. Stephan. Lowness for the class of Schnorr random sets. *SIAM Journal on Computing*, 35:647–657, 2005. [537, 554, 559, 560, 561, 591]

[208] S. C. Kleene. General recursive functions of natural numbers. *Mathematische Annalen*, 112:727–742, 1936. [23]

[209] S. C. Kleene. On notation for ordinal numbers. *The Journal of Symbolic Logic*, 3:150–155, 1938. [13, 14]

[210] S. C. Kleene and E. L. Post. The upper semi-lattice of degrees of recursive unsolvability. *Annals of Mathematics. Second Series*, 59:379–407, 1954. [17, 32]

[211] A. N. Kolmogorov. Three approaches to the quantitative definition of information. *Problems of Information Transmission*, 1:1–7, 1965. [xiii, xx, 111, 112, 115, 637]

[212] A. N. Kolmogorov. Logical basis for information theory and probability theory. *IEEE Transactions on Information Theory*, 14:662–664, 1968. [113]

[213] L. G. Kraft. *A Device for Quantizing, Grouping, and Coding Amplitude Modulated Pulses.* M.Sc. thesis, MIT, 1949. [125]

[214] S. A. Kripke. "Flexible" predicates in formal number theory. *Proceedings of the American Mathematical Society*, 13:647–650, 1962. [93]

[215] A. Kučera. Measure, Π^0_1 classes, and complete extensions of PA. In H.-D. Ebbinghaus, G. H. Müller, and G. E. Sacks, editors, *Recursion Theory Week. Proceedings of the Conference Held at the Mathematisches Forschungsinstitut in Oberwolfach, April 15–21, 1984*, volume 1141 of *Lecture Notes in Mathematics*, pages 245–259. Springer, Berlin, 1985. [259, 323, 324, 325, 326, 330, 336, 337, 338, 347, 609]

[216] A. Kučera. An alternative priority-free solution to Post's problem. In J. Gruska, B. Rovan, and J. Wiederman, editors, *Mathematical Foundations of Computer Science 1986. Proceedings of the 12th Symposium. Bratislava, Czechoslovakia. August 25–29, 1986*, volume 233 of *Lecture*

Notes in Computer Science, pages 493–500. Springer, Berlin, 1986. [90, 91, 92, 337]

[217] A. Kučera. On the use of diagonally nonrecursive functions. In H.-D. Ebbinghaus, J. Fernandez-Prida, M. Garrido, D. Lascar, and M. Rodríquez Artalejo, editors, *Logic Colloquium '87. Proceedings of the Colloquium Held at the University of Granada, Granada, July 20–25, 1987*, volume 129 of *Studies in Logic and the Foundations of Mathematics*, pages 219–239. North-Holland, Amsterdam, 1989. [92, 93, 373]

[218] A. Kučera. Randomness and generalizations of fixed point free functions. In K. Ambos-Spies, G. H. Müller, and G. E. Sacks, editors, *Recursion Theory Week. Proceedings of the Conference Held at the Mathematisches Forschungsinstitut, Oberwolfach, March 19–25, 1989*, volume 1432 of *Lecture Notes in Mathematics*, pages 245–254. Springer, Berlin, 1990. [371]

[219] A. Kučera. On relative randomness. *Annals of Pure and Applied Logic*, 63:61–67, 1993. [531]

[220] A. Kučera and A. Nies. Demuth randomness and computational complexity. To appear in the *Annals of Pure and Applied Logic*. [315]

[221] A. Kučera and T. A. Slaman. Randomness and recursive enumerability. *SIAM Journal on Computing*, 31:199–211, 2001. [231, 409, 410, 418]

[222] A. Kučera and T. A. Slaman. Low upper bounds for ideals. *The Journal of Symbolic Logic*, 74:517–534, 2009. [93, 550]

[223] A. Kučera and S. A. Terwijn. Lowness for the class of random sets. *The Journal of Symbolic Logic*, 64:1396–1402, 1999. [489, 508, 509, 510, 524, 526]

[224] M. Kumabe. *On the Turing Degrees of Generic Sets.* Ph.D. dissertation, University of Chicago, 1990. [102]

[225] M. Kumabe and A. E. M. Lewis. A fixed-point-free minimal degree. *Journal of the London Mathematical Society*, 80:785–797, 2009. [349, 618]

[226] M. Kummer. Kolmogorov complexity and instance complexity of recursively enumerable sets. *SIAM Journal on Computing*, 25:1123–1143, 1996. [649, 728, 729, 730]

[227] M. Kummer. On the complexity of random strings. In C. Puech and R. Reischuk, editors, *STACS '96. Proceedings of the 13th Annual Symposium on Theoretical Aspects of Computer Science held in Grenoble, February 22–24, 1996*, volume 1046 of *Lecture Notes in Computer Science*, pages 25–36. Springer-Verlag, Berlin, 1996. [738, 740, 743]

[228] S. A. Kurtz. *Randomness and Genericity in the Degrees of Unsolvability.* Ph.D. dissertation, University of Illinois at Urbana–Champaign, 1981. [xii, 105, 107, 254, 255, 256, 259, 269, 285, 286, 287, 288, 295, 315, 323, 356, 360, 361, 362, 380, 381, 382, 383, 385, 386, 392, 394, 401, 496]

[229] S. A. Kurtz. Notions of weak genericity. *The Journal of Symbolic Logic*, 48:764–770, 1983. [105, 107]

[230] A. V. Kuznecov. On primitive recursive functions of large oscillation. *Doklady Akademii Nauk SSSR (N.S.)*, 71:233–236, 1950. In Russian. [69]

[231] A. H. Lachlan. Lower bounds for pairs of recursively enumerable degrees. *Proceedings of the London Mathematical Society*, 16:537–569, 1966. [47]

[232] A. H. Lachlan. Distributive initial segments of the degrees of unsolvability. *Zeitschrift für Mathematische Logik und Grundlagen der Mathematik*, 14:457–472, 1968. [364]

[233] A. H. Lachlan. Wtt-complete sets are not necessarily tt-complete. *Proceedings of the American Mathematical Society*, 48:429–434, 1975. [333, 334]

[234] R. E. Ladner. A completely mitotic nonrecursive r. e. degree. *Transactions of the American Mathematical Society*, 184:479–507, 1973. [207]

[235] R. E. Ladner and L. P. Sasso, Jr. The weak truth table degrees of recursively enumerable sets. *Annals of Mathematical Logic*, 8:429–448, 1975. [207]

[236] J. I. Lathrop and J. H. Lutz. Recursive computational depth. *Information and Computation*, 153:139–172, 1999. [304, 305]

[237] H. Lebesgue. *Leçons sur L'intégration et la Recherche des Fonctions Primitives.* Gauthier-Villars, Paris, 1904. [592]

[238] S. Lempp and M. Lerman. Priority arguments using iterated trees of strategies. In K. Ambos-Spies, G. H. Müller, and G. E. Sacks, editors, *Recursion Theory Week. Proceedings of the Conference Held at the Mathematisches Forschungsinstitut, Oberwolfach, March 19–25, 1989*, volume 1432 of *Lecture Notes in Mathematics*, pages 277–296. Springer, Berlin, 1990. [67]

[239] S. Lempp and M. Lerman. The decidability of the existential theory of the poset of recursively enumerable degrees with jump relations. *Advances in Mathematics*, 120:1–142, 1996. [67]

[240] M. Lerman. *Degrees of Unsolvability. Local and Global theory.* Perspectives in Mathematical Logic. Springer-Verlag, Berlin, 1983. [72, 475]

[241] L. A. Levin. *Some Theorems on the Algorithmic Approach to Probability Theory and Information Theory.* Dissertation in Mathematics, Moscow University, 1971. In Russian. [xiii, 121, 125, 133, 145, 146, 154]

[242] L. A. Levin. On the notion of a random sequence. *Soviet Mathematics Doklady*, 14:1413–1416, 1973. [xiii, 145, 146, 169, 227, 232, 239, 240]

[243] L. A. Levin. Laws of information conservation (non-growth) and aspects of the foundation of probability theory. *Problems of Information Transmission*, 10:206–210, 1974. [xiii, 121, 125, 129, 133, 227]

[244] P. Lévy. *Théorie de l'Addition des Variables Aléatoires.* Gauthier-Villars, Paris, 1937. [235]

[245] A. E. M. Lewis. A single minimal complement for the c. e. degrees. *Transactions of the American Mathematical Society*, 359:5817–5865, 2007. [93]

[246] A. E. M. Lewis and G. Barmpalias. Random reals and Lipschitz continuity. *Mathematical Structures in Computer Science*, 16:737–749, 2006. [442]

[247] A. E. M. Lewis and G. Barmpalias. Randomness and the linear degrees of computability. *Annals of Pure and Applied Logic*, 145:252–257, 2007. [420]

[248] M. Li and P. Vitanyi. *An Introduction to Kolmogorov Complexity and Its Applications.* Texts and Monographs in Computer Science. Springer-Verlag,

Berlin, 1993. [xi, xx, 110, 113, 114, 116, 122, 132, 136, 137, 150, 227, 238, 260, 265, 304, 738]

[249] E. H. Lieb, D. Osherson, and S. Weinstein. Elementary proof of a theorem of Jean Ville. Unpublished manuscript: arXiv:cs/0607054v1, July 2006. [246, 249]

[250] D. W. Loveland. A variant of the Kolmogorov concept of complexity. *Information and Control*, 15:510–526, 1969. [117, 118, 122]

[251] J. H. Lutz. Category and measure in complexity classes. *SIAM Journal on Computing*, 19:1100–1131, 1990. [270]

[252] J. H. Lutz. Gales and the constructive dimension of individual sequences. In U. Montanari, J. D. P. Rolim, and E. Welzl, editors, *Automata, Languages and Programming. 27th International Colloquium, ICALP 2000. Geneva, Switzerland, July 9–15, 2000. Proceedings*, volume 1853 of *Lecture Notes in Computer Science*, pages 902–913. Springer, Berlin, 2000. [xiii, 594, 596, 597, 599, 603, 654]

[253] J. H. Lutz. Dimension in complexity classes. *SIAM Journal on Computing*, 32:1236–1259, 2003. [594, 596]

[254] J. H. Lutz. The dimensions of individual strings and sequences. *Information and Computation*, 187:49–79, 2003. [xiii, 594, 596, 597, 598, 599, 603, 654, 658, 662, 663, 664, 665, 666]

[255] J. H. Lutz. Effective fractal dimensions. *Mathematical Logic Quarterly*, 51:62–72, 2005. [596]

[256] W. Maass. Characterization of the recursively enumerable sets with supersets effectively isomorphic to all recursively enumerable sets. *Transactions of the American Mathematical Society*, 279:311–336, 1983. [90, 215]

[257] A. Macintyre. Omitting quantifier free types in generic structures. *The Journal of Symbolic Logic*, 37:512–520, 1972. [206]

[258] D. A. Martin. Classes of recursively enumerable sets and degrees of unsolvability. *Zeitschrift für Mathematische Logik und Grundlagen der Mathematik*, 12:295–310, 1966. [80, 97, 575]

[259] P. Martin-Löf. The definition of random sequences. *Information and Control*, 9:602–619, 1966. [xiii, xix, 231, 233, 234]

[260] P. Martin-Löf. Complexity oscillations in infinite binary sequences. *Zeitschrift für Wahrscheinlichkeitstheorie und Verwandte Gebiete*, 19:225–230, 1971. [136, 260]

[261] Y. V. Matijasevic. The Diophantineness of enumerable sets. *Soviet Mathematics Doklady*, 11:354–358, 1970. [101]

[262] E. Mayordomo. A Kolmogorov complexity characterization of constructive Hausdorff dimension. *Information Processing Letters*, 84:1–3, 2002. [598]

[263] Y. T. Medvedev. Degrees of difficulty of the mass problem. *Doklady Akademii Nauk SSSR (N.S.)*, 104:501–504, 1955. In Russian. [344]

[264] Y. T. Medvedev. On nonisomorphic recursively enumerable sets. *Doklady Akademii Nauk SSSR (N.S.)*, 102:211–214, 1955. In Russian. [69]

[265] W. Merkle. The Kolmogorov-Loveland stochastic sequences are not closed under selecting subsequences. *The Journal of Symbolic Logic*, 68:1362–1376, 2003. [310]

[266] W. Merkle. The complexity of stochastic sequences. *Journal of Computer and System Sciences*, 74:350–357, 2008. [304, 305, 306]

[267] W. Merkle and N. Mihailović. On the construction of effective random sets. In K. Diks and W. Rytter, editors, *Mathematical Foundations of Computer Science 2002. 27th International Symposium, MFCS 2002, Warsaw, Poland, August 26–30, 2002. Proceedings*, volume 2420 of *Lecture Notes in Computer Science*, pages 568–580. Springer, Berlin, 2002. [325, 326, 484]

[268] W. Merkle, N. Mihailović, and T. A. Slaman. Some results on effective randomness. *Theory of Computing Systems*, 39:707–721, 2006. [243, 244, 279, 280]

[269] W. Merkle, J. S. Miller, A. Nies, J. Reimann, and F. Stephan. Kolmogorov-Loveland randomness and stochasticity. *Annals of Pure and Applied Logic*, 138:183–210, 2006. [276, 309, 311, 312, 313, 314, 328, 330, 357]

[270] W. Merkle and F. Stephan. On C-degrees, H-degrees and T-degrees. In *Twenty-Second Annual IEEE Conference on Computational Complexity (CCC 2007)*, pages 60–69. IEEE Computer Society Press, San Diego, CA, 2007. [120, 437, 456, 457, 458, 500]

[271] J. S. Miller. Contrasting plain and prefix-free Kolmogorov complexity. To appear. [743]

[272] J. S. Miller. Deriving Muchnik's Theorem from Solovay's manuscript. Unpublished notes. [155, 168]

[273] J. S. Miller. Extracting information is hard: a Turing degree of non-integral effective Hausdorff dimension. To appear in *Advances in Mathematics*. [610, 612, 615]

[274] J. S. Miller. Two notes on subshifts. Unpublished notes. [601]

[275] J. S. Miller. Π^0_1 *Classes in Computable Analysis and Topology*. Ph.D. dissertation, Cornell University, 2002. [368]

[276] J. S. Miller. Kolmogorov random reals are 2-random. *The Journal of Symbolic Logic*, 69:907–913, 2004. [261, 262]

[277] J. S. Miller. The K-degrees, low for K-degrees, and weakly low for K sets. *Notre Dame Journal of Formal Logic*, 50:381–391, 2010. [263, 713, 714, 715, 716]

[278] J. S. Miller and A. Nies. Randomness and computability: open questions. *The Bulletin of Symbolic Logic*, 12:390–410, 2006. [xiii, 319]

[279] J. S. Miller and L. Yu. Oscillation in the initial segment complexity of random reals. To appear in *Advances in Mathematics*. [131, 329, 481, 484, 485, 486, 487]

[280] J. S. Miller and L. Yu. On initial segment complexity and degrees of randomness. *Transactions of the American Mathematical Society*, 360:3193–3210, 2008. [229, 250, 251, 252, 332, 465, 466, 473, 474, 475, 476, 477, 478, 479, 480, 481, 487]

[281] R. Miller. The Δ^0_2-spectrum of a linear order. *The Journal of Symbolic Logic*, 66:470–486, 2001. [43]

[282] W. Miller and D. A. Martin. The degrees of hyperimmune sets. *Zeitschrift für Mathematische Logik und Grundlagen der Mathematik*, 14:159–166, 1968. [67, 68, 69, 100]

[283] A. Mostowski. A generalization of the incompleteness theorem. *Fundamenta Mathematicae*, 49:205–232, 1960/1961. [93]

[284] A. A. Muchnik. On the unsolvability of the problem of reducibility in the theory of algorithms. *Doklady Akademii Nauk SSSR (N.S.)*, 108:194–197, 1956. In Russian. [32, 34, 36]

[285] A. A. Muchnik. Isomorphism of systems of recursively enumerable sets with effective properties. *Trudy Moskovskogo Matematicheskogo Obshchestva*, 7:407–412, 1958. In Russian. [86]

[286] A. A. Muchnik. On strong and weak reducibilities of algorithmic problems. *Sibirskii Matematicheskii Zhurnal*, 4:1328–1341, 1963. In Russian. [344]

[287] An. A. Muchnik. Lower limits of frequencies in computable sequences and relativized a priori probability. *Theory of Probability and its Applications*, 32:513–514, 1987. [472]

[288] An. A. Muchnik and S. P. Positselsky. Kolmogorov entropy in the context of computability theory. *Theoretical Computer Science*, 271:15–35, 2002. [155, 168, 739, 744, 745, 752]

[289] An. A. Muchnik, A. L. Semenov, and V. A. Uspensky. Mathematical metaphysics of randomness. *Theoretical Computer Science*, 207:263–317, 1998. [304, 305, 309, 310, 311, 312, 313]

[290] J. Mycielski. Algebraic independence and measure. *Fundamenta Mathematicae*, 61:165–169, 1967. [478]

[291] J. Myhill. Creative sets. *Zeitschrift für Mathematische Logik und Grundlagen der Mathematik*, 1:97–108, 1955. [21, 22]

[292] A. Nabutovsky and S. Weinberger. The fractal nature of Riem/Diff. I. *Geometrica Dedicata*, 101:1–54, 2003. [420]

[293] A. Nerode. General topology and partial recursive functionals. In *Summaries of Talks Presented at the Summer Institute for Symbolic Logic*, pages 247–251. Cornell University, 1957. [21]

[294] K. M. Ng. Beyond strong jump traceability. To appear in the *Proceedings of the London Mathematical Society*. [672]

[295] K. M. Ng. *Some Properties of D.C.E. Reals and their Degrees*. M.Sc. thesis, National University of Singapore, 2006. [219]

[296] K. M. Ng. On strongly jump traceable reals. *Annals of Pure and Applied Logic*, 154:51–69, 2008. [672, 689]

[297] K. M. Ng. *Computability, Traceability and Beyond*. Ph.D. dissertation, Victoria University of Wellington, 2009. [672, 693]

[298] A. Nies. Calculus of cost functions. To appear. [528]

[299] A. Nies. Low for random reals: the story. Unpublished manuscript, `http://www.cs.auckland.ac.nz/~nies/papers/LRpreprint.pdf`. [510]

[300] A. Nies. Lowness for computable and partial computable randomness. To appear, preprint available at `http://www.cs.auckland.ac.nz/CDMTCS/researchreports/363andre.pdf`. [586, 590]

[301] A. Nies. Intervals of the lattice of computably enumerable sets and effective Boolean algebras. *The Bulletin of the London Mathematical Society*, 29:683–692, 1997. [419]

[302] A. Nies. Lowness properties and randomness. *Advances in Mathematics*, 197:274–305, 2005. [473, 508, 518, 523, 524, 525, 527, 528, 529, 530, 586, 591]

[303] A. Nies. Reals which compute little. In Z. Chatzidakis, P. Koepke, and W. Pohlers, editors, *Logic Colloquium '02. Joint Proceedings of the Annual European Summer Meeting of the Association for Symbolic Logic and the Biannual Meeting of the German Association for Mathematical Logic and the Foundations of Exact Sciences (the Colloquium Logicum) Held in Münster, August 3–11, 2002.*, volume 27 of *Lecture Notes in Logic*, pages 261–275. Association for Symbolic Logic and A K Peters, Ltd., La Jolla, CA and Wellesley, MA, 2006. [504, 523, 530, 700, 701]

[304] A. Nies. Non-cupping and randomness. *Proceedings of the American Mathematical Society*, 135:837–844, 2007. [534, 535]

[305] A. Nies. Eliminating concepts. In C. T. Chong, Q. Feng, T. A. Slaman, W. H. Woodin, and Y. Yang, editors, *Computational Prospects of Infinity: Part II. Presented Talks, National University of Singapore, Institute for Mathematical Sciences*, volume 15 of *Lecture Notes Series. Institute for Mathematical Sciences. National University of Singapore*, pages 225–248. World Scientific Publishing Company, Singapore, 2008. [536]

[306] A. Nies. *Computability and Randomness*, volume 51 of *Oxford Logic Guides*. Oxford University Press, Oxford, 2009. [251, 316, 364, 376, 377, 504, 526, 533, 535, 538, 586, 591, 669]

[307] A. Nies and J. Reimann. A lower cone in the wtt degrees of non-integral effective dimension. In C. T. Chong, Q. Feng, T. A. Slaman, W. H. Woodin, and Y. Yang, editors, *Computational Prospects of Infinity: Part II. Presented Talks, National University of Singapore, Institute for Mathematical Sciences*, volume 15 of *Lecture Notes Series. Institute for Mathematical Sciences. National University of Singapore*, pages 249–260. World Scientific Publishing Company, Singapore, 2008. [611]

[308] A. Nies, F. Stephan, and S. A. Terwijn. Randomness, relativization, and Turing degrees. *The Journal of Symbolic Logic*, 70:515–535, 2005. [136, 229, 260, 261, 262, 349, 350, 351, 356, 382, 712, 713, 715]

[309] D. Nitzpon. *Lowness Properties and Randomness*. Doctoraal examens, University of Amsterdam, 2002. [586]

[310] P. Odifreddi. *Classical Recursion Theory. The Theory of Functions and Sets of Natural Numbers*, volume 125 of *Studies in Logic and the Foundations of Mathematics*. North-Holland Publishing Company, Amsterdam, 1990. [xiii, xix, 8, 28, 85]

[311] P. Odifreddi. *Classical Recursion Theory. Vol. II*, volume 143 of *Studies in Logic and the Foundations of Mathematics*. North-Holland Publishing Company, Amsterdam, 1999. [xiii, xix, 8, 28, 72, 208, 209]

[312] J. C. Owings, Jr. Diagonalization and the recursion theorem. *Notre Dame Journal of Formal Logic*, 14:95–99, 1973. [14]

[313] J. C. Oxtoby. *Measure and Category. A Survey of the Analogies Between Topological and Measure Spaces*, volume 2 of *Graduate Texts in Mathematics*. Springer-Verlag, New York, second edition, 1980. [4]

[314] J. B. Paris. Measure and minimal degrees. *Annals of Mathematical Logic*, 11:203–216, 1977. [381, 401]

[315] D. B. Posner and R. W. Robinson. Degrees joining to $\mathbf{0}'$. *The Journal of Symbolic Logic*, 46:714–722, 1981. [64, 65]

[316] E. L. Post. Recursively enumerable sets of positive integers and their decision problems. *Bulletin of the American Mathematical Society*, 50:284–316, 1944. [22, 32, 82]

[317] E. L. Post. Degrees of recursive unsolvability. *Bulletin of the American Mathematical Society*, 54:641–642, 1948. [25]

[318] M. Pour-El and J. I. Richards. *Computability in Analysis and Physics*. Perspectives in Mathematical Logic. Springer-Verlag, Berlin, 1989. [199, 224]

[319] A. Raichev. Relative randomness and real closed fields. *The Journal of Symbolic Logic*, 70:319–330, 2005. [219, 224, 424]

[320] A. Raichev. *Relative Randomness via rK-reducibility*. Ph.D. dissertation, University of Wisconsin-Madison, 2005. [219, 224, 424]

[321] A. Raichev and F. Stephan. A minimal rK-degree. In C. T. Chong, Q. Feng, T. A. Slaman, W. H. Woodin, and Y. Yang, editors, *Computational Prospects of Infinity: Part II. Presented Talks, National University of Singapore, Institute for Mathematical Sciences*, volume 15 of *Lecture Notes Series. Institute for Mathematical Sciences. National University of Singapore*, pages 261–270. World Scientific Publishing Company, Singapore, 2008. [437, 439]

[322] J. Raisonnier. A mathematical proof of S. Shelah's theorem on the measure problem and related results. *Israel Journal of Mathematics*, 48:48–56, 1984. [555]

[323] S. Reid. *A Class of Algorithmically Random Reals*. M.Sc. thesis, Victoria University, Wellington, 2004. [606]

[324] J. Reimann. *Computability and Fractal Dimension*. Doctoral dissertation, University of Heidelberg, 2004. [330, 604, 605, 609, 611, 636, 637, 638, 641]

[325] J. Reimann. Effectively closed classes of measures and randomness. *Annals of Pure and Applied Logic*, 156:170–182, 2008. [335]

[326] J. Reimann. Randomness—beyond Lebesgue measure. In *Logic Colloquium 2006*, volume 32 of *Lecture Notes in Logic*, pages 247–279. Association for Symbolic Logic, Chicago, IL, 2009. [264, 265]

[327] J. Reimann and T. A. Slaman. Measures and their random reals. To appear in the *Transactions of the American Mathematical Society*. [7, 21, 265, 331, 334, 335, 336, 713]

[328] J. Reimann and T. A. Slaman. Probability measures and effective randomness. To appear. [21, 336]

[329] J. Reimann and T. A. Slaman. Randomness for continuous measures. To appear. [21, 336]

[330] J. Reimann and F. Stephan. Hierarchies of randomness tests. In S. S. Goncharov, R. G. Downey, and H. Ono, editors, *Mathematical Logic in Asia. Proceedings of the 9th Asian Logic Conference Held in Novosibirsk, August 16–19, 2005*, pages 215–232. World Scientific Publishing Company, Singapore, 2006. [465, 605]

[331] R. Rettinger, X. Zheng, R. Gengler, and B. von Braunmühl. Weakly computable real numbers and total computable real functions. In J. Wang, editor, *Computing and Combinatorics. 7th Annual International Conference (COCOON 2001). Guilin, China, August 20–23, 2001. Proceedings*, volume 2108 of *Lecture Notes in Computer Science*, pages 586–595. Springer, Berlin, 2001. [217]

[332] H. G. Rice. Classes of recursively enumerable sets and their decision problems. *Transactions of the American Mathematical Society*, 74:358–366, 1953. [13]

[333] R. W. Robinson. Jump restricted interpolation in the recursively enumerable degrees. *Annals of Mathematics. Second Series*, 93:586–596, 1971. [67]

[334] H. Rogers, Jr. *Theory of Recursive Functions and Effective Computability*. McGraw–Hill Book Company, New York, 1967. [xiii, 8, 28]

[335] H. L. Royden. *Real Analysis*. The Macmillan Company, New York, 1963. [264, 365, 400, 639]

[336] W. Rudin. *Principles of Mathematical Analysis*. International Series in Pure and Applied Mathematics. McGraw-Hill Book Co., New York, third edition, 1976. [219]

[337] A. Y. Rumyantsev and M. A. Ushakov. Forbidden substrings, Kolmogorov complexity and almost periodic sequences. In B. Durand and W. Thomas, editors, *STACS 2006. Proceedings of the 23rd Annual Symposium on Theoretical Aspects of Computer Science, Marseille, France, February 23–25, 2006*, volume 3884 of *Lecture Notes in Computer Science*, pages 396–407. Springer-Verlag, Berlin, 2006. [601]

[338] B. Y. Ryabko. Coding of combinatorial sources and Hausdorff dimension. *Soviet Mathematics Doklady*, 30:219–222, 1984. [598]

[339] B. Y. Ryabko. Noiseless coding of combinatorial sources. *Problems of Information Transmission*, 22:170–179, 1986. [598]

[340] B. Y. Ryabko. The complexity and effectiveness of prediction algorithms. *Journal of Complexity*, 10:281–295, 1994. [598]

[341] G. E. Sacks. *Degrees of Unsolvability*. Princeton University Press, Princeton, NJ, 1963. [65, 66, 323, 358, 363]

[342] G. E. Sacks. On the degrees less than $\mathbf{0}'$. *Annals of Mathematics. Second Series*, 77:211–231, 1963. [39, 40, 58, 72, 373, 534]

[343] G. E. Sacks. A maximal set which is not complete. *Michigan Mathematical Journal*, 11:193–205, 1964. [83]

[344] G. E. Sacks. The recursively enumerable degrees are dense. *Annals of Mathematics Second Series*, 80:300–312, 1964. [58]

[345] G. E. Sacks. Forcing with perfect closed sets. In D. S. Scott, editor, *Axiomatic Set Theory. Proceedings of the Symposium in Pure Mathematics of the American Mathematical Society held at the University of California, Los Angeles, Calif., July 10-August 5, 1967.*, volume XIII, part I of *Proceedings of Symposia on Pure Mathematics*, pages 331–355. American Mathematical Society, Providence, RI, 1971. [645]

[346] G. E. Sacks. *Higher Recursion Theory.* Perspectives in Mathematical Logic. Springer-Verlag, Berlin, 1990. [711]

[347] A. Salomaa. *Computation and Automata*, volume 25 of *Encyclopedia of Mathematics and Its Applications.* Cambridge University Press, Cambridge, 1985. [8]

[348] C.-P. Schnorr. A unified approach to the definition of a random sequence. *Mathematical Systems Theory*, 5:246–258, 1971. [xiii, 236, 237, 257, 269, 270, 271, 273, 276, 280, 350, 594]

[349] C.-P. Schnorr. *Zufälligkeit und Wahrscheinlichkeit. Eine algorithmische Begründung der Wahrscheinlichkeitstheorie*, volume 218 of *Lecture Notes in Mathematics.* Springer-Verlag, Berlin–New York, 1971. [xiii, 146, 236, 237, 257, 269, 270, 271, 272, 273, 276, 280, 303, 594, 599, 654]

[350] C.-P. Schnorr. Process complexity and effective random tests. *Journal of Computer and System Sciences*, 7:376–388, 1973. [xiii, 125, 145, 146, 227, 232, 239]

[351] D. Scott and S. Tennenbaum. On the degrees of complete extensions of arithmetic. *Notices of the American Mathematical Society*, 7:242–243, 1960. [87]

[352] D. S. Scott. Algebras of sets binumerable in complete extensions of arithmetic. In *Proceedings of the Symposium on Pure and Applied Mathematics*, volume V, pages 117–121. American Mathematical Society, Providence, RI, 1962. [84]

[353] A. Shen. On relations between different algorithmic definitions of randomness. *Soviet Mathematics Doklady*, 38:316–319, 1989. [303]

[354] J. R. Shoenfield. On degrees of unsolvability. *Annals of Mathematics. Second Series*, 69:644–653, 1959. [24, 25, 65]

[355] J. R. Shoenfield. Applications of model theory to degrees of unsolvability. In J. W. Addison, L. Henkin, and A. Tarski, editors, *Theory of Models (Proceedings of the 1963 International Symposium, Berkeley)*, pages 359–363. North-Holland, Amsterdam, 1965. [54, 56]

[356] J. R. Shoenfield. *Degrees of Unsolvability*, volume 2 of *North-Holland Mathematics Studies.* North-Holland Publishing Company, Amsterdam-London, 1971. [71]

[357] J. H. Silver. Counting the number of equivalence classes of Borel and coanalytic equivalence relations. *Annals of Mathematical Logic*, 18:1–28, 1980. [478]

[358] S. G. Simpson. First-order theory of the degrees of recursive unsolvability. *Annals of Mathematics. Second Series*, 105:121–139, 1977. [364]

[359] S. G. Simpson. Mass problems and randomness. *The Bulletin of Symbolic Logic*, 11:1–27, 2005. [345, 346, 347]

[360] S. G. Simpson. An extension of the recursively enumerable Turing degrees. *Journal of the London Mathematical Society. Second Series*, 75:287–297, 2007. [346, 347]

[361] S. G. Simpson. Mass problems and almost everywhere domination. *Mathematical Logic Quarterly*, 53:483–492, 2007. [347]

[362] R. M. Smullyan. *Theory of Formal Systems*. Princeton University Press, Princeton, NJ, revised edition, 1961. [86]

[363] R. I. Soare. Cohesive sets and recursively enumerable Dedekind cuts. *Pacific Journal of Mathematics*, 31:215–231, 1969. [199, 201]

[364] R. I. Soare. Recursion theory and Dedekind cuts. *Transactions of the American Mathematical Society*, 140:271–294, 1969. [198, 204]

[365] R. I. Soare. Automorphisms of the lattice of recursively enumerable sets. I. Maximal sets. *Annals of Mathematics. Second Series*, 100:80–120, 1974. [83]

[366] R. I. Soare. *Recursively Enumerable Sets and Degrees: A Study of Computable Functions and Computably Generated Sets*. Perspectives in Mathematical Logic. Springer, Berlin, 1987. [xiii, xix, 8, 10, 14, 27, 29, 36, 43, 44, 57, 58, 65, 503, 517]

[367] R. I. Soare. Computability and recursion. *The Bulletin of Symbolic Logic*, 2:284–321, 1996. [8]

[368] R. I. Soare. Computability theory and differential geometry. *The Bulletin of Symbolic Logic*, 10:457–486, 2004. [420, 421]

[369] R. J. Solomonoff. A formal theory of inductive inference, I and II. *Information and Control*, 7:1–22 and 224–254, 1964. [xiii, xx, 111, 112, 133, 145, 146]

[370] R. M. Solovay. A model of set theory in which every set of reals is Lebesgue measurable. *Annals of Mathematics*, 92:1–56, 1970. [296, 555]

[371] R. M. Solovay. Draft of paper (or series of papers) on Chaitin's work. Unpublished notes, May 1975. 215 pages. [xi, xii, 137, 138, 139, 140, 141, 142, 143, 144, 155, 156, 160, 161, 162, 163, 164, 166, 167, 234, 251, 262, 288, 404, 405, 408, 409, 413, 466, 467, 468, 469, 470, 501, 732, 743]

[372] R. M. Solovay. On random r.e. sets. In A. I. Arruda, N. C. A. da Costa, and R. Chuaqui, editors, *Non-Classical Logics, Model Theory and Computability. Proceedings of the Third Latin-American Symposium on Mathematical Logic, Campinas, July 11–17, 1976*, volume 89 of *Studies in Logic and the Foundations of Mathematics*, pages 283–307. North Holland, Amsterdam, 1977. [732]

[373] A. Sorbi. The Medvedev lattice of degrees of difficulty. In S. B. Cooper, T. A. Slaman, and S. S. Wainer, editors, *Computability, Enumerability, Unsolvability. Directions in Recursion Theory*, volume 224 of *London Mathematical Society Lecture Note Series*, pages 289–312. Cambridge University Press, Cambridge, 1996. [347]

[374] C. Spector. On degrees of recursive unsolvability. *Annals of Mathematics*, 64:581–592, 1956. [70]

[375] C. Spector. Measure-theoretic construction of incomparable hyperdegrees. *The Journal of Symbolic Logic*, 23:280–288, 1958. [358]

[376] L. Staiger. Kolmogorov complexity and Hausdorff dimension. *Information and Computation*, 103:159–194, 1993. [136, 598]

[377] L. Staiger. A tight upper bound on Kolmogorov complexity and uniformly optimal prediction. *Theory of Computing Systems*, 31:215–229, 1998. [598, 636, 637]

[378] L. Staiger. Constructive dimension equals Kolmogorov complexity. *Information Processing Letters*, 93:149–153, 2005. [598, 636]

[379] F. Stephan. Martin-Löf random sets and PA-complete sets. In Z. Chatzidakis, P. Koepke, and W. Pohlers, editors, *Logic Colloquium '02. Joint Proceedings of the Annual European Summer Meeting of the Association for Symbolic Logic and the Biannual Meeting of the German Association for Mathematical Logic and the Foundations of Exact Sciences (the Colloquium Logicum) Held in Münster, August 3–11, 2002.*, volume 27 of *Lecture Notes in Logic*, pages 342–348. Association for Symbolic Logic and A K Peters, Ltd., La Jolla, CA and Wellesley, MA, 2006. [337, 339]

[380] F. Stephan and G. Wu. Presentations of K-trivial reals and Kolmogorov complexity. In S. B. Cooper, B. Löwe, and L. Torenvliet, editors, *New Computational Paradigms. First Conference on Computability in Europe, CiE 2005. Amsterdam, The Netherlands, June 8–12, 2005. Proceedings*, volume 3526 of *Lecture Notes in Computer Science*, pages 461–469. Springer, Berlin, 2005. [411]

[381] F. Stephan and L. Yu. Lowness for weakly 1-generic and Kurtz-random. In J.-Y. Cai, S. B. Cooper, and A. Li, editors, *Theory and Applications of Models of Computation. Third International Conference, TAMC 2006. Beijing, China, May 15–20, 2006. Proceedings*, volume 3959 of *Lecture Notes in Computer Science*, pages 756–764. Springer, Berlin, 2006. [582, 583, 584, 585]

[382] J. Stillwell. Decidability of the "almost all" theory of degrees. *The Journal of Symbolic Logic*, 37:501–506, 1972. [323, 359, 360, 363, 365]

[383] M. Stob. Index sets and degrees of unsolvability. *The Journal of Symbolic Logic*, 47:241–248, 1982. [83]

[384] D. Sullivan. Entropy, Hausdorff measures old and new, and limit sets of geometrically finite Kleinian groups. *Acta Mathematica*, 153:259–277, 1984. [639]

[385] K. Tadaki. A generalization of Chaitin's halting probability Ω and halting self-similar sets. *Hokkaido Mathematical Journal*, 31:219–253, 2002. [602, 603]

[386] S. A. Terwijn. *Computability and Measure*. Ph.D. dissertation, The Institute for Logic, Language and Computation (ILLC), University of Amsterdam, 1998. [98, 303]

[387] S. A. Terwijn. Complexity and randomness. *Rendiconti del Seminario Matematico di Torino*, 62:1–38, 2004. Notes for a course given at the University of Auckland, March 2003. [5, 610, 611]

[388] S. A. Terwijn. The Medvedev lattice of computably closed sets. *Archive for Mathematical Logic*, 45:179–190, 2006. [345]

[389] S. A. Terwijn and D. Zambella. Algorithmic randomness and lowness. *The Journal of Symbolic Logic*, 66:1199–1205, 2001. [99, 100, 554, 555, 559]

[390] B. Trakhtenbrot. On autoreducibility. *Soviet Mathematics Doklady*, 11:814–817, 1970. [340]

[391] C. Tricot, Jr. Two definitions of fractional dimension. *Mathematical Proceedings of the Cambridge Philosophical Society*, 91:57–74, 1982. [639, 657]

[392] A. M. Turing. On computable numbers with an application to the Entscheidungsproblem. *Proceedings of the London Mathematical Society*, 42:230–265, 1936. Correction in *Proceedings of the London Mathematical Society* 43: 544–546, 1937. [198]

[393] V. A. Uspensky. Some remarks on r.e. sets. *Zeitschrift für Mathematische Logik und Grundlagen der Mathematik*, 3:157–170, 1957. [69]

[394] V. A. Uspensky. Complexity and entropy: an introduction to the theory of Kolmogorov complexity. In O. Watanabe, editor, *Kolmogorov Complexity and Computational Complexity*, EATCS Monographs on Theoretical Computer Science, pages 85–102. Springer-Verlag, New York, 1992. [238]

[395] V. A. Uspensky, A. L. Semenov, and A. Kh. Shen. Can an individual sequence of zeros and ones be random? *Russian Mathematical Surveys*, 45:121–189, 1990. [246]

[396] V. A. Uspensky and A. Shen. Relations between varieties of Kolmogorov complexities. *Mathematical Systems Theory*, 29:271–292, 1996. [122, 147, 170]

[397] M. van Lambalgen. *Random Sequences*. Ph.D. dissertation, University of Amsterdam, 1987. [xix, 110, 227, 265]

[398] M. van Lambalgen. The axiomatization of randomness. *The Journal of Symbolic Logic*, 55:1143–1167, 1990. [110, 257, 258]

[399] N. Vereshchagin. Kolmogorov complexity conditional to large integers. *Theoretical Computer Science*, 271:59–67, 2002. [263, 471]

[400] N. Vereshchagin. Kolmogorov complexity of enumerating finite sets. *Information Processing Letters*, 103:34–39, 2007. [732]

[401] J. Ville. *Étude Critique de la Notion de Collectif*. Monographies des Probabilités. Calcul des Probabilités et ses Applications. Gauthier-Villars, Paris, 1939. [xviii, 230, 235, 246]

[402] R. von Mises. Grundlagen der Wahrscheinlichkeitsrechnung. *Mathematische Zeitschrift*, 5:52–99, 1919. [xviii, 229]

[403] A. Wald. Sur la notion de collectif dans la calcul des probabilités. *Comptes Rendus des Seances de l'Académie des Sciences*, 202:180–183, 1936. [xviii, 230]

[404] A. Wald. Die Wiederspruchsfreiheit des Kollektivbegriffes der Wahrscheinlichkeitsrechnung. *Ergebnisse eines Mathematischen Kolloquiums*, 8:38–72, 1937. [xviii, 230]

[405] Y. Wang. *Randomness and Complexity.* Ph.D. dissertation, University of Heidelberg, 1996. [275, 286, 287, 290, 303, 349, 350]

[406] Y. Wang. A separation of two randomness concepts. *Information Processing Letters*, 69:115–118, 1999. [349, 350]

[407] G. Wu. Prefix-free languages and initial segments of computably enumerable degrees. In J. Wang, editor, *Computing and Combinatorics. 7th Annual International Conference (COCOON 2001). Guilin, China, August 20–23, 2001. Proceedings*, volume 2108 of *Lecture Notes in Computer Science*, pages 576–585. Springer, Berlin, 2001. [206]

[408] C. E. M. Yates. A minimal pair of recursively enumerable degrees. *The Journal of Symbolic Logic*, 31:159–168, 1966. [47]

[409] C. E. M. Yates. On the degrees of index sets II. *Transactions of the American Mathematical Society*, 135:249–266, 1969. [210]

[410] C. E. M. Yates. Initial segments of the degrees of unsolvability, II. Minimal degrees. *The Journal of Symbolic Logic*, 35:243–266, 1970. [72]

[411] L. Yu. Lowness for genericity. *Archive for Mathematical Logic*, 45:233–238, 2006. [378, 586]

[412] L. Yu. When van Lambalgen's theorem fails. *Proceedings of the American Mathematical Society*, 135:861–864, 2007. [276, 357]

[413] L. Yu and D. Ding. There are $2^{\aleph_0}$ many H-degrees in the random reals. *Proceedings of the American Mathematical Society*, 132:2461–2464, 2004. [465, 478]

[414] L. Yu and D. Ding. There is no sw-complete c.e. real. *The Journal of Symbolic Logic*, 69:1163–1170, 2004. [442]

[415] L. Yu, D. Ding, and R. G. Downey. The Kolmogorov complexity of random reals. *Annals of Pure and Applied Logic*, 129:163–180, 2004. [262, 464, 465, 475, 478]

[416] D. Zambella. On sequences with simple initial segments. Technical Report ML-1990–05, The Institute for Logic, Language and Computation (ILLC), University of Amsterdam, 1990. [98, 501, 508]

[417] X. Zheng. On the Turing degrees of weakly computable real numbers. *Journal of Logic and Computation*, 13:159–172, 2003. [218]

[418] X. Zheng. *Computability Theory of Real Numbers.* Habilitationsschrift, BTU Cottbus, Germany, 2005. [217]

[419] X. Zheng. Classification of computably approximable real numbers. *Theory of Computing Systems*, 43:603–624, 2008. [217]

[420] X. Zheng and R. Rettinger. Weak computability and representation of reals. *Mathematical Logic Quarterly*, 50:431–442, 2004. [217]

[421] M. Ziegler. Algebraisch abgeschlossen Gruppen. In S. I. Adian, W. W. Boone, and G. Higman, editors, *Word Problems II. The Oxford Book, Outgrowth of a Conference on Decision Problems in Algebra Held in Oxford, Summer 1976*, pages 449–576. North Holland, Amsterdam, 1980. [206]

[422] M. Zimand. Extracting the Kolmogorov complexity of strings and sequences from sources with limited independence. In S. Albers and J.-Y. Marion, editors, *26th International Symposium on Theoretical Aspects of Computer Science. STACS 2009, February 26–28, 2009, Freiburg, Germany*, volume 3 of *Leibniz International Proceedings in Informatics*, pages 697–708 (electronic). Schloss Dagstuhl–Leibniz Center for Informatics, Dagstuhl, Germany, 2009. [635]

[423] M. Zimand. On generating independent random strings. In K. Ambos-Spies, B. Löwe, and W. Merkle, editors, *Mathematical Theory and Computational Practice. 5th Conference on Computability in Europe, CiE 2009. Heidelberg, Germany, July 19–24, 2009. Proceedings*, volume 5635 of *Lecture Notes in Computer Science*, pages 499–508. Springer, Berlin, 2009. [635]

[424] M. Zimand. Two sources are better than one for increasing the Kolmogorov complexity of infinite sequences. *Theory of Computing Systems*, 46:707–722, 2010. [627, 628, 629, 635]

[425] A. K. Zvonkin and L. A. Levin. The complexity of finite objects and the development of the concepts of information and randomness by means of the theory of algorithms. *Russian Mathematical Surveys*, 25:83–124, 1970. [xiii, 116, 146, 150, 151, 237, 238, 265, 266, 267, 282, 598]

Index

$2^{<\omega}$, **2**
2^n, **2**
$2^{\leqslant n}$, **2**
λ, **2**
$|\sigma|$, **2**
$\sigma\tau$, **2**
$\sigma^\frown\tau$, **2**
$\sigma <_{\mathrm{L}} \tau$, **2**
χ_A, **2**
$\mathbb{N}$, **3**
ω, **3**
2^ω, **3**
$A =^* B$, **3**
$A \upharpoonright n$, **3**
$A \upharpoonright S$, **3**
$\overline{A}$, **3**
$\langle n_0, \dots, n_k \rangle$, **3**
D_n, **3**
$[x, y]$, **3**
(x, y), **3**
$(x, y]$, **3**
$[x, y)$, **3**
$A^{[e]}$, **3**
$f^{(k)}$, **3**
$\log n$, **3**
$O(f(n))$, **3**
$o(f(n))$, **4**
$f \sim g$, **4**
$\exists^\infty$, **4**
$\forall^\infty$, **4**
$\exists^{\geqslant k}$, **4**
$\lambda x\, f(x, y_0, \dots, y_n)$, **4**
$\mu n\, R(n)$, **4**
$x \vee y$, **4**
$x \wedge y$, **4**
$[\![\sigma]\!]$, **4**, 618
$[\![A]\!]$, **4**, 618
$\mu(A)$, **5**, 618
$\#(r)$, **8**
Φ_e, **9**, 17
$\Phi(n)\downarrow$, **9**
$\Phi(n)\uparrow$, **9**
$\emptyset'$, **11**
$\Phi_e(x)[s]$, **11**
$\Phi_e(x)[s]\downarrow$, **11**
$\Phi_e(x)[s]\uparrow$, **11**
W_e, **11**
$W_e[s]$, **11**
$W_{e,s}$, **11**
$X[s]$, **13**
$\equiv_{\mathrm{R}}$ (for a reducibility $\leqslant_{\mathrm{R}}$), **15**
$<_{\mathrm{R}}$ (for a reducibility $\leqslant_{\mathrm{R}}$), **16**
$|_{\mathrm{R}}$ (for a reducibility $\leqslant_{\mathrm{R}}$), **16**
$\leqslant_{\mathrm{T}}$, **16**

deg, **16**
$\mathbf{a} \leqslant \mathbf{b}$, **16**
$\oplus$, **16**
$\mathbf{a} \vee \mathbf{b}$, **17**
$\bigoplus$, **17**
$\mathbf{0}$, **17**
Φ^A, **17**
$\Phi_e^A(n)[s]$, **17**
φ^A (for an oracle machine Φ), **17**
A', **18**
$A^{(n)}$, **18**
$\mathbf{a}'$, **18**
$\mathbf{a}^{(\mathbf{n})}$, **18**
$\emptyset^{(\omega)}$, **18**
$\leqslant_{\mathrm{m}}$, **19**
$\leqslant_1$, **20**
$\vDash$ (for truth tables), **20**
$\leqslant_{\mathrm{tt}}$, **20**
$\leqslant_{\mathrm{wtt}}$, **21**
$\sqcup$, **39**
$A^{[<e]}$, **58**
$[T]$, **73**
$\Vdash$, **100**
$\leqslant_{\mathrm{pb}}$, **107**
$C_f(\sigma)$, **111**
$C(\sigma)$, **111**
$C(n)$, **112**
$C(\sigma, \tau)$, **112**
σ_C^*, **112**
$C(\sigma \mid \tau)$, **114**
$C^A(\sigma)$, **115**
$I_C(\sigma : \tau)$, **116**
Kd, 122
$\mathcal{U}$, **123**
$K(\sigma)$, **124**
$K(\sigma \mid \tau)$, **124**
$K^A(\sigma)$, **124**
$K_M(\sigma)$, **124**
$K(n)$, **124**
σ^*, **124**
$K_s(\sigma)$, **124**
$\widehat{K}(\sigma)$, **129**
$Q_M(\sigma)$, **133**
$Q(\sigma)$, **133**
$I_K(\sigma : \tau)$, **134**
$I(\sigma : \tau)$, 134
$K^t(\sigma)$, **139**
$\mathcal{D}_n$, **141**
F^* (for a finite set F), 141
Ω, **142**
Ω_s, **142**
$\mathcal{M}$, **146**
$\mathcal{D}$, **146**
$Km(\sigma)$, **146**
$Km_D(\sigma)$, **146**
$Km_S(\sigma)$, **146**
$KM(\sigma)$, **150**
M_L (for a monotone machine L), **151**
$\mathcal{V}$, **154**
L_n, **157**
$m_C(\sigma)$, **161**
$m_K(\sigma)$, **161**
$\leqslant_{KM}$, **169**
$\leqslant_{Km}$, **169**
$L(\alpha)$, **197**
$\mathcal{I}(\alpha)$, **208**
$\mathbb{R}_2$, **219**
$\widehat{\Omega}$, **229**
$S[d]$, **235**, 243, 594
$E[X]$, **242**
$E[X \mid A]$, **242**
$s_f(\alpha, n)$, **246**
$S_f(\alpha, n)$, **246**
$S(\alpha, n)$, **246**
$G(n)$, **252**
Ω^X, **257**
$\oplus_X$, **259**
C^g, **261**
μ_ρ^*, **264**
μ_ρ, **264**
$(\sigma)_\nu$, **266**
$(\sigma)_{\nu,s}$, **266**
$\mathrm{seq}_\nu(\alpha)$, **266**
$S_h[d]$, **271**
S_M^n, **281**
$\mathbb{P}_n$, **297**
$A \vDash \varphi$ (for a sentence of arithmetic), **297**
$\Vdash$ (in effective Solovay forcing), **297**
$=_I$, **340**
$\leqslant_{\mathrm{s}}$, **344**
$\leqslant_{\mathrm{w}}$, **344**
$\mathcal{P}_{\mathrm{w}}$, **345**
$\mathbf{r}_1$, **345**
$\mathbf{r}_2^*$, **346**
$A^{\leqslant_{\mathrm{T}}}$, **358**
$\leqslant_K$, **404**

$\leqslant_C$, **405**
$\leqslant_S$, **405**
$\leqslant_{cl}$, **420**
$\leqslant_{ibT}$, **420**
$\leqslant_{rK}$, **421**
$A \otimes f$, **461**
$\sigma \otimes f$, **461**
$\leqslant_{Sch}$, **462**
$\leqslant_{stt}$, **463**
$\alpha(n)$, **467**
$\alpha^X(n)$, **467**
$s(n)$, **467**
q_f, **472**
$\leqslant_{vL}$, **473**
$\leqslant_{LR}$, **473**
$\leqslant_{Km\oplus}$, **473**
$\widehat{\oplus}$, **477**
$\ll_K$, **486**
$\gamma(n)$, **487**
$\widehat{\gamma}(n)$, **488**
$\leqslant_{LK}$, **494**
$KT(c)$, **505**
$G(c)$, **506**
$KT(c,n)$, **506**
J^A, **523**
c_α, **528**
$S^\diamond$ (for a class S), **535**
MLR, **537**
W2R, **537**
$\mathcal{K}$, **538**
Low($\mathcal{C}, \mathcal{D}$), **537**
Low($\mathcal{C}$), **537**
$\leqslant_{uT(tu)}$, **577**
$\leqslant_{T(tu)}$, **577**
g_A, **578**
A^*, **578**
ML2R, **591**
CompR, **591**
SchR, **591**
W1R, **591**
H^s_n, **592**
H^s, **593**
$\dim_H$, **593**
$\widehat{H}^s$, **598**
$\widehat{H}^s_n$, **598**
Ω^s, **603**
Q^*, **606**
h^ω, **618**
h^n, **618**
$h^{<\omega}$, **618**
μ^h, **618**
$\dim^h$, **619**
$\dim^{[0,1]}$, **620**
Q^b_a, **623**
P^c_a, **624**
$\overline{\dim}_B$, **635**
$\underline{\dim}_B$, **635**
$\underline{\dim}_{MB}$, **636**
$\overline{\dim}_{MB}$, **636**
$\dim_{MB}$, **636**
$D^{[n]}$ (for $D \subseteq 2^{<\omega}$), **637**
$\underline{\dim}^1_B$, **637**
$\overline{\dim}^1_B$, **637**
H_A, **637**
$A^{\text{i.o.}}$, **637**
$A^{\text{a.e.}}$, **637**
$\mathcal{H}_1$, **637**
$\mathcal{H}^{\text{str}}_1(C)$, **637**
$\mathcal{P}^s_n$, **638**
$\mathcal{P}^s_\infty$, **638**
$\mathcal{P}^s$, **639**
$\dim_P$, **639**
Dim, **641**
dim, **597**
$\dim_{comp}$, **654**
Dim_{comp}, **654**
$\dim_S$, **656**
Dim_S, **657**
$\mu_{\vec{p}}$, **657**
$\square$, **663**
$d[m]$, **664**
$\dim^n_d(\sigma)$, **664**
$d_\square$, **665**
$\dim(\sigma)$ (for a string σ), **665**
Ω^A_M, **707**
Ω_M, **707**
$\leqslant^A_S$, **709**
$\Omega_U[S]$, **712**
Spec(Ω_U), **717**
S^c, **722**
$P_W(A)$, **731**
$P(A)$, **731**
$H(A)$, **732**
$I(A)$, **732**
$\overline{R}_C$, **738**
O_Q (for a complexity measure Q), **739**

$\overline{R}_K^{\mathrm{str}}$, **743**
$\overline{R}_K$, **743**
$\overline{R}_K^U$, **744**
O_K^U, **744**
$\overline{R}_Q^U$ (for a complexity measure Q), **749**
Km_M, **750**
$\overline{R}_i^M$, **750**
O_{Km}^M, **752**
O_{KM}^U, **761**
$O_{Km_D}^U$, **761**
$O_{Km_S}^U$, **761**

a priori
  entropy, **150**
  probability, **238**
a.n.c., *see* array noncomputability
Ackermann's function, **29**
adaptive selection function, *see* selection, function, adaptive
Ageev, M., 732
algorithm, 7
Allender, E., xv, 738, 743, 749
"almost all" theory of the Turing degrees, 365
almost computably enumerable set, **200**
  and computable enumerability, 201
  and left-c.e. reals, 200
"almost everywhere" behavior, xxii
  and CEA sets, 386
  and density, 385
  and hyperimmunity, 381
  and initial segments of the degrees, 401
  and minimal degrees, 401
  and minimal pairs, 359
  and nth jumps, 363
  and 1-genericity, 383, 385
  and randomness, *see* randomness, and "almost everywhere" behavior
  and Turing degrees, 360
  and 2-randomness, 394
  and weak 2-genericity, 380
almost everywhere domination, *see* domination, almost everywhere
almost recursive degree, *see* hyperimmune-freeness
almost simple
  martingale, *see* gale, martingale, almost simple
  randomness, *see* randomness, almost simple
α function, **467**
  and initial segment complexity, 489
  and Ω, 469–470
  and relativized complexity, 469
  and the s function, 468
  and 2-randomness, 470
  growth rate, 467
α-computably enumerable set, **28**
Ambos-Spies, K., xv, 15, 16, 53, 91–92, 201, 215, 217, 219, 270, 277, 303, 307–308, 349, 554
Ample Excess Lemma, xxi, **250**
analytic set, 711
Anderson, B., xv
Andrews, U., xv
anti-complex set, **576**
  and c.e. traceability, 576, 578
  and domination, 579
  and minimal programs, 579
  and plain complexity, 579
  and Schnorr triviality, 576, 580
  and (uniform) reducibility with tiny use, 579
  and wtt-reducibility, 576, 578, 580
approximation, 24
  and the halting problem, 24–25
  notation, 13
  restrained, **695**
  to a c.e. set, 12–13
  to a Δ_2^0 set, 24–26
  to a left-c.e. real, *see* real, left computably enumerable, approximation
  to a real, *see* real, approximation
arithmetic
  genericity, *see* genericity, arithmetic
  hierarchy, **23**
    and index sets, 26
  randomness, *see* randomness, arithmetic
  set, 23
array

strong, *see* strong, array
very strong, *see* very strong array
array computability, xxiv, **94**, *see also* array noncomputability
and c.e. traceability, 99
and cl-reducibility, 444, 447, 448
and definability, 99
and effective packing dimension, 649–650
and GL_2ness, 97
and hyperimmune-freeness, 98
and ibT-reducibility, 444, 447
and initial segment complexity, 730
and Kummer complex sets, 730
and lowness, 98
and low_2ness, 97
and pb-genericity, 107–108
and strong minimal covers, 100
and superlowness, 98
array noncomputability, **94**, *see also* array computability
and identity-bounded reductions, 96
and permitting, 94, 445
and separating sets, 94
and the halting problem, 94
and very strong arrays, 94–96
relative to a very strong array, **94**
Arslanov's Completeness Criterion, **89**
Arslanov, A., xv
Arslanov, M., 27, 89
asymptotically equal, **4**
Athreya, K., 636–641, 654
atom
of a computable measure, 266
of a measure, **265**
atomic measure, *see* measure, atomic
autocomplex set, **366**
and diagonal noncomputability, 367, 369
and extending partial functions, 585
and Kolmogorov complexity, 366
and 1-randomness, 368
and Turing completeness, 368
and weak computable traceability, 369
automorphism machinery, 83
autoreducibility, **340**
and indifferent sets, 341
and nonmonotonic randomness, 341
and 1-randomness, 340
avoiding
a class, **101**
a string, **601**
power, *see* randomness, and computational strength, avoiding power

Barak, B., 642
Barmpalias, G., xiv–xv, xxii–xxiii, 69, 315, 323, 339, 358, 362, 377, 420, 442, 444, 447–448, 489–491, 499, 536, 541–542, 689, 731
Barzdins' Lemma, **728**
Barzdins, J., 122, 728
base
for a notion of randomness, **531**
for computable randomness, 534
for difference randomness, 535
for 1-randomness, 531
and K-triviality, 531
and lowness for K, 533
and lowness for 1-randomness, 531
for Schnorr randomness, 534
for weak 1-randomness, 359
for weak 2-randomness, 359, 531
basic open set, *see* set, open, basic
basis for the Π^0_1 classes, **77**
and PA degrees, 86
nonexistence of a minimal basis, 80
basis theorem, 77
computably enumerable, **77**
hyperimmune-free, 78
jump inversion, 81–82
for classes of positive measure, 373
Kreisel, **77**
low, 77
with cone-avoidance, 78
low for a given 1-random, 334
low for Ω, 713
non-CEA, 79
pseudo-jump inversion, 376–377

Scott, **84**
superlow, 78
weakly low for K, 715
Bayes' rule, 238
Bayes, T., 238
Becher, V., xv, 229, 257
Bedregal, B., 560
benign cost function, *see* cost function, benign
Bernoulli measure, *see* measure, Bernoulli
betting strategy, 235, 269
nonmonotonic, **309**
and computable enumerability, 313
c.e., 311
capital function, **309**
payoff function, **310**
scan rule, **309**
scan rule, oblivious, **319**
stake function, **309**
success, **310**
bi-immunity, **295**
Bickford, M., 530
Bienvenu, L., xiv–xv, 138–139, 254, 263, 298–301, 327, 329–330, 333, 412–413, 471–473, 484, 504–505, 591, 642, 643, 714
Binns, S., 497
boolean algebra
effectively dense, 419
Borel
Determinacy, 7, 336
σ-algebra, *see* σ-algebra, Borel
Borel, E., 5, 12, 592
Borel-Cantelli Lemma, **5**
bound, *see* traceability, bound
bounded
injury, *see* priority, method, bounded injury
machine, *see* machine, bounded
Martin-Löf test, *see* test, bounded Martin-Löf
request set, *see* KC set
Bounded Request Theorem, *see* KC Theorem
bounding, **72**
Bounding Lemma, **481**
box, 674
amplification, *see* box, promotion
k-, 674
meta-, 674
promotion, 673–674
box counting dimension, *see* dimension, box counting
branching degree, **458**
Brodhead, P., xv, 319
broken dimension question, **610**, 612
for m-degrees, 611
for wtt-degrees, 611
Buhrman, H., 743, 749

C-complexity, *see* complexity, plain Kolmogorov
C-degrees, *see* degrees, C-
C-independence, *see* independence, C-
C-randomness, *see* randomness, C-
C-reducibility, *see* reducibility, C-
C-triviality, **504**
Cai, J., 598
calculus of cost functions, *see* cost function, calculus
Calhoun, W., 147, 432, 459–462
Calude, C., xi, xv, 12, 142, 200, 203–204, 228, 333, 405, 409, 413, 501, 604–605, 627–628, 706
Cantelli, F., 5
Cantor space, 3, **4**
and $[0, 1]$, 265–266
as a continuous sample space, 145
basic open set, *see* set, open, basic
measure, *see* measure
Cantor's diagonalization argument, *see* diagonalization argument
Cantor, G., 31
Cantor-Bendixson derivative, *see* class, Π^0_1, Cantor-Bendixson derivative
capital function, *see* betting strategy, nonmonotonic, capital function
cappable degree, **91**
and prompt simplicity, 92
Carathéodory, C., 400, 592, 635, 639
Cauchy sequence, 198
c.e., *see* computably enumerable
CEA set, xxii, **79**

and "almost everywhere" behavior, 386
and hyperimmune-freeness, 103
and 1-genericity, 104, 392
and Π^0_1 classes, 79
and 2-randomness, 386
and weak 2-randomness, 393
CEA(X), *see* computably enumerable, in and above a set
Cenzer, D., xv, 74–76, 373, 377
Chaitin's Ω, *see* Ω
Chaitin, G., xiii, xv, xxi, 12, 118–121, 125, 128–131, 133–134, 142, 145, 148, 227–229, 233, 250, 456, 467, 500, 504, 627, 705, 731–732
characteristic function, 2, 11
Chernoff bounds, 629, 633
Chisholm, J., 368
Cholak, P., xv, 83, 496, 668–670, 673, 680, 685
Chong, C., xv, 386
Chubb, J., 368
Church stochasticity, *see* stochasticity, Church
Church, A., xviii–xix, 8, 230
Church-Turing Thesis, **8**, 29, 358
cl-degrees, *see* degrees, computable Lipschitz
cl-reducibility, *see* reducibility, computable Lipschitz
class
Δ^0_1, **74**
uniformly, **74**
diamond, *see* diamond class
of positive measure
and mass problem reducibilities, 344
Π^0_n, **75**
and open Σ^0_{n-1} classes, 255
and $\Pi^{0,\emptyset^{(n-2)}}_2$ classes, 287
and relativized Π^0_1 classes, 255
closed, 255
index, *see* index, for a Π^0_n class
null, and $(n-1)$-randomness, 260
of positive measure, 297
of positive measure, and n-randomness, 259
of positive measure, and weak n-randomness, 382
relativized, 76
uniformly, 76
0-1 law, *see* 0-1-law, for Π^0_n classes
Π^0_1, **73**, 201
and CEA sets, 79
and complete extensions of a theory, 84
and Hausdorff dimension, 608
and hyperimmune-freeness, 78–79
and hyperimmunity, 81
and incomplete c.e. degrees, 81
and intersections, 73
and jump inversion, 81–82, 373
and low sets, 77–78
and minimal degrees, 79
and pseudo-jump operators, 376–377
and superlow sets, 78
and unions, 73
approximation, 74
as an effectively closed set, 74
basis, *see* basis for the Π^0_1 classes
basis theorem, *see* basis theorem
basis, and PA degrees, 84
Cantor-Bendixson derivative, 75
countable, and effective packing dimension, 648–649
countable, and never continuously random sets, 336
finite, 75
forcing, *see* forcing, with Π^0_1 classes
in ω^ω, 73
in ω^ω, computably bounded, **73**
index, *see* index, for a Π^0_n class
of complete extensions of PA, 84
of 1-random sets, 234, 324
of positive measure, 347
of positive measure, and jump inversion, 373
of positive measure, and 1-randomness, 259

of positive measure, mass problem, *see* mass problem, of a Π^0_1 class of positive measure
rank, **75**
rank, of an element, **75**
relativized, and LR-reducibility, 497
special, **81**
special, and jump inversion, 81
special, cardinality, 75
strong degrees, *see* degrees, strong, of Π^0_1 classes
thin perfect, 373
uniformly, **74**
universal, **84**
weak degrees, *see* degrees, weak, of Π^0_1 classes
with upwards closure of positive measure, mass problem, *see* mass problem, of a Π^0_1 class with upwards closure of positive measure
Π^0_2
and almost everywhere domination, 496
and Hausdorff dimension, 608
as an intersection of uniformly Σ^0_1 classes, 77
closed, 76
$\Pi^{0,X}_n$, *see* class, Π^0_n, relativized
Σ^0_n, **76**
and closed Π^0_{n-1} classes, 255
and relativized Σ^0_1 classes, 255
and $\Sigma^{0,\emptyset^{(n-1)}}_1$ classes, 286
and $\Sigma^{0,\emptyset^{(n-2)}}_2$ classes, 287
index, *see* index, for a Σ^0_n class
null, and $(n-1)$-randomness, 260
open, 255
relativized, 76
relativized, generators, 76
uniformly, 76
0-1 law, *see* 0-1-law, for Σ^0_n classes
Σ^0_1, 269
Σ^0_1, 73, 201
and diagonal noncomputability, 582–583
and hyperimmune-freeness, 582–583
approximation, 74
as an effectively open set, 74
generators, c.e., 74, 76
generators, computable, 74
index, *see* index, for a Σ^0_n class
relativization and density, 582–583
relativization and having measure 1, 582
relativized, and LR-reducibility, 489
uniformly, **74**
uniformly, and prefix-free complexity, 127
Σ^0_3, 289
and mass problems, 346
Σ^0_2
and Hausdorff dimension, 608
as a union of uniformly Π^0_1 classes, 77
of 1-random sets, 324
relativized, and LR-reducibility, 497
$\Sigma^{0,X}_n$, *see* class, Σ^0_n, relativized
clumpy tree, *see* tree, ε-clumpy
co-c.e.
function, *see* function, real-valued, co-c.e.
set, **11**
coding
constant
for plain complexity, **111**
for prefix-free complexity, **122**
effective, 8
Gács, **326**
into the natural numbers, 8
Kučera, **332**, 374
marker, *see* marker, coding
method, 42–43
string
for plain complexity, **111**
for prefix-free complexity, **122**
the halting problem, 10
Coding Theorem, xx, **133**, 731
for continuous measures, 151
for continuous semimeasures, 150–153

Cof, *see* index set, Cof
Cohen forcing, *see* forcing, Cohen
Cohen, P., 297
Cole, J., 347, 696
Coles, R., xi, xiv–xv, 42, 203–204, 405, 501
collection of nonrandom strings, *see* nonrandom strings
column of a set, **3**
  and n-randomness, 259
comparable strings, *see* string, comparability
completeness, 12
  computable Lipschitz, 442
  criterion
    Arslanov's, *see* Arslanov's Completeness Criterion
    Friedberg, *see* Friedberg Completeness Criterion
  many-one, **20**
    and creative sets, 22
    relative to a class of sets, **25**
  NP-, 19
  1-, **20**
    and creative sets, 22
  relative to a class of sets, **25**
  Solovay, xxii, **408**
    and halting probabilities, 409–410
    and initial segment complexity, 410
    completeness, and 1-randomness, 409–410
    relative to an oracle, **709**
  truth table, 89
    and wtt-completeness, 334
  Turing
    and effective immunity, 80
    and fixed-point freeness, 89
    and Π^0_1 classes, 81
  weak truth table
    and fixed-point freeness, 89
    and tt-completeness, 334
completions of PA
  mass problem, *see* mass problem, of completions of PA
complex set, **366**
  and C-degrees, 457
  and cl-reducibility, 441
  and diagonal noncomputability, 367
  and effective dimension, 599
  and hyperavoidable sets, 368
  and hyperimmunity, 368
  and K-degrees, 457
  and Kolmogorov complexity, 367
  and 1-randomness, 368
  and wtt-completeness, 368
  Kummer, *see* Kummer complex set
  relative to a function, **366**
  shift, *see* shift complex set
complexity
  bounds
    for computable measure machines, *see* machine, computable measure, complexity bounds
  C-, *see* complexity, plain Kolmogorov
  decision, 122
  extraction, 608, 629, 635
    and polynomial time Turing reducibility, 642
    for effective dimension, 609
    for effective packing dimension, 642
    for Hausdorff dimension, 643
  K-, *see* complexity, prefix-free Kolmogorov
  KM-, 150
    and fast-growing functions, 238
    and monotone complexity, 153, 169–170
    and 1-randomness, 239
    and optimal c.e. supermartingales, 238
    and strong s-Martin-Löf randomness, 605
    and universal monotone machines, 151
    collection of nonrandom strings, *see* nonrandom strings, for KM-complexity
    overgraph, *see* overgraph, of KM-complexity
    relativized and limit, 473
  Kolmogorov, xi, xx–xxi
    applications, 114

foundations, 110
notation, xii, 110
plain, *see* complexity, plain Kolmogorov
prefix-free, *see* complexity, prefix-free Kolmogorov
with respect to a function, **111**
monotone, 122, **146**
and computability, 148
and concatenation, 148
and KM-complexity, 153, 169–170
and 1-randomness, 227, 239, 460
and prefix-free complexity, 147–148, 459
and process complexity, 147
collection of nonrandom strings, *see* nonrandom strings, for monotone complexity
failure of subadditivity, 148
overgraph, *see* overgraph, of monotone complexity
relativized and limit, 473
plain Kolmogorov, xii, xx, **111**
and addition, 425
and c.e. sets, 115
and cl-reducibility, 440
and complexity of minimal C-programs, 112, 115
and computability, 117–120
and computable functions, 112
and concatenation, 113, 136
and effective dimension, 598
and effective upper box counting dimension, 638
and finite sets, 115
and immunity, 114
and 1-randomness, 252–254
and packing dimension, 641
and prefix-free complexity, 136, 154–156, 160–169
and process complexity, 147
and Turing reducibility, 120
and wtt-reducibility, 440
collection of nonrandom strings, *see* nonrandom strings, for plain complexity
conditional, **114**
counting strings of low complexity, 117, 119–120
critique, 121
failure of subadditivity, 113
information content, *see* information content, plain
lack of computable lower bounds, 124
monotone approximation, 578
of a number, **112**
oscillations, 137
overgraph, *see* overgraph, of plain complexity
relativized, **115**
relativized and limit, 471
relativized, and Turing reducibility, 115
symmetry of information, *see* Symmetry of Information, for plain complexity
time-bounded, 261
time-bounded, and 2-randomness, 261–262
upper bound, 112
upper bound for initial segments of sets, 136–137
prefix Kolmogorov, *see* complexity, prefix-free Kolmogorov
prefix-free Kolmogorov, xii, xix–xx, **124**
and addition, 425
and cl-reducibility, 440
and computable functions, 124
and concatenation, 132, 135
and dimension of strings, 665
and effective dimension, 598
and effective upper box counting dimension, 638
and KC sets, 126
and Martin-Löf tests, 232–233
and maximal c.e. discrete semimeasures, 133
and monotone complexity, 147–148, 459
and 1-randomness, 229, 250–252
and packing dimension, 641
and plain complexity, 136, 154–156, 160–169

and presentations of left-c.e. reals, 411
and process complexity, 147
and Turing reducibility, 456
and universal prefix-free machine output probabilities, 133
and wtt-reducibility, 440
approximation, 124
collection of nonrandom strings, *see* nonrandom strings, for prefix-free complexity
computable upper bound, 138–139
conditional, **124**
counting strings of a given complexity, 140
counting strings of low complexity, 129, 131, 140
Counting Theorem, *see* Counting Theorem
information content, *see* information content, prefix-free
lack of computable lower bounds, 124
lowness, *see* lowness, for K
minimality as an information content measure, 129–130
monotone approximation, 467
of a finite set, **141**
of a number, **124**
overgraph, *see* overgraph, of prefix-free complexity
quadratic time version, 139
relativized, **124**
relativized and limit, 472
relativized, and n-randomness, 257
subadditivity, 132
symmetry of information, *see* Symmetry of Information, for prefix-free complexity
time-bounded, **139**
time-bounded, and Solovay functions, 139
upper bound, 127–129, 131
upper bound for initial segments of sets, 137
process, 122, **146**
and computability, 148
and monotone complexity, 147
and 1-randomness, 227, 239
and plain complexity, 147
and prefix-free complexity, 147
collection of nonrandom strings, *see* nonrandom strings, for process complexity
failure of subadditivity, 149
overgraph, *see* overgraph, of process complexity
strict, **146**
strict process
collection of nonrandom strings, *see* nonrandom strings, for strict process complexity
overgraph, *see* overgraph, of strict process complexity
theory, xxv, 19, 114, 743
uniform, 122
compression function, **261**
low, 261
computable
analysis, 231
approximation, *see* approximation
function, **8**
and continuity, 31
and primitive recursive functions, 28–29
partial, *see* computable, partial function
rational-valued, *see* function, rational-valued, computable
real-valued, *see* function, real-valued, computable
relative to an oracle, **16**
uniformly, **11**
Hausdorff dimension, *see* dimension, Hausdorff, computable
index set, *see* index, set, computable
Lipschitz degrees, *see* degrees, computable Lipschitz
Lipschitz reducibility, *see* reducibility, computable Lipschitz
martingale, *see* gale, martingale, computable
measure, *see* measure, computable

measure machine, *see* machine, computable measure
model theory, 368
packing dimension, *see* dimension, packing, computable
partial function, **9**
domain emptiness problem, 10
enumeration, 9
index, *see* index, for a partial computable function
uniformly, **11**
universal, **9**, **111**
universal by adjunction, **111**
permutation, 21–22
randomness, *see* randomness, computable
rational probability distribution, **279**
real, *see* real, computable
set, **11**, 16
and fast-growing functions, 504
and monotone complexity, 148
and plain complexity, 117–120
and process complexity, 148
and the arithmetic hierarchy, 23
relative to an oracle, **16**
relativization and measure, 358
uniformly, **12**
stochasticity, *see* stochasticity, Church
traceability, *see* traceability, computable
weak, *see* traceability, weak computable
computably bounded Π^0_1 class, *see* class, Π^0_1, in ω^ω, computably bounded
computably dominated degree, *see* hyperimmune-freeness
computably enumerable
continuous semimeasure, *see* semimeasure, continuous, computably enumerable
degree, *see* degrees, Turing, computably enumerable
discrete semimeasure, *see* semimeasure, discrete, computably enumerable
function
real-valued, *see* function, real-valued, computably enumerable
in and above a set, **65**, *see also* CEA set
martingale, *see* gale, martingale, computably enumerable
operator, **731**
optimal, **731**
permitting, *see* permitting, c.e.
real, *see* real, left computably enumerable
set, **11**
almost, *see* almost computably enumerable set
and cl-reducibility, 435–436
and effective dimension, 611
and effective immunity, 80
and ibT-reducibility, 447
and initial segment complexity, 440
and minimal degrees, 72
and Π^0_1 classes, 81
and plain complexity, 115
and rK-reducibility, 436
and Schnorr Hausdorff dimension, 660
and Schnorr packing dimension, 661
and Schnorr randomness, 660
and settling times, 18
and Solovay reducibility, 435
approximation, *see* approximation, to a c.e. set
as a Σ^0_1 set, 23
entropy, 731
enumeration probability, xxv, **731**
gap phenomenon, *see* gap phenomenon, for c.e. sets
high, *see* high set, c.e.
index, *see* index, for a c.e. set
initial segment complexity, xxv, 728–730
lattice of c.e. sets, 83
low, *see* low set, c.e.
minimal pair of C-degrees, 457
modulus function, **421**

pair of incomparable degrees, 36
relative to an oracle, **18**
relativization and measure, 358
splitting, *see* splitting, c.e.
superhigh, *see* superhigh set, c.e.
thick subset, *see* thick subset, of a c.e. set
Turing completeness, 89
uniformly, **12**
uniformly, and prefix-free complexity, 127
wtt-completeness, 89
splitting, *see* splitting, c.e.
supermartingale, *see* gale, supermartingale, computably enumerable
traceability, *see* traceability, computably enumerable
Computably Enumerable Basis Theorem, *see* basis theorem, computably enumerable
computably finite
Martin-Löf test, *see* test, computably finite Martin-Löf
randomness, *see* randomness, computably finite
computably graded test, *see* test, computably graded
computably layered machine, *see* machine, computably layered
computational paradigm, *see* randomness, paradigm, computational
Conder, M., xiv
condition, *see* forcing, condition
conditional
expectation, *see* expectation, conditional
plain complexity, *see* complexity, plain Kolmogorov, conditional
prefix-free complexity, *see* complexity, prefix-free Kolmogorov, conditional
Conidis, C., xv, 642, 648
conjunctive truth table reducibility, *see* reducibility, truth table, conjunctive
constant of K-triviality, *see* K-triviality, via a constant
constructive
Hausdorff dimension, *see* dimension, Hausdorff, effective
termgale, *see* gale, termgale, Σ^0_1
continuity and computability, 31
continuous
measure, *see* measure, continuous
semimeasure, *see* semimeasure, continuous
convention
hat, *see* hat, convention
on logarithms, *see* logarithm conventions
on reals, *see* real, convention on reals
on uses, *see* use, conventions
Cook, S., 19
Cooper, S., xiii, xv–xvi, 8, 72
correspondence principle
for effective dimension, 608
for packing dimension, 648
for Schnorr Hausdorff dimension, 608
cost function, xxiii, 492, 502, 508, **526**, 672
and Δ^0_2 1-random sets, 692
and K-triviality, 527–528
benign, **689**
and ω-c.e. 1-random sets, 692
and jump traceability, 690–691
and strong jump traceability, 690
calculus, 528
for lowness for K, 526
limit condition, **526**
monotone, **526**
obeying, **526**
standard, **526**, 689
and K-triviality, 527
countable predecessor property, **464**
Counting Theorem, xx, **129**
Improved, **131**
tightness, 131
cover, **5**
effective box, **637**
n-, **592**
effective, **598**
Σ^0_1-, **386**
proper, **386**
tight, **386**

tight, and 1-genericity, 386
coverability, Martin-Löf, *see* Martin-Löf, coverability
creative set, **22**
and completeness, 22
Csima, B., xv, 379, 420–421, 458, 551–552
cuppability
Martin-Löf, *see* Martin-Löf, cuppability
wtt-, *see* wtt-cuppability

d-minimal program, *see* program, d-minimal
d-shift complex set
d-shift complex set, *see* shift complex set
d.c.e.
real, *see* real, left-d.c.e.
set, **27**
and effective reals, 201
test, *see* test, d.c.e.
Daley, R., 304, 305
Damle, V., xvi
Day, A., xiv–xv, xx, 146–147, 149, 151, 153, 169–170, 282–283, 341, 749, 752, 761–763
de Leeuw, K., 323, 358
decanter method, 511, 517–518
decidable machine, *see* machine, decidable
decision complexity, *see* complexity, decision
Dedekind cut, *see* real, left cut
deficiency set, 503
degrees, **16**, 21, *see also* reducibility
C-, 426
and complex sets, 457
and joins, 479
and Turing degrees, 457
branching, 458
cardinality, 465
density, 426
minimal, *see* minimal, degree, C-
minimal pair, *see* minimal, pair, of C-degrees
nonsplitting, 426
splitting, 426
computable Lipschitz
and array computability, 444, 447
and ibT-degrees, 443
and joins, 444
computably random
and upwards closure, 340
discrete monotone, 460
identity bounded Turing
and array computability, 444, 447
and cl-degrees, 443
and joins, 444
K-, 426
and complex sets, 457
and joins, 477
and Turing degrees, 457–458
branching, 458
cardinality, 465, 478, 495
density, 426
minimal, *see* minimal, degree, K-
minimal pair, *see* minimal, pair, of K-degrees
nonsplitting, 426
splitting, 426
LR-, 489
and c.e. sets, 491
minimal pair, *see* minimal, pair, of LR-degrees
many-one
and effective dimension, 611
and the broken dimension question, 611
monotone, 432
antichains, 460
density, 432–433
minimal pair, *see* minimal, pair, of monotone degrees
uncountable, 461–462
1-random
and upwards closure, 338–339
relative K-, 424
and infima, 424
density, 424
minimal, *see* minimal, degree, rK-
nonsplitting, 424
splitting, 424
Schnorr random
and upwards closure, 340

Solovay, xi, 413
and infima, 414
density, 415
minimal pair, *see* minimal, pair, of Solovay degrees
nonsplitting, 415
splitting, 415, 419
theory, 419
undecidability, 419
strong, 344–345
of Π^0_1 classes, 345
strong weak truth table, *see* degrees, computable Lipschitz
truth table
computable traceability, *see* traceability, computable, of a tt-degree
Turing, **16**
and "almost everywhere" behavior, 360
and C-degrees, 457
and effective dimension, 612
and infima, 17
and K-degrees, 457–458
and second order arithmetic, 364
and the broken dimension question, 612
cardinality, 17
computably enumerable, **16**
computably enumerable, density, 58, 66
decidability of the "almost all" theory, 365
effective dimension, 610
incomparable, 32
incomparable, c.e., 36
initial segments and "almost everywhere" behavior, 401
join, **17**
jump, *see* jump
minimal, *see* minimal, degree
minimal pair, *see* minimal, pair
notation, 16
theory, 364–365
undecidability, 364
upper bounds, 58
van Lambalgen, **473**
and decidability, 474
and joins, 474
maximal, 474
minimal, *see* minimal, degree, van Lambalgen
theory, 474
weak, 344–345
of Π^0_1 classes, 345
weak truth table
and effective dimension, 611
and the broken dimension question, 611
c.e. traceability, *see* traceability, computably enumerable, of a wtt-degree
weakly 1-random, 290
and upwards closure, 340
Dekker deficiency set, *see* deficiency set
Dekker, J., 503
Delahaye, J., xv
delayed permitting, *see* permitting, delayed
Δ^0_n
set, **23**
and the $(n-1)$st jump, 25
test, *see* test, Δ^0_n
Δ^0_1 class, *see* class, Δ^0_1
Δ^0_3 method, 542
Δ^0_2
dimension, *see* dimension, Hausdorff, Δ^0_2
permitting, *see* permitting, Δ^0_2
randomness, *see* randomness, Δ^0_2
real, *see* real, Δ^0_2
set
and computable approximability, 26
and hyperimmunity, 67
and the halting problem, 26
relativization and measure, 358
splitting, *see* splitting, Δ^0_2 sets
$(\Delta^0_2)^\diamond$, *see* diamond class, $(\Delta^0_2)^\diamond$
Demuth
randomness, *see* randomness, Demuth
weak, *see* randomness, weak Demuth
test, *see* test, Demuth
strict, *see* test, strict Demuth
Demuth's Theorem, xxii, 21, **333**

Demuth, O., xxii, 21, 103, 199, 231, 265, 315–316, 333, 364, 380, 409, 418–419
dense simple set, **574**
and highness, 575
and Schnorr triviality, 574
density, xxii, 385
along a set, **723**
and 2-randomness, 385
and "almost everywhere" behavior, 385
in a partial ordering, **645**
of a set, **5**
of a set of strings, **104**
pb-, **108**
uniform wtt-, **108**
Density Theorem, 57, **58**
description, *see* program
system, xx, 111
descriptive set theory, xxv
diagonal noncomputability
and autocomplex sets, 367, 369
and c.e. traceability, 584
and complex sets, 367
and effective dimension, 610, 624–625
and fixed-point freeness, 87
and hyperimmune-freeness, 369, 582–584
and lowness for computable randomness / weak 1-randomness, 591
and lowness for Kurtz null tests, 583–584
and lowness for 1-randomness / weak 1-randomness, 591
and lowness for Schnorr randomness / weak 1-randomness, 591
and lowness for weak 1-genericity, 583–584
and lowness for weak 1-randomness, 584
and minimal degrees, 618
and 1-genericity, 103
and 1-randomness, 336, 347–349
and Σ_1^0 classes, 582–583
mass problem, *see* mass problem, of DNC functions
of a degree, **87**
of a function, **87**
$\{0,1\}$-valued
and PA degrees, 89
diagonalization argument, 31
diamond class, 289, **535**, 689
and jump traceability, 689, 693–694
$(\Delta_2^0)^\diamond$, 689
low$^\diamond$, 689
(ω-c.e.)$^\diamond$, 689, 693, 694
superhigh$^\diamond$, 694
superlow$^\diamond$, 689, 693–694
$\emptyset'$-trivializing$^\diamond$, 536
Diamondstone, D., xv, 693–694
difference
hierarchy, **27**
randomness, *see* randomness, difference
differential geometry, 420
dimension
box counting, **635**
and countable stability, 636
and Hausdorff dimension, 636
effective, and effective Hausdorff dimension, 637
lower, **635**
lower, effective, **637**
modified, **636**
modified, and countable stability, 636
modified, lower, **636**
modified, upper, **636**
modified, upper, and packing dimension, 639
upper, **635**
upper, effective, **637**
upper, effective, and effective packing dimension, 641
upper, effective, and entropy rates, 637
upper, effective, and initial segment complexity, 638
effective, *see* dimension, Hausdorff, effective
Hausdorff, xiii, xxiii, **593**, 596
and box counting dimension, 636
and effective dimension, 608
and measure, 593
and packing dimension, 638
and Π_2^0 classes, 608

and s-(super)gales, 594
and Schnorr Hausdorff dimension, 608
and Σ_2^0 classes, 608
and (super)martingales, 594
and unions of Π_1^0 classes, 608
computable, **654**, *see also* dimension, Hausdorff, Schnorr
computable, and Schnorr Hausdorff dimension, 656
computable, correspondence principle, *see* correspondence principle, for computable Hausdorff dimension
constructive, *see* dimension, Hausdorff, effective
countable stability, 593
Δ_2^0, **600**
effective, xiii, xxiii, **597**, 598–600
effective, and C-independence, 629
effective, and c.e. sets, 611
effective, and c.e. supermartingales, 598
effective, and complex sets, 599
effective, and complexity extraction, 643
effective, and diagonal noncomputability, 610, 624–625
effective, and dimension of strings, 666
effective, and DNC_h, 625
effective, and DNC_n, 624–625
effective, and effective box counting dimension, 637
effective, and effective packing dimension, 641, 643, 649
effective, and entropy rates, 637
effective, and Hausdorff dimension, 608
effective, and initial segment complexity, 598
effective, and m-reducibility, 609, 611
effective, and 1-randomness, 599, 601, 609
effective, and Π_2^0 classes, 608
effective, and shift complexity, 601
effective, and the halting problem, 609
effective, and Turing reducibility, 612
effective, and unions of Π_1^0 classes, 608
effective, and weak s-randomness, 603
effective, and wtt-reducibility, 611
effective, correspondence principle, *see* correspondence principle, for effective dimension
effective, in h-spaces, **619**
effective, in h-spaces / in [0,1], 620–622
effective, in h-spaces / in Cantor space, 623
effective, in [0,1], **620**
effective, of Turing degrees, 610
effective, stability, 598
monotonicity, 593
relative to a complexity class, **596**
Schnorr, xxiv, 600, **656**, 657
Schnorr, and c.e. sets, 660
Schnorr, and computable Hausdorff dimension, 656
Schnorr, and computable measure machines, 659
Schnorr, and Hausdorff dimension, 608
Schnorr, and left-c.e. reals, 660
Schnorr, and Schnorr randomness, 657
Schnorr, and Σ_2^0 classes, 608
Schnorr, and stability, 661
Σ_1^0, *see* dimension, Hausdorff, effective
of a string, xxiv, **665**
and prefix-free complexity, 665
relative to a termgale, **664**
upper bound, 665
packing, 638, **639**
and Hausdorff dimension, 638
and martingales, 639

and upper modified box counting dimension, 639
computable, **654**, *see also* dimension, packing, Schnorr
correspondence principle, *see* correspondence principle, for packing dimension
countable stability, 639
effective, xxiv, 636, **641**
effective, and array computability, 649–650
effective, and c.e. traceability, 649–650
effective, and complexity extraction, 642–643
effective, and countable Π^0_1 classes, 648–649
effective, and dimension of strings, 666
effective, and effective Hausdorff dimension, 641, 643, 649
effective, and effective upper box counting dimension, 641
effective, and genericity, 641
effective, and initial segment complexity, 641
effective, and left-c.e. reals, 649
effective, and Schnorr packing dimension, 662
effective, and Turing reducibility, 642
effective, 0-1 law, *see* 0-1 law, for effective packing dimension
Schnorr, xxiv, **657**
Schnorr, and c.e. sets, 661
Schnorr, and computable measure machines, 659
Schnorr, and effective packing dimension, 662
Schnorr, and hyperimmunity, 661
Ding, D., xv, 262, 442, 464–465, 475, 478
discrete
machine, *see* machine, discrete
monotone degrees, *see* degrees, discrete monotone
semimeasure, *see* semimeasure, discrete
DNC, *see* diagonal noncomputability
DNC_h, **618**
and effective dimension, 625
and minimal degrees, 618
DNC_n, **618**
and effective dimension, 624–625
Dobrinen, N., 495–496
domain
of a finite assignment, *see* selection, domain
of a set of pairs, **3**
dominant function, **97**
and highness, 97
domination, **19**
almost everywhere, xxiii, 315, 380, **495**, 509–510
and highness, 496
and lowness for 2-randomness / 1-randomness, 496, 591
and LR-reducibility, 496–497, 499
and Π^0_2 classes, 496
and $\emptyset'$, 496–497, 499
uniform, **496**, 509–510
and GL_2 sets, 97
and highness, 97
settling time, **421**
Doty, D., 643
Downey, R., xi, xiv–xv, xxiv, 42, 53, 70, 72, 82–83, 93–98, 103, 107–109, 138, 204–210, 212, 215, 218, 240, 262, 275, 277–280, 288–295, 319, 321, 323, 327, 329, 334, 340, 349–350, 357–358, 360–362, 373, 379, 386, 406–408, 412–416, 418–427, 430, 432–436, 440–442, 444, 447–448, 462–465, 475, 478, 484, 501, 503–506, 511, 526, 528–530, 537, 539–542, 562–565, 568–569, 581, 586, 590, 606, 618, 642, 645, 649–650, 655–656, 658–661, 668–670, 673, 680, 685, 689, 700, 705, 707, 709–714, 716–721, 723–724, 726–727, 731
downward density, **394**
drip-feed strategy, 212

dump set, 503
Durand, B., 601
dynamic definition, *see* reduction, dynamic definition
dynamical systems, xxv
Dzhafarov, D., xv

e-splitting tree, *see* tree, e-splitting
e-state, 384
effective
  box cover, *see* cover, effective box
  coding, *see* coding, effective
  dimension, *see* dimension, Hausdorff, effective
  Hausdorff dimension, *see* dimension, Hausdorff, effective
  immunity, *see* immunity, effective
  lower box counting dimension, *see* dimension, box counting, lower, effective
  n-cover, *see* cover, n-, effective
  packing dimension, *see* dimension, packing, effective
  s-dimensional outer Hausdorff measure, *see* measure, s-dimensional outer Hausdorff, effective
  upper box counting dimension, *see* dimension, box counting, upper, effective
effectively
  dense boolean algebra, *see* boolean algebra, effectively dense
  inseparable pair, **73**
    and PA degrees, 86
    separating set, 86
  0-1-valued formula, **365**
Embedding Lemma, **346**
Enderton, H., 84
entropy
  a priori, *see* a priori, entropy
  of a c.e. set, *see* computably enumerable, set, entropy
  rate, **637**
    and effective Hausdorff dimension, 637
    and effective upper box counting dimension, 637
enumeration probability, *see* computably enumerable, set, enumeration probability
Enumeration Theorem, **9**
  for oracle machines, 17
ε-clumpy tree, *see* tree, ε-clumpy
Epstein, R., 28
equivalence under a notion of reducibility, **16**
Ershov hierarchy, **27**
expectation, **242**
  conditional, **242**
exponential order, *see* order, exponential
extended monotone reducibility, *see* reducibility, extended monotone
extendible element of a tree, **75**
extension, *see* forcing, condition, extension
extraction
  complexity, *see* complexity, extraction
  randomness, *see* randomness, extraction
extractor, 632, 642

F_σ set, **77**
f.a., *see* finite assignment
Falconer, K., 639
Federer, H., 635
Feferman, S., 100
Feller, W., 250, 629
Fenner, S., 454
field
  of left-d.c.e. reals, 219
  real closed, **219**
    and rK-reducibility, 424
    of computable reals, 224
    of Δ^0_2 reals, 224
    of K-trivial reals, 721
    of left-d.c.e. reals, 219
Figueira, S., xv, 120, 229, 340–341, 523, 668–671
filter, **645**
  generic, **645**
Fin, *see* index set, Fin
finitary independence, *see* independence, C-

finite
  assignment, **309**
    domain, *see* selection, domain
  extension method, 32
  game, 745, 746, 762
  injury, *see* priority, method, finite injury
  Martin-Löf test, *see* test, finite Martin-Löf
  randomness, *see* randomness, finite
    computably, *see* randomness, computably finite
  Solovay test, *see* test, Solovay, finite
  total Solovay test, *see* test, Solovay, finite total
Fitzgerald, A., xiv–xv, 341
fixed point, 13
Fixed Point Theorem, *see* Recursion Theorem
fixed-point freeness, xxii, **87**
  and DNC functions, 87
  and joining to $\emptyset'$, 93
  and minimal pairs, 92
  and prompt simplicity, 90
  and Turing completeness, 89
  and wtt-completeness, 89
  n-, **371**
    and $(n+1)$-randomness, 371
flexible formula, 93
fluctuation about the mean, **249**
follower, *see* priority, method, follower
forcing, 7, 100
  Cohen, 297
  condition, **645**
    extension, **645**
  Gandy, 478
  notion, **645**
  Solovay, 296–297
  with Π^0_1 classes, 374
  with computable perfect trees, 68, 645
Fortnow, L., xi, xiv–xv, 132, 229, 303, 642
FPF, *see* fixed-point freeness
Franklin, J., xv, xxiii, 273, 316–317, 534, 535, 564, 570–572, 574–580, 591
Freivalds, R., 303
fresh large number, **37**
Friedberg Completeness Criterion, 64
Friedberg, R., 32, 34–36, 38, 42, 64, 82
Friedberg-Muchnik Theorem, **36**, 44
Fubini's Theorem, 365
full approximation, 384
  method, 72
function
  computable, *see* computable, function
  partial, 8
  partial computable, *see* computable, partial function
  polynomial time computable, 16
  primitive recursive, *see* primitive recursive function
  rational-valued
    computable, 203
  real-valued, 202
    co-c.e., **203**
    computable, **203**
    computably enumerable, **203**
    Σ^0_1, *see* function, real-valued, computably enumerable
  total, 8
  tree, *see* tree, function
    perfect, *see* tree, perfect function
functional
  truth table, **21**
  Turing, **17**
  weak truth table, **21**

G_δ set, **77**
Gödel number, **8**
Gödel's Incompleteness Theorem, 73, 84, 93
Gödel, K., 8
Gaifman, H., 287, 361
gale
  Hitchgale, **321**
  Kastergale, **321**
  martingale, xiii, xxi, xxiii, **235**
    additivity, 235
    almost simple, **308**
    almost simple, and simple martingales, 308
    and Hausdorff dimension, 594
    and null sets, 235

and packing dimension, 639
and s-gales, 594
co-c.e., and computable martingales, 280
computable, 236, **270**
computable, and bounded Martin-Löf tests, 280
computable, and computable randomness, 270
computable, and computably graded tests, 280
computable, and enumerations, 276
computable, and rational-valued martingales, 270
computable, and Schnorr randomness, 273
computable, and weak 1-randomness, 290
computably enumerable, xix, **236**
computably enumerable, and 1-randomness, 236
computably enumerable, and Martin-Löf tests, 236
computably enumerable, and optimality, 240
computably enumerable, nonexistence of enumerations, 240
computably enumerable, universal, **237**
condition, **235**
etymology, 321
h-success, **271**
h-success set, **271**
in probability theory, **242**
in probability theory, and martingales / martingale processes, 243
Kolmogorov's Inequality, *see* Kolmogorov's Inequality
multiplication by a constant, 235
operator, **587**
partial computable, **303**
process, *see* gale, martingale process
rational-valued, 270
s-randomness, *see* randomness, martingale s-
s-success, **597**
savings property, **238**, 273
savings trick, 237, 273
Σ_n^0, **257**
Σ_n^0, and n-randomness, 257
Σ_1^0, *see* gale, martingale, computably enumerable
simple, **308**
simple, and almost simple martingales, 308
simple, and von Mises-Wald-Church stochasticity, 308
Space Lemma, *see* Space Lemma
strong s-success, 639
success, **235**
success set, **235**
success, relative to an order, *see* gale, martingale, h-success

martingale process, **242**
and 1-randomness, 244
and Schnorr's critique, 269
Kolmogorov's Inequality, *see* Kolmogorov's Inequality, for martingale processes
rational-valued, 245
success, **243**

nonmonotonic, *see* betting strategy, nonmonotonic

s-gale, **594**
and s-supergales, 597
and Hausdorff dimension, 594
and martingales, 594

s-supergale, **594**
and s-gales, 597
and Hausdorff dimension, 594
and supermartingales, 594

supermartingale, xiii, 150, **235**
additivity, 235
and continuous semimeasures, 238
and Hausdorff dimension, 594
and null sets, 235
and s-supergales, 594
computably enumerable, **236**
computably enumerable, and 1-randomness, 236

computably enumerable, and effective dimension, 598
computably enumerable, and Martin-Löf tests, 236
computably enumerable, optimal, **237**
computably enumerable, optimal, and KM-complexity, 238
computably enumerable, optimal, and optimal c.e. continuous semimeasures, 238
for h-spaces, **619**
h-success, **271**
h-success set, **271**
Kolmogorov's Inequality, *see* Kolmogorov's Inequality
multiplication by a constant, 235
partial computable, **303**
rational-valued, computable, and enumerations, 276
s-randomness, *see* randomness, supermartingale s-
s-success, **597**
savings property, **238**
savings trick, 237
Σ^0_n, **257**
Σ^0_n, and n-randomness, 257
Σ^0_1, *see* gale, supermartingale, computably enumerable
success, **235**
success set, **235**
success, relative to an order, *see* gale, supermartingale, h-success
termgale, 662, **664**
constructive, *see* gale, termgale, Σ^0_1
induced by a semimeasure, **664**
optimal, **664**
optimal, and semimeasures, 664
s-, **663**
Σ^0_1, **664**
terminology, 321
game
finite, *see* finite game
γ function, **487**
and the s function, 487
and 2-randomness, 488
Gandy, R., 478
gap phenomenon
for c.e. sets, 730
for K-triviality, 551
for 1-randomness, 250
lack
for Church stochasticity, 327
for 1-randomness, 327–329, 484
Gasarch, W., 69, 303
Gauld, D., xiv
generalized high$_n$ set, **19**
generalized low$_2$ set
and array computability, 97
and domination, 97
generalized low$_n$ set, **19**
generalized Martin-Löf test, *see* test, generalized Martin-Löf
generally noncomputable function, **92**
$\{0,1\}$-valued, 92–93
generators of an open set, **4**
genericity, xxii
arithmetic, **101**
and initial segments of the degrees, 102
of degrees, 102
Cohen, 378
for a filter, *see* filter, generic
n-, 101
and effective packing dimension, 641
and existence results, 102
and finite extension arguments, 102–103
and jumps, 102
and Turing reducibility, 379
and van Lambalgen's Theorem, *see* van Lambalgen's Theorem, for n-genericity
and weak $(n+1)$-genericity, 105
and weak n-genericity, 105, 107
forcing definition, 101
of degrees, 102
1-, 101
and "almost everywhere" behavior, 383, 385
and CEA sets, 104, 392
and diagonal noncomputability, 103
and generalized lowness, 102
and hyperimmune-freeness, 103

and initial segments of the degrees, 401
and jump inversion, 103
and Omega operators, 723–724
and 1-randomness, 380
and PA degrees, 103
and pb-genericity, 108–109
and tight Σ_1^0-covers, 386
and 2-randomness, 385, 393
and weak 2-genericity, 379
and weak 2-randomness, 385
and weak 1-genericity, lowness, *see* lowness, for 1-genericity / weak 1-genericity
lowness, *see* lowness, for 1-genericity
relative, and Turing reducibility, 379
pb-, **108**
and array computability, 107–108
and effective packing dimension, 650
and 1-genericity, 108–109
and 2-genericity, 108–109
Solovay n-, **297**
and weak n-randomness, 298
2-
and effective packing dimension, 641
and pb-genericity, 108–109
and Turing reducibility, 379
weak n-, **105**
and $(n-1)$-genericity, 105
and n-genericity, 105, 107
and relative hyperimmunity, 105
weak 1-
and hyperimmunity, 107
and 1-genericity, lowness, *see* lowness, for 1-genericity / weak 1-genericity
and Schnorr randomness, 356
and weak 1-randomness, 356
lowness, *see* lowness, for weak 1-genericity
weak 2-
and "almost everywhere" behavior, 380
and 1-genericity, 379
Gengler, R., 217
GH_n, *see* generalized high$_n$ set
GL_n, *see* generalized low$_n$ set
global independence, *see* independence, global
GNC function, *see* generally noncomputable function
golden
pair, **697**
run, **520**, 698
method, 511, 518
graph of a function, **3**
Greenberg, N., xiv–xv, xxiv, 323, 348, 379, 442, 444, 447–448, 496, 526, 562–564, 576–580, 584–586, 591, 609, 618–626, 642, 645, 649–650, 668–670, 673, 680, 685, 689–695, 700, 731
Griffiths, E., xiv–xv, 240, 275, 277–280, 290–295, 349–350, 462–463, 562, 564–565, 568–569, 581, 658
Grigorieff, S., 229, 257
Groszek, M., 79
guess, *see* priority method, guess
Gács, P., xv, xx–xxi, 133–134, 138, 143–144, 147, 153–154, 169–170, 172, 174, 252, 323, 325–326, 484
Gács coding, *see* coding, Gács

h-space, **618**
and $[0,1]$, 620
h-success, *see* gale, (super)martingale, h-success
Hölzl, R., 139, 689, 729
Haas, R., 28
halting probability, **142**, 201
and initial segment complexity, 410
and Solovay completeness, 409–410
relativized, *see* Omega operator *and* Ω, relativized
halting problem, 9, 11, 21
and computable approximations, 24
and Δ_2^0 questions, 33
and Δ_2^0 sets, 26
and effective dimension, 609
and finiteness of trees, 75

and index sets, 15
and Ω, 228
coding, *see* coding, the halting problem
completeness, 20
computable enumerability, 12
relative to an oracle, 18
unsolvability, 9, 31
Hanf, W., 84
Harizanov, V., 368
Harrington's golden rule, 36
Harrington, L., 83, 478
Harrington-Silver Theorem, 478
Hartmanis, J., 598
hashing, 632
hat
convention, **57**
trick, 57
Hausdorff dimension, *see* dimension, Hausdorff
Hausdorff, F., 592, 635
Hertling, P., 200, 203–204, 405, 409, 413, 706
high set, xxii, **19**
and domination, 97
and lowness for computable randomness / weak 1-randomness, 591
and lowness for Schnorr randomness / weak 1-randomness, 591
c.e., 42
and computable randomness, 349
incomplete, 53–54
measure of the class, 535
high$_n$ set, **19**
highness for a notion of randomness, 591
Hirschfeldt, D., xiii–xv, xxiv, 96, 207, 289, 334, 340, 357, 360–361, 368, 379, 406–408, 413–416, 418–427, 430, 432–436, 440–442, 447, 501, 503–504, 511, 524, 526, 528–531, 533–536, 539–542, 689, 694–695, 705, 707, 709–713, 716–721, 723–724, 726–727
Hitchcock randomness, *see* randomness, Hitchcock
Hitchcock, J., xv, 242–245, 321, 597, 608, 636–642, 654
Hitchgale, *see* gale, Hitchgale
hitting power, *see* randomness, and computational strength, hitting power
Ho, C., 199
Hofstadter's Law, xii
hungry sets construction, 531
hyperavoidable set, **368**
and complex sets, 368
hyperdegree, 358
Hyperimmune-Free Basis Theorem, *see* basis theorem, hyperimmune-free
hyperimmune-freeness, **67**, *see also* hyperimmunity
and array computability, 98
and CEA sets, 103
and computable traceability, 100, 555, 559
and diagonal noncomputability, 369, 582–584
and lowness for Kurtz null tests, 583–584
and lowness for weak 1-genericity, 583–584
and lowness for weak 1-randomness, 584
and 1-genericity, 103
and 1-randomness, 356
and Π^0_1 classes, 78–79
and Σ^0_1 classes, 582–583
and tt-reducibility, 69
and Turing reducibility, 69
and weak 1-randomness, 356–357
and weak 2-randomness, 357
cardinality of the class, 68
hyperimmunity, *see also* hyperimmune-freeness
and "almost everywhere" behavior, 381
and complex sets, 368
and Π^0_1 classes, 81
and principal functions, 69
and 2-randomness, 382
and weak 1-genericity, 107
and weak 1-randomness, 356
and weak 2-randomness, 382

of degrees, **67**
and of sets, 69
of noncomputable Δ_2^0 degrees, 67
of sets, **69**
and of degrees, 69
relative to $\emptyset'$
and weak 2-randomness, 362
relativized
and weak n-genericity, 105
hypersimplicity, **69**
and c.e. splittings, 83
and wtt-cuppability, 82

ideal, **4**
generated by a set, **530**
principal, **531**
Σ_3^0, 541
tt-, 574
Turing
low upper bound, 550
low$_2$ upper bound, 541
wtt-, **208**
Σ_3^0, 208–210
identity bounded Turing
degrees, *see* degrees, identity bounded Turing
reducibility, *see* reducibility, identity bounded Turing
ignorance test, 229
immunity, **12**
and plain complexity, 114
bi-, *see* bi-immunity
effective, **80**
and Turing completeness, 80
k-, **454**
and (weak) 1-randomness, 455
Impagliazzo, R., 642
incomparable strings, *see* string, incomparability
Incompleteness Theorem, *see* Gödel's Incompleteness Theorem
independence
C-, **627**
and effective Hausdorff dimension, 629
and global independence, 628
and initial segment complexity, 628
and left-c.e. reals, 628
and relative 1-randomness, 628
finitary, *see* independence, C-
global, **627**
and C-independence, 628
and initial segment complexity, 628
and K-triviality, 628
and relative 1-randomness, 628
of sources, xxiv, 627
of strings, 635
index
for a c.e. set, **12**
for a partial computable function, **9**
for a Π_n^0 class, **76**
for a Σ_n^0 class, **76**
set, **13**
and levels of the arithmetic hierarchy, 26
and $\emptyset'$, 16
Cof, **26**
computable, 13
Fin, **26**
Inf, **26**
Tot, **26**
uniformly Σ_3^0, **541**
indifferent set, **341**
and autoreducibility, 341
for a member of a Π_1^0 class, **341**
for a 1-random set, **340**
for genericity, 341
Inf, *see* index set, Inf
infinite injury, *see* priority, method, infinite injury
infinitely often
C-randomness, *see* randomness, infinitely often C-
strong K-randomness, *see* randomness, infinitely often strong K-
information content
measure, **129**, 133
minimal, 129
plain, **116**
prefix-free, **134**
initialization, *see* priority, method, initialization
injective randomness, *see* randomness, injective

injury, *see* priority, method, injury
bounded, *see* priority, method, bounded injury
finite, *see* priority, method, finite injury
infinite, *see* priority, method, infinite injury
set, 57
unbounded, *see* priority, method, unbounded injury
injury-free solution to Post's Problem, *see* Post's Problem, injury-free solution
inner measure, *see* measure, inner
interval determined by a string relative to a measure, **266**
interval Solovay s-test, *see* test, Solovay s-, interval
investment adviser method, 428
Ishmukhametov, S., 98–100, 650
isolated path, *see* path, isolated

Jech, T., 297
Jockusch, C., xv, 15, 41–42, 64, 69, 72, 77–79, 81–82, 84, 86–89, 91–98, 101–102, 104–105, 107–109, 207, 215, 295, 368, 370, 374, 376, 401, 414, 530, 534
join, **4**
Jones, V., xiv
jump, **18**
class, 19, 731
inversion, xxii, 64–66
and c.e. sets, 65
and Δ^0_2 sets, 65
and 1-genericity, 103
and 1-randomness, 373
and Π^0_1 classes, 81–82
basis theorem, *see* basis theorem, jump inversion
for higher jumps, 66–67
Sacks, *see* Sacks, Jump Inversion Theorem
Shoenfield, *see* Shoenfield Jump Inversion Theorem
nth, **18**
and "almost everywhere" behavior, 363
ω-, **18**
operator, **18**, 38, 64–66
and 1-genericity, 103
traceability, *see* traceability, jump
strong, *see* traceability, strong jump
ultra, *see* traceability, ultra jump
well-approximability, *see* well-approximability, jump
strong, *see* well-approximability, strong jump

K-complexity, *see* complexity, prefix-free Kolmogorov
K-degrees, *see* degrees, K-
k-immune, *see* immune, k-
K-reducibility, *see* reducibility, K-
k-set, **514**
weight, *see* weight, of a k-set
K-triviality, xxiii–xxiv, 305, 359, **425**, 501, 668
and addition, 529
and array computability, 510
and bases for 1-randomness, 531
and computable enumerability, 527, 530
and cost functions, 527–528
and Δ^0_2-ness, 456, 500
and difference randomness, 533, 550
and downward closure, 525
and global independence, 628
and joins, 530
and jump traceability, 523, 680, 685, 689, 700
and left-d.c.e. reals, 721–722
and lowness for generalized Martin-Löf tests, 538
and lowness for K, 508, 524, 525, 541
and lowness for left-d.c.e. reals, 722
and lowness for 1-randomness, 510, 525, 533
and lowness for 1-randomness / computable randomness, 591
and lowness for weak 2-randomness, 537–538
and lowness for weak 2-randomness / computable randomness, 591

and lowness for weak 2-randomness / 1-randomness, 537
and Omega operators, 719–721
and ω-c.e.-ness, 523
and real closed fields, 721
and Solovay functions, 505, 689
and strong jump traceability, 680, 685, 700
and superlowness, 518, 530
and the standard cost function, 527
and Turing incompleteness, 511
and wtt-incompleteness, 512
cost function, *see* cost function, standard
counting, *see* K-triviality, via a constant, number of K-trivials
gap phenomenon, *see* gap phenomenon, for K-triviality
incomplete upper bound, 542
listing the K-trivials, 538–540
low upper bound, 550
low_2 upper bound, 542
Σ^0_3 ideal of K-trivial c.e. degrees, 529
Σ^0_3 ideal of K-trivial degrees, 530
via a constant, 539
number of K-trivials, 501, 506–507
Kach, A., xv, 658
Kallibekov, S., 209
Kanovich, M., 366, 368
Karp, R., 19
Kastergale, *see* gale, Kastergale
Kastermans randomness, *see* randomness, Kastermans
Kastermans, B., 311, 319–321
Kautz, S., xiii, xxii, 79, 255–257, 259, 265–268, 287, 297–298, 330, 333, 359, 361–364, 382, 385–386, 393
KC request, *see* KC Theorem, request
KC set, **126**
and prefix-free complexity, 126
weight, *see* weight, of a set of KC requests
KC Theorem, **125**
and the recursion theorem, 127–128
request, **125**
weight, *see* weight, of a KC request
Khoussainov, B., xv, 200, 203–204, 405, 409, 413, 706, 746
Kjos-Hanssen, B., xv, xxiii, 335–336, 348–349, 366–369, 489–490, 494, 497, 499, 537, 554, 559–560, 576, 581, 591
Kleene, S., 13–14, 17, 23, 28, 32, 34
Kleene-Post
method, *see* finite extension method
Theorem, **32**
KM-complexity, *see* complexity, KM-
KM-reducibility, *see* reducibility, KM
Km-reducibility, *see* reducibility, monotone
Knight, J., xv
Kolmogorov complexity, *see* complexity, Kolmogorov
Kolmogorov's 0-1 Law, *see* 0-1 law, Kolmogorov's
Kolmogorov's Inequality, **235**
for martingale processes, 243
in h-spaces, **620**
Kolmogorov, A., xiii, xx, 6, 111–113, 115–116, 637
Kolmogorov-Loveland
null set, *see* null set, Kolmogorov-Loveland
randomness, *see* randomness, nonmonotonic
Koucký, M., 743, 749
Kräling, T., 139, 689, 729
Kraft's Inequality, 125
computable version, *see* KC Theorem
Kraft, L., 125
Kraft-Chaitin Theorem, *see* KC Theorem
Kramer, R., 28
Kreisel Basis Theorem, *see* basis theorem, Kreisel
Kreisel, G., 77
Kripke, S., 93
Kučera, A., xiii, xv, xxi–xxii, 89–93, 103, 231, 234, 259, 277, 315, 323–326, 330–331,

336–338, 346–347, 364, 367, 371, 373–374, 376–377, 380, 409–410, 418, 474, 489, 508–510, 524, 526, 531, 533–534, 550, 554, 609
Kučera coding, *see* coding, Kučera
Kučera's universal Martin-Löf test, *see* test, Martin-Löf, universal, Kučera's
Kučera-Gács Theorem, xxi, **326**, 330, 332
  bound on the use, 326, 441
Kučera-Slaman Theorem, xxii, **410**, 444
  and cl-reducibility, 454–455
  relativized, 709
Kumabe, M., 102, 349, 618
Kummer complex set, 366, **729**
  and array computability, 730
Kummer's Gap Theorem, **730**
Kummer, M., xxv, 303, 501, 649, 728–730, 738–740, 743–744, 761
Kurtz
  array, **294**
    and Schnorr randomness, 294
  n-randomness, *see* randomness, weak n-
  null test, *see* test, Kurtz null
  randomness, *see* randomness, weak 1-
Kurtz, S., xii–xiii, xxi–xxii, 105–107, 254–256, 259, 269, 285–288, 295, 303, 315, 323, 356, 360–362, 380–383, 385–387, 394, 401, 496
Kurtz-Solovay test, *see* test, Kurtz-Solovay
Kuznecov, A., 69

Lachlan, A., 47, 58, 333–334, 364
Ladner, R., 207
LaForte, G., xiv–xv, 42, 206, 208, 210, 215, 240, 278–280, 349–350, 377, 406, 419–424, 433–436, 440, 442, 462–463, 564–565, 568–569
Lathrop, J., 304–305
lattice, **4**
  of c.e. sets, *see* computably enumerable, set, lattice of c.e. sets
law of iterated logarithms, 230
law of large numbers, xviii, 230, 232, 303
Lebesgue Density Theorem, **5**
Lebesgue measure, *see* measure, uniform
Lebesgue, H., 5, 592
left computable real, *see* real, left computably enumerable
left computably enumerable real, *see* real, left computably enumerable
left cut, *see* real, left cut
left semicomputable real, *see* real, left computably enumerable
left-c.e. real, *see* real, left computably enumerable
left-d.c.e. real, *see* real, left-d.c.e.
Lempp, S., xv, 67, 72, 311, 319–321, 349
length of agreement, 39
  maximum, 48
length-lexicographic ordering, **2**
Lerman, M., 67, 72, 87, 370, 475, 497, 517, 534
Levin, L., xiii, xv, 116, 121, 125, 129, 133–134, 145–147, 150–151, 154, 169, 227, 232, 237–240, 265–267, 598, 601
Levy, P., 235
Lewis, A., xv, xxii, 93, 323, 339, 349, 420, 442, 448, 489–491, 499, 618
Li, M., xi–xii, xx, 110, 113, 116, 122, 132, 136–137, 150, 227, 238, 260, 265, 304, 738
Lieb, E., 246, 249–250
limit condition, *see* cost function, limit condition
limit frequency, **472**
  and discrete semimeasures, 472
Limit Lemma, **24**, 29–30
  strong form, **25**
limit randomness, *see* randomness, limit
limited dependence, 635

Lipschitz transformation, 420
LK-reducibility, *see* reducibility, LK-
loading measure, 513
logarithm
  conventions, 3
  factor, 627
Loveland, D., 117–118, 122, 305
Low Basis Theorem, *see* basis theorem, low
low cuppable degree, **92**
  and prompt simplicity, 92
low_n set, **19**
low set, **19**, 507
  and Π^0_1 classes, 77–78
  and array computability, 98
  and joins, 93
  c.e., 38
low_2 set
  and array computability, 97
$\text{low}^\diamond$, *see* diamond class, $\text{low}^\diamond$
lower
  box counting dimension, *see* dimension, box counting, lower
  modified box counting dimension, *see* dimension, box counting, modified, lower
  semicomputable real, *see* real, left computably enumerable
  semicontinuity, **723**
lowersemilattice, **4**
lowness
  for a class, **507**
  for a notion of randomness, **507**
  for a pair of classes, **537**, 590
  for a test notion, **507**
  for computable measure machines, **562**
    and computable traceability, 562
    and lowness for Schnorr randomness, 563
  for computable randomness, xxiii
    and computability, 586
    and hyperimmune-freeness, 560
  for computable randomness / Schnorr randomness, 591
  for computable randomness / weak 1-randomness, 591
  for Demuth randomness, 590
  for difference randomness, 535
  for generalized Martin-Löf tests, 537
    and K-triviality, 538
    and lowness for weak 2-randomness, 537, 538
  for K, xxiii, **507**
    and bases for 1-randomness, 533
    and jump traceability, 680
    and K-triviality, 508
    and K-triviality, 524, 525, 541
    and LK-reducibility, 508
    and lowness, 541
    and lowness for 1-randomness, 508, 525, 533
    and strong jump traceability, 680
    cost function, *see* cost function, for lowness for K
    reducibility, *see* reducibility, LK-
    via a constant, 541
    weak, **713**
    weak, and lowness for Ω, 714
    weak, and 2-randomness, 715
    weak, basis theorem, *see* basis theorem, weakly low for K
  for Kurtz null tests
    and computable traceability, 581, 584
    and diagonal noncomputability, 583–584
    and hyperimmune-freeness, 583–584
    and lowness for weak 1-genericity, 584
    and lowness for weak 1-randomness, 584
  for left-d.c.e. reals, **722**
    and K-triviality, 722
  for Martin-Löf tests, 507
  for Ω, **712**
    and Omega operators, 712
    and 2-randomness, 713
    and weak lowness for K, 714
    basis theorem, *see* basis theorem, low for Ω
  for 1-genericity, 586
  for 1-genericity / weak 1-genericity, 583
  for 1-randomness, xxiii, 473, 507–510

and bases for 1-randomness, 531
and computable traceability, 555
and K-triviality, 510, 525, 533
and lowness for K, 508, 525, 533
and LR-reducibility, 508
reducibility, *see* reducibility, LR-
relativized, 509
for 1-randomness / computable randomness, 591
for 1-randomness / Schnorr randomness, 591
for 1-randomness / weak 1-randomness, 347, 591
for partial computable randomness / computable randomness, 590
for Schnorr randomness, xxiii, 554
and computable traceability, 561
and hyperimmune-freeness, 560
and lowness for computable measure machines, 563
and lowness for Schnorr tests, 561
and lowness for weak 1-randomness, 584
and Schnorr triviality, 564
truth table, **570**
truth table, and computable traceability, 572
truth table, and Schnorr triviality, 572
for Schnorr randomness / weak 1-randomness, 591
for Schnorr tests, 554
and computable traceability, 555
and lowness for Schnorr randomness, 561
for 2-randomness / 1-randomness, 591
for weak 1-genericity, **581**, 586
and diagonal noncomputability, 583–584
and hyperimmune-freeness, 583–584
and lowness for Kurtz null tests, 584
and lowness for weak 1-randomness, 584
for weak 1-randomness
and diagonal noncomputability, 584
and hyperimmune-freeness, 581, 584
and lowness for Kurtz null tests, 584
and lowness for Schnorr randomness, 584
and lowness for weak 1-genericity, 584
for weak 2-randomness
and K-triviality, 537–538
and lowness for generalized Martin-Löf tests, 537, 538
for weak 2-randomness / computable randomness, 591
for weak 2-randomness / 1-randomness, 537
for weak 2-randomness / Schnorr randomness
and c.e. traceability, 591
for weak 2-randomness / weak 1-randomness, 591
truth table for Schnorr randomness, *see* lowness, for Schnorr randomness, truth table
LR-degrees, *see* degrees, LR-
LR-reducibility, *see* reducibility, LR-
Lusin, N., 711–712, 718
Lutz, J., xiii, xv, xxiii, 242–245, 270, 304–305, 594–598, 603, 636–641, 654, 658, 662–666

m-completeness, *see* completeness, many-one
M-pullback, *see* pullback
m-reducibility, *see* reducibility, many-one
Maass, W., 90, 215
machine
bounded, **282**
and computable randomness, 282
as a decidable machine, 298
computable measure, **277**, 292
and Schnorr Hausdorff dimension, 659
and Schnorr packing dimension, 659
and Schnorr randomness, 277

and weak 1-randomness, 292
as a decidable machine, 298
complexity bounds, 278
lowness, *see* lowness, for computable measure machines
relativized, **562**
subadditivity, 278, *see* subadditivity, for computable measure machines
with domain of measure 1, 278–279
computably layered, **291**
and weak 1-randomness, 291
decidable, **298**
and 1-randomness, 298
and Schnorr randomness, 299
and weak 1-randomness, 300–301
dependence, 21, 112, 124, 140, 142, 228, 408–409, 507, 705, 744, 749
discrete, **145**
monotone, **145**
and c.e. continuous semimeasures, 151
discrete, *see* machine, process
universal, 146
universal, and KM-complexity, 151
universal, and optimal c.e. continuous semimeasures, 151
universal, output probability, 257
oracle, *see* machine, Turing, oracle
pinball, *see* pinball machine
plain, *see* machine, Turing
prefix-free, **122**, 705
and measure, 232
KC Theorem, *see* KC Theorem
universal, **122**
universal by adjunction, **122**
universal oracle, **123**
universal oracle, $\mathcal{U}$, **123**
universal, and Solovay completeness, 409
universal, counting programs of a given length, 140
universal, counting short programs, 140
universal, fixed points, 139
universal, halting probability, *see* halting probability
universal, output probability, **133**, 229, 409
universal, output probability of a set, 229
universal, output probability, and maximal c.e. discrete semimeasures, 133
universal, output probability, and prefix-free Kolmogorov complexity, 133
universal, set of short halting programs, and Ω, 142
universal, set of short halting programs, complexity, 141–142
process, **146**
quick, **282**
universal, 146
s-measurable, **606**
and strong s-Martin-Löf randomness, 606
and tests for strong s-Martin-Löf randomness, 606
self-delimiting, 122
strict process, **146**
Turing, xix, 8
oracle, 16
universal, **9**, **111**
universal by adjunction, **111**
universal oracle, **17**, **114**
with infinite outputs, 145
majority vote, 358
majorization, **67**
Mandelbrot set, 636
many-one reducibility, *see* reducibility, many-one
marker, 59
Marker, D., 478
Martin's Conjecture, xxiv, 706
Martin, D., xxiv, 67–69, 80, 97–98, 100, 104, 288, 381, 496, 555, 575, 578, 706, 732, 735, 738
Martin, G., xiv
Martin-Löf
coverability, **534**
and $\emptyset'$-trivialization, 536
cuppability, **534**

and (strong) jump traceability, 685
and $\emptyset'$-trivialization, 536
weak, **534**
null set, *see* null set, Martin-Löf
randomness, *see* randomness, Martin-Löf
test, *see* test, Martin-Löf
bounded, *see* test, bounded Martin-Löf
computably finite, *see* test, computably finite Martin-Löf
finite, *see* test, finite Martin-Löf
generalized, *see* test, generalized Martin-Löf
Martin-Löf, P., xiii, xvii, xix–xxi, 113, 136, 227, 231, 233–234, 254, 260, 269, 378
martingale, *see* gale, martingale
mass problem, **344**
and classes of positive measure, 344
and Turing reducibility, 344
of a Π^0_1 class of positive measure, 345
of a Π^0_1 class with upwards closure of positive measure, 346
of completions of PA, 345
of DNC functions, 347
of 1-random sets, 345–347
of sets that are 2-random or completions of PA, 346–347
reducibilities, *see* reducibility, weak *and* reducibility, strong
Matijacevic, Y., 101
maximal
computably enumerable discrete semimeasure, *see* semimeasure, discrete, computably enumerable, maximal
set, **83**
maximum length of agreement, *see* length of agreement, maximum
Mayordomo, E., xv–xvi, 16, 270, 277, 308, 598, 636–641, 654
McNicholl, T., 368
measurable function, **242**
measure
and computability, 358
and computable enumerability, 358
and Δ^0_2-ness, 358
and Turing reducibility, 360
atom, *see* atom, of a measure
atomic, **265**
Bernoulli, **657**
computable, **264**
atom, *see* atom, of a computable measure
computable rational probability, *see* computable, rational probability distribution
continuous, **265**
induced by a premeasure, **264**
information content, *see* information content measure
inner, **5**
interval determined by a string, *see* interval determined by a string relative to a measure
Lebesgue, *see* measure, uniform
loading, *see* loading measure
of relative randomness, xxii, *see* randomness, measure
outer, **5**
probability
representation in a Π^0_1 class, 335
representation of a real by a sequence, *see* representation, of a real by a sequence relative to a measure
resource-bounded, 270
risking, *see* risking measure
s-, **592**
s-dimensional, **592**
s-dimensional outer Hausdorff, **593**
effective, **598**
s-dimensional packing, **639**
theory, xix, xxiii, 495, 592
trivial, **265**
uniform, **5**
and Hausdorff dimension, 593
for *h*-spaces, **618**
measure-theoretic paradigm, *see* randomness, paradigm, measure-theoretic
Medvedev
degrees, *see* degrees, strong
reducibility, *see* reducibility, strong
Medvedev, Y., 69, 344

meet, **4**
meet-irreducibility, **346**
meeting a class, 100
Merkle, W., xv, 120, 138–139, 243–244, 251, 254, 276, 279–280, 298–301, 304–306, 309–314, 325–326, 328, 330, 357, 366–369, 437, 456–458, 484, 500, 505, 576, 581, 655–656, 658–661, 689, 729
meta-box, *see* box, meta-
Mihailović, N., 243–244, 279–280, 282, 325–326, 484, 562–564
Mileti, J., xv
Miller, J., xiii–xv, xx–xxiv, 121, 125, 131, 155, 166, 168–169, 229, 250–252, 261–263, 276, 289, 309, 311–316, 319, 323, 327–330, 332, 334, 340–341, 348, 357, 368, 373, 379, 465–466, 473–481, 484–489, 494–497, 499, 505–506, 528, 535, 537–538, 584–586, 591, 601, 609–612, 615, 618–627, 635, 642, 651, 705, 707, 709–724, 726–727, 743
Miller, R., 43
Miller, W., 67–69, 100, 555
Mills, C., 530
mind-change function, *see* real, left computably enumerable, mind-change function
minimal
  C-program, *see* program, minimal C-
  degree, **70**
    and Π^0_1 classes, 79
    and "almost everywhere" behavior, 401
    and c.e. sets, 72
    and c.e. traceability, 650
    and diagonal noncomputability, 618
    and DNC_h, 618
    and GL_2-ness, 72
    and joins, 93
    and jump inversion, 72
    and lowness, 72
    and 1-randomness, 259
    C-, 458–459
    K-, 459
    of effective dimension 1, 626
    of effective packing dimension 1, 645
    rK-, 437, 459
    rK-, and 1-randomness, 439
    rK-, and initial segment complexity, 439
    rK-, cardinality of the class, 439
    van Lambalgen, 474
  information content measure, *see* information content measure, minimal
  K-program, *see* program, minimal K-
  pair, **47**
    and "almost everywhere" behavior, 359
    and fixed-point freeness, 92
    of C-degrees, 457
    of K-degrees, 458, 550–553
    of c.e. degrees, 47
    of c.e. degrees, and c.e. splittings, 53
    of high c.e. degrees, 56
    of K-trivial degrees, 504
    of LR-degrees, 491
    of monotone degrees, 460
    of Solovay degrees, 415
Minimal Pair Theorem, 44
Minkowski dimension, *see* dimension, box counting
modified box counting dimension, *see* dimension, box counting, modified
modulus function, *see* computably enumerable, set, modulus function
monotone
  complexity, *see* complexity, monotone
  cost function, *see* cost function, monotone
  degrees, *see* degrees, monotone
  machine, *see* machine, monotone
  reducibility, *see* reducibility, monotone

Montalbán, A., xiv–xv, 335–336, 458, 551–552
Moore, E., 323, 358
Moscow school of algorithmic information theory, 120
Mostowski, A., 93
Muchnik degrees, *see* degrees, weak
Muchnik reducibility, *see* reducibility, weak
Muchnik, A., 32, 34–36, 86, 344
Muchnik, An., xx, 155, 168, 263, 304, 305, 309–313, 471–473, 507–508, 738–739, 744–745, 749, 752, 762
multiple permitting, *see* permitting, multiple
music, 715
Mycielski, J., 478
Myhill Isomorphism Theorem, **21**
Myhill's Theorem, **22**
  randomness-theoretic version, 410
Myhill, J., 21–22

n-c.e.
  randomness, *see* randomness, n-c.e.
  test, *see* test, n-c.e.
n-computably enumerable set, **27**
n-cover, *see* cover, n-
n-fixed-point freeness, *see* fixed-point freeness, n-
n-FPF, *see* fixed-point freeness, n-
n-genericity, *see* genericity, n-
n-packing, *see* packing, n-
n-randomness, *see* randomness, n-
Nabutovsky, A., 420
NCR, **336**
NCR_n, **336**
Nerode, A., 21, 121, 746
never continuously random set, 7, 335–336
  and countable Π^0_1 classes, 336
Newton's Method, **222**
Ng, K., xiv–xvi, xxii, 219, 316–317, 319, 323, 339, 358, 362, 377, 535, 590, 650, 672–673, 689, 693
Nies, A., xi, xiii–xv, xxi–xxiv, 69, 120, 125, 228–229, 254, 258, 260–262, 276, 288–289, 309, 311–316, 319, 328, 330, 333–334, 340–341, 349–351, 356–357, 376–377, 382, 407–408, 413, 415–416, 418–419, 425–427, 430, 432, 473, 501, 503–505, 508, 510–511, 518, 523–531, 533–542, 554, 559–560, 562–564, 586, 590–591, 611, 668–671, 689–695, 700, 706–713, 715–721, 723–724, 726–727
Nitzpon, D., 586
Niveaufunktion, 600
nonascending path trick, **586**
noncappable degree, **91**
  and prompt simplicity, 91
nonmonotonic betting strategy, *see* betting strategy, nonmonotonic
nonmonotonic randomness, *see* randomness, nonmonotonic
nonrandom strings, xxv
  for KM-complexity, 749
  for monotone complexity, 749
  for plain complexity, 738, 740, 743, 749
  for prefix-free complexity, 743–745, 749
  for process complexity, 749
  for strict process complexity, 749, 761–763
nontrivial pseudo-jump operator, *see* pseudo-jump operator, nontrivial
notion of forcing, *see* forcing, notion
NP-completeness, *see* completeness, NP-
nth jump, *see* jump, nth
Nugent. R., xvi
null set, xix, **5**, 231
  and (super)martingales, 235
  Kolmogorov-Loveland, **310**
    and finite unions, 313
  Martin-Löf, **231**
    relative to a measure, **264**
  Martin-Löf ν-, *see* null set, Martin-Löf, relative to a measure
  Π^0_n, *see* class, Π^0_n, null

Π_2^0, 537
Schnorr, **272**
and Schnorr tests, 272
Schnorr s-, **654**
and total Solovay s-tests, 655
Σ_n^0, *see* class, Σ_n^0, null

O-notation, **3**
obeying a cost function, *see* cost function, obeying
oblivious scan rule, *see* scan rule, oblivious
Odifreddi, P., xiii, xix, 8, 28, 72, 85, 208–209
Ω, xxi–xxii, 12, **142**, 227–229, 408–410, 705
and Demuth randomness, 315
and initial segment complexity, 410
and K-reducibility, 469–470
and sets of short halting programs, 142
and Solovay reducibility, 408, 415
and the α function, 469–470
and tt-incompleteness, 333
and 2-randomness, 469–470
and vL-reducibility, 475
and $\emptyset'$, 228
approximation, 142, 228
as an operator, *see* Omega operator
initial segment complexity, 469–470
left computable enumerability, 228
1-randomness, 228
rate of convergence, 467–468
relativized, 257, *see also* halting probability, relativized
and C-reducibility, 479
and K-reducibility, 477
and vL-reducibility, 475
Solovay completeness, 408
wtt-completeness, 228
Omega operator, xxiv, 386, **706**
and continuity, 723
and K-triviality, 719–721
and left-c.e. reals, 716–719, 721
and lower semicontinuity, 723
and lowness, 708
and lowness for Ω, 712
and 1-genericity, 723–724
and 2-randomness, 711, 724
failure of degree invariance, 718
range, 712, 724–727
spectrum, **717**, 719, 726
and 1-randomness, 717
$(\omega\text{-c.e.})^\diamond$, *see* diamond class, $(\omega\text{-c.e.})^\diamond$
ω-computably enumerable set, xxiv, **25**, **27**
and identity-bounded mind-change functions, 27
totally, *see* totally ω-c.e. degree
ω-jump, *see* jump, ω-
Ω-like real, **409**, *see also* completeness, Solovay
1-completeness, *see* completeness, 1-
1-genericity, *see* genericity, 1-
1-randomness, *see* randomness, 1-
and Solovay functions, 254
1-reducibility, *see* reducibility, 1-
only computably presentable real, *see* real, left computably enumerable, only computably presentable
open
set, *see* set, open
Σ_n^0 test, *see* test, Σ_n^0, open
open question, xxi, 19, 122, 140, 145, 147, 150, 205, 263, 290, 311, 322, 333, 341, 357, 362, 394, 424, 426, 432, 433, 459, 462, 473, 486, 488, 507, 534, 535, 541, 550, 553, 590, 591, 597, 604, 606, 627, 628, 650, 670, 672, 680, 689, 694, 700, 701, 715, 721, 723, 731, 732, 743, 761
operator
computably enumerable, *see* computably enumerable, operator
martingale, *see* gale, martingale, operator
Omega, *see* Omega operator
pseudo-jump, *see* pseudo-jump operator
opponent, 31
optimal
computably enumerable
continuous semimeasure, *see* semimeasure, continuous,

computably enumerable, optimal
operator, *see* computably enumerable, operator, optimal
supermartingale, *see* gale, supermartingale, computably enumerable, optimal
termgale, *see* gale, termgale, optimal
oracle, 16
machine, *see* machine, Turing, oracle
prefix-free machine, *see* machine, prefix-free, oracle
Turing machine, *see* machine, Turing, oracle
order, xiii, **271**
complex set, *see* complex set
exponential, 599–600
ordinal notation, 27
Ordnungsfunktion, 271
Osherson, D., 246, 249–250
outcome, *see* priority method, outcome
outer measure, *see* measure, outer
output probability, *see* machine, prefix-free, universal, output probability *and* machine, monotone, universal, output probability
overgraph, **739**
of KM-complexity, 761
of monotone complexity, 752
of plain complexity, 744
of prefix-free complexity, 744–745
of process complexity, 761
of strict process complexity, 761
Owings, J., 14
Oxtoby, J., 4

PA, *see* Peano Arithmetic
PA degree, xxii, **84**
above a low degree, 93
and bases for Π^0_1 classes, 84, 86
and c.e. degrees, 87
and computable trees, 86
and effectively inseparable pairs, 86
and jump classes, 93
and lowness, 87
and minimal degrees, 87
and 1-genericity, 103
and 1-randomness, 337–340
and separating sets, 86
and $\{0, 1\}$-valued DNC functions, 89
upwards closure, 85
packing, **638**
dimension, *see* dimension, packing
n-, **638**
Paris, J., 381, 401
partial
function, *see* function, partial
randomness, *see* randomness, weak s- *and* randomness, strong s-
partial computable
function, *see* computable, partial function
randomness, *see* randomness, partial computable
path, **72**
isolated, **74**
computability, 74
Pavan, A., 642
payoff function, *see* betting strategy, nonmonotonic, payoff function
pb-density, *see* density, pb-
pb-genericity, *see* genericity, pb-
pb-reducibility, *see* reducibility, pb-
Peano Arithmetic, 73, 84
mass problem of completions, *see* mass problem, of completions of PA
perfect function tree, *see* tree, perfect function
permitting
and array noncomputability, 94, 445
c.e., 43
delayed, 61
Δ^0_2, 43
multiple, 94, 445
simple, *see* permitting, c.e.
permutation
computable, *see* computable, permutation
randomness, *see* randomness, permutation
Π^0_n

class, *see* class, Π^0_n
set, **23**
test, *see* test, Π^0_n
Π^0_1 class, *see* class, Π^0_1
Π^0_2 null set, *see* null set, Π^0_2
piecewise
computable set, **56**
trivial set, **53**
thick subsets, 54
thick subsets, and highness, 53
pinball machine, 517
Pingrey, S., 368
Pippinger, N., 125
plain
information content, *see* information content, plain
Kolmogorov complexity, *see* complexity, plain Kolmogorov
machine, *see* machine, Turing
symmetry of information, *see* Symmetry of Information, for plain complexity
polynomial time
computable function, *see* function, polynomial time computable
Turing reducibility, *see* reducibility, polynomial time Turing
Porter, C., xvi, 333
Positselsky, S., 738, 752
Posner's trick, **48**
Posner, D., 48, 64–65, 72, 101
Post's Problem, **32**, 34, 36, 82–83, 501, 511
injury-free solution, 502
priority-free solution, 91, 502
Post's Program, 83
Post's Theorem, **25**
Post, E., 17, 22, 24–25, 32, 34, 80, 82–83, 90
prefix Kolmogorov complexity, *see* complexity, prefix-free Kolmogorov
prefix-free
function, **122**
computable, universal, **122**
computable, universal by adjunction, **122**
information content, *see* information content, prefix-free
Kolmogorov complexity, *see* complexity, prefix-free Kolmogorov
machine, *see* machine, prefix-free
set, **74**, 121–122
weight, *see* weight, of a prefix-free set
symmetry of information, *see* Symmetry of Information, for prefix-free complexity
premeasure, **264**
rational representation, **264**
presentation, *see* real, left computably enumerable, presentation
preservation
of the use, *see* use, preservation
strategy, *see* Sacks, preservation strategy
primitive recursive function, **28**
and computable functions, 28–29
principal
function, **69**
and hyperimmunity, 69
ideal, *see* ideal, principal
priority
method, 34–36
bounded injury, 38
finite injury, 34–36
follower, 36
guess, 44
infinite injury, 47
initialization, 35
injury, 35
outcome, 44
priority tree, 44, 55
protecting a set, 37
requiring attention, 36
restraint, 37
restraint function, 41
strategy, 44
true outcome, 46
true path, 46–47
unbounded injury, 39–40
visiting a node, 46
ordering, 35
tree, *see* priority, method, priority tree

priority-free solution to Post's Problem, *see* Post's Problem, priority-free solution
probabilistic method, 632
probability
  a priori, *see* a priori, probability
  halting, *see* halting probability
  measure, *see* measure, probability
  output, *see* machine, prefix-free, universal, output probability *and* machine, monotone, universal, output probability
  theory, xxv
process
  complexity, *see* complexity, process
  machine, *see* machine, process
productive set, **22**
program, **118**
  counting programs, 118
  d-minimal, **141**
    counting, 141
  minimal C-, 112, 578
    complexity, 115
  minimal K-, 124
    complexity, 143–145
    for a finite set, **141**
prompt simplicity, **90**, 215
  and cappability, 92
  and fixed-point freeness, 90
  and low cuppability, 92
  and noncappability, 91
  and superlowness, 694
proper Σ^0_1-cover, *see* cover, Σ^0_1, proper
protecting a set, *see* priority, method, protecting a set
pseudo-jump inversion, *see* pseudo-jump operator, inversion
pseudo-jump operator, **41**
  inversion, 41
    basis theorem, *see* basis theorem, pseudo-jump inversion
    for 1-random sets, 376
    for wtt-reducibility, 377
  nontrivial, **41**
pullback, **606**

quick process
  machine, *see* machine, process, quick
  randomness, *see* randomness, quick process

Raichev, A., xvi, 219, 224, 424, 437, 439
Raisonnier, J., 555
random variable, **242**
randomness
  almost simple, **308**
    and simple randomness, 308
  and "almost everywhere" behavior, xxv, 359, 381
  and computational power, xxiii, 228–229, 288–289, 317, 326, 332, 339, 360, 363, 370–371, 533, 713, 715
    avoiding power, 370
    hitting power, 370
  and stochasticity, 303
  arithmetic, **256**
    and $\emptyset^{(\omega)}$-computability, 324
  C-, **112**, 743
    and strong K-randomness, 161–164, 715
    and weak K-randomness, 133, 251
  computable, xxi, **270**, 600
    and bounded machines, 282
    and bounded Martin-Löf tests, 280
    and Church stochasticity, 303
    and computably graded tests, 280
    and existence of limits for computable martingales, 270
    and highness, 349–351
    and initial segment complexity, 304–305
    and left-c.e. reals, 351
    and nonmonotonic randomness, 311
    and 1-randomness, 275, 351
    and 1-randomness, lowness, *see* lowness, for 1-randomness / computable randomness
    and partial computable randomness, lowness, *see*

lowness, for partial computable randomness / computable randomness
and quick process randomness, 283
and relative tt-Schnorr randomness, 571
and Schnorr randomness, 275, 351
and Schnorr randomness, lowness, *see* lowness, for computable randomness / Schnorr randomness
and ultracompressibility, 305
and upwards closure, 340
and van Lambalgen's Theorem, *see* van Lambalgen's Theorem, for computable randomness
and von Mises-Wald-Church stochasticity, 307
and weak 1-randomness, lowness, *see* lowness, for computable randomness / weak 1-randomness
and weak 2-randomness, lowness, *see* lowness, for weak 2-randomness / computable randomness
base, *see* base, for computable randomness
lowness, *see* lowness, for computable randomness
computably finite, **318**
and total ω-c.e.-ness, 319
Δ_2^0, **600**
Demuth, **315**
and Δ_2^0-ness, 316
and difference randomness, 318
and generalized lowness, 316, 364
and hyperimmunity, 316
and Ω, 315
and ω-c.e.-ness, 315
and 1-randomness, 315
and 2-randomness, 315
and weak 2-randomness, 316
lowness, *see* lowness, for Demuth randomness
difference, **316**, 339, 534–535
and K-triviality, 533, 550
and Demuth randomness, 318
and martingales, 318
and 1-randomness, 317–318
and strict Demuth tests, 317
and the halting problem, 317
and weak 2-randomness, 318
base, *see* base, for difference randomness
lowness, *see* lowness, for difference randomness
extraction, xxiv, 608, 609, 618, 627
for strings, 635
extractor, *see* extractor
finite, **318**
and 1-randomness, 318
Hitchcock, **322**
infinitely often C-, **260**
and infinitely often strong K-randomness, 262–263, 715
and 1-randomness, 260
and 2-randomness, 261–262
infinitely often strong K-, xxiv, **262**
and 2-randomness, 716
and infinitely often C-randomness, 262–263, 715
and 3-randomness, 262
and 2-randomness, 262–263
injective, **319**
and 1-randomness, 319
Kastermans, **321**
Kolmogorov-Loveland, *see* randomness, nonmonotonic
Kurtz, *see* randomness, weak 1-
Kurtz n-, *see* randomness, weak n-
limit, **315**
Martin-Löf, xix, **231**, *see also* randomness, 1-
and 1-randomness, 232
martingale s-, **604**
measure, 404, 464
n-, xxi, **256**
and C-reducibility, 479
and columns of a set, 259
and initial segment complexity, 257
and jumps, 324
and K-reducibility, 477

and $(n-1)$st jumps, 363–364
and $(n-1)$-fixed-point freeness, 371
and $(n+1)$-randomness, 257
and nth jumps, 364
and 1-randomness relative to $\emptyset^{(n-1)}$, 256
and open Σ^0_n classes, 254
and open Σ^0_n tests, 256
and Π^0_n classes of positive measure, 259
and Π^0_{n+1} null classes, 260
and plain complexity, 263
and prefix-free complexity, 263
and Σ^0_n classes, 254
and Σ^0_{n+1} null classes, 260
and $\Sigma^{0,\emptyset^{(n-1)}}_1$ classes, 254
and (super)martingales, 257
and Turing reducibility, 332, 475
and vL-reducibility, 474
and weak $(n+1)$-randomness, 360
and weak n-randomness, 288, 361–362
and $\emptyset^{(n)}$-computability, 324
and 0-1 laws, 259
relative, 257–258
relative to a continuous measure, 336
relative to a measure, 264
relative, and joins, 257–258
single gap characterization, 487
n-c.e., 316
n-ν-, *see* randomness, n-, relative to a measure
nonmonotonic, xxi, **310**, 319
and autoreducibility, 341
and initial segment complexity, 312
and 1-randomness, 311, 314
and (partial) computable randomness, 311
and total betting strategies, 310
and van Lambalgen's Theorem, *see* van Lambalgen's Theorem, for nonmonotonic randomness
of a closed set, xxv
of a continuous function, xxv
of a degree, **227**
of a string, xx, 110–112, 132–133
collection of nonrandom strings, *see* nonrandom strings
relative to a function, **111**
1-, xix, xxi, **227**, 600
and addition, 419
and approximations to left-c.e. reals, 416
and autocomplex sets, 368
and autoreducibility, 340
and C-reducibility, 425
and c.e. degrees, 337
and cardinality of K-degrees, 495
and Church stochasticity, 232
and cl-reducibility, 441, 448, 455
and complex sets, 368
and computable enumerability, 324–325
and computable functions, 299
and computable randomness, 275, 351
and computable randomness, lowness, *see* lowness, for 1-randomness / computable randomness
and computing c.e. sets, 289
and decidable machines, 298
and degrees computing $\emptyset'$, 330
and Demuth randomness, 315
and diagonal noncomputability, 336, 347–349
and difference randomness, 317–318
and downward closure, 333
and downward closure under strong reducibilities, 333
and effective dimension, 599, 601, 609
and finite randomness, 318
and hyperimmune-freeness, 324, 356
and hyperimmunity, 455
and ibT-reducibility, 447
and indifferent sets, 341
and infinitely often C-randomness, 260

and initial segment complexity, 229, 250–254, 466, 477, 479, 481, 484–485
and initial segments of the degrees, 333
and injective randomness, 319
and joins, 339
and jump inversion, 373
and K-comparability, 486
and k-immunity, 455
and K-incomparability, 480–481
and K-reducibility, 425
and Kastermans / Hitchcock randomness, 322
and KM-complexity, 239
and left-d.c.e. reals, 410
and lowness, 324
and Martin-Löf randomness, 232
and martingale processes, 244
and measure, 234
and minimal degrees, 259
and minimal pairs, 359
and minimal rK-degrees, 439
and monotone complexity, 227, 239, 460
and nonmonotonic randomness, 311, 314
and 1-genericity, 380
and 1-randomness relative to a measure, 267
and PA degrees, 337–340
and partial computable randomness, 304
and Π^0_1 classes, 234, 324
and Π^0_1 classes of positive measure, 259
and plain complexity, 252–254
and presentations of left-c.e. reals, 411
and process complexity, 227, 239
and pseudo-jump operators, 376
and rK-reducibility, 424–425
and Schnorr randomness, 349–351
and Schnorr randomness, lowness, *see* lowness, for 1-randomness / Schnorr randomness
and shift complexity, 601
and Solovay completeness, 409–410
and Solovay functions, 412
and Solovay randomness, 234
and Solovay reducibility, 419
and strong K-belowness, 486–487
and (super)martingales, 236
and the law of large numbers, 232
and tt-reducibility, 333
and Turing reducibility, 259, 326, 332, 475–476
and 2-randomness, lowness, *see* lowness, for 2-randomness / 1-randomness
and upwards closure, 338–339
and vL-reducibility, 474
and von Mises-Wald-Church stochasticity, 303
and weak K-randomness, 227, 251
and weak 1-randomness, 290, 356
and weak 1-randomness, lowness, *see* lowness, for 1-randomness / weak 1-randomness
and weak 2-randomness, lowness, *see* lowness, for weak 2-randomness / 1-randomness
and wtt-reducibility, 326
as a Σ^0_2 class, 324
base, *see* base, for 1-randomness
computable characterization, 243
gap phenomenon, *see* gap phenomenon, for 1-randomness
lowness, *see* lowness, for 1-randomness
mass problem, *see* mass problem, of 1-random sets
no gap phenomenon, *see* gap phenomenon, lack, for 1-randomness
plain complexity characterization, 252–254
plain complexity characterization, and Solovay functions, 327
relative to a computable measure, 264

relative to a continuous measure, 335–336
relative to a measure, **264**
relative to a measure, and 1-randomness, 267
relative to a measure, and noncomputability, 334
relative to a measure, for atomic measures, 268
relative, and C-independence, 628
relative, and global independence, 628
relative, and minimal pairs, 337, 533
relativized, **245**
relativized, and generalized lowness, 708
relativized, and n-randomness, 256
relativized, and Turing reducibility, 475
Schnorr's critique, *see* Schnorr's critique
subsets, 347–349
1-ν-, *see* randomness, 1-, relative to a measure
paradigm
computational, xx, 226–227
measure-theoretic, xx, 226, 229–231
stochastic, 226, 229–231
unpredictability, xx, 226, 234–236
partial, *see* randomness, weak s- *and* randomness, strong s-
partial computable, **303**
and computable randomness, lowness, *see* lowness, for partial computable randomness / computable randomness
and initial segment complexity, 304–305
and nonmonotonic randomness, 311
and 1-randomness, 304
and von Mises-Wald-Church stochasticity, 303
lowness, *see* lowness, for partial computable randomness
permutation, **319**
quick process, **282**
and computable randomness, 283
relative, **257**
measure, *see* randomness, measure
relative to a measure, xxi, xxv
Schnorr, xxi, **271**, 600
and c.e. degrees, 350
and c.e. sets, 660
and Church stochasticity, 330
and computable martingales, 273
and computable measure machines, 277
and computable randomness, 275, 351
and computable randomness, lowness, *see* lowness, for computable randomness / Schnorr randomness
and decidable machines, 299
and finite total Solovay tests, 294
and highness, 349–351
and initial segment complexity, 658
and Kurtz arrays, 294
and Kurtz null tests, 294
and left-c.e. reals, 350–351
and 1-randomness, 349–351
and 1-randomness, lowness, *see* lowness, for 1-randomness / Schnorr randomness
and Schnorr Hausdorff dimension, 657
and Schnorr tests, 272
and total Solovay tests, 275
and upwards closure, 340
and van Lambalgen's Theorem, *see* van Lambalgen's Theorem, for Schnorr randomness
and weak 1-genericity, 356
and weak 1-randomness, 286, 290, 356
and weak 1-randomness, lowness, *see* lowness, for Schnorr randomness / weak 1-randomness

and weak 2-randomness, lowness, *see* lowness, for weak 2-randomness / Schnorr randomness
base, *see* base, for Schnorr randomness
lowness, *see* lowness, for Schnorr randomness
relative to a computable measure, 658
relative to $\emptyset'$, 315
truth table lowness, *see* lowness, for Schnorr randomness, truth table
Schnorr Δ_2^0, **600**
set-theoretic, 297
simple, **308**
and almost simple randomness, 308
and Church stochasticity, 308
Solovay, **234**
and 1-randomness, 234
strong K-, **132**, 744
and C-randomness, 161–164, 715
strong s-Martin-Löf, **605**
and KM-complexity, 605
and s-measurable machines, 606
and supermartingale s-randomness, 605
and weak s-randomness, 605
in h-spaces, **619**
supermartingale s-, **604**
and strong s-Martin-Löf randomness, 605
3-
and infinitely often strong K-randomness, 262
truth table Schnorr relative, **570**
and computable randomness, 571
2-, xxi, xxiv
and "almost everywhere" behavior, 394
and CEA sets, 386
and Demuth randomness, 315
and density, 385
and generalized lowness, 363
and hyperimmunity, 382
and infinitely often C-randomness, 261–262
and infinitely often strong K-randomness, 262–263, 716
and initial segment complexity, 470, 478, 487–488
and K-reducibility, 469–470
and lowness for Ω, 713
and mass problems, 346–347
and Ω, 469–470, 478
and Omega operators, 711, 724
and 1-genericity, 385, 393
and 1-randomness, lowness, *see* lowness, for 2-randomness / 1-randomness
and the α function, 470
and the γ function, 488
and the s function, 487
and time-bounded plain complexity, 261–262
and Turing reducibility, 475
and 2-randomness relative to a measure, 268
and vL-reducibility, 475
and weak lowness for K, 715
relative to a measure, 268
single gap characterization, 487–488
2-ν-, *see* randomness, 2-, relative to a measure
weak, 308
weak Demuth, **315**
weak K-, **132**
and C-randomness, 133, 251
and 1-randomness, 227, 251
weak n-, xxi, **286**
and $(n-1)$-randomness, 360
and n-randomness, 288, 361–362
and Π_n^0 classes of positive measure, 382
and $\Sigma_1^{0,\emptyset^{(n-2)}}$ classes, 287
and Σ_n^0 Kurtz null tests, 287
and Σ_{n-1}^0 classes, 287
and $\Sigma_2^{0,\emptyset^{(n-2)}}$ classes, 287
and Solovay n-genericity, 298
and weak 1-randomness relative to $\emptyset^{(n-1)}$, 286
and $\emptyset^{(n)}$-computability, 360
and $\emptyset^{(n-1)}$-c.e. degrees, 361

as strong $(n-1)$-randomness, 288
weak 1-, 271, **285**
and bi-immunity, 295
and c.e. degrees, 295
and computable martingales, 290
and computable measure machines, 292
and computable randomness, lowness, *see* lowness, for computable randomness / weak 1-randomness
and computably layered machines, 291
and decidable machines, 300–301
and hyperimmune-freeness, 356–357
and hyperimmunity, 289–290, 356
and k-immunity, 455
and Kurtz null tests, 286
and Kurtz-Solovay tests, 293
and left-c.e. reals, 295
and 1-randomness, 290, 356
and 1-randomness, lowness, *see* lowness, for 1-randomness / weak 1-randomness
and only computably presentable left-c.e. reals, 411
and Schnorr randomness, 286, 290, 356
and Schnorr randomness, lowness, *see* lowness, for Schnorr randomness / weak 1-randomness
and upwards closure, 340
and weak 1-genericity, 356
and weak 2-randomness, 357
and weak 2-randomness, lowness, *see* lowness, for weak 2-randomness / weak 1-randomness
lowness, *see* lowness, for weak 1-randomness
weak s-, **602**
and effective dimension, 603
and Solovay s-tests, 603
and strong s-Martin-Löf randomness, 605
and (super)martingales, 604
and weak s-Martin-Löf randomness, 602
Martin-Löf, **602**
Martin-Löf, and weak s-randomness, 602
Martin-Löf, in h-spaces, **619**
weak 2-, 232, 287–288
and CEA sets, 393
and computable randomness, lowness, *see* lowness, for weak 2-randomness / computable randomness
and computing c.e. sets, 289
and Δ_2^0-ness, 288
and Demuth randomness, 316
and difference randomness, 318
and generalized Martin-Löf tests, 287
and hyperimmune-freeness, 357
and hyperimmunity, 382
and initial segments of the degrees, 357
and 1-genericity, 385
and 1-randomness, lowness, *see* lowness, for weak 2-randomness / 1-randomness
and Schnorr randomness, lowness, *see* lowness, for weak 2-randomness / Schnorr randomness
and the halting problem, 288–289
and van Lambalgen's Theorem, *see* van Lambalgen's Theorem, for weak 2- randomness
and weak 1-randomness, 357
and weak 1-randomness, lowness, *see* lowness, for weak 2-randomness / weak 1-randomness
and $\emptyset'$-hyperimmunity, 362
base, *see* base, for weak 2-randomness
lowness, *see* lowness, for weak 2-randomness
relative, and minimal pairs, 337, 359
rank, *see* class, Π_1^0, rank

rational representation, *see* premeasure, rational representation
rational-valued
  function, *see* function, rational-valued
  martingale, *see* gale, martingale, rational-valued
r.e., *see* computably enumerable
real, **2**, 197
  approximation, 198–199, 217
    rate of convergence, 198
  computable, 31, **197**, 198
    as a real closed field, 224
    uniformly, **202**
  convention on reals, 3
  Δ^0_2, **199**
    as a real closed field, 224
  left computably enumerable, xxi–xxii, 197, **199**, 201–202, 705
    and addition, 202, 419
    and almost c.e. sets, 200
    and C-independence, 628
    and C-reducibility, 425
    and cl-completeness, 442
    and cl-reducibility, 448, 455
    and cl-upper bounds, 442, 444
    and computable randomness, 351
    and effective packing dimension, 649
    and ibT-reducibility, 447
    and initial segment complexity, 440
    and multiplication, 202
    and Omega operators, 716–719, 721
    and 1-randomness, 448
    and Schnorr Hausdorff dimension, 660
    and Schnorr randomness, 350–351
    and Solovay completeness, 408–410
    and strongly computably enumerable reals, 201
    and von Mises-Wald-Church stochasticity, 328
    and weak 1-randomness, 295
    approximation, 199–200, 203, 206
    approximation, and monotone reducibility, 432
    approximation, and 1-randomness, 416
    approximation, and rK-reducibility, 422
    approximation, and Solovay reducibility, 405, 407–408, 415–416
    C-degree, *see* degrees, C-
    cl-degree, *see* degrees, computable Lipschitz
    ibT-degree, *see* degrees, identity bounded Turing
    initial segment complexity and addition, 425
    K-degree, *see* degrees, K-
    mind-change function, **422**
    minimal pair of Solovay degrees, 415
    monotone degree, *see* degrees, monotone
    1-randomness and initial segment complexity, 410
    only computably presentable, 206, 210
    only computably presentable, and 1-randomness, 411
    only computably presentable, and weak 1-randomness, 411
    presentation, **206**
    presentation, and initial segment complexity, 411
    presentation, and prompt simplicity, 215
    presentation, and wtt-ideals, 208–209
    representation, **203**
    rK-degree, *see* degrees, relative K
    settling time, 422
    Solovay degree, *see* degrees, Solovay
    standard reducibility, *see* reducibility, standard
    uniformly, **202**
  left cut, **197**

left-c.e., *see* real, left computably enumerable
left-d.c.e., **217**
and K-triviality, 721–722
and 1-randomness, 410
as a field, 219
as a real closed field, 219
lowness, *see* lowness, for left-d.c.e. reals
right computably enumerable, **199**
and Solovay reducibility, 420
uniformly, **203**
strongly computably enumerable, **200**
and left computably enumerable reals, 201
real closed field, *see* field, real closed
real-valued function, *see* function, real-valued
Recursion Theorem, **13**
and the KC Theorem, 127–128
for prefix-free machines, **123**
with parameters, **14**
recursive, *see* computable
primitive, *see* primitive recursive function
recursively enumerable, *see* computably enumerable
reducibility, 15, 404, *see also* degrees
C-, xxii, **405**, 427
and addition, 426
and cl-reducibility, 420
and n-randomness, 479
and 1-randomness, 425
and rK-reducibility, 421
and Solovay reducibility, 405
and the countable predecessor property, 465
and Turing reducibility, 425, 456
and vL-reducibility, 479, 480
cl-, *see* reducibility, computable Lipschitz
computable Lipschitz, xxii, **420**, 427
and array computability, 444, 447
and C-reducibility, 420
and c.e. sets, 435, 436
and complex sets, 441
and ibT-reducibility, 443
and initial segment complexity, 440
and joins, 442, 444
and K-reducibility, 420
and 1-randomness, 441, 448, 455
and rK-reducibility, 422, 435–436
and Schnorr reducibility, 462
and Solovay reducibility, 433–435
and the Kučera-Slaman Theorem, 454–455
and tt-reducibility, 436
completeness, *see* completeness, computable Lipschitz
equivalence, *see* equivalence under a notion of reducibility
extended monotone, **473**
ibT-, *see* reducibility, identity bounded Turing
identity bounded Turing, **420**
and array computability, 444, 447
and cl-reducibility, 443
and differential geometry, 420
and joins, 444
and 1-randomness, 447
K-, xxii, **404**, 427
and addition, 426
and cl-reducibility, 420
and m-degrees, 464
and n-randomness, 477
and 1-randomness, 425, 480–481, 486
and rK-reducibility, 421
and Solovay reducibility, 405
and strongly K-belowness, 486
and the countable predecessor property, 464
and Turing reducibility, 456
and vL-reducibility, 477, 480
measure of lower cones, 478
Km-, *see* reducibility, monotone
KM-, **169**
LK-, xxiii, **494**
and lowness for K, 508
and LR-reducibility, 494
low for K, *see* reducibility, LK-
low for 1-randomness, *see* reducibility, LR-

LR-, xxii, **473**, 509
and LK-reducibility, 494
and lowness for 1-randomness, 508
and non-GL_2-ness, 491
and Π^0_1 classes, 497
and relative Δ^0_2-ness, 495
and relativized Σ^0_1 classes, 489
and Σ^0_2 classes, 497
and the countable predecessor property, 491
and Turing reducibility, 491
and (uniform) almost everywhere domination, 496–497, 499
and universal Martin-Löf tests, 489
and van Lambalgen reducibility, 473
m-, *see* reducibility, many-one
many-one, **19**
and effective dimension, 611
and the broken dimension question, 611
and Turing reducibility, 20
completeness, *see* completeness, many-one
polynomial time, 19
Medvedev, *see* reducibility, strong
monotone, **169**, 432
and approximations, 432
Muchnik, *see* reducibility, weak
1-, **19**
pb-, **107**
polynomial time, *see* reducibility, many-one, polynomial time *and* reducibility, Turing, polynomial time
relative K-, xxii, **421**, 427
and addition, 424
and approximations, 421–422
and C-reducibility, 421
and cl-reducibility, 422, 435–436
and computing with advice, 421
and K-reducibility, 421
and 1-randomness, 424–425
and plain complexity, 421
and real closed fields, 424
and settling times, 422
and Solovay reducibility, 422, 435
and Turing reducibility, 423
rK-, *see* reducibility, relative K-
S-, *see* reducibility, Solovay
Schnorr, **462**, 564
and cl-reducibility, 462
and strong truth table reducibility, 463
Σ^0_3, **427**
Solovay, xxii, **405**, 427
and addition, 408, 413
and approximations, 405, 407–408, 415–416
and C-reducibility, 405
and c.e. sets, 435, 436
and cl-reducibility, 433–435
and K-reducibility, 405
and multiplication, 414
and 1-randomness, 419
and right-c.e. reals, 420
and rK-reducibility, 422, 435
and Turing reducibility, 406
and wtt-reducibility, 406
completeness, *see* completeness, Solovay
relativized, **709**
standard, **427**
and density, 427, 430, 432
and splitting, 427
strong, 206, **344**
and weak reducibility, 345
strong truth table, **463**
and Schnorr reducibility, 463
strong weak truth table, *see* reducibility, computable Lipschitz
sw-, *see* reducibility, computable Lipschitz
truth table, **20**
and cl-reducibility, 436
and hyperimmune-freeness, 69
and 1-randomness, 333
and totality, 21
and Turing reducibility, 69
and weak notions of randomness, 570
and wtt-reducibility, 334
completeness, *see* completeness, truth table
conjunctive, **739**

tt-, *see* reducibility, truth table
Turing, **16**
and C-reducibility, 425, 456
and effective dimension, 612
and hyperimmune-freeness, 69
and K-reducibility, 456
and LR-reducibility, 491
and m-reducibility, 20
and mass problem reducibilities, 344
and 1-randomness, 259
and rK-reducibility, 423
and Solovay reducibility, 406
and the broken dimension question, 612
and the countable predecessor property, 17
and tt-reducibility, 69
and vL-reducibility, 474
and wtt-reducibility, 70
completeness, *see* completeness, Turing
measure of upper cones, 358
polynomial time, 16, 19
polynomial time, and complexity extraction, 642
relativization and measure, 360
uniform Schnorr, 462
van Lambalgen, xxii, **473**
and C-reducibility, 479, 480
and joins, 474
and K-reducibility, 477, 480
and LR-reducibility, 473
and n-randomness, 474
and 1-randomness, 473, 474
and Turing reducibility, 474
vL-, *see* reducibility, van Lambalgen
weak, **344**
and strong reducibility, 345
weak truth table, **21**
and effective dimension, 611
and initial segment complexity, 440
and Solovay reducibility, 406
and the broken dimension question, 611
and tt-reducibility, 334
and Turing reducibility, 70
completeness, *see* completeness, weak truth table
with tiny use, **577**
and anti-complex sets, 579
and bounding orders, 577
and computability, 577
and wtt-reducibility, 577
uniform, **577**
uniform, and anti-complex sets, 579
uniform, and computability, 577
uniform, and domination, 577
uniform, and highness, 578
wtt-, *see* reducibility, weak truth table
reduction, 15, 29–30
dynamic definition, 29
rules, 30
static definition, 29
regularity, Schnorr, **657**
Reid, S., xv, 290–295, 581, 606
Reimann, J., xv–xvi, 7, 21, 265–266, 276, 309, 311–314, 328, 330–331, 334–336, 357, 465, 603–605, 609–611, 636–638, 641, 655–656, 658–661, 713
relative K-
degrees, *see* degrees, relative K-
reducibility, *see* reducibility, relative K-
relative randomness, *see* randomness, relative
relativization, 18, 245
relativized
computable measure machine, *see* machine, computable measure, relativized
hyperimmunity, *see* hyperimmunity, relativized
KM-complexity, *see* complexity, KM, relativized
Kučera-Slaman Theorem, *see* Kučera-Slaman Theorem, relativized
lowness for 1-randomness, *see* lowness, for 1-randomness, relativized

monotone complexity, *see* complexity, monotone, relativized
1-randomness, *see* randomness, 1-, relativized
Π^0_n class, *see* class, Π^0_n, relativized
Π^0_1 class, *see* class, Π^0_1, relativized
plain complexity, *see* complexity, plain Kolmogorov, relativized
prefix-free complexity, *see* complexity, prefix-free Kolmogorov, relativized
Σ^0_n class, *see* class, Σ^0_n, relativized
Σ^0_1 class, *see* class, Σ^0_1, relativized
Σ^0_2 class, *see* class, Σ^0_2, relativized
Solovay reducibility, *see* reducibility, Solovay, relativized
Remmel, J., xvi, 74
representation
of a left-c.e. real, *see* real, left computably enumerable, representation
of a real by a sequence relative to a measure, **266**
and continuous measures, 267
request, *see* KC Theorem, request
requirement, 31–32
requiring attention, *see* priority, method, requiring attention
resource-bounded measure, *see* measure, resource-bounded
restrained approximation, *see* approximation, restrained
restraint, *see* priority, method, restraint
function, *see* priority method, restraint function
hatted, 57
Rettinger, R., 217, 410, 722
reverse mathematics, xxiii, xxv, 349, 495, 499
Rice's Theorem, **13**
Rice, H., 13
right computably enumerable real, *see* real, right computably enumerable
risking measure, 323, 381, 401
rK-degrees, *see* degrees, relative K-
rK-reducibility, *see* reducibility, relative K-
Robinson, R., 58, 64–66
Rogers, H., xiii, 8, 28, 82, 209
Ronneburger, D., 743
Royden, H., 264, 400
Rumyantsev, A., 601
Rupprecht, N., 294
Ryabko, B., 598

s function, **467**
and the α function, 468
and the γ function, 487
and 2-randomness, 487
S-degrees, *see* degrees, Solovay
s-dimensional
measure, *see* measure, s-dimensional
outer Hausdorff measure, *see* measure, s-dimensional outer Hausdorff
packing measure, *see* measure, s-dimensional packing
s-gale, *see* gale, s-gale
s-supergale, *see* gale, s-supergale
s-m-n Theorem, **10**
s-measurable machine, *see* machine, s-measurable
s-measure, *see* measure, s-
s-randomness, *see* randomness, weak s- *and* randomness, strong s-
S-reducibility, *see* reducibility, Solovay
s-success, *see* gale, (super)martingale, s-success
s-termgale, *see* gale, termgale, s-
s.j.t., *see* traceability, strong jump
Sacks
Density Theorem, *see* Density Theorem
Jump Inversion Theorem, 65
uniformity, 66
preservation strategy, 40
Splitting Theorem, 39
Sacks' Theorem, **358**, 531
Sacks, G., 39–40, 58, 65–66, 72, 83, 209, 323, 358, 363, 373, 534, 645, 711
Salomaa, A., 8

Sasso, R., 207
savings
  property, *see* gale, (super)martingale, savings property
  trick, *see* gale, (super)martingale, savings trick
scan rule, *see* betting strategy, nonmonotonic, scan rule
Schaefer, M., 77, 454
Schnorr
  Δ^0_2 randomness, *see* randomness, Schnorr Δ^0_2
  Hausdorff dimension, *see* dimension, Hausdorff, Schnorr
  null set, *see* null set, Schnorr
  packing dimension, *see* dimension, packing, Schnorr
  randomness, *see* randomness, Schnorr
  reducibility, *see* reducibility, Schnorr
    uniform, *see* reducibility, uniform Schnorr
  regularity, *see* regularity, Schnorr
  s-null, *see* null set, Schnorr s-
  s-test, *see* test, Schnorr s-
  test, *see* test, Schnorr
  triviality, xxiii, **564**
    and anti-complex sets, 576, 580
    and bases for randomness, 575
    and computable enumerability, 565
    and computable traceability, 572
    and dense simple sets, 574
    and highness, 564, 575
    and joins, 574
    and lowness for Schnorr randomness, 564
    and plain complexity, 580
    and tt-lowness for Schnorr randomness, 572
    and Turing completeness, 564
    and wtt-completeness, 568
    and wtt-reducibility, 574
    as a tt-ideal, 574
    size of the class, 575
    tt-downward closure, 569
Schnorr's critique, xxi, 243, 269
  and martingale processes, 269
Schnorr, C., xiii, xxi, 125, 145–147, 227, 232, 236–240, 243, 257, 269–273, 276, 280, 303, 321, 350, 587, 594, 599, 604–605, 654
Scott Basis Theorem, *see* basis theorem, Scott
Scott, D., 84, 87
selection, 302
  domain, **309**
  function, 230, **246**, 301
    adaptive, 230
    and martingales, 302
  rule, *see* selection, function
self-delimiting machine, *see* machine, self-delimiting
Semenov, A., 246, 309–311
semicontinuity, lower, *see* lower semicontinuity
semimeasure
  continuous, xiii, **150**, 264
    and discrete semimeasures, 150
    and supermartingales, 238
    computably enumerable, **150**, 170
    computably enumerable, and monotone machines, 151
    computably enumerable, optimal, **150**
    computably enumerable, optimal, and Bayes' rule, 238
    computably enumerable, optimal, and optimal c.e. supermartingales, 238
    computably enumerable, optimal, and universal monotone machines, 151
    subadditivity, 150
  discrete, xiii, **133**
    and continuous semimeasures, 150
    and limit frequencies, 472
    computably enumerable, 129, **133**
    computably enumerable, maximal, **133**

computably enumerable, maximal, and prefix-free Kolmogorov complexity, 133
computably enumerable, maximal, and universal prefix-free machine output probabilities, 133
separating set, **73**
and PA degrees, 86
for an effectively inseparable pair, 86
sequence, **2**
set, **2**, *see also* computable, set; computably enumerable, set; etc.
cover, *see* cover, of a set
density, *see* density of a set
domain, *see* domain, of a set of pairs
eth column, *see* column of a set
k-, *see* k-set
of generators, *see* generators of an open set
of nonrandom strings, *see* nonrandom strings
open
basic, 4
generators, *see* generators of an open set
theory, 297, 555, 613
settling time
domination, *see* domination, settling time
function, *see* computably enumerable, set, modulus function
of left-c.e. reals, *see* real, left computably enumerable, settling time
Shannon, C., 323, 358
Shannon-Fano codes, 125
Shapiro, N., 323, 358
Shelah, S., 478, 555
Shen, A., xvi, 122, 147, 170, 246, 263, 303, 471–473, 601
shift complex set, **601**
and 1-randomness, 601
and effective dimension, 601
and prefix-free complexity, 601
1-, 601
Shoenfield Jump Inversion Theorem, 65
Shoenfield's Limit Lemma, *see* Limit Lemma
Shoenfield, J., 24–25, 29, 54, 56, 58, 65, 71
Shore, R., xvi, 15, 41–42, 64, 72, 91–92, 215, 376, 392, 421, 650
σ-algebra, **241**
Borel, **242**
generated by a class, **242**
Σ^0_n
class, *see* class, Σ^0_n
Kurtz null test, *see* test, Σ^0_n Kurtz null
(Martin-Löf) test, *see* test, Σ^0_n
randomness, *see* randomness, n-
set, **23**
and m-completeness, 25
and relative computable enumerability, 25
and the $(n-1)$st jump, 25
Σ^0_1
class, *see* class, Σ^0_1
cover, *see* cover, Σ^0_1-
function, *see* function, real-valued, computably enumerable
Hausdorff dimension, *see* dimension, Hausdorff, effective
martingale, *see* gale, martingale, computably enumerable
set, and computable enumerability, 23
supermartingale, *see* gale, supermartingale, computably enumerable
termgale, *see* gale, termgale, Σ^0_1
Σ^0_3
class, *see* class, Σ^0_3
ideal, *see* ideal, Σ^0_3
reducibility, *see* reducibility, Σ^0_3
wtt-ideal, *see* ideal, wtt-, Σ^0_3
Silver's Theorem, 478
Silver, J., 478
simple
martingale, *see* gale, martingale, simple
permitting, *see* permitting, c.e.

randomness, *see* randomness, simple
simplicity, **12**, 43
and c.e. supersets, 83
prompt, *see* prompt simplicity
Simpson, S., 69, 345–347, 364, 495–496, 696
Slaman, T., xv–xvi, xxii, 7, 21, 79, 93, 231, 243–244, 265, 279–280, 331, 334–336, 345, 349, 409–410, 550, 713
Slowdown Lemma, **15**
Smith, C., 303
Smullyan, R., 86
Snir, M., 287, 361
Soare, R., xiii, xvi, xix, 8, 14–15, 27, 29, 36, 43, 44, 57–58, 65, 69, 77–79, 81–84, 86–89, 91–92, 198–199, 201, 204, 215, 370, 374, 420–421, 503, 534
Solomon, R., xxiii, 494, 497, 499
Solomonoff, R., xiii, xx, 111–112, 133, 145–146
Solovay
completeness, *see* completeness, Solovay
degrees, *see* degrees, Solovay
forcing, *see* forcing, Solovay
function, **139**
and K-triviality, 505, 689
and Ω, 412
and 1-randomness, 254, 412
and plain complexity characterizations of 1-randomness, 327
nondecreasing, 413
Solovay's, **139**, 252, 505
n-generic, *see* generic, Solovay n-
randomness, *see* randomness, Solovay
reducibility, *see* reducibility, Solovay
test, *see* test, Solovay
total, *see* test, total Solovay
Solovay, R., xi–xiii, xvi, xx, xxii, xxv, 85–89, 137–145, 147, 155–156, 160–164, 166–168, 229, 234, 251, 262, 275, 288, 296, 340, 370, 404–405, 408–409, 413, 466, 468–471, 487, 501, 503, 505, 534, 555, 715, 728–729, 732, 743–744
Sorbi, A., 347
Soskova, M., 489–491, 499
Space Lemma, **325**, 331, 350
sparsity, 437, 456
special Π^0_1 class, *see* class, Π^0_1, special
Spector, C., 70–71, 358
spectrum of an Omega operator, *see* Omega operator, spectrum
splitting
c.e., **39**
and cone avoidance, 40
and minimal pairs, 53
of the left cut of a real, 203–205
Δ^0_2 sets, 40
theorem, *see* Sacks, Splitting Theorem
tree, *see* tree, e-splitting
Staiger, L., 136, 598, 604–605, 636–637
stake function, *see* betting strategy, nonmonotonic, stake function
standard
cost function, *see* cost function, standard
reducibility, *see* reducibility, standard
static definition, *see* reduction, static definition
statistical test, *see* test, statistical
Stephan, F., xvi, xxi–xxiii, 120, 229, 260–262, 273, 276, 303, 309, 311–314, 328, 330, 337–339, 349–351, 356–357, 366–369, 382, 411, 425–426, 437, 439–440, 455–458, 465, 491, 500–501, 503–504, 510, 511, 523, 526, 529–531, 533–534, 537, 539–542, 554, 559–560, 570–572, 574–585, 591, 605, 628, 643, 668–671, 708, 711–713, 715
Stephenson, J., xvi
Stillwell's Theorem, xxii, **365**
Stillwell, J., xxii, 323, 359–360, 363, 365

Stob, M., 83, 93–98, 107–109, 205, 530
stochastic paradigm, *see* randomness, paradigm, stochastic
stochasticity, xxi
 and randomness, 303
 Church, xviii, 230, **302**
  and computable randomness, 303
  and 1-randomness, 232
  and Schnorr randomness, 330
  and simple randomness, 308
  no gap phenomenon, *see* gap phenomenon, lack, for Church stochasticity
 computable, *see* stochasticity, Church
 for a class, **302**
 time-bounded, 308
 von Mises-Wald-Church, 230, **302**
  and computable enumerability, 305
  and computable randomness, 307
  and initial segment complexity, 306, 328
  and 1-randomness, 303
  and partial computable randomness, 303
  and simple martingales, 308
strategy, *see* priority method, strategy
strict Demuth test, *see* test, strict Demuth
strict process
 complexity, *see* complexity, process, strict
 machine, *see* machine, process, strict
string, **2**
 as an oracle, 16
 comparability, **170**
 incomparability, **170**
 nonrandom, *see* nonrandom strings
 random, *see* randomness, of a string
 terminated binary, **663**
strong
 array, **69**
  very, *see* very strong array
 degrees, *see* degrees, strong
 jump traceability, *see* traceability, strong jump
 jump well-approximability, *see* well-approximability, strong jump
 K-randomness, *see* randomness, strong K-
 minimal cover, 100
  and array computability, 100
 reducibility, *see* reducibility, strong
 s-Martin-Löf randomness, *see* randomness, strong s-Martin-Löf
 s-success, *see* gale, martingale, strong s-success
 truth table reducibility, *see* reducibility, strong truth table
 weak truth table degrees, *see* degrees, computable Lipschitz
 weak truth table reducibility, *see* reducibility, computable Lipschitz
Strong Thickness Lemma, *see* Thickness Lemma, Strong
strongly K-below, **486**
 and K-reducibility, 486
 and 1-randomness, 486–487
strongly computably enumerable real, *see* real, strongly computably enumerable
subaddivity, **132**
success
 of a martingale process, *see* gale, martingale process, success
 of a nonmonotonic betting strategy, *see* betting strategy, nonmonotonic, success
 of a (super)martingale, *see* gale, (super)martingale, success
  relative to an order, *see* gale, (super)martingale, h-success
 s-, *see* gale, (super)martingale, s-success
 set
  of a (super)martingale, *see* gale, (super)martingale, success set
  of a (super)martingale relative to an order, *see* gale,

(super)martingale, h-success set
strong s-, *see* gale, (super)martingale, strong s-success
Sullivan, D., 639
superhigh set, **42**, 694
c.e., 42
superhigh$^\diamond$, *see* diamond class, superhigh$^\diamond$
Superlow Basis Theorem, *see* basis theorem, superlow
superlow set, xxiv, **21**, 693–694
and array computability, 98
and joins, 530
and jump traceability, 523
and Π^0_1 classes, 78
and prompt simplicity, 694
and strong jump traceability, 694
c.e., 39
superlow$^\diamond$, *see* diamond class, superlow$^\diamond$
supermartingale, *see* gale, supermartingale
svelte tree, *see* tree, svelte
sw-degrees, *see* degrees, computable Lipschitz
sw-reducibility, *see* reducibility, computable Lipschitz
Symmetry of Information, xx
for plain complexity, **116**
for prefix-free complexity, **134**

Tadaki, K., 602–603
tailset, **6**
Tennenbaum, S., 87
termgale, *see* gale, termgale
terminated binary string, *see* string, terminated binary
termination symbol, 121, **663**
Terwijn, S., xv, xxi–xxiii, 5, 99–100, 209, 229, 260–262, 303, 345, 349–351, 356, 382, 474, 489, 508–510, 524, 526, 554–555, 559, 599, 604–606, 610–611, 712, 713, 715
test
bounded Martin-Löf, **279**
and computable martingales, 280
and computable randomness, 280
and computably graded tests, 280
computably finite Martin-Löf, **318**
computably graded, **279**
and bounded Martin-Löf tests, 280
and computable martingales, 280
and computable randomness, 280
d.c.e., **316**
Δ^0_n, **256**
Demuth, **315**
strict, *see* test, strict Demuth
finite Martin-Löf, **318**
finite total Solovay, *see* test, Solovay, finite total
for strong s-Martin-Löf randomness, **605**
and s-measurable machines, 606
in h-spaces, **619**
for weak s-Martin-Löf randomness, **602**
in h-spaces, **619**
generalized Martin-Löf, 231, **287**
and weak 2-randomness, 287
lack of a universal test, 289
lowness, *see* lowness, for generalized Martin-Löf tests
ignorance, *see* ignorance test
Kurtz null, **286**, 294
and Schnorr randomness, 294
and weak 1-randomness, 286
lowness, *see* lowness, for Kurtz null tests
Kurtz-Solovay, **293**
and weak 1-randomness, 293
Martin-Löf, xxi, **231**, 269
and prefix-free complexity, 232–233
and (super)martingales, 236
bounded, *see* test, bounded Martin-Löf
computably finite, *see* test, computably finite Martin-Löf
finite, *see* test, finite Martin-Löf
generalized, *see* test, generalized Martin-Löf
lowness, *see* lowness, for Martin-Löf tests

nested, 231
ν-, *see* test, Martin-Löf, relative to a measure
relative to a measure, **264**
Σ^0_n, *see* test, Σ^0_n
universal, **233**, 409
universal oracle, 245, 489
universal, and LR-reducibility, 489
universal, Kučera's, **331**
n-c.e., 316
Π^0_n, **256**
Schnorr, **272**
and Schnorr null sets, 272
and Schnorr randomness, 272
lack of a universal test, 276
Schnorr s-, **654**
Σ^0_n, **256**
open, **256**
open, and n-randomness, 256
Σ^0_n Kurtz null, **287**
and weak n-randomness, 287
Solovay, **234**, 256
finite total, **294**
finite total, and Schnorr randomness, 294
total, **275**, 294
total, and Schnorr randomness, 275
Solovay s-, **603**
and weak s-randomness, 603
in h-spaces, **619**
interval, **604**
total, **655**
total, and Schnorr s-null sets, 655
statistical, xix, 231, 233
strict Demuth, 317
and difference randomness, 317
total Solovay, *see* test, Solovay, total
theory
"almost all", *see* "almost all" theory of the Turing degrees
complete extensions, *see* class, Π^0_1, and complete extensions of a theory
of the Solovay degrees, *see* degrees, Solovay, theory
of the Turing degrees, *see* degrees, Turing, theory
of the vL-degrees, *see* degrees, van Lambalgen, theory
thick subset, **53**
of a c.e. set, 56, 58
of a piecewise trivial set, 54
and highness, 53
Thickness Lemma, **56**, 57
Strong, **58**
weak form, **54**
tight Σ^0_1-cover, *see* cover, Σ^0_1, tight
time-bounded
prefix-free Kolmogorov complexity, *see* complexity, prefix-free Kolmogorov, time-bounded
stochasticity, *see* stochasticity, time-bounded
tiny use, *see* reducibility, with tiny use
Tot, *see* index set, Tot
total
function, *see* function, total
Solovay s-test, *see* test, Solovay s-, total
Solovay test, *see* test, total Solovay
totally ω-c.e. degree, **319**
and computably finite randomness, 319
trace, *see* traceability, trace
traceability
bound, **98**
computable, **100**, 555
and c.e. traceability, 560
and diagonal noncomputability, 584
and hyperimmune-freeness, 100, 555, 559, 560
and lowness for computable measure machines, 562
and lowness for Kurtz null tests, 584
and lowness for 1-randomness / Schnorr randomness, 591
and lowness for Schnorr randomness, 561
and lowness for Schnorr tests, 555
bound independence, 100, 555

of a tt-degree, 572
of a tt-degree, and c.e. traceability of wtt-degrees, 576
weak, *see* traceability, weak computable
computably enumerable, **98**
and array computability, 99
and computable measure machines, 563
and computable traceability, 560
and effective packing dimension, 649–650
and extending partial functions, 585
and hyperimmune-freeness, 560
and initial segment complexity, 649
and lowness for 1-randomness / Schnorr randomness, 591
and lowness for weak 2-randomness / Schnorr randomness, 591
and minimal degrees, 650
and null sets, 559
bound independence, 99
of a wtt-degree, 576
of a wtt-degree, and anti-complex sets, 578
of a wtt-degree, and computable traceability of tt-degrees, 576
jump, **523**, 669, 700–701
and benign cost functions, 690–691
and joins, 673
and K-triviality, 523, 680, 685, 689, 700
and lowness for K, 680
and ML-cuppability, 685
and Π^0_1 classes, 694
and superlowness, 523
for an order, **523**
strong jump, xxiv, **669**
and benign cost functions, 690
and completions of PA, 695
and computable enumerability, 700
and joins, 673
and jump well-approximability, 670–671
and K-triviality, 680, 685, 700
and lowness for K, 680
and ML-cuppability, 685
and (ω-c.e.)$^\diamond$, 689, 693, 694
and Π^0_1 classes, 694
and strong jump well-approximability, 670
and superhigh$^\diamond$, 694
and superlow$^\diamond$, 689, 693–694
and superlowness, 694
downward closure, 670
ideal of s.j.t. c.e. sets, 672
index set, 672
plain complexity characterization, 671
trace, **98**
universal, **99**, 691
ultra jump, **672**
weak computable, **369**
and autocomplex sets, 369
Trakhtenbrot, B., 340
trash quota, 513
tree, **72**
e-splitting, **71**
ε-clumpy, **646**
function, **68**
perfect function, **646**
svelte, 584
Tricot, P., 639
trivial measure, *see* measure, trivial
triviality
K-, *see* K-triviality
Schnorr, *see* Schnorr, triviality
trivialization, **535**
$\emptyset'$-trivializing set, 535–536
and LR-reducibility, 535
and ML-coverability, 536
and ML-cuppability, 536
and (uniform) almost everywhere domination, 535
$\emptyset'$-trivializing$^\diamond$, *see* diamond class, $\emptyset'$-trivializing$^\diamond$
true
outcome, *see* priority method, true outcome
path, *see* priority method, true path
truth table, **20**

functional, *see* functional, truth table
ideal, *see* ideal, tt-
lowness for Schnorr randomness, *see* lowness, for Schnorr randomness, truth table
reducibility, *see* reducibility, truth table
strong, *see* reducibility, strong truth table
Schnorr relative randomness, *see* randomness, truth table Schnorr relative
tt-completeness, *see* completeness, truth table
tt-ideal, *see* ideal, tt-
tt-lowness for Schnorr randomness, *see* lowness, for Schnorr randomness, truth table
tt-reducibility, *see* reducibility, truth table
tt-Schnorr relative randomness, *see* randomness, truth table Schnorr relative
Turetsky, D., xvi
Turing
completeness, *see* completeness, Turing
degree, *see* degrees, Turing
functional, *see* functional, Turing
jump, *see* jump
machine, *see* machine, Turing
reducibility, *see* reducibility, Turing
Turing, A., 8, 198
Turing-Church Thesis, *see* Church-Turing Thesis
2-genericity, *see* genericity, 2-
2-randomness, *see* randomness, 2-

ultra jump traceability, *see* traceability, ultra jump
ultracompressibility, **305**
and computable randomness, 305
unbounded injury, *see* priority, method, unbounded injury
uniform
almost everywhere domination, *see* domination, almost everywhere, uniform
complexity, *see* complexity, uniform
measure, *see* measure, uniform
reducibility with tiny use, *see* reducibility, with tiny use, uniform
Schnorr reducibility, *see* reducibility, uniform Schnorr
wtt-density, *see* density, uniform wtt-
uniformly
computable
functions, *see* computable, function, uniformly
reals, *see* real, computable, uniformly
sets, *see* computable, set, uniformly
computably enumerable sets, *see* computably enumerable, set, uniformly
Δ_1^0 classes, *see* class, Δ_1^0, uniformly
left-c.e. reals, *see* real, left computably enumerable, uniformly
partial computable functions, *see* computable, partial function, uniformly
Π_n^0 classes, *see* class, Π_n^0, uniformly
Π_1^0 classes, *see* class, Π_1^0, uniformly
right-c.e. reals, *see* real, right computably enumerable, uniformly
Σ_n^0 classes, *see* class, Σ_n^0, uniformly
Σ_1^0 classes, *see* class, Σ_1^0, uniformly
Σ_3^0 index set, *see* index set, uniformly Σ_3^0
universal
by adjunction, *see* machine, prefix-free, universal by adjunction *and* machine, Turing, universal by adjunction
c.e. martingale, *see* gale, martingale, computably enumerable, universal
computable prefix-free function, *see* prefix-free, function, computable, universal
generalized Martin-Löf test

nonexistence, *see* test, generalized Martin-Löf, lack of a universal test
Martin-Löf test, *see* test, Martin-Löf, universal
monotone machine, *see* machine, monotone, universal
oracle
Martin-Löf test, *see* test, Martin-Löf, universal oracle
prefix-free machine, *see* machine, prefix-free, universal oracle
Turing machine, *see* machine, Turing, universal oracle
partial computable function, *see* computable, partial function, universal
Π^0_1 class, *see* class, Π^0_1, universal
prefix-free machine, *see* machine, prefix-free, universal
process machine, *see* machine, process, universal
Schnorr test
nonexistence, *see* test, Schnorr, lack of a universal test
trace, *see* trace, universal
Turing machine, *see* machine, Turing, universal
unpredictability paradigm, *see* randomness, paradigm, unpredictability
upper box counting dimension, *see* dimension, box counting, upper
upper modified box counting dimension, *see* dimension, box counting, modified, upper
uppersemilattice, **4**
use, **17**
computable, *see* reducibility, weak truth table
conventions, 17
identity, *see* reducibility, identity bounded Turing
up to a constant, *see* reducibility, computable Lipschitz
notation, 17
preservation, 34
tiny, *see* reducibility, with tiny use
Use Principle, 18
useless information, 715
Ushakov, M., 601
Uspensky, V., 69, 122, 147, 170, 238, 246, 309–311

van Lambalgen
degrees, *see* degrees, van Lambalgen
reducibility, *see* reducibility, van Lambalgen
van Lambalgen's Theorem, xxi, **258**, 473
for computable randomness, 276, 357
for n-genericity, **378**
for nonmonotonic randomness, **314**
for Schnorr randomness, 276, 357
for weak 2-randomness, 358
van Lambalgen, M., xix, xxi, 110, 227, 257–258, 265, 508
van Melkebeek, D., 743
Vereshchagin, N., xvi, 263, 471–473, 732, 737
very strong array, **94**
Ville's Theorem, xviii–xix, xxi, 230, **246**
and the fluctuation about the mean, 249–250
finite version, **246**
Ville, J., xviii–xix, 230, 232, 235–236, 246
Vinochandran, V., 642
visiting a node, *see* priority method, visiting a node
Vitányi, P., xi–xii, xvi, xx, 110, 113, 116, 122, 132, 136–137, 150, 227, 238, 260, 265, 304, 738
vL-degrees, *see* degrees, van Lambalgen
vL-reducibility, *see* reducibility, van Lambalgen
von Braunmühl, B., 217
von Mises, R., xvii–xix, 229–230, 301
von Mises-Church-Wald stochasticity, *see* stochasticity, von Mises-Church-Wald

Wald, A., xviii, 230

Wang, F., 642
Wang, Y., 200, 275, 286–287, 290, 303, 308, 349–350, 409, 413, 706
weak
  computable traceability, *see* traceability, weak computable
  degrees, *see* degrees, weak
  Demuth randomness, *see* randomness, weak Demuth
  K-randomness, *see* randomness, weak K-
  lowness for K, *see* lowness, for K, weak
  Martin-Löf cuppability, *see* Martin-Löf, cuppability, weak
  n-genericity, *see* genericity, weak n-
  n-randomness, *see* randomness, weak n-
  1-randomness, *see* randomness, weak 1-
  randomness, *see* randomness, weak
  reducibility, *see* reducibility, weak
  s-Martin-Löf randomness, *see* randomness, weak s-Martin-Löf
  s-randomness, *see* randomness, weak s-
  2-randomness, *see* randomness, weak 2-
weak truth table
  functional, *see* functional, weak truth table
  ideal, *see* ideal, wtt-
  reducibility, *see* reducibility, weak truth table
Weber, R., xv–xvi, 288–289, 537
weight
  of a k-set, **514**
  of a KC request, **126**
  of a KC set, *see* weight, of a set of KC requests
  of a prefix-free set, **201**
  of a set of KC requests, **126**
Weihrauch, K., 201, 217, 219
Weinberger, S., 420
Weinstein, S., 246, 249–250
Welch, L., 53
well-approximability, **670**
  jump, **670**
    and strong jump traceability, 670–671
  strong jump, **670**
    and strong jump traceability, 670
Wigderson, A., 642
window lemma, **57**
witness, 33
wtt-completeness, *see* completeness, weak truth table
wtt-cuppability, **82**
  and hypersimplicity, 82
wtt-ideal, *see* ideal, wtt-
wtt-reducibility, *see* reducibility, weak truth table
wtt-topped degree, **207**
Wu, G., xv–xvi, 206, 218, 377, 411, 576–580

Yates, C., 47, 72, 210, 650
Young, C., xvi
Yu, L., xiv–xvi, xxi–xxii, 103, 131, 229, 250–252, 262, 276, 288–289, 327, 329, 332, 356–357, 378, 442, 464–466, 473–481, 484–487, 505–506, 534, 537, 582–586, 591
Yue, Y., xvi

Zambella, D., xxiii, 98–100, 501, 505, 508, 524, 554–555, 559
0-1 law, 5
  effective, xxi
  for complexity classes, 642
  for effective packing dimension, 642
  for Π^0_n classes, **259**
  Σ^0_n classes, **259**
  Kolmogorov's, **6**
$\emptyset'$-trivializing sets, *see* trivialization, $\emptyset'$-trivializing sets
$\emptyset'$-trivializing$^\diamond$, *see* diamond class, $\emptyset'$-trivializing$^\diamond$
Zheng, X., xvi, 201, 217–219, 308
Zimand, M., xvi, xxiv, 627–629, 635
Zvonkin, A., 146, 266

Printed in the United States
By Bookmasters